INDONESIA HANDBOOK

Second Edition

Indonesia Handbook is the first and only published survey covering the geography, flora and fauna, history, ethnology and culture of all the main Indonesian island groups, including the outer islands. A gypsy's manual for the cheapest places to eat and sleep; ancient ruins and historical sites; wildlife and nature reserves; spiritual centers; arts and crafts; folk theatre and dance venues; money-making and money-saving tips; slow boat, bus, horse and foot connections through the cities, mountains, beaches and villages of the largest archipelago in the world.

INDONESIA HANDBOOK

Second Edition

INDONESIA HANDBOOK

Published by
Moon Publications
P.O. Box 732
Rutland
Vermont 05701 USA

Printed by
Multiprint Services, Singapore.

Distributor
Apa Productions (Pte) Ltd
Suite 1021, 10th Floor International Plaza,
10 Anson Road, Singapore 2
Tel: 2205288/2205323.

Second Edition
October 1978.

ISBN Number 0–8048–1268–3

nks to: Iwan Roberts, William Gouw Jr., Jim Snedden, Michael Van Langdenburg, Sue Piper, suddin, Michael White, Tony Appleton, Graham Simmons, Emily, Rene St. Goddard, Anang Spriggs, Henno and Marianne Oudejans, Colin Brooks, David Stanley, Oka Kartini, Randy, Kim Kaminis, Frank, Magnus Lindgren, Stefanie Mooney, Susan Ritz, Dave Wilson, Mike Benckert, David Leake Jr., Ela Orzechowska.

this b
Singapo
14, Petalir
912115. Hon
Netherlands
Germany — Geo.
Lascelles, 3 Holland
Tuttle Co., Inc., Post Of

from: **Australia** — Bookwise (Australia) Pty. Ltd., 104-108 Sussex St., Sydney, 2000, tel. 29 6537. okstores, 63 Robinson Rd., or 71-77 Stamford Rd. **Malaysia** — MPH, Jaya Supermarket, Section lumpur. **Thailand** — Chalermnit Bookshop, 1-2 Erawan Arcade, Bangkok, tel. 58759, 510630, Hong Kong University Press, 94 Bonham Road, University of Hong Kong, tel. 5-468161. Lamm B.V., Pampuslaan 212, Postbus 195, BTW. 11/510607, Weesp, tel. 02940, 15044. lag, 8000 Munchen 45, Schleibheimer Str. 371b, tel. (089) 351 5786. **United Kingdom** — Roger nsions, 16 Holland Park Gardens, London, W14 8DY, tel: (01) 603 8489. **USA** — Charles E. wer F, Rutland.VT 05701, tel: (802)-773-8930.

TABLE OF CONTENTS

INTRODUCTION

THE LAND   1
AGRICULTURE   2
FAUNA AND FLORA   3
CLIMATE   3
HISTORY   4
GOVERNMENT   12
THE ECONOMY   15
THE PEOPLE   19
LANGUAGE   21
RELIGION   23
EVENTS   26

CRAFTS   28
CONDUCT   31
ACCOMMODATION   34
THEFT   35
FOOD   36
GETTING TO INDONESIA   39
TRANSPORT WITHIN INDONESIA   41
HEALTH   44
MONEY   48
VISAS   49

JAVA

INTRODUCTION   51
WEST JAVA   73
CENTRAL JAVA   99

YOGYA   110
EAST JAVA   147

BALI

INTRODUCTION   177
CENTRAL BALI   196
EAST BALI   204

SOUTH BALI   207
NORTH BALI   220

NUSA TENGGARA

INTRODUCTION   227
TIMOR   228
ISLE OF ROTI   233
SOLOR AND ALOR   234
FLORES   237

KOMODO ISLAND   242
SUMBA   245
SUMBAWA   249
LOMBOK   254

SUMATRA

INTRODUCTION   259
SOUTH SUMATRA   263
RIAU PROVINCE   272
WEST SUMATRA   279
THE MINANGKABAU   285
ISLE OF NIAS   295

NORTH SUMATRA   299
THE BATAK   306
SAMOSIR ISLAND   313
THE KARO BATAK   318
ACEH PROVINCE   324

KALIMANTAN

INTRODUCTION   327
THE DAYAKS   331
SOUTH KALIMANTAN   336

CENTRAL KALIMANTAN   340
EAST KALIMANTAN   341
WEST KALIMANTAN   356

CELEBES

INTRODUCTION   359
NORTH CELEBES   360
CENTRAL CELEBES   371

SOUTH CELEBES   376
TORAJALAND   384

MOLUCCAS

INTRODUCTION   397
CENTRAL MOLUCCAS   399

SOUTHEAST MOLUCCAS   407
NORTH MOLUCCAS   410

IRIAN JAYA

INTRODUCTION   417
THE NORTHERN PROVINCES   424
SOUTHERN COASTS   427

EASTERN HIGHLANDS   430
CENTRAL HIGHLANDS   432
BALIEM VALLEY   435

APPENDICES

A. PRACTICAL INDONESIAN   441
B. HINDU LEGENDS — HINDU GODS —
   OTHER INDONESIAN LEGENDS   445

C. MOUNTAIN-CLIMBING IN
   INDONESIA — INDONESIA BY RAIL   449

ANNOTATED MAPS OF INDONESIA

TRAVEL   56-57
HISTORY   116-117
ARTS, CRAFTS AND LITERATURE   188-189

NATURAL PHENOMENA   252-253
ETHNOLOGY   350-351

BOOKLIST   451

GLOSSARY   457

INDEX   473

INDONESIAN GEOGRAPHIC ABBREVIATIONS
USED IN THE TEXT AND ON MAPS

D.   — Danau (lake)
G.   — Gunung (mountain)
Jl.   — Jalan (street)
Kb.   — Kebun (garden, plantation, estate)

Kec. — Kecamatan (district)
Kep. — Kepulauan (archipelago, islands)
S.   — Sungai (river)
Tg.   — Tanjung (cape, point)

INTRODUCTION

THE LAND

The outer limits of this 6400 km stretch of islands ('dari Sabang ke Merauke') is as far as California is from Bermuda or as far as Perth, Australia, is from Wellington, New Zealand. Indonesia has a total area of 5 million sq. km (about 1 million sq. km more than the total land area of the USA) of which more than 2 million sq. km are land. Its sea area is 4 times larger than its land area, and Indonesians are one of the few peoples in the world who include water within the boundaries of their territory, calling their country *Tanah Air Kita* or 'Our Land and Water'. Of the 10 largest islands in the world, 5 are in Indonesia; in addition there are about 30 small archipelagos. Of the 13,677 islands that make up its territory, only 992 are permanently settled and some 6000 are named. A country of incredible and diverse beauty, there are mind-stupifying extremes: from the 5000 meter snowcapped mountains of Irian Jaya to sweltering lowland swamps of eastern Sumatra, open eucalyptus savannahs of Timor, lush rainforests of West Java, with lava spewing volcanoes the whole length. Most Indonesians live and die within sight of a volcano. In the part of the western Pacific this archipelago sprawls through ('The Ring of Fire'), there are over 400 with 70-80 of them still active, registering 3 earthquakes per day. Each year there's an average of 10 major eruptions. This volcanic activity doesn't only destroy, but also brings gigantic benefit to aid growth and life. The ancient Hindu monuments constructed for over 750 years on Java were mostly built from cooled lava rock, ideal for carving. The whitish ash produced by an eruption, rich in chemicals, reaches a wide area of surrounding land. Rivers carry ash even further by way of irrigation canals to the crops. Thus Indonessia has some of the most fertile land on the planet. In places it's said you can shove a stick in the ground and it'll sprout leaves. A serious pursuit not to be missed in Indonesia is volcano climbing-Keli Mutu, Rinjini, Gunung Agung, Bromo, Merapi, Papandayan, Sibayak-each offering haunting desolate landscapes, cold invigorating hikes, and sometimes a hotsprings bath after. There are numerous remote and wildly pristine high mountain lakes made from volcanic cataclysms eons ago.

AGRICULTURE

Indonesia is an agricultural nation. 4 out of 5 Indonesians work the soil. The *desa* is the entire productive community of a small village. In the western sense, the *desa* is an authoritarian undemocratic system. It can be likened to a sort of oriental kibbutz. Wooden houses are loosely scattered around vegetable plots and fruit trees– papaya, mango, quava, coconut, *kapok* and various palms with narrow pathways winding in every direction. Sometimes there is a community meeting place, barns, and fishponds. The *desa* is often surrounded by dry or wet ricefields, hedges, bamboo groves, with forests beyond. People work hard all day, then return home to pray, sing, dance, smoke *kretek*, gossip, watch *wayang*, sleep, rising at 4 am again to labor in the fields. Controlling everything in the *desa* is a council of elected villagers. The headman is called the *kepala desa*. An ancient cooperative system (gotong royong) manages the parceling out of land, community seed beds, the growing of crops, and the irrigation and storage of rice. There are mainly two systems of cultivation used in Indonesia, *ladang* and *sawah*.

LADANG

Shifting-cultivation. Characterized by prodigious human labor using uncomplicated pre-industrial implements, it's estimated that as much as ⅓ of all Indonesians still work *ladang*. This method of farming was practiced in Europe during the Middle Ages when Europe was underpopulated, its inhabitants beating back the forests. *Ladang* could be very complex, a stable, well-balanced system in which man and his environment co-exist in harmony. Basically, it is an imitation of nature itself. Unirrigated arable land is prepared by slashing and burning jungle, clearing it, then planting and harvesting a wide variety of quick-growing, predominantly food crops. They plant in rows, working upwards over fallen trees and rough ground. The men poke holes with sharpened sticks, the women follow behind dropping in unhusked rice seeds, a few per hole. After some days green shoots appear from 99% of the holes. *Ladang* is usually practiced on the non-volcanic soil of the outer islands, so that the soil soon becomes exhausted. The plot is then abandoned. At least 10 years are needed for the jungle to overgrow the cultivate plot and replenish the soil with growth elements. The *ladang* farmer then returns and cultivates the plot for another 2 years, repeating the cycle. If the cycle is shortened and the forest doesn't take root again, tenacious *alang2* grass takes hold and depletes the soil of all nourishment, becoming useless for any kind of farming. In most parts of the world, shifting-farming means moving villages or a nomadic existence, but in Indonesia most shifting farmers live in permanent villages. The system requires roughly 10 times the area needed than wet rice growing and large tracts of land are held by relatively small numbers of farmers. *Ladang* usually fosters clans or genealogical communities as are found on Flores, Sulawesi, and Timor. Because of the pressure of population and the introduction of improved agricultural methods, this dry fields type of cultivation is giving way to the more intensive wet rice cultivation, called *sawah*.

SAWAH

This type of wet-rice cultivation is a spectacular form of agriculture which often looks like a green soft stairway climbing into the sky. Although it can be utilized up to 1600 m above sea level, *sawah* is most usually found in the monsoon areas of the low-lying plains because of the more plentiful and more regular water supply. Because such complicated irrigation systems have always needed a despot to manage them efficiently, *sawah* cultivation has given rise in Indonesia's history to strong territorial agrarian communities supporting an aristocratic hierarchy headed by kingships based on divine right. Technically very intricate and delicate to manage, this system of complex waterworks is more economical than *ladang* in terms of rice output per acre, able to support some of the highest rural population densities in the world. Nowhere has *sawah* been better perfected than on Java and Bali because nowhere is there so little land available to accommodate the high birthrate. Two or 3 ricecrops a year may sometimes be planted, and *sawah* has the capacity to produce undiminished yields year after year. Water is of supreme importance in *sawah* growing: it decomposes the soil, checks weed growth, aerates the soil, and generally works like an acquarium. During the wet season the *sawah is* planted with rice, and during the dry it's often planted with corn and cassava. Backbreaking planting, weeding, plowing and harvesting are all done by hand, elbow and knee deep in mud, with iron and wood tools. Plows are worked by *kerbau* (water buffaloes) except on smaller fields close to the edges of the terraces. But by using a hoe, the farmer can in effect transfer the food the buffalo would eat directly to himself. The many animist

rites practiced today persist from the old time when people were bound by such strong religious ties to their communal land. When rice is planted on Java or Bali a small plaited figure of a fertility goddess is placed under an umbrella and incense is burned in her honor so that there will be good crops the following year. This rice goddess, Dewi Sri, literally dwells in the rice stalks. At harvest time the stalks must be cut in a certain way so as not to offend her. Wood mounted razor-like handblades (ani ani) are used by women who deftly conceal them in their palms. Only 3-4 stalks at a time are cut so the rice soul will not be frightened. This method also has its use in reaping the largest percentage of yield and it leaves the greatest amount of harvested crop on the field to refertilize it. Though it's gruelling work, rice harvesting is a happy time.

FAUNA AND FLORA

There are 40 different kinds of animals scattered throughout the archipelago and 115 state-supervised game parks and nature reserves. Also, if you can handle the *karma,* many hunting areas. Bird species number in the thousands: peacocks, pheasants, partridges, turkey-sized pigeons, jungle fowls which incubate their eggs in volcanic steam, black ibis flying in V-formations, and the hornbill which sounds like a puffing locomotive when it flies. There are fabulously colored butterflies, praying mantises like bright green banana leaves, submarine diving grasshoppers. Reptiles include giant monitor lizards, the reticulated python (world's largest snake, 9 m long), deep croaking gekkos. Among its mammals are great apes such as the orangutan with its blazing orange shaggy coat, deep black wild cattle, miniature deer (350 mm high), clouded leapords, mountain goats (serow), wild wart hogs, the sun bear with a large white circle on its chest, long snouted tapirs which gallop like stallions, tossing their heads and whinnying. The fauna of Irian Jaya (West New Guinea) resembles that of Australia: vividly colored Birds of Paradise, spiny anteaters, mouse-like flying possums, bandicoots. In Indonesia's seas are found the world's most expensive shell (The Glory of the Seas), crabs (birgus) which

can clip down coconuts and open them on the ground, fresh-water dolphins, fish that climb mango trees looking for insects. Due to its extreme geographic fragmentation, Indonesia is richer in plant species than either the American or African tropics. Its total number of flowering plants number more than 35,000 species. To cite only a sample of Indonesia's floral wealth, there are 250 species of bamboo, 150 species of palm, and in the more fertile areas flowers are rampant-hibiscus, jasmine, allamanda, frangipani, bougainvillea, lotus lilies 1 ½ m wide. There are 5000 plant species on Java alone and twice as many species of plants on Borneo as in all of Africa. There are tall hardwood rainforest trees of Irian Jaya which rival the Sequoias of California; *banyan* trees, connected with authority and populated by hordes of spirits, planted outside the royal cities of Central Java; the Corpse Plant of Sumatra which smells like putrifying animal flesh; the biggest flower in the world, the *reflesia* (1 meter wide); the luxurious vegetation of Borneo where the seductive colors of orchids glow in the perpetual twilight of the jungle. Because of the unbelievable humidity, strong sunlight and volcanic soil, when you build a fence in Indonesia 6 months later it is not a fence. It is a living wall of vegetation.

CLIMATE

Indonesia straddles the equator and days are all the same length. This country has a typical equatorial climate with only 2 seasons: the wet season and the hot season. The hot season is slightly hotter and not quite so wet as the wet season and the wet season is slightly wetter and not quite so hot as the hot season. The wet season lasts from about Nov. to

Mar. or April (sometimes it rains so hard it's like falling into a swimming pool), and the hot season from May to October. Locales east of Solo, Java, have sharply defined dry seasons, the duration increasing as the area gets nearer to Australia. In Kupang on Timor the dry season lasts up to 7 months; it's the only island that gets cyclones. Sumatra and Kalimantan, lying closer to the equator and far from Australia, have no dry seasons. In Indonesia it's always hot but due to mountain breezes and altitude, there's roughly one degree of cooling for every 90 m elevation. Humidity is always high. When it rains the dust on the roads is kept down, flowers are bursting, it's fresher, and everywhere it's green like dripping wet paint. If you're caught in the rain, just cut down a banana leaf to make an ideal umbrella, or in Irian Jaya, use grass. In many places good umbrellas are made from bamboo coated with wax paper and fat; Rp3-400. Slips easily through the top of a pack. Asians have a different appreciation of climate then people of the west; warm is associated with 'hard work, pain, terror, bad' while we think 'pleasant, cozy, secure, healthy'. Most Indonesians socialize and promenade in the cool of the evening.

HISTORY

When you read Indonesian history, you read world history. This country is a subtle blending of every culture that ever invaded it — Chinese, Indian, Melanesian, Portugese, Polynesian, Arabian, English and Dutch. Indonesia's history is a story of wave after wave of migrations of peoples who either absorbed earlier arrivals, killed them off, or pushed them into less favorable regions such as deep forests, high mountains, or remote islands (where they are found to this day). This explains Indonesia's astounding ethnic diversity.

PREHISTORY

Java was one of the earliest places in the world where man lived. In 1891 a fossil skull of an ape man was discovered at Trinil in Central Java. This erect near-man lived at a time when Europe was under ice and most of Indonesia was a part of Asia. He walked to Java when the Sunda Shelf was above water. Java was then a high mountainous island covered in jungle. This species of man ranged from Africa all the way to the glacial border of Europe and east to China 500,000 years ago at the very beginning of the Pleistocene Period. Charcoal and charred bones indicate he used fire and made crude flint heads. This *homo erectus* was not an ancestor of present-day Indonesians but a race all its own that has vanished; either he couldn't adapt or was destroyed by a more advanced species. Excavations at Sangiran (north of Solo, Central Java) uncovered an even more primitive type than *homo erectus*. In 1931 at Ngandong (near Trinil), 11 skullcaps were found, more advanced than *homo erectus*, the so-called Solo Man. All eleven skullcaps had been deliberately cracked open at their bases: Solo Man was probably a cannibal. Found with him was an astonishingly rich fossil bed of 23,000 mammalian bones, mostly of extinct oxen, elephants and hippos. Also uncovered were scrapers, borers, choppers, and stone balls used in slings. Negritos, a pygmy people who began to radiate through the islands 30,000 years ago, were the first known human migrants into Indonesia. No one knows from where they came. There are still genetic traces of these wooly-haired round-headed people in the jungles of East Sumatra, the uplands of the Lesser Sundas, and in the remote highlands of New Guinea. They were the First Wave. More advanced than the Negritos were the two human skulls found at Wajak along the Brantas River in East Java. The first true ancestor of present-day Indonesians, Wajak Man was the earliest known *homo sapiens* found on Java; he lived about 10-12,000 years ago. Wajak Man might have been an Australoid type, who replaced the Negritos.

THE ANCIENT PEOPLES

Ancestors of the present-day Malay peoples of Indonesia had been living in Cambodia and Vietnam and were pushed towards Indonesia by population pressure from the north. Anthropologists say they came in two great waves, spreading through Sumatra, Borneo, Celebes, and Java. First came the so-called proto-Malayans (caucasoid Malays), possessing a neolithic level culture, and represented today by the Batak of Sumatra, the Torajas of Celebes, and the Dayaks of interior Borneo. Next the deutero-Malays (more of a mongoloid type) arrived. These were carriers of the more advanced bronze-age civilization from Indochina. They are represented in all the ports and coasts of the Greater Sunda Islands of Sumatra and Java. Both waves originate from the same stock of people, but the proto-Malay people were a culturally retarded stock who fled Indochina before they learned civilization. Today, generally speaking, the proto-Malays occupy the agricultural interiors while the deutero-Malays have settled the coastal regions. These two types in turn greatly mixed with the non-Malay earlier immigrants. Indonesian life was already well-established before Christ was born. Bronze and iron have been in use in some parts of Indonesia since at least 2500 B.C.; these neolithic peoples made huge bronze drums and chopping hoes. They knew how to grow rice, use bamboo pipes for irrigation, and buffaloes for drawing plows. These were matriarchal societies and organized villages under *adat* law. They could navigate by stars as far as India. They had animist beliefs and worshipped ancestors. There was puppetry, music, coil pottery, cloth, fighting arts. They absorbed war fleets, political systems, and religions.

THE HINDU PERIOD

Indian chroniclers wrote of Java as early as 600 B.C. and the ancient Hindu epic, the *Ramayana*, also mentions Indonesia. By the 2nd Century A.D. Indian traders had arrived in South Celebes, Sumatra and Java. At this time the stage was set for Hinduism. Bronze Age Indonesians had many culturally similar traits that made the Indian culture easier to absorb, they could assimilate Indian civilization and religion without feeling hopelessly backwards. Indonesians were ready to go beyond the confines of their culture, to advance. At the time of its colonialization, India was considered the pinnacle of civilization, at the apex of its cultural vigor. The local rulers of Indonesian feudal states most likely invited high caste and learned Brahmans to migrate and work as a literate bureacracy. Indian influence touched only the ruling classes, it had no significant impact on the rural people who have always leaned more towards animism. By the 4th Century, Indonesians were using the South Indian Pallava script to carve Mahayana Buddhist inscriptions. Sanskrit loan words found in the Indonesian language today indicate the specific contributions Indians made during their period of influence in the archipelago which lasted 1400 years: healing practices, astronomy, navigation techniques, the potter's wheel, horses and elephants, textile dyeing, plank boats and wheeled carts, figure sculpture and decorative arts, written literature, monumental architecture, spices for cooking (tumeric and cardamon). Many legal practices were carried to Indonesia, as well as numerous titles relating to social rank and regal pomp. The Indians spread the use of wet rice cultivation, which the Tamils themselves had mastered by 450 B.C. Sanskrit words such as *angsa* (duck) and *gembala* (shepherd) show that they introduced techniques of animal husbandry. Glass was also brought by the Indians: *kaca*, or mirror, is a Sanskrit word. But their most far-reaching and significant exports were metaphysics, philosophy, and the Hindu concept of a divine ruler with unchecked magic powers. The Indians practiced a more integrated religious system than what the Indonesians possessed at the time, a heirarchy of gods with specific roles to play. Indian missionaries took Buddhism to Indonesia at a time when it was declining in India itself. Though Hinduism and Buddhism were hard and fast enemies in India, in most instances in Indonesia these two religions lived in peace, blending and borrowing from each other. On the fertile ground of S.E. Asia, Mahayana Buddhism evolved into a new kind of polytheism. Sumatra remained primarily Buddhist, but Hinduism eventually took over on Java. In the 5th Century, Brahmanist cults worshipping Shiva had sprung up on Java and Sumatra. Temples were built to confirm the authority of the Hindu religious beliefs. By the 9th Century syncretism appeared on Java. That is, its followers regarded both Shiva and Buddha as incarnations of the same being. In the 10th Century students were sent to the great Buddhist University of Nalanda in N.E. India and Indonesians even went as far as Tibet for learning and philosophy. The Sriwijaya Hindu Kingdom rose in southern Sumatra during the 12th and 13th Centuries and exercised a wide sphere of influence over all of S.E. Asia. On Java, early Hindu states rose and fell — Pajajaran, Saliendra, Kediri, Singosari — most of them, although very rich and powerful, were mainly coastal empires. The Indonesian-Indian era reached its apogee in the 14th Century Javanese Majapahit Empire, the Golden Age of Indonesian history. Though it thrived for barely 100 years (1292-1298 A.D.), Majapahit was Indonesia's greatest state because it aimed at Indonesian unification and an Indonesian identity. Gadja Mada, the famous prime minister of this East Javanese empire, worked so hard in his life to unite all the islands that it took 4 people to do his job when he died. It was during this last great Hindu kingdom when Indonesian sculpture and architecture suddenly veered away from Indian prototypes and a revitalized native folk art re-emerged. When Islamic traders arrived in the 15th and 16th Centuries, they found all the great islands of Indonesia were a complex of well-established Indianized kingdoms. Even though Indian cultural traditions had ostensibly disappeared from the island of Java by the 16th Century (as a result of Islamization), much is still visible from Buddhist-Hindu times. The *kràton* courts of Solo and Yogya are today hardcore enclaves of Java-Hindu culture. The religion and culture of Bali, the *gamelan* orchestra, and the 5-note scale were also inherited from India. Many motifs and styles of the previous Hindu-Javanese culture permeate Indonesia art and on Java you can see gates leading to the mosques and cemetaries of the Islamic high saints constructed in Hindu-style. Indian epic poems have been adapted into living Indonesian theatre and their heroes dominate the plots. Place names of Indian derivation are found all over Indonesia. Indian scripts persisted until Indonesian was latinized in the 20th Century, and Sanskrit words still abound in many Indonesian languages. Indonesia's present state motto is a Sanskrit phrase. The national emblem of Indonesia, the largest and most populated Muslim state in the world, is the mythical bird *Garuda*-the mount of the Hindu God Vishnu!

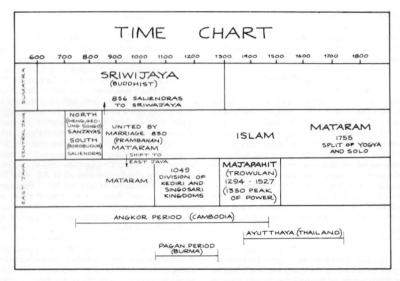

TIME CHART

	600	700	800	900	1000	1100	1200	1300	1400	1500	1600	1700	1800
SUMATRA		SRIWIJAYA (BUDDHIST) 856 SALIENDRAS TO SRIWAJAYA											
CENTRAL JAVA		NORTH (DIENG, GEDUNG SONGO) SANJAYAS SOUTH (BOROBUDUR) SALIENDRAS	UNITED BY MARRIAGE 830 (PRAMBANAN) MATARAM SHIFT TO					ISLAM			MATARAM 1755 SPLIT OF YOGYA AND SOLO		
EAST JAVA			EAST JAVA MATARAM		1049 DIVISION OF KEDIRI AND SINGOSARI KINGDOMS			MAJAPAHIT (TROWULAN) 1294 - 1527 (1350 PEAK OF POWER)					

ANGKOR PERIOD (CAMBODIA)

AYUTTHAYA (THAILAND)

PAGAN PERIOD (BURMA)

ISLAM

Arabs started arriving in Indonesia as far back as the 4th Century A.D., even before the birth of Mohammed (about 571 A.D.), to take part in the trade between India and China. In the 14th Century, the Mohammedans consolidated their hold in Gujerat in India and began to expand their trade considerably in Indonesia. This was the beginning of the Islamic period in the islands. Islam caught on in far northern Sumatra first, then spread to Java. The capture of Melaka by the Portugese in 1511 scattered Muslim merchants all over the archipelago, taking their faith with them even further afield. Islam took hold most solidly in those areas of Indonesia which had been least affected by the Hindu civilizations of the past: the north-central Java coast, Banten in West Java, and the Aceh and Minangkabau regions of North and West Sumatra. The Hindu princes of Java were probably first converted to Islam by a desire for trade, wealth and power. Principalities on the north Java coast employed skilful Arab harbormasters to merchandise for them and to run shipping warehouses. The *raja* would be converted first, then the people would take up the faith of the ruler wholesale. The converted rulers adjusted to indigenous pre-literary sentiments by permitting sultans to be worshipped as saints after death. Pre-Islamic signal towers became Muslim minarets and the native Indonesian meeting hall was transformed into a mosque. Rulers placed their royal

gamelans in the mosques and people came to listen, and stayed to be converted to the new religion. Demak in Java was the first important city to turn Muslim (in 1477), followed by Cirebon (in 1480). In 1487, a coalition of Muslim princes attacked what was left of the Hindu Majapahit Empire. By the end of the 15th Century there were 20 Muslim kingdoms over the entire archipelago and Islam was here to stay. What was the attraction of Islam? Indonesia is one of the few countries where Islam didn't supplant the existing religion by military conquest. Its appeal was first and foremost psychological. Radically egalitarian and possessing a scientific spirit, when Islam first arrived in these islands it was a forceful revolutionary concept that freed the common man from his Hindu feudal bondage. He lived in a land where the king was an absolute monarch who could take away his land and even his wife at whim. Islam taught that all men in Allah's eyes are made of the same clay, that no man shall be set apart as superior. There were no mysterious sacraments or initiation rites nor was there a priest class. Islam had great simplicity with its direct and personal relationship between man and god. Everyone could talk to Allah. Though Mohammed was His only Prophet, each follower was an equal of Mohammed. Islam also had a great political attraction. It was adopted by coastal princes as a counter to the threat of Portugese and Dutch Christianity, as a rallying point of identity. Islam first caught on in the early 16th Century as a force against Portugese colonial domination, then 100 years later as a force against the Dutch, always spreading just ahead of the foreign overlords. Islam is ideally suited to an island nation, a trader's religion which stresses the virtues of prosperity and hard work. It allows for high individual initiative and freedom of movement in order to take advantage of trade opportunities everywhere. The religion is tied to no locality and God can be worshipped anywhere, even on the deck of a ship. It was (and is) an easy religion to join, all that was needed was a simple declaration of faith, the *syahadat*: 'There is no god but Allah and Mohammed is His only Prophet.' It compelled a man to bathe and to keep clean, encouraged him to travel out to see the world (to Mecca), and, in short, exerted a modernizing, civilizing influence over the peoples of the archipelago. During the process of Islamization in the 15th and 16th Centuries, the arts were also deeply affected. The Indian period is known for its emphasis on the performing arts, but during the Islamic period the emphasis shifted more to the written arts. Arabic literary styles (and some themes) provided models upon which a local literature could be based. Stimulated by the sultans of the new central and north coast Javanese Islamic states, the textile-decorating arts and armoury flourished, as well as some high-quality decoration in plaster, stone and brick (at Sendangduwar, near Bojonegoro; and at Matingan, near Jepara). *Wayang* and *gamelan* went through their most refined development during the fully Islamic 18th Century. Because Islam prohibited the worship of idols (most of the seated Buddha heads at Borobudur were knocked off by Muslim vandals) and portraits of human beings, early Islamic art in these islands had to be made stiff and formal. Only trees and flowers could be represented, never living creatures. This prohibition has been the main source of uniqueness and intrigue in Indonesian art forms and even on today's *batik* you often see wings of birds and antlers of deer, but not the animals themselves. Because of the puritanism of Islam, Indonesia has a short tradition in painting and the public is still down on nude drawing and painting.

THE PORTUGESE PERIOD

The Portugese were the first bearers of European civilization to Indonesia. Carrying their god with them to be embraced by the heathens, they arrived in Indonesia a full 100 years before the Dutch. The Portugese period lasted only a century, from about 1512 A.D. Portugese was the *lingua franca* in the archipelago in the 16th Century and even Dutch merchants had to learn it in order to trade. Portugese involvement was strictly commercial and did not involve territorial expansion; they set up fortified outposts in sheltered harbors of islands to guard their trade routes and to offer respite and repair facilities for their fleets. Keeping the upper hand by virtue of their superior striking power and better navigation techniques, the Portugese were simply pirates who acquired tribute and booty, exploiting whatever commodities they came upon: slaves, pepper, gold, spices, ivory. The Portugese period was of small significance economically and had little effect on the great intra-asian trade route that stretched like a giant artery from Arabia to Nagasaki. In 1570, they murdered the sultan of Ternate in the hopes that they would gain favors with his successor. The inhabitants revolted and threw them off the island, the beginning of Portugese decline in Indonesia. What did they leave behind? For their numbers and for the brevity of their visit, they had a deep impact. Much musical influence is evident (*kroncong*, named after guitar strumming), and the Indonesian language is sprinkled with hundred of Portugese loan words: *mentega* (butter), *pesta* (festival), *garpu* (fork), *sepatu* (shoe), *gereja* (church), *meja* (table); as well as many geographic locations (Flores, Celebes, etc.). Tobacco was first brought from the New World by these medieval adventurers in the 16th Century. Portugese ship-building techniques and designs are still adhered to in Celebes and in many places in the eastern islands old Portugese helmets and spears are kept as family heirlooms by descendants. Large numbers of Florinese and Amboinese have Portugese blood. Scores of 16th and 17th Century Portugese forts are scattered around the Moluccas and the Lesser Sundas. East Timor, their last anachronistic stronghold in the area, gave out when Indonesian troops invaded and occupied that territory in late 1975.

THE ENGLISH PERIOD

In the early part of the 17th Century the English were direct rivals to the Dutch in the exploitation of the East Indies; they even kept outposts alongside each other in Banten, Macassar, Jakarta, and on Ambon. Although treaties made in Europe dictated that cooperation between the two companies were to be peacefully regulated, in the actual theatre of conflict the two were far from amicable partners. The underlying rivalry and enmity erupted at last on the island of Ambon in 1623 when all the personell of the English factory were tortured and executed. This 'Ambon Massacre' was heatedly blown up by the diplomatic circles of the time and vivid woodcut illustrations were printed in popular pamphlets which duly enraged the English public. Almost 200 years later during the Napoleonic Wars, Java was occupied (1811-1816) by English Expeditionary Forces and the sultan's *kraton* of Yogya was stormed and subdued. A young energetic Lord Raffles was appointed Governor. He immersed himself enthusiastically into the history, culture and customs of Indonesia, uncovering the famous Borobudur Buddhist temple and meticulously recording the cannibalistic habits of the Batak of northern Sumatra. But because England wanted to prepare Holland against attack by France and Prussia, most of the Indies were handed over again to the Dutch in 1816. Raffles tried to perpetuate British interests in the islands and to keep order; but within several Sumatra, but eventually the English abandoned Indonesia altogether and by 1824 had shifted their focus of power to Singapore. It is a fiction of English historical scholarship that during the English period many significant economic, land and humanitarian reforms were introduced. They made another brief and ignominious appearance on Java in 1945 to accept the official Japanese surrender of the islands and to keep order, but within several months they were accused by the Indonesians and the world of being pawns of the Dutch and had embarrassingly extricated themselves from their awkward role by 1946. The English presence lives on today in hundreds of words of English derivation found in *Bahasa Indonesia: stop* (stop), *bis* (bus), *mobil* (car), *universitas* (university), *pena* (pen); and in the name of Yogya's main street, Malioboro, a corruption of Marlborough, a victorious English general in the Napoleonic Wars.

THE DUTCH PERIOD

By the time European traders reached the East Indies in the late 16th Century, it had cities, monumental temples, government, irrigation systems, handicrafts, orchestras, shipping, art, literature, cannon-fire, harems, astrological systems. It was Europe that was undeveloped at this time, not Asia. The Dutch started as only a trading company, first entering Indonesia at Banten in 1596 in 4 ships which had lost 145 out of 250 men on the journey from Europe. When these ships with their valuable cargoes of spices returned safely to Holland, it touched off wild speculation. Backed by private companies, 12 expeditions totalling over 65 ships were sent to the East Indies between 1598 and 1605. To avoid rival Dutch companies from competing amongst themselves, the Vegeenigde Oost-Indische Compagnie was chartered in 1602, a private stock company empowered to trade, make treaties, build forts, maintain troops, and operate courts of law in all the East Indies lands. The Dutch did everything they could to isolate this closed world from all outside contact. They gained their first foothold in Batavia and within 10 years they were sinking all vessels in Indonesian waters, whether they be Indian, Malay, Javanese, Portugese, Japanese, Chinese, Siamese, Ammanese. The Dutch opened strategic fortified 'factories', or

trading posts, over the length of the archipelago to protect their interests. Internal Indonesian dynasties, continually feuding amongst themselves, were easy prey for such a strong external force, and by the 17th Century the Dutch found themselves the new masters of huge amounts of unintended and unexpected territory. Using a combination of arms, treachery, treaties and puppets, they became more and more involved in the internal affairs of Indonesian states. When sultans asked for Dutch arms and assistance to help put down a rival sultan or usurper, the Dutch would always gain more land in exchange for the help that they gave. Not content with mere trading as middlemen and carriers, the Dutch began to seek control of the very sources of production. New crop plants were introduced and a plantation agriculture was established and expanded. It was during their efforts to develop a coffee crop in West Java in 1723 when the Dutch first appointed supervisors to organize production, the beginning of a Dutch administrative system in Indonesia. A forced cultivation system, called in history the Culture System, was instituted by the Dutch in 1830, and soon not only coffee, but also sugar, indigo, pepper, tea and cotton were raised to supply the demand in Europe. During this period all of Java was turned into a vast state-owned labor camp run somewhat like the 17th Century slave plantations of southeastern USA. Javanese farmers were even starved to produce cash crops: In 1849-50 serious rice famines occured in the great rice producing area of Cirebon. The island of Java made the Dutch such profits that they were able to build railways, pay off national debts, and even to start a war with Belgium. The history of Dutch colonial rule was based on a racial caste structure: swimming pool signs read 'No Natives or Dogs'. Pick up any of the old phrase books: 'Master, children have entered the garden, sir.' and 'Don't just stand there! Answer me when I speak to you! Be off with you! Wash it again!' The formal position from which to address a Dutch master was from the floor. The Dutch regarded Indonesians as 'half-devil, half-child'; they carried their White Man's Burden with pride. In exchange for their work and for the wealth of their land, the Dutch would bestow upon them all the benefits of white civilization: their education, technology, social order, their arts, even let the Indonesians love their god. The hangover of the Dutch 350 presence is still with the people to this day. It is especially evident on Java which was colonized for the longest period. Tourists are still greeted with *Belanda! Belanda!* which originally meant Hollander, but now has come to mean any white person. And boys still call male travelers by the honorific *'Om'* which is Dutch for 'uncle'. The Dutch softened later in the early 20th Century with their humanitarian inspired Ethical Policy which showed more of a desire to begin a true partnership with the Indonesian people. By 1938 the Dutch owned and controlled over 2400 estates equally divided between Java and the outer islands. They never really thought about handing these regions over to the indigenous peoples and did little to educate them. Under Dutch rule no higher education was available until the 1920's when 3 colleges were finally started. By 1940 only 630 Indonesians were attending them and just 240 Indonesians graduated from high school. About 90% of the people were illiterate and only 2 million children were in schools in a country of 68 million. There was only one university in the whole archipelago, opened in Batavia in 1941.

NATIONALISM

Intellectuals and aristocrats were the earliest nationalists, the peasants have always accepted authority in Indonesian history, no matter whose. Diponegoro, the eldest son of a Javanese sultan, would have to be the first nationalist leader. In 1825, after the Dutch had built a road across his estate and committed various other abuses, he embarked on a holy war against them. The man was a masterful guerilla tactician, and both sides waged a costly war of attrition and scorched earth policy in which 15,000 Dutchmen and 250,000 Indonesians died, mostly from diseases. At one point during this war the Dutch even considered pulling out of Java. Diponegoro fought for 5 years until he was treacherously lured into negotiating and arrested. His face is now on coins, and street signs and an Army Division are named after him. Certainly he's become the nationalists' most important symbol. But it was the daughter of a nobleman, Raden Kartini, who first expressed publicly in the beginning of this century the right of Indonesians to have the same access to knowledge and western ideas as Europeans had. Although filled with self-pity at being a pampered princess, her *Letters* written to a liberal Dutch couple and first published in 1911 were sensitive, visionary and full of fire. They cause people in both Europe and Asia to wake up to the new spirit that was in the air. Indonesians knew that something was in the wind for Asia when little Japan defeated the colossus Russia in 1905. Indonesia didn't pass completely into Dutch hands until 1911, and as soon as the Dutch got it altogether, they started to lose it. In the mistaken belief that to-know-us-is-to-love-us, Indonesians were sent to Holland for education, and by providing education for Indonesians, the Dutch had made themselves redundant. By the time WW I came, a number of nationalist organizations had sprung up suddenly and almost simultaneously, indicating the extreme dissatisfaction that the Javanese masses had for the colonial regime. The Javanese were waiting for a *ratu adil*, a Righteous Prince who would free them from their oppressors. Budi Utomo (High Endeavor), formed in 1908, was a society whose members came largely from the western-educated Javanese elite. A religious organization called Muhammadiyah followed in 1912, an attempt to blend western technology and culture with Islamic thought. But these were intellectuals' societies and had little to do with the ordinary man. An organization of middle-class traders started the Sarekat Islam (Muslim Society) on a nation-wide basis in 1912. Originally intended to help Indonesian *batik* and textile businessmen meet growing Chinese competition, Sarekat Islam grew at a spectacular rate into the first mass political organization in Indonesia; by 1917 it had 800,000 members. Momentum was building up. The PNI (Indonesian National Party) was started in 1926, an ex-engineer named Sukarno as its chairman. With his oratorical power and dominating charismatic style, Sukarno soon emerged as Indonesia's most forceful political personality. PNI wanted complete independence for the Indonesian people, a government elected by them and responsible to them. It advocated this right through non-cooperation. But with the world depression of 1929, the Dutch were determined to make up for all their losses by increasing the exploitation of Indonesia's natural resources. A police state was imposed throughout the islands and increasingly repressive measures against nationalist leaders were becoming effective with men like Sukarno, Hatta, and Sjahrir arrested, exiled, released, then re-arrested. Anti-Dutch feelings grew. The Dutch broke up political parties and waived petitions. In January 1942 the Japanese landed troops on Celebes and Borneo and by early March they had overrun Java. The Indonesians were at first gratified that these other Asians had overthrown the Dutch. The Japanese at once backed the nationalists and orthodox Muslims, the two groups who had been most opposed to Dutch rule. The new masters even spoke reassuringly of one day granting Indonesia its independence. But the Japanese soon showed themselves to be even more ruthless, fascist and cruel than the Dutch had ever been. They were an occupying military power; workers were made to bow to Japanese soldiers and forced to wear identification tags. They conscripted tens of thousands of slave laborers who never returned and rounded up Indonesian women to work as prostitutes. Indonesia was included in their 'Greater Southeast Asia Co-Prosperity Sphere' which just meant that it was to be exploited of every possible resource. Jakarta was stripped clean of tons of wrought iron fences and ornament to be sent back to Japan and smelted down to make pig iron for the war machine. During their occupation, the Japanese encouraged Indonesian nationalism and allowed political boards to form, but only with the intention of using them for their own war aims. Sukarno was retained by the Japanese to help them govern the people and he used the opportunity to educate the masses, injecting them with nationalist fervor at every chance. The Japanese promoted *Bahasa Indonesia* in order to use it to spread their propaganda to the smallest villages. But the language only grew to become a gigantic symbol and became disseminated on an ever wider basis, unifying the islands even more tightly. The Japanese also created an armed homeguard which was later to become the revolutionary militia which would fight the Dutch upon their return. As the war progressed and the Japanese began losing the battles, more and more power passed into the hands of Indonesians. Eleven days after Hiroshima, on Aug. 17, 1945, Sukarno and Hatta declared independence and the Republic of Indonesia was born. The war ended, the British

were charged with the thankless task of disarming the Japanese and maintaining order. The shattered Dutch colonial army, weakened by the war, tried desparately to regain a foothold on their precious islands and even duped the English into fighting for them, culminating in the furious month long Battle of Surabaya. In January 1946, Sukarno considered Jakarta too vulnerable and moved the republic's capital to Yogya where he could depend more upon Yogya's powerful sultan for support. In April of that year negotiations began between the Dutch and the Indonesians to decide the question of independence, the Dutch only using the resulting pacts and treaties to buy time and to gain international support. Dutch troops embarked on 'pacification' exercises, attacking many key cities on Java and Sumatra in July 1947 and butchering thousands. In Dec. 1948 Yogya was bombed and strafed, then occupied by Dutch shock troops, Sukarno taken into protective custody again. End-

Panca Sila: *Indonesia's Coat of Arms. The Five Principles put forth by the state as a foundation of political and social rule; comparable to USA's Bill of Rights and England's Magna Carta. The 'Five Principles' are: 1) Belief in God. It doesn't matter which one — the Christian God, Allah, Budda, Magumbubingi — but you must believe. The mass support of this principle made the killing of a million 'atheist' communists much easier. The symbol is the star. 2) Nationalism: Symbolized by the head of a wild buffalo. All ethnic groups must unite and prosper. 3) Indonesian Democracy. Distinct from western-based democracy. Takes place on the village level to promote mutual help, discussion, agreement. Citizens must believe that Indonesia is a democracy. The symbol is the banyan tree. 4) Humanitarianism: The un-* *broken unity of mankind. Indonesia takes its place among the family of nations. Its symbol is the chain. 5) A just and prosperous society that will give adequate supplies of food and clothing for all, the basic requirements of social justice. Represented by sprays of rice and cotton. The Panca Sila is a synthesis of all the main intellectual movements of the modern world, another expression of the famous blending of philosophic and religious ideologies which have been operating in Indonesia for thousands of years. Rather than to actually promote the unity of the Indonesian people, different political groups have always interpreted these 5 principles to serve their own purposes. The Panca Sila has to be defined over and over again.*

less guerilla attacks were launched against the Dutch. Outraged, soon world opinion was rallying behind the new republic and the United Nations was applying pressures. It was also discovered that the amount of money the Dutch were spending to regain the islands and to crush the patriots was embarrassingly close to the sum which the USA had given Holland in Marshal Plan war reconstruction aid. After the US Congress decided that its backing was against US principles, the USA withdrew its support. Indonesian republicans controlled the highways, the food supply, the villages, and what they could not control they burned or blew up. Finally, on Dec. 27, 1948, the Dutch transfered sovereignty to a free Indonesia.

POST INDEPENDENCE

When the Dutch were at last ousted in 1948, the Indonesians had nothing — no teachers, no higher level civil service class, no national income, the mills and factories were closed or destroyed, there was serious fighting against secessionists and religious fanatics. As a constitutional democracy in the early 50's, the new republic turned over cabinets rapidly. The fifties are known for the chaotic bickering and dissension amongst the military, religious, left wing and conservative factions in the government. In 1955, there were 169 political parties formed up fighting for only 257 seats. In 1956, Sukarno declared his policy of 'Guided Democracy' and the creation of a National Council made up of members he would handpick himself. Sukarno stated that the age-old Indonesian tradition of *gotong royong* (decision through concensus) would be best suited for Indonesia as a way of hastening the cumbersome decision-making process. Political parties were abolished. The outer islands continued to prove unruly, claiming rightfully that the central government was neglecting them, and that Jakarta was becoming too leinent towards the communists. In Feb. 1958 West Sumatra and North Celebes revolted against the Jakarta centralist government, demanding more outer island Muslim-oriented autonomy. By calling themselves anti-communists they received aid, equipment and arms from the USA. A full-scale, though lachadaisical, civil war was under way and 70 army battalions had to be mobilized to suppress the insurgents. Sukarno landed troops on the eastern coast of Sumatra and in April 17, 1958 Jakartan troops took Padang, West Sumatra, and on May 5, Bukittingi fell. By the late 50's Sukarno was augmenting more and more power, press censorship was introduced, politicans and intellectuals were jailed. The Irian Jaya question was brought to a head in 1961 when the Indonesian president ordered amphibian landings and paratroop drops into this Dutch-controlled territory of West New Guinea. These forays stirred the UN to action, who prevailed upon the Netherlands to turn the territory over to Indonesian administration. Sukarno's government grew violently anti-American and militant, initiating a *konfrontasi* campaign against British controlled sections of Malaysia and North Borneo. Raiders were sent to attack the Malaysian peninsula and skirmishes broke out in northern Borneo between Indonesians, British and Australian troops. Sukarno alligned himself with Communist China, parroting their official anti-imperialist line, even cutting ties with the UN. For 20 years this visionary and mesmerizing leader had welded the islands together by adroitly playing off powerful groups against one another, his government a hectic marriage of widely disparate political ideologies. Sukarno had squandered billions on colossal stadiums, conference halls, and soviet-style statuary. The inflation rate was running at 650% per year, mammoth foreign debts had accumulated, opposed factions of the military, communists, Muslims and other groups were grappling for control of government. Prompted by the failing health of Sukarno, the rumor that the army was planning a purge against them, and partly because of the USA's increasing build-up in Vietnam, the communists made their move. In Jakarta on the night of Sept. 30, 1965, they abducted and brutally murdered 6 top generals and their aides. This abortive coup triggered one of the most massive relatiatory bloodbaths in modern world history. An unknown general named Suharto found himself at the end of the telephone, took the initiative, and mobilized the armed forces against the conspirators. Fanatical Muslim youth groups with army backing burned the PKI (Communist) headquarters in Jakarta to the ground. By the end of October, the army had crushed the communists' grip on Indonesia's cities. Over the following months all of Java ran amuck, resulting finally in the mass political murdering of perhaps one million people who were shot, knived, strangled, hacked to death. The Communist Party was obliterated and the army assumed leadership of the country. A complete ideological reversal then took place (and is still taking place). In 1966 Indonesia's *konfrontasi* with Malaysia was called off and a neutralist foreign policy was adopted. The Indonesian Congress announced plans to rejoin the UN. Although his implication in the plot was never made clear, Sukarno's power was systematically undermined by the army until his death in June 1970. Pragmatic, cautious, reliable, Suharto was born of humble parents in 1921 in a village near Yogya. A family man with 6 children, he is a mild-mannered speaker and keeps a low profile, a style which stands out in stark contrast to the flamboyant Sukarno . Suharto was just what Indonesia needed at the time.

GOVERNMENT

Indonesia has tried them all, practically every political reality: absolute kingship, extreme cultural conservatism, outlandish noisy political radicalism, noble revolution, Stalinist mass political butchering, parliamentary democracy, civil war, total anarchy, a hero against international aggression, and now generals with modern weaponry. You can't talk about any of Indonesia's beliefs, practices, ideals or institutions as being modern or old-fashioned because at the same time it is a progressive and a backward state — believing in myths, false messiahs, Marxist prophecy, solid traditional custom, archaic magic, chilling rationality. In modern times the concept of *Panca Sila* (Five Prin-

ciples) has become the foundation of civilized rule. These principles include: Nationalism, Humanitarianism, Democracy, Social Justice, and the Belief in God — a super-condensed constitution. Each regime tends to interpret each of these concepts in a way that will further their political goals. The old joke about Indonesian politics is 'If you understand the situation, you're obviously badly informed.' Indonesia is easily the most broken up country in the world and by its sheer expanse awesomely difficult to govern. There have been revolts in one part of Indonesia or the other for the past 25 years (presently in West Kalimantan). To bring all the diverse peoples of this

corruption: *Corruption is rampant in the Indonesian bureaucracy. President Suharto himself has always denounced komersialisasi jabatan (abuse of office). It is a difficult country to do business in. You must pay extra fees for business licences, for passports, for import licences, for customs clearance once the goods have arrived (if an Indonesian gets a job in the customs house, he's rich). As many as 18 different clearances might be needed on a document, all from different officials. Many foreign corporations are told to mail their cheques to numbered accounts in Switzerland. Everybody wants their cut. In order for Suharto to do something about this situation, he would have to begin by first dismantling his whole administrative apparatus.*

sprawling island nation together within the political and geographic entity called 'Indonesia' is still the greatest single problem facing its leaders. The 40-60,000 political prisoners only shows how much is below the surface and how deep this country's social disunity and differences are. On the state crest are the old Sanskrit words *Bhinneka Tunggal Ika*, 'We are many but we are one'. This line is played hard. One way the government chooses to spread national consciousness is through their fitness program *senam pagi* (morning exercise), practiced even in the most remote hill villages. The Indonesian language is another great unifying force. There is definitely a shared feeling of being an Indonesian, a pride in things characteristically Indonesian (Indonesianasi), and in their vast and beautiful native land. The gigantic conservatism of the masses — and the army — keeps the government in power. According to the 1945 Constitution,

elections for the two highest legislative bodies, the Parliament and the Peoples' Representative Council, are to take place every 5 years. But since 1945, general elections for these offices have been held only 3 times. Suharto was voted into his third term in May, 1977 (until 1983) and younger army officers are now being prepared for leadership. In the international politics game Indonesia is perhaps the only country in S.E. Asia with the potential of a major world power. The cannons and troops of its army coerced Portugese Timor (and its oil) into joining the Republic, neglecting to extend to that small state the right of self-government which Indonesia itself had fought so hard for 30 years previously. The country is changing fast, its isolation fast becoming a myth. The trans-Indonesian telecommunications system, completed in 1977, is putting Indonesia in even closer touch with the world and with itself.

PROVINCES OF INDONESIA

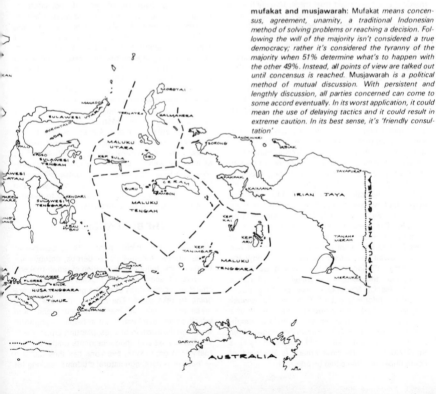

mufakat and musjawarah: Mufakat *means concensus, agreement, unamity, a traditional Indonesian method of solving problems or reaching a decision. Following the will of the majority isn't considered a true democracy; rather it's considered the tyranny of the majority when 51% determine what's to happen with the other 49%. Instead, all points of view are talked out until concensus is reached.* Musjawarah *is a political method of mutual discussion. With persistent and lengthly discussion, all parties concerned can come to some accord eventually. In its worst application, it could mean the use of delaying tactics and it could result in extreme caution. In its best sense, it's 'friendly consultation'*

THE ARMY

As is the case in many developing countries, Indonesia is a warrior's society. Although their soldiery often display a banana-republic appearance and lack of discipline, the military is this nation's only credible political power at present. The army calls itself the 'New Order' and the concensus is that eventually the country will be ready for permanent civilian rule, the military looking upon itself as a sort of temporary reform regime. Dads love to dress their little sons up in generals' uniforms adorned with medals and braids, and half the streets are named after soldiers or revolutionary heroes. Everywhere in Indonesia you see army officers in their Mercedes or shiny jeeps with furled flags cruising past the burdened peasants. Aristocrats with a new face. The army's continuing power and presitge is a leftover from its role in the early days of the republic when the civil administration was still disrupted after the rebellion against the Dutch. The army fought side by side with the people for their freedom and the people trust them. Usually there's an army level of command which corresponds to each function of the civil government from the village right up to the province. The army not only considers itself as a watchdog of the state, but also as a socio-political force which stabilizes the state and defines its objectives. But anybody knows that politics is much too serious a business to leave up to mere generals. The army is only a miniature Indonesia and it's just as regionalist and corrupt as the civil service and the business world. At its best, it's the peoples' friend. At its worst, it's a terrorizing and intimidating secret police. On Jan. 16, 1974, eleven students were shot dead in the Jakarta riots which were staged by a powerful general to discredit his rival; the rival subsequently lost his job. (The army has a history of organizing mobs of civilians demonstrators to get its way). All Indonesian dynasties since the 14th Century Majapahit have maintained their power through appearances. Each must only appear strong and invincible. The present government artificially suppresses the price of rice so that the people are at least able to feed their bellies. If the price of rice were allowed to go its own way and follow the careening inflation rate, there would be unrest throughout the land. As a traveler you'll notice definite fascist tendencies (like blacking pages critical of Indonesia out of Time and Newsweek magazines). And even if you stay as a guest of a family they must register you with the neighborhood police or the R.T. (Rukun Tetangga) within 24 hours. Reason? To avoid suspicion (and a Rp50,000 fine). The government is paranoid of communists and you could be one.

MUSJAWARAH AND MUFAKAT

Political life is built on very ancient customs of Javanese origin, *musjawarah* (discussion) and *mufakat* (agreement), methods of resolving political and policy differences by prolonged discussion ending in unanimous decision. It is each person's responsibility to state his views, taking part in all negotiations. This method goes very slow, but all points of view are brought together in one compromise agreement. Indonesia is not heir to the democratic tradition and Indonesians don't believe in the western-style type of democracy where the majority of 50 plus one gets their way. They think that this system isn't fair to the remaining 49 or less percent. The will of the minority is just as important as that of the majority, so everyone just talks himself out until all parties come to some accord, too exhausted or too hoarse to argue any further.

GOTONG ROYONG

Indonesia is made up of tens of thousands of villages and the tradition of *gotong royong* (village socialism) is the real basis of political rule. Having its roots in much earlier times, it is an all important principle in Indonesian life and it is greatly stressed. *Gotong royong* means the joint responsibility and mutual cooperation of the whole community to each of its members. When fire, flood, earthquake, volcanic eruption strike, when pipelines carrying water break down or a new dam needs building or an old dam needs repairing, *gotong royong* goes immediately into effect. Men usually work with their own tools and without pay. Sometimes neighboring villagers are expected to help. If a village follows this communal organization, no household will be at anytime without land to work or without employment to subsist. Anyone in trouble will receive help. A nation can be run in the same way and *gotong royong* could also be expanded to mean a military agreement as between two states.

THE BUREAUCRACY

You'll also find ample opportunity to observe at close quarters Indonesia's ponderous, octopus-like bureaucracy. Indonesia is a nation of graph-makers, builders of scale models, makers of production charts and projections of all the projects which are *going* to take place. The making of these charts takes many valuable manhours, labor and time which could have been spent in fields digging mud from canals, building bridges, planting crops. Plans are formulated and announcements made, but actually little get's done. Everyone has their uniform — harbormasters, agricultural students, parking lot attendants, etc. (this penchant inherited from the Dutch). Petty officials proliferate. For 350 years of their occupation the Dutch had given Indonesians virtually no experience in administration and government service above junior levels. Indonesian officials were allowed to decide most inconsequential departmental matters, but for the weightier decisions in affairs of high finance and politics the Dutch decided for them. Over 350 years there evolved a tradition of invariably allowing the more important decisions to go to the top and to settle only minor problems lower down the hierarchy, resulting in the extreme patriarchalism and painfully slow decision-making process in the Indonesian bureaucracy today.

JAKARTAN CENTRALISM

Government is centered on Java and it is also intensely Java-centered. Of the army's 47 top officers, 35 are Javanese. The Javanese are the new colonialists. It has been said that an elite of perhaps 2000 men manipulate Indonesian politics. With only a dozen or so exceptions, they all speak English, drive Mercedes, live in Jakarta, and are Javanese. There has always been tension and conflict between the seafaring mercantile Muslim states of the outer islands and the Hinduized bureaucratic powerful forces of Java. Java has come to represent the political interests of all the Indonesian islands, whereas the outer islands want a looser federation to ensure a more just distribution of the national wealth. Java's 80 million can't possibly survive on their own and if any of the richer outer islands get's uppity, Java sends bombers into the sky and assault troops ashore to quell at once any secessionist uprisings. There were serious revolts in 1958 in Sumatra and in North Celebes since Java took the revenues these islands were earning for its own survival and improvement. Recently the Javanese have been able to actually enforce their demands, for example, against the smuggling of goods from the outer islands to bordering countries for higher profits. The Javanese are transporting Balinese in *transmigrasi* schemes in the outer islands, then moving in and buying up land on Bali. It's now a deliberate government (Javanese) policy to constantly rotate all provincial chiefs of police as well as heads of military districts throughout Indonesia. This is aimed at preventing too much power from becoming consolidated in one man (Bapakism) and to check the possibility of any further costly challenges to the central Javanese government. The army maintains this same method of changing command posts of field officers in order to keep provincial power from becoming invested in army commanders. Not a single outer island command post is held by a native son.

THE ECONOMY

There is no doubt that the present government has pushed the nation upwards since the near economic collapse in 1965. Even a cigarette seller on the streets of Jakarta can now make Rp8000 a day. But this is only Jakarta. The average Indonesian still earns less than US$150 a year. Indonesia is one of the poorest of S.E. Asian countries because its wealth is distributed too unevenly and too many of its people are concentrated in only certain fertile areas. About 1.4 million Indonesians join the labor force each year (375,000 young men in Jakarta alone), and there is rising unemployment. The amount of 14 year old girl in Sydney spends on a pretty ring while shopping on Saturday morning a Javanese farmer must work for two weeks under the sun in a ricefield up to his armpits in mud. He walks over potentially one of the wealthiest countries in the world, though Indonesia's turbulent political history has so far prevented realization of its full economic capabilities. The Indonesian government receives considerable help — financial, technological, educational — from the Have Nations, almost to the point where they have come to expect it. This same attitude you'll meet with on the street when a man will ask you for a job or for money only because you appear richer than he. An old Indonesian proverb goes unheeded: 'He who gives rice for planting is greater than he who gives rice for eating. And he who teaches how to plant and grow rice is greater than either.'

NATURAL RESOURCES

Indonesia is one of the earth's richest mineral areas. Only 5% of its total land area has been mapped geologically in detail and offshore surveys haven't even got off the ground yet. Indonesia lies in the tin belt of the world, being the 4th largest producer Freeport Copper Co. mines copper in the rugged Ertsberg Mountains of Irian Jaya, probably the world's largest base metal reserves (33 million tons of high grade ore), producing over 65,000 tons of concentrates each year. In a time of growing petroleum shortage, Indonesia is a petroleum producer of great potential. Revenue from oil has increased ninefold since 1965. Indonesian oil has a relatively low sulphur content and is thus less polluting. Its easy access from relatively shallow pools and its close proximity to Japanese, Australian and S.E. Asian markets, all cause it to be in great demand, especially since the Oct. 1973 Middle East War and the subsequent oil embargo. Until 1975, Indonesia's mammoth state-run oil company (Pertamina) had grown rapidly, accounting for 65% of the government's non-aid revenue and roughly 70% of Indonesia's gross export earnings. This huge conglomerate empire had about 30 subsidiaries: real estate, shipping and port development, tourism and hotels, insurance, oil marketing, steel complexes, office buildings, 80 aircraft, and its tankers at one time added up to more tonnage than the Indonesian Navy. In 1975-76 it was disclosed that Pertamina had incurred international and domestic debts totalling over US$10 billion. Indonesia is still staggering from the collapse of this multi-billion dollar conglomerate, and the country has a long way to go before it digs itself out of the Pertamina recession. There are even more shocks

to come when additional debts of Pertamina fall due. In order to make up for the losses, the government in early 1976 pressured about 35 foreign oil companies into 'renegotiating' their production-sharing contracts so that the government's cut is now 85%. This move will net the government more income, but the Indonesian investment climate has soured as a result of it. Indeed, the whole S.E. Asian region is affected. Oil companies have laid rigs up, sent their oil survey ships home, called off contracts, and only a few are still looking for oil. This situation will drastically decrease oil production as existing wells run dry. As the demand for petroleum products increases over the next few years, Indonesia will have less and less of its most ready foreign exchange-earner at a time when it is most needed. Forests cover 300 million acres of Indonesia's total land area of 475 million acres (60%

RESOURCES OF INDONESIA

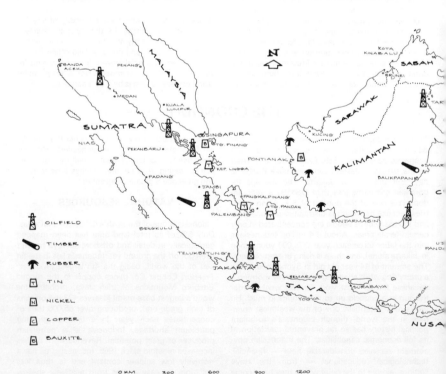

OILFIELD

TIMBER

RUBBER

TIN

NICKEL

COPPER

BAUXITE

0 KM   300   600   900   1200
KUALA LUMPUR   JAMBI   JAKARTA

of Sumatra, 77% of Kalimantan, 52% of Sulawesi, 75% of Irian Jaya and the Moluccas), and are now being rapidly plundered and not replanted. From only US$6 million in timber exports in 1967, there was a dramatic increase to over US$330 million in 1973 (12% of exports). At the present rate, in 28 years there will be *no* forests left. Agriculture constitutes approximately half of the GNP with about 35% of all arable land devoted to cultivation. Four out of every five Indonesians work the soil, the majority small farmers in rice growing villages. Of 40 or more commercial crops, only rubber, tobacco, sugar, copra, palm oil, hard fibre, coffee and tea are of national importance economically.

FOREIGN INVESTMENTS

Since 1966 the military government of Indonesia has been making a full and dangerous bid for foreign investment capital. International investment in Indonesia is taking place mostly in the robber industries: timber, oil, tin, bauxite, nickel, copper, all of which only go to feed hungry western manufacturing. One third of the industrial investment in Indonesia is American. Next to the US, Japan is its biggest foreign investor (the largest sign on the tallest building in Jakarta is TOYOTA). Obviously, all the new found revenue for Indonesia doesn't filter down to the people and foreign enterprises only participate in the consolidation of an unequal society. There's little sense of nationhood where big wealth is concerned. It's every man for himself. The very operations which are able to help, don't. Pertamina does precious little for the natives of the outer provinces from where they're ripping out so much wealth and profits in oil. Balikpapan is run-

the riches of Indonesia: *Indian traders were drawn to this lush archipelago as early as the 3rd Century. Beginning in the 13th Century Arab traders began to arrive, searching for riches and converts to Islam. Legends of the fabled spice islands of the Moluccas was the incentive behind the great waves of European exploration during the 16th Century, including Christopher Columbus. The Portugese, the Dutch, and the English all fought for control of these islands, with the Dutch at last emerging on top. They ruthlessly exploited Indonesia, first for its spices, later for its plantation crops such as coffee, sugar, rubber, tobacco, and finally, starting in the late 19th Century, for its untold deposits of offshore oil and other minerals: copper deposits on remote primitive Irian Jaya, bauxite in Kalimantan, coal deposits in Sumatra. Though the development of its petroleum resources has slowed over the last several years, the exploitation of the crucial mining sector — nickel, copper, bauxite, tin and coal — has increased to speed up the momentum of development.*

down and dirty, likewise anywhere else where the government sponsored robber industries operate — Irian Jaya, Billiton, Central Sulawesi. One often gets the impression that Indonesia isn't a nation, it's a private enterprise run by generals, or ex-generals turned businessmen. There are hundreds of foreign-based companies. These US, Japanese, Filippino and Australian industrial centers have become enclaves of foreign activity, not at all dependent upon the domestic economy. What is called a 'dual economy' is created, their own and the society's outside. The labor-saving technology of foreign companies doesn't create employment opportunities and they increase inequality by over-paying their employees. These companies have also become ideal springboards for US and other foreign multinational ventures. The absence of strikes gladdens them. Indonesia presents a potentially huge market for the manufacturing industries: transportation equipment, steel, telecommunications hardware, agricultural machinery, foodstuffs such as wheat and dairy products ('Peter's Ice Cream: The Health Food of Two Nations'). Surplus or out-dated commodities are dumped on the Indonesian market so that foreign companies can earn large profits. Many of their products like hair rinse, ice cream, white flour, are completely alien to village Indonesia, displacing local handicrafts, skills and products. Coca Cola (rots your teeth) factories are built in a society where delicious natural fruit drinks are available, potato chips are produced when Indonesians have nutritious *krupuk*, boot polish is sold on islands whose people have gone barefoot for eons.

CORRUPTION

Not only does corrpution exist in Indonesia, but it's a complex art; the perfection of rottenness. It is this rot that is eating away at the foundations of the nation's economy. You can be philosophical about the problem and argue that corruption is found in every country in the world, and that it's purely a western concept. But in Indonesia it permeates every level of government, from the lowliest post office clerk right up to the highest government echelons. Even the President's wife's business ac-

tivities are diverse and far-reaching. Using Chinese middlemen who handle most of the money, Mrs. Tien Suharto is rumoured to be involved in everything from flour mills, to cement plants and land speculation. For years she has been nicknamed Madame Tien Per Cent, though recently because of inflation she has become known as Madame Fifty-Fifty. There are further charges that other members of Suharto's family have used their well placed connection with 'Pak Harto' to gain profits, i.e. his brother was recently awarded a multi-million dollar clove importing deal. Corruption in part stems from the traditional Asian attitude of paying deference and presenting gifts to your superiors. Low salaries are another cause of corruption, as civil servants feel compelled to look for other sources of income to buttress their official salaries. A man of standing in the community must maintain an appearance of affluence — clothes, a car, comfortable living quarters, a ritual feast every so often. Furthermore he has weighty responsibilities on his Rp20,000-30,000 per month salary; to support relatives, send his kids to schools, etc. He *must* accept and seek bribes. Thus, Indonesia is a land where oil-king generals earn US$100 a month, then blow US$50,000 on a daughter's wedding. You can buy the captaincy of a ship (Rp500,000), or to send off a letter extra-fast at the post office (Rp100 extra). You must even pay the teacher in order that your child graduate from the 4th to the 5th grade. To get your child in to a government high school, the only channel by which he or she may enter a university, it'll cost Rp55,000 in Surabaya, Rp35,000 in Central Java, and as high as Rp75,000 in Jakarta for the privilege. The right amount to the right person at the right time is like putting oil on the big unwieldly machine. The government's 1,200-3000% pay increases which took effect in April 1977 were aimed at cutting down corruption and to narrow the gap between high and low income groups. Before April, the highest basic public salaries were 25 times the pay of the most junior civil servants. In April the salary of the lowest paid civil servants, about Rp4000 a month, soared to Rp120,000. About a million civil servants, armed forces personnel and pensioners benefited under the new salary scheme.

THE PEOPLE

Indonesia has the 5th largest population in the world — about 139 million — which equals the combined population of all the other S.E. Asian countries. There has been such an influx of peoples from China, Arabia, Polynesia, S.E. Asia, Indochina, and later from Portugal and Holland, that you can't say that Indonesia has produced one people. The country is in fact an ethnological goldmine, the variety of its human geography (366 ethnic groups) without parallel. Being a collection of local nations, many Indonesians identify themselves in local terms: *Orang Toraja, Orang Sawu, Orang Mentawai*, etc. This sense of local identity for one's tribe has fostered an attitude of tolerance towards other cultures summed up in the Indonesian expression *'Lain desa, lain adat'* or 'Other villages, other customs.' There are regional differences (between the devout matrilineal Minangkabau and the syncretic hierarchal Javanese); class conflicts (animist villager and orthodox Muslim landlord); racial minorities (Chinese, Eurasians, Indians, Negritos); religious minorities (Christians, Buddhists, Hindus); and local minorities (Kupang Buginese, Surabaya Madurese, Jakarta Amboinese). Indonesia has all the Asian cultures, races and religions; they worship Allah, Buddah, Shiva, and the Christian God — and in some places an amalgam of all four. Shades of skin vary from yellow to coal black. Many of Indonesia's ethnic pockets have remained isolated because of the archipelago's size, its jungles, swamps, highlands, complex customs. You can find ways of life which are 5000 years apart, a journey through time. Cross-sections of the people live in the Neolithic, Bronze, Middle, and Nuclear Ages. Some Indonesians wear rings and rats' ribs in their noses, others read Kafka and dance The Bump. If they have mingled at all, it took place from the sea. Many of the mountain tribes have never recovered from past invasions or migrations when they were scattered into the hills by conquerors who took over the richer valleys and coasts. The Kubu and Mamak tribes of Sumatra, the Punans of Kalimantan, and the Alfuros of the Moluccas, are all descendants of the so-called Veddoids from Central Asia who drifted into the archipelago from 7000-8000 B.C. They are still considered savages by the present local inhabitants of these areas. A theme in much Indonesian folklore and *wayang* is the constant struggle between highlanders and lowlanders, or between the good noble princes and the 'black giants' (the aboriginals of the jungles and mountains). Indonesians can be quite color conscious and many are outright racists. Village women and their little girls smear white powder on their faces to 'beautify' themselves and Indonesian women take all possible precautions against exposing their skin to the sun to prevent a fieldworker's complexion. It's thought that the darker the skin the more primitive the person is and the lower his or her class. People from Biak look down upon the Papuans from the mainland, urban Timorese regard the mountain people as stupid, and Jakartans hold themselves above the farmers of the countryside.

RICE

Ever since nomadic Malay hunter-gatherers turned settled farmers and started cultivating rice in the fertile ashes of burned forests and on the slopes of volcanoes, transforming their migratory society some 4500 years ago, rice has been at the very center of Indonesian culture. Grown virtually everywhere in Indonesia, it's considered the tastiest of all grains and is eaten at least 3 times daily. Rice is always saleable and can be stored up to 3 years. It's believed that rice has a soul without which it lacks the power to germinate. *Ani-ani* blades are hidden so as not to offend the rice goddess, Dewi Sri, during the harvest. The structure and pressure of this intensive form of cultivation has given rise to very close-knit families all over Indonesia, particularly on the island which supports the bulk of the population — rural Java. A family could include grandparents, grandchildren, father's relatives, mother's relatives, nieces, nephews, cousins. The nation as a whole is a family; presidents, *bupatis* and schoolmasters are often referred to as *Bapak* or *Pak* (father) or else *Bung* (brother) by the public. School mistresses are addressed as *ibu* (mother) by their pupils. The heart and soul of Indonesia is the village. 80% of the people live in 60,000 agricultural communities throughout the archipelago. Village life has changed only very superficially over the past thousands of years. The village council of elders is the foundation on which the Indonesian version of democracy is based. Village and family loyalties come before all others. City dwellers, only 15% of the total population, are the exception. But even the capital of Indonesia with a population of 5.7 million has all the habits and manners of a village, or actually, of hundreds of villages.

ADAT

This is the word Indonesians utter when you ask them a question about a custom which they practice and they don't know why or how it began. They just say, 'It is *adat*.' The closest thing to *adat* we have in the west is Common Law. Although it might not be obvious to the casual observer, this unwritten, unspoken traditional village law covers the actions and behaviour of each inhabitant in every village and city *kampung* in Indonesia. Evolving from a distant time when villages were largely self-governing, its dictates and taboos decide what foods are eaten and when, ceremonies and duties to the ill or dead, ownership of land and irrigation systems, architecture of family houses and granaries, criminal and civil cases such as theft and rights of inheritance, relations between older and younger brothers and sisters, the order in which daughters will marry, who they will marry, how they will marry, how guests are to be treated — everything, the total way of life. Over a period of thousands of years all the more elaborate and cultic *adat* have been ignored and only those are left now which cover the necessities of life. *Adat* helps to ensure peace and tolerance between all the various religious communities because they all have many *adat* in common. Being a self-contained law-of-the-village, *adat* is especially forcible at times of economic or political insecurity. It even serves as a sort of social welfare organization for new migrants to the city. *Adat* is rooted in religion, though it is not a religion. Indonesians say, 'Religion comes in from the sea, but customs come down from the mountains.' Islam was in many instances radically modified to fit in with *adat*-law. Rules and behaviour from imported religions have also become a part of *adat*. Some say that *adat* is a stranglehold on the people because it encourages superstition instead of reasoning, and that there is no progress because all actions are based on precedents. The product of centuries of habit, the original meaning of many acts and gestures may be lost, yet are rigorously performed without question. Change from within Indonesian society is very slow.

THE CHINESE

Indonesia's most important ethnic minority and largest alien group. In the Riau Archipelago Chinese make up more than one fifth the total population, and in Pontianak, West Kalimantan, the Chinese form 3/5's of the total. Although only 3% (3.5 million) of the total population of Indonesia, the Chinese control about 70% of the economy. They succeed in all fields: as professionals, bankers, moneylenders, traders, artisans, plantation overseers, shopkeepers, machine shop workers, mechanics. Chinese migrants were first brought in by the Dutch during colonial times to work as coolies. Later they were introduced to create a merchant class, enjoying many more privileges in the Dutch multi-caste society than Indonesians enjoyed. In the 20th Century, Nationalist fighters remember with bitterness the indifference and opposition with which most Chinese looked upon the revolutionary struggle. It's this very class of Indonesians who today form the civil bureaucracy and officer corp in the army. Thus there is much hostility against them. Other Indonesians resent and envy them for their wealth and business skills. Periodic purges — economic, social, physical violence — are perpetrated against them. The government prevents Chinese from settling in rural areas in large numbers nor are Chinese allowed to run their own schools, newspapers, or political parties. They may not keep dual citizenship and must even take on Indonesian surnames. Chinese characters have been erased, by government order, from all of Indonesia's Chinatowns. But you can't really define Chinese in Indonesia by racial, legal or cultural criteria, but solely on their social identification. The Chinese have adapted in different ways to the Indonesian environment. Hokkiens (found in West Sumatra and throughout East Indonesia), whose decendants came from southern Fukien, are today merchants and traders; Teochius (found in East Sumatra and in the Riaus) originally come from Swatow and operate most of the market gardens. Cantonese, mineworkers initially, have become skilled tradesmen, restaurant owners and hardware store owners. The Hakkas, an historically aloof mountain people from Kwangtung Province in China, were miners; now they have settled in West Java, Borneo, and on Bangka Island. In West Kalimantan the Hakkas have abandoned their age-old wet rice cultivation from China which used the plow, sickle and threshing box and have taken on the local Malay harvesting blade and the Dayak digging stick! Other Chinese have become thoroughly Indonesianized, having intermarried with Indonesians, many often illiterate in Chinese languages. The name for these Chinese-Indonesians is *peranakan* (Children of the Indies), a group which has evolved its own customs, law, dialect and cuisine. *Peranakan*-Chinese have lost more of their Chinese-ness than have most of the world's 23 million or so overseas Chinese; they are looser, funkier, less inhibited and reserved than for example Singaporean or Taiwanese Chinese.

LANGUAGE

Throughout these islands there are some 250 distinct languages spoken (about 40 language clusters), with many of these separated into different dialects. Often the inhabitants of the same island don't speak the same native tongue such as the Javanese and Sundanese on Java, and alone on the tiny island of Alor there are some 70 separate languages. Fortunately one language, *Bahasa Indonesia*, is taught in all schools from at least the 3rd grade. Each ethnic region of Indonesia speaks its own accented form of *Bahasa Indonesia;* the Javanese speak it very slow and monotonous while the Sundanese very sing-song, and the Irianese an archaic form taught by missionaries. The Indonesian language is the one cultural element that unifies the entire population. It is the only language used in official and popular publications, road signs, advertising etc. Just as you can use American in Scotland, if you learn Indonesian well you can use it all over Malaysia, Singapore, and in the Malaysian portions of northern Borneo. English is the most spoken foreign language in Indonesia. Many people over 40 on Java can speak Dutch, but not many can on the outer islands (except Ambon and Minahasa).

HISTORY

Bahasa Indonesia started as a trader's language for use throughout the Malay archipelago, a prototype of the old Melayu language which you can still hear spoken in its almost pure form in the Riau and Lingga archipelagos off the central-east coast of Sumatra. Sumatra's 12th Century Sriwijaya Empire caused the language to be widely spoken in the archipelago through its early and broad influence in the region. The Dutch from the start, deigning not to speak their own language, used Malay as the native language of government. In the 1920's a new literature sprang suddenly into existence with native poets such as Yamin, Effendi and Pane writing traditional sonnets but using Indonesian. Indonesian nationalists realized the need for a national language when they found themselves addressing their meetings in Dutch. They adopted *Bahasa Indonesia* mainly as a political tool in 1927 with the cry 'One Nation, One Country, One Language!' When the Japanese army occupied Indonesia from 1942-1945, they found it impossible to substitute their own language, so for purely political reasons they encouraged the use of Indonesian in native writing and art, and also in order to disseminate their propaganda over the islands. When the war ended, the proclammation of Independence was written and broadcast to the world in Indonesian. When Indonesia achieved nation-status in the 1950's, a modern version of the language was quickly developed and extended to apply to all the higher requirements of a fully modernizing, developing country — technical, abstract, literary, as well as serving all the needs of administration, law, scholarship and commerce. Today Indonesian has grown more involved, polite, dynamic than the Malaysian language. In modern Indonesian literature Indonesian has served quite satisfactorily for the expression of Muslim (Karta Mihardja's *Atheis*, The Atheist, 1949), Christian (Sitor Situmorang's *Si-nak Hilang*, The Lost Son), and Hindu (I Gusti Njoman P. Tisna's *I Swasta Setahun di Bedahulu*, I Swasta's Year at Bedahulu, 1938) beliefs and feelings. In its history it has devoured thousands of words from Indonesia's local languages, as well as from Arabic, Chinese, Dutch, Portugese, Sanskrit, Tamil, and English. A super-onomatopoetic language, *layang-layang* means 'kite' and *cemplung* means 'to drop into the water'. It is a poetic language: *matahari* means sun' or literally, 'the eye of the day', and it is picturesque: *bunga uang* means 'bank interest' (from *bunga* or 'flower' and *uang* or 'money')

LEARNING

A language can't be taught, it must be learned. The only way to learn to speak a language is to never speak your own. Avoid Indonesians who speak to you in English; they are your worst obstacles for learning their language. If you live with a non-English speaking family, you'll be semi-fluent after one month. You have to learn it, *to survive*! You must hear Indonesian spoken and practice it yourself every chance you get. It takes only several weeks to learn the sound system properly. Spoken Indonesian has the quality of song, especially when the 'r's' are rolled Spanish-like and when it's spoken in anger or joy. For conversation practice just head over to any *warung* and have a free 2 hour Indonesian lesson with the people. *Warungs* are the best classrooms in the land. Indonesians love to teach you and they are very patient, writing words out and breaking them down for you. They are also very encouraging, crying *'Wah, pintar sekali!'* (Wow, very smart!) if you just utter a few words. Using this method of studying with the people all you really need is just your dictionary. Find one that suits you (buy them cheaper in Indonesia). Don't go anywhere without it. Use it in combination with a good oral method and a good grammar book. Australian high school texts are usually good. For other helpful books, check the language section of the Booklist. An outstanding way to learn is with children; learn as they learn. Childrens' readers are well suited for learners because they are scaled down from the 8th or 9th grades to the first grade level. The language used is idiomatic and the contents have everyday applications. The lower the number (1 B opposed to 3 A), the simpler the text. Some you can almost follow by looking at the pictures; they cost only Rp100-200. When learning a regional Indonesian language, use *Bahasa Indonesia* as your learning medium: always ask for the Indonesian word for the *bahasa daerah* (local language) word. **Intensive Language Cour-** se: Each year from Dec. 20th, the Satya Wancana University of Salatiga in Central Java holds a one month course for Rp130,000. Registration closes in September. Some previous experience with Indonesian is a requirement. The cost pays for teaching materials, room and board, and group excursions to places like the Dieng Plateau and Prambanan. Contact either George Quinn, Dept. of Indonesian and Malayan Studies, Univeristy of Sydney, N.S.W. 2006, Australia; or Dr. Toisuta, Satya Wancana University, Salatiga, Java Tengah, Indonesia.

GRAMMAR

At first Indonesian might appear extremely simple to learn. It's a non-tonal language and there are no tense suffixes or prefixes, no cases, genders, or definite articles, no declensions, no conjugations, not even a verb 'to be'! Plurals are formed by just repeating the word (*desa*, a 'village', or *desa-desa*, 'villages'); or to amplify a condition (*pagi* means 'morning' and *pagi pagi* means 'early morning').

---

pantun: A very old traditional form of poetry handed down orally. Spreading throughout the Malayan-speaking world since Hindu times, some pantun are more than 500 years old. A pantun is a quatrain intended to be sung, sometimes to the accompaniment of musical instruments. Or the pantun could stand alone as a poem. Usually it takes the form of satire, to point out a moral, to humor, or to instruct. Often the first pair of lines describes a scene, an object, or an event, while the second pair describes an emotion. Both pairs of lines, contrasting greatly in feeling, are linked by a parallel being drawn between the external or tangible world and the internal emotional world. Some pantuns are quite elegant and contain the passionate impact of a haiku, others are reminiscent of love poems found in all of the world's great languages. There are also pantuns which are like the Psalms of the Bible, they have that same evocative supernatural religious power.

> Buah berembang masak ranum,
> Masak di-peram dalam gua.
> Kumbang lalu bunga tersenyum,
> Sa-ekor belalang tumpang ketawa.
>
> The berembang fruit is fully ripe,
> Kept till ripe in a cave.
> The flower smiles as the bee passes by,
> The grasshopper joins in laughing.

This pantun employs at least 5 symbols. The fruit is an Indonesian girl. Masak di-peram is the keeping of a marriageable girl cooped up at home. As the boy passes by her house he may not speak, but he looks, and the girl smiles at him, and an odd little fellow who happens to be with him joins in the glory of that smile. The grasshopper is the symbol of a small person of no significance.

Unlike English the adjective comes after the word refered to, for example *kopi manis* means 'sweet coffee'. Indonesian was designed to be simple and streamlined for the masses, and to learn enough to get by is easy. But to speak it well, it is as difficult and as sophisticated as any of the world's great languages. It has its complexities: there is a vast jungle of prefixes and suffixes with consequential consonantal changes that work very puzzlingly on you for months. Finding the root of the word is troublesome. But in one month you'll be talking the 'market talk' or *bahasa pasar*, all that you'll need for bargaining, dealing with the environment, relating to people. You can get along for weeks with just *sudah, belum, sekarang, sebentar lagi, terlambat, mandi, tidur, makan* (already, not yet, now, in a little while, too late, wash, sleep, eat) but the very lack of obvious rules in the language makes it more difficult to speak it correctly and to express yourself in a natural way.

spelling: Indonesian is written in the Latin script and has 21 letters. Spelling is strictly phonetic and small children after only 2-3 years at school can read adult literature aloud to their grandparents. In 1972 Indonesia simplified its spelling, though the pronounciation remains the same. Sometimes the old spelling is still used on road signs, maps, and in publications. In the new spelling, every '*j*' becomes 'y' (as in yarn), every '*dj*' changes to 'j' (as in jam), every '*tj*' to 'c' (as in chair), '*ch*' to 'kh', '*nj*' to 'ny', and '*sj*' to 'sy'. There are variations in spelling everywhere you go. Many Javanese words change 'o' for 'a' when translating to Indonesian; Diponegoro becomes Dipanegara and Solo becomes Sala, etc. If you come across any Indonesian words on maps or signs which were transcribed using Dutch sounds — like Bandoeng — then 'oe' becomes 'u'; except peoples' names, being sacred, don't change.

RELIGION

All of the world's great religions have come to these islands at one time or the other and the Indonesians have absorbed them all, in some cases making them even more complex, in other instances making them almost unrecognizable. Islam is the professed religion of 90% of the Indonesian population. Despite the fact that Protestant and Catholic missionaries have been going full at it for centuries, there are only 8 million Christians in various pockets throughout Indonesia. In Flores, which has had strong Portugese influence, the majority of the inhabitants are Catholics. In Minahasa, North Celebes, 90% are Christians; in Ambon, South Maluku, 50%; and in the Mentawai Islands off the west coast of Sumatra, 50% are Christian. The Chinese of Indonesia are either Christians, Taoists, Confucianists or Buddhists. The 2½ million people of Bali are Hindu, or to be more precise, Bali-Hindu. There are huge areas where just animists live. Animism, the belief that everything that exists has a hidden power, cuts through everything most Indonesians do and think, no matter what their professed religion. All over Indonesia people are strongly influenced by the spirits of rice, trees, rocks, rivers, the sun, the rain, and other natural phenomena. Mountains in many places are still considered seats of the gods, full of mysteries, the source of fertilizing water and soil, the border between the human world and the world of the dead. Mountains are dangerous, always to be appeased. In Indonesia the sea unites and the land divides; coastal Muslims have much more in common with each other than they have with their more animistic fellow believers inland. Many of In-

donesia's highland, jungle, or swamp people have been cut off from the coastal peoples for centuries, retaining their own superstitions and singular methods of slash and burn cultivation or hunting and gathering (the Kubus of Sumatra and the Alfuro of Ceram). Other animist group such as the Badui and Tenggerese of Java and the Torajas of Celebes retired to the interiors long ago rather than adopt the newer Muslim faith which came to the archipelago progressively from the 13th Century onwards.

HISTORY OF ISLAM

Mohammed, the founder of Islam, was born in 571 A.D. and began his teachings in 612 A.D. This man meditated in caves to gain wisdom, and he was also a fierce and skilled swordsman. By welding together an early Hebraic kind of monotheism with a latent sense of Arab nationalism, this religion began to gain adherents in Medina, Arabia, around 622 A.D. Mohammed didn't claim any supernatural powers but preached that he was God's only teacher and prophet, charged with the special divine mission to interpret the word of God. The scripture of Islam is the sacred book, the *Koran*, said to be a legal document inspired by God Himself, 'the will of Allah'. Compiled from oral and written records of the revelations and utterances of Mohammed put together shortly after his death, the *Koran* is a medium-sized book divided into 14 chapters. All its verses are preceeded by the phrase 'God has said...' to indicate that Mohamed's role was only passive. Every word in the *Koran* is believed to have come from Mohammed's own lips: 'God is as close to you as your jugular vein.' Much of this holy book outlines codes of behaviour. Themes emphasized in it are God's mercies to man, man's ingratitude and misuses of God's gifts, evidences of God's creative powers in nature, bliss of paradise (where every Muslim male will receive 13 virgins), the dead being reborn, the Day of Judgement, punishment of followers who go astray and the horror of hell, the missions of former prophets (including Christian prophets). Mohammed's teachings were heavily influenced by Judaism and Christianity and even today there are uncanny similarities between the two religions. Every man must account for all his earthly deeds. There is a hell and a heaven. There is only one true god and one true prophet. There are even Judaeo-Christian myths present in the *Koran* such as Noah's Ark and Aaron's rod. The Story of Creation in the Koran is strikingly similar to the Christian account, with an expulsion from the Garden of Eden and the eating of the forbidden fruit. Basic social institutions like marriage, divorce, and inheritance are defined in great detail, somewhat like a law book. This holy book contains much wisdom. Once, when someone asked The Prophet how he could best serve the memory of his dead wife, Mohammed answered him, 'Build a well.' The *Koran* was put into final form in 644-655 A.D. Starting in the 7th and 8th Centuries, a fury of holy wars expanded the borders of Islam far beyond Arabia to Spain, the Middle East, Persia, India, Indonesia and even as far as the Philippines. Although originally designed to foster a religious community and to overcome the different factions and jealousies of 7th Century Arab tribalism, gradually over the centuries a system of theology and law evolved. Initially there were no sacraments, formal rituals or priesthood, but in time Islam evolved *imam*, who lead prayers in mosques, and *mullah*, who teach the word of Allah. A distinctive Islamic civilization was created. *Kathis* and *shariah* courts administering Islamic law came into being, and rituals were introduced such as the washing of hands and face, divine congregational worship 5 times a day at a mosque, recital of the creed, fasting annually in the month of *Ramadan*, almsgiving, and the pilgrimmage to Mecca. Islam reached Indonesia in the 13th Century, carried into the region by peaceful Gujerati merchants and not by fanatical Arabs, more than 600 years after its birth in the Middle East. Islam had really mellowed out by the time it had reached Indonesia, dipping into Persian and Indian philosophies along the way. When it came it wasn't as austere a form as was found in the Middle East, but a more personal, mystical salvation-conscious sect from Persia called Sufism which practices a more emotional approach to God. It wasn't until 1869 with the opening of the Suez Canal when orthodox Islam finally entered Indonesia. More and more Indonesians could then visit Mecca, bring back with them the Arabic Islamic way of life, setting up theological seminaries upon their return. The areas in Indonesia today which practice the most orthodox forms of Islam are far away from the regions where the ancient Hindu-Java civilizations developed: Ternate in Maluku, the north coast of Java, Banten in West Java, Aceh Province in the northern tip of Sumatra, and the Minangkabau region of the west coast of Sumatra.

WHAT IS ISLAM?

The best possible preparation you could have in the understanding of this religion is simply to read the *Koran*. There's been little change in the core of Islamic religious thought over the past 500 years. The word Islam means 'submission'; this oath demands that you unconditionally surrender to the highest wisdom of Allah. This religion is much more than just a belief system, it's a way of life, a system of society, philosophy, law, science, art. At its best, it's democratic and egalitarian. Devotion is the responsibility of the individual and there are no social prerequisites or hierarchal structures. Islam is bound to no locality since a man may worship in a ricefield, home, prayerhouse, or on a mountaintop. It compells people to travel to Mecca and to use individual initiative and thereby independence. The confession of faith in orthodox Islam, *La ilaha illa llah*, means 'There is no God but Allah.' It's a fatalistic religion, if something goes wrong, 'Allah willed it.' Islam is a moralistic religion and its followers are required to lead moralistic lives. If done correctly, the reading of the *Koran* and the postures of praying demand great precision.

ISLAM IN INDONESIA

All aspects of Indonesian life reflect Muslim traditions. Friday is a half-working day to allow worship in the mosques from 11 am. Many men have more than one wife. Arabic is learned in all Muslim schools so that the *Koran* may continue to be read and studied by successive generations. There are Muslim greetings and gestures. Scrupulous attention is given to cleanliness. The pig is considered unclean and is not found in Muslim areas. The white *peci* wearers, *haji*, who have been to Mecca and kissed the black stone in the Ka'ab seven times, are greatly respected men. Though many younger men would rather buy a Suzuki motorcycle or travel to West Germany with the money, there are also those who save up constantly for this pilgrimage. Every town on Java has a *santri* (orthodox) quarter, called the *Kauman*, usually near both the main mosque and the central market and most often inhabited by traders and craftsmen. Roughly ⅓ of all Javanese are *santri* Muslims. There has always been conflict in Indonesia over those who want to see it turned into a more fundamentalist Islamic state and those who want to promote modern life. Orthodox right wing Muslims demand that the whole population observe religious holidays and that the government protect and encourage Islam. Two of the most serious rebellions since Indonesia gained independence have been Muslim-fomented, and several times Muslim extremists tried to assassinate President Sukarno. Since the 1972 elections, however, when there was a forced merger of 4 Muslim political parties into the United Development Party (PPP), Muslims have lost much influence. Senior generals around Suharto view Muslim militants as security risks and dislike the idea of a potent Islamic bloc in the People's Representative Council, the nation's highest policy making body.

ISLAM AND ADAT

Dogma has never had the importance to Indonesians as the ritual and social aspects of religion. Today Indonesian life conforms more to pre-Islamic animist and Hindu-Buddhist ways of life than it does to the precepts of the *Koran*. Indonesians are preoccupied by mystical and devotional matters, their spiritualism eclipses the

basic rationalism of Islam. Indonesia is a country where even its president believes in mystics and omens. Subversive groups have often masked themselves behind religious sects and gained much influence because the Indonesian masses are so spiritually vulnerable. In Oct. 1976 a mystic bent on succeeding Suharto secured the signatures of prominent figures such as Dr. Hatta, the co-signer of the Independence Proclammation, in order to give authority to his cause. High public officials in Java still seek *wahyu* (divine revelation and guidance from above) through meditation and seclusion. Suharto avidly sought and won re-election in 1977 in an attempt to restore *kerukunan*, a sense of harmony to his heavenly mandate to rule, which has been shaken after 11 years on top by such omens as earthquakes and two plots against the government in 1976. In Yogya, Central Java, the sultan is still looked upon as a god. Although the official state religion is Islam, many Christians sit in the cabinet and in high army commands, while Sunday is the official government holiday. Everywhere in Indonesia, Islam is practiced with a peculiar twist of its own. Many Indonesian mosques lack minarets and instead have cupolas shaped like onions. Few Indonesians can actually understand Arabic. Not many Javanese Muslims perform strictly the precepts of Islam: the 5 prayers a day, almsgiving, fasting, pilgrimmages, and so on. The word for prayer, *sembahyang*, comes from the Buddhist

'The dalang *and the puppets, the* gamelan, *the banana trunk that holds the puppets, the screen, the lamp — are all united in one being. The* dalang *is life itself. The body, acting and speaking, is the puppet appearing on the screen of the world and moved by that life, the* dalang. *The entering of the* suksma *(soul) into the body is the entering of the* dalang *into the puppet. So we are all dominated by the* suksma *in us, which is life itself. Our life story is the plot of the* wayang. *We are the spectacle ourselves. Who is the spectator? The spectator is the witness of all that lives...'*

Wiratjapa, a wandering 19th Century
Javanese mystic

sembah which describes the hands pressed together with the fingers extended, touching the chest, lips or forehead. *Puasa*, the Indonesian word for the Muslim fast, is actually a Sanskrit word still used in India. Respect for the dead in most of Indonesia isn't shown by veils but is expressed by wearing one's traditional dress. The Indonesian woman is more advanced socially, economically, and politically than any of her Islamic sisters in other 3rd World countries. They are not in *purdah* (wear facial veils), they are not segregated, and they are not considered 2nd class citizens. Sometimes special mosques are built for women. There are also numerous matrilineal and matriarchal societies. The *adat* laws of the devout Minangkabaus of West Sumatra allow matriarchal rule which conflicts sharply with the male supremacy inherent in Islam. Throughout Indonesia the female initiates divorce proceedings. This agreement between spouses is part of the marriage contract, a heresy in any other Islamic country. Java was a Hindu-Buddhist island for over 1000 years and there are strong traces left of Buddhism and Shivaism. In spite of the fact that East Java is overwhelmingly 'Muslim', everywhere you see the Hindu split-temple gateway (candi bentar) copied from Hindu times. Although the Hindu-Buddhist blend reached its zenith in the 15th Century Majapahit Empire, the faces on Indonesian Christian crucifixes seen today have the same knowing half-smile as Buddah. The fertility symbol Dewi Sri of animistic origin is dressed in Hindu clothing. Among some Islamic groups of Sumatra trance dances are connected with Islamic mysticism. Mysticism is today very much alive and well on Java and there's still a very brisk market in newly published or reprints of old editions of Javanese esoteric wisdom and other mystico-religious books. In Bali and Solo, Central Java, travelers may study meditation under Buddhist and Sufi teachers. Ritual meals, *selamatan*, are attended by neighbors and friends to appease the spirits. Witch doctors, *(dukuns)* exorcize evil spirits from grandaries and temples. Thieves use black magic to rob houses. There are devils and satans, ghosts which steal children (wewe), and lure young men (puntianak). There are daylight spirits (banaspati), angels of God, and even one angel who went astray, Idyadril. In isolated Kalimantan, like 5th Century Europe, wraiths of smoke are taken for ghosts. On Ambon, priests (mauwang) work harmoniously right alongside Christian or Muslim religious leaders of a village. The staunchly Islamic Makassarese of South Celebes worship ancient pieces of regalia such as large stones, flags, swords, umbrellas, plows, making regular offerings of food and betelnut, and on important occasions animals are even sacrificed to them. Catholics of Yogya use *gamelan* music to celebrate mass and many Christians of Kalimantan pay homage to God by spitting. Christians of Torajaland, Celebes, sacrifice bulls to the memory of a dead *raja*. It's easier to learn when religions began in Indonesia than it is to know when they ended.

EVENTS

90% of Indonesians are nominal Muslim and their religious holidays dominate the festival calendar. First off, get ahold of a calendar of events for the current year at the Government Tourist Bureau; the regional tourist offices might hand out a list of annual events as well. A good Javanese calendar also has the observations shown on it. The European calendar is based on the earth going around the sun whereas Muslims base theirs on the moon going around the earth. Thus their festivals move backwards through the solar months, the dates varying from one year to the next by approximately 11 days. For example, one year *Leberan* is held on Sept. 3rd and the next year it's on Aug. 23rd. The Balinese calendar is based on yet a different system. Being Hindu, Bali has festivals all its own. And this goes for all the ethnic groups of Indonesia; each holds their own celebrations. On Good Friday, Portugese descendents on Flores carry a statue of the Virgin Mary in a barefoot procession with grass pompoms, black costumes, and triangular shaped caps — a tropical slant on this Roman religion. The Tenggerese of East Java throw live bulls and chickens into a molten crater to placate the gods in the once a year *Kasada* Festival. And on remote Sumba Island mock battles and jousting matches are held each April, harkening back to an era of internecine warfare. Because of the heat, Indonesians celebrate most of their ceremonies early in the morning or late at night. On holidays people come out in resplendent white clothes or bright new *sarungs* or *kebayas*, immaculately groomed. Some of the more important, Java-oriented, holidays are:

Ramadan (or *Puasa*): The 9th month of the Javanese calendar. It is preceeded in Java by *Padusan*, a cleansing ceremony to prepare the spirit for the coming fasting month. Islamic fasting is more subtle than the drastic Hindu custom of total abstenance from all food and drink, Gandhi-style. Muslims are more into a moon-cycle. The whole family rises at 4 am, gorges themselves, then eats nothing during the daylight hours. Many visit family graves and royal cemetaries (Kota Gede and Imogiri on Java) where they recite prayers, strew flowers and holy water, burn incense. Special prayers are said at mosques and at home. Brand new velvet *pecis* are sold everywhere on the street. *Ramadan* is practiced with varying severity throughout the islands. Usually the only places to eat during this time in Islamic areas are dark, hidden, secretive back alley places.

Lebaran (or *Hari Raya*): The Arabic Idul Fitri. The first day of the 10th month of the Arabic calendar marking the end of the Muslim fast. *Lebaran* is an outburst of celebrations climaxing a month of pent-up tension and austerity. After tom-tomming all night long, the celebrations usually begin at 7 am when everyone turns out for an open-air service in the village square. Women dress in white, like nuns, and mass prayers are held early in the morning of the first day followed by 2 days of continuous feasting and public holidays. Verses are sung from the *Koran* and sometimes there are religious processions. Gifts are exchanged. A householder buys new clothing for his servants and the children are given new clothes. *Leberan* is a joyous time for mutual forgiveness when pardon is asked for all wrongs done during the past year; kind of like Christmas, Valentine's Day, and the New Year's resolutions all rolled into one. With everyone dressed in their finery, this is a time for Muslim Indonesians to visit and revisit neighbors and relatives, bringing gifts of specially prepared food, the best the family can afford. At each house a cup of tea is served with a sweet doughy cake and helpings after helpings from selections of bright cookies until you burst. *Lebaran* continues until all the visits to relatives are ended. A big family could celebrate *Lebaran* for as long as a week.

Al'qur'an: Sacrificial ceremonies. A famous festival which corresponds to an Arabian event. In Yogya it is called *Garebeg Besar*; it's celebrated on a lesser scale also in Solo, Jakarta, Cirebon, Demak (centering around Demak's ancient mosque) in Java. In Medan, North Sumatra, the Sultan of Deli takes part in a traditional Malay court.

Idul Adha: The Muslim day of sacrifice held on the 10th Day of the 11th month of the Arabic calendar when devotees visit the mosque. Those who are able, attend special ceremonies in Mecca.

Maulid Nabi Mohammed: The birthday of Mohammed held on the 12th day of the Arabic calendar. Also called *Hari Natal*.

Mi'raj Nabi Mohammed: Celebrates the Ascension of The Prophet.

Proklamasi Kemerdekaan (Independence Day): A public holiday which marks the anniversary of Indonesian independence from Holland, declared in 1945. On August 17th, celebrations take place all over Indonesia. *Proklamasi* is the biggest Indonesian national holiday, celebrated differently on each island. In Aceh there are Arab ceremonies; in Wamena, Irian Jaya, Papuan tribal dancing and athletic events; in Manado, North Celebes, parade floats applaud the growth of industry. There are dances, public entertainments, performances. The tradition is for kids and youth organizations to take part in the festivities with parades and marches, and for the older generation to look on. Go out to the *kampungs* where village sports and games take place. Many of the resort towns and hill stations are crowded with domestic tourists at this time.

Bersih Desa: Takes place at the time of rice harvesting. Houses and gardens are cleaned, fences white-washed, village roads and paths repaired. Once enacted to remove evil spirits from the village, *Bersih Desa* has lost most of its ritualistic significance and now expresses gratitude to Dewi Sri, the rice goddess.

Kartini Day: Kartini was Indonesia's first womens' emancipationist. Her collection of published letters written to close Dutch friends at the turn of the century are now a modern classic. In them she poured out her feelings about the restrictions imposed on her life by the feudal Javanese *adat*-system. She had had a formal Dutch high school education and was offered a Dutch scholarship. Then, instead of continuing her education, she was given in marriage. Kartini died in childbirth, age 24. There are parades, lectures, programs, and social activities attended by women, schoolgirls, university teachers, female workers, members of womens' organizations, all wearing their regional dress. Like Mother's Day, mothers aren't allowed to work, kids and fathers do the cooking, washing, housecleaning, etc. Many go on a pilgrimmage to the grave of Kartini near Rembang, Central Java.

CRAFTS

With its giddy variety of insular environments, Indonesia is unique as a place where so many beautiful things are made. Because of the tropical climate, stone temples and megaliths are the only remnants of their ancient art, the art of priests and aristocrats. The art of the common peoples' everyday lives—cloth, papyrus, palm leaf offerings, wood structures—have long since decayed. But the motifs survive. Designs and techniques of prehistoric painters and sculptors are still widely used in textiles, metal objects, and woodcarvings on houses and *prahus*. Fish with human faces which were carved on Prambanan stone reliefs 1000 years ago can be seen today in South Balinese paintings. Nothing is destroyed and everything is preserved in Indonesia. Superb craftsmanship and the longest traditions are best seen in the simplest crafts: the palm woven designs of Bali, the flutemaking of the Torajas, the basketry of the Rotinese, the lizard motifs on Batak magic wands and houses, and infinite other examples of traditional domestic and cultic art. **Note:** Visit ASRI (Schools of Fine Arts) in the larger cities where painting, sculpture, drawing, graphics and the decorative arts are taught.

BUYING AND TRADING

Go directly to the town or island where the item is produced because there's a much wider selection and the artisans are more agreeable to bargaining than shopkeepers. Many villages specialize in their own crafts. Don't let anyone take you into a shop because their commission will be tacked on to the price you pay, and they sometimes make a lot of trouble demanding their cut. Shops which are working on a low overhead don't want anything to do with them. You can spend 3 hours in an Indonesian shop unfolding and examining every single piece of *batik*, then leave with just a *terimah kasih* and no hard feelings (try this in money-fixated Singapore). Bring western clothes only for trading, and just one change of clothes to get on the plane with. Eventually you'll replace all your clothes with really cheap and lovely Indonesian-style garments which you can have tailor-made (be your own designer). Your safari-style jean jacket could fetch as much as Rp7000 in Indonesia, either in cash or in trading value, but jean trousers don't have such a high barter value any longer because everyone's got them.

TEXTILES

At one time over much of Indonesia, textiles had a religious importahce. Sundanese women weren't allowed to marry until they had woven a *samping* and Pekalongan women used to spend half the night meditating and burning incense before starting work on a *batik*. Organic dyes were sometimes made from the blood of human sacrifices. Even today *sarungs* are often wrapped around the bride and bridegroom to symbolize unity, spread over a seriously ill person to increase his power of resistence, and the dead are honored by being covered with precious textiles. Indonesian artists love animal motifs, buffaloes, elephants, crocodiles, snakes, lizards; dragons, lion birds, and other mythological creatures. You can see these motifs vividly represented in Indonesia's most renowned craft, *batik*. These beautiful hand done works of art on cloth are made by using a wax-resist method whereby wax is applied to the cloth in order to resist the dye. The wax can be applied by hand (*tulis*) or it can be applied by a metal stamp (*cap*). On Yogyanese *batik* the colors on both sides are equally as vibrant because the wax is applied to both sides, whereas in *cap batik* the inside colors are duller because wax has been applied to one side only. A fine art has been developed by using the *batik* wax-resist technique. It is called *batik* painting. In this case, usually the wax is applied by using the traditional tool, *canting*, or by using a brush (as in oil painting). The quality of the cloth used is an important determinant of the price. In Yogya, Central Java, where there are over 900 *batik* factories, you can study under Javanese masters. For more about *batik*, see 'Java'. **Australian duty:** *Batik tulis* or hand-embroidered designs on natural cloth (like cotton) are duty free; they come under 'handicrafts' at the Australian customs gate. Have the seller verify the fact that they are hand-drawn on the receipt. On plain white cotton and for hand-written designs on synthetics (dacron, nylon, orlorn, etc.), you pay duty. For satin and velvet they hit you with the most duty. You can often get around paying duty on Indonesian goods by sending them in just 1 kilo packages.

WEAVING

First brought from India, weaving still shows heavy Hindu influences. In these islands fabrics aren't only woven in 2 directions but sometimes even in 4, and some fabrics are interwoven with gold thread. Each completed handloomed fabric represents a collosal amount of human labor and now most of these tribal agricultural crafts only survive in the more remote parts of the archipelago (Nusa Tenggara, Kalimantan, Sulawesi) where imported cloths aren't readily available yet. There are many regional and island differences: the ancient applique technique of the Dayaks, the magnificent 'Ships of the Dead'

batik tulis (Hand-drawn batik): Hot wax is poured into this small 12 mm copper crucible called a canting. With 1, 2 or even 3 spouts of varying thicknesses, it's used like a pencil to apply a wax pattern upon a fabric. In this wax resist method, all parts of the cloth not covered in wax take up the dye. Although several 'wax-writings' inscribed with a canting date back to the 16th Century, batik did not reach its zenith until high quality white cotton was first introduced from European factories. The technique achieved its highest level in Central and East Java during the 17th Century with the making of batik of unbelievable detail and quality. In the kraton-courts of Central Java, see priceless old batiks on soft worn silk behind glass cases.

POTTERY

Since bamboo is so easily made into vessels, pottery and firing techniques have never developed into advanced crafts in these islands. Indonesia was once a big center for Chinese pottery and you can find well-preserved pieces in the far reaches of the archipelago: dug out of old Chinese graves on Sumba, in the Dayak longhouses of Borneo, in dusty souvenir shops in Ambon. The further away from the tourist centers, the cheaper. As well as the finer court ware, you also find 'Kitchen Ming', so named because it was utilized for everyday use by the Chinese 3-400 years ago. Giant Tang vases cost Rp50,000 in Ambon, and whole sets of Kitchen Ming perhaps as little as Rp25,000. Transport this venerable and expensive China *on your lap* on the plane.

ANTIQUES

The markets and shops of Indonesia are a hidden mine of antique hunters. Marvelous ice shaving machines. Ming China, old coins, bottles and ink-wells, embroideries, 300 year old trading beads, also antique Dutch lamps, Delftware, enammeled bed pans, and a wealth of other period artifacts are left-over from the Dutch years. The best antique markets are on Java, in particular in Solo and on the

textiles of the Kroe country of South Sumatra, brilliant flaming *ikat* cloths of the Bali Aga villages of East Bali, the pure silk *sarungs* of Samarinda, East Kalimantan, that last 20 years.

north coast. To view a sampling of the most incredible antique dining room and bedroom furniture, visit Jane's House in Surabaya, or stay in the Chinese family-run Hotel Megawati (sleep Rp1000 a night) on the main road coming from Surabaya, 1 km from Malang's city center.

CARVING

The detail on the carving of buffalo horn, bone, ivory and hornbill beak can be so extreme you need a magnifying glass to see the work. For carved tortoise shell and seashells go to the outer islands (Ambon) for the cheapest and the best. Leatherwork is done mainly in buffalo hide, the best known being the carved and gilded puppets used in *wayang kulit*. So strongly stylized that they look barely human, the eyes, nose and mouth are carved out last 'to break open' the puppet, i.e. to give the puppet life. Wood available is mostly teak, ironwood, and young ebony from which demons, *naga*, fish, etc. are carved. Dragons and other mythological creatures are popular on gong stands, prows of boats, beams of houses, and on temples. Many traditional handicrafts would have disappeared long ago if it weren't for tradition-loving souvenir-seeking tourists. And this is also why they've become so expensive. A good Balinese carved statue now costs up to US$250. Find almost any form of wood-carving: *si gale gale* life-sized wooden puppets which the Bataks of North Sumatra jerk to life at a childless person's death, eerie 2 m high ancestor figures of the Leti Islands in the Moluccas, handsome striped ebony chillums on Bali.

METAL WORKING

Indonesian artists excel in the precious metalworking crafts, especially in silversmithing and in the setting of semi-precious stones such as quartz, agate, moonstone, onyx, jasper, carnelian in silver and gold. Metalworking is still thriving in the areas where Hindu influence was once strongest: in the prosperous seaports of Java, Bali, South Celebes, coastal Borneo, and all over Sumatra. Precious metals are often mixed with other metals to obtain different nuances of color (and also to save money). In Aceh, North Sumatra, acid is even used to discolor ornamental gold. Stones are seldom polished so as to preserve their natural look and sometimes even nut casings or shiny green wings of beetles are set in gold; for the beauty of it, not for the 'value'. Silver, contrary to popular belief, is quite cheap, especially cheap the way they cut it in Indonesia— as little as US$4 an ounce. No matter what the silversmiths of Bali, Yogya and Bukittingi say about all the excruciating handtooled work it took to make a particular piece, never pay more than Rp600-1500 for a ring, small brooch or pendant.

PLAITING

Indonesia's oldest craft. Woven containers are still made where tin or plastics haven't yet penetrated. Bamboo, rattan, sisal, *nipah*, or *lontar* palm are ingeniously utilized all over Indonesia, probably most creatively by the Dayaks of Borneo. Bamboo tubes are used to store tobacco or as life-preservers, arrows, quivers, jars, bridges, knife sheaths, fishing rods, betelnut boxes, walking canes, flutes, animal cages. Split bamboo is made into nets, hats, wicker-work, mats, unbrella frames. Since iron hatchets, axes, machetes, small planes and knives are needed to gather bamboo and to work it, this craft is best developed in western Indonesian and not in more inaccessible eastern Indonesia.

SHIPPING

You can't buy something that morning and ship it out that afternoon in Indonesia like you can in Singapore. Just look at the freight regulations to see what I mean. It's very difficult to export objects in bulk, and seamail could take up to 6 months. There are air express companies on Java and Bali who arrange air-freight for you, so it's better if you're buying a lot in the outer islands to wait until you get back to Bali or Singapore to ship it. This way, you make sure it gets there. On Bali, try P.T. Golden Bali Express, Jl. Kartini 52. This company is about the most together out of the 5 or so shipping companies operating on Bali. Minimum 5 kg by air: US$22 plus airway bill ($1), packing ($3.75), clearance ($1.50), and handling ($5.50). Total: US$33.25 for 5 kg to the USA; takes 1 week. If you pack it yourself, get the price down to US$28 (only about $7 more than sending it by sea). There are two freighters which regularly deliver GMH spare parts from Australia to Jakarta and to Surabaya; in Jakarta call Tel 40323 or 40948. If you want to transport crafts from one part of Indonesia to another, overland bus companies offer quite cheap freight-only charges: Rp500 up to 5 kg, then Rp50 for each kilo over 5 kg. Try Elteha, Jl. Tanah Abang Timur 16 A (Jakarta) or right behind the Denpasar Post Office (Bali), with other branches in all the main cities. On Bali, Balimas, Jl. Hasanudin 27, Denpasar, charges Rp10,000 to transport 200 kg from Denpasar to Jakarta.

CONDUCT

Only by making yourself dependent on help and advice from Indonesians can you start to understand them. Travelers realize that to experience the people is not to have ballboys fetch their tennis balls at the Amburrukmo Palace Hotel all morning long for 17½ ₵. Tourists must first get it out of their heads that the man in front of them is only an Indonesian and that 'he's so small and I'm so big' (the little-man-in-the-village syndrome). You've got to stay a month in a *kampung* before you can even get a glimpse of what it's like to be an Asian. One of the most valuable gifts you can be given as a westerner is a new way to structure your time. You learn not only that time is not money but that life is better than money. You learn how to wait and be patient.

DEALING WITH THE BUREAUCRATS

You don't always need permission and clearance to do something or go somewhere. The more questions you ask, the more questions will be asked of you. Just go and do it. In offices, open up with a conversation first, then after a friendly exchange bring up business, 'Oh, by the way ...' When confronting the Immigration Department, be extra respectful. 'And what would *you* recommend in this matter?' Play the game. If you're trying to get some paperwork through or get something cleared through customs, say as little as possible and be courteous. In places unaccustomed to tourists such as parts of Sulawesi, Kalimantan, and Nusa Tenggara, the police can be almost harrassing at times. As well as wanting to know who you are and what you are doing all alone in their territory, they will quickly let you know that they run the place, and also grab the chance to show off their English, especially if there are other functionaries about who have no command of *Bahasa Inggeris*. If you get into any hassels with annoyingly officious cops, customs, or *imigrasi* officials, just act stupid, meek, friendly, and innocent. In most cases, they just want you to acknowledge the fact that they are real and that they have the power. Bypass petty officials if you can and go right to the top; often these higher placed men are more intelligent, reasonable, and understanding.

INDONESIAN ATTITUDES

There's no place for the individual in this society as there is in the west. Individuals aren't admired and are even laughed at. If you say you're over 20 years old and haven't any children yet, Indonesians pity you. In fact, to say an outright 'No!' in answer to

such queries is too blunt; say instead *belum* (not yet). They think that the man or woman who stands alone is unnatural and a little absurd. Loyalties to family, village and friends are more important than self-advancement. *Wayang* shows, circumcision feasts, *gamelan* music, happy *selamatans,* and lovely *batik* give more joy than getting ulcers and getting rich in the heart attack machine. While traveling through Indonesia always suspend judgement rather than get mad. You can't get mad at 130 million people. Asians rarely show anger and when they do, they go and stick a knife in someone. *Amuk* (blind terror) is an Indonesian word. They believe that Westerners get angry so quickly because they eat too much meat, that they take themselves far too seriously and don't know how to laugh at themselves. To stand with your hands on your hips while talking with people is regarded as insulting, being the traditional attitude of defiance in *wayang* theatre. Don't bring any sentimental attachments towards animals with you. This is Asia. Balinese children jump up and down with glee while dogs die horribly from rifle shot. Don't try extreme dances in Indonesia. The modern Indonesian youth who has received western education has no objection but the older generation considers modern dancing in which couples touch each other blatant and vulgar sexuality. Never kiss in public. Not even relatives. Don't beckon to anybody with your forefinger, it is rude. If you want to beckon with your fingers make a motion using the cupped fingers turned downwards. Neither should you point with your forefinger, use your thumb for pointing. With the disarming smile of a little girl, some Indonesians are skilled at coaxing you into doing things that you only half want to do. If you don't want to do what Indonesians want you to do just say, *Bukan adat kami,* or 'It is not our custom.' Don't jump into the bathwater, it's for throwing over you. If you have to shit in the open do it in running water. If males need to piss in crowded places, just squat down in a ditch with knees spread to cover you. About 1000 million people in 3rd World countries piss in this manner onto the earth. Try not to sit with the bottom of your feet pointing at people. Cover your mouth with your hand when picking your teeth. Except for such Indonesian social etiquette, don't change · your whole life-style for them. If you're the really outrageous and flamboyant type, go ahead and show them who you are. These cultures aren't as fragile and delicate as many tourists make them out to be: there's at least 8 civilizations buried under their soil. In Australia you wouldn't ask an Indian woman to take the ring out of her nose, a Thai not to remove his shoes, or ask an Indonesian to take off his *peci* inside a building or not to board with his 3 wives just so that they be like us. Likewise, they shouldn't except you to change for them. Frayed jeans and a relaxed sexual mores are *our* culture. They will love you for providing them with your own brand of street theatre. They expect it from *orang barat* (westerners). There's plenty of *kasar* characters around, great characters and not really frowned upon. These types usually qualify for the gesture of the forefinger held vertically in front of the nose and between the eyes which means that you, he, or she are mad, stupid, or 'does not speak his brain'. Most Indonesians generally leave outrageous behavior to the village idiot, the traveling gypsy theatre, and to *becak* drivers.

RELIGION

Respect their religions, they're really locked into God. Indonesians aren't offended easily, but they have opinions. Don't tell everybody you're an atheist; people will react with confusion, disbelief, even scorn, thinking you're a commie. While the *Koran* is being read, don't drink or smoke; never put a book or anything else on it. Remove your shoes when you enter a mosque. Don't pat a kid on the head, especially if he's Buddhist. In fact, never touch anybody's head. Most Indonesians see the head as the seat of the soul and therefore sacred.

DRESS AND GROOMING

You'll be the object of constant scrutiny. Adhering so strongly to local customs, Indonesians are very conservative and slow to change. So be fairly careful about what you wear. Shorts, singlets, braless jerseys and thongs in the main streets of even the smallest village could be insulting, something only the lower class people do such as fieldworkers and *becak* drivers. A *sarung* tied above the breasts is only acceptable on the way to bathe. Long hair is no problem because many Indonesian freedom fighters vowed not to cut their hair until they had won independence from the Dutch (the struggle went on for 4 years!) If you wear a beard you'll be known as *Bapak Jenggot,* Father Beard. Indonesians want to know how you keep from getting food caught in it, mothers will tell their children you'll eat them up, and others will think you're angry all the time, like a *raksasa.* Whether you wear a beard or not, children will often be afraid of you and older people too, though they will not show it. Children only see white men when they shoot, kill and punch in the movies; this is why many start crying when they see you.

INTERACTIONS

Don't get too uptight about constantly being asked where you're going. Think up some zany answers, or use the standard ones like exactly where you're going, if you know, or just *jalan jalan* (out walking). Or try the Malay response, *Saya makan angin,* 'I'm eating the wind.' The custom is carried on from the time when you called out who you were and where you were going as you walked through a strange village just to assure people everything was alright, maybe you could do something for them on the way. On Bali people ask you repeatedly, 'How are you?' or the same old questions they asked the day before. To them just reply, *Pakai rata,* which describes the usual position during sexual intercourse (flat). In other words, 'Same as usual, man!' It deserves a reply such as this because so often this greeting is not sincere but only used as an opening line to get you to buy something. If people join you on the path or road, make conversation; they're not latching on to you forever (not usually). When you hear *Belanda!* behind you and turn around and come back with *Bukan Belanda! Saya orang Selandia Baru!,* or some such reply, the fixed look of suspicion turns to a smile or a look of surprise at being spoken to in roughly recognizable Indonesian, and the information seems to travel on far ahead of you.

HASSELS

The 'colonial complex' is still with Indonesians and there remains an underlying resentment and envy of the west: witness the ferocity in which Indonesians play chess with westerners in Yogya. Don't freak out if a pickpocket probes your pocket or bag for money, just take the strange fingers out, point at him, and announce to everyone, *Pencopet!* (Pickpocket!). On occasion in South Sumatra, Flores, or in South Celebes you could get taunted by young boys who just want to see how you'll react. It's absolutely essential not to get angry, this is what delights them all the more. A good method is to ask bystanders where the boy's father is, go to him and complain of his son's disrespectful behavior. With all the neighbors looking on and with the fahter having to uphold his honor in the *kampung,* the boy will be taken care of, perhaps before your eyes for all to see and hear. Single traveling ladies are much more likely to get raped in the USA or in Australia than in Indonesia, but you can expect men and boys to touch you indecently. If this happens just spit out at him, *Kau babi!* (You pig!), the aim being to humiliate him in public so he doesn't do it again. Indonesian males could fondle a male traveler's penis when the traveler is taking his leave. In most cases this is only intended as a friendly parting gesture, to reaffirm his affection for you. If a western male travels with an Indonesian girl through Indonesia, expect a lot of hassles. She has to report to the police in every town and since you don't have the same name many hotel owners won't allow you to sleep together in the same room; it opposes Islamic law and makes it look like his hotel is a whorehouse. Normally, if a couple is unmarried there is no problem sleeping together in the same room, as long as they're both from the west. If you're traveling with a child in Indonesia, especially a fair male child, the problem is not in finding a free babysitter for the day but the problem is getting your child *back* from the babysitter.

STAYING WITH PEOPLE

Conversations on buses, trains, and boats often lead to great places to stay. You may never have to stay in a hotel if you're friendly and patient with yourself and with others. Staying with a family means absolutely no privacy, often sharing a bed. This could get old fast since you're always in the spotlight. As a visitor you must take on many unwilling roles, acting somebody you aren't. All friends and relatives will come to see you, and anyone in the *kampung* who speaks English will come around to practice. You'll be invited to do things with the family so that they can parade you around the village or city street, to show you off to everyone. On occasion you're only used as a vehicle to boost someone's standing amongst his peers or to somehow increase his status in the community.

VISITING

The best time to visit Indonesians in their homes is between 4 and 6 pm after work, food, and siesta; and in Islamic areas, before the evening prayers. Visitors are never turned away. If you are kept waiting for your host to appear, it's a compliment: he's changing into nice clothes to receive you. Conversely, he'd be offended if you visited him only in a *sarung* or a singlet. It is polite to introduce yourself when meeting strangers and not to wait for someone else to do the introductions. Do shake hands when greeting people; women and men will offer their hand. Respect is shown by bowing from the waist when passing in front of people, especially older people. Never eat with the left hand. Use it with water instead of toilet paper. Wash your hands, in particular your right hand, since you will be eating with the right hand fingers in a village. Your Indonesian hosts will certainly do so and you are expected to follow suit. In the cities people eat more often with a spoon in the right hand and a fork in the left hand. If you are invited by an Indonesian to eat or drink, watch your host since a guest may not start if not invited to do so by the host, with *silahkan* (sometimes 20 minutes later). Take a small helping the first time around because you'll be expected to eat a 2nd helping. Your host will be offended if you don't. It is polite to keep pace with your host. (If you empty your plate, it means you want some more). Don't ask for salt, pepper, soya sauce, or *sambal*. It is an insult to the cook, implying that the cook did not know which spices to add while cooking the dish. Be careful not to offend your Indonesian friends, 90% of whom are Muslims, who are forbidden to eat pork. In their company never ask for or offer dishes prepared with pork or lard. Share the meal you're eating when a visitor arrives in your house, office, or park bench. Share your cigarettes around and if you've been into town bring back some biscuits for the kids (if you've got the money). *Do* talk politics (except with the army or with the police), who else is going to tell them? Travelers should be prepared to make of the night, the day. Many forms of entertainment, prayers, and religious festivals run all night long. In some places people stay up all night on the night of the full moon simply for the coolness and for the magic of it. There's plenty of magic left in Indonesia.

ACCOMMODATION

If you're paying more than US65¢ to US$3 a day for a room, you're being culturally deprived of first-hand experience with the Indonesian people, the *rakyat,* the masses. You can live in neo-colonialist splendor relatively cheaply in Indonesia, but the more you're spending the more distance is created and the less of an Indonesian experience your visit will be. How good a time you have in a place depends frequently upon the friendliness and location of the *losmen* you stayed in, so choose your *losmens* carefully. It makes quite a difference in expenses if two people travel together and split rooms. A double room could cost Rp750 while a single room costs Rp600; or in many places you pay a flat rate for the room no matter how many people occupy it. Ask at bus or train stations immediately upon arrival in the towns for cheap places to stay. *Becak* and taxi drivers always know of some. In the smaller villages ask the *hansip* (district civilian militia) for sleeping quarters. The same person who tells you that a hotel or *losmen* in this book no longer exists, will also be able to tell you where another cheap one is. Most of the typical low-cost Indonesian style staying places have short beds and low doorways for westerners. If there are prostitutes around it will probably prove noisy at night. Indonesian hotels are good about waking you up early to catch a train, bus or plane. Here are some types of Indonesian-style accommodations, their functions and prices varying from region to region:

a) stay with people, everywhere: Muslims take care of strangers, it's part of the Islamic code. Someone is almost always in the mood to take you home to their family. If you stay with a family in a *kampung* in the village or city, it's polite to drop in on the *kepala kampung* or the *kepala desa* (headmen) to introduce yourself and to register (pay sometimes a charge of Rp1-200). His house is usually the largest one in the village with a big verandah for holding meetings. If the village is very small and you have no other place to stay, the *kepala* will fix you up for free or for a nominal charge. Often you're obliged to stay with the *kepala desa* and not in a less-ranking household. If you're hard up, crash on village platforms or in fields at the side of the road (but never in Sumatra).

b) the police: If places are too expensive or there are none, go to the police explaining that you're a poor student. Some hotels might refuse to put you up even though they have empty rooms because there are too many police forms for them to fill out and too many hassles and even suspicions if they do; plus they must pay the police too much of a cut for putting up tourists. In these cases, since they're causing all the inconveniences, go to the police and request accommodation. In exchange for entertainment and English-speaking practice, sleep for free on their floor or pitch your tent in their yard.

c) penginapan (lodging house): Very basic facilities. Even more basic than the *losmen,* but often even cheaper. See them all over Indonesia in little back lanes, sometimes with just a sign 'Peng-X' with the owner's name.

d) losmen: A cheaply run hotel but still quite livable. Often concentrated around train and bus stations. A bathroom is usually shared. Room service depends on the *losmen* or on the *ibu* (your hostess). Here's where you find the most interesting people-wandering merhants, students, Indonesian travelers, other travelers. *Losmens* run anywhere from Rp150-750, but prices differ from

Sumatra right on through to Irian Jaya (the most expensive). On Bali, where you even see signs 'Hotel Ex-Losmen', it means living with a family. In Jakarta and other places on Java, a *losmen* could mean a brothel and they are considered somewhat downgrading.

e) wisma (sometimes called *pondok*): A bit more expensive still. This is an indonesian lodge or small guesthouse. Pretensions of grandeur in the high sounding name. Usually it's one storey, efficiently run, privately owned or owned by a family. The *wisma*-class hotel is actually the best accommodation for the money in Indonesia. Running usually about Rp1000-2500, they are remarkably comfortable and homey. *Wismas* often have flush toilets and a simple breakfast is often included in the price of the room. The name *wisma* is also used for ordinary buildings or for office blocks; could be anything.

f) hotel: Although it could also be quite cheap and dirty, a hotel infers more expensive accommodation with the European connotation. Room service depends on the price. Every room should lock (except in Yogya). The owner sometimes does the cooking, errands, managing and bookkeeping himself. In very cheap hotels, meals are not included in the price. Some hotels are just *losmens* with another name; the others you'll recognize easily and avoid. There are mercifully few of the 'international standard' hotels in Indonesian, perhaps 25 in the whole archipelago.

g) YMCA's and Youth Hostels: Though quite comfortable because they have to live up to a standard, these are frequently more expensive than cheaper hotels and *losmens*. YMCA's run Rp1000-2500, but are quite centrally located, clean, usually have dining rooms, and are run much like an inn. Youth Hostels, of the few that exist, are small, plain, regimented.

h) asram: Students live here in dormitory accommodation or share a room. Often you can find spare beds, especially during school holidays.

i) pasangrahan or rumah2 kehutanan: Their functions are nearly interchangeable. They are government forestry huts or government lodges in parks, nature or wildlife reserves. You can stay in them if not occupied by government people. Usually they are quite cheap, sometimes even free. Found mostly in the outer islands–Moluccas, Celebes, Kalimantan, Sumatra. There could be several of them in one locale, therefore by asking for a *rumah2 kehutanan* you may be directed to a different one than the one you're looking for. *Pasangrahan* could also mean a commercial lodging house, frequently in more out-of-the-way places.

THEFT

There are thieves the width and breadth of Indonesia–snatch thieves, pickpockets, cat-burglars, and on the buses of Sumatra travelers have even been drugged in order to make them easier to rob. Take all imaginable precautions because practically anything you have, they want. Indonesians themselves are very seldom stolen from. At night they accord their motorcycles the ultimate honor: they put them in their *bedrooms*. The best is to travel through the islands without jewelry, watch, or camera. The less you travel with, the less there is to be stolen, the less resentment is aroused, the less restricted your bargaining position. Money belts, designed to go *under* your clothes, are recommended for Java and particularly if you're going beyond Indonesia (India?). Never take a room without strong bars on the windows. If you do, either take all your valuables with you when you go out, or hide them very well. Take your own lock and key along. If you're worried at all about security, the best is to always stay in a more expensive hotel. As much as you'd like to trust the Indonesians you're staying with, the word that a whitey (connotes 'rich') is in town spreads instantly throughout the whole *kampung*.

Quick and quiet, thieves will enter your room through the window while you sleep and steal the camera from the hook above your head or the backpack from underneath your very bed. Purses and bags could be snatched from your shoulder by motorcyclists as you walk along, wet wash is stolen from the line. When writing letters see to it that stamps get postmarked or else they get ripped. When trains stop at stations, never leave anything valuable or unattended on the seats or on the table while the window is open. Another Indonesian specialty is slitting into packs, purses, shoulder bags and pockets with razors. When big interisland ships dock, avoid at all cost passenger crushes. Make money pouches slit-proof with steel line backing or leather reinforcement. Never keep valuables in side pockets or on the top layer of packs. It's no good going to the police. It's gone, that's all. In fact if you go to the police it often costs you *more*. Before the investigation they could ask to talk about it over dinner, which you pay for. Other accounts are of travelers appealing to the police upon theft of their casette recorder; when the police recover it by sheer accident they ask that the traveler give Rp500 'for finding it'. Indonesians borrow things—surfboards, sunglasses, rings, guitars, books, and 'forget to return them' (pinjam lagi, trus hilang). The Indonesians you are forced to move amongst traveling on the cheap frequently confuse generosity with abundance, taking advantage of your good naturedness and your desire to be friendly.

FOOD

There's much less foreign food served in Indonesia than in most ex-colonies, lucky for you. All traditional Indonesian food is designed to complement or to be complemented by rice. Indonesian cuisine is known for its deliberate combination of contrasting flavors and textures: spicy, sour, and otherwise flavor-assertive dishes. Indonesia taught the world the use of exotic spices. In Indonesian cooking spices are used less than in the curries of India, yet more than in Chinese food. Tumeric, a yellow root that resembles a small carrot, is used often in Indonesian recipes. Soybean is the vegetable cow of Indonesia. Coconut, coconut milk, chilis, ginger, and peanuts are used more than in other Asian cooking. Freshly grated coconut is kneaded and sieved, then blended with water. As it cooks, the coconut milk thickens and with the addition of flour or corn starch it becomes a sauce. Bananas are used frequently to season meats and stews. The basic diet on most of the islands is rice, lots of it, supplemented with a bit of fish, often fried, and once in a while savory meat, eggs, and vegetables. Anything with the word *nasi* in front of it means that it's prepared or served with rice. Indonesian food is delicious at *all* levels. You can eat unbelievably cheap. Often the country people eat more healthily than the rich who gorge themselves and their children on status foods such as meat, carbohydrates, beer, soda and chocolate. Country people eat hearty organic foods such as *tahu* (soybean cake), *tempe* (fermented soybeans), or coconut candy and cane syrup which are all 'poor man's food' and much more nutritious. The traditional way to eat is with the fingers of the right hand touching the food; fingers taste better than metal. Always eat with the right hand, the left hand is used in the toilet. (They used to cut the right hand off thieves, thereby preventing him from ever eating in public again.) Meals are often served on a banana leaf which tastes better than plastic or glass. The appearance of the dish counts for a lot. If it doesn't look good, Indonesians can't eat it. Great care is taken at markets to make the food attractive so as catch the shopper's eye: flowers are sprinkled over fruit, dishes are brightly garnished, and green leaves spread under vegetables. As you'll notice on any busride, Indonesians have very delicate stomachs. When they visit Australia and eat Colonel Sander's chicken for the first time, they throw up. For those who are into cooking, there's tremendous diversity in the markets: grains, beans, brown and black rice, palm sugar, all kinds of fruits and vegetables, spices, and where there are Chinese people, *ginseng* (organic speed).

REGIONAL FOODS

A great variety of regional foods are found over the whole archipelago. Always sample the homecooking in each region. In some regions mice and dog are eaten. You never see pork in Muslim areas, which is a favorite of the Chinese and the Hindus. Pigs run all over Bali, but are absent on Java. Central Java's food is sweet and spicy while in East Java it's saltier and hotter. Sumatran food is very spicy hot, and in the eastern island groups cassava and sago are the main diet. Cassava, which looks like a shriveled turnip, has a ridiculously low protein content (1% as compared to 10% in rice); a starchy unappetizing fibrous mass, it's the staple food of millions. Westerners know it only in its refined form as tapioca. Sago is sometimes served in unusual ways such as Ambon's glue-like *papeta*.

NATIONAL DISHES

The following dishes are found all over Indonesia. *Gado2* is a very healthy vegetable salad with added spices and a rich peanut sauce. Get it at roadside stalls, Rp75-100. *Nasi goreng* (fried rice) and *mie goreng* (fried noodles) mean rice or noodles fried in coconut oil with eggs, meat, tomato, cucumber, with shrimp paste, spices and chilis added; these are common breakfast dishes for Indonesians. If *istemiwa* ('special') is written after a dish, it usually means it comes with an egg on top. Another nourishing dish is the Chinese *cap cai,* a kind of Indonesian meat and vegetables chop suey. *Soto* means that a thick *santen* (coconut cream) is added to the soup; this is also a breakfast dish. *Sop* is more like a meat and vegetables stew; it means only that water is added. Chilies and soybean sauce (kecap) are the favorite spices. When in doubt as to whether the dish is spicy hot or not, just ask '*Pedas atau tidak?*' There are many kinds of hot chili sauce (sambal) and spiced chili pastes; the one from Padang, West Sumatra, is the hottest in the world. *Kretek* cigarettes help cool down your throat after a chili burning. Or if it's too hot just squeeze lemon with some salt over the dish to make it less so.

FISH

Indonesia, consisting mostly of sea, offers a staggering amount of fresh fish to eat: tuna, shrimp, lobster, crab, anchovies, carp, prawns. You can eat real bargain (average about Rp400-800) fish and shellfish dinners in Indonesia's ramshackle restaurants and roadside *warungs* at about half the Singapore price. Many rice farmers raise a supplementary fish crop by letting fish loose to spawn in flooded ricefields; dinner is caught by just opening up the sluice gates. Some fresh-water fish are bred in compounds such as the buttery *belanak* (gray mullet): take the bones out, mix with coconut milk and spices, then wrap it into the skin and bake.

WARUNGS

When you're hungry just follow your nose and head for the day and night markets where you'll discover a collection of smoky *warungs*. A *warung* is a kind of poor man's restaurant and by far the best food for the money is served in these makeshift foodstalls with canopies, hardwood benches or stools, and glowing hissing gas lamps. Hundreds line the streets of Indonesia's cities, towns and villages, especially at night. If you eat US50¢ of this roadside food you're making an absolute glutton of yourself. *Warungs* usually specialize in *soto, sate, nasi goreng, mie goreng, lontong,* or *cap cai.* After eating and before paying your bill, ask first how much and make sure that it's correct, then pay. Don't just hand the money over and except to be given the correct change.

DRINKS

About the only drink that Indonesians take with their meals is warm or cold tea (for unsweetened drinks, say *pahit*). There are many natural drinks, both hot and cold. *Bajigur* is a drink made of coconut milk thickened with rice and sweetened with palm sugar. Go to ice juice stands for delicious fruit drinks: citrus juices (air jeruk), *es zirzak,* and the incredible avovado drink blend, *es pokat.* Alcoholic *tuak* (palm wine), brewed a month before it's drunk, gives you a mellow kind of slow-motion high. *Brem* is rice wine made from glutinous rice with coconut milk. Old *brem* (more than 3 days old) is sour and has more alcoholic content, new *brem* (under 3 days) has a sweet taste and has less alcoholic content; costs Rp175-200 per bottle for either. Bintang beer, made by Heinekins of Holland, is Rp350-600 a bottle. Because of the lack of refrigeration, it's often served with ice bobbing in it. Powerful Indonesian coffee, first introduced by the Dutch in 1699, is grown in Java, Bali and Sumatra. The best is cultivated south of Semerang. Indonesian *kopi* is sometimes laced with chicory or chocolate. Served pitch black, sweet, thick and rich, grounds are still floating on top of the glass; costs in most places only Rp20 a tall glass. Makes you take a big beautiful shit first off in the morning and sends a blast of energy through you that lasts all morning long.

FRUITS

There are some splendid fruits you should try for you may never get another chance. Often, stands selling fruit stay open until late at night. Besides really cheap oranges (on Java, after bargaining, 4-6 small sweet *jeruks* cost only Rp100), pineapples, tangerines, there are mangoes, *salak, rambutans,* guavas, lychees, jackfruit. !ndonesia has 15 varieties of bananas of all shapes, flavors, textures and sizes from the tiny finger-like *pisang tuju* to the prized 1 m long *pisang raja,* seedless ones and ones with big black seeds, wild species, some big and fat and red-skinned, others with edible skins, and some that are edible only when cooked. The *durian,* spiked like a gladiator's weapon, tastes like onions and caramel fluff at the same time. It's believed to be an aphrodisiac ('When the *durians* are down, the *sarungs* are up.') There are many other sweet, gooey, sumptuous fruits such as the *langsat* and the *marquisa.* When you bite into the jelly-like *tuih* fruit, it tastes like sweet fine coconut milk. *Jambu air* fruit, though tasteless, is a good thirst quencher.

VENDORS

The *sate* man comes with his kitchen on his shoulders. Listen for the sound of his feet rhythmically hitting the mud. He squats in the gutter and fans the embers of his charcoal fire, turning out sizzling skewered beef, pork, chicken, turtle meat or mutton with different sauces, the style varies from place to place. *Krupuk,* the Indonesian pretzel, is a big crispy misshapen cracker made from either shrimp paste, fish or fruit mixed with rice and dough. After being dried to look like thin hard colored plastic, it unfolds, blossoms, when fried in oil. Served cold, it's very tangy. The *krupuk* man carries on a bamboo pole two huge containers which look like big milk cans. Since bread is seldom eaten, being too expensive and not to their taste, Indonesians use *krupuk* for bread.

RESTAURANTS

When you see the word *restoran* it usually means it's expensive. *Rumah makan* just means 'eating place' and it could be good. Most major towns and cities have Chinese restaurants. If you ask for a *mie goreng* in a Chinese restaurant, although it could be superior to that found in a *warung* or in a *rumah makan*, it is not Indonesian cooking. Restaurants or *warungs* catering exclusively for tourists are generally shitful. They are typified by western casette music, menus written in English, sterile food, brightly neon-lit, overpriced, and Chinese-run. Most tone down the spicy hotness and eliminate many of the 'funny tasting' spices in order to make it palatable for the tourists who come there to listen to the great tapes. Consequently they serve uninspired, bland, prostituted food.

NASI PADANG

The Minangkabaus from West Sumatra are some of the best cooks in Indonesia and it is in one of their *rumah makan nasi padang* where you'll meet with the most bonafide and the tastiest Indonesian cooking, though sure to be very spicy. They will set many dishes in front of you and you pay only for what you eat. So get the prices straight for each dish before you dig in, otherwise it could prove embarrassing. The sauce from each dish is free so if you find a restaurant that gives plenty of rice just eat a couple of the dishes and use the sauce from the rest, like Indonesians do. If you ask for *nasi campur* instead of taking the 'a la carte' dishes, it's often cheaper.

Nasi campur is a quite filling plate of steamed rice with either fish, beef, chicken or mutton, plus a mixture of eggs and/or vegetables heaped on top. The best value eating in Indonesia. Get your best *nasi campurs* before the lunch crowd starts coming at around 11 am.

DESSERTS

Bananas steamed, fried or boiled, cost Rp15 each and are found everywhere. *Ketan* is rice pudding cooked in coconut milk and sugar syrup. *Bubur santen* is rice porridge made with coconut milk. *Lontong* is rice cooked in banana leaves and tastes somewhat like cold 'Cream of Wheat'. There are many special holiday desserts. During *Hari Raya* pastries and all manner of cookies are served. On *Asjura*, a Muslim holiday on the 10th day of the first month, *bubur asjura* is prepared, a rice porridge with peanuts, eggs, and sweet beans. Indonesians love their sweetmeats and you'll see them everywhere: lentil pastes, coconut cakes, crunchy peanut cookies, sticky banana cakes, mung-bean soups, and other bizaare munchies. Ice cream comes in *durian* and lychee fruit flavors; sweet corn kernel ice cream is another Indonesian treat.

GETTING TO INDONESIA

The following are the currency exchange rates used
in this section:

US$1 = Rp400-415	US$1 = S$2.46
M$1 = S$0.99¢	B$1 = S$1.00

FROM MALAYSIA

When it's operating, take a cargo boat (Agent Soo
Hup Seng, 165 Victoria St., Penang, Malaysia)
every 2 or 3 days from Penang overnight to Medan,
North Sumatra, for Rp8000. Or for nearly Rp15,000
or M$84 fly with Merpati or MAS from Penang to
Medan; you land while the aftertaste of the
fruit juice is still in your mouth. In Penang, take the
yellow bus no. 66 from Maxwell Road out to the airport. There are sometimes *prahus* carrying charcoal
(and passengers) from Melaka to Dumai for M$30,
takes 1 day, then from Dumai travel by road to
Pekanbaru, East Sumatra. There's also an occasional hydrofoil out of Kelang (Kuala Lumpur's port)
to Medan.

FROM EAST MALAYSIA

Straits Steamship Company, Ocean Bldg. 1, 16th
floor, Singapore, Tel. 76071 ext. 152, operates ships
from Singapore to: Kota Kinabalu, S$97 deck class
on the M.V. Keningau; Sandakan, S$112 deck;
Kucing on the M.V. Perak, S$92 cabin class or S$66
economy class; Tawau or Lahad Datu, Sabah,
S$220 first class only on the M.V. Kimanis. Quite
often there's plenty of room on deck class and you
don't need to book, but for cabins always book at
least two weeks in advance. From East Malaysia
(Sarawak or Sabah), or from Brunei, take landrovers, jeeps, walk overland or take *longbots* or
coasters down into Indonesian territory (see 'Kalimantan'). Another approach is via Kuching to West
Kalimantan Province: take the Straits Steamship
Co. boat from Singapore to Kucing (S$69), then
from Kucing to Pontianak it's M$69 by plane; also a
ferry plies this route. Because of communist insurgents, West Kalimantan is an uptight region at present.

FROM SINGAPORE

Ships taking passengers don't leave regularly for
Indonesia from Singapore but from Tanjong Pinang, an island about 4 hours south of Singapore by
motorboat. From Tg. Pinang take a ferry or fishing

boat to Pekanbaru, East Sumatra, for Rp3000 and
up; boats could leave anytime. On Tues. the Pelni
Lines ship the Tampomas leaves for Medan from
Tanjung Pinang; the price S$118 deck class from
Singapore includes the motorboat from Singapore
to Tg. Pinang and the transfer by *sampan* from Tg.
Pinang's harbor to the Tampomas. Each Sat. this
same ship, on its way back from Medan for Jakarta,
stops in Tg. Pinang to take on passengers arriving
from Singapore. The fare S$115 from Singapore to
Jakarta also includes the motorboat from Singapore to Tg. Pinang and the transfer by *sampan* from
Tg. Pinang's harbor to the ship, accommodation on
the KM Tampomas according to the class booked.
Meals are provided free of charge. For 2 B class,
S$163, you get a 4 berth cabin and communal facil-
ities shared with deck class. For 2 A class, S$171, a
4 berth cabin and communal facilities. For 1st class,
S$184, a 2 berth cabin with private facilities. Ger-
man Asian Travels, Straits Trading Bldg., 9 Battery
Road, 13th floor, Tel. 915 116; and Intra Express
Pte. Ltd. next to the entrance to the Indonesian
Embassy in Wisma Indonesia, 435 Orchard Road,
Singapore, both sell through boat tickets from
Singapore to either Jakarta or Medan (but not to
Pekanbaru). Or you can do it on your own. First
take a launch to Tg. Pinang from Finger Pier, Prince
Edward Road, Singapore. This launch is more like
an excursion boat featuring a continuous picnic; the
normal fare is S$40 but you could possibly pay as
little as US$10 if you pay it in cash to one of the
crew. In Tg. Pinang you can buy your ticket on the
weekly Pelni boat for Rp11,500 to Jakarta. On the
Tampomas, the top deck is the breeziest, the least
crowded, and not as noisy as belowdecks which
look like an immigrant ship. For deck class you
sleep in your own sleeping bag or mat on deck. It's
only a 2-day passage and just when you're starting
to get sick of it, it's over. There will be 20-30 other
Euros in lines of sleeping bags. A beautiful trip, see
14 sail sailing ships on your way through the Java
Sea. Don't fall for the officers' mess meals offered
by the crew for Rp750 which aren't that much
better than the food served free deck class. **by air
from Singapore:** The usual student fare (ID
card needed) from Singapore to Jakarta is S$160

either way; the ticket is open for one year. Garuda Airlines offers a flight Singapore-Jakarta-Yogya-Denpasar-Singapore for S$460, but it's good for only one month. Thai International's regular flight Singapore-Jakarta-Singapore is S$320, and is also good for one month. Some cheap travel agents: MAS, 5th floor, Suite 544, Tanglin Shopping Center, Singapore; Sunseekers (Pte.) Ltd., Suite 310, Orchard Towers (opposite the Hilton Hotel), Orchard Road, Singapore, Tel. 2354427; also Mansfield Travels, 15th floor, Ocean Building (same bldg. as Straits Steamship Co.), Singapore.

FROM AUSTRALIA

Hitch to Darwin via Townsville, or take a train from Sydney or Melbourne with student discount (50% off) to Alice Springs, then hitch to Darwin from there in 1-2 days. On flights from Darwin, Australia, straight to Bali you must book 1-2 months ahead, especially during university vacation in Australia, Dec. and January. From Darwin there are sometimes cattle boats US$75-150 one way, or private yachts a bit cheaper, that shuttle irregularly between Darwin and the Indonesian islands, but you can't depend on them. Merpati is the only airlines handling the Darwin-Bali route now and charge an exorbitant Aus$228, having capitalized on the Darwin-Dili (Portugese Timor) flight stopped because of war. With the airfare being so expensive, it now works out usually cheaper to fly from Sydney direct to Jakarta for Aus$3-400. Unless you have extraordinary luck hitching and snag a ride straight through to Darwin, you must consider how much you'll spend on food and sleep getting there. It is even more dismal a prospect during the wet. Might as well fly from Perth, Western Australia, it's only about Aus$25 or so more expensive than flying from Darwin. There are flights for around Aus$256 from Perth to Jakarta. Cathay Pacific costs Aus$308 from Perth to Jakarta; a morning flight, only 4 hours, good meal, free grog. Or fly this route with A.U.S. for only Aus$160. **tours from Australia:** Be wary of pre-packaged travel agencies advertising 'Cheap Tours to Indonesia'. Bad reports. Make sure you get the best value for your money. You pay for places and services sight unseen. Occasionally, agencies don't pay their bills so when you arrive hotels could refuse to put you up. Or else they could be really out of the way and have expensive food. If you're taking the Easy Rider Tour, book at different times if you're a husband and wife or close friends and you want to travel together, yet separately. Even though they say you'll each get a motorcycle for the 28 days, when you arrive in Bali you'll only receive vouchers for one machine and you must share it. You can always rent your idle bike out to another tourist and make money from it. A reliable travel agent in Australia? Try Bali Tours,

34 Raleigh St., Windsor, Melbourne; or Palmii, 49 Park Street, South Yarra, Melbourne, run by Pat Price. Good reports. These both offer cheap package tours from Australia right on through to Penang, Malaysia. All tickets are open-dated and you're on your own.

FROM PAPUA NEW GUINEA

A unique way to enter Indonesia is through the back door via Papua New Guinea to Irian Jaya (West New Guinea), a much less frequented route of mountain Papuan tribes and snowcapped peaks. It costs about Aus$372 to fly all the way to Ambon in the Moluccas Islands from Cairns (Queensland) via Port Moresby, Madang, Wewak (P.N.G.), Jayapura, Biak, Ambon (Indonesia). You can do it even cheaper if you start taking boats from Port Moresby (P.N.G.) instead of flights. But remember, this eastern region of Indonesia is 2-3 times more expensive than Java and Bali, and there are a few more bureacratic hassels to deal with.

OTHER APPROACHES

from the Philippines: Because of an agreement between the two governments aimed at curtailing gunrunning, travelers can't go by sea from the Philippines into Indonesia or vice versa. You can only fly. Either take a flight from Manila to Kota Kinabalu (Sabah) with MAS for about US$138 (Brunei Air could be cheaper); or catch a flight with Swift Air Co. from Zamboanga, Mindanao (southern Philippines) to Tarakan each Tues. for US$135. Merpati operates a charter for US$150 from Manila to Bali 'x' number of times per month; very irregular. Although boats to East Malaysia from the Philippines aren't that regular, they are cheaper: from Manila to Palawan Island (get a stretcher to sleep on), then another boat to the small island of Labuhan. From Labuhan to Brunei it's only Brunei $5 by motorboat. **from Thailand:** Jay's Travel Agency in Bangkok (near the Malaysia Hotel) sells fake student cards for US$6. Vingh Thai Hotel and Liberty Hotel issue A.U.S. tickets (on good authority) to any age; cheap fares to Indonesia and to the rest of Asia (also, if you're interested, Kuala Lumpur to Copenhagen, US$240). **from Europe:** Fly charters from Amsterdam to Singapore for S$630-650 one way which is cheaper than to fly from Sydney to Singapore (about S$900); then from Singapore, Indonesia is only S$115 away by launch and ship. **from USA:** Some companies sell tickets for as little as US$760 round trip, good for a year. T.I.A. Airlines from Seattle to Hong Kong is US$313. Charter flights round trip from L.A. to Bali for US$750 just started up in 1977. Or, cheaper than any of these, take a ship from Vancouver to New Zealand, then up to Indonesia via Australia.

'Family Outing'
by Otto Djaja
1956

TRANSPORT WITHIN INDONESIA

HITCHING

Simplify and travel light. When your shirt gets dirty, wash it. Get down to just one piece of baggage and a shoulder bag if you can. Not only does this cut down chances of theft, but it changes your whole philosophy towards travel. When you arrive in a town, it relieves you of having to set up a base right away. You are able to walk around, sightsee, and if you don't like it, just blow through. Hitching is fair to good on Java, northern Sumatra, South Celebes, and is quite enjoyable besides, but slow. Hitching is easiest of all on Bali. Meet the people. Practice your Indonesian. Engineers, the military, merchandisers, truckies, Colombo Plan workers, tourists will pick you up in jeeps, cars, landrovers, motorcycles, and there's even a story of an oil company helicoptor landing by a highway in South Sumatra to pick up a hitchhiker.

MOTORCYCLE

A bike is great to have but best to buy one of the local Hondas for around Rp40-80,000 and then re-sell it later for maybe half that. Rent them on Bali or Yogya, Rp1000-2500 per day. In his book, *S.E. Asia on a Shoestring* (1975), Tony Wheeler claims that taking a lightweight (because you load and unload it frequently) machine through the islands is quite feasible (he did it) and well worth it. Freighting costs aren't that high and petrol is cheap. Top up at Pertamina, they sell the cheapest petrol. Tony says

that you need a carnet which is a deposit you leave with an Automotive Association at home to ensure that you don't sell the bike in Indonesia. So you don't get bogged down by hours of paperwork at the customs dock, try just driving right off the ship and right through the gate saying hello to everyone without stopping. You might make it.

PUSHBIKE

Bicycles here serve as packmule, jalopy for dating, family car, vendor's shop, and what someone uses until he can afford to buy a motorcycle. The places in Indonesia where it's the most pleasant to ride pushbikes (Yogya, Kuta and Legian) they are plenti-ful and fairly cheap to rent. Buy a used bicycle for around Rp10-15,000 to travel overland or to use for a period of time in the cities. Read Hunt Kooiker's *Bali By Bicycle*. It could be dangerous to ride a bicycle on Java and Bali because of the driv-ing attitudes of the drivers. In East Java you could handle it but traffic is too heavy from Solo to Jakar-ta. It really freaks you out to have horns blown at you all the time. The physical shock of riding corru-gated Indonesian roads long distances is a huge strain. If you're not a physical fitness freak and dis-like the torment of the highway, it's suggested that you load your bicycle on top of a bus for the long hauls to the main centers of interest so that you don't arrive too exhausted to enjoy cycling around the local sights once there. Indonesia is a bargain place to get your bicycle repaired, but bike parts in Indonesia are near to impossible to get (except for a few well-stocked *toko sepedas* in Denpasar) so have a care package of parts most likely to break down mailed ahead. Most cycylists don't bring camping equipment because you can stay in *losmens* so cheaply and people are so struck with the novelty of a lone bicycle rider that you are always guested in peoples' homes along the roads. Some police stations are hospitable, some are not.

GETTING AROUND CITIES

Helicaks and *bemos,* 3-4 wheeled vans which carry 6-15 or more people, run along all the main routes in the cities. There are 3 ways you can die in a *bemo:* a head-on collision, suffocate, or die of fright. Hail them over, they cost usually Rp30-50 for a 1-3 km ride. Ask the passengers how much, then ask the driver or the driver's assistent. All over Indonesia you find the *becak* (trishaw) which looks like a big painted rocking chair with wheels. *Becaks* are more expensive than the *bemos*; they cost Rp50-200 for a 1-5 km ride. When asking directions, if people say yes too quickly it probably means maybe or else they don't know. They don't want to disappoint you. Interpret rather the way he says it to determine what he really means. Never ask a leading question such as, 'This is the right way, isn't it?' but instead 'Which is the right way?' Ask at least 3 people, then take a mean average. **car rental:** Nitour, found in all the bigger towns, is the only trustworthy car rental agency. They charge the correct prices and their cars are less likely to break down than other agencies. Always use a driver (sopir) because if there's an accident he'll be liable. *Sopirs* also clean, polish, and do maintenance on the car. If you hire a car privately, *sopirs* usually come with the car.

BY BUS

Bus costs are Rp2-5 per km (but in Kalimantan, Irian Jaya, and Celebes, more). Bus fares for short distances (especially on Java and Bali) are extraordinarily cheap. On the local buses, anywhere you're standing when the bus comes by, that's the bus stop. Traveling by night buses (bis malam) is cooler, faster, and more expensive than regular day buses because they are non-stop. If you roll into a town or city during the day you may store your things safely in the *bis malam* office or even in the local bus station office for the day while you wander around. Some bus companies keep brand new Mercedes buses out front to lure you in, then when you show up for your 30 hour journey it's in an old crate crammed full with as many people as there's standing room. Bus companies very seldom give discounts.

TRAINS, OPLETS, AND COLTS

In South Sumatra and across Java trains are the best, huge black lumbering puffing coal-burning locomotives. For the longer distances, trains are more comfortable than buses. They give up to 35% off for students at the ticket window, though this only applies to the cheaper day-trains. Trains have different prices at different times of day; travel in the more expensive but infinitely better trains (even 3rd class is OK). In Sumatra, an *oplet* is a multi-colored Chevrolet bus, while on Java it's a canopied pickup truck with seats. Mitsubishi Colt (pronounced 'Kol') minibuses travel all the major and secondary roads all over Java, Bali, Sumatra, South Celebes, and South Kalimantan; they usually cost Rp50-100 more than buses. For the shorter distances, they're fast and more comfortable than trains and the bigger buses. Colts are always departing (as soon as they're full) and arriving; like a taxi, they will often take you right to the doorstep of your destination. This is well worth the extra money that would otherwise be spent after hasseling for a *becak* or *bemo.* When you reach a town and you want to find the bus, *oplet,* or Colt station in order to continue on to your destination, just ask, *Dimana stasiun ____?,* with the name of your destination put after.

BY AIR

In Kalimantan, Irian Jaya, and Sumatra, frequently you can take flights on missionary or oil-company aircraft. You could be lucky and get a free ride with a lone charter, but most often you have to pay. If you have to go through an Indonesian mediary, you might have to pay for a ride which ordinarily would be free. Garuda is the largest of all the Indonesian airlines, flying major international routes plus to 26 domestic airports (mostly DC 9's and Fokker F27's). In Indonesia fares are a bit more efficient than other Indonesian airlines though 15-20% more expensive. Or by world carrier standards, Garuda's services and reliability are below that of other international carriers and their international flights are dearer than most international airlines. Mandala Airlines flies main points on Java and Bali, plus Sumbawa, Ambon, and most of the principal towns of Sulawesi. Merpati Airlines covers 53 destinations inside Indonesia plus flies to Darwin, Penang, Kuala Lumpur, and Kucing. Zamrud only operates in Nusa Tenggara. Check Mandala and Zamrud airlines first, they may be cheaper in places. Pelita, a subsidiary of Pertamina, has a fleet of 80 helicopters and 30 fixed winged aircraft which mostly serve Pertamina and the 37 foreign oil companies in Indonesia, but they also regularly carry paying passengers such as from Jakarta to the Thousand Islands and to Pelabuhan Ratu, both in West Java. Bouraq Airlines serves Jakarta and Surabaya on Java, many points in Kalimantan, Sulawesi, Ambon, Ternate; Davao and Zamboanga in the southern Philippines (only by charter), and Tawau in East Malaysia. To charter an aircraft costs approximately US$220-800 per hour depending on the type.

MAPS

The most extensive collection of maps for sale in Australia is at Angus & Robertsons, 107 Elizabeth St., Melbourne, or at Sydney's Angus & Robertsons, Pitt St., or at Dymock's on George St. in Sydney. Get good US Airforce maps of all the main Indonesian islands in the map room of the Adelaide Public Library blown up on their photocopy machine for free. An atlas of all the tropical Netherlands territories (*Atlas van tropish Nederland*, Batavia, Topographical Survey of the Netherlands Indies) was printed in 1938 and many of its social, economic, and political assertions have long been outdated. Still, this pre-war atlas is the most general and thorough available. If you have photostat copies made of this atlas, you'll possess the best.

PAPERS AND BOOKS

Get an international driver's licence in Australia (Aus$2) if you want to rent a motorcycle on Bali or in Sulawesi; a licence on Bali costs Aus$9! The International Student Identification Card is still useful for discounts on trains and planes. Counterfeit ones on Bali sell for US$4 and US$2 for each yearly stamp; these are also for sale at Jay's Travel Agency near the Malaysia Hotel, 54 Ngam Duplee Rd., Rama 4, Bangkok. If you want to do some reading up beforehand, Mitchell Library in Sydney has one of the largest collections of books in the world on Australasia, perhaps surpassed only by Cornell University's collection, Ithaca, N.Y., and the collection at Leyden University, Holland. The Adelaide Public Library's Asian collection is also outstanding. The Indonesian Embassy, 8 Darwin Ave., Yarralumia, Canberra, has an information section and a small library. A.N.U. University of Canberra puts out a monthly acquisitions list of all publications relating to Indonesia; they are sent material by their agent who travels around Indonesia and does nothing but acquire books, pamphlets, and periodicals. Buy books on Indonesia outside of Indonesia because imported books cost about 3 times more there. Many titles appearing in Indonesia in the Indonesian language are not distributed outside of Indonesia; for these go to the big bookshops of Jakarta (see 'Jakarta'). MPH Bookshop, 71-77 Stamford Road, Singapore, has a wider selection of books on Indonesia than any bookshop in Indonesia itself–history, culture, politics, anthropology, language study, travel. For further reading, see 'Booklist'. Most of the really useful, interesting, and accurate travel info you'll get from other travelers along the way–

the cheapest *losmens,* where to eat and drink (in detail), the most isolated beaches, the most unusual things to do. 13,000 islands should keep you busy for awhile.

TRANSPORT BY SEA

Boats and ships go everywhere, even up to 900 km inland from the mouths of rivers (in Kalimantan). Surabaya and Jakarta are the nerve centers for shipping in Indonesia. Take either small sailboats (prahus), large sailboats (kapal layar), coasters (kapal motor) or sea-going ships (kapal laut). Kalimantan, a big part of a giant equatorial swampy island, has its own genus of river boats. Most ferrys for river and channel crossings are owned by the railway system; this is why connections between railheads, rivers and channels are so much smoother. Check with the *syahbandar* (harbormaster) in the thousands of ports of Indonesia about the coming and going of boats and their prices. Most carry cargo with limited room for passengers. Often it's cheaper to go directly up to the captain himself and pay him your fare; if you go to a ticket agent it could be 10-15% more expensive. Usually there's no student discount on vessels, but always try (especially in the southeast islands and in Sulawesi). At a ticket office have the ticket seller carefully itemize for you each 'extra' charge on your ticket; he might not have had lunch yet. Don't fall for the *asuransi* bit; by the time you collect you'll be too old to enjoy it. Pelni, the largest shipping company, is state-owned and connects most of the fair-sized ports of Indonesia. Other big shipping companies are Arafat and Sriwijaya; always check with them, they could have smaller ships, friendly crews, cheaper fares and better food than Pelni. Always call to confirm embarcation time on the day of departure. At ports, custom officials don't want to hassel anyone who's talking friendly to them. Take a big *durian* through customs; it creates such a conversation piece if a westerner is seen carrying one that the police and the customs guys forget to be mean.

sea travel: You definitely must be open-ended with your schedule if traveling by sea; in other words, don't have one. Indonesians call it *jam karet* (rubber time). Sometimes you wait 30 hours on deck for your ship to leave port. Most smaller boats don't carry flares, radios, or spare parts and you could be riding anchor 2 weeks in the middle of the Makassar Strait with a missing propellor before help comes. Take along a woven rattan mat (*tikar,* costs Rp200) with which you stake out your territory; the *tikar* serves as your carpet by day and mattress by night. Or sometimes you can rent a folding bed from the crew, Rp2-300, or crew members could even give over their own cabin for rent. Go onboard early or the night before to get a good place to avoid sleeping in piss and mire amongst masses of people; also much of the available space could be taken up by merchandise. Though the food is monotonous, deck class is not only the cheapest but often superior to the small hot cabins. On the big ships unless you fancy chunky white rice and fishheads, bring your own victuals. They only serve meals twice a day. Some smaller boats serve freshly caught fish but most give you salted dehydrated fish which smells like wet dog fur. For sustainance and divergence through the voyage bring fresh fruits and vegetables, canned cheese and fish, sago cakes, dried toast, biscuits, nuts, candy, coffee, tea, and sugar. There's always hot water. Bring your own tin cup, plate, and eating utensils, these are seldom provided. Cork up a couple of bottles of drinking water. On bigger ships sometimes you can slip the 2nd class kitchen or the officer's mess some money or a shirt and they'll deliver you food even if you're traveling deck class. You get a lot of mileage out of your white skin in Asia. If you pay a bit more to go 2nd or 1st class, the Indonesian islands are a place where you can still experience leisurely, luxurious 19th Century travel in ocean-going ships; by the time you buy your 6 kilos of peanuts, oranges, etc. to sustain you through the deck class journey, you might have spent more!

kapal layar: It's harder than you think getting on one of the bigger Bugis *kapal layar* cargo boats to the outer islands from Surabaya or Jakarta. Unless you just show up with all your luggage and sit on the boat, a lot of times they sail off without you. They make enough money shipping their cargoes and don't really need your piddly 5000 rupes to take you to Ujung Pandang or elsewhere. Besides you might prove more trouble than you're worth. These huge motorless boats, which look like a fat, round bilged sailing hippopotamus with an enormous and unweildy lateen sail, are sometimes stuck out on a windless sea for a week. You could get sick or get washed overboard. It's much easier to get on the big sailing boats on the outer islands to *other* outer islands (from Flores to Sumbawa, for example) where they depend more on passenger fares. Try to get on one just for the sheer medieval experience of it. A little grass and a bottle of Chinese wine is enough to guide you in the night like the north star.

HEALTH

A traveler is more likely to get hurt or killed riding a motorcycle on Bali his very first week in Indonesia (snuffs out 3 Aussies a month) than he's likely to get some hideous tropical disease. Most illnesses among travelers are resistence-diseases, a result of their health running down, smoking too much dope, eating poorly, etc. While in Indonesia take local or Chinese medicines and treatments for what ails you, they know best what it takes for a cure. Make up your own medical kit before you go of antiseptic, gauze, surgical tape. Indonesia's fruits provide your multi-vitamins. **Note:** You need up-to-date typhus and cholera shots to get into Indonesia.

VITAMINS

Vitamin tablets, when available, are fiendishly expensive in Indonesia. Take iron and calcium because of the lack of dairy procucts. If you feel run down or have trouble with menstruation, eat much liver. If you eat too much rice, you'll lack vitamin B; take vitamin B12 and B6 because they work as a catylyst for each other. It's also advisable to take 2 nevoquin tablets weekly or Fansidar by Roche (take 3 once a month) to prevent malaria, though it customarily isn't a problem over 1800 m.

COMFORT

For plain comfort, wear what Indonesians wear like cool *sarungs* and *kains,* and do what they do. Besides its most common use as a colorful wraparound skirt, a *sarung* is also an all purpose garment used to carry fruit or babies, as a baby hammock, to cover yourself while bathing, as a nightgown or bedcover, as comfortable informal wear tied over the breasts, as an umbrella, etc. Man-made chemical fabrics (nylon, rayon, etc.) are too hot and sticky, so just wear drip dry cotton clothes. At night Indonesians of all ages love to cuddle a long skinny sausage-shaped pillow, the *bantal guling* ('Dutch Wife'), which looks like a punching bag. This pillow absorbs the sweat so that you can sleep sounder while it delightfully fits the contours of arms and legs. In cheap hotels keep mosquitos off by moving your bed under a fan or by using mosquito coils (obat nyamuk) which are quite effective, slightly nauseating, and can be bought anywhere for Rp75-100. If you lay your mattress out in strong sunlight, bed-bugs will vacate it. Take a *mandi* to stay cool, though if it's too hot it'll give you a headache. When you're hot, bring your inner body temperature up to the outside temperature by drinking hot tea; cold cokes just make you all the the thirstier. It's good to be out in the sun's torrid heat sometime during the day; it has a purifying effect.

HOSPITALS

If you get bronchitis, get into dry country. If you're seriously ill, get to Jakarta (which has Indonesia's best medical facilities), Semarang, Bandung, Surabaya, Medan, or Singapore, cities which have the best equipped hospitals. You can buy most medicines in Indonesia without a prescription but you'll need to bargain heatedly in the drugstores (apotek). Keep all medicines out of reach of Indonesians; it's like candy to them. Doctors cost much less in Indonesia (Rp1000-2000) than say in Thailand. As a general rule, if you have to go to a doctor at all, go to a Chinese one. All reports indicate that Bali has really freaky medical services and that malpractice is widespread. There's a hospital in Kediri, East Java, run by American 7th Day Adventists. If you need an operation, go there or to Singapore. In many of the outer islands the only treatment available is from small foreign supported missionary clinics or poorly staffed and outfitted government health centers.

SKIN AILMENTS

Phisohex is best for rashes and sores. For fungus, buy Mycolog in Indonesia. Whenever the skin is broken, clean it, treat it, and cover it. Bacteria breeds very quickly in this climate and the tiniest cut could become a festering tropical ulcer which necessitates prolonged antibiotic treatment. Since antibiotics break down your resistence, only use them as a last resort. Antibiotic Cicatran Cream and penicillin powder are good for cuts and mosquito bites that have gone septic. Sepso-tupf from Germany heals small cuts by morning. Bacitracin is a very good bacterial ointment available in Indonesia. Outstanding ointments used against tropical ulcers are F.G. Ointment (Meiji) and Neosporin Ointment. Native herbal treatments include *bajamduri* (spiny spinach) for treating burns, and Cap Pagoda Cream for tropical ulcers. Eat garlic for worms and the odor keeps mosquitoes (and people) off your skin. *Lular* paste, made from rice mixed with pulverized bark and flowers slows the wrinkling and aging process. *Mangir* is a yellow powder put on the skin to makes it clear, fragrant, refined.

MUSCLEACHES, PAINS, AND SPRAINS

Indonesians think it ludicrous that westerners take aspirins for a headache when the only sensible thing is to get a massage. The Danis of Irian Jaya tie smoked charmed grasses around the neck and some Indonesians wear little white tapes which contain an anesthetic on their temples. There's also a green paste to smear on the forehead to cure a headache. The *krok*-treatment consists of rubbing I-Ching coins on the skin in combination with eucalyptus oil to produce a friction rash so that the pores open to let out the pain and heat (and evil). *Kayumanis* is a stick which is chewed for throat ailments; it tastes sweet but is expensive at Rp2000 a bundle. For sprained ankles and wrists, apply ice for the first 24 hours, heat the next 24 hours. Also use *daun kelor* which can be bought in the market for Rp10; enough to fix you up. Mix it up yourself (add salt) and apply it like a mudpack. Swelling and pain goes down within 2 days. A species of dogbane (strophanthus) yields cortizone which reduces pain and swelling. Irianese rub the skin with big nettle leaves which causes it to burn and blister, but the cramp goes away. Bring baby powder to prevent rashes because you're always splashing your ass with water. *Kayuputih* oil is a native oil (but not greasy) used for the treatment of skin diseases, rubbed on for colds, headaches, stomach aches, ideal for massages, soothes mosquito bites, skin rashes, clears up nose and head during bouts of influenza, is good for your skin and gives your hair back its health if it's too dry. A little bottle costs Rp100 (it's the cheapest in Maluku). The Chinese call the all-purpose salve, Tiger Balm, the 'Ten Thousand Uses Ointment'. If rubbed on the center of the forehead it brings out your spiritual 'third eye', plus works wonderous other cures. It can be used as an insect repellant, and if you put it on mosquito bites it stops the swelling and itching. Smear Tiger Balm around the legs of your bed, it keeps the bedbugs away. If rubbed vigorously on the temples its heat draws out the pain of headaches. If rubbed on teeth and gums, it relieves toothaches. For mentholated joints, roll grass over Tiger Balm smeared on the palm of the hand. Or coat it inside of a chillum. If put under the nose, it clears the nostrils. Put a lighted match under the jar and inhale the fumes to blast away sinus congestion. It increases the circulation of blood in the muscles and makes for extraordinarily sensual toe massages. Put very lightly on the eyelids for clearing eyes reddened by city smog. If you have arthritis, rub it in really hard. It also helps to alleviate the discomfort of rheumatism and muscleaches. Buy it on Dixon St. (Chinatown), Sydney; or at Nusa Indah, Barton Highway, Hall, A.C.T. There are two kinds, white and red. The red is stronger but more expensive and stains clothing.

THE SHITS

Before you consider eating in a *warung* or restaurant look closely at the faces of the cooks and the people who will serve you. They also eat the food they sell you and if their faces reflect ill-health and their establishment is unkempt, walk on by. Eat hot chili peppers with your meals to kill the bacteria. Cardamom are peppery seeds used as a carminative and as a digestant. If you do get the shits, go on a diet with sugarless light tea for a day, then afterwards add biscuits until you're well. Indonesian families drink *jamu* and eat the young *jambu* fruit and plain rice if they eat at all. Opium drops are also excellent. The best thing of course is just to shut down and starve those mothers out. If you believe in white man's medicine, Loperamid-hydrochloride is the best. Enterovioform, mexaform are dangerous. After a serious attack of the shits your body is dehydrated and there could be painful muscular contractions in the stomach; fruit juice with a teaspoon of salt dissolved in it will counteract this. If you're shitting out a litre an hour be sure to drink that much H_2O because it could be cholera; you might need intravenous feeding. If you see blood in the diarrhea (black-colored stools) you probably have dysentery. Seek medical attention as this disease can cause severe damage to the intestines and to general health. Against mild dysentery or fevers, 10 papaya or pumpkin seeds a day should do it. Don't overconsume fruits, especially during Dec. and Jan; even the Balinese get the infamous Bali Belly' during this epidemic season.

HEPATITIS

Often you're just hasseling your head if you worry about hepatitis because this consciousness overlaps into other things, 'How were these dishes washed? Was the tea boiled long enough?' If it's your turn to get the Hep, you're gonna get it. Hepatitis is a debilitating liver disease which turns the skin and the whites of the eyes yellow, you feel mainly a dramatic loss of appetite and sleepiness, your shit turns whitish, you piss deep orange or brown. See a doctor. Relax in the shade of a hill climate. Never drink alcohol while under treatment. Though it doesn't prevent the disease, a gammaglobulin shot beforehand ameliorates the symptoms if you do get hepatitis.

GONNORHOEA

This venereal disease is not very serious, but could be if ignored or not recognized. Like getting a runny nose except easier to clear up. Just go to an outpatient clinic as their treatment is often much cheaper than private doctors. A public hospital usually charges you a mere Rp150-250 for a 1.500.000 unit injection of penicillin or tetracycline. You need two injections plus a course of ampicilline. A private hospital or a hospital run by a church group could charge you up to Rp10,000 as atonement for this very routine and simple treatment. **vaginal in-**

fections: Try Canesten, made by Bayer, a broad spectrum anti-fungal. Fungus is caused by a bacterial imbalance and yoghurt is a bacterial culture, so yoghurt on a tampon neutralizes the fungus and soothes the itch.

LEECHES

Smelling the perspiring odor of men, leeches wait insidiously at the sides of tracks, cling to trees or hang from leaves overhead along dense jungle tracks used by deer and wild pigs, waiting to fall into your hair or beard (they love darkness), push their suckers through boot eyelets, get under your belt and into the groin area, and even penetrate the anus. They also attack at night while sleeping. Clothes only offer a catchhold for leeches; it's better to walk barefoot and go half naked like the Dayaks of Kalimantan who cover their bodies with mud while hiking. Also effective is to put soap on your skin and let it dry. If you're naked you can just pick them off as you see them; they usually can't be felt until they drop off saturated with your blood, or you feel a trickle of blood or a warm sticky spot under your clothes or inside your boot. Either burn them off with a cigarette or apply salt to make them fall off, then use cigarette paper to help stop the flow of blood as they inject a substance which keeps blood from coagulating. Don't tear them off, off, bites could become inflamed.

DUKUNS

Great numbers of Indonesia's 135 million people put their faith in the *dukun* (folk doctor). For the villager he is cheap and he's on the spot; they go to him first before they would go to any hospital. In the cities often you see them standing or sitting in parks or on street corners inside circles 5 people deep, giving their sales talks on their special medicines. Long established opponents of western medicine, these barefoot doctors have used locally made remedies and treatments for thousands of years Though many of the *dukun's* medicines have never been tested (obat serasi), some of his remedies have a sound scientific basis in modern medicine. Dukuns were the first to use quinine to cure malaria. The *dukun* often receives no consultation fee but gets his income from the sale of herbs only. They are men who supposedly have supernatural powers. It's believed that some *dukuns* contain souls of dead people who talk through them, speaking in tongues of the spirit or in Old Javanese. Among them are witch doctors who can exorcize evil spirits from houses and heal illnesses by faith. They can rid people who have been secretly poisoned or purge them of spells cast on them by less powerful *dukuns*. These native medicos believe that mind rules over matter; for psychosomatic sicknesses they dispense psychosomatic cures. Often secret Islamic sayings and prayers are written on pieces of paper then dunked in a glass of water. When drunk, the patient is cured of his ailment. *Dukuns* can also improve a client's sex appeal; a diamond blown onto the lips by a *dukun* will give his customer an irrestible smile and fascination for the opposite sex.

JAMU

Herbal medicines, called *jamu,* are derived from plants, grasses, minerals, fungi, roots, barks, parts of mammals, birds, and reptiles. They come in the form of pills, capsules, powders, beans, peas, flat seeds, or else look like tea leaves. See tri-colored *jamu* stalls in the markets painted up like barber poles with lots of packages, little jars and bottles in them. Go up and act out your illness or pain and they'll know what you'll need. *Jamu* is cheap, about Rp25 a packet; the 'super' is served with egg, 2 sorts of wine, a cup of sweet tea and a lolly afterwards, Rp100. Most *jamus* have real pop names like Rooster (Cap Jago) or the Fountain of Youth (Air Mancur). There are hundreds of different *jamus* for every conceivable malady. Javanese women look astonishingly well preserved after having 6 kids because new mothers take up to 10 *jamus* internally and externally over a period of 40 days after delivery to remove any excess blood from the body, to contract abdominal muscles, for slimming, to restore vigor, to reinforce sex appeal. Patmosari or Jamu Galian Singset makes women between 20 and 50 younger looking, causes the vagina to become tighter, revitalizes and slims her. Women over 50 drink a special *jamu* to keep themselves from getting too thin. Jelok Temu is given to one year old babies for strength. Jantung fortifies the heart. Ginjal is for inflamed appendix, making an operation unnecessary. Kumis Kucing (cat-whiskers) is for urinary tract infections. Beras Kencur peps you up all day. If you're tired, on a bad depressing trip, take a 40-day course of the curative Colasan which really blasts you right out of whatever it is that's hanging you up; like an organic speed clearing. There are mens' tonics to increase strength and if rubbed on at night all feeling of tiredness and stiffness are gone by morning. There are also herbs to strengthen and increase health of the hardworking woman, *jamus* for colds, tightness or dizziness of the head, runny nose, sore throat, bronchitis, flu, 'starryeyes', anti-cough herbs, others for sore bones, backaches and listlessness. *Jamus* can quickly smooth out wrinkled skin, cure bloodshot eyes and hangovers, intestinal tapeworms, stomach sickness, indigestion and overeating, pimples, skin diseases and rashes. Girls take Kokok after menstruation, cleansing the blood, beautifing, making the eyes and face bright. Other *jamu* are for late menstruation or taken before to ensure that it comes on time (but be warned that it can cause abortions if 1-2 months pregnant). Special aphrodisiacal *jamu* are available to increase virility'. For women, especially mothers with many children, there is 'magic formula No. 125'; they will find that their husbands will become more considerate.

MONEY

Indonesian money is called *rupiah* (Rp). US$1 = Rp400-415. The rates for foreign currencies depend on the bank and even on the *branch* of the bank. Check with the money changers in Singapore's Change Alley near the G.P.O.; they could give a good *rupiah* rate for Australian or US cash. The best rates in Indonesia are usually found in tourist towns. US currency has the most fixed rate of exchange because the *rupiah* is based on it. But don't make the mistake of always translating Indonesian prices into US currency; think in *rupiahs*, not in dollars. It doesn't cost 'just' 80 American cents, it costs 300 goddamn *rupiahs*! Swaggering with your money in Indonesia is super-uncool. To the man-in-the-street a dollar's worth of *rupiahs* has the same emotional impact as US$5 has to us. US$300 is enough to keep a rural Indonesian family of 6 for a year. There's no black market so bring travelers cheques for safety. Buy American Express or Cook's T.C.'s because these companies have branches in Jakarta, Singapore and all over the world, in case you lose them. Some of Australia's savings banks and other lesser known banks without agents in Asia will let you starve before they replace your lost chequeo. Traveler's Cheques usually carry a better rate than cash, but carry some US$1's and US$5's in case you need quick money when banks are closed. In the outer islands such as Maluku and Irian Jaya, foreign cash fetches a higher rate than foreign T.C.'s. Or better still, since the best rates are found on Java, buy Indonesian Bank Bumi Daya T.C.'s to take to the outer islands. Bank Negara is typical of Indonesian commercial practices: they keep the money you have wired for up to 2-3 months and invest it. Bank Bumi Daya has a better reputation; they take most Aussie and the better known T.C.'s. If you're on the move, count on living for about US$3 a day or in places like Jakarta, and in Irian Jaya and Maluku about US$5 a day. If you're staying put, much less. There are tens of thousands of villages where you can live for US50¢ a day if you do it like the people. On account of the intense competition the cheapest places are right along the traveler's trail-Bali, Yogya, Lake Toba, etc. Unless it's a village, more off-the-track places are usually more expensive. Mountain resorts are the most expensive. Don't think that because it's so cheap in the tourist ghettoes that you won't get extravagant. Often you spend more. Instead of buying one of it, you buy three of it. If you have an Indonesian buy your tickets for boats, flights, buses, vehicle charters, also fruits, food, shoes, etc., they get better prices than you. Always try asking for *harga belajar* (student's price). If you speak the national language, *Bahasa Indonesia,* they reckon you already know the prices ad usually they won't charge as much. Sometimes guards try to make you pay a fee to enter a parking lot, historical site, temple or museum; plus Rp75-100 for your camera. If you can't afford it, put the camera in a bag, go around the side and get in free. Or demand a ticket with the price on it, otherwise don't pay it (unless only a 'donation' is asked for, then Rp50 is enough). If you can spare it, give something; the attendants make their living from tourists. In Indonesia there's a price for everything-a better seat on the bus, for extra sugar or ice in your drink, to urinate at the market, for the use of a fan, for each and every application form at a government office, and even to pick up letters at Post Restante (Rp10 per) - everything. Be prepared for *korupsi;* perhaps 30% of the salaries of civil servants come from bribes. You known when it's coming, 'The official is out . . . , or 'The matter must be referred to another department . . . or 'No more forms.' You can pay your way out of almost anything in Indonesia: for forgetting a cholera shot at Bali airport, Rp800: for a dope buot on Java, Rp2U,UUU; for killing a man in Medan, Rp60,000, and so on; prices subject to inflation. Bring watches, flashy shirts, and trendy clothes for trading, making it possible to strike up some good deals for artwork, fabrics, jewelry, etc. Even wool is coveted.

BARGAINING

Bargain hard always for everything everywhere including medicine in drugstores, hospitalization, immigration fees, entrance charges to museums, no matter what it is. The more Indonesians overcharge, the less communication there is and the more impoverished the communication becomes. Ask the price of everything first; don't ever assume anything or take a bystander's word for it. For luxury items like carvings and paintings (never show your *true* interest), start out with ¼ the price they ask; for services like buses, *becaks,* laundry, photo prints, start out at ½ of the price they ask; for essentials like canned groceries, room rental, soap, start off at ¾'s of the price they ask-roughly. Bargaining is a leisurely and friendly exchange. Make the first offer so that the trader doesn't start out too high. Go up only Rp 10-25 at a time, fight for every decimal. When they smile it means your offer was too realistic, when they frown the bargaining's reaching its conclusion. Don't try to get the same prices as the locals, you can't. You pay according to your station in life. If you say you're poor, they just laugh. If you're poor, how come you're there?

WORK IN INDONESIA

Get jobs in the oil and timber companies with profit-sharing contracts in Indonesia by applying in the companies' offices in Houston, Dallas, Jakarta, or Singapore. You have a chance in Singapore, but don't go to the offices, go to the bars: Gill's Grill in the Shaw Center, Genieveve's in the International Bldg., the Tropicana Club next to the Shaw Center, the Ambassador Hotel and the Country Club Hotel in Katong, and other places where the oilies and chippies hang out. Get your interview, medical examination, work visa, and sign the contract all in Singapore; in Indonesia all this is too much of a tiring ordeal, including questions like 'Where were you and what did you do on 30 Sept. 1965?' Jobs going in the timber companies are for heavy equipment operators and mechanics. Those with oil companies usually are for offshore rig operators as a roughneck (on the floor of the rig), derrickman (on top of the mast), or as a loadmaster (relaying instructions to coptors building rigs from the air)–all

unskilled jobs, just takes a knack to do them. Some companies give 1 week on the job and 1 week off, others 2 weeks on, 2 weeks off. They fly you in and out of Singapore for free. The basic wage for most jobs is about US$1800 and you could even land a job as Head Gardner in Balikpapan at US$1600 per months. **others:** Caucasian women can work as magazine and advertising models in Jakarta, quite well paid. English teaching in Jakarta and Surabaya is big business. No qualifications, they'll take anyone who speaks intelligible English. In some schools, classes read American dialogue, listen to the Aussie accent on tapes, while learning under a German teacher! The school gets to use you to draw the students in and the students have a bit of fun communicating with a real live native speaker in a real live language lab (though most have fake or faulty technical equipment). You're obliged to stay a little while, the course is usually 3 months. You are paid an average of Rp750-1000 per hour, though in Bandung the wage is Rp1500 per hour, or Rp2000 if you speak Indonesian. I.E.C. Schools (Intensive English Course) will arrange a work permit for you after 3 months on the job.

VISAS

If you have a passport, you're rich. Visas are issued in Australia at the Indonesian Government Office, 6 Bridge St., Sydney; Indonesian Consulate, 8 Darwin Ave., Yarralumla, Canberra; Indonesian Consulate, Grain Pool Bldg., King St., Perth, W.A. They say Canberra is kind of slow at issuing one. In Singapore, 1st floor, Wisma Indonesia, 435 Orchard Road, they're just too busy to care who or what you are so it takes only 2 days. In Penang, Malaysia, the Indonesian Consulate is on 9 Beach Road, right next to the Hongkong Shanghai Bank, and they're real bitchy, asking embarrassing questions like how much money you have and for tickets, etc. In Kuala Lumpur, the new Indonesian Embassy is on Jl. Pekeliling. In Colombo, Sri Lanka, it costs just Aus$1.50 for your Indonesian visa. If everything is in order most consulates take only 3 days to get your visa ready; visas are valid for 90 days.

SOME TIPS

If you're a writer or a journalist, don't say so. If you think there's going to be any trouble at all, submit your passport with a big travel agency who'll get it processed for you; there's a better chance of getting through since they do 100's of passports at a time. These travel agents charge extra for the mailing and legwork; about Aus$10 for a 28 day or around Aus$26 for a 5 week visa. At the Indonesian consulate you might be asked for air tickets into

and/or out of Indonesia before you're issued a visa. In this case the cheapest is to just buy a MAS ticket for Aus$38 from Medan, North Sumatra, to Penang, Malaysia. The TAA office in Darwin won't sell you tickets for this flight because too many freaks cash it in and take the Medan-Penang boat, which is only Aus$20 (when it's working). One way to get around the onward ticket bit is to get a Miscellaneous Charge Order (MCO) which looks like an air ticket but is really just a receipt for money which you deposit with them. Just write in the travel details space 'Medan-Penang' or 'Jakarta-Singapore' or the like. This is acceptable to consulate officials and if bought from a large international airlines it can be cashed in any airlines office in the world whereas an air ticket can usually only be cashed in the office where you bought it. If you want a student discount, tickets usually have to be paid in cash thus you can only use an MCO towards full fare purchases. Going east to Indonesia, Singapore is the last place you can cash in a TAA ticket.

TYPES OF VISAS

A four week visa costs Aus$3.20 and a five week visa costs Aus$23.20 (Aus$20 extra for the so-called Landing Fee). Pay for this Landing Fee in the country you get your visa in and get it over with; make sure that 'Landing Fee Paid' is stamped or written in your passport no matter *where* you get it. For the 6 month Visitor's Visa, fill out a special application form and show a letter from a sponsor or a guarantor in Indonesia. On this sort of visa you still have to pay the Landing Fee but you pay only the ordinary price for each of your 5 extensions which you should receive automatically. Bring the sponsor's letter with you because the *imigrasi* officer in Indonesia sometimes asks to see it for extensions. Work visas such as for teachers are issued for up to 2 years. Research visas (anthropology is easier to get than archaeology) usually run a year or 2, although at times given for only 3 months. All research visas must go through LIPI (Lembaga Ilmu Pengetahran Indonesia), a body in Jakarta that arbitrarily clears each one. Often LIPI makes more difficulties for you than they actually help you. You could hassel with them in Jakarta for weeks, the real run around. And even if LIPI authorizes your request for a research visa, BAKIN (the security arm of the government) could block it. An indefinite residency permit will run you about US$1000; cheap for such a startlingly exciting place to live, especially if you have a steady income. Inside Indonesia itself it's almost impossible to change over from a tourist visa to a resident visa through official channels. Some travel agents can fix up resident permits for you for a fee.

VISA EXTENSIONS

If you stay in Indonesia more than 28 days or 5 weeks, you have to start haggling with *imigrasi*. You can always get a 3-4 day extension over your 28 day visa to meet a ship or plane (if you show them your ticket) but anything longer than that you have to pay the infamous Landing Fee. In each *imigrasi* office it's a personal business transaction between the official and you and the price that he finally decides upon for a visa extension ranges from Rp2000-3500. In many offices you can even get away with bargaining a bit, especially for the more expensive extensions of work or resident visas. Get visa extensions only in provincial capitals, *Ibu Kota*, on each island. To get more than 3 months could be difficult and sometimes a letter of recommendation from a government official or a respected property-owning sponsor is necessary. If you stay over 3 months then you must 'register as an alien' and pay Rp750 (plus Rp200 for 2 forms) and be fingerprinted. Organizations like Sumarah in Solo, Central Java, have been known to make it easier for travelers to get extensions in order to study their religious discipline. It's easier for Europeans to get extensions than it is for North Americans or Australians, and for some reason, easiest of all for Germans. Right now Bandung, Ujung Pandang, Lombok, (Mataram), and Jayapura are the most sympatico *imigrasi* offices in Indonesia and still fairly cheap; people even get a 5th month in those places. In Surabaya and other places unofficial monthly extensions, if you've already spent 4 months in Indonesia, cost Rp15-20,000; if you pay the Rp20,000 each month you can stay in Indonesia indefinitely. You can get visa extensions to remain in Indonesia (to export handicrafts and textiles, for instance) if you have an Indonesian sponsor you or if you start up a company with an Indonesian, then 'the company' will sponsor you. If you can no longer get visa extensions and still want to spend more time in Indonesia, every 5-6 months or so go to Singapore, Tawau (East Malaysia), Port Moresby (P.N.G.), Australia, or Penang (peninsular Malaysia) to get a new visa, then return to Indonesia for another round of visa extensions.

JAVA

INTRODUCTION

When fossil remains of the erect ape *pithecanthropus* were found on Java in 1891, scientists guessed that Java was the original location of the Garden of Eden. This island is one of the richest, lushest, most densely populated, and ranks among the loveliest regions on earth. Theatre-stage scenery. Never forget it. The sun rising over Java is deep red, then orange, then bright yellow, as big as a barn. Deep purple, fiery volcanoes tower over a land of intense green plains, rice terraces, twisting mountain passes, cool hillside resorts, remote crater lakes, wild game parks, botanical gardens, serene beaches, dense rainforests, limestone hills, thick bamboo groves, teak forests. Many areas of Java can be compared to India because of the congestion, the rice paddies, the explosive colors: 'I see India everywhere, but I do not recognize it.' said the great Bengali poet Tagore when he visited Java in 1927. Its people belong to the oceanic branch of the Mongoloid race with light brown skin, straight black hair, high cheekbones, small and slender builds. Here live primarily two ethnic groups, the Sundanese of West Java (15 million) and the Javanese of Central and East Java (about 65 million). The Dutch concentration of all their resources on Java for several hundred years greatly increased the differences between it and the other islands of Indonesia. Educationally, it's the most advanced. Java's technological institutes form the backbone of Indonesia's tertiary education. Java is top heavy with industry, the island of opportunity where young men flock to find jobs. Yet, because of its giant population, Java could never survive if it were left to its own resources: it would be a head without a body. Java is both young and old. It was the genesis of Indonesia's most powerful martime and agricultural kingdoms, and contains by far the best preserved and highest number of monuments, many completed centuries before Columbus discovered America.

transport: No problems getting around. Java has 3/4's of all tarred roads in Indonesia. Each district has its own type of bus, cart, wagon, gig, carriage, *oplet* and *becak* with their own harnesses, designs, colors. Hitching is fairly good. **trains:** Take trains on Java, day-buses are too tiresome and hot. Student discounts are given only on the cheap trains (25%-33% off). The *senya* (dusk) trains leave Surabaya and Jakarta around 6 pm and reach the center of Java (Yogya) around 8 or 10 am. They also leave from Central Java at dusk for Jakarta and Surabaya. Two parallel railways run the whole length,

along the north coast and another through the center via Yogya and Bogor. Krupp locomotives commissioned in 1881 are still running. No point is more than 80 km from a RR station. **boats and ships:** Nor can you get more than 160 km from the sea. There are hundreds of ports on the north coast. Surabaya and Jakarta are the best ports from which to catch *kapal motors* and ships to the outer islands. **buses:** For the really out of the way places, take buses rather than trains. Always ask the guys in the white shirts in the bus station information office about which buses to where and when. Most helpful. Leave your gear safely with them so you can wander around town before catching your bus out. On Java the bus and taxi stations are often called by the old Dutch name: *stanplatz*. On some of the long-distance buses or *bis malam* (night bushes) meals, snacks, and drinks are included in the fare.

the land: A volcanic chain of mountains extends the whole length of the island: 15 volcanoes are above 3000 m and 44 are between 2-3000 m. There's a vast contrast between the sluggish muddy isle-enclosed Java Sea of the north coast, and the wild deserted shoreline of the South Sea, where the continental shelf drops off sharply into the Indian Ocean and tremendous waves crash against steep dangerous beaches. Most manufacturing and processing in Indonesia takes place on Java. The main manufactured products of Java are tea, tobacco, foods, beverages, rubber, textiles, timber. In East Java there are many sugar cane plantations. Java's level of fertility is without parallel in any equatorial land elsewhere and most of its people make their living by farming. Because of the miraculously rich volcanic soil, farmers often harvest 2 or even 3 rice crops a year; maize grows in 7 weeks and a banana tree in 10 weeks. Some irrigation systems are over 2000 years old. There isn't enough land to go around and, since large families are common, land is split up many times among sons and daughters. Javanese farmers must make a living for their families of 5 and 6 children from the same space that an average Australian farm family uses to park its cars and tractors. The average holding has now dropped to 0.6 hectare of land per family (about 2 acres) with 0.3 being for rice, and the rest the family uses as fruit and vegetable gardens, house and stables. Only 7% of Java's land is cultivated by estates as compared to about 93% managed by smallholders. Steep hills are laboriously terraced, sometimes only one meter wide, by handtool methods. Everything that grows on Java has its use and nothing is thrown away unless it's made into compost or used to feed chickens. Rocks and stones are removed by hand and stray soil is swept up with brooms and returned to the paddy. In principle, land is village owned and established villagers have a right to work land which was cultivated by their ancestors. Shifting cultivation is almost unknown, cattle are seldom raised. Java has been without arable forest land since before WWII, since all its forests have been cut down to make room for people and for rice-growing. No more forests can be cleared for farming or for firewood without increasing the very serious erosion problem even more. It is already a race against time. The funds which are directed for re-forestation and extensive terracing only get siphoned off as they travel down the long pipeline of offices and departments. The Javanese farmer won't begin terracing a whole hillside for Rp2000. Meanwhile the topsoil of Java is sliding into the sea; the whole island might be a desert by the year 2050.

flora and fauna: There exist 500 species of butterflies, 100 varieties of snakes, 400 species of birds, including the Fairy Bluebird of Java. Also rhinoceros, tigers, panthers, deer, wild buffalo. Java's frogs sound like birds. There are at least 5000 plant species including about 35 kinds of fruits, 20 of them found nowhere else. There are giant strawberries, turpentine mangoes, scarlet hibiscus (Kembang sepatu); moonlight orchids, water lilies, frangipani, the lotus (padmasna) flower. Gossamer beards hang down from kapok trees, showers of brilliant flowers sit atop cassieas and trees-of-fire. High forest regions have azaleas, rhododendrums growing wild, yew trees, heather, lily of the valley, myrtle, honey-suckle, even edelweiss.

climate: It's a myth of temperate peoples that the tropics have perpetual bright blue skies. Since this island is so mountainous (121 volcanoes), it's often cloudy. Though the sun doesn't stay hidden for long, bright clear days are rare. From Dec.-Mar. it's rainy, especially in the northern parts of Java. It rains heaviest in February. Java's 'winter' is June, July and August, one of the most pleasant times to visit.

history: Because of such large surpluses obtained from wet rice cultivation throughout its history, great pre-colonial empires have arisen on this island: Majapahit, Singosari, Kediri, Mataram. On all the major islands but Java the major centers of population and power have been located in coastal areas. Java is in the center of all the islands and has always been the trading focus and tne metropolitan island of the archipelago. It is the golden mean in both size and location, for long the most favored of all Indonesian islands for human habitation. It has a fantastic wealth of documents and monuments compared to the poor archaeological record on the outer islands. Java's history is long. It had a Buddhist king as early as 502 A.D. Ancient Java was a land of peasants and princes with the peasants producing and laboring for the palace cities and temples, providing the massive agricultural wealth for their maritime and export trade. For centuries Indian culture overwhelmed Java and is still very much in evidence today-names of noodles, mystic vocabularies, even trains (the Bima) are named after heroes of the Indian epics. There are still Buddhist and Hindu religious symbols everywhere you turn. Islam extended itself first over the north coast starting in the 14th Century. The first strongholds eventually grew into a series of powerful commercial Islamic city-states. The days of the Hindu kingdoms were numbered. Then for a period of 200 years, beginning in about 1723, Java became the key island in the Dutch East Indies empire, paying its shareholders in Europe an average dividend of 18% per annum. For 40 years during the 19th Century all Java was cultivated like a huge work farm, run by a system of enormously profitable forced deliveries of cash crops. The peasants starved. The Javanese have said that the Dutch had good heads but cold hearts, and claim that they had lost all their lands because it was exactly the reverse with them.

kraton: When the temple-city idea arrived from India, the *kraton* was the Indonesian outcome. These walled fortified palaces of Javanese rulers became the center of political power and culture. Containing several thousand people, each of these self-contained regent cities was tied to a dynasty and each new dynasty founded a new *kraton*. As in India, these fortresses incorportated all that the surrounding region would need in the way of commerce, art, religion. There were banks, baths, shops, temples, massage chambers, schools, workshops, scribes, concubine quarters- everything, both body and soul, the royalty haa a use for. Only the *kratons* were open to all the new values and attractions which the new Indian civilisation had to offer. The further away from the *kratons*, the more the indigenous customs and animism held sway among the rural population. The *kratons* adopted, and then modified, first the caste system of Hinduism, then the philosophical structure of Islam. Being the home of the leisured aristocracy, it was only in these courts where enough wealth existed so that architecture and handicrafts could flower. Craft objects were made as ornaments and utensils for the king and members of the court. The finest *wayang* puppets, masks, and dance costumes in Indonesia were produced here and are still being produced. The

Jakarta is found a monument built to commemorate this Eurasian who in cooperation with a Javanese nobleman planned an indigenous uprising aimed at overthrowing Dutch rule in 1721. Deep rooted Dutch phobia and hysteria over possibilities of Eurasians allying themselves with the native peoples against the Dutch regime is reflected in the severity of the inscription. On top is a skull pierced by an iron spear as a sign of dishonor, and underneath a plaque with the words: 'In loathsome memory of the punished traitor Pieter Erberveld, no one may build, carpentar, lay bricks, or plant on this place either now or on any further day. Batavia, April 14, 1722.'

by a Dutch governor, Jan Pieterszoon Coen, in 1619. Now this despot lies buried under the Jakarta City Museum on the site of an old Church. Agrarian Muslim Mataram armies attacked Dutch controlled Batavia in 1629, but since the Mataram troops couldn't be supplied by overland routes and their supply ships had been sunk by the Dutch, famines and exhaustion defeated them and they withdrew. Batavia then grew to be the center of Dutch power in the archipelago for over 300 years.

HISTORY OF JAVA

Trowulan Museum: Contains relics dating from the 13th Century when East Java was a stronghold of ancient Javanese-Hindu kingdoms. All around Trowulan village is the Majapahit kraton complex, a few remaining gates, temples, and bathing places.

shape with its perfect peak surrounded by 4 minor peaks at a lower level and 4 more tops near the foot, 9 peaks in all. Ruins are spread all over its slopes. The most important groups are on the western slopes. The Hindu bathing place Jalatunda, built in 977 A.D., is well hidden in the forest high on Mt. Bekel, a western peak of Penanggungan. Jalatunda's basin used to receive its water supply from the mountain, the water looked upon as an elixir of immortality. Ashes of an unknown royal person (Airlangga?) are interned under the actual basin. The site once had waterworks, pools, spouts and 16 stone relief panels depicting scenes from the Mahabharata, now most are scattered and in ruins. Belahan bathing place, with its spouts and statues, is another very ancient hermitage, the site of a prehistoric megalithic monument. 500 meters N.E. of Belahan there's a Shivaite temple with only terraces and gateways left. At the southern point of the complex are two four-armed female images 2 m high, representing the goddesses of Lakshmi and Shri, the two incarnations off Vishnu's shakti. Once the bathing place of deities who lived in the mountains, this spring has always been regarded as a sacred site.

the Culture System: The ruthless Dutch Culture System was based on the assumption that only the government could own the land and the native population be allowed only to lease and to work it. The rich Prianger coffee plantation area, 50 km south of Jakarta, has the distinction of retaining this forced cultivation system in Indonesia for the longest time (for 200 years, until 1916). The east Priangan area around Garut is the oldest tourist region in Indonesia. During the colonial administration, Dutch entrepreneurs owned vast plantations in this area, spending their leisure in mountain villas and luxurious hotels that dotted the hills.

Banten, history: Chinese, Indian, and Arab traders poured into Banten after being driven out of Melaka in 1511. Banten was conquered for Islam in 1527 by Hasanuddin, son of a great religious leader. It has been strongly Islamic since that date. Lancaster, an Englishman, loaded spices here in 1602. At the time of the Dutch lust for power through the islands, the ruler of Banten had European captains sailing his ships as far as Macao, Persia, and the Philippines. He plotted against the Dutch in all the islands but when his son rebelled against him the Dutch sided with the son militarily. After winning their battles, the Dutch placed the son on the throne as their vassal in 1684. A revolt broke out in 1750, which was crushed by The Company who reinstated their own ruler. This area today has many historical sites such as Surosowan Palace and an old Dutch fortress built in 1682.

cave hermitages: A peculiar feature of East Javanese archaeology is the presence of many cave hermitages. Traditionally, Javanese kings have become recluses during their reigns. Airlangga became a hermit before and at the end of his reign, and the Majapahit Queen Mother retired to a royal hermitage when she became old. Two interesting cave hermitages which date from the Kediri period are found near the town of Kediri and near Tulungagung. They show Arjuna being tempted by nymphs and celestial dancers. The Tulungagung cave, 30 km south of Kediri, legend says is the cave of the hermit king Rajasanagara. Both caves are called selamangleng, grottoes dating from Buddhist times. In the same village outside of Kediri where you find the cave hermitage, there's also a Catholic church built in the Majapahit style.

the Madiun Revolt: Took place on Sept. 18, 1948, at 3 am. This rebellion was crushed in surprisingly short time by loyal troops of the Siliwangi Division. There were many parallels between this rebellion and the Sept. 1965 coup: a common prelude of rising political tensions and minor clashes in the country; a common technique of power seizure including the abduction of opponents; the close cooperation between progressive revolutionary officers and communists; the premature opening of both revolts; the hopes of a popular uprising throughout Indonesia; the quick suppression of the rebellions by staunch anti-communist troops; the mass killings in clashes between communists and anti-communists (mainly Islamic and nationalist groups) at the end of both rebellions.

kratons were their origin, but soon crafts spread beyond its walls and into the villages. Dance also found a home in the *kratons*. The four princely courts of Solo and Yogya, including the Paku Alam and Mangkunegaran courts, all created a theatre of their own and their dance styles all evolved differently. During the colonial period, a time of peace when money wasn't going to war, artistic expression was even more intense. The princes, though politically powerless, were still extremely wealthy and indulged in all the more pompous, grandiose ceremonial occasions. During the years of the Forced Cultivation Period (approximately 1830-1869), the twin *kraton* regents of Java were partners with the Dutch in the ruthless exploitation of their own people. Yet the *kratons* have always been regarded as the center of the world for the masses, symbolic of spiritual power. They were even built in such a way as to represent a microcosm of the universe. Cities have grown up around them. The titles of the hereditary rulers who live in them today testify to their supernatural cosmic function: the Susuhunan of Solo is called *Paku Buwana* (Axis of the World) and the Sultan of Yogya is called *Hamengko Buwana* (He Who Cradles the World in His Lap).

ARCHAEOLOGY

Traces of Hindu-Buddhist temples have been excavated at Cangkuang and at Cibuaya in West Java. But by far the highest concentrations and the best preserved have been uncovered in Central and East Java, a region known as the 'Realm of the Dead'. For more than 750 years (732 A.D. to about 1405 A.D.) temples were built all the way from the Dieng Plateau in Central Java to Candi Kedaton, near Bondowoso in East Java. Ruins are still being unearthed. Most of the art of the early Hindu period has perished and relatively little is known of the development of art until the 8th Century, the beginning of the Hindu-Indonesian period. Because of the tropical climate, only the work of the stone sculptors and the megalith builders has survived, leaving remains of temples not only on Java but all over Sumatra, on Sulawesi, and even as far as Borneo. When searching for ancient monuments there's most always a sign on the roadway and an arrow pointing the way to the *candi*.

candi: This word is derived from the Sanskrit *Chandgrika* (House of the Goddess of Death) or *Candika*, another name for Durga (Goddess of Death). The present-day meaning of *candi* is roughly 'temple', regardless of the temple's purpose or its religious source. Outwardly, *candis* don't differ from temples serving for regular worship of Hindu deities, but many Javanese *candis* were dedicated to the cult of the dead. On some supposedly 'Hindu' temples on Java, there's a combination of Hinduism plus a monument to a god-king, ancient nobleman, ancestor, sire or teacher whose ashes are buried underneath the *candi*. In some temples the dead king is actually depicted as a Hindu god, his spirit presiding in a statue of a god which can be contacted ritually. Thus, *candis* were magic centers radiating power. Irrigation farming long ago created on Java an intensely cooperative society where villages grouped together under strong district rulers who were needed to control the flow of water. The ability to support luxurious pastimes as immortalizing oneself or one's god by erecting such impressive monuments which required decades to build, massive human toil and suffering, indicates a gigantic agricultural wealth. The *candis* you see today were once surrounded by flowering trees, high walls, and tall gates opening to inner courtyards. All around these sumptuous temple complexes were shady lanes, ricefields, and the bamboo homes of the people. Seldom do you see any of these ruined temples venerated today. *Candis* were rich Brahmins' structures, the temples of the people were built of just wood and bamboo. But the temple-builders created the seeds of their own destruction. Working the peasants too hard was the most likely reason why power shifted from East Java in the 10th Century and did not return until the 16th Century. Temple construction had all but stopped by the end of the 15th Century with the Mount Lawu group being one of the last remnants in stone of the Java-Hindu era.

candi construction: Plans of most temple construction probably originated in India, but this has never been proved. There are no monuments in India quite like the *candis* of Java. Indonesian artists and sculptors struck out on their own, coming up with a new way of building, sometimes even surpassing architectural works in India. Hindu-Java religion, cosmology, monotheism and aboriginal cult worship all come together in the construction of these monuments. The ground-plan of many complexes reproduces the human body laying face downwards on the earth, the foot, body and head. This is related to the parallelism between the micrososm and the macrocosm- i.e. in the very small you see the very big. Many *candis* were built in the shape of the Buddhist sacred mountain, Meru. In their simplest form, these sepulchral monuments consist of 3 parts, base, temple, and temple roof, forming a cube-like terraced pyramid with a platform for walking around to view the carved pictures. A stairway often leads up to the terrace. In the more elaborate *candis* there are more platforms, niches, porches and bases. Hindu-Javanese temples were often re-enlarged, their foundations replaced or annexes added on.

This happened frequently and it makes for much confusion among scholars. Their technique of building made little use of pillars or true arches. One striking characteristic of classical Hindu-Javanese stone architecture is that the amount of hewn stones required for walling in space is usually very large. Often the enormous masses of stones making up the straight walled temple body contain just one small inner chamber (cella) in which is placed the cult image of the god or ancestor in whose memory the whole structure was erected (these are almost always missing). There is room for only a single priest to pray. Mass is always given more emphasis than space, the structure often piled high with heavy overlapping layers of big stone blocks. Borobudur is stunning example of this, a huge ponderous mass of stone covering the top of a hill with only a small room in its central *dagob* where the relics are kept.

reliefs: The characters and themes from the Indian epic poems on basreliefs of temples are very common because in the 12th Century a courtly *kakawin* poem was written (inspired by the Indian version) which became immensely popular, greatly stimulating the plastic arts of Java. Indonesian narrative poems carved in relief aren't nearly as sexually explicit as in India. The everyday life of ancient tropical Java is made abundantly clear with pots, pans, small lizards, ropes, birds robbing grain bins, fruit markets, parading priests. Archaeologists can derive the date of a monument by 'reading' certain animals somewhere on the structure; such as 3 frogs, 2 crabs, 3 iquanas and an eel = 1451 A.D. Highly durable 'diamond plaster' enabled carvers to add extreme detail, helped to preserve the carvings, and provided a base to paint bright colors upon. Equatorial wind and rain have worn smooth the now exposed carvings and ornamentation to such an extent that many reliefs have lost much of their vividness and definition even in the mere 40 odd years since they were first photographed in the 20's and 30's. The most superb example of Java-Hindu art, Borobudur, is now being eaten by lichen, cracked by seeping water, all its classical carvings disintegrating and nearly illegible. The monument is slowly but surely sliding off the hill on which it was built, as bungling bureacrats try vainly to save it. The finest sculpture of the Central-Javanese period makes up today part of the royal collection in Bangkok, plus other outstanding collections in Leyden and Amsterdam.

Candi Puntadewa, Dieng Plateau: *The oldest Hindu relics in Central Java are found on this plateau near Wonosobo. Surrounded by spectacular mountain scenery, this ruined 8th Century Shivaite Hindu temple city is located on a 2135 m high filled-crater where the temperature sometimes falls below freezing. All temples still standing are named after the Pandava brothers of the Hindu* Ramayana *poem, the source of many of the wayang heros. All temples are still strongly revered. Candi Puntadewa is a tall slender building whose small delicate decoration is comparatively simple and more refined than the other monuments of Dieng. Instead of the demon itself, only its paws are seen growing out of curls, scrolls, and leaves — much more sinister. In its sculpture, the gods ride on the shoulders of seated human figures with heads of animals (a bull, a goose, or a bird).* **Candi Bima:** *A 5-tiered temple at the southern end of the plateau. Its roof is the most interesting because it's a synthesis of two different styles (north and south India). Looks a bit like the Prambanan Temple. Bima contains horseshoe-shaped niches with heads of human beings in each. Beautiful, eerie.* **Candi Arjuna:** *Tall and graceful with hills sweeping up behind it. The mossy entrance and niches in the walls are enclosed by monstrous kala-heads sculpted without their lower jaws. Also diabolical heads resembling mythological aquatic animals (lion or bird). A spout below the niche in the north wall lets out water and other liquids which were shed over the worshipped* lingga. *The 2 ruined temples beside Arjuna were for the king's wives.*

Bima Express: *Named after a Ramayana warrior. Built in East Germany, the Bima has flush toilets and is diesel-fired. First class cabins have two berths and wash basins, dinner and breakfast included in the fares. Costs Rp12,000 between Surabaya and Jakarta; economy class costs Rp9000. Takes 16 hours. Another (airconditioned) night express, the Limex (Economic Limited Express), operates between Surabaya and Jakarta via Cirebon and Semarang. Takes 15½ hours. The Jaya train also runs between Jakarta, Yogya, and Surabaya. Takes 15 hours and costs Rp1700 economy class.*

Pekanbaru: *Hotel Dharma Utama goes for Rp1000 double; there are a number of cheaper penginapans, but you get what you pay for, and even Rp1000 doesn't get you that much. Merpati, Sempati and Garuda fly Pekanbaru to Tanjung Pinang, then you can take a ferry to Singapore. Merpati is cheapest at Rp14,500, on Tue., Wed., and Sundays. Merpati is a hell of a slack airline. Getting your money if a flight doesn't jadi is like getting water from a rock. If you get stuck with an MCO (because otherwise you'd have to hang around Jakarta waiting and waiting), many agents won't touch it, including their sole agents in such towns as Pekanbaru.*

Parangtritis: *Hire a bicycle in Yogya and take the fantastic 28 km ride south to this beach and village. Or take the bus to Kreteg, Rp75, takes 1 hour. Get poled across the river in a long boat, or ford the river, then walk or take a horsecart 3 km into Parangtritis. Losmens still cost only Rp50 a head. Can also rent stone cottages. Food is very cheap. Surfing however is bad because of a vicious undertow. Watch men gather birds' nest soup. Nests are built by swifts (much like our chimney swifts) on the side of the cliffs around Parangtritis.*

fighting mosquitoes: *In malarial areas contact local health officials or missionaries whether the preventative drug in your bag is efficient against their plasmodia. Start swallowing when you enter infected area; stop 1 or 2 months after leaving. The most delicate areas for bites (difficult to heal) are feet and ankles, so rub them before going barefoot in the dark with a good repellent, or better: wear woolen socks and long jeans in tropical darkness. Tropical ulcers and sores are mainly due to mosquito bites. Mosquito coils, though effective, could be dangerous; you see mattresses burning. Why do so few travelers use a mosquito net? You can get them single or family (just for a song, and they only weigh 100-200 grams. Fix one up anywhere, but the strings must be long enough. Makes sleeping in the tropics great!*

tourism in Indonesia: *In 1970 only 90,000 foreign tourists visited Indonesia. In 1971, 180,000. In 1975, 300,000, the last year for which there are figures for. Next to Bali, the area forming a triangle between the 3 cities of Yogya, Solo, and Semarang is the most popular region for tourism in Indonesia.*

travel up the Kapuas River: *At every town you have to report in to the imigrasi, police, army, Laksus (military intelligence), and camat if there is one. If you don't, at the next town they'll be highly suspicious and possibly send you back. In one month, travelers in this region could get as many as 33 chops (stamps) in 11 stops (coming and going, too). That means 33 offices. The military has an eye on you the whole time, they've nothing else to do. If you want to take a walk in the country, they send gun-slinging soldiers with you. With this option, you'd rather not, not wanting to terrorize the local population. Why all this? This whole border region between the Sarawak border and W. Kalimantan Province is an anti-communist 'operations area'. The Indonesians are afraid that the terrorists they've pushed back into Sarawak are going to come back.*

Kuta Beach: *Wanna buy a Pentax camera with lenses real cheap? How is the gado2 here, good? When is your flight to Darwin booked for? Have you seen Jerry and Amanda? Would you like to look at some jewelry? Is it windy up on the beach now? What losmen did you stay in at in Ubud? You paid too much for that sarung, didn't you? How do you get to that cockfight from here? Are you out of lobster already? Hey does anybody know what the train costs from Surabaya to Solo? Have you been to Kintamani yet? Anybody wanna change Australian dollars for rupiah? Are there bemos going to the airport at 11 o'clock at night? Is it OK to drink the water here? Where have you come from last? Would you mind swapping cassettes for a couple of days? Can I rent that motorbike when you get through with it? You better do something about that mosquito bite, huh? What, you haven't left yet?*

ONESIA

mbok berek: In the village of Prambanan, 17 km from Yogya, try this fried chicken specialty (yard-fed chicken that actually tastes like chicken) of Central Java. The original mbok berek restaurant is here, plus there's 4 others along the road back to Yogya (Jl. Solo). Eat with boiled rice, sambal, and a bottle of cold Bintang Baru beer.

Sangir Islands: The largest village on the island of Siau, Ulu, sits at the foot of a luxuriously vegetated volcano. After you make the climb, see red and white vapor clouds and sulpherous smoke drifting inside the crater. Surrounding the volcano are pink cliffs and on the lower part, a yellowish-green lake. In the distance Tamata Peak and the Island of Makawehi can be seen. Start back down in good time before sunset, being sure to take the path because if you go down the Kiawang Village side, you'll run into thickets and deep gullies.

Transport on Java: There's a dense network of [roads] on Java, leaving from the smallest towns. [Wai]ting goats are tied on the back and chickens [squ]awk overhead or in your lap. At each stop [ther]e's a burst of activity with endless curries and [swe]etmeats, while peoples' dress and the geog[rap]hy changes from region to region. Each district [has] its own style of transport. For instance, be[twe]en Garut and Tasikmalaya, the becaks are more [colou]rful than ever with outlandish riotous decora[tions]. In this area horses pulling carriages have shiny [Nap]oleonic regimental style harnesses. In Malang, [the] becaks are bright yellow. Around Karangbo[lon]g, oplets are made out of old Chevrolet station [wag]ons, and at Kutowingangun, horse harnesses [hav]e grenadier-like feathered plumes. Occupations [like] wheelwright, blacksmith, and wainwright are [still] prevalent on Java.

sandiwara: New Indonesian drama patterned on western theatre. This form of theatre was the first where the Indonesian language was used. Sandiwara plays are not restricted to a specific era or tradition in Indonesian cultural history (as in wayang), but are about contemporary situations, legend and historical episodes. Many of the earlier plays were just translations of classical European dramas, but original plays by Indonesian authors are becoming more popular. Many sandiwara groups, amateur and professionals, are found throughout the cities of Indonesia now. The film industry, started in the 1930's, drew its actors and actresses from sandiwara players

Biak: The city of scrap metal, surrounded by a garden of rusting tanks and trucks, all overgrown with flowering jungle creepers. See the pier near Wisma Titawaka, built entirely out of tanks and covered with a shroud of shells and coral. There are wonderful beaches (good swimming) on Biak. Visit the pasar, fish market (coral fish and tuna). All hotels in Biak charge you a 10% Development Tax and a service tax of 10%. Stay at Losmen Juranga. Eat at Chinese Restaurant near the cinema. From Biak to Jayapura, the capital of Irian Jaya, there are now daily Garuda flights. You fly over a mass of tropical kale where you see only about 10 villages (each pop. 300) along rivers or on lakesides, completely isolated because of jungle and mangrove.

Dieng Plateau: On G. Prahu 128 km from Yogya, 3½ hours by car or 5 hours by bus. Glorious landscapes. On the way up you pass steep gorges, steeper and wilder the higher you climb, tall mountains all around. See Lake Pengilon and bubbling Condrodimuko crater. Go up through the high mountain pass of Kledung, where mountain lakes are the source of the wide Serayu River. On Dieng itself hire horses for Rp5-600 for 3 hours and ride around the plateau to look at unusual natural phenomena and ancient temples of classical simplicity. There are sulphur springs cascading down rocky hillsides, stagnant ponds, marshy fields, muddy lanes, cool air, horses crazing on luxuriant green grassy valley floors, shady trees, woodland paths. A very fitting place to contact ones' ancestors. It's too cold to grow rice here. Small boys collect horse droppings in baskets for fertilizer. Once a hermitage for Shivaite priests, there are ruins of a monastery to the west, now covered by a mushroom farm. On the southeastern edge of the plateau is Lake Warna and nearby is Semar Cave, an ancient meditation chamber.

Australia and Indonesia: You would be hard put to find a country more opposite to Australia than Indonesia. Australia is flat, white, wasp, capitalist-materialist, Christian, rational, scientific, new, western, post-industrial, empty, unborn, sleeping. Indonesia is made up of hundreds upon hundreds of mountainous islands, some of them very crowded. It's Islamic, mystical, multi-racial, irrational, Asian, preindustrial, agricultural, poor, dynamic, with thousands of years of history, infinite styles of art, sculptural expression and theatre forms all its own. The unique and famous uniformity and monotony of Australian landscape, culture, ideals, values, and speech, is in startling contrast to Indonesia's complexity where customs, skin color, music, language, clothes, smells and food changes every 50 kilometers.

POPULATION

Population is purely a Javanese (and to a lesser extent, Balinese) problem. Thus it's an Indonesian problem. With a birthrate of 1½ million people per year, Java is a precise working model of the Malthusian Theory in which the positive check of death operates to keep the total population within the means of subsistence. In 1805 Java had a population of only 5 million. While Asia as a whole doubled its population between 1800 and 1950, Java's increased 7 times. Now Java has 80 million people in an area about the size of the state of New York and will most likely double its present population in 20 years, becoming a virtual island city. 65% of Indo-

nesia's total population is concentrated on this 1000 km long grossly overpopulated island, its land area amounting to only 7% of the total land surface of Indonesia. Java today has Indonesia's biggest and most crowded cities, yet 85% of it is rural. It has the densest agricultural population in the world with over 1500 people per square km, one vast village. Because the countryside is so economically depressed and politically insecure Indonesians surge into the cities. But even the countryside is now feeling the pressure; the incredible absorption capacity of the Javanese village finally breaking down. If population growth and urban immigration levels continue at the current rate, Jakarta's population alone is expected to grow to more than 21 million by the end of this century. Java's population leaps ahead of measures to limit it. The government has begun

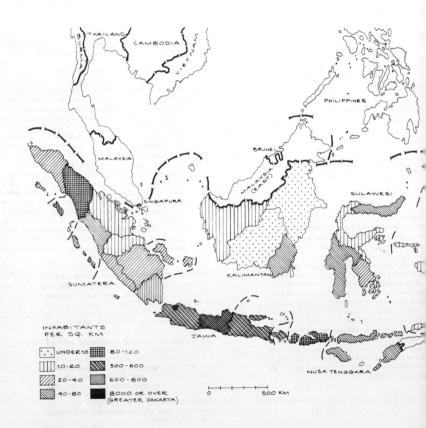

INHABITANTS
PER SQ. KM

- UNDER 10
- 10-20
- 20-40
- 40-80
- 80-120
- 300-600
- 600-800
- 8000 OR OVER (GREATER JAKARTA)

0 — 500 KM

family-planning programs and the new Rp5 coin, the lowest monetary unit and circulated widely amongst the rural masses, has on the reverse side a neat couple with two kids and the motto *Keluarga berencana menuju rakyat sejahtera* ('Family Planning leads to a Prosperous People'). There are folk traditions used in limiting family size, and in some Javanese villages elections for the 'King of the Condom' and the 'Queen of the Diaphragm' are held. But the absence of a welfare system or of any social security program almost necessitates having children who'll take care of you when you grow old. The Javanese give as the solution to the over population and erosion crisis the magic word, *transmigrasi*. These transmigration schemes, the shifting out of Java's overpopulation to resettlement agricultural camps in the outer islands, have never real-

ly worked. It's like transplanting a malignant cancer from the breast onto the leg. There will be gigantic problems with regards to education and natural resources in the years to come.

poverty-sharing: Because of Java's unbelievable population density, a phenomenon known as 'shared-poverty' is often seen. It means basically that for what jobs there are, there are too many people. So, many do a job that takes few. Half a dozen people work on a car, 3 men milk a goat, bales of tobacco are shared by buyers as a way of spreading risks if they're not sold quickly, *becak* drivers share territories, and stall owners haggle and peddle intensively, or else trade goods constantly in order to keep business and money circulating at all times. Everyone survives just below or just above the poverty line by dividing, for example, the per hectare gains when there's a declining ratio of rice-growing land to each man as population increases. Good professors are so scarce that they are flown around the outer island universities giving lectures. In Solo, Central Java, there are so many university teachers that each teacher is allowed to teach only 4 hours per week, or full-time, 8 hours a week. This unique system is able to absorb most everyone, providing all with at least some kind of work to earn their daily bread. Instead of some being really poor, everybody's just a little poor.

population: *Indonesia has the 5th largest population in the world. In 1930, this island country had only 7 cities with more than 100,000 people, 6 of them on Java. By 1961, it possessed 21 — eleven on Java, 6 on Sumatra, and 2 on Borneo and Celebes. Containing already some of the most densely inhabited areas on earth, Indonesia's population is expected virtually to double, to 250 million, by the year 2000. It has the worst possible combinations: one of the highest growth rates in the world, approximately 2.8% per annum; a high population density, particularly on Java, Bali, and Madura; and a very large population base, nearly 139 million. A vigorous government birth control program is hardly slowing the rate.*

CUSTOMS

The Javanese pride themselves on being one of the most refined, polite and cultivated peoples on earth. Even children are awesomely well-behaved. Their cultivation has stemmed from the so-called *priyayi* tradition. *Priyayi* is the gentry class of Java, the old Hindu-Javanese aristocracy who guard and hold such values and ethics as extreme politeness, deference to the aged (you may not differ with your elders), softspokenness, proper conduct, sophistication, social arts and graces, artistic skills (dance, drama and music), and verbal eloquence. Although considered Muslim, this ruling class of Javanese are preoccupied with mystical religious views and metaphysical philosophy (traditionally, many of Java's kings became hermits when they grew old). Manual labor is considered undignified; if you read and write, then you must 'have clean hands'. This official class eventually became the civil servants under the Dutch. Today, they are white collar workers, the business community, the newly educated, and the civil administrators. All their values still have a strong hold on peoples of all ages on Java. The Javanese always try to keep control of themselves. Loud voices, flamboyant behaviour, bragging, roars of laughter, wails of sorrow, are

considered bad-mannered. Passion or anger is only expected of children, wild animals, peasants, the retarded, and foreigners. The Javanese keep it all inside; you only see the placid exterior and a calm smile. On this overcrowded island everyone would be at each others' throats if people were too intimate, too loud, too vulgar, or too blunt. The granny won't ask outright for her cup of tea if someone has forgotten it, but will only say, 'It's awfully hot and dusty, isn't it?' It's a virtue for a Javanese not to say what he really means, i.e. 'to talk Javanese'. Thus, when a Javanese says 'yes', interpret the way he says it to determine what the man really means. A complicated Javanese etiquette dictates eye direction, position of hands, the way one sits, stands, points, greets people, laughs, walks, dresses. They even have certain smiles for anger, sorrow, suffering and grief. Most Javanese art forms reflect this discipline and patience: *wayang, batik, pencak silat, gamelan.* Java's classical dances are unbelievably intricate, demanding great dignity and perfect self-control. Its elaborate cultural traditions have always set Java apart from the other islands of Indonesia which are all looked upon as 'outer islands'.

language: As a direct result of the strong influence of the Indian caste system on Javanese life, their language is known as the most intricate linguistic device ever devised to show social rank. Many Javanese in fact prefer to speak *Bahasa Indonesia* because then they won't have to speak up or down to people. Because its population is the densest of all the islands, people are organized into a tighter heirarchy on Java. There are high, middle and low levels for speaking to your inferior, your equal and to your superior. There are also separate languages for the goods and for ritual feasts, an ancient poetic language, a classical Old Javanese, and special formal vocabularies for the royal court. This means that a sultan always has to use the low language and the servants the high language when talking to each other. Village school teachers address pupils in *ngoko* and the pupils answer back in *kromo*. Their language also shows the Javanese to have an obsession with politeness. You never ask a tailor outright 'How much?' but instead 'What will it be in exchange for the thread?'. For your wife you say 'friend in the back of the house.' Two different speech tones, *alus* (polite) and *kasar* (crude) are used. One is very soft, slow, tender, the other hard, loud, rough, rapid. In *wayang* performances you can easily hear the difference between the good guys and the bad guys, the well-bred knight and the uncouth giant.

religion: Once again, out of sheer numbers the religion of Java is no doubt the most potent political force in Indonesia. In its early years, Javanese

Islam was a merger of Sufism (Islamic mysticism) and native superstition rather than of Islam and Hinduism proper. For centuries Javanese feudalism was the true religion, not the law of the *Koran.* Only in the 19th and 20th Centuries did Islam penetrate rural Java so deeply as to upset the traditional patterns of authority. *Agama Jawa* (Religion of Java) has evolved into a totality of religious beliefs and practices, an incredible blending of doctrines. In the Javanese story of creation, all the world's major religions have been taken into account. The Javanese today practice their own slant, their own interpretation of Islam, shot through with animistic rites. Javanese *pamongs*, black magicians, mystic teachers and *dukun* (healers) are famous for their oracular powers and often influence powerful politicians. Incense is burned before beautiful works of art such as a *topeng* mask, a *kris*, a gong, or a famous bronze *gamelan.* They could be objects of worship to individual families or to villages, often forming legends around themselves. These *pusaka* can charm people, ward off sickness and evil, make the rains come on time.

BATIK

Java produces the finest *batik* in Indonesia. *Batik,* a traditional method of decorating cloth, is an art of great antiquity. The word is derived from a Javanese word meaning 'fine point' but in everyday usage it means 'wax printing' or 'wax-resist painting'. Formerly, *batik* fabrics were mainly used to make *sarungs,* women's skirts, scarves, and mens' headgear, and even had a cultic function. But now *batik* is used in long dresses, housecoats, blouses, ties, sport jackets, as well as for interior decorating, wall carpet designs, lampshades, tablecloths and runners, napkins, bedspreads, coverlets, shopping bags, umbrellas, fans, belts, slippers, hats. Even school uniforms in Indonesia have subdued *batik* patterns in them.

history: Indonesia has been trading in *batik* since the days of the Arab and Indian merchant fleets of the early 16th Century. The craft was probably introduced into Indonesia during the 12th Century; no one knows from where exactly. Possibly it originated in Turkey or Egypt. Most *batik* can be traced back to Javanese influence and some believe that it evolved on Java and Madura out of an ancient way of painting on textiles. At one time, only persons of royal rank were allowed to wear some patterns and *batik* kerchiefs (kain kepala) are still draped over the tombs of Javanese princes and Islamic saints. This art was considered a spiritual discipline and the making of *batik* was once only the pursuit of ladies of the nobility. *Batik* as a folk art was nearly destroyed by the import of Japanese cotton prints in the 1930's and 40's.

figure of a bird in
batik *design*

garuda *wing motif
on batik design*

batik motifs: Batik *is very striking patterned cloth made by a wax and dye technique. Indonesia is conceded to produce the highest quality in the world. For 700 years this art was confined to women of royal families. Since it took many months to produce a single fabric, batik-making was once considered a spiritual discipline and a form of meditation. To design and dye a piece took great inward concentration; one would 'draw a batik design on the heart'. However, copper stamps (cap) devised in 1840, are much in use today and* cap-*printed batik is usually much less expensive and painstaking than the older hand-done method. Yogya and Solo, Central Java, are still the twin capitals of both kinds of batik. Soelardjo in Yogya has the best collection of original* batik *from which modern designs, seen everywhere today, were taken from. He was one of the first (about 15 years ago) to get the idea to turn cloth* batik *into paintings. Today, many famous artists' original pieces hang up in his house. He has the very first Amri painting.*

batik tulis: *Batik tulis* is the most prized and expensive *batik,* usually printed on fine cotton, linen, or by those who can afford it on silk. Fine designs are first drawn free-hand with a pencil on the textile, then hot liquid wax, impervious to dyes, is applied by a pen-like instrument (canting) with 1, 2 or even 3 spouts and a small bowl on top which is dipped into the hot wax. The areas not to be colored are filled in with wax. The cloth is passed through a vat of the desired color, such as blue. Next, the areas to be kept blue are waxed over. The wax is removed from the parts of the dried material that are still to be dyed in the next step by soaking the cloth in hot water and scraping it off. This process is repeated during each phase of the coloring up to 4, 5 or more times until the overall pattern and effect is created. Women generally do the designing and waxing, both of which require great care and skill. Men normally do the dyeing itself. A *batik tulis* cloth could take up to 40 days to complete. Really high-standard *batik tulis* can take as long as 6 months, especially if deep-toned vegetable dyes are used which take time for the colors to come out. *Batik,* when new, is stiff to the touch. Until recently there's been a tendency away from the time-consuming painstaking *batik tulis* work towards the quicker but usually inferior stamped-process (cap) which can be produced on a larger commercial scale. But as the knowledge and sensitivity of tourists towards Indonesian art forms increases, hand-drawn *batik* is now always in demand.

cap: A type of *batik,* a faster and cheaper method which uses the same traditional patterns. Some *cap batik* is in fact far superior to *batik tulis* work of the more simple and imitative designs. Copper stamps (cap) are used to impress wax patterns onto the fabric. *Caps* are made from strips of metal and wire carefully soldered together, in themselves collector's items and art objects. This process, in use since 1840, is making *batik* more and more a male industry, a craft of young men.

designs: As infinite and as variegated as Indonesian society itself. There are basically 3 types: horizontal (called 'soft rain'), vertical, and diagonal. Some designs are non-symmetrical and free, others are much more rigid. Diagonal designs of motifs are considered less harsh than either vertical or horizontal. Most artisans copy from patterns but the older and more talented designers can draw intricate floral, geometric and wildlife patterns from memory- flowing designs filled with beautiful colors. The motifs of Central Java vary greatly from those used on the north coast of Java. Other regions and cities prefer western motifs, and still others have ancient stylized motifs which are so simple yet so mysterious. You find crazy quilt patterns, checkered and round patterns, intersecting circles, ovals, rosette shapes, stars, rhombuses, wavy lines, S-like flourishes, swastikas, bird tails or wings. Even partly completed *batik,* just a cream or white background with some unfinished patterns, is very striking. Sometimes the waxed cloth is crackled by hand to create a shattered effect. In the Central Javanese sultanates certain patterns reflect the position of the wearer. Court officials, bridal couples and important people wear a special *sarung* (dodot) which is much larger than that worn by ordinary people. It usually has an overall pattern or is divided in sections showing a double row of triangular designs, symbolic of fertility (tumpal).

colors: There are striking regional differences in the colors used. Blue-indigo, made from the plant, is the oldest. Human blood was at one time a prized natural dye. The Central Javanese sultanates in Yogya and Solo keep to indigo, dark browns and deep blues, colors of dignity. Maroon (soga), the official court color, is also popular. Mauve is unsuitable for any but young unmarried girls. In the northern coastal districts and on Madura, bright reds, yellows and greens are most dominant. West Javanese batik has more light browns, golden yellows and rich deep blackish-blue backgrounds. Cirebon has its 'shadow technique'. Modern batik makes more use of multicolored combinations: crimson, yellow and green mixed with blue and yellow and black are the main

colors used. Batik looks brilliant in summer sunshine which brings out the colors that much more. Darker colors look stunning next to dark complexions or on deeply tanned skin. Note: Don't ever use strong detergent when washing batik, only a mild handsoap. If chemical dyes are used (usually really bright colors), batik lasts 25-30 years; for organic dyes, which fade into a rich deep color, 45-50 years. Sometimes the fabric is dipped into an organic dye up to 25 times.

KRIS

A wavy bladed dagger. Its use in ceremonial occasions on Java still persists; it's worn at weddings and by young boys to their circumcision ceremony. There are rules pertaining to the wearing of it. On Java it must be stuck in the belt in back so that the end of the sheath points to the left and the hilt

kris: Indonesia's traditional dagger and an organic part of this culture and of this culture alone (40 different types). It's used as a weapon, an ornament, an object of cult, or it could be a family's Coat of Arms, an enshrined heirloom, or stand proxy for a bridegroom marrying a girl of lower caste. Its wavy snake-like blade makes it easier to bypass bones and ribs (like a saw) and because of the shape of the puncture the wound doesn't close. Its presence brings luck, relieves pain of women in labor, it rattles in its sheath when danger is near, averts fire and flood. A prince's kris can affect the whole nation. At one time a kris was something every adult Javanese male had to possess, and different handles stood

for different classes of people. You still see this dagger as part of the uniform in the kratons of the Central Javanese sultanates, but now the rarest and most beautiful specimens are in museums or in the possession of old families. Masterfully made kris blades inlaid with gold and meteorite in antique shops cost around Rp100,000-250,000 although rare and prized kris handles of noblemen sculpted of gold and set with rubies, diamonds and sapphires could cost 1 million rupiahs. Cheaper souvenir models start at about Rp5000. The pande-caste (kris-makers) are now mostly panel beaters in garages.

points to the right. A very high mystic value is given this instrument of death. Traditionally, old *kris pusaka* are part of the family's heirlooms kept in the back of the house with other objects of the cult of the ancestors. Once a year at a rite the *kris* is taken out, a sacrifice shown to it, incense burned, and the blade rubbed down with ointments. This ceremony is still practiced in Central Java. Carved out of gold and silver and studded with gems, a *kris* was at one time the exclusive right of the noble class. The *kris* must suit the wearer's disposition and character exactly, it was the ideal alter ego. The number of times it had drawn blood added to its power and this dagger was once used in the execution of criminals by sultans who plunged the blade through the shoulder to the heart of the kneeling man. The owner may bring the blade into contact with the entrails and brain of a snake to also increase its power. A *kris* has a spirit and is capable of sorcery. It can talk, fly, swim, turn into a snake, even father human children. Designs on the blade were intended to ward off demons and they rendered the wearer unwoundable. Its invisible venom kills men simply by pointing it at someone or by stabbing it into the shadows or footprints of intended victims. When danger is near, the *kris* has been known to rattle in its sheath.

kris-making: This unique Indonesian weapon was made by the *empu* or *pande* (smiths and armourers) who exercised a secret and holy craft. Though he usually came from a poor and humble family, the *pande* was addressed as an honored lord. The smithy was considered a hallowed place and the *empu* always carried out a very detailed ritual before work was to begin on each *kris*. These deadly weapons were forged by beating and folding alternate layers of meteorite iron and nickel. The blade was polished and treated for weeks with lemon juice, coconut water and arsenic. Then a secret formula would blacken the iron and whiten the nickel to make a strange pattern of rivulets. The art of cutting and folding these contrasting metals is now lost; the best nickelous iron from several meteorites embedded on Java was exhausted over 100 years ago. The metals later used were of inferior quality. Gradually over the 19th Century the superior arms of the Dutch made the *kris* obsolete in battle.

design: On the best *kris* the grips often have exquisite carving in ivory or metalwork with such decorations as *raksasa* figures (demonic images to drive off evil spirits), little gnome-like men, or monkeys. There were sometimes up to 31 undulations and over 30 motifs on the blade. Some *kris* handles of noblemen were sculpted of gold and set with rubies, diamonds and saphires. The ornaments on

the blade are also there for protection: delicate leaves, *Garuda*, or *kala*-figures representing time, and very frequently a *naga*. One model of the *kris* handle on Bali is the chrysalis of a big beetle with long antennae set in ebony. In Solo, you find the painted scabbard. The *Majapahit Kris,* of which you see only facsimilies nowadays, had both its blade and hilt forged out of a single piece of metal.

FOLK DRAMA

Java's performed literature is exciting and diverse with each locality boasting its own folk drama. The best place to see popular theatre is in the small villages where the admission is low and performances are spiced with lots of humor. In the cities people have been conditioned too much by modern film, the faster pace of life, and want their entertainment *hebat* (terrific, violent, sensational). When an entertainment troupe arrives in a small village, it's a big night. Actors and actresses just barely make a living from their profession, living like gypsies with their pots, pans, bedding, and children all in tow. Most come from poor families, have had little education, and work at unskilled jobs when not touring. The actors are professional improvisors. They seldom have time to rehearse. The director distributes the roles and gives a brief expose of the story about an hour before the performance. For villagers who can't read and have no TV, these dramatizations of folk tales, proverbs and poems give them new ways of thinking and behaving. They are also used as a political vehicle. Almost all troupes nowadays are financed by army officers. THR (Peoples' Amusement Parks) in all of the biggest cities of Java regularly stage the following folk drama forms.

Ludruk: A modern-day, mostly East Javanese, theatrical form. Plays aren't based solely on Javanese mytholoy and history but are taken also from everyday life with many satirical allusions to contemporary events. There's no definite repertoire, the actors improvise. All roles are taken by male actors renowned for their flawless ability in imitating women. In the countryside of Java, *ludruk* performances cost as little as Rp15 entrance. Get backstage if you can.

Ketoprak: A folk melodrama originating in Yogya. A more traditional theatre form than *ludruk*, yet it's more movie-like and more costly to stage with technical devices often utlizied. *Ketoprak* is most often performed in the Javanese language accompanied by *gamelan*. Dancing and singing is used in the beginning and at the end, but not in the middle. A show usually begins at 9 pm and ends at 1 am. Serials are frequently divided into 7 installments to last throughout the week. This form takes its stories mostly from East Javanese folklore and history as well as from Chinese and Arab sources. Traditional moral lessons with contemporary social commentary are woven into the performance; it informs, instructs and entertains at the same time, passing on new trends and ideas in subtle ways. *Ketoprak* tells much about current Javanese society. Past, present and future are all incorporated into the plot—kings, court scenes, enchanted rings, magic incantations, village doctors, political elections, bandits, dwarves, battle scenes on man-powered horses. You could see anything. If the Christmas story is enacted, it's with traditional Javanese dress and mannerisms. Hamlet can even be adapted to *ketoprak* with all kinds of local elements mixed in to Javanize it so it will be a success. Clowns do mimicry of the courtly *Serimpi* dancers, including all the simpering expressions. Audiences roar with laughter at this slap-stick comedy. It's truly a theatre of the people. *Ketoprak* is sometimes so popular that local authorities must close these shows down because villagers are spending too much money, neglecting family responsibilities and local taxes.

GAMELAN

The native Javanese orchestra used as accompaniment in *wayang* and dance performances. This type of orchestra is found in other forms in Thailand, Philippines, Madagascar, Cambodia, and you find predecessors of the *gamelan* on 10th Century Borobudur basreliefs. It is seldom played outside Indonesia because of the expense of transporting an orchestra so heavy that it takes up to 80 people to carry one. Rows of small bronze kettle-shaped discs of varying sizes with raised nipples are hit with cudgel-like sticks. These bronze instruments give the *gamelan* its highly distinctive sound, ranging from thin tinkles to deep booming reverberations. The inimitable harmonic quality of *gamelan* has attracted western composers ever since Claude Debussy first 'discovered' it at the end of the 19th Century. Every Javanese orchestra is tuned to a certain tone system, either *slendro* or *pelog*, each with a different feeling. Generally the *slendro* is more festive and cheerful while the *pelog* is more solemn and sad. *Gamelan* can't be compared with the compositions of the west's great polyphonic composers such as Bach whose music is so mathematically laid down. Javanese music is strange to the European ear because the scales are divided into unfamiliar intervals. *Gamelan* has over 14 different layers of sound and can construct scales appropriate to any kind of performance. It is much looser, freer, more flighty and unpredictable. Modulations aren't found and melodies aren't based on a fixed key note and the tonal material is very flexible. Like in jazz there's no written score, though *gamelan* is more rigidly structured. Neither is there as much

solo playing as in western bands but more of an integration of sounds. The playing technique is handed down through successive generations and very outstanding *gamelan* which are handed down often carry such proper names as 'Venerable Dark Cloud' and 'Drifting in Smiles'.

instruments: The main theme is carried by the *saron*, a set of convex metallic resonating keys which are beaten with small mallets. This sound is given more depth and is paraphrased by the xylophone-like *gender*, a row of small bronze slabs suspended by 2 cords over a similar row of resonant tubes. Then there are the short flat dull accents of the *ketuk*, while the *kenong* has deep resounding notes. The various gong tones and subtle drum beats are difficult to distinguish at first. The gongs reverberate with incredible shimmering echoing notes. There are half a dozen drums. The *kendang* provides the beat for the melody, accelerating or lowering the tempo as the composition requires. The beat of the *keprak* (wood-block) provides the rhythm for the dancers. The sorrowful violin-like two-stringed *rebab* accompanies the chorus who sings in unison or recites speeches of the plot of a a *wayang* in nasal tones. Light magical flutes (suling) are the only wind instruments in the *gamelan*, paraphrasing the nuclear theme in a higher key.

kecapi: A unique Sundanese instrument used as a part of the *gamelan* in West Java. This boat-shaped plucked zither (found in two sizes) often has a *suling* or vocal accompaniment. **angklung:** A portable instrument made from bamboo tubes cut to different lengths and freely suspended in a frame. Although restricted to only 4 notes, a strange xylophonic sound is produced when the frame is shook. The *angklung* was used in ancient times for marching into battles. It has now been adapted to western scales and large *angklung* orchestras can play European as well as Indonesian songs. The *gamelan angklung* orchestra, very popular in West Java, combines these bamboo instruments with gongs and drums.

gamelan* with dance and drama: The music which accompanies a *wayang* performance remains constantly in harmony with the sequence of events unfolding on stage. There is appropriate music for each of the different main characters, music which accompanies battle scenes, love scenes, melancholy or tender music played at the demise of a hero, spiritual music, heroic music, dance music. There is such a close inter-relationship between *gamelan* and dance that 'dances' are sometimes broadcast over the radio in Java whereby the audience is able to follow and visualize perfectly the movements of the dancers.

> 'Gamelan *is comparable to only two things: moonlight and flowing water. It's pure and mysterious like moonlight and always changing like flowing water. It's a state of being, such as moonlight itself which lies poured out over the land.'*
>
> Jaap Kunst in Music in Java

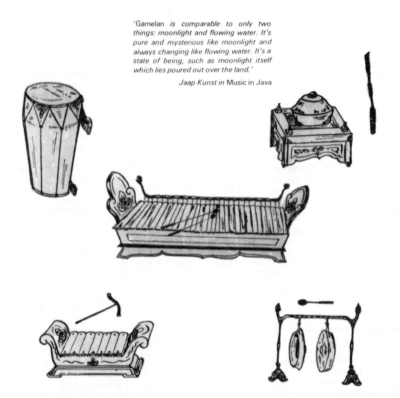

gamelan: *The native orchestra of Indonesia with a 1500 year old history. The names of the instruments suggest the sounds and rhythms of this remarkable music-making group. Certain instruments have the role of carrying the main theme, others play counter melodies and keep the tempo, while still others do the musical paraphrasing (gongs). The leaders are the drummers, the better musicians of the group. The* kendang *usually follows the movement of dancers or puppets, the role of conductor in European orchestras. The* demung *has rows of small bronze slabs, while the* gambang *has blocks of resonant wood which are beaten with wooden sticks to make a snapping, cracking sound through the music. The* kenong *is like an overturned brass bowl with a raised nipple, set in a red, blue or gold frame and beaten with small mallets to produce a sharp metallic ring. The total sound of the gamelan is like the beating of insect wings or the sound of a river trickling over rocks at night. Said to stimulate the growth of flowers. Keep your eye out for* KOKAR, *music academies where you can study gamelan and other regional instruments, as well as watch dance rehearsals.*

JAVANESE DANCE

There are both classical and popular. Because of the split of the Kingdom of Mataram into vassal states in 1755, the art of court dancing evolved differently in the two central Javanese *kratons*. These Javanese capitals have always been rivals: Solo thinks that Yogya dancers are too stiff and Yogya considers Solo dancers too slack and casual. The differ-ences today in the two schools are still recognizable though unimportant. In the court dancing, emphasis is on angular graceful poses and smooth, subtle gestures. This type of dancing is far removed from western theories of art and reflects the Javanese court's ultra-refinement. Having evolved at a time of warring states, classical dancing is executed with all the delibation of a slow march and the precision of a drill manoevure. Sometimes years of arduous muscular training is required to execute gestures such as the bending of the hand until the fingers touch the forearm, i.e. to imitate the opening of flower petals. Dancers are incredibly detached. Their inaction and long periods of immobility are just as important as the action. All the pauses, silences, motions arrested in space, with the eyes lowered and the meditative poses, make Javanese dance hypnotic to watch. The tradition of classical dancing was once looked upon as a sacred heirloom by the courts. Dancers selected from the lower class families of the *kraton* population could take part only in supporting roles in the royal plays. It wasn't until 1918 that the Krida Beksa Wirama Dance School was founded outside the walls of the Yogya *kraton* in order to perpetuate the Javanese arts by teaching any pupil the dances practiced in the court. The royal monopoly on dancing was at last broken. Many village groups have since imitated and dilluted the courtly style. **dance hire:** Private dance groups will perform on occasions of anniversaries, wedding receptions, or *selematans.* A group can be hired from anywhere between Rp 2000 and Rp50,000 (average, around Rp10,000-15,000). If you hire a group to perform you'll thus repay the family you're staying with for their kindness, their prestige in the village or *kampung* would rise, and their neighbors would share in the pleasure.

Serimpi: A slow, graceful, disciplined classical dance of Central Java using super-controlled movements of arms, hands, fingers and head; perfected over centuries. Its sources are drawn from the same sources as the *Bedaya,* the old *Amir Hamzah* stories, depicting a battle between two rival princesses. Impersonal poise, subtle restraint, and an intense inward meditation is maintained throughout with the face tilting downwards, staring fixedly at the floor. The dancers carry out unrealistic movements such as a fish flowing through water or tip-toeing over the floor and gliding (called 'flying'), with a dagger in one hand and a fluttering scarf in the other – a sort of stylized combat. Dancers' heads move slowly from side to side in a regal manner while executing 'bird movements' or 'make-up miming', the hips arch back slightly, the torso leaning forward. Hands usually stay at hip level, breaking a little at the elbow. *Serimpi* ends in a sitting position with a Hindu blessing.

Bedaya: Many different versions. One of the oldest and most sacred forms is *Bedaya Ketawang,* performed on the anniversary of the Susuhunan of Solo's ascension to the throne on the 2nd day of the month Ruwah by the Javanese calendar. It has its beginnings over 400 years ago. This dance is dedicated to the dreaded South Sea Goddess Nyah

Loro Kidul who was said to have appeared to the first ruler of the dynasty, Sultan Agung (1613-1645) and expressed her love for him by dancing and singing before him. The dancers, also called *Bedayas,* are traditionally selected from families related to the sultan. They belong to the innermost ceremonial life of the *kraton,* where this dance form reached its highest development. Their period of training is long and they must also sing. The 9 dancers (girls aged 15-16 years) are dressed like brides with their hair piled up in a bun on top of their heads. They wear beautiful intricate haircoils of gold and precious stones and jasmine buds. They must fast before the dance to purify mind and body, nor must any of them be menstruating. First, offerings to the gods (sajens) are made. The dance lasts 90 minutes. A female choir sings a litany while dancers move languidly, punctuated by chanting and hypnotic bell-like sounds, incense and flicks of long sashes and gentle kicks with long swirling trains. Dancers are like priestesses in their detachment, solemnity and gestures, their gowns undulating like sea waves. Showers of petals are thrown over the audience. Performances are kept secret so as not to anger the goddess if photographs were taken. The South Sea Goddess is invisibly present and if the dance displeases her, she carries one of the dancers off to the bottom of the sea. You might get in on one of the rehearsals, which lasts a week.

Reyog: A *wayang topeng* masked dance in which a great leering tiger's head or monster's headmask with peacock feathers on top is worn. Sometimes weighing 50 kilos and up to 500 mm tall, it rests on the nape of the neck and is held by the teeth. Though they only have small builds, *Reyog* dancers have unbelievably strong neck muscles due to dancing many hours wearing this heavy highly-decorated headpiece. It's said to be impossible to strangle these dancers with your hands. The story features a local king desiring the daughter of a neighboring king. She doesn't desire him, so after some fighting takes place she assigns her prospective husband an impossible task: to dig a tunnel from his palace to her father's palace. You may be bored by the story of the success of good over evil, but the average villager sits enthralled and wide-eyed for 4 hours. This dance is now encouraged by the East Java Tourist Development Board to attract tourists. You can hire a whole performance for about Rp6-7000 per hour. The Balinese *Barong* dance might have been derived from the *Reyog.*

Kuda Kepang (or *Kuda Lopeng*): East Java's famous horse-trance dance in which dancers ride black cut-out bamboo weave hobbyhorses to the rhythm of drums, gongs, flutes, and a man who beats a steel pipe with a hammer. There are 4, 6 or 8

performers. Many variations in different parts of Java in which more masked players (even a role for a dragon), monsters, and mysterious rites are involved. There's no stage or enclosure for this dance. It could be dangerous, requiring the presence and aid of *dukun* (medicine-man) who uses mantras to control the dancers. Drugs, hypnosis or alcohol are never used. Sometimes there's a sham battle, then suddenly one of the dancers becomes possessed (jadi), thinking that he's a horse. This state is usually induced by the pain of cracking each other with whips, sometimes drawing blood. The dancer gallops, canters, rears and prances like a circus pony. There's a bundle of hay in a corner which 'the horse' chews. A dancer often loses control while behaving like a horse- shrieking, twitching, slurping water from a pail, running wild and whinnying, rolling in the grass, charging with stiff body and blank voided expression. An old mystic teacher calms him and brings him out of the trance with incense and incantations.

WAYANG

A Javanese word meaning literally 'shadow' or 'ghost'. *Wayang* is a theatrical performance of living actors, puppets, or of shadow images held before a lighted screen from behind. The word could also refer to the puppets themselves. In most forms, the dialogue is in Javanese or in Sundanese; sometimes the Indonesian language is used. Most often the chants are in *Klaten* (or Kawi), Old Javanese, as archaic a language as Shakespearean English. Performances are held when some transitional event happens in a person's life: birthdays or weddings, an important religious occasion, or as ritual entertainment during family feasts or *selamatans*. Promotions in rank, the building of a new swimming pool, coming of age (puberty) or a circumcision ceremony, all could be an excuse for a show. *Wayang* stories are both entertainment and protection against the spirits; while you're in the audience the spirits can't get at you. *Wayang* drama forms reflect all aspects of Javanese culture. Characters are judged not by their actions but by their devotion to what is appropriate to their castes, their predetermined roles in the drama. Gestures are appreciated more than commonsense, style more than content. Courage, loyalty and refinement always win out in the end and fate is accepted without question. As a foreigner you won't be able to follow all the stories, but you could never miss the atmosphere. The audience is the best show of all. Made up of just 20 people or as many as thousands, Javanese sit up all night long in a theatre reeking with clove cigarette smoke and packed to the overflowing. Babies fall asleep on mothers' laps, people tip off chairs in hysterics, while kids alternately come awake and giggle in front of or behind the screen until dawn. Though they already know all the stories and roles backwards and forwards and are constantly moving around eating, sleeping and talking, the audience never loses the thread of the story. A show is like eavesdropping on neighbors, or on friends and relatives. The suspense is excruciating and they lose all sense of time. This 3000 year old mythology applies to today, it's living and dynamic. The gods themselves — not their shadows — are on the screen. *Wayang* characters provide types to be emulated, giving the young an idea of what qualities and virtues to strive for. It is a character chart by which to judge people and Indonesians even use the names from the Indian epic poems to refer to real live people they meet: 'He's a Suyudana.', the ambitious and decitful leader of the 99 korawa brothers; or 'He is just like Gatutkaca!' (brave). The shape of a person's face and body could designate him: 'He walks like a Raksasa!' threatening and lumbering! Arjuna typifies tenacity and dedication to duty; Yudistira is pure, righteous and compassionate; Krishna exemplifies clairvoyance and magic powers, and on and on.

history: This art dates from before the 9th Century. *Wayang* came before Indian influence, the present-day heroes having evolved from ancestral spirits. In ancient pre-Hindu times, *wayang* puppets were perhaps portraits of deceased ancestors who came down to earth to visit and communicate with their descendants during the performance. Its function was to exorcize, placate, and please the gods so as to increase fertility. The moving flickering silhouettes were considered the very souls of the dead and the puppeteer (dalang) probably was first a shamanistic priest, the medium between the dead and living. During the time of intense Hindu influence (8th to 15th Centuries), Hindu teachers used the *wayang* medium to propagandise and popularize their religion. Indian epic heroes, gods, demons and giants supplanted all the ancestor figures (except the clowns). Records tell of a remote King Airlangga enjoying puppet performances at his court in Java in the 11th Century. These shows had a strong influence on Java-Hindu sculpture. On 13th Century basreliefs you can see figures similar to those of the *wayang* puppets of the time, portraying all the same persons and events as the characters do today. When Hinduism started to give way to Islam in the 13th Century, Indonesian Muslims simply made heroes of Islamic literary figures and turned them into puppets. Shadow plays were used by sultans to flatter themselves and their courts, to glorify and perpetuate the feudalistic court ritual of the Javanese royalty. *Wayang,* by reinforcing the class system, has always kept everyone exactly in their place. Since Muslims banned the reproduction of the human form both good and evil puppets were made ugly and grotesque so that they wouldn't resemble living beings, and the puppets' faces, coloring, hairdoes, clothes and jewelry are to this day so strongly stylized that they are more symbols than actual human figures. *Wayang* figures are the only figural representations left over from the graphic arts of the early Islamic period. The Javanese colonialists have gradually transmitted *wayang* and its ethical system all over the archipelago.

lakon: The plot of a *wayang* performance. Divided into 3 principal phases, each with many scenes. Often lasting 10 hours, *wayang* plays are more exciting and spectacular than tragic and funny. Everything is illusions, symbolism, dreams, fairytale or mysticism. Stories are a combination of old sacred myths, ancient Javanese poetry, and the newer Indian epic tales of gods and princesses, made almost unrecognizable after having been put into the Indonesian blender. Sometimes modern stories, the adventures of noblemen, historical plays and social problems are acted out. Illiterate peasants will guffaw all night long at two of the oldest poems in the world, the *Ramayana* and the *Mahabharata* epics. For many Indonesians these classic stories are the holy books, not the *Koran.* Themes are usually variations of the struggles between these gods and demons with men choosing sides *(Barata-yuddha).* Man either shares the glory with the gods or is destroyed. Often the men help the gods to ward off demons' attacks *(Arjuna Wiwaha).* Some plots are drawn from the old Arab story, the *Menak cycle,* but have been completely Javanized and 'improved' upon; even old Javanese folk tales such as the *Panji* cycle have been worked over extensively. There are *wayang* plays about the shrewd, brave little mousedeer (Wayang Kancil) who outwits stronger animals of the jungle. Mystics use *wayang* to propagate their cult: *wayang madya* plays are based on the 19th Century epic poetry of Ranggawarsita who recorded the reign of an East Javanese prophet-king, Jayabaya (now confined to the Solo court and rarely performed). *Wayang* is also utilized by Christian missionaries to spread the

word of God; *Wayang Josuf* is about Joseph and his brothers. Despite the differences, all themes emphasize absolute good against absolute evil. Plots became more politicized after World War II during the independence struggle when the need arose to politically indoctrinate the masses. *Wayang* was then used to applaud heroism in guerilla warfare. *Wayang* plays have since been utilized to explain the meaning of 5 year economic plans to the people. Communists had Arjuna use the hammer and sickle as a weapon. In *Wayang Panca Sila,* the history of the republic is glorified: the 5 Pandava brothers from the *Mahabharata* symbolize the 5 Panca Sila Principles of the government. Although western and Chinese cinema have had a strong influence on all forms of *wayang* theatre (Kung Fu fighting in the battle scenes), its popularity remains strong.

dalang: The *wayang* puppeteer. This art was once passed down from father to son. Now it's taught only in special schools in Central Java. The *dalang* is the playwright, producer, principal narrator, conductor and director of this shadow world. He must be intimately versed in history, including complex royal genealogies; music (melodies, modes, phrases, songs); recitation (both *gamelan* and spoken); eloquence (an extempore poet creating a warm or terrifying atmosphere); have a familiarity with metaphysics, spiritual knowledge and perfection of soul. He's an expert in languages and highly skilled in the techniques of ventriloquism. He must be familiar with all levels of speech according to the *dramatis personae,* modulating his voice and employing up to 9 tonal and pitch variations to suit each of their tempermments. The *dalang* has a highly developed dramatic sense and if he has a good voice, his chants are beautiful and captivating to hear. Sometimes he carves his own *wayang,* maintaining a cast of up to 200 which are kept in his big wooden box. A man of unbelievable physical endurance (some chew betelnut for strength) and amazing detachment and self-control, he must be able to work his many characters for 6 hours or longer, keeping up to 6 cut-out puppets moving and talking at the same time. With movements of arms, hands, fingers, feet and voice, the *dalang* must maintain different body rhythms all at once. Battle scenes show best of all the degree of the *dalang's* skills. Small children sit in the front rows and sometimes the *dalang* increases the number of battles in the plot in proportion to the number of children in the audience. He has as many fans as a film star.

characters: The easiest way to pick out the speaker is to watch the puppets' or actors' arms. If they stretch out, they are speaking; if they hang down, they are silent. You can tell the good and evil characters as easily as you can in any American cowboy film by observing the placement and shape of eye, nose, mouth, the absence or presence of body hair or chin whiskers, the pose of the head, the coiffure, the headgear, clothing, jewelry. All of these immediately identify who the character is. Soft or raging voices also assit in zeroing in on a specific type of character. The most easily recognizable *wayangs* are those of the Hindu epics; Brahma, Vishnu (the gods who create and sustain life); Shiva (the Great Teacher), Durga (consort to Shiva), and Ganesha (the elephant-headed son of Shiva). Each of these heroes has his own melody played for him at his appearance. Facial and body colors (6 in number) show individual characters, temperment and mood. Vishnu's face is black, Shiva's face is gold, Krishna's enemy brother Baladewa has a red face. Black stands for inner maturity, adulthood, virtue, calmness. A black face with gold body depicts a refined warrior in a state of determination. Red shows uncontrolled passions and desires; gold indicates beauty or royalty or glory; white indicates noble descent, youth, beauty; a blue or green face means cowardice. Gods wear long cloaks, a shawl and footwear; kings wear a pleated *kain* that sticks out. Warriors wear a belt for their *kris*. Priests and high nobility have eyes almost closed. The clowns Semar, Gareng and Petruk are the deformed sidekicks of the hero. With their short-legged ugly shapes, fat stomachs, sagging breasts, jutting jaws, limping or clowning or fighting, they are the most lovable and laughable characters. The size of each puppet depends on whether they be demons, giants, gods, or just ordinary people. Puppets representing the highest deities are smaller than those of the noble heroes who in turn are smaller than their opponents, the demons, who are the largest puppets of all. This same proportion is followed in the classical relief sculpture on ancient Javanese temples. Big sizes like Bima and Kumbarkarna are an indication of physical power but not necessarily of greatness or passion or violence. Generally, the large figures belong to the negative 'left' side, the bad guys, while the smaller good guys belong to the positive

'right' side of the screen or stage (though with many exceptions). The posture with the legs held wide apart is found with warriors and rough characters while females are shown with legs close together. There are different shapes of eyes and noses denoting nobility, patience, crudeness, steadfastness, power, loyalty, clownishness, wisdom. Also a dozen shapes of mouths to express emotion and about 25 varieties of stylized coiffures and headgears which represent priests, princes, fighters, queens, deities, high kings, or gods. At least 3 types of hair buns dilineate different characters. Arjuna and his twin brothers Nakula and Sadewa wear their hair in an upward curl like a scorpion's tail or a lobster's claw, showing their royalty. Basically, almond eyes and pointed noses mean beneficient puppets while bulging round eyes and bulbous noses identify crude ones with their pompous display of ornamentation and the cocky angle of their heads, typified by a character like Burisrawa. Arjuna epitimizes aristocracy and refinement with his almond-shaped eyes, finely turned long pointed nose in a straight line from the tip to forehead, slightly bowed head showing his humility, no moustache, and absolutely no jewelry or finery.

WAYANG KULIT

A shadow-play using flat two-dimensional puppets chiselled by hand out of buffalo parchment. Known in Central and East Java, and on Bali. By far the most popular *wayang* form, it is a spellbinding medium for storytelling. Since a *wayang kulit* puppet is a stylized exaggeration of a human shape, it's really a shadow of a shadow. *Wayang kulit* is difficult to compete with, it's the cheapest *wayang* form to present on stage. *Wayang kulit* is often heard on the radio with just the voice of the *dalang* and the *gamelan* music. **history:** The Javanese have been cultivating the shadow play for more than 2000 years and this very sophisticated type of theatre is one of the strongest cultural traits to have survived throughout the recorded history of Indonesia. Originally it was connected with ancestor worship and from the very first has had a religious significance. South India was probably the original source of influence for Indonesia. Recorded in Pali canons, it existed there as far back as the 1st Century. Forms related to *wayang kulit* are found today from the Nang plays of Thailand all the way to Turkey in the Mediterranean. The earliest written record in Indonesia of a shadow play was found on a stone insciption in Central Java dating 907 A.D., a performance of dances, music, buffoonery and songs dedicated to Bima. At present these plays, after a long evolution, are based on the Indian epics, native East Javanese legends, and stories adopted from Arabian tales.

wayang-making: A complete set of *wayang kulit*, including duplications of a single character to show different ages and moods, could number 350-400 puppets, the smallest only 230 mm high and the tallest over 1 meter. *Penatah,* the *wayang*-making artist, first cuts out contours from leather hide, or more recently, goatskin. All the cutting out and coloring is done with the help of a special pattern book using 12 different motifs which help make the figures more recognizable. Before painting, the hide is rubbed smooth, then given a plain white background. Gold or yellow paint gives puppets the effect of gilding. Of very delicate and grotesque design, stiffened with glue and coloured with organic ingredients, the best look like exquisite filigree. Each leather figure is held by a stem of split buffalo horn or a wooden rod which is stuck in a banana trunk when not in use. Thin sticks are attached to the puppets' elbows and shoulder joints to manipulate the arms. Faces of the puppets are always in profile, the body turned to the front and both feet turned in the same direction as the facial profile. Performances are quite realistic with the characters jabbing each other in the chests and waving their arms about human-like to punctuate the action or to fit the type of character who's speaking or acting. The puppets can tilt, advance, retreat, fall, pivot, dance, fight, rise, hover, come down from the sky, fly up like a bird. By moving the puppets towards or away from the screen, the shadows themselves become sharp black lines or blurry greys, always fading and wavering; this is done for its outerwordly effect. Small boys love to sit in back on the *dalang's* side of the screen to watch his deft hands and appreciate more the designs and the colors of the puppets.

lakon: There are predominantly two types of repertory. *Wayang gedok* has heroes who date from the late Java-Hindu era and stories that revolve around the East Javanese legends (Prince Panji). This form is most popular in East Java but rarely seen in Central Java. *Wayang purwa* draws its themes from episodes and heroes of Indonesian prehistory and the Hindu *Mahabharata* and *Ramayana* epic poems, these mythological tales being the most frequently seen and best known of all shadow plays. All the themes share the same plots and the same typology of heroes runs through them all. The setting is always Java. The traditional 10 hour performance is divided into 3 principal parts. In each of these periods a different *gamelan* musical pitch is employed to heighten the mood. The leading character seldom appears before midnight, usually a little after. Only then can the audience be sure which story is being staged. The first time period, from about 8 pm to 12 am, is said to stand for the youthful period of human life, from infancy to adolescence. The *dalang* takes this opportunity to instruct on refinement of manners and moral and ethical advice. At midnight there is always a great climax (gara-gara), a clash between the good and bad forces. After this, the 2nd period opens which lasts until around 3 am. In this period the clowns play a large part, giving comic relief while the heavy plot unfolds. This phase symbolizes the young adult's struggle in society. Finally, the *gamelan* switches the mood (3rd phase) to a lighter pitched music as the hero slays his enemies, good triumphs over evil, and peace is regained. There's a joyous victory dance (tajungan) by Bima or his father Blaju (God of Wind). Then the sun comes up in both worlds. This last period represents the wisdom and maturity of old age.

WAYANG GOLEK

Puppets in-the-round. Since *wayang orang* is only the imitation by human actos of the movements of the shadow puppets, the 3-dimensional *wayang golek* puppets imitate human beings imitating the shadow puppets. These puppets are much more like our western puppets except that rods are used to manipulate them, not strings. No shadow screen is used. The audience faces the *dalang* and watches realistic people in minature. This *wayang* form is most often performed in the daytime; it has a less ceremonial, less magical, more wordly atmosphere than the shadow puppets. In each period a different *gamelan* musical pitch is employed to heighten the mood. The original source lies in China over 2000 years ago. The most recent form of popular theatre on Java, the idea might have been borrowed from the round puppets of the Chinese in the northern coastal ports.

puppet-making: There is no room for innovation in the sculpting of a *golek* puppet, the artisans are strict copyists. Puppets consist of a trunk and head plus arms that rotate at the shoulder and elbow joints, moved from beneath by means of thin rods attached to the palms. Since a *dalang* must stand for so long with his arms upraised, the puppet is carved from strong but light *arbasiah*-wood. The neck is elongated and the head swivels on a central bamboo pole hidden under the flowing *kain* or *sarung,* the real clothing of the figure. Puppets are dressed by the local seamstress, often the wife of the carver. Costumes include court dress of a European lord of the 18th Century or perhaps a dashing Arabian knight. The shape of the head, face, headdress and color are the same as the leather puppets, though less stylized and more individulaistic. Puppets are *batiked* and bejeweled and have surprisingly human features, much more so than the *kulit* forms. Their heads are enammeled and sometimes set with stones. *Golek* faces are like masks, meticulously painted, showing all types of expressions: smiles, hideous mean-tempered scowls, foolish dumb staring. You can see the puppets pant and shake with fright, their heads turning in all directions and their arms going a mile-a-minute. A 180 mm (7 inch) miniature of a *golek* puppet might cost Rp750-1000; a 450 mm tall (1 ½ ft.) one, about Rp3000.

lakon: *Wayang golek* is something of a morality play, a social commentary, and a magical mythmaking — all in one. In Central Java this form is used often in plays connected with the penetration of Islam into Java, based on the stories and adventures of Mohammed's uncle, the Arabian prince Amir Hamzah. Stories could also be about the chivalrous Prince Menak who prepares the world for Mohammed. In West Java, *wayang golek* draws its heroes more from the *Mahabharata* and *Ramayana* legends (*purwa*-repertory).

WAYANG TOPENG

Masked theatre which mimes the stories of the *wayang golek,* employing dancing by men acting like puppets wearing shiny beautiful masks with big mysterious eyes which seem suspended in the air. *Wayang topeng* is known all over Java in many forms, each region has a different style of masks, costuming and dancing. The most active centers are in East Java. Sometimes the dancers themselves speak their roles, other times the *dalang* speaks for them while the actors just marching on and off the stage. Although classical Javanese language is the most often used, it's spoken in a less stylized form than in *wayang orang.* Masks are very similar to the heads of *golek* puppets. Carved out of light wood, they are held in position by the actor biting a leather strap or wooden prong in the back. Face, hair and headdresses are painted in a color according to who the character is. Faces are generally round and the nose depends upon the personage for its size and shape. Troupes consist only of male dancers. Female roles are taken by boys from 8-14 years old, before their voice changes. The entire troupe has perhaps 20-25 people and a set of *topeng* contains traditionally 40-80 pieces. Some masks are very rare and prized, found only in collections of princes and in museums, guarded as *pusaka* (sacred heirlooms). The ones on display at the Sonobudoyo Museum in Yogya reach this classic standard, the acclaimed Reni masks.

history: This theatre form stems from the ancient Javanese practice of masked dancers performing at death rites. Origin of the modern form is the 16th Century, invented by an important historical person, Sunan Kalidjaga. When Islam became entrenched on Java, masked dances were banned from ritual life but persisted in folk plays in villages put on by wandering masked players. Even today *topeng* persists more as a popular theatre than as a court tradition. **lakon:** The plots are derived mainly from the *Panji* cycle, centering on the legendary Prince of Jenggala. See the solo performance of the *Topeng Tua* which portrays the wistful meditative movements and attitudes of an old man. Usually involves 3-4 actors and up to 40 fascinating masks.

WAYANG ORANG

Wayang wong in Javanese. Abstract, symbolic dance plays with or without masks, employing people who dress up like puppets. Masks are usually worn only by animals such as monkeys, birds, or monster roles (for example, the King of Demons in the *Ramayana).* A *dalang* could recite and chant, but the dialogue is most often spoken by live actors and actresses. *Wayang orang* is more intelligible and more of a spectacle to tourists with its rich costuming, *gamelan* music, highly sophisticated dance, and the antics of the clowns. Shiny costumes of gold and black and rich deep-colored-*batiks* and silks are worn. This *wayang* form is by far the most expensive to stage. A boxful of leather or wooden puppets is much cheaper to maintain than a whole troupe of live actors who have to be fed, clothed and given salaries. Consequently, *wayang orang* is the rarest seen.

history: *Wayang orang* has an ancient pre-Islamic source as perhaps a cremation celebration, male initiation rite, war dance, or chant recital, with the *dalang* acting as a kind of priest. The modern form first flowered in the 18th and 19th Centuries, put on solely for the aristocracy. Many of the best dancers are to this day pure nobility. The present style reached its peak in the years 1900-1940 when huge extravagant performances were presented in the royal courts of Central Java. Presided over by the sultan, Javanese and Dutch dignitaries and splendidly dressed court ladies sitting in long rows would attend an opulent feast and glittering dance drama lasting 3 days. Now only the 4-day long dance festivals held at Prambanan in Central Java and at Pandaan in East Java each year from June to Oct. can compare with them .

dancers: *Wayang orang's* highly controlled and stylized dance style so closely imitates the gestures and movements of leather cut-out marionettes that the dancer, especially the male, seems to move on a flat 2-dimensional plane; feet, knees and thighs are separated at extreme angles so that his body appears flat. Thus the term *wayang orang*, or 'human puppets'. There are many parallels between *wayang orang* and *wayang kulit*. The actors' waiting room is called *katok*, the same name as the chest in which the *dalang* of *wayang kulit* keeps his puppets; the shape of the stage is similar, being long and narrow; the dancers usually show only their profiles to the audience, just as the *wayang kulit* puppets do; the postures, costumes and make-up of the actors are also very similar. *Wayang orang* actors are so heavily made up that their faces look like they have a coat of enamel over them. Arms and shoulders are covered with a fine yellow powder. Dressing for the *Tari Gatotkoco*, a dance portraying manhood, can take as long as 2 hours. Observe the amazing jewelry and tall headdresses, the same shapes as those worn by the little *wayang kulit* puppets. Almost complete impassivity of facial expression is the requirement. Facial gestures are strictly limited to just 3 levels, each expressing different states of the soul. Likewise, most strong emotion and moods are expressed within a particular mode of dance; you don't see inner conflicts. Dancers have to learn a meticulous, painstaking iconography. Each mode of dancing is adjusted to the physique of an individual dancer and characters can be picked out by just the way they walk. A small man will play the part of a smooth, flowing, slow-moving and soft-speaking dancer, the *alus*-style, whereas a big round-faced man is chosen for a hostile, crude and booming-voiced part, the brusque *kasar*-style. In the battles, all combatants fight in strictly their own styles. An actor always remains 'in character' with even the movements of monsters technically very highly controlled. The crux of the male-style is the snappiness and angularity in which all movements are carried out. His hands form the Hindu *mudras*. Female dancers play subtle, graceful parts, always dancing with legs held close together, the steps small and tight-fitting with knees slightly bent. Fingers are at times extended by artificial fingernails to accentuate their dramatic impact. Dance scarves (*sampur*) are used often to express sadness or to symbolically topple an enemy. Love scenes are enacted powerfully without players ever touching each other but with all the tension and passion put across by just looking. The Javanese *wayang orang* comic servants (panakawans), Semar, Petruk, Gareng and Bagong, are not found in the more faithful and sedate Indian original of the *Mahabharata* by Valmiki; they are a pure Javanese creation. The Hindu God Shiva is often played by a woman, dilligently taught from 5 years of age. Taunted by bearded devils and other demonic creatures, she glides, dances, fights, makes speeches, cries, sings, and wins.

lakon: *Wayang orang* combines the glamorous mythology of the Hindu epics with classical Javanese dance, both interwoven with many tribal myths. Like a good Shakespearean play there's a little something for everyone — clowns, demons, magic, juggling, tricks, bawdy jokes, a mixture of circus vaudville and the grace of ballet. The dialogues are spoken in High Javanese, intoned with melodic, almost ecclesiastical monotony except for the extremely stylized high-pitched cackle of mockery or a sudden roar of anger. 50 different scenes are sometimes played out and *wayang orang* could last from 6 hours to 3 days. Nowadays you could see a girl putting on makeup, a boy flying a kite, a woman weaving - anything could happen in *wayang orang.*

WEST JAVA
(JAWA BARAT)

UJUNG KULON RESERVE

This completely untamed wilderness lies on the far western tip of Java, cut off from the rest of the island by a narrow marshy isthmus. There are two separate parks, one located on the peninsula and the other on the small island of Panaitan across a narrow strait. The reserve has open broad meadows, waterfalls, ready swamps, estuarine shallows with crocodiles, steam rising from *alang2* grass, flocks of peacocks, rooting wild pigs, hornbills flapping through the air, gibbons leaping from trees, squeaking otters in the rivers, miniature deer, *sambur* stags with huge sets of antlers. There are also wild buffaloes, tigers, panthers, herons, wild ducks and numerous other varieties of birds. Skindiving near the island of Peucang. Sandy beach at Nyiur where the rare one-horned Javanese rhinoceros sometimes hangs out (also on the peninsula part). Now 45 protected rhinos are left. Similar to its Indian relative which is found now only in very small pockets in Assam and Nepal, the armor on its back is divided into four sections. His little pig eyes don't see well, but he'll attack blind anyway. Look out for fresh 3-toed hoofmarks, making sure that a tree is always nearby.

getting there: Best time to visit is April-Oct. for in this dry season the rhinos make their way to clay pits to sun themselves. Get an entry permit first from the Forestry Office, Jl. Juanda, Bogor - it's rumored that it's a hassle. Travel agents can fix it up for you, but more expensive. A 4-day tour to Ujung Kulon costs Rp40,000 and up, including accommodation in a guesthouse on Peucang island, a photo safari with guide, entrance fee, all meals, two nights at the Carita Beach in Carita. Contact Mangiring Tours, Jl. Tueku Cik Ditiro 45, Jakarta; Tel. 50128. Tours are often advertised in the *Indonesia Times.* By road from Serang there are 3 ways to get to Labuhan from where you can take boats out to the volcanic isle of Krakatoa and to Ujung Kulon: the northern route (70 km) via Cilegon, the intersection for Merak, and Anyer is the quickest; the central route (80 km) passes through Mandalawangi; and the southern route (65 km) goes through the mountain village of Pandeglang. The motorboat from Labuhan to Ujung Kulon takes 12 hours; or take a *prahu,* much cheaper.

KRAKATOA VOLCANO

40 km from the West Java coast. Blown to pieces in the 19th Century in the most violent explosion the world has ever known. Tidal waves 30 m high. Debris landed in Madagascar on the other side of the Indian Ocean. The boom was heard in Brisbane over 4000 km away. Special masses were held in Spain. Tennyson wrote a poem. It rumbles still occasionally and Anak Krakatoa (Son of Krakatoa) has already risen 500 m above the sea since its first appearance in 1928. Seventeen years after the explosion, which took place in 1883, the isle of Krakatoa was again astonishingly covered in plant life though virtually bereft of fauna except for snakes, lizards, spiders, rats, bats and birds. Scientists estimate that it will take 2-3 million years before animal life returns in numbers.

getting there: The Rp30,000 boat trip from Labuhan takes only 4 hours; 5-6 people to a boat. To circle the island by boat takes 3 hours. Each time you go, the volcano is in a different mood. Water could be 60 degrees C. (hot). Hot ash blackens your face, boulders the size of basket-balls are tossed out, the roar is deafening, while black smoke clouds the sky. Can also hire a boat from Pasauran. No regular services in monsoon season, Nov.-March.

BANTEN

The Bantenese are a culturally distinct people. Banten town is on the coast 10 km north of Serang. The first haggard Dutchman set foot on Java at Banten in 1596 after a 14 month voyage in a fleet of 4 ships in which 250 men died. Along with the Mataram Empire, Banten was one of Java's two dominant states in the 17th Century. It was so continuously rebellious towards Dutch rule that it was known as 'The Aceh of Java'. There are many well-preserved 16th and 17th Century buildings in Old Banten. See Mesjid Agung in Pecinan village. Istana Surosowan is a heavily fortified compound with 4 m high crumbling walls and a museum of weapons, clay pipes, old bottles. Also visit the ruins of 17th Century Spellwijck Fortress. Kelenteng, a 200 year old Chinese temple on the west side of the fortress, has a sacred chair in a glass case. See the renowned Debus Players, ascetics who can control fear, pain, the heat of fire, the sharpness of weapons. They perform before tourists, undergoing torture, burned and buried alive, cut, slashed, etc. - surviving unharmed. Observe them slide down a rope from the Chinese-style minaret of Banten's Great Mosque. **stay:** Base yourself in Serang, Merak or Cilegon. Wisma Kasihsayang, Jl. Tirtayasa, Serang, Rp500 single.

from Banten: Pantai Suralaya (Florida Beach)

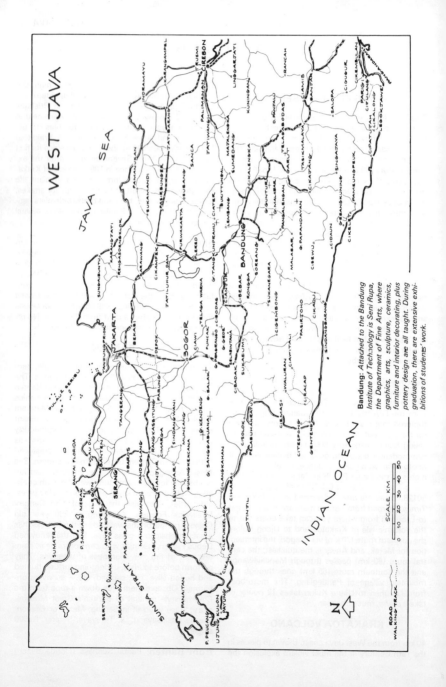

WEST JAVA

JAVA SEA

INDIAN OCEAN

SUMATRA

KRAKATOA

SUNDA STRAIT

PULAU SERIBU

SERANG

JAKARTA

BOGOR

BANDUNG

CIREBON

Bandung: Attached to the Bandung Institute of Technology is Seni Rupa, the Department of Fine Arts, where graphics, arts, sculpture, ceramics, furniture and interior decorating, plus pottery design are all taught. During graduation, there are extensive exhibitions of students' work.

SCALE KM
0 10 20 30 40 50

ROAD
WALKING TRACK

N

has many good cafes. Visit the giant cave of Karang Bolong. Anyer Kidul is an old lighthouse with a good view over the Sunda Strait. Hire a fisherman to take you out to the deserted island of Sangiang: lonely coral beaches, mangrove swamps, abandoned Japanese shore batteries, brown monkeys, delectable fruit. Bird sanctuary islands off N.W. coast of Java are all within reach of Banten: Rambut, Bokor, Dua. Along with Peru's guano islands and the Norwegian Bird Cliffs, Pulau Dua is one of the world's chief bird islands. It is reachable by *prahu* one hour from Karanghantu harbor in Banten Bay. From a distance it looks like a green umbrella. From March-July each year its 20 acres are a favorite breeding ground for 40-50,000 migratory birds (even breeds of ice birds). Take care when walking under nesting places because birds will spew you with slimy vomit and jets of guano.

BADUI PEOPLE

Held in awe by common Javanese and politicians for their mystic and clairavoyant powers; they predicted both World Wars. Suharto safely ignores them. This small tribe of Sunda-speaking people live in a 50 sq. km forest territory on G. Kendeng, S.E. of Rangkasbitung. For 400 years they have maintained complete isolation from the outside world, preserving intact their religion, moral code, kinship, hierarchial system and general way of life. Now their isolation is breaking down with the increasing population of the plains to the north of Kendeng encroaching more and more on traditional Badui lands. Their villages are divided into *Badui Dalam* (inner 3 villages) and the *Badui Luar* (outer 22 villages). The Inner Badui, or White Badui, consist of 40 families (Kajeroan), the purest of Badui stock. This inner clan dresses only in white and follows rigorous rules of conduct which were first laid down by an ancestral divinity called Batarratunggal. They are forbidden to kill, steal, lie, commit adultery, get drunk, eat food at night, take any form of conveyance, wear flowers or perfumes, accept gold or silver, touch money, cut their hair. Other taboos relate to defending Badui lands against invasion: they may not grow *sawah,* use fertilizers, raise cash crops, use modern tools for working *ladang* soil, keep large domestic animals. The *Badui Dalam* live in the villages of Cibeo, Cikaratawarna, and Cikeusik in *tanah larangan* (forbidden territory) where no stranger is permitted to spend the night. Outside this 'sacred inner circle' are the Outer Badui (Kaluaran). This outer clan wears bluish black turbans and sashes, lives less strictly, bargains on behalf of the Badui Dalam, are permitted to sell their crops, and serve as go-betweens for the White Badui and the rest of the world. These men oversee not only the entry of strangers into the Badui lands but also the exit of Badui people. In the past no one

was allowed to leave their jungle fastness, but now you sometimes see Badui men in the streets of Jakarta or even as far away as Bandung. But two things are certain: they have a good reason for going there and they have come on foot. The Baduis consider records of their progeny as sacred living things. There's a grove of hallowed family trees at Arcas Domas.

history: Their origins are uncertain. Dr. B. van Tricht's expedition in 1928 to gather medical and anthropological data on the Badui was a complete failure. They could be descendants of the aristocracy of the Sunda Kingdom of Pajajaran who lived near Batutulis in the hills around Bogor; their domestic architecture follows most closely traditional Sundanese architecture. Pakuwan, the capital of Pajajaran, was destroyed by invading Muslims in 1579. To preserve their basic animism (with Buddhist and Hindu overtones), their ancestors could have fled to this mountain retreat. Another theory traces their origin to northern Banten; pockets of people in the northern hills still speak the archaic dialect of Sunda that the Badui use.

getting there: The rigid *buyut* taboo system makes it difficult for tourists to visit the inner territory, but you can get to the outer villages of Keduketug, Kadujangkung and Karakal. You could catch a glimpse of an Inner Badui man visiting an Outer Badui village for the day, the flash of his white garments moving between the houses. Get permission first from the Kantor Kabupaten in Rangkasbitung to visit the Inner Badui village of Cibeo on a walk-in, walk-out basis; speak with the *pu'un* (leader) in Cibeo. Best is to find a Badui guide in Rangkasbitung who is going back home on foot to Cibeo. The jungle track leads from Rangkas up to the hills to the Muslim villages of Cisimeut and Kemancing. Cross the 100 m wide river at Cisimeut. Spend the night at Kemancing and start next morning at dawn. From Kemancing it takes 3½ hours to reach the Outer Badui village of Keduketug, which is strikingly different physically as well as in atmosphere from the Muslim villages. From Keduketug, it's a 2 hour hard climb to Cibeo, the very heartland of the Badui.

TASIKMALAYA

57 km east of Garut; or Rp800 by minibus from Bandung. Tasikmalaya is the center of rattan and *pandanus* woven goods, and a special *batik* style (batik tasik) with mostly a red background. If buying quantity buy here: purses, trays, handbags, floormats (medong), bowls, strawhats, paper umbrellas. For even cheaper prices and more unusual purchases try Rajapolah village 12 km north where the weavers actually work. **stay:** Hotel Merdeka,

Jl. Siliwangi 54, four minutes walk from the train station, Rp750 single or double; an OK place. Hotel Tasik, Jl. Komala Sari 18 (a back street), is Rp1200 per room with *mandi;* clean. Hotel Selamat, Jl. Empang 26; Rp900 for single, Rp1500 for three, clean and central. The cheapest is Hotel Pusaka, Jl. Yuda Negara 32, Rp500, Rp750 double, 3 people for Rp1000. **eat:** Banda Pulai, right across the street from Hotel Kencana, has *nasi padang.* Many good *warungs* on Jl. Pemuda; *ayam goreng,* Rp150 for a drumstick. Restoran Hobby and Rumah Makan Combinasi are further down, near Hotel Tasik. Rumah Makan Saderhana, Jl. Mesjid 16, has *gado2, gule, mie telor, sop buntut,* etc. all well prepared. Resmi, next door, is good too. At Tasik, Jl. Mustafa 35, see live pythons in the kitchen, excellent snake soup.

crafts: Check Kandaga Art Shop, Jl. Dr. Suharjo, near Bioskop Garuda. Batik Bordil, Kotaresik, Jl. Seladarnia, Tel. 335, sells *batik tulis* for Rp2-7000. The GKBI (Batik Cooperative) is on Jl. R.E. Marta Dinata (taller building). Try also Miss Herna Sarbini's, Jl. Gudang Jero II/17. Or Toko Batik, Jl. Cihideung. **vicinity of Tasik:** Good pottery *pasar* at Majelang. Gede Lake is 3 km from Tasik, and Panjalu Lake is 25 km from Tasik. Papandayan Crater is fantastic but it's only accessible by foot.

PANGANDARAN

This tiny fishing village is at the entrance of a small peninsula which is surrounded almost completely by beach. On the very tip of the peninsular is a wildlife reserve. Hike your stiff legs or swim in the gentle surf here. Cagar Alam Pananjung Nature Reserve is 525,025 hectare and 3 km long. Rp50 entrance fee, or walk along the beach and get in free. Stuffed mounted animals taken from the wildlife reserve are for sale everywhere in *warungs* before entering the park; live squirrels and civet cats are also for sale. It's a 10 km walk around the entire peninsula at low tide. An intriguing place. Some segments of the beach are right out of *Treasure Island;* can really get away. By motorboat it can be done in 1 ½ hours for Rp6000; 15 to a boat. They want Rp1500-2000 an hour for a motorless *prahu* and it's hard to budge them. The park's got everything: caves to crawl into, hollows of deep silence, teak forests, grazing fields and scrub areas, wild buffaloes, black monkeys, deer, porcupines, peafowls, hornbills, and you could even come upon a 10 m long python. Costs Rp100 to get out on the reefs by sailboat. While surfing the break, see big silver fish riding the waves alongside your board. During school or other holidays (especially *Hari Raya*), Pangandaran is swamped with people.

Pangandaran: *Spend a memorable night in the watching towers of this reserve. These watching towers are raised off the ground, built for observing the grazing bulls. You have the company of a full moon and a full frog orchestra which comes to a dead halt at a particular time in the night. In the early morning, the rising sun creeps above the tree tops where you can watch black monkeys breakfasting on young leaves. The figments of imagination of the night before also disappear with the rising sun. The dancing figures which you thought you saw were merely jungle trees with vines wound like snakes around the tree trunks.*

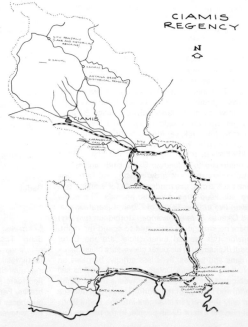

CIAMIS REGENCY

N

getting there: Take bus to Pangandaran from Banjar, 42 km east of Tasik, but take the train for the return trip; it's more comfortable and more scenic. From Yogya it's 7 hours on the 'day-express' train to Banjar, Rp1800. If you get stuck in Banjar, stay at Peng. Asli right near the train station or at Peng. Galuh just after the bridge. Usually as soon as you come out of the train station in Banjar the Colt drivers will be on you; Colts cost Rp3-400 for the 2 hour 63 km drive south to Pangandaran and the last Colt leaves at around 8-9 pm. Taking the train all the way takes a good bit longer. An alternative route to Pangandaran from Yogya is to take the train to Kroya, bus or Colt to Cilicap, *prahu* to Kalipucang, then a minibus Rp125 to Pangandaran.

stay: From Pangandaran's *stanplatz,* the row of hotels is 2 km away, Rp75-100 by *becak.* No matter which hotel you stay in you can hear the waves breaking on either side of the peninsula. The beach on the eastern side is dangerous but the beach to the west is safe (more sheltered) and clean. At least 30 *losmens* and bungalows. Some places want as high as Rp1500 for a room but talk them down. There are several *rumah makan* with rooms for rent on their upper storeys. Yan's Accommodation is popular with travelers, Rp300 single, Rp500 double. Across the street, Rumah Makan Saderhana Bandung has small but comfortable rooms up the ladder, Rp300; *nasi goreng* and other meals for Rp1-250. Peng. Putra Asli, Wisma Sawargi and Wisma Dinar are all right on the beach, all Rp1000 per room. Peng. Setia Famili, Rp300 single, Rp500 double; a pleasant place, you can order meals, and get a cheaper rate if you stay longer. Next door is Losmen Itikurih, but more expensive. One km into the forest near the beach is Pasangrahan Rengganis, but you must first go to Kantor Seksi, Jl. Oto Iskandardinata 427, Bandung, to get permission. See the map on the porch of this *pasangrahan* before setting out in the peninsula.

eat: Best deal is to buy fresh fish Rp250 a kg on the beach and have the restaurants or *losmens* cook it up for you. *Warungs* down in the village past Yan's towards the reserve or your left serve tasty *nasi campurs* for Rp75 with vegies or Rp125 with meat. Another convivial *warung* is right on the western beach; serves coffee and snacks, and is open until late at night. Delicious *mangosteens* when in season, Rp15 each. Also try Rumah Makan Sumedang with a good *sate* place next door.

from Pangandaran: Big surf pounds long stretches of deserted beaches to Batu Hiu. There are many less accessible but quieter beaches with fewer people than Pangandaran: Batu Hiu, Parigi,

and Batu Karas beaches. For Batu Karas, get a taxi from Pangandaran to Cijulang, Rp125, then walk down to the beach. There are three coastal villages easy to reach from Pangandaran. Just start walking west and you reach the first village before it gets really hot. The headman will put you up. For Cilicap go first to Kalipucang by bus Rp100, then do the very nice boat trip to Cilicap. Train (more to look at than on the bus) leaves Pangandaran for Banjar at 2 or 3 pm, costs Rp200, takes 5-6 hours.

JAKARTA

Indonesia's capital city, center for government, politics and business – the brain of Indonesia. This is where the world's ideas, technology and fashions first touch Indonesia; Java grows the finest coffee in the world, yet in Jakarta they drink Nescafe. It's the literary center and headquarters for the mass media: ¼ of all Indonesia's newspapers are printed here. It has a film industry, a modern theatre academy, and a prestigious university. Jakarta is where all the big contracts are signed, the strings pulled, the rakeoffs happen. 80% of all foreign investments come through here and most of the money in Indonesia is spent and earned here. And it all stays here. This is why everything is 2-3 times more expensive in Jakarta than anywhere else in Indonesia. For Rp300 you get a 3-course meal in Yogya, but only a one course meal in Jakarta. It costs Rp7500 to see a Deep Purple or a Susi Quarto one-group concert, and even a 2nd rate western movie costs Rp2500. A slice of pineapple puts you back Rp50, a Toyota Corona Rp9 million, a suburban house with modern amenities Rp100,000 a week. The chief drama of Jakarta is its contrasts, a fascinating collision of East and West. It has Indonesia's highest and most expensive buildings and by far its murkiest slums, the most highly and the least educated people. Ultra-modern and ultra-traditional, fast and slow, are side by side. Airconditioned diesels hurtle by the peddler; skyscrapers throw shadows across hovels made of cardboard, plastic and tin cans; shiny new Holdens park by squatter's passageways filled with flies. It's Indonesia's most dynamic, problem-ridden city. **climate:** Lying on the flattest, least interesting coast of Java, it could be suffocatingly humid. Because of the city's outdated sewerage and drainage system, two-thirds of Jakarta is inundated each rainy season when all municipal and central government offices close down, there are traffic snarls, stranded vehicles, petrol shortages, and up to 250,000 people in need of shelter.

history: From its beginnings as a fortified warehouse in the early 1600's, it has the longest continuous history of any modern Indonesian city (440 years). Jakarta was built on the site of the Javanese village of Jayakarta which the Dutch governor burned and razed to the ground in 1619. To remind them of home the Dutch renamed the site in honor of a medieval Netherlands Kingdom, Batavia, then built a completely new city of intersecting canals, small houses with tiny narrow windows and burnt red tiled roofs. a Little Holland in the Tropics. Dutch governors based here sent out voyagers to open up new trading routes; in 1642, Abel Tasman named an island in the southern oceans 'Van Diemen's Land', resulting in the discovery of Australia. Jakarta was known as the Pearl of the Orient with massive agricultural wealth flowing through here. Then long-distance European sailing ships carried malaria to this once healthy seaport and it became one of the pestholes of the world. Known for 100 years as the Graveyard of the Orient, its canals became ideal breeding places for diseases. The modern city was built before WW II for 600,000 people and now contains 5.7 million. Since 1619, Jakarta has had a reputation for being rundown, decayed, hectic, a city of stinking canals, potholes and cracked sidewalks. Its water tastes like a rusty mug. A gung-ho mayor and tough ex-marine, Ali Sadikan has transformed Jakarta over the last 11 years with his iron broom into not only an industrial and trade city, but into a tourist and cultural city as well. Bang Ali stepped down July 11, 1977.

people: The original inhabitants were slaves, but today it's the only true Indonesian city, a melting pot for Sundanese, Javanese, Chinese, Balinese, Batak, Minangkabaus, Maluku Islanders, Europeans, etc. The population is so mixed that it comprises a separate race of people (the Dutch called them 'Batavians'). Jakartans speak their own vivid dialect, Jakartanese. 200,000 migrants enter Jakarta each year from the economically depressed countryside of Java and from the outlying islands of Indonesia. Four-fifths make their living as laborers, becak drivers, one-man manufacturers, hawkers, servants, warung cooks, etc. – all contributing to the substratum world of its bazaar economy. One-fourth of Jakarta's people are squatters, sticking close to shopping centers for the money income or close to rivers and ditches for cleaning and washing. Thousands sleep in the streets, known as orang gelandangan ('always on the move'). Jakarta is a city of a million villages. You can walk through the kampungs of Jakarta one after the other all day long (visit Kampung Arab, Krukut; and Kampung Portugis, Tugu), each with its own bridges, shops, schools, police, midwives, dukuns, customs, manners.

arriving: If by sea at Tanjung Priok, just walk 2 km from the docks to the Tanjung Priok Bus Station and take a bus (Rp30) to Benteng Station in the middle of the city. Or share a taxi (between 5 people), Rp1500 into the city; have him drive through Chinatown on the way. Arriving by air, it's Rp1500 from the airport by taxi to most hotels. Be forewarned of the so-called taxis from Jakarta's airports, locals call them sistem Jakarta (rip-off system), the drivers claim that their meters are mati (dead). From Jakarta's Halim International Airport, take bus into the city for Rp30. transport: One of the most congested cities of Asia. Keystone Cops. Stay iow from 11-5 or you'll collapse from heat exhaustion. Crowded intercity buses are the cheapest at Rp30; the main terminal is Lapangan Benteng. Get ahold of a map at the tourist bureau (Jl. Thamrin 9) which shows all the main bus routes in Jakarta. Most buses radiate from L. Benteng and most you jump on will eventually end up there. Next cheapest are bemos or oplets which go along the main drags, Rp50-100 for an average run. Becaks cost Rp100-200 for a 1-3 km ride, but are banned from the downtown. If you take a helicak, Rp2-300 for short distances, make sure that they take you all the way and not drop you off at 'the border'.

stay: Wisma Delima, Jl. Jaksa 5, Rp600 for dorm beds or Rp500 with a Y.H.A. card. This hostel has the most traffic of any. You could meet anyone here. Have mail sent here and buy charter flight tic-

JAKARTA

1. Jalan Jaksa
2. National Museum
3. Gambir Train Station
4. Presidential Palace
5. Jakarta Post Office
6. Benteng Bus Terminal
7. Borobudur Hotel
8. Bungur Youth Accommodation
9. Senen Train Station
10. Senen Market
11. Sarinah Department Store
12. Hotel Indonesia
13. Immigration Department
14. T.I.M. (cultural center)
15. Oasis Restaurant
16. Cikini Fruit Market
17. Jalan Surabaya antique stalls
18. Hotel Inkopak
19. Gedung Polo
20. Glodok District
21. Kota Train Station
22. Jakarta City Museum
23. Wayang Museum

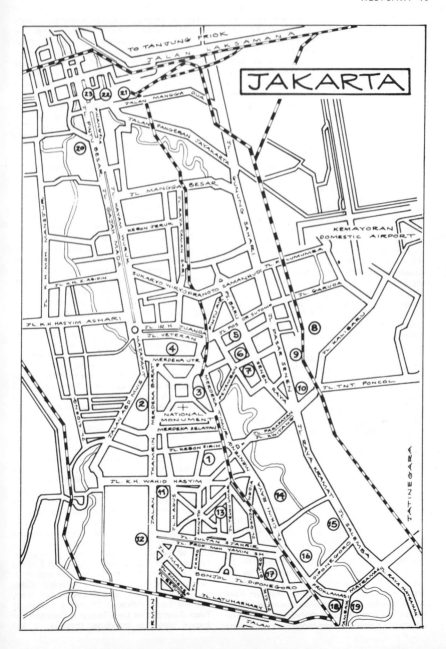

kets to Singapore and Pelni boat tickets to Medan, etc. Though quite central (one km south of Gambir Station), it has bad lighting and it's quite stuffy and cramped in most of the rooms. Pure money trip: there are so many travelers that they hardly smile anymore; you order a drink and they reach out for the money first. Heed the sign: 'Don't go outside in your underpants.' Semi-European breakfast, Rp400, and good 3-course meals, Rp500. Everyone gets sick from the food at Jl. Jaksa 40, a horrible place, so filthy, needs painting, hot; Rp600 for a dorm bed. You'd be lucky to get into Fru Brouwer's place (but only has two rooms) at Jl. Jaksa 27, Rp1500 double. Worth paying the little extra; a very nice lady, and you're taken right into the family. Do your socializing down at no. 5. If she's full, try Bali International between Jl. Jaksa and Sarinah Dept. Store; special student price to share a room, Rp1000. Another excellent place nearby Jalan Jaksa is Kebon Sirih 23 with new rooms for Rp2000 double including breakfast; a pleasant lady, a bargain place right behind a Pelni booking office. Hotel Hai Kok, 300 m from Kota Station, is Rp750 per person, double Rp1500, but very dirty, stinks. Street outside is frequently flooded with water. Hotel Inkopak is the central office for the YHA, Jl. Tambak 2 (follow Jl. Cikini Raya south); peaceful place, Rp450. Dorm's usually empty, good value. Wisma Esther, Jl. Mataram Raya 113; Rp600, 2 3 people to a room, good music, clean. Get an oplet from Senen Market (Rp30), Wisma Esther is about 4 km from Hotel Borobudur. An organized losmen with many foreigners, free tea all day, and free breakfast (banana and cake). Bungur Youth Accommodation, Jl. Bungur Besar Gang IV/3 (less than 10 minutes walk from Pasar Senen), Rp500. Very loose losmen in a typical Javanese kampung run by young guys. All day long food trips are going on out on the alleyway: baked corn, mie soup (Rp50), ice cream. It's only a short walk from here to Senen Station for trains to any point along the northern coast of Java to Surabaya. Catch bus easily from just down the street on Jl. Mataram Raya to Tanjung Priok Harbor, Rp30.

eat: Sate Blora, Jl. Jen. Sudirman, serves the best sate in town. Kapuran Blora, near Sate Blora, is almost as good. Other famous sate houses are: on Jl. Pakubuwono 6; the Satay House on Jl. Kebon Sirih 31 A., Rp1000 for unequalled sate. Trio Restaurant, Jl. Gondangdia Lama 29, is a bargain shack near the RR tracks, good Indonesian food, cheap for Jakarta. For the rare Javanese restaurant, try Bu Citro's, Jl. Cikanjang, Kebayoran (another at Senen Raya). For Padang food: Roda, Jl. Mataram Raya 65; or Natrabu, Jl. Haji Agus Salim near the Quantas office. Cahaya Kota, Jl. Wahid Hasyim 9, is one of Jakarta's finest Chinese-Indonesian restaurants

and the no. 1 big shot restaurant where the capital's rich and powerful go. Rp1500-2500 per person for matchless Chinese food (the best frog legs). Other good restaurants are: Oasis, Jl. Raden Saleh 47; and Liong Liong, Jl. Hayam Waruk 116, for tasty Chinese food at budget prices. Cheap foodstalls in front of Menteng Theatre. Try the night market near Pasar Boplo, Jl. Teuku Umar north of the G.P. O. for good warung food. Another excellent night market where everyone goes, rich and poor, for Chinese food and seafood, is Pecengongan. For cheeseburger freaks, repair to Hotel Borobudur's Coffee Shop. For Rp900 (!), you get toasted bun, lettuce, tomato, onion, coleslaw, great fries, plus condiments like Delmonte catsup, tobasco sauce, and lip-smacking mustard.

markets: Most markets are open 7 days a week 8 am- 10 pm. Orchid gardens: Jl. Serang, Jati Petamburan, Cilandak, and Cipete. Biggest fruit markets at Pasar Minggu and Pasar Cikini. Pasar Baru (near G.P.O.) is best for fabrics. Jl. Surabaya in Menteng is Jakarta's densely packed flea market: silver filigree, leatherwork, batik, Mario Lanza records, Delft, old coins, sets of false teeth, Kalimantan spears, teak chests; best in the late afternoons when they want to make last sales and go home. Flowers and tropical fish on Jl. Sumenep in Menteng. There's another flower market near Pasar Majestic in Kebayoran. Birds from all over Indonesia in front of Jatinegara market, Jl. Raya Jatinegara, 8 am-4 pm, from Rp75 to 2500 (for macaws and parrots); Jl. Stasiun Senen is another bird market with bird auctions. Sarinah Car Park is the tourist bird market; more fun to look at the tourists. Newest and biggest bird market is on Jl. Pramuka, 8 am-6 pm. Buy felt baseball caps by the G.P.O., at least Rp1500 cheaper than sunglasses and equally as effective. Bargain them down to Rp300. **shopping:** Cheapest batik in Jakarta is at GKBI, Jl. Agus Salim 39; a producers' cooperative, with a large assortment of all qualities, both contemporary and classic designs. Precious stones specialist and salesman, Mr. Spiro, Jl. Kebon Sirih 13. The cheapest tapes in the world are sold in Indonesia: tapes (2 albums on one) which cost Aus$9 in Australia cost only Rp500 (Aus $1.25) in Jakarta (though better quality in Denpasar). The Sarinah Dept Store has fixed prices and you don't have to wade through all the cheap crap in Yogya expecting to be ripped off. Instead buy Indonesian arts and crafts at Sarinah's and you'll at least get what you pay for. **bookshops:** Gunung Agung, Jl. Kwitang (near Pasar Senen) is the largest bookshop in Indonesia (even has a branch in Jayapura). Other good bookshops are: Sarinah Department Store, near the Tourist Office, Jl. Thamrin 9; Tropen, Jl. Pasar Baru; not far from Tropen is Gramedia, for English books on Indonesia; Bhratara, Jl. Oto

Iskandardinata III/29. Foreign books are quite dear and newspapers arrive weeks late; instead read them at the Lembaga Indonesia-Amerika, Jl. Teuku Umar 9, or at the British Council. **antiques:** Antique and curio shops are along Jl. H.S. Salim (parallel to Jl. Thamrin) and on Jl. Kebon Sirih. For old Dutch bottles and jugs, Tanjung Priok is the place. Chinese antique porcelain shops are also found on Jl. Majapahit. For old Chinese *kebayas,* go to Glodok (Chinatown).

interesting areas and sights: Jatinegara was the most exclusive Dutch residential area; still see villas with white stucco walls, tiled roofs and floors, great shaded porches, reflecting the wealth and mentality of the colonialists. See the millionaires' row of Kemang, the Sport's complex Senayan built with Russian money, the posh residential district of Menteng where all the diplomats live. An old Dutch colonial mansion on Jl. Gajah Mada 111 now houses the national archives. Medah Merdeka (Freedom Square) is between old and new Jakarta with it's phallic marble monument 137 m high covered with 35 kilos of highly inedible gold leaf; for the knockout view, they ask Rp1000 to go up to the top. Sometimes called Sukarno's Last Erection, this monument is suppose to last 1000 years. Its base has an historical museum. In the very best tradition of Soviet-style social realism, the Chainbreaker status commemorates the 'liberation' of West Irian from the Dutch; crude, but you'll never forget it. Now all these monuments, symbols of Sukarno's extravagant and megalomaniacal sense of nationalism, have been dubbed with nicknames by the residents, i.e. The Mad Waiter. Glodok (or Kota) around Jl. Pintu Besar is the home of Jakarta's 150,000 Chinese, an area laced with Amsterdam-like canals, old Dutch warehouses, European-style bridges, old white-washed gabled houses with bright red-tiled roofs and diamond-shaped windows. This was the waterfront swamp where the Dutch first settled and stayed 350 years. Heavy Old World atmosphere. See the Bridge of Sighs. Temples along the narrow back streets. Best time is evening when hundreds of little *warungs* line the street. Walk out of the Museum Kota, Jl. Pintu Besar 34, and turn left, crossing the 17th Century Dutch drawbridge over the Kali Besar, to see the only 17th Century shop left from Old Batavia; owned by P.T. Satya Niaga. See remains of Kasteel Batavia, an old fort and Dutch East Indies Co. trading post built in 1652; great view of the old and new worlds from the top of the watchtower near the bridge over the Kali Besar. Nearing the cooler coast, go at dawn to Pasar Ikan (fish market) when the night's catch is auctioned off. Infinite small alleys, stalls and shops selling stuffed exotic animals, birds, skins, turtle shells, seahorses, coral trees, seashells, and 19th Century boating and fishing equipment. The old port area of Tanjung Priok is the home of fishermen and sailors, handling 70% of Indonesia's imports. Hire a boat to cruise the waterfront, Rp5-600; a must. The wharf juts out a mile into the sea, a forest of masts around it, wooden hand-made shallow drought ocean-going Makassar-type schooners row on row.

Indonesian sealife: *The oceans that surround these thousands of islands are habitats of the strangest sealife imaginable: the dreaded gigantic rock-grouper, kerapu, which can swallow a man; killer whales and seasnakes; silimpat that coil on the surface of the water like rope; the tundak which will spear a swimmer with its razor-sharp nose; snailfish; venemous sea bream; scorpion fish, lion fish, rabbit fish (poisonous but edible); eels banded like seasnakes; walking catfish; the puju-puju which can travel overland and climb trees; the most transparent of fish ('glass fish'); fish that fight each other called betah ('enduring fish'), fish that knock down flies by squirting water at them; and mud-skippers with frog-like faces. Plus all manner of unusual acquarium fish that sparkle like jewels. The ikat lawari batu of the Banda Sea guides its way through the blackness of the ocean bottom by sending out twin beams of light like those of a car at night from luminous bacteria in glands behind each eye.*

Thousand Islands (Pulau Seribu): To visit these actually only 600 islands, disembark near Tanjung Priok. Board a boat to P. Seribu (P. Air) from Sanggar Bahari, Rp1000. Leaves at 8 am, returns 3 pm, a 90 minute passage. Or take a boat from Kartika Bahari pier to Pulau Puteri. The nearest islands are only 10-15 km from Jakarta. P. Genteng for the best skindiving. Reefs of P. Opak Besar and P. Puteri are filled with tropical fish, multicolored corals and shells. Go clamming on P. Barat. On P. Onrust, Captain Cook's ship the Endeavor put in for repairs in 1770; an old shipyard is here plus a fort's ruined foundations in the woods with 200 year old moss-covered headstones. Visit the bird islands of P. Bokor and P. Rambut. More remote and unpeopled islands: Pabelokan, Sibaru Kecil and Sibaru Besar with fine beaches and coconut plantations. On P. Kelor find big 1 ½ m long black lizards. The Thousand Islands are really a tropical paradise, hard to believe that Jakarta's so close. Now being 'developed as a paradise'

others: Bina Ria for casinos, discos, nightclubs, bright lights, a wealth of flashy ladies, and a great swimming pool with a wave-making machine and gigantic 20 m long fibreglass slides, Rp300 weekdays, Rp500 on weekends. Also an oceanarium here and rigged Basque games of Jai-Alai. There's a gambling casino opposite Sarinah Dept. Store; cheapest bet is Rp100 on the roulette table. No cover charge, informal dress permitted, free drinks and cakes. For the Presidential Palace Tour, get permission from the chief of the Presidential Household, Istana Negara, Jakarta. Give it two weeks. Must wear a dress, and shirt and tie. Dutch Colonial furniture and lavish interiors. The biggest zoo in Indonesia is in Jakarta (but not as good as Surabaya's); open 8-6 pm. Komodo lizard, tapir, *anoa,* Java tigers and native birdlife in natural settings. Horseracing at Pulo Mas; paramutual betting on Wed., Fri. and Sundays. Really a sight to see Indonesians playing the horses. Indonesia is created in miniature at the 'Mini-Indonesia' tourist project near Halim Airport. Rp100 entrance. Go by bus from Benteng to Ciililitan, then change to 'Indonesia Mini'. Super-Indonesian kitsch. Sliding electric doors and air-conditioned Batak 'traditional' buildings. Take a cable car over a 22 acre artificial lake and look down upon a scale model of the whole archipelago, regional architecture, etc. Each pavilion represents a different culture area of Indonesia, all 27 provinces. On Sun., dances and cultural performances. Indonesians will tell you that there will be no need to see the rest of Indonesia if you visit here.

museums: On Jl. Taman Fatahilah (the old City Hall) is the City Museum, Museum Kota; Rp50 entrance. Like a huge 17th Century Amsterdam house chock full of period paraphernalia: maniacal tyrant faces of past Dutch governors, porcelain used by the Dutch aristocracy, timepieces, exquisitely carved furniture, as well as sections devoted to the different sultanates and eras of Jakarta's history. The canon Si Jagur ('Mr. Sturdy') is believed by women to be a cure for sterility because of its phallic shape, its clenched fist (a symbol of fertility on Java) and the Latin inscription on it: *Ex me ipsa renata sum,* or 'I am reborn from myself.' Barren women offer it flowers, then sit on top of it. **National Museum:** Or Gedung Gajah. Located on Jl. Medan Merdeka Barat 12; only 10 minutes walk from Jalan Jaksa. Open Tues.-Thurs. 8:30-2:30, Fri. 8:30-11, Sat. 8:30-1 pm. Every Sun. from 9:30-10:30 am, visitors may enjoy *gamelan.* Closed on Monday. Richest collection of Indonesiana in the world: its Hindu Javanese antiquities section even rivals Leyden Museum's in Holland. There are 8th-15th Century bronze icons, reliefs, friezes, statuary, bronze age tools and weapons. Ask to see the giant granite penis from Candi Sukuh kept in the back. Fantastic coin exhibit (including cloth money), scale models of houses, villages and *prahus* showing the miraculous variety of building styles throughout these islands. World's largest exhibition of Chinese Han, Tang and Ming ceramics dating back to 200 B.C. To help understand the hugh ceramics room, buy Egbert Willem van Orsey de Flines's 'Guide to the Ceramic Collection' (Rp2000) at the book counter. There's a king-size relief map to learn what mountains on Java to climb and a great ethnic map of many of Indonesia's 450 different societies – their culture, dress and locations. The Gold Room, with its statuettes, crowns, and medallions, protected by guards and steel gates, is open only on Sunday. You could spend one day each in just the prehistory and ethnographic sections of this museum. In order to use the magnificent library of Indonesian and S.E. Asian subjects, you need a letter of introduction to get a card (Rp200); captivating old tomes and titles: Camping and Tramping in Malaysia', 'A Diplomat's Wife in China', etc. **Museum Wayang** (Puppet Museum): For *wayang kulit* and *golek* exhibits. Near the City Museum on Jl. Pintu Besar Utara 27. Open Tues., Wed., and Thurs., 9 am-1 pm. Rp50 entrance, students Rp25. *Wayang kulit* performances are held from 9 am-12:30 pm for Rp50 (students, Rp25) on Thurs., Fri. and Sat. and Sunday. Costs Rp500 to take a photo, although postcards are only Rp50. **Museum Pusat Abri Mandala:** A temple dedicated to the Armed Forces Brotherhood. From Blok M, take a bus along the road to Ciililitan and Manggarai and let everyone know where you want to go so the bus doesn't overshoot the museum. Dioramas in the hundreds depicting events in Indonesia's military history since 1942. Their commandos were most skilled at night

TAMAN
ISMAIL MARZUKI

A.   entrance gate
B.   planetarium
C.   residential units
D.   water basin
E.   river

1.   open-air theatre
2.   closed theatre
3.   movie theatre
4.   exhibition hall
5.   studios and workshops
6.   arena theatre
7.   dance studio

operations so the inside of the museum is very dark to accentuate these scenes. A guidebook, Rp150, explains the dioramas in English. Like most of Indonesia's ships and planes, the MiG21 jet on display here has been out of use since the abortive communist coup of 1965 when the Russians discontinued the supply of spare parts for all the war material sold to Sukarno during his armed confrontation with Malaysia in 1963. This building was the late Sukarno's Japanese wife's home. What fitting irony. **Gedung Pola:** Jl. Proklamasi 56. The Proclamation of Independence was read out here on Aug. 17, 1945, by President Sukarno after the urging of students who had kidnapped him at gunpoint.

mosques and churches: Mesjid Jami Tambora, built in 1762 by Muslim exiles from Sumbawa; a mixture of Hindu and Arab roof design; ancient Arab graveyard in back. Immanuel Church, Jl. Pejambon, is an old Dutch Protestant church in the late Renaissance style. See the organ inside, only two others like it in the world. The Kathedral, Jl. Kathedral, unique in its sad gothic glory with three black steel spires. Sion Church (1693), Jl. Pangeran Jayakarta, is the oldest standing house of worship in Jakarta. Filled with intricate 17th Century woodcarved pillars, baroque pulpit, ornamental pews. See the largest mosque in the world in downtown Jakarta. With its minarets and grandiose lines, you can't miss it. Unfinished for years, one of Sukarno's pets abandoned. This city still very much wears his mark.

arts and crafts: Get ahold of a program at the Taman Ismail Marzuki Cultural Complex, Jl. Cikini Raya 13. So many cultural goings on: photo exhibits, ballet, painting shows, rock bands, orchestras, violin concertos, lectures on folklore, shadow play theatre, *wayang golek* and *wayang orang*, Rendra staging *Hamlet,* poetry readings, film showings, childrens' programs, contemporary dances. Admission is low. Try to catch drama and music indigenous to Jakarta: *kroncong* groups (Portugese influenced); *terbangan* (Islamic music adapted to Indonesian culture); and *Lenong,* a comical satirical play accompanied by the *gambang kromong* orchestra. At Bakti Budaya, Jl. Bugu 5/A (off Jl. Mataram Raya), study Sundanese traditional dancing, *gamelan, wayang, topeng, suling;* get there for the 11 am performances. School of Folk Art, Jl. Bunga V, Jatinegara, is where you can see teachers and students playing music, Cirebon-style, dancing, *wayang topeng, wayang kulit* and *golek* puppet theatre from 10:30-12 pm each day. Radio Republic Indonesia holds regular performances of *wayang kulit* every second Sat. 9 pm-4:30 am at the National Museum on the western side of Medan Merdeka. *Wayang golek* is put on each alternate Sat., same hours, same location. At the National Museum, each Sun. 9:30-10:30 am, performances of Javanese *gamelan* for the classical dance drama, *wayang orang.* Visit the Erasmus House, Jl. Cikini Raya, the Dutch Cultural Center with many activities offered. Really old-fashioned colonial atmosphere: Indonesian ladies in their finery speaking High Dutch *kouwekak* ('cold shit'), classical concerts, *kroncong* bands, social nights. Sometimes free beer. Huge well-stocked library.

miscellaneous: Beware of West Jakarta's *imigrasi* office, they'll try to make you pay a second landing fee. If you're running out of time wait until Tanjungkarang (South Sumatra) where extensions cost the usual Rp3500. Jakarta's *bancis* (or 'sister boys') are female impersonators who hang out on Taman Suropati, Jl. Latu Har Hari and on Jl. Sumesep at night; be careful of hustlers. Some others beat between Hotel Indonesia and Kartika Plaza. If they like you, they pay you- you don't pay them! Hotel Indonesia for camp guys after 7 pm. This is not so money-oriented. More money-oriented is Hotel Borobudur, between 9 and 10 at night. After 10 pm, go to the 2nd floor bar; this is no substitute gay scene but real. Halfway between Bogor and Jakarta is Boker where 500 girls work. Tanamur Disco, near Taman Merdeka Utara, opens at 9:30 pm; happening. Many expats frequent here. Teach English? See Graham James at the 'English 900 Course' on Jl. Kartini Raya 26 (near Jl. Pintu Besi). Also try the I.E.C. (Intensive English Course) on Jl. Merdeka Timur, Tel. 49217. Or any school as you're walking along the street drop into and ask for a job. You get up to 12 hours a week at Rp1200 an hour, though you make most of your money on private lessons, Rp4-5000.

from Jakarta by train: There's a number of different train stations in Jakarta, but most trains leave from Gambir Station (centrally located) and from Kota Station (not central, so allow time to get there). Train prices vary greatly depending on class, speed and/or comfort. Student discount is 25%. From Senen Station, the Gayabaru II leaves for Semarang at 5:30 pm, arrives at 3 am; costs Rp1750. This same train arrives the next day in Surabaya at 10 am; costs Rp2200. Buy tickets at Senen at 4 pm on day of departure. This is the scenic 'northern route' of Java. The other train to Surabaya from Kota Station is the cheaper Mutiara, Rp8500; departs 3:30 pm and arrives at 6:15 am. Only one class, has reclining seats, and the price includes two meals. Always book your tickets at 10 am the day you want to leave because both these trains are most always full. The cheap train to Surabaya is the Gaya Malam, leaving at 2 pm from Gambir Station, arriving at noon the next day so you'll be able to find a place to sleep. Gambir Station handles most trains for the south: Yogya and Solo (Central Java); the Jaya leaves for Yogya 4 times a day: 2 pm, arrival at 2 am; 4:45 pm, arrival at 4 am; 6:17 pm, arrival at 6 am; 7:30 am, arrival at 7pm; economy class, Rp1700. From Kota Station, the Bima leaves at 2:30 pm, arrives in Surabaya at 7:30 the next morning; 1st class Rp 12,000, economy class Rp9000; takes 16 hours. Lousy food, dirty toilets. 1st class has two berths while economy class has 3 berths to a cabin. **for Bandung:** Most people go by bus, but the fast train Parahiangan ('Abode of the gods') is also convenient, getting you there 3 hours faster than the 'express train'; it's well ventilated and there's no standing passengers; you can buy tickets only for Rp1700 seats. At least 6 trains a day for Bandung, leaving mostly from Kota station.

trains for Sumatra: Leave only once daily from Kota Station at 3 pm and once a day from Tanah Abang Station at 5:10 am. You ride with it first to Merak, West Java, and then board the ferry across the Sunda Strait to Panjang, South Sumatra, from where you continue northwards by train 400 km to Palembang. A through ticket from Kota Station, economy class, is Rp2500; from Tanah Abang economy class is Rp 3750. You can do it cheaper by train if you do it in stages. Or take a bus Jakarta-Merak, Rp400, 3 hours, then board a ferry (6 hours) for Panjang; Rp 750 for the afternoon ferry, Rp1000 for the night ferry. Take the ferry from Merak that leaves at 6 pm if you want a through connection on train to Palembang. If you want to hang around Panjang all day long (not much to do), catch the ferry from Merak that leaves at 10 pm.

buses: These prices vary quite a bit too. All buses to the north (Cirebon) and east leave from Benteng Terminal, while buses to the west and south leave from Cililitan Bus Station. Sample fares: Bandung, Rp560; Bogor, Rp180 (train is cheaper, Rp150); Semarang, Rp900; Solo, Rp2400; Blitar, Rp4500; Yogya, Rp2200; Surabaya, Rp4500. *Bis malam* (night buses) travel at night and are faster and more expensive than the hotter day buses; these usually leave from where the company's offices are situated. **bus companies:** 4848, Jl. Prapatan Kwitang 34, has small (seats only 10) fast buses to Bandung, door to door, for Rp1850. Cheaper are suburban taxi companies, Rp750 to Bandung. Elteha minibus Co., Jl. Tanah Abang Timur 16 A: Semarang, Rp1800; Solo, Rp3200. Kembang Express, Jl. Krekot Raya, or Damri (government-run), Jl. Mataram Raya- both have buses to: Surabaya, Rp4000-5000; Yogya, Rp2200-3000. **by road:** Instead of the main highway, take the back road to Bogor via Depok for an unfrequented ride in the country; rice paddies, vegetable plots, rubber and sugar plantations, a more hopeful introduction to the island of Java.

from Jakarta by sea: Get vessels to virtually anywhere in the archipelago or the world. The Arafat Lines office is located at Jl. Johan 8. Pelni Lines sells tickets at 158 Pasar Baru, 2nd floor, or at Senen Raya 26; they give student discounts (even for cabin class!) but only at the head office in Jakarta on Jl. Wachid Hasyim 1/A. Pelni has 3 boats a month to different ports of Irian Jaya (stops in 3-4 ports along the way), Rp40,000. Mersk Lines has regular shipping to west coast USA if you're interested. Be systematic about checking all the ships at the docks everyday and you can work your way to anywhere. Try Norwegian ships. **for Padang** (west coast of Sumatra): Get ready for cooler weather. Kalimantan Shipping Lines, Jl. Tanah Abang II/123, Tel. 43296. Don't need to go to the office, just buy your ticket on the boat itself; pay (Rp9750) money to Mr. Soenardi or Mr. Rusmaui only. Embarks from Pelabuhan Nusantara, Pos. 1, Number 004. Leaves every Wed., takes 60 hours, 2 good meals are served, the bathrooms are clean, and the chief officer is a great guy. Pelni has launched a new ship on the Jakarta-Padang run, the Nukori, with tile bathrooms, hand showers, even decent food; costs Rp9280 deck class from an agent or cheaper if you buy at the docks. Don't buy at Jalan Jaksa 5 (Rp11,500!). Should disembark on Sat. at noon, but usually doesn't get away until 8 pm. Not that crowded.

by sea to Singapore and Medan: Pelni's Tampomas does the trip to the North Sumatra city of Medan for Rp13,500, stopping off at the little island of Tanjung Pinang on the way (continue on to Singapore by regular launch, Rp4500). Leaves Jakarta usually each Mon., 6-7 pm, arrives Tanjung Pinang 6 am Tues., and arrives Medan Wed. 9 am. Head up to the top deck where it's windier and cleaner. You can buy 1st class food (Rp1000) or 2nd class food (Rp750) even if you're deck class. If you have shoes, go into the 1st class bar and have a drink. Get boats to Singapore and Medan cheaper by going around the Jakarta docks and checking different shipping companies. Maybe get to Singapore one day less than the Pelni ship and you could pay only US$10 a day or about Rp10,000 all the way. Try P.T. Wasesa Line, Jl. R.E. Martadinata, Jakarta; their ship the Telanaipura has cabins on the forecastle; leaves for Singapore about every 10 days (takes 3 days). Eastern Orient Lines, Pos 1, Tanjung Priok, has ships to Medan for as cheap as Rp8000.

by air: Cheap air fares to Europe, Asia, USA, Canada, and Australia, at Setia Travel, Jl. Biak 45, Tel. 44161. On the flight from Jakarta to Padang you see fantastic views of the Kerinci volcano (3812 m) in South Sumatra looming up through the clouds. From Jakarta the cheapest flight to Europe right now is with Aeroflot, in the Sahid Jaya Hotel, Jl. Sudirman 86; travel via Tashkent with a one day stop in Moscow. It's Aus$200 cheaper to fly round-trip to Australia from Jakarta than it is to fly to

Jakarta round-trip from Australia. From Jakarta for Singapore, go to Continental Tours (Sempati Airlines), near Jl. Jaksa 23; Rp22,000 plus Rp1250 airport tax, instead of the regular fare of US$114. Against irregular boat services fly with Merpati to: Padang, Rp32,000; Palembang, Rp18,500; Ujung Pandang, Rp42,000. To get to the airport take a *bemo* from Benteng Terminal, Rp200. Airport tax is Rp1250. At Kemayoran domestic airport, good and cheap food in the cafeteria. **Airlines offices:** Merpati, Jl. Patrice Lumumba 2; Garuda, Jl. Ir. H. Juanda 15; Bouraq, Jl. Kebun Sirih 13; Mandala, Jl. Veteran 34; Pelita, Jl. Abdul Muis 15.

BANDUNG

180 km S.E. of Jakarta. Third largest city in Indonesia (1.3 million), surrounded by mountains covered in tea plantations and a great tangle of high volcanic peaks. Bandung has perfect weather — high altitude climate, cool fresh air. Equatorial dusks. Brightly colored *becaks*. West Java accounts for 60% of Indonesia's textile production, mostly concentrated here. The native people of West Java, the Sundanese, make up the majority of this city's population. Acclaimed for the beauty of their women, their dreamy melancholy music, and for their evocative poetic imagery, the Sundanese tend to be more light-hearted and earthier than the refined tired old Javanese race of Central and East Java. In Sundanese history there's no ancient palace tradition of ruling Hindu princes; they practice Islam with devotion and strong faith. The Dutch loved it here and their long occupation is seen in the sombre middle class architecture such as found in early 20th Century West European cities. Unfortunately, Bandung has lost much of its glamour and nowadays appears dilapidated and covered in dust. Bandung's women wear western dress, very style-conscious. In Aug. 1975 the first Indonesian rock festival took place here featuring groups like Voodoo Child, God Bless, etc. Many of the young grow their own. **transport:** All *bemo* and *oplet* rides within the city, Rp40. Buy a push-bike new or used on Jl. ABC.

stay: Wisma Remaja, Jl. Merdeka 64 (near the British Council), is only 1 km from the city center; Rp1500 double or Rp500 for dorm rooms (6 to a room). Also Rp750 rooms for just two people. A new building, very comfortable, the focus of youth activities and youth conferences. When Indonesians arrive in numbers, could be boisterous. In the cafeteria: good *gado2*; *nasi rames* with chicken, Rp250; *mie goreng,* Rp150. Book train tickets right across the street at Panti Karya instead of going to the train station. At night the market opens up across the street. Hotel Malabar, Jl.

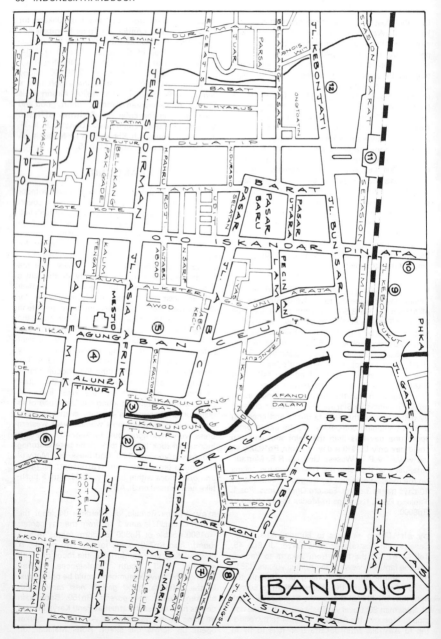

BANDUNG

Kebun Jukut 3; turn left after emerging from the train station, walk over the RR overpass and you'll see it. Rooms cost Rp1250 double or other rooms Rp750 single or double; Rp2000 for 3 people. About the cheapest in this area but quite adequate and clean. Meals served, but some reports the food isn't that good. Free tea. There's an even cheaper hotel behind Pasar Baru, but it stinks. Hotel Sahara, Jl. Oto Iskandarinata 3, Rp2000 double, clean and simple and also close to train station. Peng. Bungsu, Jl. Bungsu, Rp750 per person; very central. Hotel Gania Plaza is next door; newer, brighter and a bit more expensive. Hotel Lugina, Jl. Jen Sidirman 526, Rp150 by becak from the train station, is Rp1000 for YHA members, 3-4 to a room but probably have it all to yourself. Nice gardens, quiet, off the main road. Hotel Brajawijaya, Jl. Pungkur 28, Rp2000 single or double with coffee or tea. Very close to bus station, every room has a bath. Wisma Department Social, Jl. Ciumbuluit 197, Rp600 single, a nice place but you must have a YHA card to stay here.

eat: Local delicacies include sate, gado2, bajigur (coconut juice), and bandrek ginger drink. Oncom is fried beancake, peanuts and yeast, Rp50 for a small one. Peyeum is made out of cassava with yeast added (a little sour); buy it at any market for Rp100 per kilo, more than enough for two. For western delights: T-bone steaks, bread, cookies, crackers, in fact, anything you can think of, try Tizi, Jl. Hegarmanak 14; take a Ledeng bemo. Rp40, to Tizi. Also try other European dishes like mixed grill and Spaghetti Bolognaise (Rp1500) and puddings at Sukarasa Steak and Eggs, Jl. Tamblong. A good place for Sundanese food is Balai Kambang, Jl. Bungur. There's a small Javanese restaurant near the RR Station on Jl. Tera near Jl. Merdeka. Ponorogo

Restaurant, Jl. Batot Subroto 58, has good sate ayam, Rp250. Tjoen Kie, Jl. Jen. Sudirman 46, is as good as Queen Chinese Restaurant but less expensive; Rp1000 for a luxury meal. A good value cheap restaurant is Rumah Makan Sakadarna, Jl. Kebun Jati 34, near Peng. Semarang, 10 minutes walk from Hotel Malabar; nasi goreng, Rp150, sop sayur only Rp75; ask for the 'special sauce'. PLN Complex at night has delicious martabak and side dishes; for around Rp200 eat your fill. Many warung and night markets downtown for Bandung specialty soto ayam. Indonesians eat along Jl. Cikapundung: ayam goreng, ikan bakar (expensive), soto ayam, sate, gado2 tahu petis (hot). For ice cream, P.T. Rasa, Jl. Tamblong, make their own. Well known also for ice cream is Panorama, Jl Setia Budi; from there see Bandung alit at night. Try liscious comro sweets; they'll laugh at you when you ask for them because they're for kids. Jl. Braga for sidewalk cafes, pastries, marzipan, and ice cream. Dago Teahouse: Catch a Colt at beginning of Jl. Jr. H. Juanda for Rp40, get off at the end of the line, then walk ½ km. The best view of the city from the top. Food served out on the terrace; a nice place to eat. Just behind the teahouse is the waterfall. University students who run the teahouse will point out the path to Maribaya for you, a lovely one hour's walk through rice paddies and over rivers.

arts: Culturally speaking, this city is the 'Yogya' of the Sundanese. At Yayason Pusat Kebudayan, Jl. Naripan, at 9 pm each Sat. night until morning, are wayang golek performances, Rp2-300 entrance. West Java is the home of this wayang medium (larger puppets than Central Java's) and the Sundanese would rather see wayang golek than the shadow play. Each night at Gedung Kesinian, Jl. Baranang Siang 1, there are performances at 7 pm, Rp1-100. Could be anything: wayang orang, orchestras, western theatre productions, ballet, kroncong bands, drama, Reog, etc. For Sundanese music and dance, Konservatori Karawitan Indonesia, Jl. Buahbatu 212; listen to traditional Sundanese orchestra, the kecapi suling, with its soft-toned flutes and the long vibrating notes of the kecapi. Also the angklung, an instrument used in olden times to create excitement while marching into wars, or to announce the arrival of a ruler. Bandung has many commercial landscape painters and art fairs now and then. One of its finest landscape artists is Wadhi, born 1917. Pak Ujo's School: Jl. Padasaka 8. See wayang golek performances from 4-6 pm. Almost every day 3-6 pm there are also Sundanese dancing and other performances here; costs Rp400 entrance, also Rp1000 seats but you can get a student discount. Pak Ujo's sells angklung, a whole set for around Rp5000.

BANDUNG

1. Tourist Office
2. Asia Africa Building
3. PLN Complex
4. Alun2 Square
5. Post Office
6. Queen Restaurant
7. Sukarasa Steak & Eggs
8. to Peng. Bungsu and Hotel Gania Plaza
9. Hotel Malabar
10. Hotel Sahara
11. railway station

crafts: Jl. Braga for souvenirs, leather, art galleries, antiques. The Leather Palace is a more expensive shop but has fine wares; cheaper shops on other streets. Bandung is a good place to buy shoes; have them made very well and cheaply. Canadian, Jl. Markoni, is the best known shoemaker, Rp10,000 for a pair of boots. Also for homemade leather shoes try Lucia, Jl. Martadinata 21. For wooden shoes (Rp2000) try the place on the corner of Jl. Pacinan Lama and Jl. Banceuy, only 500 m from the tourist office. Kenangan, Jl. Banceuy 37, is a good shop to buy *wayang* puppets. High standard Chinese porcelain fakes are sold at the Ceramic Research Center. Handicrafts and wooden puppets are for sale at Luwes, Jl. Braga 44; and Sukama, Jl. Braga 88-two of the biggest shops.

sights: In 1955 at the Afro-Asian Building, Jl. Asia Afrika, Sukarno invited leaders of 29 underdeveloped non-aligned nations to a solidarity conference — Nehru, Nasser, Ho Chi Minh, Chou En Lae — all attended with Sukarno acting as the Grand *Dalang*. In this building the Theory of the New Emerging Forces was first formulated (called NEFOS by Sukarno) who are mainly dark-skinned people comprising three-quarters of all mankind; against the Old Established Forces (called by Sukarno OLDEFOS) comprising ¼ of all mankind. A *wayang* show was once made of this famous meeting yet there are no records of it here; if you ask you'll be told to go to Jakarta (in other words, forget it). Now this movement counts as members 83 nations; the last conference was held in Sri Lanka in 1976. Bandung is the technological capital of Indonesia. 30,000 students attend 17 higher educational institutions here, Indonesia's biggest technical schools, colleges and training centers. Visit the Bandung Institute of Technology, founded in 1920; spectacular ship-prowed Minangkabau architecture. Geological Museum, Jl. Diponegoro 57, has a huge floor space of fossils, a *pithecanthropus* skull, rocks, minerals, models of volcanoes, maps, in all 400 geological displays. The Army Museum, Jl. Lembong, near Istana Hotel; open in the mornings. Also you may visit the Blind and Deaf Institute.

Sundanese music and drama: *The most characteristic Sundanese orchestra is the* kecapi-suling, *consisting of just two instruments and a singer. The* kecapi *is like a predecessor of the zither except the strings are plucked with the fingers; the* suling *is a soft-toned flute which fades in and out of the long vibrating notes of the* kecapi; *the singer sings love songs in a high clear voice. The Sundanese orchestra sometimes includes a* rebab, *the Indonesian violin. They play as well the* degung, *a gamelan orchestra made up of typical Sundanese instruments, such as* suling *flutes.* Angklung *is also widely played, an ancient traditional device of one short and one longer bamboo pipe slotted upright in a wooden frame with an 8-note scale;* angklung *has a deep hollow echoing sound which can play the western octave as well. Plus there are Bandung-made iron gongs,* gendang *drums, also bamboo phones, bass-bamboos, and the bamboo wave instrument, which is several octaves of bamboo suspended together from a high frame and played in quick succession by a single performer.*

BANDUNG
REGENCY

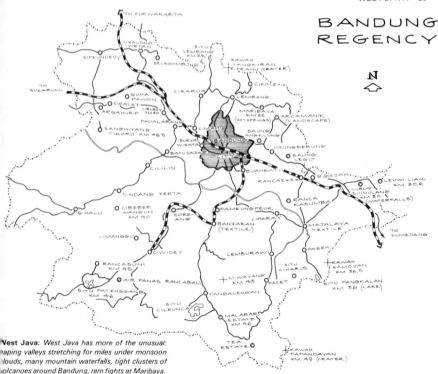

N

West Java: *West Java has more of the unusual: aping valleys stretching for miles under monsoon louds, many mountain waterfalls, tight clusters of olcanoes around Bandung, ram fights at Maribaya.*

miscellaneous: Tourist Information Center for West Java is in the Asia Afrika Building, Jl. Asia Afrika 65, open 8 am-2 pm. Ask where cockfights are held; cocks fight without razors here. Kantor Imigrasi, Jl. Diponegoro 34, Jalan Sumatra is where all the prostitutes hang out. For camp guys, pay a call at the rotunda at Taman Merdeka Park at night. For something different in the way of nightclubs? Saung Kuring, Jl. Braga 9, open 5 pm-1 am. Good *gamelan* music and warm atmosphere; a nice mixture of traditional and modern. Rp250 entrance (ask for free tickets at Wisma Remaja), Rp1500 per hour for a hostess. Mostly Indonesians go here. Sip a hot *bajigur* (Rp150) all night and dance with women dressed in Sundanese trad attire. Bandung's Boromeus Hospital, Jl. Ir. H. Juanda 100, has an outpatient clinic and doctors, only Rp500 per consultation, plus cost of medicines.

from Bandung: If you take the 5 am train from Bandung to Jakarta it costs Rp750 (or Rp550 student), but if you take the 5:30 am train it costs Rp1750! All you get for that extra money are better

seats, it takes the same amount of time (3 ½ hours). Trains to Surabaya (stops in Yogya also), class I, Rp4200; class II, Rp2250, leaves at 5:30 pm; class III, Rp1850 (can get student discount), leaves at 3:30 pm. To Bogor, no trains. Don't take a local bus to Yogya which takes 18 miserable hours; take the train. To Yogya (starts from Bandung), only class III, Rp850, leaves 5:30 am, arrives 2:30 pm, nice scenery on the way. Or for Yogya just get on any train to Surabaya. **buses:** Terminal Bis, Jl. Mohammed Toha, has buses to: Jakarta, Rp600; Puncak, Rp400; Bogor, Rp450; Garut, Rp300; Plered, Rp250; Pameungpeuk, Rp700 (two connections); Sumedang, Rp250; Purwokerto, Rp1000; Semarang, Rp1250; Pekalongan, Rp900; Cirebon, Rp400. To handicrafts center of Tasikmalaya, Rp400 by Colt. **night buses:** Remaja Express (Mercedes), Jl. Oto Iskandardinata 19, Rp1300 to Yogya. Elteha (minibus) Co. is on Jl. Kebonkawang beside the Pertamina gas station.

Lembang: 16 km from Bandung, uphill all the way. Hotel Grand is on the main road; grand beds, garden view and central: Rp2500 single, Rp3000 double. Outstanding market for fruit, mouth-watering corn on the cob (jagung bakar), refreshing *bajigur* drink, the best avocados. Sometimes at night a circus is held at the market with dancing dogs. Lembang's planetarium (Bosscha Observatory) is open to visitors on Sat. afternoons; see Prof Hidajat. For Tangkuban Prahu, 'Capsized Boat', take a bus or *oplet* from Lembang 3 km Rp75 to the turn off, then walk up to this smouldering 2000 m wide tourists' volcano. (Other craters furhter up mountain on foot). Smell stinking sulpher 2 km away. Trees are bleached snow white, thick bright yellow crust, boiling pools. Descend into the crater and walk around in smoke and bubbling lava. Go in the morning. Leaving, take the path, not the road, on the way down through a steamy spooky forest. When you come down from the crater take a left on the main highway, flag down a Colt, and travel on a road overhanging with flowers 5 km to Maribaya. Also a very touristy spot but worthwhile visiting. Nicely-landscaped, a wooded garden of cascading streams, cacti and tall evergreens. Bathe in colored volcanic water; bring a *sarung,* a bit chilly. Can spend the night here, but kind of rundown rooms for Rp1000 with a very noisy waterfall. Expensive restaurant in Maribaya, but a woman comes around with *sate* and snacks in the parking lot. Another thermal spa at Ciater. Traditional Sundanese ram-fights are held eaoh Sun. at 10 am about one km from Maribaya (also held at Pasundan); their impact resounds through the bamboo forest. The rams' testicles are tweaked each time before they take up combat. Wild betting.

vicinity of Bandung: 80% of the world's natural quinine (pel bandung) comes from this area. To get away from the congestion of urban Java there are boarding houses, holiday hotels, park and garden resorts all around the hilly outskirts of this city. To the north are palatial old Dutch villas at Ciumbuluit (Rp40 by minibus). **mountains:** All around Bandung volcanoes are packed close together, some to be climbed, others to be gawked at: Mt. Cereme can be seen from 50 km because of it's almost perfect summit. Also there's Bukit Tunggul (The Lonely One), G. Malabar (3000 m). To the S.E. lies the mountain crater Papandayan, even more outerworldly than Mount Bromo of East Java but more difficult to reach; only by landrover, jeep or foot. On the main road between Bandung and Garut, turn south at Cicalengka towards G. Guntur, a fairyland wood on the way up to its billowing crater. Situ Patenggang is a natural cold water high mountain lake surrounded by forest and tea plantations 46 km S.W. of Bandung. **Gunung Telaga:** Climb G. Telaga where there's a sulphur lake, wild oxen and peacocks; 4 hours by *oplet* from

Bandung, then walk. A very bad road to get there, but definitely worth the trip. Completely free nature, bubbling noisy lava pools and bright green water like a chemical. Only a simple *warung* serving food there. **the watershed:** Travel over the watershed of Java where the rivers Citarum and Cimanuk (Ci = 'river') run northwards towards the Java Sea while other streams run southwards to the Indian Ocean. Once every 3 days a bus leaves Pangalengan via Kertasari for Garut. Spend the night in Kertasari, then the bus starts rattling and crashing up the mountains of the Papandayan. Remnants of the original tropical forests of Java are here with wild pigs and deer, spices and herbs growing wild. From Cikajang, the road winds down to the fertile sunny valley to Garut.

Garut: 57 km east of Bandung, center for tobacco, oranges. This is the oldest tourist region in Indonesia where wealthy Dutch planters vacationed in their fashionable hotels. Check out the horse harnasses. Hot water geysers here. Stay at Hotel Nasional, Rp500. From Garut, follow the mountain road down to the white sands and rolling waves of beautiful Pameungpeuk Bay. Along the way watch men make charcoal from forest timber (40-60 million people in Indonesia cook on charcoal). Grapes and citrus grow wild. It looks near but takes a full day to get to Pameungpeuk from Garut. Immaculate beaches all along this coast, but the swimming is dangerous. Near Garut is the hot bathing place Tarogong.

Purwakarta: A scenic area 70 km north of Bandung, a holiday resort where the huge Jatiluhur Dam stretches 1200 m across a river. Nearby Purwakarta, visit the art center in Sukaraja. Ask to be taken to Bu Machmud's. Fine *batik*, traditional themes but modern colors. Kerajinan Banjarnegara is a small town notable for its ceramic products — vases, ashtrays, jars, wall decorations; sold all over Java. Rawgogo village museum is known for its antiques. In Sumedang, which you must pass through on the journey from Bandung to Cirebon, see the Y.P.S. Museum Restoran Tampomas Baru is good; Sumedang is applauded for its *tahu*. Lovely mountain scenery around this little town. Wild pig hunting in the Ujungjaya area. Colonial architecture at Jabelang. At Cangjuang and Cibuaya, traces of Hindu Buddhist temples. At Banjaran, a *pencak silat* dance form can be seen; in these mountains between Bogor and Bandung the fighting art approaches a religion. Mental discipline, fasting periods and prayers are all used to increase inner power. Adherents can smash coconuts with blows of their wrists; they can deal with 12 assailants at once, the attacker stamping the turf before the fight. At Plered, 64 km north of Bandung, a center for earthenware crafts; clay is pounded in stone troughs. *Warungs* at Weru sell rattan furniture.

BOGOR

60 km south of Jakarta, one hour busride, Rp200. A smog-filled city of pretty villas, bush shrubs, banana, mimosa and wild almond trees, giant size fruits and vegetables. Being in the more exposed uplands, Bogor maintains a cooler climate. Probably leads the world in thunderstorms. Rain comes precisely at 4 pm two out of every three days year round. **stay:** Being so close to Jakarta, accommodation is generally lousy and costly. Peng. Pasundan, Jl. Veteran 19, is just off the busy road and close to the bus station; Rp1500 single or double with outside bathroom, or with inside bathroom, Rp2000. Whores work here. Damai Hotel, Jl. Jayaatmaja 29, Tel. 512, Rp1000 single or Rp1500 double, coffee included. Close to the train station, an OK place, superior to Peng. Pasundan. Hotel Salak, Jl. Juanda 8, right opposite the Bogor Palace, Rp1750-2500 single. Enormous rooms but

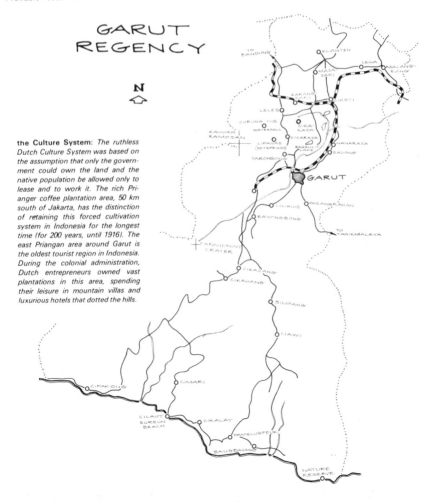

GARUT REGENCY

N

the Culture System: *The ruthless Dutch Culture System was based on the assumption that only the government could own the land and the native population be allowed only to lease and to work it. The rich Prianger coffee plantation area, 50 km south of Jakarta, has the distinction of retaining this forced cultivation system in Indonesia for the longest time (for 200 years, until 1916). The east Priangan area around Garut is the oldest tourist region in Indonesia. During the colonial administration, Dutch entrepreneurs owned vast plantations in this area, spending their leisure in mountain villas and luxurious hotels that dotted the hills.*

the whole place (except for the newer A.C. rooms in the back, Rp5000) is fast going to seed. Get buses to Jakarta and other places from here; they also arrange tours to Istana Bogor. **eat:** Known for its black radishes (talas), *salaks,* one meter long bananas, sweet small pineapples, Rp25. Restaurant Lautan, Jl. Jen. Sudirman 15, good. Rumah Makan Bogor, up from the Gardens, eat pretty well for Rp300; nice rice soup, Rp200. **crafts:** One of the few remaining gongsmiths on Java is Pak Sukarna, Jl. Pancasan 17, one km from the Istana down Jl. Empang. Carpets made from plant fibres (*rami* and *mendong*) can be bought at Parung, just N.W. of Bogor. **souvenir shops:** Manan, Jl. Bondongan 30; and P.P. Dobbe, Jl. Kantor Batu 19.

Presidential Palace: The road from Jakarta runs smack into this former Governor's Mansion with deer roaming over undulating lawns under big shady trees. This was the official residence of the Dutch Governor-Generals from 1870-1942. While Baron Gustaf Willem van Imhoff, Governor-General for the Dutch Each Indies Company, was making a duty tour around the country in 1744 he came across the peaceful village of Bogor which fascinated him. He had a small resthouse built here and named it *Buitzenzorg* ('Without a Care'), A road was built twisting uphill for 60 km from his residence in Batavia leading right into the 25 hectate resthouse yard. Many huge glamorous parties were held here, the Dutch elite coming

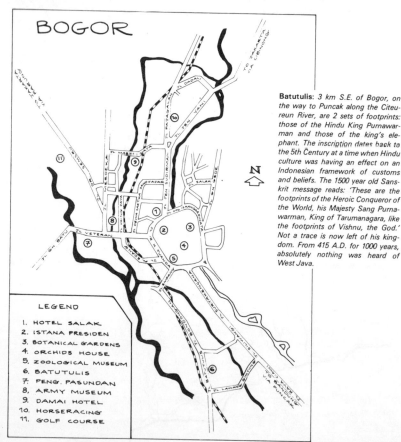

BOGOR

N

Batutulis: *3 km S.E. of Bogor, on the way to Puncak along the Citeureun River, are 2 sets of footprints: those of the Hindu King Purnawarman and those of the king's elephant. The inscription dates back to the 5th Century at a time when Hindu culture was having an effect on an Indonesian framework of customs and beliefs. The 1500 year old Sanskrit message reads: 'These are the footprints of the Heroic Conqueror of the World, his Majesty Sang Purnawarman, King of Tarumanagara, like the footprints of Vishnu, the God.' Not a trace is now left of his kingdom. From 415 A.D. for 1000 years, absolutely nothing was heard of West Java.*

LEGEND

1. HOTEL SALAK
2. ISTANA PRESIDEN
3. BOTANICAL GARDENS
4. ORCHIDS HOUSE
5. ZOOLOGICAL MUSEUM
6. BATUTULIS
7. PENG. PASUNDAN
8. ARMY MUSEUM
9. DAMAI HOTEL
10. HORSERACING
11. GOLF COURSE

up from Batavia for riding, hunting and dancing. The deer were fattened by the Dutch to provide venison for banquets. Pleasant Bogor village eventually developed into the noisy city of today and the country estate into a splendid colonial palace. Inside the mansion is the late President Sukarno's private collection of paintings by Indonesia's most famous painters some of whom he 'improved' to suit his tastes: there are 219 paintings and 136 sculptures, with many voluptuous nudes representing every race. Hotel Salak, opposite the palace, arranges tours.

Botanical Gardens: These world famous gardens, right behind the Presidential Palace, were the inspiration of the English Governor General of Indonesia during the Napoleonic Wars, Sir Stamford Raffles, an avid botanist. His wife is buried on the grounds. This incredible 111 hectare estate has been here for over 160 years and the city of Bogor has risen up around them. See plants (15,000 varieties) and trees from as far afield as Ceylon, the Himalayas, Philippines; open-air cactus gardens, great twisting foot-thick overhead vines,

river paths, ponds, enormous waterlilies. Visit the orchid hothouses with 3000 registered hybrids (open daily 8-1) for black orchids, the giant orchid *grammatophyllum speciosum* which can bear 3000 flowers at one time, orchids no bigger than a thimble, orchids with experimental scents such as antiseptic and toilet soap. Also a well-stocked botanical library, a Zoological Museum (open 8-12) where they have a 27 meter long skeleton of a Blue Whale, skeleton of the giant Japanese crab, plus other displays of Indonesian wildlife. Early Dutch researchers used these gardens to develop cash crops (oil palm, vanilla, sugar cane, corn, beans, taro) shade trees and timber in order to provide profits for the mother country during the so-called Forced Cultivation Period (1830-70) when all of Java was turned into one vast work camp. Cassava was encouraged as a 2nd food crop on Java to support an increasing agrarian population so as to increase productivity. There was even famine in many parts of Java because rice was being exported to Australia and to Europe in the early 19th Century.

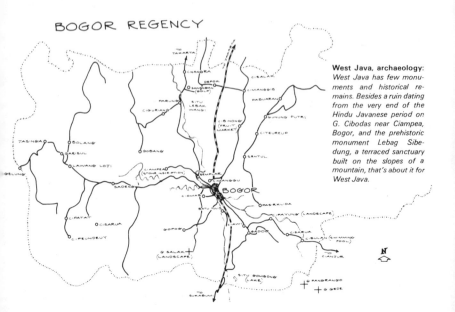

BOGOR REGENCY

West Java, archaeology: *West Java has few monuments and historical remains. Besides a ruin dating from the very end of the Hindu Javanese period on G. Cibodas near Ciampea, Bogor, and the prehistoric monument Lebag Sibedung, a terraced sanctuary built on the slopes of a mountain, that's about it for West Java.*

vicinity of Bogor: At Batutulis, just out of Bogor in Ciaruteun, see 1500 year old Sanskrit stone inscriptions and the footprints of a Hindu King and his elephant; the first written record of man on Java. Bogor was the capital of Pajajaran (12th-16th Centuries), an historic rival of the Central Javanese kingdoms. Hike up the green pyramid of G. Salak (Snake) from Cimelati, 6 km south of Lido. At Cibadak, 20 km south of Lido, the cave of the Hermit King Siliwangi. Visit the pass between G. Salak and G. Pangrango: rubber trees, *dokar* wagons that look like 1940 autos, a quaint old power station reminiscent of a castle, tea plantations, valleys, luxuriant hills. Up until the end of the 17th Century all of West Java was just a continuation of the Sumatran jungle (rhinos were still shot around Jakarta) but this area is all that's left of it. Another lovely hill station is Ciawi, 9 km S.E. of Bogor, a far cry from Jakarta's steamy heat; stay at Hotel Sindanglaja and eat at Happy Valley in Gadog. Cigonbombong-Lido, 23 km south of Bogor, has hotsprings, and canoeing on the lake in the hills nearby. More mountain scenery at Selabintana, 7 km north of Sukabumi. In Cipanas is the elegant Victorian presidential country house, Istana Cipanas, with gardens, triple canopy jungle and hotsprings; try Pendawa Hotel and Hotel Sanggabuana, Rp1200, Rp2400 double; eat at Roda or Padang Sati. In Cipayung, stay at Hotel Cipajung, Rp1200. Indonesian, Chinese and European food is served at Tamah Cibogo.

Puncak Pass: If you take the bus from Bogor to Bandung, Rp400, on the way you pass over this spectacular 1500 m high pass. At Puncak, lunch at Roda Restaurant right on Jl. Raya Puncak; *ayam goreng* and soups superb, 1000 rupes just well spent. Many mountain waterfalls in this area. Climb Megamendung for the view. Gaping valleys stretching for miles under monsoon clouds. Telaga Warna is a lake of changing colors (red, green or yellow) due to the changing daylight. The best tea thrives on these mountain slopes up to 800 m because cooler air slows growth and increases flavor. Constant pruning keeps plants short and bushy. Harvesters, mostly young girls, take only the young leaves and buds; they can pick up to 25 kg. daily, enough to make 5 kg of dried tea.

Botanical gardens: 5 km south of Cibodas, 41 km S.E. of Bogor, on the slopes of the twin volcanoes Pangrango and Gede, visit this branch of the Bogor Botanical gardens, a beautiful park with cooler climate specimens of tropical mountain trees and plants including 15 m high tree ferns (also-

Puncak Pass: *There are some beautiful hikes in this area, especially near the towns of Cibodas, Tugu, Cisarua and, once over the pass, at Cipanas. From Cipanas it's a short ride to the turnoff to the Cibodas Botanical Gardens (4 km from the main road). Near the parking lot at the gardens is the beginning of the hiking trail up to Gunung Gede, a volcanic peak overlooking the entire area towards Bandung. The hike to the peak takes 6-12 hours. An hour on the trail brings you to a fork; one trail goes to the top and the other descends to a waterfall. Following the trail to the mountaintop, you'll come to some hotsprings with a waterfall cascading down a rock edifice and steam rising from the gorge below. Start the hike before dawn if the moon is full. Not recommended during the rainy season Nov.-February.*

Cianjur: *See the West Javanese Kuda Kosong, held on May 20th, a unique and colorful parade of riderless horses dressed up in ceremonial umbrellas.*

phila). It's an 8 hour climb up the forest reserve behind this park to the summit of G. Pangrango and the broken crater of G. Gede; maybe see Jakarta harbor or even Pulau Seribu.

Pelabuhanratu: A fishing village 90 km south of Bogor. Really cheap tuna and lobster when in season. Take walks along beaches and high hills on West Java's dramatic, dangerous and deserted southern coastline. A Sea Festival. *Pesta Nelayan,*

is held here in June. In the Samudra Hotel (Rp5000 single), a room is always kept unoccupied for the Queen of the South Seas. At Cipanan Cisolok, 10 m high spouting geysers. Five km west of the hotel at Pantai Karang Hawu, giant cliffs, ragged reefs, crashing waves, and hazardous swimming; the Bulgarian Ambassador drowned here a few years back. At Pengumbahan, 7 km from Ujung Genteng Game Reserve, ride on the back of giant sea turtles.

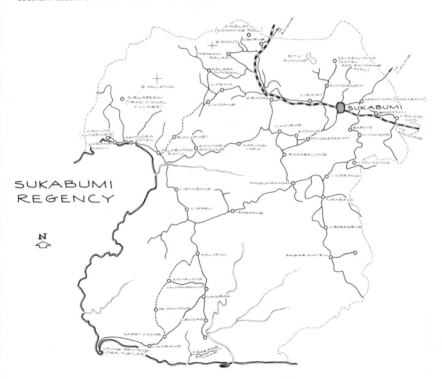

SUKABUMI REGENCY

CIREBON

The name Cirebon derives from the Javanese word *Caruban* which means 'mixture'. A harbor town on the border of West and Central Java, Cirebon is the meeting point of the Sundanese and Javanese cultures. It was here where advancing Muslim power first gained a foothold in the territory of the older Hindu-Buddhist Kingdom of Pajajaran. Have a look at the palaces of Cirebon to realize this city's history: the architecture, interiors, furnishings are a

conglomeration of Sundanese, Javanese, Islamic, Chinese and Dutch cultures. Since the sultanate here was split into two houses, Kanoman and Kesepuhan, there are two palaces open to visitors with ceremonies, dances and *gamelan* still taking place. **transport:** In this small city the *becaks* sound like sleigh bells; take one for a full hour for Rp150-200, or a good long ride for Rp50.

stay: The best for the money is Hotel Asia, Jl. Kalibaru Selatan 11, 11A and 15. Rp1500 single and double. Quite central and clean, down a quiet street opposite a green canal. Mosquito nets even. Hotel Eng Hwa (close to Hotel Asia) is Rp600 double, the very cheapest in town but smells of piss. The old woman here will speak Dutch to you even if you have a British flag pasted on your forehead. There's a rash of other cheapies around the intersection of Jl. Siliwangi where it runs into the

alun2 in front of Grand Hotel: Hotel Baru, Jl. Siliwangi 157; the cheapest rooms are Rp1000, Rp1800 double. Hotel Islam, Jl. Siliwangi 126, Rp600 single, Rp800 double, no fan, no bath- but quite comfortable. Hotel Damai, Jl. Siliwangi 130, Rp1000 or 1500 double (with outside toilet and bath) but no fan; fairly clean. Hotel Semarang, Jl. Siliwangi 132,

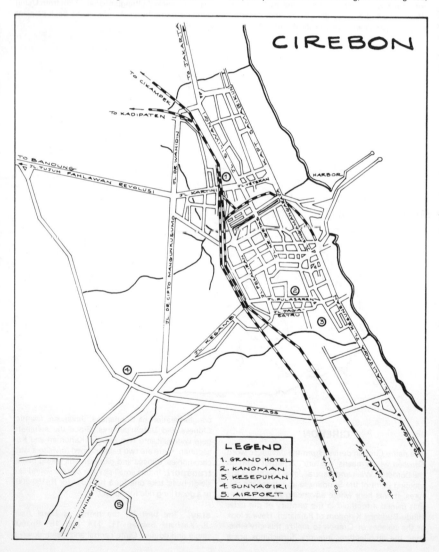

CIREBON

LEGEND
1. GRAND HOTEL
2. KANOMAN
3. KESEPUHAN
4. SUNYAGIRI
5. AIRPORT

Rp1000 per person. Also try Losmen Kuningan, Jl. Lawanggade, only Rp500. At the Grand Hotel, Jl. Siliwangi 110, the cheapest room is Rp1500 in a dorm with the drivers. Next cheapest is Rp4000, on up to Rp20,000 for the 'President' suite. **eat:** Known as the Shrimp City (Kota Udang), Cirebon has excellent seafood. Experience some of the local specialities: *nasi lengko* (rice and *tempe, tahu, sambal,* lemon, onions, meat); also *nasi rames, nasi ayam, nasi langi.* For all kinds of baked goods, Toko Famili, Jl. Siliwangi 96. Pasar Pagi, open till evening, is a good place to eat. For excellent Padang-style food and delicious ice juices (Rp150-250) and hi-fi music go to Sinar Budi, JL. Karanggetas 22. Kopyor Restaurant, Jl. Karanggetas 9, has tasty meals.

Kraton Kanoman: Ride through Pasar Kanoman to this *kraton* with its *pendopo* walls embedded with antique plates. Find the man with the key to the Gedung Pustaka (Heirloom Building) inside the *kraton* and see the Paksi Naga Liman coach (*Garuda,* dragon, elephant — symbols of the Indonesian airforce, navy and army) and also a coach on which the queen sat in the middle of her wooden 'cloud puff'. *Seni Debus* stakes, which are driven into a man on Mohammed's birthday each year, decorate the walls like a torture chamber; this ritual is a sort of mystic self-injury for God. Istana Kanoman has a restful courtyard of shady *banyan* trees and kids flying kites; remnants of the old Javanese *priyayi* world lie decaying in overgrown plazas. You can rent out the *gamelan* played on the premises, but must give a week's notice. **Kraton Kesepuhan:** From Lapangan Kesepuhan, walk directly down the lane leading to the palace. Find it yourself, don't let an old man 'guide you'. The crafty old men around the *kraton* are always tapping you for bread; ignore them. Pay Rp200 to get inside the palace, see the coach (a zoological wonder), suits of mail, royal guards' bayonets, old muskets, get a douse of holy water, and view the dead sultan's 400 year old clothes. A comatose place very much smelling of age, and it's poorly lit, all the grounds and *pendopos* overgrown with grass, goats and ducks wandering, rotting woodcarved pillars, earthen floors, forecourts and whitewashed walls stuck with blue and white Delft tiles. **others:** Thay Kak Sie Chinese temple of Cirebon is one of Indonesia's oldest.

crafts: Unique Cirebon art shows Chinese influences both in its motifs ('rock and clouds') and in the lacquer technique used. Chinese characteristics are also evident in stone, wood, jade, and ivory carvings. Nuances of Cirebon *batik* are found nowhere else on Java. All the finest pieces in the *kratons'* museums have been sold for mere money,

only small collections left. Most of the traditional *batik* is sent to Jakarta, being too expensive for the local market (Rp7-15,000). Buy *batik* in the following places: 1) around Pasar Pagi, on Jl. Karanggetas, there are many *batik* shops: Toko Batik Permana, Jl. Karanggetas 18; and Toko Batik Saudara, Jl. Karanggetas 46. For *batik kain,* most of these shops start out at Rp5000 but you can knock them down to possibly as low as Rp1500. You'll also find many examples of the Indramayu-*batik* (more involved patterns), plus examples of Solo and Pekalongan styles; 2) Pasar Balong, until 4 pm; 3) the G.K.B.I. (Batik Cooperative), Jl. Pekarungan 27, open Mon.-Thurs. 8-12, and 1-4; Fri. 8-11 and 2-4; Sat. 8-12. Many varieties of *batik*; 4) Some of Cirebon's best *batik* is made in Trusmi, 5 km west. For Trusmi, take a *becak* first to Gunungsari Station, then take a Colt to Plered, then walk 1 km to Trusmi from Plered down a country lane full of *batik* waving and drying in the sunlight. Try Mr. Masina's workshop where some 14 women work. Also Budhi Tesna's for *batik* painting and printing. Many other workshops in this village. Although the *batik* is actually made here, it is not necessarily cheaper-you just have more of a selection. They want Rp15-20,000 for the finer pieces; the highest priced are Rp60,000.

from Cirebon: From Taxi Stasiun *stanplatz,* Jl. Gunungsari, catch taxi buses to Bandung, Rp500, and to all towns in the surrounding areas. From Stasiun Bis, nearby on Jl. Gunungsari, catch buses to: Indramayu, Rp150, 1½ hours; Subang, Rp500, 3½ hours; Semarang, Rp1200, 6-7 hours; Bandung, Rp450, 4 hours; Pekalongan, Rp475, 2½ hours; Jakarta, Rp850, 7 hours. **outskirts of Cirebon:** 5 km from town along Jl. Kesambi is the old meditation grotto Sunyagiri built of red brick, concrete and plaster, sitting in the middle of a small lake. Once a fortress hermitage which sustained attacks by the Dutch, there are secret stairways, tiny doors and tunnels. Monkeys climb over the cemetary of Kalijaga, 5 km from Cirebon.

Gunungjati: Take a Colt taxi bus Rp125 from Cirebon (but only Rp75 return) 7 km down the main road to Jakarta to this tomb of Falatehan. He was the 9th *wali* who conquered Banten and then ruined the Hindu Kingdom of Pajajaran by conquering Jakarta. After subjugating the Kingdom of Cirebon he died. His tomb is still one of the holiest places on Java. Being a place of consecration, take off your shoes to enter. If you're going to give money, give only to the *juru kunci* (Keeper of the Shrine). Buy an empty bottle (Rp25) to fill up with holy water for sickness or to give to relations. Gunungjati's grave is closed to the public except for Kliwon (Fridays) of the Javanese calendar. Nearby, walk to the hilltop covered in graves next to the highway to get a view of the sea. Very pleasant on top with wild squirrels and silence; feel what Java used to be like.

others: Visit other museums in West Java; at Kuningan (Madrais Palace), Tasikmalaya, Sumedang (Cadas Pangeran). In Linggarjati is the building where negotiations took place between the Dutch the rebel government of Indonesia in 1946. At this conference the republic's *de facto* authority over Java and Sumatra was recognized, though the ambiguity of the terms did little to clarify the West

Irian question which was to explode in armed conflict 15 years later. Near this building is a museum of ancient relics discovered around Cigugur. Nature reserve Panjalu is in the middle of Nusa Situ Lengkong, 42 km north of Ciamis. At Karang Kamulyan, between Ciamis and Pangandaran, is a well-maintained wooded area inhabited by monkeys and birds, with ruins of old buildings believed to be the former royal palace of Ciung Wanara. For rattan crafts, visit Tegalwangi in Kedawung. Hot-springs at Jonggean (rheumatism) and at Palimanan (skin diseases) at the foot of Mt. Jeremai where you get an unreal view of the northern Java Plain.

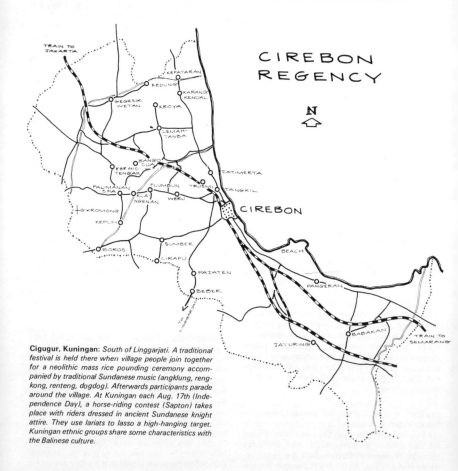

Cigugur, Kuningan: *South of Linggarjati. A traditional festival is held there when village people join together for a neolithic mass rice pounding ceremony accompanied by traditional Sundanese music (angklung, rengkong, renteng, dogdog). Afterwards participants parade around the village. At Kuningan each Aug. 17th (Independence Day), a horse-riding contest (Sapton) takes place with riders dressed in ancient Sundanese knight attire. They use lariats to lasso a high-hanging target. Kuningan ethnic groups share some characteristics with the Balinese culture.*

CENTRAL JAVA
(JAWA TENGAH)

PEKALONGAN

Known as *Kota Batik* (Batik City), 99 km east of Semarang, Rp450 by bus from Cirebon. If you bargain, *becaks* cost Rp50 to anywhere in town. A billiard-crazy northern coastal town and a main textile center famed for colorful hand-waxed, stamp-waxed, and machine-printed *batik* of specific motifs: red and blue birds and flowers on white or pink backgrounds; *batik pekalongan* is immediately recognizable. **stay:** Three quite convenient cheap hotels are right opposite the train station. Best is Hotel Gadjah Mada, Jl. Gadjah Mada 11 A, Rp750 for singles or doubles, quite comfortable. Hotel Damai, Jl. Gajah Mada 7, Rp910 for singles or doubles. Hotel Ramayana, Jl. Gajah Mada 9, Rp1020 for singles or doubles. If all these are full, try Hotel Hayamwuruk, Jl. Hayam Wuruk 158 (right in the center of town), Rp1000 single or Rp1250 doubles; or Hotel Putra, on JL. Bendan, Rp700 doubles. Hotel Nirwana, Jl. Dr. Wahidin 11A, on main highway. Tel. 745; Rp1750 or Rp2500 double, very relaxing and the girls on the front counter are helpful. **eat:** Typical *makan asli* of Pekalongan include *jangan asam* (sayur asam), *semur, sambal tempe*, etc.

batik pekalongan: Weavers used to keep awake and burn incense through the night before starting work on a new fabric. Now they're in it more for the bread. Numerous *batik* factories and shops. As in Yogya, peddlers with their bundle of *batik* come up to restaurant tables and there's always a guy around the hotels who has *batik* of every variety to show you. Coming directly from the *kampungs* where the *batik* is made, they are generally cheaper (starting price Rp750 each) than at the shops on the main streets Jl. Hayamwuruk and Jl. Hasanudin, especially if you buy 3 or more. Visit Tobal Batik, Jl. Teratai 7a, Klego: rayon and cotton kaftans with bright flowers, Rp2500; Losem pieces with the Phoenix bird on beige background Rp1000 each; fairly long scarves, Rp350; bikinis and skirts. Also Megamandoon cloud-patterned *batik*, most beautiful, for about Rp5000. Princess Munroh Batik Gallery, run by Salim Alay-adrus, Jl. H.A. Salim 31, Tel. 575, sells *batik* 4-5 m long for about Rp800 per meter. Most of the really fine Pekalongan-style *batik* comes from the village of Kedungwuni, 9 km from town, Rp40 by *bemo*. For really superb work visit the Leonardo of *batik*, Pak Oey Tjoen in Kedungwuni, Jl. Raya 104. He uses 8-9 colors on one piece. Real close up or at a distance it looks just as good. A *sarung* costs Rp75,000 and a *kain* Rp95,000, starting and ending price. Unbelievably intricate designs. Other workshops in the following places: Kampung Pesindon, see Mr. Yahya who speaks English; the *Kauman* (Old Town), and Kampung Arab around Jl. Surabaya where there are many *batik* factories and sellers; Kampung Sampangan, off Jl. Hasanudin; the Chinese *batik* factory Rinbun Jaya, Jl. Urip Sumohardjo; Mr. P. Bahur on Jl. Java; Krapyak; also visit the Batik Museum, use it as a standard when buying.

vicinity of Purwokerto: Wangon is known as the neatest town in all of Central Java. **Banyumas:** A small town of wide streets and white 19th Century buildings. Banyumas has its own particular *batik* design. Mountain retreat of Baturaden on slopes of Mt. Slamet (3428 m). The 85 km road which links Banyumas and Wonosobo runs besides a foaming rocky river called Kali Serayu. **Tegal:** North of Purwokerto on road running from Cirebon to Pekalongan. Here brassware and handcrafted red ochre pottery are produced. Bargain at roadside stalls. **Karangbolong:** South of Gombong on south coast of Java. Best quality birds' nest on the whole coast is found here. Birds' nest soup is a consume made from the nests of two species of cane swifts or sea swallows. Their nests, built solely out of their saliva, are reaped every 3 months when men climb down cliff-faces on rope ladders hundreds of meters above crashing waves to collect the nests which they sell later to Chinese restaurants as delicacies.

SEMARANG

Fishing port and administrative capital of Central Java, Rp350 from Pekalongan by bus. 120 km north of Yogya via Magelang. Population 800,000, including about 150,000 Chinese. More a commercial center than a city for tourists, but a good starting point for many holiday resorts in the mountains to the south. The silting up of this harbor in the 10th Century might have been a factor in the shifting of power from Central to East Java by cutting off the ruler's income through sea trade. For long known as 'The Red City', the center of socialist activity in the archipelago. The Communist Party of Indonesia was born here in 1920 (first introduced by a Dutchman in 1914) and finally grew into the largest in the world outside communist-controlled countries. Good night life in Semarang, many clubs and massage parlors. Pasar Johar next to the main square, and Jl. Bojong, are the main shopping centers. Be-

SEMARANG

JAVA SEA

TO SURABAYA

JL. R. PATAH

TO JAKARTA

JL. SILIWANGI

JL. PEMUDA

JL. PANDANARAN

G.O.R.

JL. A.YANI

JL. MAJAPAHIT

TO PURWODADI

JL. VETERAN

JL. SRIWIJAYA

JL. SULTAN AGUNG

TO BOROBUDUR

JL. JETIABUDI

LEGEND

1. RAILWAY STATION
2. GAREJA BLENDUK
3. SHOPPING CENTER
4. BUS STATION
5. BAITURAHAN MOSQUE
6. TUGU MUDA MONUMENT
7. AIRPORT
8. SAM PO KONG TEMPLE
9. SNAKE GARDEN
10. GOLF COURSE
11. LIGHTHOUSE

events of Semarang: Hari Pembangunan *(Development Day)* is an annual festival in the city's main public square Simpang Lima held on July 2nd. It features shows and cultural performances to commemorate the start of 'the restoration and development of Central Java'. Dugderan *Festival* marks the beginning of the Muslim fasting month. It's highlight is the night bazaar in the public square in front of the city's Grand Mosque *(Baiturahan)*; souvenirs and folk toys made of paper, clay, cotton, and rubber are sold at the bazaar. On Sept. 14th the Five Days War Commemoration is held. First there's an official ceremony around the Youth Monument *(Tugu Muda)*, then a solemn pilgrimmage to the city's war cemetary in memory of the youth of the city who fought against Japanese occupation troops for 5 days in 1942.

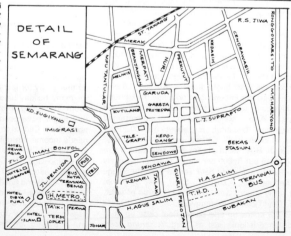

DETAIL OF SEMARANG

cause of its large Chinese community, Semarang has been a center of *jamu* production for hundreds of years. Masterfully made brass gongs are produced here, US$5000. A comparitively easy-going *imigrasi* office is on Jl. Regang 4 (off Jl. Pemuda) for extensions. Best bookshop is Merbabu, Jl. Pandanaran. Nitour Office is on Jl. Pemuda 11. **transport:** All *bemos* within the city cost only Rp30. *Bemos* start out at Terminal Bemo on Jl. Pemuda right in the center of the city (near Pasar Johar) for these directions: Karangayu, or to Kalibanteng Airport; to Tegalwareng (the tropical zoo); to Peterongan or Joblang (Sri Wanito Theatre); to Candi, Rp50 (the residential quarter for the rich).

stay: On Jl. Iman Bonjol there are hotels of every class; Hotel Singapore, Jl. Iman Bonjol 12, Rp1200 or Rp1600 double. Losmen Pontjol, Jl. Iman Bonjol 60, Rp500 or Rp750 double, dirty but cheap. Hotel Ardjuna, Jl. Iman Bonjol 51, Rp1500 single or double. Swank new Hotel Rahaju, Jl. Iman Bonjol (next to Hotel Ardjuna), Rp2500 for two. Hotel Oewa-asia, Jl. Iman Bonjol, Rp1000– a former big colonial hotel. One of the guards will offer the services of a masseuse (male or female) for Rp500. Inclusive in the price, get served weakened coffee and a watery egg the next morning. Closer to the bus station is Losmen Srimulia, Jl. Raden Ratah 76, Rp600; and Hotel Jerita, Jl. Let. Haryono, Rp1800. Both are comfortable. **eat:** The buffet right next door to Hotel Oewa-Asia serves good *es buahs.* Santana Restaurant and ice cream shop, excellent. For European, Chinese, and Indonesian food try Oen Restaurant, Jl. Pemuda. Good meal for Rp750, also the lightest cookies you'll ever taste and other outstanding baked goods. At Hotel Dibaya Puri, beefsteak Rp950. Chinese food is best on Jl. Gajah Mada, try restaurant Gadjah Mada for their seafood. Good cheap place to eat is Pasar Ya'ik (open at night) next to Pasar Johar (open in the daytime) for special Semarang dishes such as *soto ayam* (Rp25), *sate ayam, sate kerang* (oyster sate, Rp25 per stick). Tropical fruits at Pasar Johar; *rambutans, salak, blimbing, durian* (big one for Rp250). You got to try *masrochan* at Rp10 each, like a banana fritter taco; originates in Semarang. Lots of small restaurants around Klinteng Chinese temple. Gang Lombok off Jl. Pekojan for great Chinese food. Jl. Depok is also popular for its eating stalls at night.

sights: The tourist office is on Jl. Pemuda 11 next door to the Dibaya Puri Hotel; see Mr. Soetjipto B.A. for specific questions. **Candi:** Semarang's hill town with cooler weather, lovely houses, gardens, and a view over the mountain scenery to the east, south and west; visit Gombel Park. See the city lit up at night while sipping cocktails. **Tugu**

Mudu Monument: Commemorates the struggle against Japanese soldiers at the end of WW II. Reliefs on the foot of the obelisk show the sufferings of the people during the Japanese occupation, painted communally by one of the oldest artists' organizations in Indonesia. On Oct. 14 each year, two months after Proclamation Day, the *Pertempuran Lima Hari* ceremony is held around this monument to honor the 5-day battle between Indonesian youths and Japanese soldiers. **Gedung Batu:** This great stone cave is found in the western part of the city on the road to Kendal. Walk from the tourist office on Jl. Pemuda or take a *becak,* Rp100. One of the largest and most honored Chinese temple complexes in Indonesia, it houses the spirit of a 15th Century Chinese admiral and his men who landed on Java in 1424 A.D. during the Ming Dynasty with a fleet of 62 vessels and 27,000 sailors. Get your fortune told. Twice a month, on Jum'at Kliwon (Fri.) and on Selasa Kliwon (Tues.) of the Javanese calendar, multitudes of visitors arrive at this cave. **Klinteng Sam Poo Kong Temple:** On Gang Lombok in the Pekojan area. Contains 18 Buddah images which appear quite impassive. The positioning of their arms and hands, however, shows that they are ready to kill. The only light comes from tapers kept lit 24 hours a day; beautifully carved beams. **Tegalwareng Zoo:** See especially the Snake Garden for its many varieties of tropical snakes. **mosques and churches:** Mesjid Baiturahan is the largest and most elegant mosque of Central Java, modernly designed, located N.W. of Simpang Lima. The second oldest church on Java is on Jl. Jen. Suprapto south of Tawang Station. Gereja Blenduk (or Gereja Belanda) was built in 1753; unique dome roofs. The Catholic church of Semarang recites its liturgy to *gamelan* music. Nothing much else to do or see but old Dutch warehouses and architecture; check out the buildings, houses, and shops around Jl. Let. Jen. Suprapto. Walking's best.

theatre and dance: Regional folk dances include Kuda Lumping (dancers ride on matted bamboo horses), the *Reyog,* and the *Gambang Semarang* Every Sun. morning at 9 am, see the *Kuda Lumping* at Cofe Eva coffee shop in Bedono, 45 km from Semarang south on the road to Magelang, Rp150 by bus. Drink coffee and take in the performance for free. This village looks down on Ambarrawa. View this dance also at Temanggungi, 50 km from Semarang. *Reyog* performances are staged at the zoo in the THR's *rekreasi* portion, but only on Sun.; also *wayang orang*. The *Gambang Semarang* is sometimes performed at Loyola Junior High School in the rear of Gedung Olahraga (Sports Stadium); contact the principal. Ngesti Pandawa, a professional theatre company on Jl. Pemuda 116, holds nightly performances of *Ketoprak, wayang orang,* and other stage ballads based on the Solonese style using traditional *lakon.* Tickets for the better seats cost Rp250, 2nd class Rp100, 3rd class Rp75. Begins at 8 pm. From the tourist office, get a *daftar cerita* (programme) which lists performances for the coming 2 weeks. Ngesti Pandawa is known for its outstanding dancers, creative lighting, staging and supernatural effects. This company also tours in the countryside performing in large bamboo theatres. Actors are given just an outline of the plot on the morning of the performance with a list of the cast and their actions, that's all. A script is rarely used, the dialogue often improvised right on stage. At the Sri Wanito Theatre, Jl. M.T. Hardjono, all *wayang orang* roles are played by women. From Terminal Bemo take *bemo* on road towards Pekongan, Rp30. Performances begin at 8 pm; about the same prices at Ngesti Pandawa. **crafts:** A wide selection of Pekalongan and Cirebon *batik* is found at GKBI Batik Cooperative, Jl. Pemuda 52. Most souvenir and artshops are found in Jl. Pemuda: Galendra, Mustika Mas, Toko Semarang, etc. Also try Andy's on Jl. Gajah Mada and Micky Mouse on Jl. Depok.

from Semarang: Catch small freighters to Surabaya and Jakarta. Elteha Minibus Company, Jl. Karangsaru; to Jakarta, Rp1200; to Surabaya, Rp850. **flights:** Merpati office, Jl. Gadjah Mada 23. **vicinity of Semarang:** Semarang is a center for *kebatinan,* a spiritual discipline through breathing exercises. On the outskirts of the city is Watugong at Srondol. From Bubakan Terminal Bis, take a bus Rp50 down the Semarang-Magelang Road. Here lives an old Chinese who practices Theraveda Buddhism and owns a big rambling garden property with meditation grottoes and a Buddhist temple. Part deaf, he shouts a lot and seems very happy. Has a good library and the most incredible collection of papaya and *durian* plants. He teaches *pranayama* (how to regulate breathing), a 10 day course for Rp2000. Peaceful nice hilly country.

other sights: An immaculate Dutch civilian cemetary is 2 km west of Semarang, for those who died in camps during WW II. At Weleri, surviving teakwood forests, grey monkeys scamper over roadsides. On Seprapat Island in the estuary of the Silugonggo River 12 km from Pati, N.E. of Semarang, wild monkeys and the fairytale tomb of Ki Ludang. The only cog railway on Java can be enjoyed on the railway mountain tour from Ambarawa, a small town 40 km south of Semarang, to Bedono, a village nearby. Antique coaches, remodeled after the original designs, are hauled by a steam locomotive built in 1903. The tomb of R.A.

Kartini is 18 km south of Rembang. Patol Sarang is a small village near Rembang where wrestling games (patol) are performed by fishermen during moonlit nights. Rawapening Lake, the largest lake in Central Java and surrounded by mountains and green hills, has a most unusual great marsh of floating rice paddies.

Demak: 25 km east of Semarang on road to Surabaya. The first Islamic kingdom on Java which grew powerful in the years 1500-1546. In 1478 the ruler built Demak's wooden mosque, the oldest one on Java, a prime example of the joint architectural influences of the Java-Hindu and the Islamic cultures. The Demak mosque is so holy that 7 pilgrimmages to it are the equivalent to a pilgrimmage made to Mecca. The mosque has many relics; nearby is a burial ground for 60 sultans. On Besar 10 (Javanese calendar) thousands gather here to celebrate Idhul Adha Day. Although it once was a prosperous seaport, Demak is now 12 km inland and all its old boats grounded or laid up.

Salatiga: A typical Javanese country town, fruit and vegetable growing area with many schools and colleges. This well-laid out city is located in the highlands. Universitas Kristen Satya Wacana here organizes an Intensive Indonesian Language Course each Dec. and Jan. for U3$325 full room and board (see Language section). **stay:** Student dorm accommodation at Asrama Mahasiswa Universitas Satya Wacana, Jl. Kartini 11 A., Rp500. A student kitchen is also available. **vicinity of Salatiga:** Near Salatiga is a camp for 600 political prisoners; first built by the Japanese. Indonesia probably stands in history as the first country to ever accept concentration camps from another country (also bequeathed was the notorious Boven Digul camp at Tanah Merah, South Irian Jaya). **Kopeng:** 15 km from Salatiga. Sequestered retreat (1400 m above sea level, 400 m higher than Puncak and Sarangan) on slopes of Mt. Merbabu. Stay at Hotel Victoria, Rp1200; restaurant next door. Climb Merbabu from here.

temples in the Semarang area: Candi Pringapus, on east side of Gunung Sendara north of Parakan, is a Shivaite group of temples with well-crafted arabesques and porch decorations, *kala*-heads with lower jaws, petting scenes, and pot-bellied dwarves. Take a bus from Semarang to Magelang, Rp150, then from Magelang to Parakan, Rp100. **Gedong Sono** (Nine Temples): Go first by bus to Magelang, get off at Ambarrawa (Rp200), then change to public taxi to Bandungan (Rp100). Or take bus from Semarang to Lemahabang, then a taxi-truck or *andong* 5 km further to hilly Bandungan, a holiday resort with bungalows Rp1000-3500.

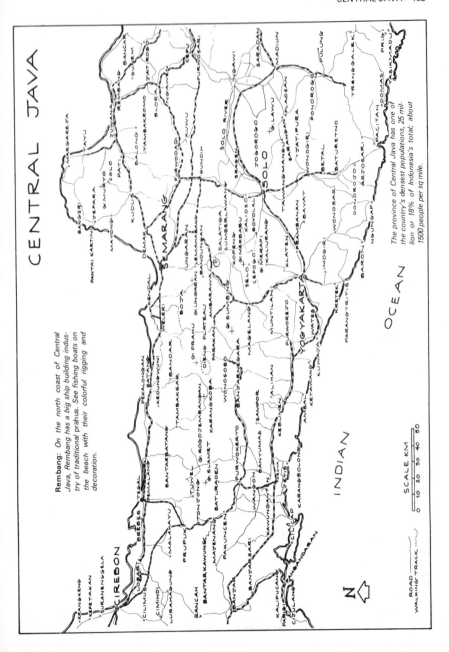

CENTRAL JAVA

Rembang: On the north coast of Central Java, Rembang has a big ship building industry of traditional prahus. See fishing boats on the beach with their colorful rigging and decoration.

The province of Central Java has one of the country's densest populations, 25 million or 18% of Indonesia's total; about 1500 people per sq mile.

N

SCALE KM
0   10   20   30   40   50

ROAD ▬▬▬▬
WALKING TRACK ·······

The quite comfortable PJKA Railways Guesthouse is Rp1000. About 3 km after this village, take horse or walk up road which turns up the mountainside where 9 minor temple groups stand on tops of 6 different hills. Most beautiful temple location on Java. This Shivaite-Hindu complex dates from the 8th-9th Century and clusters around ravines and sulphur springs. Includes a Vishnu temple, very rarely worshipped on Java. Most are elaborately built and in excellent condition. See Temple II with its well preserved *kala-makara* relief on the portal. Place chosen with great care; sweeping view high over the central Javanese plain plus 3 of its most towering volcanoes. Wander about. Walk the ancient pilgrims' paths; takes about 3-4 hours to visit all the sites.

KUDUS

Founded by a saint. 55 km east and Rp150 by bus from Semarang. A rich clove-town, famed as a center for the clove cigarette industry (25% of Indonesia's annual output). Though a staunch Islamic town (funny vibes if you wear shorts), some old pre-Hindu customs prevail: cows may not be slaughtered and schoolboys still spend a night at the shrine of Sunan Muria (at Colo, 18 km north) to improve their chances in exams. The Kiajis of Kudus (in the Old Town) can throw stones in the air which become balls of fire; they have a reputation as healers. **transport:** It's quite easy to get around town, guys always offer you rides on their bikes and trucks.

stay: Cheapest is Hotel Amin, Jl. Menur 448, Rp400 or Rp750 double; lies Rp50-75 by *becak* from Simpang Tujuh (the town center, where Tosera Shopping Center is); weak electricity and rooms are very small; like a drab motel. Hotel Devi Tungal, Jl. Kenari, Rp500; not very clean. An OK place is Hotel Slamet run by Frits Ong Tjinghap, Jl. Jen Sudirman 63, Rp600 or Rp1200 double (bigger room); some rooms alright, some not. Eat at the Flamingo Cafe. If you bring Frits a nice big picture of a flamingo he'll give you a night free at the hotel. Hotel Notosari, Jl. Kepodang 12 (off Jl. Bintinganbaru), Tel. 245, Rp1500 single and double. Very central, well kept, and a nice quiet courtyard. Hotel Duta Wisata, Jl. Sunan Muria, Rp1800 for double, is in a residential neighborhood, a fine out-of-the-way place, so book ahead. Has a TV. **eat:** Try *jenang kudus* made of glutinous rice, brown sugar and coconut. It can keep 10 days, though it hardens. Another specialty is *soto kudus* made from chicken. In the Kudus Bus Terminal ask for Pak Denuh's, the most famous of all the *soto kudus* soupmakers, Rp50 only. Or try it and other traditional dishes at Rumah Makan Hijau, near the bus terminal; Indonesian/Javanese food at its best. Rumah Makan

Intan, Jl. Sunan Kudus 2/A; delicious *bakmie goreng* Rp300 and other Chinese-style meals, Rp3-500. A fancy place is Garuda Restaurant, Jl. Panglima Sudirman 1, for Indonesian, Chinese and European food. Don't miss the *masrochan* carts, Rp10.

sights: See the 16th Century 20 m high red brick minaret which looks like a Javanese Hindu temple. It combines Hindu and Islamic architecture. This *menara* is so radically different from the traditional Muslim minaret in Saudi Arabia or Egypt that it is really just a modified *kulkul* tower (watchtower) which was added to fortified temples during Hindu times to warn rice farmers of catastrophe. Now it is used to announce the 5 daily prayers. Nearby is the tomb of Sunan Kudus. See men lose themselves while praying and chanting. Lawang Kembar, ancient Javanese writing on the gate of the mosque. There's also a *rumah adat* house near the mosque.
kretek factories: Clove cigarettes were invented here by a guy who claimed they ameliorated his asthma. Indonesians now smoke up over 35,000 tons of cloves a year, even importing them from Zanzibar. Visit Kretek factories Djarum, Noryorono, Seokun, Jambu Boh, etc. Free tours. Chinese-owned Djarum is the biggest, having made spectacular ground on Gudang Garam over the past several years. Djarum has 17 factory buildings producing *kretek,* each factory turning out one million hand-rolled cigarettes per day. Five hundred people work in the rolling shed; one roller gets Rp75 per 1000 cigarettes; some roll 5000 a day. In the packaging building there are 2000 women working like ants, all dressed so fine in dainty *kebayas* and jewelry.
Kauman: The Old Town. Ruins of Mesjid Bubar here; dates from the Hindu period. These back streets have the atmosphere of Zanzibar; narrow, winding, stark white.

from Kudus: Kembang Express, quite near Tosera Shopping Center, has night buses to Surabaya leaving 9:30 pm, arriving at 4 am, Rp1500; to Jakarta, Rp3200; to Bandung, Rp1500; to Denpasar, Rp3250. Meals served free onboard. **vicinity of Kudus:** At Sumber, 8 km east of Kudus, holy turtles were once human beings who desecrated the praying pond. **Colo:** At the foot of G. Muria. High, healthy, cloudy weather. Catch a Colt from Simpang Lima in Kudus and ride up the mountain on a narrow road lined with pine and willow trees, the rice paddies like luxuriant steps against the sky. Visit Montel Falls alone in the forest one hour's walk from Colo. Climb up a thousand steps to the grave of Sunan Muria. The *pasanggrahan* is on top of the hill, lovely location, Rp900 per room. *Asli* meals are served here such as *ayam panggeng,* Rp200; and *nasi pecel pakis* with fish, Rp200.
Bleduk Kuwu: 25 km east of Purwodadi. See

the Eternal Flame and other strange volcanic phenomena in the form of mud volcanoes and vapor exploding out of the ground. The mud is brackish and since time immemorial (even mentioned in Chinese dynastic records) the population has made its salt from the salt wells it forms. From G. Kuwu to Dander on the border of Central and East Java, there's an arid chain of limestone hills, called Gunung Kendang. Along this road is Gua Teras, a one km long cave.

JEPARA

A small town 90 km N.E. of Semarang on the north coast of Central Java. Jepara was the main port of the 8th Century Hindu Mataram empire; now a small town whose claim to fame is its woodcarving. Best traditional woodcarvers on Java work in this area (in Yogya, they're more academic). Except for the hinges, no nails, screws, or metal joinery is used. Nice ride to get here on the bus or minibus from the Kudus Terminal Bis, Rp150, 35 km. You know you're getting close because you see trucks and *dokar*s rumbling by piled high with carved chests and cabinets. Men come in from the surrounding villages to work in the shops as carvers.

To see carvers in action visit: Tahunan village, 4 km from Jepara on the highway to Kudus; Mantingan, before Ratu Kalinjamat; Blakang Gunung, 10 km from Jepara (they specialize in a caged lion carved from a single piece of wood). Purchase furniture such as beds, bookcases, writing desks, jewel boxes, and round or heart-shaped wooden buttons (Rp600 for 12). Fine quality furniture sets cost from Rp250,000 to ½ million. *Kursi gadjah,* another design known as the 'elephant chair', costs up to Rp125,000 a set (costs Rp30,000 alone for the labor). You can get the price down, but not by much, maybe by only Rp5-10,000. There are cheaper models: for one set of *Kursi Antik,* Rp25,000-70,000. The carvers are paid by each meter they carve. The wood comes from Blora and Cepu (East Java); teakwood for the most part, but also find *kayu mahoni* (mahogany) and *kayu meranti*; statues are usually made of *sono* wood. Learn carving? S.T.M. (Bagian Ukir) gives a three-year course both modern and traditional styles. **stay:** Jepara is a restful place. Losmen Asia, Jl. Kartini 32, Rp600. Losmen Jakarta, Jl. Pemuda 16, Rp600 or Rp750 double. These are the only two *losmens* so if they're full you must make it just a day-trip and return to Kudus.

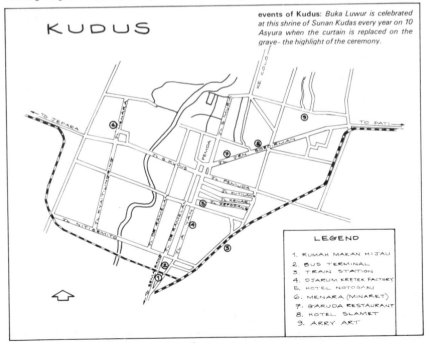

events of Kudus: *Buka Luwur is celebrated at this shrine of Sunan Kudas every year on 10 Asyura when the curtain is replaced on the grave- the highlight of the ceremony.*

KUDUS

TO JEPARA

TO PATI

LEGEND

1. RUMAH MAKAN HIJAU
2. BUS TERMINAL
3. TRAIN STATION
4. DJARUM KRETEK FACTORY
5. HOTEL NOTOSARI
6. MENARA (MINARET)
7. GARUDA RESTAURANT
8. HOTEL SLAMET
9. ARRY ART

vicinity of Jepara: The birthplace of Kartini is in Mayong, 25 km south of Jepara on the way to Kudus; the house is only 50 m from the highway. Kartini wrote the most important Indonesian literary work of this century– written in Dutch. She died in childbirth at age 24. Pilgrimmages are still made to her grave near Rembang. At Mantingan, near Jepara, there are remains of an old mosque and cemetary with reliefs on tombstones. Examine reliefs on the tomb of Ratu Kalinjamat, by *dokar* Rp500 up and down hills about 4 km from town. She was a warrior-queen of Jepara who attacked the Portugese fortress in Melaka twice in the 16th Century. What appears as leaf decorations close up, when viewed from a distance you can make out a figure of a monkey. Although Islamic religious laws forbade representing living creatures, the desire to draw people and animals was so great that the sculptors composed them of leaves and flowers. Three km from Jepara is Pantai Jepara, or Pantai Kartini, for swimming. Bangsri is known for its Javanese women 'of beautiful profile'.

DIENG

The oldest temples of Java lie on this pear-shaped plateau 26 km N.W. of Wonosobo. The name comes from *Di Hyang* ('Abode of the Gods'). Because of its silent invigorating mountain heights, skudding clouds, mineral lakes, cool misty atmosphere, this area has been a sacred spot since early times. Gets only 1500 tourists a year. No telephones. **getting there:** Approach Dieng either from Semarang (S.E. 132 km) or from Yogya (north 135 km). From Yogya, take bus first to Wonosobo, Rp300. In Wonosobo, stay overnight at Losmen Jawa Tengah (Railway Guesthouse), Jl. Agung 45 near the bus station, Rp400; this *losmen* is about the most convenient. Losmen Baru, Jl. Kawedanan 2/A, Rp800 double, Rp500 single. Hotel Petra, Jl. Agung, Rp400. Pleasant Hotel Merdeka, Rp2000 double. Restaurant Asia is expensive. For information, see the man in the blue and cream *rumah makan* in back of the bus station. Next morning take a truck, *oplet* or hitch up to the 2093 m high village of Dieng. The road passes tobacco plantations, rugged steep landscapes with clouds below the road, bamboo aquaducts, pale eucalyptus, sleeping volcanoes. See Kawah Si Kidang, a crater with smoking boiling sulpher mud, and Kawah Si Leri, another large crater with whitish smoke and water. Telaga Merdada Lake, surrounded by green hills, has cool weather, misty pines, wild roses.

the temples: Only 8 out of perhaps 40 original temples have been restored. The others have only their foundations left. The temples are scattered over a 10 sq. km area in a crater whose rim collapsed eons ago. Now a marshy plain and high mountain meadows cover the hilly crater floor where horses graze beside the lichen-covered *candis.* Inscriptions date from as far back as 809 A.D. All monuments are dedicated to the Hindu God Shiva and were built as places of worship and not to glorify kings as were the later Buddhist-Hindu monuments of Central Java. Archaeologists first believed these remains indicated that Dieng was a ruined city, but realized later that it was just a flourishing temple city of hermitages, priests, attendants, and visiting pilgrims. Many of the temples share uncanny resemblances to temple architecture of South India, in particular a group of 7th Century temples at Mamallapuram. All extant temples on Dieng were given their names (members of the Pandava clan from the *Ramayana* epic) by the local population one thousand years after they were constructed. The *candis* are each very compactly built, none over 15 m high, have sparse ornamentation, and are still in fairly good condition after standing 10 centuries. The Bima Temple in the south is entirely unique in all of Indonesia; faces in the roof seem like spectators looking out of windows. Also peculiar to the Dieng site are its sinister animal mounts.

stay and eat: About 8 *losmens* in Dieng village, some with wooden balconies overlooking it all, some provide quilts. Go to the biggest *warung.* This man runs the tourist info service and also rents rooms in a house up on the hill above his *losmen*; they cost Rp200 (half the *losmen*'s price). This hill is the best place to stay because of the view, and you live with the family. He serves *tahu* so rich and creamy that it tastes like cheese! Another popular *losmen* is the Gunung Mas, Rp400-800. Has electricity. A-Sri, Mekarsopi, and Losmen Sederhana all have Rp500 rooms. Eat at Hotel Soto, *nasi goreng,* Rp100. The restaurant next to the new *losmen* serves *nasi sayur* for Rp50 and vegetable and mushroom soup, Rp175.

others: Traces of a palace can be seen in the center of the plain east of Semar meditation cave and Arjuna temple. Stone staircases used to lead up to this site, and you can still see remains of an underground tunnel which once drained the crater floor. Along a rocky woodland path 2 km south of the lakes, a pool of hot bubbling mud, geysers and sulphur fumes shooting from the earth. Bring paints, charcoal or crayons; this plateau is a favorite artists' subject.

faces of Indonesia

vicinity of Dieng: Very mountainous walking in this region. The ground is often waterlogged and it's damn cold at night (as low as 4 degrees C.), so dress accordingly. Can hire horses, Rp6-800 per hour. **Gua Semar:** There's a whole ritual to go through to visit this holy cave. Bathe first at Bimolukar (gives you 'a pliable heart' and 'a swift mind'), then walk deep into the cave where incense burns and it's very dark and warm because of the sulphur. The cave is said to be the exact physical center of Java. Suharto spends the night here when things are piling up. **Trappist Monastery:** This farm is 10 km beyond Dieng village. They make their own cheese. There's a guesthouse set aside for visitors, but women aren't allowed to enter the monastery itself. **from Dieng:** A unique exit from Dieng plateau is the 13 km walk north down to Bawang. Steps are cut into the path; you lose all that altitude in 4 hours. Pass through villages which have seldom seen foreigners. From Bawang take a regular bus to Pekalongan, Rp150.

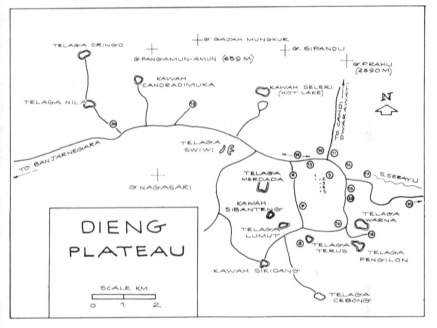

1. Candi Semar
2. Candi Arjuna
3. Candi Srikandi
4. Candi Puntadewa
5. Candi Sembadra
6. hermitage ruins
7. Candi Gatotkaca
8. Candi Bima
9. palace ruins
10. museum
11. taxi terminal
12. Tourist Information Office
13. Losmen Sederhana
14. hotels, restaurants, losmens
15. old palace wall
16. flower gardens
17. Bimolukar
18. Gua Semar
19. Gua Jimat (Death Valley)
20. Sumur Jalatunda
21. to Wonosobo
22. mushroom factory

YOGYA

Yogya lies in the center of Java's 'Realm of the Dead', a city surrounded by ancient ruins. The Mataram Empire of Central Java fell apart under Dutch pressure and formed the two states of Surakarta (Solo) and Yogyakarta in 1755. The Yogya Kraton is the highest ranking court in Indonesia and 'Special Region Yogyakarta' is to this day responsible directly to the central government in Jakarta and not to the provincial head of Central Java. The layout of the city still reflects the formal, traditional relationship between the sultan, marketplace, and mosque. To the Javanese, Yogya has always been a symbol of nationalist passion and resistence to alien rule. During the Dutch occupation of 1948, the sultan of present-day Yogya locked himself in his *kraton* and when he finally consented to negotiate with the Dutch it was from the top of his palace wall looking down on them with his people watching. Yogya was from 1946-50 the grass roots capital of Indonesia and the headquarters of the revolutionary forces; its people were scorched earth fighters. At last in 1948 the Dutch launched an all out attack on the city, dropping 900 paratroopers, heavy bombs and rocket fire while US and British planes strafed the city streets. With all of the republican leaders captured and its ministries closed down, the rebel forces retired from Yogya to the countryside and carried out a peoples' war. The US Senate, whose Marshall Plan rehabilitation money appeared to be supporting Holland's fight against the Republican Army, threatened to withdraw support. Finally in Dec. 1949, Holland recognized the new republic. Today Yogya is a center for higher learning and the Javanese language is said to be spoken in its purest form here. Yogya is the cultural capital of Java, Java's Kyoto. In a town of only 400,000 there are over 75 art organizations. The city has numerous music and dance schools, brilliant dance choreographers, drama and poetry workshops, folk theatre and *wayang* troupes, its artists excell in the plastic arts. It's one of the best places to shop in S.E. Asia, if you look. Along with Solo, Yogya is a major *batik*-producing center and because of increased tourist awareness this art is becoming of even higher quality. Its painters and sculptors are Indonesia's elite, strongly individualistic and increasingly commercialized. It's one of the biggest villages in the world.

transport: The best way to see the city is to walk. Next best is by bicycle, like everyone else. The back streets are filled with friendly hellos and the main street with the sound of bicycle bells.

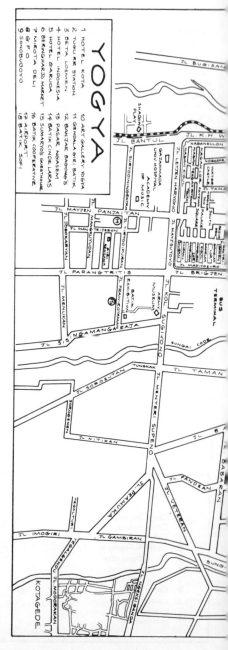

YOGYA

1 HOTEL KOTA
2 TUGU KK STATION
3 BETA LOSMEN
4 HOTEL INDONESIA
5 HOTEL GARUDA
6 BERINGHARJO MARKET
7 MIROTA DELI
8 GPO
9 SONOBUDOYO
10 ART GALLERY YOGYA
11 GENDALA GIRI BATIK
12 BANJAR BAGONG'S
13 PASAR NGASEM
14 BATIK CINDE LARAS
15 SUMARYOS GUESTHOUSE
16 BATIK COOPERATIVE
17 AIRPORT
18 BATIK SOFI

Yogya's history: Yogya was named after the city of the heroes of the Ramayana, Ayudhya, by Mangkubumi, who was proclaimed sultan by the Dutch in 1745. The main street, Malioboro, is a corruption of Marlborough, a British general who fought in the Spanish Wars. During the war of independence against the Dutch after WW II, Yogya was the main focus of revolutionary activity.

Bikes are much cheaper than taking *becaks*. Rent them for Rp150-200 per day; or one week, Rp1200; one month, Rp3-3500. Rent from: Malioboro Restaurant, Jl. Malioboro; Hotel Kartika, Jl. Sosrowijayan 10; and from Hotel Indonesia. If you lose a bike or it gets stolen, it could cost you Rp20-25,000, so take care. Parking fees for pushbikes most places around Yogya run Rp15-25. Buy a bicycle or a motorcycle at Pasar Sepeda Tandjung, Jl. Mesjid; hundreds row on row. Good used motorbikes run about Rp200,000; bicycles Rp15-20,000. By *andong* is a nice way to get to Kota Gede, Rp300. Take buses out to Borobudur and other sites around Yogya; cheapest and more fun. Minibuses and taxis are a bourgeoise bore.

stay: The Pasar Kembang area around Jl. Sosrowijayan is the cheapest. This area is so close to the train station that it sounds like little toy trains all night long. Most of the *losmens* here charge Rp250-350 single, Rp400-600 double. On the small lane running between Jl. Pasar Kembang and Jl. Sosrowijayan there are 6 small *losmens*. Beta, in its own *kampung*, is the biggest; Rp300 single, Rp500 doubles. Run by 5 women who sing all day long, it is quiet, friendly, and almost always full. Losmen Bu Purwo's, Rp250 for a small bed and Rp350 for a room with a big bed; or Rp500 double. Losmen Lima is opposite Hotel Indonesia behind the Aziatic; cheap, clean, and quiet but the best thing about it are the people. Hotel Aziatic, Jl. Sosrowijayan 6, Rp1000 single or double. Big rooms and very cool if you want to get away from the heat. Hotel Indonesia consists of a maze of rooms surrounding a garden courtyard; Rp300 single, Rp500 double, also a more expensive row of rooms, Rp1000. Very popular, many travelers. Bike rental is Rp150 per day. Towards the station is Hotel Asia Africa, Jl. Pasar Kembang 25; Rp1000 single or double with *mandi* and private patio. Room service. Losmen Trimulya, next to the railway, where mostly Indonesians stay. Never a dull moment, American soul music, and Indonesians invite you out to the movies or out to eat. Hotel Kota, Jl. Pasar Kembang; Rp600 single, Rp1000 for very big twin rooms. Even has a washroom. Eggs and toast served; food prices are fixed. Sumaryo Guesthouse, nearer the Kraton on Jl. Prawirotaman 18/A, Rp2000 single including breakfast. Rp500 meals. Subardjo Guesthouse is just next door, Rp2400. Prambanan Guesthouse, Jl. Sosrokusuman 18-20, very central, Rp1200 single or double. Also rooms for Rp1500. Tea, coffee twice daily. T.V., refrigerator, water, telephone (Rp50 per call) — nice place. The more modern Intan Hotel is on the same small street (no. I/16), single Rp1000, double Rp1500. Old fashioned colonial-style Hotel Garuda, Jl. Malioboro 72, way overpriced at US$11 single.

Ambarrukmo Palace, out of town a bit on the road to Prambanan (Jl. Solo) is US$19 single (cheapest) up to US$100 for the Presidential Suite. Free *gamelan* concerts 10:30-12:30 and 3:30-5:30 pm. Pineapple Brasilia with marashino cherries by poolside, Rp550. Pool is open 9-6 pm, but costs Rp550 for the privilege. Fine Indonesian dancing in Borobudur Restaurant. In back is a complex of 3 buildings built in traditional 19th Century Javanese classical architecture. A *pendopo*, courtyard and some royal relics. Pasar Kembang is a great area, very colorful, but not the place to settle if you're going to be in Yogya for awhile. The Chinese guy who manages Mirota is the real estate man of Yogya who can help you find a house to rent for longer periods. Or scan or put an ad in the town rag *Kedaulatan Rakyat*, Jl. Mangkubumi 42, to find a house, flat, or room with a family. **note:** During the Ramayana Ballet (4 days only, each May, June, July and August), Yogya's hotels are packed.

eat: An excellent town for vegetarians: beancakes, *rempeyek* (peanut cookies) and vegetable soups galore. The *makan asli* of Yogya, *gudeg*, is jackfruit cooked in coconut milk with a mixture of eggs, soya beancake and chicken. Also tasty Javanese *opor ayam*, slices of chicken simmered in coconut milk; and sumptuous *mbok berek*, one whole fried chicken for Rp5-600. Colonel Sanders can't hold a candle to it. The best *mbok berek* restaurants are in Prambanan village and along road between Yogya and Prambanan. Yogya's wide variety of street stalls serve other Javanese specialties; try duck egg special *ronde* (spicy warm drink), Rp100. Bustami's *warung* (Sumatran people), Jl. Pasar Kembang 27, just two doors down from the Asia Africa Hotel on the right; try their fried vegies, Rp175. For *nasi padang,* Rumah Makan Wiena, Jl. Mangkubumi 2 (just over the RR tracks). Sinar Budi, Jl. Mangkubumi 41, for *nasi campur,* Rp175, very tasty; try their *rendang.* Minang Mini, Jl. Mataram, a bit expensive and stingy with their rice, but good food. The sauce is free, so just eat one dish and use the sauce from the rest. Bagong's Dance Studio, Jl. Laksamana; relax, have a meal (the best *gado2*) and look at the paintings. Go in the afternoons when there are dance rehearsals (4 pm). Pasar Gandekan, Jl. Jen. A. Yani, for fruit: apples from Malang, *anggur* (grapes), *dondong* (sour taste), pineapples (Rp100), giant *blimbing* from Demak, lemons from Australia. Mirota Delicatessan, Jl. Malioboro 73, open 9-1:30, 6-8:30, for delicious sandwiches with the works on rye bread, Rp150; really fills you up. Pack a lunch for the train. **restaurants:** At Colombo's, Jl. Malioboro 25, the food is too dear and much of it (like the fried rice) is pre-cooked and turned out on an assembly-line basis to the music of Moonlight Serenade; not a persohalized place, they've gotten lazy with success. For this class of food it's cheaper in Malioboro Restaurant, Jl. Malioboro 87, a more cheerful place with bargain dishes and they have the best black rice pudding in the mornings. Watch it though, a lot of pickpockets. The real tourist hangout is Helen's, Jl. Malioboro 44, which is likewise a rip-off place where Javanese hipcats waste time. At Happy's, Jl. Malioboro, you at least get what you pay for; the *cap cai*, Rp250, is very satisfying; consistently good food and service. Mama's by the RR Station, on Jl. Kembang Pasar, for big helpings for good prices. Try speed-drink ginger-coffee. Superman's on the lane between Jl. Pasar Kembang and Jl. Sosrowijayan is one of the cheapest restaurants and the best breakfast place; scrambled eggs, Rp150, omelet, Rp125; toast and jam, Rp100, *mie goreng* with egg on top, Rp200. Always good music, good lighting (no neon), and relaxed atmosphere. Creamy ice cream at Tip Top, Jl. Mangkubumi 28, for flavors like tutti fruitti and lychee. Open 9-1:30, and 5-9. Ice cream cup, Rp100; or in a plate Rp100-175. Also by the litre, Rp1000.

the kraton: Classical Javanese palace-court architecture; the finest in existence. Open daily until noon. Don't let them rush you through; sometimes the guide tries to turn visitors in and out in 10 minutes – for Rp150! Original buildings date from 1756, one year after the founding of the sultanate. Looted by the English in 1812. During the war of independence 1947-49 guerilla-commander Suharto, the current president of Indonesia, used to dress as a barefoot peasant and peddle vegetables at the rear of the *kraton* in order to confer with the sultan on guerilla tactics to use against the Dutch. The *kraton* is enclosed by 4 white walls 3 m thick, each one km long, their construction imitating European fortifications. The population of this small city within a city is about 25,000 including jesters and 200 gracious elderly court attendants. The *kraton* has *batik* and silver workshops, mosques, schools, markets, offices, and two museums. See ornate and heavily gilded Bangsal Kencono (Golden Pavilion) with its carved solid teak pillars. The Glass Pavilion combines Hindu motifs, Buddhist lotus flowers, and stylized opening words of the *Koran;* marble floors, vortex ceilings. The sultan's collection is made up of *wayang* puppets, royal carriages, Raden Saleh portraits, a saddle made with gold and silver thread, royal heirlooms exuding an odor of sanctity (at the Proboyekso), huge 600 year old brass gongs, a *gamelan* that was founded during the Majapahit Empire – and much more. In the dances put on by this court, even the jangle of bells is considered coarse; anklets are used only for monkey and animal roles played by men. The Yogya dance style was created by Sultan Hemeng Kubowono I (1755-1792) in time of war and reflects an almost military discipline of mind and body. Dancers are awesomely distant and withdrawn with all the pauses, silences, meditative poses and motions arrested in space. At Uyon Uyon Hadiluhung, performances of traditional dances are held on Sat. 2-4 pm, Rp200 including a meal. *Gamelan* rehearsals without dancing take place on Mon. and Wed. 10:30 pm –

wayang: *A Javanese word meaning literally 'shadow' or 'ghost'. Indonesians believe that drama is the shadow of life and that man is a mere puppet of God. Wayang is the main vehicle of drama in Indonesia, using live people or puppets to enact scenes from the lives of Javanese ancestors or from the Hindu epic poems. This art is 1000 years old and on Java you may see figures on 13th Century basreliefs similar to those used in* wayang *today. Some* wayang *forms have completely died out. These are only a few of more than 200 diverse characters: gods, noble and cruel kings and princes, demons, giants, vile monsters, beautiful princesses, wise men, servants, lovable clowns and fools. The almond-eyed slant-nosed chalky faced ones are the heroes and the pop-eyed bulbous-nosed ones are the villains. All characters win approval no matter what their personality or appearance. Everyone watches and enjoys* wayang, *from becak drivers to government ministers. It's a mixture of mysticism, slapstick comedy, morality play, social commentary, and magical myth-making—all in one. Audiences sit up all night for 10 hours watching live plays in immense bamboo theatres following every word with laughter or boos, tense silence or crying. Wayang is also used for social change; clowns have now begun to ad lib about family planning. Movies, TV and rock groups only provide more themes.*

the Yogya Kraton: *Entrance fee Rp 100. This royal palace of the sultan is the archtype of classical court architecture on Java in which old fashioned ideals of courtesy and etiquette are practiced. There are many rituals and activities still taking place and part of the university medical faculty is here. Gamelan and dance rehearsals are open to the public and guided tours are offered. Within this kraton a classical dance school has recently begun classes again after a 30 year break. Performances in one corner of the palace (Sasono Hinggil) are staged on the 2nd Sat. of each month. The kratons have always been centers of artistic creation.*

structure: *The kraton is 1 kilometer square with walls 4 m high and 3 m thick, a walled fortress town 4.83 km in circumference. Its external walls were imitations of European castles' glacis, parapats, moats, bastions, and drawbridges (now vanished). There are 5 gateways. The main entrance is through a great ornamented ceremonial gate on the northern wall which has two great snakes facing in opposite directions with their tails intertwined. Visitors must enter through a little side portal. On the alun2 (large plaza) to the north and south of the palace complex grow the sacred old waringan trees which still receive offerings. These alun2 also serve as sportfields and grounds for large annual fairs, parades, and religious celebrations. Mosques are usually located on a Javanese kraton's eastern side, facing west towards Mecca.*

pendopos: *This kraton is famous for its pendopos (open sided pavilions with marble floors) incorporating European and Indonesian court design, with Hindu, Buddhist, and Islamic motifs all combined. All its pavilions are ornately and heavily gilded with painted rafters and panels, platforms supported by finely carved wooden beams, cast iron columns. Check out the carved solid teak pillars on the Bangsal Kencono, once famed for its grand-scale wayang wong performances in the 1930's when all the royal courts of Java were competing for distinction in artistic pomp and skill. See also the small bandstand pavilion, and the Glass Pavilion with its marble floors, vortex ceilings, red beams with carving all over them, the main pavilion for ceremonies, balls, and banquets on state occasions. Mixed European and Indonesian court design. The museum contains paintings and photos of the royal lineage of sultans and their families, and gifts from foreign diplomats.*

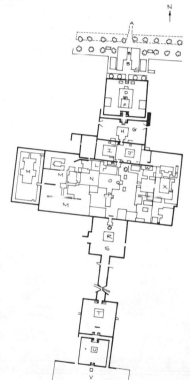

staff: *The gamelan musicians of the kraton wear special court costumes of batik and dark blue pranarkan (close-fitting high necked coats) and a destar headcloth, a neat Javanese turban with a bun in the back. The kraton women wear high collared black batik kebaya dresses with special gelung hairdos. In the Great Garebeg procession, 800 palace guards fire rifles in the air while accompanying mountains of food (gunungan) which are distributed to the poor. Soldiers use whips to keep the crowds back. These volunteer guardsmen serve without pay and they are drawn from every class: workers, students, noblemen, farmers.*

the interior: *The ultimate in 18th Century palatial decor. Peacocks strut around the dusty yard. Extensive renovations were done in the 1920's by the sultan of that time. There's quite a mixture of gifts from Europe: Italianate bronzes, carvings, stained glass, gild-formed mirrors, crystal chandeliers, Murano glasswork. There are sacred krises in shrines with lamps burning before them, wooden litters, horse-drawn carriages, venerable gamelan instruments. On Tues. and Fri. hundreds of wayang puppets—some of the best—are taken out from their boxes for an airing.*

Hamengko Buwana: *A thunderbolt came from a blue sky when this sultan of Yogya returned to support the revolutionaries' struggle against the Dutch. Since then he's shown himself to be one of the more enlightened leaders, a man-of-the-people, a sort of aristocratic republican. When Gadjah Mada University sprang up during the war of independence he allowed students to sit down for lectures in his throne-room, and the palace grounds he gave over to the people for recreation. For more than 20 years the sultan has been a minister in several national governments, and he's now Indonesia's vice president. Hamengko Buwana is the last hereditary ruler to retain loyal status and his bathwater is considered holy. Although his father died young, he has 31 brothers.*

12:30 am. On the 2nd Sat. of each month an all night *wayang kulit* (8 pm-5 am) takes place at the Sasono Hinggil Hall in the Alun2 Kidul. To visit all parts of this palace, first put in an application at the Kraton Office. To take motion pictures you must get permission from the tourist office. **others:** The Pakualaman on Jl. Sultan Agung is a princedom founded within the sultanate of Yogya by Paku Alam I in 1813. This court also receives visitors. *Gamelan* concerts are held there about once every 5 weeks.

THE YOGYA KRATON

A. *Alun2 Lor (Northern Square)*
B. *Tratag Pagelaran*
C. *Bangsal Pangrawit (Pangrawit Pavilion)*
D. *Tratag Sitinggil*
E. *Bangsal Manguntur Tangkil*
F. *Bangsal Witono*
G. *Kemandungan Utara (Keben Courtyard)*
H. *Bangsal Ponconiti*
I. *Bangsal Srimanganti*
J. *Bangsal Trajumas*
K. *Gedong Purworetno*
   (Office of Sultan's Private Secretary)
L. *Gedong Kuning*
   (Yellow House, sultan's living quarters)
M. *Living quarters for the sultan's family*
N. *Bangsal Proboyekso*
O. *Bangsal Kencono (Golden Pavilion)*
P. *Bangsal Manis (Sweet Pavilion)*
Q. *Tratag Bangsal Kencono*
R. *Bangsal Kemagangan*
S. *Kemagangan*
T. *Bangsal Kemandungan Kidul*
   (Southern Kemandungan Pavilion)
U. *Bangsal Sitinggil Kidul*
   (Southern Sitinggi Pavilion)
V. *Alun2 Kidul (Southern Square)*
W. *Gedong Kopo (Museum)*
X. *Bangsal Kesatriyan*

FESTIVALS OF JOGYA

Keep an eye out for these. Most center on the *kraton.* In the past their main purpose was to reinforce the prestige of the reigning sultan and his court. Even today the bathwater of the Sultan of Yogya (Indonesia's current vice president) is considered holy and his fingernail clippings are kept for their latent power. But since the now reigning sultan is a reformed, democratic one, Yogya's festivals aren't nearly as grandiose as they were once and are now held more in the style of a folk festival. The *Garebeg* Procession, held 3 times within the Muslim year, was at one time a pre-Islamic cultic charity feast that was carried over and grafted onto the Islamic feast days of Mulud and Idul Fitri. The following are the more important events.

Seketan: Mohammed's Birthday. Big fairs are held on the great open square north of the *kraton* and there is continuous prayer in the mosque compound to the west of the *kraton.* Two ancient *gamelan* (Sekati) dating from the 16th Century are played alternately mornings and evenings for 7 days. Ceremonies start at noon with great processions carrying the beehive-shaped *gunungan* on bamboo frames. These 'Mountains of Food', representing the tree-of-life symbol (like our Christmas tree) are escorted by 800 palace guards (prajurits). These guards, all dressed in zany uniforms with zebra-striped shirts, slipper shoes, Napoleonic and top hats, armed with bows and arrows, spears, rifles, swords, parade in 100 platoons while firing rifles in the air. The *gunungan* are borne from the *kraton* to Mesjid Agung on the northern square. Accompanying the *gamelans,* bulky *female* kraton guards march with *kris* in their sashes, and *kraton* officials in white turbans and flowing white robes sit on thick cushions. The fair includes folk theatre forms such as *Ketoprak.* Vendors sell sweets, balloons, pin-wheels.

Garebeg Besar: A religious festival based on the Muslim alqur'an. Mass prayers are held in mosques and public squares, then goats, sheep, lambs, cows and buffaloes are ceremoniously slaughtered (korban) to commemorate Abraham's willingness to sacrifice his own son for God. The meat is distributed to the poor. The Sultan, with a retinue of nobility and court dignitaries and large floats of *gunungan,* takes part in a procession from the *kraton* to Mesjid Agung. A big bamboo theatre is set up in the northern *alun2.*

Labuhan: Means 'offering'. An annual ceremony, the day after the sultan's birthday. At 8 am offerings leave the *kraton* and are taken to Parangkusumo (1 km west of Parangtritis) on the south coast of Java where the sultan's old clothes are dedicated to the Queen of the South Seas, Loro Kidul, and put out to sea on a raft. Other offerings, nail clippings and hair trimmings, are buried in the sand. (Each Juma'at, every 35 days, Chinese women come and offer sacrifices as well.) Similar offerings are sent to the volcanoes Merapi and Lawu, and once every 8 years, to the village of Dlepih near Wonogiri.

recorded history of Indonesia: *The first westerner to write about these islands was the Greek geographer Ptolemy; they were on his world map in 160 A.D. In modern times most of the studies of Indonesian history, culture, and geography were written in English, French, German, but mostly in Dutch. The language difficulties and high price of these publications made them inaccessible to Indonesians until independence in 1945 when these books started to be translated into Bahasa Indonesia.*

history of Hinduism in Indonesia: *Early Indonesians believed only in old spirits and in the supernatural unpredictable people who had lived before them. But when Indian traders arrived, they brought a whole pantheon of gods, each of them having names, forms and functions, and a cosmic relationship with man. The Hindus also brought the doctrine of karma. The Hindu religion was based on a caste system with every human being occupying a fixed place in society, both on earth and in heaven. The highest place was reserved for the king, or maharaja, worshipped as a god on earth. The king shared power with the royal family and the princes. He had palaces with sacred heirlooms, which protected the welfare of the state. In the 15th Century Muslim state of Melaka on the southwest coast of Malaysia became powerful and this gave Islam a firmer base from which to spread throughout the archipelago.*

West Sumatra: *At Kamang on the coast near Padang, and at Surien in the district of Solok, shards of earthenware used by men 2000 years ago were found in front of caves, showing that this was one of the oldest settlement areas of Sumatra. In the 18th Century, West Sumatra was a big collecting center for pepper and gold.*

Riau, history: *During the 17th Century, the Riau lands were subject to Johore on Peninsular Malaysia, but in 1745 the Sultan of Johore surrendered his claims to the Dutch East Indies Company.*

Dieng Plateau: *The first of the great Central Javanese monuments dating from the 8th and 9th Centuries. Some of the temples were erected during the dynasty preceeding that of the Saliendras (builders of Borobudur and Angkor Wat), indicated by the fact that they were all dedicated to Shiva. Built by King Sandjaja, a king of Mataram who forced the various regional rulers of Central Java to give him obedience and tribute. He might have extended his authority over West Java, parts of Sumatra, and even Bali. A religious community flourished here, then it was deserted for 1000 years. Raffles' engineers in the early 19th Century reported 40 groups of temples, 25 years later Junghuhn mentioned 20 odd. Today there are 8 monuments more or less intact, smaller temples with simpler ornamentation than the temples of Central Java. Kala-makara motifs are found over mossy entrance gates and sometimes over the recesses of the temple itself. After the Indian style, they were probably built around a single central edifice. In India temples were built to the Hindu gods but on Dieng they were just a part of the ancestor worship from earlier times built to contain ashes of dead princes, or sometimes a carved stone god, a prince incarnated, was placed in the candi. Their manner of construction is Indian, but Dieng temples also have many Javanese characteristics that show even longer traditions. Indonesia only took from Hinduism what it needed or what inspired them, ignoring the rest.*

for numerologists: *Take note of all the momentous years in Indonesian history that end with 5: 1945, Independence; 1955, General Elections; 1965, bloody coup; 1975, the Jakarta Riots; 1985 ...?*

Jakarta, history: *Jakarta was built by a Dutch governor, Jan Pieterszon Coen, in 1619. Now this despot lies buried under the Jakarta City Museum on the site of an old Church. Agrarian Muslim Mataram armies attacked Dutch controlled Batavia in 1629, but since the Mataram troops couldn't be supplied by overland routes and their supply ships had been sunk by the Dutch, famines and exhaustion defeated them and they withdrew. Batavia then grew to be the center of Dutch power in the archipelago for over 300 years.*

Krakatoa volcano: *Blew in 1883, shooting debris 27 km into the air. The whole of the northern and lower portions were blown away leaving a submarine cavity 300 m deep and 41 sq km. Waves sent boats in the straits to the top of mountains. Volcanic ash and dust shot up so high that dust clouds could be seen in South America. Weeks of amazing sunsets all over the world. Tidal waves washed away all tall vegetation on all land facing the strait which remained denuded of vegetation and animal life and is still so in many parts. Two other volcanic islands are found in this area.*

The F-111 Mentality: *American warplanes were purchased by Australia to counter the threat of Indonesian expansionist policies in the early 1960's when the Indonesian Communist Party (PKI) was gaining more and more influence. Since 1914 the PKI had an active record of militance against foreign rule until banned in 1967. At one point it was the 3rd largest communist party in the world.*

Sriwijaya Empire: *A around 400 A.D. modern-day Palemba Strategically situated the entrance of the Sea beside one of the ern world's greatest tra routes for virtually years, this kingdom c ruled not only coa Sumatra but the w Malay peninsula, West mantan, and Java. An A historian once noted tha parrots could speak Ara Greek, Persian and Hir stani. Sriwijaya emplo the first economists a consultant to an establis government and had a liant collection of scho Here also in the 17th C tury were the first tang signs in the archipelago Mahayana Buddhism. great teacher Atisha Tibet arrived in Palemb in 1012-1022 to study C passion under Dharmab In the 13th Century empire finally broke up city states.*

Taman Sari *(Watercas Means 'Lovely Gardens 'Fragrant Gardens'. Buil the same court archi who constructed the ton. It was completed years later than the kra (1765). The story goes the architect who Taman Sari was execu to keep its secret passa secret. The park was u as a recreation area for sultan and his family. O nally it had gardens, se swimming pools, can pavilions, waterbe aquatic palaces, avenue mango and spice tre flower pots of exotic pla Wander about and try imagine. Now young b fish in the ponds formed these ruins, and kampu are scattered through the area among the m art galleries. It's informa to go through with a s dent guide, who'll cha you about Rp200 for a t*

waruga: *Pre-Christian stone tombs used up to the 19th C. as coffins by distinguished Minahasan families. Looks like a small Chinese temple and was made by scooping out sandstone. Saddle and pyramid-shaped roofs are adorned with human and animal figures in relief with widespread arms and legs. Corpses are buried inside the waruga in a sitting position together with household valuables; many have been plundered. See these sacrophagi around Lake Tandano sticking up out of ricefields. Also at Kema, Airmadidi, Likupang, Kokoleah, Wangurer, Batu, Tatelu, Matungkas, Maumbi, Tumaluntung, Kaasar, Kaima, Tanahwang, and many other sites.*

Irian Jaya: *3rd Century Bronze Age objects from Indochina have been found as far east as Lake Sentani on the northern coast of West New Guinea, but the civilization responsible has long since vanished. This island was first discovered by Portugese navigators in the 16th Century and named Papua which is early Malay for 'black, fuzzy hair'. Jan Carstenz sailed along the south coast of Irian Jaya in 1623, writing in his journal that he saw very high mountains which appeared covered in snow. When he returned to Europe he was laughed at. The whole of the interior was terra incognito until the 1930's when a Dutch expedition first penetrated and reported finding a chain of 'ice mountains'. They named the highest peak after Carstenz, the Dutch captain who first saw them.*

Singosari: *This shows best the of the medieval e builders. Origi-Singosari stood g a large complex e temples (like at aran), perhaps ne of nine. What usual about this e is the fact that aner sanctum is ed in the base the body of the e doesn't contain ual cella, thus it's a cellar temple. ne images origi-at Candi Singo-e now in Leyden, ed, with the ex-n of Guru ya in the south-che of the tem-ingosari has been ed clean of all its culpture.*

Pattae Cave: *East of Maros, South Celebes. A painting of a leaping boar with a spearhead through its heart is found on the ceiling of this cave. Discovered in 1950 by a Dutch professor, this magical artwork was never meant to be seen. There are also 7 hand stencils in the same cave. Hands were pressed against the wall with fingers spread wide apart and red ochre paint spat over them. Dates from the early Toalian culture of the Mesolithic era (10,000-2000 B.C.), the oldest evidence of art in Indonesia. Spreading through the islands by means of rafts and canoes, this modern man gathered wild plants and clams and probably followed the migration of large vertebrates into the archipelago.*

The Makassans: *For a period of 200 years, from the beginning of the 18th Century to around 1907, the Makassans visited Arnhem Land and the island of Groote Eylandt, northeastern Australia. Here they bartered for trepang (beche-de-mer) and introduced the Australian aboriginals to the metal axe, dugout canoes, the totem northwest monsoon wind-god, Bara; also, many words from the Makassan dialect were absorbed into the aboriginal languages of this region.*

HISTORY OF INDONESIA

women in Indonesian history: *Women have been portrayed hugely in Indonesian traditional literature. As in the biblical Adam and Eve fairytale, gods needed the help of women in Indonesian mythology. In genesis tales, Batak's Paragara, Borneo's Uniang, Bali's Ibu Pertiwi (Smitten Grandmother), and also in Aceh and Minahasa, it's usually a legendary woman who first gives mankind rice, though she often has to die first. She is sacrificed to give the earth fertility. From her death comes life. Even though Indonesian societies were polygamous in olden times as many are now, women held an important position in old Java. Once a land of female warriors and amazons, female dancers are seen with swords and shields on Prambanan basreliefs, and the Mataram kings once appeared in state surrounded only by a bodyguard of women. The Mataram line, in fact, might have shifted its palace and base of power from Central to East Java because the king's wife, Sindok, who ruled jointly with the king, feared an attack from the Sriwijaya Kingdom of South Sumatra. As recently as the 19th Century, Sultan Buwana of Yogya had a troupe of female calvary.*

the Moluccas Islands: *1000 islands clustered around a beautiful inland sea. Maluku was the focus of early trade in spices long before the Europeans started their legendary search which drove Columbus across the Atlantic and Magellan around the world. Here's where Sinbad the sailor found his pearl divers and cannibal kings. Luxurious plumes were exported from the Banda Islands to ornament the robes of oriental emperors. Captain Kidd sailed peacefully through Maluku on his last voyage before returning to American waters to be hanged. Children here are sometimes given humiliating names like 'Fart Odor' so that evil will not bother them.*

Francis Xavier: *Francis Xavier tore through the Moluccas in 1546 and with his usual Jesuit zeal hiked clear across the mountainous island of Ceram looking for souls to save. Ten years later there were 20,000 Catholics on the island.*

the Spice Islands: *Cloves were first mentioned in Chinese Han Period literature (206-220 A.D.) when officers of the court used to make their breath fragrant before the emperor. Traveling by way of the Malabar coast, India and Alexandria, cloves were used in the Roman Empire for cooking, temple services and funerals. During the 13th and 14th Centuries spices were taken overland from China by caravan, skirting the borders of Tibet, then through Burma and India to the Mediterranean where they became extremely costly. The Europeans were lured to search for their source and the race for the Spice Islands was on. This search resulted in the discovery of the Cape of Good Hope by Diaz and of America by Columbus. Magellan's crews took on a load of cloves here on Ambon at 3¢ per 28 grams to help pay the cash expenses of their past years of suffering, starvation and death. Two ships went on to Seville, Spain; this first shipment of cloves to Europe made a profit of 2500%.*

Garebeg Poso: Takes place close to Idul Fitri, the big Islamic feast day that closes the fasting month *Ramadan*. On the eve of Garebeg Poso, parades of white-robed children, each carrying a burning torch, file through the streets of Yogya on their way to Mesjid Agung. Later on, fireworks and skyrockets. At 8 am next day the climax of this festival is the parade from the sultan's palace to Mesjid Agung.

Siraman (Bathing Ceremony): This cleansing of the *pusakas* (royal heirlooms) takes place once a year. Spears, flags, sacred gold *gamelan,* royal armory, banners and *kris* of the sultan's ancestors are washed and blessed. The water used is believed to have supernatural powers. Not open to the general public. Royal golden coaches inside the *kraton* are cleaned, the water enthusiastically drunk by commoners as a panacea afterwards. Large vases of holy water at Imogiri are emptied, cleansed and refilled. These last two ceremonies are open to the public.

Galungan: The local Balinese community celebrates this Hindu festival every 210 days. The formal ceremony is at the Balinese temple at Magelang, 42 km N.W. of Yogya. Several days later there's Balinese dancing at its best in Yogya.

Sendangsano Pilgrimmage: During May a religious ceremony is obsreved by the Catholic devotees at Sendangsano, 32 km N.W. of Yogya. A statue of the Virgin Mary lies in a cave on the slopes of the Menorah mountain range. Sendangsano is the Javanese Lourdes; the well water here is considered holy. On the way you pass through Boro, a Catholic village where people have names like Josuf, Petrus, Maria, etc.

THE ARTS

batik courses: *Batik* is a great deal more technical than imagined and without the technique artistic development is impossible. Courses average about Rp5-7000 per week including materials, but not meals and accommodation. So you don't become a *batik* illiterate, take a *batik* course in which you learn about the dyeing. Most tourists who study *batik* in Yogya are quite satisfied with the low-standard courses offered because they are able to actually produce something – a moon rising over ricefields, a peasant's hut cane stalks, a soaring Garuda – crap like that. Down in the Watercastle (Taman Sari) area one-week courses are offered for Rp5000. These are generally rip-off because the artists are too young and inexperienced, it's a village of apprentices. For beginners, Tops, right around the corner from Superman's, teaches *batik*

for only Rp350 per day. Can't get any cheaper. Opens at 8:30 am. Learn the very basic skills, see how you like it, then take a more expensive and intensive study course with a skilled artisan and really get into it. At Tops you listen to Indonesian yippy music, lots of air, good lighting. Ask questions constantly. The most thorough-going course with the best facilities would have to be Balai Penelitian Batik Kerayinan (The Batik Research Center), Jl. Kusumanegara 2. They offer one month courses, 6 days a week, 9-12 pm, a maximum of 3 persons, which costs Rp25,000 per person. The emphasis at B.P.B.K. is more on the industrial approach, experimenting with new dyes and methods of wax application, etc. At least visit this large institute to gain a familiarity before taking a course elsewhere. Open until 2 pm. It has a permanent exhibition of *batik* which amounts to a history and introduction to *batik*-making. The processes involved can be seen, both hand-painted and cap-printed *batik*. Buy *batiks,* stamps, waxes, and color chart booklets showing all the possible colors and how to mix them. *Buku Penuntun Batik,* Rp700. *Motief Batik* (Batik Design), Rp500. *Batik Manual,* Rp2250 is a thick book of *batik* specimens and photos of the processes. Beware of courses taught by the 'world masters'. Students are supposed to get a charge out of studying under such prestige names, but you learn nil. Banjar Bagong's course, run by the dance choreographer Bagong Kussudiardjo, Jl. Laksamana, costs Rp6000 plus Rp1200 per day for bed and breakfast. But the teacher doesn't teach and employs boys who don't speak English to teach you. For the same reason Kurswadji's course, Kadipaten (Mangkubumen) 1/342, is poor at Rp7500 per week; he puts his 'assistants' on you and you don't learn a thing unless you speak Indonesian. Bambang Oetero in Babadan village gives courses but it depends on his schedule. This acclaimed modern *batik* designer charges Rp5000 per week. Courses run for one month, 9 am-3 pm, 6 days a week. He doesn't take any more than 6 students at a time and he really teaches you. Born in 1936, he's exhibited all over the world from Rhodesia to Ohio. He was chief designer for the Government Batik Research Center for 14 years. Bambang sticks to classical themes and uses classical colors, a symbolic style. He lives in a quiet Javanese *kampung* out of town, an ideal work environment. Hadjir, an older teacher, uses a big blackboard to instruct. He really goes into detail, mixing dyes, etc. Plays nice music. Join his intensive course at Gapura Batik, Taman Kraton Kp. III/1777; begins at 2 pm, lasts 7-10 days.

batik factories and shops: The really fine *batik* you can't buy in the markets. In *batik* factories, watch families and artisans at work plus visit showrooms where you can buy materials. Most close at around 8 pm. Just as important as getting *batik* cheap is being able to trust your agent, that it is what he or she says it is. There's a big difference in quality of *batik tulis;* not every artist who takes it up can do it well. There are 3 qualities of *batik* cloth; given here with comparative prices: *biru,* Rp 1000; *prima,* Rp 1600; *primisima,* Rp2200. **Jl. Tirtodipuan:** South of the Kraton. There are over 25 *batik* factories alone on this street. For Chinese-style *batik,* try Plentong, Jl. Tirtodipuran 28. On the same street is Mr. Lod E.A. — Philosopher, Artist, Your Friend'; open 10-1, 5-6, where you can see the *batik* process. Visit also Batik Winotosastro, Jl. Tirtodipuran 34. **Batik Sofi:** Past Hotel Ambarrukmo towards Solo, take a left up Kledokan in Kec. Depok (Slemon). She's an agent for *batik* materials from all over Indonesia, but specializes in the Pekalongan style. Some really creative clothing. *Batik tulis* for Rp9-13,000, for which many other shops ask Rp25,000. **Terang Bulan:** This is Yogya's *batik* supermarket, on Jl. Jen. A. Yani 76 (exactly opposite Happy's Restaurant). This shop is especially rewarding if you don't know anything about *batik.* Has a really fine selection from Rp650 *sarungs* to Rp35,000 *pekalongans.* All kinds of material at fixed honest prices. Gives you an idea of what you should be paying. Compare the different prices for *cap* and *batik tulis* work. Browse and learn. Terang Bulan also sells fine locally-made *lurik batik* material for Rp860 for 2½ m and Rp1050 for 3 m; comes also in green, beige and orange; when *lurik* is banded it's very striking.

galleries: Look around before you buy. *Batik* paintings, cheaper than oils, run US$10-200. It's worth paying a bit more if it helps to improve the art. Oil paintings cost US$50-1000. Visit the dynamic young Sumatran artist, Amri Yahay, Jl. Gampingan 67. In Babadan, Bambang Oetero's pieces run US$25-300. Seni Soto Art Gallery is one of the biggest in Yogya. Saptohudojo Art Gallery, Jl. Sala, for aluminum sculpture collages. Arjoyo Art Gallery, Jl. Gampingan (near the art academy) for *batik* wall hangings. The Sumatran artist, Batara Lubis, Sentul Rejo 1, uses Indonesian farm life and traditional culture as themes. Affandi, Indonesia's best known contemporary artist, was born in 1908 in Cirebon. He lives in an airy bizaare studio house on Jl. Solo 167 just before the river. See his bright yellow GTO Galiant parked out front. Meet him possibly late in the afternoon. Vital, genial old man. When the Japanese asked him to paint a poster to help recruit more Javanese forced labor for Burma, he submitted a canvas showing starving men slaving in a hellhole jungle. Try to see his private collection. Amazing self-portraits from the 30's and 40's. View his paintings best from a distance because he's farsighted. Affandi doesn't have a studio but finishes his paintings on the spot, most of them within 30 minutes to an hour. Affandi's daughter, Kartika, has a gallery specializing in Irian Jaya artifacts further down Jl. Solo towards the city.

Taman Sari (The Watercastle): A funky part of town where young artists scrape and try to survive

panakawans: *Dwarves, albinos, and grotesquely deformed persons have always been regarded as special wards of the* kraton-*palaces even up until the 1930's. Called* polowijo *(weeds), they used to parade in the retinue of the sultan and make happy comical attendants, messengers, court curiosities. In wayang plays these clowns are mythological beings and are the most revered and loved of all* wayang *characters. Given the status of servants, they are actually very powerful. Panakawans take pity and even defy the gods because they are only gods, and generally bring the audience down to earth with their sense of humor. Some say they represent the humble, wise, miserable, strong villagers of Java's prehistory*

blencong (9): On Bali, red, is the white screen (kelir, 5), bordered by red, is the visible world, illuminated by the blencong, an oil lamp which hangs above and a little forward of the dalang's head behind the screen to flicker and create a livlier and warmer atmosphere than the cold glare of an electric bulb, bringing to life the shadows on the other side. It is The Lamp of Life, The Sun. Ki Dalang is often protected from the heat of this lamp by a sheet of iron that's attached to it, reflecting the light towards the screen.

WAYANG KULIT

Various devices are used in wayang kulit, not only for the audience's entertainment and instruction, but also for cueing the musicians. The props also represent different dimensions of reality. The light which projects the puppet shadows onto the screen represents eternal life, the shadows themselves are the peoples' souls, while the puppets are their bodies. The dalang (1), during the performance, is actually symbolic of God, the 'interpreter of the universe'. In fact, god is sometimes nicknamed, 'The Supreme Dalang'.

gamelan: the orchestra which accompanies the play. Its motives and melodies are fixed in accordance with the various persons and events projected on the screen. The gamelan accentuates the moods, animates the drama, carries the imagery across. Music represents the harmony and mutual relationship of everything that occurs in the world.

kotak (4): A chest in which the puppets are kept and transported. During a performance it is almost empty and sits to the dalang's left within reach of his right foot. With a wooden mallet he knocks upon this as a warning at dramatic moments and to also signal his musicians changes in melodies or rhythms. A kotak could also mean a set of wayang puppets.

gunungan (7): On Bali, Babad, or The Story. Consisting of a peaked, triangular or pentagonal plate of complicated openwork design which is set before the screen, this is the dalang's only stage prop, serving as a divider between scenes. This same motif was used to separate scenes on Borobudur as well. The gunungan is solemnly removed by the dalang at the beginning of the wayang ceremony. At the end of each scene the placement of the gunungan is different. Before midnight its apex is turned to the left, at midnight it points straight up, and after midnight it inclines to the right. These different positions represent the way man turns from the sensual and material pleasures of life towards spiritual values. The gunungan, during the performance itself, could represent a mountain, a river, a forest, a palace, a gateway to a palace or a temple, a valley, the earth, clouds, a tempest, fire, wind or water, an ocean. If it stands still, it indicates the beginning or the end.

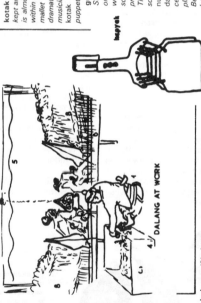

wayang

DALANG AT WORK

the puppets: The puppets are arranged in an orderly fashion at both edges of the screen at the beginning of the play. Because the puppets represent magic powers, the dalang usually opens a play with offerings of rice, flowers, water and incense, reciting prayers and chants. Sheaves of rice are traditionally hung at each end of the screen. Even today, wayang kulit is frequently performed to make it rain or to bring good luck at weddings. The reason for all the elaborate detail on the puppets is because the men sat at one time on the same side of the screen as the dalang and could enjoy the full splendour of the puppets' colors, while the women, who sat in front, could only see their shadows projected on the screen.

kebyak (2): A bundle of metal plates suspended from the wall of the wooden puppet box (kotak, 4). The dalang hits them with a wooden knob (cempala) inserted between the toes of his right foot, to make a thunderous clashing noise. The sharp raps of the cempala are used to underscore the dramatic action, especially when a battle is raging. Sometimes the whole stage just dissolves in chaos, portentous storms, clashing symbols, the cosmic order of nature upset.

dodogan (3): A percussion instrument which the dalang beats during the whole performance to produce a single rhythmical motive (called in musicians' slang: derogdog).

gedebog (6): The banana trunk into which the dalang sticks his puppets whenever they have no role to fulfill in the play. The gedebog stands for the surface of the earth.

in an area of tumble-down dustfilled alleys, broken pathways and bridges, trees sprouting from windows. They make multiple copies of their best sellers and rip off more renowned artists' ideas. But some of their paintings show startling effects and are cheap. Taman Sari was once a pleasure park built in feudal splendor for the sultan and his family at his behest in 1758. Like the Hanging Gardens of Babylon, it once had lighted underwater corridors, underground mosques, meditation platforms in lily ponds, *gamelan* towers and galleries for dancing, all in Spanish architecture. Princesses bathed in flower-strewn pools, streams flowed above covered passageways and boats drifted in man-made lakes. Now wheeling, squealing, shitting bats have it. Much of the ruins are being renovated at present, the swimming pools and crumbling walls rebuilt and many of the gates have been replastered. It's now a renewed ruin, built along the old lines, the life and drama going out of the place. Shops selling *batik* materials here are being updated as well, some of them even look a bit classy. **ASRI** (School of Fine Arts): On Jl. Gampingan. Sculpture, painting, graphics, commercial and industrial arts, art education, primitive, symbolic and decorative paintings (even nude drawing classes) are all taught here. ASRI is re-discovering the lost Javanese art of stone sculpture. A big art carnival is held in the 2nd half of January each year and a permanent exhibition of paintings is always on sale. Good honest young art; into amazing things.

puppet theatre performances: At Sasono Hinggil, Alun2 Kidul, *wayang kulit* is staged the second Sat. of each month, 8 pm-5 am, Rp100. At Agastyua Art Institute, off Jl. Bantul about 3 km from the city in Gedong Kiwo village, shadow play performances take place every day except Sat. from 3-5 pm. Sometimes the Horse Dance (Kuda Kepang) is held in the same place. Buy tickets beforehand, Rp3-400. In Sentolo, 20 km west of Yogya, the famous *dalang* Pak Widi can be hired out for his *wayang golek* performances, Rp15,000. See a *dalang* trained? Habiranda Dalang School, Gedung Kiwa Med. 111/221 at the Pracimisno (near the *kraton*); nightly at 7 pm, except Sunday; also short *wayang kulit* performances on Mon.-Fri., 3-5 pm, and on Sat. *wayang golek* at the same time.

dance and drama: Be wary of some dance teachers. They could ask for money in advance (Rp17,000 or more), then set up a hassel with you (like they want to sleep with you), then there's a confrontation whereby you don't get your money back. Even the more renowned teachers are known to pull this. A superb dancer, Bagong Kussudiardjo, Jl. Laksamana, teaches his own interpretation of modern jazz ballet. Rehearsals 4-8 pm except Friday. Vishnu Wardhana, Jl. Suryodiningratan 13, teaches a whole range of dance styles, from traditional Indonesian to modern improvisational. Krido Mardawa, sultan's palace, for classical *Serimpi* and *Bedaya* in the Yogya and Solo styles; rehearsals every Sun. 10 am-2 pm. Arena Budaya, Jl. Suryodiningratan, also welcomes visitors. There are many dance companies. Ask at the tourist office about those operating, times and addresses. ASDRAFI, near the Watercastle, Jl. Sompilan 12, for drama study and cinematography. Each Sat. at 9 am you can see performances of the horse trance dance (Kuda Kepang) near Candi Sewu in Prambanan village; the whole bit: eating glass and hay, slurping water from a pail. Sometimes it takes the leader two hours to bring the dancers out of trance. At Krido Beksa Wirama School, Jl. K.H. Wakhid Hasyim, classes are packed. Watch old Java come alive in the story of *Ken Angrok,* episodes from the *Ramayana,* mask plays. Rehearsals are from 8-9 pm on Sunday on the Tejakusman *pendopo.* Classical Javanese dancing was the exclusive prerogative of the courts until the Krido Beksa Wirama school opened in 1918 outside the walls of the *kraton.* At the THR each night, 9 pm to midnight, view the theatre of the people; *wayang orang, Ketoprak, kroncang* bands, satirical *Ludruk* comedies in which men dress up as women. Tickets cost between Rp75-125 depending upon whether you stand or sit. Go after dark. Loudspeakers blast out hit tunes. Saturday nights are wild.

Ramayana Ballet: These DeMille-like spectacles take place on the enormous stone stage of the Lorojonggrang open-air theatre near Prambanan Temple complex on the four successive full-moonlit nights in each month of the dry season June to October. This 6-episode contemporary ballet is based on traditional *wayang orang* dancing of the classical Javanese theatre. Each is a modernization and dramatization of episodes from an Indian epic poem. The Prambanan Temple panels are, in effect, re-enacted live. The Shiva temple serves as the floodlit backdrop. Taking part are two entire *gamelans,* 60 singers, hundreds of beautifully and grotesquely costumed dancers, singers and musicians; with monkey armies, strutting menacing *rawanas,* acrobatic miracles, giant kings on stilts, clashing battles, *real* fire. Bring cushions or a sleeping bag to soften hard stone seats. Nitour Travel, Jl. Malioboro 16; Hotel Garuda, Hotel Ambarrukmo on JL. Solo, plus many other agents charge Rp2000 and up for transport and tickets for this performance. But it's cheaper to take the local bus yourself to Prambanan village, Rp75. The most expensive seats are in the center (Rp1250), while the cheaper ones are to the sides (Rp150). Buy the next cheapest seats for Rp300. The second night in the four-part series is the most spectacular: The Invasion of Alengka and the Burning of the White Ape's Tail. The performance lasts from 7-9 pm.

museums: Museum Angkatan Darat (The Army Museum), Jl. Bintaran Wetan, in the southern part of the city near the Biology Museum. Open mornings, closed on Fridays. Records the Indonesian revolution: documents, historical articles, homemade weapons, uniforms, equipment from the 1945-49 struggle. Museum Biologi, Jl. Sultan Agung 22, has a collection of plants and animals from the entire archipelago. **Museum Sonobudoyo:** Open Tues., Wed., and Thurs. 8-1; Fri., Sat., and Sun. 8-12. Built in the classical style. A first rate collection of Javanese, Madurese and Balinese arts and crafts. The most intriguing room is the one devoted to Bali. Big library. Archaeological objects such as an 18 carat gold Buddah and

---

DANCING AND GAMELAN VENUES

K.H.P. Krida Mardawa (Classical Dancing)
place : Bangsal Kasatryan Kraton Yogyakarta
day : Sunday
time : 10:00-2 pm

K.H.P. Krida Mardawa (Gamelan)
place : Bangsal Kasatryan Kraton Yogyakarta
day : Monday and Wednesday
time : 10:00-12 pm

Krida Beksa Wirama (Classical Dancing)
place : Dalem Tejokusuman, Jl. K.H. Wakhid Hasyim
day : Sunday
time : 8-9 pm

Siswa Among Beksa (Classical Dancing)
place : Dalem Poerwodiningratan, Kadipaten Kidul 46
day : Friday
time : 8-10 pm

Mardawa Budaya (Classical Dancing)
place : Dalem Pujokusuman, Jl. Brig. Jen. Katamso 45
day : Thursday and Sunday
time : 5-9 pm

Bagong Kussudihardjo (Contemporary Classical Dance)
place : Singosaren Utara, Jl. Wates 9. Tel. 2982
day : Monday : student group, *putra campuran* (mixed female)
       Saturday: student group, *putri* S.D. (male)
       Thursday and Sunday: student group, *putri* S.M.P. (male)
time : 4-6 pm
day : Tuesday: professional group, *putra* and *putri* (male and female)
     : 6-8 pm

Habiranda (Dalang training)
place : Pracimasono, Alun2 Utara
day : every night except Thursday and Sunday
time : 7-10 pm

another Buddah with gold lips. Best exhibits are *wayang golek* puppets, woodcarvings including marvelous wood sculptural screens and figures, two very old *gamelans*, models of *prahus*, a renowned collection of the Reni *wayang topeng* masks from Malang; there are also coins, instruments, ancient Chinese spearheads, Bronze Age Hindu household relics. The weapons room has many varieties of *kris*. Give a contribution when you enter (Rp50). **Monumen Diponegoro:** 4 km west of Yogya at Tegalrejo. Hire a bicycle to get out there, 10 minutes ride from town. Or round trip by *becak*, Rp500 return. This museum was built to honor Prince Diponegoro (1785-1855) who led partisans during the Java War (1825-30). His *krises* are hung with flowers in glass cases, there are photos of his other sacred possessions, and a big commemorative *pendopo*. See the hole through which Dionegoro escaped to go into hiding in his retreat at Gua Selarong, 8 km S.E. of Yogya. After 5 years of bloody war he was at last cunningly tricked into negotiations and arrested, then sent into exile in South Celebes for his remaining 25 years. At Magelang, 42 km from Yogya, visit the room where Diponegoro was captured; see his belongings, and the chair scratched by his nails as he tried to control his fury. Stay at Wisma Sosial at Matesah.

mosques and churches: Best to visit mosques during non-praying time between sunrise and noon. Dress straight. 200 year old Mesjid Agung on the western side of the Alun2 Lor where the *kraton's* royal *gamelan* are kept during *Sekaten* week and where the famous *Gunungan* Procession ends up, held only 3 times a year. Mesjid Soko Tunggal, in Taman Sari and built in the *kraton* pavilion-style, has stories from the *Koran* carved on its pillars. Hear ethereal beautiful Batak hymnsinging at Huria Kristen Batak Protestant Church, Nyoman Oka 22, Kota Baru, early Sun. mornings. Visit the Indonesian-style Catholic mass in the oldest church in Yogya, St. Francis Xavier, Jl. P. Senopati near the main P.O.; masses are held 5:30 pm on Sat. and all day long on Sunday.

Gadjah Mada University: In the northern part of the city. Merapi volcano smokes behind the uni complex. The largest in Indonesia with 17,000 students. Poetry readings amongst the students are very popular, although sometimes interrupted by the army and poets arrested. Don't hire a jeep from the Department of Economics, their interest rates are the highest in town. Opened in 1949 with a total student body of 463, many part-time guerilla fighters among them. Its first medical faculty was set up on the *pendopos* of the Crown Prince's palace, the *gamelan* store was turned into a dispensary. At Jl. Karangwuni 16, near the uni, an artists' colony

offers cottage accommodation; bed and breakfast, 3 to a room, Rp500. At the beginning of the university year, browbeating of junior students by seniors is quite brutal and out of perhaps 2000 students who take part 50 or 60 are admitted to the hospital. Students from the lower classes receive the most abuse, it's their ticket-of-passage to the elite class of students. An informal place to meet students is Colombo Swimming pool, off Jl. Demangan, Mon.-Wed., Rp150, Sundays Rp200, closed Thurs. and Fri. and in the evenings.

crafts and markets: Tan Jam An, Jl. A.A. Sangaji (near Tugu Monument); and Tjokrosuharto, Jl. Panembahan 58, are silverware shops in the city center. Both do modern settings for semi-precious and precious stones. Old Chinese *kebayas* at Busana Dewi, Jl. Dr. Sumtomo 9/B, and perhaps cheaper from the sidewalk sellers in front of Malioboro Restaurant and along Malioboro Street; Rp6-8000 for the finer ones. Have fine embroidery work done on pants, shirts, Rp300-500, at some clothing shops. The best *Kuda Kepang* (flat hobbyhorses made from plaited bamboo) are made near Candi Sewu in the Prambanan Temple complex. For stone sculpture visit Prumpung village, about 25 km from Magelang; statues, temple deities, gate reliefs, lawn decorations. Also noted for stonecarving is Muntilan. The leatherwork of Yogya is unreal; you seldom see leather as cheap as this. Fully embossed suitcases, Rp6-8000; roomy duffelbags, Rp8-9000; shoulder bags, Rp2500-3000. Make sure that the leather is thick and that you treat it after you buy it. Sometimes the embossing work is shithouse and cardboard backing is used. Watch carefully how buckles are fastened, they tend to break off first. In Indonesia you can still sit down with a craftsman and decide together on a design, what hide will be used, reinforced stitching if any, etc. - it's a creative process between the two of you. Try Pomo Wahono's Leather Factory, Jl. Suhartono 7 (near Bethesda Hospital), Rp150 round trip from Colombo Restaurant by *becak*. Besides bags and purses, you can have a pair of high boots made to order here for around US$45 that would cost you US$150 in Italy. On the sidewalks of Malioboro are leather lampshades with *wayang* characters stenciled out, very cheerful looking, glinting with color from the light behind it; starting price Rp2000. High quality *kulit* puppets are made at Moelijosoehardjo's, Jl. Taman Sari 37/B. For the most part the *wayang kulit* puppets of Yogya are made from goats' skin, not buffalo hide. *Wayang golek* are made at Pak Warno's on Bantul Road, 8 km south of Yogya. At Pasar Beringharjo, off the southern end of Malioboro, one km of market stalls swarming with brazen rats and selling everything from macrame, mutton and mangoes. Leathergoods are for sale in front of the market at reasonable prices. **Kasongan:** A potters' village one hour's busride from Yogya. Pots are fired with blazing straw, then carried 16 km to market. Well known for their brightly painted children's moneyboxes made to look like roosters, lions, elephants, Garudas.

miscellaneous: Ride a bike or take an *andong*, Rp300, out to Gembira Loka Zoo, a nicely landscaped zoological and botanical gardens 4 km east of Yogya in a valley by a river; Rp75 entrance. Two giant Komodo lizards (who don't move a muscle), a vicious Mandril monkey (good collection of monkeys), a legendary (smart) orangutan, and a 5 legged cow are the main features. On Sundays and holidays the animals get to see the most people. Outside the zoo are cheap *warungs; nasi rames* only Rp50. Pasar Ngasem (Bird Market) north of Taman Sari has orioles, parrots, roosters, and singing turtle doves (perkutut) in 9 m high ornamental cages; dogs and kittens are also for sale as food. There's a *warung* (the big one) serving outstanding Indonesian food in this market. The tourist office is halfway down Jl. Malioboro towards the P.O., take a left into the complex of government buildings known as Ketatihan, Danurejan. For bachelors, a little ways outside of Yogya is Buntilan village. The *imigrasi* office is near the airport, Rp40 on the Solo bus. Easy-going compared with hardass Denpasar (Bali) office; extensions are Rp3000. It's no good saying that you're studying *batik* anymore; too often tourists pretend, and the Indonesians are afraid that too many students will take the art out of the country. On holidays change money at Mutiara Hotel, cash or cheques. Bank Bumi Daya is more reputable than corrupt Bank Negara Indonesia. Old women give massages (Rp3-500) on the lane off Jl. Sostrowijayan; some claim more gratifying than on Bali.

from Yogya by local buses and Colts:

The bus station is near the THR. No buses run in the city itself, but they leave all day long (5 am-6 pm, every 10-15 minutes) for all the towns in the immediate area: Magelang, Rp150; Muntilan, Rp100; Kreteg, Rp75; Imogiri, Rp50; Klaten, Rp100; Wates, Rp150; Semarang, Rp350; Solo, Rp200 (or catch a Colt in front of the bus stn.); Kaliurang, Rp100 (or take a Colt from Gedung Serba Shopping Center south of Pasar Beringharjo); Kartosuro, Rp175; Samas, Rp75 (or *bemo* from Serba Guna); Prambanan, Rp75 (or get a Colt in front of the bus stn.). Express buses to Surabaya leave fairly regularly.

from Yogya by long-distance bus:

Many night-bus companies, located mainly around the train station. Check them all out for cheaper fares and better buses. Mutiara Express, Jl. Kyai Mojo 8, for night buses to Surabaya, Rp1300; departs 9 pm, arrives 4 am. Kembang Express, Jl. Diponegoro 16, Rp1400 to Surabaya, leaves at 8:45 pm, arrives at 5 am. Damri also has buses to Surabaya, Rp1300; departs 8 pm, arrives 5 am. **to Bali:** Kembang Express has buses leaving at 8:45 pm. Legowo, Jl. Diponegoro 47; and Gita Bali, Jl. Sosrowijayan 31, both cost Rp3000. Gita Bali is one of the best companies; you get reserved seats, there are no standing passengers, and they really move along. Their buses leave Yogya at 7 pm and arrive in Denpasar at 3 am (20 hours). Gita Bali's other fares, to: Probolinggo (Mt. Bromo), Rp1900; Surabaya, Rp1350. **to Jakarta:** Muncul Express, Jl. Diponegoro 16, leaves at 4 pm, arrives 6 am; Remaja Express, Jl. Mangkubumi (Rp2500 with a snack) leaves at 3:30, arrives 6 am. Barankarya, Rp2000, leaves 3 pm, arrives 6 am - one of the best outfits for this run. Damri Express, Jl. Mangkubumi 8-10, also has cheap buses to Jakarta for Rp2000, departs 4 pm, arrives 4 am. Unbearably crowded. Buy tickets at least one day before. **others:** Pemuda Express is on the corner of Jl. Jen. Sudirman and Jl. Mas Sangaji; Elteha minibus Company, is at Jl. Perwalian 7.

trains from Yogya:

The RR station is right in the middle of town just off Jl. Malioboro. Trains to West Java are generally bad and more expensive than buses, but trains to East Java are cleaner, faster and less expensive than buses. **to Surabaya:** A train leaves 12:53 am, 3rd class only, Rp1050, 6 hours. The Bima leaves 2:09 am, Rp8100 1st class, Rp6600 2nd class. Mutiara leaves 3:17 pm, Rp3300 1st class. Rp2500 2nd class, Rp1650 3rd class. Also the Purbaya to Surabaya, leaves at 11:10 am, 3rd class only, Rp725. Another day express departs at 2:32 pm, Rp1150, 3rd class seats only. **to Jakarta:** 12 hours by train. Best to catch the late train to Jakarta because you get there early in the morning. The Bima departs 9:44 pm, Rp8100 first class, Rp6600 for 2nd class. The Senja train leaves Yogya at 6 pm, Rp3100 for 1st class, Rp2600 for 2nd class, Rp1650 for 3rd class. The Gayabaru train leaves 8:06, 3rd class only, Rp1550 (can get student discount). **to Tasikmalaya:** Take the Mutiara, Rp1650 for 3rd class; the 'Day Express' costs Rp1150. Or the 'Fast Train', Rp625. **to Bandung:** The Mutiara leaves at 10:44 pm, Rp3300 for 1st class, Rp2600 for 2nd class, Rp1650 for 3rd class; takes 10 hours. An express train also leaves for Bandung at 11:30 am, Rp1150 for 3rd class only. Another train leaves at 7:50 am, Rp825 for 3rd class only; very crowded. **Note:** There's a 25% discount for students on trains, but not for the more expensive trains like the Bima, Senja or the Mutiara.

For the Bima, buy your ticket 2-3 days before departure. During holidays buy Bima train tickets one week before. For the Senja (dusk) trains, buy your ticket at 9 am on the same day it departs. Mutiara train tickets are sold only one hour before departure. **to Bali:** Cheapest is to do it step by step. Take train to Surabaya, then train to Banyuwangi, minibus to ferry, ferry (Rp100), then hitch to Denpasar.

Kota Gede: Pronounced 'Gee-day'. 5 km S.E. of Yogya's city center. Peddle the back way via the zoo down Jl. Gembira Loka through the countryside. Kota Gede was once the capital of the old Mataram Kingdom. Many royal personalities are entombed in Makam Senopati under ornamental parasols. Take the first left after the market beyond Tom's Silver and enter the mossy burial ground (Rp100) and ancient mosque. Must wear conservative dress. Don't go to the graveyard any other day but on Fri., 1:30-4 pm when there's activity; otherwise there's not much to see, just turtles in a dirty pool. Give a donation. **silver-working:** Many busy clanging silverware shops here. In this small village 25 tons of silver are consumed annually. You're free to wander around through big workrooms full of men and boys hammering on anvils, filing, polishing, heating and soldering on strips of bright silver, using the simplest of handtools. Buy embossed hand-heaten and chased bowls, exquisitely designed miniature butterflies and flowers, *sirih* containers, repousse work, some modern jewelry, filigree work, etc. Silversmiths use fine viscid ductile ash from volcanic eruptions in their moulds. Most of the silver shops have much the same stock, they seldom deviate from the sure sellers. At Tom's Silver (everybody knows where it's at), they bargain only if you buy wholesale. Pay anything from Rp600 for a filigree silver ring up to Rp1,300,000 for a complete silver dinner service for 12. If you make enough purchases they might even lay a 'Tom's Silver' T-shirt on you. SH800, Jl. Kartanegara 65, is a bit cheaper than Tom's Silver. Kresna Arts, just past the *sekolah desa,* specializes in tortoise shell.

Imogiri: A cemetary for the royal houses of Yogya and Solo 20 km south of Yogya 30 minutes busride, Rp50. Open to the public Mon. Thurs. 10 am-1 pm, Fri. 1:30-4 pm, Rp100 entrance. A pilgrimage place of ancestor worship. Do as the Javanese do. Hire a *kemban* for women and a *kain batik* for men (Rp50), or bring your own. Climb barefoot up the 345 warm stone steps of a great rising sundappled staircase to the burial ground on the top. Looks like a ladder leaning up against the sky. Incense bowls burn, there's praying, chanting, flower petals strewn everywhere. Some graves are 400

years old. To the left are the sultans of Solo, to the right the sultans of Yogya. In the center the Mataram kings. Crawl into Sultan Agung's tomb and pay your obeisance, make a wish. From the highest point through palm fronds Mt. Merapi is visible to the north, plus a fantastic view over the Indian Ocean 15 km away.

Mt. Merapi (Fire Mountain): One of the most destructive volcanoes in the world, it erupts about once every 5½ years. Merapi needs 6 volcanologists' posts high on its slopes to keep an eye on it. When it blew in 1006, it covered Borobudur 48 km away and devastated the land around the monument to such an extent that it remained uninhabited for generations. Since that year, volcanoes in Indonesia (two volcanic belts spread over a total length of 5500 km) have killed over 150,000 people. Ruling princes of Central Java today throw precious silk textiles into Merapi's crater because it's believed that high volcanoes have a life and spirit of their own. When Merapi erupts, tigers are sometimes driven down into the lower slopes. During its hot-lava stage, Yogya's normally tranquil river is turned into a cocoa-colored torrent. **getting there:** Climb Merapi safest from its eastern side. From Yogya take a bus to Kartosuro, then change to Boyolali, Rp175. Then take an *oplet* to Selo where a guide for the climb can be hired at Pos Pengawasan for about Rp1200-1500. On its slopes there are many mountain forest tracks. The summit, usually with a cloud cutting through it, is 2911 m high, a 7 hour climb. The very steep climb takes you through a countryside of lantana flowers and misty ridges, then up through rasberry country to the barren peak. Experience this crater at night with its rivulets of orange-red molten lava, sparks spilling over the rim, black acrid smoke, enormous clouds of steam. Bring a sleeping bag.

Kaliurang: A mountain resort 25 km north of Yogya 900 m high on Mt. Merapi's southern slope. Get bus near Yogya's G.P.O., Rp100. Go up during the week, they've got a different price list during the weekends. Pick a cloudless day. **stay:** Tell the driver you want to get off at Hotel Garuda, most of the other hotels are Rp1000 and up. As you go up the hill see the big sign, then walk 400 m in from the road. Hotel Garuda is spotlessly clean, Rp500 double; bargain if they don't give you this rate. Get room number 2 with the French windows so you can sit in your hotel room and watch the volcano spit fire. Honking geese wake you in the mornings. In back of Hotel Garuda there's a swimming pool and a track that leads up to Merapi, a shorter but harder climb than the most trodden path. **eat:** Food is expensive compared to Yogya, Rp200 for a square meal. Buy eggs, bread, and make sandwiches. Bananas are cheap, Rp3 each. Go to the big grocery store down the road; fried rice, Rp150.

vicinity of Kaliurang: There are 3 tracks to choose from, one to a waterfall 100 m away, another for bushwalking, and the other to the volcano. The beginning of the path up the mountain is at the end of the road where the bus stops. Pay Rp50 to get through the gate; you can't lose your way up to the post, a climb of only two hours. Merapi's smoking crater can be seen from a telescope near the seismographic station, 45 minutes

walk or 2 km from the crater. Bring food up the mountain if you plan to spend the night. The *warung* near the top sells drinks and biscuits. Stay at the volcanologists' post, an unforgettable night. Just sleep on the floor. Friendly guys. See their photos of the last big 1954 eruption.

PARANGTRITIS

28 km south of Yogya on the Indian Ocean. Take bus to Kreteg, Rp75. Wade to the other side of the river and take an andong, or *ride* on the back of a motorcycle for Rp100. Then walk the remaining 3

rice: *In most of Indonesia, life revolves around rice. Four out of 5 Indonesians work ricefields. Religious festivals and marriages are scheduled to fit in with planting and harvesting. Rice is often cut with tiny hidden knives so that the spirits in the fields won't be offended. Government employees are paid partly in rice and the price of rice is known as the 'Mother Price'—it affects prices of all other commodities. From rice-stems come paintbrushes, paper, baskets, mats, Rice is so important that the language has 3 words for it: when it's growing it's called* padi, *when the grains are re-moved from the stalk it's called* beras, *and when it's been cooked it is* nasi. *The word* nasi *is often used as a synonym for food in general. Just a mound of cold boiled rice with chili peppers and a little fish is enough to keep most Indonesians going The rigid organization, labor, and control required of* sawah *(wet rice) cultivation has given rise to a long tradition of despotic rule in Asia, with kingships having absolute power over the waters, the earth, the crops, the life and death of the people.*

km into the village. Or rent a bicycle in Yogya and ride it down all the way. In the wet season you must take a small ferry across the river, Rp50. Parangtritis is the place if you want to get away from Yogya for awhile. Life is simple here and very quiet (except for hollidays). Just take your *sarung*, that's all you need. A very superstitious place; when it's half deserted it feels like a ghost-town. Pitch black at night under a million stars like inside a planetarium. An area of many jagged cliffs and beaches of meadow-like grey sand dunes. This is the domain of Loro Kidul, the Queen of the South Seas. Like Queen Neptune, her hair is green and full of shells and seaweed, she holds court over sea nymphs. Loro Kidul is summoned by a gong on the evening of the Muslim day of rest (Thurs.) when a bamboo tray of rice, bananas, jasmine flowers, cosmetics, and coconuts are offered to the eternally youthful goddess. Don't wear green; that's her color. Buy magic mushrooms (Rp50 per package) from little old ladies or kids on bikes: 'Hello, mushroom!' Freshest in the afternoons. Take them to a warung and have them cooked up for you in a soup or omelet. The last bus goes back to Yogya around 4 pm.

stay and eat: Perhaps you can stay for free in a *warung* if you buy all your meals there. There are also places to sleep without roofs, Rp50. About 20 *losmens* line the main road down to the beach. They all look the same. No electricity. Rooms rent for Rp150-250. Right at the entrance of the village on the left is Suharjo's, the headman's, with Rp200 (mattress and window), Rp150 (no window but mattress), and Rp100 (with window, no mattress) rooms. A big *warung* with drinks and food (*cap cai,* Rp100) served. Try the coconut and egg cookies (Rp10 each), black rice pudding, etc. Many other good eating *warungs*. Widodo's is Rp250 single, Rp400 double, and has good cheap food. A couple of doors down from Widodo's is Rumah Makan Soponyono which has rooms for Rp100 (only 2 with padlocks). Peng. Parang Endong is a little beyond the village, Rp4-500 per night for one or two; sleep on mats. Has a well-kept and clean freshwater swimming pool.

vicinity of Parangtritis: Just before the village one km there's the hot bath Parang Wedang, entrance Rp50. The walk to the caves is through undergrowth; rough getting there but upon your arrival they may have a pot of tea waiting. Ceremonies are often held at the cave; strange Javanese arts of witchcraft. Swim in the pools, Rp150, beneath Diponegoro's hilltop place of meditation fed by spring water flowing through two bamboo pipes; seems a place for nymphs and satyrs. Watch men gather the ingredients for birds'

nest soup (a Chinese delicacy) on far out elastic-like bamboo scaffolding over steep cliffs. The soup isn't actually made from the whole nest but from the saliva which is used by birds to glue their nests together. **Parangkusomo:** 1 km down the beach where legendary Sultan Senopati lived for some months with Loro Kidul in the 17th Century. The sacred spot of their rendevouz is enclosed by a fence, contains a symbolic tree and lamp, with remains of flowers and incense offerings from Javanese (including the mayor of Jakarta) who come to ask direction and aid from Loro Kidul. You may enter this area by asking for the *juru kunci* (mystic caretaker) who will offer your questions to the Queen for Rp100, plus offerings of flowers and incense. Take a translator or learn Indonesian. **Samas:** A beach 25 km south of Yogya. Violent surf, hot black sand, lagoons, steel colored dunes, several *warungs*. **Baron Beach:** 60 km S.E. of Yogya. Get bus Rp150 to Barong through Wonosari then an *oplet* the remaining 25 km to Baron. Relatively isolated. A long narrow beach and ridges inside a sheltered cove with shallow water and safe swimming. **Kukup:** A white sand beach east of Baron. The Kukup turnoff is 1 km before Baron. Be careful of currents while swimming.

BOROBUDUR

The ruins of this 1100 year old temple lie 42 km N.W. of Yogya, one hour by 2 public buses from Yogya, Rp125. This colossal man-made cosmic mountain is one of the most imposing creations of mankind. There's nothing in the world quite like it, there's no *2nd* Borobudur. Put up 200 years before Notre Dame and Chatres cathedrals, it preceeds the Buddhist temple of Ankor Wat in Cambodia by 300 years. Built with more than 2 million cubic feet of stone, it's the world's largest stupa and the largest ancient monument in the southern hemisphere See it on a rainy day when water spews out of the mouths of gargoyles.

history: Its name is probably derived from the Sanskrit, *Vihara Buddah Uhr. Vihara* means monastery, *Uhr* means high, translated 'Buddhist monastery on a high place.' The structure has many characteristics of the Central Javanese style (700-950 A.D.) and has been compared with nearby temples that have inscriptions. It's related to both the Indian monuments of northwest India (the terraced bases of Indian stupas) and also with the terraced sanctuaries of prehistoric Indonesian art. A complicated, cluttered example of a stupa and replica of the universe, it has little else in common with other Buddhist temples in India or S.E. Asia. Persian, Babylonian and Greek influences can be seen in Borobudur's art and architecture. Planned by men with a profound knowledge of Buddhist philosophy, on it Buddah and Shiva are spiritually the same being. This giant monument served the purpose of veneration, worship and meditation, an achievement of the Vajrayana sect of the Tantric School of Buddhism which emerged in the 7th Century and found acceptance in Indonesia around 700 A.D. The feudal Sailendra princes erected it with peasant labor between 778 and 850 A.D. The monument took perhaps 10,000 men 100 years to build. They were not elite savages but highly advanced technicians who constructed it. No nation or group of men could possibly build it today. If they had had the technology to build an Apollo rocket, they would have done it. Thousands of laborers, slaves, carvers, sculptors, carriers, and expert supervisors worked for decades with only their hands and arms, rolling logs, using ropes, levers, hammers, mallets and chisels. Records indicate that the population of the countryside of Central Java became drastically reduced after the completion of Borobudur in the 9th Century. It exhausted 5 generations. Artisans and specialists undoubtedly visited the area from India. Borobudur was abandoned soon after completion. The Shaliendras were finally overthrown by Hindus on Java in 856 A.D. It might have started to collapse just when the sculptors were putting on the finishing touches; there's evidences of work started to reinforce the base, and some panels have trace marks begun on them. The monument became buried under a thousand years of volcanic eruptions until discovered by an English colonel during the British occupation of Indonesia in 1814. Though it was buried, it was not unknown: a 19th Century Javanese historical work mentions that a Yogya prince went out to visit 'the 1000 statues standing on a natural hill, and a holy man in a cave'. In 1855, Borobudur was cleared of all ash, earth and forests.

location: The approach is about as unBuddhist-like as you can get, the roadway is choked on both sides with souvenir stalls. Many Indonesian visitors look upon Borobudur as just an object to have their pictures taken in front of; loud transistor radios and hawkers wreck the atmosphere. The best part of the monument is now cordoned off, there's signs all over telling you where to go and what to do, barbed wire everywhere. Some people leave after 5 minutes. It was built on the confluence of two rivers, always considered a holy spot in India. The view from the top of the stupa takes in lush green hills and meadows of palm trees rising up around it with the mountain peaks Merbabu and Merapi beyond. The background looks like a miniature Himalayas. According to tradition, the architect who designed it was Gunadharma, whose face you can see to the right of the largest pinnacle in the Menorah mountain range just behind the monument.

Kenari trees were planted around Borobudur in 1840. At the foot of the east stairway stands a sacred fig tree descended from the original Bodhi-tree under which the Buddah attained enlightenment. This particular tree was brought to Borobudur in 1928, a shoot of the holy tree in Ceylon which was itself a shoot of the original tree brought from India in the 3rd Century B.C.

shape: Borobudur is in the form of a giant Buddhist prayer symbol, the *mandala.* It's an unspectacular almost impassive shape, found nowhere else; like something carved out of solid rock, or like a bursting fruit. It was constructed to look like the holy Mount Meru of India, a mythological model of the Universe. Its famous silhouette can only be appreciated when viewed from the air. You can't enter this stupa because it consists of just terraces built over the top of a hill. Greek columns and Gothic cathedrals of Europe have a vertical structure, but in Asia the pattern is horizontal. Temples are laid out in square or rectangular enclosures and they rise up to a gently culminating pyramid. This massive perfectly symmetrical stupa is only one of 84,000 all over Asia which are said to contain the remains of Buddah. But it is a stupa with a difference. This unique building combines symbols of the circle (heaven), of the square (earth) and of a stupa into one coherent whole. There are many projections, making in all 36 corners. The foot is 122 sq. m and the temple goes up tier by tier. Enter on your right, *pradaksina,* which means that you pay tribute to the gods. The widest and lowest terraces are used for processions. The 5 galleries above it have but one internal and one external wall. There are 10 square and round terraces from the base to the main top-most stupa, each representing the individual stages towards perfection in a man's life. The pilgrim's walk takes you around the temple 9 times before reaching the top. There are 4 stairways, in the middle and to each side, leading up to the top. The east side's third gallery has the best preserved and most beautiful gateway visitors are swallowed up symbolically by the *kala*-monster upon entering, then given new spiritual life. Each sphere shows striking differences; from the richly decorated square terraces full of reliefs, Buddahs, niches, stupas, ornaments, to the circular terraces devoid of all decorations. The higher you climb the more heavenly the reliefs become until you reach the pinnacle or *nirvana* (literally 'blowing out', extinction). At the top, there's a much wider spaciousness and more simplicity. As you climb, you can feel yourself rising, then flying off into space, a release from the endless chain of rebirth. The topmost central stupa has a diameter of over 15 meters. This pinnacle was once 10 meters higher than it is now, seen for miles away to guide the pilgrim.

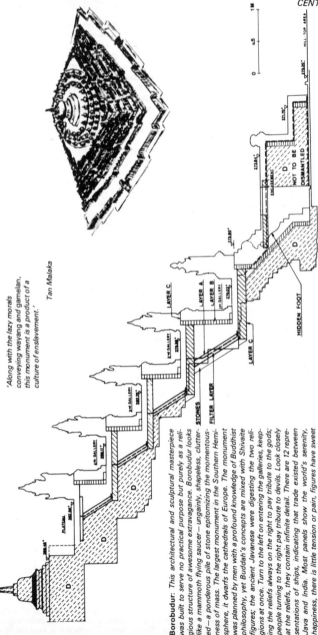

'Along with the lazy morals
conveying wayang and gamelan,
this monument is a product of a
culture of enslavement.'

Tan Malaka

Borobudur: This architectural and sculptural masterpiece
was built to serve no practical purpose but purely as a religious structure of awesome extravagance. Borobudur looks
like a mammoth flying saucer— ungainly, shapeless, cluttered— a ponderous pile of stone epitomizing the momentous-
ness of mass. The largest monument in the Southern Hemisphere, it dwarfs the cathedrals of Europe. The monument
was planned by men with a profound knowledge of Buddhist
philosophy, yet Buddah's concepts are mixed with Shivaite
figures; the ancient Javanese were digesting the two religions at once. Turn to the left on entering the galleries, keeping the reliefs always on the right to pay tribute to the gods;
people turning to the right pay tribute to devils. Look closely
at the reliefs, they contain infinite detail. There are 12 representations of ships, indicating that trade existed between
Java and India. Most panels show the world's serenity,
happiness, there is little tension or pain, figures have sweet
detached faces. 72 defaced Buddah statues are inside small
stupas; touching one by reaching through the lattices is said
to bring luck. Kenari trees around the monument give it an
age old charm and to the northwest are ruins of a monastery
for pilgrims. See Borobudur during the full moon or in the
early morning when layers of mist fill the valley and surround
the lush mountains, while conical volcanoes shine in the
morning sun.

reliefs: One of the largest and most complete ensembles of Buddhist reliefs in existence, amounting to a virtual textbook of the Mahayana Buddhist doctrine in stone. There are 1500 pictorial relief panels of Buddah's teachings, plus 1212 purely ornamental panels. Once glistening with bright purple, crimson, green, blue and yellow paint, over 8235 sq. meters of stone surface are carved in high relief. These high quality bas-reliefs tell scholars much about the material culture of 8th-9th Century Java. There are lessons on history, religion, art, morality, literature, clothing styles, family life, architecture, agriculture, shipping, fighting arts, dancing – the whole Buddhist cosmos. See jugbands and dancing drummers, kings in high court, trees heavy with fruit, elephants trampling people, babies being born, female warriors throwing spears. The distance through all the galleries to the summit is a walk of over 5 km, a labyrinth of narrow corridors. Because of so many right angle corners, you are able to see only a few steps ahead. This forces you to take in each phase of the story a frame at a time, like 9th Century TV. The best-known relief panels of the historical Buddah are today cordoned off, awaiting restoration. This 5-storied pyramid is subdivided vertically into 3 spheres of Buddhism. The base-terrace or the 'hidden-foot' wasn't discovered until 1885. Originally it was buried under the earth and covered with stone to hide its reliefs from view. It contains a series of reliefs showing man shackled to greed, a world dominated by desire, lust and death. Lower richly-adorned square terraces are for the senses, the round top terraces are for the soul. The lower terraces are full of scenes of *karma* and earthly existence, woe and desire, good and evil deeds, rewards and punishments – all the *samsara* of the world. But as you climb to the higher levels, reliefs become more heavenly. By the time you come to the square terraces nearer the top, man has eliminated desire, though he is still tied to the world of the senses. Man finally attains perfection and is released from all his earthly bonds when he reaches the round terraces.

Buddah-niches: There are over 400 Buddah niches sculpted in the round. Small bell-shaped stupas, which look like inverted lotus blossoms or like bells of stone lattice-work, each contain a sitting statue of an athletic young Buddah. Through the apertures the Buddah can be seen only half in sunlight, half in shadows, each statue only partly visible. This is calculated to bring home to the visitor both the formless and the absolute reality, the two faces of god. Each one of the hands are in different positions to represent various *mudras* or symbols for Buddah's different actions such as teaching, blessing, preaching, etc. Reaching in through the lattices and touching Buddah's hands brings good luck. In the niches above the 4 galleries are statues of reincarnated Buddahs, each pointing to a different direction of the compass. There are subtle differences between the latticed bells of the first and 2nd rows and those of the third. Most of the heads are missing. They were knocked off or destroyed by Muslim vandals. You can find them in museums in Holland, Paris, London, Boston.

restoration: It took almost 100 years (1814-1911) to uncover it and bring it back to life, but just in the past 60 years it has been deteriorating rapidly. This stupa is in an almost continual state of anastylosis, a method of reconstruction (used at Ankor) which consists of taking the ruin apart stone by stone, numbering the stones and blocks, then putting all of the pieces back together again like solving a maddeningly complex jigsaw puzzle. The monument is crumbling now under its own weight. Since it was made by virtually wrapping a gigantic pile of geometrically massed rocks around the top of a natural hill, the rubble and soil from underneath presses against the mantle and gives the structure a very insecure foundation. Inadequate drainage and water seepage has caused monsoonal runoffs to pass through the delicately carved stone reliefs, slowly but surely destroying and cracking the panels. This process of oxydization deposits a hard layer that covers the porous reliefs with mould (not unlike smallpox), eating away at them. The foundation must be reinforced and the lower galleries completely dismantled section by section and rebuilt on a solid foundation with adequate drainage. The whole restoration project has fallen prey to bureacratic ineptitude, corruption, and financial mismanagement. Although begun in 1969, the project will probably cost another US$20 million and last for 10 more years, even though Borobudur may not.

Waicak Day: An event which usually falls on the most auspicious day in May. This annual Buddhist full moon ceremony commemorates the day that Buddah received enlightenment under the Bodhi Tree in Bodh Gaya, India, 500 years before Christ. Waicak Day also commemorates Buddah's birth, death, and final ascension to *nirvana,* the inaugeration of new monks, etc. It is attended by Indonesian Buddhists and also by many from abroad, especially Theravada Buddhists from Sri Lanka. The climax comes at 4 am when all the worshippers converge on the temple. Each carrying a lighted candle, thousands of followers in saffron robes (for men) and white saris (for women) move barefoot in a slow nocturnal procession up the stairs of Borobudur while chanting and praying. Then they circle the temple clockwise towards the main stupa at the top. **Note:** Since Borobudur is now being extensively restored, Waicak Day has been shifted to Mendut Temple.

MENDUT

3 km east of Borobudur. It's really a pleasure to walk from Borobudur to Pawon, then on to Mendut. This temple's location is like a breath of fresh air after Borobudur's garish trinket stalls and uncouth peddlers. Mendut stands alone in an empty courtyard, it's quiet, there's a little grass about. This temple is a genuine 9th Century temple of worship, not a *candi* to the dead. It faces Benares, where Buddha spoke his first words of deliverence. Originally it was over 27 m tall. Mendut was only a mound of rubble with cows eating grass on top until 1836 when it was cleared of all the dirt that hid it. It dates from about the same time as Borobudur, 850 A.D. The temple has extensive galleries, terraces, and a stupa on top of the main structure. A very sophisticated knowledge of Buddhist and Shivaite texts, Indian iconography, symbolism, and monumental architecture was crucial to build it. Its builders no doubt visited the Indian Holy Land.

relief panels: Mendut's 30 relief panels are among the finest and largest compositions of Hindu-Javanese art. The stories are drawn from the *jatakas,* old Buddhist folk myths about the previous reincarnations of Buddha. There are Trees-of-Heaven at the entrance to the ante-chamber and folktale decorations on the stairs. **statues:** The stone images in the temple interior are very well preserved. A 2½ m high Buddah is seated and relaxed in between two of his Bodhisattvas, the Congretation between The Law. These collosal statues

weren't ripped off simply because of their sheeer weight. Buddah's feet rest upon a stylized lotus blossom and his hand is held in the gesture of a preacher (mudra: dharmachakra). Architects put a shaft on one side of the chamber to let in moon and sunrays in order to illuminate the main Buddah image. Buddah's back support is flanked by an elephant, a lion, a *makara.* What was once holy to the ancestors of the Javanese is still holy and there might be fresh offerings of flowers and food in the laps of the statues and incense smoking at Buddah's feet. The empty niches in the interior used to contain four *dhayani* Buddah statues. A profound air of tranquility inside.

vicinity of Mendut: All these temples belong to the Borobudur complex. Mendut Temple, Borobudur, and Candi Pawon all fall along a straight east to west axis which connects them all to the Deer Park in Benares, India, where Buddha gave his first lecture. Pilgrims had to pass each temple to reach the main monument of Borobudur. **Candi Pawon:** 1150 m from Borobudur or 2 km N.E. of Mendut, near Muntilan. Could be a porch temple of Borobudur dedicated to Kuvera, God of Riches. A little jewel of a temple with tiny windows and dwarves pouring riches from bags above the door. Beautiful body decoration. **Candi Ngawen:** Also walking distance from the Borobudur-Mendut complex near the village of Muntilan. The corners of its base are decorated with lions. Candi Ngawen is actually a collection of 4 temples in a row, about 3 m apart. Only one temple has been restored. **Gunung Wukir:** On a plateau just south of Muntilan. Ask directions. These temple remains could date from as early as the 8th Century (732 A.D.?), making

Mahayana Buddhism: *Called the 'Greater Vehicle' because of the universality of its tenets and intentions. Its canon is Sanskrit. It's called a vehicle because its doctrine,* dharma, *is conceived like a raft or a ship carried across the oceans of this world of suffering to salvation beyond,* nirvana. *The ones who reach* nirvana, *Bodhisattvas, don't grasp it. They renounce* nirvana *in order to take it further so that everyone on the planet can become a Bodhisattva. The nucleus of the Buddhist-Hindu outlook on life and the world is the doctrine of the transmigration of souls,* samsara, *which became enshrined. It also teaches that Gautma was only one in a long series of Buddahs from previous ages. Mahayana Buddhism believes that celestial beings were sent to earth on rays of light emanating from Dhyani Buddahs and it also postulates saints, heaven, and the power of faith. Popular gods and ancient magic conceptions became accepted, as well as sundry other gods, spirits, and demons in between the celestial and terrestial spheres. Since Mahayana accepted local gods and beliefs, it spread far — to China, Japan, Tibet. This tantricism also adapted very well in Indonesia, especially on Java.*

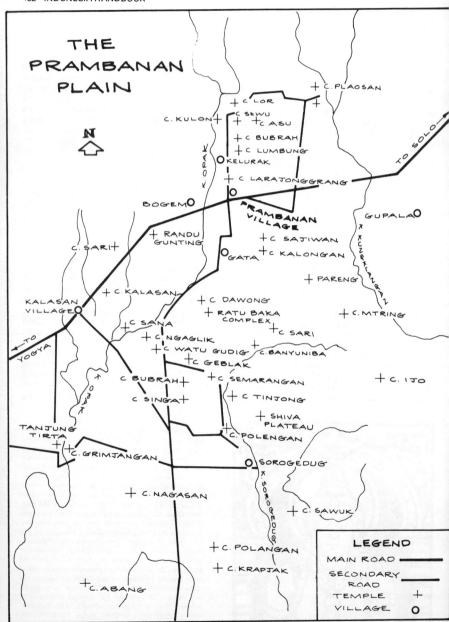

THE PRAMBANAN PLAIN

N

+ C. PLAOSAN
+ C LOR
C. KULON + C SEWU
+ C ASU
+ C BUBRAH
+ C LUMBUNG
O KELURAK
TO SOLO
+ C. LARAJONGGRANG
BOGEM O
PRAMBANAN VILLAGE
GUPALA O
+ RANDU GUNTING
+ C SAJIWAN
C. SARI +
+ C KALONGAN
O GATA
K. KUNGKLANGAN
+ PARENG
+ C. KALASAN
KALASAN VILLAGE O
+ C DAWONG
+ RATU BAKA COMPLEX
+ C.MTRING
TO YOGYA
+ C SANA
+ C SARI
K. OPAK
+ C NGAGLIK
+ C WATU GUDIG
+ C.BANYUNIBA
+ C GEBLAK
C BUBRAH +
+ C SEMARANGAN
+ C. IJO
C SINGA +
+ C TINJONG
+ SHIVA PLATEAU
TANJUNG TIRTA +
+ C. POLENGAN
+ C. GRIMJANGAN
O SOROGEDUG
K. SOROGEDUG
+ C. NAGASAN
+ C. SAWUK
+ C. POLANGAN
+ C. KRAPJAK
+ C.ABANG

LEGEND
MAIN ROAD ———
SECONDARY ROAD ———
TEMPLE +
VILLAGE O

it the oldest identified Shivaite sanctuary on Java. Only foundation stones remain under a tree. Volcanoes in the distance.

THE PRAMBANAN PLAIN

17 km east of Yogya, Rp75 by bus. It's an easy 17 km pushbike ride from Yogya through the countryside to Prambanan village. Or you can sling your rented bicycle on top of the bus, then use it to tour the temples once there. Lying among villages and green ricefields with the sharp peak of Merapi's volcano in the background, these temples were built at the beginning of the 10th Century. They were abandoned when the Hindu-Javanese kings moved from Central to East Java. Around 1600 A.D., all extant temples were toppled by an earthquake. In the 19th Century, their blocks were carried off to pave roads, build sugar mills, bridges, railroads. In ancient times this area was a vast cemetary, not a city; people couldn't populate a place of death. Since these many *candis* were mausolea of dead kings, Central Java has become known as the Javanese 'Valley of the Kings'. It took a staggering agricultural productivity to enable pompous feudal monarchs to erect temples to their own glorification. Thus the rich Prambanan Plain has the most extensive Hindu temple ruins in all of Indonesia. There's no telling how many more are still under the earth.

Prambanan temple complex: The central courtyard contains 3 large temples, a main temple dedicated to Shiva flanked by those of Brahma (south) and Vishnu (north). Besides these, this complex originally contained 244 minor temples (candi perwara), all of them arranged in 4 rows. Only two of these have been restored. The two small *candis* at the side of the main terrace were probably the treasuries where jewels and gold were kept. **Shiva Temple:** The largest central temple was dedicated to Shiva the Destroyer, built to contain the remains of a king of Mataram who claimed himself to be a reincarnation of this God. A wonder of the analzotized process, this tall elegant temple is a synthesis of both North and South Indian architectural styles. Almost 50 meters high, for 1000 years it was the tallest building on Java. It's lavish decorations, panels, motifs, statues, details of architecture all show an outstanding sense of composition. The whole structure is perfectly balanced and fit together; walking around its 20 sides it never seems to change. See it late in the day when the angle of the sun turns it gold.

reliefs: Candi Prambanan's relief sculptures, very realistic and humerous at the same time, are among the finest in Indonesian art. Four stairways lead up to the walk-around gallery that goes entirely around the temple; they face the 4 points of the compass. The body of the terrace is decorated with the unique 'Prambanan-motifs'. Steps are lined with part-fish, part-elephants, little niches of smiling dancers, frontal lions with Trees-of-Heaven on each side. On the lower foundations are seated deities flanked by attendants. On the outer walls are 62 panels of dynamic dancing figures and celestial musicians taken from the *Manual of the Indian Art of Dancing.* See the beautiful haunting cosmic dance of Shiva. In order to follow the story, go up the east stairway first, walk down to the left after the gallery, then start to walk slowly around the temple proper. On the inner wall gallery the *Ramayana* scenes are even more dramatic, expressive and down-to-earth than Borobudur's. There's an amazing harmony and technical skill in evidence. Humans and animals are anatomically flawless. Rama stories, of an unknown version, were first depicted on this temple in the 9th Century. Sprinkled throughout are Christmas tree-like Trees-of-Heaven flanked by animals, pots of money, half women and half birds (kinnaras), also rams, deer, cats, monkeys, geese and comic hares with oversized ears. Trees, rocks and water are more stylized, more earthy and responsive than Borobudur's with monkeys in fruit trees and busy kitchen scenes. Here and there on the reliefs you can even see traces of Buddhism (many stupas). In the office at Candi Prambanan, ask to see the erotic basrelief.

sculpture: A 3 m high statue of the 4-armed Shiva in royal dress is enshrined in the main eastern chamber; there are also minor rooms for the Divine Teacher, Ganesha, and in the northern cell the goddess Durga kills a demon-bull. Prambanan temple is often called Candi Lorojonggrang after the statue of the 'slender cursed virgin' in the north room, her nose missing and her breasts worn shiny smooth by hands for hundreds of years. In the courtyard in the small shrine opposite Shiva's great temple is a statue of Shiva's bull, Nandi, the only free-standing stone statue of an animal in ancient Indonesian art; sculpted in a very simple, powerful, yet natural style.

TEMPLES IN THE VICINITY OF PRAMBANAN

Take bus or ride a pushbike to Prambanan village. In Prambanan, horsecarts (andong) can be hired at Rp600 an hour to visit the outlying temples, but it's more enjoyable walking down lanes through fields of sugarcane, rice, tobacco and palms. Costs Rp25 to enter each site, plus extra to take photos. Temples Sambisari, Kalasan and Sari lie between the airport and the town of Prambanan. Follow the road signs. For temples Lumbung, Bubrah, Sewu, Asu, Kulon, Candi Lor and Candi Plaosan, they are all more or less north along the same side of the road from the Prambanan complex. To start, follow road signs pointing towards Candi Lumbung.

Candi Kalasan: Lies on the left bank of the Opak River near the Yogya-Solo highway. One of the easiest of the outlying group to visit. Kalasan is the oldest Mahayana Buddhist temple in Indonesia to which a date can be set: 778 A.D. The present exterior was done much later. In fact there are actually 3 Candi Kalasans: the present one is still standing, which turned out to be the third building erected on top of and around the second one while within the second building the remains are to be found of the first. The inscription (778 A.D.) refers to the construction of the first building. This Buddhist royal mausoleum is set in a lush garden landscape, bats flutter in the inner chambers. The temple, like Borobudur, was once completely covered in multi-colored shining stucco. Unique niche decorations, and probably the most beautiful *kala*-head in Central Javanese art is surrounded by heavenly musicians. Partly composed of leaves and roots, lions spring up from the corners of its mouth. Exquisite craftsmanship. A sensual 2½ m high bronze image of the goddess Tara, built by priest-architects and teachers who were also master-sculptors, has disappeared.

Candi Sari: Near Candi Kalasan N.E. of Kalasan village in the middle of coconut and banana groves. Its design is woven together superbly, like a basket. The second floor served as a priests' dormitory; see notches cut into the walls which supported wooden beams. There are famous decorations on the panels between the windows with 36 large semi-divine beings dancing and playing instruments.

Candi Sewu: The 'Thousand Temples', 1 km north of Prambanan. Dates from the first half of the 9th Century. Largely in ruins, scattered in piles of stone blocks. It consisted once of a central temple and 250 minor temples and shrines with two rows of side chapels. To assist pilgrims in their meditations, the whole complex is shaped like a *mandala*. Many niches, dark passageways, and 2 m tall *dwarapala* (Sanskrit for 'gateguard') demons leaning on one knee, and armed with swords and clubs, guard the entrances.

Candi Plaosan: 3 km east of Candi Sewu. See restoration work in progress. Attributed to a 9th Century Sailendra princess. Plaosan combines the function of both temple and monastery. There are statues of pilgrims and well-preserved reliefs show portraits of donars and groups of devout pilgrims in procession with downcast eyes. The *kala*-heads over the windows are in mint condition. Both Hindu and Buddhist religious symbols and ornamentation exist here side by side, indicative of peaceful co-existence of the two religions on Java at the time.

Candi Sajiwan: S.E. of Prambanan. Turn south at the sign on the eastern outskirts of Prambanan village and walk about 2 km. The site is near village of Sajiwan. This 9th Century Buddhist temple's base and staircase are decorated with animal fables.

Ratu Baka: A few km south of Prambanan village. Take a right turn up the path from the 'Yogya 18 km' signpost. Watch for the sign at the foot of the ridge. Climb for 15 minutes to reach the entrance at the top. Ratu Baka lies on the ridge of Gunung Sewu (Thousand Hills). Once the site of a huge fortified 9th Century *kraton*-complex, it overlooks the luxuriant rolling green fields, bamboo groves and feathery palms of the whole Prambanan Plain. An extraordinarily tranquil view. This entire plateau is full of ruins, some not yet completely excavated. There are remains of monumental stone platforms, exquisite floors of large pillared halls, paved stone passages, bathing places, gates, stairways, shrines, chambers, deep cisterns. Once a retreat for royal hermits, a stone discovered here had an inscription on it which showed that a Sailendra princess who ruled in Java between the 8th and 9th Centuries was related to a reigning dynasty of ancient Ceylon. Sinhalese monks lived in a fortress monastery here more than 1000 years ago.

Candi Banyuniba: S.E. of the Ratu Baka complex. After Ratu Baka, turn left and walk 1 km. You'll see the temple near a small village on the other side of a gully. Beautifully carved double *makara*-motif is above the niche which frames a seated female deity. Three stone oxen stand in a row. You can see the spaces where the most important sculpture has been robbed. Most of the roof is missing. A statue of a goddess points to Java's ancient links with Ceylon, some believe, in its strong facial and bodily form, very reminiscent of India. An almost duplicate goddess can be found in a niche above the entrance of the House of Pilgrims behind the Temple of the Tooth in Kandy, Sri Lanka. Other temples on this ridge line are reached by crossing the river beyond Candi Banyunibo and climbing the hill: Candi Ijo, Candi Mtring, Candi Tinjong.

Candi Barong: All that is left of this temple is a headless deer inside a *kampung*.

Candi Sambisari: 2 km from the road near the village of Sambisari at the end of a country lane. This 8th and 9th Century Shivaite temple was discovered in 1966 when a farmer broke the blade of his plow against a stone. It is still being unearthed from underneath 5 m of volcanic ash; Sambisari could be a part of a larger complex. The ornamentation on the outer walls is in flat relief. See stone images of Durga and Ganesha, a lovely Tree-of-Life motif, and a *makara*-ornamented doorway. The remarkable thing about Sambisari is that it can be studied in a perfectly preserved state, unmarred by plunderers and unaffected by the elements. The lintels are roughly cut and the *kala*-heads are unchanged from what they looked like on the day they were chiseled.

SOLO

65 km east of Yogya, 2 hours by bus, Rp200. Often spelled 'Sala' but pronounced 'Solo'. 500,000 population (larger than Yogya's). The oldest Javanese cultural center and considered the least westernized city of Java; a *priyayi* stronghold. Solo was the capital of the Mataram Kingdom from 1745 until the petitioning of the realm in 1755 when the sultan's uncle shifted out and made his own capital in Yogya. During the Diponegoro revolt, 1825-30, most of the *priyayi* families of Yogya had supported Diponegoro while those of Solo had remained loyal to the Dutch. Over 120 years later when the Dutch occupied Solo in their 2nd Police Action during the fight for independence, the Sunan even held a reception for them in his *kraton*. All this was remembered when the Sunan of Solo lost his authority in 1950 when Indonesia became a republic, whereas Yogya continued to be semi-autonomous because its sultan had played such an active part in the independence movement. In the 1960's Solo was the focal point for the Communist party in Central Java where the PKI consolidated their sturdiest and most tenacious support. The court dances of Solo, *Bedaya* and *Serimpi,* are the last vestiges of the old ceremonial dances of the Central Javanese palace compounds of the 13th and 14th Centuries. Solo has everything that Yogya has but without all the tourists — art galleries, theatres, mystical fraternities, dance and music academies, extensive markets, Chinese temples, cheap *losmens,* good restaurants, and a frivolous night life (the girls of Solo are said 'to walk like hungry tigers'). Solo never sleeps, people roam the streets 24 hours a day. There are two *kratons,* one even larger and more venerable than Yogya's. Solo is an ideal place to live from the traveler's point of view, centrally located on Java halfway between Jakarta and Bali. Mountain resorts and forest wilds are within easy reach. Although a noisy city, you come across some streets and intersections which are extraordinarily village-like. Religion is soft and flowing here, not the fanatic frontier Islam of the outer islands. There's tradition of religious tolerance and you could even find a mosque and a church in the same yard. Yet the Solonese are devout; there's even real-life *muezins* and *mushollas* (prayer rooms) in even the smallest hotels. Many Muslims in Solo go to a special sermon (Kuliah Subuh) on Sunday morning. A city of famous philosophers (Ronggowarsito and Josodipuro), in place of the usual victory statue of Indonesians killing Dutchmen, Solo's town monument is a burning candle. There are a half dozen social institutes treating crippled, maladjusted and orphaned children, also deaf and mute and orthopaedic institutions. Six tertiary colleges were formed together in early 1976 to make a university in which 500 teachers teach 7000 students. **climate:** In the wet season, Oct-March, the Solo River often overflows its banks. In 1966 the dike broke and the city lay 2 m underwater.

stay: In the area between Jl. Ahmad Dahlan and the little lane Gang Keprabon Wetan (right off Jl. Slamet Riyadi), you'll find the cheapest and most convenient accommodation, only 6 minutes walk from the G.P.O. Also lots of good places to eat in this area. Peng. Timur, down the alleyway right next to Hotel Central, is Rp350. A small, Javanese traders' hostel, very quiet with a nice long sitting room. Ask Murdi if you can borrow or rent his pushbike. Hotel Wigati, Gang Keprabon Wetan IV/14, Rp500 single or double, Rp700 for a larger single or double. A maze of rooms, food is served by vendors in the halls all day long. Hotel Keprabon, Jl. Ahmad Dahlan 12-14, Rp800 or Rp1000 double, quiet and clean, rich wood grain everywhere. Other hotels in this area cost Rp600-1500. Losmen Kemuning, on the corner of Pasar Surakarta, clean beds, Rp400 double. There are other hotels close to the train station, though a bit far from the center of town, Rp100 by *becak.* Hotel Jayakarta, Jl. Balapan 122, Rp1270 single or double (cheapest rooms) on up to Rp2300; very plush. Down the lane next to Hotel Jayakarta, the best one is San Francisco, Jl. Marjurjo Kulon 8, Rp750 single or double. Also try Hotel Wismantara in the vicinity of the train station on Jl. Pasarnongko 53, Rp1500 double or single, quiet clean and comfortable with a bathroom in each room. Hotel Soeboer, on Jl. Gadjah Mada 172; near the RR station; new, clean, and each room has a bath; Rp1500 single or double.

eat: For the cheapest food, learn the different sounds which serve as trademarks for the sellers; they'll come and feed you- ice cream, *bakmi, beras kencur* drinks, etc. Exactly opposite Hotel Central

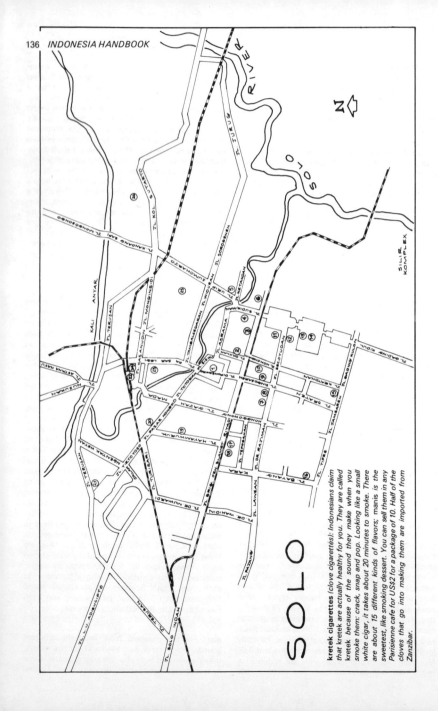

SOLO

kretek cigarettes (clove cigarettes): Indonesians claim that kretek are actually healthy for you. They are called kretek because of the sound they make when you smoke them: crack, snap and pop. Looking like a small white cigar, it takes about 20 minutes to smoke. There are about 15 different kinds of flavors; manis is the sweetest, like smoking dessert. You can sell them in any Parisienne cafe for US$2 for a package of 10. Half of the cloves that go into making them are imported from Zanzibar.

on Jl. Ahmad Dahlan is a small *warung* serving *kopi, pisang goreng, nasi campur* (Rp100). Down the same street is Rumah Makan Populair, Jl. Ahmad Dahlan 52; great food, meals Rp250-300; their *cap cai* is hard to compare, enough for two. Aneka Rasa, Jl. Slamet Jiyadi 101; good food but average meals cost Rp4-500. Many small *warungs* in Kampung Purwosari make specific Solonese dishes, Rp150 per portion. Rumah Makan Parta, Jl. Nonongan (in front of Hotel Islam) for original Javanese food. Rumah Makan Miroso, near Bank Bumi Daya at the eastern end of Jl. Slamet Riyadi, has unusually good Chinese food. Go here if you're hungry because they really feed you, Rp300 for an average meal which is as good as Solo's ritziest restaurant, The Orient, but half the price; only open at night. The best *sate* is opposite Hotel Nonongan on the corner near Aneka Rasa. The Ramayana Restaurant, Jl. Ronggowarsito 2, also has excellent chicken *sate*, Rp250, Rumah Makan Centrum, Jl. Kratonan 151, has a menu which is like a magazine, so much to choose from. Here you get what you pay for (Rp250-500); delicious meals. Along Jl. Secoyudan: Seger Ayem, Jl. Secoyudan 16, has outsanding ice juices and a *combinasi buah*, Rp150, which includes fresh tomatoes. Rumah Makan Puas, Jl. Secoyudan 30, has excellent *gado2* and *racikan selat*, both Rp100. Another place down the street sells *loket yogya* (similar to *gado2*) for Rp75, fantastic and healthy; look for the sign. There's cheap eating places around the train station for Solonese specialties like *nasi liwet* (sweet salty), *nasi rawon, nasi langgi* and *nasi pecel tumpang,* all Rp50-100, all different combinations of rice with completely different tastes and condiments. There are many night markets: Pasar Lagi, Pasar Gede, Pasar Senggol, etc. At night on the sidewalks try the local dessert, a portion of rice custard on a cripsy pancake with banana slices on top (also chocolate sprinkled ones); best hot. On Jl. Teuku Umar at night the hot milk tents open up; Rp75 with honey; Rp90 with honey and egg yoke; Rp95 with honey, egg and chocolate. Other goodies to munch on, a warm meeting place. For homesick westerners, Elysium, near the museum; cafe atmosphere and taped music. The only place in Solo that doesn t have flourescent lights. Arabs and Chinese frequent here and they could buy you a drink and a meal. Service is quite good but meals (Rp600) are a rip-off and taste like TV dinners. Madukoro, 12 km west of Solo in the little town of Kartosuro on road to Yoga, has the best *ayam goreng* or *seger ayam* around; try also the 'madukoro drink'.

SOLO

1. Mangkunegaran Palace
2. Hotel Central
3. Rumah Makan Miroso
4. Post Office
5. Pasar Gede or Pasar Besar
6. Dutch fortress remains
7. Danar Hadi Batik Factory
8. Pasar Singosaren
9. Suraji's Batik
10. Batik Keris
11. the Grand Mosque
12. Pasar Klewar
13. Sasono Mulyo
14. Susuhanan's Palace
15. Harjodaksino Bus Terminal
16. Art Shop Trisni
17. Solo Museum
18. Sriwedari Amusement Park
19. Srimpi wayang-maker
20. Batik Semar
21. cockfighting arena
22. Balapan Railway Station
23. Radio Republic Indonesia
24. Hotel San Francisco
25. Conservatory Karawitan
26. Prof. Dr. Soeharso Rehabilitation Center

---

batik: Solo *batik* is noticeably different and more traditional than Yogya's with its Central Javanese designs and its sombre classical colors of indigo, brown and cream. (Also some of the finest *tritik* work is produced here.) Look for *solo malam,* a particular local style of *batik* with bright colors against a black background. At Pasar Kliwon buy *batik sarung* for Rp1000-10,000. Visit the *batik* factory Danar Hadi, centrally located right next to Singosaren Market to see the *batik* process; some of their pieces are cheaper than Pasar Kliwon. Pasar Klewar (The Hanging Market) on Jl. Secoyudan near the Susuhanan's palace, for bright Pekalongan *batik,* some with gold and velvet borders and embroideries, modern designs and colors as well. Court dress of sash, *kain,* and butterfly-shaped headdresses, Rp500-1000. In terms of value, the 2nd floor of Pasar Klewar has the best *batik*. Buy 2nd hand *batik sarung* right at the side of Klewar. Don't worry, they'll find *you*. Don't pay more than Rp250-300 for used *cap batik* (look it over carefully for holes), or Rp800-1000 for second hand *batik tulis*. Most textile factories are on Jl. Adisucipto. Batari (the Batik Cooperative owns it), Garuda Tex, Arjuna Textiles, etc. Batik Semar, Jl. Pasarnongko 132, is worth a visit. Trisni Batik and Art Shop, Jl. Bayankara 2, has some very elegant, high quality and expensive *batik* pieces. Batik Keris, Jl. Yos Sudarso 37, has fixed prices: cotton and nylon *batik* T-shirts only Rp720-1200; long-sleeved batik shirts, Rp3000-5700; kains that range from Rp1200 up to Rp42,000. If you ask, they'll explain all the differences between them. Pasar Gede (or Pasar Besar), Jl. Urip Sumoharjo, is another well-stocked market for materials; a very wide range of batik with 360 degrees of stalls. Suraji, Jl. Tembayan Tengah 39, also sells fine batik at reasonable prices. You can take batik courses in Solo; they are usually offered in someone's house privately. Yogya is cheaper for courses.

Pasar Triwindu: Off Jl. Diponegoro. this is the Flea Market of Solo, an easy walk from Kraton Mangkunegaran. Bric-a-brac of every description: brass inlaid belt buckles, uniform buttons, hanging oil lamps, stoneware bottles, old bell jars, ornate cruet sets, statuettes, goblets, tiles, teakwood furniture and carvings, rare antiques (many Chinese antiques), lamps, pottery, porcelain, teacups, and much more from the gilt and candelabra decades of the 20's and 30's. (The Dutch were settling in for keeps!) Triwindu is cheaper than most markets on Java. Some prize items but a lot of worthless junk as well, so bargain hot and heavy for everything.

wayang crafts: A craftsman, Subandono, still makes the almost extinct form of the scroll-like wayang beber at Carangan Ft. 15/52, Baluwarti, inside Kraton Hadinigrat. He wants Rp8000 for a 2 m scroll painted on cloth; 12 scrolls make up the complete Panji tales. The most ancient wayang form, the dalang unrolls long illustrated scrolls while reciting the tales, the audience laughing and crying according to the poigency of the scenes. For theatrical supplies and dancers' costumes try Toko Serimpi on corner of Jl. Hayamwuruk and Jl. Ronggowarsito: wayang wong masks, gold gilt headdresses, kris, painted armbands, monkey topeng masks. Visit R.L. Dutosudamo (ask for Duta Pradonggo), the official Haningrat Kraton gamelan instrument maker, a hereditary profession. His workshop is on Jl. Gambuhan 30, a little lane in Kampung Baluwarti, within the walls of the kraton. Five kencong (one complete set) costs Rp175,000. Rebab (two-stringed zither) for Rp16,000. Big gongs, Rp75,000 with a Rp60,000 dragon-stand. Iron gongs, Rp400,000 for a whole set, but iron doesn't sound nearly as resonant as the brass gong. Kendang, Rp12,000. Gender, Rp45,000. Browse around the work yard and play the instruments or have them demonstrated for you.

other crafts: For one of the largest collections of ancient kris in Indonesia, visit Pangaran Hardjongogoro, Jl. Kratonan 89; his Chinese name is Gu Tik Swan. To see this private collection, first meet the Pangaran in Kraton Hadinigrat. Some quite famous kris he has. Only in Solo do you find the painted

kris scabbard. The goldsmith street is Jl. Secoyudan with many small toko mas who set precious stones in gold; they also sell antique jewelry, cufflinks, cameos, sapphires. Have gold weighed and tested by guys outside the shops on the sidewalk, Rp100 for the service. There's a toy market every day until 10 pm in the same yard as the Solo Museum. On Sunday the best selection; homemade toys are cut from scrap metal which make a clicking, clacking noise; 19th Century doll's house furniture; small painted tea sets; orange clay dolls; cardboard wayang kulit puppets; miniature gamelan sets with silver xylophone keys, painted wooden frames, and perfectly tuned to slendro key, Rp200-250. Restored, renovated and reproduced antique furniture at Toko Parto Art, Jl. Slamet Riyadi and at Mirah Delima, Jl. Kemasan. Fascinating curios and antiques at Toko Singowidoyo, Jl. Urip Sumohrjo, including fossils and uncut semi-precious stones.

Kraton Hadinigrat (Susuhanan's Palace): In the city center. Susuhanan means 'royal foot placed on the head of vassals paying homage', a title dating from the conquering King Agung of Mataram who reigned in the 1600's. This kraton is less overun with tourists than the one in Yogya and many people enjoy it more. Open 9-12. Rp300 entrance, Rp200 for students. Listen to the gamelan on Sun., Wed., Thurs., and Sat., beginning at 12 pm, for 3 hours. Cameras are forbidden inside and you must walk barefoot. There's a cool inner courtyard of shady trees and singing birds, antechambers, royal halls, leafy pathways. Pendopo Pegelaran has shining marble tiles, crystal chandeliers, wrought iron pillars, stained glass screens. A phallic-shaped tower is the sultan's trysting place with the Goddess of the South Seas. Pay for the guide at the ticket office, Rp100, a well-conducted tour. Museum Radyapustaka has a lavish collection of regal pomp, a model of a dalang and his puppets, an odd international assortment of statues, quite valuable collections of old Hindu-Javanese bronzes, ancient Chinese porcelain, a diorama of Prince Diponegoro fighting the Dutch, and superb 18th Century European Cinderella royal coaches with plush interiors. See large demonic gargoyle figureheads which once graced the splendid royal barges that used to journey up and down the Solo River from Solo to Gresik in the 18th Century. Also bull-fighting muzzles with spikes attached. Full of surprises. Take your time. In the pendopo in front of the kraton, there's a female canon with a curtain around it. She goes by the name of Meriam Setom. Her husband, Setomo, is in Jakarta's City Museum.

Sasono Mulyo (or PKJT): The Music and Dance

Academy of the Hadinigrat Kraton. Anything could go on at Sasono Mulyo: Malaysian and Balinese dances, art exhibits, etc. On Tues. at 7:30, dance music; on Thurs. at 3 pm the *Bedaya* Dance and at 7:30 pm classical dance; on Fri. at 1:30 the *Serimpi* Dance. There's no entrance fee. The zenith of the refined court dance forms are practiced at this dance school and here you can see the emphasis the Javanese place on composure and perfection. The Hadinigrat Court is the origin of many lyrical dances such as *Golek* and *Bondan* (or 'mother tending her baby') which is a fusion of professional (taledek) and classical solo dance styles. The body movements in Solo dance are more liquid than the rigid, disciplined Yogya-style in which dancers move like puppets. In Solo, even Rama is danced by women. Most of the *Ramayana* Ballet dancers of Yogya come from the Solo area. You can also study music at PKJT. On Wed. and Thurs. University students study *gamelan* from 8 am-6 pm. In the Solo-style *wayang* performance, orchestral compositions (gending) belong to a different class of melody; they have a rhythmical opening melody (buka) instead of a melodic one. **ASKI:** On Jl. Keptichan. Over 60 years ago this famous music conservatory devised a system of ciphers to mark traditional Javanese *gamelan* notes so that songs and music were able to be preserved. Before this, musicians learned the songs and meters by heart. Rehearsals every morning except on Sundays.

Kraton Mankunegaran: Built in 1787. Not actually a *kraton* but a Javanese home on an extra large and splendid scale, the palace of the junior line of the royal family. This is a smaller court with its own set of aristocracy, artisans and dancing masters, even its own *gamelan* factory. It has equally extravagant architecture and furnishings as the Susuhanan's palace, but just a scaled-down version. Open for tourists only since 1968. Rp300 entrance, Rp150 for students. Taking photos in the Dalem, the palace proper and the King's residence, is not allowed. The giant *pendopo* (or *puro*) with is zany painted ceiling of zodiac signs, is one of the finest examples of stately Javanese wood architecture. All the buildings were made from teakwood; no nails were used. The floor was laid with Italian marble in 1925, and there are European chandeliers. On Wed. mornings the *pusaka gamelan* is played, and dance rehearsals begin at 10 am on the main *pendopo*. This *gamelan* orchestra is one of the finest on Java and it's older than the palace itself; its name means 'Drifting in Smiles' Swallows dip and dive as the *gamelan* plays. There's also a library of old Dutch books. In this palace you are allowed to go right inside the royal residence where glass cabinets hold relics from the Java-Hindu era,

displays of 14th Century jewelry, dance costumes, a solid gold chastity belt, silver *sate* skewers, lovely *Bedaya* and *Serimpi* body ornaments, old portraits of haughty sultans, bridal beds, and a matchless collection of masks from different regions of Java and Madura. Perhaps you'll see the queen answer her telephone, or smile at you through her garden window (this means luck).

events of Solo: On the eve of Asyura I, the first day of the Javanese year on the Javanese calendar, a traditional ceremonial procession takes place in which royal heirlooms (*kris*, lances, etc.) of both *kratons* are carried around the city in order to be observed and blessed by the people. In Yogya, this ceremony is called *Seketan* and although it's more lavish and more famous, tourists are as thick as flies. Try to see a traditional Solonese wedding and 'meeting-ceremony' (temu) in which the groom crushes an egg with his foot and the bride then washes the foot in flowery water. During *Puasa,* Solonese make pilgrimmages to graves in order to visit bathing places (at Cokrotulung and Pengging) to take ceremonial baths (padusan)

The Solo Museum: Next to the Sriwedari Theatre. Open 8-12 everyday, closed on Mondays, Rp25 entrance. A diverse and fascinating display of classical Javanese architecture, Mataram artifacts (8th-10th Century), weapons, old tattered Dutch and Javanese books (some gems), exquisite *krises,* a model of Imogiri, Indonesian money from the revolutiuon, high standard *wayang kulit,* Java Hindu statues of Shiva and Durga on the porch. Old charts show the various uses of ritual umbrellas on Java. See ceremonial hats and hairy figureheads (an incredible blend of *Barong* and Sealyham) which topped the royal *prahus.* The City Library right next door is open from 9-1 pm. but on Fri. only until 11 a.m.

Sriwedari Amusement Park: Jl. Slamet Riyadi. Open 9-12 each day but Saturday; Rp60 to enter. Uncrowded park-like pleasant atmosphere. Good cheap *warungs* and drink stalls. Lie on the grass. At night, a number of music trips going on: rock groups, female vocalists, string quartets, etc. Also the celebrated Sriwedari Dance Company's home base. *Wayang orang* tickets range from Rp100-350. Buy the 2nd cheapest seats, Rp200, or stand for free at the side of the building and look through the wire mesh. Starts at 7 pm but takes them time to warm up. Over by 12 am. They use realistically painted stage props such as a palace hall, a dense wild forest, ricefields or mountains. Besides the *Ramayana* and *Bharatayuda* epics, Sriwedari also stages more popularized productions. The style of its dancers is sometimes learned 2nd and even 3rd hand from the court dancing masters down the lane at the *kraton* dance schools.

other sights: Kantor Parawisata, just east of Bioskop Dhady on Jl. Slamet Riyadi 86, for more details or where to get more details. There's a small museum on Jl. Kratonan 101 west of the palace, the home of Hardjonagoro. See Mesjid Besar with its front veranda (pendopo) and minaret, a combination of Javanese and Muslim styles. The Catholic Church at Purbayan is built in the old cathedral style. There's a small Hindu *pura* at Tamtaman Gang I, Baluwarti. Also a Morman church in Solo. The Buddhist community is found in Prawit in the northern fringe of town. Other ethnic communities in Solo include a Confucius group in Chinatown who gather each Sun. at the main temple, Lithang, on Jl. Jagalan. The Arab quarter is around Pasir Kliwon. There are beautiful merchants' houses in the Lawiyan neighborhood, but surrounded often by high walls. Recreation Park Ronggowarsito (Jurug) has camping grounds, fresh air and relative quiet.

miscellaneous: *Wayang orang* is occasionally held at RRI (Radio Indonesia) near the the RR Station, Rp100 by *becak* from the city center. As good as the Sriwedari, better acoustics, and the dancers are generally younger. Rp250 for 1st class tickets, comfortable seats. Keep your ears open or ask the tourist office because these performances are excellent. For fossils, rocks and stones, go to Singowidoyo, Jl. Urip Sumoharjo 117, on road to Surabaya. Cockfighting at Arena Pandji Putoro, Jl. Let. Jen. M. Haryono (Jl. Terusan) each Wed., Sat., and Sun. at 10 am. Much gambling; razors aren't used, only the cocks' natural spurs. Study Tai Chi? Tai Chi is an ancient form of Chinese martial arts which, through gentle exercise, improves blood circulation and conditions the body muscles. Mr. Tan (ask for him at Hotel Kota) is one of the best teachers around. There are 3 discos in Solo at last count. Amigo Disco, inside Sriwedari complex, has strobe lights and a foot stomping sound system. If you sit at the bar, there's no cover charge and you can save yourself Rp300; dance hostesses, Rp1000 an hour. Pop concerts in Solo occur at least once a month, most groups try to emulate Deep Purple. Visit a clove cigarette factory? Try Menara, Kerbau, Djitu, etc. Menara is the biggest. Want to call home? Kantor Telpon, opposite the G.P.O., has a nice courtyard setting. See sentimental melodramatic Indian films at Trisakti Theatre, Jl. Kratonan. Biggest bookstore in Solo is the Deluxe in front of Mangkunegara Palace; also good is Midi, Jl. Slamet Riyadi. At the Billyard Sport Hall, Jl. Secoyudon 103, hostesses will play eight ball with clients who don't have a partner (and will probably beat you),

for only Rp200 an hour. Includes the game and the hostess' company. Great company. Silir is a prostitutes' village 4 km from town, a little *desa* in the middle of rice paddies. If you don't have your own transport must go by *becak,* Rp200 from the city center. Far more easy-going than Surabaya's circuses, the girls here even go home each weekend to visit their parents in the country. Study Yoga? Contact the old Hindu sage Mr. Harjanta, Pradjapangarsa, Jl. Baluwarti II/5 near the palace.

meditasi: Solo is a center for spiritual and occultist groups. The Sumarah Association and the Theosophical Society are among the best known. The Theosophical Society is on Jl. Gadjah Mada; the sign just says 'Theosophe'. There are many long-term resident European students practicing spiritual exercises through meditation under the guidance of a *pamong,* or 'guide'. These sessions are held in *pamongs'* or students' houses, sometimes in the mornings, sometimes in the evenings. To make ends meet, most of the meditators teach English in language schools or give private lessons for Rp750-1000 per hour.

Sumarah: A white-magic mystical fraternity founded by a bank clerk in 1937. Its name is an acronym for *Sujud Marang Allah,* which means 'devotion, dedication and surrender to God'. It accepts aspirants from all creeds; Christians, Buddhists and Muslims are members. Hindu terminology is used to describe points on the body the soul has reached (chakran), from the genitals to the crown of the head. Each *pamong* uses a different technique. Hardjanto is into having his students immerse themselves in water for several hours a day for periods of up to 40 days. Pak Sri gives spellbinding talks. Some believe that you can't understand the occult without going without food or sleep. None of the *pamongs* practice levitation or spectacular public demonstrations of their faith, believing that any outward manifestation of God's favor is irrelevant. The idea is to maintain a spirit of humility and self-surrender and to constantly worship God. Followers try to cut off all senses in order to enter a world 'filled with light but no shadows' (semadi). Another characteristic of this discipline is the 'testing' of the student by the *pamong* to determine if any progress is being made in 'opening him up'. Commands and instructions used by *pamongs* during meditation sessions are revealing: *Jangan notol!* (Don't be overeager!); *Jangan melihat!* (Don't look! Be one with the observed!); *Lapaskan!* (Let go of remaining energy, relax instantaneously!); *Dengar saja!* (Just hear!). Admission into a meditation group is by invitation. Go along to a meeting or two to see how you like it. Spiritual groupies need not apply. First visit Pak Sujono, Jl.

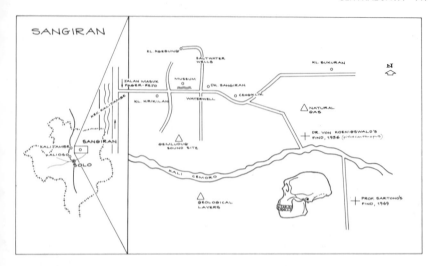

SANGIRAN

pithecanthropus erectus *(Java Man): Remains of an ape man found at Sangiran and at Trinil, near Solo, Central Java. One of the earliest known hominid fossils, Java Man was an upright giant creature whose skull fragment and leg bone were found along the Solo River. This discovery in 1891 made all existing theories of man's evolution obsolete at the time. His bones closely resemble Peking Man and also species who lived in Africa, Europe and Asia half a million years ago.*

Ronggowarsito 60. There's a registration fee of Rp1000, payable after one week of attending sessions. You must also pay a monthly dues of Rp1000. Direct questions also to Sri Sampoerno (or simply, Pak Sri), Jl. Yosodipuro 106. Read some folders at Sujono's to familiarize yourself with the technique. Sumarah Association keeps a current list of all hotels, cheap and expensive, plus rooms-for-rent (about Rp5000 a month) for the long term meditators. Sumarah's library at Sujono's house is outstanding, most books having been contributed by former western students. There are metaphysical, para-psychology, Buddhist, Hindu , Islamic and mystic writings, including a diverse collection of fiction and non-fiction. If you're registered you may borrow books and take them back to your quarters.

from Solo by bus: The main bus station is Hardjodaksino. Buses to: Yogya, Rp200; Tawang-mangu, Rp125; Salatiga, Rp150; Pacitan, Rp325, leaving often; Malang, Rp1200, leaving once a day at 7 am only, a 6 hour ride; Bandung (Samijaya Co.), Rp1600, leaving at 10, 12, 1 pm and 5 pm, takes 8 hours. Many buses to Jakarta until 8 pm, Rp1800, 12 hours. **bis malam:** Many *bis malam* companies on Jl. Veteran near the bus station with buses to: Surabaya, Rp850; Bogor, with the Bogor Express, Rp1750. Best bus to Malang is the Agung Express; catch it at Sari Restaurant, Rp1800. Buy tickets 2 days before. The nicest way to get to Jakarta is to take the Bima train, Rp7000. But the best bus company is Bhayankara, Rp2800; ride in air-conditioned buses.**Colts:** Stasiun Colt is on Jl. Veteran in front of the bus station to: Pacitan, Semarang, Madiun, Yogya, Rp250. Or catch a Colt to Yogya in front of the bus station (Rp250) or in front of Hotel Central on Jl. Ahmad Dahlan anytime 6 am-6 pm, for Rp300. Or just flag one down going south on Jl. Slamet Riyadi. Colts drop you off right at your door in Yogya.

vicinity of Solo: There are two beautiful mountain roads leading out of the city. One is to the east over Mt. Lawu via Sarangan to Madiun. The other is to the west passing through Boyolali (the milk center), Cepogo, Selo, and finally to Borobudur. There are palace ruins at Kartosuro, 12 km west of Solo, the old capital of the Mataram Kingdom. At Penanggungan, 34 km from Boyolali, a mountainous village with luscious scenery. **Bayat:** Near Klaten. Visit the tomb here of one of the nine legendary saints, the *walis,* who brought Islam to Java. Built in 1633 A.D., it's situated on a hill and is entered through a series of gateways. The tomb has a split gate made of stone, very much like a Balinese temple of today. *Wali* is an abbreviation for *Wali Ullah* or 'one close to God', which reflects Indonesia's emphasis on the mystical side of Islam. Even though Islam opposes the worship of saints, *walis* are regarded as great magicians and miracle-working apostles. Many legends have been woven around them. In reality they were tough, hard-working, devout, and wealthy merchants. When the *walis* arrived in the late 16th Century, each made skilful use of the Hindu *gamelan* and *wayang* dances to win and soften the people for Islam. (One of them, Kalidjaga, a coastal prince of the 16th Century, reinvented mask plays, *wayang topeng.)* Their tombs are looked upon as sacred places and are mostly found on hilltops between Demak and Surabaya on the north coast of Java. In Indonesia, ancestors have traditionally been venerated on mountaintops.

The Solo River: The longest river on Java (560 km) which flows right through Solo. You can cross this river on a regular poled ferry south of the city. For thousands of years an important waterway, the only navigable link between rich agricultural inland Java and the coastal ports of Gresik, Sedayu and Surabaya. Imperial Cleopatra-like barges up to 13 m long and 7 m wide with dining halls, banners, and *gamelan* orchestras once traveled up and down the Solo River in the 18th Century. Along the banks of this river was one of the first places in the world where man lived. Today you can dig out with your own hands mastodon (early elephant) tusks, sabre toothed tiger teeth, giant ox vertebrae or maybe even a *homosoloensis* skull. **Sangiran:** Get a Colt from Balapan Train Station to Kalioso, Rp50. Then from Kalioso walk 3 km to Sangiran. For students of paleontology, geology, and natural history, visit this site in a picturesque valley 16 km north of Solo. A small but unique museum here exhibits fossils and various kinds of plant and animal life hundreds of millions of years old. There are fragments of stegodon and mastodon, rhinoceros, crocodiles, deer, pigs, apes, and molluscs. See different layers of soil dating back to the Lower Pleistocene, Middle Pleistocene and the Pliocene eras. This is where a *pithecanthropus erectus* (Java Man) skull was found by a Dutch professor in 1936.

Tawangmangu: A pretty retreat nestled on the slopes of Gunung Lawu 42 km, Rp125 by bus from Solo's bus station. It's 900 m high (300 m higher than Bandung). There's a herbal laboratory here: spices grow better in this colder climate. Nice place to just get away to, does your soul good. Hilly woodsy walks. Flowers of every description from tiny ones beside the trails to giant bushflowers, plus berries, strawberries. If you don't want to walk, hire horses Rp3-500 an hour. See the Thousand Falls (Grojogan Sewu). Visit a 100 m high waterfall, Rp100. Descend down to the pool to swim, nobody else uses it. **stay:** Quite expensive accommodation because many rich people live here. Cheapest

hotels are Rp1500 a day. **from Tawangmangu:** To Sarangan on very crowded *bemos,* Rp250, 14 km. Or, a cool 5 hour walk on a very precipitous road that climbs over 1800 m, one of the highest roads on Java. Even steeper than the road to the rim of Bromo. Quite an unspoiled area. Climb the trails up to Mt. Lawu. On top is the tomb of Sunan Lawu, a much visited pilgrimmage spot. In the mornings the mountain is clear. Because of its isolation and its height (3265 m), Mt. Lawu can be seen from as far away as Solo and Madiun.

SARANGAN

Best to go in the dry season. A picturesque hill sta-

Labuhan: *An event of Yogya taking place in Parangtritis on the morning after the sultan's birthday. Offerings are made to the South Sea Goddess, the queen's trousseau being the main offering. It is made up of* kain batik, *and dark blue, red and white checked breastcloths smeared with nutmeg ointment, the queen's favorite scent. This bride's outfit is then packed on rough flat lattice-worked frames of bamboo lined with banana leaves, with heavy stones set on top. Next the sultan's old clothes and linen are laid down (being holy, they couldn't be thrown away). The procession leads to Parangkusomo where the clothes are offered up to the sea. The sultan's nail clippings and hair trimmings, religiously preserved over the past year, are buried deep in the sand.*

tion between Solo and Madiun. A placid crater lake sits right in the middle of the town with *losmens* and hotels overlooking the lake. There are two approaches: from Solo it costs Rp125 to Tawangmangu, then board a *bemo* for Rp250 over the mountain to Sarangan; or else approach from Madiun, Rp250 to Sarangan. Not many low-budget tourists visit Sarangan. In the tourist season July, Aug. and Sept., there are many elderly Dutch tourists; and every Sunday, Indonesian day tourists come by the droves, like Blackpool! There are many more Colts shuttling between Tawangmangu and Sarangan on Sundays. Sometimes *Ludruk* performances are held in the former old Dutch palace.

stay: Even hotels with very basic *losmen* facilities want at least Rp1000; many others hire out rooms for Rp5000 and up. But if it's the slow season, then you have a much better bargaining position. The higher priced have hot water. Hotel Lawu, above the town, is Rp2500 (one or two people), Rp3000 (3 people), Rp4000 (4 people). Indonesian, European and Chinese food served, *komplet* meals, Rp600. Electricity and wood for fires provided. Very nice location and comfortable small apartments. Hotel Rahayu, down the hill, Rp3500 full board; or for 2 people Rp5000 full board. Sleep without food, Rp2500 double. At Losmen Lestari, they'll first ask Rp3000 for a room with a TV, hot water, etc. But he'll come down to Rp1500 which is not a bad deal

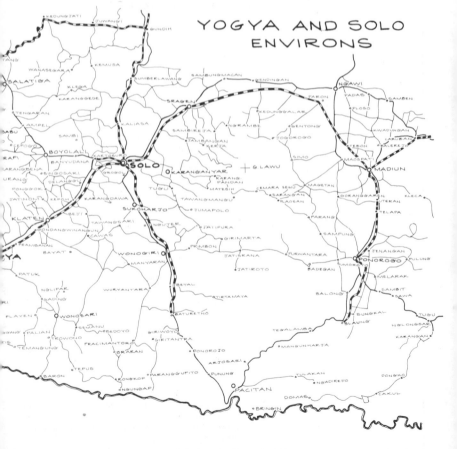

considering all you get. Cheapest places: At Villa Angkasa, run by Sarip, dumpy rooms for Rp1500 single or double. Losmen Kartika, Rp1000 single or Rp1500 double; smaller rooms for Rp1000 for two. Quite close to town and nice enough, near a small roadway down to the lake. Right next to Shinta Restaurant, Rikastuti has a Rp1000 room with its own *kamar mandi*, but 'only for her friends' (this means only in the off-season). **eat:** At Asia or Shinta restaurants, Rp175-400 for a good meal, Rp175 for *gado2*. *Warungs* sell soups, fruit, *sate kambing*, *nasi pecul*, Rp50, *nasi rawon*, Rp75, *nasi soto*, Rp75.

from Sarangan: To Madiun by Colt, Rp250. If there are no *bemos* from Sarangan back to Tawangmangu and you want to get back to Solo, take a Colt Rp200 to Maospati, then a bus to Solo for Rp350. Going back this way you see the mountain you just went over. Or walk over the mountains to Solo through wild misty passes of firs and pines, meeting middle-Javanese mountain people with deep black eyes and dark skins along the way, carrying giant vegeatables (pumpkin and lettuce) down to market. Big beautiful flowers in this area: roses, bonfire salvia, jerbera.

ANTIQUITIES OF CENTRAL JAVA

candi	religion and century	remarks
1. Kalasan	Buddhist, 8-9th C.	Though founded in 778, the temple's present structure is of a later date.
2. Dieng	Shivaite, 9th C.	8 Shivaite temples still standing. Earliest inscription dates from 809 A.D.
3. Borobudur	Buddhist, 9th C.	Consecrated in the early 9th Century (824-850 A.D.). Largest stupa in the world.
4. Mendut	Buddhist, 9th C.	Belongs to the Borobudur complex and is the same period as Borobudur.
5. Pawon	Buddhist, 9th C.	A porch temple of Borobudur.
6. Banyuniba	Buddhist, 9th C.	Known for its very fine double-makara motif.
7. Sewu	Buddhist, 9th C.	250 minor temples, a large complex.
8. Plaosan	Buddhist, 9th C.	This temple complex incorporates a mixture of Buddhist and Hindu elements.
9. Pringapus	Shivaite, 9th C.	Remains of a small complex.
10. Ratu Baka	Traces of both Shivaite and Buddhist adherents.	Remains of a fortified palace-monastery (a former kraton) with hermitages, dance platforms, gateways, pillars in the vicinity.
11. Prambanan	Shivaite, 9th C.	Large temple complex including one of the most beautiful Shiva temples on Java.
12. Sari	Buddhist, 9th C.	From the same period as Kalasan. See the reliefs of the dancers.
13. Ngawen	Buddhist, 9-10th C.	Originally consisted of 4 sanctuaries.
14. Sukuh	Bima cult, 15th C.	Although built late in the Hinduized 1400's, this high-altitude temple includes many Javanese aboriginal elements that would appear to pre-date the arrival of Hinduism.
15. Ceta	Bima cult, 15th C.	Similar to Sukuh, but even higher altitude.

vicinity of Sarangan: Hire a motorboat for the lake, asking price Rp750 an hour. Rent sturdy, healthy, handsomely groomed horses for Rp500 an hour. But walking is best of all. Walk entirely around the lake, 3 km. For the Sarang Sari flower gardens and waterfalls, a 1 ½ hour walk. Visit the Nagadilojo Waterfall, 1 hour's walk in good weather; start on the path from Ujung Telaga. There are interesting walks to villages nearby. The highest village in the vicinity is Cemorosewu, 2116 m, a 2 hour 5 km walk or by horse Rp800 return. To Kawah Lawu (the crater), it's 5 hours on foot or Rp1500 by horseback which takes 3 hours. Lake Warung is a smaller lake 2 km down the road. It's one hour's walk to Ngerong towards Madiun by the old road (shorter than the new road), or Rp50 by Colt. Nice walks and rivers near this village, but not as pretty as Sarangan. In Ngerong accommodation is much cheaper. Indrawati, Rp600 doubles, Rp800 for 4 persons. Losmen Tirto Taman, Rp750 for singles or doubles. Losmen Burbaya, on a hill, Rp1000-1500. Eat at Rumah Makan Anyar. There's market everyday at Plaosan, 6 km from Sarangan, Rp75 by Colt. Climb Mt. Lawu? Get a guide at Blumbang village near the top halfway between Tawangmangu and Sarangan. A guide costs

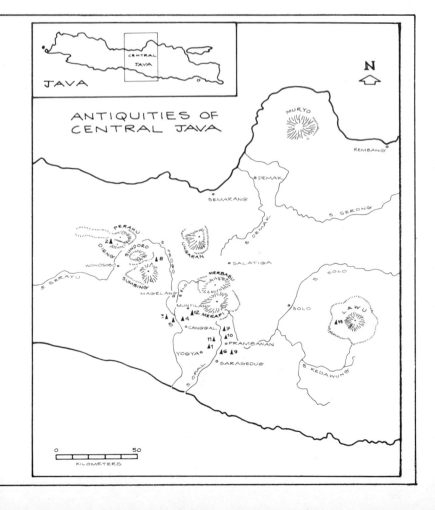

Rp2500 for 2 days and one night. If it's a full moon then you can climb up and back in one day and a night. If you spend the night on the 3265 m high summit, light a big fire because it's near 40 degrees C.

MT. LAWU TEMPLE GROUP

Two terraced pyramids and megaliths are found high in the pine forests on the western side of Mt. Lawu, a sacred site since early times. These mysterious mid-15th Century temples, with their stark, crude, and moving sculptural reliefs, have often been compared with the ruins of ancient Mexico and Egypt. Both are dedicated to Bima, the giant warrior god of the *Mahabharata's* Pandava brothers. Built during the final days of Hinduism when the last Hindu Kingdom (Majapahit of East Java) was toppling, these temples are strikingly distinct and considerably less ornate than other Hindu-Buddhist monuments of Central Java. Though they are the most recent (15th Century) Hindu-Buddhist temples in the region, they mark a resurgence of a pre-Hindu fertility and mountain-god cult prevalent in the archipelago over 1500 years ago. These prehistoric 'aboriginal' cults reappeared when Hindu influences started to weaken. **getting there:** Approach either from Madium via Sarangan and Tawangmangu. Or from Solo take road to Tawangmangu, then get off at Karangpandan, 29 km east of Solo where you'll see a sign pointing to Candi Sukuh. Walk up slopes of gaseous sulpherous ravines. The site was chosen with great care. These temples overlook the whole central Javanese plain, an unforgettable location.

Candi Sukuh: Approached in ancient times from the plains by a long flight of steps. To Sukuh, 910 m above sea level, it's about a 7 km very steep walk, or take *andong, oplet* or horse. Rp50 entrance. The shape of Candi Sukuh with its flight of steps leading to the upper part of the temple looks like the Maya temples of Guatemala. Walk up three grassy pyramids until you come to the main structure, a large flat unadorned powerfully carved stepped pyramid of rough hewn stone. Sukuh's narrow stairway leads into a dark inner chamber. There are many phallic symbols; Sukuh is said to be the only explicitly erotic temple in all of Java. On a stone floor at the top of the steep stone tunnel a large realistic penis faces a lovingly sculpted, swollen in excitement vagina carved in relief. The first representation of a *kris* in Indonesian art is shown in one panel; Bima forging one with his bare hands while using his knee as an anvil. These strongly carved figures are so intriguing because they are done in the *'wayang*-puppet style'. There is a statue of Bima, plus carvings of crabs, lizards, tortoises, bats, *panakawan* clowns, nasty underworld creatures, decorated tortoise statues, and guardians holding their clubs in one hand and their penis in the other. Pylons and obelisks nearby are decorated with the story of Garuda. Sleep in the hut near the temple grounds. There's also a *kampung* nearby with excellent goats' milk. On Sukuh's mountain the last king of Majapahit, Brawijaya, is said to be buried; offerings are placed on this site by the Sultan of Yogya each year. **Candi Ceta:** A 15 km walk from Candi Sukuh. You pass through a small village, then it's 6 km beyond. At 1500 m altitude, it's 600 m higher than Sukuh, but not as fascinating. Ceta is in poorer condition, not having the statues and monuments that Sukuh has, just guardian figures and *linggas.*

EAST JAVA
(JAWA TIMUR)

Mojokerto: Rp150 from Surabaya's Joyoboyo Bus Station. Visit the small but important museum next to the Kabupaten, Jl. Achmad Yani 14, open 7 am-1 pm, closed on Sundays. Give a donation of what you think it's worth. There's a fascinating series of reliefs around the main room with a magnificent sculptural group of Vishnu being carried on Garuda's back as the centerpiece. Taken from the Belahan bathing place near Trawas, it was probably carved as early as the 11th Century. Contains many other life-like statues, relics, sculptures, stoned carved reliefs showing daily scenes, and umpteen plaques with ancient writing on them. Wander through the alleys of the old quarter of town. **stay:** Peng. Barat, Jl. R.A. Kartinin GG/II no. 93, down a quiet path along a canal, is the nicest; Rp750 single or double. Losmen Merdeka, Jl. Bamudji 6, Rp600, Rp1200 double, is quite adequate; eat down the street near the bridge. Peng. Mutiara, Jl. Setia Mulio Gang 5 no. 8 (behind the Colt station on main street, Jl. Mojopahit), is a cheerful workingmans' place; Rp400 for a small room or Rp600 for a big room. Also try Losmen Slamet or Losmen Tegalsari. From any of these *losmens,* it's an easy walk to the museum. **eat:** The *stanplatz* (the Colt and minibus terminal) on Jl. Mojopahit metamorphoses into Pasar Kriwon at night; good eats in this night market. Also dine at Depot Murni, Jl. Mojopahit 72; a gracious man and he serves savoury food. **from Mojokerto:** Catch taxis from the Colt terminal or from the bus station to Surabaya, Rp200; to Trowulan, 12 km S.W., Rp75.

ANCIENT EAST JAVANESE ART

There are many differences between the *candis* of Central Java and those of East Java. In Central Javanese art, mastery is shown in the handling and modifying of Hindu traditions and styles. But characteristic Indonesian elements are much more dominant and obvious in East Javanese ruins. The nationalistic East Javanese Majapahit Kingdom, which lasted the lifetime of one man, Gadjah Mada, was the only ancient indigenous empire which controlled nearly all of Indonesia including Irian Jaya. When it arose in the 14th Century, there was a sudden emergence and Javanization of styles, a return to a flatter, less 3-dimensional, highly stylized method of carving to the point where the figures resemble shadow puppets used in *wayang* shows today. Expressions are more subtle and human than anywhere else in ancient Indonesian art. The figures' bodies, sculpted delicately with scant clothing and *wayang*-puppet caps, are seen from the front while the head and feet are turned sideways. Thus the name '*wayang*-style', which is used often to describe ancient East Javanese basreliefs. Many times there are magical or supernatural settings. Central Javanese basreliefs are hollowed out deeper, whereas in East Java they are much shallower. The East Java architectural style was likewise more slender. Temples have narrower bases, are less symmetrical, and are comparatively smaller than the large complexes of Central Java. East Javanese temple art was less religious, and syncretism actually went so far as to show both Buddhist and Hindu symbols on the same building. At *candis* Kedaton, Panataran, and Surawana, you can best see the '*wayang*-style'; and on large-scale *candis* Jago, Singosari and the smaller Kidal you can see best the active and unusual blending of Buddhism and Hinduism. Humans and animal statues were also modeled more freely and show more movement in East Java. The fierce guardian images in the *alun2* west of Singosari are done in a typical naturalistic East Javanese style, while the Central Javanese guardians at Prambanan and at Kalasan are much more peaceful in appearance.

TROWULAN

Rp75 by Colt from Mojokerto. 60 km S.W. of Surabaya or an hour's busride. Get dropped off right in front of the Trowulan Museum where you see huge stone demons close to the highway. This small agricultural community was once the capital of the mighty Majapahit Empire (1292-1389 A.D.) which under the ruthless and efficient Rasputin-like Gadjah Mada, controlled most of the islands of the archipelago in the 14th Century. This ancient capital was completely surrounded by a high red brick wall with deep pools, palaces, tournament fields, plazas, Shivaite and Buddhist temples, and lavish pavilions for the god-kings. Now there are just the remains of walls, bases, temples, and *gapuras* (gateways) scattered over a 15 sq km area.

Trowulan Museum: Noted for its well displayed collection of *terra cotta* figurines and small heads, tile fragments, shards, also vats, toys, fired clay portraits of girls and comic caricatures, bronze statues, *prasasti* (ancient engraved messenger plates) — a museum of fragments, so you really have to use your imagination. Good lighting. A big map of the area is on the porch. Thousands of bits and pieces of statues and stone images are strewn in the garden. **other sights:** Pendopo Agung is an exact reproduction of a 14th Century Majapahit building. Gapura Waringan Lawang, south of the highway, is a split gateway that once led towards the palace of Gadjah Mada. The cemetary of Trolojo is 2 km south. Though these members of the royal family had become Muslims, some of their graves are decorated with the 6-point Sun of Majapahit. Possibly the oldest Muslim grave on Java is here; dated 1376 A.D. Another grave is that of a Champa princess from Cambodia (1448 A.D.). The gateway of Bajang Ratu with its glowering *kala*-heads in one of the best preserved ruins; surrounded by papaya trees. Candi Tikus, S.E. of Bajang Ratu 500 m, was a splendid bathing place with terraces, turrets and bathing spouts along the walls of the basin.

transport: Hire a *becak* to see the different temple sites. Keep your pack in the souvenir shop and guard's house at the entrance of the museum before setting out, Rp50 for the service. Starting price to 5 sites: Candi Berahu, Candi Waringan Lawang, Makam Trolojo, Candi Tikus and Sanggar Pamelengai, is Rp1500 (or even lower if you bicker). This *komplet* tour is a good deal because just for Candi Tikus and back they want Rp1000. By foot it

would take you about 3-4 hours to see all the more important temples, or 2-3 hours by *becak*. No matter which temple you visit, a visitor's book will materialize and you'll be asked to donate money. Kids will come up and sell you authentic 500 year old Majapahit relics and *terra cotta* figurines for Rp100-500. The walk or ride to each temple down lanes of laughing children and people working *padi* is at least as satisfying as the temples themselves. **stay:** Spend the night in Mojokerto, 12 km N.E. of Trowulan, because there's no *losmen* in Trowulan village. If you're really keen perhaps you can stay on the open-air Pendopo Agung or sleep in the house of the head of the museum.

from Trowulan: If you're headed for Malang there's a much nicer road via Jombang and Batu than if you were to take the bus back through Mojokerto and Surabaya again (Rp400). Take a Colt first into Jombang, then from Jombang to Kandangan (Rp200) from where you connect with another Colt the rest of the way over the mountains to Malang (Rp400). There's another beautiful sylvan road leading from Trowulan to Pacet, a little visited mountain resort, then through to Tretes. But occasionally this road is cut. Make inquiries first.

*basrelief,
Candi Surawana*

East Javanese Art: *Starting in the 12th Century (to the 15th), East Java suddenly rejected the classicism of Indian traditions and went back to native ideas. Temple art became earthier, more realistic and decorative with lively flaming scenes from everyday life, wild flaming motifs, spirals, leaves, flowers, and animals. With the rise of this revitalized folk art, it is much more difficult and intriguing to understand the symbols in the temple art of East Java. Not as easy as in Central Java where the iconographic and religious symbols, though modified, are so well known from the study of Indian arts. In East Javanese ruins it's often impossible to distinguish between Buddhist and Hindu elements.*

PACITAN

S.E. of Solo on the southern coast. Pacitan is a fair-sized but easy-going village. Super beautiful beaches in this area; can't be compared with anywhere. Not so accessible though. Bring good books, food and lover. Place is all your own. **stay and eat:** Losmen Sidomulyo, Jl. Soedirman 25, Rp400 double or single, and Rp550 for bigger rooms. Right next door is Depot Makan, good curries and *nasi*

campurs at quite reasonable prices. At night, *sate kambing* is grilled on one side of the market, and on the other side, delicious *sate ayam* with rice for only Rp150. Another, less peaceful, place is Rumah Penginapan right inside the bus station, Rp250 or Rp375 for two. Lots of eating places. In Desa Tamperan, 5 km out of Pacitan down the coast, is a *pasanggrahan,* but only has two rooms and is often filled with *pegawi.* Tamperan is in a little cove and the *pasanggrahan* is up on a hill with a swimming pool and nice gardens. A *warung* in the *desa* serves

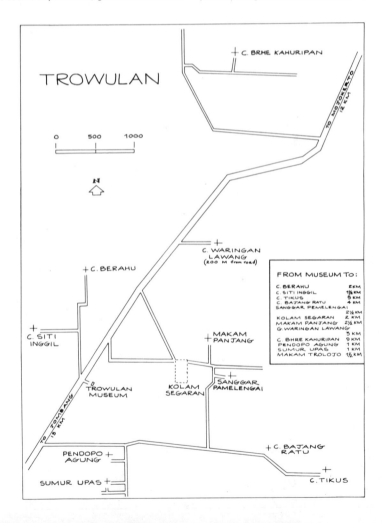

TROWULAN

+ C. BRHE KAHURIPAN

TO MOJOKERTO 12 KM

0   500   1000

N

+ C. WARINGAN LAWANG
(200 M from road)

+ C. BERAHU

FROM MUSEUM To:

C. BERAHU   2 KM
C. SITI INGGIL   1½ KM
C. TIKUS   5 KM
C. BAJANG RATU   4 KM
SANGGAR PEMELENGAI
                   2½ KM
KOLAM SEGARAN   2 KM
MAKAM PANJANG   2½ KM
G. WARINGAN LAWANG
                   3 KM
C. BHRE KAHURIPAN 9 KM
PENDOPO AGUNG   1 KM
SUMUR UPAS   1 KM
MAKAM TROLOJO   1½ KM

+ C. SITI INGGIL

+ MAKAM PANJANG

TO JOMBANG 3 KM

+ SANGGAR PAMELENGAI

TROWULAN MUSEUM

KOLAM SEGARAN

+ C. BAJANG RATU

PENDOPO + AGUNG

SUMUR UPAS +

+ C. TIKUS

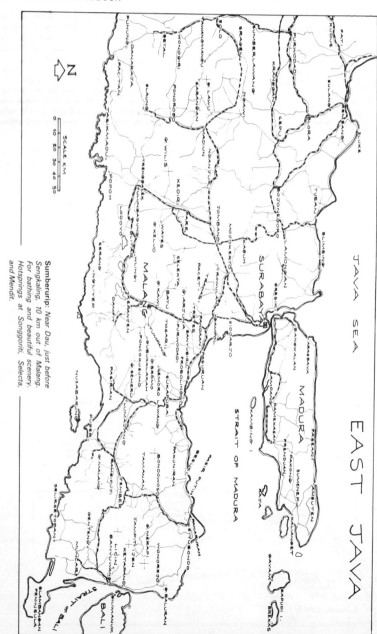

Sumberurip: *Near Dau, just before Sengkaling, 10 km out of Malang. For bathing and beautiful scenery. Hotsprings at Songgoriti, Selecta, and Mendit.*

rice, fish and vegetables, Rp100. The *dokar* ride out there and back for Rp500 is a joy. On the way you pass a classical Greek mortuary temple. **from Pacitan:** To Solo by bus is Rp350 (pay Rp50 extra for a good seat), 105 km, 4 hours. The last bus leaves at around 2 pm.

vicinity of Pacitan: The best view of the coast is from a rocky hillside 15 km south of Pacitan on the road to Wonogiri. The ocean sweeps in and out of bays and foamy waves smash on rocks. Punung is 30 km from Pacitan, Rp100 by bus. Three km beyond Punung Village is Gua Tabuhan, the Musical Cave (Rp50 entrance) which was once a hideway for the 19th Century guerilla leader Prince Diponegoro. Just follow the signposts down a dirt track to the cave. A boy will guide you through slippery 50 m high caverns. In the main chamber listen to a unique *gamelan* orchestra played by striking rocks against stalactites, each in perfect pitch, the melody vibrating and echoing at each blow (only 3 tunes). In this area, in Danaraja village, lives one of the last *wayang beber dalangs* on Java, Pak Sarnen, who performs and reads using 16th Century scrolls. This is also agate country where cut and polished stones sell from Rp200 to Rp5000. Have them set by the skilled silversmiths of Bali, or bring your own gold and have Balinese craftsmen set them for you. Kolak Caves are 12 km south of Punung near the south coast; some say the finest caves on Java. Baksoka River Valley, 4 km from Punung towards Pacitan, has silicified woods; many neolithic stone tools have been found here. **Wonogiri:** 45 km S.E. of Solo. Known for its *gamelan* instrument-making. Climb the peak behind Wonogiri and look out over the plains to see the cones of 3 southern volcanoes, Merapi, Merbabu and Lawu. Ngadirojo, near Wonogiri, is known for its beautiful Javanese women.

PONOROGO

S.E. of Solo or 25 km south of Madiun. Warlock area here (and around Wonosobo). Thick with sorcery and black magic. Let care be taken, some bad dudes. Spirits include: *memedi*, phantoms who walk at night; *lelembut*, invisible spirits who enter people and possess their souls, bringing calamity, and death; *tujul*, who mediate between man and devil and whose followers must propitiate with dead bodies. It's said that *dukuns* of this region have psychic - sinister powers. They can inflict curses and sickness on enemies, kill a man with chants or by touching his Achilles' Heel. In Ponorogo, find well-known *batik*, and lampshade hats. The *pencak silat* form, *Delima* (named after a fruit), is practiced here even by small girls and boys.

dance: The dance drama Reyog originated in Ponorogo hundreds of years ago. It portrays a legend of a king who loses his lover to another but wins her back through a disguise and a hobbyhorse army who frightens away his opponents. Entranced dancers drop from exhaustion. *Reyog* dances are occasionally held (last ½ day) at the Kebupaten on Jl. Kebupaten north of the *alun2*. Free admission. Or contact Pak Rusmin, Jl. Diponegoro 30, for *Kuda Kepang* and the *Reyog* dances; performances cost Rp6-7000 per hour to charter. **stay:** Losmen Gembira, near the bus terminal on Jl. Gadjah Mada, is Rp650. Losmen Aman, in the center of town on Jl. Pemuda, Rp500. Losmen Pantes, Rp50 by *becak* from terminal Colt, on Jl. Diponegoro, Rp500. **from Ponorogo:** Pacitan is Rp500, 80 km south of Ponorogo by Colt. The Colt Terminal is by the *stanplatz* in the center of town.

GUNUNG PENANGGUNGAN

A revered 9-peaked mountain S.E. of Mojokerto that is shaped like a natural miniature replica of the mythical Mount Meru of India. In 1935, eighty-one monuments and ruined sanctuaries were discovered under dense jungle grass and rainforests covering G. Penanggungan's slopes: hermitages in caves, altars, old water systems, steps, terraced temples, gateways, reliefs of marching elephants, and *Panji* scenes carved into big rocks. These ruins, most dating from the 15th Century, encompass many different and peculiar East Javanese styles. Most are found on the western slopes from 750 m to 1500 m altitude. This sacred mountain was to the ancient Javanese what Besakih (the 'Mother Temple' of Bali) is to the present-day Balinese. **getting there:** Heading north from Malang, take the highway just before Gempol going in the direction of Mojokerto. Pass the Pabrik Korek Api Kejapanan on your left and 2 km further is Watukosek. Take the 2nd left after the BRIMOB Camp and climb up the mountain about 7 km until you come to a clearing. Here you'll find a guide who will lead you up to the Belahan and Jalatunda temple sites.

Belahan: A bathing place in a quiet clearing in the jungle on the west side of G. Penanggungan. It dates from 1049 A.D. King Airlangga spent 13 years in a hermit's cave before taking the throne; this could be his burial monument. Belahan sits on 3 shady overgrown terraces and is still used as a bathing place. There are two 4-armed statues of goddesses, Lakshmi and Shri, in location. The water trickling from their nipples is looked upon as the nectar of the gods by the locals who call this place *Sumbergambar,* literally 'the spring from the sculptures'. These statues once flanked the splendid statue of Vishnu carried by Garuda which you can now see totally out of context in Mojokerto's Museum.

Jalatunda: Also on the west side of the mountain, 4 km higher up on a rough steep road. This bathing sanctuary is on the slopes of Bekel, a western peak of G. Penanggungan. You can also reach it by a 3 hour walk from either Trawas or Mojosari. Built at the end of the 10th Century, it's probably the earliest *candi* in East Java. Sixteen large relief panels depicting the Pandava's story are scattered in ruins. Very down to earth simple tales. There are evocative, lithe, thin-limbed females and some of the male figures are dancing. Most of the figures' heads are too large for their bodies. Reliefs on the outside of the spout panels depict a fictitious genealogy of a prince. **other sights:** The mountain resorts Pacet and Trawas are on the slopes of Welirang, 30 km S.E. of Mojokerto; visit the hotsprings. At Trawas, a *lingga* has been dragged from Jalatunda. In the neighborhood of Nagara on the northern slopes of G. Penanggungan is the gateway of Jedong, dating from 1385 A.D., which resembles the facade of a temple; also another gate in the area.

KEDIRI

Check out the famous Kediri Bonnet. It's more ex-

ANTIQUITIES OF EAST JAVA

candi	religious affiliation	Century	dedicated to
1. Jalatunda	Shivaite	10th	bathing place
2. Selamangleng (Tulungagung)	Buddhist (Tulungagung)	10th-11th	cave hermitage
3. Selamangleng (Kediri)	Buddhist	10-11th	cave hermitage
4. Belahan	Vishnuite	11th	King Airlangga
5. Kidal	Shivaite	13th	King Anushapati, 2nd king of Singosari
6. Jago	Buddhist	13th	King Vishnuvardhana, 4th king of Singosari
7. Bara	Shivaite	13th	A giant image of Ganesha
8. Singosari	Shivaite-Buddhist	13th-14th	King Kartanagara, last king of Singosari
9. Jawi	Shivaite-Buddhist	13th-14th	King Martanagara, last king of Singosari
10. Sumberjati	Shivaite	14th	King Martarajasa, first king of Majapahit
11. Panataran	Shivaite	14th	possibly the state temple of Majapahit
12. Surawana	Shivaite	14th	a prince of Wengker
13. Tigawangi	Shivaite	14th	Prince Matahun
14. Kedaton	Shivaite	14th	
15. Trawulon	Hindu	14th-15th	Majapahit relics and remains
16. Mt. Penanggungan	Tantric-Shivaite	14th-15th	remains of bathing places

pedient to base yourself in Kediri for the temples near Pare. **stay:** Close to the bus station is Losmen Doho I, Jl. Panglima Soedirman 91, Rp425 but only little rooms. Further down the street is Losmen Doho II, Jl. Panglima Soedirman 43, which has bigger rooms for Rp850 single or double. Losmen Jawa near the train station, Rp300 single. Hotel Panataran, Jl. Basuki Rachmat. Rumah Peng. Wilis, Jl. Brawijaya 71. Hotel Merdeka, Jl. Basuki Rachmat 4, in the other end of town from Losmen Doho, a big palace of a hotel built in the old Dutch style; Rp1700 for 1st class rooms, Rp2350 for 2nd class,

or 4 people for Rp3000. **from Kediri:** There are 2 buses a day from Kediri to Malang via Kandangan, in the morning and afternoon. This is a much prettier way to travel to Malang than the road via Surabaya.

vicinity of Kediri: Kediri is a coffee-growing district. It's also known for whip-fighting, though today it's seen only at festivals or ceremonies, especially during the S.E. monsoon season when the weather in intensely hot and the land droughtstricken. It's believed that the whip action will make

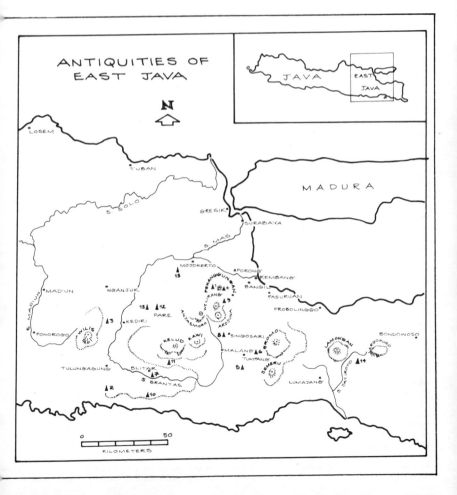

it rain. Men can sustain whip lashes on their arms without pain and are able to whip off shirt buttons precisely. In the Jember area they crack tiles and rocks. Kilisuci Cave is 15 km from Kediri. Seludo waterfall is 40 km from Nganjuk. Negetos temple is 25 km from Nganjuk. Ngebel is a natural crater lake 39 km from Madiun. **Pemenang:** 6 km from Kediri. A remnant of the Kediri Kingdom from the reign of King Jayabaya. King Jayabaya was an oracle-king who lived in the early history of Java. A famous prophecy of his which gave tremendous strength and faith during the brutal Japanese occupation of this century predicted that a white buffalo (the Dutch) will come to rule Java, followed by a yellow monkey (the Japanese). Jayabaya's prophecies have all been fulfilled without exception and are believed to be still valid.

Pare: 24 km N.E. of Kediri, Rp150 by Colt. If you want to make it just a day trip to see the outlying temples, Colts go back to Kediri from Pare until 7 pm. **stay:** Losmen Sederhana Jl. Kediri close to the train station, Rp300; but Losmen Selamat, Jl. Kandangan, Rp400, is the better of the two. Quite close is Restoran Sari Rasi, Jl. Pasar Lema, where you can eat decently for Rp2-250.

Candi Surawana: 6 km from Pare. Get a *becak* from the bus station, Rp500 there and back. Or take an *andong* for Rp150, Rp300 return. It's Rp1000 if you charter a Colt from Pare to see the temple; several can share expenses. This burial temple of a prince dates from 1400 A.D. All that remains is the lower part. Surawana belongs stylistically to the 'wayang-style', the reliefs coming the closest to Balinese puppets of today. The handling of nature in these reliefs is some of the most exciting in East Javanese temple art. Panels show animal stories, lively reliefs of the temptation of Arjuna, erotic scenes, funny and obscene pictures: Arjuna is seen shooting a wild boar, a lady rides a big fish, animals copulate. Dwarves decorate the corners.

Candi Tigawangi: An unfinished Shivaite complex not far from Candi Surawana, built in the latter half of the 14th Century. Take a Colt, Rp75, seven km to Desa Tigawangi; the *candi* is one km from the road. A magical death monument, the story is introduced by drummers. There are scenes of people delivered from dangers and spells, and also humerous stories from the *Sundamala* epic. Scenes go around the corners without a break. On the northern wall there's only a half finished man and woman. See the panel depicting Sadeva (one of the Pandavas) threatened by Shiva's consort Durga while tied to a tree.

TULUNGAGUNG

30 km south of Kediri. There are about 30 old Buddhist-Hindu statues in the Halaman Kabupaten on Jl. R.A. Kartini. For unique *batik tulungagung* try Kalangbret, 6 km from Tulungagung, or Rp50 by Colt from Pasar Wage. Here a whole *kampung* specializes in *batik tulis* and *batik cap.* Visit Pak Sutomo's *industri batik;* his prices range Rp3000-5000 though some creations go up to Rp15,000. For antiques, there's a shop on Jl. Wakhid Hasyim in Tulungagung. Antiques are also found in Pasar Wage, Jl. Kapt. Kasinhin. **stay:** Losmen Centrum is the best, right in the *kauman* on Jl. Akhmad Yani Barat 37; Rp550 rooms downstairs double or single, small Rp400 single rooms upstairs. In this area a thief doesn't dare enter. At night down the street there's a great *mie kua* and *mie goreng warung* and a little place where you can enjoy hot ginger drinks, arabian-style coffee, etc., and hang out with the boys. In the mornings, very cheap *nasi pecel.* Losmen Indonesia, Jl. Kapt. Kasinhin (on a little lane off this street), Rp3-500 single, Rp600 double. A poor man's house, modest but cheap. Losmen Surakarta and Peng. Rahayu, both cheap and near the train station; eat at Warung Sederhana nearby. Out of town 6 km, Rp100 by Colt, is higher-altitude Pasanggrahan Argo Wilis, Rp300 a night. **eat:** Rumah Makan Sumber Rasa, Jl. Teuku Umar. Depot Apolo, Jl. Wachid Hasyim, good *mie* dishes. Rumah Makan Kenongo, Jl. Adisuptjipo, also good. **from Tulungagung:** It's Rp75 from Losmen Centrum by *becak* to Tamanan, the Colt and bus station near the Pertamina gas station. To Pacitan it's Rp100 (30 km) by bus first to Tereng, then change to another bus for Rp160 further (52 km) to Ponorogo through the hills. From Ponorogo, take a Colt Rp500, 3 hours, down to Pacitan. Popok Beach is 28 km south of Tulungagung, Rp200 by Colt from Tamanan Station. Rent a small house ('villa') there with 3 rooms and a toilet for Rp2000.

Hermits' Caves: Cave hermitages, which ancient Javanese rulers and mystics used as recluses, are a curious feature of East Javanese archaeology, not found in the rest of Java or in Sumatra. At Selamangleng, 10 km S.W. of Kediri, there are rare examples of basreliefs carved on the walls of a cave. Dates from the 10th Century. Four rooms show mountains, mysterious clouds, and burial scenes. See here the first version of the *Mahabharata* epic. There's another hermit's cave 10 km S.E. of Tulungagung; both are called 'Selamangleng'. Catch a Colt from Tamanan on Jl. Diponegoro in Tulungagung for Rp100 to Sanggrahan village. Ask at the police post or at the *camat's* how you get to Gua Selamangleng. This cave lies at the foot of the Wajak Mountains; use the great pinnacle of rock as a landmark. A gang of kids will show you the way through ricefields and across a small river. (Also visit Candi Cungkup while in the area). The Story of Arjuna is carved on the wall of this hermit's cave. Voluptuous heavenly nymphs descend on clouds from heaven to earth to seduce him while he's meditating. A deer and a monkey are hidden in the lush vegetation and one of the nymphs is urinating in a stream. Steps lead up to it and you see an enormous *kala*-head over the cave's mouth. Gua Pasir, 4 km further, also has scenes of Arjuna being tempted (but not as good). Shows the love life of the comic and deformed dwarves, the *panakawans*. note: The area around Boyolangu is a black and white magic center (called *goona2* in Indonesian, *tenung* or *santet* in Javanese). In Balairejo call in on the most renowned magician of them all, Gipowikromo.

PANATARAN COMPLEX

North of Blitar 10 km, S.W. of Malang 80 km, or 170 km S.W. of Surabaya. This is the largest complex of ruins in East Java and one of the largest temple sanctuaries in all of Indonesia. The Panataran temple group took 250 years to build, starting in about 1197 A.D. Work must have begun during the Singosari Dynasty though the most important parts were erected during the rule of the Majapahit. There are 3 gradually rising, walled courtyards laid out on a long flat field; see dance-play platforms, terraces, shrines. Temple reliefs show the transition from the 3-dimensional to 2-dimensional representations, figures tend to take 2nd place to the decorations. The design and arrangement of this complex is similar to temples of Bali and Panataran's sculpture is like an old version of Balinese art. The whole complex is very well-maintained. **getting there:** Wait for an antique Chevrolet to depart Blitar bus station to Nglegok village, Rp100. From Nglegok, take a *dokar* to Desa Panataran, 6 km, Rp200 roundtrip. The road out to it is a delight.

The Dated Temple': So called because of the date 1291 (1369 A.D.) over the entrance. A fine example of East Javanese *candi* architecture, this vertical temple is richly decorated with extreme exuberant detail. Carvings show a test between a vegetarian and a meat-eater, the left and the right paths of the yogi, the fat Bubuksah and the thin Gagang Aking. The bands in the roof are filled with animals. **Naga Temple:** Used to store sacred objects. All around it are colossal carvings of coiled serpents carried by priests and on its base are reliefs of animal tales. **Main Temple:** On its basreliefs the Monkey General Hanuman leads his army through

the air past the flying wounded, clouds of fighting monsters, battles, and monkeys building a dam across the sea. Notice the harmonious, lovely medallions, what this site is acclaimed for. **bathing place:** 1515 A.D. Southeast of the main temple. Panataran was built more for the taste of the commoner than for Brahmans, and this bathing place shows flying tortoises, the bull and crocodile fable, winged snakes, ornate birds and flowers, and a lion plowing a field. These reliefs depict the Indian *Tantri Tales,* the Indonesian equivalent of *Aesop's Fables.*

BLITAR

A characteristic middle-sized Javanese community. A useful town from which to make tours of the surrounding countryside's sights and temples. In comparison to West Java, East Java is friendlier because it is more rural. **stay and eat:** The nicest are any one of the 3 small *penginapans* down an alleyway inside a typical East Javanese *kampung* off Jl. Merdeka. Only 5 minutes walk from the P.O. Stay in either Peng. Sederhana, Rp200, Peng. Pantes, Rp200, or in Peng. Tentrem. Peng. Tentrem is the most organized, Rp200 rooms with kero lamps. Hot coffee is served in the *warung* outside in the mornings, Rp20. There's a great little *sate ayam* place around the corner and up the street, Rp200 for 10 sticks. Peng. Aman, Jl. Merdeka 128, right on the main street one km from the bus station; Rp425 single, Rp850 double, is not bad for the money. Hotel Sri Lestari, Jl. Merdeka 123, across the street from Peng. Aman, Rp550 for singles, Rp1500 for doubles, Rp2200 for three. It has big rooms and it's central. Losmen Darmar Wulan, Jl. Anjasmoro 66, Rp100 by *becak* from the bus station, out of town a bit but comfortable; Rp900 single, Rp1200 double.

Sentul: On the way out to Panataran temple you pass Sukarno's plain unmarked grave, Sentul, located outside Blitar in Taman Makam Pahlawan War Cemetary. It's the one under the ceremonial umbrella with the words 'Here lies Sukarno, mouthpiece of the Indonesian People'. A hero's burial was awarded this ex-engineer, double-gemini, lecherous leader of Indonesia from 1949-1965. Starting shortly after the 1965 coup, in which he was implicated, the army began to systematically dismantle his power right up until his death in 1970. When he was a young political activist on Java the Dutch called him 'The Fighting Cock'. Sukarno was a mad jumble of contradictions — prophetic powers, immense charm and learning, with a dangerous totalitarian leaning. Appointing himself a crusader against the economic and political might of the post industrial nations, he initiated aggressive territorial expansionist policies against Malaysia in his *Konfrontasi* campaign of 1962-65. Known affectionately as Bung Karno, he had spellbinding oratorical powers, championing the cause of the ordinary man. Yet he was a preposterous hypocrite. He owned 19 motorcars, kept scores of mistresses, and used to hover in his helicoptor over streams of naked women bathing. It was Sukarno who inspired most of the super-kitsch monumental architecture of Jakarta. The man was adulated as a god, a reincarnation of Vishnu, the ancient Hindu god. On the night Sukarno died, Indonesians say that you could see his face in the full moon, and that there were electrical storms for 3 days. His birthplace was in Bu Wardoyo's (his sister's) house, Jl. Sultan Agung Gebang, Blitar.

temples in the Blitar area: To the south there's the smaller Candi Gedo and Arja, and along the highway from Wlingi to Malang, remains of Candi Selaraja. Candi Pamotan (only the foundations are left) is near Sidoarjo; Candi Pari, N.W. of Porong (14th Century); Candi Sumur, near Candi Pari; Candi Gunung Gangsir, 6 km from Bangli; Candi Indrokilo, 7 km south of Tretes. There are many more temples scattered over G. Kelud to the north: Gambar, Gambar Wetan, Tuban or Domasan, Bacem, Sumbernanas (Brahman). The majority are in bad shape, but no wonder. Though only 1731 m high, Mt. Kelud is one of the most treacherous volcanoes in East Java, quite often on the very dangerous list; it has a very hot crater lake. In 1919 it killed thousands of villagers as far away as the banks of the Brantas River and in 1951 it erupted again, raining ash all over Central Java.

Bara Ganesha: Take a *bemo* from Blitar out to the village of Bara where this gigantic 3-dimensional 14th Century statue of the elephant-god Ganesha stands in a garden. Dates from 1239 A.D. On his back is a large protective monster-head of *kala*. The elephant-god holds a fly whisk and a hatchet; tusks and skulls ornament the lower frieze.

Candi Sewentar: N.E. of Blitar. Since the top third of this 13th Century temple has caved in, it's now only 10 m tall. This Vishnu temple was dug out of lava, buried until the 19th Century. The base is quite well-preserved.

vicinity of Blitar: For seascapes and shining beaches, Pantai Serang is 60 km south of Blitar; take a Colt to Lodoyo (Rp100), then another Colt to Bangunredjo (Rp100), then on to Serang (another Rp100), a 3 hour ride in all. Krisik is a quiet retreat 15 km north of Wlingi Rp75 or by Colt Rp100, then on to Krisik by Colt, Rp100. To Tulungagung, it's Rp125 by bus or Rp150 by Colt from Blitar. **The Holy Gong of Lodoyo:** 12 km south of Blitar (also numerous small temples surrounding Lodoyo). Best time to see this sacred gong, called *Mbah-pradah* in Javanese, is during all the pageantry that goes with a big Islamic holiday such as Mohammeds Birthday (Maulid Nabi Muhammed) on the 12th day of the 3rd month of the Arabic calendar. Otherwise it's locked up and you have to find the *juru kunci* (caretaker).

Madiun: There was an abortive communist revolt in Madiun in Sept. 1948, the first serious attempt by the communists to sieze power by force, but not their last. The Indonesian Communist Party (PKI) under Sukarno grew to 3 million members and had gained some 20 million supporters by indoctrinating youth and worker groups, labor unions and rural workers, until banned in 1967. Their abortive coup in 1965 had many uncanny parallels with their 1948 Madiun revolt. The most respected *pesantren* (a religious boarding school for Muslims) in Indonesia is in Madiun, Pondok Gontor. **sights:** Check out the 19th Century locomotives in the railyards of Balai Yasa P.J. Keretapi in Madiun. See the oldest locomotive still running on Java, commissioned in 1881. If you're a steamrail enthusiast, Indonesia's railway stock is said to be the most diverse and archaic anywhere in the world.

PROBOLINGGO

On the north coast, Rp300 from Surabaya or Rp700 from Banyuwangi by bus. Justly famous for its mangoes (arun manis) and its grapes. The town whores ride around in *becaks* propositioning males. **stay:** Hotel Ex-Losmen Luxor, Jl. D.R. Soetomo 70, Rp900 or for two, Rp1600. OK, but a bit expensive for the rooms you get. Hotel and Restaurant Kemayoran, on the main street Jl. Jen. Soedirman 75, Rp700 or Rp800 double with coffee or *teh pahit;* clean and central. Hotel Victoria, Jl. Suroyo

1, on the Bromo end of town, quite comfortable, 1 or 2 persons Rp2000. The award for the cheapest (Rp300) goes to Hotel Rela Hati, Jl. Mesjid 1, near the train station under a mosque loudspeaker. **eat:** Restoran Malang on the main street Jl Jen. Soedirman 104-106, has good *cap cai* and other Chinese-Indonesian dishes. The *warungs* in back of the bus station are cheaper than those in front.

from Probolinggo: From the bus terminal in the eastern end of town, catch buses to Denpasar, Bali, Rp1750. They leave at 7 pm and arrive in Denpasar at 3 am just in time for the Nusa Dua sunrise. Take daily buses all the way to Sumenep on Madura Island, Rp1050. Or take a bus just to Bangkalan on Madura for Rp500. From Probolinggo to Banyuwangi, Rp600. To Yogya with Bis Malam Damri, Rp1750, 19 hours, leaving at 7 pm each day. To Pasir Putih, Rp250 by bus. The terminal Colt station is only 5 minutes walk from the bus station; these minibuses provide faster transportation than buses. Colts cost Rp350 to Surabaya and Rp350 to Malang.

vicinity of Probolinggo: Start climbs to Mt. Bromo and Gunung Bermi on the Hyang Plateau from Probolinggo. Hyang Plateau still has heavy forests. Visit lovely seacoast and beaches of Puger; take bus first to Kasian, Rp300, then a taxi to Puger for Rp100. At Rembangan, 30 km north of Jember via Baraton, breathless scenery; Rp500 by bus. Candi Jabung, east of Pasuruan, is a queerly-shaped temple made of bright red brick. Colonial architecture and a good market at Pasuruan. Bathing places Banyubiru and Umbulan. Grati Lake, 15 km east of Pasuruan, near Bratiunon. Around Pasuruan is one of the few cattle raising regions of Java. At Besuki, decorated megalithic burial cists have human and animal figures carved on the outside.

Pasir Putih: Rp250 by bus from Probolinggo. A fine beach between Panarukan and Besuki with surf, coconut palms, coral sea gardens, dazzling white sand- like on a desert island. Good family place, or alone. Sometimes you got the beach all to yourself. No peddlers hasseling you as you find on crowded Kuta. Rent boats for Rp500 per hour in the off-season; graceful painted outriggers line the shore. Try your hand at night-fishing. Use their equipment, not your own, or you won't catch a damn thing; rent out fishing equipment, Rp500 for 4-5 hours. If the weather is good, be assured of a good catch. **stay and eat:** Has about 5 hotels of varying prices, all lying between the highway from Probolinggo to Banyuwangi, and the sea. Pasir Putih Inn (Papin) is the best of the Pasir Putih hotels; bedrooms for Rp2750 and Rp2500. One

room with two double beds, Rp3650. Or rooms right on the beach for Rp2000. A restaurant serving delicious Padang food is nearby. At Wisma Bhayangkara, the cheapest rooms are Rp1000-1500. Pasangrahan Sidho Muntjul, Rp1750, 1-3 persons. Hotels serve charcoal broiled fish.

The Tengger: A mountain people with almost Tibetan features, numbering about 300,000 , who live in approximately 40 villages ranging from 1500 to 2745 m altitude around Mt. Bromo. When armed conflict broke out between insurrecting Islamicized coastal district and the Majapahit Empire of inland Java at the end of the 1300's, the nobles, priests and artisans fled to Bali, but the ordinary people withdrew to the Tengger Highlands. Esteemed by other Javanese as unquarrelsome and sincere. Theft is rare. You're invited deep inside Tengger houses next to the hearth because traditionally visitors must be kept warm to combat the cold outside. The Tengger are famous for their expertly cultivated market gardens on the steep mountain slopes which surround every village in these highlands. The gardens themselves are amazing feats of engineering. **religion:** Tenggerese call their religion *Agama Buddah*, but it's more a mixture of Buddhism and Hinduism. Although the Tengger don't believe in reincarnation, their caste system and calendar are similar to that of the Balinese. They have their own priests. There's an altar in each home, and a general place of worship (Dayang or Punden) located usually on a hill overlooking each village, most often a neatly fenced-in tree, sometimes strewn with flowers and crowded with people saying their prayers. Inside Widodaren in the Bromo crater complex are buried the legendary ancestors of the Tengger, Roroanteng (wife) and Jokoseger (husband), who produced 25 children. They had to throw the last child into the crater to thank the gods for their fecundity. This sacred couple still lives in a cave on Widodaren, Gua Adam, where the Tenggerese go to say their prayers and to ask for things.

MT. BROMO

The 2200 m high sandsea of the caldera has 3 mountains within it: Widodaren (Bride), Batok (Cup) and Bromo (Fire), which are really craters within craters. The whole crater is said to have been dug out by an ogre with just a half coconut shell in a single night to win the hand of a princess. When the king feared that the ogre would succeed, he ordered all his servants to pound rice at which time the cocks started to crow, thinking that dawn had broken. The ogre didn't finish the job so died of grief and exhaustion. In the early morning inside the mammoth crater, there's just the sound of wind while the sun rises over the sand sea and silvery grass waves on the windswept hills. It looks like a landscape on the moon, a science fiction place where you expect to see a rocket ship land. Tiny clusters of Tenggarese tread across the sand which stretches far away. The ideal time to visit is in the dry season when you have a better chance of seeing a blood-red sunrise. Over Christmas there are as many as 100 tourists standing on the rim. During July and August, there are often 50 people each night. The temperature on the top of Bromo is around 5 degrees C.; in July it could drop to 0 degrees C. Climb Gunung Penanjakan before sunrise. You can see the whole crater from its summit and perhaps see the sun rising over the island of Bali.

Kasada Festival (or the 'Karo Feast'): Like a Tenggerese All Soul's Day and a New Year's feast combined, this event is held in the Bromo crater on Buddah's birthday, the last month on the Tengger calendar. The Surabaya tourist office will be informed of when it is to take place. Before dawn, priests prepare their offerings to the God of Fire which are carried on bamboo poles by worshippers who hold coiling oil torches and climb to the top of Bromo by foot and horseback. All the way up the mountain are clusters of lights, rainbow colored Buddhist prayer flags, incense, flickering fires, and chanting saffron-robed priests. Thousands of people perch all along the razor-thin edge over roaring jets of steam 200 m below. There's a fantastic air of unreality, like a Black Mass, until the sun comes up dispelling the magic and fear. So far it works. This volcano last erupted in 1930.

getting there: Probolinggo to Sukapura, 30 km; Sukapura to Ngadisari, 14 km; Ngadisari to Cemoro Lawang, 3 km; Cemoro Lawang to the Bromo Crater, 3 km. From Probolinggo there's sometimes a bus at 9 am to Sukapura, but a more dependable one leaves at 2 pm. Takes 2 hours, costs Rp150. Another way is to take a Colt from Probolinggo's terminal Colt to Ngadisari; Colts leave every hour or so until noon. From Ngadisari to Cemoro Lawang, walk or take a horse (Rp1000-1500) either the day before or start out very early in the morning. **hitch**? Stand at the Ngadisari turnoff 12 km from Probolinggo or at another turnoff 4 km from Probolinggo. Travel up a tree-lined road of acacia forests to Sukapura. **from Tosari:** Another way is to approach Mt. Bromo from the west. Take a bus from Pasuruan to Tosari, Rp150. Tosari is 36 km from the main highway connecting Malang and Surabaya, and 19 km from Bromo. There are resthouses at Tosari. Most take a horse, led by the guide's flaming torch over a narrow trail past silent villages and deep ditches. Hills are bare except for low scrub. Choking fine red dust rises from the track. Getting nearer, this dying volcano smells of rotten eggs. The horse could become skittish on entering the caldera. The track then turns to undulating waves of sand. Although on the equator, it's very chilly. You have to stamp and walk up and down and throw your arms about to stay warm. The sun rises as you reach the top.

Sukapura: The first big town you come to coming up the valley from Probolinggo. If there's no transport to Ngadisari, don't sweat it. Just spend the night here, really good views and bracing climate. **stay:** Hotel Ex-Losmen Sukapura, Rp850 per room, no matter how many people. Another nice *losmen* is Hotel Bromo, Rp300 a night in big double beds. **from Sukapura:** Hitch a ride on a vegetable truck or with a tourist. Or hassel the taxi or *bemo* drivers down to the proper fare (Rp300) up to Ngadisari.

Ngadisari: Visitors must report to the *Hansip* (village homeguard) Post where you ask about horses. Keep your rucksack in the post. Very friendly, but refuse to pay Rp100 to pass. Horse-hire from Ngadisari to the Bromo crater is about Rp1000. It's a 3 km walk further straight uphill to the crater's rim where you can also find accommodation. **stay and eat:** Try new Wisma Utji guesthouse, but cheapest is to have the villagers put you up in their houses, such as Pak Manut's next to Lapangan Ngadisari, Rp3-400. Eat in the *warung* behind the police station, but bargain the price of the dishes.

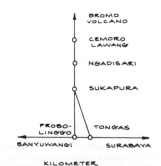

KILOMETER

PROBOLINGGO – BANYUWANGI	=	200 KM
PROBOLINGGO – SURABAYA	≈	100 KM
PROBOLINGGO – SUKAPURA	≈	30 KM
SUKAPURA – NGADISARI	≈	14 KM
TONGAS – SUKAPURA	≈	19 KM
NGADISARI – CEMORO LAWANG	=	3 KM
CEMORO LAWANG – BROMO	=	3 KM

Cemoro Lawang: 3 km higher than Ngadisari and only one hour's walk away from Bromo. From here it's just a 20 minute descent into the crater. On the edge of the crater pitch a tent or if you have a warm sleeping bag (it's as cold as Sydney in dead winter), sleep outside. Villagers will offer you a Rp600 bed, for which you can haggle them down to Rp500. Or stay at Motel Bromo Permai, 30 meters from the crater's edge. This 'motel' is actually similar to a youth hostel for all classes and ages. Some rooms facing the crater are as high as Rp3000, quite decrepit with dirty *mandi* water and kero lamps. It's a far better bargain if you stay in the row of rooms in the backyard for Rp1200 or 4 to one room, Rp300 apiece. Wait for someone else to happen along to share a room, otherwise you might talk to one of the waiters (see Hadi) to sleep in the 'special room' beside the kitchen, Rp600. Cozy campers' gatherings at night. Get a shot of Johnny Walker (Rp200) to brace you up against the cold; or a hot ginger drink, *sekotang*, Rp75. *Sop sayur* (vegetable soup) is the cheapest and neatest thing on the menu.

the climb: No matter how much you've heard of Mt. Bromo, you won't be prepared for this. You don't really need a guide, just follow the road. Get up at 3:30 or 4 am; you can hear the horses arrive outside. Take a flashlight. For this early morning climb, the best thing against the cold and wind is simply a blanket from the motel. When you reach the crater floor, head straight up through the corridor of white painted rocks which leads between The Cup and Mt. Bromo. If you get lost, wait for the horses to go by, then follow. At the top of a rise you'll find a concrete staircase up to the rim. If you don't feel like taking the walk the next morning, some people think that the sunrise from the motel is more sweeping. Just sit on a bench and take it in.
from Cemoro Lawang: To Tosari (19 km), it's 5-6 hours walk. To the village of Gubukklakah on the other side of the crater complex, it's 4-5 hours walk. Stay in the *kepala desa's* house or else in the other houses of the *kampung*. From Gubuklakah it's another 2-3 hours to Tupang where you can catch Colts or *oplets* into Malang for Rp200.

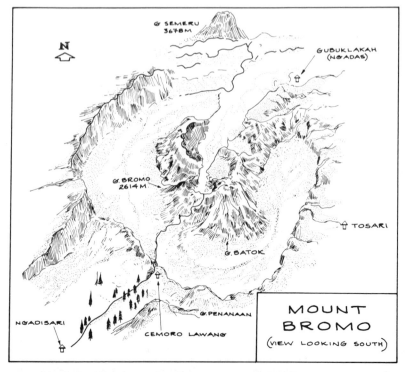

MOUNT BROMO (VIEW LOOKING SOUTH)

MALANG

90 km south of Surabaya. A nice, cool, clean city in the hills. Well-laid out square and parks. Trees everywhere. Big villas with large glass windows; old Dutch architecture. Coffee and tobacco growing area. Army Museum Brawijaya on south end of Jl. Besar Tjen for relics, photos, weapons, documents; open Sat., Sun., Tues., 8-12 pm only. South of the main square is Pasar Besar for fabrics, 2nd hand wares and antiques, good bronze and copper sections. An outstanding *jamu* shop is on Jl. J. A. Suprapto. Spiritual center Krishnamurti Foundation, c/o Mr. M. Dalidd, Jf. Singkep 14. For information: Robert Jan Waworuntu at the Tourist Development Board, Jl. Basuki Rachmat 72-76, is very helpful. Buy good maps and books at Toko Atlas, Jl. Basuki Rachmat. Flower market down on Jl. Majapahit. Children are also for sale further down in the *kampung* by the Brantas River. **transport:** Malang is not so big that you can't walk to anywhere in the city worth going to. **arts:** See Javanese *Ketoprak* performances 8-11 pm in the Wijaya Kusuma Building on Jl. Kabupaten, Rp280 for first class tickets. Shows are held nightly. Right down the street from Hotel Santosa *Ketoprak* performances are held 8-12 pm, Rp100-400, depending upon where you sit. Malang has long been a center of *topeng* culture and has a number of troupes. Go to Kepanjen, S.E. of the city, and to the Senggreng area, where shows are put on to celebrate marriages, circumcisions or village festivities.

stay: Hotel Simpang Tiga, Jl. Kasinkido 56, is the best for the money; clean and only Rp550, or Rp1100 double. It's far from the bus station but close to the Sawahan Colt Station. Hotel Miranda, Jl. K.A. Zainul Arifin (Kidul Dalem), Rp1500, for 4 people Rp3000. A palatial hotel, quite clean, big rooms. Meals served just next door in Depot Murni; *mie goreng* Rp175, etc., are quite good. Losmen Agung, Jl. Belakang Loji near the Malang Theatre, Rp950 for 2, Rp1500 for 3. Small rooms in the back for Rp500, clean and quiet. Losmen Montana, Jl. Kahuripan, Rp1250 for the cheapest rooms, single or double; with bath, Rp1500; fairly clean. Hotel Sriwijaya near the Penjara Perempuan, Rp1210 for 1 or 2, Rp1815 for 3. Nice view out the back over the river and *kampungs* in the distance. Single girls are advised to avoid Hotel Santosa, really *kasar* management. At Hotel Semarang there's a genuine Indian Swami who reads palms of young women, locking the door and looking down their blouse as they lean over. For the splash, Splendid Inn near Alun2 Bundar, Jl. Majapahit 4, is recommended; Rp5250-6500 double including breakfast, tax and service. The YMCA on Jl. J.A. Suprapto is comfortable at Rp2500 single including breakfast.

eat: For Padang food at its best, eat at Minang Jaya on Jl. Basuki Rachmat 22 near the YMCA, or Minang Agung, also on Jl. Basuki Rachmat. Indonesian *warung* food is served at Pasar Besar until 8 pm; good fruit here during the day (avocados Rp30 each). On Jl. Pegadaian at Depot Marhaen, good *warung* food. Tasty *sate* at Warung Nikmat, Jl. K. A. Zainul Arifin 61. Food stalls at night are found near Merdeka Bioskop at the bottom of Jl. Basuki Rachmat; *martabak, mie, sate,* etc. Other stalls on corner of Jl. H. Agus Salim and Merdeka Station. For *mie* dishes try Depot Pangsit Mie, Jl. Kahuripan 24. For other Chinese food, Nikmat-Lezat and Dirsa-Surya, both close together on Jl. Pertukangan; okay meals for Rp5-600. If you want to splurge on Chinese food, go to Taman Sari, Jl. A. Dahlan, where the dishes are superb; crab claws are the best you'll ever have. Eat well for Rp1000-1500. Everyone goes to Tiga Putra, Jl. Pasar Besar — but it's not as good, just cleaner and brighter.

MALANG

1. *to Museum Brawijaya*
2. *Toko Atlas*
3. *Pattimura Bus Station*
4. *Splendid Inn*
5. *YMCA*
6. *antique shop*
7. *Losmen Montana*
8. *Hotel Sentosa*
9. *Sawahan Bemo Station*
10. *Pasar Besar*

---

pasars: Be sure to visit the *pasars* of Malang. Anything that the Javanese doesn't need for his own consumption, such as extra rice, is sold in the *pasar* for cash. These markets are the major channel for villagers to acquire cash income to buy items of technology and pleasure - combs, mirrors, tobacco, cassettes, radios, furniture, cooking oil, kerosene, sugar, textiles, fertilizers, etc. The *pasar* is the climax of the pre-industrial life, its whole focus and center.

from Malang by road: There's an incredible road (but very bad) of variegated landscapes running N.E. from Malang for 75 km, passing by pine forests, ricefields, waterfalls, rickety old bridges, mountain passes, orchid farms, riverbeds. **bemos and minibuses:** The biggest *bemo* station in Malang is on Jl. Pasar Besar in front of Pasar Besar. Sawahan Station, on the corner of Jl. Sulawesi and Jl. Julius Usmat, is the big Colt minibus station. Some fares: Jember Rp600 (189 km); Kediri, Rp350

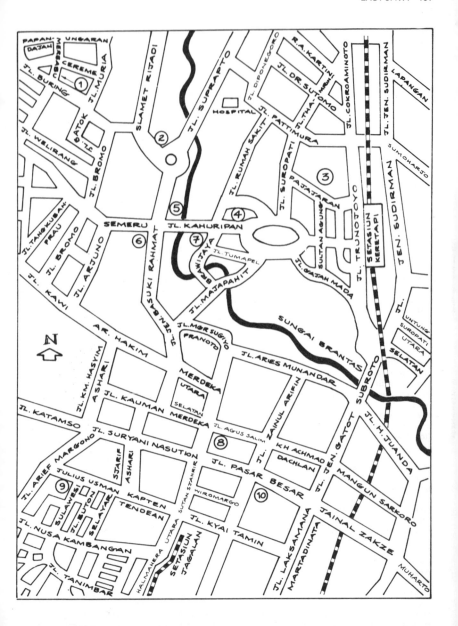

(100 km); Blitar, Rp300 (78 km); Banyuwangi, Rp1200 (400 km). Take a minibus to Surabaya, Rp350, on a road with volcanic mountains rearing up on both sides. The minibus to Blitar (Panataran temple complex) is 80 km, a refreshing road through the mountains. **buses:** Stasium Bis Pattimura, Jl. Pattimura 54, is about Rp100 from the city by *becak*. Some fares: Bali, Rp1850, leaving at 5 pm and 7 pm; Kediri, Rp375, 3 times in the morning starting at 6:25 am; Banyuwangi, Rp970, 9 times a day; Surabaya, Rp250, starting at 6:30, every 10 minutes; Blitar, Rp250, every 10 minutes; Semarang, Rp1300, starting at 4:40 am; Yogya, Rp1270, 6 times a day; Solo, Rp1100 (same bus as the Yogya bus); Probolinggo (Climb Mt. Bromo?), Rp300. **night buses:** For Bali, Agung Express, Jl. Gereja, close to the bus station, leaves 7 pm, arrives in Denpasar 5 am. This same company has buses to Yogya, leaving at 8 pm, arriving at 4 or 5 am (arrives in Solo at 2 am). Also try Pemuda Express, Jl. Kidul Dalam 22; for Bali, Rp1850, leaving at 5 pm arrives at 5 am; for Yogya, Rp1600; Semarang, Rp1600.

vicinity of Malang: Using Malang as a base, there are many points of interest to visit. Jabung, N.E., of the city is known for its handsome *langgar* (prayer-houses) and large well built stone houses. **Mt. Buring:** 3 km south of Malang towards Bululawang. Good view of Malang from its 631 m height. Start climbing from Kedungkandang. Sometimes see Javanese Hindu women carrying morning offerings to the gods up this hill, just as on Bali. A Hindu-Java revival is taking place in East Java, now 400,000 strong, focusing around Malang. **Mendit Lake:** 7 km N.E. of Malang. There's no train anymore. Take a *bemo* to Blimbing, then it's 3 km further by Colt. Has monkeys, ruins, a hermitage with a hermit, a clear water pool; very relaxing. **Gunung Kawi:** A pilgrimmage place 40 km from Malang on the southern slopes of G. Butak. Go to Kepanjen 18 km south of Malang, then by horseback (or walk) up to Gendogo, and from there by foot a further 3 km. Or if you go on Thurs. there are many Colts doing the trip from Malang; board one at Sawahan station, Rp500. Crowds continuously worship Mbah Jugo's grave here; sometimes number in the thousands. All faiths visit this site from all over Indonesia seeking healing, fertility, blessing the mother of the paddyfields, for plain good luck, etc. Each individual has his own idea of Mbah Jugo. **Ngliyep:** A getaway beach 60 km south of Malang. Take a minibus or bus Rp75 in the direction of Blitar and get off at Kepanjen 18 km from Malang. In Kepanjen, arrange for a ride on a vegetable truck the rest of the way, Rp250. There's a *losmen* in Ngliyep for Rp250, but it's kind of ratty and has no toilets. You can possibly crash in the radar station 4 km from Ngliyep.

Mt. Semeru: South of Mt. Bromo. One of the most beautiful volcanic peaks in the world and the highest on Java (3680 m). Named after the Indian World Mountain, Meru. According to myth, all the other mountains of Java fell away from Semeru on its journey from India. A very strenuous 3-4 day climb. Only for the experienced. Approach from Tumpang, Rp125 from Blimbing Station. From Tumpang take a *dokar* to Poncokusomo, Rp350. Start climbing. Reach Ranupane in one day. From Ranupane it's another 2 day's walk. You must time your arrival at the summit by 7 or 8 pm because of the release of deadly gases. Inside the crater you walk in white and up to your knees. Not only can you see the Java Sea and all the mountains of East Java from the top but if the weather is clear, you even see Bali. **Mt. Arjuna:** Takes 20 hours to climb. It's 4 hours to reach Wonosari, then 16 more hours to reach the summit. There's no water, so take a gallon.

Batu: This 2000 m high mountain resort is 17 km north of Malang. Take a Colt or taxi-truck from Jl. Kauman near the *alun2* in Malang for Rp125-150. Batu is a small quiet town with few other travelers. Batu is dry, Selecta is wetter. Even during the rains there's always 1 or 2 hours of sunshine at Batu. **stay:** Central and homely Losmen Kawi, Jl. Panglima Soedirman 19, Rp1000 for 1 or 2; if it's not crowded you can bargain her down to Rp500 single. Hotel Mutiara, Jl. Soedirman 9 IV/146, Tel. 192, is down a small lane right under Gunung Arjuna; Rp1500 single or double, Rp2000 for 3 people. Clean and quiet except for a terrific sound system. Penginapan Metropole, Jl. Soedirman 93, Rp1000 for YHA card holders. Has a 8000 m garden in the back with ½ kilo apples, juicy avocados. This woman, who knocked a Japanese soldier off his feet during the war, can tell you some stories. She cooks excellent Javanese, Chinese, Greek and Dutch food. Losmen Maru near Cine Solo, Jl. Agus Salim 234, is the cheapest at Rp600 single, Rp800 double. About 20 working girls live here (first price: Rp2500), so don't expect to get much sleep. **eat:** Restoran Kenangan, located beside the market, has Chinese food; *cap cai*, Rp250. Another quite small, cheap restaurant for Chinese-Indonesian cooking is beside the Garuda Theatre near the police station.

vicinity of Batu: From Batu to Kandangan and Trowulan, Rp275 in all. Half-way between Batu and Selecta is Punten, Rp50 by taxi. Renowned for its citrus fruits. Much lower-priced than Selecta. Stay in Losmen Punten, Rp750 single or double. Or Peng. Pondok Asri, Rp500. Wisma Viva, further up the hill, is where all the girls are. There's a sulphur springs at Songgoriti, an easy walk from Batu. It costs Rp600 for the 'nice bath' and Rp200 for the other one. There's a hotel in Songgoriti and next to

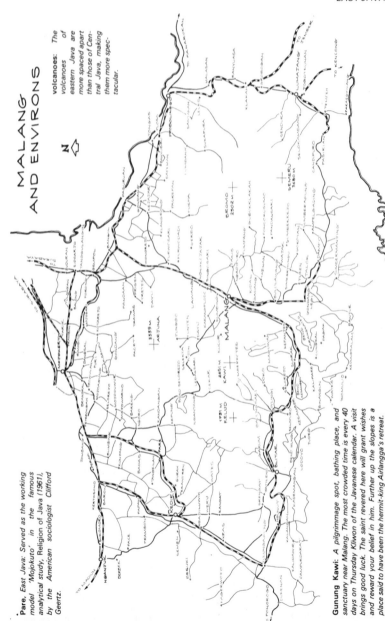

MALANG AND ENVIRONS

volcanoes: The volcanoes of eastern Java are more spaced apart than those of Central Java, making them more spectacular.

Pare, East Java: Served as the working model 'Mojokuto' in the famous analytical study, Religion of Java (1961), by the American sociologist Clifford Geertz.

Gunung Kawi: A pilgrimmage spot, bathing place, and sanctuary near Malang. The most crowded time is every 40 days on Thursday Kliwon of the Javanese calendar. A visit brings good luck. The saint revered here will grant wishes and reward your belief in him. Further up the slopes is a place said to have been the hermit-king Airlangga's retreat.

it is a *losmen*. Sebalwung Falls is 6 km from Batu, and Joban Rondo Falls is 1½ hours south on foot. From the top of Panderman (3037 m), a great view.

Selecta: A haven in the Java hills, 6½ km from Batu, Rp75 by taxi. A spectacular view of the volcano from here. Some of the attractions of Selecta are snack bars, roadside markets, good tennis courts, cold water swimming pools, hill walks, fresh air, and an astounding variety of plants, wild orchids, trees and fruits, with alpine and tropical plants growing side by side. Gladiolas flower in February. To enter the park and the rock garden, Rp100. Stay at Hotel Selecta, Rp3000 double. Hotel Sentosa is Rp3000 with meals. **from Selecta:** North of Selecta visit the little mountain town of Sumber Brantas, and the source of the Brantas River. Climb Mt. Arjuna on horseback via Lalijiwo. Mt. Welirang (3156 m) can be climbed as well. Mt. Anjasmoro (2277) is an easy 3 hours climb.

Lawang: 18 km north of Malang. Visit the grand 5-storey art nouveau mansion built by a Brazilian architect at the turn of the century, now taken over by Hotel Niagara. It has 10 m high ceilings, painted wall tiles, terrazzo floors, etched glass, brass railings, teak paneling. Go up to the rooftop for a new look at Gunung Arjuna. **vicinity of Lawang:** Many small guesthouses in the surrounding area of Lawang. Baung Falls is 5 km from Lawang. Kebun Raya Purwodadi, established in 1914 as a branch of the Botanical Gardens of Bogor, is a big, dry-climate botanical gardens, 300 m high, just 5 km north of Lawang on the lower slopes of G. Arjuna. **Nonkojajar:** 15 km S.E. of Purwodadi by car in the Tengger Mountains; see the Coban Waru Falls, Veth's and Lawangan Hills, and 100 m high Rambutmogo Falls. Riding horseback is the best. Ride all the way to Tosari in 3-4 hours, rest, then ascend for 19 km to the Bromo volcano.

TEMPLES IN THE VICINITY OF MALANG

Malang is about the most advantageous base from which to visit the astonishingly rich Hindu Java ruins of East Java. Allow at least a week. Chronologically, the sequence is: 7th Century Candi Badut, 3 km to the west of Malang; 10th Century Candi Gunung Gangsir, about 64 km N.E. of Malang; 13th Century Candi Kidal, about 20 km S.E. of Malang; 13-14th Century Candi Jago, 16 km S.E.; 14th Century Candi Jawi, 40 km north; and finally Candi Singosari, 10 km north of Malang. **transport:** Your own vehicle or motorcycle would be ideal. If you go by *bemos* and Colts, allow more time. All you need to visit most of the temples is just an early start each day and a pocketful of change. Stand out on Jl. Basuki Rachmat in front of the YMCA and tell the *oplet* drivers you want to go to Blimbing,

which is a northern suburb of Malang, the focal point for *oplets* and Colts whose routes pass by the various temple locations. The drivers will drop you off at the right places.

Candi Singosari: The local name is Candi Linggo. 12 km north of Malang in the town of Singosari. Take an *oplet* Rp30 to Blimbing, then pay another Rp30 by *oplet* to Singosari. Walk 1 km down a side road. This Shiva shrine, built around 1300 A.D., is the most imposing monument left of the murderous Singosari Dynasty. It was built in a fierce monumental East Javanese style to honor a king and all his priests who were killed in a palace revolt while feasting with his prime minister. This monarch, King Kartanagara, mortified Kubla Khan's Chinese emissaries by cutting off their noses and tatooing 'No!' across their foreheads, an act which precipitated (in 1293 A.D.) the launching of 1000 Mongol troop ships to Java in retaliation. Most of the statues originally at Singosari now form the backbone of the world famous Hindu Javanese collection at the Leyden Museum in Holland, including the masterpiece of Singosari iconographic art and perhaps of all Hindu-Javanese religious sculpture, the renowned Prajnaparamita image. Architecturally, what makes Singosari unique is that the so-called base is actually the central *cella* of the temple; the inner sanctum of the temple is situated in the base. Thus it's called a cellar-temple, or tower-temple by archaeologists. Only the top of Singosari has ornamentation. Because of time, finance or catastrophe, ornamentation wasn't completed on the remainder. Carving was always begun at the top of a *candi* and worked downwards so as not to damage lower finished sculptures with falling pieces. See 3.8 m tall *raksasas,* and the statue of Guru Agasty in the yard. In a field to the east just 200 m further down the road going away from the Malang-Surabaya highway, are a pair of enormous terrifying guardian statues wearing snakes and skulls.

Candi Sumberawan: 6 km from Candi Singosari. Go towards the guardian statues, then turn to the right down a country road and walk northeast until you reach this bell-shaped *stupa,* one of the only two *stupas* in all of East Java. A *stupa* symbolizes Buddah's death and his attainment of *nirvana* (heavenly bliss).

Candi Indrokilo: 5 km N.W. of Purworejo or 2 km north of Purwodadi. Walk or take a pony

Candi Jago: 18 km east of Malang. From Blimbing take a Colt or an *oplet* to Tumpang, Rp125-150. Candi Jago is close to the road near the *pasar.* People will point out the way. Although the roof and body have caved in, it's still one of the most remarkable temples from the East Javanese period. Made of andesite stone. Effusive decoration. Although Jago dates from 1269 A.D., it has distinct connections with the prehistoric monuments and terraced sanctuaries found in the mountains in which the very high base is brought into prominence. There's one beautiful door-opening intact and a flight of steps decorated with complicated arabesques and curls, also Buddhist sculptures, Krishna reliefs, Arjuna's fretful night in his hermitage, and some of the first grotesque *panakawan* carvings. There are also reliefs of the Pandavas going into exile, set in a frame of cloudy sky and rocky earth; the *jataka* animal fables; the *Mahabharata* story decorates the side panels. See clearly the shift towards 2-dimensional figures that occured during this dynasty. *Wayang*-like moving picture sculptures are placed right next to each other like figures in stiff parade. The action unfolds clockwise. Temple reliefs are bolder, more vigorous than any earlier style. Definitely a change was taking place. Sumberwringin watering place is nearby.

Candi Kidal: A very characteristic East Javanese temple. At Tumpang's market, rent a *dokar* Rp600 to the temple and back. The village of Kidal is 7 km west of Tumpang on the road back to Malang via Tajinan. A nice road to get down to it On the far side of the village you'll see the sign. Small but lovely, this 12.5 m tall burial temple honors a Singosari king who died in 1248 A.D. To the left of the steps are well-crafted episodes of Garuda carrying the nectar of immortality. The building appears more slender since the base towers up so high, the temple tapering at the top to form a pyramid. It has elaborate carvings of medallions and *kala*-heads on the main body. Statues of Garuda guard its base.

Yang Mountain: Built on these slopes during the megalithic stone age are terraced pyramids used as burial places for ancestors.

Candi Kedaton: West of Mt. Yang near Bondowoso. Completed at a much later date (14th Century) than the megaliths. Reliefs depict scenes from Arjuna's adventures and the story of Garuda. The walls on the base look like stories from a Balinese *lontar* book. Graceful figures.

Candi Jawi: On the right-hand side of the road from Pandaan up to Tretes. An early 14th Century gem in masonry, built on a terrace surrounded by a moat. Most of its blocks have been hauled off and used for local buidling. Inexplicable, unidentified quite realistic reliefs are carved all around the temple, a mixture of Shivaite and Buddhist elements. In an *atap* hut nearby there's a portrait of Shiva, kept there to keep it safe from robbers.

BALURAN GAME PARK

In the N.E. corner of Java 12 km from Wonorejo in a dry country of open beach forests, scrubland, coastal marshes, swampy groves, and crab-eating monkeys. This is one of the most accessible of Indonesia's game parks, lying just 5 hours by bus, 264 km from Surabaya on the road to Banyuwangi. Baluran is unusual for Java because it is a mountainous area, yet it has beaches. Go in the drier months (April-Oct.) to see herds moving to the waterholes. **getting there:** Get first to Wonorejo, Rp200 by Colt from Situbondo, or Rp125 by Colt from Banyuwangi. At the park's entrance report to Pos Gabungan Abri (Military Post) and pay the entrance fee of Rp75. It's compulsory that someone accompanies you from Pos Gabungan Abri the 11 km to Bekol in the park's center, Rp250. Or you can arrange with the soldiers to rent a truck for Rp2000-3000. Keep your heavy luggage at the Pos Gabungan Abri for 2-3 days if you want; it's safe because there they lock up thieves. Take food along. Binoculars are available from the park attendant in the park.

stay: In Bekol the Forestry Authority runs a *pasangrahan* (guesthouse), Rp500 per night. Meals come to about Rp500 per day. There's a guard at the *pasangrahan*, so your stuff is safe. No electricity but acetylene lamps. There's a spring nearby where you can see the animals come to drink. The beach is only a 2½ km walk from the watchtower and park centre. **sights:** For someone to guide you within the park itself, Rp500. On Mt. Bekol there's a 6 m high watchtower with a telescope for viewing the animals. Most animals are seen at dawn or dusk. The landscape looks like Africa. See peacocks prancing, wild wart hogs thunder across savannahs of acacia trees with solitary crowns, and grasslands of wild oxen that weight up to 2 tons and stand as high as a man. Don't get out of the jeep or off well-trodden tracks. Climb up through the mahogany and teakwood forests of Madura Strait. **from Baluran:** There are two other wildlife parks on the S.E. coast of Java, Maelang and Meru Meru, which are like smaller versions of Baluran. Visit the long white beach between Ketapang and Menang, both north of Banyuwangi, where there's a holy stone (Watu Dodol) and the grave of an unknown hermit nearby This coastline facing Bali is rich copra country with miles upon miles of jungle slopes covered in stands of coconut trees.

BANYUWANGI

On the far east coast of Java: Banyuwangi's very beautiful mosque, Mesjid Baiturrachman, is Rp50

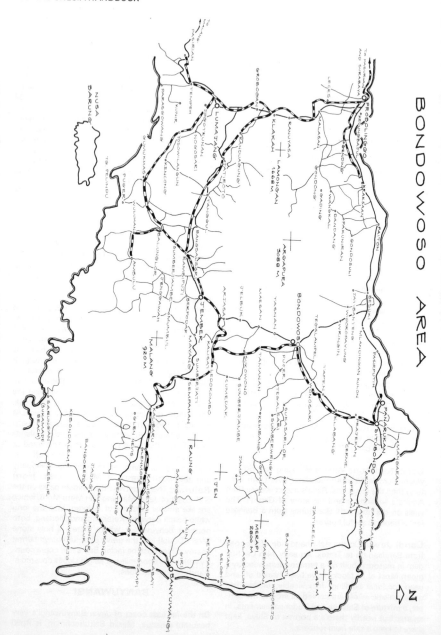

BONDOWOSO AREA

by *becak* from the bus station. Nitour Office, Jl. Raya 43 C, Tel. 678, can advise about tours to the Ijen Plateau. **stay:** Get to Bali where the living is better. In Banyuwangi the nicest cheap place, usually quiet but it's often full, is Hotel Wisma Blambangan, Jl. Dr. Wahidin 3, Tel. 299. Rooms are as low as Rp750 and Rp850, or for 2, Rp1700 and Rp2000. Hotel Berlin Barat, a noisy whorehouse, is on Jl. Pertukangan, Rp600 for a little room, Rp700 for a 'grand room'. Cheap tasty meals are available at Depot Mama and Papa a block away (soto ayam, Rp150); meet their daughter Vivik before she gets married off. Hotel Baru, Jl. Pattimura 2, has small rooms for Rp750 single, or Rp850 for a double bed. Rooms range up to Rp1250 for 3 beds or Rp2000 for 5. At Kaliklatak Plantation, 20 km from Banyuwangi, there's a guesthouse.

from Banyuwangi: Catch ferries to Bali from Ketapang, 4 km north of town Rp50 by taxi or Colt. Ferries cross 8 times a day, Rp125. Then it's 3 more hours by bus from Gilamanuk (port on Bali side) to the capital of Bali, Denpasar. If you're too late for the regular ferry, just go through the hole in the fence and walk down the bench 250 m to the LCM depot. Catch one of these converted WWII landing crafts which leave for Bali quite often up to 8 pm. They cost less (Rp100) and are just as fast. From Banyuwangi Colt station to: Pesanggaran, Rp250; Licin (from where you climb to the Ijen Crater), Rp100; Situbondo, Rp300.

vicinity of Banyuwangi: 78 km south of Banyuwangi is Sukamade Beach with its deep green water, 250 kilo sea turtles, and a blinding, long beach, most of the time empty. Take bus first to Pesanggaran, Rp200, then from Pesanggaran to Sukamade by taxi, Rp150. The last remaining Java tigers are in a wildlife reserve nearby; also black monkeys and sleek long-bodied panthers. Bawean Bird Park, where there's waterfowl species including pelicans and cormerares, is south of Sukamade on a small islet along the coast. Each New Year's Day of the Javanese calendar (1st of Sura), there's a mass-bathing ceremony on this coast. **Blambangan Peninsula:** A remote peninsula located on the far S.E. corner of Java. This region was the last stronghold of institutionalized Hinduism on Java (until the 17th Century), the legendary kingdom of Menak Jonggo. An unexplored archaeological region, now a wildlife reserve.

Bondowoso area: Use the *losmen* in Bondowoso as a base. Coffee plantations dot this valley floor. Bondowoso and Situbondo are both renowned for their bullfighting contests (bull against bull). You might catch one. Visit the livestock market in the village of Wonosari and the two volcanoes Gunung Hyang and Gunung Ijen. Walk to the placid Lake Kawah 150 km in diameter in the mountains. Ijen Plateau has a dormant volcano with crater lakes and savannah landscapes. Tourists haven't made it here yet, not at all built up. **getting there:** Approach the plateau from Banyuwangi. First take a taxi to Licin, 14 km, Rp125, then from Licin walk or take horse Rp1000 the 16 km to the *pasangrahan*. Shorter is to take a bus from Banyuwangi to Situbondo, Rp300, then from Situbondo to Wonosari, Rp100. From Wonosari travel up to Pondokraja by bus. Then just follow the trail. From the crater, climb Gunung Merapi with its dark forests and 170 m deep crater lake. Go wandering. **other sights:** Prajikan, 12 km south of Situbondo or 24 km north of Bondowoso, is a pilgrimmage spot — the holy grave of Kiai Emas Atmari. South of Mt. Semeru from Pasirian to Dampit there's a 50 km long scenic highway. Time it in the wet season, more color. Candi Puro at Pasirian has been almost ruined by eruptions of Mt. Semeru. There are nice seascapes at Bambang and at Parasgowang south of Pasirian. A bathing place is at Selokambang, 5 km north. At Jember, stay at Pak Handojo's, Jl. Wachid Hasyim 148 (Tel. 148), Rp1200 room and board. Beautiful beaches at Puger and at Watu Ulo, 30 km south of Jember.

SURABAYA

Surabaya is the industrial city of Indonesia, the biggest city in East Java (2.6 million population) and the 2nd largest city in Indonesia, its bustle and noise contrasting with the serene countryside around it. The idea that Surabaya is a dirty port city full of pickpockets just isn't true anymore. The people are friendlier and the city is generally cheaper than Jakarta. Tunjungan, Surabaya's shopping center, often has better bargains than Singapore. And take a look at the new two-storey airconditioned super-flash passenger terminal at Tanjung Perak, Surabaya's port. This is an active city for theatre and East Javanese dance forms. Try to see the astounding horse trance-dance, *Kuda Kepang. Imigrasi*, Jl. Kayoon 50, is only 10 minutes walk from the Bamboo Denn. Pay Landing Fee of Rp8000 and extension fee of Rp3000 (or only Rp2000 if they've already eaten their lunch). **history:** Alleged to have been founded on the spot where a legendary battle between a shark (sura) and a crocodile (buaya) took place. Surabaya has been the trading center and chief harbor of East Java since the fall of the 14th Century Majapahit Kingdom. Formerly it consisted of islands and swamps where King Wijaya of Majapahit did battle with Kublai Khan's Chinese army in 1293 A.D. After World War II, nationalist forces fought the British Occupation Army here and when things weren't going their way, beginning on Nov. 10, 1945, the British bombed this defenceless city for 3 days and 3 nights (read *Surabaya* by Idrus about this battle). The Tugu Pahlawan monument commemorates this guerilla war against the Dutch and their allies. During the political upheavals of 1965-66 there were street executions, bodies clogged up under the bridges, and Surabaya's canals flowed red for months. Outside the city near the airport was the site where thousands of 'communists' were massacred by villagers cranked up on *jihad*. The captives were led to believe that they were being driven to the airport to be deported but were murdered on the way. Very messy. There's even a special onomatoepoetic verb in Javanese for 'killing by cutting the jugular vein'.

transport: *Becaks* cost Rp50-100 for an average fare. Even cheaper are *Bis Kota* (city buses) which travel all the main routes of the city, Rp30. Take *bemos* near the Bamboo Denn for the big Joyoboyo Bus Station just past the zoo. Quite a good *bemo* system, the fare is Rp30, with routes all over the city. The two biggest *bemos* stations in Surabaya are at Wonokromo (near Joyoboyo) and at Jembatan Merah (The Red Bridge). A *bemo* from Wonokromo Station to Jembatan Merah Station is Rp30. **arriving by air:** At Juanda Airport taxis want up to Rp5000 to take you into the city. Instead, walk to the bus station at Waru, one km from the airport and take 'Bus H' into Joyoboyo Station in the middle of Surabaya for only Rp30, then another Rp30 by *bemo* or bus to the Bamboo Denn, the cheapest hotel.

stay: Best for the money is Bamboo Denn, also called the Transito Inn, Jl. Pemuda 19; Rp375 for dorm beds, Rp1000 for a double room. Many advantages to staying here: it's open all night, it's central (750 m from Gubeng Station), and you get all kinds of information from other travelers (about 5 different versions of the Bromo trip every day!). Meals are too expensive (one egg, Rp250!) and there is a constant communication breakdown between the guests and the kitchen, so eat for less than Rp100 up the street in front of the *rumah sakit*, 5 minutes walk, or in front of Gubeng Station at night. Read 'Regulations to the Students of the Webb Language Institute' — a gas! Go to the Jungle Bar at night. It's Rp150 by *becak* to a hotel with resident prostitutes at Jl. Bangun Sari 2, about 3 km from the Bamboo Denn; Rp500 singles. Hotel Wisma Nirvana, Jl. Jen Basuki Rachmat 124 A; has twin-bedded rooms with bathrooms and fans, Rp2750 double. Hotel Paviljoen, Jl. Genteng Besar 94, Rp2000 for 1 or 2. Wisma Ganeca, Jl. Sumatra 34 A, is very comfortable and only 200 m from Gubeng Station; Rp1750 per room. For something different, there's a number of cheap hotels all along Jl. Mansur right in the midst of the Arab Quarter (Kampung Sasak), a busy warehouse and

market neighborhood only a short walk from Jembatan Merah. Not bad are Hotel Mesir, Rp500 single, Rp1000 double; Rumah Peng. Santosa, Jl. Mansur 57, Rp550 single or double; Hotel Kemajuan, Jl. Mansur, Rp500 single or Rp750 double.

eat: Try the East Javanese specialty *bumbu rujuk*, chicken in chili sauce. Kampung Sasak is a great place to eat Chinese, Arab, and Indonesian food at night. Open until 5 am. At Warung Pojok, *kopi medina* (Arabian coffee) with ginger and anisette, healthy and gives you energy; *nasi kebuli, sate kambing* (goat), Rp15 per stick, and *caac* (Arabian-style ginger bread). Eat roast goat, Rp250 per serving, at Restoran Atika; opens in the late afternoon. For Chinese cooking, dine at the Phoenix, Jl. Genteng, Kali Petak 1-2; or at Kiet Wan Kie, Jl. Kembang Jepun 51. More Chinese restaurants are along Jl. Kendung Doro. The oldest *jamu* shop in East Java is also on this street; hand-beaten fresh drinks served in coconut cups. Surabaya is a good place for fried things like puffy *cemblem* (jam donuts). Buy kilos of *krupuk* wholesale in the Sitoarjo District. Best seafood and cheap is the Shinta, Jl. Besar; watch for the big Pertamina neon-sign. Also the Miami, Jl. Urip Sumohargo 43, has great seafood, but a bit more expensive than usual; lobster fried rice, Rp500, and other meals are up to Rp2000. Excellent Indonesian food at the Bibi-Baba Restaurant at Tunjungan or at the Zoo Corner Restaurant at the Zoo. Eat anytime in the *warungs* known Kuputran; other good *warung* areas are along Jl. Basuki Rachmat and around Tunjungan. Probably the number one *martabaks* in all of Indonesia are made in and around the THR complex at night. For the best ice cream try Turin Italian, Jl. Kayoon 10 A; Yoly, Jl. Progo 7; and Zangrandi, Jl. Yos Sudarso 15.

SURABAYA

1. Bamboo Den Hotel
2. Tourist Office
3. Governor's Residence
4. Branch Post Office
5. Gubeng Train Station
6. Rumah Batik Danar Hadi
7. Elteha Bus Company
8. Wisma Ganeca
9. Immigration Department
10. to the zoo and Joyoboyo Bus Station
11. bemos *and buses to the harbor*
12. K.M.S. (Municipality Office)
13. Kembang Express Bus Company
14. Tanjungan Shopping District
15. T.H.R. (People's Amusement Park)
16. Pasar Turi
17. Kota Train Station

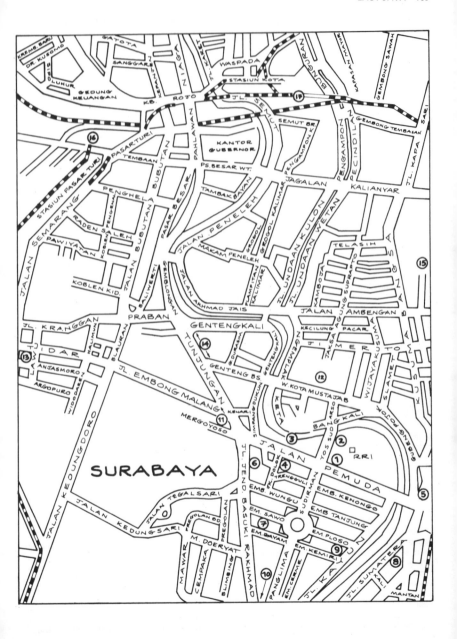

becak: The *becak* drivers of Surabaya stretch plastic bands under the seats that hum in the wind like riding a flying saucer. In other parts of Java drivers tie bundles of metal discs and iron gears under the seat that sound like sleigh bells (Cirebon). Original, colorful and zany works of art are painted on the sides of *becaks* by *kampung* artists in just 40 minutes: scenes of erupting volcanoes, ricefields, mountain lakes, airplanes, villages, dance and circus scenes, fantastic winged horses and men with wings fighting saber-jets, mythical birds, pagodas, junks, ships, Apollo moon landings, characters and events from Indian epics, sexy girls, breathtaking landscapes of paradise. The drivers love to be photographed posing beside their machines. Often *becaks* are given names like Krishna, Apache, Rocket Man, Voodoo. Few men work harder for their bowl of rice than the *becak* driver. His thighs are enormous, his shirt is wet with sweat, his life longevity averages about 35 years.

shopping: Check around Tunjungan Shopping district for cameras, sound systems, casette recorders and other electronic goods at prices often as much as 25% below Singapore's. Buy casette tapes (hot jazz, heavy classics, hillbilly, rock, Javanese *gamelan*, and Balinese dance music), for only Rp6-700. A *batik* showroom, Rumah Batik Danar Hadi, is at Jl. Basuki Rachmat 9. The GKBJ, on Jl. Kranggan 102, is where all *batik* styles can be purchased. For *batiks* and *sarungs*, some good buys are found on Jl. Panggung and on Jl. Sasak. The most capable tailors in the city are found on Jl. Embong Malang. The Kayoon flower market is interesting. The best antique shops are on Jl. Urip Sumoharjo, for carriage lamps, old bottles, coins. For gold and silver, try *kampungs* Gipo and Nyamplungan. A good general market is on Jl. Kuputran.

sights: The tourist office, Jl. Yos Sudarso 3, specializes in East Java; very helpful. Get their 77-78 Events booklets. For information about when the Madura bullraces are held (or about anything), see Pacto Tours on the opposite corner to the Bamboo Denn. AKSERA (Academy of Fine Arts) for performances. Gay spot Kota Braja (nicknamed Paradise Park) 400 m from Bambo Denn. Best saltwater acquarium is at the zoo; there's another smaller one at Pasar Kembang on Jl. Kayoon. Ngampel, near Semut Station, is the tomb of the first Islamic settler in East Java, Sunan Ampel. This sacred cemetary with its Hindu-style gates sits right in the middle of an orthodox Islamic neighborhood. Jolo Dolog ('fat young man') is a Buddhist stone statue of King Kartanagara seated on a pedestal inscribed 1289 A.D. This magic place lies opposite the governor's residence. Bring flowers and a few rupes. Visit the Kali Mas wharf area in the northern part of the city with its motorless Makassar schooners, many weighing over 200 tons. Also see the Chinese neighborhood. **museums:** Near the zoo, on Jl. Taman Mayankera 6, is a small historical museum. Open 9-1, closed on Sundays. There's also the inevitable Army Museum, but it's a long way out.

Surabaya Zoo: Only an hour's walk from the Bamboo Denn. Or take a *bemo* down Jl. Jen. Soedirman, Rp30. One of the most complete zoos in Southeast Asia, specializing in exotic birds and nocturnal animals. Go early to watch them feed the animals. On Sundays, sit and feast your eyes on the women in their dazzling native dress. Eat *gado2* (Rp65) under trees of swinging monkeys. There are 500 species of animals including mongolian bears. See the aviary (with its great collection of pheasants) and the cassowaries (world's largest flightless bird). The Nocturama (Rp50 entrance) houses slow lorries, marvelous flying squirrels and flying cats. The Dolphinarium features the freshwater Mahakam River dolphins from Borneo. The hoofed and ruminant enclosures for the rare Chinese wapiti, the *babirusa*, and the *anoa* (dwarf buffalo). There are 18 komodo dragons devouring raw meat in a sandbed enclosure. In the Reptilium see King Cobras. The canopy dwellers exhibit, with its Proboscis monkeys, black-crested macques from Sulawesi and pig-tailed monkeys, is one of the best. The Sea Acquarium is also a must.

Jane's House: Jl. Dinoyo 100. They don't like just anybody tramping through so ask permission at the reception desk first. Souvenir sellers are not allowed entry, nor is anyone allowed to take photographs. This hotel (US$15 per day single) contains one of the best private antique and traditional arts collections in Indonesia: the whole facade of an exuberantly carved Jepara house is on display in the bar, 18th Century Javanese beds, Spanish and Raffles chairs, French mirrors, Chinese offering altars. There are often concerts and folk songs at dinner, barefoot boys in *sarungs* serve you just like during the Dutch era. Handles a lot of package tour groups from Europe and Australia.

THR: The Luna Park of Surabaya, Rp150 for two by *becak* from the Bamboo Denn. Don't go in the big flash entrance. The one to the left, Rp30 entrance, is the part with the best and cheapest small restaurants and most of the theatres. Nighly performances of *wayang orang, Ludruk* and *Sri Mulat* open stage shows which sometimes feature live *Kroncong* pop-bands. Most productions are really bastardized with Bruce Lee-type sensationalist combat styles, giving the audience their money's worth. The Sri Wandowo Theatre has Rp200 seats right down to quite adequate Rp50 seats. 'The War' happens around 10 pm, otherwise it's all dialogue and you yawn. *Palawa* (comedy) and *Ketoprak* shows are Rp150, Rp100 or Rp50. The park is open from 6 pm to mid-night. Most shows begin at 8 or 8:30 pm.

Charak and Bungunrecho: World renowned prostitute districts of Surabaya. Take a *bemo* to Wonokromo Bus Station, then another *bemo* from there to Kupang. Cross the railway tracks to the left and walk a kilometer. Charak is like a huge honky tonk Mexican border town in the orient. Best take a mate along, more fun and safer. Upon entering the complex a fake cop tries to touch you for Rp150. See roving minstrel groups, and once in awhile even a *ronggeng* (street dancer) who sings and dances for small change. There are row upon row of gaudy little doll-house shanties where 15,000 girls and women (of all sizes, shapes, ages, races, humors, prices) work and live. Lanterns are strung out in the night, muddy streets filled with *becaks,* milling people, hustlers, and carts selling antibiotics. Don't need pimps, just go straightaway into the houses. The village on the island of Pucetcherie is much cheaper, but higher incidence of gonorrhoea.

from Surabaya by ship: Pelni Shipping Lines office is at Jl. Pahlawan 20. Sriwijaya Lines is at Jl. Prapat Kurung 7. There's at least 15 ships a day sailing from Surabaya to outer island ports. Get boats to anywhere: Celebes, Kalimantan, Nusa Tenggara, Maluku, Irian Jaya. For Singapore or other countries you must have clearance from the *imigrasi* and the harbormaster. Check the 'Shipping News' of Surabaya's English language newspaper, the *Daily News.* Bargain for at least 75% cheaper than air costs. **for the harbor:** Turn to the right upon emerging from the Bamboo Denn and walk 1 km to the 2nd set of traffic lights. Stand near the overpass on Jl. Tunjungan and take a bus Rp30 directly to the harbor or, usually faster, pick up a *bemo* and take it to Jembatan Merah, Rp30. Then change *bemos* at Jembatan Merah for the harbor, 10 minutes, Rp30. Jamrud is the harbor for the bigger inter-island ships to Sumatra (Belawan), Jayapura, Sangir Islands, etc. Kalimas is the *kapal layar* and *kapal motor* harbor, just behind the Port Authority Building at Tanjung Perak. *Kapal motors* to Balikpapan, East Kalimantan, take 4 days, a boat leaves at least once weekly; Ujung Pandang, at least once weekly, Rp7-9000; Ambon, one boat weekly.

for Kalimantan by sea: A Pelni boat leaves weekly. Reserve places prior to departure. Their boat takes a week to work its way up the east coast to Tarakan, then it returns. For Tarakan and Balikpapan, also contact Panca Daya, Jl. Kalimas UDJK I/56; has boats leaving weekly. For Banjarmasin and Balikpapan, P.T. Pelayaran Meratus, Jl.

Alon Priok 27. For Samarinda, Balikpapan, Tarakan, try P.T. Dwijayaja, Jl. Slompretan 31, or P.T. Linie Java Shipping, Jl. Pasar Besar 57. **for Sumatra and Singapore:** See P.T. Sriwijaya, Jl. Prapat Kurung, for ships to Sumatra. For Singapore (one every 2 weeks, takes 9 days), try P.T. Eja, Jl. Taman Jayeng Rono 1, near Jembatan Merah; their ships also stop in Belawan, North Sumatra. Also for Singapore, try P.T. Bahtera Adhiguna, Jl. Kalimas Baru 192, Tel. 293751 or 291180; departs once every 2 weeks, takes 9 days. **for Nusa Tenggara** (The Eastern Islands): Ask P.T. Pelayaran Nusa Tenggara, Jl. Tg. Perak Timur 426, if they have ships going out. Also contact P.T. Pepana, Jl. Tg. Perak Timur 540. For Waikelo and Kupang, try P.T. Peldan, Jl. Tg. Peldan, Jl. Tg. Perak Timur 162. Pelni ships to Kupang, Timor, depart about every 10 days, Rp18,500. For Ende (Flores), Solor, and finally Alor via Lombok, try the mission boat Stella Maris at Jamrud; sails every 2 weeks, Rp10,750. **for Sulawesi:** For Bitung and Donggala, see P.T. Surya, Jl. Tg. Perak Barat 14, boats leave about once a month. For Ujung Pandang, go to Pelayaran Sulawesi Selatan, Jl. Tg. Perak Timur 426. The Pelni boat to Ujung Pandang costs around Rp10,000 and takes 3 days, 2 nights. **for Ambon** (Maluku): Try P.T. Perusahaan Maluku, Jl. Telur Lampung 16.

buses from Surabaya: From Joyoboyo Bus Station, buses leave for the east and west; Madiun, Rp450; Pandaan, Rp125, takes one hour; Mojokerto, Rp150, leaving all the time; Malang, Rp275, leaving every 5 minutes; Probolinggo, Rp300, leaving often; Jember, Rp500; Banyuwangi, Rp900, takes 4-6 hours; Solo, Rp1100, leaving every 20 minutes and takes 5 hours; Yogya, Rp1200, leaving at 8 am, 10 am, 12 pm, a 7 hour drive; Jakarta, Rp3800-4000, departing at 4 pm, arrives at 8 am next morning, about 7 buses at day. From the Jembatan Merah Bus Station, buses west to: Tuban, Rp325 (3½ hours); Lamongan, Rp150, leaves often; Semarang, Rp1000; Jakarta, Rp3000, takes 9-12 hours; Cepu, Rp400. **night buses:** If you get in Surabaya early, just leave all your luggage with the bus company for the day. For Bali, most night buses leave Surabaya at 5-7 pm and arrive in the early misty morning, Rp1750. Departure at 5 am with Elteha Bus Co., Jl. Embong Sawo. Departure at 4 pm, 6 pm or 7 pm with Kembang Express from their Jl. Tidar 58 office. Artha Mas Express office is at Jl. Makam Peneleh 77. Bali Express is on Jl. Makam Peneleh 88; Tel. 41586. **for Mt. Bromo:** Take the 10 am morning bus, Rp300, 98 km to Probolinggo. This gets you there with about 1 hour to spare before the afternoon bus leaves from Probolinggo to Sukapura. **to Yogya:** Kembang Express Bus Co., Jl. Tidar 58, has buses departing at 8 pm. **minibuses from Surabaya:** Colts leave from

Taxi Jurusan on Jl. Sumatra for Gresik, Rp100; Sedayu, Rp250; Sembayat, Rp150; Lamongan, Rp150; Babat, Rp250; Tuban, Rp350; Malang, Rp300; Mojokerto, Rp175; Jember, Rp600; Probolinggo, Rp300.

trains from Surabaya: For Bali, trains depart at 10:15 am and at 10:15 pm from Gubeng Station. The box office is open 1 hour before. It's a 370 km run to the Bali ferry at Ketapang, takes about 16 hours, Rp2500. This train might be better than the grueling bus comfort-wise and you'll also have the rare opportunity of riding on possibly the only train that runs on time in Indonesia. **to Yogya:** The Jaya departs at 5 am, take the economy class. The Purbaya departs at 10 am, the cheapest at Rp850. The Bima departs from Gubeng Station at 4 pm, Rp6600 second class. The Mutiara costs Rp1650, 3rd class. **to Jakarta:** The Gayabaru departs at 5 am, Rp2200. The Bima departs at 4 pm. Rp12,000 first class (and not worth it). Both of these trains depart from Gubeng Station. The Mutiara departs 5 pm from Pasarturi Station, Rp8500, only one class. **flights:** To Ujung Pandang, Mandala Airlines is the cheapest. Merpati fares, to: Ujung Pandang, Rp21,500; Maumere (Flores), Rp32,000; Waingapu (Sumba Island), Rp27,000; Balikpapan (Kalimantan), Rp22,000; Tarakan, Rp40,000; Jakarta, Rp19,000; Denpasar, Rp10,000. The airport tax is Rp1000. The airport is 15 km from Surabaya; take the bus to Waru, then walk. Costs a criminal Rp5000 to get into the city by taxi. Airlines offices: Bouraq, Jl. Urip Sumoharjo 52; Garuda, Jl. Tungungan 29; Merpati, Jl. Urip Sumoharjo 68; Mandala, Jl. Sulawesi 28.

vicinity of Surabaya: Seludo Waterfall is 3 hours by bus from Surabaya on the slopes of Gunung Wilis near Nganjuk. Considered to be a fountain of eternal youth, it gets 50,000 Javanese visitors annually. **Pandaan:** A cool and exhilarating mountain resort one hour's drive from Surabaya. The large open-air Candrawilwatika amphitheatre sits at the foot of the flawless cone of Mt. Penanggungan. During the 4 nights of the full moon May-Oct., East Javanese classical dances and dramas dating back to the 8th and 9th Centuries are staged here: *Ken Angrok,* the Meditation of Arjuna, *Menak*

kerbau *(water buffalo): Since the soil is sacred the farmer doesn't ride over his land impersonally in a noisy smelly tractor, ripping and tearing up the earth. Tractors not only cost too much, but could never be used on such tightly worked and terraced land, some terraces being only one meter wide. Water buffaloes are used instead, just like in the times of the ancient Malays. Some flooded sawah of West Java are over 2000 years old. Most plows are still made of wood.*

Jonggo Leno, and others. Costumed players mime ballets and temple rituals. There's no dialogue, so concentrate just on the music and dancing. **Tretes:** A 850 m high mountain resort 55 km south of Surabaya. From Pandaan, take a taxi up to Tretes for Rp150. Good quiet living. With a volcano behind and the silvery curving coastline of the North Java Sea far below, swimming, waterfalls, walks, horseback riding, Tretes is much less hectic than the city. About 1000 girls live here. Find an older house and rent a room in it for as little as Rp500. The villages (such as Prigen) on the lower slopes of G. Welirang are the cheapest to live in. Good food at Abadis. At Ibu Jaya's shop on the road from Tretes to Pandaan, bizaare antiques and kitsch junk. **Sendangduwur:** Along the north coast of Java near Tuban, Rp300 by bus from Surabaya. An early Islamic cemetary, mosque, gateways with wings, and a wooden building containing the tomb of a legendary apostle. This could be Java's oldest mosque, built on what may have been a pre-Islamic temple ground. Early Islamic art is very similar to Balinese art, both having been derived from late Hindu-Javanese styles.

Gresik: 20 km N.W. of Surabaya. The biggest woodworking compex in all of S.E. Asia was opened here in mid-1976, processing the razed forests of Kalimantan. 80% of the factory's products are exported. See the old Arab Quarter's narrow streets and women in white shawls and veils. There's an ancient cemetary inside the town where Muslim heroes are buried. The ruins of the first Muslim settlement on Java are here, dating back to the 13th Century. There's also a very old school where Islamic texts are studied (pesantren). Visit Sunan Giri Hill, a holy mountain guarded by two Hindu mythological creatures. Many steps lead up to the bathing places of the *walis,* men who (it is said) were able to fly and work miracles. A shirt is brought once a year, the 'flying jacket'. If you wear it, you can fly. The mystic saint Sunan Giri's grave has fine laces, Persian tapestries, Chinese carvings, gateways in the Majapahit-style. **crafts:** Many small textile factories are hidden away in Gresik's back streets. Just wander through and you'll be invited in to view a selection: 2½ m *ikat* cloths cost about Rp3000, after bargaining. Very colorful and the quality of the weave is outstanding.

MADURA

A large island 160 km long by 30 km at its widest across the strait separating it from Surabaya. East Java. Madura is usually included in the statistics of East Java. The best day to visit Madura is on Sunday, the market day. This island is famous for its bullraces. These colorful, crowded farmers' festivals are held frequently and attract visitors from all over the world. Traditional races are put on between April and Aug. in bullracing stadiums in villages all over Madura. Races are also held on weekends and public holidays. For schedules, contact Pacto or the Tourist Board of Surabaya. There's a new stadium in Bangkalan, 16 km north of the ferry port of Kamal, where bullraces are staged at least twice a month, usually coinciding with the arrival of tourist cruise ships. Sometimes bullfights are also staged in open clearings, but the animals are separated before they can do real damage to each other.

getting there: From Kalimas, near the port of Tanjung Perak, Surabaya, it's only 30 minutes and Rp100 by ferry across the narrow strait to the town of Kamal on Madura. Or buses leave Joyoboyo Bus Station in Surabaya from 7 am until evening for Pamekasan, Madura. Or you can just take a bus from Joyoboyo to as far as Kamal.

transport: Take Colts to practically anywhere on the island worth going to. A Colt costs, for instance, Rp750 from Kamal to Pamekasan. *Oplets* or *bemos* run along the main highway that encircles the island. Hitching is slow; there's not much private motor traffic. It's possible to catch freighters from Kalianget on the far east coast back to Bangkalan or Sampang.

the land: Madura belongs geographically as well as geologically to East Java. The strait between them flooded over during the ice age. Otherwise, they are very similar. Madura is a flat, dry island of many treeless, infertile limestone slopes. There's a narrow strip of lowland along the southern coast. See interesting volcanic phenomena and wierd landscapes of mounds, rock caves, and over 50 hotsprings on the island. Madura produces much of Indonesia's salt; its hot dry climate is perfect for it. There are great tracts of salt at Nambakor and around Kalianget. Its wealth also includes poultry and goat farms, rambling fruit gardens, tobacco estates. Madura is still a center for the spice trade, and superb *jamus* are made here. Fishing is extensive along the south coast where vividly-painted twin outrigger canoes are used.

the people: Madurese are well-known for their hot-temperedness, energy and thrift. Their mystic form of *pencak silat* has no sporting application and is used only in seriousness: to kill. The women of this island are small and dark and have very fine features. They are renowned for a special style of movement and massage during lovemaking, called *goyang madura.* But don't go looking for any there;

MADURA

Madura's fighting arts: Men of this island practice a physically exhausting and acrobatic combative system. But the knife (pamur) is much preferred. The Madurese use very long and vicious curved blades which can be swung under the armpit or between the legs to catch you off-guard. As if this ain't enough, they also cast spells. Madura's becak drivers practice a grappling judo-like fighting art called okol.

vicious knives are very sharp. (Thousands of Madurese women reside in Surabaya). The best stockbreeders of Indonesia live here, producing 1600 studbulls each year. One of the purposes of the bullraces is to find the best bulls for breeding in order to improve the stock. The faster a bull can run, the faster he can plow. A major cattle exporting island, you see immaculately groomed cattle with long eyelashes and sheeny brown coats being driven along the roads in braces of four.

crafts: Madura's *batik* has rich glowing red-brown coloring, winged *naga*-snakes, crocodiles, sharks, rays, airborne horses with fish tails, and other strange animal representations associated with the ocean. Fantastically gnarled, lucky seaweed (black coral) bracelets are made here. Worn to ward off sickness, it's said they can cure rheumatism. *Tempet kue* are bamboo containers with 3 legs; they're used to store cakes. Very pleasing to the eye. Found only on Madura. Buy one in the morning *pasars* for about Rp500. Unusual pre-Malayan pottery is made at Sodara in the mountains N.W. of Sumenep. **eat:** A fruit and vegetable island with the best armadillo-like fruit *salak*, and lots of other sweet, juicy, and sour fruits. Madura's chicken *sate* and other kinds of *sate*, plus *soto madura* (a rich spicy soup) are prepared all over Indonesia.

Kerapan Sapi Races: The word *kerapan* stems from an old Madurese word 'to work the soil' The idea caught on from racing plowing teams. Like something out of Ben Hur, these thrilling high speed spectacles of sleek racing bulls are held during the dry season at the time of the annual harvests, Aug.-October. The first rounds are small friendly village events (Kerapan Desa) with no requirements about the size and strength of the bulls, or the skill of the handlers. These elimination trials could run for months. Next are the subdistrict races held under government supervision. For these, the bulls are fed special foods like raw eggs (up to 50 a day), honey, medicinal herbs, and beer. The winner may take part in the district races and then, if he wins, becomes eligible for the more important regency races (Kerapan Kabupaten). The first races usually begin in April and the runoffs in May. Then comes the Grand Final (Kerapan Besar). Like Derby Day or the Melbourne Cup, this great fair is held in the town square of the island's capital, Pamekasan. During the week prior to *Kerapan Besar,* traditional games, ceremonies, parades of decorated bulls *gamelan* orchestras, and night bazaars take place in all of the provincial towns. The night before the big race cattle raisers choose their best bulls and sing them to sleep. The next morning these animals are bathed, brushed, and tenderly massaged. Their coats get like shiny burnished copper. Magificently adorned with ornaments, flowers, ribbons, and elaborate headdresses, they are paraded through the town under ceremonial parasols to the accompaniment of drums, gongs, flutes, bells. There are often up to 200 participants. Around 9 or 10 am the field is cleared and a signal given for the first race to start. The bulls look heavy and awkward, but watch. On the grassy strightaway, 24 pairs of bulls are matched up. Ornament is then stripped off the bulls and they're lined up with their brightly dressed jockeys. Each is given a huge tot of rum from a bamboo tube. *Gamelan* music is played to excite the bulls. A 3-man judgin g panel takes its place. Dead silence before the race begins. Then the starters drops his flag and the teams charge forward, the riders straddling skids slung between two yoked bulls, the rear of the skid trailing along the ground. Jockeys prod bulls with wooden sticks or flog them mercilessly with thorns and spiked rods. They can cover 100 m in 9 seconds flat, faster than the world's track record. Animals win by getting front legs, not noses or heads, across the line first. The triumphal team then parades around the stadium. After, the bulls are rubbed down and soothed to quiet *gamelan*. Those with the finest performances are used as stud. The owners of the winning bulls are held in quite high esteem in their villages.

Pamekasan: 100 km east of Kamal. A showroom for the local arts and crafts is located near the public square. **vicinity of Pamekasan:** Api Abadi (Eternal Fire) is 5 km south of Dangka village. Fire spouts out of the earth and neither rain nor wind can put it out. Legend has it that it comes from the mouth of a giant, sentenced thus by the gods. See it on a moonlit night. The Tomb of Pangeran Jimat with its rainbow motif is in a cemetary near Kalpajung Laut north of Pamekasan. Other old graves. The village of Kardulak is a center for Madurese arts and crafts, from furniture to toy sailboats. Good swimming at Camplong Beach. **Ambunten:** The most beautiful spot on the whole island are these rolling yellow dunes and beaches directly to the N.E. of Pamekasan 60 km, or only 13 km north of Sumenep. The north coast road to Ambunten passes through tobacco country and in places comes dangerously close to the sea. Ambunten can also be reached via Pakong, the highest point on Madura. At Ambunten sleep on the beach with a sleeping bag and a tent. Only a small village here.

Sumenep: 53 km N.E. of Pamekasan. On the road from Pamekasan, stop to see the tides at Prenduan, and look out over the island of Gilidua. More hills as you approach Sumenep. Sumenep is a collanaded town mindful of the Roman Forum, a more interesting place to base yourself after mundane Pamekasan. It has more history and is more remote. See the 17th Century Sumenep mosque and the small local museum opposite the *kraton* with a 300 year old ornately carved Chinese bed, Chinese porcelain and earthenware, weapons and *kris*, stone and wood sculptures inside and outside the museum. In the temple opposite the mosque, there's a legendary truss of grass which originated from a story of a grasscutter (Damar Wulan) who fell in love with a princess. Visit the royal graves outside of Sumenep. Bullraces are held at Sumenep's stadium; you could catch a local meet on the 750 m track, usually from 9 am - 1 pm. **stay and eat:** There's a guesthouse (pasangrahan) but also cheaper places: Hotel Matarhari, Jl. Diponegoro, Rp1750. Hotel Damai, Jl. Diponegoro, Rp600. Eat at Rumah Makan 17 Agustus.

vicinity of Sumenep: At Pasongsongan and at Pasean, there are small fishing villages with rainbow colored *prahus,* dazzling beaches and sandhills to slide and run down. In Dasuk, north of Sumenep, *goyang madura* is still practiced as an honorable profession. The best hotel here is Garuda at Rp2500 but there are many other, cheaper hotels besides. To reach Arasbaya, allow plenty of time because the stretch of road in the N.W. is really rough. **Sapudi Islands:** Off the eastern end of Madura. Catch a *kapal motor* from Kalianget. Natives here are fearsome spear and staff fighters.

Air Mata: Old Muslim cemetaries often have a decaying musty air of glamor about them. The earliest and most beautiful cemetary of Madura is located on a hill on the north coast of West Madura at Arasbaya, 11 km north of Bangkalan. Knockout views. Ravines on all sides with a flight of steps up the middle. On the highest terrace is the tomb of Ratu Ibu, a descendant of Sunan Giri, the great East Javanese saint. A finely carved *gunungan* screen makes up the backpiece of a Hindu-Javanese throne.

BALI

INTRODUCTION

This tiny Bali Hindu island of nearly 3 million, surrounded by a Muslim sea of 135 million, is just 2 km from the far eastern tip of Java. When the first Dutch war-yacht pulled into Bali in the late 16th Century, immediately the whole crew jumped ship. It was heaven on earth. It took the captain 2 years to round up his men again before he could set sail back to Holland. They reckon Bali was really put on the map back in the 30's when a few documentaries were made of this paradise-like island. Then the world knew. Bali has been degenerating into a tourist colony for well nigh 50 years now, an Isle of Capri of the Western Pacific. Numbers of tourists and earnings from tourism have doubled each year since 1970 and the industry is now aiming for one million tourists a year, more than one third of Bali's total population. At last their unbelievably complex social and religious fabric is breaking down under the onslaught. Now you see signs: 'Cremation! Rp2000! Book here!', and Hindu priests wear Mr. Natural t-shirts. When groups of men go to pray, some wear a hibiscus in their ear, a clean bright *sarung,* and their crisply-pressed soulfully faded Levi jacket. Old men will tell you that only two things haven't changed yet, the cockfights and the betelnut. Bali has known travelers- Chinese, Javanese, Polynesians. Japanese, Europeans, and now freaks and tourists, absorbing and synthesizing them for hundreds of years. But big business tourism is now being foisted upon the Balinese by the Javanese and hotels are built without the consent or consultation of Balinese villagers. The money earned from the swank hotels doesn't remain on Bali to benefit the people but is siphoned back to

Java or overseas. You used to be able to leave your bag in the open anywhere on the island for 3 days and nothing would move it but the wind. Not anymore. Recently the first Balinese boy OD'd on heroin, and for the first time in its history you see rubbish piles; banana leaves rot away, plastic doesn't. Its art is living on borrowed time. Soon communities won't be willing to subsidize the high cost involved in the sumptuous ceremonies, music and dance troupes, new costumes and masks for actors, etc. but for the more desirable comforts of western technology. Prices are getting higher, money-minded people in the tourist ghettoes like Sanur, Kuta, and Denpasar hassel you, the sound of motorbikes is constant, quality of paintings and carvings is declining, etc. etc.-you've heard it all before. But travelers and tourists haven't caused one eighth of the cultural pollution that the four movie houses in Denpasar have; so misleading and poisonous (i.e. all white women ask you for a screw). People who were there during the 30's can't bear to go back now; it's too painful to see. What's left? Although an island only 144 km long by 80 km at its widest, you can get as lost as you want on it. There are still hundreds of villages on the island which haven't changed since Covarrubias's book (written in the 30's). You don't need directions, just head for the hills. The best things are still free: orange and gold tropical sunsets, an astoundingly rich culture, the dynamite smiles of the children, the sound of the palms. You can still get into hundreds of temple dances free, and live well for US$3 a day or less.

getting there: Board the ferry in Ketapang, East Java, Rp125 across the channel to Bali. If you're too late for the ferry, just go down the beach to the LCM depot. From the ferry depot in Gilamanuk on the N.W. corner of Bali, take a *dokar* or a *bemo* Rp50 to the terminal where you can board a bus (Rp400) or a Colt (Rp500) for Denpasar, the capital. Or walk to the edge of town and start hitching. If you want to go to Singaraja instead and avoid the touristic south, the distance is 87 km, Rp400 by bus. If you take the last boat across and come into Bali at first light you see the whole island come to life: mists lifting over tiered pagodas, ducks off to the fields under flags of herders, women yawning in doorways, pots boiling on early morning fires, lines of shadowy people going off to the market. **arriving by air:**   Don't take a taxi from the airport, but rather walk 50 m where there's always cheaper buses or *bemos* until 10 pm. Or just walk down the beach from the airport about 3 km to Kuta Beach. Where the surfies and bikinis are the thickest, turn in.

history: Historically speaking, Bali is a fossilized Java, a living museum of the old Indo-Javanese civilization. Over 400 years ago all of East Java was like Bali is today. Prior to 1815 Bali had a greater population density than Java, suggesting that its Hindu-Balinese civilization was even more successful than Java's. The Indian culture was present on Bali as early as the 9th Century and the Balinese language is derived from the Palava script of South India. Bali today provides scholars with clues about India's past religious life in old sacred texts that have long ago vanished in India itself. When Gadja Mada of Java's Majapahit Empire conquered Bali in the mid-14th Century, East Javanese influences spread from purely religious and cultural spheres into arts, sculpture, architecture. When this empire fell in the 15th Century under pressure from the military and economic invasion of Islam, there was a mass migration of the cream of Majapahit's scholars, dancers and rulers to Bali. Priests took with them all their sacred books and historical records. Here they found refuge and developed unique Bali-Hindu customs and institutions. But Hinduism is only the veneer. The adopted Hindu practices of the new masters were merely superimposed on the deeply rooted aboriginal animism of the Balinese natives who hold beliefs dating back to the Bronze Age and even as far back as the Megalithic Age. In the early 19th Century, Bali's sole export was its highly-prized slaves, and its imports were gold, rubies and opium. Bali remained obscure for so long because of its lack of spices and ivory, its steep cliffs rising from the sea, the deep straits and treacherous tidal currents and reefs which encircle it. Surprisingly, the incredibly fertile

lava-rich lowlands of Bali were among the last areas to be occupied by the Dutch and only came under their colonial rule following prolonged resistence. When a wrecked cargo ship off Bali's south coast was looted by the Balinese at the turn of this century (a traditional practice of island peoples), the Dutch used this incident as a pretense to implement their control over the island. One sunny morning in 1908 at Puputan Square, Denpasar, Hindu princes and their families, wearing splendid ceremonial costumes and waving priceless *krises* at the invaders, charged deliberately into Dutch rifles. This mass suicide (puputan) resulted in the annihilation of the entire royal family.

the land: Bali is like one big sculpture. Every step is manicured and polished, every field and niche is carved by hand. Once a part of Java, Bali is a geographic extension of it, mountains and all, with much the same climate, flora, and fauna. There are few flat areas, hills and mountains are everywhere. The surface of the island is marked by deep ravines, fast-flowing rivers and in northern Bali a west to east volcanic chain (1500-3000m), an extension of the central range in Java. In the southern part of the island you see ricefields exquisitely carved out of hills and valleys, sparkling with water or vividly green. All seasons are one: in fields side by side there is rice that has just been planted, rice that is still growing, and rice that has ripened. Terracing and irrigation practices are even more elaborate and sophisticated than on Java with remarkable systems of aquaducts, small dams, underground canals, and water is sometimes carried by tunnels through solid rock hillsides. A village organization, *subak*, controls distribution of water coming from a reservoir or main pipeline. In South Bali, besides rice (grown extensively up to 700 m), there are crops of tea, cocoa, groundnuts, tropical fruits. As you leave the southern plains and drive north, the landscape changes from tiers of ricefields to gardens of onions, cabbages and papaya which grow better in the cooler climate. Thatched palm huts change to sturdy cottages made of wood, tile and stone to withstand the heavy rains. There's alpine country with mountain streams, moss, prehistoric ferns, wild flowers, creepers, orchids, leeches, butterflies, birds, and screaming monkeys. The western tip, known as Pulaki, is the unspoiled, uninhabited wilderness of Bali. Legend has it that Bali's original people had their origins here in a lost, invisible city.

**Indonesian
houses of worship**

the banjar: The community extension of the house and family. Each Balinese village is like a little republic, self-contained and independently run by the *banjar*, a sort of town council. More than any other factor, this village organization has kept intact the Balinese way of life after the decline of the local *adat* princes and chieftans. Each family pays a subscription fee and when a man marries, membership is compulsory or else he's considered morally and spiritually dead. Attendance of all household heads are required at regular meetings; absentees are fined. The *banjar* runs its own communal bank from which villagers may borrow to buy farm equipment, cattle or other necessary purchases. The *banjar* supports and maintains village temples, owns a *gamelan,* handles taxation, cockfighting, divorces, duck herding, helps to arrange and finance weddings, family celebrations, temple festivals, cremations, community feasts; labor is shared. It will advise all villagers on matters of religion, marriage and morals, which are all regulated carefully by elected members of the *banjar.* Each *banjar* has its own meeting house to gather in the evenings to drink, talk and gamble, each man taking turns to act as cooks and waiters. The leader of the *banjar* is elected by members and approved by the gods through a medium. No other political system has yet broken through the patriarchal shield of the *banjar,* though recently its cohesiveness is being weakened by the consumerism and the 'modern' lifestyles of the growing towns and the travel industry. Many now send a monetåry contribution in lieu of their presence.

the people: 90% of Bali's population practices Bali-Hinduism. There is also a sprinkling of Muslims in the coastal towns, Buddhists in the mountains, and Christians everywhere (Belimbingsari is a small Christian village in the far western part of Bali). Five hundred Arabs and Indians, who mostly deal in textiles, live in Denpasar. Ten thousand Chinese are found in the main trading centers of Denpasar, Singaraja and Amlapura, running most of the businesses. There are also hundreds of resident European artists, aid workers, English teachers, jewelry and clothes makers, etc. The Balinese are small people with round delicate features, long sweeping eyelashes, heart-shaped lips. Extraordinarily creative people who practice a highly theatrical culture, Bali's cults, customs, and worship of god and nature is animist, their music warmblooded, their art as extravagant as their nature. Culturally, the Javanese lean more towards refinement, keeping themselves in check in life and art, whereas the Balinese enjoy more the flash sensations, big meals, laughs, terrors. He's more lavish in his colors and decorations, likes explosive music and fast jerky dancing. Today there's still a distinction made between the *wong majapahit* or descendents of 15th Century migrants from the fallen Majapahit Empire of East Java, and the Bali Aga, the secluded original inhabitants of the island who retreated into the mountains where they are found to this day, still hostile to outsiders. Caste is indicated by name on Bali with the classical Hindu division into 3 main classes: the Brahmans with the title *Ida*, the Kshatriyas with the title *Deva*, and the Vaishyas with the title *Gusti*. The indigenous population, Bali Aga, are sudras, or casteless though none are untouchable. Women often have independent incomes and are in charge of not only cultivating the fields, but also of all the landmarks in her family's life considered important or magic: birth, the first cutting of nails and hair, filing of teeth, piercing of earlobes, marriage, and death. Women carry loads of up to 30 kg or more and 1 ½ m tall on their heads, while men take up the rear empty handed. A young Balinese girl can train herself to carry up to 40 coconuts, stacks of fruit, or great water jars on her head without even using her hands, all this while riding her bicycle down a bumpy country road. Women delousing themselves or each other is a great social pastime. They wear bras like European women do bikini tops. Unmarried girls often have a loose lock of hair hanging down the back over one shoulder with a flower (gonjer) dangling in it. As in many Indonesian societies, women are sent out of their homes while menstruating to board in a special house set aside for the purpose. A Balinese man believes that if menstrual blood ever touches his scalp he will become impotent for the rest of his life, following his wife around like a dog. The birth of boy or girl twins is a calamity in a village, an evil omen. It's thought that the twins had committed incest in the womb and rigorous purification ceremonies are carried out. If a child is sick too often its name is simply changed. The Balinese believe that each part of the house corresponds to a part of the human anatomy: the arms are the bedrooms and the social parlor, the navel is the courtyard, sexual organs are the gates, the anus is the garbage pit in the backyard, legs and feet are the kitchen and granary, and the head is the family shrine.

structures of Indonesia

BALI HINDUISM

The way the Balinese practice their island form of frontier Hinduism is still their greatest art. The Balinese call their own religion–*Agama Tirtal* (Science of the Holy Water), an interpretation of religious ideas from China, India, and Java. Hinduism originated in India, though it has developed along lines all its own. Hinduism doesn't have a single founder nor has it a single prophet, but instead a whole parthenon of gods. This religion is at least 3000 years old and dates from the writing of the *Upanishads* (600 B.C.) But the Bali-Hindu religion is much closer to the earth and more animist than Hinduism proper. The two sects are as different from each other as Ethiopian Christianity is from Episcopalean Christianity or from the Catholicism practiced by the Irish and the Catholicism practiced by American Indians. If a Hindu from Benares visited Bali, he'd think them savages. Although the Hindu epics are well-known, forming the basis of their favorite dances, the deities of the Hindu parthenon (Vishnu, Shiva, Brahma) worshipped in India are here considered too aloof and aristocratic. Often Balinese don't even know their names. The Balinese have their own trinity of supreme gods which is a deity in itself called 'The Shrine of the Three Forces' which corresponds to the well-known Indian trinity. Because of the caste system, 100 million people are shunned in India, though on this largest Hindu outpost in the world outside of India, only the older people still believe in it, the young ignore it. In India a Hindu must be cremated at once in order to get to heaven, but on Bali because of the expense sometimes a whole village will temporarily bury its dead and then stage a mass cremation. In India widows must not remarry but on Bali they do again and again, and even high priests marry. In India, worship at home is all important but on Bali group worship at temples is practiced.

Durga

Balinese animism: The Balinese are scared witless of ghosts, goblins, and the like who disguise themselves as a black cat, a naked woman, a crow. Spirits dominate everything they do and their life is constantly taken up with offering fruit and flowers to appease angry deities. If put in our society they would show all the classic symptoms of paranoia and neurotic disorder, but on Bali it's ritualized and institutionalized. There are sun gods, totemic gods, secretaries to the gods, deer gods, mythical turtles, market deities. Clay figures of the animist fire god are put over kitchen hearths and bank clerks place *pandanus* leaf offering trays on their desks. *Ngedjot* are seen in the courtyards of every house for the spirits which haunt that house; these house offerings consist of little squares of banana leaves with a few grains of rice, a flower, salt, and a pinch of chili pepper. No one eats before these *ngedjot* are placed in front of each house each and every day. Though the dogs follow and eat it as soon as it touches the ground, the essence has already been consumed by the spirits. The gods and goddesses inhabit stone thrones and statues or are simply in the air. They protect or threaten every act performed by a person during his lifetime. Gods are often invited down to visit earth and are gorged with offerings and entertained with music, but eventually must go back home because they are too expensive to maintain. The Balinese always try to stay on the good side of all the forces there are and if the spirits are kept happy, they can relax and even be light-hearted. Children carry flowers to shrines and learn to dance at an early age to please the gods. Feasts mark special periods in the infant's first year: 3 days after birth, 42 days after the first bath, 105 days after birth and finally 210 days after birth- his first birthday celebration. At each stage of the agricultural cycle ceremonies are held, offerings are made and holy texts chanted. Even cockfighting was originally a temple ritual, blood spilled for the gods. During the 1965 political bloodletting in which 50,000 people died on Bali, victims and suspects would dress up in spotless white ceremonial attire before being led voluntarily away to be executed. Devils were believed to live in the communists and their deaths were necessary in order to cleanse the island of evil. The Balinese religion divides most concepts into polarities: heaven and earth, sun and moon, day and night, gods and demons, man and woman, clean and unclean, strong and weak, hot and cold. The interaction of all these contrasting pairs works in harmony with each other, runs the world and determines one's fate. Thus the Balinese witch, *Rangda*, who symbolizes evil, plays her useful role guarding the temples. In Balinese folk medicine, headaches are cured by spraying the head with a mixture of crushed ginger and mashed bedbugs; a heated or irritated condition is cured by a cooling medicine. It's said that the Balinese are one of the few island peoples who don't turn their eyes towards the sea, but upwards towards the mountains. The Balinese believe that everything high like mountains are good, powerfully magic and healthy, whereas the ocean below is sinister, filled with poisonous fish, sea snakes and sharks. Their sacred mountains are 'north' and the sea 'south'; these are the cardinal points so their villages are alligned in these directions. Heaven? The Balinese believe that heaven will be exactly like Bali.

festivals: There's an unending chain of festivals, over 60 religious holidays each year. The basic tenet of Balinese religion is the belief that the island is owned by the supreme god *Sanghyang Widhi*, and that it has been handed down to the people in sacred trust. For this trust the people show their gratefulness by filling their lives with symbolic activities and worship, devoting most of their waking hours to an endless series of religious observances, offerings, purifications, temple festivities, processions, dances, cremations and dozens of other religious rites. Festivals are held dedicated to the art of woodcarving, to the birth of a goddess, for percussion instruments; there are temple festivals, fasting and retreat ceremonies, parades to the sea to cleanse villages, celebrations to wealth and learning. The festivals of East Bali are unique to the island. Get a Balinese calendar; besides being faithful pictorial examples of simple, realistic folk scenes, they show all the most propitious days for religious activities.

cremation: On this extravagant occasion you'll see much of their popular art and all of the more important religious symbols. Cremation is meant to liberate the soul of the dead, allowing it to journey to heaven to rejoin the Hindu cycle of reincarnation. Bodies are often buried twice on Bali, the villagers waiting for a mass cremation to be held where the vast expenses can be shared. These funerals are a time of tipsy hilarity, gossip, offerings and dances, all brightened by continuous *gamelan* music. First the deceased is 're-awakened', the grave opened and the remains put on a giant decorated wood and bamboo tower, a fantastic creation of tinsel, paper, flowers, mirrors, silk and white cloth. The corpse is then taken from the home in a noisy procession to the cremation grounds. On the way it's spun around on top of mens' shoulders so as to confuse the soul, not enabling it to find its way back to its house where it might cause mischief to the living. Tourists trip over themselves taking pictures. The splendid tower, offerings and coffin are then set ablaze with a magnifying glass, as matches are considered unclean. After the cremation the eldest son rakes the ashes to make sure all the flesh is burned. To free the soul, the ashes are then carried out to the sea and scattered.

temples: At least 20,000 on Bali: If you see *pura* in front of a word, it means temple. You must wear a sash to enter. Notice the exuberant ornamentation; carvings on them are like the flowers and the trees. Bring binoculars to observe the extreme detail on some, such as the Gerta Gosa in Klungkung and the bronze drum of Pejeng. There are temples everywhere- in houses, courtyards, marketplaces, cemetaries, rice paddies, beaches, on barren rocks offshore, on deserted hilltops and mountain heights, deep inside caves, within tangled roots of *banyan* trees. At most intersections and other hazy dangerous places temples are erected to prevent mishap. Even in the middle of jungle crossroads incense burns at little shrines. There are simple domestic temples, island temples, and even some social groups have temples of their own. The Mother Temple of Bali, Besakih, is the state temple. It lies on the slopes of Gunung Agung, the holiest mountain of Bali where all the gods and goddesses live; the Navel of the World.

ARTS OF BALI

The island's very well-organized cultivation system and its astounding fertility has given the Balinese leisure to develop their arts for centuries. It's incredible that so many people on such a small area of the earth's surface (3200 sq km) pour so much energy into creating beautiful things. Their worship of life and the gods encompasses a wide range of art forms, making an art out of even very simple necessities of everyday life. Fruit salad is served with flowers strewn on top and coils of pigs' intestines are used for temple decoration. Influenced by incoming European artists, modern Balinese art only began about 1927 when for the first time artists gave the date and signed their paintings. Before this, all art was for god. If the painting or sculpture was too innovative, it might not have qualified in the service of god and the artist was considered a failure. Still there is no word in their language for 'art' or 'artist'. A sculptor is a 'carver', a painter is known as a 'picture maker', a dancer goes by the name of the dance she performs. The Balinese have never allowed artistic knowledge to become centralized in a special intellectual class. Everyone is an artist on Bali. The simplest peasant and the most slow-witted create something or else are aesthetically conscious as critical spectators. A field laborer will chide a clumsy instrument maker for a job poorly done. Even *dagang,* young girls who run small foodstalls, are skillful practitioners of Bali's classical dances. The Balinese are very susceptible

to fads: fashions, themes for theatre, new painting styles and dance forms often sweep the island. They are unabashed and uncanny copyists and some of their stone temple carvings such as a hold-up or a plane crash are copied right out of magazines. Stone carvings and paintings show pregnant women, boys playing, beer drinking, seductions, even atomic bombs going off in heaven. The purest and oldest example of Balinese art is the ancient mosaic-like *lamak* which last only for a day. These are woven for Balinese feasts by women from strips of a palm leaf, bamboo, and yellow blades of sugar or coconut palm pinned or folded together to form fancy borders, rosettes, and little tree designs. There are hundreds of different *lamak* designs. After hanging a day on an altar or rice granary, they're wilted by night. Other of their perishable arts include 5-layered stacks of temple offerings, outrageous adornment on cremation towers, cones of fruits and cakes, long rectangular panels of sculptural tapestry hung on temples and shrines. Hourglass-shaped fertility figures of girls (cili) with round breasts and long thin arms are made from palm leaves, and start to appear when rice seeds first sprout about 3 months after planting. The Balinese form of *wayang kulit* has the same repertory as on Java but puppets are smaller and more realistic than Javanese *wayang* puppets, which were made more stylistic because Islam forbade portrayal of the human form. On Bali *wayang* shows are held in the open air and the men aren't separated from the women as on Java. In addition, Balinese theatre forms aren't as strongly in-

fluenced by the one-dimensional shadow play as the Javanese are. On Java *wayang topeng* is a dying art, but on Bali it's still going strong. More expressive and typical of the characters than *topeng* masks of Java, these performances act out deeds of local kings and warriors in Balinese history with usually 2-3 players impersonating the heroes of the stories in pantomime.

sculpture: The Balinese sculpt with natural media such as wood, stone, bone, horn, and even gnarled roots of trees. For the most part, purely a souvenir variety of woodcarving is turned out now; successful creations are often assembly-line produced. There are only half a dozen places at most in Mas, the main woodcarving center, that sell high quality carvings and they want as much as US$250 for one. The other places sell pure shit. Wood is often left unpainted. Using very simple tools, top class woodcarvers are paid only Rp1000 a day. Often Balinese woodcarving is grotesque, almost psychotic, expressing so well their fear of the supernatural. The features of a subject are distorted to heighten its special character- a frog's eyes, the sleek movement of a fish, the graceful legs of a deer, a farmer's toiling back, the prancing of a bird. Figurine carving is still unique with faces of painstaking detail. Still frequently met with are examples of the slender fluid form of figure sculpture with elongated arms and faces, a leftover from a style born one day in the 30's when the artist I Tegelan of Belaluan refused to cut a long beautiful piece of wood in two. Mythological creatures such as Hunuman wrestling the serpent, dancing Sita, are still quite often sculpted. Painted wood carvings of a mythological bird to hang from your ceiling, Rp1500. Called 'The Bird of Life', it's used in cremation ceremonies as the bearer of the deceased person's soul to heaven. Chess sets of carved teakwood or bone pieces are quite distinctive; Vishnu riding on the shoulders of Garuda is the King. On Kuta the starting price is Rp40,000 but they'll come down to Rp20,000 or even less; in Celuk, could be cheaper. For something different, the woodcarvings of the Bali Aga (aboriginal Balinese) villages in the uplands are more tribal and ancestral than those produced in the Hinduized portions of the island. Stone carving belongs to the craft of woodworking and, since soft volcanic rock is used, the technique is very much the same. Because they believe that constant maintenance of their stone temples is a moral obligation, stone sculpture survives today as the only Balinese art with a religious function. Stonecarving is relatively unaffected because it hasn't been influenced by a buyer's market since it's so expensive to ship.

PAINTING

Painting had virtually died out on Java when the last Hindu civilization there fled to Bali in the 15th Century, but on Bali it has been practiced continuously for the last 400 years. For centuries Java was the Mother Country and this is reflected even today in the subject matter of traditional Balinese art. Now most Balinese artists work solely for money, reasoning that it's senseless to go to the trouble making a good painting when a bad painting will sell for just as much, just as fast. Avoid guides and agents. Better is to visit the home of the artist (which you can find after persistent inquiry), saving yourself a percentage of the painting which goes to the guide, driver, or agent. The exact same paintings which sell for US$2500 in the art shops on the main road of Ubud, the artist himself sells for US$25 just down the path in the *kampung* in back of the art shops.

traditional painting: These religious narrative paintings derive from the 14th and 15th Centuries, when the Hindu population of East Java fled to Bali. They are characterized by a flat, stiff, formal style, painted according to a very strict traditional formula which lacks all emotion. Figures of Hindu gods, demons, and princesses in limewater colors are placed row on row in high state in the realm of the gods. Each god is distinguished by details of dress which sets him or her apart. Shading to indicate perspective is traditionally not used. These paintings are to be read like a comic strip, the characters and events

represented in separated space cells, the scenes all taking place in a divine cosmic world. Cloud and wind patterns and flame and mountain motifs separate the scenes. Sometimes up to 15 m wide and 4 m long, these paintings are hung along temple eves as festive decoration. Modern examples of these cloth paintings are still turned out, especially around Klungkung (try Kamasen village). Although much influenced by western art, Balinese painters have retained many traditional features in their paintings which stem from their Javanese cultural ancestors. Balinese painting is still limited in subject matter, in treatment, in symbolism, and especially in the colors used: blue, yellow, black, white, and Chinese red, with dull browns and greens mixed from the pigments.

modern painting: The period between the two world wars brought heavy changes. Balinese artists stopped painting according to rules and started to recreate their own visual experience. During the years 1933-39, the European artists Walter Spies, Rudolph Bonnet and others demonstrated to Balinese artists that painters can be free of set formulas and painting to a single stylistic convention. At the same time they allowed them to unfold individually. These Europeans also taught them the concept of the 3rd dimension. You can still see Rouseau, who influenced Spies greatly, evident in Balinese painting. Artists are now working mostly for a European market and the tourists' demand for paintings 'suitable for framing' has again changed the technique and contents of their painting style. Full face representations are rare and profiles rarer still. Balinese painters are filled with stories and myths from childhood up and sometimes dozens of stories are happening all at once in many of their paintings. They never lack a theme to paint about. In their paintings of jungle scenes there's elaborate, riotous decoration of leaves, flowers, and animals, with every leaf and tree carefully outlined. Mindful of Persian miniatures or of the English artist Beardsley, tiny blades of grass and insects are found in the furthest corners of their paintings. The cost of high standard paintings, if you can find them, is roughly US$50-100 per square meter. For the usual paintings you'll often find that when you take them back to Australia, USA or Europe, the frame will cost more than the painting did. To familiarize yourself with high quality work, visit the Puri Lukisan Museum of Ubud. Many of Bali's finest painters live in and around this village.

classes of painters: First class painters include I Bagus Made, Sobart, Kobot, I. B. Nadra, and Lempad. **I Bagus Made:** Sixty-years-old, looks like a Balinese farmer with tobacco-stained teeth, was trained by Bonnet. You'll never find his paintings in an art gallery. His simple house is located under bamboo trees behind Oka Kartini's in Ubud. Eccentric and very uncomplicated, money doesn't impress him. Some paintings of his are US$5000 and others are just 'not for sale'. Leave your guide behind; he doesn't like guides because he has to pay part of their percentage. **Sobart:** Lives in Padangtegal, Ubud. Specializes in market scenes. Is more business minded than I Bagus Made. During the 1930's Sobart headed a group of painters in an association called Pithamaha. These artists were the first to execute paintings on any subject matter, not only on religious myth and legends. This group brought about the secularization of painting on Bali. **Kobot:** In Pengosekan, a village down the Monkey Forest road. This artist does paintings of harvests and paddy fields. **I. B. Nadra:** Another senior painter

living near Tegallingga. He likes to paint *Barong* dances, prefering larger paintings. **Lempad:** 100 years old. His paintings are like a sketch; done only in black and white; little detail. Paints on paper. His son sometimes copies his paintings to sell. **second class:** Barwo and Turun—young men, but already producing good quality paintings. **third class:** Sadia and Atjin. **fourth class:** Includes the Young Artists, a term which doesn't mean that the artists are actually young, but refers to a recent style only, started in 1961 by the Dutchman Harry Smit who now lives in Denpasar. This style centers around Ubud and Penestanan. For something unusual that depicts quite a cross section of Balinese culture, Balinese calendars show daily scenes: a farmer plowing his fields, women going off to the market, rice harvestings, offerings placed at shrines, etc.; Rp 500-1500.

'Birth' by I.B. Rai, 1956

CRAFTS

Due to the extravagant amounts package-tourists have paid for Balinese artifacts, prices have become ludicrously high and the Balinese have developed a pathetically inflated notion of the true value of their crafts. Clothing, woodcarvings, bonework, and *batik* are much cheaper in India and other countries, and often better quality. Although Bali's silversmiths are more inventive, silverwork is usually cheaper in Yogya. On Bali, the first asking price in a local market or by a peddler is not necessarily lower than that of the exclusive shop. They both start out at an equally escalated price. If you're trading clothes for good bargains, there's a glut of AMCO and Levi jeans now and you can seldom trade them for anything anymore. For other fashionable clothes you don't usually get the whole amount in cash but rather its value in painting or carving. From March-June, crafts are about ¼ to ½ the usual price.

French tourists start raining down around mid-year and the Aussies overrun the island during X-mas holidays. But during these four months, a small *Garuda* carving, for example, is down to Rp500 (sometimes up to Rp15,000 in the tourist season); full length kaftans in Ubud go for 3 for Rp3500 (other months they cost Rp3000 each); Rp12,500 paintings are only Rp2500; small wall-hangings only Rp500 (down from Rp2000 and up). There are mass produced handicrafts all over the island now so if you don't like it or can't afford it say vehemently, 'Sing ngeleh pipis!' (Balinese for, 'I'm dead broke!'). If you let a guide take you into a crafts shop, he gets a commission of 20% or more; that's what you have to pay extra for each item. North Bali (such as Singaraja) has cheaper crafts than in more touristy South Bali. For handicrafts at their cheapest, and for the widest range, go to different villages.

Babat — Sandstone carvings; silver and goldwork.

Bangli and Tampaksiring — Coconut, cattle bone and buckhorn carvings.

Batuan — Woven goods. Known for traditional woven cloth and carved and decorated painted wooden panels. Also some painting. These art shops will offer you tea and Balinese sweets and cakes. Eat to the rhythm of the shuttle and loom.

Batubulan — Stone sculpture center. Lining the roadsides are fantastic stone figures and statues of divinities and demons sold as protective figures of family shrines, to be placed at crossroads or at entrances to temples and houses. Also stone basreliefs of mythological heroes. Watch the stonecarvers and their apprentices at work without buying anything. They've got packing and shipping agents here as well. Quite regular and well-staged *Barong* dances are held in Batubulan.

Blaju and Gianyar — Weaving. Where most of the good *sarungs* come from. An excellent place to shop for textiles.

Bona — Near Gianyar. A center of the plaiting industry. Baskets, hats, sandals, bags, fans. They build bamboo chairs and tables, bamboo birds and flowers.

Bratan and Celuk – Weaving, gold and silverwork. In Celuk the tourist buses digorge the hordes on the main road shops, but it's the back lanes where it's all happening. If you find the right shop, have your personal designs made up for you really inexpensively: ornaments, rings, bracelets, pendants, brooches made to order. Must leave a deposit.

Gua Gadjah — Baskets, shell carvings and other curios. Cheaper than Denpasar.

Klungkung — Wood and horn handicrafts, bone carvings, fine woven silk. Also several antique shops sell Chinese porcelain, ornamental gold and silver jewelry, and old Gelgel Dynasty relics.

Mas, Peliatan, and Ubud — Carving and painting centers. Some of the best known Balinese carvers live in Mas, old masters who are still working and teaching apprentices. Visit Ida Bagus Nyana, Rodja, Ida Bagus Glodok, the last being noted for his carved wooden masks. Visit the home of Ida Bagus Tilum and his museum of carvings and panels.

Puaya — Near the village of Sukawati. Puppets are made from old Chinese coins. Leather puppets are also made here.

jewelry: Find a *kampung* craftsman whose workshop is just a dirt floor and work with him directly. Trade silver for jewelry or give silver coins with a high silver content and get back hand done jewelry. They usually want a little cash-in-hand too. Balinese silver is often only 60-70% pure and they cut it as thin as a razor. Buy gold in Bangkok (cheap) and have it reworked into rings, brooches, necklaces on Bali. Also bring stones for setting; very striking backgrounds. There are dozens of westerners selling their own personalized jewelry around Kuta Beach, either by word of mouth or else approaching you in restaurants. Want to learn silversmithing? Some *losmen* owners do silversmithing on the side. Gold and Silversmith Artha in Kuta charges about Rp1000 per week. *Akar bahar* (root) bracelets are in the shape of a serpent. You can further shape them if you heat them over a flame, then tie with wire. Or shape them while still wet then dry in the sun. Polish with ash until very smooth and shiny. Some say they have a definite therapeutic effect, giving relief from rheumatism and arthritis. These seaweed bracelets (actually a sea tree) grow on your wrist from the heat and perspiration; you're wearing something that lives.

textiles: Chinese *kebayas* (womens' blouses) have rich hand-embroidered edges and a swooping decolletage. Some are very old, others are manufactured to meet the demand. Can't get the real fine oldies anymore for under Rp6000 (on Kuta, Rp10-12,000), and they won't come down. In fact, sometimes you can get good ones cheaper in Australia than in Indonesia. Take advantage of the inexpensive pants and shirts that you often see peddlers carry. They cost only Rp800-1250 to have a perfect fit made to order in a tailor shop in 4 days, so you shouldn't ever pay more than that amount. Keep a lookout for *kain prada* fabrics woven of silk or cotton and decorated with silver or gold threads or gold leaf. These very colorful kerchiefs are worn during festivals by temple girls. A ceremonial cloth 2 m long could take 3 weeks to a month to weave depending on the intricacy of the design. Not washable. Clean by dusting, then let it air in the sun.

shells and trinkets: 150-200 year old perforated Chinese coins (kepeng) with Chinese characters on one side ('Year of the Corn') and Pali script on the other, are used in casting I Ching. Find them at river mouths or kick them up as you walk along the beach. On Kuta, they cost Rp100 each. Inland, Rp10 each. Pukkah-shells are small, round, white (sometimes dotted with brown) shells found only in Hawaii, the Philippines and Bali (almost cleaned out on Hawaii). The best ones are the small necklaces with all uniform size shells. On Kuta you pay Rp350-400 for a small pukkah-necklace, but out at the surfers' hangout Ulu Watu's souvenir *warungs* you get really long chains much cheaper. Turtle Island has the most gorgeous seashells. Conical shaped straw hats used by fieldworkers cut out the sun exactly below the eyes and also make a good umbrella, Rp150-200.

dance in Indonesia: *Due to the drastic isolation of many of the tribes of so many islands, dancing in Indonesia has been able to maintain through to modern times its original ritual form. There's a great variety of styles of accompanying music and also of rich colorful costumes. See every kind of dance imaginable from the most courtly and austere dance-dramas using complex polyphonic music of Central Java to the wild ritualistic dancing and chants of the Irianese of New Guinea. On the Isle of Nias, dancers fly into the air, and on Bali they glide and flutter along the ground. Elbows are double-jointed and wrists are loosened until they can duplicate the profile of a swan. Dancers have been known to break and reset bones in order to execute difficult limb movements. Many dances tell stories of struggles between the gods, princesses and giants, or of conquerors or founding fathers and heroes who have come and vanished. You can see dances which celebrate harvests, ward off evil spirits and illnesses, or catatonic surrender to go beyond oneself and contact supernatural powers or mediums. In the great majority of Indonesian dances the participants are all males; male and female dancers appear together mainly in courting dances only. In the larger cities visit ASTRI (dance academies) to view their performances and for study.*

Chairil Anwar: *This war-poet had no time for symbols and sentimentality. After WW II he wrote a collection of harsh, angry poems about the Japanese occupation. As an intense nationalist he tried to find a distinctive place in world literature for the Indonesian artist who he believed was highly original, deriving his sources from all over the world. Anwar died of typhus at the age of 27 in 1949.*

mandau: *A traditional Dayak weapon made of bronze or steel, a combination of axe, sword, machete. Possesses a powerful spirit. Exquisite handles made of ivory, ebony or staghorn are designed into reptiles or human heads with tufts of hair on the ends, oiled and well-combed. One side is 7 mm thick to give it weight, while its curved razor-sharp edge is ideal for beheading.*

Rendra: *A gifted poet, dramatist, actor, stage director, who has translated and staged 'Waiting for Godot'. Now living in Yogya. Believes in the poetry of body movement. Has the most avant garde troupe in Indonesian theatrics, the Bengkel Theatre (bengkel means workshop, plays last from 15-20 minutes). The government doesn't allow him to put on his own plays, he now directs and acts in Greek tragedies. Rendra has staged plays such as Oedipus Rex with powerfully designed masks and also dabbled in the theatre of the absurd. Practically no props are used, merely a chair or two, a box, a ladder. Actors wear simple dark dress. Dialogue is reduced to a minimum, with words used as pure sound (mini-kata, or 'theatre of mini-words').*

pencak silat: *This fighting art originates in Sumatra. Pencak silat is a stylized form of self-defence performed also as a spellbinding dance form. It derives many of its combative stances from early proponents having observed enraged monkeys, the wing beatings of a stork, actions and skills of bats, tigers, snakes, swallows, otters, the motions of a newborn baby, and even the weavings of a drunkard — all giving rise to deadly attacks and evasions. A master-teacher (pandekar) has powers of mental telepathy, mind-reading, and mystic healing through touch alone and is considered invincible.*

Affandi: *Sukarno disliked abstract painters, so Affandi, Indonesia's greatest living painter, wasn't allowed to display in the Hotel Indonesia or at the Asian Games Stadium during the Sukarno era (20 years). Today there are two galleries of his oil paintings in Yogya. In his peculiar cave-shaped gallery many of his works are for sale. No one paints the many expressionistic moods and phases, realistic folk dramas, and blazing color landscapes like Affandi does, though many try. See his painting of his mother-in-law, painted in April 1976.*

Niah mortuary figurine

folk drama: *See the folk drama forms of Java: the extemporaneous Ludruk of Surabaya, the slapstick Ketoprak of Yogya, the super-stylized wayang orang, the hilarious wayang kulit of Solo, and the masked wayang topeng of Malang.*

Ramayana Ballet: *This story, a series of re-enactments of the Prambanan temple panels, is the Odyssey of the Javanese people. It goes back to a Hindu legend from the 10th Century B.C., telling of a symbolic struggle between good and evil. The length of the adaptation has been cut and some dialogues thrown out as repetitious and unsensational; sequences which were too drawn-out have been eliminated. This type of dance theatre without words is called sendrateri. Read an outline of the Ramayana story in the appendix (pg. 446) before going so you can follow it.*

wayang golek: *Three-dimensional puppets. Faces are very meticulously painted and surprisingly human with all types of expressions: smiles, hideous mean-tempered scowls, foolish dumb staring. Batiked and bejeweled, costumes could include the court dress of a European lord of the 18th Century or a dashing Arabian knight. Usually evil puppets are on the left, good guys on the right, the characters as easily recognizable as in any American cowboy film. Most always a blue face means cowardice. The puppets are moved by thin rods attached to the hands while the neck and head swivel on a central bamboo pole hidden under the flowing kain or sarung. See puppets pant and shake with fright, their heads turning in all directions and arms going a mile-a-minute.*

Sumbanese dancing: *Men dance like horses with the 'mane' hanging over their eyes similar to a pony's mane, and around their shins tawny hair of horse's tails are tied. Also see Sumba's renowned sword and ceremonial war dances, used at one time to inflate and psyche up warriors for battle.*

be guling *(guling means 'to turn'):* Stuffed suckling pig roasted on a spit. Kill pig. Pour boiling water over it and scrape the skin with a coconut shell. Open mouth and scrape tongue also. Cut open belly big enough for the hand and remove vicera. Wash inside of pig well with cold water. Stuff to taste with lombok (red chili pepper), garlic, red onions, kunyit, tumeric, jahe (ginger), salt, tinke (nuts resembling ginger), cokoh (aromatic roots of ginger), merica (black pepper), saladam (aromatic leaves), and ketumbah (peppercorn). Chop all these ingredients fine and mix them with coconut oil. Stuff the pig and put a piece of coconut bark inside as well. Sew it up. Run pointed stick through the mouth and anus. One end of the stick must be crooked to serve as a crank. Coat the pig in crushed tumeric in water to give the skin a brown color. Make a big wood fire and place the pig to one side of it, not over it, on a spit supported with forked branches. Turn the pig constantly and fan the fire to direct smoke and flame away. You want the heat to be concentrated on the head and tail and not on the middle so that the stomach skin doesn't crack. Roast for 2 hours to make pork juicy and tender. Skin should be brittle and covered with a golden-brown glaze. Eat.

coins: *V.O.C. coins (Dutch East Indies Company) sell for 100 marks each in Germany, cost only Rp100 in Indonesia. Buy 50 and pay for your passage to and from Germany.*

ochtar Lubis: *Former editor of the newspaper 'donesia Raya' which has been closed along with dozen other newspapers and magazines by the vernment. Lubiş began his career in journalism ring the Japanese occupation and the war of in-pendence from the Dutch. He was one of the ur men who developed the early Indonesian ess. Lubis continuously criticized politiking and rruption in Jakarta in the 1950's during the re-nstruction period. When he publicized that the e President Sukarno had taken a 2nd wife, he s thrown into jail immediately. When released er 5 years, he went to Israel (then forbidden to Ionesians by their government), spoke out ainst Sukarno, and upon returning home was own into prison again. After 9 years he was re-sed in 1966 when General Suharto gained wer. In 1969, he led a campaign against rruption in the state-owned oil company, Per-mina. During a visit by the Japanese prime-nister in Jan. 1974, Jakartan students rioted, using the government to suppress the intellec-ls and the students. Lubis was arrested in the orning of Feb. 4th, 1974, when he arrived home m a game of tennis. The news was on Radio ustralia before the security men left the house.*

dance on Sawu: *The original dances of Sawu, the Ledohawu and the Pedoahawu, are put on for excursion ships that call here, or for special occasions. Participants thrust and stab their swords in mock battles, and there are mounted manoeuvres with two-up riders in elaborate dress. Other dances are performed which were once used to comfort the infantry before battle. Orchestras on Sawu consist of a 3-man band playing instruments with strings stretched across a section of thick bamboo, and with a palm leaf bowl at the bottom acting as a resonator. Men dance with a small wooden box filled with rattling seeds tied to their ankles.*

ARTS, CRAFTS, LITERATURE OF INDONESIA

Indonesian fairytales: *The tiny kancil (mouse-deer) plays a role similar to the fox in western folk-lore, a cunning creature seemingly helpless but uses trickery to get the better of stronger animals. Crocodiles, found in many of Indonesia's rivers, swamps, mango forests, play the part of the big bad wolf, and are often refered to by a venerable name which means 'scholar', hoping that he'll let the traveler who shows such respect pass. The tiger represents power and majesty, and the snake earth and eternity. Wild cattle of Indonesia (ban-teng) are symbolic of freedom. The snail is the symbol of poverty.*

Bugis boatwrights: *There are many shipbuilding towns in South Celebes where ships have been built after the same pattern for centuries. Have a 2-2-rudder sailing prahu built in about 2 months for Rp1 million (Aus$2500) plus another Aus$2000 for hull, cabin, compass, rigging, motor. Half-schoo-ner, half-Chinese junk with jib sails, these seagoing ships are 12-20 m long and very wide. They weigh up to 150 tons (with one to six sails) but their aver-age size is 14 m long and 25 tons. Planks are hewn out of solid logs of teak. Not a single nail is used, only wooden pins. Amazing joinery techniques. Sides are built first, then the ribs are put in last. Measured only by eye with a piece of knotted string, timbers are cut, chipped and fitted by hand through all the phases of building. Strange old tools made of bronze and iron are used. Choose your man: don't have a housebuilder build your boat.*

note: *Be aware when buying crafts in Irian Jaya or the eastern islands of Indonesia that feathers, bows and arrows, mud (as on masks), untreated cowhide (lamp-shades of Yogya), or anything with shells embedded on it, won't be let in Australia (Australia doesn't have hoof and mouth disease yet).*

Greek and Indian influences in Indonesian art: *The invasion of Alexander from the west into India had two effects on Indonesia. Many Sumatran rulers henceforth claimed that they descended from Iskander or Al-iskander. The brief invasion also brought Graeco-Buddhist art which allowed deities to be represented by sculpture. Sculptures of Indian sages with typical classical folds of the robe began to appear. The stupa, which used to be just a mound containing Buddah's ashes, became elaborate with stone hemispheres. Indianized Malays carried the image of the elephant-headed god to New Guinea where it lingers on today in carved figures with grotesquely elongated noses. But the further you move west from New Guinea, the more detailed the trunk becomes until you find statues of Ganesha on Java and Bali identical to those found in India. In this sprawling mass of islands which had no individual artistic expression, Indonesian artists have created in just over 20 years since independence a modern national art that uses every idea that ever came their way. Indonesians will absorb the European influences now taking place in painting, sculpture, and dance just as they did with Greek, Hindu, Chinese and Arabian forms — coming up with art forms all their own.*

THE PERFORMING ARTS

music: Truly loved by the people. The sound of
echoing zylophones, drums, and clashing cymbols
are heard all hours of the night and day throughout
the island. Bathers sing in the rivers, rattles clack in
the fields, looms tingle with bells, kites vibrate in the
wind, little boys walk along lanes imitating the
sound of gongs, and flocks of pigeons circle
overhead with whistles attached to their feet.
Among the finest *gamelan* are made on Bali and
cost up to US$3000. Every village has its orchestra,
all its players being unpaid amateurs. Anyone may
play and a musician might hand over his *gendang* to
a spectator during a performance. The Balinese
gamelan is played more vigorously and passionately
than the slower, more aimless and haunting
Javanese *gamelan.* The Balinese like their music
electrifying, very loud, with sharp changes in tempo
and volume. Similar instruments are tuned slightly
out of pitch with each other to make the sound
shimmer. Old men play flutes in the background,
dogs prance across the dance floor, children play in
the audience, the musicians oblivious to it all. Many
gamelan orchestras practice in the evenings; free
entry. Look for *genggong,* the Balinese jaw's harp,
a short thin strip cut from the rib of the sugar-plum
leaf in which a tongue is cut. Tugging a string
causes the instrument to vibrate; you 'breathe' the
tune. There's a whole repertoire of jaw's harp
pieces played by orchestras of up to 24 *genggong*
players: 'Crow Steals Eggs', 'Frog Song' which
sounds like the blissful rhythms of frogs' breeding
chorus, etc. These instruments can bleat, trill,
croak, laugh, or lull you to sleep. Perfect music for
spells and animist spirits. Another unique instrument of Bali is the *rejog:* two deep gongs
fastened to hang vertically at each end of a stick.

dancing: Balinese dance will probably be the
most impressive sight you'll see and remember.
With over 2000 dance troupes on the island, it's at
the very center of Balinese life. On Java dance is in
large part the prerogative of the courts, but on Bali
it's most active in the ordinary villages. The Balinese
think that Javanese dancing is boring and the Javanese think that Balinese dancing is noisy and vulgar. Dancers on Bali perform pleasingly before the
gods, for prestige, for the entertainment of friends
and family, and for tourists for money. Many dance
performances are staged especially for tourists at
exorbitant prices (Rp800-1500) and many dances
have been shortened to please the fickle foreigners.
Rather, try to see performances connected with a
temple festival or other local ritual events which are

much cheaper (Rp4-600) or free. On any night of
the week within a radius of just a few km you could
see a number of different dance dramas and ballets
to honor a local temple god, to celebrate a wedding,
a tooth-filing ceremony, a cremation. The stage
could be an open dusty courtyard in front of a temple gate or at a crossroad with the open starry sky
and the towering palm trees as the roof. The dance
area will be encircled by hundred of squatting, sitting, standing people of all ages. The mood is electric. Balinese dance is generally easy to understand,
all you need is just the thread of the story. In their
classical dance all movements and limbs speak: the
joints, features of the face, fingers, wrists, neck,
eyes, hips, knee, foot, ankle. Balinese dance styles
stem from the work they do; they are just working
gracefully and wearing beautiful clothes when they
dance. Men climb coconut trees with prehensile toes
which you also see utilized in some dance steps.
Pikulan - carrying is excellent training for male dancers, the work giving them rhythm and a breathing
sense, allowing them to rise and fall in dance almost
without noticing them. Women carry burdens on
their heads, flicking their eyes in the same way as in
dance, to greet each other and to watch where they
step. Their fingers are trained from childhood to
make small things, thus flutter with such agility expressing feelings in dance. Womens' dance is pure
form. Only in the mens' dancing is the content of
the dance open to interpretation. The Balinese
don't dance upwards and away from the earth, but
move along its surface in slow zig-zagging circles.
Female postures are characterized by an outcurved
spine and buttocks pushed out with the shoulders
off-center. In both female and male dancing the
limbs form angles with elbows pointing upwards
with the head sinking down so far that the neck
disappears. Sudden changes of direction and
precise jerky steps are marked features of Balinese
choreography. They dance with a mesmerizing intensity like they're always being startled. The only
exception to this intensity are the comic or
grotesque characters who show shocked surprise
or fear. Violence is shown on stage during a dance
where it's not permitted in real life. You must have
fire to dance, and it must come from the eyes. The
complete lack of emotional expression of their
facial features can be likened only to a state of trance. It's said that experts can tell immediately who a
dancer's teacher is by the style in which she dances, and good Balinese dancers can be judged
solely by the complexity and suppleness of a girl's
little finger.

dance study: To seriously study Balinese
classical dance at the KOKAR Dance Academy in
Denpasar you have to have a permit from LIPI in
Jakarta as a 'guest student'. You can't really get in-

to it on an ordinary tourist visa. An average course lasts 1-2 years; they'll ask Rp2000 an hour but it's highly negotiable. For short term, it's more rewarding to go out to a village to study. Stay for several weeks; they'd be glad to have you. When you leave give a donation to the *gamelan* orchestra. Quite informal. **KOKAR:** This dance academy is on Jl. Ratna, 3 minutes walk from Jl. Soedirman. Take a *bemo* in the direction of Ubud, then get off just out of Denpasar. At this dance college sit in on classes held many times a day. There are 3 classes: beginners, intermediate, and advanced. The Music Conservatory is right next door. The *Legong* and *Gambuh* dance drama rehearsals are from 1-6 p.m. The most accomplished *Legong* dancer on Bali, and the only woman who knows the complete two-hour repertoire of the dance, is Ketut Renung. Watch this 60 year old woman teach her young students out in the villages on Sundays and Thursdays, starting around 6:30 pm. The interpersonal dynamics between teacher and pupil are captivating. Contact Wayang Sinti at KOKAR and perhaps he can arrange for you to go with him.

BALINESE DANCES

There are over 200 different kinds of dances, many still religious, and each is a composite of not only dance, but also of drama, music, spoken poetry, ballet. Here are some of the more popular.

Kecak: This dramatic pre-Hindu dance is said to derive from the choral element of the trance dance, *Sangyang Dedari*. Also called the 'Monkey Dance' because of the savage ape sounds the performers make, 200 or more seated men are shaking, clapping and shouting as one being. *Kecak* takes place in a big shadow-filled area at night with only burning torches around the all-male choir. No *gamelan* accompanies it, just the massed voices chattering in perfect unison, compassionate or fearful or all voicing shock, despair or panic. Fierce eerie hissing and moaning, bellows, and other wierd outerworldly primeval sounds. All the bodies appear as black, throwing their arms out at once in the night and shaking their fingers wildly. *Kecak* has borrowed some typical Kuntao movements, a secret Chinese fighting art imported into Indonesia. The story is taken from the *Ramayana* and concerns Rama, his brother, and Sita, exiled in the dark forests of Sri Lanka (Ceylon). The monkey armies of Hanuman and Sugriwa later help rescue Sita.

Barong (or 'Kris Dance'): A dance pantomine of a fantastic dragonlike holy animal, the *Barong*, in pitched battle against the machinations of a witch, *Rangda*. This is the most violent of Balinese dances and is often used as an exorcism. The open-air *Barong* is held usually in the middle of the road. *Rangda* is Queen of the *Layaks* (witches), her sawdust-filled breasts sagging and her tongue lolling wickedly. She is the female principal, a ruthless child-eater and a black magic expert

the Barong dance mask: *Both the* Rangda *and* Barong *dance masks are considered sacred. When not in use, they're wrapped in a magic cloth and kept in the temple of the dead. Sacrifices are presented before the masks and priests keep a close eye on them lest they 'escape'.*

belonging to the 'left' side, The Night, bringing sickness and death. *Rangda's* mask is painted white with a horrible expression of round bulging eyes and tusks protruding from the mouth, with long hairy pieces of rope hanging down to the ground. A white cloth is her only weapon. She runs away but never dies. Some scholars say her origin is Shiva's wife Durga in her evil aspect. *Rangda* and *Barong* have a long-standing feud. *Barong,* a hairy, eerie, mythical lion, sides with human beings against *Rangda* to thwart her evil plans. Without him, humanity would be lost. He is The Day, the Light, The Sun, the Male Principal, the force that overcomes evil, the 'right' side. The huge and frightening *Barong* has a beard of human hair decorated with flowers, long hair, feathers and bells all over his body. Strength is concentrated in the beard. Manipulated by two men who take the *Barong* through comic yet very complex dance movements that make people laugh—but not *too* loud. At its conclusion, *Rangda* turns the humans' power against them and you see men trying to willfully impale themselves on sharp *krises.* After the dance is over and when they come out of the trance, there is no trace of injury, bruising or bleeding.

Legong: Considered the most dazzling of all Balinese dance-ballets. Swathed in cocoons of gold plaited fabrics with their hands palpitating and their eyes flashing, these dancers perform an interpretation of a literary classic. A pair of 8-12 year old girls are chosen for their natural good looks and for their physiques. If they can be found to look alike, all the better. They are chosen before they begin menstruation because only then are they considered pure and limber enough to perform all the necessary movements. Training begins at 4 or 5; they retire at about age 13. *Legong* dancers were once a Balinese prince's private property. Extraordinary muscular control and great physical endurance is required in this dance. Dancers are first dressed in gorgeous costumes: head to toe in silk and goldleaf with a headdress of frangipani and earplugs of gold. Their bodies are tightly girdled from chest to hips with many meters of heavy cloth and covered with rich beautiful silks decorated with gold. This clothing helps to support their backs and gives them a graceful line. They both have heavily powdered faces with a white dot (priasan) on their foreheads which stands for beauty in dancers. Their eyebrows are shaved and given a new line with black paint. These young nubile girls dance to rapid staccato rhythms with wide open eyes, hips shifting and back arched, all of their movements executed in perfect unison. Enacting the story of *Malat*, the Balinese 'Thousand and One Nights', this is a drama of a princess kidnapped by a despised suitor.

Sangyang Dedari: Held only in time of trouble to alleviate sickness or misfortune in a village this celebrated shamanistic dance is a way of contacting the gods. The 'Virgin' or 'Trance Dances' offered by tour agents are not the *Sangyang Dedari*, but a laughable sham of it. The real article is often closed to tourists, so you'd be fortunate to see it. The dance steps are the same as in the *Legong.* Two auto-hypnotized little girls become possessed by a spirit of a god and dance on the top of mens' shoulders. They never open their eyes, yet their performances coincide perfectly. Once awake, the girls don't remember any of the performance nor have they ever had formal dance lessons. When the performance is over the dancers are revived by priests who bring them out of the trance by means of incense, chants, and rhythmical movements.

Kebyar: An interpretive dance of man's many moods. Performed from the squatting position with only the knees changing position. Moving just from the waist up, the audience's attention is forced to focus on movements of the torso and arms, hands and facial expression of the dancer. Darting glances, gentle swaying. Many different styles.

Janger: A modern-style dance performed in a large square with two rows of young men and two rows of women opposite each other. The story tells of a prince's search for a magic arrow. Led by a man, those at the side accompany the dance with rhythmical movements, tinkling music, and singing.

joget: A popular Balinese dance. Each girl who performs chooses a partner from the audience by tapping him with her fan. Partners are changed every 5 minutes. Especially hysterical when a French clerk or an Australian crayfish fisherman is tapped on the shoulder, with all his mates egging him on.

Baris: A stately un-Javanized native war dance performed on occasion of festivals and ritual feasts. Very typical of the most masculine aspects of Balinese life. The 10-12 men who perform dress in all white, black or checkered clothes. Could also be performed by 8 or 9 year olds who wear triangular headdresses of flowers. There are heroic poses, expressive faces, sham battles, duels, and violent music. *Baris* goes through all the emotions: passion, pleasure, rage, tenderness, love.

Tari Tenum: A typical example of contemporary dance that describes a woman making a *sarung.*

MISCELLANEOUS

folk medicine: If you have a friend who gets possessed or trips out on mushrooms, ask for *Orang Sakti* and he'll fix them up. The *balian* (folk doctor) combines practical medicine (sage, barks, herbs, roots) with religious magic. These inspired mystics have developed massage into a high science, even for orthopaedic problems and headcolds. A paraplegic friend, after being internally massaged by a *balian*, felt in his legs the first sensations in 8 years. It's claimed they can heal a broken leg in two weeks. They use horoscopes and can practice both 'right' and 'left' magic, also love-magic using amulets and medicinal recipes. If you want to improve circulation and muscle tone, try Balinese masseuse for Rp4-500. These old women with incredibly strong hands massage your body with coconut oil and *boreh*, a yellow paste made from mashed leaves, flowers, aromatic roots, cloves, nutmeg and *kunyit* (tumeric) for coloring. Tingles and refreshes the skin when hot or gives it heat after being out in the rain. Come out smelling like a flower. Buy 'Lidah Buaya' (crocodile tongue) shampoo in Denpasar; has an inimitable fragrance.

cockfighting: Can be seen in almost any village or town usually in the morning. You'll hear of them. You only see men at the cockfights, though women may enter the tourist ones. Fighting cocks are given the greatest loving care, being massaged, bathed and trained everyday. Their feathers, combs, earlobes, and wattles are trimmed so that none protrude to provide a beak-hold for the opponent bird. The owner concentrates on its diet so that it becomes lean and little subject to fatigue. Pet, mascot, child, dreams, income, the bird is always carried with him around his courtyard and to the *warung* or *banjar* clubhouse, taking up as much attention as a new wife. Their bellshaped cages are

placed at roadsides so that the cocks may be amused by the passerbys and not get lonely. A village will put up as much as a million *rupiahs* on their favorite cock. Two cocks eager to fight must be decided upon then equal or unequal bets are placed. The fight is blessed. Evil spirits receive an offering which hopefully satisfies them and also assures a good harvest. Brokers squabble. The birds are teased by their handlers, tails pulled, feathers ruffled, and palm wine sometimes spit down their throats, all to arrouse the fighting spirit. Razors are strapped to their spurs. The fight is often finished in 15-20 seconds. Amazing ferocity even when crippled with wounds. If they both refuse to continue the fight they're put inside an upside down basket, then one almost always kills the other. Often a badly wounded cock can be revived by artificial respiration or by special massages, then fights again, and wins. The devotion, gesticulating and hysteria of the audience is fascinating to watch.

bullraces: At Negara, West Bali, regional bullraces are held. Trained bulls are dressed up in silk banners with painted horns and big wooden bells. Each team is judged by speed and style. Like Roman charioteers they come thundering down to the finish line, whipping, shouting and mud flying. Jockeys twist the bulls' tails. Much gambling. This festival is to please the god of harvest. In Negara, stay at Hotel Ana, just off the main road.

accommodation: Homestays or *losmens* (family-run hotels) are the finer experience. You live right inside the family compound and participate in the life of the family: learn how to make *lamak* from the grandmother, flute-making from the father, kite-making from the small ones, learn how to cook *bebek tutu* (smoked duck) from the mother. The grandfather will take you to the next cockfight and the daughter will show you the shortest way to the market or how to sew a *sarung* into a skirt. Kuta and Legian don't have a monopoly on the best homestays. Some excellent ones can be found in the villages of Ubud, Peliatan and Penestanan (near Ubud), also in the vicinity of Amlapura, in Singaraja, and even in Denpasar itself. Quite often around Kuta and Legian you'll be approached by locals with offers of a room. These could be good, newly opened and eager to please. You used to be able to stay as a guest in a Balinese house anywhere on the island, but now families are not permitted to put you up as long as there's a hotel or *losmen* in the same village; and they're building hotels in all the towns and villages now. Some of the *losmens* and 'Beach Inns' remind you of old peoples' homes the way the rooms are all set in a row; tourists have no choice but to sit and have breakfast together. Coffee, tea and bananas are often included in the room price. Try Balinese-style accommodation (bale); its *atap* roof keeps your room cool all day.

eat: Balinese food is very spicy and peppery. Often it's served cold. Grated coconut meat (nyuh) is an essential ingredient in their cooking. Thick rich coconut cream, made by squeezing grated coconut over and over, is used in many native dishes; it doesn't keep so must be used the same day. *Sate* is often kneaded into the cream. Frying is done in coconut oil. Markets in most villages take place every 3 days; a cornucopia of grains, beans, greens, and fruit. Tropical fruits include: *zirzak, salak* (best from Rendang), *nangka, jeruk* (pink are better), *durian* (stinking aphrodisiacal soul food), *blimbing* (starfruit), breadfruit, *mangosteens*, passion fruits (from Kintamani), white mangoes (melt in your mouth). Also exotic vegetables like acacia leaves (twi), greens (kangkung), edible ferns (paku), etc. Most of Indonesia is Muslim but on Bali pigs are bred and cooked magnificently. Try Bali's famous delicacy *babi guling*, stuffed suckling pig roasted on a spit and stuffed with red chili, garlic, tumeric, *jahe*, ginger, aromatic leaves, pepper-corn. The flesh is juicy and tender, the skin is brittle and covered with a golden brown glaze. Sweet potatoes (ubi) with coconut, palm sugar and ketchup, are found at every *warung*, Rp15-25. Balinese also eat worms, frogs, flying foxes, snakes, porcupines, anteaters, lizards, wild boars, centipedes, grubs, birds (bones and all), and ricefield eels which look like baby snakes. A Balinese kid will take you out dragonfly catching using a long thin pole with a sticky end. Take the wings off, fry the bodies in coconut oil until crisp and eat with spices and vegetables. Also try some very mellow homemade native brews: *arak* (distilled rice brandy), *tuak* (sweet palm beer), and *brem* (rice wine).

imigrasi: Located off Jl. Diponegoro in Denpasar; the *bemo* knows where. Australians and North Americans get only two 30 days extensions on their initial one month visa. Your 2nd extension plus the 'Landing Fee' (payment is mandatory) costs in all Rp10,000. These arrogant self-important small-minded men are really into power games. For your 2nd extension (3rd month), they delight in stamping Last Extension' in your passport. It's possible to get a 4th, even a 5th month extension elsewhere (Bandung? Pekanbaru? Ujung Pandang?) but if you get your 2nd extension in Denpasar you're obliged to leave the country earlier than expected. If you're willing and able to fly to Singapore to get a new visa, *imigrasi* won't mind; more foreign currency is brought into the country. Everyone must follow the graphic dress code chart in front of Denpasar's *imigrasi* office (no indecent shorts!), otherwise they

won't even talk to you (unless you're white-haired and wealthy). More humanistic *imigrasi* are on the neighboring island of Lombok and in Surabaya, East Java.

jail: Go straight to jail and do not collect for: overstaying your visa, shameful nudity (the Javanese, who administer Bali, can't handle it), or dope busts. As any intelligent person knows cannabis causes blindness, insanity and death. You could get up to 30 days and fined as much as Aust$100 for possession (a little or a lot) of the noxious weed. Police don't bust you out of any moral compunction or even to do their duty. They bust you to make money out of you. Beginnings now of narc cunning and stealth (trained by Aussies). Jails, euphemistically called 'detention centers', are found in Denpasar and Singaraja. But jail need not be so bleak on Bali; they treat you humanely. If you can pay, get cigarettes or *batik* equipment. Visitors only on Sunday afternoons.

TRANSPORT AROUND BALI

The best way to see Bali is to just start walking. Take half-hidden narrow pathways at roadsides and follow them inland sometimes 15 km. You'll reach places about as outlandish as you want to be in. Children pop up and yell out a sing-song 'hellow!' or you could come across infants who start screaming at the sight of you. **cars:** Huge chauffeured American cars ('Heavies in the Chevies') are the most expensive to hire: about US$20-25 a day. **boats:** Buy a 30m teakwood hull for about US$3000. Look around Benoa harbor. When buying anything smaller such as an outrigger, watch it— might be rotten. Know what you're doing. Sailfish-shaped *prahu* (gadjah-mina) look like a sort of elephant-fish with long double trunks and big bloodshot eyes that see you through the night. Costs about Rp30,000 used. Sail it around the islands. It takes two people to handle one.

pushbikes: When riding a bicycle around Bali, there's appreciably more contact with the villagers than if you were on a speedy smelly noisy motorbike. They rent for only Rp2-300 per day. For a full week, Rp1200-1400. For a month, cheaper still. The fewer the bikes they have left, the higher the rental fees. Or buy a bike for around Rp20,000 from a *toko sepeda* in Denpasar, then arrange to have them buy it back from you for Rp15,000 or so after you use it for several months. Because the seats are so hard and uncomfortable, buy a cushioned saddle for Rp900 and a seat post to heighten your seat for long-distance riding. To get to the highlands of Bali take *bemos* or buses, then when you get ready to come back it's just 2 days downhill through the breeze, touring all the way. If you throw your bicycle on the back of a *bemo*, Colt, or on top of a bus, it'll usually cost you just an extra passenger's fare. Be sure to bring your bike inside the *losmen* at night; lot of rip-offs and you could pay up to Rp12-25,000 for a lost rented bike.

buses and bemos: Cheapest motorized transport are buses. To anywhere on the island, Rp50-350. The local buses such as the one from Gilamanuk to Denpasar or from Amlapura to Denpasar are often unbelievably slow (48 stops in 1 hour) but excellent for drinking in Balinese native life. Colts are much faster. The *bemo* and bus system on Bali is now so extensive that you can go virtually anywhere worth going to on day-trips from Denpasar. Do it in stages. For example, if you want to go from Ubud to Gianyar, go to the Sakah intersection first for Rp50, then flag down another *bemo* for the rest of the way for another Rp50. Charter a whole *bemo* for Rp3-4000 per day between 5 or 6 people. Just stand out on the roads and hitch-hike whatever comes by. Hitching on Bali is the best in all of Indonesia, getting rides with tourists, mail trucks or on the back of motorcycles.

motorbikes: Motorbikes may appear the best but they often prove more trouble and expense than they're worth. Intrusiveness in quiet villages, pollution, breakdowns, and injuries all go against them. Even experienced bikies, properly clothed, get shattered nerves after just a week of riding on Bali where trucks drive right down the center of the roads, chickens and dogs are everywhere. Driving at night is especially hazardous; lot of insects and

very dark. You have to worry about petrol (Rp75 a litre) and oil money, as well as parking fees (Rp25-50) at nearly every tourist site. Off-season rates are Rp1000-1500 per day, or from Rp7,000-10,000 per week. The more powerful and new, the higher the rent; the longer the rental period, the lower the rent. Rental charges rise when the French or Australians arrive in numbers in Aug., Dec. and Jan. You'll constantly be approached by guys offering to rent their bikes. Or go in front of Asia Restaurant on Kuta and bargain with the different bike-owners. Be wary of motorbike rip-offs in dealing with these local Kuta Honda Hells Angels. They overhcharge for faulty equipment, bad tires, etc. The bike repair shops on the road from Kuta into Denpasar, just before town, have bikes-for-rent in much better condition than private rentals. Rent a motorbike for a week and ride it instead all around Java. You need a Balinese driver's licence because there are occasional police roadblocks and the fine is Rp10,000. For a driver's licence take a *bemo* from the Guardian Statue on Jl. Gadjah Mada to Komdak XV, Jl. Supratman, Denpasar. It's all a hype. Not only is it expensive (Rp6000) but it's also a hassle. Wear long pants and shoes lest you grievously offend the police.

climate: Bali lies only 8 degrees south of the equator and has an eternal summer, warm sea breezes, high humidity. Dry season is May-October. Don't worry if it rains because tropical showers can quickly give way to blinding sunshine. Rainfall is usually not heavy and continuous, coming mainly in the late afternoon and night. From Nov.-Ap. the rains really come with the wettest days being in December and January. From June to the end of September, very pleasant.

Gunung Kawi Temple Complex

CENTRAL BALI

Gianyar: Shop for your textiles and *sarungs* here. Just before entering town from Denpasar there are 4 shops right in a row. Quite cheap prices. *Sarungs* sells for Rp1500-1800 (the more you buy, the cheaper). Colorfully decorated t-shirts go for only Rp1000, but the selection is often picked clean by the hordes dumped out by tourist buses. Try Pertenunan Cap Togog. The clerks at Togog can come down 15% automatically; anything more than that they have to ask the boss. Togog pays the 30-40 young girls in the back loom sheds Rp175 per day (7am-3pm); all these female workers are too poor themselves to wear *sarungs*, they wear cheap dresses instead. It takes about 6 hours to complete one *sarung*. Also look in at Meru, Jl. Kesatri 5.

vicinity of Gianyar: Exceptionally beautiful temples in this area. Between Kutri and Klungkung are lush river gorges, valleys of farming villages, and country tracks down to the sea. **Pura Puseh:** In Batubulan 150 m from the highway. On its gate are Hindu deities next to a meditating Buddah with Balinese facial features. **Pura Gaduh:** At Blahbatu. Its massive head is a portrait of the fearsome mythical giant, Kebo Yuwo. Though it dates from the 14th Century, it doesn't resemble Hindu-Javanese iconography of that time; might be

a native Balinese creation. There are numerous carvings inside the gate on the main stairway. Opposite the *pura* is the road leading straight to Kutri and Bedulu. **Bukit Darma:** At Kutri, 4 km south of Bedulu. Take the steep path through a *banyan* forest leading up to this sanctuary on top of a rock sheltering the worn but arresting statue of King Airlangga's mother, Gunapriadarmapatni, who came to Bali to rule until her death in 1006 A.D. This famous widow, in the shape of the goddess of death (Durga), cursed and plagued her own son's kingdom. She could be the historical origin of the witch Rangda seen in the *Barong* Dance. **Pura Dalem:** A small but exquisitely carved temple in Sidan, 3 km north of Gianyar on the road to Kintamani. A fine example of a Pura Dalem (Temple of the Dead), the *kulkul* tower has reliefs showing tormented evil-doers being punished by devil giants. Gates are flanked by deities of death and the witch-queen Rangda.

Tampaksiring: Sleep for free at the police station, the only place to stay. The top cop speaks top speed English. Good restaurant in this town, and really nice people. Pura Bukit is on a hill coming into Tampaksiring; a grand location. **Tirta Empul:** People journey from all over Bali to bathe at this

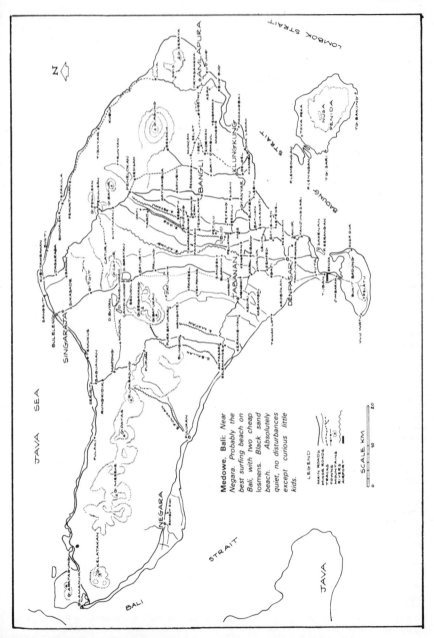

Medowe, Bali: *Near Negara. Probably the best surfing beach on Bali, with two cheap losmens. Black sand beach. Absolutely quiet, no disturbances except curious little kids.*

sacred cleansing spring in Tampaksiring. It was created by Indra who pierced the earth to tap *amerta*, the elixir of immortality For 1000 years villagers worshipped a holy stone here on a precise day each year without ever knowing the origin or the whyfor, only that it was *adat*. It wasn't just a coincidence that Sukarno built his secret retreat on a hill near this fountain of eternal youth, a spendid twin palace connected by a footbridge. Krushehev once watched a *Kecak* Dance on these palace grounds at a time (1965) when Sukarno's government had incurred debts of US$2477 million, half of that on loans for purchases of war material from Russia. It's now a govenment resthouse.

Gunung Kawi: 1½ km from Tampaksiring towards Denpasar. One of the more impressive historical sites of Bali. In this blinding green watery canyon are ancient blackened tombs hewn from solid rock. These very well-preserved temples in two rows within two cliffs facing each other with a river running between are all royal memorials for a king and his wife, son, concubines, and his son's concubines. Gua Gadjah and these temples are the earliest monuments of Balinese art. A legendary giant carved them all out in one night with his fingernails.

UBUD

Most Indonesians who live on Kuta are there to serve you or to rip you off, but in Ubud you are a visitor in a Balinese village which closes down at 8 pm. People are more approachable and even Bali's apocalyptic dogs play in the streets. Well worth it to stay awhile. Go here, not Kuta, to acclimate yourself to the real Bali. Higher and cooler, there are fewer flies and mosquitoes. Ubud is to Bali what Yogya is to Java, culturally speaking. In and around this village are where the most accomplished dancers, musicians, painters, weavers and carvers live. The main road into town strikes one as a big commercial scene with its many art galleries, studios, craft and souvenir shops, yet Ubud is often very quiet with few tourists (there's a lot of desparate shopkeepers during these times). Those who come only stay for an hour or so. There's a dance school here (Ubud is the home of the renowned graceful *Legong* Dance), you can learn how to make a bamboo jaw's harp, learn the art of the *dalang*, see cockfights, and take scenic nature walks around the village.

stay: Walk along the back lanes of the various *kampungs* as here are where all Ubud's best *losmen* are located. Depending upon what you're interested in there are at least 15 *losmens,* each of which offer different specialities to their guests. Painting? Oka Kartini's *losmen* is just opposite the big Garuda Art Gallery just as you're entering Ubud.

Nice place to stay, a *kampung* in a small forest atmosphere; Rp3-400 single, Rp5-600 double. For tourists she speaks an abbreviated, quite easily understood form of *Bahasa Indonesia*. Oka worked for 6 years as a guide in the Puri Lukisan Museum and knows painting. She will give you good prices on paintings, clothes and artifacts, prepare good meals which are sometimes served free, and store your luggage while you're traveling around. Dancing? Masih Accommodation (like a homestay) is on Gang Padangtegal; Rp400 single, Rp600 double. She teaches dance at Rp400 per one hour lesson: the *Gabor, Oleg* (Bumblebee Dance), and the classical weaving dance, *Tari Tenun*. Watch dance rehearsals right in the flowered courtyard; guests are sometimes treated to special demonstration lectures. Stay with a *dalang*? Homestay Sukadana, B. R. Padangtegal; Rp400 single, Rp600 double. He'll take you to some of the performances he's staging. Stay with a painter? Homestay and Painter Wayang Lantur, Rp400 single, Rp600 double; turn off the main road and walk 400 m up an unmade road, then see his sign. **others:** Homestay Made Badera, Rp400-600, breakfast Rp200. Stay here 5 weeks for US$22! Homestay Geria Taman Sari is on a little hill above the main road; 5 rooms, some with mosquito nets. Tjanderi's is the livliest and the longest established *losmen*; Rp3-400 single, Rp7-800 double. She has two places: at the main *kampung* (8 rooms), then another quieter place down the street (4 rooms). Homestay Okawati, up the lane from her restaurant, Rp400 single, Rp600 double with bath and toilet; banana sweets in the mornings. But she puts so much time into turning out good food in her *warung*, that her *losmen* is run-down and dirty. There are many more quieter homestays in the back lanes, hunt them out. Warning: you need a flashlight to wend your way at night along the rutted muddy back lanes of Ubud.

eat: Tjanderi lays out delicious and abundant meals. Her vegetable tacos, and banana coconut tacos, and spicy omelettes are acclaimed. Gregarious gatherings in the evenings. A bottle of *arak,* Rp300. Several foodstalls by the market serve the cheapest food. Nadi's Restaurant is on the main road opposite the theatre; good menu including B.L.T.'s for Rp175. At the roadside restaurant opposite the clothes shops, try *nasi bumbu*, a substantial beef, gravy and rice dish, Rp250. Oka Wati's *warung* is still going strong; the best scrambled eggs you'll ever have, spices and everything, Rp100. Her roast pork serves 4 or 5, Rp5000; roast duck oven-cooked with rice, serves 2 or 3, Rp2000- scrumptious but need to order these two items 24 hours in advance. Excellent *brem* wine (great with ice) is also served here by the bottle or by the glass, Rp100. The 'old' *brem* (brem tua) is Rp350 a bottle and *brem manis* (sweet *brem*), Rp300 a bottle.

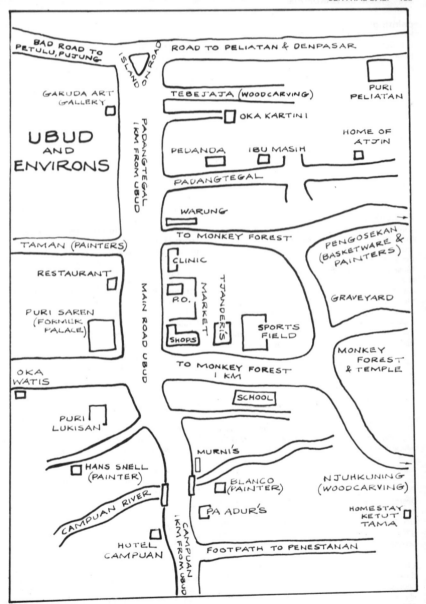

painting: Ubud is noted for its painters. Ask locals where they're all at. Visit galleries of A. D. Gd. Sobart, Gusti Nyoman Lempad, I Gusti Ketut Kobot (in Pengosekan), I. B. Made Poleng, and Atjin—all fine artists, men to learn from. If you allow yourself to be led around to the different and numerous art shops of Ubud, your driver will get 10% and your guide up to 15% of the amount you pay for a painting. This means you're paying 25% more than you need to; it's sometimes 1000% (or more) cheaper if you seek out the artists yourself, avoiding business with the galleries. There's a small European and Australian artist colony here as well; visit studios of Donald Friend, Hans Snell, and the Catalan artist Blanco whose thing is erotic art and illustrated poetry. Some charge Rp100 just to enter their showrooms.

Puri Lukisan: Ubud's Art Museum. Situated in a garden with rice paddies and water buffaloes out the back windows, Rp100 entrance fee. This museum houses the island's finest selection of modern paintings, drawings, and sculptures (Bali Museum in Denpasar specializes mainly in traditional art). The establishment of this museum in 1956 was the first deliberate separation of the arts from the communal religious life. Thus Puri Lukisan is a monument or a tomb, whichever way you want to look at it. Over the 10 years of frenzied activity in the 1930's, young painters broke away from the old Balinese traditional formalistic painting of mythological scenes and Hindu epic stories. It was in Ubud where Balinese artists first started painting subjects such as village scenes, funerals, landscapes. The old style was combined with realism, many rules were discarded, and natural figures were set against natural backgrounds (in sculpture as well). This naturalism has been maintained to this day. In Puri Lukisan see sculptures and paintings exhibited in chronological order covering the whole modern movement and the evolution into modern idiom with paintings of dances, temples, feasts, rice harvests. Some artists include Hondas and transistor radios in scenes along jungle paths. Puri Lukisan was also designed to record for posterity untarnished, unvulgarized Balinese art before the tourist industry finished it off for good. Use this museum as a standard to buy in the galleries and studios below. Ask to see Muning's private collection.

crafts: See the headman Anak Agung Raka for flutes of all tones and sizes, from the shrill little chorus flutes to ones about a meter long that sound like an oboe and takes long arms to play, Rp500-2000. The huge finely-made *suling gambuh* belongs to the *gamelan gambuh* and isn't played very much now (only in Batuan). He also sells homemade bamboo jaw's harps, Rp500. Raka is the leader of the *genggong-suling* band and the *gamelan*. He doesn't live far from the *banjar* (village council) and sometimes can be found in the *warung* next to Oka Wati's. **Pengosekan:** Near Ubud. A village of the arts where about 70 painters live. On the path from Ubud stop in the first *wurung* just before Pengosekan. Here a woman works making ten baskets that all fit within each other, very ingenious, cost US$50. Also visit the woodcarver's village of Nyuhkuning.

from Ubud: All around this small village are deep river gorges, lush vegetation, tarzan pools, and even a monkey forest (they'll piss on your shoulder and savage you if you touch the young). If it rains the night before, go down the path towards the monkey forest and pick mushrooms. The bluish ones are the best. Various homestays will cook them up 'in secret' into a tasty dish for you. **walks from Ubud:** Walk to the monkey forest, then on to Pengosekan, Peliatan and back to Ubud; this one takes about 2 hours. Or walk through the monkey forest to Nyuhkuning-Penestanan-Campuan-Ubud; takes 5 hours. Both are nice walks. **for Kintamani:** If you leave from Ubud at 5 am and go through Payangan, you reach Kintamani around 5 or 6 pm. Another way, a bit longer, is from Ubud through Taman and Sebatu to Kintamani via Penelokan; all the mountains can be seen on this beautiful walk. On the way up to Penelokan by way of Sebatu stop and stay on one of the village platforms when it starts to get dark. It's a big event in the village when a car drives by, when a plane flies over, and when you arrive. From Ubud to Penelokan it's a 7 hours walk, steadily uphill. **Petulu village:** 6 km from Ubud. Time your arrival to the afternoon so you can see all the white herons come in to rest in the trees. **Pujung:** A woodcarving village ¼ km from Ubud. Knockout panorama. Carved *garudas* here cost only Rp4000. **Sebatu:** A village high on a ridge with a miniature temple complex like Gunung Kawi. Good *gamelan* and lovely scenery. Also a bathing place separated into mens' and womens' sections.

Campuan: 1 km out of Ubud. Walk down the road between huge green embankments with fireflies and dripping water, then over a swaying antique iron bridge. Former residences of Walter Spies and Rudolph Bonnet, both of whom gave canvas, paints and many suggestions to Balinese artists during the 30's. Colorful dancing dragonflies hover everywhere. **stay:** Take a stroll through the Campuan Inn, the former home of Walter Spies; US$20 per day for full room and board. Costs Rp3000 for an unreal Indonesian lunch or dinner.

They'll pack you a lunch for the day if you're traveling around the island. One half km uphill from the main road is W. Munut's Homestay, Rp500 or Rp1000 double, Rp1500 full board. Nice garden setting on a hill next to rice paddies. Has electricity. San Michelle package tourists stay here. See Tony and Kody if you need info or a guide. Pa Adur's place is high on a hill overlooking the road, breezy with a view of the volcanoes, Rp500 single, Rp1000 double. For breakfast he serves papaya, eggs, bananas, toast and butter, coffee or tea, Rp300. Homestay Sadri, also up on a hillock off the roadway, has big pavilion-type Balinese style houses; Rp1000 per person or cheaper rooms for Rp500. Tea or coffee in the mornings. Komplet breakfast (eggs, bread, fruit salad), Rp500. High up in the ricefields, the panorama is great with Gunung Agung looming up in the distance. Really quiet, couldn't be better. **eat:** Murni's Warung, just before the bridge on the left walking from Ubud to Campuan, is No. 1: yoghurt, chili con carne, sweet and sour pork, great french fries, ice cold beer, and very jegeag (pretty) waitresses.

Penestanan: From Campuan, turn in at the sign. Penestanan is only a 1½ km walk in from the main road. Stay at Reka's losmen in the artist's own compound, 2 rooms only, Rp300; nasi campur, Rp150. He's a member of the Young Artist's School. Another painter, Ketut Tama, runs a homestay; Rp300 single, Rp600 double. Especially ideal for nature lovers, this is probably the most beautiful natural losmen setting on Bali. A lovely set of 3 rooms right in the rainforest; one is just a platform with a shutter you roll up. Descend down a path through a bamboo forest to the river below to bathe under a water spout. Meals available. Good stock of books (Thoughts of Confucius and Angkor Wat). Perfect for hermits, yet it's only 20 minutes fast walk to Tjanderi's conviviality. If full, check out Ketut's relative's place. Largest banyan tree in Bali, 100 m across, is in Bonangkas, near Sayan. Ask permission, it's on private property.

Peliatan: Two km before Ubud. Very well known dance troupe and gamelan here; so much dancing going on. This village puri teaches dance to 5 year olds and up. Usually on Sundays (if enough pupils show up) there's a dance rehearsal beginning around 9 am at the puri. Listen to the old raja's memories. Peliatan is also a center for carving and painting. Young boys have no worries in life, they just carve. **stay:** There are 12 losmens in this village, most of them down paths and lanes running off the main road. Losmen Puri Agung, Rp400 per person, is so bright, clean, spacious and peaceful that people stay for months on end. Cockatoos and

parrots cackle in the attractive courtyard. Anom will tell you of her dance troupe that toured the world. Mudita Inn c/o Toko Netera Remaja, has a very nice courtyard, 4 quiet rooms; Rp400. For breakfast they serve black rice pudding, Rp100; komplet breakfast is Rp200. Prepares lunch and dinner with 2 hours notice. Smoked duck (Rp1500) must be ordered 24 hours in advance. Mandala Homestay and Genggong Service, Rp300 single or Rp600 double. Quiet little back lane place, 5 minutes walk down from the main road. Free coconuts for guests and 'special coffee'; also the use of a kerosene fridge. See Togog if you want to learn to play the genggong (jaw's harp), the first Balinese instrument. Sells for Rp700 (on Kuta they cost Rp2000). Learn to play well in two weeks. If there are many guests, Togog holds big tuak and suckling pig blowouts (Rp200 per person). Gado² down the road, Rp25. Homestay W. Durus is across the street from Mandala's; Rp400, but cheaper the longer you stay. A restful place, a painter's homestay. **eat:** At Jero Arso Warung under the banyan tree on the main road, meals for Rp1-200. Also some bubur (Rp25) stalls nearby. Mandala Boutique Restaurant is right outside the village puri, at night sets out tables under the stars. Excellent nasi campur, Rp150. They specialize in banquet style Balinese food: babi guling (roast suckling pig), Rp10,000; bebek tutu (smoked duck), Rp1600; angsa guling (roast suckling goose), Rp5000; sate empol (Balinese port sate), Rp1000; lawar (Balinese salad), Rp400.

Yeh Pulu: Between the Petanu and Jurang Rivers (near Bedulu) are the ruins of this 14th Century high relief carving on a low cliff face. Not excavated until 1925. Rarely visited because it's a walk inland along borders of ricefields. An enigmatical frieze 4 m high and 25 m long shows the elephant god, a fight with a tiger, and a woman pulling at a horse's tail.

Pejeng: The location of the government archaeological offices. Also there's a superb example of Bronze Age art here, the monumental bronze drum, the 'Moon of Pejeng'. It hangs in a pavillion in Pura Panataran Sasih. Considered a masterpiece in the art of bronze-casting, this is thought to be the largest kettle drum in the world cast in a single piece. Legend says that it fell from the sky (a meteorite?) and landed in a tree. Because it was so bright it stopped the work of a thief, so he pissed on it and it exploded (thus the crack). A highly revered object, the drum even looks like a legend with its supernatural charged moonstruck faces. Dates from 300 B.C., the beginning of the Bronze Age in Indonesia, though no one is sure if it originates in Bali or comes from overseas.

cave monastery,
Gua Gadjah

Gua Gadjah (Elephant Cave): West of Bedulu. Very similar to the hermits' cells of East Java. Formerly a Buddhist monastery, it dates from the 11th Century. There are carvings on the outside of the cave of forests, waves, animals, and people running in panic. An enormous demon head above the entrance splits the rock apart with its hands. A boy holding a candle will take you inside to see t-shaped niches which probably served as monks' meditation chambers or sleeping compartments for ascetics. Deep silence. Bathing pools in front where carved nymphs and goddesses hold waterspouts. Clamber down rocks and rice terraces to see fragments of a fallen cliff face with broken basreliefs and a small cavern containing two ancient Buddah statues.

vicinity of Pejeng: There are over 40 old temples in this area. South of Pejeng is Pura Kebo Edan, the Mad Buffalo Temple. Small but significant, it features a 3 m high masked image of Bima fighting a buffalo. Nearby is the bigger Pura Puser Ing Jagat (1329 A.D.); interesting reliefs. There's a rock temple at Kalebutan, near Tatiapi, west of Pejeng. Gua Garba, The Womb (an old hermit's cave) is east of Pejeng on the bank of a river. Another 6 m high rock temple is at Krobokan (12th Century) north of Gua Garba at the meeting of the two rivers near Cemadik village.

Gunung Batukau (Coconut Shell Mountain): A mountain sanctuary and state temple built to venerate deities of mountains and lakes. Take the rough road up the southern slopes leading to Pura Luhur near the peak. This seven-tiered pagoda is somewhat like a Thai stupa and lies in a solitary clearing with gigantic uninhabited forests all around it. Shrines are surrounded by a pond, green moss everywhere. Nearby is the holy hotsprings Air Panas bubbling from the riverbank. Often on Bali, any wierd natural phenomena are given spirits. Temple Wanggaja Gede overlooks a small lake. These uplands have sublime landscapes. The view from the mountain village of Jati Luwih takes in the whole of South Bali and the mountain range which extends to the heavily forested western tip.

Sangeh: 20 km north of Denpasar is this Holy Monkey Forest with towering 30 m tall trees and hundreds of monkeys crawling over lichen covered Bukit Sari Temple. There are 10 hectares of *pala* trees here, a species which is not native to Bali and whose presence has never been explained, thus contributing to the holiness of the place. Buy a bag of peanuts and watch for the King of the Monkeys; also watch out for their claws and teeth. Walk down a pathway by the river gorge in back. From Sangeh, take a rocky side road that crosses over to Mengwi.

Mengwi: Visit the art center. Also see the 2nd largest temple complex on Bali here. Located on high ground, a wide moat surrounds it. Feels like you're in the middle of a lake. Very beautifully crafted stone carved gate; small wooden doors of the shrines are masterfully carved as well. Most impressive. Candi Bentar has a ½ *kala*-face on each side of the gate. Give a donation. Also in the vicinity are neolithic stone thrones. At Marga stands a monument honoring a regiment of guerilla fighters who were killed in the battle of Marga by the Dutch in 1946. Hundreds of small stupa-shaped headstones. A strange feeling to the place.

BANGLI

10 km north of Sidan in the cool rich farmlands of Central Bali. This capital of an ancient kingdom has great views of volcanic Mt. Batur. Bangli has a history dating back to 1204 A.D.; a document tells of a feast being held in that year at the great state temple, Pura Kehen. It's claimed that Bangli's climate is number one in all of Bali which makes it even more of a pity that it lacks a good *losmen*. A

friendly place, there are temple ceremonies and dances (*Barong* Dance and *wayang kulit*) put on free for 'the people, not only for the tourists. San Michelle Travel puts on 3 dances each Monday in Bona which cost Rp1800: The Fire Dance, *Kecak*, and a ballet; must book at the Irama Hotel in Denpasar.

stay: Homestay Darmaputra, Jl. Brahmaputra 1, Rp300 single, Rp600 double. A dirty and disorderly place with mediocre, expensive food. Most of its drab rooms are occupied by women and children, the yard is full of chickens and snarling dogs; maybe okay for one night. You'll never learn any Indonesian from Mr. Ngurah, he speaks fluent English. His hospitality is a bit unctious and overwhelming, though to be sure quite informative. He's really got a thing for maps of Bali with about 7 giant ones on the premises. He'll show you about the town. Try to enjoy the silence. The Rai Inn, located down the alleyway next to the *warung* opposite Homestay Darmaputra, is run by Agung; Rp350 single, Rp700 double. It has seven big rooms and is quieter than the homestay, but sometimes the W.C. is broken and the electricity is off. Food is available.

sights: Meet the royal family painter A.A. Gd. Bagus Ardhana at Puri Kilian Bangli. See his dramatic allegorical paintings of the *Ramayana* epic. The one with all the monkeys on Rawana's back took 5 years to paint. One of the biggest *gamelan* on Bali is in Bangli; it costs Rp9000 for a performance. The Dutch captured it from the Klungkung Dynasty when they went to war with them, then gave it to Bangli. Art Center Wisata Budaya, one of the largest cultural complexes on Bali, is about 2½ km from the town center. Puts on theatre performances (*Kecak*, *wayang* forms) plus art exhibits. **Pura Kehen:** Thousands visit this temple located north of town at the foot of the hill, Rp50 to get in. One of the finest examples of its kind on Bali, a big temple consisting of 3 parts. At the foot of the stairway is a museum. Its splendid closed gateway is called 'the great exit' and above are the splayed hands and hideous face of the *kala-makara* demon. His function is to prevent evil spirits from entering the temple grounds. *Wayang kulit*-like statues line the 1st terrace. The first courtyard is shadowed by a giant *banyan* tree and its walls are inlaid with Chinese porcelain. Ornamentation on the highest temple is so overdone and uncontrolled that it's even rare for Bali. The inner sanctuary has a

shrine of 11 tapering *meru* roofs, the highest honor that can be offered, resting places for the visiting gods.

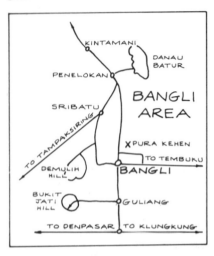

vicinity of Bangli: If you freak out on mushrooms you're sent to the psyche-hospital in Bangli (seen from Demulih Hill) where they still use 18th Century methods such as the infamous 'water treatment'. It's a nice walk to Sidembunut village where you'll find the *kampung* of I Ketut Lebah, the only man on Bali who does cassowary egg carvings; he also carves ivory, bone and wood. For any work, place an order. Sell him an elephant tusk (gading) for Rp25,000 which you buy on Timor for Rp15,000. **Bukit Demulih:** A one hour walk. Mr. Ngurah will instruct you on how to reach it. From the top you can see the 'Balinese Pyrennes', a range of 9 mountains to the west named after the nipple-like *trompang* percussion plates in the *gamelan* orchestra. Also visible is Pura Kehen under a *banyan* tree north of Bangli, the whole Bukit Peninsula to the south, and the ugly box of the Bali Beach Hotel along the east coast. Don't bathe under the waterfall on the way to Demulih Hill, it's sacred. An Australian lost Rp600,000 after he did it. **Apuan village:** 5 km walk from Bukit Demulih. The house of the *kepala desa*, with its gold leaf decoration, is as beautiful as a king's palace. **Bukit Jati:** Another hill to the south of Bangli. Take a *bemo* first to Guliang, then walk or take a motorbike 500 m to the top of the hill.

EAST BALI

Besakih: Bali's most austere, yet impressive temple group 60 km northeast of Denpasar on the slopes of Gunung Agung. A real money trip to get up to see it. Dates from before the 11th Century invasion of Hinduism on a site where animist rites, ceremonies and feasts took place. Long stone steps lead up through 7 rising terraces; a godly view from the top. Besakih is a very complex architectural structure incorporating the holy triad of temples venerating the Hindu trinity. It's a 10 km climb to G. Agung's peak from where you can see Singaraja and the whole north coast. This mountain is to the Balinese what Mt. Olympus was to the ancient Greeks. East of Klungkung the countryside is still blackened by lava streams of the '63 eruption in which 1600 were killed and 86,000 made homeless. One quarter of Bali was covered in lava. Hot choking dust was scattered all over the island for a week and clouded up the whole of East Java. Besakih's temples were covered in ash, stone and ruin. Hindu priests rushed into the lava, hoping to appease the angry gods. This eruption occured at the time of the greatest of Balinese sacrifices, Eka Dasa Rudra, which takes place only once every 100 years. It was the first time this sacred volcano had blown since 1350 A.D. The Balinese don't take such coincidences lightly.

KLUNGKUNG

39 km from Denpasar by bus, Rp150. An old royal cultural center for music, drama and fine arts, the seat of the Gelgel Dynasty which ruled Bali for 300 years. Most of the Balinese nobility draws its descent from the royal family that settled here, and even today the King of Klungkung is regarded as the most exalted prince among the Balinese aristocracy. **stay:** Hotel Wishnu, Jl. Kunti, 3 minutes walk from Stasiun Klungkung and back from the main road; Rp600 single or Rp800 double. Rooms upstairs are nicer and breezier. This is the cleaner of the two hotels in town. Ex-losmen Sudihati, Jl. Karangasem 101, is 8 minutes walk from the *stasiun;* Rp350-500. Grubby but cheap. **eat:** Across the street from the courthouse in Kertha Agung Bar and Restaurant; meals Rp350-750. Hot tea, Rp125 (the same tea at Klungkung Station is Rp10). Many *warungs* at Pasar Malam Singol or at Statiun Klungkung, Rp150 for *nasi campur.* **crafts:** Visit the marketplace for handicrafts. In the Klungkung area many of the old crafts are still produced. Right by Pasar Klungkung are 4 antique shops, open 8-12, 4-9 pm. Kamasen village for traditional Balinese painting.

Gerta Gosa: This Royal Court of Justice was constructed in the 18th Century. Once the High Court of the land, there are terrifying episodes and scenes of the horrors a defendent would meet after his death depicted on the walls and ceilings as a warning to evildoers and the guilty: thieves boiling in oil, decapitated whores walking a plank over fires, liars being clawed by tigers, and women who have aborted themselves having their breasts gnawed away by rats, and on and on. Bring binoculars for more detailed study. Above hell's miseries and agonies, the beauty of heaven and the joys of marriage are seen. The highest panelling shows the rewards of heaven when good souls are attended by councils of divinities.

vicinity of Klungkung: 4 km south is the village of Gelgel, the early capital of the old kingdom. Megalithic stones under *waringan* trees. On the road from Klungkung to Kusamba, pass one of the many lava flows which are seen throughout Karangasem district. Where there were once ricefields, rivers, villages, now is just a wide strip of volcanic rubble down to the sea. Lines of fruit trees rising out of the ash once marked a village street and tops of old crumbling brick temples and shrines stick out of rocky barren stretches. At Bukit Jambul, 8 km north of Klungkung, a wide unbroken view of Klungkung Valley and of Nusa Penida Island. **Gua Lawah** (Bat Cave): Just north of Kusamba. Said to extend all the way to the base of Gunung Agung. In 1904 the kings of Bali held an historic conference in this cave to plan action against the encroaching Dutch armies. At Candi Dassa, near the Bat Cave, is a private homestay-ashram with a very nice panorama and quiet.

NUSA PENIDA

Nusa Penida was once the Siberia of Bali, a penitentiary isle of banishment for criminals and undesirable subjects from the Kingdom of Klungkung. This strait roughly marks the division between Asia and Oceania. As the Balinese say, 'Here the tigers end.' Such a contrast to Bali. Nusa Penida is a dry hostile land where arid hills, big cacti, low trees, patches of green, small flowers, thorny bush and a few marsupials live—or rather, survive. White cuckatoos swarm in the trees. Coral gardens and white sand shores; many houses are made of jagged sea stones. There are two islands offshore, Lembongan and a smaller one Geningan (walk out to it at low tide) with their lazuli and cobalt blue coral pools, and starfish. Because of the shortage of vehicles in the out-areas, the best way to travel is by horse.

getting there: You can see the island looming offshore from Kusamba, 7 km or Rp50 by *bemo* from Klungkung. From this small Muslim coastal village take a *kapal motor* or *kapal layar* over to Nusa Penida for Rp350-375; with favorable winds about a 1½-2 hour passage. Fishermen carry peanuts, fruit and rice to the island; what they're carrying depends on the season. A boat leaves at least once a day, as soon as there are enough passengers. When you arrive in Montigi harbor, sign the police report book, then take a Colt to Toya Peka for Rp50. You can also sail to Nusa Penida from Benoa.

sights: From Toya Peka ride down the tree-lined road along the sea to Pura Ped, a temple complex consisting of a garden pond with a miniature island and a shrine in the middle of it. In Toya Peka, stay with the *kepala desa*. About 1 km north of Swana is a big cave, Gua Karangsari. Descend through a small trap-like opening down into tremendously deep vaulted halls with stalactites; so still and silent it's like being inside a hollow mountain. To the south of Swana are two pagoda-like temples. Pura Batukuning is on the beach. **others:** There are also villages in the mountains. Tanglad is a rocky mountain village of steep-roofed stone houses sprawling on different levels of hills. See the throne for the sun-god Surya supported by a huge stone woman; reminiscent of the style of Candi Sukuh on Mt. Lawu on Java. Across the plateau at Batukandik are shrines, one 'male' and the other 'female'. This unique temple has a prehistoric stone alter: a woman with enormous breasts supports a stone throne on her head and has two roosters standing on her shoulders. The Holy Forest of Sahab hides a temple, the exit of a mythical tunnel connecting Bali with Nusa Penida; it apparently starts from a hole in Pejeng. In the village of Salak, on the south coast, stand on a yellowish rock cliff and watch the dazzling green of the sea 200 m below.

TENGANAN

An original Balinese settlement (like Trunyan), long a stronghold of native Bali Aga traditions. Tenganan has its own culture and way of life. There is not a lot of selling of souvenirs to tourists; people are quieter and more dignified. For many years even the *joget* was forbidden here. The most striking thing about this walled-in isolationist town is its layout, totally different from elsewhere on Bali. There are two parallel streets with the walled living compounds, all nearly identical, on both sides of the wide stone-paved avenues. One gate is so narrow that a fat man could never get through it. Spacious lovely lawns grace this village. On the widest street is the administrative building, meeting hall, school, playing field, and rice barns. At one end of the street is a big square (the *banjar*) where all the important village events take place. In Tenganan live only 180 families, about 400 people. Seldom do the young people marry outside the village; evidence of inbreeding and retardation can be seen. *Kawin pandan* is practiced here once a year: a young man throws a flower over the wall and whoever catches it (even a one-eyed girl), he must marry. The *gamelan selunding*, a sacred archaic orchestra, is peculiar to the ancient cloistered conservative villages of East Bali, and is seldom heard outside of this village. *Rejeng* is a ritual offering dance originally performed by virgin boys and girls. Also see the boy-meets-girl mating dance, *Abuang*.

getting there: To reach Tenganan from Padangbai, expect to walk at least some of the way. First get out to the main road 2 km, then catch a *bemo* down to the Tenganan turn-off. Walk a further 3 km from the main road into the village. Or catch a Colt, an *oplet*, a truck, or anything that's going along the way.

crafts: A guide will volunteer his services to show you the village. He'll lead you to the *kepala desa* who makes *lontar* books. The *kepala desa* will pose for a photo and you may buy one of his books for Rp2500; he'll tell you that half of the money goes to the village. The guide also asks for a donation. The craft shop is near the gates when you first come into town. The guy who works there (speaks English) sells *gringsing*, woven fabrics, handsome tassled shawls, baskets, betelnut containers, woven reeds. Tenganan is the only place in all of Indonesia where both the warp and the weft are played into the weaving design; this is called the double-*ikat* method. Very loosely woven, this so-called 'flaming cloth' (kamben gringsing) is said to immunize the wearer against illness. Reddish or dark brown backgrounds are used to show up whitish and yellow designs. Threads were once dyed in human blood. These cloths are used now for ceremonial purposes: weddings, teeth-filings, covering the dead, or for a child's first haircut. You can't buy the 'perfect ones' anymore which have just the right tones. There's only one old lady who still weaves *gringsing* on her small make-shift loom.

events: A special ceremony is held once a year in June or July when a crude ferris wheel is erected. The women sit on chairs and it's revolved for hours on end. See this ferris wheel at the start of the road to Padangbai. At this time there is also a trance procession. **vicinity of Tenganan:** The penis of the famous hourse (Outje Seraya), turned to stone, is on top of a nearby hill. The dancers of Asak wear their hair in great coils to the side of their heads; their orchestra consists of the old *gamelan gambang* with wooden keys.

AMLAPURA

Its old name is Karangasem. The name was changed to mislead evil spirits from burying the town again under a volcanic eruption. You can't cash money here so bring enough, or go to Klungkung where the nearest banks are. See Puri Kanginan, the last *raja's* famous palace. A combination of European, Chinese, and Balinese designs, the large verandah on the main building is called *Bale London*. This is an enormous complex though the fountains have stopped spouting; dragons and serpents sit stonily with wide open mouths. South of town only 3 km at Ujung is the majestic old waterpalace, now being fully restored. Further on, black sand beaches. **stay:** Losmen Sidah Karya is at the beginning of town on Jl. Nasamudin, Tel. 43; Rp500 single, Rp800 double, has electricity, is clean and efficient. A sign greets you upon entering: 'Attention. You must be well dressed on the road. Violating this rule you will be seized and confiscated. Police.' No meals, but coffee, tea, and bananas are served in the mornings. The *pasar* and the bus, *bemo* and Colt stations, are all about 1 ½ km walk from this *losmen*. Another hotel up on the main street has Rp400 dormitory beds. **eat:** At Rumah Makan Sedap try the *garian-*fish, a specialty of the area, Rp1500. There are many *warungs* around the bus station serving Javanese and Balinese style *nasi campurs* on a banana leaf, Rp75.

from Amlapura: Take bus to Iseh, Rp150, or to Rendang, Rp350, from Jl. Selat or from the *pasar*. Abang is 11 km, Rp100 by *bemo*. For the waterpalace in Ujung (only 3 km from town), get a *bemo* from the *pasar*, Rp50. For Denpasar, take Colts or *bemos* for Rp350, 2½ hours; buses cost Rp300 but are painfully slow (4-5 hours). Buses go all the way to Singaraja up the east coast via Culik and Tianyar over a pockmarked and dusty road; they start at 4, 5, or 6 am, Rp350, 4-5 hours. Throw your motorbike or bicycle on top. Spectacular volcanic washouts along the way.

vicinity of Amlapura: There's a fighting system practiced in the Karangasam District, called *ende*, which originated in West Flores. Using sticks or whips, and shields, the combatants wear hoods for protection and take turns to formally attack each other (3 blows each). Iseh, on a dirt road north of Amlapura in the foothills of Gunung Agung, is *salak* growing country. This road continues on to Klungkung; unique landscapes. At the eastern extremity of the island is Seraya Volcano, now a vast ruin. Walk to it from the village of Ngis, a 6 hour climb. Buddahkling, between Amlapura and Tirtagangga, is a Mahayana Buddhist colony on the slopes of G. Agung. There live two different castes of Buddhists here who have retained prehistoric feasting traditions.

accommodation near Amlapura: Some of the finest places to stay on Bali are within easy reach of Amlapura. **Abian Soan:** Homestay Lila, 5 km west of Amlapura on the road to Bebamdem, Rp50 by *bemo*; Rp800, or Rp1000 double with a continental breakfast. Small Balinese cottages sit only 50 m from the road on the edge of a small ravine beside a river with rice paddies beyond. They'll prepare meals, or you shop in Amlapura and cook at the homestay yourself. In the morning the mountain G. Agung is clear. From the homestay walk ½ hour to Bukit Kusambi. Every 3 days in Bebamdem there's a cattle market. **Putung:** The government has built a miniature tourist resort at Putung, 11 km beyond Bebamdem. From Amlapura, take a *bemo* to Bebamdem, Rp100, then Rp100 more by *bemo* to the turnoff, then walk 1 ¼ km. A whole bungalow with closets, a *mandi*, and porch costs Rp1000, or Rp1500 for two. There are also some bamboo and *alang²* roofed *lumbung* (rice-barn) style bungalows. The bottom part is the *mandi* and sitting room, the top part is for sleeping. All the bungalows sit on the edge of a high terrace over a deep chasm which cuts its way down to the sea. Truly a breathtaking view over the coastline with Nusa Penida in the distance. Very cool fresh air; it doesn't get warm until noontime. Restaurant meals are Rp4-500 (plus 10% government tax), but you can get a *nasi campur* for Rp100 across the road. Nice walks in the area.

Tirtagangga Water Palace: From Amlapura it's Rp25 by *bemo* or bus to the highway turn-off to Tirtagangga. Then it's 5 km further by *bemo*, Rp50. One of the nicest *losmens* and prettiest places in all of Bali, Peng. Dhangin Taman Inn has its own entrance to the water palace; Rp700 double with gigantic rooms and big double beds, sunlight streaming through the windows. Swim laps in big flower-strewn pools that are filled from freshwater mountain streams. Run by Nyoman Dauh, the one with the ear to ear smile. Nyoman cooks huge meals for Rp2-300. Eating stalls near the *losmen* have cheaper food; *nasi campur*, Rp75, peanuts, fruits and such. **from Tirtagangga:** Climb the hill in the back and walk 1½ km to the village where there are occasional cockfights. Come back by way of the road which winds up through the valley; coconut palms, ricefields, the sea in the distance, and the biggest mountain on Bali towers right above. For Singaraja, buses pass right in front of Dhangin Inn at 3, 4, 5, and 6 am, doing the 87 km trip for Rp350. Have Nyoman wake you up.

Padangbai: A perfect pearl-shaped bay and tiny Muslim port of transit to the neighouring island of Lombok and beyond. Stay in Hotel Madya, Rp450 single. Listen to travelers' tales from the Southeast Islands, Nusa Tenggara. If you're facing the bay, there's a sandy beach with palm trees over the hill to the right. People seldom go there; very quiet. **from Pandangbai:** A Pelni office is right

by the pier. Many *kapal laut* shuttle between Padangbai and Lembar (on Lombok), a 5-6 hour crossing. Lembar is about 35 km south of Ampenan, Rp150 by Colt. Passenger and cargo vessels depart Padangbai each morning except Sunday; smaller boats generally cost Rp1200, bigger boats, Rp1500. Take the larger boats if you're prone to sea sickness. A new car ferry, in operation since Aug. 1976, is more expensive still. The K.M. Kuda Putih leaves Tues., Thurs., and Sat. at 11 am and arrives at 4 pm; Rp1500 including *sampan* service from the ship to Lembar. The Tiga Mas is too small and grubby. The K.M. Garuda leaves every Mon., Wed., and Fri. at 11 am, Rp1200. From Padangbai to Sumbawa Besar (on Sumbawa Island) catch a boat here on Sat., 12 hours, Rp3500, arrives Sun. morning.

SOUTH BALI

Sanur: 9 km east of Denpasar. A really fine lagoon; the coral reef stretches for hundreds of meters out to sea with tide pools and swaths of sand. The specialty of Sanur is shrines carved in white coral. This area is known for its painters, orchestras, and performances of *arja*, a traditional opera of courtly romances. Sanur is billed as one of the most popular international resort areas of the East, yet most of its premier hotels are running at a terrible loss with only 40% occupancy level (except Texan-owned Hyatt: 90%). The drift is over to Kuta; it's naughtier. **stay:** At the end of the *bemo* run to Sanur are several shops on the left. Immediately behind these shops is a small complex of inexpensive rooms. After bargaining rates, should be about Rp4-500. There is also bungalow-style accommodation on Jl. Sanur for Rp1800-2000 with private bathroom; try Hotel Puri Mass, Jl. Sanur 27. If you want to get away from Bali, go to the Bali Beach Hotel. Has a staff of 1000, airconditioning, telephone room service, self-opening doors. Sterilized double units, Aus$22; luxury suites, Aus$68. This hotel is 20 storeys high on an island where no buildings are now allowed to exceed the height of a palm tree. Costs Rp500 to

launder a pair of socks, Rp3000 for breakfast, and Rp900 to jump in their pool. **eat:** At Swastika, close to the intersection of the main road to Denpasar, sample their pork spare ribs, Rp500, or their *nasi goreng*, Rp200. The Taverna serves Rp1800 meals that would be hard to equal in Paris for triple that price. At Jojo's, outstanding seafood, Rp600-2000. The only Italian restaurant on Bali is the Trattoria Del Marco (or simply 'Marco's'), open from 6 pm. Great food but expect to spend Rp2000 at least. Try the fillet steak or Spaghetti Viennese; also fine wines.

Serangan (Turtle Island): Off the S.E. coast of Bali. Reached by *prahu* from Sanur, Nusa Dua, or Benoa. The most beautiful seashells are on this island; women come up with trays full to show you. But the reefs make it dangerous to dive for them. Giant sea turtles are caught and kept to be fattened on sea grass until sold as a specialty to restaurants. On a moonlit night watch them lay eggs on the beach. The children of this island fly huge kites hoisted into the air from outrigger canoes. Pura Sekenan (Turtle Festival) is held here once a year when droves of people cross over the sandbars bearing offerings to the sea temples. Towering giant puppets, *barong landung*, are carried by canoe in a water procession.

Bukit Peninsula: A dry rough land connected to the mainland by an isthmus. This tableland had once been at the bottom of the sea but is now 100 m above sea level, its sides rising straight up. Arid stunted bushland with cactus; very windy. Miles of open beach and volcanic caves. On some clifftops there are remains of foundations of ancient sea temples. Although hilly, it's possible to ride a pushbike around the peninsula. **Ulu Watu:** The road leads right by it. An unbelievable temple on a cliff overhanging the Indian Ocean 90 m below. Legend says that this temple is a ship turned to stone. Best time is at sunset. Watch sea turtles swim below in a hundred shades of churning sea water. The surf under Ulu Watu sometimes reaches 8 m in height, purported to be one of the best lefthanders in the world and the most challenging surf on the island. Go 1 km past Ulu Watu and ask farm boys, *'Dimana gua?'* and they'll show you where they are. Isolated and lovely beaches are 45 minutes descent down cliffs; run naked in the sun. Though totally out of the stream, to live here presents a logistics problem: no water.

Nusa Dua: *Bemos* leave Kuta from near the intersection at the start of Bali Beach road when enough people want one. Nusa Dua has just as nice a beach as Kuta but no *losmen* to stay in yet (maybe in 1977-78). The government is building a giant tourist project. From Nusa Dua to Benoa it's 8 km, then cross over to the fisheries and the Pelni Office side, Rp50 by boat (plus Rp50 extra for your pushbike), then on to Denpasar.

KUTA

10 km south of Denpasar, Rp50 by *bemo*. A longer beach than Sanur's, arching out of sight. Splendid tropical sunsets, equinox low, wide, and psychedelic. At least 4 out of 10 visitors are Australian. Peak vacation time is December. Although hundreds of travelers, vacationers, and tourists are turning Kuta into a middle class resort, it's still one of the cheapest travelers' enclaves in the world. Package-tourists high on money have metamorphosed this village. They pay too much money for services and crafts, drive prices up, spoil the people, use the beach as a drag strip for their motorcycles. It gets more hectic as the August holiday season nears with increasing numbers of French and German charter flights. Electricity is

bale: *The basic model of all Balinese construction. Very sturdy, even in high winds. Lasts more than 50 years. Roofs are made of ½ m thick* lalang *grass which keeps the structure cool; long ribs of coconut leaves are interwoven like shingles and lashed to the bamboo skeleton with super-strong cords of sugar palm fibre. The roof is combed with a special rake and all edges are trimmed with a knife. The end nearest where the roots were in the tree must correspond to the bottom part of the posts. Engraved beams (tiang) holding the roof are fitted together with pegs of coconut wood, no nails are used. Not built with any master plan, the builder has the design and the scale already worked out, as the Balinese say, 'in his belly'. On domestic* bale-*platforms are low wooden beds with bamboo springs on which the family sits cross-legged to eat, sleep, work, play, rest, read, talk. The Balinese kitchen has a simpler roof of coarse thatch that's supported by 4 posts with a bamboo platform at one end (the kitchen table), and a mud stove at the other. The dirt floor keeps food inside the clay pots hot for hours, and is easy to clean and smooth.*

Balinese temples

gradually coming in and most of the roads are now paved. In the dark undulating back lanes of Kuta at night you could meet pubescent pushers selling smack, pimps and Javanese hookers, bearded bicycle riders off to the beach, middle-aged Swiss couples on their way to Poppies, white children going home with flashlights, night walkers, Balinese and Javanese roaring by on their motorcycles, village fishermen setting off, farmers going home. Anybody. You might meet the guy who started the *sarung* craze in southern California, or your ex-husband. The whole complex of this bamboo city is like Ibiza or Mallorca, just without the wine. Kuta is now expanding towards Legian, and Legian is now but an extension of Kuta. There are still good *Kris* Dances with gas lamps glowing, but it now costs Rp4-700 to get into many of the dances. Watch your gear. You might meet the stealing's getting bad (the Balinese say, 'It's the Javanese.'). You can see the prices go up by the week. The place is thick with sellers; always someone wanting to sell you something. In fact, you could end up spending more money on Kuta than anywhere else on the island simply because there are more things to buy. Unless you're in a group, it's not safe anymore to walk along the Kuta-Legian beach late at night. Already Kuta needs a better trash disposal system than the dogs. Covarrubias says that its dogs are the one thing which keep Bali from being perfect. The miserable *anjings* abound — mangy, flea-bitten bags of skin, bones, and open sores. Don't die on Bali. You might come back as a dog.

surfing: Good body surfing with crystal clear water and top to bottom tubes. The best months are during the Aussie winter, March-July. Waves seldom get over 2 m high. During the summer, the weather is changeable, from glass to cyclone and then back to glass in five hours. Watch out for sneaky undertows and cross-currents. Take a *prahu* out to the reef, it's safer. There's a wide range of boards for rent (Rp400 per day) and for sale leaning up against *losmen* walls. Buy wax for your board at Sunshine Surfboard Shop, Jl. Legian, near Legian, but it's expensive so bring your own. There are many loud arrogant Aussie surfies acting like they never left Manly or Ceduna; even down to the Aussie manhood thing of throwing girls in the water. Already a breed of young hip Balinese surfers have evolved, wearing neck pendants, talking about their boards, and calling you 'mate' or 'Hey, Spunky!'.

dope: The Sumatran connection and Buddah's Noble Path flow through here and many smoke large quantities of cannabis in an attempt to get up to the level of the Balinese who are so naturally high all year around on that good ol' time religion. Pop-

pies back lane is a real Sin Alley: wine, women, and dope; where 12 year old pushers call you by your first name. If you buy grass from Indonesians, don't be deceived by the wrappings; they make it look convincingly like authentic Buddah weed. *Half* the time they burn you, no exaggeration. Best is to do business only with westerners or with the waiters in the restaurants. The price varies from Rp1500-2000 per stick for Sumatran or top Thai weed, although the troubles in Thailand have slowed down the flow now. Sometimes there's a lot of grass, other times only Nepalese hash (Rp1000 per gram), or deadly smack. It's unwise to be penniless, raids and busts do occur. Police and *imigrasi* are into 6 am sweeps for users and sellers. Watch the *ibus* who come around selling clothes and materials, many are paid police informers. Also Indonesian pushers and the police work very close together. They'll turn in a tourist pusher in a flash because he cuts into their sales. Then the tourist pusher's whole stash is mysteriously selling up on the beach two days later. Savvy? If you get busted, it just means that it's going to cost you money (Rp20,000-Rp50,000), and your possessions might be confiscated. Although a law passed in 1976 allows them to throw you in jail for 6 years, there's still corruption; settle it right off. If you're broke perhaps it's safer to drink earthy *tuak* with the old man stroking their fighting cocks in the back lanes of Kuta.

miscellaneous: Bring reading material. Unless you swap, books are hard to come by on Bali. Shops and *warungs* in Kuta charge up to Rp2000 for old beat-up 2nd hand books jettisoned by former travelers. In Kubu Krishna's, you can read books on the premises for Rp25. There's a bulletin board at Kuta Post Office advertising for passengers on private boats, travel bargains, for-sale notices, yacht sales and crews, room and traveling mates, lost, found and stolen, all and everything. Many of the better known restaurants have bulletin boards as well, like Tama's, Poppies, etc. Massages cost Rp4-500 for adults, Rp150-200 for kids. Even the massage ladies speak English now. Bicycle rental is Rp200 per day (at Surata's) on Kuta Beach. *Arak* (palm gin) costs Rp200 a bottle in the market. Have letters addressed to Post Restante, Kuta Beach. This P.O. is on the road to Legian.

stay: There are literally hundreds of *losmens,* so many that no more are allowed to be built. Official prices are Rp300-500 single, Rp500-800 double. Also some beach front bungalows, Rp5000 for a twin bedroom with all facilities; unreal splendour. If you consider the sunsets, the restaurants, and the beach, Kuta is about the most comfortable place to stay in Indonesia. Lots of times you're waylaid at the airport or along the road and brought to a *losmen* on Kuta, this often turns out good. Some *losmens* offer rewards (Rp150) to their European boarders for each new customer they bring in. The nicest places are on the wings of Kuta village, just where it starts to get quiet again. These *losmens* tend to be lower priced, more relaxing, and there are fewer sellers. Each lane is actually a little neighborhood by itself, with its own eating *warungs* and strip of beach where the neighbourhood gathers at sunset. On the Legian village side of Kuta there are more *kampungs*, more trees and bushes, more life, more foodstalls and it's generally cheaper and closer to the sea. On the Kartika Plaza side there are only coconut groves, cows grazing, the *losmens* are further apart and more isolated. There are so many *losmens* now and so much competition that travelers are beginning to choose their *losmen* by the services and extras offered, i.e. if the family teaches silversmithing, dancing, *Bahasa Indonesia*, offers a bicycle, a bigger and better breakfast, or an outstanding collection of books to read. There's little spirit of neighborliness between *losmen*-owners where money is concerned. There's a lot of jealousy and many bad feelings when *losmens* 'lose' customers to their neighbors. Many *losmens* try to buy a motorbike because there's more money in renting it out than they get for renting out rooms. During March and June, *losmen* prices drop from Rp600 to Rp500. **south side of Kuta:** Towards the airport, Petala Beach Inn is Rp600 or Rp1000 double. Komara Losmen, Jl. Bakung Sari, Rp600 double, Rp400 single Losmen Pendawa is in back of Kartika Plaza, Rp600 single, Rp1000 double with private bath and shower; out of the way. Puspa Sari between Kartika Plaza and Sunset Inn, facing a beautiful courtyard and great old *banyan* tree; Rp1200, or Rp1000 per day if you stay a week. **Kuta village:** Three Brothers Losmen, two minutes walk back from airport-Kuta Beach road intersection, super beautiful garden, central, Rp400 single, Rp600 double. Losmen Artha, Rp400 and Rp600 double, including a Balinese breakfast (*bubur* with coconut), very nice place. For something more posh, Yasa Samudra's hotel is close to the beach at the end of Kuta Beach Road. Prime location. Cheap (Rp4500) for what you get; big breakfast included and delicious *nasi gorengs* only Rp110. East and West, also right on the beach, rents out bungalows from Rp400 (in the back) up to Rp2000-2500; a quiet relaxing place. Smack in the middle of Kuta behind the Bamboo Den is small, clean and quiet Homestay Ibu Dewi; Rp400 or Rp600 double; so much in Kuta's eye it's hidden. No stealing, good vibes, and close to the dance rehearsal platform. **Legian side:** You'll find most of these *losmens* on the same lane as Poppies Cottages. Nyoman Gora, quiet and leafy. House Dewa, Santhi Graha, Pension Dua Dara, near Nyoman Gora; and especially good is Losmen Cempaka in its

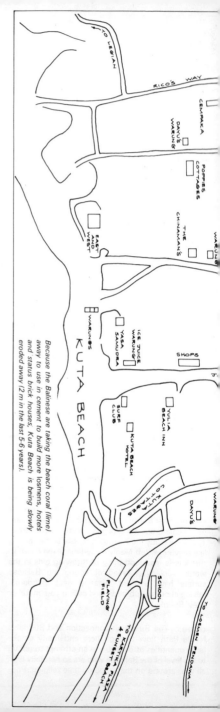

Because the Balinese are taking the beach coral (lime) away to use in cement to build more losmens, hotels and status brick houses, Kuta Beach is being slowly eroded away (2 m in the last 5-6 years).

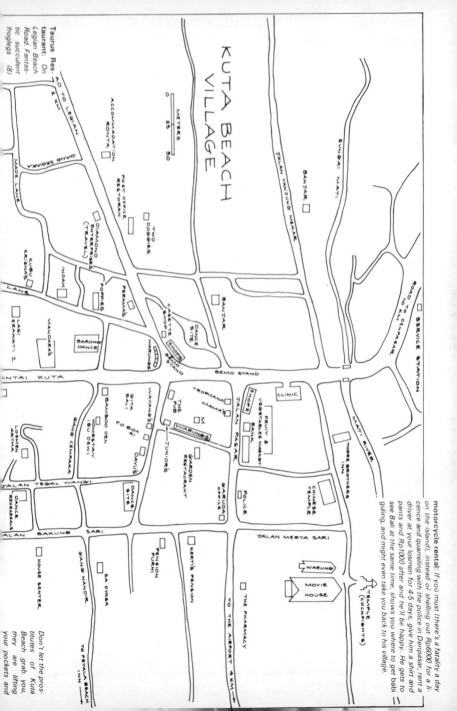

KUTA BEACH VILLAGE

METERS
0   25   50

TO LEGIAN ← 1 KM

GANG SEGARA
MADE LANE

ACCOMMODATION KONTA

POST OFFICE
RESTORAN

DIAMOND
ENTERPRISES
(TRAVEL)

TWO
DOGGIES

POPPIES

PERAMA'S

CASSETTE
SHOPS

SHOPS

DANCE
SITE

WARUNGS

SHOPS

BEMO STAND

BEMO STAND

INDAH

KUBU
KRISNA'S

LANE

MANDARAS

LASI,
ERAWATI I.

BARONG
DANCE

ANTAI KUTA

GANG CEMPAKA

LOSMEN
ARTHA

BAMBOO DEN

GITA
BALI

HOMESTAY
IBU DEWI

PO. BOX

DAYU'S

WAYANE'S

THE PUB

3

JUNIOR'S

GARDEN
RESTAURANT

TROPICANA
MAMA'S

JALAN PASAR

FRUIT &
VEGETABLES MARKET

SHOPS

BANK

CLINIC

SANTAR

JALAN TANJUNG MEKAR

SUNGAI MATI

ROAD TO DENPASAR

SERVICE STATION

MATI RIVER

THREE BROTHERS
INN

CHINESE
TEMPLE

ROAD TO DENPASAR 10 KM →

JALAN TEGAL WANGI

JALAN

DANCE
REHEARSALS

DANCE
SITE

GARUDA
OFFICE

POLICE

BAKUNG

SARI

GANG NANDUR

SA DYASA

KEETI'S PENSION

PENSION
PURNI

JALAN MERTA SARI

HOUSE SENTER

TO THE AIRPORT 4 KM →

TO PETALA BEACH

THE PHARMACY

WARUNG

MOVIE
HOUSE

TEMPLE
(COCKFIGHTS)

Taurus Restaurant: On Legian Beach Road. Fantastic succulent froglegs (8)

motorcycle rental: If you must (there's a fatality a day on the island, instead of shelling out Rp6000 for a licence and quarreling with the police in Denpasar, rent a driver at your losmen for 4-5 days, give him a shirt and pants and Rp1000 after and he'll be happy. He gets to see Bali at the same time, shows you where to get babi guling, and might even take you back to his village.

Don't let the prostitutes of Kuta Beach grab you, they are lifting your pockets and own *kampung*. Towards Kuta village, but all by itself, is Losmen Waringan, Rp400 and Rp600 double. Towards Legian about one km is Nyoman Jony 200 m from the beach. Further still is Lusa Accommodation, halfway between Kuta and Legian; it's only 75 m from the road and 50 m from the beach. Surfboards and bicycles for hire on the same lane.

eat: Easily as many restaurants and *warungs* as there are *losmens*. Go to different places for different specialties—the best vegetable soup at the Bamboo Den, Rp75 (also great enchiladas); best *gado2* and *nasi campur* at the Post Office Restoran; best prawn salad at the Free Bar and Restaurant; best banana daiquiries at Poppies, etc. If you get misty for home some places serve toast and vegemite or peanut butter and honey sandwiches, Rp100 None of the food on Kuta is really first class; only in Sanur are there really fine (and expensive) restaurants. Even Kuta's better restaurants have their off-days. Some dishes, like 'vegetable pie', somehow get lost in the translation. 'Vegetable pie' could end up as just a pancake with vegies inside. For the cheapest food: fried *tahu* carts, Rp25-50; goose and noodle soup carts, Rp50; sweet mungbean soup, Rp10-25; baked corn, Rp25 per. The back lane *warungs* are good for the money, heaps of food. Most *nasi campurs* cost Rp150 in the *warungs*. Though it costs Rp2000 for a mediocre meal at Yasa Samudra's Restaurant, you can eat quite satisfyingly in the *warungs* out in front of it for Rp150. Buy big papayas for Rp125-150. Buy wedges of *tempe* (Rp10 each) in Kuta Market and take them to Dayu's or the Chinaman's on Poppies Lane and have them cook you up some fried rice. Several places prepare magic mushroom soups and omelettes, either the Rp500 strength, or if you just want to get a little bit disturbed, the Rp300 strength. The in place for breakfast is Allang's; also the very best jaffles, chili con carne, and yoghurt. Lenny's is an exceptionally good seafood restaurant near the beach, but not for the impecunious: Rp1500 for a small tasty chicken lobster or Rp2000 for a large fish (big enough for two). Good service without them falling all over you. The best restaurant food is at Jenik's Poppies, which has become a singles pick up bar and a hangout for Indonesian pimps. Try fish and chips, Rp500, the fish chowder, Rp400, and Mexican dishes like bean tacos, Rp300. About one-third more expensive than the cheaper restaurants, Poppies plays the Ritz of Kuta. Mama's, right next door to the Tropicana, has the tastiest vegetarian smorgasbord going every evening; all you can eat for Rp300. Get there early before all the best dishes are snapped up. Sit out front and take in the street life. Tropicana has the best bean tacos and breakfasts. Both Tropicana and Perama's make the best deep pan apple pie and

ice cream, Rp300. They stay open late to cater for people who roll in after a heavy night of smoking. Drink *tuak*, Rp25 for a container full, in the *warung* on the same lane as the dance rehearsal platform (on the lane parallel to Kuta Beach Road) on the left-hand side going towards the beach. Spike your fruit juices with gin, rum or vodka, a cheap and refreshing buzz. For banana and pineapple pancakes, the best fruit salad and fruit juices, go to the last *warung* on the right on Kuta Beach Road going towards the sea; always crowded. Lasi Erawati's is the place for rye bread sandwiches and yoghurt drinks, etc. Kubu Krishna's for vegetable tempura, Rp200, four bowls of good food, can hardly finish it. Also Bombay curry and brown rice, potato salad, and loaves of wholewheat bread (Rp225). Best Australian jaffles (baked filled sandwiches) are at Ayu's Juice Shop on the main road, also for plain good cheap Indonesian food. Ayu's features a suckling pig supper including rice, soup, vegetables, fruit salad, *tuak*, eat your fill for Rp1000. Dayu's Warung, opposite Poppies Cottages, serves good *tahu* burgers, tasty vegetable salad and cheese sandwiches, Rp75. Drink beer from frosted glasses at The Pub ('Cares for you') near intersection of Kuta Beach Road and Legian Road; convivial, and the best location for people-watching.

crafts: For buying anything from coconuts to stone carvings, the 'morning price' is the lowest first price of the day because the sellers believe that if they make a sale right off then the day will go well for them. Bring t-shirts, especially ones with cartoons or messages on them, to sell or to swap for good *batik*. Parish t-shirts go over the biggest for trading, getting up to Rp3000 in value.

dance: The *Kecak* and *Legong* Dances are put on for tourists, Rp600. The Balinese won't let you peep at the performances around the side of the dance like the rest of the people; tourists must go through the front and pay. Because it takes place usually from 11 pm to 5 am, few westerners ever attend *arja* (opera), Rp200. You see tour companies advertising the Fire Dance and the Virgin Dance, both for Rp2000. The Virgin Dance is actually a much watered down version of the famous trance-dance, *Sangyang Dedari*. To learn dance it's generally cheaper to study in Ubud (Rp400-500 an hour) than in Kuta (Rp500-600 an hour).

from Kuta: There's a path running parallel to Legian Road that starts from just beside Kubu Krishna and leads all the way through ricefields and *kampungs* to Legian. **Tanah Lot:** Walk eight hours up and back from Kuta to this pagoda-like temple sitting on an eroded rock offshore. Reach it

Balinese festivals: Njepi *is an annual Balinese festival held to purify the whole island, a time when demons and evil spirits are driven out of the villages. All work stops for the procession to the seacoast. The evil ones are lured to great offerings set up at crossroads and then expelled by curses of the high priests (pedandas). The unclean earth is purified by the spilling of cock's blood and at sunset the villagers, es-* *pecially the children, bang bamboo sticks together and beat on gongs or tin cans to frighten away any evil spirits who are lingering still. The Saraswati Festival is an annual Hindu festival held in honor of the Hindu Goddess of learning, science, and literature. Literary manuscripts receive offerings. No one may read on this day.*

also from Kediri by taking a side road which ends on a green hill that slopes down to the beach. (Snakes sleep in the rocky holes along the beach.) Tanah Lot looks like a Chinese painting. Ironically, this temple was built by one of the last priests to come to Bali from Java, Sang Hiyang Nirarta, a man remembered for his successful efforts in strengthening the religious beliefs of the people. Anything even faintly resembling a spiritual atmosphere is dissipated by money-obsessed Balinese at the temple who ask you for money to park your bike (Rp25), hire a sash to enter ('It's up to you.'), enter the temple, and at the Shiva shrine in the temple ('It's up to you.') On this south coast of Bali there's a whole series of sea temples: Pura Sekenan, Pura Ulu Watu, Pura Rambut Siwi, Pura Petitenget. All pay homage to the guardian spirits of the sea. **tours:** Tour companies offer minibus tours of the island, 7 or 8 people to a bus. Sample tours: On the Singaraja Tour, Rp2000, you visit Bedugal, Lake Bratan Temple, Gitgit, Singaraja, Sangsit, Kubutambahan, Sanih Beach. Leaves Kuta at 8:15 am and gets back around 4 pm. On the Besakih Tour, Rp1600, visit Batubulan, Celuk, Batuan, Mas, Gianyar, Klungkung, Gerta Gosa, Bukit Jambul, Besakih. Leaves at 8:15 and ends at 4 p.m. **for Java:** Long-distance buses leave Kuta from the Gita Bali Office on Kuta Beach Road; to Surabaya, 12 hours, Rp1750; Yogya, 20 hours, Rp3000. Honey Holidays, Jl. Bunisari, also has buses to Yogya, Rp3000, starting from in front of their office at 4:30 pm, arriving 22 hours later; to Surabaya, Rp1750, departs at 4:30 and arrives 10 hours later. The Sari Express is just as fast, but it's air-conditioned so it's twice as expensive.

LEGIAN

Rp60 from Denpasar by *bemo*. Or a pleasant two km walk north of Kuta Beach. This little village is still out-of-the-way from the speedy Kuta vibe; visiting Kuta after Legian is like going into the big city. For people who want to stay for several weeks or months, they usually spend a couple of days on Kuta then move down to Legian. Legian has got the worst reputation for stealing. They will steal stuff above your head or from under your very bed while you sleep, so lock your windows and doors at night. If there are bars on the windows move all valuables out of reach. Many of the rip-offs are inside jobs or tip-offs by the guys who work in the *losmens*. They usually wait right up to the day before you plan to leave so it's too much hassel for you to complain to people or track your goods down. So never tell your *losmen* when you're leaving. Legian is really being pushed by the trendy fun-in-the-sun Australian travel agents now, a playground for young travelers. It also has it's share of resident smack freaks. There's good music (sometimes live performances at Tama's), outstanding cheap food, two bicycle repair shops, two laundries. There are dances at least every other day: *arja* (opera), *Barong, Kecak,* and the *Ramayana,* all Rp600. For mushrooms, go down to the cow paddocks near the beach, but really early before the locals pick them clean. Families have even begun to cultivate mushrooms in their backyard gardens for the wholesale market. Change money at Chandri's.

stay: There are about 30 *losmens* in and around

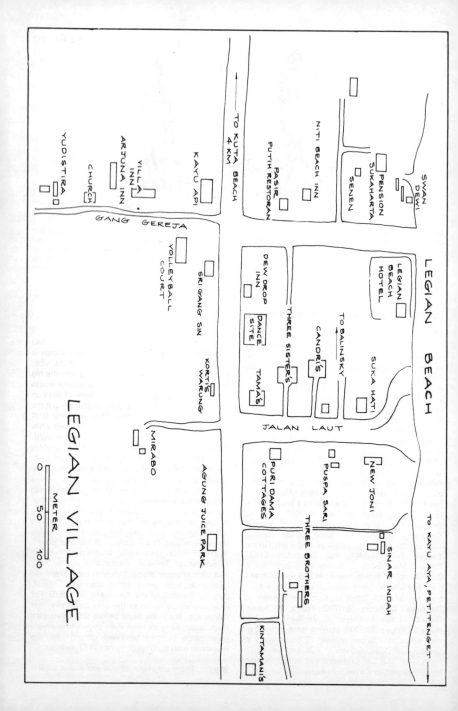

Legian, some quite unique, tucked away in hard-to-find places. Legian Beach Hotel has luxurious facilities; Rp7500 singles, Rp15,000 doubles; Rp300 for outsiders to use the pool. Accommodation Sinar Indah is one of the quietest *losmens*; Rp400 single, Rp600 double. Nice sea breeze and exactly on line with the US$20 a day Legian Beach Hotel, and just as adequate. Puspa Sari, Jl. Laut, Rp500 or Rp600 single, Rp1000 double; a bungalow for four, Rp2000. This is the place for the socializers; lot of strays. Excellent food served, jaffles, ice drinks, etc. Has electricity and offers a package-deal of 'room, full board and motorcycle'. Mirabo is another central yet hidden *losmen* off the main Legian road and down a path through the rainforest. Off-season rates are as low as Rp500 double. Surrounded by jungle, you just hear the birds, insects and gekkos. Your things are quite safe here; constantly guarded. About 300 m from the highway down Gang Gereja (opposite Legian Beach Hotel Road) is Yudistira, a fine *losmen* that's usually empty, enclosed by bright green ricefields and coconut trees, very quiet, and only 200 m from a river. Arjuna Inn and Villa Inn are on the same lane. Play volley ball each afternoon at the beginning of the lane with the boys. Losmen Suratha, Rp300; very kind, Christian, the brother of the owner is a cop, the grandmother makes great flower arrangements, *bubur hitam* is served for breakfast. At Korti's *losmen* out in the cow paddocks, black rice pudding, bananas, toast and jam, plus coffee and tea anytime are included in the price of a room, Rp3-400 (a bargain!). Great service and it's halfway between the beach and the road. Pension Sukaharta is on the south side of Legian; Rp400 single, Rp600 double. Sits by itself, is close to the beach, and you can rent bicycles for Rp300 a day. **north side of Legian:** Three Brothers Inn, Rp400 single, Rp600 double with private bathrooms and a large garden; you can see the ocean. Ideally located, Legian Sunset Beach Cottages is about two km beyond Legian; units rent for Rp1500 double. But the guys who run it are obnoxious and someone gets something stolen practically every day. Also has a snack bar. Tama's has opened a new flash restaurant that will offer needed competition to Sunset Cottages. In the same area as Sunset Beach are the Roby Inn (only four rooms), and Made's, which are nearly as quiet. Blue Ocean has little bamboo huts, Rp700. Belgi's is another place, standard prices, many rooms; Belgi acts like a mother hen to single girls. The most isolated and remote *losmens* are beyond Sunset Cottages. Rent a bicycle to make Legian and Kuta more readily accessible. Kayu Aya's cottages, an enterprise which went bankrupt after the manager absconded with the funds, is about 2½ km beyond Legian; rent villas here for US$5-10 daily. The bar is deserted, dusty and gone to weed. There are other *losmens*

even more remote charging standard prices; search for them. The last two *losmens* are in Petitenget, one hour's walk from Legian; an unreal area. One is called 'The Ricefield Losmen', Rp400 single or Rp600 double, but is highly in demand and often full.

eat: Food is better in Kuta. It's too bad Tama's got spoiled, but the smorgasbord every Saturday night, 6-8 pm, Rp350, is still usually good. Dine to the music of Humble Pie. Check out the health food menu but avoid the onion and garlic ice drink; they make it too strong. Kayu Api s is run by two prim English women who sell health food such as muesli, cheesecake, fresh milk, but small portions. Korti's *warung*, near Tama's, is right on the road like a cafe; good everything. Lover's, also next to Tama's, is a beautiful place but has a lousy cook. Mini Restaurant is the best for Chinese food. *Warungs* serving *babi guling*, rice cakes, and other goodies, are set up outside the dance hall on Mon. and Thurs. evenings; pay the peoples' prices. Agung's Juice Park is right on the main road, has a soft garden setting, and incomparable ice juices, especially carrot, but his waitresses are unbearable to single white women. Ratu's is a small bargain place down the road, best for guacamole. Many of the fancier bamboo restaurants sell expensive rip-off food, especially their western dishes. Happy's has very good food but caters mostly to Australian arranged tourists and give shitty service to others. Kintimani's Indonesian menu isn't that bad. Good cheap beer at the Dew Drop Inn; their pepper steak with garlic and potatoes is cooked perfectly. At Sri Gang Sin, opposite Dew Drop Inn, the turtle steak (Rp250) and other seafood is nice. The only Javanese restaurant is Legian (with a whorehouse behind it) lies on the road to Losmen Baleka, and serves quite respectable *nasi campurs*.

DENPASAR

Capital of Bali and the largest city on the island. The local name is Badung. This typical middle-sized Indonesian community is still small (pop. 100,000) but growing. It's like Luna Park 24 hours a day, a hot dirty smelly noisy dusty city that gives you a headache when you visit it for a morning from Kuta Beach. Few charms. Buy quality pre-recorded tapes for only Rp500 along the main street. The best bank to have your bread sent is Bank Bumi Daya, Jl. Veteran; they will cash most kinds of traveler's cheques.

stay: Wisma Taruna Inn, Jl. Gadung 27, on a quiet rubbly back street. Two km from the city center (Rp35 by *bemo*) or a 20 minute walk. Walk up Jl. Hayamwuruk and turn in at Arya Hotel, then it's

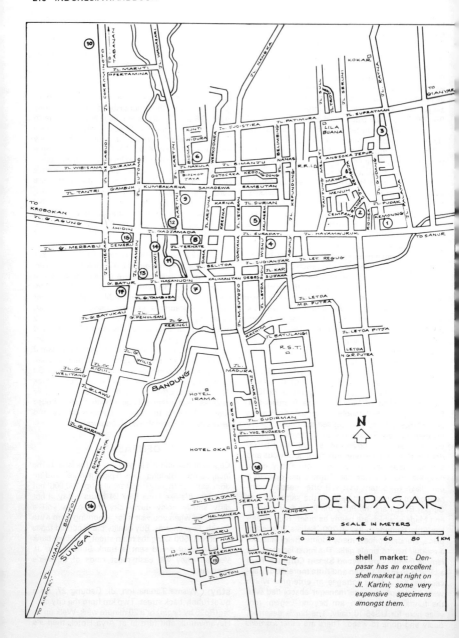

DENPASAR

SCALE IN METERS

0   20   40   60   80   1 KM

N

shell market: *Denpasar has an excellent shell market at night on Jl. Kartini; some very expensive specimens amongst them.*

only a short walk from there. Costs Rp400 with a YHA card or Rp500 without. Rent a motorcycle from them for Rp1500 a day or a pushbike for Rp500 a day. Also offers laundry service, beverages and food. This hostel is only ten minutes walk from the Kreneng Bus Terminal which provides transport to all of eastern Bali. It's also about a five minute walk to the Lilabuwana Theatre (Rp250 entrance) where there's a night market and vast food trips at cheaper prices. Watch *dukuns* mesermerize crowds. Sumertha Centre, which holds performances of the *Kecak, Ramayana,* and *Legong* Dances (Rp600 for a one hour performance) is also nearby. Two Brothers Inn, Jl. Banjar Tegal, lies 100 m down a lane running off the main road to Kuta Beach, Jl. Iman Banjol; Rp400 single (one bed), Rp500 single (two beds), or Rp600 double. Quiet, clean, safe, has electricity, sitting toilets, showers, fragrant flowers. You can easily walk or take a *bemo* into town, Rp25. Just stroll down the lane in your swim gear with your towel over your shoulder and thumb a *bemo* to Kuta Beach for a swim, Rp50. Breakfast *komplet*: fruit salad, boiled eggs, banana pancakes, toast, coffee, etc.—Rp300. Try local meals in the *banjar* (meeting house) down the lane, *mie* and *nasi goreng* for Rp200, two *sate* for Rp25. Also very early in the mornings black rice pudding with shredded coconut, syrup, a delicious way to start the day for Rp5! Two Brothers will always tell you of an event going on in Denpasar — funeral, cockfight, dance, ceremony, or the like. Hotel Arjuna 24, Jl. Ardjuna 24, Langon (enter right by the jeweler's shop) was the home of the late I

Gusti Putu Timur, now run by his daughter, Tantri; Rp500 or Rp1000 double. Quiet, clean, central location, private bathrooms, drinks are served. Eat at Ada Sedia *warung* just down the street. Losmen Puri, Jl. Ardjuna 10, Rp500 single, Rp1000 double. Communal bathrooms, quite central and quite ordinary. Hotel Adi Yasa, Jl. Nakula 11, charges Rp300 single, Rp600 double, or Rp1500 for two with a bathroom. Rooms could be kind of close and hot at times but there is a bar. Adi will play 'Blowin' in the Wind' on his guitar; he might take you to a cockfight, a real treat. For long term stay at Hotel Yasa, Jl. Tanimbar (not very central), Rp10,000 a month. If you're with an Indonesian boy or girl go to Hotel Arta on Jl. Diponegoro (just before the Kantor Imigrasi) where they don't ask questions; other places, there could be problems; Rp1500 a night with showers and a toilet. Note: don't ride with an Indonesian girl in a *dokar*; the police might follow and ask for a payoff.

eat: There are a large number of foodstalls everywhere in Denpasar; eat good for Rp200-250. On Gang Kresna, opposite the traffic police station on Jl. Gadjah Mada, *warungs* serve *cap cai* and *mie goreng*, Rp100. Go to the open-air night market on Jl. Kartini after 6 pm for noodle soups, fried rice, excellent *martabak* (Rp50-100), roast pork (Rp150), good chocolate donuts. Try steaming *kue putu*, smothered in coconut shavings, Rp10. A splendid place to visit at night with thousands of milling people of all ages, races and nations; fresh whole goats hang above grills, boys play Balinese checkers with beercaps and stones on the sidewalk. For Javanese food, try Warung Indonesia, Jl. Veteran. For *nasi padang*, Pagi Sore, Jl. Gadjah Mada, is about the best. Go to Babi Guling Gianyar, Jl. Hasanudin in front of Pemucutan Hotel, for *babi guling*, Rp200. Sumber Rasa, Jl. Gadjah Mada 34; and Rumah Makan Ria, Jl. Gadjah Mada 102, for dove (burung dara), Rp800; also tasty pork and chicken dishes. Atom Baru, Jl. Gadjah Mada 98, good. At Delicious Restaurant, Jl. Kartini, the turtle steak and frogs' legs are still excellent. For Chinese food try Polaris, Jl. Sulawesi; or Sie Fu, right behind Bank Negara. For lashing out or to escape the heat and sellers, go to Restoran Puri Seleri, right opposite Bank Rakyat Indonesia on Jl. Gadjah Mada, or the Bali Sky, Jl. Kartini. Puri Ice Cream Palace on Jl. Beliton serves outrageous sundaes.

sights: Bali Museum contains a survey of Balinese art from prehistoric times to the early 20th Century: masks, woodcarvings, cricket cages for fighting crickets, neolithic stone implements, miniature scale models of ceremonial events. This museum's architecture combines the two principal edifices in Bali, the temple and the palace, a

---

DENPASAR

1. tourist bureau
2. Kreneng Bus Station
3. Wisma Taruna
4. Bali Museum
5. Post Office
6. Adi Yasa's
7. Suci Station
8. Rumah Makan Pagi Store
9. Delicious Restaurant
10. to Ubang Station
11. pasar
12. bemos to Sanur and Ubud
13. Candi Pemecutan
14. bemos to Kuta Beach
15. Zamrud Airlines
16. Two Brothers Inn
17. bemos for Kuta Beach
18. Hotel Arta
19. Immigration Department

blending of building styles of north, east and west Bali. Wear long pants. Visit Puri Pemecutan near the central bus station on the corner of Jl. Thamrin and Jl. Hasanudin. Above the St. Joseph Catholic Church, Jl. Kepundung 2, are angels dressed like *Legong* dancers and in a stone basrelief of Christ, Pilate studies the scrolls by electric light and a motorbike sits in the background. At the University Library near the Central Hospital, there's a collection of masterpieces of illustrative art and caligraphy, called *lontar*. These palm leaf 'books' and the *candi* of Java are the only record of ancient Indonesian culture, history and literature. Meredith Memorial Library on the main road between Kuta and the airport for good English travel books and Christian literature. There are cockfights near the Kuta Bemo Station every Fri. and Sat. from 11 am to 4 pm, Rp50 entrance. Even in Denpasar, teethfiling ceremonies, *Barong* Dances, and cremations and weddings take place. Keep your eyes and ears open. **tourist offices:** For information about the island of Bali go to Kantor Parawista, Jl. Kemoning 1. Ask them about any events that are to take place in the countryside. For the city of Denpasar go to the tourist office on Jl. Surapati, only 5 minutes walk from the central P.O. heading away from the city.

crafts: At the Jl. Kresna market, off Jl. Gadjah Mada opposite the traffic police, t-shirts, bone carvings, beads, shell crafts, basketware and masks are sold. Visit the Sanggraha Kriya Asta Handicrafts Centre at Tophati on the outskirts of Denpasar to view all aspects and styles of Balinese handicrafts. This center will give you a good indication of the prices you should be paying as it is government-run and all prices are fixed. Nyona Dhewi will offer advice on which crafts-village to visit, and will even write letters of introduction to artists on your behalf. **dances:** Most dances in Denpasar are strictly tourist events. The *Kecak* is held at the Sumertha Centre each night from 6-7 pm. The *Ramayana* Ballet is held at the Hyatt Hotel every Wed., 7-8 pm. The *Barong* Dance is staged especially for tourists at Batubulan every morning 9-10 am; jammed with hundreds of Europeans, buses and cars, and suffocated with sellers. For cheaper, longer and more traditional dances, try to view celebrations and festivites in the villages. At the Conservatory of Instrumental Arts and Dance (KOKAR), Jl. Ratna, watch or learn Balinese music and dance. *Wayang kulit* is staged at the Pemecutan, Mon., and Thurs., 6-7 pm; plus many other venues in the city. Most cultural performances cost Rp600.

local transportation: The *bemo* fare to anywhere in Denpasar city is Rp25. There are two *bemo* stations, on Jl. Kartini and on Jl. Camboja

(Pasar Baru); and 3 bus stations. No bus fare to any town on the island is more than Rp350. All buses to eastern Bali leave from Kreneng Station, Jl. Hayamwuruk. From Kreneng also catch minibuses to: Padangbai (and a boat further to Lombok), Rp350; Klungkung, Rp150; Amlapura, Rp300; Gianyar, Rp100; Kintamani (1500 m highland town), Rp250. All buses to western Bali depart from Stasiun Ubang, Jl. Cokroaminoto; minibuses to Singaraja from here too, Rp350. Board *bemos* at Stasiun C.V. Giat near the Kuta Beach Bemo Station, to: Tanjung Benoa, Rp200; Ulu Watu, Rp250. They leave when they're full. Take a *bemo* from Jl. Kartini (off the main street Jl. Gadjah Mada) during the day to: Ubud, Rp125, and Sanur, Rp50. To Klungkung, catch a *bemo* from Jl. Camboja (Pasar Baru), Rp175, 40 km.

inter-island buses: These leave from Stasiun Suci for Surabaya, Yogya, Jakarta, and Semarang. Buy tickets in advance otherwise seats get booked out. For Java: Elteha Bus. Co., Jl. Durian near Hotel Bali, offers fares from Denpasar to Surabaya, Rp1750, and to Banyuwangi, Rp750. Leaves at 6 pm from their office and arrives in Surabaya at 5 am. Gita Bali Express are about the best and most efficient. For Yogya their bus leaves at 5:45 am, arrives 4 am (22 hours), Rp3000 including 2 meals (*nasi campur* and drinks), served in the afternoon and night. For Surabaya, Gita Bali buses leave at 3 different times: 5:45 am, arriving at 4:30 pm; 4 pm, arriving 3:30 pm; and at 6 pm, arriving at 5:30 am. Costs Rp1750 with meals. Mutiara Express, Jl. Diponegoro in Sangiah (also another office in Kuta village) offers bus and train connections from Bali through to Java. Cheaper than the bus companies, especially with a student card. First to Surabaya, Rp1750, then from Surabaya to Jakarta on the Gayabaru train for another Rp2200. For Malang direct, the Anugerah Express costs Rp2000, but it's a night bus so you see nothing. Kembang Express, Jl. Diponegoro 43, goes to Surabaya for Rp1750. Balimas, Jl. Hasanudin 27 (Tel. 2590), has the same price to Surabaya (7 am to 7 pm) and also has buses straight through to Jakarta for Rp5500.

hitch: First to Gilamanuk, then take the ferry to the other side. Ask the vehicles on the boat for a ride onward through Java. **motorbike:** Can travel north to Singaraja via Mengwi in a day but that's rushing it. This road through Bedugal is in better condition and faster than the one through Penelokan. Bring warm clothes because in the highlands the temperature drops by as much as 10 degrees. **hiking:** North of Celuk take the path that runs parallel to the river all the way to Ubud, 10 km. In this strip of land between the Oos and Petanu

Rivers there are numerous antiquities: broken basreliefs, rock monasteries, Hindu statues scattered over fields; some dating from the early Balinese period which began in the 11th Century.

by air: Airport tax is Rp800. Often during the months Dec., Jan., and Feb. all flights out of Denpasar are booked solid. Merpati, Jl. Veteran, has flights to: Bima (Sumbawa), Rp17,500; Yogya (Java), Rp11,300; Kupang (Timor), Rp27,300; Waingapu (Sumba), Rp15,600; Ende (Flores), Rp17,600. If you're under 26 and have a student card get a 25% discount on these flights. For example, to Ujung Pandang (South Celebes), instead of paying Rp16,000 pay only Rp12,000. They have to give it to you because the discount is on their price-list. Merpati has now monopolized the lucrative Aus$228 route from Bali to Darwin, Australia, but they offer a much better value albeit irregular charter from Denpasar to Manila, Philippines, for US$150.00. Zamrud Airlines, which flies mostly within Nusa Tenggara, is based in Denpasar on Jl. Dr. Wahidin 1, at the very start of Jl. Gadjah Mada. Zamrud flights to: Ampenan, 3 times week, Rp4200; Bima, twice weekly, Rp16,000; Sumbawa, 3 times a week, Rp10,500; Ruteng (Flores), once a week on Thurs., Rp26,200; Maumere (Flores), every Mon., Rp25,250; Sumba (Waingapu) every Sat. and back again on Sun., Rp16,250; Kupang, every Sat., Rp25,100; Surabaya (if enough passengers), Rp11,000. For chartered flights you must book one week before; per hour cost is US$350, including catering and meals.

by boat to the Southeast Islands: Freighters which ply between Bali and Timor call at Benoa Harbor fairly regularly. Pelni has a boat to Kupang, Timor about once every 3 weeks, takes 4-10 days depending on how many islands the boat calls at along the way; costs Rp13,000 including meals. Nusa Tenggara Lines also does inter-island trips. Try hustling around Benoa Harbor for a lift on a boat or a yacht; there could be a lot of competition from other travelers. For Lombok, from where you island-hop east, board the ferry at Padangbai on the east coast of Bali; leaving each morning circa 11 am. For Sumbawa direct, the Shipping Office Darma Karya in Stasiun Suci sells tickets on the ship Kuda Putih. Sails every Sat. at 10 am and returns to Denpasar on Sun. afternoon. Takes 20 hours to Badas Harbor close to Sumbawa Besar on the western end of Sumbawa, and costs Rp4000.

for Komodo Island: Darma Karya Shipping Office in Stasiun Suci sells tours to Komodo Island on the Garuda I from Padangbai to Komodo and return; charter 7 days (maximum 20 passengers) for Rp1 million (about Rp50,000 per person). Plus you must pay for food: 7 days, Rp15,000; or 10 days about Rp20,000. The company graciously pays for the goat. Much less expensive is to fly to Bima, then negotiate for a motorboat. It's more expedient to get your permit to visit Komodo Island in Singaraja rather than wait until you get to Labuhanbajo. Get this written permission from Departemen Pertainian Dirjen Kehutanan Seksi Perlindugan Dan Pengawetan Alam Bali, Jl. Gadjah Mada 2, Singaraja. Takes a couple of days. After you get your papers from Singaraja, take them to PKN DAK XV/NUSRA (close to the stadium) for a stamp and the commander's signature. On Kuta Beach travel agents who sell tickets to Komodo, using local transport, have sprung up. The price ranges from US$125-150 depending upon how much you fly.

NORTH BALI

The Dutch occupied North Bali and ended the feudal rule of the local *rajas* a full 60 years prior to their colonization of the south. Thus North Bali is more European, the class system isn't as strictly adhered to, and the social order centers more around the individual family than in the more communalized agricultural *banjars* of the south. Women here wore the Malay blouse first ('to protect the morals of the Dutch soldiers'). **temple art:** South Bali has small shrines and *meru* towers with classical lines, but the soft pink sandstone quarried near Singaraja in the north allows sculptors more exuberance. Tall gates have a dynamic flowing style covered with spiky, flame-like shapes. Steep flights of narrow steps lead up to airy thrones and shrines. On basreliefs see plump Dutchmen cramped into a motorcar, people copulating in the bushes, and a man riding a bicycle composed of leaves and flowers.

PENELOKAN

The name means 'place to look'. From Kuta Beach it's Rp350 by 3 *bemos*. Take a *bemo* first to Denpasar, then on to Bangli or Gianyar, then up to Penelokan. At 1450 m altitude this village perches under the sacred, smoking Gunung Batur volcano. One can see Gunung Agung and sometimes even beyond to Gunung Rinjani on Lombok from here. Penelokan used to be located at the base of the volcano which erupted in 1917, 1926, and again in 1963. The villagers finally decided it would be advisable to move to the higher cliffs overlooking the lake. Penelokan has a high fresh climate, the *losmens* are cheap, there are some good walks across the mountains, and the views of Lake Batur are unequalled. Sometimes the colors of the crater lake below change from glassy blue to platinum, a perfect mirror of the sky and mountains. At night see the moon sail over the volcano. The Japanese are the big spenders here, arriving by the busloads. If you want to see what the tourists are doing to Bali, this is also the place to look. Life is very poor in these mountain villages and probably the most aggressive, money-hungry people in all of Indonesia live around Penelokan. At least down in Kuta you can laugh and joke a little, but not here. Being very isolated and thus inbred, they are likewise not very pretty to look at. In fact, they scare the shit out of you. Dishonest people with a real streak of meanness. Lock up your motorcycle inside the hotel at night. If you leave your bike down in Kedisan, it costs Rp50 'to keep it' for you. They could steal the key and try to 'sell it' back to you for Rp2000. If you stop your bike on the road they crowd around and turn your key off and hassel you. If you get into a price-disagreement with them, your tank could get filled with sand. If you get stuck in the cold rain in Kedisan, they'll ask Rp1500 to take you up the hill to Penelokan (but just walk, it takes about an hour). Must be what living under a live mountain does to you.

stay: Lakeview Homestay is Rp300-400 single, Rp600-800 double; there's also a deluxe row of rooms for Rp1500. No electricity. They've got a drink and food menu, but the food isn't fit for pigs. A *warung* that serves dishes at one half the price of Lakeview is just around the corner about 5 doors down; excellent *nasi campurs* morning and night. Their *cap cai* is highly recommended, Rp150. Fresh lake fish often and when the proprietress gets to know you she'll give you extras. Losmen Gunawan, for better food, sleep and a more hassel free location, is Rp300-500 single, Rp600 double. Bargain for possibly Rp800 for 3 to a room. The smaller rooms are warmer. A homey place with electricity in each room, and good lighting in the eating room for writing aerograms or for reading. Here you'll learn that the most pleasant activity in Penelokan is just to sit and look at the mountain and the lake. Meals at the Kintamini Restaurant, 2 km up the road, are delicious but costly; cheapest thing on the menu is chips, Rp400. Their many waiters have got to be paid.

vicinity of Penelokan: Hike to the rainforest on top of Gunung Abang in about 5 hours. Eat raspberries along the way to quench hunger and thirst. Rendang is 14 km to the south. Go first by motorbike to Kedisan, then travel over a fascinating dirt road running high above the lake across the foothills of G. Agung through far out villages. Not many tourists on this very bad road, the Balinese are surprised to see you. A little before Rendang is the turnoff to Besakih. Besakih is about a 7 hour walk from Kedisan. Southwest of and downhill from Penelokan is Taro near Jati on the road to Peliatan. In these mountaineer Bali Aga villages, the *bale agung* (or council-house) is the heart of the political and religious life of the community. In Taro, the longest council house on Bali is located. In the highlands between mountains Batu and Catur, and also between Gunung Agung and Gunung Batukau, are more Bali Aga villages; Selulang, Batukaang and Catur, with remains of pre-Hindu primitive monuments, stone statues, and small megalithic pyramids.

GUNUNG BATUR

When this volcano is erupting, it glows red at night and bellows, throwing out rocks and showers of volcanic debris. This happens fairly regularly. Drop everything and get up here to see it. **getting there:** This mountain area can be reached by highway out of Denpasar, or by back road from Ubud through Pujung. Or, even wilder, from Ubud via Payangan with a 100 cc or more motorcycle (carries two) through the deep interior of Bali: variegated scenery, bamboo forests, remote hilly pre-Hindu walled villages. From Ubud via Payangan, it's about a 12 hour walk. The higher you ascend the more it changes. The natives of the G. Batur region look different from those of the coasts; darker, shorter, more wiry bodies, pinched faces, direct gazes.

stay: On the western shore of Lake Batur is a *losmen* and hotsprings; a very lovely setting. Swim Finnish-style from the warm-water pool straight into the icy cold lake. The hotsprings just bubbles up under the lake to the surface and is not really that hot. This hotsprings *losmen* might not be open, the guy only comes there about once a day. Sutan Takdir Alisjahbana, a pre-1945 Sumatran poet, has started a dance academy just above the *air panas*

where new dances are being created and old ones preserved. Rich people pay for this dance school by renting out the cottages. Take the path from the *losmen* to the north crossing over black lava rocks; newer lava flows are along the way.

climbing it: You don't really need a guide if you don't mind losing your way a couple of times. If you do get lost, don't expect anyone to show you the way without exacting payment. Pay no more than Rp500 for the guide to the top. You need a young boy because it's an arduous ascent. Start out real early before it gets hot, and when the locals are still sleepy; not as many hassles. Approach the summit of G. Batur from the hotsprings. From Kedisan to the hotsprings it's a 1½ hour walk over rough ground, black-grey sand, big rocks, long gullies. Then from the hotsprings it's a 3½-4 hour climb to the top. Or take the boat trip from Kedisan to the hotsprings, walk up the volcano, get back down to the hotsprings again, then back to Kedisan — all in one day.

LAKE BATUR

the lake trip: Be warned that the waiters and con artists at Lakeview Homestay speak with forked tongues, so it's better to buy your boat tickets in Kedisan rather than at Lakeview Homestay or on the roadway. From Penelokan down to Kedisan on the crater floor where the boats leave, take a horse

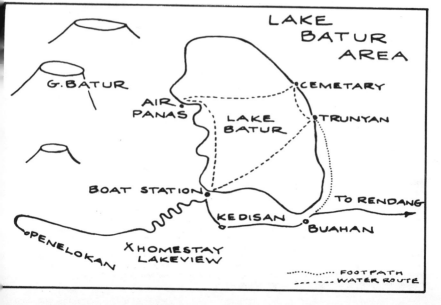

or donkey (Rp1000), get a lift on a motorcycle (Rp500), or walk it in 45 minutes. Five people can hire a motorboat (Rp3000) for the 2½-3 tour of Trunyan, the cemetary, *air panas* (hotsprings) and back to Kedisan. If you get an offer to take you around the lake for under Rp2000, it's probably a canoe even through they say it's a motorboat. The cheaper (Rp1500-2000) 5 hour canoe trip is sceptical. After bargaining intensely for an extra low price, they could drop you off at Trunyan, then suddenly they jack the price up. If you don't go along with the new and revised price, they *leave* you. The canoe could embark Kedisan at 3 pm and return around 8 pm, freezing your ass off. No matter what kind of boat you take or no matter when you leave, take jeans and a jumper. **alternative route:** You don't have to hassel for a boat across to Trunyan, you can also walk it. Take a *bemo* from Penelokan to Buahan, Rp100. From Buahan, it's a 2 hour hike along the lakeshore path to Trunyan. After your visit in Trunyan, negotiate for a ride back to Kedisan. They ask Rp1500 and *you* also paddle; sometimes they put up the price once you've embarked. Or just walk back.

Trunyan: If the truth be known, it ain't much. You're not really welcome in this village, you're an intruder. Don't stay overnight if you can help it, it's cold and scary. You don't see the ancient ways of the Bali Aga tradition, and there are a lot of money hustlers. The Bali Aga are the oldest inhabitants of Bali, aboriginals who lived here from before the Majapahit invasion (1343 A.D.). At Trunyan, you just get out of the boat, go up to a temple which you're not allowed to enter, sign the visitors' book, pay Rp100, then you're marched right back down to the boat again and taken next to the cemetary. The cemetary is full of skulls and bones and bush, but hasn't had a body in it for 7 years. Don't believe them when they say there's a freshly rotting body there. This is the tourist cemetary anyways, the real Bali Aga cemetary is in another, hidden place. It's not worth it, only the setting is spectacular. Hidden away in Trunyan is Bali's largest statue, Ratu Gede Pancering Jaget, but you'll be lucky to see it. **from Trunyan:** There are 4 other villages on the shore of Lake Batur; equally as unfriendly as Trunyan and harder to reach. Walk over the mountains to the north coast in 6-8 hours with a guide, Rp1200-1500. Visit sequestered monasteries and mountain Balinese villages of Abuan, Abang and Sonyang with their brick houses and flower gardens. Big temple at Abang.

volcanoes in Indonesia: *With dense island populations, volcanoes could be very disastrous. Indonesia has a greater number of volcanoes than any other country in the world. Out of its total number, 71 still show activity. There are 3-4 earthquakes a year (4 on the Richter scale) of which one or two are destructive. Every year an average of 10 major volcanic eruptions occur and every 3 years an eruption with loss of life and property. The chances of seeing a volcano blowing its top is remote. There's black acrid smoke, sulphur fumes, enormous clouds of steam, boulders weighing hundreds of tons being tossed into the air like matchsticks, and in the middle a gushing, spitting river of orange-red lava. All of this, plus the accompaniment of distant thunder that shakes the ground beneath your feet, is known as the hot-lava stage. This is often followed by a cold-lava flow, an avalanche of boulders. These boulders, formed when the lava cools, encircle the mountain's cone in a series of precariously balanced heaps. Only a minor storm could send them toppling, sometimes into rivers. These lava cooled boulders are broken and ground down, then used for building materials and road surfacing. Were it not for active volcanoes the fertility of the soil over great tracts of Indonesia would be nothing like it is today.*

KINTAMANI

A windblown little town on the top of a ridge, Rp125 by *bemo* from Bangli. There's a big market along the highway every 3 days when mountain people come in from all the surrounding villages. In this damp climate, a variety of vegetables and fruits (score passionfruit) not found elsewhere on the island are grown. In Kintamani *Sangyang* Trance Dances, seldom seen in other parts of Bali, are practiced but often barred to tourists. Kintamani has more angry dogs per square meter than any other place on Bali. But many people prefer to stay in Kintamani instead of in Penelokaɲ. There are fewer annoyances from the locals, you're treated more like a human being. Get up early to watch a superb sunrise.

stay: Most *losmens* are on the main street. They offer cubicle-like, cold, damp-smelling rooms, though this is somewhat compensated for by a crackling log fire at night. Hotel Ex-losmen Miranda is Rp500 single, Rp1000 double. For the bigger and nicer rooms in the front they'll ask Rp1500, but just counter-bargain down to Rp1000 for two. Price includes a good breakfast of eggs, toast and tea; also a good menu for dinner. Most people eat at Losmen Lingga Giri next door, Rp400 single, Rp600 double. Small rooms but OK. Homestay Kintamani, in the middle of town, has 5 clean and well-kept rooms at Rp500 single or Rp800 double. At the bottom of the town is Hotel Batur Sari, cheapest at Rp300, Rp600 double, but rather cramped quarters. Wisma Ardi, at the top of the town, is a *losmen* with a difference. Turn down the road just before the radio tower and walk 1 km. It almost hangs over the volcano. Pelni Shipping Lines runs it. For single Rp750, two persons Rp1500, and there's one room for 3 for Rp1500. Only coffee and tea are served. Has electricity. The rooms aren't really friendly, but the location and the sitting room (like a hunting lodge!) make it worth it and you have the run of the place. Eat in the *warungs* up the sandy lane or do your own cooking. Lots of good walks in the area. For G. Batur, start climb at 6 am, return at 12 pm.

Penulisan: 8 km north of Kintamani at a bend in the road. Take a gigantic broken stairway up a hill to lonely Pura Sukawana temple on the top, surrounded by mountains. This is the highest temple on Bali and one of the five holiest. Not visited by a European until 1881. Most sculptures date from the 11th Century. On a clear day you can see half the island all the way to the Java Sea.

BEDUGAL

A small village in the central highlands east of Gunung Batur, as near to paradise as you can get. Good road to get there. At 2500 m above sea level, Bedugal is even higher than Kintamani. Lake Bratan fills the crater of G. Bratan. Children fish for minnows, and canoes cross the lake carrying firewood to villages on the far side. Take lakeside walks through pine forests with shrines along the shore. Chilly swimming. On a small promotory above the lake is peaceful Uludanu temple. Just below Bedugal is the market of Bukit Mungsu; sells live and stuffed birds (parrots and cuckoos), wild orchids, vegetables, pomegranates, corn-on-the-cob. Many species of orchids are seen in the area of Lila Graha.

stay: Government Resthourse Wisma Lila Graha sits on a hill with a magnificent view of the lake. Wisma Bali is right on the road. Hotel Bedugal, on the shore of the lake, is Rp800 double. Three km south of Bedugal is Peng. Hadiraharjo Bar and Restaurant, out by its lonesome in a bushy area. **from Bedgul:** 2 km north is the Muslim village of Candikuning. Walk from here all the way to Munduk via the two other tranquil lakes inside these mountains: Buyan and Tamblingan. You can cover the 27 km in approximately 6-8 hours. At Gitgit, 10 km north of Bedugal, is a beautiful view over the coast and the Madura Strait. Also a waterfall in this area. It's possible to walk to the 3 lakes, Bratan, Tamblingan and Buyan, from here. Another retreat is Baturiti 4 km south of Bedugal. At the 'Denpasar 40 km' sign at Baturiti, a dirt back road will take you to just before Mengwi. But it's so full of boulders that it'll shake the guts out of you. Not any fun.

SINGARAJA

On the north coast. Take buses to Singaraja out of Kintamani until 1 pm, Rp200. Or from Stasiun Suci in Denpasar, catch a Colt to Singaraja for Rp400. Go through a mountain pass, descend from a point 1200 m above sea level, and there it is. Holland fought powerful *rajas* at a great battle in the village of Jagaraga and finally took control of this northern Buleleng region in 1849. Singaraja was the Dutch capital for all of Nusa Tenggara during colonial times. Today it's a main cattle export center and a coffee-growing district; Indian corn and oranges are also grown in this area. Many ethnic groups live in Singaraja, a blending of Islamic, European, Indonesian, and Chinese customs and cultures. There's still much 18th Century colonial architecture around. A city of tree-lined avenues, a wide market street, a square with rows of Chinese shops, and horse drawn *dokar* everywhere; prettier, quieter and cleaner than Denpasar. Delicate orchids are sold in the market, also the island's best, richest, stinkiest *durian*. It's amazing the way the prices go down the further you move north. A package of Commodore cigarettes in Kuta Beach costs Rp200, in Ubud, Rp125, and in Singaraja only Rp100. The climate here is drier than the south.

stay: More pleasant is to stay out at Lovina Beach. In Singaraja the best for the money is Hotel Singaraja, Jl. Veteram 1, Rp2000 for two for gigantic rooms, very clean. A breezy location as it's a little elevated above the city. The cheapest is Hotel Seranta, 100 m down Jl. Mangoa, a small street off Jl. Diponegoro. A good Christian-run hotel is Hotel Mertayadnya, Jl. Ahmad Yani 2, Rp400 single, Rp600 double; quite central (*too* central). Hotel Sentral, Jl. Jen A. Yani 48, is Rp400 or Rp800 double; a noisy billard hall and hotel combination. Hotel Ratna, Jl. Iman Bonjol 33, Rp450 single, Rp800 double. Fairly clean, near to the harbor. Out of town a bit is Hotel Sakabindu, Jl. A. Yani 26, Rp400 or Rp600 double. Family atmosphere and comfortable. **eat:** Nearly opposite Hotel Mertayadnya is Rumah Makan Kartika serving Balinese-style *nasi campur,* Rp200. Also try Rumah Makan Mertasari or Taman Lila. In the market, sweet mung-bean soup is sold in the mornings.

sights: View *lontar* books, miniature pictures and texts incised on palm leaves and framed by ornamental wooden panels, at Gedong Kirtya (open 8 am to noon) down the street from Hotel Singaraja. The *lontar* in this historial library records the literature, mythology and history of North Bali. There are also examples of *prasastis,* metal plates inscribed in the Balinese language, among the earliest written documents found on the island. In the warehouses around the harbor see women sorting out trays of coffee beans by hand and coffee being loaded on freighters for export to Europe and the east. There are beautiful sunsets over this harbor with its fishing boats and faraway to the west, the mountains of East Java.

crafts: Try Puri Agung on Jl. Veteran for distinctive handwoven *sarungs* or *kains.* In this *kampung* there's a loom in practically every house. Starting prices for different pieces are Rp1000, Rp1500 and Rp2000; they come down only Rp1-200. Also try Bali Bhusana Sari, Jl. Veteran 20, right up the street from Hotel Singaraja; enter next to Gedong Kirtya. Have a look in the factory to see the *kain tenun,* a typical Balinese weave, being produced; starting price, Rp1650.

from   Singaraja   by   bemos   and buses: From Stasiun Banyusari, a little outside (east) of Singaraja, catch buses, Colts and *oplets* to the eastern part of the island. Bus fares to: Gilamanuk, Rp350; Seririt, Rp75. For Surabaya, buy tickets at Toko Tridadi, Rp1500. If you ask them beforehand they'll pick you up at Lovina Beach on the way. From Stasiun Gitgit near the main intersection Simpang Empat Prapatan catch *bemos* to: Gitgit, Rp75; Panca Sari, Rp125. From Stasiun Kampungtinggi, Rp50 by *dokar* from Simpang Empat Prapatan, catch a Colt to Kintamani, Rp300 (or bus, Rp250); Tianyar, Rp250; Lemukih, Rp200; Denpasar, Rp350 (Colt, Rp400). Also catch *oplets* at Stasiun Kampungtinggi for points east. For the east coast trip to Amlapura (old name: Karangasem), a bus leaves once daily at 4 am, arriving in Amlapura at 11 or 12 pm, for Rp600. If you take it just as far as Tejakula, it costs Rp150. For Denpasar, catch a Colt early in the morning on Jl. Diponegoro, Rp400.

from Singaraja by ship: Chinese companies operate cattle boats to and from Hong Kong, their schedules depending upon if Hong Kong wants cattle or not. Costs about US$100 for your own cabin plus 3 meals a day. A ship sails from Singaraja for Nusa Tenggara perhaps twice a month. Most of these ships come from Surabaya and do mail stops here, but on their way back from Nusa Tenggara the ship usually doesn't stop in Singaraja. They take 8-10 days to do the round-trip from Surabaya to their destination in Nusa Tenggara. Contact Shipping Office Nusa Tenggara, they know one week in advance when a ship is due. Some sample fares: Ampenan, Rp5400; Sumbawa Besar, Rp6670; Bima, Rp8000; Waingapu, Rp9430; Ende, Rp10,650; Kupang, Rp13,000; Kalabahi, Rp14,100; Reo, Rp10,350; Maumere, Rp12,750; Larantuka, Rp13,200. Coffee boats to Surabaya, Rp5000.

vicinity of Singaraja: On the way to Amlapura see the famous horse bath at Tejakula, 35 km east; even more elaborate than the baths for people. There's a nice view of the seacoast further on at Culik. **Sawan:** In this small village S.E. of Singaraja is the small temple of Jagaraga. Basreliefs show two corpulant Europeans in a model-T Ford held up by an armed bandit, aircraft falling from the sky into the sea, Dutch steamers being attacked by sea monsters. Also incredible flamboyant statues of *Rangda* the witch, and of a dazed mother burried under a pile of children. The temple is surrounded by big trees. Gongs are made at Sawan village where there's also a bamboo *angklung* orchestra. **Sangsit:** 7 km east of Singaraja. See Pura Beji dedicated to the goddess of agriculture, Dewi Sri. A perfect example of the northern baroque-style

dalang (wayang *puppeteer):* A man of extraordinary physical endurance, he must stand the strain of working many characters (up to 6 rods with his 10 fingers) in a cross-legged position under a burning lamp from sundown to sunrise. He is highly skilled in ventriloquism, dramatization, storytelling, stage direction, and production. His voice can create any mood in the audience — contentment or chaos, tragedy or danger, grief, mystery, magic, or inner voices. The leading performer, he must know by heart all the ancient legends and have a deep understanding of the Javanese mystique and attitudes, interjecting his own comments as the tale unfolds. He has wit and repartee, often using crude village humor which contrasts hilariously against the snobby airs of kings. He has spiritual and metaphysical knowledge, magical powers, and many practice the art of semadi. The dalang is responsible for buying and maintaining his huge cast of puppets, must organize the erection of the special covered stage for each village performance, and hire the gamelan for orchestral accompaniment. During the performance itself, traditional ways are used to cue his musicians. These signals (sasmita) are expressed by the dalang either musically, visually or verbally — puppets hit their chests, raise their arms in the air, or utter verbal cues. Even requests for drinks, cigarettes, or betelnut are made indirectly through the mouths of the wayang puppets.

temple carving, see stone vegetation growing in and out of the carvings. Strange off angle symmetry. There's a spellbinding gateway of *naga*-snakes and imaginary beasts, devils, demon guardians, also wooden statues, wierd guardians, and a throne of the sun god. **Kubutambahan:** Visit the unusual Pura Medruwe Karang, The Temple of the Owner of the Land, worshipped to ensure success of crops grown on unirrigated land. Carvings show ghouls, home scenes, lovers, noblemen, an official riding a bicycle with flowered spokes, a riot of leaves, tendrils, all on top of an almost *stupa*-like structure.

Yeh Sanih (local name is Air Sanih): Deserted beaches and sea temples are found all along the northern coast of Bali. Catch an *oplet* from Stasiun Kampungtinggi, Rp100, and travel down a road sentinelled with trees east of Singaraja to this shady spot with its big globular-shaped, enclosed natural swimming pool of clear fresh water fed from underground springs, Rp50 to enter. Sometimes this retreat is stampeded by 150 screeching schoolchildren and at other times it's virtually empty for 3 days in a row. Next to the pool is the rather expensive Restoran Puri Sanih, *nasi goreng*, Rp300. In the *warungs* across the street the meals are cheaper; *nasi campur* and *mie goreng*, Rp200. **stay:** Hotel Ginza Beach Inn has nice cottages with electricity and giant private baths under trees facing the ocean and overlooking lily ponds. Quite a good deal for Rp1000 per 'house'. No disturbances, just the birds. Meals and drinks are available in the bar, where males might meet young Javanese women to converse with on various levels. From Yeh Sanih, a rough road south along the eastern coast leads to Amlapura.

LOVINA BEACH

11 km west of Singaraja on the road to Seririt. Catch a *bemo*, Rp50, anywhere on Jl. A. Yani on the road west out of Singaraja. For pure relaxation, this is the place. Most people who arrive here are refugees from Kuta Beach who wanted to get away from the rip-offs. They pick a place as far away and as completely opposite Kuta as they could find — no sellers, no flash menus, no motorbikes, no music, few dogs (a Muslim village), no 'scene' — and quite cheap. You can actually live on about US$1.50 a day here easy, a tourist economy hasn't set in yet. But it's growing. Already there are 4 *losmens*. There's nice swimming inside at bay of Lovina Beach, quite safe and tame compared to the volatile southern coast; the water just laps lazily at the shore. At night fishermen take their lanterns on their boats and fish out all along the ocean to the front.

stay: Manggala Homestay is the first accommodation you come to on the road from Singaraja. Rp500 double, Rp300 single. Rainbows lie quietly across the ricefields through the window. A nice family with children and crowing roosters. Not much privacy, but a cheery atmosphere. The food, which you eat in a cafe-like setting, is excellent (as a rule). Though a bit damaged by the July '76 earthquake, Tasik Madu ('Sea of Honey') next doors is more like a proper hotel, a bigger place with more room to roam around and to be by yourself. You don't have to go to the beach for the sunset, just walk out on the verandah. There are rooms with your own balcony facing the ocean for Rp400 and other more expensive double units with a sitting porch, virtually a small house, for 1500 or Rp800 single. People from Tasik Madu go over to Manggala's to eat (better food) and people from Manggala's go over to Tasik Madu to mix. In the middle of Lovina village is Lituhayu Homestay, Rp300 single, Rp500 double; black rice pudding, Rp50, yellow rice, Rp100, are served. In Kalibukuk village, 1½ km from Lovina towards Singaraja, is the Ayodya Inn. **eat:** Here coconuts cost Rp25 each (down on Kuta, Rp200). Each day at 7 am a sweet mung-bean cart comes by on the street outside, Rp25 per bowl. Later in the morning a *sate* and *rawon* cart trundles by; eat your belly full of tangy soup and spiced meat for Rp100. Ibu Alimah's *warung* (the future 'Mama's') is just down the street near the bridge exactly opposite the mosque. *Ibu* serves tasty *nasi campurs,* Rp100, and *pisang goreng,* Rp5; the smiles and the playfulness are free.

from Lovina Beach: Walk to Singaraja along the beach, crossing about 6 small rivers, in a couple of hours. For the waterfalls, take a *bemo* down to Pamokas, 3 km from Lovina towards Seririt. Or walk it in 45 minutes. The waterfalls are a 1 km walk from Pamokas. Good eating stalls along the way, whole meals of crispy boiled vegetables and *gado2* dressing for Rp15! Boys will show you the way to Sing Sing Waterfall, where you can swim naked (with the boys looking on) while cool fresh water cascades over you. There's another bigger, better and more isolated waterfall up a path to the left (east).

Buddhist Monastery (Brahma Vihara): Go first to Banjar village, 15 km west of Singaraja. From the highway where the *bemo* lets you off, walk 2 km and then turn in at the road going uphill just before Banjar's market. Climb another 2 km to this gleaming storybook monastery high on a hill. A breathing technique (pranayama) and a 'slow walking technique' are practiced here, the aim being to produce clear comprehension and mindfulness. Resident *bhikkus* (Buddhist teachers) guide you on your way to equanimity. Talk to Bhikku Giriraakkhito. The course is 14 days but stay as long as you want; count on about Rp2-3000 for two weeks. Quite comfortable with plenty of *mandi* water and good vegetarian food. Unsurpassed views on all sides. At night in these highlands of Bali, stars reflect in the rice paddies, and in between, fireflies fill the air. From Banjar's market, there's a hotsprings one hour's walk away.

raksasa and meditator

NUSA TENGGARA
(THE SOUTHEAST ISLANDS)

INTRODUCTION

These southeast islands, sometimes called the Lesser Sundas, include 5 main islands: Lombok, Sumba, Sumbawa, Flores, and Timor, plus many smaller islands such as Roti, Sawu, Alor, Lembata, etc.—all together comprising less than 4% of Indonesia's total land area.

the land: One volcanic belt runs all the way down from Sumatra, through Java and Bali, continuing on through Sumbawa and Flores, ending up on the island of Banda in the Banda Sea. Another belt, made up of the islands Sumba and Timor, contains no active volcanoes. Forest areas are much less widespread and tangled in eastern Indonesia, most of the land being covered in eucalyptus, savannah-type plants, grassland, scrub, and monsoon forests. In interior parts of Sumba and Timor the old *ladang* system of growing taro and yams still exists. **flora and fauna:** Large Asian mammals such as tigers, rhinos and elephants cut off suddenly at the Wallace Line between Bali and Lombok, although many Asian birds, insects, and reptiles are found still further eastwards to the Weber Line (east of Halmahera in Maluku) when even these types stop for good.

climate: These islands are characterized by prolonged dry seasons with semi-arid even desert-type climates interrupted by rainy spells. Dry months are Aug. and Sept. (the driest island is Timor) and wet months are Nov.-June. The Timor archipelago is the only region of Indonesia that gets tropical cyclones, at the rate of 3-5 a year.

economy: There's no modern industry. Most goods are imported from Java and paid for by the export of cattle and horses. Besides some sulphur, there are few minerals. Oil is found in East Timor. Tourism is scant and roads are few. Economic development won't affect these islands and Nusa Tenggara will be the way it is now for many years to come.

people: Estimated population is 7 million. There are considerable linguistic and cultural differences. Racial types are very complex, especially on Flores and Timor where not only Malays and mixed-blood Portugese are found but also descendants of even earlier arrivals of Veddoid, Negrito, archaic Melanesians, and Australoids. All of these people still show rudiments of ancient cultures with widespread beliefs in spirits, ancestor cults and the use of magic. The staple food is corn and sago; little rice is grown due to the dry weather and generally poor soil.

religion: Most are Christian. Muslims are in the minority, found mostly in the urban centers such as Kupang and Sumbawa Besar. Having been settled by the Macassans of South Celebes, Sumbawa is the most Islamicized of the islands. On many of the more remote islands gods representing the sun and the moon are worshipped, some groups believing that they are constantly copulating to make the world go round.

crafts: Only weaving and plaiting crafts are practiced, and these are strictly cottage industries. *Ikat*-woven textiles are their most important branch of art. Cotton is being introduced, so these crafts will eventually die.

travel: Visa renewals are obtainable only in Denpasar (Bali), Mataram (Lombok), and in Kupang (Timor). The people of Nusa Tenggara are very conscious about you registering with the police. Especially now. Obviously the Indonesians don't feel secure in eastern Indonesia. Soldiers are everywhere and any private vessels sighted east of Kupang could be sunk by the Indonesian Navy as suspected gun-runners. Be careful of what you wear in East Lombok, Sumbawa, and on Flores; travelers represent a cultural threat and could get stoned if dressed 'indecently'. There are no herbal intoxicants, so stock up. In the dry season, carry water. Other times, carry an umbrella.

TIMOR

EAST TIMOR

Called Tim Tim (Timor Timor), the new designation. Contrary to Jakarta's claims, the war in east Timor isn't over. Resistance and terrorism are still waged against Indonesia's clumsy annexation of this former Portugese territory and rumor has it that Jakarta's hospitals are filled with Indonesian wounded, whom close relatives are not allowed to visit. Indonesia has claimed that it sent in 'volunteer' troops in late 1975 at the request of an anti-Fretilin coalition which later set up a 'Provisional Government of East Timor'. This government consequently opted for integration with Indonesia. A spokesman for the east Timor independence movement in mid-September 1976 stated in the United Nations that 75-85% of the territory is still ruled by the left-leaning 'Revolutionary Government of the Democratic Republic of East Timor' established by Fretilin in Nov. 1975 shortly before the entry of Indonesian regular army troops. It was alleged by the spokesman that the war in East Timor has cost Indonesia 10,000 casualties and more than US$100 million so far. Although there are now flights twice weekly between Kupang (West Timor) and Dili (East Timor), tourists may not enter the territory without military clearance.

WEST TIMOR

the land: Its land forms are very different from the rest of Indonesia. Western Timor is quite mountainous with 60% of the land consisting of rugged hills, high plateaus cut by deep valleys, and loose soiled terrain mostly covered in grass. One of the most characteristic features of the Timorese

NUSA TENGGARA
LESSER SUNDA ISLANDS

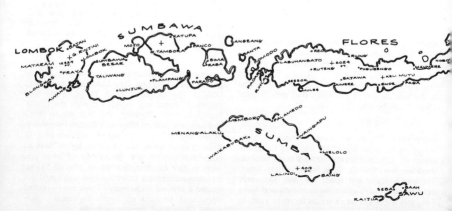

landscape is the acacia tree with its solitary flat-topped crown and wide branches. There are many man-made savannahs and higher up stands of original evergreen forests. Indonesian Timor's open rainy grasslands make natural grazing regions and its economy today is tied up in cattle raising. Cattle were first introduced by the Dutch on a large scale in the 1930's and distributed among the *rajas*. Herds run in the thousands and heads of cattle number twice the human population. 25,000 head are exported each year, mostly to Hong Kong.

climate: A transition point between humid tropical Indonesia and the more temperate climate of Australia. Very heavy rains fall from Nov.-Feb., and for the remainder of the year droughts occur. During the dry season the Timorese make salt, fell wood, collect beeswax, build houses, repair roads, tap palm juice, transport cattle, relax, feast, dance, visit, make journeys, be merry, the criminals come out, the taxman comes. Landscapes during the dry are similar to the Aussie bush, parched and brown, leaves fall, rivers and wells dry up, soil cracks, wind

blows all day long. Later in the season dust and smoke from *ladang* and grass fires fill the air. The first rains turn the dry savannahs into a vast garden, dust disappears, skies clear– this is Timor at its best (Jan.). At the beginning of the wet season people move out to the *ladangs* and live in shelters; villages are practically deserted except for old people and children. When the rains really set in, Timor is impassable. Much more rainfall occurs in the north than in the south and west. The end of the rainy season is the high season in Indonesian Timor when the maize is harvested, the *pasars* all over the island are alive with news and gossip. People travel, tourists pass through, kids go to school, new houses are inaugerated, and there are more marriages, funerals, and births. *Lontar* palm produces a strong alcoholic drink (sopi) and during this time it's drunk everywhere and plentifully.

history: Sandalwood has been Timor's 'Tree of Destiny' and traders discovered it early. The Hindu-Javanese imported the water buffalo and the horse; the Portugese brought maize and potatoes;

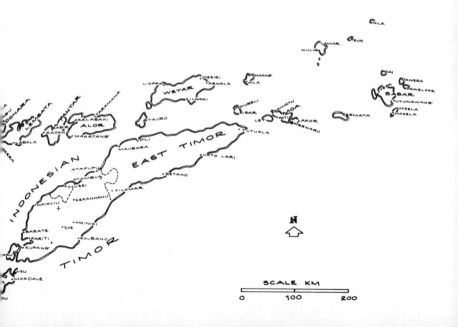

the Chinese arrived with their fruits, vegetables, and gold; and the Dutch brought coffee, cassava, livestock, firearms, dice-playing and distilled liquor. (The *rajas* of West Timor have a stunning history of alcoholism). An expedition which was sent out by the Dutch in 1821 to search for the legendary *Noil Noni* (River of Gold) failed. But in 1829, with an escort of 1200 men, they finally penetrated the interior, first opening up this territory to the outside world. Later in the 1920's it was learned that the gold that was seen had been brought into Timor by the Portuguese and Chinese sandalwood merchants hundreds of years previously for barter purposes. High quality sandalwood is still being exported.

people: Population 900,000. Most live from the sea or from subsistence level farming; life inland is very hard. Timor is racially divided into two groups, the Timorese, and an old Melanesian element, the Atoni, who were pushed by the more recent intruders (the Belunese and Rotinese) into the mountains of the interior. The Atoni are the native people of Indonesian Timor who belong to 10 traditional princedoms (swapradja) and speak several different languages. Although the Indonesian government has de-politicized them, some *rajas* are still quite powerful. The patrilineal Atoni are short with dark brown skin and frizzy hair like Papuans; also Negrito types are often met with. All ethnic groups on Timor chew *sirih* after meals and especially on ceremonial occasions. An adult chews 15 betelnut seeds a day; children start chewing it age 7 or 8. Timorese have never accepted the plow and fields are tilled by driving herds of water buffaloes over the wet *sawah* until it turns into a smooth sea of mud. Wild bees build huge honeycombs 1 m in diameter suspended from branches of the highest trees. Bees are first smoked out, then the giant nests are lowered to the ground. Honey and beeswax have been an important produce for local consumption and for export, causing violent border disputes since early times. Borders move with the bees.

crafts: Traditional arts and crafts such as weaving, plaiting, and basketry are still widely practiced inland. Atoni women decorate betelnut baskets (oko) with elaborate vivid colored patterns. The *ikat* method is found in the Amarasi area. Fabrics often have very naturalistic designs: crocodiles, lizards, gekkos, or sometimes humans mounted on horseback. Both men and women wear 2 m long and 1 m wide *tais (kain and sarung),* the patterns indicating the princedom they derive from. Colors could be solid black (Amfoan and Insana areas) or red, black, and white cloth (Soba district). Timor has one of the largest reserves of antique ivory in the world. Originally brought by the sandalwood merchants, ivory is still used as part of the dowry price. Buy a whole antique tusk for Rp12,000 or an old bracelet

for Rp800 (on Bali Rp3-3500). Aged ivory is like a fine dark polished wood, taking years to turn brown from the oil in your skin. Don't get caught taking any ivory out, the police confiscate it on the spot. Clubs with stone heads like tomohawks (gada) are still used in places. Boomerangs occur along southeastern coastal regions.

travel: There could be bureacratic hassels now while Indonesia is pilfering Portuguese Timor. A backpack is crucial for all the walking you might be forced to do. Because West Timor is so little visited it's still intact. You could see hunters on horseback with bows and arrows gallop alongside your taxi truck, or wake up from a nap with 100 people staring at you. In the wet, landslides are common and are constantly wiping out roads. The rainy season turns mountain paths slippery and roads and plains to mud; it's even difficult to travel by 4-wheel drive. In the dry season, roads and trails are strewn with stones, and riverbeds are even used for traffic. For this terrain, Timorese horses as a mount and pack animal can't be bettered. Take horses down trails of eucalyptus savannahs and through mazes of foot and bridal paths which are very narrow and sunken into the earth hiding both man and beast; it's like walking down a winding mole tunnel - all you can hear are the voices. Food is scarce in Jan.-Mar., a season known as *lapar biasa* (time of hunger), so take your own.

KUPANG

The largest urban center in Nusa Tenggara lying only 483 km from the coast of N.E. Australia. Darwin is closer than Jakarta. Population is 50,000 plus perhaps as many as 4000 soldiers armed with grenades, bayonets, rifles. In the harbor are Indonesian destroyers and troop carriers. **history:** Early in the 17th Century the Dutch established a trading post in Kupang and for more than a century there was fighting between the Dutch and the Portugese. The Dutch were almost repulsed from the island in 1749 when a 'Black Portugese' *raja* from the northern Portuguese enclave of Oecusse threatened Kupang with a band of 200 angry men, but were thrown back just in time. Irascible Captain Bligh ended his epic 6500 km journey here mighty pissed off after the mutiny on his ship 'The Bounty' in 1791. In the first half of the 19th Century, Kupang was a port of call for English and American whalers. Somerset Maugham wrote novels of Timor set here. The mood and pace of life is easy in this capital city of west Timor, it didn't get street lighting until 1971. The city has no industry, only a local ice factory and an electricity plant. Everybody wants to get to a job in the civil service, the army, the police, or on the hospital staff. **people:** Kupang has a highly mixed population, most from the surround-

INDONESIAN TIMOR

N

SEMAU
KUPANG
NAIKLIU
BARATE
PARITI
BAUN
CAMPLON
SOE
NIKINIKI
KAPANO
MUTIS MOUNTAINS
EBBAN
UOLO
NOIMUTI
FORMER PORTUGESE TERRITORY
MANAMAS
KEFANNANU
MAUBESI
MANUFUI
PUTAIN
KOLBANO
BETUN
SEON
MANUFUI
ATAPUPU
ATAMBUA
LALIAN
KADA
BESIKAMA

ROTI
ROTI

RIVER
ROAD
TRACK

ing islands: Atoni (orang asli), Rotinese. Sabunese, Chinese, Javanese, Macassans, Florenese, Kisarese, Solorese, Alorese, Ambonese, Waiwerangese, ex-Portugese Timorese, Eurasians. It is predominantly Christian with a small minority of Muslims, descendants of Arab traders.

stay: Wisma Salam in only 2 minutes walk from the taxi terminal, Rp400 a night. Tree-covered Losmen Fatu Lu is peaceful and has nice rooms; Rp400 to split a room, Rp500 per person in a double room, Rp750 for a room with a private bath and toilet. Get to it by asking for 'Losmen Winston'; a 15 minute walk from the city. Winston, the manager, speaks English but is not the man to do business with (where are Randy's gongs, Winston?). Winston also runs a travel agency which arranges flights 'while the more lazy traveler lies in bed' and has a swimming pool which you can pay to have filled. Or try Losmen Isabella. **eat:** Dine at Panta Laut. Rice is imported into Kupang from other islands and fruit and vegetables are limited. In the uplands, mandarins and oranges are so abundant that they're fed to pigs. The people of Amarasi make a cheese from buffalo milk (susuritis), precipitating the cassein with vegetable juices.

from Kupang: If you're heading east, take a truck direct to Atambua, a 200 km trip on really terrible roads; Rp1500-2000. At about the halfway point is Kefannanu where there are 2 *losmens*. The best is Losmen Beringen, Rp750 double; also serves food. The finest rugs in West Timor are sold in Kefannanu. From Kefannanu to Atambua, there may be few trucks so you might have to wait or walk (takes 2 days); a truck costs Rp500. **by boat:** A major dock city. Bear in mind that boat fares aren't fixed and you must haggle with the captain. There are many ships heading west but much fewer going east. Ask around Kupang harbor for missionary planes or for a mission boat named Stella Maris bound for Surabaya via the island of Alor. Barges travel fairly frequently from Kupang to Ende, Flores, Rp5000. Also from Kupang to Waingapu, Sumba, Rp5000, 250 km. The ship Ratu Rosari calls in Kupang every 3 weeks or so, heading back and forth from Surabaya. Or you can take the ship Permata along the northern route from Kupang to: Atapupu, Kalabahi, Larantuka, Maumere, Reo, Bima, Sumbawa Besar, Ampenan- 9 days in all, Rp15,000. For the 'southern tour', take the ship Bogar from Kupang to: Ende, Waingapu, Weido, Labuhanbajo, Bima, Sumbawa Besar, for around Rp10,000. But these go by very loose schedules,

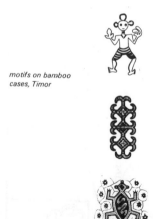

motifs on bamboo cases, Timor

Bamboo: *A whole civilization is seen through this towering 30 m high weed. Bamboo has at least 50 uses: water piping, scaffolding, sails, toothpicks, whisks, flutes, xylophones, mats, animal cages, boxes, beds, ladders, chopsticks, arrows, quivers, pens, fishing rods, water pipes, sunhats, multi-purpose baskets; for cooking, tying, thatching, messenger dispatch cases, carrying and storing liquids, decoration, bridges. Shoots are good to eat while other parts* *are used for medicines. Poison can be made out of new leaves. Bamboo has the strength of steel and the qualities of the lightest wood. The plant can be woven into light movable screens, and plaited bamboo walls of houses last 10 years if they are coated annually with a lime wash. Narrow strips are cut when green then are lashed together to form a framework which closes together rigidly when dry.*

departing once every 2-3 weeks, and are slow since the copra is all loaded by hand. If there's no copra to be picked up in a given port the ship just bypasses it. **alternative route:** A roundabout way to island-hop west is to ask agents, captains, crews, and custom officials in Kupang for a *kapal motor* to Ujung Pandang, South Celebes; Rp9-12,000, takes 2-3 days. Buginese *prahus* also trade at Naikliu, a Rotinese settlement on the northwest coast of Indonesian Timor; possibly catch a *prahu* to South Celebes from there too. **flights:** Merpati fares to: Denpasar, Rp27,500; Alor, Rp12,350; Ende (Flores), Rp14,500; Surabaya, Rp33,500; Ruteng, Rp18,000; Waingapu (Sumba), Rp21,150. Check out Zamrud fares as well, might be cheaper.

Atapupu: On a narrow bay extending deep inland, 20 km from Atambua which is on the border to east Timor. One of Timor's busiest cattle ports. Mentioned on Riberiro's world map of 1529. Sleep at the *stasiun polisi*. **from Atapupu:** A boat leaves at least once weekly for Kupang or other destinations such as Roti, Sawu, Sumbawa, Lombok, and Surabaya, etc. If you're lucky you'll find a boat all the way to Bali via Kupang. Kupang is about a 2 day busride from Atapupu. To Atambua it's Rp150 by bus. There's an Indonesian check point and a couple of good *losmens* in Atambua. Though there's no entry now into eastern Timor, Atambua is a more pleasant town to hang around in

than Atapupu. Stay at Losmen Sahabat.

others: The Mutis mountains, much wetter than coastal or plain areas, are Indonesian Timor's highest. Climb isolated Mt. Lakaan. You still see beehive huts in the Miumafo area, and in the mountain village of Lamaknen dwellings have roofs that reach right down to the ground. Around Amanuban and Amanatun is very rugged terrain with gigantic rocks rising suddenly hundreds of meters above the surrounding countryside, looking like ruins of ancient castles or like giant antheaps. Timorese mountain folk call them *fatu* and give them myths, believing that souls of the dead gather there and that the rocks are where the first marriages took place.

Soe: A typical Dutch government settlement built along the trunk highway in the 1930's. Quite different in its layout and in the makeup of its population than other Timorese towns. **South Belu Plain:** The most fertile region of Timor where a wide variety of crops grow: maize, sorghum, tobacco, rice, onions, cassava, cotton, and fruit trees such as papaya, banana, coconut. Some places produce 3 crops a year. **Nikiniki:** Natives here have remarkably strong teeth and use biting tactices when fighting, going for the neck and throat. They're able to tear off chunks from wood planking with their teeth and likewise, from human flesh.

ISLE OF ROTI

Separated from Timor by a 10 km wide strait navigable by *prahu* 2-3 hours from Kupang harbor. (Or fly with Merpati, Rp7500.) Because of monsoonal turbulance during July and Aug., this strait is called the 'Grave of the Rotinese'. Roti is a densely populated island whose overflow lives in Kupang (one third of Kupang is Rotinese). The lighter-skinned Rotinese have had longer contact with western Indonesia and are agriculturally, educationally and politically more sophisticated than the Timorese. Their myths say that the present inhabitants of Roti stem from Ceram in the Moluccas Islands to the north. The Rotinese were keen allies with the Dutch, accepting Christianity and even fought some battles for them against the rebellious natives. Covered in palm savannahs, this island is geologically and climatically much the same as Timor. **crafts:** The Rotinese musical instrument, *sesando*, is like a bamboo zither with 10-36 copper strings and a hemispheric resonator made of *nipah* palm. Decorated antique axes with cast handles and blades are products of the Bronze Age; the date of their origin in Roti is unknown.

lontar-culture: The drought resistent *lontar* palm is the tree-of-life for the Rotinese. Life is surrounded by this tree's products; furniture and household articles are made from it and there are also many different kinds of *lontar* baskets. Derived from 16th and 17th Century Portugese helmets, there are 8 different kinds of hats made from *lontar* leaves. Each hat has its own use in everyday life: hats to store tobacco in, to work in, to dance in, etc. Each costs about Rp200. This tree is their guarantee against famine. Even newly born babies are fed *lontar* sugar with water. From it the Rotinese make food and many varieties of drinks are concocted from its juice such as their famous sweet *tuak*, also *sopi, gula air, gula lempeng*, and *laru*. Some men drink an average of 10 bottles of *tuak* daily. Rotinese are skilled *lontar*-palm tappers. Twice a day, in the morning and afternoon, the tapper climbs a tree using a rope made of *lontar* leaf stalks, and on his belt are the *arit* tool to cut the spadix and a basket to collect the juice. This advanced food gatherer takes only 15-20 minutes to climb and tap a tree and he works 25-30 trees per day. But fatality awaits the inexperienced: you often hear someone's death was caused by 'a fall from a tree'.

Isle of Ndau: A lonely rocky island west of Roti. Here live the traditional silversmiths of the Timor archipelago who have had long contacts with Javanese artisans. Wandering silversmiths make anklets and bracelets which are much less elaborate and adorned than Yogyanese or Kendari work. In most cases the customer supplies the silver in the form of old coins or jewelry to be re-worked. **Sawu:** An island like the Garden of Eden 100 km N.W. of Roti. Sawu has strong historical ties with Hindu-Java and the people consider themselves of Hindu origin. Travel from Seba (Sawu's capital) back to Kupang by motorized *prahu* in 24-36 hours. Or return to Roti and fly from there to Waingapu (Sumba) with Merpati, Rp18,250.

THE SOLAR AND ALOR ARCHIPELAGOS

ISLAND OF LEMBATA
(LOMBLEM)

Every district has its own language, its own customs, its own brand of animism. The quality of the weaving arts and richness of Lembata's fabrics can only be compared with Sumba Island. There are two districts worth visiting in the northern part of the island, Iliape and Kedang, where villages are scattered under the shadow of volcanoes, dotting the coasts. The best *sarungs* are in the Iliape District but you won't find them very easily (only for ceremonial use) and they cost up to Rp20,000. In the Kedang District much porcelain can be found, even in the back villages, plus ivory (including whole tusks) which came from Sumatra originally. Very fine *ikat* is woven on this island.

getting there: From Tanjung Perak in Surabaya take the ships Ratu Rosari or the Stella Maris, one of which leaves for Lembata every 2 weeks. From Surabaya to Ende it take 4 nights and 3 days, costs Rp12,200. Make sure that you have at least a month visa because you need a month to do Lembata properly. From Ende take either the mission boat M.V. Teresia or the Ama, one of which leaves every 2 weeks for Larantuka, Rp3000. Lowolava is only Rp400 by boat from Larantuka. You can reach Larantuka from Kupang for about the same price. The Ama also calls at Kupang.

people: Most inhabitants are Melanesian-looking, some look Portugese, others are unmistakably Papuan. A quite superstitious people with spooky beliefs and practices. Some villages on Lembata still display human ancestors skulls in full public view. No one ever goes out at night. It's also a trait of the people that they're difficult to get to know after the initial meeting. The men are fond of drinking *tuak* and often ask you to stop and drink with them along the trails. If you share *tuak,* you are not an enemy. Most will call you 'father' because the only Europeans they ever meet are priests. Thirteen peoples' throats were slit on this island during the communist coup; the police were fulfilling a quota. A Catholic father had to take the confessions.

transport: The chief of police in Larantuka in west Flores will issue you a *pas jalan*. The island of Lembata is all walking or horseback. Put a pack on your back and take some gifts along. The horses from the lowlands can't take the highlands and the highland horses can't take the lowlands. Go to a priest and he'll get you a horse for a short while, or buy one for about Rp15,000. Every 10 km or so there's a good-sized mission which you should use as much as possible; they'll always feed you and give you a nice bed. If you meet one priest, he'll fix you up with an introduction to another. Mostly Dutch priests are assigned here though now they're changing over to Indonesians; when the Dutch on the island die, there will be no more. Father Schmitz (an American from Chicago) is in the south, and Father Giust's village is only 12 km from Lowolava. Father Giust has an excellent map of Lembata on his wall. You can also stay quite comfortably with the *kepala desa* in each village. Register with the police at each police post, they're keen on you doing it because they want most of all just to meet you.

Lowolava: The *losmen* here is very nice, run by a Chinese family. For room and board Rp1100, 2 meals a day; you get a whole roast fish, baked corn, and fishball soup (3 dishes of fish!) and 2 coffees a day. They feed you royally and will even make you a meal wrapped in banana leaf to travel. There are *warungs* around but food at the *losmen* is unbeatable. **from Lowolava:** To Balauring it's 5 hours by boat, Rp500. Or walk it in 3 days, 80 km, through a fabulous looking country of rolling tall grassy fields, big green hills, marshy, swampy damp lowlands with volcanoes constantly dominating the landscape.

Balauring: See Pak Giap. He might put you up or arrange for you to stay with someone else. Leaving Balauring, walk out to a back trail up through corn-fields and high above the cliffs, then drop down to the villages on the shore again. East Lembata is very rocky and quite beautiful. From Balauring continue on to Alor by *prahu;* a motorboat for Alor also comes in once in awhile. **Hadakewa:** If you're walking, ask along the way where Father Van de Leur lives. He might even be by to pick you up before you reach Hadakewa. Fascinating man. He can tell you a good bit about the people and the animism in the mountains. Hear his tape of the ritualistic night chanting. From Van de Leur's place, cross the mountains all the way to the whaling village in South Lembata, Lamalerap.

Lamalerap: A whale-hunting village of only 3000 on the southern coast. Though it is a Catholic village, there are other temples around for worship of spirits. Lamalerap is made up of settlers from the Kai Islands, Melaka, Ceram, Flores; each clan has its own boat and boathouse. Few other villages on Lembata are so dependent on fishing and so poor agriculturally. Their boats (pledang) are painted, named, and decorated on the bow and sides with slogans in *Bahasa Indonesia* or in Latin. Built completely without nails (only wooden pegs and rattan are used), the planks are cut with the necessary curve instead of being artifically bent. To keep the flow of life force, wooden ends which correspond to the original trunk of the tree always lie towards the front of the boat. There's a feast when all the largest planks of a new boat have been fitted, and pigs' blood is smeared on the tools. Some boats have eyes painted on the bow for protection and vigilance. When a manta ray is caught they 'feed' the brain to the boat, and each year before the fishermen to go out to sea to hunt sperm whales for the first time, chicken blood is sprinkled on the joints of the boat. The villagers also hunt seacow, turtle, porpoises, but will always go after a whale first. The fishing season is from about May towards the end of the rainy season when the seas aren't so rough and sperm whales begin to arrive, and lasts until the coming of the rainy season in November. Manned by 7-14 helmsmen, oarsmen and harpooners, after spotting a whale and before they go in for the kill, they all urinate, pull down their sails, and say a communal *Pater Noster.* From platforms extending out over the water the harpooner jumps into the ocean to give the harpoon added thrust. If the whale spouts bright crimson, this signifies a fatal wound. Sometimes a boat is pulled all the way to Timor by a maddened runaway whale. These villagers capture 30-60 whales a year and the skulls are placed at the village gates.

SOLOR, ADONARA, AND ALOR

Island of Solor: Lies between Flores and Lembata. For many years the rendevouz point for Por-

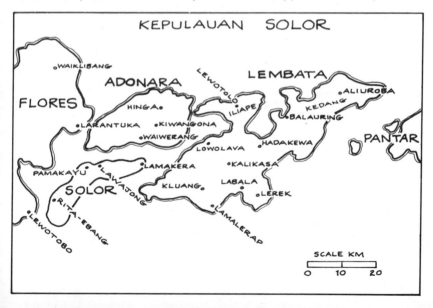

tugese sandalwood traders. In 1566 Dominican monks built the stone fortress of Henrique on the north coast near the present-day village of Lawajong, a well-chosen spot which provided good anchorage. Although the fortress itself lies in ruins, the walls and its cannon still stand. The small Muslim village of Lamakera on the east shore of this small island is one of only two whaling villages in all of Indonesia (the other is Lamalerap, South Lembata). Generations of expert boatmen, fishermen and hunters of large sea mammals have lived this way for 140 years. Being a volcanic island where only a few scanty crops are raised from the stony soil on the coast, the women of Lamakera tramp up to the mountain villages to barter whale meat and whale oil for maize, rice and cassava.

Isle of Adonara:
A narrow strait separates Flores and Adonara. Known also as the 'Isle of Murderers', two mountain clans, the Demons and the Padjis, have had a deadly running feud here for hundreds of years. No one could stop it or discover its ringleaders for often the old men behind the frequent massacres nominated young men to confess and go to prison in their places. Though now thoroughly a Catholic island with Portugese-style religious celebrations and practices, the coastal villages still fear the mountain people. Full-dress war dances with men wearing war paint and palm fronds as battle camouflage and brandishing spears are still staged once or twice a year. Many pearl divers live on this island.

Island of Alor:
North of Timor. Kalabahi is the main town with a population of 120,000.Warriors of Alor once used war a arrows with chicken bone barbs which splintered when they hit, the original dum dum bullet. Seventy languages are spoken on this small island, most of them unintelligible to anyone living more than 20 km away; several Papuan languages linger. Luckily most of its people have learned *Bahasa Indonesia* in the mission schools. A heavy Catholic trip here, but the people aren't fooled. The *naga*-snake cult persists on Alor with sacrifices of meat and rice made to this protective deity. In the villages, woodcarved *nagas* on posts, often surrounded by piles of stones, are endowed with magic powers. Small islands off the coast of Alor still don't use Indonesian currency but rely on the barter system, trading fish for corn and tapioca. Women spend most of their time weaving fine *ikat*-style cloth. **getting there:** Can be reached from Kupang in a 6-seater mission plane (fairly regular), Rp6000. Or by mototboat twice weekly from Kupang harbor, 18 hours, Rp3-4000. Another way is from Balauring (Lembata) by *prahu* or motorboat.

moko drums:
Small megalithic bronze kettle drums (moko) decorated with Hindu motifs are found nowhere else in Indonesia in such extraordinary numbers as on Alor. Their origin could be North Vietnam, the seat of the so-called Dongson Culture whose skills of bronze-casting and artifacts making entered Indonesia 500 years before Christ, reaching as far as New Guinea. On Alor, *moko* drums have been used until quite recent times as a ceremonial object. They are still used as an unofficial form of population control. Every time a male wants to get married he must give a *moko* drum to his inlaws. But since there's only a limited number of drums left and no new ones made or imported, there aren't enough to go around and often the unlucky couple must leave the island. The drums also play a part as a symbol of wealth and as currency to buy land (and once human heads). Needless to say, outsiders can't buy *moko* drums for any amount of money; they've been valued as high as US$3500. Hundreds are said to be buried under the earth.

FLORES

the land: A very pretty island which few travelers visit. The interior and eastern parts are covered in rolling heavy tropical forests. One rugged spectacular ridge of mountains runs down the middle with ten volcanoes lazily smoking. The peaks of this central range are all over 2100 m and the highest peak, located in the western half, is 2600 m. **history:** There was once a species of elephant on Flores, but now extinct. Some scientists connect ancient Flores with the Balkans because of the similarity of musical instruments, others connect it to Easter Island in the Pacific. Over a period of thousands of years, waves of migrations have passed through Flores. Hindus migrated here and even today Indian beads are very popular and valuable. The eastern point of Flores was sighted by a Portuguese trader from Melaka 400 years ago and named Cape of Flowers, though this island has few flowers. The Portugese stopped here on their way to Maluku and set up several bases.

people: With one million people, Flores is the most populous island in Nusa Tenggara. Many of its inhabitants look more Papuan than Indonesian with dark brown and sometimes almost black skins, heavy brows, wide flat noses, stockily built, their hair often black and curly, sometimes fuzzy. Life is simple. Most Florenese live from fishing, hunting, and simple agriculture. A man's daily routine is oriented to planting, harvesting, and protecting his crops from rodents. His animals forage for themselves. Rainfall is irregular so sometimes water shortages occur. In the rainy season roads frequently get washed out. Though the terrain is quite fertile, the markets in West Flores are impoverished because of too much or not enough rainfall, coupled with pests, which wipe out crops. Megalithic cultures are still extant in places and indigenous peoples of the inland areas could still be defensively hostile. It was not until 1936 that the Dutch considered the inland safe enough to be transfered from military to civil control. Traditionally, village houses had to be built over the body of a child buried under one of its main stumps, so every child was alertly guraded. This happened as recently as 19 years ago.

religion: At least ⅔'s of the population are Roman Catholics, the largest single R.C. community in Indonesia. Catholicism was first introduced by the Portugese trading fleets and when control of the island passed to the Dutch it continued to grow. The Dutch brought out their own priests and refused entry to all other Christian denominations. Now, from the central towns to the most remote villages you find tall reinforced concrete churches on hilltops with pointed spires, large beautifully appointed structures, all funded by churches and donations from the country of origin. The missions are quite strong and rich on Flores and you must depend upon them for transportation and accommodation. Everybody seems to work for the missions. But don't be deceived; not all Florenese accept wholeheartedly this western religion. You see in the villages sites for pure animist rituals, round grass areas surrounded with stones where the people dance to celebrate the planting and harvesting of crops and for weddings and burials. Peculiar organic arrangements like scarecrows of dried branches and leaves dressed with various articles are placed around the villages to keep away evil spirits. Outside villages, stone pillars are set up to receive offerings to the gods, and to perpetuate the power of those who erected them. You can still find graves consisting of Stonehenge-like clumps of stones surmounted by a large slab. Muslims are found mainly in the ports.

music and dance: Flores in an espącially rich island musically. In the districts of Ende and Lio, harvest songs are popular. The Florenese sing in complicated 4-part harmonies with lilting melodies and irregular rhythms. The people of Manggarai yodel. In eastern Flores folk songs originating from 17th Century northwestern Europe are sung. Instruments include horizontal flutes of various tones, an end-blown bamboo instrument which plays a deep thumping note, a primitive one-stringed lute played with a bow, and bamboo zithers. But percussion-type instruments are dominant with bamboo slit drums, small gongs, panpipes, simple zylophones, and drums made from parchment stretched over the end of a hollow piece of coconut-trunk and played with the hands. War dances are still practiced (though not for war) and women perform graceful 'round dances'. A solo dancer, man or woman, holds a long scarf before them and dances with shuffling steps around a grass area surrounded with stones, their hands fluttering and their bodies gyrating, advancing retreating, and encircling other dancers. Large groups also dance in a circle with arms linked, revolving counter-clockwise. **caci whip duel:** A test of skill and an ordeal of courage. Dancers use leather shields and painted wooden helmets decorated with horsehair to protect the face like a welder's mask. There's whistling, drum beats, and snapping whips hissing through the air. Towels protect the arms from the blows. At intervals the two men trade weapons. *Caci* is performed only at festivals now in the Manggarai and Ruteng areas.

crafts: Exquisite cloths are made on Flores. European influences from the 15th and 16th Centuries when the Portugese were here are still in evidence; see peacocks and European architecture in the fabrics' designs. In eastern Flores (and on Solor Island) are found intricately-worked, fantastically ornamented and colored fabrics, *sarungs* and scarves done in the *ikat*-technique. Blue, reddish-brown, and yellow designs are arranged according to what clan has woven it.

transport: Flores is long and narrow, about 400 km in length and only 70 km wide. It has a 640 km road from one end of it to the other. There are few vehicles, and the few there are owned by the missionaries. Zamrud and Merpati airlines services connect the main towns. In the dry season there's regular transport everywhere on Flores except between Labuhanbajo and Reo (but there's a weekly boat between these two towns). From Reo to Ruteng, there's a daily truck, and from Ruteng to Ende, a truck about twice a week. But during the rains, nothing is reliable and the going could be tough. If the roads are muddy you get sometimes only 1 km in 24 hours. Although you see lots of boats they never seem to be going where you want to go. Mission trucks usually cost the same as *bemos*. Bring penicillin and an antibiotic drying powder; could get many infections, and no medicine is available. **warnings:** Women shouldn't travel alone through any of the villages. Everyone stay away from Lekluo on the east end; the kids stone you.

accommodation: Catholics have long ago built way stations on the island which have been turned into priests' parishes where you can stay and eat, or else most ot the missionaries keep rooms in the back of their houses for poor travelers. Where there aren't missions stay in the army barracks or go to the local police station and sleep on the floor. Give them a tip. Police on Flores (around Ende) are quite uncorrupted in their dealings with Europeans and will help you; just don't talk politics or religion. The Florenese as well are refreshingly honest in comparison to the remainder of Indonesia. How you will be treated in a given area depends on the local missionary. If he's hated, then the people will not care for you either and rip you off.

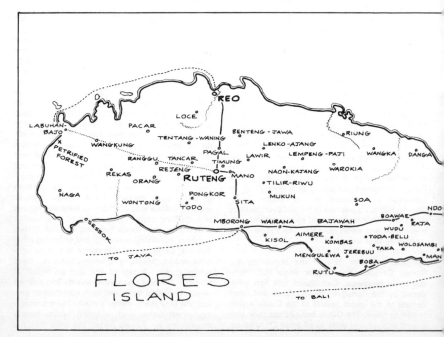

OVERLAND EAST TO WEST

Larantuka: A lovely port Rp1500 by truck or jeep from Maumere. Fabulous old houses, all stone and stucco. Very colorful market with nice blankets for sale. The religious life of Larantuka follows old Portugese traditions with Portugese names, prayers, Good Friday processions, devotional clothes and 17th Century helmets, statues, jewelry preserved in bamboo chapels. An old Portugese cannon and a bell hangs outside the Church of Kepala Maria. **stay:** Only 2 places to stay here. Losmen Ora et Labora is rundown but cheap; Rp300 single if you bargain. The food is decent. The other *losmen* is by the bank. **from Larantuka:** Boats depart regularly out of Larantuka. For example on Mon. and Fri. boats leave for Lowolava (Lembata), returning on Tues., Thurs., and Saturday. To Adonara (Waiwerang), only Rp250. To Solor (Pamakayu), Rp150; try the boats Taruna (a small motorboat covered in goats and chickens) and the Teresia. You can also catch boats to Surabaya from Larantuku for around Rp15,000. **vicinity of Larantuku:** There's an interesting graveyard to visit. Swim at the beach just outside of town.

Maumere: A port west of Larantuka. There's not much to do except on Christmas morning when you can see a Portugese play. Maumere blankets start at about Rp1000 (sell for Rp25,000 in Bali). There's an open end that you can finish yourself. Don't wash them because it's indigo dye and your bath will turn purple. **stay:** Losmen Bogor is near the river, Rp500 single; very clean. Also try Losmen Beng Goan behind the market. At night eat in the market or at Restoran Wura Laran. **from Maumere:** To Reo by boat costs Rp2500-3000; but boats aren't very regular. Fly from Maumere with Merpai to: Kupang, Rp13,000; Ende, Rp7200; Ruteng, Rp10,000.

Ende: The capital of Flores, Rp1000-1500 by boat from Kupang. In the dry season boats can't come in all the way to Ende, but go to Ipi (2 km from Ende), then a *sampan* will take you ashore. He'll try to charge you Rp500 but only pay Rp50 (with a reasonable amount of luggage). At the mission talk to some of the priests, such as Pater Petu. He knows Flores really well, its customs and laws. In the market buy the *leo sarung* from an area N.E. of Ende for Rp1500-2000. Very thin, stark black and yellow with triangular motifs made by continuous

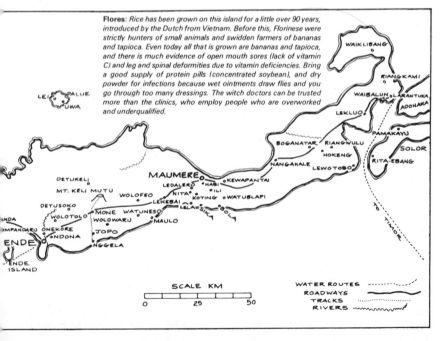

Flores: *Rice has been grown on this island for a little over 90 years, introduced by the Dutch from Vietnam. Before this, Florinese were strictly hunters of small animals and swidden farmers of bananas and tapioca. Even today all that is grown are bananas and tapioca, and there is much evidence of open mouth sores (lack of vitamin C) and leg and spinal deformities due to vitamin deficiencies. Bring a good supply of protein pills (concentrated soybean), and dry powder for infections because wet ointments draw flies and you go through too many dressings. The witch doctors can be trusted more than the clinics, who employ people who are overworked and underqualified.*

SCALE KM

0   25   50

WATER ROUTES
ROADWAYS
TRACKS
RIVERS

lines; looks like a triangular maze. They say that in Manokwari (Irian Jaya), where it's used as part of the bride price, they pay up to Rp80,000 for one of these fabrics. **stay:** Losmen Karya is right on the beach and close to the *dermaga;* they tell you it's Rp750 but you end up paying more like Rp1200. More expensive is Hotel Flores and Hotel Solafide, Rp1200 single, Rp1800 double. Stay instead in the place on top of the hill, a real hole but cheap. Eat at Rumah Makan Anugrah near the pier, quite good food. **from Ende:** Take the weekly *kapal motor* from Ende to Waingapu, Sumba, for Rp2500. Fly from Ende to Bima (Sumbawa) with Merpati, Rp12,900.

Mt. Keli Mutu: One of the more outerwordly sights in all of Indonesia. The 3 lakes on top of this mountain have different colored mineral-dyed waters. Legend has it that in the burgundy lake live the souls of sinners, in the green lake the souls of young men, virgins and the pure of heart, and in the deep-black lake the souls of the elderly. **getting there:** Start out up the mountain from Mone, a small village on the main road. Either hire a jeep in Ende for Rp2500-3000 and travel the 60 km N.E. of Ende to Mone, or else take a *bemo* to Mone from Ende, Rp500. In Mone a guide will volunteer himself readily. The road up to the volcano is 3 km before Mone. When you reach the barrier it costs whitey Rp250 to enter, Rp50 for Indonesians; no way to get around it. Walk 14 km up the very steep mountain, borrow or hire (Rp500) a horse, or charter a jeep (Rp1000) for the ascent. If walking, start early and take water. **stay:** Sleep in one of the *warungs* in Mone; they usually have a bed in the front room for which they'll charge Rp250. There's a hot-springs down near the river.

Wolowaru: 12 km from Mone on the road to Maumere. The *bemo* from Ende to Wolowaru is Rp500 (also Rp500 from Mone!). In Wolowaru there's a very nice *losmen,* Rp300, which serves family-style food for Rp250 (noodle-soup, rice, vegies). Zillions of kids, every window and doorway is filled. Contact Frederick who works at the agricultural department. He speaks English and knows a lot of the local *adat.* **from Wolowaru:** Mission trucks go through quite often and even go beyond Wolowaru to Maumere, but *bemos* don't that often. Visit the village of Lekebai, northwest of Wolowaru, for the market on Sat. mornings.

the Jopu area: The best weaving from Central Flores comes from Jopu and the surrounding 6 villages. Beautiful tapestry-like *sarungs* and other very richly-dyed fabrics; all you do is unthread the seam and you have a wall-hanging. Also *selandang* (shawls) for wrapping the dead in during former times, for carrying things, and to keep warm with.

getting there: Cross the river from Wolowaru to get to Jopu, a 4 km walk. You can also reach Jopu from Mone by walking, but an American girl was stoned to death on this route a few years ago. She didn't mention that she had been struck, returned to Ende, and that night she started hemorrhaging. Jopu is an old-style Florenese village with steep roofed *adat* houses and a distinctive looking Belgium-like church. Also a small hospital here. The people on the Wolowaru side grow food and the people on the Jopu side do the weaving; this is a time-old trade agreement between them. **walks from Jopu:** An interesting area, a very hilly part of Flores with big volcanoes. Walk down to Nggela over the cliffs. At Nggela a similar weaving technique but yet another style is practiced. You can climb Mt. Keli Mutu from Jopu, but it's a longer and steeper climb than climbing it from Mone.

Bajawa: Quite idiosyncratic boxing matches are popular at festivals in this area; just the middle knuckle of a semi-clenched fist is used and partners steer their fighter from behind into the fray like a puppet. The isolated society of the So'a in this sub-district number about 6000. **stay and eat:** Only two *losmens* in Bajawa. Stay at Losmen Sinazia or at Rumah Makan Anugrah, but cheaper than both is the army barracks. Eat at Rumah Makan Paradiso.

Ruteng: In West Flores. Nice surroundings, many volcanoes. This village is so high (1200 m) that it could *snow.* On a commanding height sits the headquarters of the Divine World (a German mission) where the Florenese are taught technical skills. Ruteng has very nice Losmen Karya, Rp400, with good food. From Ruteng, take a truck twice a week to Ende, though it's much less tiresome to take a plane. Merpati has flights from Ruteng to: Ende, Rp10,000; Bima, Rp13,000. From Mborong, south of Ruteng, cattle boats which take passengers leave for the slaughterhouses of Java.

Wairana: A little paradise in a small valley with streams running through it. Houses are built in the Swiss-chalet style. The priest, Rene Daen, arrived 20 years ago and built his house on a swamp where a man had been murdered by being staked to the ground. Rene's bed shook for years. People here are the nicest because the missionary is so good natured and kind. **vicinity of Wairana:** If he's got time, Rene will take you out to a former headhunters' village in the hills; the chief's house has human skulls all around it.

Reo: On the west end of the island, by bus from Ruteng Rp500. Or, if you're lucky, a boat will be heading for Reo from Maumere for Rp2500-3000.

The port of Reo, Kendindi, is 5 km from town. Stay at Losmen Teluk Bayur, Rp750 double. Quite good food at the *rumah makan.* Reo has a lovely beach. From Reo catch a boat to Labuhanbajo, Rp1000-1200. The road from Reo to Labuhanbajo seen on most maps doesn't exist; it's what the Dutch would have built had not WW II broken out.

LABUHANBAJO

On the far west coast of Flores. A miserable place, dirty, no good food, and there could be difficulties getting it together for the Komodo Island trip. **stay and eat:** The townspeople will offer to put you up for a modest price. The only *losmen* in the whole village is Losmen Mekar for Rp750 a bed run by Leo, a ship's captain. Leo will try to get Rp900, but just point at the sign. Not very appetizing meals consisting of only rice and dried fish are served. though in the wet season there's fresh fish. Go down to the market each morning and buy coconuts, Rp50 each; sometimes bananas, Rp100 a bunch, and sometimes papayas. If not, look for other food in the countryside up in the mountains.

from Labuhanbajo: There are boats to Sape (Sumbawa) once a week, Rp4000. Walk to Ruteng in 6 days from Labuhanbajo. In the dry season, it's quite easy to get boats from Labuhanbajo to Reo (or it takes 4 or 5 days to very pleasantly walk it). Or charter a boat for Rp15,000-20,000. There are also boats from Labuhanbajo to Waingapu (Sumba) for Rp3000. **vicinity of Labuhanbajo:** If you're going to be stuck in Labuhanbajo for several weeks rent a small sailboat for Rp500 a day and go out to

an inhabited island (buy a mosquito net first); many nice islands to explore around this port. There's a petrified prehistoric forest 5 km south of Labuhanbajo, acre upon acre of trunks lying in tangled broken heaps. Komodo dragons are found anywhere in the eastern end of Flores (also *anabas,* a land-creeping fish); just go out in the forest and wait. However, to the west across a channel only a few km wide are 3 islands, Komodo, Rinca, Padar, where the giant lizards live in much larger concentrations.

others: Spirit cults persist on Flores today. The island is steeped in witchcraft. Meet the *roh,* the local shaman and healer; often old women. At Soa village, Central Flores, is a site of Stone Age rites and symbols of the animist faith with endows every object with a spirit. Needle-like stones, with flatter stones on top serving as altars, are built around a natural amphitheatre. In the center stands a *peo* totem fetish shaped like a wooden doll; another pole is topped with the Virgin Mary. When the harvest is in, the Feast of Carabao is celebrated. A buffalo is tied up in an open arena and spears and knives are thrown at it until it's wild with pain and finally bleeds to death. The buffalo is meant to suffer for the sins of the people who have breached tribal custom and is used as a scapegoat to keep sickness and rat plagues away from the village. In Mengulewa, south-central Flores, a wooden post is carved with the face of the Buffalo Man, another one of the many features of ancestor worship and animist belief present on Flores.

Toke lizard *(cik cik): Small insect-eating harmless lizards seen on inner and outer walls of buildings, a lonely traveler's ideal companion and entertainment. The cik cak walks upside down or at any angle. Goodyear once spent US$25,000 trying to find out how they grip (by vibrating). They make their rubbing croaking sound only at night. When heard, Indonesians keep quiet and start counting. Seven croaks means wealth, five means happiness, more than seven means that the last person who spoke lied. Objects of mystical belief, toke sounds are also used as a means of making difficult decisions. A Balinese might decide to go to a cockfight or not by counting yes-no the moment a cik cak starts croaking. The gekko is larger, the lizard you hear making the unbelievably deep slow croaking sound. This creature living in the roof of your house insures good fortune for that house. Besides that, it eats mosquitos and other insects. There also exist somewhat larger species of lizards in Indonesia.*

KOMODO ISLAND

Only 36 km long and 20 km wide, this island home of the Komodo dragon is nestled in between Sumbawa and Flores. The giant lizards of Komodo were only a myth until the turn of the century when a few pearl fishermen were forced to land here one night in a storm. A desolate inhospitable island with only one mountain on it, Gunung Arab (Sataliso), which no native will climb believing that it's possessed with evil spirits and their reptile companions, the *nagas*. The few fishing families on Komodo today are descendants of convicts sent here from Flores as punishment. These convict colonists and their women were scared shitless on this island of thirst, crawling with 4-legged monsters, and built their *kampung* on posts as near to the sea as possible. Today they fish from outriggers, it being impossible to grow rice (too dry). **the land:** Nearly all the island's 76,601 arid acres are covered in coarse grassy slopes, stunted scrub bush, volcanic ridges, and *lontar* palms. Cave bats hover in black hollowed cliffs and the island swarms with snakes. In places the land rises 600 m from the sea. **climate:** The torrential monsoon season is Nov -Mar., and beginning in April through the rest of the year it's scorching hot.

Komodo lizard: There are over 2000 on this island. Natives call it *buaya darat* (land crocodile). It takes its scientific name *varanus komodensis* from the ancient belief that they warn of the presence of crocodiles. It belongs to a group known as monitor lizards found through Asia, Africa, and Australia, this species being the world's largest. Not discovered until 1912, only about a dozen of this rare species are found in the world's zoos other than in Indonesia, and outside of the wild they look like sleeping logs and usually die within a few years of amoebic parasites. Fossils strikingly similar to this lizard have been unearthed from chalk deposits dating back 130 million years, about the end of the great Age of Dinosaurs. All other places in the world this creature has been extinct since the Jurassic Age. The Komodo weighs up to 150 kilos and has a barrel-like, battle-scarred body up to 3 m long, enormous, rough, fearsome-looking jaws, muscular legs and sharp claws to support the heavy body. Its skin is dappled grey. Females are about 1 m shorter than males; she lays 30 eggs at a time. The fiercest lizard known, the Komodo can down a deer, goat or wild pig, ripping them apart with sawtoothed teeth. Sometimes it comes into the village in broad daylight to steal goats, though it likes putrefying meat the best. Their stomach juices are so strong that they can digest bones, hair, maggots,

hoofs, eyes — everything. They plunge their heads into the bellies of carcasses to eat the intestines; they also devour birds' eggs (waterfowl), insects, shellfish. Small water buffalo are sometimes swallowed whole, no chewing; its jaws are inarticulate like a snake's. Young dragons are the most unpredictable, the speediest, and the most skillful tree climbers; sometimes you see 1 and 2 m subadult dragons perched in trees preying on monkeys. Adults run through the grass with their tails lifted off the ground lashing it about. They can also wind their tails like snakes and deliver mighty blows with it, the tail being the Komodo's most dangerous weapon. While coming towards you they raise their heads up out of the grass like a periscope, then disappear down rocky holes without a trace. Their tongues protrude up to ½ m, it's an organ of both touch and smell. Historians believe that the Chinese dragon was modeled after such a creature because its long, forked, yellow-orange tongue was thought to be fire. Komodos are stone deaf; you can fire a rifle 2 m away and it won't flinch. No one has accurately determined their average life-span; it's thought they could live as long as 150 years. There's a legend of a 300 year old lizard living on top of Gunung Arab. Only one native has ever died; he speared one, consequently got bitten in the thigh and bled to death.

preparations: Apply for a permit (Rp500) at the Wildlife Conservation Office in the opposite end of town from the market in Labuhanbajo, a village in far western Flores. It's more convenient to obtain this permit in Singaraja, North Bali, before you arrive. In Labuhanbajo the permit takes 3 days to get since 9 copies have to be made. Don't accuse them of corruption otherwise they'll raise the fee to Rp5000 and won't give you a receipt. For baiting the lizards, buy a goat in Labuhanbajo for Rp2-3000 (the *losmen* should arrange it) and have it slaughtered before you go so that the carcass will be sufficiently rotted by the time you get to Komodo Island; Rp600 worth of stinky old fish will also suffice to capture their olfactory attention. You must also take along a guide from Labuhanbajo, Rp1000 a day. Bring some rice and vegetables because food is neither plentiful nor varied on the island. Take a telephoto lens.

getting there: Best time to visit is in the dry season Mar.-Sept. as during that time there's a regular weekly boat plying between Sape (East Sumbawa), Komodo Island, and Labuhanbajo (West Flores),

KOMODO ISLAND

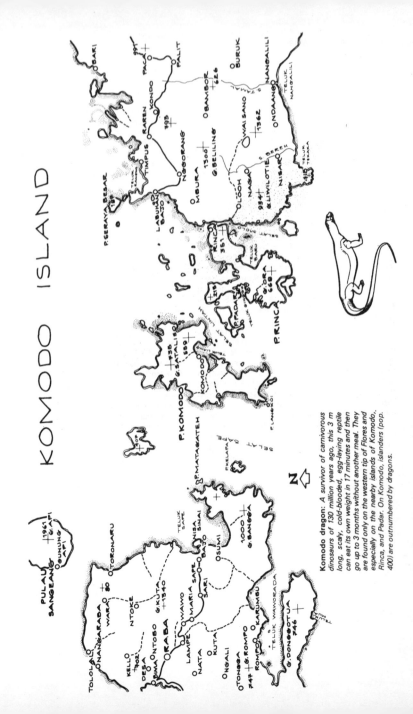

Komodo dragon: A survivor of carnivorous dinosaurs of 130 million years ago, this 3 m long, scaly, cold-blooded, egg-laying reptile can eat its own weight in 17 minutes and then go up to 3 months without another meal. They are found only on the western tip of Flores and especially on the nearby islands of Komodo, Rinca, and Padar. On Komodo, islanders (pop. 400) are outnumbered by dragons.

which costs Rp4000 or just Rp2000 either way to Komodo. Alternatively, count on between Rp5000 (as low as that) or up to Rp18,000 to charter a small sailing boat from Labuhanbajo. Share expenses with several people. The boat rental is usually for 3 nights only, you won't get a permit from the Forestry Department longer than 5 nights anyways. Because of the reefs, seldom do big boats go out to Komodo but you can take a small sailing boat which takes 36 hours; going back takes only 12 hours. You might meet with some reluctance; there are hazardous rip tides, sand bars, and some currents around Komodo can attain a speed of 13 knots. In places the sea bubbles, boils and foams like a river below a waterfall. Boats sometimes just disappear, even in calm weather. First your chartered *prahu* will go out to a small 500 sq m island where the crew dives for pearls and you stay overnight. Next morning you reach Komodo Island. It could be such a hassel getting out to Komodo in the rainy season (Nov.-Mar.) that you might as well buy a macro lens and find a couple of willing gekkos. There's a house to stay at in Komodo village for free, or sleep on your boat, or on the beach. This village has the only water on the island, so you must stay in the vicinity or bring water with you. To carry your dead goat 2 km to the place where you view the dragons the villagers will want you to pay for another guide besides the one you've already hired from Labuhanbajo, but just refuse. If you want to hire a boat at Komodo village to explore the island, the headman charges your ass. **dragon-watching:** Take water. You can find their borrows along the banks of dry riverbeds but the villagers know of the best places to watch them. The dragons don't as a rule come out of their holes in the earth and rocks until after 10 am when the air really begins to get hot. Build a hidden shaded platform, tie the rotting carcass to a stake, and quietly wait.

other sights: Liang Bay or Loho Liang is about one hour's punting from Komodo village. Pitch a tent on this semi-circular little bay, a pristine area of white sulpher-creasted cockatoos, jungle fowls, bush turkeys, *wili wili* birds, bellowing Timor deer, snorting boars crashing through the grass. Orchids grow in clumps at the tops of high trees and hills of *lontar* palms and shady trees rise up behind the beach. Don't swim because the water could have sharks, and sea snakes which can kill as quickly as a green viper or cobra. Other isolated bays in the northern part of the island are Loho Boko and Loho Buaya (Crocodile Bay). Ferocious and rare species of seawater crocodiles 10 m long still turn up in bays and deserted beaches such as these, throughout the archipelago. **Gunung Arab:** With clouds enveloping its top and evil spirits lurking, this mountain is covered in bamboo woods, monkeys, wild buffalo. Once a handful of Arabs tried to live on Komodo and there are relics of their settlement on this mountain; the wild buffalo found on this island are descended from the Arabs' cattle. Climb up through the well-trampled tracks of wild pigs and deer to the top. High *alang-alang* grass hides rubble and blocks of lava, so avoid it. Marvelous landscapes can be seen from the summit with chains of valleys in the distance. Bring binoculars. **Loho Shrikaya:** A bay on the northern side of the island with rocky lava cliffs and a thick wood. *Buaya darat* are much larger here than those found on the Komodo village side of the island. Though a land reptile, the dragon is also a good swimmer. (How else could he have gotten here?) Lizards stride on Loho Shrikaya's beach and swim like sea monsters, sometimes staying submerged up to 5 minutes.

SUMBA

This outlying, flat, barren island is the source of some of the most handsome fabrics in Indonesia as well as the country's strongest horses. The famous, sturdy 'sandalwood breed' of horse is exported to Java and to other islands for drawing carts. Sumba practices mostly subsistence agriculture. There's not much vegetation, but there are widespread savannahs of eucalyptus and large tracts of grassland for grazing cattle. Its forests produce sandalwood and cinnamon. On this island, buffaloes in groups of 20-30 are driven over the flooded fields until they are of uniform mud consistency, a method of plowing. The rivers aren't navigable, but provide irrigation. There are fish runs at the approach of the rainy season with plentiful sea fish in the rivers. Megalithic cultures are still extant in some locales. An isolated society survives in the Kodi subdistrict, the Bukambero people; about 6000 left. **loluk:** Every village has a spokesman (wunang) who are masters of the ceremonial language of *loluk.* They are cho-sen for their melodious voice and fast clear speech rhythms. Set in couplets of parallel meanings, *loluk* is used in traditional ritual songs, love ballads and animal stories, often containing moralistic or amusing comments on human nature.

travel: Most travelers just visit Sumba in transit going to and from other islands in the area. Lying so far off the track, it could be a difficult island both to reach and to get away from. Take plenty of thinky books to read during 1 day to 1 week layovers in sleepy port towns. If you can't hitch a ride on a jeep or a truck, you got to walk on some roads which are so overgrown even the squirrels can't get over them. In East Sumba where there are many rocky hills travel is difficult even on horseback. You hear some reports of not so friendly people; most are OK, but reserved. Besides blankets, horses and graveyards, there's not much else on Sumba except huge mosquitoes.

Ikat: *A tie-dye method of ornamenting fabrics. Threads are stretched out on simple looms and women hand-dye them each with natural colors (A). Either the warp or weft threads (rarely both) are tied up then dipped into a dye. The parts of the thread that have been tied up remain untreated (B, C, and D). When the next color is applied the already dyed parts are bound up and the parts left blank receive the coloring. The process is repeated as often as required by the design and the number of colors desired (E). There are many regional and island differences.*

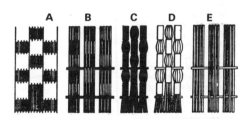

IKAT SUMBA

Ikat is a very ancient tie-dye method of decorating rugs, shawls, blankets, each completed fabric representing a colossal amount of human labor. Some pieces take 2 years to make. Only feudal, isolated, tribal, agricultural societies such as Sumba's produce these *ikat* textiles now, and they have reached an unusually high level here. These large, rectangular cloths are traditionally used in festivities and to wrap around the dead. **the process:** Either the warp or the weft threads (rarely both) are tied up and then dipped into a dye. The parts of the thread that have been tied up remain untreated. When the next color is applied, the already dyed parts are bound up and the parts left blank receive the required coloring. This process is repeated as often as required by the design and the number of colors.

colors: Many different shades can be derived from just 2 colors, depending upon how often the fabric is dipped into the natural dye. In East Sumba the bark of the *kombu* tree is used and in West Sumba the color from the indigo plant (wora) is prefered, the age old colors used for the blankets being blue, red, white and brown. Sometimes the artist must wait for one particular week in the year when a certain berry comes out to make a certain natural dye. After the fibres have been dyed they are woven on a loom consisting of simply 4 bamboo sticks stuck in the ground. There are about 4 classes of Sumba blankets (selimut sumba) which are usually made and sold in pairs.

motifs: Designs differ greatly. The fabric could be woven together unevenly and inexactly which gives the cloth a strange 3-dimensional shimmering effect. East Sumbanese *sarungs* (lau) have light figures standing out on dark backgrounds. The most frequent motifs used on Sumba are animals: birds, snakes, stags, crayfish. The Tree-of-Life is also a recurrent pattern. The 'skull-tree' motif, seen often, dates from headhunting days when skulls of captured heads were hung on the branches of a tree in the village center. This tree ensured fertility and was the main religious object ot the village.

purchase: At the airport in Waingapu (the capital) you are greeted with *ikat* cloths strung out along lines like confetti-like washing. If you settle on the price for one it doesn't mean that you pay the same for each; you have to bargain for each and every blanket. They can be bought cheaper in villages along the coast south of Waingapu for possibly as little as Rp5000-6000 a pair from merchants who come up with the blankets wrapped all around their arms and shoulders. In Waingapu, they want Rp10,000 a pair: avoid Chinese shop owners if you can, they're too inflexible. You can sell a blanket for 500% profit in Bali or Jakarta, or up to 1000% in Australia.

other crafts: In eastern and western districts *hinggi kombu* scarves are rust-brown in color. Sometimes travelers come across tortoise shell combs with designs of stags and cocks engraved on them. Much of Indonesia's precious Chinese porcelain originates in Sumba, dug up from old Chinese graves. Since the most valuable possessions of the deceased (ivory, gold, China, fabrics and coins) are buried with the corpse, there are hoards of China here. They could search you at the airport but some people manage to get away with a few plates stuck down their pants or skirts.

SIGHTS OF SUMBA

Waingapu: Catch a boat from Ende, Flores, to Waingapu for Rp3000. Nusa Tenggara Shipping Co. has *kapal motors* from Sumbawa Besar to Waingapu for Rp5850. Or fly from Kupang, Rp31,150. Besides marvelously woven Sumba blankets and shawls (see them actually woven in nearby village of Prailiu), there are beautiful *kains*, *sarungs* and blankets from Sawu Island for Rp2000; a few cost as high as Rp8000-10,000. If Waingapu's bank doesn't offer you a good enough rate, bargain your exchange rate with the bank manager. **stay and eat:** There are 3 *losmens*. Although the manager is a bit slimy, Losmen Lima Saudara is quite

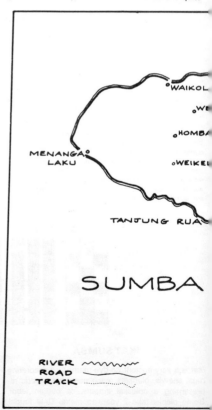

good; Rp200 to sleep in a big shed. Losmen Cemara, Rp400, is also quite comfortable and they serve decent meals. Fairly good food is served everywhere in the *warungs*. Nice tomatoes and grapefruits here. **from Waingapu:** Hire a horse in Waingapu and ride it through the villages on the southern coasts. Flights to Ende, Rp9100; Maumere, Rp13,800; Sawu (a small island east), Rp12,000.

Kupundak: On the north coast live the Kupundak people, a society of subsistence farmers among whom class distinctions are still hereditary: royal (maramba), free clansmen (kabihu), and servants (ata). Kupundak divide themselves into patrilineal clans, each claiming descent from a single founder (marapu). Bride prices are exceptionally high, a way of maintaining loyalty and class rigidity. **Maru:** In this village are several Marapu high-peaked houses, a type peculiar only to Sumba. Major ceremonies take place in and around these houses, and inside treasures sacred to the deities from the old capital are stored. This village sits at the foot of the former hilltop priestly capital, a royal walled village. Different clans, including a warrior clan, once clustered around the king's residence. Now deserted, all having moved down to the Maru river valley. During the Ratu Festival of prayer, sacrifices and myth narration open the planting season.

West Sumba: Every April, a tribal war takes place in this region, the staging of which is a long deep cultural tradition. It's a hell of a walk to the battle area. There will be charging horsemen, spear-throwing and deaths. Spectators are tolerated. Being excellent bareback horsemen, Sumbanese combatants charge along circular runways tangential to each other. When their courses intersect they try to club their opponent from his mount, slamming him to the ground with the butt end of a spear. Women

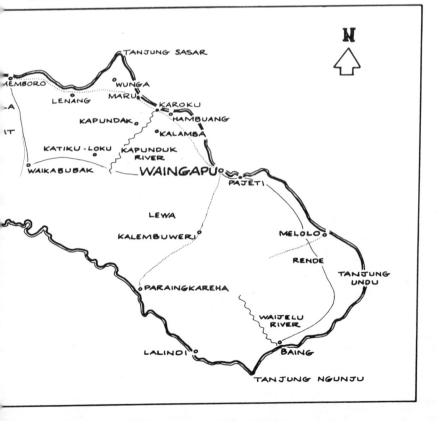

are the chief observers and supporters of these combats, each cheering loudly for her favorite. (The 'vibrated shriek' songs of the women of Sumba were once used ritually to welcome their husbands back from headhunting expeditions.) **Sumba boxing contests:** Prior to combat each fist of the combatants is wrapped in a wild grass leaf, the barbed edges of which can produce vicious wounds. Swipes across the eyes are highly prized as blood flowing from such wounds blinds the opponent and usually causes his defeat.

Anakalang: The focal point of this whole village is a massive graveyard. Sumbans believe that the present world is just an antechamber to the palaca of the next world and that death is the most important event in life. Also see the flawlessly built thatch homes with their high conical roofs. **Prai Bokul:**

The heaviest stone on Sumba weighs 70 tons and sits like a fallen meteor in this village. This giant sepulcher is owned by the richest man on the island who hired 2000 workers to chisel it out of a remote mountain. It cost US$50,000 to complete the project, took 3 years and 3 lives to transport it. 250 buffaloes were sacrificed and 10 tons of rice were consumed in the ritual accompanying the movement, a fullblown medieval pageant in the belief that the stone will ensure his entrance into heaven. **Wunu-Mutu:** In this village buffalo horns and pigs' jawbones hang on each and every house. Villagers here hunt on horseback in the surrounding forests. Men of Sumba are farmers with weather-beaten faces who ride horses bareback, drape color rich handwoven fabrics over their shoulders, and carry long knives with buffalo horn hilts stuck in their waistbands.

pangolin: *Malayan for 'one who rolls up'. This nocturnal anteater has a narrow head which it tucks inside its tail, winding it so tightly around its body that you can't get your fingers between the tip of the tail and the body. The pangolin can be lifted and carried like a bowling ball without the finger holes. With a long scaly tail and sharp digging claws, the upper part of the body is protected by hard overlapping scales. The pangolin digs its way into ant or termite* heaps, licking the insects up with its long sticky tongue. It has no teeth though its digestive track has miniature ones which chew up its food. Sometimes it plays dead on an antheap, with its tongue sticking out, letting the ants crawl over it, then eats them. Ants will also crawl underneath the pangolin's scales; it later drowns them in the river, then eats them when they float up to the surface. To harm one is to ask for 40 days bad luck.

SUMBAWA

the land: Made up of rolling uplands, eroded foothills, volcanic ridges, and ancient crater walls. Australian climatic influence is evident: spiny bush, acacia, thorn, cactus, and extensive savannah areas. Its entire southern coast is lined with extinct volcanic peaks that plunge straight into the Indian Ocean. The north coast consists of plains and river basins. In the north near Teluk Saleh is the jagged 2820 m peak of G. Tambora, towering 915 m above any other point in Sumbawa's central mountainous spine. Some of these mountains are volcanic, but none are now active. Eastern Sumbawa is a rocky, dusty, parched country of stubbly growth and bamboo villages on stilts.

history: As early as the 14th Century Sumbawa had become very wealthy through its natural resources of timber and horses. Along with Timor this island was the source of the fragrant woods, *sapan* and sandalwood, which European and Asian trading powers exported for over 300 years. For two centuries the Makassans of southern Celebes indulged in pillage and slaving raids along its north coast. It was they who first brought Islam to Sumbawa. The political system and the descent of the royal sultanate families of the north coast derive from the Kingdom of Gowa near Ujung Pandang. The most violent event in Sumbawa's history was the 1815 eruption of G. Tambora; its rain of ash either directly killed or eventually starved to death most of the island's population.

people: Population 320,000. From prehistoric times, Sumbawa has been inhabited by 2 linguistic groups who couldn't understand each other for centuries: the Sumbawa-speaking states to the west and the Bima-speaking clans of the east. The sultan has remained the ultimate civil and religious authority and Sumbawa is a very heavy Islamic island. Many of the women still cover their faces. The western part is a mixture of multiple cultures and customs. Mountaineer rustics live in distinct mountain villages in the interior of the western peninsula's foothills. You can see them come down to the more prosperous urban lowlands to trade their horseloads of woven mats and baskets. Male Sumbawans of the uplands carry large machete-like knives (berang), ornamented with carved dragons. Sumbawan men are skilled archers and still hold matches occasionally, firing their arrows into a target which moves along a high wire. The Dompu area is well known for its cloth worked with silver thread. Mock battles can be seen here with men wearing Arabic rolled turbans. Sumbawan orches-tras, made up of drums and flutes, sound like bagpipes. Fine violins which sound similar in pitch to violas are made. *Kulkus* or long hollow drums are still used for sending messages.

travel: Besides the road transversing Sumbawa from Sape to Jareweh, the island is covered in foot tracks. A twisting bumpy trail follows Sumbawa's north coast. During the wet months Nov.-April, there are many washed out, rotted bridges. Floods sometimes occur between late Nov. and Feb. which could carry shacks, fences, and cattle down to the ocean. Sumbawa is well known for its honey and eggs, both of which are said to increase potency. Try green bananas deep fried in fresh coconut oil, and cool melons for thirst. Medicinal paste *seme* is effective in treating cuts.

mountain villages: From Sumbawa Besar, visit Rarak and Lawang about 2½ hours walk. Take the narrow rutted road which winds its way into the island's interior mountains to the southwest. Old Dutch stone posts mark the kilometers as far as Kayu Sengkal, 24 km up in the high foothills. The road slowly climbs towards the pinnacle of Sumbawa's western peninsula, the twin peaks of the Batu Lante Mountains. Catch glimpses of the Flores Sea 300 m below. Closely clustered villages are found in this area. Hear the musical rhythmic thumping of women working the rice boat (rantok) and beating thistles. In the evenings during the monotonous chore of threshing they sing humerous or nostalgic verses to alleviate the work. These villages are closed up tightly at dusk for fear of *setan* (bad spirits). On Sumbawa, as in many of the backwater regions of Indonesia, witchcraft is rampant.

BIMA

On the eastern end of the island. A strongly Muslim town, take care on Fridays with your dress and demeanor; you could get stoned (with *rocks*). Darul Islam, a group which wanted Indonesia to become a completely Islamic theocratic state, conducted a terrorist guerilla campaign in West Java from 1949-1962, which amounted to open rebellion. In 1957, three fanatics from Bima tried to assassinate President Sukarno at Cikini School, Jakarta, but only managed instead to kill 13 schoolgirls with grenade fragments. Bima is still in the doghouse with Jakarta. Try to enjoy yourself here. **stay:** There are 4 *losmens*. Quite close to the bus station but extremely nasty is Losmen Merdeka, Rp300; they are

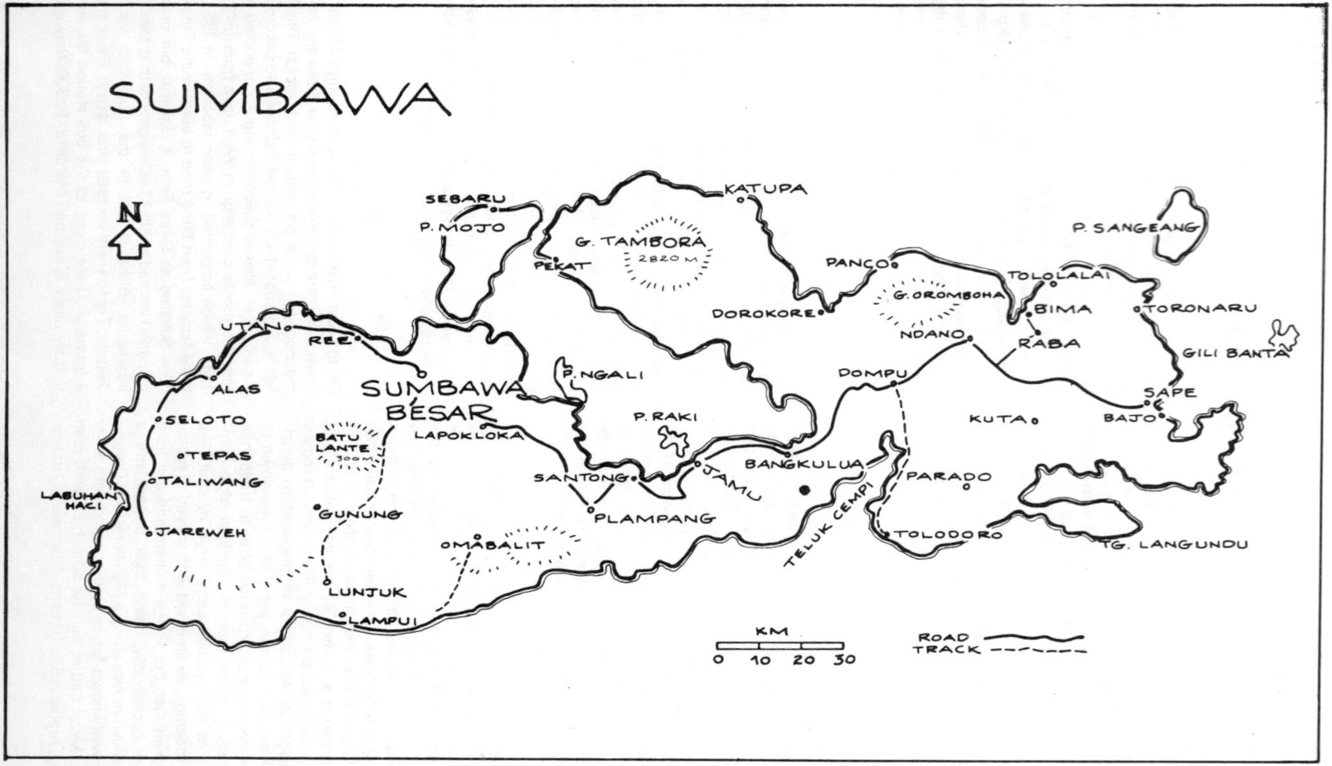

SUMBAWA

N

SEBARU
P. MOJO
PEKAT
G. TAMBORA
2820 M
KATUPA
DOROKORE
PANÇO
P. SANGEANG
TOLOLALAI
TORONARU
GILI BANTA
BIMA
RABA
NDANO
G. OROMBOHA
SAPE
BAJO
KUTA
DOMPU
PARADO
TOLODORO
TG. LANGUNDU

UTANO
REZE
ALAS
SELOTO
TEPAS
TALIWANG
JAREWEH
LABUHAN HACI
BATU
LANTE
300 M
GUNUNG
LUNTUK
LAMPUI
OMÁBALIT
SUMBAWA
BÉSAR
LAPOKLOKA
P. NGALI
P. RAKI
SANTONG
JAMU
BANGKULUA
PLAMPANG
TELUK CEMPI

ROAD ―――――
TRACK ------

KM
0   10   20   30

a boat and bus agency as well. Losmen Komodo costs Rp1000 but 4 people are allowed to share a room; this is the best. They serve fried rice for Rp200, slightly more expensive than other places, but more than palatable. This *losmen* lies near the sultan's palace which is now a university. Rumah Makan Nirvana and Rumah Makan Anda, both near the bus station, have long menus and serve so-so Chinese food. **vicinity of Bima:** Visit the traditional village of Donggo outside of Bima. There's also a swimming pool in the hills. On Banta Island, between Bima and Komodo Island, giant turtles swim in a jade lagoon. Utter solitude. Makes you wish you had your own boat.

from Bima: Take buses to Sumbawa Besar on Tues. and Sat., Rp1500. It's quite easy to get a boat from Bima to Labuhanbajo, Flores, but most don't stop at Komodo. Bargain with the captain; a fair price is Rp3000-4000. There are also boats from Bima to Lombok's port of Lembar, Rp4000, but they could take up to 8 days. Sometimes a Pelni ship runs from Bima to Kupang. There are about 3 ships per week from Bima to Surabaya carrying cattle, copra, rice and passengers. **for Komodo:** Losmen Merdeka sells tickets for an outrigger *prahu* equipped with a Johnson called the Mekar which leaves once weekly (Tues.) from Sape to Komodo (3 hours) and then on to Labuhanbajo; costs Rp4000 for the whole trip or Rp2000 just to Komodo. The busride from Bima to Sape is Rp400. The only place you can stay in Sape is the police station; it's free. Friendly police, but the people aren't. **by air:** Bima's airport is 40 km out of town on a terrible road. Start quite early in case the bus breaks down, could take 4 or 5 hours to reach, Rp400. For both Merpati and Zamrud flights, buy tickets in Bima. Zamrud fares to: Ampenan (Lombok), Rp11,500; Denpasar, Rp15,000 (slightly more with Merpati); Ruteng (Flores), once weekly, approximately Rp10,000.

SUMBAWA BESAR

The lowland capital in West Sumbawa. See the old, collapsing, barn-like former sultan's palace with its rusty cannon. A wrinkled 100 year old woman with snow white hair, Sultan Jalaluddin III's widow, 4th and only surviving wife, still lives in this palace (built in 1931). Inside are creaking carved doors, carpets full of dust, a huge wall with a row of nupital couches on either side; frayed red and white tapestries hang sadly on the wall, rows of spider webs clutch the ceilings. Now village children take care of her, coming each day with food and water. They clean her room, wash her *sarungs,* and generally help her live in her memories. **stay and eat:** Many good *losmens*. Losmen Sudara, Rp600, is clean, central, and the management is quite pleasant. The *losmen* located on the other side of the road is just as good. If Losmen Saudara is full, try Losmen Bahagia at the end of town, Rp400 single. Eat in the *warungs* in front of the sultan's palace. Alright food is served at Rumah Makan Anda or Rumah Makan Gembira. **vicinity of Sumbawa Besar:** At Taliwang, Rp500 by bus from Sumbawa Besar, go 10 km past to Labuhan Haci, a natural harbor surrounded by beautiful scenery. A fantastic *losmen* here.

buses from Sumbawa Besar: To Bima there are buses (two companies) only twice weekly on Wed. and Sun., Rp1500. The trip takes 12-18 hours, depending upon how many breakdowns there are. The road is very bad but the scenery is quite spectacular. Buy tickets at the bus station or the *losmen* will send a boy. Avoid getting a seat over the rear axle and don't ride on top of the bus because there are too many branches. If the buses on this route are full they don't stop but plow right through, so it's no good jumping off halfway because the buses won't stop to pick you up and you might end up walking to Bima. **boats:** Catch a boat to Padangbai (Bali), Rp3500. No food onboard. It leaves from Badas (Harbor) near Sumbawa Besar on Sun. at 4 pm and arrives Mon. morning at 3 am. For Lembar Harbor on Lombok, buy tickets at Losmen Saudara, Rp1000. Start out from Sumbawa Besar by bus at 5:30 am for Alas so you'll have plenty of time to reach the boat which leaves at 9 am. **flights:** From Sumbawa Besar to Bima take Zamrud's Monday flight, Rp6250, but book one week ahead.

the durian: *An enthusiast knows that there are various tests to put the durian through to determine if it is ready to eat. Observe the length of the spikes on the shell, look at the shape, bounce it on the ground, shake it up and down and listen to the sound it makes, examine the color, feel for the 'soft spots', and so on. To eat, just suck the provocative fruit from the pods. It's impossible to truly describe the taste. It's a combination of flavors like cream with a hint of onion, and smooth port wine, butter-almond pudding. When durian freaks get together, they exchange recollections of unforgettable durians they've had in the past. A true durian fanatic can't leave the fruit unfinished; once opened, he eats it. It's meant to be super-nutritious as well as a potent aphrodisiac. The Dayaks of Borneo have been known to kill for this fruit in questions over ownership of certain trees. Sometimes one tree yields up to 100 durians. It's the only fruit that tigers eat, ripping the spiky shell open with their claws. Rhinoceros are fond of it too. If you drink alcohol while eating durian it could be dangerous (mabuk sekali).*

the Hairy Sumatran Rhinoceros: *One of the rarest mammals. Whereas the African and Indian rhinos live in open savannah and dry tablelands, the Sumatran rhino is a swamp animal and haunts one of the oldest and most inaccessible tropical jungles in the world. It's the smallest of the three types of rhinos, has a hairy hide, is fiery and ill-tempered. Very nimble, it moves in and out between roots, trees and tangled undergrowth, able to stop and turn around almost instantly to charge at you. They make a shrill, whimpering, whispering sound, something between the sqeak of a little pig and the whine of a big dog. Powder made from rhino horn distends erectile tissue and fetches US$1000 in Singapore. The Chinese demand for this powder almost resulted in the total extinction of the Asian rhinoceros.*

Pulau Dua: *Located on the N.W. coast of W. Java. This migratory bird island attracts birds from as far as Australia, India, China, and many points in Asia. See flocks of white and orange cattle egrets, red night herons, snake birds, doves, ibises, spoonbills, storks, purple herons, naked night herons (or 'gangster birds') which steal newly-hatched young birds from their nests. The whole bay is very shallow with long legged birds wading in lines. The highest land point is only 3 m above sea level.*

dhole: *A reddish wild dog found in Siberia, Java and Sumatra. Looks like an Irish terrier. Its Indonesian name ajak means 'urging on' because the dhole chases and pulls down its prey when it becomes exhausted. They hunt in packs and attack buffalo, snapping and biting at its flanks until it collapses.*

mango trees: *In the villages of Java, the coolest spot is often under the deep dark shade of a mango tree. Vegetables and other fruits are hung in the lower branches to keep them 'refrigerated'.*

macan tutul: *A sleek, long-bodied, spotted wild cat. The Java Tiger is called harimau macan jawa; find him in a reserve near Sukamade, East Java.*

the climate of Indonesia: *There's little variation of temperatures and the annual range of average monthly temperatures is a matter of only 2-3 degrees. Days and nights are almost all the same length with only 48 minutes difference between the longest and shortest days of the year.*

remarkable
beetles of
Kalimantan

Sumatran leopard cats: *Smaller than a housecat, spotted, graceful, lovely to watch, and very playful. Always die in captivity.*

banyan trees of Bali: *All over this island banyan trees' aerial roots hang down and take root in the ground, sometimes covering an area of 0.6 hectares. The shady banyan trees are named after native banians (merchants) who used to trade under them.*

Pasar Ngasem: *The Bird Market of Yogya is on Jl. Ngasem, where you can buy Javanese singing birds (perkutut). Small shops in the vicinity sell charcoal braziers, moneyboxes from Kasongan, pottery and water jars.*

the Solo River: *This 560 km long river has the longest flow of all Java's rivers. It starts in the extreme south of the island, then flows through the Solo Valley, reaching the Java Sea north of Surabaya after twisting through swamps near its mouth. This river is used for floating logs downstream from upland teak forests. A city was named after it.*

East Java: *The population of East Java is 27 million. Because of restricted rainfall and the quality of the soil, maize is grown widely. Sugar cane is also a major crop; cassava and sweet potatoes, which require East Java's drier climate and more sunshine, are also grown. There are few dry ricefields in the prolonged drier areas. Many parts of the region are covered by infertile limestone ranges. The most eastern part of Java (such as the Ijen Plateau) has savannah landscapes and mountain lakes.*

scarlet hibiscus: *While frangipani blossoms dazzle their whitest at midday, the scarlet hibiscus seems even brighter in the first morning sun. The Indo-Malayan region's richness of plant life derives from its warm moist climate and partly from the highly varied topography, separated by seas, which have caused such a diversity of insular environments. 30% of Indonesia is still dense jungles.*

: *Beautiful black ibis with long legs and fusiform bodies fly in V-nations. Their plumage has a allic sheen, especially at twilight. y look black only from a distance.*

phins *(ikan pusat): Live in the shwater Mahakam River of East imantan. You can see a specimen the Surabaya Zoo, the first one m this area was captured in 1976.*

volcanoes of Moluccas: *With 70 volcanic eruptions in the last 400 years with much loss of life and property, the Moluccas region is one of the most unstable regions in the world geophysically. One eruption in 1840 destroyed every house in Ternate town. Great slopes of hard lava and rugged volcanic debris stretch from the peaks to the sea on the northern side of the island. See Batu Hangus where a river of white-hot molten lava burned a path from the crater down to the sea in 1763. Seen even miles away at sea.*

reticulated python: *Found from the Asian mainland to the Tanimbars. The world's largest and longest snake reaching up to 9 m in length. Feeds mainly on wild birds and mammals such as pheasants and small deer. It has spectacular swimming skills, able to swim and drift for days. These creatures swam from Java or Sumatra to Krakatoa volcano soon after it erupted in 1883, being one of the first creatures to take up life again on the devastated island.*

cassowary bird: *Has no enemies but human beings. It lays giant grass-green coloured eggs with a strange granular surface.*

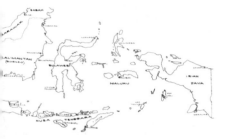

Island of Waigeo: *Off the N.W. coast of Irian Jaya. The only place on earth where the Crimson Bird of Paradise is indigenous. Although by far the largest number of species live on New Guinea, 4 species of the Bird of Paradise are found in Australia, one species lives in the Moluccas (has long golden brown wings and tail, and a gleaming green coat); and one species has even reached Sulawesi. Hybrids are extraordinarily common amongst them, two examples being Queen Carola's Six-Wired Bird of Paradise and Mayer's long-tailed Astrapia. Birds become more colorful and their plummage explodes the more easterly you travel in Indonesia.*

gor: *The governor's mansion unded in 1817) was complete-destroyed by an earthquake in 34, when the present palace as built and made the official sidence of the Dutch gover-r-generals from 1870-1942. he finest and most famous otanical gardens in Asia are be-nd the mansion. There are ady trees 30 m high, a river owing through it which ends in e black mud of Pasar Ikan, akarta, the oldest and tallest oil alm brought from West Africa 1848, huge banyan trees, and library with 75,000 books. ome of its plants take 50 years bloom. See the insect-eating flesia which blooms once very October to over a yard in iameter. There are also thou-ands of breeds of orchids in arefully tended hothouses.*

the goura: *Giant turkey-sized pigeons found in the thickly vegetated forests of the eastern islands. They are a delicate blue and mulberry with a lacy crest of feathers on their heads.*

Puncak Jayawijaya: *The highest mountain between the Himalayas and the Andes and easily the highest in Indonesia at 5030 m. This vicinity Irianese call Dugundugu which means 'reed flower' because of the white hanging flowers of the reed plants which grow all over the marsh-lands here. Other snow and glacial covered mountains present on the equator in other parts of the world include the Chinborazo (6477 m) in the Ecuadorian Alps, and the Rowenzori (5080 m) in Central Africa.*

flora of Irian Jaya: *There are many species of liana, beech trees, tree ferns, tree orchids, and the so-called 'ant-house plants', potato-shaped and honeycombed with tunnels inhabited by sharp-biting ants, tree frogs, and lizards. From the lagenaria comes a gourd used by the Irianese for centuries as bottles, dippers, and other containers. Libodedrus is an incense tree found in high altitudes. At night the mould of the forest floor glows and flickers in the dusk from the decomposing bacteria it contains.*

scorpions: *Although they can get up to 50.8 mm long, scorpions in Indonesia are pretty harmless. Feels like a bee sting and swells.*

mudskippers *(ikan tembakul): This fish with a frog-like face chases insects along the ground and climbs mango trees. It wets its eyes by wiping its fins over them and wets its body by rolling in mud puddles.*

LOMBOK

Lombok means 'chili pepper' in Javanese. It's a small island, slightly smaller than Bali, with untouched white sand beaches the whole way around it. The 3 towns in the west, Ampenan, Mataram, and Cakranegara, are almost all one continuous town 6 km long. There's an intact Balinese culture in the western part with amazing temples. Though this lush non-commercialized island is just beginning to be discovered, tourists and travelers are still a rarity. Everywhere you go on Lombok people stop and stare; sometimes whole villages full of kids trail after you. It's best not to believe the stories of black magic, etc. that the Balinese tell about Lombok; they just don't want to loose your patronage to their sister island.

getting there: The main port of Lombok is Lembar, 35 km south of Ampenan. Take the daily 11 am ferry from Padangbai, the east coast port of Bali, for the 5-6 hour crossing to Lembar, Rp1500. They charge you heavily to transport your motorbike, Rp600 (it's bargaining time). From Lembar to Cakranegara by bemo, Rp100. Or fly from Denpasar to Ampenan airport in Mataram for Rp4200 plus Rp800 airport tax. The imigrasi office is only a 10 minute walk from the airport. **transport:** There are some acceptable roads around Ampenan but there's only one good one, the road from Ampenan to Labuhan Lombok. The remainder of the towns are interconnected by awful roads. It costs Rp300 and takes 3 hours to get across the island from Ampenan to Labuhan Lombok by bus. You can charter a taxi for Rp800 per day, a motorcycle for Rp1500 per day, a minibus for Rp25,000 per day, a bemo for Rp500 per hour.

the land: Like Bali, Lombok has a chain of volcanic mountains in the northern half of the island and the same climate and soil for its variety of crops, mainly rice, coffee, and tobacco. Gunung Rinjini rises to 3775 m from a high plateau area with a large lake, Segura Anak. The south, similar to Bali, has fertile alluvial plains except in the extreme south where there are scrubby barren hills; quite dry and strikingly different. The continuous alluvial fan (a continuation of the slope of the mountain) gets little rain and sometimes droughts last for months; the rice crop often fails. In 1966 fifty thousand people starved to death in 150 villages all over the island.

the people: Lombok has a fairly large population (1.5 million), a mixture of Islamic Sasak and Hindu Balinese. The Balinese conqured Lombok and en-

slaved its native peoples, the Sasaks, in the 18th Century. The Sasaks are a hill tribe of a different racial stock with dark skin, long heads, wavy hair and more caucasian facial features. This was a result of migration streams at an earlier date than most Indonesian ethnic groups, the Sasaks coming overland from N.W. India or Burma. Today the Balinese make up 20% of the population and live mainly in the west. To the east are the Sasaks, heavily Islamicized and poorer. Most of the Chinese in the east were killed off in 1965-66. Though Muslim, Sasak boys are carried in a circumcision ceremony borrowed from Hindu Bali to the west. The boy rides on a lion with a tail of palm fronds. No anesthetic is used; each boy must be willing to suffer pain for Allah. There's much pageantry in Sasak courting rituals. If a girl accepts a gift from an admirer, she must marry him. The native Sasak dances include: Cupak, Cepung, Tawa-Tawa, Gendang Belek, Rudat, Kroncang Sampi. You can charter a dance troupe for Rp15,000 a show. Gorgeous cloths and ceremonial fabrics are woven on this island. The men wear a batik kain with an attached ikat (sapuk) border. The women of Lombok, who aren't allowed to wear gold ornaments, don the black baju lambung with a black kain and a red shawl (beberut).

MATARAM

The administrative capital of Lombok, just a series of new government offices, pre-fab homes, and many many soldiers. Compared to Bali there's an easy imigrasi here, located 1 km from town, Rp25 by bemo (but they'll try to sock you for Rp200). Stay in very nice Losmen Kamboja, Rp800 double. Delicious filled pancakes in this town. **from Mataram:** To Cakranegara it's Rp25 by bemo. Fly from Mataram with Merpati to Bima (Sumbawa), Rp14,500; to Sumbawa Besar, Rp8000. **vicinity of Mataram:** Visit the floating istana with surrounding gardens at Mayura, the water-palace and bathing place of the old sultan. The Miru Temple group is the largest on Lombok. **Purbasari:** A weaving center on Jl. Ukir Kawi where the native kain purbasari is produced. **Pantai Pemenang:** A sea garden 25 km north of Mataram with coral diving and all sorts of tropical fish. **Aikbukak:** 25 km east of Mataram, a swimming pool and a pasangrahan. **Sukaraja:** An Islamic weaving center of Lombok fabrics 45 km south of Mataram.

Kuta Beach: A gleaming white sand beach 45 km south of Mataram. Each year on Feb. 2nd and 3rd, youths gather here for singing and poetry recitals. Really off the beaten track, a splendidly deserted coastline. *Bemos* go to Sengkol (Rp75) which comes within 7 km of the little village of Kuta, then you take a truck, Rp100. Rent a small house for Rp400 a night from the *kepala desa*. Few facilities, very few visitors, and simple food. Stacks of *cumi cumi*. Watch out for stinging seaweed while swimming. **Pagutan village:** An historic temple in Lombok where an ancient *lontar*-manuscript is kept, the *Nagarakertagama*. Written about 1365 A.D. by the poet Prapantja, it's one of Java's *kawi* classics.

AMPENAN

Cattle are exported from Ampenan to Jakarta, Surabaya, Hong Kong and Singapore. **stay:** Ratih, Jl. Selaparang 71, is Rp600-1200 single, Rp900-1800 double. Pusaka, Jl. Merpati, Tel. 519, is Rp600

single, Rp1210-1500 double, Rp4500 triples; a breakfast of *nasi goreng,* eggs and milk is included in the price. Hotel Kamboja, Jl. Kamboja 10, is now being remodeled and is more expensive. Hotel Cempaka, Jl. Cempaka 31, is Rp1215 and Rp1875 (with fan), or Rp3850-5000 double with A.C. Hotel Meraja is on Jl. Mareja 3. Hotel Tigamas is on Jl. Pabean Ampenan (but too close to a mosque); Rp725-900 single, Rp900-1100 double. Hotel Pabean is at Jl. Pabean 146; Rp850 single, Rp1000 double, get rooms upstairs for Rp500 double. Cleaner and cheaper than Tigamas. There are 3 good Chinese restaurants opposite Hotel Pabean, Rp2-300 a meal.

from Ampenan: To Pemenang, Rp150 by bus or *bemo;* to Cakranegara, Rp25 by *bemo;* to Labuhan Lombok, Rp300 by bus. Catch a ferry from Lembar, 35 km south of Ampenan, to Bali's Pa-

lontar palm *(or fan-palm): A palm tree that can endure long dry periods and grows very slowly. This tree flowers twice a year, once at the beginning of the dry season and once at the beginning of the wet. It's only climbed in the dry because the trunk is too slippery otherwise. Once it produces a juice, it remains productive for 70-100 years, producing an average of 600 liters of juice a year. Besides palm juice (tuak) and syrup (gula air) for alcoholic drinks and sweetening, this palm also provides raw materials for making many everyday articles. Its large fan-shaped leaves are used in roofing, to make baskets, water buckets, sleeping mats, hats, footwear, musical instruments, bags, and cases for sirih. Leaf stalks 1-1½ m long are used to make fences and leaf stalk fibers are utilized to make harnesses and strings. Trunks are used for house and bridge building, horse stalls, cowsheds, pig sties.*

lontar literature: *Java has a rich literature mostly in the form of old legends inscribed on* lontar *(palm leaf) documents, themselves reaching small master-pieces of the engraver's art. These little books record old Indonesian myths, history, and the Hindu epics of Rama and Sita. They have been made out of this palm leaf for centuries, the text and illustrations engraved with a fine stylus and then darkened by rubbing the soot of burned palm-leaf spines into the groves. Then the individual palm leaves are cut into strips and sandwiched between pieces of ornamental wood. These inch wide 'books' fit neatly into narrow wooden boxes carved and decorated with animal heads or made completely in the shape of animals. Each box holds several books, a 'volume'. This whole procedure is still used by* lontar *copyists today. It's thought that the curlique appearance of many ancient Asian scripts came about because scribes were forced to inscribe straight lines on the ribbed surface of* lontar *palm strips so as not to split them.*

dangbai each day, Rp1200-1500. Buy your ticket at the harbor. Tickets for the Kuda Putih (a better boat(can be bought just past where they sell tickets for the Tiga Mas. Try for a student discount. **vicinity of Ampenan:** Along the coast are temples and holy places, but nothing spectacular. There's a nice beach outside of Ampenan; take your bicycle, walk or take a *bemo*, Rp50. Rent motorbikes for Rp1000-1250 per day; pushbikes are also available for rent. Ride around both towns of Ampenan and Mataram by pushbike. Get a lift up the Lombok mountains by *bemo* (Rp100 extra for the bicycle), then just coast back down. It's a fine motorbike trip too. **Batu Bolong:** 2 hours by pushbike from Ampenan. A temple sits on a cliff that juts out over a quiet beach. The 'Hollow Stone' temple is underneath. **Gunung Pengsong:** 7 km south of Mataram. Climb up to the monkey temple on a hill 1 km from the mountain; very quiet and a beautiful panorama looking over the towns below.

CAKRANEGARA

The shopping and market center of Lombok, a big dusty central street like Morocco. A wealthy city with many Chinese living here. Cakranegara is a busy crafts center, but not just to look at, these crafts are functional as well. Very well-known for its basketware, which is bought up by the Balinese and sold to the tourists on Bali at ridiculous prices. Unique fabrics and fantastic cheap *sarungs* woven with gold thread are for sale here but go to the workshops (try Slamet Riyadi) where they are actually made. You could also come across clay animal figurines and elegant ceramics. **stay and eat:** Not such an out of the way place to stay with 2 *losmens*, Rp1000-1250. Many good eating *warungs*. Try spicy-hot buffalo meat curries. **vicinity of Cakranegara:** Nearby is Balimurti where they produce weaving in the Purbasari-style.

from Cakranegara: Lying right on the main road, Cakra is a focal point for transportation to all over the island. Take buses, Colts, and *bemos* to: Mataram, Rp25; Ampenan, Rp25; Narmada, Rp25; Labuhan Lombok (on the east coast), Rp300; Praya, Rp100; Selong, Rp250; Sukaraja, Rp200 by bus. If heading for the east coast, it's better to get a bus straight through to Labuhan Lombok rather than stopping in Selong, a nasty place with a lot of thieves. Officially, it's said that thieves are killed, but in reality a boy can't marry until he's stolen something successfully. **for Sumbawa Island:** Stay in Cakranegara overnight (Labuhan Lombok hasn't much to recommend it) and get up to catch the 6 am *bemo* to Labuhan Lombok as the boat leaves from there at 9 am, costs Rp2000 (possible to get student price of Rp1500 if you buy ticket from the captain).

OTHER SIGHTS

Narmada: 10 km from Cakranegara, Rp25 by *bemo*. A restful 3-tiered swimming pool, a part of the old *raja's* kingdom where he used to make his selection from the village lovelies. Worth a couple of hours walking around and swimming. The lakeside park is surrounded by somewhat dilapidated, terraced, ornamental gardens. Don't need to take a picnic lunch as there's a *warung* inside the complex and plenty more in town. **Suranadi:** 7 km out of Narmada. Take a *bemo* from Cakranegara to Narmada, Rp25, then pick up another *bemo* for Suranadi for Rp50. A small temple and gardens are here. See the rebuilt ruined baths of kings carved in the Balinese style. Really cold water bubbling up. At the temple of the Holy Eels, eels will swim out of conduits if you drop an egg in the water for them to eat. Stay at flash Hotel Suranadi that has a swimming pool, Rp7000 a day. Sesaot forest is 3 km from Suranadi. There's an old Balinese temple at Lingsar, west of Suranadi or 4 km from Narmada, which combines Hindu and Islamic motifs.

Tetebatu: 50 km east of Mataram up in the mountains, about 4 km north of Kotaraja. From Cakranegara they drop you off on the turn-off to Kotaraja. Just wait for a *bemo* (quicker and cheaper than a *dokar*) to take you to Kotaraja. Then from Kotaraja it's Rp50-200 per person by *dokar* further on a rocky road straight up to Tetebatu. Or about a 2 hour nice easy walk going through some beautiful countryside. Exquisite ricefields. See Sumbawa. **stay:** Wisma Soejono in Tetebatu is an old colonial-style house run by a very civilized lawyer; Rp500 single or Rp750 double, with brass beds! Ice cold pools for swimming. They fix excellent home-cooked suppers (Dutch, Indo, or Javanese) for Rp2-300, laid out on the table in feudal splendor. They'll also give you food to take up the mountain with you. **from Tetebatu:** You can't actually reach the summit of Mt. Rinjani from here (there's no track) but take a walk up the thick screaming jungle full of black monkeys swinging from trees. Meet the mountain people on the way up, cutting heavy mahogony in the forest. They are really freaked out about meeting Europeans. Really spectacular forest views.

Mt. Rinjani: Tackle it only in the dry season because it's too dangerous to attempt it in the wet. This is the 2nd highest mountain in Indonesia, a rough but beautiful climb. For the Balinese it's a holy place on top. You're supposed to have a permit first from the police office in Mataram. **getting there:** It's best to approach Rinjani either from the north or from the east from Sapit. Catch bus first from Ampenan to Bayan, Rp400. Or get a truck leaving from Cakranegara just opposite the rice market at 11 am for Rp200 to Bayan. The road is terrible. Bayan is a traditional muslim village, quite isolated, with Hindu-style dances still practiced. Stay with the *kepala desa,* a greedy man who wants you to buy 2 kilos of rice from him for the journey. Or stay with the Swedish anthropologist in Bayan. From Bayan to Sembulun Lawang it's a one day walk. A really young (23 years) *kepala desa* and his vivacious wife live here. There are actually two 'Sembulans', 5 km apart, with 500 people living in each. Stay in Sembulan Lawang, not in Sembulan Bunbum. A fantastic valley, very cold. From Sembulan Lawang to Sapit it's a 5 hour walk. Or from Sembulan Lawang to the summit a 12 hour walk in all. It's so out of reach that no one lives on top of Gunung Rinjani. Just a high mountain lake there with conifers, wild nature, *babi hutan,* buffaloes, and deer.

Labuhan Lombok: A very strong Muslim town on the N.E. coast. For Rp300 a night there's a stinking rip-off *losmen* here, the Sudimampir. Not much to entertain yourself with in this town, but some of the finest blankets are produced in the vicinity. In the evenings a few *warungs* open up around the bus station. Sleep the night on a *warung* bench; the owner and his wife live under the table. **from Labuhan Lombok:** To Ampenan by bus, Rp300. If you're headed for Sumbawa Besar on Sumbawa Island, it's better to stay overnight on your last night in Cakranegara rather than in Labuhan Lombok. Then catch a *bemo* real early from Cakranegara so you can reach the 9 am boat from Labu-

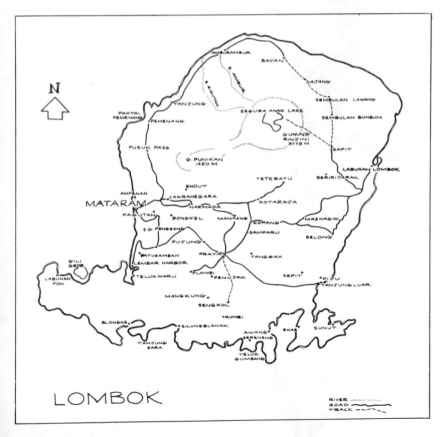

LOMBOK

RIVER ~~~~
ROAD ━━━
TRACK ━━━

han Lombok over to Alas on Sumbawa, taking 3 hours. From Alas take a *bemo*, Rp400, 3 hours, to Sumbawa Besar. **for Mt. Rinjani:** Take a *bemo* from Labuhan Lombok a few km, then walk the rest of the way to Sapit. From Sapit, it's a one day hike to reach the top. Sapit is the best place from which to go around the mountain, where you can join up with the road that goes across the island below the mountain.

The Wallace Line: Because of melting ice caps about 120 million years ago, Bali and Lombok separated. The channel between these two islands marks the so-called 'Wallace Line', named after the great naturalist Sir Alfred Wallace. Sir Alfred ob-

served, after 7 years of zoological and botanical research, that on all the island west of Lombok you find tropical vegetation, monkeys, elephants, Bengal Tigers, wild cattle, and straight-haired Asiatics, while on the islands east of Bali are thorny arid plants, cockatoos, parrots, giant lizards, marsupials, frizzy-haired Papuans, all typical of Australasia. The more advanced placental animals and flora which were beginning to evolve at that time in Asia proper were prevented entery over this turbulant 300 m deep strait. Thus, zoological Model T-Fords such as kangaroos and echidnas were allowed to proliferate on the islands east of Bali because of the absence of flesh-eating mammal predators.

the drongo

for ornithologists: *In preparation for Indonesia's diverse birdlife, visit first Singapore's Bird Park in Jurong (bus 209 from South Bridge Road). You need one day; this bird park is one of the best in the world with its great 2½ hectare cages. Get acquainted with species, what they sound like, etc. There are Argus pheasants, Birds of Paradise, hornbills, 3 species of Crown Pigeons breeding.*

SUMATRA

INTRODUCTION

An island 1760 km in length and up to 400 km wide, it covers 25% of the total Indonesian land area. With its grass huts, lake tribes, steamy jungles, swift clear rivers, spectacular waterfalls and immense forests full of tropical trees 60 m high, Sumatra is like the Africa of Southeast Asia. Here live some of the most ancient cultures of Indonesia. The traditional architecture of Sumatra is magnificent: large rectangular buildings on wooden pilings 1-2 m off the ground have saddle-shaped roofs with high gables at both ends which rise to a point and are adorned with buffalo horns and carvings. Called the Isle of Hope or the Isle of Gold, Sumatra's natural wealth is fabulous. It's the mainstay of the Indonesian economy supplying the total output of tin, most of its petroleum, as well as coal, bauxite and gold. Essentially it's a mercantile island; it's oil accounts for nearly 40% of the Indonesian government revenue. 30% of Indonesian exports — oil, rubber, palm oil, tea, sisal, and tobacco — are from North Sumatra alone. Sumatra has only 9% of Indonesian industry, but in a very unindustrialized country as Indonesia, 9% doesn't mean much. You can imagine how unpolluted an island it is. Underpopulated with only 21 million people on the 5th largest island in the world, only 18% of the people live in the towns. Sumatra has about 25-30 persons per sq km while Java has over 1200 per sq km. On Java you see people everywhere you look, but on this island you can often travel for 20 km or more without seeing anyone. You'll feel a vast difference between Sumatra and neighboring Java. With its cash crops and mineral wealth, people are better off in Sumatra; meals laid before you are enormous. There are trees, wooden houses, green grass, space — a grand beauty. It's far wilder and more rugged, harder to get around; people are shorter, darker, and more wirey, a jungle people. Islam entered some coastal regions of Sumatra more than 300 years before it ever reached Java. On Sumatra they take the fasting month seriously and their mosques are built more in the Indian Islamic style. Rather than the fedualistic rule and the caste system of Java, on Sumatra free election by local chiefs has been traditional. Although it's one of the richest culture areas of S.E. Asia with a great diversity of tribes (puak) and numerous matriarchal societies, on this gigantic island there are only 4 museums.

getting there from Singapore: Check out the cheap travel agents for flights to Jakarta, about S$160 student; then from Jakarta take the train with through connections on the ferry across the Sunda Strait, then straight up to Palembang, South Sumatra. Or take the Pelni boat from Jakarta, Rp10,000 deck, to Padang, West Sumatra. Another way from Singapore is take a launch (S$40) 4 hours to Tanjung Pinang Island. From this small island board a boat to Pekanbaru, East Sumatra, for around Rp3600. From Pekanbaru, it's only 6-8 hours by bus to Bukittinggi, West Sumatra. From Tg. Pinang you can also board the Pelni ship on Wed. for Medan, North Sumatra; costs about Rp13,000. **from Malaysia:** Many prefer to enter Sumatra from the north at Medan so that they can travel the island lengthwise, continue on to Java and Bali, and exit finally out of Jakarta to Singapore; this itinerary fits nicely into the usual 3 month allotted visa. Penang is S$24-27 (S$2.46 = US$1) from Singapore on the train. In Penang, stay at Pin Seng Hotel, 82 Love Lane, M$7.35 (M$2.48

= US$1) single; an OK place. Or at the New Asia Hotel at 110 Rope Walk; double rooms, M$10.50, a real palace and more central, only 2 minutes walk to the Prangin Road Bus Station. The best cheapie in Telok Bahang is Miss Low's, M$1.50 per head, but clear out by the first Sat. of every month when immigration officials sweep using SS police tactics at 1 am, stamping S.H.I.T. (Suspected Hippy in Transit) in your passport, giving you 72 hours to get out of the country. From the Prangin Road Bus Station in Penang, take Bus 66 out to the airport for M65¢. Each day either a Merpati or MAS flight departs Penang at 8:55 am, takes 20 minutes to Medan, costs 14,500 (US$36) plus M$5 airport tax. Perentis Lines, 165 Victoria St., Penang, has a boat across for Rp8000, but is less reliable; takes 1 night. There are also charcoal boats from Melaka to Dumai, East Sumatra, for around M$30; takes 1 day.

the land: Almost ⅓ of Sumatra is continuous swamp extending some 1370 km down the whole east coast. There's an unbroken mountain wall ranging in altitude from 1575 m to 3700 m stretching along the entire west coast, Bukit Barisan (Parada of Mountains), including 93 volcanic peaks, 12 of them still active. On the western side of this range mountains plunge right into the sea. There's a chain of islands off the west coast, most with rocky reef-enclosed coasts, where the old *ladang* system of cultivation of taros and yams is still practiced. Most of the inhabitants on these islands of Nias, Mentawai and Enggano have been bypassed by the mainstreams of the 20th Century.

flora: In its rainforests are trees, such as the *ketapang*, which are over 60 m high supported on 6 m tall buttress roots. Vines called 'wait-a-minute' are tipped with spines and snare at people using jungle tracks. Strangler figs send long tendril roots to the ground from branches of tall trees; as the tree grows, it gradually suffocates its host tree. The Corpse Plant, a huge foul plant that smells like putrefying animal flesh, consists of a central spike over 2 m high which rises from a bowl of giant leaves. Its stench attracts beetles and other insects which help it pollinate. The *reflesia*, the biggest flower in the world, grows up to 1 m in diameter. Found on the west coast, this fascinating plant rises from the fungus-like leaf-littered forest floor. A bud develops which grows and reaches the size of a large cabbage, brown in color. Nine months later the flower opens, spreading out brilliant white-spotted orange petals. Finally it rots to a spongy mess on the mossy, damp ground, its large sticky seeds are carried to new soil by animals that eat or brush against them.

fauna: Sumatra has always been famous for its animals. Besides tigers, rhinos, and wild oxen, there are orangutans, many species of apes, tapirs, wild dogs and pigs, sun bears, flying foxes, the rare goat antelope, the Sumatran Hare, Sumatran leopards, and civet cats. In its mangrove swamps are found the flying lemur (culogos) and the Proboscis monkey. Other unique animals of Sumatra are the Black Baboon (cynocephalus niger), the fox-nosed monkey (taraius), and the Slow Lori (nycticebus). There's a difference between fauna

Black
Baboon

of the north and that of the south; the orangutans, rhino, wild pigs are only found in the north, while the tapir and certain species of monkeys are found only in the south. Birdlife includes dazzling parrots and cockatoos, hornbills, the Great Argus Pheasant and the Crested Partridge, the Rose Crested Bee-eater, woodpeckers, and pigeons. There are 900 elephants left, moving in herds of 20-30.

history: Sumatra was sending gifts to China as early as 441 A.D. By the 7th Century, it was the most important island in the archipelago and the cultural heart of S.E. Asia. Two sea-going piratical mercantile empires were based at present-day Jambi and at Palembang. The Sriwijaya Kingdom was an 11th Century Buddhist offshoot of the Hindu Sailendra cult of *devaraj* (God Kings). Guarding one of the main waterways of the ancient world the (Straits of Melaka), this kingdom at its height controlled an area which included Sumatra, the western end of Java, the east coast of Malaya, extending their commercial and political influence as far as Formosa and Hainan. A Sriwijaya prince even became ruler of Cambodia. In the 13th Century, the empire finally broke up into city states, mainly on coasts and mouths of rivers. The Sriwijaya was much more concerned with its control over the Straits of Melaka and international trade rather than in controlling the interior. Thus no great monument complexes were produced as are found on Java, and what few temples and stupas that exist are in such a state of ruin that they don't grab you like the ones on Java. Accounts of Indonesia's first Muslim community, Perlak, were brought back to Europe by Marco Polo who visited the northern tip of Sumatra in the 13th Century. He also recorded that Sumatra was 'Java the Less' though it is 3 times larger than Java.

music and dance: Sumatra's heavier Islamic influence is reflected in their musical instruments: a primitive type of oboe, *serunai*, is almost identical to the Persian original, the *surnai*. A type of drum, *rebana* (like a tamborine) found here is also popular in other Islamic areas of the world. Each region of Sumatra has its own choreography and dance forms, performing primarily dances of the feet. Sumatran dancers are known for their *gaya* (grace), very smooth, soft, willowy movements. Candle-dances (*tari lilin* or *tari piring*) are danced all over the island. Girls with tassled caps carry lighted candles affixed to saucers. As the dancer dips and rises, their open palms describe in space semi-circles and figure eights. Music is accented by the clicks of rings against the bottom edge of the plates which are turned over and under very quickly,

though the flame never quite goes out. When *tari lilin* is over, the girl blows the candle out and silently leaves. In the Handkerchief Dance, men and women hold one end of a large white square of cloth. They do a kind of maypole dance, winding in and out and turning around, tying the handkerchiefs in a series of knots. At the conclusion, they can untangle it immediately and faultlessly. Sometimes they let it drop on the floor and pick it up with their teeth. They say there's a different dance for every one of Sumatra's 100 districts and as many dancers as it has single girls. When a woman dances at her wedding ceremony it's for the last time.

TRANSPORT IN SUMATRA

The chief interest of Sumatra is the journey through it. Don't be put off by tales you hear of the Jambi-Palembang run, the country in between more than makes up for the suffering. One of the last true adventures, you could travel on a bus with gunny-sacked pigs, casks of coconut wine, and occupied coffins resting on the shoulders of relatives. warning: Beware of men who come up asking to share a smoke with you, then when you turn them on claim they are cops and demand a pay off or else they'll turn you in. Also, if you're holding, beware of searches on your way back from Aceh Province into North Sumatra Province.

climate: The equator cuts this island in two equal halves. Heaviest rains north of the equator are Oct.-April and the dry season is May-September. South of the equator the rainy season is Dec.-Feb., making the southern roads impassable (they're bad to begin with). Best time to travel is September and October; the rains have started, but not heavily so that the roads are still good and, unlike in the dry season, there's no dust.

bus travel: Beware of pickpockets who are thick on the buses of Sumatra. Indonesians' sense of garishness is reflected in their multi-colored Chevrolet 'chicken-catcher' private buses which are often painted bright colors to make them distinctive. They often have names such as *Guntur* (thunderbolt) and *Kilat* (lightening), thus *Bis Malam Kilat* is Lightening Night Bus. If you take local buses they pick up all the locals even if the bus is already full. If you take the Mercedes buses, they don't pick up many extra passengers and they have better suspension (also cost Rp1-500 more). You can cross Sumatra lengthwise in the dry season in 5 or 6 days if you meet all your connections. If you don't want to rupture you spleen, however, 2 weeks should be allowed. In the wet season it might take you a solid month. There could be many lengthly delays during the rainy season when river levels at ferry crossings are swollen too high for the vehicle to board the unweildy rope-bound wooden rafts which are used as ferries, hauled across the river along a steel hawser slung between the two banks. If bridges are out in South Sumatra you can often catch the next barge downriver, a memorable journey, to a town where you can wait more comfortably for another bus. Swim in the rivers while waiting (up to 3 days) for your bus to cross. Try A.N.S. bus company, about the most reliable, but their seats are built for bigger asses. Next best is A.L.S. For less wear and tear on your big ass, it's imperative that you get a seat *in front* of the back axle of the bus. Also your luggage is safe from theft up front where the whole bus can keep an eye on it. Sometimes a rope is strung out in front of you to lean on for relief or to sleep on, if you can. On a Sumatran bus you'll have a guaranteed breakdown at least once, a comic repair show, and endless Indonesian music played right over your head at full distorted volume. You're bogged in mud, driven over log-strewn cow paddocks, your head crashed against the ceiling (if you're over 5 ft. tall), your ass resting on spikes. Like being inside a cement mixer, you spend more time airborne than on the seat. Bus sickness is rampant and companies thoughtfully dispense plastic bags. A stoker usually rides with the driver to do running repairs, errands, and to collect fares. The driver eats 5 times a day at Padang-style restaurants along the way and there are untold stops for drinks. On some North Suma-

tran runs, the drivers even race each other with passengers as unwilling spectators. If you're coming up from the south by bus, break the ride up and take 1-2 day rests. This way you can appreciate South Sumatra and enjoy your trip more and not have it associated only with pain. The first leg would be Tanjungkarang to Palembang, then from Palembang to Padang, then from Padang to Lake Toba or Medan. Book immediately on your bus out as soon as you get in a town. Always ask the local people or other travelers what the true fare is before buying your ticket. On long bus journeys you could pay as much as Rp1000 over the usual fare.

trains: Trains run in South Sumatra between Tanjungkarang, Palembang, and Lubuklinggau in North Sumatra between Medan and Aceh; and in West Sumatra between Padang and Bukittinggi. Don't reserve train seats on a train that's going to arrive because the seats are already full and people won't move. Only reserve seats on a train which is beginning from the station you're in. **flights:** Caltex runs charter flights out of their oilfields in South Sumatra and you could get a free ride such as from Jambi to Tanjung Pinang (Riau) or from Jambi to Jakarta. Mobil Oil Co. works most of North Sumatra and they have the same thing going. Sometimes Indonesian air controllers will ask for money to get on one of them or charge you before they'll tell you about them. But it really could be free.

Sumatran death mask

SOUTH SUMATRA
(SUMATERA SELATAN)

There are many high plateaus, rift valleys, interior basins and ranges, and also more volcanoes in the southern half of the island (west coast) than in the northern half. The highest peak is Mt. Kerinci (3800 m). The Batanghari, the longest river in Sumatra, starts at Mt. Kerinci and runs through the Jambi Plains and the town of Jambi itself. A belt of coastal marshes runs down the whole southeastern coast. The 'Green Deserts' of South Sumatra are up to 250 km wide, some of the largest swamps in the world and as extensive as the infamous Sudanese Sudd. Some of Indonesia's biggest oilfields are located in South Sumatra around Palembang Province. This is also elephant country. When crossing a river in this region, be sure to address a crocodile as 'grandmother' and call a tiger 'grandfather'. Tigers' claws are a powerful good luck charm and their whiskers grated in alcohol will make a man as strong as 10 men. Antarruang Tours and Travel, Jl. Tanah Abang Dua 53, Jakarta Pusat, offers 15-day tiger-hunting safaris in South Sumatra (staff included) at rates from only Rp2-6,000,000 plus 5% commission for a minimum of 6 persons.

people: The population of this province is 4 million, the so-called Rejang Complex of peoples, a blending of Javanese, Malay and Minangkabu races and cultures. Houses along rivers and in jungles in Southern and Eastern Sumatra are pole cottages with ladders (tigers can't climb ladders) situated on hilltops surrounded by hens, skinny dogs, banana trees, children, and mud. If someone does something for you, he often asks for *uang rokok* (cigarette money). Not much to eat here but *pisang goreng* (fried bananas). Camp guys can expect to make a lot of friends in South Sumatra, especially in places with extreme shortages of women combined with Islamic code like the jungle oil towns and camps in between. Purely for love and lust; no money exchanged.

Telukbetung: The ferry from Java comes in at Panjang. If you get stuck in Panjang, stay at Losmen Kastari, Rp500 single. In Telukbetung, stay: Hotel Kenanga, Jl. Kenanga 5, is very good but costs nearly Rp5000, or Rp6300 double. Try also Hotels Kesuma and Kencana. The Shintana, Jl. Selat Berhala 95, has 15 rooms at Rp2500 including breakfast. **vicinity of Telukbetung:** Hire a boat (they want as much as Rp30,000) to view remains of the stupendous volcano Krakatoa which blew in 1883 and killed 36,000 people, darkening the sky for months.

Tanjungkarang: A few km north of Telukbetung, this town is the starting point for the journey north. There's a direct bus service from Tanjungkarang all the way to the northern Sumatran city of Medan (Rp9000) in 4 days and 4 nights, but only for masochists and fugitives. **to Bukittinggi and Padang:** Buses usually leave 2-3 pm for Bukittinggi and Padang. The fare varies, some days it's Rp4000, some days Rp4500; depends on the demand. Bus takes 24-36 hours, about 680 km to Bukittinggi: the first 390 km is over a reasonable dirt road (only about 50 km is really bad), then 290 km on the Trans-Sumatran Highway, the best sealed road in Indonesia. Get front seat of bus. Sometimes the bridge is out in Lukuklinggau, then you might have to change buses. **for Jambi:** In Tanjungkarang, they'll tell you that it's going to be a magical 24 hour trip on the A.L.S. or Sari 'Express' to Jambi, but it's more like a 48 hour trip. There is no such thing as an 'express' bus service in Indonesia.

from Tanjungkarang by train: The train departs after the ferry arrives. From Tanjungkarang to Palembang, Rp1300, 10 hours of green trees, leaping monkeys, lazy flowing rivers. When the train stops, it fills suddenly with humid jungle-laden air. From Tanjungkarang to Perabumulih by the morning train is only Rp750 with student card, arriving around 5 pm. Either continue on to Palembang, arriving 1 hour later, or if you don't want to visit Palembang only pay to Perabumulih and wait for the train which comes back from Palembang at 10 pm. Board the train again and ride it until 5 am when it arrives at Lubuklinggau. If you're still not totally whacked, there could be a place on buses leaving from Lubuklinggau at 7 am for Bukittinggi, or to Padang for Rp3500. Or go from Lubuklinggau by bus to Bengkulu Rp400 (4 hours, one change), then from Bengkulu take a boat or bus up to Padang.

Perabumulih: The night train from Tanjungkarang to Perabumulih with a student discount costs Rp2250. There are great showers in this small midway transit town for Rp25, and the cheapest and best meals in the dozen or so restaurants in the village. This is a pineapple growing area so you get as many as 10 for Rp100. Sederhana Losmen is only Rp400. There are many *losmens* but don't pay more than Rp400. **from Perabumulih:** The 3rd class train is Rp450 with a student's card from Perabumulih to Lubuklinggau, leaving at 10 am or after, and arrives about 11 hours later; the seats are horrible.

Lubuklinggau: Take the morning train, Rp1350, from Tanjungkarang all the way to Lubuklinggau, really slow, all day long. There are many *losmens* in Lubuklinggau; most cost Rp750 double. Hotel Indonesia is a dirty place and they don't have single rooms. Losmen Subur, near the RR Station on th^ main street, Rp400, is quite alright. *Nasi padan*ͅ and *sate* places are everywhere. **from Lubuklinggau:** There are no buses actually starting from Lubuklinggau to Bukittinggi or to Padang. Buses to Bukittinggi and Padang start from Tanjungkarang and pass through Lubuklinggau to collect extra passengers so you may have to put up with a bad seat. The fare to Bukittinggi is Rp3500 on the A.N.S. regular bus. By train to Palembang, Rp1200. Buy a ticket for the meal car, Rp350 and worth the price. It's the least crowded; stay there for the whole trip.

the Kubu People: Remnants of a 5 ft. tall race of nomadic negrito peoples, the Kubus live in small bands of 20-30 along the swamps and dense jungles of the eastern coast of South Sumatra and in Central Sumatra. A pure branch of the first inhabitants of the archipelago who began to migrate in about 3000 B.C., the Kubus even preceed the Bataks of North Sumatra and the Torajas of Celebes. So primitive that they learned of the bow and arrow from later migrations of peoples, the Kubus are quite distinct from the Mongoloid race. This tribe doesn't practice agriculture nor do their children enter the school system. They use spears and stones in their search for food. To meet them, trek into the jungle and wait patiently in small villages where they come to trade. Or see these naked aboriginals come out from the forest and stop the bus between Jambi and Palembang and beg for money and food. They are considered savages by the present local inhabitants of these areas.

Muntok: A small town on the west coast of Bangka Island, lying off the southeast coast of Sumatra. Mostly Chinese inhabitants. This island, along with Belitung and Singkep (in the Lingga Archipelago), together produce 100% of Indonesia's total tin output and supply 8% of the world's tin market from deposits of unusually high metal content. **getting there:** Reach Muntok on the overnight riverboat from Palembang, Rp2500. The Pelni boat from Jakarta stops a couple of hours at Muntok on its way to Tanjung Pinang and Medan; costs Rp11,500 from Jakarta to Muntok. It works out to about Rp18,500 to reach Singapore by taking boats from Palembang-Muntok-Tanjung Pinang-Singapore; might as well fly from Palembang to Tanjung Pinang with Garuda for Rp13,000, then on to Singapore by launch for Rp4200. **stay and eat:** Losmen Muntok is recommended,

Rp300, really clean, private rooms, mosquito nets. Losmen Jakarta is also Rp300. Hotel Muntok is the same price but pretty decrepit. There's *lontong* made from coconut milk, but *mie* is predominant. Fruit's cheap. **vicinity of Muntok:** Walk to the lighthouse 45 minutes along the beach; several wrecked ships, some 30 m long. Nice beach beyond the lighthouse; dead calm. Very picturesque around the central part of the southern coastline but quite expensive to get around the island by boat or jeep.

LAMPUNG PROVINCE

The 500,000 Lampungese call themselves Orang Pablan. Prior to Islam they practiced a syncretic Buddhist Hindu ancestor cult. The Lampungese have always had close contact with the Banten culture of West Java and took the Islamic faith early. Since 1932 when the Dutch started *transmigrasi* schemes here in order to cut down on Java's overpopulation, modern Javanese agricultural pioneers have settled in these areas by the tens of thousands. In this province you find *sawah* very similar to Java's and in many areas where the Javanese have settled, the same overpopulation and work-sharing problems as in a typical village on Java have arisen, but without the corresponding high fertility of soils, efficient drainage and water control as is found on Java. In North Lampung, 10% of the population are Javanese transmigrants, in South Lampung 60%, while in Central Lampung, 75%. These Javanese have of course brought their *gamelan* and *wayang* with them. **archaeological remains:** Often these are far from the main roads. Stone inscriptions are found at Palas, South Lampung; Talangpadang (south-center); Liwa (north-east). Megalithic sculpture at Batu Badad and Bojong. Hindu stone sculpture at Gunung Sugih Besar. At Kenali (northwest) there's a menhir. A slender Bodhisattva is still *in loco* at Pugung Raharjo, Central Lampung.

Lampung fabrics: Two types of cloth are widespread in this district. The *tampan,* found especially in the Kroe Region, is made by the floating weft technique with brown and blue designs. This fabric covers dishes, gifts, and sacrificed offerings during festivities. *Tapis sarungs,* made by women for ritual occasions, have ancient simple and complex designs of human, land and water animals. But the principal motif is the Ship of the Dead. This so-called ship-cloth survives from an earlier culture, people who believed that the souls of the dead journeyed to the land of souls by ship. Big pieces of ship-cloth are used in circumcision ceremonies and weddings; for important conferences they are hung up on the wall to spread good vibes.

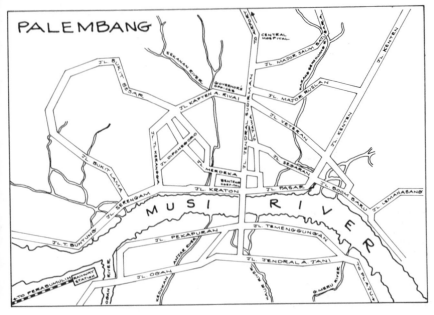

PALEMBANG

The main market and oil export center of South Sumatra located on both sides of the Musi River 200 km upstream from the sea. After Medan, Palembang is the 2nd most populous city of Sumatra, population 600,000. Its neon strip is not that interesting. Strong Muslim. Could get very sticky and hot. Much of the city is built on piles over the water and tidal mudflats. Floating houses are moored along the bank with river traders paddling about, shops line the waterfront like a shopping and promenade street. This area is known for forest products, oil wells, tin mines, rubber and coffee plantations. See the oil refineries at night down the Musi all lit up like a space city. 40% of the total Indonesian government revenue comes from this oil province alone. The monstrous Sungei Gerong Refinery has a daily capacity of 75,000 barrels; also a huge US$200 million petrochemical complex at Plaju. Pertamina has built a large sports stadium here and also given the city a town clock, a handsome minaret for its mosque, and a TV station. **getting there:** All roads, rivers, and railways in South Sumatra end up eventually in Palembang. Ships up to 10,000 tons can voyage this far upriver. The daily slow express train from Telukbetung departs around 8 am, arrives at 4 or 5 pm; elephants have the right of way.

Take the bus from Padang to Palembang for around Rp4-5000. To fly from Jakarta, Rp17,000.

history: This city was born on pepper, raised on tin, grew rich on oil. By tradition an old oriental trading center, for 500 years up to the 13th Century Palembang was one of the principal ports of the world, a central point for the bulk of the Indonesian islands' trade. In the first quarter of the 7th Century here was the first tangible signs in the whole archipelago of the arrival of Mahayana Buddhism (a full 100 years later it shows up in the inscriptions of Candi Kalasan in Central Java). On his way to India a Chinese-Buddhist pilgrim, I Tsing, arrived at Sriwijaya University in 671 A.D. and spent 6 months studying Sanskrit. On his way back to China in 685 A.D. he stayed 4 years, writing his memoirs and giving a valuable description of the city. As a predatory power, Palembang was once the capital of the Sriwijaya Empire (7th-12th C.), 'The Phoenicians of the East'. Tamil, Persian, Arabic, Greek, Cambodian, Siamese, Chinese and Burmese were spoken in its giant marketplace. A thousand ships laid at anchor and it sent its mercenaries as far as Mesopotamia. It had a huge money bazaar. Thousands of scholars and monks learned Buddhist teachings and translated Sanskrit texts here. It reached its zenith at the beginning of the 11th Century. Then in

1028 A.D. it was brutally attacked by a jealous Chola king from South India and it never recovered. By the end of the 13th Century Sriwijaya had splintered into 8 smaller kingdoms, the largest of which, Malayu, was centered on Jambi and became a strong maritime power. Finally, with the rise of Melaka in the 14th Century, Sriwijaya became a remote backwater. There are few physical remains of the kingdom. The region around Palembang still produces fine woven fabrics and performs unique Hindu-like dances, though these are a sad remnant of its past great days. South Sumatran dancers wear elaborate tree-like headdresses with glittering pendants and festoons, or crowns, and carry gold gilt fans. Wedding costumes are still patterned after the royal courts of the old medieval empire with a flap on the groom's headdress preventing him from looking at the bride.

stay and eat: Cheap *losmens* are down by the river. Hotel Segaran, Rp800 double. Peng. Aman, Jl. Lematang, Rp900 for rooms with twin beds and private *mandi*. Hotel Sukabumi, Jl. Sajangan, Rp500. Hotel Malaysia, Rp1100. Hotel Asiana, alright. Hotel Sumatra, Jl. Major Ruslan, is definitely the worst hotel in Sumatra. Peng. Riau, Rp1100 double, quiet. The government-owned Swarna Dwipa, Jl. Tasik 2, just off Jl. Merdeka, has rooms Rp2600-8600, including breakfast. Hotel Sintera, Jl. Jen. Sudirman 30-38 is central but noisy, Rp2700 for quite small rooms, Rp4000 doubles. Eat at Hotel Sanjaya, Jl. Kapten A. Rivai, which has better food than the Swarna Dwipa. Jl. Jen Sudirman has many small good restaurants **miscellaneous:** Palembang's red light area is Kampung Baru, an amazing place Rp100 by *oplet*. Single males will be caressed and solicited and have kisses constantly thrown at them by homosexuals if they go out walking alone at night in Palembang. Sometimes you won't be required to pay at restaurants because you are 'a beautiful boy'. There are even stories of travelers rejecting advances (masturbating in front of them), and then being stoned. Could be quite heavy.

sights: See the Sultan's graveyard. Historical relics in Limas House. Palembang's crowded original Chinese quarter, Pasar Illir, down on the river, is 2 km of funky market selling anything and everything. Also visit smaller Pasar Kuto. See the old *benteng* built in 1780 with its tall withewashed walls, now occupied by the army (invariably the army occupies historic forts in Indonesia). **Rumah Bari:** A small but important museum with the 'largest and the best of the sculptures from Pasemah, a plateau near Lahat which contains some of the most important megalithic statuary in S.E. Asia. On the front lawn is a stone elephant, a stone

Buddah, and about 5 other sculptures. The first building of the museum contains ethnography and archaeology!: stone implements from the Mesolithic period (15,000-3000 B.C.), ancient spears, daggers, old native guns, wooden sculptures from Kayuagung, a headless statue from Candi Gedung, house lamps, weaving models, Chinese blue and white porcelain, royal oars, bright gilt and red Palembang chests, fish traps, basketry. Bring a flashlight because the lighting is atrocious. The building in back houses the Natural History Muesum: a stuffed tiger, iquana, Malayan black bear, Slow Loris, many birds such as the *elang laut* (white-bellied sea eagle), Great Argus Pheasant, *ular sawah* (ricefield snake). **Gending Sriwijaya:** This dance is the only remains of the 7th Century kingdom, a welcome dance which traditionally greets V.I.P.'s arriving in the city. Elaborate headdresses are worn with slivers and spears of gold and draped in thick multi-colored brocades. Fingertips have long arching gold fingernails from which trinkets dangle. Seven girls ('princesses') kneel before the guest, never looking him in the face. At the end they offer him betelnut.

from Palembang: If you take a bus to Padang, there's up to 5 river crossings, you are tortured by raucous local music for 48 hours with your knees rammed up your throat and kids spewing in your lap. Merpati flights to: Padang, once weekly, Rp15,000; Jambi, 5 weekly, Rp7000; Jakarta, Rp17,000. There are also Garuda flights from Palembang to the small island of Tg. Pinang, Rp13,000, from where you can catch a launch further to Singapore for Rp4200. **for Singapore, Jakarta, Medan:** Some cattle boats to Singapore take passengers, but you almost sleep with the cattle and their flies. Quite a cheap fare though. Takes a long time to get out of the Musi River, the delta of which is 380 km wide. Or catch a riverboat, about 4-5 times a week, overnight down Palembang's ancient highway to the sea to Muntok, Rp2500. Then take the Pelni boat on Tues. up to Tg. Pinang for Rp11,800. This 4 hour trip from Muntok to Tg. Pinang is the most expensive boat fare in Indonesia for the distance, it actually costs *less* to travel all the way up to Medan. (There are also less regular cheaper boats.) On Sat., the same Pelni boat returns from Medan and stops in Tg. Pinang on its way back to Jakarta. **trains for Jakarta:** Take a *bemo*, Rp50, across the bridge over the river to the Kertapi Train Station in Palembang. There's a daily train from there to Panjang. From Panjang take a ferry across the Sunda Strait to Merak on the Java side and then on to Jakarta for around Rp1200-2000 (depending on the train). The ferry takes 4-5 hours, Rp600. **for Jambi:** The bus to Jambi from Palembang costs at least

Rp3000, takes 36 hours. You pass through a flat ghostly country full of oil derricks and dry tufted grass or rolling meadows of yellow flowers and swamps, and more swamps. An alternative is to ask around the river pier for a barge via Banjunglincir to Jambi. Two days through dense riverine jungles with fireflies, flying foxes and lemurs, exotic birds, crocodiles, plenty of monkeys; an Amazon-like, untraveled region. Hazy departure schedules, Rp2-2500. From Banjunglincir you can also go by river to Nyogan through heavy jungles, then take the track from Nyogan to Palembang. This same route is possible from Jambi.

vicinity of Palembang: From the shore of the Musi River, hire a *sampan* for Rp50 to cross over to

the other side. At the small town of Kayuagung on the banks of the Komering River pottery is made in the Kedaton quarter across the river from the Mangunjaya residential district. A big pot fired in the open air under a kiln of brushwood costs Rp50. Also traditional style gilt and red cabinets and chests are still made here. **Pagaralam:** Take the train first to Lahat, then take the local bus to Pagaralam, a mountain village as high as Bukittinggi. Lots of *ganja* grows wild. Also found are halucinegenic fruits of South Sumatra such as the *kepayang* which is like smoking *ganja* ('you fly, you fly') and the plant *kadui*. Fermented *durian* eaten here acts as a dramatic aprodisiac. Gunung Dempo, on which this town sits, erupted in September 1976 and killed 8 people.

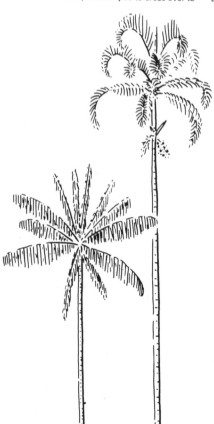

*Arecoid palm
(or arenga or sugar-palm)*

betelnut *(sirih):* The meat of the Areca nut. All classes indulge in betelnut-chewing but the older the person, the more they like their betelnut as these scarlet seeds are mildly narcotic. Even the toothless enjoy a crushed form of sirih. To chew betelnut, a piece of the green nut is dabbed with a little lime, wrapped in pepper leaves, and then chewed together with a wad of tobacco; all of this is stuffed under the lower lip. These ingredients are kept in a special box or in a woven pandanus palm. The combination of betelnut and lime makes you salivate and spit crimson splotches; royalty has a golden spitton, peddlers use the street. The wad (or 'nut') is supposed to strengthen the teeth but it stains them red after years of chewing. In fact, the aristocracy used to deliberately cover their stained teeth with black varnish. Chewing sirih is very symbolic and ritualistic, a sign that one is acting or speaking truthfully and in humility according to the norms and values of civilized society. Families use it when discussing possible marriages between their children, or it's used by a headman and two quarreling farmers when trying to resolve an issue. If brought out in front of guests in a home, it's a sign of welcome.

JAMBI

Population about 160,000. Very mixed ethnic complex — Minangkabaus, Chinese, Sundanese, Javanese, Bataks, Arabs, Indians, Pakistanis, Japanese, Malaysians, Kubus. The East Sumatran region has always been known as a boiling pot because of so many ethnic differences resulting from lying on one of the main water channels of Asia and the world. You can feel the jungle press in on you from all sides in this city; tigers sometimes come into town and carry people away (over 40 people have been devoured by tigers in South Sumatra Province in the last 2 years) Very heavy rainfall. Get extension at *imigrasi*, down near the harbor. Walk along the waterfront of the wide Batanghari; take a narrow *sampan* across the river to visit the fanatic Muslim village of Olak Kemang. See the Sriwijaya and the local 'maypole' dance when colored ribbons are wound together by dancers who then untangle them perfectly; sometimes dances are held at the Gedung Nasional. **stay:** Hotels average Rp1500. Hotel Mustika, Rp1100, is 2 km from the bus terminal; small rooms but big beds. Single people may stay for free in Jambi at Ibu Waga's, Pago Lebar, Jl. Palembang. **vicinity of Jambi:** Many untouched aboriginal societies around this area such as the Sarolangun in the Bangko, Tanjab, Bungo or Batanghari Districts; separate tribes numbering in all about 9000. In the isolated village of Bukit Tembesu (a rubber-growing area), a nomadic group of the Batin Lima aboriginals have been given government housing.

from Jambi by boat: Catch a riverboat up the Batanghari (the longest river in Sumatra) all the way to Sungaidareh; except to spend Rp2-3000 for this slow hot trip. Down on the river front you can also find boats to Jakarta, Singapore, and Banten. **hitching:** From Jambi to Palembang the going is slow. Mostly oil tankers travel this route and you get only 40-50 km along the jungle road when you're forced to flag down a taxi-bus. **by bus:** Daily buses to Palembang cost Rp2500-3000 inclusive of river ferries. Sometimes you get out and walk up to 12 km while the bus is pulled by winches, or you help repair bridge planking so that the bus can cross. Sometimes see tigers shitting in headlight beams then scurrying off into the jungle. See bridges bombed out by the Japanese and barefoot men carrying engines on poles like dead animals. **for Lake Kerinci:** Take bus first to Bangko (Rp 1000), then by jeep across the mountainous jungles of South-central Sumatra for 2 days to Sungaipenuh for Rp1800-2000. **flights:** Merpati flights to Palembang, Rp7000. Also fly to Singapore for

around Rp30,000. For free flights the best thing is to get up in the control tower and talk to the planes coming in to see if you can get a ride when they leave. The guys working there don't mind. If you get a ride with Pertamina (Pelita Airlines) be sure to bargain; they may offer a seat as low as half or ¾'s of a commercial flight. Pelita flies fairly regularly in and out of Jambi.

the Banjunglincir-Palembang river trip: From Jambi, take the Rp400 bus halfway to Banjunglincir to Batas, then walk the rest of the way to Banjunglincir. You have to walk it from Batas because the road is impassable. Get a hold of a *stanis stia* (stainless steel ring) to keep the tigers away. From Banjunglincir, a 10 m long boat takes 30 hours down to Palembang, Rp1500-2000 with 3 meals a day (fresh crayfish). Go past a whorehouse on stilts, monkeys swinging in trees, giant hornbills flapping up from jungle bush like B-29 Bombers. Shine your torch at night into the swamps and you can see the red eyes of crocodiles. If you don't get the boat from Banjunglincir right away; may have to wait 3-4 days. There's no *losmen* in Banjunglincir, so stay in the *warung* closest to the river. Crayfish cost Rp500 a kilo. To get back to Jambi from Batas (last bus leaves for Jambi at noon), get up at 5 am, allowing 6 to 7 hours for the walk. Don't need a guide which costs Rp1500. Because of tigers and poisonous snakes, don't travel at night.

LAKE KERINCI

Padang to Lubuklinggau is beginning to look like an interstate highway. Instead, sign up for a bus ride from Jambi or from Padang to the Kerinci District, for volcanoes, hotsprings, cinnamon trees, and a big lake. Kerinci is yet undeveloped for tourists, i.e. no fruit salad but big *jeruk panas* for Rp25 or a whole cut fresh pineapple for Rp20. **getting there:** Kerinci District goes by the name of Sungaipenuh on the Bartholomew map and on bus signs. It lies about 60 km up in the mountains from Tapan which is less than halfway (200 km plus) between Padang and Bengkulu. A.L.S. does the trip, but Habeko is recommended. They use real buses (Mercedes) which have glass windows, and rarely stop *en route*. Departure each direction at 8 or 9 am, costs about Rp1250. Padang to Sungaipenuh is 12 hours or so, a scenic drive along the coast and through small villages.

Sungaipenuh: Sits in the middle of a broad lush valley of rich green rice paddies surrounded by a ring of mountains, tea plantations, and smaller scale farming of cinnamon, cloves, coffee (Rp800 a kilo in town) and tobacco. An airport is under construction but until the Hilton crowd begins to appear you'll have to get yourself around. You might have to report to the police station if the hotel owner asks you to. **stay:** Proprietors of Hotel Jaya and Hotel Anak Gunung, each Rp350 single, Rp700 double, both speak English and Dutch and can help you get around. Tell them Mr. Djafar's bearded friend sent you. Hotel Mata Han is nicer for Rp1000-1500. There are good restaurants along the left side going up the main street (the one with the center divider).

sights: To the hotsprings it's Rp100 or less for a 11 km ride past Semurup to the *air panas* sign, then walk the last km or two. The public bath is free or a huge private room for Rp50. Boil eggs or bananas in the central pool, not suitable for bathing, and eat a couple of those Rp20 pineapples (the locals think pineapples are low class). Check out the possibility of renting a bicycle or motorbike to the lake, otherwise take a bus or *oplet* to Songgaran Agung, walk a ways, then flag another back to town. The volcano is a tough climb but nice-looking. Ask the hotel man the way.

from Sungaipenuh: Can either go back the same way and resume travel from Padang, or take a real jungle ride 160 km, Rp1800 by jeep or *oplet* 2-3 days east, right over the mountains to Bangko. You might have to wait a couple of days in Sungaipenuh for a jeep that's going through to Bangko. If the weather is bad, you can't do it. It's low gear almost all the way and there might be as many as 21 people on the combination jeep-trailer. Pay the Rp50 extra to sit in the front seat; better views. From Bangko take the bus to Jambi, Rp1100. Don't believe the price the guy first gives you. You can also continue from Bangko down to Lubuklinggau.

BENGKULU

A lovely old town on the west coast. Population 55,000. Takes 1½ days by bus from Padang, Rp4500. Garuda flies into Bengkulu twice weekly from Jakarta and twice weekly from Palembang. If you take the ship from Padang to Jakarta, it might stop a couple of hours here. Not many travelers. **history:** The British, driven from their last stronghold on Java at Banten, built a fortress in Bengkulu and stayed 150 years. The first English factory was started in 1685, but 2 years later its commander was poisoned. In 1690 Fort York was built. A French fleet destroyed most of the English forts in Sumatra in 1760 but they were all rebuilt within 3 years. Sir Thomas Raffles, founder of Singapore, arrived here in 1818 and revived the pepper trade. This brilliant and ambitious 30 year old governor tried to find a new colony for Britain and to edge the Dutch out by taking over Sumatra's west coast. But after Raffles' recall to Britain, Bengkulu was returned to the

Dutch in 1824. The United States Marines once landed here during the era of gunboat diplomacy.

stay: For the cheapies, stay in the Chinese quarter. Losmen Aman is Rp600 single, Rp1000 double. Wisma Pemuda, Jl. Indra, next to Kantor Gubernuran, is clean and new with fans, full board Indonesian food Rp400 per day. Wisma Melati, Jl. Kartini, offers all meals and sleep for Rp2000. Also try Wisma Puteri Gading. **sights:** The British Fort Marlborough still stands but is occupied by the army; they'll let you enter. Built like a castle, there are old gravestones with English inscriptions inside the gatehouse. From the top of the castle walls you get a view of the sleepy harbor and the *pasar*, oxcarts, and whirling kites. Visit Dendam Taksuda Botanical Gardens to see wild orchids and the *reflesia*, the largest flower in the world, but blooms only in October. Wander around the fishermens' streets along .the harbor by Sekolah Sint Carolus. Visit Pasar Ikan. Opposite Mushalla Nuralfalah, behind the Protestant Church, is an old Christian cemetary.

from Bengkulu: A road leads from Bengkulu across the Bengkulu Mountains towards Palembang. There are no flights north to Padang or south to Lampung from Bengkulu. Take the bus from Bengkulu to Lubuklinggau, 3 hours (stops midway at Curup), climbing up the spine of Bukit Barisan over a road of wild pigs, monkeys, giant sunflowers, ricefields, buffalo horn tipped buildings, and tea plantations (at Kepahiang). **vicinity of Bengkulu:** There's a nice beach outside of town. See Pantai Panjang's sailboats by taking a sandy path from the city. Explore Bengkulu Province by jeep or bus; the mail bus to Manna 140 km to the south takes 7 hours over a washboard road. If you're into megaliths, don't miss cool-climate high altitude Pasar Alam, on the way to Palembang, where you get a good view over Mt. Dempo. Further south in Lampung District there's Semanka Bay and the 40 km long Lake Ranau; good fishing. Curup is known for its long traditions of music, dancing and poetry. Visit the goldmining country north of Curup (N.E. of Bengkulu); 19th Century waterwheels are used for gold extraction at Muara Aman. At Lebak Sidedug, a prehistoric sanctuary.

Pasemah Highlands: On this plateau near Lahat are megalithic remains dating from as far back as 100 A.D.; said to be the most concentrated collection of monumental symbolic culture in Indonesia. Huge queerly-shaped stones are carved into fantastic figures and groups of figures: warriors mounted on elephants, men riding and wrestling buffaloes, animals copulating, men fighting an enormous snake. A great number of these menhirs, dolmens, stone cist graves, and terraced sanctuaries were erected at a time when metals were already known in the area; figures carry swords, wear helmets, rings, anklets, and men hold giant bronze kettledrums, artifacts which all belong to the Bronze Age. Warriors have bulging eyes, strong jaws, and short broad swords in their belts. The figures appear at first to be 3-dimensional but they are in fact basreliefs, the illusion being created by the skilful use of the curved surface of the boulders. Great attention is given to the carving of the heads; the rest of the body is roughly done. At Tegurwangi is a complex including the ruins of a large tomb; pillars are decorated with men riding elephants, faces have thick negroid lips. Two slab graves contain colored drawings. At Tanjungara, see the colored paintings in the inner walls of a cist grave; ferocious charging buffaloes carry warrior-riders. The modern-day people of Pasemah, who believe they are descended from a Majapahit King from Java, still use some of this statuary as vow redemption shrines, calling upon their ancestors to bestow their blessings and to stave off ill-fortune. See some examples on Mt. Dempo.

ENGGANO ISLAND

The largest of a group of 6 islands off the S.W. coast only 96 km from Bengkulu. The name means 'disappointment' or 'mistake' in Portugese, and probably refers to some ancient blunder in navigation. Native name is *soloppo*, or simply 'the land'. In the center of Enggano is its largest hill, Bua Bua (250 m). Buffaloes, pigs and cattle are found in the wild. **getting there:** Catch a *prahu* or a *kapal motor* from Bengkulu or from Bintuhan on the South Sumatran mainland. Boats out to Enggano are not that terribly frequent. Malakoni is the largest town and boats from Bengkulu arrive in its harbor. **transport:** The only tracks on the island connect the tiny north coast villages of Banjar Sari, Meok, Kaana, Kabayupu and Malakoni. River travel is out of the question since the coastline is swampy and no river penetrates more than 18 km inland. The southern monsoon lasts from July to December.

Aboriginal dwelling on Enggano

history: Stone implements were used here as late as the 19th Century. Since the Engganese are descendants of aboriginal Sumatrans who fled when Malaysians began to arrive on the mainland, there's no Hindu influence in their history. These islanders used to arm themselves with fire-hardened 2 m long spears embedded with shark's teeth or fishbones and lurk behind coral reefs in war canoes, waiting for stray adventurers. Due to cholera, venereal diseases and malaria, the Engganese have been steadily declining towards extinction since 1866; at one point, in 1928, they were down to only 162. Once compared with the Tasmanian aborigines as one of the few instances of a total genocide of a people, preventative medicine saved them. Villages used to dot the coasts, but only 5 remain.

people: Enggano is presently a rehabilitation center for juvenile delinquents from Java. The islanders suffer greatly from their lack of communication with the mainland. Many of its people have ringworms, malaria and anaemia. Most are primary school dropouts. The approximately 1200 surviving Engganese live on fishing, coconuts, sale of copra, gardening cassava and taro. Enggano exports 20 tons of copra to Telukbetung each month, but it's a Chinese-owned enterprise. There are 5 clans (suku) spread over the entire island: The Kaharuba, Kaarubi, Kaitora, Kaahuao and the Kaono. A matrilineal society, descent is traced through the female line and farmlands are usually inherited by daughters. Half call themselves Christian, the other half call themselves Muslim. But actually this society is one of the last truly animist strongholds in Indonesia. Many features are left of the old religious system. *Kowek*, good and bad spirits, are placated at times of drought or pestilence by offerings of taro, bananas, and fish. When a person dies sometimes whole villages are completely dismantled and moved elsewhere. Although regarded as pagan and undesirable by Christian missionaries, the oldest men and women can still perform the *E'aruhe* and the *Ya'udo* native dances. Now younger people are taught these dances by elders for tourists. The *E'ono Wakoroa* ritual feast is staged occasionally to reconcile parties to a quarrel, prior to a fishing expedition or hunt, or else to celebrate a rite of passage. Official public performances of folk stories include: 'The Story About Copulation', 'The Story of The Person Who Became an Earthquake', and 'How a Child Became a Flying Dog'. Engganese culture is sure now to disappear as a result of assimilation into an indiscriminate Indonesian culture. **vicinity of Enggano:** Natives of Pulau Pagai Island to the north still use bows and arrows; bowstrings are made from entrails of animals. They also build 18-20 m long canoes. Untouched beaches. Catch boat from Padang, Rp2500, 24 hours.

RIAU PROVINCE

A portion of this province is made up of the eastern coast of Sumatra (Riau Daratan); the capital of Riau Province is Pekanbaru. The other part of Riau consists of about 1000 islands, large and small, stretching from the east coast of Sumatra north to Malaysia and east towards Kalimantan (Borneo). Many islands aren't inhabited. The larger islands are covered in primary jungle with wild boar, monkeys, deer, and birdlife. The seas around Riau are very shallow and *keelongs* have been built for catching fish. In its seas are stingrays, hammerhead sharks, marlin, meter-long fish, coral fish and poisonous seasnakes (take care while diving). **climate:** The eastern islands are affected by the winter monsoon from November to March, so for swimming and diving, choose another season.

getting there: German Asian Travels, Straits Trading Building, 9 Battery Road, Singapore, offers 2-day, 2-night tours to Tanjung Pinang for S$130 return. Accommodation but not food is provided. Or just buy a Singapore to Tg. Pinang motorboat ticket from them for S$40. It's also possible to get the launch at Finger Pier at the end of Prince Edward Road; try to pay only US$10 to the crew to Tg. Pinang. Another way is to take the weekly Pelni boat from Jakarta, or from Medan to Tg. Pinang for Rp13,000 deck class. Sempati Airlines flies from Jakarta to Tg. Pinang for Rp26,050 or from Singapore for Rp6500 (plus Rp1000 airport tax). There are flights chartered by oil people operating out of Jambi (South Sumatra) to Tg. Pinang which you can sometimes get on for free. Little 2-engine Navajos with 8 seats. But the tricky thing is to get introduced to the right person. The Indonesian in the tower will charge you Rp5000 to get to meet him.

transport: In western Sumatra rivers are only navigable for short distances, but the rivers of East Sumatra are an important means of transport. Road transportation on mainland Riau connects only Dumai, Pekanbaru, Bukittinggi and Padang. To travel north or south from East Sumatra, fly from Pekanbaru's Simpang Tiga Aerodrome. An airstrip recently opened on Batam Island, 20 km south of Singapore; commercial flights now connect Jakarta with Tg. Pinang, Batam, Dumai, and Pekanbaru. The method of travel and exploration throughout insular Riau is by *kapal laut, kapal motor, spetbot* (long boat with outboard motor) or by *sampan* (sailboat). *Sampans* are the cheapest. It's quite easy to arrange boat-hire. For example, chartered boats could cost Rp5000 for 1 person from Tg.

Pinang to Penyenget Island. But just go down to the wharf and get a small sailboat across for Rp100, a delightful passage.

history: In the lowlands of Eastern Sumatra, Indian acculturation can be traced back to at least the 5th Century. But its history goes back even earlier. Today you can still see piles of shells 3 meters high remaining where Middle Stone Age peoples lived. These hunter-gatherers, who migrated with their dogs to Indonesia around 600-2000 B.C., left just these shells behind, sometimes with their dead buried inside. Since the shortest sailing route between India and China is through the Straits of Melaka, farsighted rulers have always tried to establish their authority on land to both sides of this all-important strait. Consequently, the East coast of Sumatra has had a turbulant history and many kingdoms have come and gone. Between the Rokan River and the Kampar River was the old area of the nomadic bloodthirsty Celates pirates who were employed by the Dutch to spy against the Portugese in their battle for control over the strait. From the 16th to the 18th Centuries, the Riau archipelago was the nucleus of the Malay civilization. Its capital was moved many times to avoid the attacks of ferocious *orang laut* (sea pirates) and Riau's power fluctuated with the rise and fall of the Dutch and English conflicts in the area, and especially with the fortunes of Melaka. At least 8 generations of sultans have ruled in the area. The first Malay grammar was composed here in 1859: Radja Ali Hadja's *Pengetahuan Bahasa.* Modern-day Indonesian orginated here and today in the Riau and Lingga archipelagos the purest, most classical Indonesian is still spoken. Riau has always had close economic ties with Singapore and even used Singapore money right up to the *Konfrontasi.*

economy: Fishing is the mainstay of Riau's economy with more than half the motor vessels in Indonesia's fishing fleet working out of Pekanbaru and Bagansiapiapi. There is considerable economic wealth on some islands in the form of minerals: oil on Batam, granite on Kerimun, tin on Singkep and Kundur. The mines on Bangka are Indonesia's oldest, opened at the beginning of the 18th Century. On Biliton the first mine was started in 1851 and on Singkep in 1887. Indonesia's production of tin ranks only behind Malaysia, Bolivia, and Thailand, and tin is 2nd only to petroleum as the foreign currency earning mineral. A booming oil province, Caltex Pacific Indonesia is based at Rumbai, a short drive north of Pekanbaru. The Pertamina refinery at Dumai produces 100,000 barrels a day. Bauxite, used to make aluminum, is also mined in these islands. Because of the high demand for its products and the very short distances to outside markets over the narrow reef-studded straits of Melaka, East Sumatra is also a main smuggling center. This is legitimate barter trade whose purpose is to prevent Jakarta from coming into all the wealth of the outer islands. Piracy is also said to be on the increase in this and other parts of Indonesia, a profession in which the Indonesian navy participates. Small goods trading between Singapore and Tg. Pinang is frantic.

people: Islam is the predominant religion in Riau (1,335,000 out of 1,370,000). This province is also a very rich ethnographic area. Its many tribes include: the Sakai in Muara Basung and Bengkalis, numbering about 5000. The Laut or Kuala in Sungai Asam, about 600; and in Senajang, Batam, Singkep, Santan, and Daik number about 5000. The Hutan or Asli in Sokop Sungai Pulau, Bengkalis District, number about 3000. The Akik People in Pangkalan Baru on Rupat Island, Bengkalis District, number about 2000. The Talang Mamak in Kaleso, Indragiri Hulu District, number around 6000. Of the Bonai in Kuala Kampar, Kepenuhan; and in Tanah Putih, Kampar District there are about 1500 left. The Mantang in Penuba and Kelumu, are of unknown numbers. The Baruk People in Sungai Buluh and Singkep, also of unknown numbers. Chinese, forming about 1/5 of the total population of the Riau, are concentrated on Billiton and Bangka. Originally settled in these districts to work the mines and plantations, they later became farmers and fishermen when the mines played out. On Bangka the Chinese have mixed considerably with the local culture and the Chinese here speak an almost creolized Hakka dialect.

PEKANBARU

A river port located 160 km upstream on the Siak River. By bus from Bukittinggi, Rp500, or by bus from Padang, Rp1100. If you fly in it costs Rp1000 by taxi from Pekanbaru's airport into town, after bargaining. This oil city is not what you'd imagine it would be, an unexpectedly friendly place. Many foreigners living here. See the Grand Mosque (an Nur: The Light) on Jl. Sheikh Burhanuddin, with its bright onion dome. Also stroll around the fruit market and the fish market. For a new visa first buy two Rp500 stamps at the P.O., go to *imigrasi*, Jl. J. Soedirman, then take their documents to the Jl. Singa Immigration Office to get them stamped. **stay:** There are 2 *losmens* on the main street, Jl. J. Soedirman, Losmen Muslim and Losmen Dhar-

ma Utama, both Rp1000 double. These two are about the cheapest places to stay. Grotty *mandis* in D. Utama, but their restaurant serves okay food. Losmen Pekanbaru is also cheap. Hotel Wisma Widya, Jl. Kamar, for twin beds and bathrooms, Rp1500, breakfast for Rp250. Newer and expensive Hotel Riau, because of its small size, is often full. Nearby is Wisma Indragiri Hulu, Jl. Diponegoro, Rp3000 single, but you don't get much for that price.

from Pekanbaru: For Padang or Bukittinggi, Aldilla Express has two buses daily. Take the morning bus (Mercedes) back to Bukittinggi because the afternoon bus sometimes stops overnight and leaves again at 5 am. There's at least one flight a day to Singapore from Pekanbaru by oil company planes; try to get on free. At Rumbai, apply to the Caltex public relations office for a visitor's pass which will allow you to use Caltex Club facilities like buses, hotel, air service to Jakarta and Singapore. Merpati flights to Singapore cost Rp22,000, stopping in Padang and Palembang on the way. Boats leave Pekanbaru for Tg. Pinang (enquire at the Takari Lines Shipping agent), an island 4 hours south of Singapore by motorboat, where you can catch the Pelni ship to Jakarta each Sat; the Pelni ship to Medan each Wed.; or go on to Singapore by launch for Rp4200.

vicinity of Pekanbaru: Although this is Pertamina oil country, it's still one of the least contaminated Indonesian wildernesses. The Hairy Sumatran Rhinoceros is found around Pekanbaru along the Siak River and also along the road which links Lirik and Buatan, as well as south in the muddy river country to Tenajan Ulu, and the Kampar River Districts. These sullen-faced behemoths love to take mud baths; the thick layer on their backs gives protection against attacks of bat-flies. *Durian* fruit is its favorite dessert. To make up for its poor eyesight, its sense of smell and hearing is keen, so keep alert. Big round tracks in soft mud show clear impressions of the rhinos' hoofs. In Riau Daratan there are also herds of elephants, occasional deer and wild boars, tapir, bears, tigers, explosively colored butterflies, brilliant tropical birds. Hear the black *beo*-bird's crazy laughter and the croaking of one-foot high frogs. Animals can often be seen from early morning buses traveling to and from Pekanbaru.

Bagansiapiapi (Place of Fire): On the north coast next to the mouth of the Rokan River, surrounded by swamps and jungles. This town used to be accessible by coastal steamers, but now mangrove-covered mudflats separate it from the Rokan River so goods and passengers are tran-

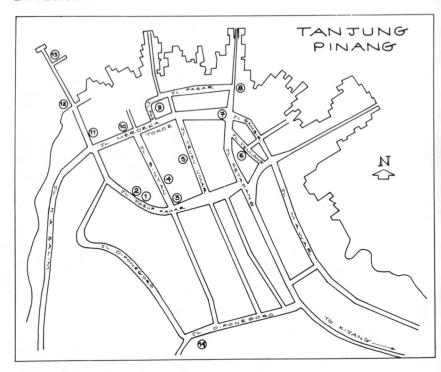

TANJUNG PINANG

N

sported by dugout. One of the richest fishing grounds in the world (only Bergen, Norway, catches more fish), this little town pulls in over 100,000 tons of fish a year. Also one of the hottest spots on Sumatra. The Hokkien Chinese of Bagansiapiapi only began mingling with Indonesians over the last decades of the 19th Century and they speak an unadulterated Hokkien. Also a major smuggling center; after dark, fast unlighted *sampans* are driven by powerful outboard motors at high speeds by captains who know their way through the reefs so well that it's difficult for Indonesian naval patrols to stop them. But it's a sign of the centralist Jakartan government's growing power that they are slowly but steadily putting a stop to smuggling throughout the islands.

TANJUNG PINANG

The principle town of insular Riau located on Bintan Island only 4 hours by launch (S$40) south of Singapore, a small Malay-Chinese trading center. Many jobless young men (as everywhere in Indonesia) who don't chose to work as manual

laborers for Rp400 per day. Many try to get jobs on the ships sailing out of Singapore. **history:** The Tg. Pinang sultan once held power over Johore, the southern island of Lingga, and ruled as far as Tembilahan on the east coast of Sumatra. Learning the use of gunpowder from the Turks and the Portugese, he reigned by virtue of a powerful sea fleet. Raffles obtained his licence to establish a trading post on Singapore island from the sultan of Tg. Pinang. This sultan actually chose to set up his kingdom on P. Penyenget, just opposite Tg. Pinang; a royal residence was built there in 1803.

stay: Tg. Pinang is a busy transit town with passengers arriving and departing all the time from Pekanbaru, Jakarta, Singapore, Medan, Palembang, most seeking out the cheap rooms. The cheapest is to stay with families; it's easy to meet people who'll take you in. The police discourage this since they are only able to extract Rp500 for their 'police report' if you stay in a legitimate hotel. Be careful of which house you stay in (beware of Kampung Jawa), there's been numerous thefts of foreigners' gear. Frank might meet you at the pier when the boats come in; he'll fix you up with a safe place. Frank is very knowledgeable about the Riau area and speaks fluent English. About the best and most central Hotel is Peng. Sampurna, Jl. Josuf Kahar, cheapest rooms at Rp1100- but remember the Rp500 for the police report. Losmen Sondang, Jl. Josuf Kahar, asks Rp1500 for a double room or for 3 in a room, Rp2400; clean, safe, well-run. Also Hotel Surya, Jl. Bintan, Rp550. Most expensive is Wisma Daerah Guesthouse, Jl. Diponegoro, at Rp4200 with a fan. Tanjung Pinang Hotel, overlooking the town, offers good economy class rooms for Rp2700; to get your bearings, there's a large relief map of the Riau upstairs.

TANJUNG PINANG

1. *Peng. Sampurna*
2. *Garuda Office*
3. *Hotel Sandong*
4. *Hotel Surya*
5. *Bank Negara Indonesia*
6. *Pelni Office*
7. *taxi stand for Kijang*
8. *Tanjung Pinang Hotel*
9. pasar *area*
10. *Post Office*
11. *Netra Service*
12. sampans *for Pelni boat*
13. sampans *for Penyenget Island*
14. *Wisma Daerah*

---

eat: Food in Riau is twice as expensive as on Java. It costs Rp175 for a *nasi goreng* and up to Rp250 for a *nasi campur*. *Gado2* and *soto ayam* are the cheapest meals, Rp100. Although Taman Sari and Restoran Bali, both on Jl. Merdeka, are good *nasi padang* places, the best eats by far are at Pasar Malam Ria Bintan with a great assortment of meals in an open square with corny band music in the background. The whole town converges here at night, a great people-watching place (take in a bottle of *arak*, Rp100). *Kepitang cinkong goreng tepung*, crab claws fried in light crispy batter are for sale at stalls, only Rp100.

sights: Males will constantly be approached in Tg. Pinang by Indonesians wanting to escort them to the renowned Batu Duabelas and Batu Enambelas villages where young men may meet young women on an extremely informal basis. They are located out of Tg. Pinang, Rp300 by taxi. **Kandil Riau Museum:** At Batu Dua, 2 km from Tg. Pinang on the road to Kijang. Take a taxi from *stanplatz auto* for Kijang and it passes right through Batu Dua; pay only Rp100, it's a regular line. Ask for *polisi* R. Razak's house. This museum contains most of the remaining *pusaka* of the old Riau Kingdom. Musty smell of history. The genealogical chart is amazing. See old *krises*, swords, guns, ceramic plates, manuscripts. Mr. Razak is an enthused and dedicated curator. **Brakit Beach:** On the east coast of Bintan Island. Reached by bus, Rp4-500, about ½ hours; or by boat Rp1500 return from Tg. Pinang harbor, 3 hours. Deserted beach and excellent diving in glass-clear water in the coral reefs during the summer months. **Pantai Trikora:** Another ovely beach but costs Rp10,000 there and oack by taxi and by boat as much as Rp30,000. Fifteen km is paved, the remaining 25 km is unpaved. **Gunung Bintan Besar:** The largest mountain on Pulau Bintan (335 m). It's a 1 ½-2 hour not too steep climb to the summit from the *kampung* at the bottom up through primary jungle with indigenous flora and fauna. From the top you can see all the surrounding islands. To get there, rent a *spetbot* across the bay and then up a small jungle river to the *kampung*. Another way is to rent a taxi for Rp2-3000 to travel the 80 km to Gunung Besar. Or take a ferry Rp500 to Tanjung Uban (leaves each day at 2 pm), then on to the *kampung* for a further Rp600. It's also possible to take a motorcycle to Tanjung Uban, but not a car, the road's in too bad shape.

from Tanjung Pinang by boat: To Singapore take a launch for Rp4200. Launches leave often and they all have the same price which includes *makan komplet*, all the snacks you can eat. A cheaper way to get to Singapore is to take a ferry first to Sambu near Pulau Batam, leaves at 10 am, takes ½ day, Rp1150; then from Sambu to Singapore, Rp2000. Ferries from Tg. Pinang to Batam Island leave each day at 10 am, takes ½ day (with coffee only, so bring your own food), Rp1000. There's a ferry twice a week to Tg. Batu on Pulau Kundur, Rp1500. Local ferries also to Daik on Pulau Lingga 2 times a week on Wed., and Sat. (allow 3 days for this trip, there and back); the *Kapal Lingga* leaves at 6-7 pm and takes 12 hours, Rp2000. There's a ruined palace and an *orang laut* settlement near Daik. **to Pekanbaru:** Every 2nd and 4th Monday of each month a Takari Lines cargo boat takes passengers from Tg. Pinang up the Siak River in East Sumatra to Pekanbaru, Rp3600 (includes food and drink), 30 hours. Their office is on the first jetty of Tg. Pinang. The time of arrival and departure depends on the cargo being carried. From Pekanbaru, take a bus to Medan, Rp2500-3000, or to Danau Toba, Rp2300-2900. There was once a powerful sultan who ruled at the mouth of the Siak at Siak Sri Indragiri, and there are ruins (more interesting than P. Penyenget) of his palace there. A nomadic aboriginal tribe, the *Orang Sakai*, trade forest products, rattan, camphor, wild rubber for salt and tobacco at nearby villages. In some East Sumatran coastal districts beach nomads use 2 m long ½ m wide mudboards (curved in front like a mud-surfboard) to cross over swamps by pushing swiftly with hands and feet for hours on end.

from Tg. Pinang by ship: The K.M. Enggano sails twice monthly from Tg. Pinang to Sambas (West Kalimantan), for Rp18,250. Pelni's Tampomas is not the only ship that sails to Jakarta from Tg. Pinang, but it's the only reliable one, the most regular. Other boats you could catch any day of the week: K.M. Mei Abeto sails from Belawan (North Sumatra) to Jakarta 2 times a month, Rp13,000 deck class. On Sun. mornings on the Tampomas there's Batak choral hymn singing below decks, the stench of the shithouse is legendary, and the crew will take a bribe of Rp2000 to let you sleep in their quarters (with hotwater showers). Most westerners naturally gravitate towards the upper decks; more air, and sweeping scenery of the Java Sea. **flights:** Sempati Airlines agents are found on Jl. Temiang (near Pelni), Jl. Bintan, and on Jl. Merdeka (Toko Djaja Baru no. 103), offering flights, ·to: Singapore, Rp6500 (plus Rp1000 airport tax) every Mon.; Jakarta, Rp26,050, on Wed. at 12:30 pm; Pekanbaru, Rp13,850, on Mondays. Call the airport in Tg. Pinang (ask for *lapangan terbang*), they usually know one day before if any charters are going to arrive, and to where they're flying. Ask the charters for free rides to Singapore, Medan, Jakarta, and to other points.

ISLANDS REACHABLE FROM TG. PINANG

Pulau Penyenget: A 20 minute *sampan* ride from Tg. Pinang harbor, Rp100 each way. Go early in the morning, cool and pleasant. Inhabited by 2000 Malay fishermen; pure Melayu is spoken here. A 170 year old ruined palace, the Kerajaan Melayu, is behind the mosque, the forest pulling it back. This old palace was made by using millions of egg whites for mortar. Very finely-crafted well and bathing place. There are surrounding palace compounds and extensive ruins along wide quiet paths through coconut groves, the ocean always glimpsed at through the palms. Also royal bathing places, ornate watchtowers, and burial pavilions (the men have penis-shaped tombstones while the womens' are shaped accordingly), some quite well attended to. Raja Hamzah Junus has a collection of momentos, a photo album, and knows well the geneaology of the local aristocracy. You can easily find a place to stay with a family at modest cost.

Try Kampung Ladi. So peaceful here, you wouldn't believe that one of the largest trading centers in the east is only 4 hours away by motorboat.

others: Besides the remains of palaces and burial grounds on several islands near Tg. Pinang, there are even more intriguing palace ruins located further out (at Tembilahan on the mouth of the Indragiri River and in the town of Daik on Pulau Lingga). Travel companies won't conduct tours to these because it takes more than one day to visit them, which would prove unprofitable, difficult to organize, and lacking appeal to the ordinary tourist. So you have to get out to the more remote sites yourself. **Snake River Chinese Temple:** On an island just across the harbor of Tg. Pinang. Take a *sampan* for Rp100, entering the small Snake River through mangrove trees. The temple is decorated with paintings. Also visit the *orang laut* settlement and the Old Town of Tg. Pinang. **Pulau Terlukai:** Beyond Pulau Penyenget. A *spetbot* from Pulau Penyenget to Pulau Terlukai costs Rp4000 return; takes 1-1½ hours; see Ramat in Kampung Datuk on Pulau Penyenget. On Pulau Terlukai there's only a lighthouse, no people, untouched white sand beaches, waving palms with shady mangrove and casaurina trees. Help yourself to all the coconuts you want. **Kota Piring** (or 'City of Plates'): On Biram Dewa Island 30 minutes by *spetbot* from Tg. Pinang or by taxi from Tg. Pinang Rp5000 for one whole day. By *sampan*, at least Rp500. Built by the 4th Viceroy of Riau, Raja Haji. The walls of this ruined palace are full of ceramic plates. Another *orang laut* village on this island.

diving for sunken wrecks: Riau is one of the few places in the world where you can dive for wrecks without a great outlay of money. Hire snorkling and scuba equipment, and maybe even a boat from the Indonesian navy. Kosional Unit, in the green building on the waterfront. See Major Sihombing. Pulau Mantang has a stunning coral reef and a 150,000 ton British freighter sunk by the Japanese, 28 m below water. Also excellent fishing. Pulau Pompong is only 35 km from the equator with no people living on it. There are 3 wrecks here, all about 18 m underwater: Kurala, Tunkuang, and the Kuangwo, all sunk trying to escape from Singapore during WW II. Very favorable conditions for underwater photography here. At the southern end of the uninhabited island of Pulau Abang lies a large freighter, sunk during the last war, that still contains some of its cargo. It's a good dive site, the depth ranging from 6-18 m. All around the island are coral reefs and many small coves and beaches.

outer islands of the Riau: For the outer islands, such as for Pulau Abang, don't hire a char-

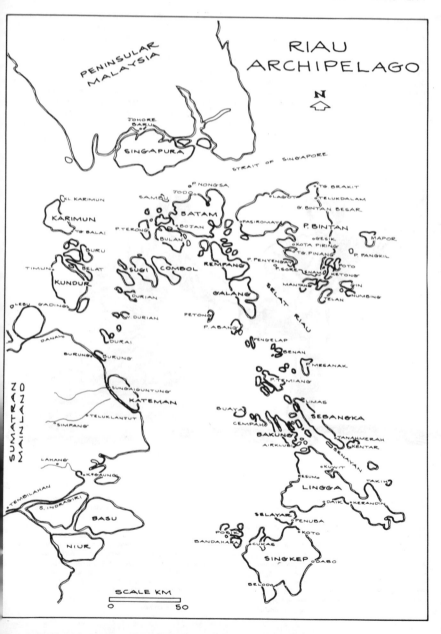

RIAU
ARCHIPELAGO

N

PENINSULAR MALAYSIA

JOHORE BARU

SINGAPURA

STRAIT OF SINGAPORE

P. NONGSA
TODO
SAMBU
SEL KARIMUN
KARIMUN
TG BALAI
BURU
TIMUN
BELAT
KUNDUR
P.TERONG
BOJAN
BULAN
BATAM
PASIROMATA
LAGOI
TG BRAKIT
TELUKDALAM
BINTAN BESAR
P. BINTAN
GESIK
KOTA PIRING
TG. PINANG
MAPOR
P. PANGKIL
SUGI
COMBOL
REMPANG
P. FENYENGAT
SORE
SENANG
KOTO
GALANG
SELAT
MANTANG
NUMBING
TELAN
DURIAN
OLEU GADING
P. DURIAN
PETONG
P. ABANG
DURAI
DANAU
BURUNG
BURUNG
PENGELAP
GENAN
MESANAK
P.TEMIANG
SUNGAIGUNTUNG
KATEMAN
TELUKLANTUT
SIMPANG
BUAYA
CEMPAHO
LIMAS
SEBANGKA
BAKUNG
AIRKLUBI
TANAHMERAH
KENTAR
SENAYAN
KUWIT
SUMATRAN MAINLAND
LAHANG
KBGAUNG
TEMBILAHAN
S. INDRAGIRI
BASU
NIUR
RESUM
LINGGA
TAKIN
DAIK
KERANDIN
SELAYAR
PENUBA
POSIK
BANDAKARA
CUKAS
KOTO
SINGKEP
DABO
BELOGO

SCALE KM
0   50

ter from Tanjung Pinang directly which would cost you phenomenal. Instead, island-hop first to Pulau Penyenget by *sampan*, then on to Pulau Terlukai, and then further to Pulau Abang. Many of the outer islands are uninhabited. On Pulau Sore you feel like Robinson Carusoe. Pulau Mapor is well known for outstanding fishing and its nice coral beaches. At the Pelni Office, Jl. Temiang, Tg. Pinang, ask about the K.M. Sirikaya which plies between most of the large and small outer islands: Tarempa (Rp7900), Letung (Rp6800), Midai (Rp8100), Bandai (Rp9400), Sedanau (Rp10,300), Serasan (Rp8350), Dabo on Pulau Singkep (Rp6600), Daik (Rp5850), Tambelan (Rp6900), and finally Dumai, 160 km N.E. of Pekan-

baru, (Rp7100). The Sirikaya does the loop about once every month but it's not known when it'll arrive at each port. Pay on the boat itself. Other freighters also visit the outer islands in the South China Sea with more or less the same prices and frequency. To buy your own *sampan layer* (small sailing vessel), it costs Rp40,000 (with the sail) to have one built for you on Pulau Penyenget. Or on Pulau Pangkil, Rp500 by *sampan* from Tanjung Pinang, they build the best *sampan melayu* (a very graceful, well constructed, bigger sailing vessel) for around Rp75,000 in only 2 months out of shorea wood (seraja) from Pulau Lingga.

pencak silat: *This fighting skill can also be a beautiful art form. The two words,* pencak silat, *are used all over Indonesia. The word* silat *has more to do with the physical culture side of it while* pencak *is more the art side. Pencak silat has a number of origins for Nepalese music, Hindu and Arab weapons, and Siamese costumes are all utilized. Priests, who used to study the actions and skills of animals to learn how to defend themselves, invented this combative technique. Though derived from Sumatra, this fighting style reached its technical zenith on Java where today you find the majority of the many styles. By the 14th Century,* pencak silat *had become a highly polished, very technical and deadly art practiced only by the Majapahit sultans and their cour* officials. Commoners were forbidden from learning its tactics. Today the tactics of* pencak silat *are used as a basis for self-defence by the Indonesian army. One characteristic of many forms is the ability to go from a standing position to a sitting posture, then springing up to tear, grab and rip like a wild monkey. Another characteristic is its natural easy-flowing circular graceful movement, with or without weapons. Sometimes trances are used during training. Hypnosis can be employed against an enemy, i.e. at close quarters taking the knife out of an enemy's hand as he blinks. Many practitioners are deft puppeteers, exercising their fingers to improve their fighting skills. The enemy is seldom despised but 'loved', even in combat.*

WEST SUMATRA
(SUMATERA BARAT)

PADANG

Main seaport of the west coast. Population 222,000. Although the 3rd largest city in Sumatra, it's not a big city but a sprawling town of low buildings, countless bicycles, and low powered Javanese motorbikes. Many bright *sarungs*. Padang used to be the chief town of the rich Minangkabau area, though the focus has now shifted inland to the highland city of Bukittinggi. The Minangkabau language is very close to the Indonesian language and you'll learn much Indonesian here. It is a very strict Muslim town and a woman could be stopped on the street for not wearing a bra. Because of the absence of tourists, as a rule people don't rip you off or overcharge you in Padang. Padang is also a good place to extend your tourist visa (Rp1700 for your 2nd extension) and to pay your landing fee (in Jakarta they rook you). The Immigration Department is on Jl. Nipah 50, a Rp30 *bemo* ride from the center. Teach English? Syahril Kasim needs native speakers at his Institute of English Service (I.E.S.) near the G.P.O. and the police station — but he can only give 'room, board and pocket money'. Perhaps one of the heaviest rainfalls in the world falls in and around Padang, over 10,160 mm per annum.

getting there: Overland from Jambi by bus is Rp3-3500, 36 hours, or from Bukittinggi by bus, Rp325. Both Pelni and Kalimantan Lines ships sail weekly to Padang from Jakarta, Rp10-11,500 deck class, takes 3-4 days. Pelni's 2nd class passage is Rp15,400, but is absolutely luxurious and well worth the US$13.50 extra if only for the unbelievable meals you get. Garuda flies from Palembang, Rp13,000; or from Jakarta, Rp30,000; or from Medan, Rp20,000. The airport is at Tabing, 9 km from Padang. Just walk out to the highway and take an *oplet* into the city for Rp50. **transport:** Take an *oplet* anywhere in town for Rp30; or take a *bendi* pulled by small scrawny horses with gaily colored pompoms, Rp100 for a 2 km or less ride.

stay: The Tiga Tiga Hotel, almost right across the street from the bus station (4 minutes walk), is perhaps the only place in Indonesia where a man and a woman may not share a room if their last names aren't the same in their passports. Rp300 for dorm beds (mixed sexes) or Rp350 per person in your own dingy room. The dorm is in the back overlooking a flooded garden of banana trees and a *kampung*; nice sunsets. Mosquitos are horrendous,

but coils are provided. Although many travelers gravitate to the Tiga Tiga, Hotel Candrawasih, right next door at Jl. Pemuda 27, Rp500 single, Rp1000 double, has better vibes and better rooms, though perhaps it's noisier. Also a travel agent here. More comfortable than either of these is Hotel Sriwijaya, Jl. Alang Lawas 15, Rp600 single, Rp1200 double. Down a quiet street, a safe, comfortable, clean hotel, Rp100 by *bendi* from the city center. Hotel Machudum near the market on Jl. Hilagoo 45, is Rp1500-4500 double, Rp500-3750 single; a little plush but has a good restaurant. Hotel Melati, Jl. Hilagoo 32, is Rp400 single, Rp800 double; central, nondescript but adequate. A friendly place on a back street is Hotel Dahlia, Jl. Jawa Dalam 3/5, Rp500 or Rp1000 double; serves *nasi campurs* for Rp100. Grand Hotel, Jl. Pondok 84, costs Rp1750 single to Rp2750 and Rp3900 double (plus 10%); nice garden and very spacious and quiet in the middle part. Meals at the Grand cost Rp1750 for European food, Rp1500 for Indonesian food. Hotel Mariani International, Jl. Bundo Kandung 25, is Rp3750. Hotel Aldilla, Jl. Damar 1/2, costs Rp3000. Hotel Jakarta, Jl. Belakang Olo 57, is Rp2500.

eat: In West Sumatra's highland areas cattle are more pentiful and thus more meat is used in West Sumatran cooking than on Java. Tumeric and red peppers are used more often as well. The most famous dish of West Sumatra is *rendang padang*, big pieces of roast buffalo or beef cooked for days in coconut milk until the meat becomes black, tough and a bit stringy. It can keep for a month; a good traveling food. It's served in a gravy so thick it's almost a paste, and hot as blazes. But *deng deng* is hotter still; thinly cut pieces of dried beef are served in a chili sauce, with more red chilies sprinkled on top. Makes your teeth bleed. But delicately flavored black tea with lime or lemon puts the fire out. Afterwards for dessert bananas, bananas, and more bananas. Sample also *gulai itik* (duck goulash), *bulai belut* (eels goulash), *gulai rebuang* (goulash with bamboo shoots), and *sambal lado* (chilies and other spices). Compared to Java and Bali, restaurant food is expensive in Padang. Kindness Restaurant, Jl. Prof. Yamin 185, is the tourist restaurant of Padang and sometimes has a sign out front that says 'We sell fruit salad'. About Rp200 a meal, but not Padang food; excellent *gado2* (Rp100) and a fair *mie goreng, es durian* (Rp 100). Kindness has a garden patio facing the street-life. Good *martabak* is served in the restaurants of Jl. Prof. Yamin. Simpang Ampat, Jl. Prof. Yamin 120, has *bistek, nasi* and *mie goreng*, real *rendang* (only

Rp50 a serving), a plate of genuine pickles (Rp50).
Also try Irama, Jl. Prof. Yamin, right next door to
Simpang Ampat, Rp100 at plate for Padang food.
Tepi Pasang, on Jl. Tepi Pasang, is an often
crowded Chinese-run open air restaurant with two
woks working full blast, turning out delicious fried
chicken, Rp500, *cap cai*, Rp350, and *bihun mie*,
Rp275.

sights: Bapparda (govt. tourist office), Jl. Gereja
34 (near Hotel Muara) for maps and info. At the Institute of Minangkabau Studies at Andalas University, a revival of Sumatran studies is taking place.
Performances of traditional•Minang dances and
music are held at Konservatori Seni Kerawitan Indonesia. Off Padang's pier is a veritable sea
aquarium with rainbows of fish in the water —
Angel Fish, Bonita, etc. But don't go swimming,
they'll eat you. There's only one niteclub in Padang
now, the town fathers closed down all the rest.
Hotel Muara, close to Taman Melati, has a bar and
restaurant. No cover charge, but a beer costs
Rp600.

from Padang by train: Take the old steam train
while you can, it's an adventure climbing up the
Bukit Barisan through Sumatra's humid tangled
jungles screaming with monkeys; fabulous scenery.
Right now this narrow gauge train only goes as far
as Kayutaman, Rp75, but sometimes as far as
Bukittinggi and beyond to Payakumbuh. 80 km in 5
hours is common; it could take you half a day to
reach Bukittinggi (Rp100). The train branches south
from the Padangpanjang junction to Solok and to
Sawahlunto. The coastal track goes as far as Naras,
beyond Pariaman. Close the windows, or soot
burns your face. **long-distance buses:** Going
overland to Jambi, Rp3500, is cheaper than the
boat and far more unforgettable. Roads are impassable during the rainy season Dec.-Feb. because
the bridges over the rivers are often down. Other
buses to: Medan, Rp2850, leaves in the afternoon
and arrives the next morning sometime; Prapat,
Rp2500; Sungaipenuh, Rp1250; Lubuklinggau,
Rp4000; Palembang, Rp5500; Tanjungkarang,
Rp7000, at least one day, one night; Jakarta,
Rp10,000, 3 days, 3 nights; Dumai (Riau), Rp1800;
Pekanbaru, Rp1100, five hours over fairly good
roads (Aldilla Express). Bunga Setangkai Bus Co.
has spacious seats. For Bengkulu, take Evy Jaya
Co., Rp4500 from Padang, 2 days, 2 nights, departs
once daily at 1 pm. For Kerinci Lake, board an ALS
or Habeko bus, Rp1250, takes 12 hours. **short
distance buses:** To Solok, Rp275, 2½ hours
over a twisting mountain road, great scenery;
Payakumbuh, Rp425; Batu Sangkar, Rp350;
Padangpanjang, Rp250; Bukittinggi, Rp325, via the
Anai Valley; Muaro Takus (near Panti), Rp750.

PADANG

1. Tiga Tiga Hotel
2. Merpati Airlines
3. Central Bus Station
4. Hotel Dahlia
5. souvenir shop
6. pasar
7. Kindness Restaurant
8. Hotel Mariani
9. Grand Hotel
10. Hotel Muara
11. Tepi Pasang
12. Bank Negara Indonesia
13. Immigration Department
14. Garuda Airlines

---

from Padang by boat: Teluk Bayur, Rp35
from the city by *bemo*, is a quiet seaport surrounded by mountains. Another harbor is Muara, Rp40
from the *stasiun bemo* near the market. For the
Mentawai Islands, try Rusco Agent, Jl. Batang
Harau at Muara harbor; has boats for Rp1500
leaving for Muarasiberut (on Siberut Island), or to
Sipora in the Mentawais. **for Jakarta:** Ships are
much less crowded from Padang to Jakarta (8 or 12
people), than they are from Jakarta to Padang (30-
40 people). Pacto Tours, Jl. Pemuda 1, keeps up
with changes in ships' schedules. Buy a mat and
bring fruit to supplement the monotonous fish diet.
Ships go down the whole west coast of Sumatra,
volcano after volcano, finally passing within 3 km of
Anak Krakatoa. Lava could be spewing forth by
moonlight. Buy your ticket at Kalimantan Shipping
Lines in Teluk Bayur. Takes 72 hours on deck,
Rp9750. Leaves on Wed. or Thursdays. Can get
cabins if you bribe the crew, women can get them
for free. A spanking new Pelni boat has just started
this route as well. Leaves Padang on Sun.,
Rp10,000. Very clean, good showers and sleeping
areas. Other cargo boats to Jakarta would probably
prove cheaper than either of these companies. For
other destinations, try Arafat Lines, which has
generally better ships than Pelni. **by air:** Merpati's
office is on Jl. Biroa 23 (tel. 54219). To Jakarta,
Rp25,000; Singapore, Rp22,000; Medan, Rp15,500
(but you miss Bukittinggi and the lakes); Palembang,
Rp15,500; Pekanbaru, Rp6750. Garuda flies weekly
to Singapore and Kuala Lumpur. Tabing Airport lies
just 9 km outside of Padang.

vicinity of Padang: Beautiful coasts are found
around Padang; little fishing villages built on piles,
with palms, wooded hills and flowering trees com-

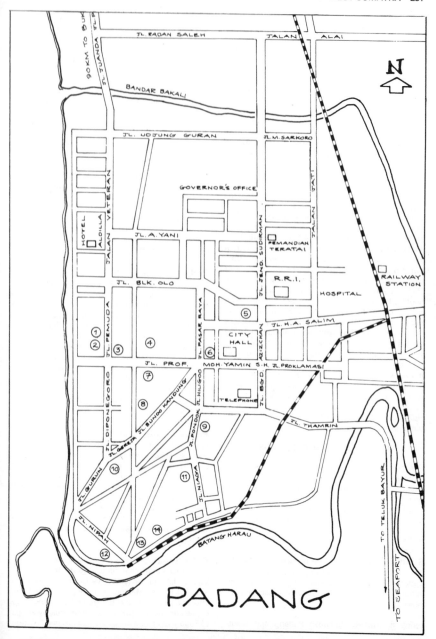

PADANG

ing right down to the sea. Water's very warm for sunset swimming. South of Padang, steep and rocky coasts with many inlets. Bungus Bay, only 1 hour's drive from Padang, for virgin beaches. There's an excellent view of Padang and its surroundings from the Chinese cemetary across the river from Muara Padang. There's a huge Japanese canon still in its concrete bunker near the river mouth. **Pariaman:** An historic port 50 km N.W. of Padang. Pariaman celebrates once a year the Tabut Festival which was originally the Syi'ah Sect's ceremonial to commemorate the death of the grandson of Mohammed in the Karbella War. **Lubukalung:** Only 1 ½ hour out of Padang. A rich district for rice, timber, and copra.

islands and beaches: If you got a few days to kill, hire a boat from Muara (Rp40 by *bemo* from the city center) for Rp5-600 out to Pulau Pisang (Banana Island); sparkling white sand beaches. But don't go on Sundays; it's too crowded. For more remote Sikakap Island, it's a 14 hour boat trip from Padang. Or stay on any of the small islands south of Padang; pitch your tent, you're the only one. **Pantai Nirwana:** A quiet out of the way stretch of open, palm-lined seashore, Rp125 by *oplet* from Padang. **Air Manis:** A fishing and boating spot south 3 km from the city center. A beautiful beach here and friendly people. **Pasir Putih:** Rp125 by *oplet* 24 km south of Padang on Bungus Bay; a memorable ride. Stay with the Djamaluddin family whose house is the first one you come to right after the park; Rp500 single or Rp1000 double. Located on a small bay with a garden overlooking the beach, it's a lovely, quiet, simple place, but all the more comfortable for it. You can borrow their canoe or rent one for Rp600 and paddle out to small islands in the bay. For a cheaper place to stay (maybe Rp200), ask around the fishing *kampung*. Or pitch a tent right on the beach.

THE PADANG HIGHLANDS

A rugged volcanic country with natural air-conditioning, peaks looming over canyons, splendid sheltered valleys, rich volcanic soil, villages perched on top of deep ravines. The home of the Minangkabau people, a densely populated area. The best mountain scenery is found around Mt. Merapi (2890 m) and Mt. Singgalang (2880 m). A nature reserve at Lembah Anai has waterfalls, wild orchids, and the *reflesia*. Tigers still inhabit the Forest of Panti. **Sungai Puar:** A center for brasswork, especially dishes and *sirih* cases. **Muaro Takus:** See 11th Century Maligai Buddhist stupa. Though very much in ruins, it's one of the few genuine stupas in Indonesia.

Lake Singarak: Between Padang and Bukit-

tinggi. Bigger and as beautiful as the more popular Lake Maninjau in the north, Lake Singarak has roads and a railway. You can see the whole lake from the train. In B. Ombilim stay in either the Jayakarta Hotel, Rp3000 double, or at Wisma Singkarak, Rp1500 double. Visit the little village of Batu Tebal on the lake, Rp350 from Padang by the longer back road to Bukittinggi. Stay in the Minang Hotel, Rp2000 double or single; good meals served including fish fresh from the lake. More remote and inaccessible lakes in this region are Danau Diatas and Danau Dibawah; good swimming in all of them. Isolated orthodox Muslim communities live on their shores.

Solok: A high mountain town. Stay at Sinar Timbulan, Jl. Pandan 41. Silungkang is a center for the best woven cloths. The road down to Lake Singarak is quite nice, but the 64 km road running from Solok down to Padang is extraordinary: pass by rice terraces, coconut palms, woodcarved saddle-backed houses, mosques with great corrugated iron domes, water mills, clove orchards.

Padangpanjang: Off the tourist path. It's got the same people as Bukittinggi, but without the tourists. On occasion, tigers come into this town and carry people away under cover of mists. For a job teaching English, ask at the Akademi Bahasa Asing. There's a conservatory of Minangkabau Dance and Music (ASKI) here devoted mainly to Minangkabau Hindu-style *gamelan* instruments. Possibly view the most famous dance of West Sumatra, the *Randai*. Padangpanjang has the highest railway station in Indonesia (1400 m). See Lake Singarak from the lookout point in this town. **stay:** Hotel Bungalow Riwung Gunung is Rp600. Hotel Makmur, Jl. Dahlan 34, Rp500 single, Rp1500 for 3.

Payakumbuh: 35 km east of Bukittinggi. A dirty town, nothing much to do except on Sunday when there's a spectacular market alive with color, noise, jostling people, odors of spice stalls, selling a large variety of bamboo and rattan products. In this area the finest horses in all of Sumatra are bred. Purnama Souvenir Shop has stuffed Sumatran wild cats, and tiger skins for Rp200,000. A nice little village to visit near Payakumbuh is Batang Tabit, with freshwater springs for swimming and *warungs* for refreshing.

Batusangkar: 56 km S.E. of Bukittinggi. Stay at Mess Kiambang, near Batusangkar, Rp500. Or at Wisma Jakarta, Rp1500. This town was once the focus of the old Minangkabau Kingdom. For a trip into the past, visit the Balairung Sari community house and the old *banyan* tree in the nearby village of Pagaruyang. Ask about the unexplained 'Written

the ruins of Muaro Takus: Many antiquities are found in central Sumatra, the most important being the ruins of Muaro Takus, which date from the 11th and 12th centuries. These temples were probably the graves of royal personages. The strange thing is that there are no statues or images of Buddah, and therefore it is questionable whether Buddhism had entered Minangkabau at that time. The 36 sided stupa base seems to be related to the 36 nat spirits of the Burmese pantheon. The form and construction of the temples indicate that Muaro Takus was a Hindu monument rather than a Buddhist one. The ruins formed part of a 12 sq km town which was entirely surrounded by an earthen wall. The central buildings (see diagram) were encircled by a sandstone wall measuring 76 sq km.

Maligai Stupa: Directly opposite a great gate, on the south side of the courtyard, stands the best preserved building: the slender, graceful Maligai Stupa (maligai = palace). Its rectangular foundation measures 9.1 by 10.62 m. On the north side ascends a flight of steps which have been twice rebuilt in the course of time. On the foundation stands a 28-sided pediment (a triangle piece used in decorating, as over a door-way, etc.). From this pedestal ascends a round tower. The body of the stupa rests on a double lotus cushion. The crown of the stupa was 36-sided, on four of which were placed sitting lions of sandstone. In the center of the tower was once a hole 2 m deep in which rested a wooden mast, bearing several sunshades, one above the other.

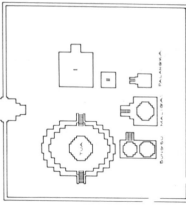

other structures: East of the stupa lies a rectangular terrace 5.18 m by 6 m with an extension and a flight of steps on the north side. West of the stupa lies a similar terrace, called Candi Bungsu (bungsu = youngest). It formerly supported a 20-sided foundation, with a stupa in a wreath of smaller stupas. It recalls the upper terrace of the Borobudur. Immediately north of Candi Bungsu stands Candi Tua (tua = old), the largest (though not the highest) building of Muaro Takus. Its greatest length is about 30.5 m, the greatest breadth 20.5 m. East of Candi Tua a sandstone foundation measuring 13.5 by 16.72 m was excavated, while south of these ruins a foundation about 6 m by 6 m came to light.

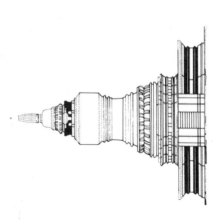

Stone' and the Batu Batikan (Stabbed Stone). There's a breathtaking view from the ridge of Tabetpatah which takes in the entire plain of Limapuluh Kota and even the Harau Canyon 35 km away. Also visit the ancient village of Pariangan near Batusangkar.

THE MENTAWAIS

An island group off the west coast of Sumatra. Long locked in its own time zone, isolated from the rest of Indonesia, the 30,000 inhabitants of Mentawai have a different language and totally different customs than the Minangkabaus of mainland West Sumatra. They lacked weaving, rice, pottery, even betelnut chewing until the start of this century. Arrange for interisland transport with the *camat* or with the missionaries. **getting there:** Catch a boat from Telukdalam, Nias, about twice weekly. A *kapal motor* leaves twice a month from· Teluk Bayur, near Padang. Boats depart more frequently from Muara, Padang's small harbor Rp40 by *bemo* from Padang. Costs Rp1500-2000 to any of the islands: 11-12 hours to Siberut (the least visited but the nearest island and the largest), 14 hours to Sipora (the central island) and 18 hours to North or South Pagai. There is no airstrip on the islands.

people: On Siberut, patrilineal clans dwell in villages along the riverbanks, 5-10 families living together in one building (uma). Wholly egalitarian, there are no headmen. Even women and children take part in discussions. Barter is preferred to cash sales. The Siberutese eat sago and bananas, the Siporese and Pagaiese prefer taro (a tubur grown in swidden gardens) and bananas, barely subsistence diets. There are also cassava, sweet potatoes, pepper, peas, *durian,* mango and pineapples. Their only exports are merchants' yokes (pikulan) which are made from a palm wood soaked 3 years in coconut oil. The government gave the people cattle but they let them wander off into the jungle. Malaria, bronchitis, gastroenteritis, malnutrition are widespread.

religion: having been active from the beginning of this century, Christian missionaries today claim perhaps half of the 30,000 Mentawains. All schools on all the islands are run by the missionaries, free of government interference, and there are now about 80 Protestant churches throughout the Mentawais. The other half believe in the usual Indonesian animism. What is most unusual about their society, however, is the strong ritual application of taboos, sometimes for months on end. The occasion of the taboo could be the building of a new house, making a boat, clearing a field, cutting down a coconut tree, an adoption, etc. During these times mens' lives could come to a complete standstill. They are prohibited from certain foods, the village could be closed to all outsiders, and the women must do all the work and obtain all the food during taboo periods. Their religion (Sibulungan), is based on nature spirits and the belief that everything, everywhere is animate- under the earth, in the jungle, in the sky, on the beach, in the sea. And everything has a soul, including floods and rainbows. No object is ever thrown away while it's still functioning for its soul would be greatly offended. They believe that monkeys are the 'chickens of the spirit' belonging to all the immortal ancestors who live in the 'Big Settlement'. Among these people the soul doesn't like men rushing about, so *moile, moile* (slowly, slowly) is one of the most common calls. It's an insult to ask someone to hurry. *Kerei* (medicine men) can communicate with spirits and heal the sick. Certain plants, called 'mediators', are employed to turn away evil spirits; entrails of animals such as pigs' hearts are used in invocations to supernatural powers. Clan ceremonies could happen anytime. During their purifying ceremonies (puliaijat), all productive work is taboo. Slit drums beating, they sing and call for hours, dance through the night, stage animal pantomines, slaughter pigs. This old religion has been forbidden by the government, yet persists.

Pagai Islands: From Muara harbor in Padang, Rp2500 and 24 hours by *kapal motor.* Another isolated culture, the Pagai people, live on these islands south of the Mentawais. Some villages still practice a stone age culture. On the islands Labuhan Bajau (Pirate's Landing) on Simeulue, and Sibajau (Pirate's Place) on an islet near Siberut, were all once dreaded places where pirates from Borneo and the Sulu area put in. There are chiefs' houses on the Batu Islands.

THE MINANGKABAU

West Sumatra is almost entirely ethnic Minangkabau, comprising about ¼ of Sumatra's population (5 million). Fervent Muslims, they are one of the best educated and most vigorous groups in all of Indonesia. Although sometimes called *Orang Padang*, they are an interior, not a coastal people. The word Minangkabau derives from *pinang kabhu* meaning 'original home', this area being the earliest homeland of this Malay people. The tourist legend says that their name means 'Victorious Buffalo' and that it has its source in a legendary fight in which steel spikes were tied to the head of a starved calf which was then let loose, gorging to death its opponent, a Javanese buffalo whom it thought was its mother. This is not so. The Minangkabaus have invented a false etymology to reinforce their popular worship of buffaloes.

history: Shards of earthenware have been found at Surien and Kamang used by men in this region over 2000 years ago. The Hindu-Malay Kingdom of Minangkabau rose in the 12-14th Centuries after the decay of the Sriwijaya Empire to the east at a time when Indian cultural influences began to spread into the highlands. Pariangan was their ancient capital. The imprint of this Brahmanic civilization is still evident in a wide range of features: Indian style scripts, agricultural skills, methods of political organization, remains of Hindu-Buddhist monuments. Minangkabaus have had a long history of brass-cutting and of mining, smelting, processing and forging weapons and farm tools out of iron or steel. They used cannons and bored matchlocks long before Europeans ever got here. (In the museum in Bukittinggi see a rifle barrel that was made by wrapping a flattened bar of iron around a circular rod and hammering it until it became a tube.) Small Muslim states ruled by sultans became powerful on Sumatra and gradually forced this kingdom into the central regions where it hung onto its independence and culture until 1825. By the time the first Europeans landed, the area was entirely under Islamic influence. In the years 1820-1837 there was a violent struggle in the Minangkabau regions between the traditional *adat* chiefs and the

Padris, religious reformers who tried to purify the Islam of the area by eliminating pre-Islamic customs such as gambling and drinking. In this rebellion against the Dutch, who sided with the *adat* chiefs, a religious and political leader Tuanku Iman Bonjol and his defenders held out until the last fortress fell at Banjol and the Padris power checked. Songs, poems and books have been written about this folk hero.

people: A strong matriarchal and matrilineal society. Even afterlife beliefs are mother-oriented, reflected in the saying, 'Heaven is below the sole of mother's foot.' (You won't get to heaven if you mistreat your mother.) Women here were once queens and women are celebrated in legends *(Kaba Cindue Moto)*. The grandmother is the grand matriarch. Houses are very much the domain of women, they also own the fields and the shops. Property belongs to a cooperate group, the matrilineage, which persists through time. Daughters inherit the property which is worked collectively and kept as family capital. In the highlands, up to 70 members can still be found living in a single house, all descended from one ancestral mother. Relatives from the mother's side hold the weight in family politics. A child is regarded as a member of the mother's family group whereas the father's group regard it as purely a blood relative without any rights of inheritance. The real father stays out of family affairs and the mother's brother (mamak) is the most important male who replaces the father and gives advice on business deals and the marrying off of children. The *mamak* is responsible for the education of his sister's children, likewise his wife's brother is responsible for the education of his own children. In this way male privileges are maintained.

merantau: The central area for Minangkabau culture is the group of valleys surrounding Gunung Merapi, near Bukittinggi, but also includes a belt along the west coast around Padang and much of the swampy lowlands extending towards the east coast. These areas the Minangkabau call *rantau*, originally meaning 'lower reaches and bay of a river', but now has evolved to mean any area where one goes to seek his fortune. Thus the word *merantau*, 'to go abroad'. The reason why this society is matriarchal is mostly economic. The Minangkabaus are a very shrewd people commercially, being the only ones who can compete successfully with the Chinese in Jakarta. From time immemorial Minangkabau men have had to absent themselves frequently from the family to do business, for scholastic study, or to search for fame, fortune, or adventure. Wives and daughters have always kept the home fires buring in his absence. There's really not much keeping a man back on the farm for he must wait politely until a girl or her family asks him in marriage through an intermediary, and all he has to look forward to is a life of working on his mother-in-law's farm. With so little industrial development and since population pressure is increasing, half the male population is driven out of the traditional homeland to the Man's World of Java, and they often remain there. This mass migration has resulted in the Minangkabau population of Jakarta being

greater than that of Padang itself. An important segment of the leadership of modern Indonesia today is ethnically Minangkabau.

religion: Having been converted by fanatical Acehnese from the north, the Minangkabau area is one of the most staunchly Islamicized regions in Indonesia. At the same time these people are known for their very strong adherence to local custom, a system which would appear in direct opposition to Islamic law. For example, it's rare that a Minangkabau husband will have more than one wife even though Islam allows him four. A man may have more than one wife but he must commute between the homes of all his wives. The mother arranges the children's marriages to ensure that the spouse comes from an outside clan, which is very strong *adat*. The bride doesn't leave home at all: she doesn't move in with him, he has to go to her. After the wedding, the bridegroom is escorted to the home of his bride, proudly taking with him all his

rumah gadang: *The 'Big House' of the Minangkabau often accommodates a number of families and is constructed on 20-30 wooden pillars. The roof is made of thick layers of black palm-tree fibres (ijuk). Each daughter is entitled to a room where she'll receive her husband when she marries and extra extensions (horns) are built onto their high roofs for each son-in-law the mother or* grandmother acquires. In front are richly decorated rice sheds (lumbung) identical to the Big House but just on a smaller scale. The more rice sheds, the wealthier the family. The Minangkabau expression derived from their house-building, 'It doesn't crack in the heat or rot in the rain ...', is used to express durability, tenacity, integrity.

possessions or his workshop to prove that he is a man of substance. In coastal areas there's even a groom price according to a man's title or rank. If he doesn't wish to move in with his in-laws, he is free to visit his new wife, asking to be let in each night. If the marriage doesn't work he usually marries another woman of the matrilineage, often his wife's sister. Sons sleep at a *serau* (mens' meeting house) from age 14 or so until they marry.

rumah gadang (big house): Traditional Minang dwellings. Their peaked roofs are reminiscent of the curved horns of water buffaloes and of the womens' ceremonial headdress. You can tell how many husbands and children a family's daughters have by the number of extensions on the roof. Bedrooms are set aside for daughters of the household and their husbnds, and there's a long common room for living and dining. Raised up to 3½ m off the ground, one must climb up and down the *rumah gadang* on a single piece of notched timber that's pulled up quickly in case of enemies, tigers, and snakes. Each cluster of houses in a village is often the locale of one matrilineage. Traditional houses are disappearing now, being replaced by brick and corrugated iron structures. In the Tanah Datar region, instead of shiny galvanized iron roofs mosques are divided into 4 or 5 pagoda-like roofs which mirror lingering Hindu influences. The old mosque of Lima Kaum has 5 storeys, symbolizing the 5 villages of the district. Because of dense foilage, drums in many Sumatran villages are beaten to announce the times of prayer, public announcements, or to give the alarm in case of emergency. A muezzin's voice would never carry.

spirits and health: Although strong believers in Allah, there are many indigenous spirits to the area: *urang jadi-jadian* can become tigers; *cindaku* are human-appearing monsters like Dracula who eat people and naughty children; *jindai* are beautiful women with long flowing hair who laugh eerily; *palasik* make children sickly and weak; *dukuns* specialize in massage, muscular disorders, and organ displacement, using a wide range of herbs and foods for medicinal purposes. Crystalized elephant sperm is an especially powerful ingredient for use in love magic.

music and dance: A popular dance is the *Tari Piring* (Dish Dance) in which entranced dancers perform on top of broken dishes. *Tari Payung,* (Umbrella Dance) portrays a young man's loving protection of his girlfriend. The graceful *Tari Lilin* (Candle Dance) is performed by girls who rhythmically juggle and balance china saucers on which lighted candles are stuck, clicking ring castanets at the same time. Though also known in Palembang, it

originated in West Sumatra. *Randai,* a combination of literature, sport, song, and drama, is held outdoors at night. It's put on by 20 young men dressed in *gelambuk* trousers and black dress, accompanied by a native Minangkabau orchestra. Using many *pencak silat* movements, this dance tells the story of a wicked woman driven from her village. *Randai* is performed best in the Pagurujung area. Also see a dance demonstrating how a *beruk* monkey climbs a coconut tree and picks choice coconuts for his owner. In the *Dabuih* Dance men stick themselves with awls (a show of faith) while in religiously induced trance. Instruments played in West Sumatra include the *rebab pasisir,* a coastal lute with 3 strings; and gong ensemble music.

pencak silat: A technique of self-defence from which a male dance form is styled. The Minang regional version is feared and admired all over Indonesia. Most of the large variety of styles are accompanied by drums and flutes. The fighting dance *Mudo* is performed by 2 men. This very technical but potentially deadly mock combat dance with dramatic pauses after each stance, is called off just before it becomes violent. Minangkabau men can kill fish in the water with blows of their feet. In the Painan area they've created a form of *pencak silat* inspired by a tiger's stalking and killing methods. Called *harimau-silat,* it's the most violent, dangerous and *kasar* form of all Minangkabau *silat*. Because it developed in wet, muddy mountain terrain, body positions are very low to the ground; fighters crawl stealthily like tigers.

crafts: Each Minangkabau village is known for its specialty—woven sugarcane and reed purses, imitation gold jewelry and silver filigree work, or intricate weaving and embroidery work. Their handloom *sarungs* woven with gold thread (very expensive) create a gleaming metallic design. The woman's traditional headdress is a turban with sharp conical points called *tanduk* (horns). Minang bridal gowns, perhaps inspired by 17th Century suits, are magnificent pieces of embroidery; to be framed in pictures or gasped at on a wall.

arts: These people have one of the highest literacy levels in Indonesia. Men are so well educated in this society because if the father dies his son is able to continue his study supported by his mother's side. Although they make up only 4% of the Indonesian population, there are more Minangkabau among 20th Century Indonesian writers than any other ethnic group. They are, afterall, writing in their native tongue: the Indonesian language was derived from Sumatra. In the only 50 years of modern Indonesian literature, such important pre-war writers as Rusli *(Sitti Nurabaya,* 1922), Muis *(Wrong*

Upbringing), Pustaka, Iskander, Pane, Anwar, Idrus, and the first noteworthy female novelist, Selasih *(If Fortune Does Not Favor)*, all came from this region. These books in their time were shattering. The first writer of importance to write Indonesian language poetry, which employed western poetic devices and concepts, was Muhammad Yamin (b. 1903). One of the earliest and best known of his poems is *Tanah Air (My Fatherland)*, published in 1920. In it, Yamin stands on the hills of his native Minangkabau country, singing of its beauty. His efforts revealed the potential of verse written in the Indonesian language. Rustam Effendi (b. 1903) is another outstanding poet of West Sumatra.

The white Sumatran beruk monkey is put on a long leash and trained to climb palm trees to pick ripe select coconuts for its owners.

BUKITTINGGI

Means 'high place'. Administrative, cultural and educational center for the Minangkabau people. One of the loveliest, friendliest, most relaxing towns in all of Sumatra with musical taxis, pompom-doured horse carts, veiled schoolgirls, elderly ladies walking sedately under umbrellas, banks of flowers, and giant Muslim meals. Set against mountain scenery, it's hilly (910-920 m above sea level) with a cool but sunny climate and healthy fresh mountain air. Bukittinggi is a real oasis after the jungles and grungy towns further south, a great place to rest up after burning your ass raw on the bus trip. It even has sidewalks. The horses here are the best looked after in all of Indonesia. Women run the show here and they really get off on relaxed females. A small university town, many people speak English. Magicians and *dukuns* are always in the streets. It's suggested not to wear shorts on Fri. and Saturdays.

stay: Grand Hotel, Jl. Jen. A. Yani 115, is very popular and geared to travelers. It costs Rp400 single, Rp900 double with sink, Rp800 double without sink. They know everything about the area; have a look at their guestbook. For information see Mr. Sulaiman or Mr. Yang. Drinks and foods such as eggs and toast are also served. You're awakened each morning by wild sounds of animals from the zoo, starting at 6 am. For something plusher next door is the Chinese-run Yany Hotel; some single rooms for Rp2000, double rooms from Rp1500-3500. Ask them about their annex (Rp500), right on the edge of the canyon, which has a kitchen to do your own cooking (only 2 of the rooms have windows and there's a key for everything). Often all by yourself, sit and watch storms move down the canyon. Hotel Zakiah, also on Jl. Jen A. Yani, is a very loose place with police sometimes gambling downstairs. Clean, cheap (Rp800 double), and coffee and tea is served (but not food). During the day all rooms are noisy except the ones in the back, but at night it's very quiet with only the sound of horses' hoofs on the street outside. Don't sit in the back set of chairs on the top floor: they have cane bugs. Opie arranges 8 am to 8 pm minibus tours of the lakes, the caves, or anywhere a group wants to go, Rp2000 per person; a good deal. Singgalang Hotel, Jl. A. Yani 130, opposite Didi's Restaurant, is Rp400 single, Rp800 double, a breakfast of coffee or tea and bread is free. Buy bus tickets here for Prapat, Lubuklinggau or Jakarta. Hotel Yogya, Jl. Prof. M. Yamin 17, charges Rp400 for dingy dorm beds, Rp850 for single rooms, Rp1700 for double rooms; very central, right next to the *oplet* terminal, but motorcycles rev up at 5 am along with the Muslim call to prayer. Losmen Roda Baru, right across from the day market and bus station, is Rp400. Hotel Nirwana, Jl. Yani, opposite Hotel Yogya, charges Rp1500 for bed and breakfast.

eat: The food in this town is worth all those hard-earned coins, a munchie's dream. If you're a vegetarian the restaurants can make *martabak* without meat. There are *sayak* (fruits, vegetables and tangy sauce) and *apam* carts all over town. Be warned that the 'tomato juice' found in Bukittinggi equals a sweet pink milk shake that tastes like baby's vomit. Rumah Makan Simpang Raya near the new market is briskly patronized by Indonesians for its *nasi padang*. Try their fried eels, Rp100 a bundle, and probably the best *soto daging* in Indonesia. Roda Restaurant nearby caters more to the western palate. French toast Rp125 and fruit salad with honey and molasses; also fruit juices Rp75 plus the usual *mie goreng* and *nasi padang;* sit by the window and look out on the market life. If you go down 3 *warungs* on the left past Roda's towards the stairway down to the bus station, get better, cheaper and thicker water buffalo yoghurt. Flop your jaws on real oats topped with yoghurt, avocado, cane syrup, and grated coconut, Rp100; afterwards it feels like you've swallowed a boulder. The Mini Corner near the Jaya is the place for Indonesian oxtail soup (sup buntut), Rp125. The Fu Yung Hai and other (expensive) dishes at the Monalisa Chinese restaurant down the street from the Jaya are superb. The food at Didi's Asia Restaurant is outrageously and blandly westernized; there's just something you can't trust about a *warung* that plays western cassettes. But with its atmosphere it makes the ideal traveler's hangout, drinking and meeting place at night. Rock music blasts out front of the Jaya, Jl. A. Yani, and the food is consistently good. Enormous *ristaffels* are set before you but you pay only for what you eat. Fish curry and *rendang* is what the Jaya is known for. Also good vegetable soup, Rp75 (but their Singapore fried rice has no taste at all), try as well the *es pokat*. Read the travelers' comments in the visitor's books, lots of sage, and hilarious advice. Meet friendly Uncle Didi if he's in town, he has a good repertoire of card tricks. Ask to see his photo album.

sights: There's a fascinating market on Sat. on steps of hills. Watch the sunset from Fort de Kock, built in 1825 on a promontory overlooking the town; see the smoking volcano and all the surrounding mountains from here. At dusk giant fruit bats come out. The highest point in town is the zoo just behind the museum, Rp60 entrance. It's a must to walk around this zoo on Sun. when everybody parades around in their best Minang apparel, shawls, and bright colorful *kebayas*. The zoo specializes in Sumatran wildlife; the animals are fantastic though despondent due to lousy care. The best is the bird collection and the animals of northern Sumatra such as the *serow* mountain goat (lives over 1500 m), and the *anoa*. Masses of birds, 150 species at least: 3 sorts of hornbills, 6 kinds of fishing owls, broadbills, and nearly all the pigeons of Indonesia. Rumah Adat Baandjuang Museum is on the grounds of the zoo, Rp30 entrance. This building, opened in 1844, typifies West Sumatran architecture. Inside are resplendent Minang wedding costumes and headdresses, old specimens of matchlock rifles (no rifling process); also models of obsolete and current architectural styles, sculptures, musical and dancing instruments.

crafts: Not all the semi-precious stones you see in the markets come from West Sumatra, many are brought by Arab traders from the Middle East. Try Aisha Chalik, Jl. Cindua Mato 94, near the museum, a new shop of West Sumatran handicrafts, typical Minang garments; household goods. Reasonable prices: hand embroidered bedcovers, 2-5 m width and length, asking price Rp10,000; *benang mas sarungs* with gold thread, Rp6000; and *benak mecau*, Rp3000, each with different qualities of thread; hand embroidered shawls (selandang gadang), Rp6000; handwoven *selandang pandai sikat*, Rp2500-3000 for a small size; pajama-like cream colored embroidered tops for men, Rp2000; *batik* trousers, Rp2000. Visit the goldsmith and antique shops street, Jl. A. Yani: find old blunderbuss pistols, Rp40,000; antique brass buttons, 10 for Rp2200; 19th Century gas lamps converted into electric lamps, US$100; 19th Century silver cased Swiss pocket watches (never seen so many in your life), Rp5000-10,000. At Nefa antique and souvenir shop, Jl. A. Yani 36, meet Mr. A.S. Majo Indo; really nice and he knows his stuff. Another small shop but loaded with prize bric-a-brac is Toko Ber-Ingin, Jl. Syahrir 52 A. Other shops are just as captivating. Visit Sulungkang village for woodcarving and handwoven gold threaded *sarung*. Kota Baru also produces gold threaded weaving. Kota Gadang for filigree silverwork.

miscellaneous: A very mellow billiard hall is located down a hidden back alley so nobody can see it, but Rp300 a game (on Java only Rp150 per game). Five new tables, fine banks. Coffee and pastries also available. Sick? Dr. Leo Lesvare, near the Grand Hotel, has lots of experience with diseased travelers. The Army Hospital also looks after you good. Or see American Dr. Applewhite (from Miss.) at the Immanuel Baptist Mission Hospital who charges Rp1000 a visit.

from Bukittinggi by long-distance bus: For bus trips south contact A.L.S., Jl. H.M. Yamin

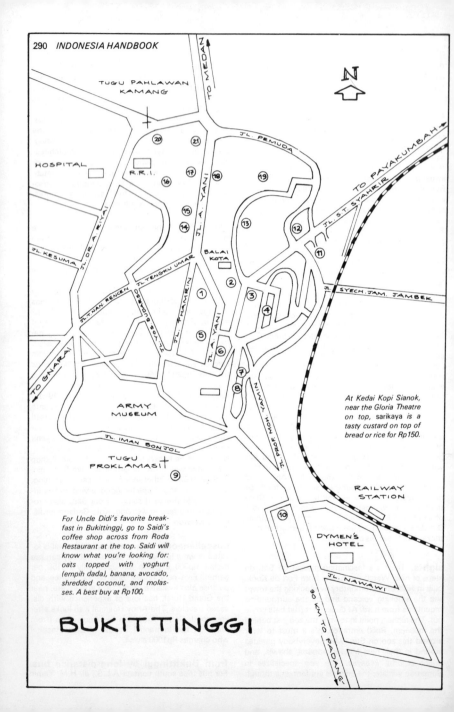

TUGU PAHLAWAN
KAMANG

TO MEDAN

N

JL. PEMUDA

HOSPITAL

R.R.I.

20
21
17
16
18
19

JL. A. YANI

15
14

13
12
11

JL. ST. SYAHRIR

TO PAYAKUMBUH

JL. KESUMA

JL. DR. RIVAI

JL. TENGKU UMAR

JL. TUAN RENCEN

JL. SUDIRMAN

BALAI
KOTA

JL. THAMRIN

JL. SYECH. JAM. JAMBEK

1
2
3
4

5
6

JL. A. YANI

7
8

JL. PROF. MOH. YAMIN

TO GNARA

ARMY
MUSEUM

JL. IMAN BONJOL

TUGU
PROKLAMASI
9

At Kedai Kopi Sianok,
near the Gloria Theatre
on top, sarikaya is a
tasty custard on top of
bread or rice for Rp150.

RAILWAY
STATION

For Uncle Didi's favorite breakfast in Bukittinggi, go to Saidi's
coffee shop across from Roda
Restaurant at the top. Saidi will
know what you're looking for:
oats topped with yoghurt
(empih dada), banana, avocado,
shredded coconut, and molasses. A best buy at Rp100.

10

DYMEN'S
HOTEL

JL. NAWAWI

90 KM TO PADANG

BUKITTINGGI

SH/41, tel. 2214. They have Mercedes buses to: Sibolga, Rp1750; Lake Toba, Rp2400; Lubukling-gau, Rp4500, 20 hours; Jakarta, Rp10,500; Prapat, Rp2400. There are also ordinary buses to: Sibolga, Rp1500; Pekanbaru, Rp500, leaving at least 4 times daily; Lake Toba, Rp1800; Lubuklinggau, Rp4250; Muaratebo, Rp2250; Prapat, Rp1800. Bus bookings can be made from most hotels and sometimes the bus will even come around and pick you up. **Lake Toba:** This 12 hour bus journey is less gruesome if you stop overnight at Sibolga, 12 hours by bus from Bukittinggi. Book a bus ticket for Prapat (a further 6 hours) as soon as you get into Sibolga. **oplets** (local Chevrolet buses): The main oplet station is at Stasiun Hotel Yogya, to: Kota Baru, Rp75; Kota Gadang, Rp60; Padangpanjang, Rp75; Solok, Rp250; Padang, Rp325 (take the more picturesque road via Solok); Payakumbuh, Rp125; Nglau Kamang, Rp75; Pandai Sikat, Rp75; Batang Palaphu, Rp50 (*reflesia* anyone?); Tanah Datar, Rp200 (also to Lima Kaum, Rp200). Another station is at Aur Tanjungkang where you can also catch Colts, *bemos* and *oplets* to most of the outlying areas of Bukittinggi. **train:** The cog wheel train to Padang actually begins about 15 km out of Bukittinggi; sometimes it's running, sometimes not. There's no passenger service from Bukittinggi to Rajutanan. Ride on top of the freight car.

vicinity of Bukittinggi: Right on the equator,

BUKITTINGGI

1. Jaya Restaurant
2. Simpang Raya Restaurant
3. Roda Restaurant
4. Pasar Atas (Central Market)
5. Bank Rakyat (change money here)
6. Clock Tower
7. Yogya Hotel
8. oplet and minibus station
9. panorama
10. Post Office
11. oplet and minibus station Aur Tanjungkang
12. main bus station
13. Aisha Chalik Souvenir Shop
14. Grand Hotel
15. Hotel Yany
16. Fort de Kock
17. Didi's Asia Restaurant
18. Singgalang Hotel
19. zoo and museum
20. Hotel Denai
21. Hotel Zakiah

---

a rugged area of gorges, mountain streams and fields. **Ngarai** (or Buffalo Hole): Just on the outskirts of town there's this 4 km long chasm with steep rocky walls; sometimes billed as 'The Grand Canyon of Indonesia'. Best seen early in the morning when covered in mists. Just after the panorama lookout in Bukittinggi, take the narrow path which descends down into the canyon. Ask the *warung* near the panorama where the path begins. Walking the gorge can be a day's trip in itself. The walls of this canyon, composed of volcanic material and layers of ashes and stones embedded from Merapi's eruptions, are an interesting geological study. It's possible to walk along the tracks made by water buffaloes as far as the bamboo bridge, 12 km upriver (walk halfway to Lake Maninjau if you care to). The track leads up the mountainsides, then back to Bukittinggi. Many small *kampungs* on the way, monkeys, etc. See the Japanese ammunition caves. **Mt. Merapi:** Bright green slopes rise up to this 2440 m high volcano, the top often disappearing in clouds; last erupted in 1926. Go first to Kota Baru village at its base. Stay overnight, then get up at 4 am to start the climb. See Bukittinggi and the whole countryside from the top. Stay in the shack near the summit.

Kota Gadang: A silversmith village one hour's walk down the gorge; take a *mandi* in the river on the way. Many flowers and a lot of birdlife, and at the end there are 80 giant steps which lead up to the village. From this one small village of only 2000 people a school has turned out a remarkable number of Indonesian cabinet ministers, diplomats and professors. Visit Denny and Dessy at 'Silverwork'; Rp1000-2500 for filigree worked brocades and rings. Tiny Minangkabau houses in silver, Rp650, etc. Get served tea, fruits, and maybe a slice of pumpkin pie while you bargain like mad. Kota Gadang is also renowned for its fine hand-embroidered shawls and weaving.

reflesia: A botanical classic grows just 12 km north of Bukittinggi at Batang Palapuh (20 minutes and Rp50 by bus). Make sure that this giant flower is in bloom before you go, otherwise you'll have to content yourself with a 30 minutes walk through rice paddies (which is not bad) and view the bulb only, the size of a softball. The *reflesia* blooms in July and August. Measuring up to 1 m across the weighing as much as 7 kilos, this thick fleshy scarlet and white flower has a putrid odor which attracts flies and carrion beetles. **Nglau Kamang:** 8 km from town. A 5 km long cave full of stalagtites and stalagmites. Take a flashlight for they charge too much to guide you. **Bukitlawar:** The orangutans in the forest here will try to steal your camera and clothing. **Pandai Sikat:** A village noted for the excellent quality and variety of its woodcarvings. For red and gold traditional carving, visit Wali Negeri's house.

LAKE MANINJAU

A retreat for famous poets and philosophers (Hamka), known for its culture, remoteness, and beauty. The best thing about this lake is the ride there and back on the bus. From Stasiun Bis in Bukittinggi, it's only 36 km and Rp200. On the way you pass white-veiled girls praying in ricefields and men with their hunting dogs along the road; wild pigs are regularly hunted for sports in this area. Get off the bus at the top, it's 1¾ hours walk and 44 switchbacks to the bottom, an incredible descent. In the village on the lake floor visit the hotsprings (only warm), about 500 m down the road from the bus stop and a short walk from the road. **alternative approach:** Take the Lake Maninjau bus but get off 17 km before at Matur. Get to the lookout about 5 km past Lawang from where you can see all the valleys to the other side of the lake. Then walk down to the lake through the jungle. **from Lake Maninjau:** The last bus from Maninjau to Bukittinggi returns at 2 or 3 and it's very crowded; scalpers sell their seats for Rp500. To hire a *bemo* for the return trip to Bukittinggi costs Rp6000! On Fri., because of the market, a bus goes back as late as 4 pm.

stay: Maninjau Indah, right on the lake, rents rooms for Rp3500; if you hit them at the right time, maybe only Rp500. Jump in the lake from your porch. Also has a bar and a restaurant. Other rooms rent for Rp1000, right next to the noisy moviehouse. The only cheap *losmen,* with only one room available, is Pasanggerahan Tanjung Raja, Rp250 per person. Quite a dingy place but only 150 m from the water which is a good thing as there is sometimes no *mandi* water. Visit the jail next door and chat with murderers and felons sitting on the steps.

vicinity of Lake Maninjau: Rent a canoe Rp250-400 per hour and go fishing. It takes 2 or 3 days to walk completely around the lake on the footpath that encircles it. For entomologists, *buprestidae* (size 4 cm) can be found around Maninjau; ask the children. From the docks by the Maninjau Indah Hotel, take small ferry boats to small *kampungs* on the lake: Tanjung Sani, Rp100; Gelapung, Rp100; Batu Nangai, Rp200. Stay with the people in the *kampungs* or else at the *kepala kampung's* house, Rp2500. **Min Mau:** Hotsprings, oranges, monkeys, and birds on the river at dusk. **Muko-Muko:** 8 km from Maninjau. Buy *durians* in season

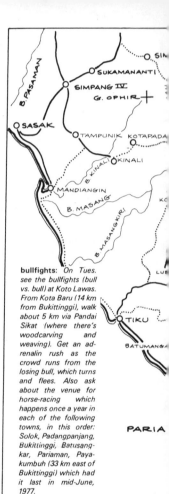

bullfights: *On Tues. see the bullfights (bull vs. bull) at Koto Lawas. From Kota Baru (14 km from Bukittinggi), walk about 5 km via Pandai Sikat (where there's woodcarving and weaving). Get an adrenalin rush as the crowd runs from the losing bull, which turns and flees. Also ask about the venue for horse-racing which happens once a year in each of the following towns, in this order: Solok, Padangpanjang, Bukittinggi, Batusangkar, Pariaman, Payakumbuh (33 km east of Bukittinggi) which had it last in mid-June, 1977.*

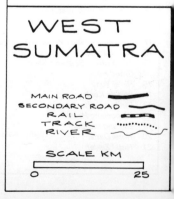

WEST SUMATRA

MAIN ROAD
SECONDARY ROAD
RAIL
TRACK
RIVER

SCALE KM

0   25

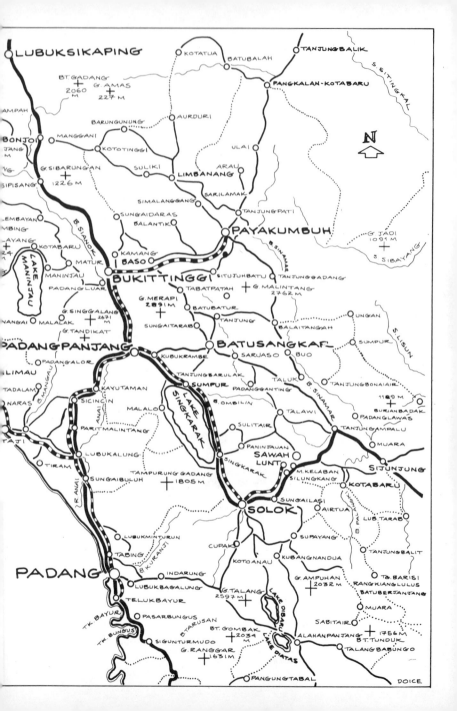

(July and Aug.) for Rp60 each (Rp250 in Bukittinggi). Many people from Bukittinggi come out to this village on the weekends to eat at Suleiman's Restoran Tanjung Alai, popular for its fresh lake fish; Rp250 for a Minang-style dinner. Stay for nothing at Suleiman's and walk down to the river one hour before dusk to watch monkeys come down to the water; also beautiful vegetation, mimosa plants, coffee shrubs.

SIBOLGA

A port town on the west coast 350 km from Medan whose main claim to fame is as the embarcation point for boats to the Isle of Nias. Amazing sunsets over the hill when coming into town; the mosque at sunset is good too. Hello Mr.'s abound. Meet the odd sleasy creep, characteristic of port towns. The water stinks like sulpher. Quiet fishing village north of town. **stay:** Hotel Indah Sari, Jl. Jen. Ahmad Yani 27-29, the most expensive joint in town; Rp4500, for 3 beds, A.C., and private *mandi;* Rp1650, 3 beds without *mandi;* Rp1100, 2 beds and no window. Cleaner, quieter and more spacious than any of the other hotels. Next best is the Rodaminang Hotel and Restaurant, next door to Sudi Mampir; rooms for Rp900 but cleaner and airier than the other cheapies. Hotel Subur, Jl. Diponegoro 19, charges Rp600, Rp900, and Rp1200 for rooms (all doubles); a flophouse with paper-thin walls, a real transient place and dirty. Losmen Sentral has rooms with 2 windows for Rp600 double;

very central, near the mosque, nothing special. Hotel Sudi Mampir, Jl. Mesjid 98, has 15 rooms available which are slightly better than Subur, but the same price. Has bigger rooms for Rp1200. Quite central, meals are served downstairs *(nasi campur,* Rp150-200), friendly. **eat:** Food is somewhat expensive. Chinese restaurant Telok Indah, Jl. Jen. A. Yani 63-65, has excellent *funjunghai,* Rp300; *cap cai,* Rp225. Medai Kopi Bali, Jl. Let. Jen. S. Parman 45, has better than usual *mie* dishes, *mie kuah,* Rp125, or with an egg, Rp200. Restoran Slamet, Jl. Katamso 30, is very clean and has quite good food.

from Sibolga by boat: Take 30-40 ton cargo boats to Telukdalam, South Nias; takes 17-24 hours. A boat leaves about once every 4-5 days for Telukdalam and every night for Gunungsitoli, North Nias. Ask at Nias Shipping Co., Jl. Iman Bonjol; Lahewa Shipping Co., or Purnama. The Karya Subur sails to Telukdalam, Rp1750, but the day it departs isn't definite. The Agape (to Gunungsitoli) holds 75 people, Rp1250; departure also not sure. Boats are often in repair. Bring food along. Paian at Rodaminang Hotel and Restaurant will call up and ask if a ship is leaving that day or when. Hurry, cruise ships started calling at Nias in March, 1974, and flights started up in March, 1977. **for Aceh Province:** The Baringan Raya sails to Sinabang, Simeulue Island, Rp2850, 4 times a month. There are also ships to Tapaktuan (Aceh Province), or you can first voyage to Sinabang, then direct to Tapaktuan. Try Baringan Lloyd Company.

Minangkabau tiger-capturing song: *A pre-Islamic song performed by certain gifted shaman who are expert in the art of silat (self-defence). In the forest these men sing to the tiger melodious ballads set to elegant poetic meters, treating the tiger as if it had all the emotions and motivations of a human being. The song is designed to entice the tiger into a cage, then it is killed with respect. Arabic prayers preceed the songs and bull roarers made out of pieces of a little boy's skull accompany them.*

ISLE OF NIAS

An island 240 km long and 80 km wide, about 125 km off the west coast of Sumatra. **getting there:** There are flights from Medan to Nias 3 times a week, about US$47, with Merpati. By boat, Sibolga is the usual port of embarcation. A boat leaves Sibolga for Telukdalam, Nias, about once every 4-5 days; costs Rp1750. Sometimes there's only 6 inches of freeboard between you and the water and much of the 12-16 hours you might spend vomiting over the side. Other boats leave Sibolga for Gunungsitoli, northern Nias, more or less every night; takes 10-12 hours, costs Rp1250. The ship Intan carries salt and cement to Nias. It leaves Padang twice a month, stopping in Sibolga, Pulau Telo (1 day only), Teluk-dalam, then on to Gunungsitoli. From Padang to Telukdalam, Rp3600. **transport:** There's malaria on Nias, so take your pills. There are buses, trucks and jeeps running along the main roads, but in the remote areas you must walk. Roads are very bad. The Niah are an agricultural people and don't use boats; mainly in the rivers do they fish. Stay in the villages for Rp250, most anybody will take you in. Southern Nias is more geared for travelers than the other parts of the island. It has been less stifled by the missionary presence, has more traditional houses, and tribal rites take place more often.

history: A magnificent megalithic heroic culture flourished on Nias until well into the 20th Century. A travel diary written (851 A.D.) by a Persian merchant, Sulayman, is the first literary record of Nias; he described the headhunters of 'Niang'. In the south part of the island during the 1800's slave raiders regularly went on the rampage. A situation existed much like in Africa, chiefs would carry off captives from neighbouring villages, selling them at huge profits for gold to the Acehnese seamen of North Sumatra. Today this same gold is used for bride prices at weddings and adorns headdresses of the dancers on Nias. In olden times, a warrior's costume was a metal armor jacket with upturned shoulder wings and toothlike spines to imitate crocodile teeth. In front of the loincloth, rattan balls studded with boar tusks, tiger fangs, and crocodile teeth were worn. Leather 'armour' jackets covered their upper bodies, the shoulder plates inspired by captured (and their owners eaten) European armour. The spears, having been patterned after European protoypes, were more sabre-like than the usual Indonesian swords. A headhunter's necklace was a shiny black ring and the traditional community greating was 'Johol!' (pronounced Ya'ahowu), or Strength!, which is still used today.

Slain enemy heads decorated the huts of the chiefs. A Dutchman, Edwin Loeb, reported that headhunting and human sacrifice were still practiced on Nias as late as 1935. The Dutch gained a foothold first in the 17th Century. Owing to Lutheran missionary work since 1907 more than ½ of the island's population has been converted, the Niah culture virtually destroyed, the people now gentle and obedient to authority. Instead of hunting heads, today they sing hymns, instead of waging war and keeping slaves, they now barter copra and pigs for bicycles and transistors, and put on diluted war dances for tourists. Where battles once raged, badminton is played on the quiet stone pavements. Children even go to school. Yet vestiges of the old culture still survive — the village architecture, war dances, incredible performances of masculine strength, and social offices are still inherited.

people: The Niah might be related to the hill tribes of Burma, their ancestors having migrated to the island from 3000-500 B.C., but their exact origin is misty. They have a culture and practices all their own. They speak a language most closely related to Malagasy, yet their sculpture shows uncanny similarities to woodcarvings made by the Nagas of Assam in the high Himalayas. Today most of the 200,000 people of Nias and Batu Islands are mainly rice growers. Besides its nutritional value, the pig is of outstanding importance as a status-symbol and as a sacrificial animal. For great cultic festivities large numbers are slaughtered. An exhorbitant fee of up to Rp100,000, plus gold, old silver coins and pigs, are all paid to the parents for a bride. The north is vastly different culturally from the south. In contrast to the megalithic culture of the south, in the north you find oval-shaped houses and idols used to drive away spirits and to treat sicknesses, resembling more a neolithic culture. In northern Nias peoples' features are finer and their skin is fair.

architecture: In case the village came under attack, southern villages consist of two long rows of houses built so as to be nearly impregnable. Bars guard windows and trap doors open to roofs. Houses are built so close together that inside doors make it possible for residents to walk the whole length of the row (over 300 meters) without ever touching the ground. Each stilted house was built by slaves to resemble the hulls of Portuguese galleons. Each house stands on piles which rest on a base of stones, resisting earth tremors that often shake the island.

religion: Although German missionaries have been here for almost 70 years, the old crocodile magic of this unique island is still adamantly believed in. Their religion today is a mixture of animism, Christianity, ancestor, and phallic worship. The people still find security in the black magic of their ancestors but they worship using Christian symbols and practices which carry more prestige. Although dogs are regularly eaten on Nias, cats are never killed and eaten because it's believed that they guard the bridge to the Land of the Dead.

music and dance: Warlike South Niah dances are the only ones in Indonesia which specialize in high acrobatic jumps. Enormous skin drums occasionally reach almost 3 m in length. They also play a bamboo 'buzzer' which is a hollow bamboo cane with two holes, the hand acting as the resonator. Two buzzers of different notes can be played simultaneously. This exists only in southern Nias, as the northern Niah culture has been all but smothered by hard-line Christians: buzzers have been replaced with trumpets to accompany European hymns.

Tulo Tulo Dance: Dancers in warrior costume hold hands and move in a ring counter-clockwise, all chanting together, the circle shrinking and expanding as if breathing. Then the tempo accelerates and the men begin to shout rhythmically, leaping frog-like high into the air and performing mock fights and armed combat dances with their spears. Then the mock battlefield dissolves in utter confusion, just like after a real battle. The Headhunter's Dance is an eerie dance-song with the rattling hypnotizing sound of shields. Niah female dancing is incredibly slow by western standards (5 seconds for a foot to touch the pavement each time), two files of women moving with down-cast eyes and completely immobile faces. They wear primary colors red, yellow, gold and black; those colors seen against expanses of gray stone make a fantastic total effect. Sometimes dances take place on large mushroom-shaped tables which act as the stage for the dance. Wearing long scarves and ear ornaments that look like bracelets, the older women are the most accomplished dancers. See the Dance of the Hawk, with its skipping, rotating, hovering movements. Then the women dance as cats, coiling and springing and clawing at each other.

stone sculpture: Though it would be difficult to find a single stonecutter on Nias today, much remains of their past megalithic culture which was of a standard found nowhere else in S.E. Asia. The people have long ago forgotten the meaning of the magical symbols adorning stone pyramids and terraces found in front of the chiefs' houses or in cere-

monial places in South Niah villages, at one time the center of sacrifices. These islanders once worshipped stone as the most important material of civilisation- for tools, utensils, pillows, even money. Stone slabs were built here similar in construction to everywhere in the early history of the planet, from Stonehenge to Easter Island. Hauled from distant riverbed quarries, all the carvings were done in a superb precision in a light grayish stone. Whole villages are paved with great flat stone tiles. Master masons constructed stone steps, throne-like chairs twisting with serpents, ornamented tables, raised stone circles, upright monolithic stone stelae and obelisks, elaborate stone seats for chiefs in the shape of hornbills, stone chests and drums, rosettes carved on stone blocks- all with little ornamentation yet very strong. Missionaries who first penetrated into the interior of the island in the 1930's came across abandoned villages in the mountains with all their stone sculpture still intact in village squares, ripping off hundreds of statues. The finest collec- ons of Niah sculpture today are in Germany.

wood sculpture: There were two phases in Niah culture, the stonework of the Ancient Peoples and the woodcrafts of the 1400's. Wooden statues were used to propitiate spirits in case of family illness. The old religion is portrayed vividly in these Easter Island-like armless statues of ancestral beings distinguished by tall Niah-style headgear, elaborate earrings, sharp features (but no chin) elongated torsos, large male organs, heads with small stuck-on beards, and right ears with distended lobes.

Siraha, a Niah
Household God

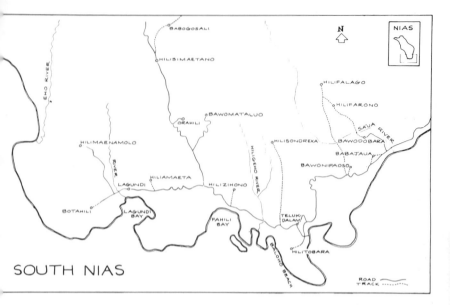

SOUTH NIAS

stone-jumping (fahombe): A famous Niah sport requiring dazzling acrobatic gyrations. A solid stone column over 2 meters high and ½ m broad stands in the village square. In front of the column is a smaller stone about 500 mm high. The young man runs from a distance of 20 metres for the smaller stone and from it launches himself feet-first high into the air over the column, twisting violently, to alight on his feet on rough heavy paving stones facing the column. In old times stones were covered with sharp spears and pointed bamboo sticks and *fahombe* was used to train young loinclothed warriors to clear walls of enemy villages at night with a torch in one hand and a sword in the other. *Fahombe* was also used to prove a young man's fitness to take a wife. Now dressed as athletes, they charge money to see it. Another Niah sport is a traditional football game which consists of keeping a rattan ball suspended in the air in order to 'keep the sun from setting'.

SOUTH NIAS

Telukdalam: Palm-fringed bay. A tourist office opened here in Jan. 1976. Check in with the police. A schoolteacher, Antonius, will try to sell you a shitty little guide book for 'one dollar'. **stay and eat:** The police take half of the accommodation price, so most cheap places have closed down. An-

tonius, the rip-off artist, has talked the government into building him a modern resthouse next to his house opposite the wharf, which costs Rp1000 per night. Another *losmen*, Cusit, has 6 quite large double rooms; Rp250 single, but they will charge you more if you don't protest. Serves food as well; a family atmosphere. Hire bikes through this *losmen*, Rp4-500 per day if you bargain. There are 3 main chinese-run restaurants serving Chinese-Indonesian food.

from Telukdalam: Visit the fascinating tribal villages Bawamatalua, Orahili, Hilismaetano. Try to reach the village near Gomo where they have tribal houses, quite untouristed. Some travelers think it's more comfortable to use Telukdalam as a base and to commute out to the villages each day. To Orahili it's Rp100 by bus; to Hilismaetano, Rp100. For Bawamataluo, get off the Hilismaetano bus at Orahili and walk. **from Telukdalam by boat:** The ship Intan from Telukdalam to Padang costs Rp3600, sailing about twice a month, takes 3 nights and 2 days. Really a good trip; the captain speaks English. Besides the regular boats leaving for Sibolga (Rp1800) about once every 4-5 days, there are also boats from Telukdalam to Gunungsitoli about twice weekly, Rp1800; takes 16 hours. Could be dangerous currents on the way north; also you hear of vessels breaking down halfway there.

Lagundi: 12 km from Telukdalam. This small Muslim village on the south coast of Nias is hard to get to, but once there hard to get away from. Take the bus (Rp50), jeep or truck to the turnoff, then walk a dirt track which leads the 6 km down to the village. Surfers appreciate Lagundi because of its great surfing beach and lagoon enclosed in coral. This village used to be the main port of southern Nias but the Krakatoa eruption in 1883 wiped it out and the port was moved to Telukdalam ('Port of Peace'), leaving Lagundi to sleep on. **stay:** The villagers really take you in, all call you by your first name. Stay right in the *kampung* in either of the 3 big houses available for visitors for Rp750 full room and board per day. Each meal is Rp200, breakfast is Rp50 (porridge), plus coffee and bananas anytime you want them.

Bawamataluo (Sunhill): The oldest extant traditional village of Nias, 14 km from from Telukdalam. Take bus to Orahili, then walk 2 km up the 480 stone steps leading to this hilltop village. The stairway has polished stone sidewalls and some segments are ornamented with reliefs. From a distance Bawamataluo has the shape of an imperfect cross. Superb fantastic carvings. Big meeting hall and tribal chief's palace 15 m high, built on wooden pillars 1 m thick, with a floor constructed of heavy wooden planks. The yard is littered with jawbones of sacrificed pigs. There are 18 ton stone chairs, round funeral tables where the dead were left to decay, and grotesquely decorated stone benches in the shape of animals. Traditional dances such as the *Tulo Tulo* are still held; hordes of warriors storm down the main wide street wildly brandishing their spears, stamping, shouting and rattling their shields, heads decorated with bird feathers. Costs Rp15,000 which is the minimum they'll do any performance for. Includes the full dance of 30 people but ·'without the stone jumping' for which you must pay extra.

Hilismaetano: 16 km inland from Telukdalam. 140 *adat* houses here. Stay in the *losmen* next to the German mission hospital, but eat at the stall oposite. Notice how friendly the missionaries are to travelers. The war dance is staged here; also stone jumping (fahombe) over stones 2 m high by young unmarried jumpers.

NORTH NIAS

Gunungsitoli: This town is the only place you can cash travelers cheques on Nias. Meet Dr. Thompson who's writing a book on the history of the island; she speaks Niah. **stay:** The tourist hotel isn't a bargain, the cheapest room is Rp2000. Stay instead at Losmen Amarasoi, 2 km south of town on the left. Or else stay at Ketilang Hotel, Rp500 per bed. **from Gunungsitoli:** There are some old *rumah adat* up the hill from Hilimbawodesolo, 13 km by bus, Rp100. For Telukdalam, a bus makes the trip to Lahusa, but it's not dependable. Lahusa isn't a tribal village, just a few houses and a store. From Lahusa walk into Telukdalam. It takes 4 days to walk from Gunungsitili 80 km south to Telukdalam. Stay in true *asli* villages with families or with the *kepala desa*. You must cross some rivers and on the way there are two sites where stone stelae and pyramids have been put to keep them together by the missionaries some 20 years ago. Ask in Gunungsitoli where the stelae are. It's about 1½ days walk to the first group. **by boat:** To Telukdalam it's 8 hours, Rp1650; try the ship Rotella, leaving twice weekly. It's a lovely trip south by boat, passing by flying fish, schools of dolphins, and dense jungle all the way down the coast.

NORTH SUMATRA
(SUMATERA UTARA)

Pangkalan Brandan: 92 km N.W. of Medan. Oil was discovered in Sumatra in 1880 by a Dutch tobacco planter, A.J. Zijlker, who was given a lease to drill by the Sultan of Langkat, striking oil in 1885 at 21 meters. The Pangkalan Brandan well was the forerunner of the giant Royal Dutch Shell oil company which started as just an exporter of exotic seashells from the Indies into Holland. The structure at Pangkalan Brandan is the first physical equipment of Permina, Indonesia's first national oil company which began with just a heap of scrap iron, a few old wells seeping oil, some rusted pumps, one leaky pipeline, and this first refinery. The monument has been bombed and burned by invasions, scorched earth fighers, and Dutch 'police actions'. Destroyed and then rebuilt 3 times, the placque states 'No reason exists to be overproud, as this ruin proves'.

BUKIT LAWANG

A relaxing village of a few hundred people 80 km west of Medan and 15 km from Bohorok on the edge of the Langkat Reserve, deep in the wilds of North Sumatra. The most memorable part of a visit here is the ride out to the reserve, and the stay in Bukit Lawang where the pace is slow and the people easy-going. On one side of Bukit Lawang are rubber plantations and on the other side rainforest and river country; the *real* Sumatra. **getting there:** It takes about 5 hours to reach, but quicker if it's not raining. The bus departs each day at 2 or 3 pm from Stasiun Sei Wampu, Medan. You bump in at dusk. A more reliable, less crowded alternative is to charter a landrover from Nitour, Jl. Prof. H. Moh. Yamin 28 A, Tel. 23191, for about Rp20,000. Before going, see DINAS P.P.A. (Perlundungan dan Pengawetan Alam), Jl. Sei Galang 26, Medan, for permission, a Rp500 charge. For Indonesians, free entry. If you haven't got the forestry permit they have forms at the *pasangrahan* in Bukit Lawang; they'll squeeze the Rp500 out of you there. Try to arrive on weekdays because up to 400 revellers and picnicers come out from Medan on Sunday.

Orangutan Rehabilitation Center (Pusat Rehabilitasi Mawas): Observe orangutans being trained to live in their original habitat; a rare opportunity. One of the great apes, the vegetarian orangutan (or mawas) is the oriental equivalent of Africa's gorilla and chimpanzee. Since they are now headed for extinction, this center and others like it were created to preserve wild *mawas* from slaughter and capture and to rehabilitate confiscated specimens. This project is sponsored by the World Wildlife Fund and is financed by the Zoological Society of Frankfurt. The reserve, situated 45 minutes walk at the end of a river trail on top of a steep hill, can only be visited from 3:30-6:30 pm daily. These *mawas* were taken as pets in Indonesians' homes. Even 'responsible' senior government officials in Medan still keep them as pets, a legacy from the Dutch times when to own an orangutan was the prerogative of a colonial gentleman. As *mawas* grow older, however, they cease being cute little babies and become large powerful adults which bite, shit all over the place, and finally have to be kept in a cage. The idea at this center is to bring them back to the wild so that they can learn how to be orangutans again. For some individuals it takes the center up to 3 months to rehabilitate. They are fed at first only on bananas and milk, but gradually their food supply is decreased, forcing them to forage for themselves. They must also learn how to build nests in the trees and how to camouflage themselves with leaves for protection. Listen for their piercing screams. When you leave they ask for a donation of Rp2000, but give them what you can. Recently there have been up to 450 tourists visiting the center each week and the government is really pushing it hard as a tourist attraction. With so many visitors the whole purpose of the center is defeated, the place now turning into a very bad zoo. Mostly domestic tourists drive out from Medan in their jeeps and landrovers, teasing the animals and leaving their garbage on the trails. So if you have a great love of nature, are silent, and will only stay for half an hour- you'll be a little bit welcome at the center.

stay: There's a government run *pasangrahan* but it's rather expensive at Rp500 per person. Swim and bathe in the clear rushing Bohorok River out the front door. People in Bukit Lawang will put you up cheaper than the resthouse. You can also stay at Peng. Achmad Gurdi's for Rp300. **eat:** Very plain food is served in the *pasangrahan* for Rp100. It's better to eat in the village, 5 minutes away on foot. There's one *warung* in Bukit Lawang at Achmad Gurdi's house; *mie goreng* (lousy), Rp75, but OK *nasi campur,* Rp75 (with fish, Rp150). The food is far superior and cheaper in the village of Gotong Royong, 1 km down the road through the rubber plantation. Warung Kopi Sederhana has outstanding *nasi campur* for only Rp50. Across the street, eat at the *nasi pecal* stand for Rp50. Delicious *pisang goreng* and *ubi goreng*, Rp15, are sold a little ways down the road.

from Bukit Lawang: There's only one *oplet* a day for Medan, leaving at 5:30 in the morning. Sometimes other *oplets* leave at around 12 noon and 2 pm, but only as far as Binjei, from where you can get a Colt the 22 km further into Medan. **vicinity of Bukit Lawang:** There are forest walks where you'll see animals in the wild such as the forest goat, squirrels, the *owa, beruk,* the jet black-monkey (lutung), *siamangs* lurching through the trees, gibbons, macaque, and much birdlife. You're out in the freedom of nature. If you want to walk upriver deeper into the rainforest ask the forestry people or the Rehabilitation Center (usually Europeans working here) where you can find *orang melayau* (forest guides). Pay Rp700 per day to the leader and to each of his men plus food (salt, rice, dried fish, *sambal*). They will catch or gather fresh food and build sleeping shelters for you each night, find or hunt anything you ask for, even carry you across rivers. Don't, under any circumstances, hire Tahir; he's a cunning thief.

MEDAN

A dominant port of Indonesia with a thriving plantation economy. This area used to be the battle site in wars between the sultans of Deli and Aceh, thus Medan means 'battleground'. Medan was first a tiny group of *kampungs* in a marshy lowland and was founded as a city under Sultan Mahmud Perkasa Alam who lived in his palace at Labuhan Deli, 10 km from Medan. Because of the immense fertility of a narrow swamp-belt only 10 km wide which faced a major shipping route of the Orient, this northeast Deli coastal area became a Dutch plantation district after 1870. The Dutch government decided to make it the capital of North Sumatra region in 1886. A small village 80 years ago, in 1910 the population was 17,500; now it is nearly one million. If you get beyond the craziness and the physical ugliness of this city, there's a fantastic confluence of cultures, even more of a plural society than the average Indonesian city. Because of its location and its trade, all races have converged on

Medan: the Javanese came to work on the plantations, the Riau people came here because it's the economic center of Sumatra. There are Sikhs, Acehnese, Arabians, and a very strong Chinese community, as well as Indian (want to learn Tamil?), also a heavy Minangkabau, Batak Islamic, Batak Christian, and a Melayu element. Each group is strongly represented. No other city in Indonesia is like it and they say that if you can make it as a politician in Medan you can make it anywhere in the world. Medan has 15 foreign consulates and many foreign business houses (even a real live English pub). Although it is known as one of Indonesia's dirtiest cities, it's also one of Indonesia's richest-handling a staggering 65% of Indonesia's exports. Rubber is the staple industry of the area, Indonesia being the world's 2nd largest producer. Most of Indonesia's annual production of palm oil comes from the huge estates around this area. Some of the finest tobacco is still grown here. Oil, tobacco and plantation products are exported from the port of Belawan, 26 km away on the coast, while the unrecorded trade such as cigarettes, *ganja,* medicines, electronics, stolen dismantled motor vehicles, centers around Teluknibung and L. Bilik which have traditionally operated as Chinese-controlled smuggling ports since colonial times.

getting there: Only 20 minutes air time from Penang, Malaysia, or overnight by ship from Penang. From the port of Belawan take a bus Rp100 to the city. Don't try to sleep at Medan airport, the officials will put the M.P.'s on you. From the airport you can easily walk into town or just walk to the outside gate and get a *becak* to the Siguragura or Irama Hotels, Rp100-150. A motorized super-powered type *becak* (becak mesin) to anywhere in the city costs Rp100-200.

stay: Watch where you stay in this city, you could be kept awake all night by traffic in an airless, mosquito filled room. Most travelers just shoot through to Lake Toba. A convenient central place is Hotel Siguragura, Jl. Let. Jen. Suprapto 2/K, less than 1½ km from the airport. Single beds in rooms cost Rp400 or dorms in the back for Rp300, or you may 'charter' a room with 3 beds for Rp1000. Siguragura is also a travel agency. Good Padang-restaurants nearby. Hotel Irama, Jl. Palang Merah 112/5, is Rp300 per person. You run smack into this hotel if you walk from the airport down Jl. Iman Bonjol. Though its rooms are hot and stuffy, it's cleaner than the Siguragura. Run by Niah people. Free tea anytime. Many *warungs* only 10 minutes walk. Hotel Waringin, across the street from the big city mosque, is the cheapest in Medan at Rp250. Hotel Banua, fairly near the P.O. and the Perentis Lines office at Jl. Serdang 23, is also a tour and travel service which sells Colt tickets to Prapat on Lake

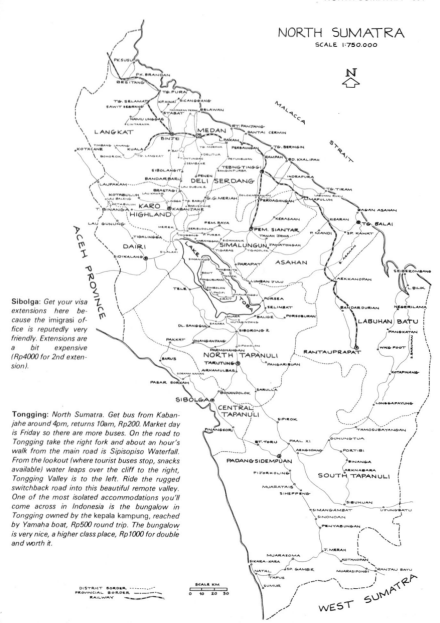

NORTH SUMATRA
SCALE 1:750.000

N

MALACCA

STRAIT

ACEH PROVINCE

PK.SUSUK
PK.BRANDAN
BESITANG
TG.PURA
TG.SELAMAT KP.HINAI SICANG KANG
SAWIT SEBRANG BELAWAN
TAMU UNGGA STABAT
LINTABUNG
LANGKAT BINJEI MEDAN PT.RANTANG
KOTACANE KUALA L.PAKAM BANTAI CERMIN
BOHOROK TG.LANGKAT P.BATU TG.MORAWA PERSAUNGAN TG.BERINGIN
TIMBANG LANANG TUNTUNGAN PETUMBUKAN RAMPAH BD.KHALIPAH
SIBOLANGIT ISMBAWE
BANDARBARU LAU DUBUK 2 TEBINGTINGGI INDRAPURA
LAUPAKAM BRASTAGI LAU BARUS TG.G.MERIAH DOLOKMASIHOL PERDAGANGAN TG.TIRAM
KOTTABULUH SERIBUDOLOK LABUHAN BILIK LIMAPULUH
KARO BERTABULUH KABANJAHE MERAH BAGAN ASAHAN
T.BINANGA HIGHLAND KERASAAN KISARAN TG.BALAI
LAU GUNUNG PEM.RAYA P.MANDI SP.KAWAT
MEREK SERIBUDOLOK PEM. SIANTAR
TIGALINGGA TIGABARAS TANAH JAWA SEIBEROMBANG
DAIRI SIMANGAMBAT SIMALUNGUN PAMATANGSAN BILIK
SIDIKALANG TIGADOLOK ASAHAN
SIMANINDO PARAPAT AEKKANOPAN NEGERILAMA
TELE AMBARITA PANGURURAN PURBA LABUHAN BATU
SIBORONG 2 LUMBAN JULU BANDAR DURIAN PANGKATAN
MUARA HUTABAYSAN PURSEA WING FOOT
SELIMBAT KOTAPINANG
PAKKAT DL.SANGGUL SIBORONG 2 BALIGE PORGOBURAN RANTAUPRAPAT
DNANGANTANG SIPOHOLON
BARUS PEMBANGAN NORTH TAPANULI PANGARIBUAN
TARUTUNG LONGGAPAYUNG
PASAR. SORKAM AIRMULBAS
SORKAM KANAN SARULLA
BONANDOLOK TAMOSUBAYANGAN
SIBOLGA CENTRAL
TAPANULI SIPIROK GUNUNGTUA
PINANGSORI PAAL XI PORTIBI
BT.TORU AEKGODANG BINANGA
PADANGSIDEMPUAN AEKNABARA
PIJORKOLING SOUTH TAPANULI
MUARATAIS SIBUHUAN UTONGBATU
SIHEPPENG
SIMANGAMBAT
SINONOAN
PENYABUNGAN
J. MERAH
MUARASOMA KOTANOPAN
SIKARA-KARA NATAL SP.GAMBIR MUARASIPONGI RANJAU BATU
TAPUS
SUMUR WEST SUMATRA

LAKE TOBA

Sibolga: *Get your visa extensions here because the imigrasi office is reputedly very friendly. Extensions are a bit expensive (Rp4000 for 2nd extension).*

Tongging: *North Sumatra. Get bus from Kabanjahe around 4pm, returns 10am, Rp200. Market day is Friday so there are more buses. On the road to Tongging take the right fork and about an hour's walk from the main road is Sipisopiso Waterfall. From the lookout (where tourist buses stop, snacks available) water leaps over the cliff to the right, Tongging Valley is to the left. Ride the rugged switchback road into this beautiful remote valley. One of the most isolated accommodations you'll come across in Indonesia is the bungalow in Tongging owned by the kepala kampung, reached by Yamaha boat, Rp500 round trip. The bungalow is very nice, a higher class place, Rp1000 for double and worth it.*

DISTRICT BORDER --------
PROVINCIAL BORDER -------
RAILWAY

SCALE KM
0 10 20 30

Toba; Rp300 for small rooms, a great *mandi* out back. Although Hotel Garuda, Jl. S.M. Raja 27, has a grand lobby, the rooms at Rp1500 up to Rp4300 double are very dumpy. Down the street at Jl. Singamangaraja 7 is the more modern and presentable Hotel Garuda, Rp4-6000, but very plain rooms for this kind of money. Much better in this price range is either: Hotel Angkasa, Jl. Sutomo 1, Rp3000 full board, recommended; or the Wai Yat, Jl. Asia 44, tel. 2757; Rp3000 or Rp3500 for doubles. Wai Yat has very big comfortable rooms with Malay *mandis*. Well worth the price if you got the money, but don't partake of their ruinous breakfast for Rp500. Hotel Dirga Surya, Jl. Iman Bonjol 6, also has very commodious doubles, Rp3500; A.C. rooms for Rp5000. Avoid super ripoff Danau Toba International, grubby and expensive.

eat: Restoran Oemoem, Jl. Jen A. Yani 116. Everything in this small, long, dark restaurant is good, *soto ayam* Rp250, *gado2* Rp100, *nasi campur* Rp150; but drinks are expensive. For Chinese food at night visit Jalan Selat Panjang, walking distance from the Siguragura Hotel. Pick out a live frog in a cage and his legs are yours; also good *pangsit mie*. Tip Top Restaurant, Jl. A. Yani 92 A, has quite good fish and meat dishes: goat's brain (Rp750 big size) and liver; also western food and bakery goods. Nice to sit in at night. Pasar Malam at Taman Ria near Jl. Binjei for *nasi goreng, babi bakar, sate,* etc. and Chinese foods. A lively little neighborhood to eat at (plus many ice cream places) is around Bioskop Metrol on the intersection of Jl. Taruna and Jl. Jen. Arifin, 10 minutes walk from Hotel Irama. A great bargain place here is Warung Ampera; stuff yourself for Rp150. Cantino Baru, Jl. Pemuda, for Indonesian food only such as *gulai, kambing, ayam goreng,* etc. For cheap and good *sate* dishes, try Rini Sate House, Jl. Mojopahit 129, 10 am-12 pm; and Memeng Sate, Jl. Irian Barat and Jl. Haryono. Hoover Mandarin Restaurant, Jl. Mangkubumi 18, Rp1000 for a superb Chinese meal, best in town. Other Indonesian-Chinese restaurants are: Micodo, Jl. Prof. H.M. Yamin 236/H; Sjarif's, Jl. Bandung; Berlian, Jl. Jen. A. Yani 118. Binjei, a town 22 km from Medan, is renowned for its *rambutans*.

sights: A basically well laid-out city with big parks and wide shady streets. Though the traffic is Asian, many downtown buildings are built in the western-style. Visit the stately residential area of Polonia near the airport. **Maimoon Palace:** This once splendid palace of the Sultan of Deli was built in 1888. Open anytime if there's no praying going on. See the Royal Dais. In a small *adat* building to the side there's a broken, holy 'male' canon, Meriam Putung; to see it, ask for the key (kunci). **old buildings:** Most of the old colonial buildings

are found around Lapangan Merdeka, the old esplanade in Dutch times. The White Society Club (Witte Societet) was the first European whites-only club in Medan, opened in 1879. Hotel DeBoer (now Hotel Dharma Bhakti) is in front of the Central P.O., built in 1880-1887. The Grand Hotel Medan (now Hotel Granada Medan), the former high class hotel for Europeans, was built in 1887. See the Nienjuys fountain in front of the Central Post Office in memory of the first Dutch tobacco planter who arrived in 1865. Deli Maatschappij (now PNP Tobacco Co.), was the first European building built by Nienhuys as his plantations office in 1869. On Jl. A. Yani is the beautifully decorated Chinese mansion of the late Chinese millionaire Chong A. Fie. The Kesawan shopping center was opened in 1874 to provide Dutch tobacco planters with an outlet. The Harrisons-Crosfield Building was, up until 1970, the tallest building in Medan. It represents the oldest British influence in North Sumatra. The City Hall was built in 1908 for the first mayor of Medan, Baron Mackay.

churches, mosques and temples: Mesjid Raya, with a pond beside it, is quite elegant. Gang Bengkok Mosque is the oldest mosque in Medan, built by Datuk of Kesawan in the 17th Century. It was partly constructed of square hewn granite stones taken from Hindu and Buddhist temples. Kramat Glugur, Jl. Putri Hijau, is a burial ground for the Muslim saint Said Tahir who died in 1570. The Roman Catholic Church on Jl. Pemuda was built in 1929. The oldest Protestant Church, the Immanuel on Jl. Diponegoro, was built in 1921. See the first Chinese temple built in Medan (1870) on Jl. Pandu. An even older Chinese temple is found in Labuhan Deli. There's also two Hindu temples and one Sikh temple. **old forts:** Medan Garnizoen, Jl. Kapt. Maulana Lubis, was the first Dutch Colonial Army fort, built in 1873 during the Sunggal War. Old guns point up the river and there's an old bridge in front of the fort. Now the army garrison Kologdam 11/BB occupies it. At Delitua, within the city limits of Medan, there are still remains of a fort and a castle built by the celebrated Princess Putri Hijau. It was destroyed by an Acehnese invasion in the late 16th Century.

crafts: Toko Bali, Jl. Jen. A. Yani 68 is well-stocked with souvenirs. Rufino, Jl. Jen. A. Yani 64, is not as junky, a lot of dusty old stuff, and some good paintings. Other shops nearby such as Mido, and Indonesian Art Shop, Jl. Jen. A. Yani III 1/A, have some wonderful stuff. Buy buffalo 'powder horns' swirling with neolithic carvings for only Rp6000 (on Java they sell for Rp25,000).

events: Cultural Center Tapian Daya, Jl. Binjei

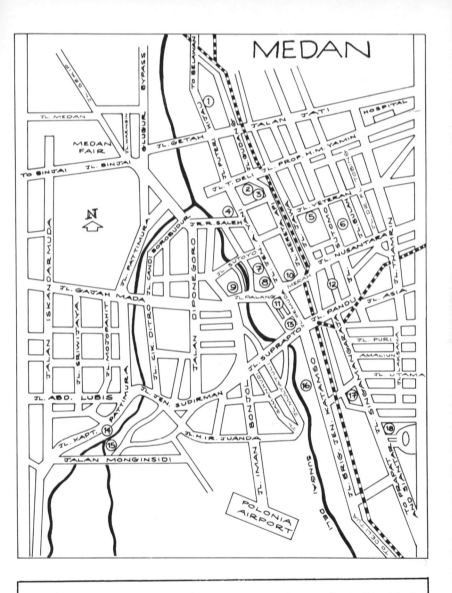

1. buses to Belawan
2. Post Office
3. railway station
4. Medan City Hall
5. Perentis Lines
6. Central Market
7. Immigration Department
8. Restoran Oemoem
9. Hotel Irama
10. Bank Dagang Negara
11. Tourist Office
12. Chinese warungs (after 6 pm)
13. Siguragura Hotel and Travel Service
14. bus station to Brastagi
15. Grundaling Tours
16. Maimoon Palace of Deli
17. the Great Mosque
18. bus terminal

Km. 6, has cinemas, open-air theatres, art galleries, restaurants, modern and traditional cultural performances. Medan takes its religious and dance festivals seriously and due to its multi-racial community there are many. One of the most exciting is *Tabut Keling* put on by the Indian community and highlighted by a colorful *tabut*-procession around the city at night time. *Leberan* is also lavishly celebrated here. The Medan Fair is put on each year in connection with Indonesian Independence Day celebrations on Aug. 15th-17th with shows and exhibitions relating to trade, industry, agriculture, and various arts, cultural and folklore performances; plus big national soccer tournaments. During May and Sept. a Malay drama festival is held at the Maimoon Palace depicting the classical themes of Malay history and the traditions of the East Sumatran sultanates. *Sri Banang* is a welcome dance for sultans or distinguished visitors. The *Pulau Putri* features intricate fast movements like a jig; in this dance women even lift up their skirts and kick their heels. Wedding costumes of Medan are among Indonesia's most sumptuous.

miscellaneous: Acupuncture Therapy Clinic, c/ Dr. C. Hembing, Widjaja Kesuma, Jl. Teruma 48. Try for a job teaching English at LIA (Lembaga Indonesia America), Jl. Yogya. *Kantor Imigrasi* is on Jl. Jen. A. Yani 74, landing fee plus first extension is Rp9900 (the usual). The Army Museum Bukit Barisan is right up from Hotel Irama just past the Medan Jaya Building. **Chinatown:** In this busy section of town all the Chinese characters above the store fronts have been erased. Goods here are twice as expensive as in Penang. See the temples. **Taman Margasatwa Zoo:** 4 km from the City Hall Open in the mornings and from 3-5 pm, for iguanas, civet cats, monkeys, gibbons, orangutans, Indian elephants, mongeese, porcupines, Malaysian bears, Indian deer, cassowaries, toucans, eagles, parrots, and the *kancil*.

from Medan by boat: A cargo boat leaves for Penang, Malaysia, about twice weekly on Tues., and Fri., for Rp8500. Contact Perentis Lines, Jl. Veteran 16 E. Get your ticket early because of limited space. Perentis' Tapanauli is often in repair or held up by customs, it runs like Russian roulette. In the wet season, Oct.-Feb., there are sometimes storms at sea and this small boat is tossed mercilessly on the ocean. In the dry season it's a very pleasant trip with fairly decent food and not too crowded. Crash on top of cargo holds carrying cabbages. **for Singapore and Jakarta:** Take the Pelni ship Tampomas on Thurs. down to Tg. Pinang (a small island south of Singapore) for Rp13,000, then from Tg. Pinang take a launch 4 hours to Sin-

gapore Rp4200. Free haircut on arrival. Or take the Tampomas straight from Medan to Jakarta for Rp14,900. Besides this regular Pelni boat, there are other cargo boats carrying passengers leaving anytime for Jakarta for Rp2-3000 less, including meals or what some might call meals.

flights: The MAS Office in Hotel Danau Toba can be helpful. Merpati Office, Jl. Jen. Katamso 35 D, operates direct flights to Kuala Lumpur plus regular flights to: Padang, Rp15,500; Pekanbaru, Rp14,000; Palembang, Rp25,000; Penang, Malaysia, Rp15,000 (or M$84), leaving at 8:55 am. Airport tax is Rp1000. From Penang, hitch down to Singapore. Hitching in Malaysia is a cinch. **hitching:** There's a conspicuous lack of traffic on North Sumatran roads (population of North Sumatra is only 7 million), so hitching is kind of slow, though possible. Faster to take buses. **to Prapat:** On shores of Lake Toba. From Stasiun Teladan direct, Rp600, 4 hours. Or take a bus first to Siantar, Rp400, then from Siantar pay Rp150 further by bus to Prapat. The longer drive via Brastagi (68 km from Medan) to Prapat is more scenic than the road to Prapat via Siantar. Or catch a Daitsu in front of Siguragura Hotel, Rp25, to Sambu Station. Then from Sambu minibuses leave all the time for Prapat, Rp750. There are also minibuses for Rp800 to Prapat leaving from in front of Hotel Garuda at 9 am and 1:30 pm daily. Minibuses also depart from Stasiun Jl. Singamangaraja 34 (besides Mesjid Raya) 6 times a day for Prapat: 7 am, 8 am, 9 am, 1 pm, and at 2 pm. Book your seat at Medan Raya Tour, Jl. Veteran 18 A.

from Medan to Bukittinggi: Rp2000 by bus from Stasiun Manur, Jl. Kawi; takes 28 hours over some really hairy roads. There are also buses Medan-Padang direct, Rp2800, 32 hours. Roads are improving; good Mercedes buses do this route now. **to Brastagi:** Grundaling Tour or Sibayak Tour has minibuses, Rp300, catch them along Jl. Pattimura. **to Siantar:** By bus it's Rp400, 3 hours, leaving often from Jl. Singamangaraja 5. (Also from here wildly painted Sumatran Chevrolet buses depart for Prapat, Rp600, 5½ hours.) **to Aceh:** Several buses operate to Banda Aceh in far northern Sumatra every day, Rp2800. Because the road is bad in places, takes at least 17-20 hours. Try A.L.S., Jl. Thamrin 27, Rp2800. Their Mercedes departs at 3 pm, arrives 9 am. Kunia Co., on the main street of Medan, Jl. Singamangaraja (coming from Lake Toba about 200 m before the water-tower) has buses departing 8 am and 5 pm. **by taxi:** The taxi stand is on Jl. Semarang, Jaya Taxi; bargain for a public taxi ride, about Rp450 to Brastagi. **train:** A narrow guage train, slow and overcrowded, operates out of Medan. In the south this line ends at

Rantauprapat and in the north the last terminus is at Banda Aceh. On the way the engineer sometimes stops the train to recapture chickens. The tracks are still damaged in places by the Japanese invasion 34 years ago.

vicinity of Medan: There's a Hindu-Buddah antiquities site in the village of Kota Cina, 5 km off the main road from Medan to Belawan. Excavations during 1971-73 uncovered many 9-11th Century Buddhist statues from 2 m underground, as well as T'ang, Ming and Sung Dynasties pottery and coins. See the basement of a Hindu-Buddhist temple and stone inscriptions. **Crocodile farm:** 6 km from Medan, were the renowned *crocodilus sumatrensis* is bred for handbags. Growing up to 10 m in length, this species is considered the most dangerous in the world. It haunts the mangrove swamps of East and West Sumatra and is able to make transoceanic voyages. Buy a duck for Rp650-700 and watch the creature eat it. Call Tel. 27249 first and ask for Mr. Wijaya. Or visit him at Jl. Palang Merah 112A, right around the corner from the Hotel Irama. **Pantai Cermin** (Mirror Beach): 40 km south of Medan via Perbaungan on the Straits of Melaka. Pine and mangrove trees. Get a bus from Jl. Singamangaraja Station, Rp300. **butterfly collection:** One of the largest in S.E. Asia is found at the Goodyear Rubber Estate in Dolok Merangir, ½ hour before

Siantar; see Dr. Diehl. His swallow-tail collection is especially outstanding. But only for avid entomologists; Dr. Diehl is a very busy man.

Botanical Gardens (Cagar Alam): At Sibolangit 40 km south on the road to Brastagi. Lying 5000 m high on the slopes of Mt. Sibayak, it covers an area of 20 hectares. Forest reserve nearby. **Bandar Baru:** 47 km from Medan, this cool and pleasant hill resort has many small resthouses and bungalows for hire. Stay at Bungalow Dirga Hayu run by R. Swistre. Much fog rolls in. Bandar Baru is also a popular prostitute center. **Sembahe:** 38 km south, the nearest hill station to Medan. Mostly just a highway stop for fruit and lunch between Medan and the Karo Highlands. Deep gorges, a river streaming over giant boulders, a wood bridge, and twisting paths leading up to steep luxurious hillside gardens (have to pay to get in). Boys wash and play naked in the river. Stay at Restoran Pemandian Sembahe, Rp1500 double. **Mt. Leuser Nature Reserve:** N.W. of Kutacane. Approach this reserve by *oplet* from Kotacane. Out of Indonesia's 115 wildlife reserves, this is one of the largest and least affected by civilization, a wild and unexplored region where herds of protected wildlife graze and hunt. There's an Orangutan Rehabilitation Center near Ketambe and also near Bohorok.

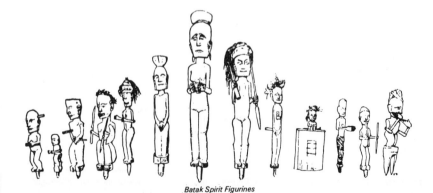

Batak Spirit Figurines

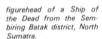

figurehead of a Ship of the Dead from the Sembiring Batak district, North Sumatra.

THE BATAK

The word *Batak* was originally a derogatory Old Malay term for 'robber'·· other translations give it as pig eaters'. This name covers a number of related ethnic groups or clans, the Karo, Pakpak, Simalungun, Mandailing, Angola, and the Toba Batak, whose dialects are different though intelligible to each other. Batak communities (huta) consist of small clusters of multi-family households. A larger unit (marga) is made up of a number of *huta,* each tracing their descent from a single male ancestor. These sturdy rice-growing people (the saying goes, 'Batak are workers, not thinkers') live in fertile mountainous valleys growing rice, cabbage, onions, tomatoes, beans, potatoes, pineapples. Their territory extends up to 200 km north and 300 km south of Lake Toba in the narrowest stretch of the island's upper neck. They are shorter than the Minangkabau because they have lived inland away from the sea and thus have kept their racial stock pure. Because of mass migrations from their heartland seeking a better life in the lowland regions and in Jakarta, modernization is slow amongst the Bataks. Each week the ship Tampomas down to Jakarta is packed, but coming back it is half empty. Many of the tribes' (esp. the Toba Batak) traditional agriculture and land tenure practices- and thus their way of life- are almost unchanged. Most homeland Batak speak an almost remedial *Bahasa Indonesia.* In modern literature, Sitor Situmorang, born of Christian Batak parents, traveled extensively in Europe in the 1950's and wrote highly charged, sad, personalized poems of existential dilemma. Well-known for their warlike traditions, Bataks have provided modern-day Indonesia with many military officers. Batak women are strong spirited and robust, not as coy as many of their Indonesian sisters. See them smoking foot long stoggies in the ricefields of South Tapanuli, dress their husbands up like dolls in the market towns of Lake Toba, and break out in vibrant hymns on the buses. Bataks are some of the best chess players in the East. Learned from age 10 or 11, every village has its expert. The loser has to scratch the winner's back. A barefoot peasant once stalemated the Dutch World Champion in the Grand Hotel in Medan in 1939, a major event in Batak history.

history: The majority of Indonesia's advance states arose in coastal valleys, rich in soil and accessible to trade, but the Bataks established their kingdom deep in the mountains. The Bataks are descendants of wandering clans of neolithic mountain dwellers from northern Thailand and Burma who, over 1500 years ago, were forced to the sea due to overcrowding from the southward migration of expanding Mongolian and Siamese tribes. Driven from their traditional homeland, they disliked the shores of S.E. Asia because they were a mountain people. They came to Sumatra in 3 waves, treking inland from the north, south and west, their faces tattooed with green 3-pointed figures. From their first settlements around Lake Toba in the interior of north-central Sumatra, their descendants spread out into villages which make up the Batak clans in the region today. There are cultural, linguistic and physical evidences of early Hindu contact, traced in the way they cultivate by irrigation, plough with the water buffalo, in the names and origins of their Hindu-derived gods, and in their script. The Karo still use an astrological chart (the Batak calendar, or *porhalaan*) which stems from the *mantirikam*-literature of Tamilnadu, South India. There are also very close similarities between Tamilnadu and the religio-magic practices of the Toba Batak. Wedged in between the two strongholds of Islam on Sumatra, the Acehnese to the north and the Minangkabau to the west, and owing to the mountains which surround them and to their reputation for ferocity and cannibalism, the Batak have retained their own way of life and isolation right up to the end of the last century. It wasn't until around the middle of the 19th Century when Dutch and German missionaries discovered and began to convert them. Although some Batak groups were united under one *raja* who was feudal and pro-Dutch, by the arrival of the Dutch in 1910 they were just beginning to evolve into a number of petty states. Today they are still very conservative by nature and foreign elements have only been accepted when they could be worked in with their original cosmic views.

traditional culture: Villages were once hostile to one another and you still find remnants of old fortified bamboo and earth settlements at Nanggar (22 km from Prapat) and at Lumban Garaga (30 km from Prapat), enclosed by hidden traps, pitfalls and long tunnel-like entrances to protect the village from marauding enemy raids. Ramparts were built of packed earth, next was a ring of prickly bamboo able to inflict puncture wounds which took months to heal. *Ranjau* bamboo stakes were planted stealthily all over the outer areas to impale unwary attackers. On towers scouts were constantly on watch from where they could fire muskets, blowpipes, arrows and spears. During a siege, Bataks could live on a potato a day for months on end though war against a *kampung* was called off if losses were too high or if it was the market season. Their dead were buried in boat-shaped stone coffins. If they misbehaved, boys were once buried in a hole up to their necks. Slavery of war captives and debtors was widespread. The only man-eaters on the island, the Bataks were in reality 'the headhunters of Sumatra'. Cannibalism was most prevalent among the Pakpak, although usually only token bits of flesh were eaten for ceremonial occasions. Cases have been reported of flesh torn from human carcasses with the teeth, and of human flesh sold in markets. Those judged guilty to the crime of incest were condemned to be eaten by their fellow villagers, the most degrading of all punishments. An old Batak curse went, 'I pick the flesh of your relatives from between my teeth!' Raffles reports in the 19th Century: 'For certain crimes, four in number, a criminal would be eaten alive. In cases of adultery the wife appeared to partake in the feast, but usually only men could eat human flesh. The flesh was sometimes eaten raw, or grilled and eaten with lime, salt, pepper, and a little rice. Blood was drunk out of bamboo containers. Palms of the hands and the soles of the feet were delicacies of the epicures. Parents were eaten when they became too old for work.'

religion: Bataks are basically animists with a veneer of education and Christianity covering very complex and sophisticated beliefs. The local pastor is likely to play the drums in a 2-day ritual to keep away Christian-type devils. Their religions are roughly divided: the northern groups are animists, the central groups are Christians (around Lake Toba), while those of the south are mostly Muslims (the Mandailing group is the strongest Muslim). The Bataks today are the largest Protestant group in the east. Out of 3 million, about 2 million are Christian. They were first converted by a fearless German missionary, Nommensen, who arrived in 1861 with only a bible and a violin. Nommensen delivered the death sentence on the old religion when he persuaded the Dutch East Indies government to prohibit the collective sacrificial celebrations (bius) and the playing of Batak musical instruments, wiping out at one blow their whole 'pagan' world. Today, regardless of their nominal faith, half the population still believes in spirits of dead ancestors, sacred trees, stones and places (parsinumbuhan), and in a Hindu-like panthenon of higher deities (begu). Since decisions must be inspired and sanctioned by ancestors, elders still sit on ancestral stone chairs for communal meetings. Bataks have an elaborate mythology and cosmology. *Tondi* (soul stuff) determines contentment, temporal wealth and power; at death it departs to dwell in another organism. Male priests and wizards (datu), skilled in sorcery and in the use of natural poisons, are also specialists in occult knowledge and divination, using Hindu zodiac and magical tables. Spirits of the dead are contacted through female mediums (sibaso) If you're lucky, you'll see a funeral. Christian Batak funerals have brass bands! **events:** There are a rich variety of male-oriented ceremonies, feasts, rituals. Even-numbers are traditionally considered ill-omened and even dangerous, so no feasts or celebrations are ever held on these days of the month. Odd numbers are more auspicious, especially the number 7 which is the number of all the Batak tribes.

genealogy: The Batak are considered to have the most clearly defined patrilineal structure in Indonesia. The bride must move into the husband's settlement and land is passed down the male line from 'the man who first cut the patch of jungle'. Genealogies are followed intensely. When Bataks meet, they rigorously *ertutur*, i.e. cross examine each other as to their lineages, clan, who is the bride-giver and the bride-taker, etc. Some of their patriclans and patrilineages (marga) extend back over 500 years. The ideal family size of a Batak is 17 sons and 16 daughters. Grandfathers are venerated almost to the station of a god and some Bataks can give the names of their grandfathers back 25 generations. At weddings not only lineages and clans of the bride and groom are involved but also those to which they are related through marriages of their lineage mates. Clans and families related by blood and marriage are called a 'drum community' (sagondang) because ancestral souls can be summoned only by the beats of a drum. All its members must marry outside the clan (infant weddings were once commonplace). One *marga* is the bride-providing group (called *hula hula* among the Batak, *kalimbubu* among the Karo), and the other is the bride-receiving group (called *boru* among the Toba Batak, *anakberu* among the Karo) The tightness of the web of kinship is unbelievably strong amongst the Batak, frequently bringing more than 1000 people together for weddings and funerals. To obstain could be dangerous to both health and welfare.

architecture: Older settlements have a distinctive type of house found nowhere else in Indonesia. Raised on piles which are soaked in mud for years, these houses are so sturdily built that they often last for 100 years. With not a single nail used, just rope and wooden pegs, the gable ends of these dynamic houses are richly ornamented with mosaics and woodcarvings of serpents, man-like figures, double spirals, snail lines, female breasts symbolising life-giving force, lizards, and elongated dark-colored monsters' heads with bulging eyes (singa). Facades of the houses and barns for storing rice and drying out produce are embellished with white, red and black colors, and covered with spiral motif carvings. The walls of their dwellings are made from heavy planks and the roof rises high, often sloping inward towards the center. Some of these steep saddle-shaped roofs are made of palm thatch *atap*, others of bright new iron. Structures often rest on a huge tree trunk running under the floor from the main door to the other end of the hall with the main entrance just above the roof. In each house lives up to 10-12 families, each in an apartment (bilik) along the two outer sides with a space in between used as a public corridor where children play, men work, women cook, and people visit each other. The family's rooms are occupied according to rank in this strongly patriarchal society- the head of the house, the son-in-law, etc., right down through the 18 m long house. A communal hall *(sopo or bale)* serves as a village council hall, trophy room and sleeping place for boys and married men.

music: Village men make their own music. A *gondang*-band is made up of cloth-covered metal gongs of different sizes, a reedy sounding clarinet-type instrument, and 2-stringed lutes made of palm fibres. Toba Bataks play a whole row of drums tuned to different pitches. Beaten with sticks, they make a zany sound to western ears. Bataks are also famous for their powerfully expressive, ethereal

*a sopa
communal house*

hymnsinging. **crafts:** Bataks are very skilled and sophisticated in the arts of metalworking, wood-carvng, and also work in bone, shell and bark. But the making of such objects as massive silver ear-rings, shell armbands, copper wire neck rings, big long-stemmed copper pipes weighing up to ½ kg, are all dying arts now. Their woodcarvings incor-porate many magic signs and fertility symbols into the decorations. Figureheads of carved hornbills adorn boats. Buffalo or mountain goat 'powder horns' are artistically made, used as containers for magical substances. Magic augery books (pustaha) are made from bark or bamboo and contain esoteric idioms spoken by priests and female mourners. These *pustahas* form the most important part of Batak written literature; old ones cost up to Rp-50,000 in the tourist shops of Medan and Prapat. Other Batak books on legendary history include *pustaha bintang* and *bilang-bilang* ('lamentation of unhappy lovers'), written on bone or on bamboo tubes with beautifully decorated ends. These are sung in a rhythmical melody, sometimes over the death of a child. The Karo script, transmitted down through the generations orally, is used only as part of the decorative motifs.

Simalungun: One of the branches of the Batak people whose name means 'he that is lonely, quiet or sad'. Simalunguns are gentle and soft-mannered and have many sad nostalgic songs. They speak with a slow lilting intonation. These people were beginning to evolve from sedentary *ladang* cultiva-tors into a feudal society by the time the Dutch first arrived. They weren't conquered until 1910. Half of them are animist, the other half Islamic and Chris-tian, though all atend animist ceremonies such as the 'group hairwashing ritual' (erpangir). Dance is particularly popular in the Simalungun district. The most macabre is a mask-dance performed at funer-als while the dead body is being washed. The hap-piest is the Marriage Dance (Sitalasari) in which the bride and bridesmaids hold flowers in one hand and slap their hips with the other while gliding across the floor in suzv-Q's. The Farewell Dance (Tading Maham Na Tading) is put on by all the young girls of the village when a man leaves, warning him 'Don't marry anybody abroad, just come back to us.'

PEMATANG SIANTAR

128 km S.E. of Medan, or a Rp200 busride from Prapat. 2nd largest city in North Sumatra after Medan. Approaching it you see endless rubber and palm oil plantations on both sides of the road. Sian-tar is like a smaller version of Medan and just as noisy. This city is the capital and the largest town of the Simalunguns, though there are many non-Simalungungs here: Chinese, Indians, Karo, and Toba Bataks. Siantar is the nearest city to Prapat for renewing your visa. Take motorized *becaks* anywhere in town, Rp75-100.

stay and eat: There's a small clump of hotels in the middle of town only 5 minutes walk from the museum or 10 minutes walk from the bus station. Hotel Garuda, Jl. Merdeka 33, is Rp600 single or Rp1200 double. Quite central and clean, it's the best for what Siantar offers in this price range; gracious Chinese people run it. Hotel Bali, Jl. Merdeka 52, Rp1000 double, is near Hotel Garuda. Hotel Dagang, right across the street from Hotel Bali, is the same price. On the other end of town nearer the bus station is Hotel Delima, Jl. Thamrin 131, Rp500 per person. Hotel Segar, Jl. Merdeka 234, Rp1000; noisy, unclean sheets, and their roof-top overlooks a *pasar* neighborhood. The Siantar Hotel is the only high standard accommodation, a bargain for what you pay (Rp3750). Has a small but select library and a nice garden. There are many Chinese shops selling fresh baked goods along the main street of town. Good *mie* places as well.

Simalungun Museum: A special exhibit of the Simalungun Batak clan. Open everyday 8-12 and 2-5 pm. Closed Sun., though Mr. G. Purba might open it for you if he's around. Check out the sculp-ture in the front yard dating from Portugese times, a purely animist powerfully carved stone group of a seated woman holding 2 children. An enormous liz-ard on the door looks like a crocodile. Inside are manuscripts in the Batak script, spears, gongs, masks, artwork, weapons and curios of Simalungun warriors, *pustaha* divination books, 300 year old iron tools, opium pipes, old Portugese guns, *topeng* masks, bygone childrens' games. All labels are in Indonesian but Mr. G. Purba will answer all your questions vividly (in German, Dutch, Indonesian or English) and also tell you some tiger stories from his boyhood days. A zoo nearby has peacocks, Suma-tran fauna, archaeological displays.

crafts: Batak and Karo Tribe artifacts are for sale in Pasar Besar; they give a good exchange rate, about Rp410 = US$1. Buy here superb homespun *kain ulos* for around Rp1200 apiece for the average quality. Up to 2 m long, these fabrics are used for wedding gifts or to spread over an ill person. Though there are different colors and patterns for each tribe, they usually run in vertical stripes with horizontal ends and have blue backgrounds with red and white designs. First go to the museum (near the zoo) and the proprietor will tell you what to look for, how fine the weaving can be, how each type should be worn, comparative prices, and show you some specimens. Also you can buy *ragidup* fabrics in Pasar Besar.

from Siantar: From Stasiun Sentral in the Medan end of town, catch Colts to: Medan, Rp550; Prapat, Rp250; Haranggaol, Rp300. Or by bus to Haranggaol from Parluasan Station 2 km from town, from Rp250. For Sibolga, Rp750 by bus. On the way you pass Balige with its riotously colorful fruit market. Bus to Bukittinggi, Rp2800. From Stasiun Parluasan, catch buses to Kabanjahe via Brastagi in the Karo Highlands for Rp300, takes 3 hours.

vicinity of Siantar: See corrugated iron churches on tops of hills everywhere in this district; stark edifices against a striking blue or stormy sky **Pematang Purba:** Carved wooden houses of Simalungun tribal chieftans are found here complete with a courtroom and execution yard. **Hutagodang:** A Batak village in Labuhan Batu. Take a train or bus to Rantauprapat, then another bus to Langgapayung. Thick dark thatched trad houses are still intact. Visit the ceremonial house which holds sacred heirlooms. All the buildings are old, worn, dark, harsh. Ceremonial drums are beaten while suspended from the railings of high platforms supported by posts blackened with age. Drum music is called by different names according to the sound of the rhythm played– 'rolling boulders', 'thundering storm', etc. **Mandailing:** The best wet rice farmers of all the Batak tribes, they live S.W. of Lake Toba to Natal on the Indian Ocean. This tribe was almost entirely converted to Islam by the start of the 20th Century. Western tertiary education is greatly valued and many Mandailing are university graduates, businessmen, civil servants, and professional soldiers in the Indonesian army. **weekly markets:** Held in rotation. Mon. at Haranggaol, Tues. at Sumbul and Merek, Wed. at Seribu Dolok, Thurs. at Sibutuon, Fri. at Tiga Runggu, Sat. at Pematang Raya. Take the special market-buses out to the markets.

Padanglawas: A collection of ruined 11th and 12th Century monuments virtually unknown to the outside world. This archaeologist's dream is found in South Tapanuli in the neighborhood of Gunungtua near the little village of Portibi, a small barren plain which was once covered in forests. Because of the area's isolation in the middle of the jungles of Sumatra, this site is very seldom visited. Out of at least 16 temple ruins there are 4 broken down but beautiful Hindu temples still standing: Bahal I, II, III, and Sipamutung. Of the other temple sites all that remain are mounds and piles of bricks. In addition, there are untold scattered and broken Hindu statues, carvings and ancient artifacts lying around

by the dozens. The statuary (but not the bricks) are thought to have come from India, transported to this site on barges all the way by river from the east coast of Sumatra. These remains are connected with East Java architecturally, though a distinct type of Buddhism was practiced by these ancient Batak peoples, a tantric cult full of wierd magic. The main vaults of the temples are left, the walls decorated with dancing *raksasas* swinging swords and clubs, lions, many warriors and guardians. Temple Bahal I is 13 m tall and has the strangest iconography: demonic Tibetan tyrannical anger and revenge scenes with thunderbolts and skulls and hideous laughter. **getting there :** From either Bukittinggi or Padang get a bus first to Padangsidempuan. This small town is known as *Kota Salak* because of the abundance of the fruit, *salak,* Rp200 for a whole basketful. From Padangsidempuan there are buses only once or twice a day, Rp300, out to Portibi village. Buses operate more frequently from Padangsidempuan to Gunungtua, Rp250, then it's easy enough to get the only 8 km from Gunungtua down to Portibi. If you want to make more than a day of it, stay with the villagers in Portibi.

TOBA BATAK

The best known Batak clan. One million strong, they are considered the most *kasar* and it doesn't bother them a bit. (Simalungun and Mandailing people don't like to be called Bataks because of this.) The oldest tribe from which all the others are believed to have originated, the Toba Batak have the purest lineages and speak the most uncorrupted dialect. Most live around Lake Toba. 80% are Christians (40% of the Christian Toba Batak live around the lake while 60% of the Christian Toba Bataks live in Tapanuli district) but their religion is mixed strongly with ancestor worship. Many isolated Toba Batak tribes, who live on the far side of the lake opposite Prapat, still haven't had much contact with the outside. **si gale gale:** Restricted only to the island of Samosir and to villages on the south shore of Lake Toba. When a childless Batak dies, in order that they may enter the realm of the dead and not haunt the living, musicians play for the *si gale gale*. A lifesize human-shaped wooden puppet is jerked to life. Attached to a box on wheels, the puppet's body is made of palm wood and has moveable head), eyeballs and hands. It goes through grotesque sudden movements while dancing with the villagers. Tears are produced from sponges set behind the eyes. **music and dance:** Toba Bataks dance wearing turbans and long shawls across one shoulder, bobbing up and down with only the hands expressing; very confined dancing, repetitious, almost solemn. Women's traditional dancing in wide flowing clothes is ritualistic and slow-moving. Dance festivals take place on certain dates fixed each year by the priest-doctors of the old religion, the 'Old Man of the Mountain'. In one, a pony is tied to a stake in the middle of the road and male dancers form a circle around it, trance-dancing to gongs and drums. This ritual dates from the time a sacred breed of horse was regularly sacrificed. Offerings nowadays are *slendang* (dance scarves).

Lake Toba: The mythical first homeland of all the Bataks high in the mountains of North Sumatra. Formed by early volcanic eruptions, Lake Toba is as big as an inland sea (800 sq. km, 80 km long), the largest lake in S.E. Asia and one of the deepest and highest in the world. Its deepest recorded depth is 450 m but for some parts they don't even have sounding equipment for. Lying 900 m above the sea, it's surrounded on all sides by pine-covered beaches, steep mountain slopes and cliffs. Though the blue-green water of this lake may look calm, due to winds (especially in Sept.) it can suddenly become like a stormy ocean. **vicinity of Lake Toba:** Trek in the mountains around the lake. Northeast of the southern shore of Lake Toba, upriver from Balige, is Asahan Falls. Siguragura waterfalls is 200 m high, the highest in S.E. Asia. G. Huta Ginjang is an extinct volcano 24 km from Prapat. Stand on its windy top with Lake Toba one mile below and see clouds drift across its surface, plunging gorges, ridges, distant villages, patchwork of ricefields, and cones of other volcanoes all around you.

PRAPAT

A small lakeside resort with spectacular views on Lake Toba, 176 km from Medan. An international airport is being built above Prapat, but you still got a couple of years left before the deluge. Package tourists from Europe have already started arriving regularly. There are no banks in Prapat, the nearest one is 44 km distant in Siantar. The rates of exchange given at Hotel Sudimampir are terrible. Some of the hotels have better rates, but for cash only.

stay: Some high-priced hotels dot the lake's shore. Of the two first class hotels, Danau Toba and the Prapat Hotel, the latter is the better value; Rp3500 for big lovely rooms looking over the water. Pago Pago Inn is over the hill 10 minutes walk from the ferry landing and about 1½ km from the main road to Padang; Rp300 single. Nice views and delicious fish dinners. Resthouse David Gurning is just off the main road to Padang down the lane next to Restoran Minang; Rp300 single, Rp500 double. The ferry to Tuk Tuk leaves from right out front of the Rest-

house each day at 10:30 am (or thereabouts). Peng. Tao Prapat, next to Resthouse Gurning, is Rp500 double. The 3 rooms out on the waterfront are the best. There are beds above Restoran Sudimampir, costing Rp300 or Rp600 double. Hotel Singalang is also Rp300 single.

eat: On the main road to Padang are dozens of good eating places, Chinese as well as *nasi padang*. Asia Restaurant, next door to the fat man's, has the best sweet and sour fish. The most expensive restaurant (Rp350-1000 per dish) is the Singgalang for Chinese meals such as prawns with bean sauce, Rp650; fish dishes are particularly good. Sinar Pagi, Jl. Pulau Samosir, has incomparable Chinese and European food (try the pancakes) at cheaper prices. In Prapat proper on the way to the ferry quay are 4 Chinese restaurants right in a row. The best is the Rose, right next to the Hong Kong, which does a fantastic sweet and sour pork, Rp300, without a stitch of fat on it. The Heart Restaurant prepares a good chicken and vegetables dish for Rp300.

from Prapat by local bus: If you take local and not express buses, there are 1 hour stops to load sacks of rice, ½ hour stops for meals, and an unspecified number of stops for fixing flat tires and to tie elastic bands around broken water pumps, etc. Spine-jarring, gut-twisting, pot-holed mountain roads. To Lumban Garaga, it's Rp150 by bus. This village, with its 10 *adat* houses, is a 1½ km walk in from the highway. By local bus to Medan, 4 hours, Rp600; by Mercedes bus, 3 hours, Rp800; by minibus (get dropped off at your doorstep), 3 hours, Rp750. **to Brastagi-Kutacane:** Regular bus to Brastagi, 5 hours, Rp800 (the last one leaves at around 11 am); to Kutacane (Mt. Leuser Reserve), 8 hours, Rp1200. **to Sibolga:** Regular bus, 6 hours, Rp1000; Mercedes bus, 5 hours, Rp1200. **long-distance buses:** Always keep one step ahead of the fat guy with the grey hair, Harun, who sells long-distance bus tickets at the Sudimampir Restaurant near the P.O. Don't let him overcharge you, especially on air tickets. Keep your luggage at the restaurant here while waiting for a bus; he can change money too, including Japanese yen. It's important that you book your seats on buses to Medan, Padang, or Bukittinggi at least 3 days in advance to ensure a good seat. Long-range night buses could be cold so take a sleeping bag or socks to prevent your feet from turning a nice shade of blue. **buses to:** Bukittinggi by Mercedes, 15 hours, Rp2500; regular bus, 22 hours, Rp200. to Padang (2-5 pm) by Mercedes bus, 19 hours, Rp3000; regular bus, 26 hours, Rp2800. To Palembang by regular bus, 3 days, Rp7500. To Pekanbaru, Rp3500. To Jakarta by regular bus, 4-5 days, Rp12,500.

by boat from Prapat: You can buy a mohogany dugout canoe in Prapat for Rp6000; ask around. The ferry landing, Kampung Ajibata, is only 30 minutes walk from the archway at the entrance of Prapat; or take a *mesin becak* for Rp150-200. From the landing catch public boats to Tomok, Tuk2, and Ambarita on Samosir Island. These ferries arrive from Samosir at about 9:30 am and usually leave around 10 or 10:30 am and at 4 pm, but they could go back anytime. Costs Rp200. A ferry leaves for Tuk2 also from the front porch of Guesthouse Gurning at 10 or 10:30 am. On Sat. market day there are many more boats and they charge half price, Rp100. On Sun. chartered tourist boats cost up to Rp5000 for 5 people; try hitching them instead. There are also boats to other villages on Samosir Island (Simanindo and Pangururan), but no one knows for sure when they arrive and depart. **Nainggolan:** 50 km from Tomok on Samosir Island. Take the ferry to Nainggolan from Prapat any day, Rp200. Accommodation is available in a couple of 200-year old traditional houses. There is also a *losmen* near the harbor. Market day is Monday.

PRAPAT

1. road to Ajibata ferry landing
2. Pago Pago Inn
3. souvenir shops
4. Chinese restaurant row
5. Prapat Hotel
6. Catholic church
7. Protestant church
8. Danau Toba Hotel
9. Sinar Pagi Restaurant
10. Resthouse David Gurning
11. Sudimampir Hotel and Travel Agency
12. Green Mosque
13. Post Office

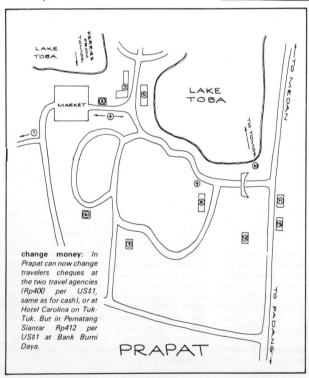

change money: In Prapat can now change travelers cheques at the two travel agencies (Rp400 per US$1, same as for cash), or at Hotel Carolina on Tuk-Tuk. But in Pematang Siantar Rp412 per US$1 at Bank Bumi Daya.

PRAPAT

SAMOSIR ISLAND

Rp200 by boat from Prapat. On a busy day boats leave from Samosir Island to Prapat at 9 am, 11 am, and 3 pm, returning with passengers. Boats could leave in either direction at anytime. No matter where you stand on the shore of Lake Toba you see this 630 sq. km island in the middle of it. Blue-grey mountain walls rise vertically from the water's edge and silver threads of waterfalls tumble into forests below. Rich dark soil. Yell *'Horas!'* and see the smiles; it means 'Lord protect you!' There's only two or three vehicles on the whole island, but motorcycles are beginning to appear. Sometimes boatloads of Indonesians, Malay, and Singaporean tourists come over from the mainland to look at the Batak houses and the European hippies living in them. During the rainy season mosquitos are vicious, so go prepared. If you're going to stay awhile on Samosir, bring good books. There's lots of music going on all the time, either casettes, or young Bataks playing flutes, guitars, xylophones, drums. Try to see the Opera of Samosir which takes place all the time but in different parts of the island. It could be a portrayal of the time when the Batak king held off the Dutch invaders, or similar to a great big night time puppet show with fireworks. It features crooning male vocalists, slapstick skits, and painted girls singing very maudlin and trilling traditional village love songs (ture ture). Indonesian soldiers sometimes have to calm the audience by firing rifles in the air. Usually costs Rp50.

lake cruises: On Sun. Gordon's boat goes around the island, departing Ambarita at 8 am, Tuk2 at 8:30, and Tomok at 9 am. On Wed., Mongoloi's boat starts from Tomok. Both cost Rp750. These pleasure cruises run from sunup to sundown and boast non-stop music and a floating restaurant. The more the merrier. They stop at villages along the way and you can visit the hotsprings. **visa extensions:** Just give either Mongoloi or Gordon money and your passport, sit on your ass, and they'll get you a one or even two month visa extension; you pay the full official price, plus their commission which is around Rp1000. **dope:** The famed Frank Sumatra or Sumatran One comes from Takingeun near Lake Tawar and from the Kutacane area in Aceh Province. But you seldom get the best. Only the third grade makes it down to the island, a coughing weed which parches your throat raw and which also turns over an enormous profit for these islanders. Mostly extended holiday makers and few actual travelers visit Samosir, so most visitors are satisfied with the low grade grass they get. A plastic 'ounce' costs Rp2000, but shop around for a 'big

ounce'. Everyone sells on the side of the island facing Prapat and they've all unionized. On Mondays the police go around to the *losmens* to collect their dues, so take care. For mushrooms head for the cow paddocks in the plateau areas on either side of the mountains south of Tomok and north of Ambarita after a little rain and some sunshine. A kid wants Rp25 for a big handful. One of the kitchens will make up an omelet and even turn out hash or *ganja* cookies if you ask them (you supply).

accommodation: You have your choice now of more than 35 different hotels and *losmens,* a whole array of 'accommodations' sprinkled all along the shore-line between Tomok and Ambarita. You get no reading lamp unless you ask, and there are no bedsheets, and no electricity so get a room with a window to the lake. You must wash in the lake. Some of the places lend you a canoe for the day. The minimum set by the police and the local government is supposed to be Rp250, though you can still get unofficial accommodation for Rp100-150 in the off-season, or if the hotel has vacant rooms. A whole *adat* Batak house can be hired from a family for as little as Rp50 a day which would make this island about the cheapest traveler's recluse in the world to live. But *adat* houses are the most popular and you must wait your turn. Ask around. Or take a tent which is ideal for Samosir because the island is a walker's paradise. Pitch it up in the hills.

eat: You eat a lot on Samosir. Although you can run into a wonderfully fresh vegetable soup, there are too many carbohydrates in Samosir's overpriced food (vegetable tacos, Rp150!). The noodles are the packaged kind. All the menus are identically as tiresome as Bali's and when you ask about many items, you get *'sudah habis!'* (out of it). It just looks good up on the menu. *Gado2* only on Sundays. Most places give 'credit'; you keep your own accounts and pay when you leave.

old graves and tombs: All over Samosir Island (good ones especially at Tomok, Huta Pangalohan, and Huta Pansur) are elaborately carved old stone sacrophagi mounted by monstrous protective heads (singa) with 3 horns and huge round devil eyes. These skull-caskets (parholian) contain the skulls of high-ranking Batak dead dug up one year after death. Scooped out of solid blocks of stone, their walls slant like the hull of a ship. Seen in fields they appear to be floating on water. Of more recent date are the Batak tribal mausoleums, solid mud brick piles with polished bones inside topped with rough cut wooden crosses. Contemporary tombs are sometimes found in the form of a brightly colored Batak house or a statue of the deceased. See the Soldier's Grave between Tuk2 and Ambarita. **burial urn:** As you leave Roongurni Huta, 1 km out of town on the right just before a stream, up above the track beside the white tomb surrounded by a brick wall, is a giant pre-Christian burial urn (with a lid) carved out of solid rock.

TOMOK

9 km across the water from Prapat. The main day-tourist entry point. Swim down in the lake in the mornings. On Sun. watch the whole Christian population turn out for church in their best. Hellfire preaching, hallelujahs and praise to *Kristus!* Up the path is a huge *hariara* tree (like an oak tree) planted in memory of King Sidabutar, pre-Christian head of the first tribes to migrate to this lake in the 4th Century, A.D., at that time one of the most remote parts of Sumatra. **crafts:** At least 100 stands are set up for the tourist boats selling artifacts, cloth and clothing . Bargain intensely. *Ulos* cloths cost Rp1500-8000, Batak calendars with memeographed English explanations (Rp500-1000), old coins, magic medicine staffs, wooden carvings, *pustaha*-bark augery books (Rp5000-10,000), whole carved doors (Rp15,000).

stay and eat: Mongoloi, 'headman' , has two high-peaked tribal houses, full board for about Rp500 per day (with mattress Rp250 or without a mattress Rp150). Righteous meals are served at night starting 7 pm, Rp250, and food is available all day. Try his *kelapa pisang choklat susu*, Rp125, an obscene and famous dessert. At Mongoloi's Sat.

night blast out (Rp150 smorgasbord, crab, etc.), he gives a talk on some aspect of Batak culture. Ask Mongoloi any questions on the Bataks, he speaks English the best and has a few good books about them too. Inquire also about his 'special accommodation' 11 km down the coast from Tomok in Simalombu with its own small jungle, monkeys, and sandy beaches; Rp250 for private rooms, Rp150 for dorm rooms. Really out of it, transport there only happens on Tues., Thurs. and Saturdays. Jogi's House is right up the path in Tomok village, homy and friendly atmosphere. Serves special omelets. Here you get no day tourists like you see down in the village. Run by a 17 year old, his mother and sister do the cooking. Blankets are provided. At Mr. Tupai's house in Silimatali, you'll be treated like one of the family. Has a nice Batak house, your own swimming spot, and a 100 year old granny. Try also Mr. Franky Silalahis, 80 m from the ferry landing and one meter from the lake; Rp500 double. Good food and music. Edison's is clean and has the cheapest food. He'll cook you a whole pig with rice and vegies for Rp3500. In 1976 Mr Oloan intimidated a Dutch couple with police arrest for possession of *ganja* if they reported the theft of their money on his property; he's a dishonest man. There's a *rumah makan* in Tomok village with a limited menu and some *warungs* up the souvenir stalls lane serving *nasi ayam* and other dishes for Rp150. Small market here too. Betty's is the best restaurant (the place is full of locals) but she only has the stuff seen on the menu in the tourist season. She features *kerbau* cheese and a smorgasbord (Rp200) but the specialty of the house is chili con carne.

from Tomok: On the way up to Jogi's meet the (supposedly) crazy man who was chained to a tree by his family for violent acts he committed 8 years ago; give him some cigarettes. It takes 8 hours to walk over to Pangururan across the mountains. (This walk is easier if approached from the Pangururan side.) The climb from Tomok to the top of the mountain in the center of the island is a mud scramble over logs and tangled tree roots. On top are stands of pine trees and one of the most awesome sights you'll ever see. Stay in the village (only 7 houses) on top overnight, simple food, give Rp150 or a gift. The children of this village walk up and down this mountain every day to attend school.

TUK TUK

Located on the tip of the peninsula, quieter than Tomok. Most of the buildings in this small village have been built for tourists, not for villagers. Tuk2 has its own ferry now. **stay and eat:** A cluster of cheap and expensive hotels, from the Matahari (Rp250) on the waterfront right up to the Tuk2

SAMOSIR ISLAND

Tomok is generally pretty empty these days. When there's wind, lousy swimming, so most people go to the losmens on more picturesque Tuk Tuk: good swimming.

ferry trip: Every Sunday there's a ferry trip around the island for Westerners, often stopping at the hotsprings near Pangururan, Rp750; serves food at jacked-up prices, so bring your own.

Pangururan: Stay at Kedai Kopi Barat, which caters to Westerners. Proprietor Richard Barat speaks English, knows the area, draws maps, cashes travelers cheques at Rp395 per US$1. Room above shop with nice balcony, Rp150 per person.

Virtually all World Travelers doing Sumatra now stop on Samosir, often for weeks because it's so restful and pleasant. Few people get sick here — those coming up from Bali and Java often arrive with the vestiges of dengue fever, dysentery or severe influenza.

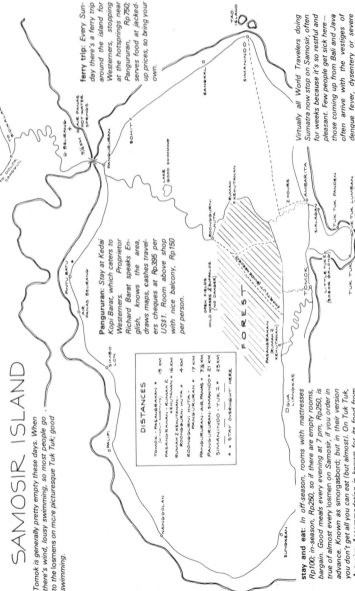

DISTANCES

TOMOK - PELANGKRAAN *
(WITHOUT SHORTCUT)   15 KM

PASANG RAHAN - RUMAH 2
KERUTANIAN *   16 KM

RUMAH 2 KERUTANIAN -
ROONGGURNI HUTA *   4 KM

ROONGGURNI HUTA -
PANGURURAN   17 KM

PANGURURAN - AIR PANAS * 3½ KM

PANGURURAN - SIMANINDO * 21 KM

SIMANINDO - TUK 2 *   25 KM

* = STAY OVERNIGHT HERE.

stay and eat: *In off-season, rooms with mattresses Rp100; in-season, Rp250, so if there are empty rooms, bargain. Good meals every evening at 7 pm, Rp250, is true of almost every losmen on Samosir, if you order in advance. Known as smorgasbord; but in their version you don't get all you can eat (but almost). On Tuk Tuk, Antonius Accommodation is known for its food from the longest menu.*

Hotel (Rp3500) on top of the hill. The best rooms at Matahari's have balconies and are the same price as the others. The Tuk2 Hotel is quite comfortable: private bath, hot water, electricity, garden out front; like any American highway motel. Bernards, Rp100-250 for rooms looking over one of the nicest beaches on the island; get a good hearty slap on the back from Pepy every morning. Carolina has 6 individual mock-Batak houses on the slope of a small hill overlooking the whole lake; Rp600-800 per house, Rp1000 for the Skyline Room. There's a good restaurant with a limited menu and a private swimming cove with a diving board. **others:** Rudy's is right around the bend from Tuk2, 6 minutes walk on the coastal path to Ambarita (turn in at the 'Munchie's' sign); beds cost Rp150-250. As tranquil as you can get. Music in the afternoons when the re-charged battery arrives back from Prapat. Mama Rudy is nice, so is her cooking and her 7 kids. From Tuk2 it's a 1 ½ km walk to Tuk Lumban Manurung where you'll find Dominic's; excellent food. Also Mr Romlan's (see Selasta) restaurant and waterside Batak house; Rp250 for cozy little rooms. At Tuk2 Pandan, about a 30 minute walk towards Ambarita from Tuk2, there are at least 5 'accommodations' hanging over the lake with spectacular surroundings and convenient ferry connections to Prapat. Rusly's is the best of them, Rp250. Nelson Vugo's is Rp250 also. Manru's is always crowded. Lastra Johnny's has number one granola, Rp150. The village of Little Tuk2 is 15 minutes walk from Tuk2 towards Tomok, all by its own in a small cove. Marpuang's and Tony's offer accommodation for Rp250. Paulus Batak house is available for travelers. Several restaurants. At Christa's you can even go in the back and cook.

AMBARITA

13 nautical km from Prapat or a lovely dramatic walk around the peninsula from Tomok. This village is a more idyllic and unfrequented spot with flowered coves, covered bridges, stony piers, graceful ship-prowed houses with 3 dimensional woodcarvings. Cannibal King's 'dinner table' and stone furniture in a courtyard include benches, chairs, and an upright stone block where captive and enemies where beheaded (the last occured in 1900). Locals all gambling in the coffee shops. Dozens of *warungs*. Why not so many fat dogs on Samosir? Dog meat is sold in Ambarita's market on Thursdays and Fridays.

Stay and eat: Rohandy Accommodation, Rp150, is right on its own peninsula. Quiet, and you can spit in the water. This is the nicest location of all the *losmens* in Ambarita, but rooms in the two Batak

houses here are smallish. They serve *pekora* (Indian pancakes), Rp200, and *guacamole* salad, Rp150. Watch the ducks paddle by. Kristen Murmi's is in the *kampung* near the landing stage. Could be noisy but couldn't be closer to the water; good food. Also try Mr. Tumpal's restaurant nearby on the corner for *mie kua* with egg, only Rp100. Gordon's, back 5 minutes from the water, has two Batak houses in a garden full of giant flowers and a 'favorites' tape collection in his restaurant. Amigo Inn and minirestaurant, clean and quiet, has a good atmosphere and is only 5 meters from the beach.

from Ambarita: There are daily ferry services to Prapat. It's a 5 km walk from Ambarita to Tomok, or to Tuk2 from Ambarita about a 1 ¼ hour walk. Get on the Sunday boat to Pangururan (from Ambarita, Rp400), then walk 2 ½ days back to Ambarita. Villagers along the way will put you up. **vicinity of Ambarita:** Some of the best mountain trails begin here. **the waterfall:** A pleasant 1 ½ hour walk to the base of this large falls which cascades down the mountain opposite Tuk2 peninsula. The walk to the falls takes you through small communities set back behind the rice paddies. The falls drops onto giant rocks which divert the water into irrigation channels for the paddy fields below. Don't try to go up the right-hand side or you'll cut your feet to shreds; try to find the path to the top on the left-hand side. **Haranggaol:** On Mon. at 6 am there's a ferry Rp300 to Haranggaol, leaving only from Ambarita. Monday is market day in Haranggaol. The ferry stops in several villages along the way. Haranggaol sits on the north shore of the lake, a really beautiful and untouristed village with the best view south of Samosir Island and Prapat on the far side. From Haranggaol, change buses for Brastagi, Rp150. The bus departs at about 1 pm (boat arrives around 10 pm). This is a different way to leave the lake, a fitting farewell.

Simanindo: 16 km after Ambarita towards Pangururan along the coastal track from Tomok, about a half day's walk from Tomok. All over the island there are superb examples of beautiful Batak houses but the former king's house in this village is by far the most outstanding. This old *adat* family house has been restored and the museum inside contains small brass pots and bowls, spears, *kris,* large Dutch and China platters, *datu* (witch doctor) charms, and sculptures of gods in the front of the house. Ten sun-bleached buffalo horns from the 10 generations of the dynasty adorn it. *Tor-tor* dances are sometimes to be seen here. Someone might try to sell you a cylindrical bamboo treasure box, or an old divination book (written in a lost language), folded up like an accordian and made of *alim* leaf by a *datu,* for about Rp1000-1500. Stay overnight in

Simanindo with the villagers, Rp250.

PANGURURAN

A ½ day hike from Simanindo. A short stone bridge in Pangururan connects the island to the mainland. Ricardo's house takes in guests but has lousy food, rats all night, a racket in the street outside, and a toilet that has to be seen to be believed. Try to find other villagers to put you up. Kedai Kopi Barat has rooms above the shop with a nice balcony, Rp150 per person. **vicinity of Pangururan:** Visit the hotsprings on the mainland. Take the right after the stone bridge, the *air panas* is halfway up the hill. Take a hot bath in any of the small pools near the bottom of the cliffs where the cascading water has cooled down. This spot overlooks the entire lake. Near the hotsprings stay for Rp100 per night on a mat on the floor of the teashop.

for Brastagi: There's a bus once weekly to Sidikalang, Rp800, then on to Brastagi. Or if you have a powerful means of transport travel to Brastagi by crossing over the narrow channel at the rear of the island and journeying through an untouched mountain area of almost total desertion and fantastic scenery. Be prepared for a sore ass. **for Tomok:** A difficult trail leads over the mountains to Tomok from here. The walk can be done from either direction but it's easier from Pangururan because you avoid the very steep climb from the Tomok-side. It takes about 8 hours or longer depending on the weather and how many times you get lost enroute. About 3 hours out of Pangururan the trail becomes difficult to follow and you must constantly confirm directions with the local people. There's a beautiful pine forest near the summit. Stop overnight in one of the local houses on the top, then descend 1-1½ hours down to Tomok the next morning. During the wet season you could wade through half a meter of mud or crawl 200 m through wet undergrowth on the way down. If walking doesn't suit you wait for the ferry to take you back to Prapat from Pangururan or return by local buses through the mainland towns.

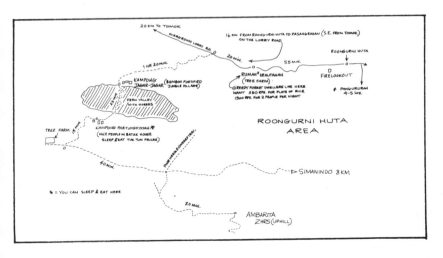

THE KARO BATAK

These 5 Batak clans and 83 subclans inhabit a high plateau of mountain slopes, rich volcanic valleys, and deep ravines north and west of Lake Toba. Possessing a temperate climate and little seasonal variation, the Karo Highlands cover an area of 2640 sq km with more than 270 villages inhabited by approximately 400,000 people. Karos run a prosperous cash crop economy with dry rice and *sawah* areas, rolling cornfields, tea plantations, vegetable patches. A strong exogamous patrilineal society, the Karos are the youngest of all the Batak tribes and are remarkable because so much of their close-knit traditional life is still intact. They are legendary for their warmness and speak a very *alus*, soft-spoken dialect, which sounds musical like Italian. Theft is an apalling offense in Karoland, the police take it *personally*. Karos dress like Tibetans in heavy broad turbans and tightly wrapped dark clothes. Many of the women wear traditional wide-brimmed tassled headdresses. Their literature consists mostly of books dealing with magic, medicine, and divination. Even goldsmiths use handbooks of divination. Other Sumatrans consider the Karo Tribe to be the most preoccupied with witchcraft and spells of all the *puaks* of Sumatra.

kinship: Islam never made deep inroads here, but the Karos have been remarkably receptive to Christianity. Under Dutch rule for only 40 years, Dutch missionaries started work in these highlands only in 1902. During the political upheavals and slaughter of 1965-66 there were mass conversions so that they wouldn't be suspected of being atheists. Now 60% are either Islamic or Christian. But the Karoness unofficial, strongest, and most widely practiced religion is actually kinship. All faiths are bound by kinship and *adat* obligations and if the lineage has been offended, illness, drought and crop failures could result. Marriage creates a totally new relationship with many people. There's an almost spiritual relationship with the wife's family, who are called 'gods that can be seen' (kalimbubu). When a Karo woman marries, the bride's father and brother become her husband's *kalimbubu* who are higher in status. They're treated ritually superior, always given honor and deference. The husband, in turn, becomes beneath them in status (anakberu). *Anakberu* serve *kalimbubu;* they do all the work at *adat* ceremonies such as weddings, feasts, etc. They must sit before them, address them very politely, never bathe in their presence, cook for them, act as legal spokesmen. The exchange of favors and obligations are mutual. The *kalimbubu* side has heavy financial committments to give presents and land to *anakberu* relatives. Since it often brings about tensions and conflict, the rigidity of this system is now breaking down. An unmarried man without sons is greviously pitied and called *bangkaren* (old bamboo) whom nobody wants; his social obligations and mission in life were never fulfilled. Couples sometimes have 3 kids before they're ceremoniously married. Karo women obey orders and work for their fathers or brothers in a almost formal relationship; joking or affection is seldom shown.

events: The Karos attend about 60 ceremonial occasions a year. If you're really interested, they are proud to take you around to them for free. Obligations to attend feasts and ceremonies in their clan brotherhood is very strong. At funerals, there's dancing to the music of the *gendang* (traditional Karo orchestra), accompanied by minor-keyed singing. Betel leaves, cigarettes, and money are often placed in the coffin. When a child dies, it's laid out in the center of the house and symbolically married: with a dead boy the *dukun* enfolds warm bamboo around his penis to simulate sexual intercourse and in the case of a girl a banana is inserted into the vagina to symbolize intercourse. This is performed before the burial so that the spirit of the frustrated deceased child (begu) will not come and disturb the living kinsmen of the village. Get in on *Kerja Tahun* (the Karonese New Years). Only at this time can you see all the *adat* at play and eat special Karonese cake *cimpa*. Ritualized offerings are often made to dead ancestors. *Nurun-nuran* is a ritual in which the bones of ancestors are washed and re-buried. *Erpangir* is a group hair-washing ceremony at which even Christian Karos attend. *Cukra Dulu, Belah Purnama* and *Bulan Raya* all have the aim of warding off evil spirits. The *Negerires Festival,* which petitions god for a good harvest, is held at the village of Batukarang near Brastagi at the beginning of the year.

BRASTAGI

A Karo township in a mountain forest region 68 km, Rp300 by minibus, from Medan. It's like taking an elevator up to these highlands, over 1300 m above sea level. Cool, healthy climate. Pine plantations. This whole region is a rich area for many descendants of European vegetables, fragrant flowers and fruits, exporting its vegetables to Penang and even flying its flowers to Singapore. Plump, ripe avocados grown here cost Rp50 a kilo and carrots are so plentiful (Rp25 a kilo) that they're fed to horses. Flies in this market town, due to all the manure

Batak magic wands *(tungkat malaikat): The most decorative and imaginative form of Batak art. Like miniature totem-poles from 1 m to 2 m long with figures of snakes, horses, buffaloes, dogs, lizards, elephants, chameleons, naga snakes, and copulating couples twisting down the pole. Tungkat malaikat are used in rain-making, protection in case of battle, to induce illness and death, and for worship. Antique ones cost up to Rp200,000; newer ones, Rp10,000.*

used, are most numerous: make sure that your room has a screen. Visit the Karo Batak market on Sat. and Tuesdays. There are no banks in Brastagi; the nearest is at Kabanjahe, 11 km down the road. **crafts:** For handicrafts from all over Indonesia try Modesty Souvenir Shop, Jl. Veteran 85, Tel. 65. Batak ornaments, antiques, stones, postcards. Mr. Sinulingga will entertain you. Practically right across the street near the Asia Restaurant is the Namaken Souvenir Shop, but not as well-stocked.

stay: Most places have immaculate flower or vegetable gardens and lawns. Guest-house Sibayak in the Kabanjahe end of town is the best for the money; a big room for Rp1000 and smaller (but still big) for Rp750. Meals also are served, about Rp400 per day. Mr. Pelawi will take time out from his English teaching to show you around. Stay the night in the trad village of Ajijahe, 10 km from Brastagi, at the courtesy of the *pengulu;* this is Pelawi's home village. Bungalow Harapan, on its own promontory, is clean, quiet, but overpriced. It looks more expensive than it really is, an impression dis-

pelled once you enter a room; Rp1000 for quite dreary double rooms, other rooms for Rp3000 (for 4 people) and Rp5000. Wisma Dieng near Guesthouse Sibayak has very nice, quiet rooms for Rp-2000. Wisma Ingin Malam is in Gongsol in back of the town; nice rooms for Rp1500 double. A little fruit market down the street plus food stores nearby. Bukit Kubu, 1 km from town on Jl. Sempurna, is very likely the most faithfully preserved old colonial-style hotel in all of Indonesia; Rp6000 double. At least you get your money's worth here. At the other extreme is dingy but livable Losmen Gunung, Jl. Veteran 98, Rp200 per night. Kind of grotty Hotel Timor hangs right over Jl. Veteran, Rp300-400 single, Rp800 double. Opposite is Ginting Sada Kata, Rp600 single, Rp800 double; watch your stuff here. Central Hotel is down a side street so it's fairly quiet; Rp500 single, Rp1000 double, but small rooms. Peng. Gundaling near the Asia Restaurant has small dark Rp600 rooms upstairs over the street. It's not that difficult to rent out a little farmhouse cheaply; ask Pelawi's students at Guesthouse Sibayak.

eat: Buy a bottle of the refreshing vitamin-rich *marquisa* juice found only here and in South Celebes. There are 3 grades, Rp350, Rp300 and Rp250. Also try exotic 'Indonesian apples', a cross between persimmons and a peach (closest description). Yoghurt (minyak susu) made from buffalo milk is available. *Babi panggang,* a traditional Karonese meal of roast pork, rice, sauce (Rp100) can be experienced in the *warung* in the market, Jl. Pasar Kios 26. Two other places serving it (for Rp150) are Terang Rumah Makan, Jl. Veteran 369, and at Jl. Veteran 366. *Tritis* is a ceremonial food made with not fully digested grass from a cow's first stomach; the Karos even say 'we eat cowshit'. Drink hot spiced ginger milk (bandrek) by night at Ora et Labora on the main street, Jl. Veteran 34; costs Rp25 a glass. Tastes as good as egg nog. Many local coffee houses and restaurants serve *tuak* and *bandrek* and have their own 'vocal groups'. For breakfast there are carts selling bean porridge (bubur kacang ijo) for Rp30. Restaurant Asia serves canned chicken! Budi Aman Nasi Islam, also on the main street, is a delicious Javanese workingmens' restaurant. Wide selection: flavorful beef soup, Rp100, garnished tasty meals, Rp250. Very cozy at night, a real personal touch, the best. Rumah Makan Minang nearby serves *nasi padang;* a *nasi campur* here costs Rp200.

from Brastagi: For Medan, Sutra Co. or Gundaling Co. minibus vans take you right to the door, but Sibayak Company doesn't. It's easy to find a private taxi for hire in Brastagi (5 people can fit in one). Some starting prices to: Prapat, Rp25,000; Barusjahe, Rp7500; Tongging, Rp7500; Lingga, a ridiculous Rp4000. Bargain vigorously. It's about 10 times cheaper using public transport. vicinity of Brastagi: The most beautifully landscaped and most typical Karo village in Karoland is Bintang Mariach. Visit the museum of Karo artifacts at Raya, 5 km from Brastagi on the road to Kabanjahe. Roam the *sawah* around Brastagi. The Maze Cave of Kamar Bingung is 3 km from Brastagi. On Gundaling Hill see the Spirit's Cave and giant totem poles of magic wands, plus traditional Karonese tribal houses. Nice view of Brastagi. On Sun. the entrance fee is Rp50. This region is great butterfly country inhabited by rarities like *troides vandepolli.* Because they fly so high, 5 m tall poles are used to catch them. Ask for Robert or Jimmy at Guesthouse Sibayak about butterflies; they'll do *anything* for money.

Kolam Renang (swimming pool): Rp100 to get in on Sun. when it's crowded, but free every other day. On Tues. and Sat. (market days) it's dead quiet. Lovely spot when you have it by yourself. Picture postcard lawn. Rent a pony Rp600 an hour. Stay on the grounds in units at Rp1000 per bed.

Perloah Prostitution Center: Up a country road in the middle of a pine forest. The only legalized prostitution in the area with fixed prices, a doctor on duty, guards and fences. Sikulikap Waterfall: 12 km from Brastagi near Lau Dubuk2. Take bus from Brastagi 8 km to the Daulu village turnoff, Rp50. Walk 3 km in from the highway to Daulu, then 2 km further to this 100 m high falls. The path down to it is very nice. Lau Dubuk2 is a large hotsprings about 500 m from the highway at the Daulu turnoff, but the water isn't as hot as the one at Radja Berne. There's also a hotsprings at Daulu village.

Lake Kawar: 30 km from Brastagi at the base of Mt. Sinabung. A private taxi costs Rp7500, but during market days (Tues. and Sat.) catch a bus after 12 am for Rp200. Taking one hour to get there, the bus waits at the lake 30 minutes, then returns to Kabanjahe. Report to the *pengulu* at Lake Kawar for accommodation . Via Lake Kawar is another way to reach the Orangutan Rehabilitation Center at Bukit Lawang. Walk over the hills through the jungles. G. Sinabung: Although the view from the top isn't as sweeping as from the summit of G. Sibayak, this active volcano is also a 4 hour climb. Tongging: A town famed for its beautiful landscapes 24 km from Kabanjahe on the north side of Lake Toba. A bus leaves only on Mon. from Brastagi. From Tongging get to the Sipisopiso Waterfall, which is only 1 hour's walk from the main road. Kotacane: A rice-growing area where high grade *canabis* was formerly grown extensively until the government destroyed most crops. It's grown now only on a small private scale. Make discreet but persistent inquiries at farms around this town, though you may have to inland over untrafficed roads. An Orangutan Rehabilitation Center is near Kotacane on the Kluet River near Ketambe.

Barusjahe: A very old, uniquely laid out village with *adat* houses, about 15 km from Kabanjahe; Rp100 by public taxi. A beautiful road out to here. Here live a cross-section of all Karo peoples and the layout of this very old village is quite unique. Monumental buildings (gertain) were used for storing skulls and bones of dead Karonese nobility; a few of the *gertain* in Barusjahe are more than 250 years old. Not a single nail was used in their construction, only rope and wooden pegs. The *pengulu* of Barusjahe, Rattim Barus, is overfriendly, a real wildman, who wears a hofberger hat and t-shirts which say

landscapes of Indonesia

'Village Chief'. Sharp guy. Takes you around on madcap rides on his motorcycle. The *penginapan* here sometimes doesn't charge you.

Lingga: 5 km from Kabanjahe and 16 km south of Brastagi. Easier to get to than Barusjahe. From Brastagi take an *oplet* to Kabanjahe Rp50, then another *oplet*, bus, or taxi to Lingga, Rp50. The bus drops you off on the highway, only a 1½ km walk from the village. Lingga is a complete Karonese village of large, painted and decorated communal Batak longhouses in which people work and live in the dark. Smoke rises to the blackened roof, the houses open at both ends to allow breezes to blow through. Stay with the *kepala kampung*.

Mt. Sibayak: An easy, beautiful 4 hour climb up to this broken crater still uppity and spitting and belching sulphureous fumes. Start early before it clouds over. Walk over a mountain, through a village, across ricefields and then straight up through the jungle with orangutans hooting all around. The ground could be treacherously slippery but worth the final achievement and the sight from the summit. Be warned that on weekends sometimes groups of 300 (yes, *300*) domestic tourists from Medan make the climb together, littering the trails with plastic drink containers and broken thongs. Bring *marquisa* fruits and oranges to quench the thirst. **getting there:** If you want to get an early start from Brastagi, you'll need a guide to lead you through the dark pathways over the mountain between Brastagi and G. Sibayak. Guides want Rp3000 to show you the way to the top of the volcano. But if you get on the earliest Medan-bound bus out of Brastagi, 8 km down the road you reach the turnoff to Daulu. From the turn off, hitch or walk the 4 km to Radja Berne village; this eliminates

the need for a guide. Get to the base by 7 am and begin the ascent. Or stay overnight in the teashop of Radja Berne and get an even earlier start. Upon returning to the village, soak your aching bones in the medicinal hot sulphur springs nearby. Afterwards, villagers will lead you to the teashop; pay Rp50. You can either walk back to the highway and catch a bus (bathe at Lau Dubuk2 on the way) or by this time it will be light enough for you to find your way over the small mountain back to Brastagi.

Kabanjahe: Rp50 by public taxi 11 km south of Brastagi. The capital city of Karoland where the *bupati's* office is. Brastagi is more scenic, more central, and has better accommodation than Kabanjahe. Visit the marketplace. Change money at Bank 1946. **vicinity of Kabanjahe:** A 52 year old painter, Rugun Sembiring, works in Kampung Kabanjahe, 1½ km from Kabanjahe. See his giant painting of refugees fleeing during the *Revolusi;* looks like a basrelief! He loves blazing yellow. A fine man with whom you can practice your Indonesian while *kampung* kids sit in the doorway. **Lau Simomo:** A leper colony 8 km from Kabanjahe that was begun by a Dutch missionary. Report to the doctor in charge first. **mawas center:** From Kabanjahe hire a landrover for about Rp10,000 between several people and travel 4 hours through smothering jungle and over hills to the Orangutan Rehabilitation Center at Ketembe. **Pematang Purba:** This 200 year old village 1 hour's drive from Kabanjahe is worth visiting for its unique Simalungun houses of tribal chiefs. Take the regular bus from Kabanjahe to Siantar, then about half way between these two points get off at Pematang Purba which is only 100 m from the highway. See the ancient courthouse, tall thatched Sumatran roofs, rice barns, palace longhouse.

watercraft of Indonesia

ACEH PROVINCE

These 2 million people are the native inhabitants of northernmost Sumatra. They are divided into the earlier proto-Malayan hill people, the Gayos and the Alas, and the more recent lowland coastal people. The Acehnese are taller, stouter and darker in complexion than most other natives on the island. The hospitality of these people could be equivalent to an abduction. **history:** The ethnic state of Aceh has been trading with Malaya, China, India, Ceylon, and the Red Sea for well over 1000 years. About 500 A.D. the Liang annals of China mentions the Buddhist state of Poli where Aceh is now. When Marco Polo visited here in 1292 A.D. he wrote the first account of an Islamic sultanate in Southeast Asia. Aceh was fiercely rebellious during colonial times. The Dutch East Indies Company broke Aceh's control of the pepper trade but when a Dutch expedition was sent to pacify Aceh in 1873, it was driven into the sea. Some say that because of magic spells when the Dutch landed they began to vomit blood. A bitter war broke out and at last when the *kraton* of Aceh fell, it had cost the lives of 250,000 men, including 2 Dutch generals. In the rebellion against the Dutch in 1877, guerilla bands fought for 10 more years during which the famous culture hero Teuku Umar went over to the the Dutch side, then escaped with whole companies of men, rifles, and ammunition. This was a holy war and Muslim priests and religious scholars (ulama) were the leaders. Intermittently the struggle for autonomy went on for more than 40 years and Dutch troops had to be stationed in Banda Aceh right up to the eve of the Japanese invasion in 1942. During the 'Police Actions' of 1947 and '48, the Dutch had learned their lesson and pointedly left Aceh alone. Even today it's a very tender area politically. Jakarta treats them with kid gloves and has declared Aceh a Special Territory where Islamic law applies.

religion: The Acehnese are socially conservative but religiously radical. The first part of the archipelago to be converted and today a rockbed of Islam, the faith is practiced in this province with unusual intensity and strictness for Indonesia. Even their games have a religious function. Rich men are not respected unless they give to Islamic causes and the poor have a right to accept what the rich have a duty to give. The interpretation of dreams and omens is widespread. It's believed in Aceh that prayer makes you into a rational being, distinguishing a man from animals and children. One's sacred duty is to pray with great precision and humility with full prostrations, touching the forehead to the ground while pronouncing Arabic prayers perfectly, even though many Acehnese have no understanding of the language (but Allah is listening). Acehnese judge strangers by the way they pray as they themselves really surrender (the true meaning of 'Islam') during prayer. Observe them praying in public places, they give no indication of knowing what happens around them. Beginning at 6 years of age, young boys learn to chant prayers from the *Koran* and learn how to write in Arabic; they practice daily from 6 am. It's because of this early training and emphasis on prayer that the Acehnese walk and stand so erectly. At 8 years a boy is circumcised and he begins to wear pants. It's considered that he reaches maturity when he experiences his first wet dream.

Acehnese society: Parents buy a house for each daughter when she gets married and usually end their lives in a shack surrounded by the houses of their daughters. Often away for long periods on business (merantau), a husband lives with his bride in her parent's house. Living like guests, husbands are powerless in the home, thus play a small role in the upbringing of children and in the maintenance of the house. The word for wife is *njang po rumoh,* 'the one who owns the house'. A woman divorces her husband by putting all of his belongings at the bottom of the steps. He is too ashamed to do anything but grant it. Women are called `brides' until the birth of their first child. At birth, if the umbilical cord doesn't come all the way out it's believed that it can crawl back into the womb and kill her. After birth women can't leave the house for 45 days and there are also many dietary prohibitions. Her body is 'roasted' over hot bricks which will make her trim and healthy again.

dance, music and games: There's a great variety of dances, most accompanied by songs: competitive verse-reciting dance (seudati), *rapai* music, a tune played by girls on percussion instruments (alle tanjang), a song and dance form from East Aceh (saman hokop), *canang kecapi, bines* and *saman gayo, guel, anjung, inen majak, sunting.* Self defence forms such as *silat tamiang* and *peulebat* are from S.E. Aceh. From West Aceh comes the sword dance *Tari Pegand,* a dance of self-inflicted ritual wounds from daggers, spears and swords. From South Aceh comes the verse dance art of *sikambang.* One of their best known dances is *Seudati Agam,* a war dance originally performed in palaces to entertain sultans and their families or to honor distinguished guests; now popular at harvest times. Nine young men leap and sing while snapping their fingers and beating their chests. The *perdito* is a modified version of an Arab dance, half danced, half spoken. Performed only by men, the dancers divide themselves into 2 groups which advance and retreat, bending the upper part of their bodies forward, while passing sarcastic remarks on the current rumors in town. Special instruments played in Aceh are the 3-stringed bamboo zither, a vase-shaped drum with a single drumhead, types of tambourines (geundrang), the flute (seurunekele). The game *geudeu-geudeu* has a religious purpose, as a kind of Acehnese anti-aggression therapy. This exercise violently purges the soul and everyone ends exhausted. Players fight and must be pulled apart. Neither side feels itself represented by its players, there's no order of play, social identity is stripped, and it's played silently.

crafts: The best markets are those in villages at mouths of navigable rivers, having better access to the interior. Finely wrought gold jewelry and gold filigree work is occasionally treated with acid to give it a reddish tint, considered more attractive than its true color. High quality cotton and silk fabrics are also produced. Lamps ornamented with large bird figures, intricately engraved copper bowls, elaborate brocades, shields with Moorish designs, and blades (rencong) of swords and *kris* with Arabic mystic markings, are all very attractive. These native arts are disappearing now.

BANDA ACEH

The capital of Aceh Province on the northern tip of Sumatra. This city was once a huge multi-ethnic metropolis with giant international markets and compounds of Indians, Arabs, Turks, Chinese, Abyssinians, and Persians. Known as the 'Doorway to Mecca', Aceh has always been a stopping off place for pilgrims journeying by ship to the Holy City. Great teachers, men of letters, poets and philosophers taught here, schools were everywhere. During the 17th Century Aceh reached its height of political power, wealth and cosmopolitanism under Iskander Muda. In Aceh's struggle to gain total supremecy over the N.W. archipelago, it engaged in great sea battles with the Portugese (1629) and almost succeeded in capturing Melaka, though destroying its fleet in the process. Today, you'd think that you were in Arabia. Some women dress in black trousers, spangled georgette veils, velvet jackets, with a garland of white flowers around the bun at the nape of the neck, fanning themselves and each other while listening to Arabian-inspired music. Banda Aceh's white buildings are stained with age. The Acehnese language is even written in the Arabic script. But no wonder.

Arabians have been trading here for centuries. Middle Eastern people are still very much in evidence. This is the strongest Muslim city in Indonesia and probably the only place in Indonesia where you cannot get food during *Ramadan,* you *must* fast. Everyone prays in Aceh, if only to keep face. But it's not heavy and people are quite friendly. Borrow a bicycle; it's very flat, an easy city to bicycle around.

getting there: Linked by air, road and rail from Medan. A plane leaves 3 times a week from Medan to Blangbintang Airport in Banda Aceh, but the cheapest is to catch a bench-seat Chevrolet bus from Medan, 20-30 hours, Rp2800-3000. Or by Mercedes bus, Rp2800. Kunia Co. in Medan, Jl. Singamangaraja, has the most comfortable buses with fans that work and a place to rest your head. They have two buses going out each day from Medan, 8 am and 5 pm, taking 17-20 hours, 610 km. Book a day or two in advance to get a good seat. The road is being improved by the oil companies, but segments are still very bad.

stay: Cheapest are Losmen Norma, Rp350 a night; down a back lane. Hotel Kiyah is Rp400. Hotel Lading is Rp600. Colonial-style Hotel Aceh, Jl. Mohd̦. Jam 1, opposite the Great Mosque, charges Rp3000 single; has communal *mandis* and each bedroom has a fan. If you get over to Sabang on Weh Island (the westerly limits of Indonesia), stay at the Sabang Hill Hotel; has a great view and a restaurant nearby. **eat:** Food's cheap if you eat in the market near the mosque; *mie rebus* and *mie goreng,* Rp100. Restaurant Aroma by the market on Jl. Palembang is very good. Aceh has fine coffee, Rp20 for a small glass, strong and sweet. Women aren't allowed to drink coffee. You ask why and they just say 'it's tradition'. *Cannabis* is a common intercrop in Aceh and the Karolands and it's traditional to cook *ganja* in with the food, as in some of the Aceh curries; very hot, spicy and potent. The *ganja* base used in curry is a light golden green, dry, and only the flowers.

sights: At the stadium native wrestling matches and bullfights are staged, also on occasion *geudeu-geudeu* and the Acehnese football game *boh awe.* At Krueng Aceh, canoe racing. See Baturrachman Mosque and the well-maintained Dutch cemetary. **The Aceh Museum** (Rumoh Aceh): Rp25 entrance. On display are distinctive collections of old brocades, tribal beds with gold canopies, a wedding set piece, household clothes, domestic utensils brought from inland areas. There is a lot of clothing but no explanations about them. A giant Chinese bell, Cakra Donya, stands in front of the museum. **Gunongan:** The baths and pleasure gardens of the former sultan's ladies; looks like Tunisian or

Algerian *ghorfas* (domed granaries). This 'Walking Palace' on the banks of a river was built for a Malay princess who married one of the sultans of Aceh. Has a terrace around it leading to the mounds which represent small hills so that she could take an evening walk, not permitted at that time in Aceh. **library:** Probably the most remote private library in the world is at Tanoe Abee near Seulimeum. Owned by Tengku Shaikh Abdel-wahhab, it contains rare 17th Century Arabic commentaries on *al-Quran al-Karim.*

from Banda Aceh: Boat to Sabang, Rp200. Ride the little steam train which runs right through the main streets of Banda Aceh, connecting Banda Aceh with Sigli and sometimes further south to Medan. **for Simeulue Island:** Take bus first to Meulaboh (sitting in the back seat for 12 hours on a dirt road), then take a boat out to the island of Simeulue (130 people crammed for 16 hours in a 30 m boat). From Simeulue it's possible to catch boats down to Sibolga. Another route is to take the bus first to Takingeun, Rp1500. There's a *losmen* in Takingeun. Then take a bus to Tapaktuan on the coast, Rp200. There are no buses past Tapaktuan. From Tapaktuan take a boat out to Sinabang on Simeulue Island. From Simeulue there are boats further to Gunungsitoli, Nias.

vicinity of Banda Aceh: Graves of famous mystics are still the objects of pilgrimmages all over Aceh; visit the tomb of the great theological scholar, Tengku Sheikh Abdurrahman (or Syah Kuala). The coastline of Aceh is really nice, clear water. The nearest beach is only 15 km away; Ihok'nga and Lampu'uk are the most beautiful beaches near Banda Aceh. The quiet sleepy port of Oeleelheue is quite pretty. Down the coast 60 km live a small group of people descended from a 17th Century Portugese shipwreck. There's some picturesque hill country around Banda Aceh with mountains up to 3660 m; see much more of the local culture out in these hinterland villages. Poppies are grown around

Langat. This province has 4 wildlife sanctuaries. When Marco Polo landed here in 1292 he claimed he saw a unicorn but it was most likely the one-horned Hairy Sumatran Rhinoceros, found now in these reserves. **Pidie Valley:** A great rice-producing area. Villages here consist of clusters of houses owned by sisters and aunts (mother's sisters); every married woman owns her own house. **Bireuen:** During the tobacco season June-August there's a bustling tobacco traders' market here. Most tobacco is grown by the Gayo living in the Takingeun area. Since Acehnese firms are non-corporate, one kilo of tobacco may have to change hands up to 6 times before it's loaded on a ship for export or smuggled by speedboat from the river mouths of Aceh.

Gayo Highlands: Northern interior Sumatra. Very similar to Batak people, the Gayos were first converted by the sultans of Aceh in the 17th Century and isolated from contact with westerners until the 20th Century. These people still practice a syncretic 19th Century Muslim animist religion, believing strongly in local spirits, transmigration of souls, omens. Women employ a peculiar cloth plaiting technique (trawang); a striking effect of black and white designs. Noted for their Pillow Dance and *didong* song. **Lake Tawar:** 17 hours by bus from Medan. Take train or bus to Lhokseumawe (heavy Muslim), then bus to Takingeun. Many Gayos live around this lake where some of the best grass anywhere is cultivated. Hassle them for a good price, about Rp3000 for ½ kilo or about Rp5-10,000 per full kilo. At Blangkejeren, cheap potent *cannabis* is also grown. There could be police searches coming back through Kutacane. There's a *losmen* on the shore of this peaceful crater lake, hidden and surrounded by primary forest. Takingeun is a bit expensive. Stay in the old Dutch hotel, Rp400 single. **vicinity of Takingeun:** Visit Ikak up in the mountains. Catch an old Dodge out to the hotsprings, 20 km from Lake Tawar. Sleep at Zany's place, Rp100 rooms.

KALIMANTAN

INTRODUCTION

Kalimantan is an Indonesian territory comprising roughly the southern three-quarters of the giant equatorial island of Borneo, the 3rd largest island in the world after Greenland and New Guinea. Kalimantan makes up 28% of the land area of Indonesia but possesses only 4% (5 million) of its population. It has one of the lowest population densities in the world, about 9 people per square km. The population is composed of one fifth Chinese, one fifth other Indonesians, plus Indian and Javanese settlers. The native people, the Dayaks, live in the interior. The most populous district is the S.E. corner; the majority of the population lives in the coastal cities of Banjarmasin, Balikpapan, Samarinda, Tarakan, and other river and island towns which make little impression on the vastness of the Kalimantan jungle. Only where there are navigable rivers or roads (most roads on maps don't even exist) has officialdom penetrated.

getting there: Take a Pelni boat from Surabaya, East Java for Rp8500, leaving weekly for the east coast, and Banjarmasin on the south coast. From Pare Pare or Ujung Pandang, South Celebes, take a *kapal motor* to one of the cities on the east coast, leaving frequently, about Rp3-4000. From Singapore, Straits Steamship Company, Ocean Bldg. 1, 16th floor, has ships to: Kota Kinabalu S$97 deck class, Sandakan S$112 deck class, Kucing S$92, Tawau or Lahad Datu S$220, first class only. From any of these towns in East Malaysia (northern Borneo) you can travel down into Indonesian territory by *kapal motor,* coasters or on foot. Most of these approaches from East Malaysia require extensive river trips, some using a combination of hiking and 4-wheel drive vehicles. **from Tawau:** There are boats to Nunukan, East Kalimantan, for Rp2000, then travel down the East coast of Kalimantan by coasters. **from Miri, Sarawak:** Take the riverboat upriver then trek overland into Kalimantan. **from Kota Kinabalu:** Do the overland trip first to Keningau by taxi 4 hours 160 km for M$17 per seat on a Landrover, then on to Pensiangan. Or take a taxi from Kota Kinabalu to Sandakan 400 km 10 hours for M$25. Or fly direct to Tawau, 5 flights a week M$51. **from Lahad Datu:** Take a taxi 160 km to Tawau, M$25, 4 hours. **from Sandakan:** By air first to Lahad Datu (only on Fri.), M$28, then take a taxi to Tawau. **from Kucing:** Take the airconditioned express-launch Mas Jaya for M$20, 8 hours to Sibu then take another launch to Kapit, M$7.50, 4 hours. From Kapit hire a longboat into Kalimantan territory, ending up about 20 km from Longnawan. This approach through Sarawak is like an Audobon wildlife documentary film; marvelous. Longhouses are all along the way. Eat on the jettys of the river towns.

the land: 80% jungle. Unlike most of Indonesia this island lies outside the volcanic belt and hasn't

overland from Sabah: From Keningau they've built a road right through the valley. Fantastic rivers. The provinsi chiefs in this region are very helpful because they've fairly good maps and they're the only ones who speak English. There's a bit of a hassle crossing the border at Lumbis if you don't have enough cash. On the Indonesian side on the Sembakung River they know you're in a bind because there's so few boats going downriver. You never know where you're going because the owners of the boats have never been more than 20 km from their longhouse. From any of the landings the boat stops at you can make short side trips into the jungle.

had a volcanic eruption for 50,000 years. Half of its total land area is under 150 m elevation and most of the interior seen from a helicoptor is a perfectly flat ocean of green right up to the horizon. Kalimantan's highest peak, Gunung Raya in the Schwaner Mountains, is only 2205 m. This range is also the source of Kalimantan's five longest and largest rivers. Much of Borneo's southern coasts and many of its river deltas are swampy. In the enormous swamplands of South Kalimantan the land is usually too flooded to be cultivated during the wet season, so rice is transplanted after the waters have dropped 10 inches and after seedlings have been prepared in the floating seedbeds. **climate:** Hot and damp. Oct.-March is the wetter period, July-Sept. the drier.

history: The Graeco-Roman geographer Ptolemy published in the 2nd Century an atlas of uncanny accuracy describing this island. Although Borneo has always been remote from the main sea lanes of world trade, notes were no doubt supplied to him by Indian traders who traveled in merchant fleets of large seagoing junks. Roman beads have been found here as well as Hindu-Javanese relics. In the area of Kutai on the Mahakam River in East Kalimantan the oldest historic record yet found in Indonesia was uncovered: 3 rough plinths dating from the beginning of the 5th Century record in Palawa script 'a gift to a Brahmin priest'. The inscriptions

are 50 years older than the oldest inscribed stones in West Java at Batutulis. These stone poles (yupas) which once stood upright were used for animal sacrifices. Hulu Sungai in South Kalimantan, the heartland of the early kingdoms of Negaradipa and Negara Daha, has been an important agricultural region for hundreds of years. But much of Borneo's history revolves around the Sultanate of Brunei (to the north) who once ruled most of the island under his powerful maritime kingdom. His royal descendants live today in the small palaces of East Kalimantan at Tenggarong and Berau, micro-kingdoms which were deprived of all political power once the Indonesian Republic gained real independence in 1950.

economy: Kalimantan is not very developed, even less so than Sumatra. Most of the territory's wealth today comes from East Kalimantan: not only is this province a major oil producing area but it handles 70% of Indonesia's timber exports, 60% alone on the Mahakam River and its tributaries. Huge rugged tracts of virgin forests are being wantonly plundered by 100 overseas and domestic forestry companies. Because of its boom economy, food and accommodation is quite pricy along the east coast.

flora: There are orchids galore, the most beautiful hidden away in the treetops of the deepest

plantlife of Borneo: *This is one of the strange forest trees of Borneo, the Tree Fern (polyalthea). There are other giant trees such as the extremely hard, durable Ironwood which is immune to insect attack and is so heavy it can't even float. Also the monstrous teakwood which takes 80 years to mature. Borneo's flora is very complex, nature's way of protecting the seeds from scavenging animals. Spiky shoot branches are found below ferns lined with thorns. Because the soil is so poor at the bottom of the sunless jungles, certain other plants become insect eaters and parasites. The insect-eating pitcher plant hangs a 450 mm long trap whose fiery red lips emit a sweet odor, attracting insects. Insects drop through slippery hairs to the bottom of the pitcher where they're dissolved by pepsins. Sometimes this plant has an insect living in it to help chew up and digest victims in a mellow symbiosis.*

There are 89 species of frogs on Borneo. One species has webs of skin between its toes and glides from branch to branch; another species never goes down to the ground but lays eggs in pools of rain held by large leaves of jungle trees. There's also a flying lizard with leathery membranes along the sides of its body enabling it to swoop between trees.

jungle. Kalimantan's Veiled Lady is a poisonous stinking fungus which shoots up out of the moist earth in only 24 hours. Its disgusting smell attracts scavenger flies and bees which spread the spores of the fungus. Although flies can walk freely on its diamond patterned hat, if you touch the coarse-meshed veil it all falls to pieces with nothing left the next day but a jelly-like mass. The luxurious vegetation which grows on Borneo is no indication of the fertility of its soil. The rainforests depend on decayed plant material for nourishment, use up the falling foodstuffs completely, and thus no deep layer of humus is ever deposited.

fauna: There are honey bears, wild cats, macaque monkeys, orangutans, 14 different kinds of flying squirrels, a snake which can flatten out its ribcage and fly, 1000 varieties of birds, and near the East Malaysian border, herds of wild elephants. The great apes of Borneo include gibbons which can whistle and make a sound like dogs barking, and the sun bear which has a large white circle on its chest (the Indonesian name for him is *beruang*, meaning 'has money'.) The Clouded Leapord of Borneo doesn't have distinct spots but rather big globby blotches of black, brown and yellowish grey which helps to camouflage him when stretched out on long branches. There are wild red dogs with white bellies which hunt in packs. A wild boar, wonderfully ugly with warts and long bristles on either side of its head, could surprise you while you're taking a bath in the river. In the interior there are animal sounds everywhere you turn. Birds include black partridges, pheasants, pigeons. The hornbill's body is mostly beak, the trunk itself is only 500 cm long. Its wings make a rhythmical sound because of interconnected air pouches beneath its skin which act as sounding boards. Borneo's

snakes, the *koele* or panther snake; *apoei*, fire snake; and the *ata-bla* or red water snake, are all as bad as they sound, but you can usually see them coming. There are queer insects: poisonous polypods, bright colored millipedes, giant walking sticks and walking leaves. Its praying mantis is like a bright green miniature banana leaf: the main stem is the body, the ribs and veins are the legs and antennae, while the stalk is the insect's head. Its skin resembles a cloth-like vegetable material.

TRANSPORT IN KALIMANTAN

There are no railways and the only 3 limited road systems in all of Kalimantan- in Pontianak, Balikpapan and Banjarmasin- are not reliable. The main lines of communication are the rivers. Aircraft and coasters are also extensively used. **visas:** There are *imigrasi* offices only at Tarakan, Banjar, Pontianak and Balikpapan. Try to get a 2 month visa in Java or in Ujung Pandang before arriving. If you run out of time on the river and go over on your visa, see the police and they'll write you out a covering letter. If *imigrasi* won't issue you another visa in Kalimantan then you must leave Indonesia by taking a boat up to Tawau, Sabah (East Malaysia) or fly to Kucing, Sarawak, then come down into Indonesia again for another 90 days or more. **jungle officialdom:** Make contact through the handing on of addresses ('I know somebody in a department ...'). Maybe you can arrange to go upriver with a government party. Check in at the local police post or *Kantor Pemerinta* (government office) at each river stop because sometimes you need their permission to travel. Police could be really heavy and officious on occasion, asking you for passes and you could even be searched for weapons. So just travel on until you find friendly ones, as you need their sponsorship.

KALIMANTAN

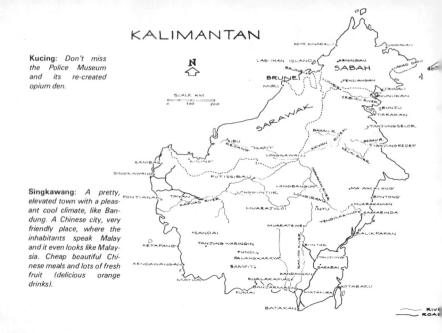

Kucing: *Don't miss the Police Museum and its re-created opium den.*

Singkawang: *A pretty, elevated town with a pleasant cool climate, like Bandung. A Chinese city, very friendly place, where the inhabitants speak Malay and it even looks like Malaysia. Cheap beautiful Chinese meals and lots of fresh fruit (delicious orange drinks).*

the interior: If you're thinking of going upriver and living in a Dayak longhouse first take a T.B. scratch in one of the bigger coastal cities, you could be a carrier and endanger others. In Dayak country the kindness and hospitality are overwhelming. They offer no excuses for their untidiness or for their simplicity. The head of the longhouse would love things like sunglasses or all your clothes; pencils and paper go down well with the kids.

river travel: The big rivers of Kalimantan are so long and wide that even amphibious aircraft can land on them. Travel into the interior is cheapest by boats up winding rivers such as the Mahakam, Barito and the Kapuas, three of the largest and most traveled. Or take coasters which ply between river mouths along the coasts. For river travel you could get anything from a trading ship (haven't changed much since Joseph Conrad), a small canoe, or else specially designed rivercraft such as a *klotok* or *stempel*. These boats might have no roof which makes it maddening in the sun's heat and they are dangerous to travel on at night when you see shadows of logs bigger than the boat, floating grass islands and uprooted palm trees pass you by. Most rivers are closed to larger craft because their courses twist so violently through swamps, their currents are very uneven, they are liable to seasonal flooding. During the rains the river could be twice its normal size. Often long thin motorized canoes

are used, their screws churning up mud from under the boat to get started. Many boats are decorated with painted bloodshot eyes to guide them along the river safely. The skipper steers by using mangrove trees as markers, and he knows what places to avoid when he sees crocodiles in the water because they mean sandbars or mudbanks. Frequently the boat goes so close to shore that branches scrape the pilot house. Whether you're going to reach anywhere that night or not will be summed up in the boatman's terse answer, *barangkali* (perhaps). *Kampungs* upriver are usually 2-3 days apart. To travel inland by river is quite dear if you're in a hurry, but if you take local boats it's as cheap as you can get, and as slow as you can get. The further inland, the less expensive it is to live: Barabai is cheaper than Banjarmasin, Tenggarong is cheaper than Samarinda, upriver Tanjung Selor is is cheaper than Tarakan, and so on. **by air:** Bouraq offers the cheapest fares and the most extensive flight network of all commercial airlines operating within Kalimantan. Try to hitch a ride on an aircraft leaving Balikpapan's airport, one of the busiest in all of Indonesia. There are missionaries and tin-mining aircraft, timber and oil company cargo carriers, Bell and Sikorsky choppers, Skyvans, Learjets, DC 3's and DC 4's, Garuda jet carriers, plus many private air companies. Could get anything to virtually anywhere in Indonesia and Southeast Asia.

THE DAYAKS

A comprehensive name for over 200 different tribes who live throughout the interior of Borneo, the island's native people. Contrary to myth, the Dayak race is light-skinned (resembling Chinese) with rounded well-featured faces and slightly slanted eyes. Numbering in all about 1 million, they live up-river in the hills where they've traditionally grown hill rice (slash and burn) and hunted. Dayaks have never been known as traders, that was the domain of Malays and later the Chinese. Other Indonesians call these people *orang bodoh* whom they think are backwards, having been headhunters for such a long period of their history. But actually the Dayaks practice responsible local government with elected members, they have provinces of their own and even have their own capital, Palangkaraya. Their traditional territory is one of the most inaccessible regions on earth. When planes fly overhead there are still some tribes who believe that the noise is made by passengers beating against the walls to keep evil spirits from getting inside. The Dayaks have no modern problems but suffer from curable diseases– malaria, dysentry, infections. Penicillin is considered the white man's magic and many die from its misuse. **history:** For centuries the Dayaks lived in splendid isolation. When the Malays started to arrive on the coasts the Dayaks moved further and further inland, not wanting to become a part of a religion that prohibited the eating of their favorite food, pork. When the Dutch finally penetrated into the interior, Dayak civilization began to decline.

Dayak society: A child follows both its father's and mother's line. The spirit of mutual help and cooperation between members of households and among relatives is very strong. Usually a man seeks a wife outside of his own village then sets up his family unit in her village. Now, mostly older people and children inhabit the villages, many of the young men have gone downriver to work in the growing towns, on the oil rigs, or at the timber camps. Dayak villages swarm with animals at all times of the day and night: there are dozens of cats and maybe twenty mongrels, hens run freely, cocks crow from the roof, pigs snort under the house catching the droppings. You sit around the hearth eating rice with your fingers that's heaped on fresh banana leaves or, in recent years, tin. Besides rice there are sauces, spices, fisn, corn on the cob, tapioca, green vegetables. The Davaks believe that only the beasts of prey in the jungle and dogs should have white teeth. So if betelnut chewing doesn't darken their teeth, they varnish them black. They also bore holes in their teeth. Perforated ear-

lobes are another sign of beauty. Sometimes only 3 days after a baby girl's birth, holes are pierced in her ears with sharp bamboo, a ring is put in which is soon followed by several more. After a time huge jangling bunches of silver rings weighing up to 8-12 ounces dangle down to her shoulders, even down to her breasts, so that young girls have to hold them when they run as not to tear their earlobes. Older women can still be seen wearing them but most of the young girls are embarrassed (malu), except in the more remote tribes. The Dayaks detest hairiness. Sometimes penis rings (palang) are worn, functioning as French Ticklers.

religion: In the old times the Dayaks were scrupulously honest. Then the missionaries invaded them with hydroplanes and high-pressure Christianity and now Christian Dayaks have to be watched. Since God has taken away all their sins they're not as honest. But outside religions have only reached Kalimantan in recent times and the Dayaks' intricate mythology, ritual order and much of their ancient spirit cults still survive. Some tribes pay homage to the gods by spitting, a way of showing that they are not neglecting them. Beginning about 300 years ago, Chinese traders sold the Dayaks huge porcelain jars with dragons on them; Dayaks believe that the dragon's spirit lives inside the jar. Many Dayaks wear charms all over their bodies: anklets, necklaces, earrings, headdresses, bracelets, and strips across their chests. Dayaks cut chicken's throats when they're putting in waterworks and sacrifice buffaloes when they're drilling a new oil rig. For really big projects they drive whole herds of buffaloes into the forests, keeping them for sacrifices. Before a cloudburst the jungle becomes deathly silent but when the rain stops it all begins again, the frogs, the cicadas, the monkeys, the men. Many of the Dayaks' ideas of good and evil are based on noises of the jungle. God is nearer in the jungle than in the noisy machine-infested towns. *Belare,* the thunder ghost, goes by the same name all over Borneo. He rides with the storm clouds and makes lightening flashes by winking his eyes. Every time he opens his mouth thunder is heard. His hands are claws with which he shatters trees and houses. *Siram,* a water-dripping ceremony, takes place at the time of the rice harvest when the rain ghosts pour water down upon the river ghosts to enable them to float home. Some Dayak tribesmen never go on hunting trips unless a certain bird flies across their tracks from right to left that day. **belawang-pole:** A grisly phallic totem pole carved from a single tree trunk and placed outside the village *kampung* to prevent evil spirits from entering the town. A fiend brandishing a sword stands on top with lesser symbols lower down the pole, along with all manner of other stinking symbols; rotting eggs, leaves, bales of grass, carcasses of chickens and pigs, all hung on it to appease the gods. Vultures circle overhead and the pole is black with flies.

headhunting: This rite is nearly stamped out now, happening only once every 5 years or so. In former times, if someone in the tribe died the men would awaken the spirit of courage, *Bali Akang*, for the headhunt. After beheading an enemy, warriors returned from their expeditions with their head-trophies in great homecomings. Heads were placed in a rattan plaited net and cured by smoking them over a fire. A dried skull was the most powerful magic in the world, a vital transfusion of energy to a village. It could save a village from plague, produce rain, warn away evil spirits, treble the rice yield. The great *Mamat Ulu* feast was celebrated by blessing the freshly taken heads. Dayaks believed that a man's spirit continues to inhabit a head after death. Surrounded by strikingly ornamented palm leaves, attention was lavished on the head-trophy, offering it food and cigarettes which were lit for it 'to smoke'

so its spirit wouldn't hold a grudge against them but feel welcome in its new home. As well as pleasing their sweethearts, the new head increased the prestige of the owner of each head. The skull's power faded as it got old so fresh skulls were always needed. Tribes without *ulu* (heads) were spiritually weak, falling easy prey to enemy poison darts and *mandaus,* or pestilence. In remote villages of Kalimantan travelers still come across old skulls.

Ship of the Dead: The dead will continue to live in the Land of the Dead, needing a *prahu* to travel there. At the elaborate ceremonial funeral a resplendently decorated and carved canoe (Ship of the Dead) containing the body is launched and allowed to drift downriver to the sea. It takes 3 days to get to heaven; the Dayaks even have *maps* of heaven. These boat-shaped coffins are modeled after the water-snake (if a man) or after the hornbill bird (if a woman). In the evening before the 'final sailing' men wear animal masks and grass cloaks and dance around the coffin. The dead are given painted hats for their trip to the afterworld. In some tribes a raft is tied to the 'ship' and it's sailed off to the Village of the Dead with the soul of the dead represented by bones, hair and nails inside.

Ship of the Dead: *A Dayak coffin, Kalimantan. The Ship of the Dead cult persists in Celebes in the form of chants and rites, while on Sumatra you can see it live on in textiles, especially in the Lampung District of South Sumatra.*

longhouse: A special feature of Dayak culture is the longhouse (lamin) which is built along the banks of rivers. These ridge-roofed structures are often up to 180 m long and 9-18 m wide. Several or more longhouses, each containing sometimes 50 families and as many as 200 doors, make up a Dayak village. There is considerable variation throughout Kalimantan in the size, method of construction, and interior arrangement of longhouses. They are almost always raised at least 3 m off the ground on wooden piles which are easier to replace than rotting floorboards. The current of air underneath reduces vermin and prevents dry rot, and pigs and chickens are kept underneath so that they won't be stolen. These stilts also provide protection against snakes, floods, and enemies; longhouses evolved from a time when the Dayaks lived in a state of almost constant intertribal warfare. Two logs with steps cut into them, or a rough ladder which bends and bucks and is pulled up at night, leads up to a

covered full-length verandah facing the river. Most of the living is done on this verandah which is used as a common room, sidewalk, for loafing, shade, parking boat paddles, fish traps, blowguns, clothing and other articles of daily use. Heads of enemies were sometimes hung on this verandah. One narrow door faces east, the direction where the sun rises which is associated with life. Sometimes the windows are stopped up with grass to impede evil spirits from entering them at night. Distant relatives live in the far ends of the building. The longhouse is often full of fleas. A loft storeroom upstairs is for keeping rice, baskets, stacks of straw mats, fishing nets and firewood. Dayak architecture is magnificent with many parts of the building decoratively carved- door frames, galleries, posts, etc. Teakwood railings are carved into dragons, snakes, demons, or birds showing detail down to scales and feathers, even lessons in sex education. The *aminaja* (chief's house) stands 2 m higher and is 15 m

orangutan *(Man of the Woods): Latin name is* pongo pygmaeus. *Found only in North Sumatra and on Borneo. About 1½ m tall with a 1½ m arm span and weighing as much as 130 kilos. Has glinting reddish-gold fur, beard, and moustache, and its long powerful arms reach down to its feet. They have been known to live up to 55 years in captivity. Wild orangutans are mild tempered and retiring and usually won't bite unless provoked. Adult males are always solitary. Its young bear a startling resemblance to the human baby. A slow-motion acrobat while feeding, the orangutan lives most of the time in tall trees and even builds a sleeping platform by weaving plant fibres together. They can travel long distances on the ground, foraging as long as 6 hours, and even take naps on the ground. Females forage together* with a subadult male. There are 200 different kinds of orangutan foods. They never eat meat, though they themselves are often eaten. They enjoy eating fruits (especially the hard pit banitan), young plants, and leaves. Since orangutans sell for as much as US$5000 to zoos around the world, hunters shoot the mother down from trees, then catch the young as they fall. Besides this slaughter by poachers, their habitat is being destroyed by logging and land-clearing agricultural operations. The Indonesian government is only now beginning to enforce a long-standing law against keeping orangutans as pets or hunting them. At Orangutan Rehabilitation Centers, which have been set up in Kalimantan and in North Sumatra to repossess confiscated young orangutans, you can see them come bounding out of the wild at feeding time.*

longer than the rest, its roof is more ornate, there are often basreliefs on the pillars, a peacock or a pheasant on the ebony door. In front of the longhouse is a sacred herb garden and a mound of genealogical ancestral stones symbolizing the wealth and lineage of a family and its warriors, also a row of grotesque household idols.

medicine-woman: Called *wadian* or *dajung.* Shamans found in Dayak societies, in most cases female, usually old women. This priestess is the *dalang* of the Dayaks. People will travel for days to see a famous *wadian* in action, lining the village street or crowding into a hot stuffy room. Many skills are required of her. She is magician-healer who must seek out the cause of sickness or evil-doing, a local historian of the origins of her people, a hypnotic entertainer who is able to dance ritually from one hour to 9 days with her huge jangling bronze bracelets and uncoiled hair. She must also be a master of spontaneous chanting which accompanies the many different ceremonies. Trance, which is usually induced by repititious movements, is believed to be the 'door of the spirit world' and a *wadian* must drop into a trance state at a moment's notice in order to communicate directly with the spirits. These witch-doctors have been known to yank out toenails without anesthesia, i.e. treating shock with shock. If a man comes down with a fever or becomes possessed a *wadian* hired by his family goes out into the jungle with a basket to implore the spirit in charge of devils to drop the man's wayward soul into the basket so that she can return it to him.

dance: Mostly held at night. Dayak dances are divided into social dances of the Malay coastal areas, and the more tribal and ritualistic dances in the Dayak areas of the interior; there's much intermingling of the two. Dayak dances are exciting spectacles with screaming dancers wearing animal skins and plumes of feathers. Ritual dances, very popular in interior Kalimantan, are peformed to mark transitional stages in life such as the coming of age, fighting and finishing wars, at planting and harvesting times, for fertility and death. In mock battle dances attackers noisily invade the village hall, then start dancing to the *gamelan.* Dancing like birds, they wheel and soar into the sky. Dayaks are also renowned for their solo sword-dances: the *Ngejiak* shows the high skill of a young man using the *mandau* sword. The *Kantet Papatai* is a mock fight between two men using *mandaus.* Accompanied by bronze gongs, hoop drums and rattles, Dayaks sometimes dance with staffs, bracelets, scarves and *engang* bird feathers (black with white tips) for ceremonies and religious rites. In some tribes animal-like demonic masks with fangs, big noses and bulging eyes are worn. The Indonesian national social dance, *joged*, is performed especially in the Ma'anjan area of South Kalimantan when a Banjar orchestra visits the village by boat. In the cockfights of Kalimantan spurs are on occasion coated with a fast-acting poison and the fight is over in seconds. Men injured by these poisonous spurs have died.

music: Certain Dayak tribes still play a curious musical instrument, the *kledi*, a mouth organ like a bagpipe with 6 or 8 narrow pieces of bamboo cane sticking out of an oval hollow gourd. The *kledi* has been known in Indonesia since the Bronze Age and is found on 9th Century Borobudur basreliefs. It survives now only in Kalimantan's interior. Also played are goblet-shaped drums made out of heavy hollowed-out tree trunks. In the northern regions magnificent dragon gongs are played. Another singular instrument used by some tribes is the *sampe*, a large flat lute with a painted wooden resonance box on which rattan strings are plucked.

DAYAK CRAFTS

Different tribes specialize in different handicrafts. Crafts are also divided between the sexes. Men are more into woodcarving and metalurgy which require more strength and knowledge of magic, while women mainly take up sewing, embroidery, weaving, tatooing and beadwork. Dayak art is more decorative than it is representational. Copying patterns are inherited and the decoration is often more ornate and detailed than that part of nature which is being reproduced. Tangled and effusive S-patterns and curlicues are very typical Dayak motifs, a mirror of their jungle world. The highly sophisticated Late Chou style penetrated this island as nowhere else in Indonesia. This style is characterized by much more typically Chinese motifs than the Dongson culture which traveled through most of the archipelago. You can easily pick out this Chinese influence in the complex decorative designs, mythological themes of the afterlife, and in the animal motifs used in Dayak art. This style is especially rich among the Iban Dayaks of the northwest. There has also been much Hindu-Java inspiration such as exuberant arabesques, the *naga* (snake) and the *harimau* (tiger) motifs; tigers aren't native to Borneo.

plaiting: Baskets for carrying larger objects are made of rattan strips of natural yellow color with black and red ornamental parts. Conical containers hold sleeping mats during travel; see woven mats with the Ship of the Dead design. Food covers are also plaited, usually from cut leaves of the *pandanus,* screw palm, or of the screw pine.

weaving: Dayaks are well known for their colorful fabrics. Most weaving is done by women on simple horizontal looms stretched out with the body. Along with the Sumbanese, the Dayaks practice the most exquisite examples of *ikat* weaving in Indonesia. Dayak *ikat* cloths aren't as stiff and formal as the *ikat* of Sumba, but very lively and multi-colored. Large pieces of *ikat* are still used sometimes to mark out sacral spots but are seldom worn; they once contained fresh heads. On occasions such as festivals you still could see the old Dayak costumes: *jawat,* a girdle of bark cloth wound around the waist and then passed through the legs; *belet,* hundreds of fibre garters clipped around the legs at the knee; kerchiefs, loincloths, plus decorated poncho-like bark coats. Women will wear *sholang*-shell skirts, or bright applique skirts, an ancient technique in which black human figures and dogs are sewn onto light-colored fabrics. All these traditional costumes are fast disappearing and are only worn now in parts of East Kalimantan.

beadwork: With their marvelous color sense the Dayaks work with glass beads much more than most other Indonesian ethnic groups do. Tobacco and betelnut containers, bark cases of swords, baby carrying baskets, lids of baskets, mens' caps, headbands, hems of skirts, are all decorated with tassels and colored bead embroidery. Kenyah tribe beadwork is in mostly black designs against a yellow background.

sculpture: Surreal, dynamic designs of sculpture in the round is seen most frequently among the Ot-Danum, Ngadju and Dusun groups in S.E. Borneo. Masks carved from a single piece of wood, *bukung* (black) and *bukong* (white), are bearded and have long eye-teeth. Some tribes fashion one meter high to lifesize sacrificial hardwood columns (temadu) with male and female figures representing the dead. Tall skinny wooden statues (always male) are set up at burial grounds with open arms, tusks, swords hanging from their waists, and accentuated penises because devils hate to see excited sexuality. *Hampatong* figures represent the live slave which once accompanied the Soul of the Dead to the other world and are designed to give protection against evil. These have deformed faces, tongues sticking out, tigers sitting on top of their heads.

metalurgy: Once Dayaks made axes, knives, and adzes out of their own iron but this art has long been forgotten, the mines, ruined forges, and smelters reclaimed by the jungle. Only a few specimens are now seen of this work. The art of diamond-cutting has also been lost. The brasswork done by the braziers of Negara, S.E. Kalimantan, still reflects Javanese-Hindu inspiration. The most important weapon of the Dayaks is the sword or *mandau*, used once for battle but now mostly for decoration or for magic purposes. Special battle swords have superb inlay work and their carved staghorn hilts are masterpieces of bone carving (the Kayans carve the best). It's rare that you'll find a good specimen today.

skin tatooing: The Dayaks' outstanding decorative sense is seen also in incredibly fine skin tatooing of half-snake, half-bird, half-plant designs. These are of the same high artistic level as the engraved decoration of their bamboo cases. Tatoo work is usually done by a woman. Male tatoos are purely for the sake of unblushing decoration and are meant to beautify a man for heaven, but tatoos on certain parts of the female anatomy are related to rank. In some tribes only wives and daughters of chiefs may tatoo their thighs. Differences in social rank are also shown in the number of lines. Small boys get their first tatoo at 12 years old. As a man grows, trips to distant villages, fights with wild bulls, and spiritual events are all recorded. At a man's death a biological map of his life is tatooed on his chest, shoulders and legs. This art is practiced by all the tribes, including the aboriginal Punans. The Kenya and Kayan tribes of the northeast have the most attractive and complicated tatoo patterns.

bamboo: Beautiful bamboo receptacles of all sizes are made at a standard found nowhere else in Indonesia. Thin bamboo containers are used to hold tobacco, sewing implements, fire-making gear, jewelry, yarn; thicker ones store arrows for blowguns. These containers could have battle scenes on them with yellowish-red flower decorations, spiral and triangular motifs, bands of intricate designs, and S-lines with the ends of the lines frequently curving around in opposite directions. The surface is often covered completely with designs.

engraved decoration of bamboo yarn case

SOUTH KALIMANTAN
(KALIMANTAN SELATAN)

Matapura: South Kalimantan province is one of the main diamond producing areas of Indonesia (*Kali* means river and *intan* means diamond), a very labor intensive industry with 30,000 people working in the mines. High quality diamonds are sold in Matapura. Near the bus station (3 minutes walk) across the playing field, see the diamond-polishing factory. 150 men, using 200 year old methods, work in each shed; see giant wheels, belts, washing sluices. It takes 2-3 days to polish a small stone and up to 30 days a large one. See the stones actually being mined by antique methods at Cempaka, 20 km away from Matapura.

Loksado area: To see the Dayaks, most tourists head off to Mandomai and to Palangkaraya where Dayaks no different from the people of Banjar live. For the real thing, go to Loksado. Arrange with Udin who can be contacted through Hotel Abang Amat in Banjarmasin to take you into the Loksado or Batu Benawa areas. Or do it alone. Take a bus

first to Barabai, a pleasant place to stay. Peng. Garuda costs Rp600 double for a neat room with a hospitable family. Take the first bus out to Kandangan the next morning, Rp150, 30 km. Dayaks from Loksado come down once a week to Kandangan weekly market for food and supplies; ask a Dayak to guide you back to his longhouse. Or from Kandangan charter a jeep yourself to Padang Batung, Rp750, 10 km. Get up at first light and walk all day perhaps 20 km to Loksado, going up and down jungle hills. There are 29 longhouses in this area, most are 2-3 hours walk from each other. *Mandaus,* spears (tombok), and blowguns (sumpit) can be bargained for relatively cheaply. It's possible to take a raft back down in only 4 hours for Rp2000; these swift rapids could be dangerous. The raft stops a few km from Padang Batung. Other isolated societies of the Dayak Banjar live in the Kotabaru District, Hula Sungai Selatan District, and Hula Sungai Tengah District, South Kalimantan, numbering in all about 5000.

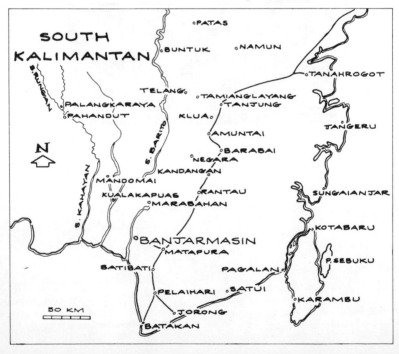

Dayak tatooing: *Flowers, hornbills, demons, dogs, dragons, bamboo trees, and hibiscus designs tell at once the tribe, family, and station in life of a Dayak. Also tales of long journeys, headhunts, feats of bravery are documented on the skin. Amazing delicacy, such as precise parallel blue lines running around their ankles. Woodcuts are usually made first* *with charcoal of fragrant dammar wood applied to it, then it's printed on the skin. The skin is punctured with brass needles hammered with a stick. Some designs take months of hard work and torture. The Kayans of the northeast have the most attractive and complicated tatoo patterns.*

BANJARMASIN

22 km upstream from the mouth of the Barito River. A strong Islamic city and the provincial capital of South Kalimantan. Canals and rivers crisscross all parts of the city which lies literally in a swamp (¼ of South Kalimantan is swamp), the water level rising and falling with the tides. Thousands live in houses built on log floats. Hire a *klotok* to go around town, about Rp1500 for two hours; this city has got to be seen from the river, which looks like blood. The Banjar, a coastal Malay people, were pirates until 1955. Today they are extremist Muslims who send over 1000 pilgrims a year to Mecca. During the *Ramadan* fasting month cigarettes will be snatched from your mouth while walking along the street, and piercing sirens announce the beginning and end of each day's fast. The Banjars are a big people; this is one of the few places in Indonesia where you'll see fat women. March is the best month to see weddings in the original Banjar style. Hundreds of brothels in this city, and beggers (ejecta of the upper river) hassel you in the markets. Banjar is a much cheaper place to hang out than Balikpapan or Samarinda and the inland towns of Matapura, Barabai and Palangkaraya, cheaper still.
getting there: Fly Bourag from Surabaya, Semarang or Jakarta. Or Garuda from Jakarta. The airport is halfway to Matapura, 20 km, or about 35 minutes by bus. From the airport into Banjar it's Rp2500 by taxi, or Rp100 by minibus (they ask for Rp200). Hitch instead.

stay: There are many *losmens* that cost around Rp400 such as Noor Arpiah, Jl. Kol. Sugiono 77, or Mess Kal Teng on the same street; built like an army barracks, also with its resident *dukun*. Losmen Abang Amat, Gang Panato 17, Rp400 is the best because it's the most central and fairly quiet; they're also used to the likes of us. The owner is a remarkably well-preserved 55 year old Indonesian Marlon Brando. Losmen Taman Sari by the bridge overlooking the busy river, is Rp600 double. Losmen Peng. Tablong, Jl. Pegadayan 68 A-68-B, 15 minutes from the bus station, Rp300, provides breakfast for Rp150; perhaps the cheapest in Banjar, not clean, not dirty. Of the higher standard hotels, the Perdana Hotel, Jl. Katamso 3, Rp2500, is quite clean and very friendly. Benua Hotel, Jl. Katamso 8, near Perdana Hotel, is Rp1500. Hotel Indonesia, Jl. Simpang Sudimampir II, charges Rp2200 for doubles. Losmen Mawar, Jl. Jen. A. Yani 8 (50 m from the bus station), costs Rp1000 double.

eat: The food is much the same as on Java, noodle soups, *sate* and such. Good Restaurants, but the best as always are the street *warungs* and night markets. Try Kelenteng Market in the middle of a fabric bazaar. Restaurants Simpang Tiga and International, both on Jl. Veteran, serve Rp3-500 meals, once you wake the waiters up. Blue Ocean, Jl. Hasanuddin 44, has quite good Chinese food for about Rp1500 a meal. Gajah Mas, Jl. Gajah Mada 1A, is an airconditioned ice cream parlor which also serves snacks. Kobana Padang Restaurant, Jl. Hasanuddin

19, has good reasonably priced *nasi padang.*

crafts: Banjar is the place for precious and semi-precious stones; amethysts, agates, saphires, even diamonds can be bought here. In Toko Makassar, Jl. Simpang Sudimampir, a nice piece of Alexander will cost you Rp500 (only Rp75 a carat). The peddlers on the sidewalk down in the *pasar* area have about the same prices. For ring freaks there are some truly stunning deep-hued stones set in old remolded Dutch silver coins selling for Rp1500-2000. Visit the Cermaic Museum (only Rp75 by *becak*) on Jl. Kuripan off the road to Matapura for Baseun's private collection of Japanese, Chinese and old Dutch Delft Blue porcelain; some of the pieces are for sale. The craft and souvenir shops are on Jl. Simpang Sudimampir. Fascinating stuff, but you pay for it. Dayak warriors carved from a rubber-like wood (Rp2-3000), lovely woven purses (Rp1000), immaculately fine Ming pieces, plus ornamental Banjar brassware, a tradition which reaches back to the Hindu-Java era.

from Banjar by road: There are two main roads in South Kalimantan Province. One connects the provincial capital, Banjarmasin, through to Amuntai and Tanjung in the north. The other road goes through the eastern area of the province. To travel up the coast to Balikpapan it's easier and faster to take a taxi-bus or jeep (unless it's raining too hard). Go first to Barabai, then on to Balikpapan. Vehicles for Balikpapan leave Barabai 4-6 pm,

cost Rp2-3000, and take one night. If you make it to Tanjung, 237 km north from Banjar, go early 8 km out of town and hitch a ride from the Pertamina oil camp to Balikpapan. They have jeeps going out everyday. **flights:** Banjar, not Balikpapan, is the focal point for Merpati flights inland to: Kotabaru, 3 weekly, Rp12,200; Sampit, 3 weekly, Rp13,400; Tanjungwarukin, once weekly; Rp14,500; Tarakan, Rp25,000; Ujung Pandang (Celebes), Rp34,800 (cheaper than Bouraq). Bouraq Airlines to Palangkaraya, 3 weekly, takes 30 minutes, Rp10,750; and to Balikpapan, Rp30,000. Two other private airlines in the city are D.A.S. Flights, Jl. Haryono M.T., to Palangkaraya, Pangkalangbun, Sampit and Kotabaru, etc. (available for charter only, 8 to a plane); and Gattari Air Service, Jl Lampung Mangkurat, but only has one aircraft (sometimes in repair).

by riverboat: To Mandomai it takes two hours upstream and costs Rp1000; stay in the mission station, Rp500. There's also a mission station at Tolong Laha, a very beautiful area. Orangutans are plentiful around Pundu. From the *dermaga* in Banjarmasin to Kualakapuas, Rp250, takes 5-6 hours, leaves morning and night; to Buntok, Rp1000, 2-3 days, leaves on Tuesday mornings. **by sea-going ships:** Catch these bigger ships by first taking a bus from Bioskop Cempaka to Pelabuhan Trisakti, Rp35. Ask the harbormaster what's happening. Sometimes you have to wait for the water to rise before your ship can leave the harbor. Ships to Pontianak are rare. At least 2-3 cargo and timber ships

nipah palms at high tide: *The* nipah *(marsh) palm is used for temporary shelters and to thatch the roofs of millions of peoples' houses in Indonesia.*

the canals of Banjarmasin

leave each week for Surabaya, Rp6500-7500, takes 35 hours. Some ships go to Jakarta as well, Rp 10,000, takes 3 days; to Semarang, Rp9000.

vicinity of Banjarmasin: At Alalak, see an old style Banjar timber mill. Takisung Beach is about 80 km east of Banjar. To visit the hill country of Batu Benawa, take a bus or minibus first to Barabai, 165 km for Rp800; then there are many taxis out to Pagat village, Rp100. Of the total area of South Kalimantan about one quarter consists of swamps, lakes and rivers — mostly tidal. The southern swamps have rivers running through almost solid walls of wood, jungle, interlocked roots, trunks of mangrove trees and *nipah* palms. Very flat land with only a small area in the eastern part of the province broken by small hills and mountains. **Amuntai:** The *Buntang* and *Ijambe* burial ceremonies are practiced by believers of the Balian religion. A buffalo is stabbed then offered to the gods at *Balai Pidara* where it will accompany the deceased in his or her journey to heaven; a very costly and cruel ceremony. **Warukin:** Dayaks hold a thanksgiving ceremony in the first week of November called *Buntang Ogong Puai.* Offerings are made to nature deities and a special rostrum is built for folk dances and celebrations.

alternative route: Another way to get from Banjarmasin to Samarinda, and also to experience a bit of Dayak country en route, is to take a *klotok* up the Barito all the way to Muaratewe, Rp10,000 (if you charter a speed boat, Rp50,000). From Muaratewe try to reach the headwaters of the Barito northeast by canoe. From the end of the line trek to Intu, which consists of just a few shacks. This is a 4-6 day walk; you need a guide, Rp2-300 a day and you must supply his food. Walk for a day over logs through swamp country; if you fall off a log, you sink up to your neck in mud (no kidding). Don't expect to cover more than 20 km maximum per day; you can usually do 10 km without too much trouble. Getting down river to Sambuan and Muaramuntai from Intu could be difficult. Allow at least 2 weeks for this alternative way to reach Samarinda.

Tamianglayang: From Magantis it's only a 15 minute walk 2 km to this Christian town which is centered on a large *pasar* area. Tamianglayang has a once a week market where you can check out the rustics coming in from the north, east and western interiors. Small merchants arrive like gypsies in ox-drawn housecarts selling knives, cloth, paper goods, bicycle parts, jewelry, etc. Much singing and dancing on market day, lasting long into the night. **from Tamianglayang:** From the market, there are roads to Ampah to the north and Klua to the east. 18 km to the west is Telang. Take the path following along the course of an old Dutch road via Sarapat and Murutuwu; very narrow and slippery in places. All the rivers flow red in this area because their tributary waters percolate through vast peat bogs. An eerie sight. Try to make it out to a Dayak Banjar village during the harvest time when the Dayaks move through silvery fields of rice with tiny knives filling their baskets. When the rice is dried out on mats and at threshing time, the songs and laughter of the women fill the air. At the end there's feasting and drinking.

CENTRAL KALIMANTAN

(KALIMANTAN TENGAH)

Barito River: For the Center, the Barito River is the way to get there; navigable up to 400-750 km upstream. The boat is always stopping and dropping off people, picking up food and goods, all the way up the Barito. Most Banjar settlements and agricultural areas are located on this river or its tributaries. In the Barito's lower course it's wide and muddy, flowing through rich marshy country. See villages of Banjars who live by fishing, rice-growing, or handsawing huge logs into planks. Traditionally, people of Kalimantan use flowers to decorate their houses. Incredible places you stop in with jungle mists in the mornings and human size monkeys lunging through trees. In the lower course all the towns are Muslim and have mosques with ornate domes and spires tucked away in the trees. When you enter Dayak territory to the north you start to notice Christian churches.

Palangkaraya: Capital of the Dayaks. Gets about 50 white tourists a year. Males will not remain lonesome for long in this upriver town. From the *dermaga* in Banjar, tugboats leave daily for Palangkaraya. When there's enough people it departs, not before. On the way up if there are not enough passengers they wait an hour or a day or two. Or a speedboat to Palangkaraya costs Rp10,000 to hire;

does the trip in 6 hours. Catch them by R.R.I. (Radio Indonesia), Banjarmasin. In Palangkaraya stay in Hotel Sakura, facing the disused 35 km highway. This famous totally empty highway was built by the Russians in 1960 during Sukarno's hectic and unpredictable regime. It runs straight for Tangkiling 35 km west to nowhere. It is a beautiful well built highway right in the middle of the Kalimantan jungle and still no one knows why it was ever constructed.
from Palangkaraya: Flights to Balikpapan on Tues. for Rp11,100; or to Pangkalangbun, Rp11,600, 2 times weekly.

Kualakapuas: This is just a day trip up a branch of the Barito River. Take the slow *kapal taxi,* Rp250, 5-6 hours. Leaves from in front of Banjarmasin's R.R.I. (Radio Indonesia) office around 8 or 9 am. In Kualakapuas the police are quite helpful. There are two *losmens,* one big and one small. To get back to Banjarmasin the same day the speedboats could ask for as much as Rp7000 per person, but you can get back for as little as Rp500. It's a nice trip in the evening with the sounds of the jungle, stars, glistening lights of villages. Peddlers come up to the boat in canoes and sell you *lontong,* cookies, and peanuts. A mini-journey through Kalimantan.

Dermaga, Banjarmasin — the start of the journey up the Barito into Central Kalimantan

EAST KALIMANTAN
(KALIMANTAN TIMUR)

BALIKPAPAN

A harbor of flaming oil flares and dozens of tankers. Its 6 m high flare can be seen from 30 km away at sea. Many American, European, and Australian oilies (oil company men) and chippies (timber workers) live here either in camps (prefab air-con and all the other mod cons on the beach near the airport) or else in housing provided by Pertamina. **getting there:** From Jakarta there are daily flights for Rp36,500. From Surabaya, Rp26,000. Bouraq is cheaper: from Jakarta, Rp33,000; from Surabaya, Rp21,500 via Semarang and Banjar. Balikpapan's airport is 8 km from town over a despicable road; costs Rp500 to get into town if you split a taxi. From Surabaya there are at least 3 ships a week for about Rp10,000. Some call also at Banjarmasin. Or by boat from Ujung Pandang, Sulawesi, Rp3000-4000. **transport:** Take *oplets* or jeep taxis anywhere in the city for Rp40-50, or go piggyback on a motorcycle to anywhere in town for Rp100. Rental fee for jeep taxis is Rp750-1000 per hour, regular taxis Rp1500, minimum of 2 hours (which is long enough to see all of Balikpapan).

stay: Look for foreign faces, maybe someone could put you up. The cheapest *losmens* are in the Kampung Baru area where you come in on the *prahus* from Sulawesi. A good one for the money is Hotel Bina Bersama, Rp1000 per person; fairly clean with a front balcony over the harbor. Hotel Beringan is Rp750, but a bit of a dump. Hotel Setia, Jl. Kb. Sayur, down the street from the Atomic is Rp1500 for a double room (quieter ones in the back). **eats:** Expensive because most of the food is imported from other parts of Indonesia; in the market a chicken costs Rp2000. The best restaurants are in Kb. Sayur. The Atomic is one highly overrated Chinese restaurant (many foreigners eat here), but has delicious chili crayfish. Sin Gheng, on the same street, has excellent meals cheaper at Rp5-750; try the crab soup. Up on the hills Mabel Steak House; Rp3500 for sirloin. Blue Sky Restaurant in Kb. Sayur is a bit expensive but has incomparable seafood, especially the abalone. For Padang-style food, eat well for Rp500-1000 at Minang Saiyo, Jl. Gajah Mada 45.

sights: Check out the fantastic difference between the housing facilities built by the overseas oil, timber, and helicoptor companies and the general environment of the people by going up the hill to Pasir Ridge (or Kampung Amerika) and looking out over Balikpapan. Pasir Ridge is a transplanted ethereal world with swimming pools smooth tarred roads, manicured gardens and neat rows of houses and shops above the sprawling hovels below. Most wives cocoon themselves for months on end inside this modern isolated city compound. In the Ray A. Burke (Union Oil) Club at Pasir Ridge there are free movies at 8 pm, a swimming pool, New York steaks, and Bingo on Sunday nights. The other glaring juxtapositions in Balikpapan include nightclubs ('Sweet Sixteen') on hills over fishing *kampungs*, long-haired Indonesian guys wearing cowboy boots and bronco belt buckles, Indonesian women in western suburban slacks, big shiny American cars cruising down muddy potholed streets. All the young guys hang out in billiard halls or ride their Yamys at ferocious speeds down the ravaged main streets. The 'Hey misters!' are a lot less because there are more misters around. You can even use US currency in Balikpapan (US$1 = 400 rupiah). There's an enormous and highly organized brothel, The Valley of Hope, in an army camp, consisting of 1 km of whitewashed huts with 300 rather worn-out Surabaya prostitutes to a hut. Little kids put covers over your licence plate numbers so no one can spot you. Get your car cleaned for Rp25. Closed on Thursdays for 'housecleaning' (see the doctor); getting ready for the big weekend. The favorite sport at the Hotel Balikpapan is to peer at all the women behind a glass wall similar to looking at a fishbowl. More relaxing is to have a drink in the bars (not whorehouses) of Banana Town. There's in addition an amazing row of houses down on the harbor where wives are for sale on a temporary basis. Very respectable, it's a service set up for Muslims who've come far away to work at the refinery or on the rigs, though now has evolved into providing a short-term 'wife' for the oilies and chippies. These teenage women (mostly from Java) cost about Rp200,000 a year, do washing, cooking, and other wifely tasks, receiving a hefty bonus when the oilies or chippies leave.

flights from Balikpapan: Garuda, Merpati, and Bouraq all have regular flights plus there are dozens of privately owned aircraft for charter. At Sepinggan Airport, 8 km from town, ask in the hangars for lifts. From Pasar Baru to the airport it's Rp500 by jeep taxi; or just to the *kampung* Rp75, then walk to the airport from there. If you connect with the right people you can fly to just about any-

LONGBAWAN
LONGBERANG
MALINAU
ATAP
MENSALONG
TIDANG PALA
NUNUKAN
TARAKAN
LONG PESOK
TG. PALAS TANJUNGSELOR
LG. PUJUNGAN
LONGGLAT
LONGLOAT
TG. BATU
DATA DIAN
LONGNAWAN
TABUR
TG. REDEP
EAST
LONGAPARI
MA. LASAN
TIONGOHANG
KALIMANTAN
LONGPAKAH
MA. MAHAW
SANGKULIRANG
LONGPAHANGHAI
TABANG
LONGBANGUN
MA. BENGKAL
LAHAM
KUTAI GAME RESERVE
BONTANG
LONGIRAM
MUARAMUNTAI
MELAK (AIRSTRIP)
MUARAKAMAN
TENGGARONG
TANJUNGISUI
SAMARINDA
HANDIL II
MA. JAWA
SAMBOJA
PENAJAN
BALIKPAPAN
LONGKALI
LONGIKIS
MA. KAMAN
BATU SOPANG
KUARO
PASIR BELENGKONG
TG. ARU

SCALE KM
0 30 60 90

timber: *Indonesia is gifted with perhaps the world's largest unexploited tropical forests, with a gigantic potential yield of timber.* Whole meranti *(shorea or Philippine mahogany)* forests provide a good, light, easily worked timber. There are hundreds of other kinds of hardwood trees such as monstrous teakwoods, plus many other oriental timbers: ballow, bilian, bintangor, chingar, damar laut, daru, ebony, ironwood, kamuning, krangi, mangrove, mirabau, russock, sandalwood, sapanwood, selangan batu, selangan kacha, serayu, tampinis, tembusu. The koompassia tree (tapang) is the tallest tree of the Indonesian rainforest and one of the tallest in the world. Due to vast tracts having been despoiled by uncontrolled logging, International Timber Corporation Indonesia (ITCI) has initiated an $80 million dollar logging operation in the Kalimantan jungles, a key experimental station for the regeneration of tropical forests. In East Kalimantan the reforested trees will take about 15 years to grow. The lease takes up 751,113 hectares of heavy jungles. This is the only large scale renewal project in process in Indonesia.

where: Celebes, Ambon, Irian Jaya, Bali, even Singapore. To take Merpati to Pontianak, Kucing, or Singapore entails flying first to Jakarta, an expensive way to do it. Better is to use Sempati (office at the airport) or Air Trust. These companies shuttle employees back and forth nearly everyday between Balikpapan and Singapore (stopping briefly in Kucing) for Rp75,000. Mandala office offers no flights inland, only to Jakarta and to Surabaya. Bouraq, Jl. Gajah Mada, flies to Samarinda, Rp15,000; to Tarakan, Rp20,000. Other possibilities include Pertamina flights to Bontong (oil base), Tanjung, Santan, Tarakan, and to the Bunju Islands. The Pertamina office is at the airport (Pelita) or near the harbor; see the Humas section of Pertamina dealing with info and public relations. Merpati office, near Pasar Baru, has been known to give student reductions of 25%. **to the Philippines:** There are two ways. Either fly first to Tawau (East Malaysia) with Merpati for Rp20,000, then fly from Tawau to Kota Kinabalu for US$25. From Kota Kinabalu to Manila a flight costs US$117.40. Or else fly with Bouraq to Tarakan for Rp20,000 (takes an hour), then from Tarakan each Tues. afternoon there's a flight to Zamboanga, Mindanao, for Rp54,000.

the interior: You can also get into the interior of Kalimantan quite suddenly by air. Missionaries fly small aircraft to Longnawan, Longiram, and to other mission stations on a space available basis. Government officers go by missionary planes because there's little other transport so deep into Borneo. Ask at the airport for CAMA (Christian Missionary Alliance). **by bus:** To Samarinda take a mini-bus Rp750 from Pasar Baru up the old coast road to the landing stage and Handil II, near the delta of the Mahakam River. Take a flat-bottomed riverboat from there to Samarinda, 5 hours, Rp500. The speedboat takes only one hour, Rp1750. You can sometimes hitch speedboats if they're chartered. Head south from Balikpapan to Banjarmasin only in the dry season. From Kampung Baru to Penajam go by motorboat, Rp150 (no more than Rp50 for your pack!). Most buses leave Penajam at 4 pm for the 12-14 hour ride south; it costs Rp3000-3500 as far as Barabai then another Rp1250 further to Banjarmasin.

vicinity of Balikpapan: Sneak into the Total Beach House (with the big shed roof) in Sepinggan right on the beach. Say, 'I'm Union Oil'. Look redneck. Bar and dance floor, free food and drinks. Get on the Union Oil boat just past Banana Town and take it over to very pretty Lawi Lawi Beach. To the south of Balikpapan 20 km at Panggar (Rp1-200 from Pasar Baru), a quiet black sand beach. But on Sundays it's crowded. If you're lucky enough to see

an oil blow-out, the whole rig and the legs start melting. Then the world famous blow-out puter-outer, Red Adair, is called.

SAMARINDA

Capital of East Kalimantan 60 km upriver from the mouth of the Mahakam River. Established 1730. From Handil II, 40 km south of Samarinda, the slowboat will give you the first taste of this sluggish mighty river which you can take over 560 km upstream. Samarinda is an old smelly, dirty trading town with a lovely location on the banks of the Mahakam. The river is wide (5 km at highwater) and deep enough at this point for big ships to come up from the coast. There's a massive *mesjid* by the river. American and Aussie timber companies work in this area; see their wives come into town to shop. Logs float everywhere on the river and traditional hand sawmills line the banks. Indonesian guys wear denim suits and boots, a real cowboy town. Be careful of snatch thieves on the street. **transport:** Take taxis to any part of the city for Rp50; they actually drop you off where you're going.

stay: If in transit sleep onboard while your boat is in port. The police station will look after your pack while you wander around. Losmen Siar, Jl. Mesjid Raya II, Rp750, is the cheapest in town and you can easily see why. Losmen Aida, Jl. Babus Salam, Rp1000, is close to the harbor. Losmen Hidayah, right down from Losmen Aida, Rp1000, central and clean. Boarding rooms in the back are better; demand a fan. There are two other clean comfortable but higher-priced hotels: Hotel Nirmala, Jl. A. Yani II, (a little way out of town, take a taxi); and Hotel Jakarta, P. Batu II, both Rp1500. **eats:** A bigger and more fascinating market than Pasar Pagi is over the bridge south of town; pet birds tied to strings, giant *nangka*, etc. Many *warungs* with hostesses serving beer are set up at night right off Jl. Niaga Selatan. Best and cheapest eats are on Jl. P. Batu with its *martabak, sate,* and *soto makassar* carts. Restaurants are expensive. Some Chinese restaurants serve roasted crocodile and turtle meat. Samarinda is well known for its fried giant river shrimp (udang galah) plus other river and freshwater lake fish *(gabus, biawan, papuyu* and *belida).*

sights: Visit Kantor Parawisata (tourist office) opposite Bank Negara, J. P. Batu 3. Sellers of gold, precious and semi-precious stones are found in the market along the riverfront. Cross the river to the other half of the city to Seberang in a *tambangan* (taxiboat) Rp50, or Rp500 per motorbike which you can drive over a road from Seberang to Tenggarong 42 km north. In Seberang, much admired *sarung samarinda* that are said to last 20 years, sell for around Rp10-15,000. Contact Haji Idris. Many designs and colors to choose from. There are at least 150 special looms (gedokan) in the village. Picturesque patchwork hills like Italian hill country are found behind Samarinda. Climb the hills N.E. of Samarinda for a fabulous view and a good look at the completely ravaged timber concessions. There's a beautiful Bugis *kampung* up there too, if you can find it.

flights from Samarinda: Bouraq flights to Tarakan (Rp21,250) and Balikpapan (Rp21,000) happen everyday; Merpati has the same prices. Merpati to Muaratewe via Balikpapan, Rp24,750. If you want to go far up the Mahakam River, a charter flight between 4 or 5 people could work out cheaper than a speedboat. Speedboats cost Rp60-100,000 to Longnawan whereas Zending Adventure has one hour flights for Rp40,000; their plane holds 8 people. Ask at the tourist office about them. **boats:** It's easy to get boats to Celebes from here; Bugis boats leave Samarinda about every 4 days, Rp4500-5000, for Donggala, Central Celebes. To Surabaya, the agent K.M. Diwi Jaya, Jl. Yos. Soedarso (on the waterfront) has a boat twice weekly Rp8500, takes about 60 hours. Also try K.M. Gelora Kaltim, Jl. Irian, for boats to Surabaya. There are ships to Korea, Japan, Mexico, Europe, etc.- some take passengers, some don't. Pelni, Jl. Yos. Soedarso, has a boat sailing once weekly to Tarakan, Rp8000, 3 days. Or if you don't want to wait try the coasters K.M. Tanjung Raya or K.M. Winaya Mulia, either of which go to Berau (Tanjung Redep) weekly. Check about these boats at Toko Gunung Mas, Jl. Mulah Warman; they cost Rp5000 and take 45 hours. From Berau there are special speedboats on to Tarakan for Rp3500-4500. Samarinda is also an excellent jumping off point into Dayak country. The first Dayak *kampung* you come to is Tanjung Isui, only Rp2000 and one day, one night from Samarinda.

Kutai Game Reserve: The 2nd largest game park in Indonesia (74,103 acres) is located near Bontong on the East coast of Kalimantan. Virtually uninhabited, it has crashing swift streams, thick undergrowth, virginal unchartered rainforests. Home of the giant manlike ape, the orangutan, this reserve is one of the most accessible places you could see him in the wild, though it's still not easy. Also the proboscis monkey, rhinos (not many), civet cats, wild pigs, and a lot of birdlife such as rainbow colored wild fowls and the peacock-like *tumbau* bird. This reserve very seldom gets tourists. Blinds are set up to view the animals from a close distance. No dangerous animals, only wild buffaloes to worry about. Get permission from the *polisi* first; bring a tent and food along. **getting there:**

Really an adventure. Take a motorboat from Samarinda to Bontong on the coast, Rp2000, then walk into the park. Or take a motorboat from Bontong which operates out of the reserve. Or journey by way of the Mahakam River, following the Sebulu River up into the park. **Bontong:** In Dec. 1975 a Bugis knife fight, in which dozens of men, women and children were hacked and stabbed to death, erupted in Bontong over a labor dispute. Down the coast the flats and forests rise out of the low tide; whole settlements appear to be floating on the water. There's a wierd looking LNG base (natural gas) in Santan, near Bontong.

TENGGARONG

Means 'Steps of the Highest'. A former sultan's town 39 km upriver from Samarinda. From Samarinda riverboats leave opposite the big mosque every hour or so from dawn until 4 pm for Tenggarong. Pass little villages with ramshackle old timber buildings while slowly crisscrossing the river; the boat stops at *kampungs* and timber loading stages along the way. If you take the riverboat as far as to Loa Kulu, Rp200, an *oplet* travels the remaining 12 km to Tenggarong for Rp150. The old wooden town of Tenggarong is at its best very early in the morning when the river mist turns the peeling pastel painted and weathered gray houses into a magic land. The town was founded 192 years ago and every Sept. 26-28th there are big anniversary ceremonies when the *Bedaya* is danced and Dayak tribes have blowpipe and rattan lashing competitions. There are two *becaks* in the whole town and many bicycles. People are really friendly and honest. They're used to tourists ('Hellow Turis!') and there's a minimum of officialdom to contend with.

stay: Losmen Indonesia, Rp600, is the cheapest and the most central but it's also on one of the main river loading stages in town. Losmen Anda I, Rp1500, is out of town a bit; peaceful and homy. Losmen Anda II, next to Losmen Indonesia, Rp750, is comfortable and has electricity. In the town of Loa Kulu there's a *losmen* right on the river for Rp550 per person with flowers through your window and just the sound of the riverboats chugging up the Mahakam. **eats:** Warung Depot Tepian Pandan in Tenggarong has good food; Rp500 for fried chicken with rice. Tasty meals are served in the *warungs* around the market. During the *durian* season try *tempuyak*, a famous dish made of preserved *durian*. Or *gangan terong*, cassava soup with sour eggplant, hot chilies, and fish paste.

sights: Tenggarong is the seat of a 71 year old *raja* (has 20 wives) who has given over his palace to the people as a museum. The original palace was demolished and the present one built by a Dutch architect in 1936; looks like what a Dutchman would have thought suitable for an Indonesian sultan: classical 1930's futurist architecture. Though not well exhibited or catalouged, the museum has a unique collection of Ming China (some giant vases), valuable South Vietnam and Cambodian pottery; silver cloth, regal thrones, and *pusaka*. The bedroom is fantastic. There are 3 not so refined Hindu sculptures from Gua Kembang (there's more left in the cave), hundreds of old Dayak stone necklaces (manik), old Indonesian money, and adzes. Outside the museum the garden of Dayak wood sculpture is worth the trip from anywhere. There's a sad neglected zoo with a neurotic orangutan, *rusa,* and sunbear, a rebuilt flimsy longhouse, bridges over stagnant ponds. In front of the palace is the tourist office with maps, photos, brochures, times of festivals, and other useful information; men who actually, it would appear, like their jobs.

crafts: In the market stalls Dayak bits and pieces are sold reasonably cheap (same stuff in Yogya is 5-10 times more). Other stalls offer you saucers full of precious and semi-precious stones. You might be lucky enough to find a piece of Ming China though most of it is from Thailand, Cambodia, and Vietnam. Some of the crafts in Depot Tepian Pandang, though purported to be 'Dayak', are actually made by Bugis people. Not bad prices for carved walking canes, spears, traditional barkwood vests and applique skirts, *mandaus,* brilliantly woven rattan knapsacks, plus China, brass teapots and boxes. Framed displays of the most common Dayak tourist artifacts in miniature go for Rp5000-20,000.

MAHAKAM RIVER

This river has been open to tourist for only 3 years. Upriver is known simply as *ulo,* an unknown traders' world. The Mahakam is a very rich ethnological region with many tribes divided into clans and subclans. There are 96 lakes in the area. Tenggarong is a good place to start your river journey into Dayak country, but it could cost you as much as Rp25-50,000 per day or perhaps as much as Rp60,000 if the boat has a Volvo engine. If going far it's better to be in a group of 3 or 4 as the petrol starts to get pretty expensive. This is if you want to get organized. Otherwise just jump on the next boat going upriver. Far upriver your journey is through mostly primary forest with impenetrable undergrowth, giant orchids and mangrove flowers, huge trees with pythons draping from branches, tropical bullfrogs, rhino-birds, kingfishers, nightbirds, fireflies, stinking mudbanks, and choking humidity. Tall trees and *lianas* hang out over the water so densely that it seems like you're going through a tunnel. The more you ascend up the river systems the shallower the river becomes and on either side it becomes more and more uneven and the vegetation grows more fertile, the river turning at last into a series of long narrow rapids. In places the boat actually fights its way uphill very slowly (1 km in 3 hours when it would take only one hour's walking).

orangutan attacked by Dayaks: *This is only one illustration from a 19th Century classic study of Indonesian flora and fauna, 'The Malay Archipelago, The Land of The Orangutan and The Bird of Paradise' written by Sir Alfred Russel Wallace. A friend of Charles Darwin and the namesake of the so-called Wallace Line, Wallace observed how shallow the seas between Java, Sumatra, and the Asian mainland were in contrast to depths further east around the Moluccas and New Guinea, concluding that elephants, big cats, and apes were geologically marooned on one side and marsupials on the other. In 1856 he wrote, '. . . I excited terror alike in man and beast wherever I went, dogs barked, children screamed, women ran away, and men stared as though I was some strange and terrible cannibal monster. . .' Things ain't changed much.*

DAYAK TRIBES
OF EAST KALIMANTAN

group	location and remarks
The Kenyah	Tabang estuary, upstream on the Belayan River; Ancalong and Wahau estuaries. Upstream on the Kelinjau River. Longiram area. Most are Christians. Well known for their fighting dances.
The Bahau	Longiram, Longbagun, Longpahanghai.
Modang Group	Longiram, Longbagun, Longpahanghai, and upstream on the Kelinjau River in Muara and Ancalong subdistricts. Dik Wuk bird dance. Unique lamin (longhouses) and their own traditional costumes.
Tanjung and Benuaq groups	Barong Tongkok, Melak, Muara, Pahu, Damai, Muara Lawa, Tanjung Isuy, Bentian Besar area, and upstream on the Kedang Pahu (a branch of the Mahakam).
Lawangan Dayaks	This hill tribe is found in the uppermost part of the Kerau River drainage when the land finally begins to rise into more rugged country.
Berusu Group	Sekatak area, Sesayap subdistrict. Still unfamiliar with money.
Putuk, Abai, Bau, and Paya groups	Malinau subdistricts, Sembakung and Sebuku Rivers. These groups are well known for their handicrafts such as rattan and woodcarving.
Kenyah groups	Kayan Hulu, Kayan Hilir, Peso and Pujungan subdistricts. Also found in Umagtukung. Tabang Subdistrict, Kutai District, numbering about 3800. Found as well around the Muller Mountains, of unknown numbers. They make mats, hats, carved shields, long knives and spears.
The Punan	Areas west of Longkemuat, Longbenato, Longpeliran, and in Batu mesjid, Ma. Ancalong Subdistrict, Nomadic hunters. The true aboriginals of Borneo.

Sept.-Dec. is the best time to travel. If the river is too shallow (May-June), you can do it only by paddleboat. When the water is swift and full of bolders, smaller canoes are used. Sometimes you must walk along the riverbank and pull the canoe or port it up and over rocks or through steaming jungle. If it's raining very hard you might have to wait 2-3 days for the river to go down again. While traveling in the upper reaches the water level could drop 2 meters in 2 hours, or rise 4 meters in 10 minutes. Thunderstorms could dump buckets of water over you and the canoe, then move on leaving you itchy, sweaty and sticky. When it really rains all you can do is sleep; it could take 3 months to get to Longpahangai. Most tourists only visit Tanjung Isui or Longiram but very seldom venture north of Longbagun, and when they do it's together in parties of 30, very regimented and expensive. The key to doing this whole river cheaply is TIME-lots of it.

Dayak crafts of East Kalimantan: Visit Tering and Keliwai for Dayak Bahal crafts: baskets, woven rattan mats, spears and shields. Old Chinese stone trading beads can be bought in Tering and Melak. For a long chain of big blue green stones (manik) Rp5-10,000; these are getting rarer now that tourists have bought them all up over the years. Females of Tanjung and Benuaq (Bentian tribe) still wear bark and tree root clothing (ta-ah). *Kelbit* (shields) and Dayak *hudog* (carved masks) make striking wall ornaments, Rp500. Also lances made of *kayu besi*. *Sumpit* (blowpipes) are made of *ulin*wood; poison darts can kill a man in 3 minutes. Dayak *biru*-leaf hats (seraung) cost Rp500-1000; also caps which have a brush-like back flap, Rp500-1000; traveling bags (anjar) last for years, Rp3000. Each tribe has its own style of painted mats. In Sabintulung village, Muarakaman, females still make *purun* mats out of long swamp grass. Baby and children carriers (aban) are covered in antique beads, Rp50-75,000 if you can still find them. Totem poles (belontong) are grisly disaster and disease averter statues of the iguana god still seen in many villages; can get ahold of smaller souvenir versions. The Bahau and Kenyah groups deep in the interior are masters of ornamental and detailed woodcarving; handles, daggers, sheaths, also bone and horn engravings. A small knife with a long handle is held under the armpit, the carved object is moved instead of the knife. For Kenyah crafts Ma. Ancalong village is best. Their *ukir mandau* are the finest, some set with precious stones and very old, Rp60,000; there are newer ones for Rp5000.

RIVER TOWNS

The first longhouse up the Mahakam is at Tanjung Isui where there are no *losmens;* sleep at the *tempat pacamat* or with the *kepala desa.* Longhouses are also found at Tanjung Disur, past Muaramuntai; stay at Losmen Taro, Rp550. Tering is the first completely ethnic Dayak village you come to. There's a church here with an American pastor, and 3 *losmens.* Find orangutans in the Binulung Daerah area, Kec. Muarakaman. Stay with the *kepala desa* and ask him where the orangutans are (about 10 km away). From Samarinda a boat leaves for Binulung daily, Rp750, takes 10 hours. Going upriver you still occasionally see huge timber-carrying rafts made of logs bound together with rattan. In the middle of the raft is a palm leaf hut for the crew, and at the stern is a steersmen with a gigantic oar. From the interior, several rafts linked to form a tow about 75 m long could take up to 3 weeks to reach Samarinda. Going to Banjarmasin? From Long Putih in Kec. Bentian Besar take a *longbot* to Randampas then walk 4 days into South Kalimantan province. Take the Barito River all the way to Banjarmasin.

Muaramuntai: Mountains and fishing villages in this area. A boat for Muaramuntai leaves from Tenggarong daily at around 2 pm, Rp500, takes 15-24 hours. Picturesque Jempang Lake is 184 km upstream from Tenggarong or 6 hours by speedboat. See dolphins (air tawar) and lots of birdlife feeding on the fish. Soft sunsets. Two other lakes to the north, but smaller.

Melak: 29 hours from Tenggarong, or 7 hours from Longiram. In Melak stay in either Peng. Bahagia, Rp750 (but bad, expensive food), Losmen Palamgoyan, Rp750, or Losmen Mulia, Rp500 (cheaper meals). There's a wild orchid forest, Kersik Luwuy, located on a plateau between Melak and Barong Tongkok, 18 km south of Melak. The Honda motorcycle taxi there costs up to Rp3000 per person (maybe get him down to Rp5000 for two). When the weather is hot and wet, flowers are exploding all over the forest's white sand floor.

Barong Tongkok: A lovely *kampung* to live in for awhile. Located in the hills with many waterfalls surrounding it. Stay at Wisma Tamu, Rp500. Eat in the *warungs.* You can make it all the way to Tering by Honda taxi, Rp3000, 3 hours from Barong Tongkok, passing many Dayak *kampungs* along the way. Or walk to Tering on this very pleasant track in 6 hours.

Longiram: Boats leave Tenggarong for Longiram each Thurs. at about 4 pm, Rp1250-1500, takes 36 hours to two days to reach. Stay in Losmen Tigadaram, Losmen Longiram, or in Peng. Sukarasa, Rp500, or with all meals, Rp3500.

Longbagun: From Longiram to Longbagun take a taxi boat, Rp1500-2000. Sometimes government boats travel the 77 km from Longbagun to Tiangohang north. There are 3 dangerous rapids north of Longbagun but they last only to Longpahangai: Udang (200 m long, 2 hours portage), Relau, and Hiddah (5 km long, 1 hour portage or 3 hours by boat).

Longpahanghai: A very scenic but difficult to get to area 480 km from Tenggarong; the locale of the Penehing tribe. From Longbagun to this village usually only *longbots* (long canoes) are available. Stay in the catholic mission here with the Dutch pastor, Sombrock. Sombrock, who has been upriver for 25 years, is hard at work on a Penehing-Bukat-Dutch dictionary for the University of Leyden. In the area live about 1200 Catholics and 50 animists. The Longpahanghai region has orangutans, tall trees with giant trunks, true Dayak *adat*-life. Not only are there Dayaks in the area, but many different tribes of Dayaks. From Longpahanghai a few day's upriver to Longapari, there are no rapids at all. Walk to Sarawak from Longpahanghai. If you make it to Longapari, they have an Indonesian *imigrasi*. Travelers walk overland from Longantoar, Sarawak, into Kalimantan in one week.

Longkemuat: Lies near the border of Sarawak in the rice-growing district of Longnawan, capital of the Apa-Kayan territory. This is one of the largest and richest *kampungs* in Apo-Kayan with a great number of resident *paren bui* (noblemen) who are thought to be direct descendants of the first man of Borneo. You're in the exact center of Borneo. Deepest blackest eyes you've ever seen. The Kayan River Valley and the Apo-Kayan (the Upper part of this valley) have been the heart and brain of Borneo for the last 10,000 years. The Kayan Dayak dialect is considered the King's English of Borneo languages. They set the dress fashions for the rest of East and Central Kalimantan, make the most skilfully constructed longhouses and generally look upon themselves as superior to all other tribes. There have been little foreign influences, except recently when missionaries invaded with hydroplanes.

Gua Kembang: A mountain cave with 5 statues from an old Hindu Kingdom which focused around Muarakaman, hidden in this mountain to keep them safe from the expanding Islamization of Borneo. Flat land all around it, just this peak. Take a boat to Jakulai village up the Kedang Kepala River 2 days, then walk all day to the cave. See 50 m high rooms with linking corridors, but hurry, the stalagmites are closing in. Be prepared to spend the night there.

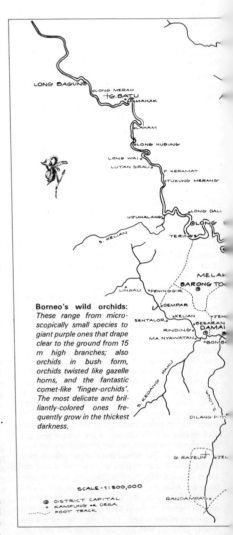

Borneo's wild orchids: These range from microscopically small species to giant purple ones that drape clear to the ground from 15 m high branches; also orchids in bush form, orchids twisted like gazelle horns, and the fantastic comet-like 'finger-orchids'. The most delicate and brilliantly-colored ones frequently grow in the thickest darkness.

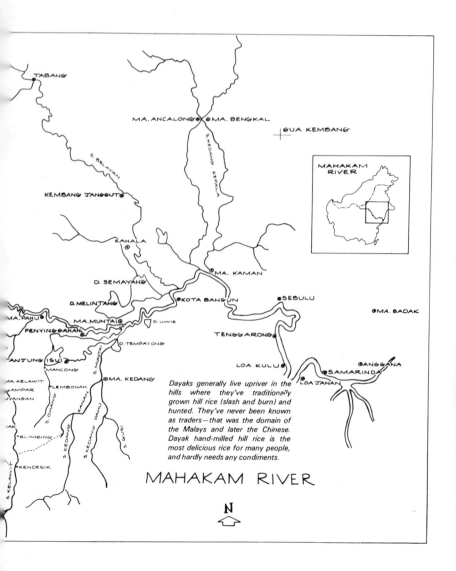

TABANG

MA. ANCALONG ⊗ ⊙ MA. BENGKAL

⊕ GUA KEMBANG

S. BELAYAN

S. KEDANG KEPALA

MAHAKAM
RIVER

KEMBANG JANGGUT ⊙

KAHALA
⊙

⊕ MA. KAMAN

D. SEMAYANG

D. MELINTANG

⊙ KOTA BANGUN

● SEBULU

⊗ MA. BADAK

MA. PAHU ⊗

MA. MUNTAI ⊙

○ D. UWIS

PENYINGGAHAN ⊙

TENGGARONG ⊙

○ D. TEMPATONG

ANJUNG ISUI

MANCONG

LOA KULU ⊙

⊕ ANGGANA

○ LOA JANAN

⊙ SAMARINDA

MA. KELAWIT
KAMPAR
NYANGAN

⊙ MA. KEDANG

PLEMBONAH

S. CHANG

S. MUARAI

S. KEDANG KAHAM

S. KEDANG PAHU

S. GUSI

AK

● BLIMBING

S. KELAWIT

KENDESIK

Dayaks generally live upriver in the hills where they've traditionally grown hill rice (slash and burn) and hunted. They've never been known as traders—that was the domain of the Malays and later the Chinese. Dayak hand-milled hill rice is the most delicious rice for many people, and hardly needs any condiments.

MAHAKAM RIVER

N

the Kasada Festival: *The Bromo volcano is still worshipped by the Tenggerese in ceremonies called Kasada which open at midnight 2 weeks of lively village festivities. Kasada begins on the 14th day of the Kasada month, the 12th (Kasada means '12') and last month of the Tenggerese calendar, which changes each year. Happens usually in April or May. Kasada is meant to celebrate Buddah's birthday. The event takes place on Bromo's fantastic, steaming desert-like crater. Festivities begin at sunset and the animist sacrificial ceremony takes place at midnight when a bull and live chickens are tossed into the crater (they used to sacrifice people). Like a carnival, across a barren plateau there are groups of bright lights, and at the foot of the highest peak Sanskrit prayers are recited and dice games are played. Childrens' faces are whitened with powder to keep away evil spirits. On the crater's edge the worshipers sway together. A mile down into the crater the volcano billows, sometimes see the fire, while sulphureous fumes burn your throat.*

unusual foods of South Sumatra: *Field rats are a delicacy of this region. They feed almost purely on rice and are very tasty and tender, unlike the town rats which feed mostly on market garbage. Dogs are also often eaten (around Palembang). Ones with short legs are selected because it shows that they haven't done much running which makes the sinews too tough and gives the meat a rank flavor. Dog must be bled and disembowelled, then put on a bamboo stick and roasted for half an hour with its skin still on (longer for older dogs). Cut the meat into pieces and remove the skin, then fry it in coconut oil with garlic and split chilis. Serve it with rice and chili sauce. Sometimes they have the dog eat a huge amount of strongly-seasoned rice and then slaughter it immediately afterwards so that the intestines are already stuffed, and thus made into spiced sausages.*

ghosts and spirits: *There are cave spirits, tree spirits, and crossroad spirits. There are devils and satans: tetekans, janggitans, ilu-ilu, all beings of the lowest order. There are musical ghandarvas (from India), the weiwess and peris (from Persia), pragangans and djinns (from Arabia), beneficial devas, angles of God. Most ghosts frequent dark and lonely places. The puntianak entices youths at night to follow her, then in a deserted place she reveals her true identity and scares them to death. This ghost probably originated to teach boys not to go near prostitutes. Likewise, the alleged existence of the banaspati which leaps out of the ground exactly at noon, running swiftly on its hands to devour any child it sees, was invented to teach children to avoid sunstroke. The gendrruwo pelts roofs with graveyard gravel, the spirit of someone killed without being prepared for death. Many of the ghosts are unhappy souls that had died a sudden or unfortunate death and weren't properly buried. Wewe (a childless woman) steals children; the peri is a disappointed virgin; the medi pocong is a carelessly buried corpse. There are also ghosts of prophecy and plague, famine and disaster, such as the rushing roaring lampor, the flaming kemamang, or the rijal, who is a ghost of sound without form. The buta causes eclipses by swallowing the sun, but as he has no body the sun reappears from his neck, and the beating of alarm gongs is said to scare him away. Also there is the deadly tenung. The sudden death of the Dutch commander-in-chief during the war of independence was popularly attributed to a patriotic tenung. Indonesians believe that if they wash their feet before going to bed, they won't have bad dreams.*

kampungs of Jakarta: *Squatters live either in the houses or in front of the houses, usually close to canals for washing purposes. Structures are built of wood, bamboo or tin containers, sometimes have a verandah, a one-room living space, kitchen, and toilet in the back. Different neighborhoods have different squatters' construction techniques. In the east, south and central parts (especially in the areas around RR stations), tightly packed shacks with narrow alleys are built of woven bamboo together with tin cans or oil drums. In other places like Tanjung Priok, parts of Cideng, Jembatan Dua, and northern parts of Grogol Bus Station, huts measure only 1-2 m and are made of cardboard, plastic, and tin cans. In the kampung ghettoes of Jakarta the streets are so small that in most cases you can only go by bicycle or on foot. Oil and kerosene lamps and woodfires are often used, just like in village life. These city kampungs rarely have sewerage and drainage systems. The longest lavatory in the world is Jakarta's Ciliwang Canal.*

bancis: *Jakarta's equivalent of Singapore's Bugis Street women. Women slumbering in the bodies of men, bancis are young foxy guys in full drag with maskara and perfume and jet black hair falling down their shoulders. Another name for these male prostitutes is 'sister boys'; most are transvestite homosexuals. Find them standing along Jakarta's streets at night, many hanging out between Hotel Indonesia and Kartika Plaza. Each year Jakarta's mayor crowns Miss Wadam (The Best Female Impersonator), the word wadam being a combination of wanita (woman) and Adam.*

the Dayaks: *The [...]rior of Kalimantan [...] habited only [...] Dayaks. Travelers [...] been known to [...] themselves ar[...] these fabulous pe[...] for years. Don't ex[...] to do anything [...] than sit in the ya[...] day sifting rice, [...] templating clouds, [...] listening to the so[...] of the jungle. [...] Dayaks can teach[...] many things and[...] help you cross the [...] tinent to the Sara[...] border or all the w[...] Pontianak, coast[...] coast.*

midwifery: *80% of village births are supervised by midwives. Midwives have a high prestige in the village but are feared for they represent an impersonal world. They could take your loved ones to the clinic where they are cut open. The midwife, dukun beranak or dukun balai, comes straight from her house, garden, or ricefield. Her services on Java cost from Rp6-10,000. She uses the traditional bamboo knife to cut the umbilical cord and hair twine to tie it, but government training of midwives is changing all this. The placenta is still kept under the mother's bed in an earthen pot for 40 days with a coconut oil lamp burning beside it. Some herbs and fruits acting as abortificients are used in Javanese folk medicine.*

rajan games: *Men ...y a semi-combat ...ne, sisemba, which ...s originally used to ...ell invasions but has ...w evolved into a ...me where hundreds ...men join hands and ...m ranks facing each ...her. Usually taking ...ce in the middle of a ...e paddy at harvest ...ne, they kick and ...w trying to tear lines ...art. There are as-...ults and many ...uries, especially to ...e face. End men are ...nt flying into the air ... centrifugal force. ...e also a dance sport, ...raga, performed by ...oups of bare-footed ...en kicking around a ...ttan ball to the ac-...mpaniment of ...andrang (drum) and ...ji pui—(clarinet-type ...strument) music.*

dagang: *Young girls who run stalls (warungs) at the markets and along the sides of the road. Usually when a girl comes of marrying age she opens a warung and becomes a dagang. The young lady then has a respectable place to hang out and to meet the boys, showing her eligibility for marriage, her cooking abilities, her social poise. A warung can be just a table with only a few odds and ends to sell. At night by gas-lit lamps the dagang makes snacks, grinds sauces, serves drinks, scrapes coco-nuts, sell mangoes, prawn pastes, sirih. The local boys hang out there and her admirers ex-change wisecracks and puns. When the dagang starts dropping the price or turning the guy on to free food and drink, that means she likes him.*

Torajan headhunting: *Taking heads was once a religious, social, and political obliga-tion; the heads were required offerings to ancestral spirits at burial and temple dedica-tions, insuring the tribe's well-being and a good harvest. A headhunting party was launched immediately after the first funeral, and the new head would be buried with the bones. It provided the deceased with a slave and a powerful source of magic. It was be-lieved that its spirit would turn into a benevo-lent ghost protecting the village.*

...ali: *One of the 9 legendary saints ...ho brought the Islamic religion to ...va. The word is an abbreviation for ...ali ullah or 'one close to God', re-...ecting Indonesians' emphasis on ...e mystical side of Islam. When the ...alis first arrived in the 16th Century, ...ach made skillful use of the Hindu ...amelan and wayang dances to win ...d soften the people for Islam. Poli-...cally, they replaced the former ...rahmanic priests. The walis con-...ecrated the princes to whom they ...ave titles of sultan. They conquered ...ngdoms and started their own wali-...ynasties. Many of their tombs have ...ringed gates such as found today on ...lindu Bali, which shows that they ...idn't destroy all that they conquer-...d. Many legends have been woven ...round these men, making them all ...ppear as great magicians, but in ...eality they were energetic and ...evout merchants. One of them, ...alidjaga, a coastal prince of the 16th ...entury, reinvented mask-plays ...wayang topeng).*

Irian Jaya: *Total population of this territory is only about 1 million. About 300,000 live in isolated or 'uncontrolled' areas and some parts have a population density of only 2 persons per sq km. Metal-working is unknown — the Bronze Age hasn't happened here yet. Some tribes burn their dead, others use burial plat-forms set up on poles with small roofs over them, and often corpses are lashed upright in trees in order to continue watching over their fields in death.*

CULTURES OF INDONESIA

Torajan burial: *Torajaland is one of the few places left in Indonesia where puppets are still used in the worship of ancestors. Corpses are sealed in rock cemetaries hewn out of mountainsides. Coffins are deposited by pallbearers who shinny up sheer cliff faces on tall bamboo poles. Life sized effigies of the dead are placed in high balconies, carved in lime-stone cliffs to protect the treasures of the dead. It's thought that wayang kulit puppets today derived from similar funeral rites in the deep past. Eerie, fascinating sight.*

cannibalism: *Cannibalism still exists in the swamps and lowlands in the southeast vicinity of Teluk Sarera and Teluk Bintuni. Men are killed usually with a spear and finished off with a bone knife. A hole is cut in the skull and the brains shaken loose or sucked out and given to the child-ren. Buttocks are a choice cut because of the amount of meat on them. Human fat is used in cooking and also utilized to grease down spears and to polish drums and bamboo horns. It's be-lieved in some tribes that a child can only grow healthy and strong if one of his kin brings home a head. The name of the victim sometimes is given to the child.*

Sibillers: *Of the Zigibi Range. These mountains are the whole world to the Sibillers (or Upi Tenna, 'worm children') who believe they descend from worms. Sibil men and boys wear a mixture of red earth and pigs' fat kneaded into their beards and hair, penis gourds, and a 10 m long black cord with magical dogs' teeth wound around the waist. During gigantic pig banquets they play jaw's harps, hourglass-shaped drums, and sing and dance all night until they fall from exhaustion. When Sibillers go to war people could die but it's more like a sporting event similar to jousting. Hostilities are suspended if a party thinks they need to work in their gardens; fighting may also be called off in case of bad weather.*

Dani ghosts, spirits, and death: *Danis believe ghosts, 'The Living Dead', live about 1½ km from their village in special ghost-villages and that they frequently come around up to no good. Danis build bridges and barriers around their village to divert the ghosts' wickedness. They believe that spirits guide the actions of everyday life, for example, if a Dani throws a banana skin on the weeds a spirit will enter his stomach and cause it to swell up. In their death rituals, the number of pigs cooked shows the status of the deceased. Heirlooms are distributed to the whole village, and to show grief female relatives smear the upper part of their bodies with mud and amputate joints of their fingers. Often you see women with only stubs for fingers.*

BERAU

The capital of the Berau regency today is Tanjung
Redep (pop. 32,000 and 200 bicycles), a secondary
harbor since WW II. The autonomous kingdom of
Berau, dating back to the 14th Century, was divided
in 1883 with the Berau River acting as a natural
boundary between new capitals which were formed
at Sabaliung and Gunung Tabur. In 1960 both kingdoms were abolished by a decree of the Indonesian
parliament. Both palaces still have small private museums. Take a canoe from Tanjung Redep for
Rp150 across the river to see Istana Sabaliung.
getting there: The waterfront of two-storey
buildings called Tanjung Redep is 59 km from the
mouth of the Berau River. About 8 boats monthly
arrive from Samarinda or Balikpapan, costing Rp
5000 either way. The only road (10 km long) is between Tanjung Redep and Teluk Bayur. **stay:**
Losmen Sempurna, Rp750, or Rp1250 with one
meal; or Losmen Sederhana, Rp1000. Food is rather
expensive in this town, Rp250 for *nasi campur*.
from Berau: It's Rp3-4000 by a fast custom built
longbot with 3 outboard engines to travel from Tanjung Redep to Tarakan, 55 km and 9 hours north.
Boats leave at least every other day. Up the unfrequented Kelai and Segan Rivers, find the Dayak
Basap, Kenya Tumbit, and Lebu tribes. Tanah Ulu
(upriver) is two hours and 40 litres of petrol by boat,
about Rp8000. And that's just the first stage.

The Punan: These tribesmen are the original inhabitants of Borneo who even preceed the Dayaks.
Very elusive aboriginals, the Punans run when they
smell you coming. About 10,000 are left in scattered
isolated pockets. Some groups have been farming
for about 5 years. Wizards in jungle craft and masters of the terrain, the Punans don't eat rice but live
off fruit and wild berries, hunt game with blowpipes
(when they fire a dart, they don't miss), and even
use packs of hunting dogs to kill wild boar. These
nomadic hunters can shoot rapids in canoes while
standing up. Their features are more Mongolian
than the Dayaks' and the Dayaks consider them
savages. They are very superstitious, into the ways
of panthers and wild boars. You could see them
come down to the villages to barter boar tusk necklaces, panther teeth and skins, bear claws, deer
horns, monkey gall bladders, snake stones,
orangutan skulls and other natural produce for salt
and tobacco (they all smoke like mad). **getting
there:** Punans are found upriver from Berau and
Balungan in the hinterlands of the Tabang subdistrict and on the Kayan from Tarakan in Peso and
Lesan subdistricts; in Longpalay, Longbanuium,
Longsuku, Berau District, they number about 500.

They are also found on the Bahau River near the
Giram Baleo river gorge (a fierce current running
through a deep central channel) and over the hills of
these forests. Punans also inhabit the areas west of
Longkemuat, Longbenato, Longpeliran and in
Batumesjid, Muara Ancalong Subdistrict, numbering in all about 2000. It's better if you arrange to go
with a government party, they could be defensively
hostile. They are fearless because they don't know
any better. One group still lives a mesolithic existence in a stone cave, the Stone Punan.

TARAKAN

An oil island surrounded by hills. Storage tanks,
which Indonesian tourist booklets describe as 'en-
chanting', gleam in the sun. It's so damn hot in this
town, every shop shuts at midday. The market is
worth exploring with lots of East Malaysian goods.
getting there: Take boats either from Samarinda
(Rp8000) in Kalimantan or else from Tawau in
Sabah, East Malaysia, where there are 5 regular
boats to Nunukan (north of Tarakan) leaving daily
around midday. Buy a ticket at the Nunukan
Express Office in Tawau before 10 am for M$10
(US$4). From Nunukan to Tarakan the fare is
Rp2000 with one good meal onboard. This boat
leaves Nunukan about 4 pm and gets to Tarakan at
dawn. **transport:** The basic transport is old jeeps,
Rp40 to anywhere in town. Get one from the wharf
when you first arrive in Kampung Bugis where
many of the cheap *losmens* are. **stay:** Try crashing
in the messes of the foreign oil companies. Most
losmens are Rp750, but Losmen Jakarta is the
cheapest at Rp500 and serves Rp300 meals. Food is
expensive in most restaurants, Rp500 for a decent
meal. Sahabat, Jl. Sudarso, has some excellent
dishes. **vicinity of Tarakan:** All along its coast
are polluted mangrove swamps but this small island
has some difficult to get to, uncontaminated white
sand beaches on the ocean side.

flights from Tarakan: Go to the airport and try
hitching oil company planes to Balikpapan or to
Samarinda. The airstrip is often closed during the
wet. Bouraq flights to Balik cost Rp20,000; to Palu,
Celebes, via Balikpapan, is Rp35,250. ARCO at
Mess. Bactera, Jl. Gereja Marconi, has one flight
each Wed. to Kucing then on to Singapore. Or try
the Mission Aviation Fellowship (MAF) on the main
harbor road for inland flights (a *longbot* could take
months); speak to the pilot himself. The missionaries aren't so friendly; you're infringing on their
private world. They'll take you only as a paying passenger, for example they ask Rp13,000 to Longnawan on the border to Sarawak. **to the Philippines:** Catch flights from Tarakan to Zamboanga
with Swift Air Co. each Tues. afternoon for

US$135.00 (Rp54,000). Australians don't need a visa for the Philippines, but the southern Philippines is now closed to tourists so you need a military permit to go outside Zamboanga.

boats from Tarakan: Take boats to Manado, Donggala, and Ujung Pandang in Celebes; Samarinda, Balikpapan, and Banjarmasin in Kalimantan; also to Surabaya, Java. The shipping office opposite Mesjid Seluruit has timber ships (the Tanjung Nurlima IV and V, Harapanan, etc.) heading weekly to Pare Pare, Celebes, for Rp5500. Food is shitty. Take their rice and put your vegies on top. Pelni's Delima sails to Surabaya twice monthly, Rp18,750; and to Balikpapan Rp12,175. From Tarakan, Japanese vessels sail to Japan or to the Philippines (get Philippines or Japanese visa beforehand). **for interior Kalimantan:** South of Tarakan at Tanjung Selor on the Kayan River is the last place to stock up for the long river journey into the interior. **for Nunukan:** Buy tickets to Nunukan each morning at the entrance to Pasir Lingkas; a boat departs at 4 pm, takes one night, arrives early the next morning. This *kapal motor* never goes out to sea but goes in and out of shady inlets with giant fronds, an amazing 'African Queen' journey.

Tanjung Selor: From Tarakan it's Rp2-2500, 4 hours and 57 km to Tanjung Selor, leaving 10 or 10:30 each morning; other boats leave around noontime. Stay at Peng. Sentosa, Rp1500. **from Tanjung Selor:** it's only Rp50 to reach Tanjung Palas by small boat. At Tanjung Palas, an old cannon is all that's left of a kingdom dating from 1503 A.D. The Dayak *Jepen* Dance (joget) is still performed here by noble girls. For upriver the Kansas Jaya departs Tanjung Selor at 10 am, Rp300, to Mara II; or to Bahankara 128 km further for Rp6000. **The Kenyahs:** Kayan and Kenyah Dayak groups are found around upstream farming villages Mara I and II. The Kenyahs still practice teethfiling. At weddings the bride and groom have their hair perfumed, they are scrubbed and oiled and decked out in new *sarungs*. Guests eat *jenei* (sticky rice), broiled pig, and *jakan* (sweet wine). Bead gifts are exchanged. Male Kenyahs pierce their penises with slivers of bone to titilate their women during intercourse, a custom practiced especially in the matrilineal Kenyah tribes. The Kenyahs play simple melodies on bamboo tubes that produce low-droning sounds. **Longglat:** In the upper reaches of the Nijam, a tributary of the Bahau, cross a 45 m long suspension bridge just before entering the boundary of this village where there are two giant phallic wooden statues, calculated to deprive evil spirits of their virility.

the hornbill: *Birds have always held an important place in Indonesian art. Upswinging curves of wings are found in shawls, dances, temple gates. Since Hindu times garuda took over as the supreme godly bird from the prehistoric hornbill, which is still venerated in Sumatra and Kalimantan. The hornbill has a featherless neck, long eyelashes, and a gargantuan oversized beak with a bony casque on top which has been carved by man, like ivory, from ancient times. The male walls up the female in the nest of a hollow tree during* *the incubation period but a slit is left open through which the male feeds its mate. It has an enormous appetite and juggles its food before swallowing. Though weak in the bite, the hornbill can drive its beak into a man's arm. They eat strychnine fruits but the seeds aren't digested in their systems, thus these birds are a symbol of fertility in Indonesia. Among the Katingan Dayaks of South Kalimantan, the hornbill is mythologically associated with the creation of mankind, a symbol of the Upper World.*

LONGPESOK AND BEYOND

Beyond Longpesok is the notorious *Giram Raya* (Royal Rapids), a 275 m long and 55 m wide gorge with rocky whirlpools and chunks of granite sticking out of the water the whole length. The boat must head straight up through the central channel or it'll capsize on the foaming cliffs. Passengers are often told to take the path along the banks. **Nahame** (Beach of Smooth Pebbles): In the middle of a primeval forest, gigantic tree trunks to every side blot out the sky. Further on still is a 48 km chain of rapids (brem-brem) with 9-12 m high waterfalls. This segment is impassable to all traffic. In order to bypass them you must slog your way through equatorial jungle to the Bahau River, a famous trek, then take to the water again and continue downstream- very slow, very painful, very hazardous. On the upper reaches of the Bahau, roughly built crash pads *(Kubu* huts) can be used as resthouses, a part of the Law of the River. The headwaters of this river are one of the few places where you still find the traditional customs of interior Borneo intact.

Longpujungan: A series of tombs are built like miniature houses with dwarf pilings supporting them. The roofs are adorned with carved and painted wooden dragons (ukir). If you're lucky you'll see some Kayan dancing; there's dance platforms set up in many villages. See masked Kayan men and women take part in rice-sowing festivities. Masks of evil spirits and demons carved of wood have big round eyes made of mirrors, teeth, lower jaws that 'speak', larger ears; the beard is made of goat's hair, and hairy bodies are covered in banana leaves. Looks somewhat like the Balinese *Barong*-dragon. Each man makes his own mask; very sophisticated use of color. Women's basket masks are less artistic with odds and ends for decoration.

Boh River: At Seniang is the Land of the Stone Men, where ancient granite Hindu statues are found in caves and grottoes along the slope of the Boh River. Go 3 days in a southwesterly direction, first down the Nawang River, then hike inland. These statues the Dayaks believe to be men and women who offended the spirits and were thus petrified. Basreliefs are covered in lime carbonate, and dripping stalactites cover the statues like white sheets. There are also traces of temples and an irrigation network. Though this region appeared in records in both China and India as far back as 200 B.C., it wasn't until the 10th Century when Hinduism penetrated the Apo Kayan region of Borneo. **from Seniang:** Further up this river you emerge

suddenly upon a great savannah like an African veldt with 2 m high tiger grass. Follow the trails cut by wild bulls (lembu). Cloudbursts are frequent, it's sopping and drizzling all the time under the tree crowns which are covered in poison vines, green slime, and mould smelling of rot. You slide over moss heaps, there are bogs under your feet, steam clogs your throat.

NORTHEAST BORNEO

Nunukan: If you leave Tarakan by coaster at 4pm you'll arrive in Nunukan early the following morning, Rp2000, 70 km. Nunukan is a timber town on a small island. You've never seen so many moneychangers per head of population in your life, though they're not heavy about it. **stay:** The cheapest is Hotel Sebar Menanti, Rp600, or else you can share a bed at Losmen Arena, Rp1500. **from Nunukan:** A boat leaves everyday from Nunukan at around 11 am to Tawau, Sabah, for Rp2000, 40 km, getting there around 3 pm. Mostly businessmen and small time peddlers going back and forth. **inland:** Dayak tribes can be reached in the area around Pembelingan, 64 km up the Sebuko River. The *tugbot* takes 6 hours to one night to reach that area, though a fast *longbot* can do it in only 3-4 hours. See the timber people P.T. Jamaker and get a letter first in order to stay at the East Malaysia Camp or the Mukah Sawmill Camp, both in Indonesian territory. Their office is in Tanjung, one km from Nunukan, the 'old town'. They might even give you a free lift up to the camp.

Tawau, East Malaysia: Get ready for the mind-blowing change between these two countries. Tawau is much faster paced, modern and bigger than sleepy Nunukan. Banks are very reluctant to take Indonesian *rupiahs.* M$2.40 Malaysian dollars, or *ringgit,* are worth US$1. Stay at Hotel Foo Guan, 152 Chester St., M$15-18 per room, clean and not crowded. Hotel Asia is a noisy whorehouse with a dozen peepholes in every room. Good food at the Islamic restaurant near The Chartered Bank. Get an Indonesian visa at the *konsulat* in Wisma Indonesia, M$1 from town by taxi. If you're in a hurry they can sometimes do it in just one morning so that you can catch the noon boat back to Nunukan.

from Tawau: Every 10 days or so Straits Steamship Company has a ship to Singapore, only 1st class tickets available for S$220, but still cheaper than the S$350 it costs to fly with MAS from Tawau to Singapore. Or you can take a bus from Tawau to Lahad Datu, M$20, then a plane from Lahad Datu to Sandakan, M$32 (road's not finished yet). Sandakan is less expensive than Tawau with hotels as cheap as M$5. From Sandakan, Straits Steamship

Co. has boats S$112 deck class to Singapore. Or from Sandakan to Kota Kinabalu, take a vegetable truck. Then from Kota Kinabalu it's S$97 deck class by ship to Singapore. **to the Philippines:** Smugglers' boats leave Tawau for Bongao, the largest town on the island of Tawitawi in the heart of the Sulu Sea. This journey, which is strictly illegal, takes 20 hours to 3 days; pick a large boat, pirates are less likely to attack it. From Bongao, sail north to Zamboanga, Philippines.

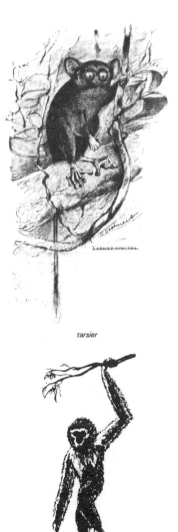

tarsier

primates of Borneo: *The tarsier-monkey comes from the Tertiary Era and stands at the crossroads on the evolutionary chart where man and ape branch off from one another. Scarcely larger than a rat with its ghostly globular eyes, the Dayaks believe that the souls of dead ancestors are reincarnated in its tiny body. Macaque monkeys will follow and abuse you as they move along the other bank while you walk down the river. Gibbons keep together in families and live up in the trees. Skilled gymnasts, they make terrifying piercing sounds which carry long distances through the jungle. Their pouch and throat swell up like a balloon which gives their call a booming quality. You can easily hear their movements through the trees, but you can't see them. The proboscis monkey (bekantan) is the Yeti of Borneo. He has an uncanny resemblance to man. Though only 1½ m tall, Dayak tribes believe that the bekantan is not an animal but a hairy man who lives in the jungle and eats fruit. The skunk monkey, no bigger than an alley cat, has a horrible stench.*

gibbon

orangutan

WEST KALIMANTAN
(KALIMANTAN BARAT)

This immense, rugged, sparsely populated province is Indonesia's Wild West where government troops and communist guerillas have been shooting it out since 1968, the year Chinese insurgents moved their bases from across the border in Malaysia's Sarawak. It is a tense region at present because of occasional guerilla raids on Indonesian military posts and transportation systems. If you stay overnight in the provincial capital of Pontianak, you must report to the *imigrasi*, police, the military, *and* the military commander; it'll take you a full day to file away your papers. Officials discourage you to go upriver now because of the guerillas in the area. West Kalimantan's economy is almost entirely based on agriculture and forestry products. It's the 2nd largest rubber producer after Sumatra and carries on a lot of trade with Singapore.

Pontianak: Straddles 0° north, 0° south of the equator. Virtually a Chinese-run trading center located on both banks of the mouth of the Kapuas River, at this point over 2000 m wide. About 230,000 people live in this overgrown village. When gold was discovered in West Kalimantan it attracted many Chinese immigrants which accounts for its large (at least 3/5's) Chinese population today. Pontianak is sometimes called the 'floating town' because at high tide most of its canals are covered in water much like Bangkok. Hire a paddler for Rp3-400 an hour and go up and down the busy crowded canals. Heaviest rainfall is between April and November. **getting there:** The cheapest way is from Singapore with the Straits Steamship Co. to Kucing, Sarawak, S$92 cabin class or S$66 economy. Then from Kucing to Pontianak it's M$70 to fly with Merpati each Friday. Or take a bus from Kucing to Stas, then it's a day's walk over the border to the river. Next take a steamer Rp500 to Singkawang, then a bus on to Pontianak. The ship from Kucing to Pontianak isn't running in Jan. and February. Or from Jakarta's Pasar Ikan take Pelni's steamer Bintang Baiduri, Rp4000-4500, to Pontianak. **stay:** Accommodation is generally expensive. The least expensive is Losmen Islam, Rp600. At Bajabaru, Hotel Anggrek, Jl. Jen. A. Yani, charges Rp800. Next is Wijaya Kusuma, Jl. Ngurairiay, Rp1100. Hotel Kalimantan, Jl. Taya Tanjung Pura, is Rp800 or Rp1650 double. Wisma Fatimah, Jl. Fatimah, is Rp300 including meals. Eat at Rumah Makan Skartika. **from Pontianak:** By boat to Jakarta is Rp4500, takes 3 days. A flight to Jakarta is Rp41,500. **vicinity of Pontianak:** South near the port of Ketapang is the little village of Teluk Batang; very quiet.

Sambas: North of Pontianak. Some of Indonesia's most beautiful cloth is produced in villages near Sambas. Go to the house opposite the mosque and inquire about the superb *kain sambas*. This cloth is hand-stitched with gold thread, takes months to weave, and it is quite expensive at Aus$10 to $100 each. Stay in Losmen Ujung Pandang. Walk among the ruins of an old abandoned diamond mine. On this west coast, the Iban Dayaks make the finest *ikat* fabrics (reddish brown color) of all the Dayak tribes: skirts, jackets, kerchiefs, and blankets are decorated with human figures.

Singkawang: A clean, pleasant, well-built town 150 km north of Pontianak. Stay at Losmen Khatulistiwa. Buy silver belts and goldwork (but cheaper in Kucing). The best thing about Singkawang are its nearby beaches. Batu Payung is a beautiful deserted beach where big bungalows rent for Rp3000. It also has *a losmen* and an outdoor restaurant which is popular with the locals on weekends. Hire a *sampan* from the fishermen. More remote is Pasir Panjang, a 5 km long golden sand beach, nicer than Bali's. Stretches out of sight. The *camat* in Singkawang, 15 km away, rents out his big cement house right on the beach for only Rp500 a day. Bring camping gear and food.

THE KAPUAS

The longest river in Indonesia. Besides the Kapuas, other navigable rivers in this province are the Sambas to the north and the Pawan to the south. Isolated societies of the Dayak Iban, Dayak Sungkung, Dayak Bukat, Dayak Kantuk, are spread all along the border between West Kalimantan and East Malaysia; they number approximately 250,000. Sarawak differs greatly from Kalimantan. In Sarawak there are much denser concentrations of the Dayaks and their culture is more in evidence- longhouses along the river banks, tribespeople in the towns- but on the Kapuas mostly Javanese settlements. You can take boats out to the very end of this river to the small Land Dayak town of Putussibau, a fishing village over 900 km upstream. Some people head all the way across the continent from Pontianak on this river; it can be done. The Kapuas is navigable by small steamer for over 300 km upriver. Then the rest is a Traveler's Delight of leeches, the slow muddy river life in canoes and rafts for weeks on end, and experiences of Dayak villages unvisited for years. The journey is in two parts. You must reach the headwaters of the Kapuas River, then cross overland through the jungle

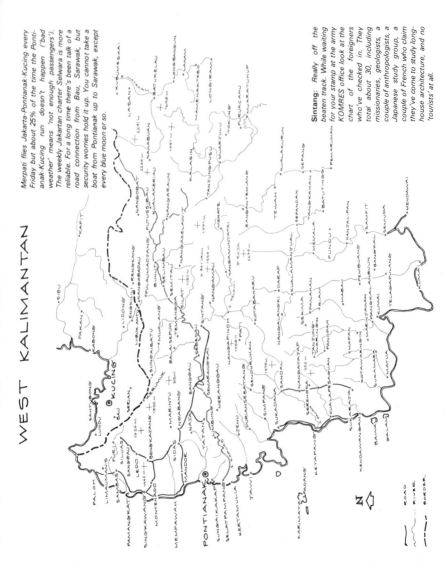

Merpati flies Jakarta-Pontianak-Kucing every Friday but about 25% of the time the Pontianak-Kucing run doesn't happen ('bad weather' means 'not enough passengers'). The weekly Jakartan charter Selwara is more reliable. For a long time there's been talk of a road connection from Bau, Sarawak, but security worries hold it up. You cannot take a boat from Pontianak up to Sarawak, except every blue moon or so.

Sintang: Really off the beaten track. While waiting for your stamp at the army KOMRES office look at the chart of the foreigners who've checked in. They total about 30, including missionaries, geologists, a couple of anthropologists, a Japanese study group, a couple of French who claim they've come to study long-house architecture, and no 'tourists' at all.

WEST KALIMANTAN

to the source of the Mahakam River from where you can descend down to the east coast in East Kalimantan Province. The Kapuas and the Mahakam are Borneo's largest rivers, forming an inverted V, the tip of the V lying in the great watershed highlands in the interior. There are no maps for this journey.

Phase 1- the water journey: The ship Selamat plies between Pontianak and Putussibau; food is included in the fare. At Tajan is a big pineapple and *durian* garden. Go out to the plantation itself; all the free *rambutans* you can eat. About 8 days upriver from Pontianak is Simitau. Then you pass several more stilted river towns such as Selimbau (see the majestic *mesjid*) and Nanga Bunut. After a 15 day long hot journey you arrive in Putussibau. Stay with the Dutch priest in the mission here. Bungan is the first village to reach, lying on a tributary of the Kapuas. To get there you need about 200 litres (Rp15,000 or US$38) of gas for the 20 hp Johnson powered power boat, plus the boatman will charge about Rp2000-2500 per day. Upstream there are raging rapids and whirlpools, the river might be swollen by the rains, and is particularly dangerous where tributaries converge. In this upriver region you only see dugouts seating 12 people who sit cross-legged beneath huge circular hats made of palm leaves. Soon the complex river network becomes quieter and calmer and giant trees hug the banks. At a certain point (about 3 days out of Bungan) you must begin the overland trek.

Phase 2- the foot journey: The first stage is through *ladang* ricefields, dense jungles, monstrous trees. The first longhouse is two days walking and canoeing away. In this settlement there are only a few cooking facilities, you sleep on mats, and burning tree sap is used for light. Hire two guides at the longhouse to lead you for Rp400 per day for a 2 day easy walk. Build a *pondok* (lean-to) from saplings at night. An elevated bark floor keeps you dry. The nights are quite cold, so there are few mosquitos. During the day mosquitos are thick; take along a net or sweet-smelling *sirih olie* to repell them. You might meet some Punan tribesmen along the way, masters at surviving in the jungle, and they have an intimate knowledge of the terrain, real beautiful walkers. Eat wild sago (quite unappetizing) that is sometimes flavored with boar fat drippings; or speared lizards with rice; *di sun; to kawat,* like a chesnut; *soar,* a red and bitter fruit; *somboloc,* like passion fruit. Containers are priceless, an empty bottle is worth Rp800-1000. The jungle in the early morning is exquisite, pungent rotting smells, clear sounds, dripping bright green trees and mists, icy baths in the rivers. About 10-15 days from the longhouse you reach the border of West and East Kalimantan, a tangled jungle plateau 780 m high. This is your turning point, about the halfway mark. Have your guides build a raft and take it down streams to reach the Mahakam. Because of rapids, the raft might overturn and even crash and the poling could become more laborious than walking. After a combination of poling and trudging along the river banks, you finally come to Longapari, the most isolated major settlement in Borneo lying at the very headwaters of the Mahakam. From Longapari you can reach the towns on the lower courses of the Mahakam by *longbot* or by regular river ferry.

Ketungau River: A tributary of the Kapuas and the original homeland of the Antu Ibans. Though individual officials are friendly, travel in the area is discouraged. Being an 'operations area' against Communist terrorists, you must first clear with a number of civilian and military offices in Pontianak and get final approval from *Laksus* (military intelligence). First take a regular Colt minibus to Sanggau (the one on the Kapuas R.) several leaving each morning, take 8 hours, expect a sore ass. From Sanggau, there's no regular road transport except for infrequent trucks or jeeps (ask at Colombo Plan road-building community near Sanggau). Hondas can be rented for Rp10,000 from Sanggau to Sintang if you don't want to wait for a boat. All river boats must report into Sanggau and Sintang as they pass (and pay bribes), so hang around the reporting stations (they invite you to sleep in at Sintang) to catch boats. Lumber company boats are often fast and empty. Cargo boats (like houseboats, owners live onboard moseying up and down river) are slow and crowded. But on either kind they are eager to meet whites; free passage and rice. Alternatively, fly from Pontianak with MAF (Missionary Aviation Fellowship), about Rp10,000 to Sintang. From Sintang take the once-a-week cargo boat up the Ketungau River to Nanga Merakai. Returning, try to hitch back to Sintang on a nice new missionary boat. You probably won't pay for any of these. In Sanggau there's a *losmen,* stay for free in the police mess in all other towns. It's tough going slogging through all the offices you're required to get stamps from in every river town. Don't expect to see anything but the towns of Kalimantan Barat, once upriver. Unlike the rest of Indonesia, the locals avoid you in this area. They seem to live in fear, after being shat on by every new kind of people to show up, most recently terrorists and now the army, most of whom consider Dayaks a close relative of the orangutan. Also, petrol is scarce and expensive. The section south is easier, Pinoh and Kayan Rivers for example, not being in the 'operations area'.

CELEBES

INTRODUCTION

The world's most peculiarly shaped island, Celebes resembles a spastic swastika or an orchid. The population of this multi-racial island is over 9 million. Joseph Conrad wrote novels set here. There are many untouched tribes, boat-shaped Toraja houses, cliff-side. graves, and unequaled carvings. **the land:** Covered mostly in rainforests and high, uninhabited, unaral le wasteland. There are 1800-3000 m mountains everywhere with unspoiled, pollution-free, spectacular tropical scenery. Monsoons heave big surf onto beaches along beautiful but treacherours coasts with hills rising abruptly up to 500 m. Few areas are more than 40 km from the sea. Lakes are widespread in the center.

flora and fauna: This island is the home of unique mammals like the *babirusa,* a pig-like animal with upward curving tusks, and the *anoa,* a rare, fierce pygmy buffalo that resembles a sort of goat-antelope that lives in the mountains of north-central Celebes. Also the Black Crested Baboon and the saucer-eyed tarsier live here. Celebes is rich in birdlife with at least 200 known species. On Lokan volcano, North Celebes, *maleos* (bush-turkeys) dig their nesting holes in ground heated by volcanic steam. The Togian Islands in Teluk Tomini are nesting grounds for giant sea turtles.

history: On the west coast at the lower course of the Karama River a neolithic settlement and prehistoric remains have been discovered. Buddhist images found at Sampaga on the west coast belong to the Indian Amarawati school of art which flourished in the 2nd, Century, indicating that Hinayana Buddhism existed in Celebes prior to the 5th Century A.D. See the famous bronze 'Celebes Buddah' in the Jakarta Museum. It shows many sculptural similarities with India such as the treatment of the open eyes, bare right shoulder, and incised lines on the robe showing the folds. Much later in the 16th Century the Portugese arrived. These seafarers thought that the 4 tentacle-like arms of Celebes were separate islands, thus they called the island Ponto dos Celebres (Cape of the Infamous Ones), their name for the cape north of Minahasa which had caused them so many shipwrecks. For centuries Celebes was a refuge for pirates who hid out in its deserted coastal mangrove swamps.

getting there: Take a ship or boat for Rp6-8000 from Surabaya, Java, to Ujung Pandang, South Celebes. Or fly from Surabaya. The cheapest is Mandala Airlines, about Rp24,000. From Jakarta to Ujung Pandang (via Surabaya), Rp27,500. **transport:** The only road networks are around Ujung Pandang, Manado, Kendari, Palu, Rantepao, and Malili. In many parts of South and Central Celebes where road surfaces resemble riverbeds, take a truck-bus whose bigger wheels make it a much less jarring ride than buses or jeeps. Always use your student card in Celebes, boats usually give a little slack and knock up to Rp1000 off the price. The airlines give discounts as well; hassle Mandala and possibly even Bouraq. In east-central Celebes you can possibly negotiate with the crews of INCO Mining Co. chartered planes for cheap lifts if they're not full and if you don't advertise to the hierarchy. There are only three *imigrasi* offices in all of Celebes in which to get your visa extended, Manado, Kendari, and Ujung Pandang.

NORTH CELEBES

(SULAWESI UTARA)

A heavily industrialized province, it has a higher living standard than most other regions of Indonesia. In fact, this very wealthy province even feels like a separate republic. The biggest *copra* production area of Indonesia (18,000 tons a month), everyone tends their plot of coconut palms, even teachers, bankers and army colonels after hours. Also the most heavily Christianized province of Indonesia. The style of North Celebes houses is unique to each region; window sills and porch railings are lined with potted plants, garden and yard vegetation is lavishly tended.

history: Legend says that the original Minahasan tribes were divided by the God Muntu Untu at a huge boulder, seen today on the slopes of the Tonderukan. On intersections of Manado you'll notice numerous statues of ferocious legendary warriors who once guarded the city. Portugese traders came first, as early as 1563. The Spainards arrived next, converting the population to Catholicism. When Dutch planters started cultivating coffee here in 1827, they brought in their wake overbearing Dutch reformist Protestants who began missionary work. By 1860 the entire population had been re-converted. Minahasa soon became known as the '12th Province of the Netherlands' because of the closeness of its religious, military and economic ties with Holland. Most aspects of Minahasan culture were obliterated by the Dutch. But once in a while you see long white haired elders in the villages; also distinctive *ikat*-weaving draws upon their vanished megalithic culture.

music and dance: June, July and Aug., harvest-time, is the festive season for pre-Christian dancing, conch shell orchestras, as well as performances of the mesmerizing wooden zylophonic *kolintang* orchestra, as exciting as the wildest Jamaican blue beat. The origin of this music is Batu on the road to Likupang on the north coast. But go out to different villages; venues change weekly. Ask the *hukum tua* (village chief) what music is happening; usually on a Sunday. The *Maengket* is a typical Minahasan cultural dance, consisting of 3 parts: *Owey Kemberu,* performed during harvest time; the *Marambak* Dance staged at the inaugeration of a newly built house; and the *Lalayaan* Dance, performed at a party when a man announces his fiance.

transport: Dry season is May to October, the rainy season Nov. to April. If you're coming from Irian Jaya and Maluku put away your *surat jalan;* you don't need one in Celebes. If you show it, every official will want to put his stamp on it. You can't travel yet by road down the North Celebes peninsula into Central Celebes. Instead fly from Gorontalo to Palu or else cross Teluk Tomini by boat from Gorontalo to Ampana, Parigi, Bunta, or Pagimana, then further by boat to Poso. Then by a combination of minibuses, trucks and walking it's 3-4 days to Wotu, from where you can get another bus south. Or from Wotu a boat leaves nightly for Malili, Rp500, 3 hours. A road is nearing completion between Wotu and Malili.

MANADO

A prosperous progressive Christian town and capital of the province. Population is about 190,000. No sharp class distinctions here and no extreme poverty. These people, the Minahasans, like and enjoy westerners. All the girls wear dresses (no traditional dress) and shops are quite fad conscious, even selling trendy denim dress overalls. At night everyone is strolling down hectic streets filled with blaring modern Chinese shops. Buy good maps of Minahasa (Rp3000) or of the city (Rp1500), plus guide books and history books of the area at Toko Cozy Corner, Pinkan. There's a Buddhist Society, Vihara Buddhayana, Jl. Yos Sudarso 8, where you can inquire about Chinese and Indian Buddhist houses of prayer and meditation groups. Get visa extensions in Manado if you think you'll run out of time before reaching Ujung Pandang to the south or if you're heading towards the easterly islands.

getting there: If you dock at the port of Bitung on the western side of the peninusla, it's 46 km, Rp250 by bus or Rp300 by *bemo* to Manado. Mapanget Airport is 17 km from Manado, Rp2000 by private taxi or Rp200 by *bemo.* Garuda and Bouraq fly to Ujung Pandang; Bouraq costs Rp70,000. **transport:** There are no *becaks* in this city so take *bendis* or *bemos* (Rp40-50), both in every direction frequently. **events:** Right away contact Kantor Parawisata, Jl. Babe Palar in Wanea, as they know what's going on- shows, music, plays, etc. Toa Peh

top: street scene, Manado
bottom: landscape, Minahasa

CELEBES

LAUT SULAWESI

TALISAI
LIKUPANG
MANADO
BITUNG
AMURANG
TANDANO

TOLITOLI
PALELEH
U T A R A
RANDANGAN
KWANDANG
INOBONTO
KOTAMOBAGU

BANGKIR
TOMINI
TILAMUTA
LAKE LIMBOTO
GORONTALO
MOLIBAGU

SABANG
DONGKALANG
TELUK
TOMINI

TAMBU
MAPAGA

— — — THE EQUATOR — — —

DONGGALA
WANI
PARIGI
AMPANA
BUNTA
PAGIMANA
MALIK
LAUT MALUKU

PALU
SAUSU
LUWUK
KEP. TOGIAN

PASANGKAYU
NAMO
POSO
BATUI

KAROSA
TENTENA
DONGGI
KEP.
BANGGAI
P. TALIABU

T E N G A H
PENDOLO
P. SALUÉ
TELUK

SAMPAGA
S. KARAMA
MANGKUTANA
TOLO

TAMALEA
MASAMBA
SAROAKO
S. MATANA

MAMUJU
WOTU
MALILI

MAMASA
RANTEPAO
PALOPO
DANAU
TOWUTI

MAKALE
TENGGARA
P.P. SALABANGKA

POLEWALI
ENREKANG
MONDRODO
P. MANUI
LAUT BANDA

PAREPARE
RAPPANG
SANGGONA
KENDARI

D. TEMPE
TELUK
KOLAKA
WOWONI

BAJOA
BONE

BUAPINANG
SELAT TIORO
P. BUTUNG

UJUNG PANDANG
BONE
P. MUNA

MALINO
WANGI WANGI

BULUKUMBA
P. KABAENA
BAUBAU

JENEPONTO
KEP. TUKANGBESI

N

SCALE KM
0   50   100   150

...ad from Polewali to Mamasa: *30 years ago the ...tch used to drive it in cars in 3 hours. Now it takes 14 ...urs (only 70 km) in a 4-wheel drive vehicle. This is the ...y it is all over Indonesia now. Cops tend to be offi-...ous in Mamasa; really want you to check in at the cop ...op.*

Kong, a traditional Chinese parade dating from the 14th Century, is seen on such a grand scale in Manado that people come from as far away as Jakarta and Tokyo to see it. It takes place usually in February.

top: **Minahasa**
bottom: **beach at Kwandang**

stay: Cheapest is Peng. Keluarga with a balcony overlooking the busy street. Located on Jl. Jembatan Singkil by the bridge, next door to Losmen Kotamobagu; Rp500 but usually full. Losmen Kotamobagu is Rp650. Hotel Kota, Jl. Singkil, is Rp1500 with coffee or tea; signs in each room warn of moral transgressions. Wenang Hotel, Jl. Bethseda, charges Rp7500 single with A.C. **eat:** Outstanding and inexpensive food is found in this city. Rumah Makan Mataram, Jl. Pier Tendean, has *sate* with the best peanut sauce, *soto sapi,* etc. Two people can eat beautifully for Rp5-700. Seafood in most restaurants is fantastic: skipjack, tuna, giant prawns. Hilman Restaurant has exotics like *burung dara goreng* (fried dove), Rp1500. Ice Palace Sumadra for special ice drinks. At shops buy sweet-sour high protein *pala* fruit (fresh raw nutmeg); Rp350 for one kilo. Jit Hien for reasonably priced Chinese food; chicken dishes and pork *nasi campurs*, Rp250.

from Manado by bus: From Stasiun Otobis or from Jenkie Market, get buses to most North Sulawesi towns. To Kotamobagu, Rp1500. **by boat:** A bus to the nearest port of Bitung takes one hour, Rp250. From Bitung, the Pelni boat Tobelo sails to Irian Jaya once monthly, Rp21,750. Then it returns to Jakarta. Get boats also to Kwandang (near Gorontalo) from Manado Harbor near the bridge about 300 m from Losmen Kotamobagu. The Albatross sails to Kwandang once weekly, Rp4500, takes 2-5 days. Other ships do this run as well. In the main towns along the coast south of Manado–Lolak, Maelang, Bintauna and Bolongitang- ask the *camat* about onward boats. Other shipping lines: Arafat; P.T. Gapsu, Jl. Yos Soedarso; Sriwijaya Raya Lines, Jl. Kol. Sugiono; P.D. Pelsutra, Jl. Sam Ratulangi. **to the Sangir Islands:** Take ships from Manado Harbor north to this island group.

Both Bouraq and Merpati Airlines have flights to the Naha-Sangir Island groups; Manado to Sangir Talaut, Rp18,000. **flights:** Merpati has flights 4 times weekly to Gorontalo, Rp12,250; to Ternate, Rp15,750. Bouraq operates flights to Davao in the southern Philippines (Rp28,000) when an automatic 3 week visa is given as soon as you enter. (Or go illegally with *copra* smugglers on fishing boats to Zamboanga, Philippines, for about Rp10-15,000.)

TOMOHON

A pretty, windy, cool, sunny mountain town with Mt. Lokan towering in the background. Pepper seeds are drying in the sun. Tomohon is a center for Christian mission groups. The few *losmens* charge Rp500. **getting there:** From Manado take a *bemo* to Wanea, Rp40, then a minibus up the mountain to Tomohon, Rp150. Pass by wonderful views of the city and see strings of lights below at night. Honky-tonk beer joints and restaurants perch on the side of the road all the way up. At Tinoor, halfway up the mountain to Tomohon, experience real ethnic Minahasan cooking: mice, dog (very peppery hot), wild pig (babi hutan), and a gin called

the fauna of Celebes: *Two unique animals found on the island of Celebes are the* babirusa *(pig-deer), a very rare boar with ornately curved tusks like the horns of a stag. To see it, take a bus from Kotamobagu to Bilalang, Rp75, walk 2 hours further to Tuduaoug, then hike 30 km further into the forest. The* anoa, *or dwarf buffalo, which developed similar to an antelope, is confined only to the remote mountain forests of Celebes.*

waruga at Airmadidi

cap tikus (like Geneva), Rp100, plus potent sago wines (*tuak saguer*) of varying strengths. Buy *durians,* mangoes, *langsat,* and other monsoon fruits at Pinelang nearby.

vicinity of Tomohon: Many places nearby to visit. There are Christian churches in the Baroa style, the Lahendong hotsprings, terraced ricefields at Leilem, and Rurukan village (1070 m) where over 100 years ago Sir Alfred Wallace was wakened during the night by an earthquake. At Kinilow, 5 km from Tomohon, hotsprings with hostesses and rubdowns; go early at 6 am. The rich clove villages of Sonder and Lahendong feature hotsprings in the middle of a pine forest. At Tara-Tara village outside of Tomohon contact the *hukum tua* for the dances *Maengket* and *Kebesaran* (War Dance), and for *kolintang* performances. A traditional watermill is still used in this village for paddy, corn and coconut milling. At Hutan Wisata, 5 km from Tomohon, there's a big forest garden. *Losmen* in Roong.

Tandano: From Tomohon take a fast bus to Tandano, Rp150, a market town with a nice river running through it. **Lake Tandano:** Many tourist resorts around this lake such as Tandengan and Eris. Visit Passo and Rembokan for ceramics and pottery; a better selection than the city (hotsprings as well). From Tandano village pay another Rp250 to travel either on the east or west shores of the lake to Kakas. There are no *losmens* in Kakas, but contact the *kepala desa* who'll turn you on to some accommodation if you're willing to speak English. Go to Kolongan Kawangkoan, Rp300 from Manado, for bullcart racing, celebrated *kolintang* musical performances, and an underground Japanese fortress. The *Maengket* Dance can be seen in Tompaso. **Batu Pinabetengan:** A memorial stone of the ancestors near Kawangkoan, its surface covered in crude, mysterious line drawings and scripts which have never been deciphered. This historical stone is located about 5 km from the village of Pinabetengan; take a *bendi* out to it. According to Minahasan history this is the place where the ancestors divided the Minahasan people into tribes: Tontemboan, Tonsea, Tolour, Tombulu, Ratahan and Bantik. Today each tribe speaks its own dialect.

other sights in Minahasa: At Kema, an old Portugese fortress. A splendid beach at Kawurukan, only a ½ hour busride from Manado; also remains of Dutch and Japanese forts. Tasik Ria and Kawarukan are well known for sunbathing and canoeing.

Longowan is a mountain village with hotsprings, *sawah*, and virgin forests. Walantaken hotsprings spurts hot steam every 3 minutes; Rp300 from Manado by minibus. Katumenga for hotwater bathing. At Tonsea Lama, a waterfall. Aertembaga is the fishing center of North Celebes. At Krawang, woven embroidered handkerchiefs. **Airmadidi:** Rp200 by *bemo* from Manado. Straightforward friendly people in this town. It's a real treat to get invited inside their rich wood grained well-built houses. In this mountain village see the best examples of *warugas*, old pre-Christian tombs of former leaders of the Minahasa people which are still venerated by some Minahasans. Having the shape of a small Chinese temple, corpses were buried inside in the squatting position with household articles, gold, and Asiatic porcelain dating back to the Ming Dynasty. Because they contained valuables, many have been plundered. There are other complexes at Sawangan and at Kema, but not as well-preserved as in Airmadidi.

SANGIR ISLANDS

90% Christian. Sangir *durians* have an exceptional flavor. A very fine fabric is woven here, the so-called *koffo*-cloth, but not pliant enough to be worn as clothing; it's used only in ceremonies. **getting there:** Take Merpati or Bourag, but it's cheaper at Rp3500-4000 by small cargo boat from Bitung. The K.M. Wirabuana and the faster, better express K.M. Marina sail from Manado's harbor to the Sangir Islands: Tahulandang (in Burias, stay at the *losmen* on the harbor), then on to Siau, Tahuna and Talaut; round trip costs Rp16,800, takes 2 days and 2 nights or more.

Siau: Has nutmeg plantations and a hair-raising volcano. The ground shakes often. The peak of G. Awu, over 1785 m (5853 ft.) high, looks like a well-turned jug from the sea. The crater, about a 6 hour climb from Ulu, is a sheer terrifying drop over a rim of jagged rocks. There are actually two craters, one smoking and the other surrounded by pink cliffs 45 m high. Stay in Losmen Serui in Siau, Rp500.

Tahuna: Miniature canoes are made in Tahuna, also embroidered blouses, bedclothes, and woven *sarungs*. Black woodcarvings and small tables are made out of *kayu besi*. In Tahuna city, stay at the *pasangrahan*. Victory Losmen or Omega Losmen charge Rp1500 per person including food. Visit the fine beaches of Manganitu near Tahuna. **Talaut:** A northern very flat island, almost to the Philippines. Praised for its black woodcarvings.

SANGIR ISLANDS

N

SCALE KM
0   25

KOTAMOBAGU

Mountain capital of the Bolaang Mongondow district, 218 km from Manado. From Manado's Stasiun Otobis, a punishing Rp1500 seven hour busride. An attractive clean Muslim town, friendly people. Gets only about 5-10 European tourists a month. Buy leather army boots here, about Rp3-4000. **stay and eat:** Losmen Lely is the cheapest at Rp1000. Losmen Tenteram, opposite Losmen Lely, Rp750 (but only Rp500 for Indonesians). Hotel Sarinah, Rp1000 for sleep or with meals Rp3000. Wisma Kabela, Rp750, has a swimming pool and a nice garden out in the back; relaxed people. Lots of market stalls for budget eating. Nasional Restaurant for Chinese-style food and drink.

from Kotamobagu: Catch buses from Kotamobagu down a forested twisting river road to Inobonto, Rp500. **alternative route to Gorontalo:** Take bus Rp500 to Doluduo, 60 km. From Doluduo, walk 20 km to Molibagu on a good easy track, a bit up and down. From Molibagu, there's a small boat leaving 2-3 times a week to Gorontalo, Rp750. It doesn't operate from July to September due to big seas and easterly winds. **vicinity of Kotamobagu:** It's a nice day-visit to Bilalang village, 3 km from town, Rp100 by *bemo*. More enjoyable is to take a *bendi* there for Rp400. Every Sun. a 1000 m horserace (with betting on the side) takes place at Togop; free entry. Ten km from Kotamobagu or 3 km from Tobonon is Modayag, a cool high goldmine village. Stay at the *pasangrahan.*

Imandi: Buses leave from Kotamobagu every morning before 9 am. Rp500. for this town in Dumoga District, passing through 47 km (takes 5 hours) of splendid river and mountain country. Imandi is a small quiet village, an ideal place to just relax. **stay:** Peng. Ingat Budi has a rocking chair, is quiet and has a garden; Rp400 for a bed and Rp250 per rather unimaginative meal. Peng. Sweetheart, right in the village itself, charges Rp500, or Rp1500 full board; better food. **vicinity of Imandi:** Walk out or take a *bendi* 7 km to Desa Bali Agung (pop. 500), the Balinese *transmigrasi* colony 1500 km away from Bali where you'll find heart-shaped Balinese faces, one *pura* (temple), a *gamelan* orchestra, Balinese *bubur* rice cakes, *Legong* dances on the occasion of the big Balinese festival, *Galungan.* Crafts are also made here. There are irrigation systems just like on Bali a further 7 km in Duluduo where you can stay in Losmen Dabar Menanti and pay for food but not for sleep. It's a 3 km walk from Duluduo to Lake Meat; a lovely view. Another smaller Balinese *kampung*, Desa Merta, is only 3 km from Imandi.

coconut palm (nyiur *or* kelapa)*: When young and green, it gives an edible soft pulp and a sweet juice (air kelapa). When mature it gives milk (santan kelapa). The tough husk is taken off on a sharp pointed stake and with a long heavy blade the brown shells are split into two halves, spilling the white milk and revealing the white meat. Then each coconut half shell is dried on a long metal floor over a fire of husks. After it's roasted, the meat comes out of the shell more easily and in uniform pieces. Then it's laid out again and dried for days more in the sun. Copra is the semi-dried meat of the coconut. Coconut flour can be processed into copracakes (bungkil) and confections. Coconut oil, extracted from the dried coconut meat, is used in soapmaking, candles, cooking margarine, synthetic rubber. Fibers from the coconut husk (sabut kelapa) are utilized for doormats and brushes, coconut shells are used as charcoal or as active carbon. The flower of the palm can be tapped for a juice from which sugar is extracted, which can also be fermented and distilled into wine.*

Labuan Uki

INOBONTO

Rp500 from Kotamobagu, buses leaving daily. A pleasant place to hang in, quiet and no motor traffic except for honking buses announcing their departures. Like Mexico, sleepy and lazy. Only half dozen travelers a month come this way. The Korean highway being built will change all this. **stay:** Hotel Tepi Laut ('Edge of the Sea') is located so close to the harbor that you can hear the waves. Joje will want Rp750 but just threaten to move to Losmen Haji Idrus right around the corner (bad lighting), which is cheaper at Rp500. Eat at Haji Idrus, Joje's food is too bland.

from Inobonto: Have tea with the harbormaster on his porch on the beach and discuss with him which boats to the north or south he expects will be arriving. You might have to wait 3-4 days, but he'll send a boy to your *losmen* when a boat comes in. It won't leave for hours anyway. Boats south to Kwandang stop in small Muslim coastal towns like Bintauna, Boroko, Buko; pay no more than Rp2500 through to Kwandang. Or from Boroko to Kwandang by *kapal motor*, Rp1000. If you speak Arabian along this west coast of Minahasa, you're in. You can also hire a horse and ride it across the rivers. There are also many boats carrying copra between Inobonto and Bitung; ride along for Rp2500-3000.

vicinity of Inobonto: At Bintauna there's an old Portugese fort. To experience Sulawesi scenery at its finest, take the trip over the mountain to Poigar village; from Inobonto, Rp600 by bus. Visit Poigar's Minahasan village on the far bank of the river for fresh fish or spiced dog. Select your dog in a cage; black are the tastiest because they have more spirit. **Amurang:** From Inobonto, Rp750 by bus, twice weekly. From Amurang, connect with a bus on to Manado. Stay in the *losmen* on the beach 10 minutes walk from the town. Or ask at Amurang's Kabupaten Minahasa if someone will put you up in their house. **Labuan Uki:** A tiny isolated village 50 km from Inobonto with clear water and a white sand beach. Go first to Lolak (stay in Losmen Gubuk), then walk 8 km along the beach or 9 km by road. There are no vehicles to Labuan Uki. Sleep at Dunkie for free, just pay for food. Build a boat in this village for Rp2-20 million; you can see the bare patches on the mountain slope across the bay where timber for boats has been cut down. Only one family lives on the white untouched beaches of Molosing Island.

GORONTALO

If you come by boat down the west coast and land

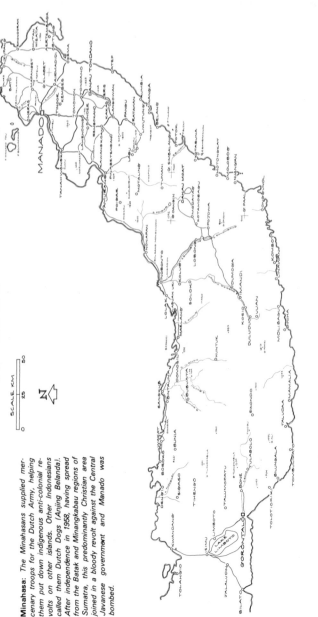

NORTH CELEBES

SCALE KM

0   25   50

N

Minahasa: The Minahasans supplied mercenary troops for the Dutch Army, helping them put down indigenous anti-colonial revolts on other islands. Other Indonesians called them Dutch Dogs (Anjing Belanda). After independence in 1958, having spread from the Batak and Minangkabau regions of Sumatra, this predominantly Christian area joined in a bloody revolt against the Central Javanese government and Manado was bombed.

at Kwandang, take a minibus Rp5-600 one hour's drive south to Gorontalo. In the rainy season it's more difficult to reach. Gorontalo is a small town, like an overgrown Inobonto. Few vehicles. Young girls use colorful *sarungs* as veils. The police send out the longest questionaire in Indonesia (9 pages); count on at least 1½ hours at *kantor polisi*. **stay:**- Namseng Losmen is Rp550; bare essentials. Cross the street to Teluk Kau which costs Rp650 but is a bit roomier with gigantic canopied double beds. Anthon Massa, Jl. Jen. S. Parman 5/37, has been known to put travelers up as well. **eat:** Meals at Teluk Kau's restaurant are a slight ripoff. Rumah Makan Dirgahaga, Jl. Pertiwi, specializes in goat:- *sate*, curry, soup. Sweet Corner nearby has a good variety of meals and drinks. Across the street from the *bemo* station, 15 minutes walk from Namseng Losmen, is a good fruit and vegetable market.

vicinity of Gorontalo: Dahawalolo, 13 km from Gorontalo, has the best panorama of 2 m deep Limboto Lake; also has a bathing place with pools of 5 different temperatures. Hire a *prahu* (Rp3-400) from boys to visit little fishing villages. Can go to the other side of the lake (about 12 km) but they want more rupes. Other places to visit in this upland plain are: Utapato, a bathing place and view over the lake; Batudia, bathe in steaming water; Lombongo, another hot bathing spot, but in the jungle. See Anthon Massa at Kasendukan Tours and Travel Service, Jl. Jen. S. Parman SK 5/37, Gorontalo, to arrange cheap or expensive travel to hotsprings around Kwandang, Limboto Lake, river travel along the north coast, pigeon-hunting, swimming, jungle walks.

from Gorontalo by ship: There are many ships of all sizes to Bitung, Rp6-7000, 20 hours; and sometimes ships to Kendari and Poso. Surya Shipping Co., Jl. Hati Mulia 3/34, has ships, to: Surabaya, Rp22,500, 5 days, about 3-4 ships a month; Ternate, Rp13,750, 2 days, once monthly. Sriwijaya Shipping Co., in the same office, has ships to Ujung Pandang, Rp21,000, 4 days, once monthly. Gapsu Shipping Lines, Jl. Pertiwi 5, has a ship going out weekly but they never know which one or where it's going: Poso, Rp7,250, 30 hours; Luwuk, Rp7-8,000, 18 hours: Ujung Pandang, Rp14,500, 3-4 days; Surabaya, Rp18,000, takes 6 days. **flights:** Merpati, Jl. Achmad Yani, has 4 flights weekly to Manado, Rp13,450. But on its flights to Poso, Palu, Luwuk, etc., you must fly via Manado which makes it very dear: to Luwuk it comes to Rp27,750! Cheaper is to fly direct to these places with Bouraq airlines. From Gotontalo Bouraq has 4 flights a week to Palu, Rp14,500, and to Balikpapan (East Kalimantan), Rp28,150. Costs Rp1000 to get out to Gorontalo's airport, 32 km north. The Bouraq people will come by to pick you up.

from Gorontalo by boat: Take a horsecart down to the harbor, Rp100. As you trundle by on the *bendi* shout out, *'Ke mana?'* down the long row of boats to find out where they're sailing. From Gorontalo there are at least 2 small *kapal motors* a week to the other side of Teluk Tomini. There are at least 3 directions to choose from:

1) The easy way is to take a boat to Parigi, then travel by *oplet* or minibus to Palu or to Donggala. You can fly from Palu. Or take a boat or ship from Donggala south to Pare Pare or to Ujung Pandang.

2) Take a boat from Gorontalo's harbor 3-5 days to either Bunta, Pagimana, Ampana or Parigi on the southern shore of Teluk Tomini. P.T. Lamala has boats going to all these points and is the cheapest company; for example, to Ampana it costs Rp3000 while other companies charge Rp4-5000. From any of these villages there are boats departing for Poso on the southernmost shore of Tomini Bay but be prepared for a wait, departure times aren't at all regular. Ampana to Poso, Rp2500; Parigi to Poso, Rp2500. Ampana is your best bet as a place to get a boat to as there is a *penginapan* there (bargain hard for Rp400 rooms) and a few places to eat; just *nasi campur,* and no ice.

3) From Pagimana, go by road to Luwuk where boats are available to Kendari to the south or north to Bitung.

CENTRAL CELEBES

(SULAWESI TENGAH)

Map 1- from Poso to Pendolo: From Poso take a minibus to Tentena, Rp750, 3 hours or so, leaving about 8:30 am. Tentena has a nice green setting on the lake. There's some rigorous but interesting hiking in the vicinity through thick rain forests with leeches. Get to go to each new town with a new 'introduction'. The eastern Toraja live around 1500 m deep Lake Poso. These Torajans make masks, *pemia* ('with handles'), and use them at funerals with a bag of cleaned bones attached. From Tentena board a small outrigger to Pendolo, Rp500, 3 more hours, leaving around 1 pm; it doesn't depart unti the minibuses arrive from Poso.

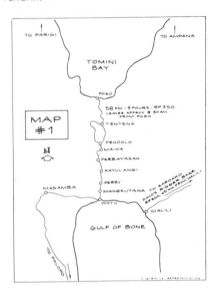

pemia-mask, Toraja-land, Central Celebes

Map 2- from Pendolo to Wotu: From Pendolo walk level for about 10 km, ascend 20 km, then gradually descend for 52 km to Mangkutana. The longest uninhabited stretch is the 18 km from Maioa village to Perbatasan. From Pendolo to Mangkutana a highway is being improved by workmen and you may get lifts part of the way in their trucks. This road is not far from completion and it's an easy-going walk. Stay at the bus depot in Mangkutana, Rp400. From Mangkutana catch a bus at 4 am for Palopo, Rp650.

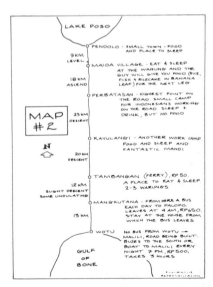

MALILI

On the N.E. shore of Teluk Bone. Merpati Airlines flies to Malili daily (about 1-1½ hours) from Ujung Pandang, Rp17,750- a shuttle flight for the miners working in the Malili area. Or take *kapal motor* from Palopo. Malili is the headquarters of Inco Mining Company. Many Americans, Canadians and Australians work here. There are sizable accommodations for 7500 employees at the Bechtel Camp in Malili and in other satellite villages. The police are quite used to Europeans wandering about Malili unless 'it' happens to wear a full beard and a rucksack with a flute sticking out of it. **stay and eat:** If you don't make a friend amongst the Inco people, stay in Losmen Satria, Rp400, or in other cheap *losmens* on the waterfront close to the harbor. Food is cheap; *mie* soup, Rp150. Or roll into the Inco camp and ask to pay for breakfast. Good food and air-conditioning; you won't believe their cafeteria. **vicinity of Malili:** One of the Bechtel barges takes a run out to the islands around the mouth of the Malili River each Sunday, coral reefs, beaches, skin-diving, etc. Book way in advance.

from Malili: There are continual buses and truck-buses for Rp500 from Malili to Soroako, the main Inco camp north 52 km. Get lifts on Inco trucks, or on Inco chartered planes if you negotiate with the crews. **by boat:** Three steel and three wooden ferries ply between Malili and Palopo. There's also a ferry to and from Malili to Wotu. Wooden boats are not so popular since one turned over recently in the Malili River (about 40 lost). They are slow and they have to steer head on into the waves for safety. The M.V. Duata is the best boat to Palopo, takes 8 hours, Rp1250. A bed below, Rp1000. Very crowded with the young ladies of Palopo on weekends and on monthly paydays. A new boat even more comfortable than the Duata has just come on this run. As boats must enter and leave Malili in daylight due to the difficult narrow channel, you sometimes arrive in Palopo as late as 1 am. Some of the boats leave Malili 12 noon, arriving in Palopo at 8 pm. Then for the return trip, they leave Palopo 10 pm and arrive in Malili at 6 am- very approximate. Rather than walking into town, get into a bus at the Palopo wharf. This way you don't get held up for questioning when you walk by the *kantor polisi* on the left going into town at the start of the wharf. No matter what hour they arrive, boats are met at Palopo by minibuses who seek charter trade to Rantepao or to Makale. The normal night fare is about Rp800 to Rantepao, or to charter a whole minibus Rp8000.

Soroako: A village about 10-15 minutes walk from the Inco camp via a creek and a buffalo paddock. Soroako is in two parts, the original tidier part and the shanty growth of the *pasar* due to the influx of Indonesians who saw a *rupiah* or two in Inco's presence. In this village you could be addressed not only as Mister, Boss, *Tuan*, but also *Mijnheer*, and even Master! But once you're down there a few times you lose your attraction as fresh meat. **from Soroako:** The lengthened strip in Soroako has just been licensed and Merpati may bring Islanders in soon. It's best not to try hitching the Manhauls and trucks near the mine site, though the drivers

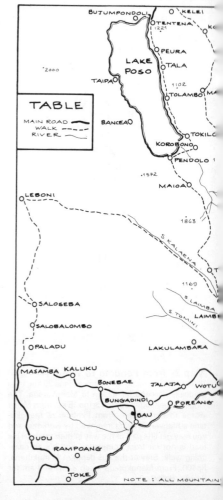

will pick you up out of sight of plant security (for 'payment', American or English cigarettes are popular). A temporary motorcycle licence from the Soroako police costs Rp1000; just 1 photo and a current foreign licence, but no test.

vicinity of Soroako: In this part of Celebes are found 2 magnificent and very deep lakes, Matana and Towuti. Lake Towuti is 48 km wide and the largest lake of Celebes, comparable in size to Lake Geneva. Mighty beautiful. Lake Matana has burial caves. Besides the bus from Malili to Wawondula

and then on to Timampu (on the shore of Danau Towuti), Inco Mining Co. has the only vehicles to the lakes. Enquire about the possibility of a launch on D. Towuti. There are recreational speedboats for Inco Co. staff on D. Matana which is excellent for swimming, water skiing, or sailing. Or you could get boats to Matana village at the head of the lake and to Nuha village across the lake.

isolated societies in Central Celebes: The Tolare people are found in Watubula, Dolo subdistrict, Donggala District, also in Lobu, Parigi sub-

district, numbering about 5000 in all. The Wana (approx. 6000) live in Ulu Bongka subdistrict, Poso District. The 500 Kahumamahoen are in Sinarang, Batui subdistrict, Luwuk Banggai District. The only native *batik* technique outside of Java and Madura is found in Central Celebes, a very ancient one-colored *batik* in which starch is used instead of wax.

Wotu: At present Inco is building a road from Malili to Wotu. Though there are no commercial vehicles doing this route yet, it is a proposition now for 4-wheel drive vehicles or motorcycles. Or walk it in 2 days, crossing several rivers by *sampan;* they ask Rp1000 but just give them Rp50. Sleep in the open in the middle of the jungle. There's a horrible hotel in Wotu, Rp500; kids stand under your rooms and look in peepholes. **from Wotu:** To Palopo by bus, Rp750. From Sabang, Rp300 by taxi from Wotu, do the short walk to Lembong on the road to Seko. An up and down trek, 3 days up, 3 days back, which means 6 days of eating only brown rice. Lake Poso, 80 km to the north, is reachable by a 3 day walk from Wotu. Take a boat across Lake Poso to Tentena, then a minibus Rp750 from Tentena, or walk 2 more days and 2 nights to Poso, then take a boat on to Gorontalo or Manado.

PALU

The provincial capital of Central Celebes. This small Bugis city has a pretty location on the edge of a deep bay surrounded by rising green hills. Although it's only 7 km from the airport they'll try to ream you for Rp500 to get into the city unless you can hitch an army jeep or a civilian; the highway is visible. **stay:** Peng. Selamat, Jl. Pasar Barat, Rp400, is for obvious reasons the cheapest. More presentable are Peng. Latimodjong, Jl. Gadjah Mada, Rp600; and Peng. Kita, Jl. Nyak Dien, Rp800. **from Palu:** Pertamina boats cross over to Samarinda, East Kalimantan; bargain with the captain or possibly ride for free. Kantor Bouraq, Jl. Mawar, has flights daily to Balikpapan, Rp15,850; to Banjarmasin, Rp29,350. Merpati operates flights to Poso twice weekly. **trips from Palu:** From Besesu Station take a minibus as far as Sirenja, 85 km north. Sirenja is also reachable by motorboat, *prahu,* or walking from Wani Harbor. To Donggala, Rp250-300 by minibus.

Wani: From Besesu Station it's a Rp250, 45 minute, and a 25 km ride to Wani Harbor. A cheaper way to get to Wani is to take the *kapal layar* (sailboat) leaving from Donggala across the bay each morning at 10 or 11 am, arriving in Wani at 2 pm. Wani is a small (pop. 6000) picturesque town with just two *rumah makan;* it takes only 10 minutes to walk through it. **prahu-building:** Have a fat-hulled Bugis *prahu* built here for Rp1-2 million. Wani's carpenter can finish the job in 2-3 months and will arrange for licences, etc. Since there's no *losmen,* the shipwrights will have a thatch hut built for you to live in or else you can live as a paying

sculpture at Bada: *This giant (4½ m) stone sculpture is found at Bada, Central Celebes. Other huge free-standing stone megaliths unique in style, and monumental stone burial vats with lizards carved in high relief on the lids are found in the same region.*

boarder with a family. Bring books to read and a radio to hear the news and music, you'll have lots of time on your hands. Everybody remembers a couple of Aussies here because they played the guitar the whole time. Most villagers speak *Bahasa Indonesia* which you can even learn in the local school, or with private teachers in exchange for English lessons. There are also shipwrights at Talise, 25 km from Wani; at Balaesong just south of Sabang to the north (can catch a daily boat from Wani 4 hours to Balaesong). Also a carpenter in Donggala. **from Wani:** There are daily motorboats to Sirenja, Rp3000, takes 12 hours. Weekly boats to Samarinda, Rp3500-400, takes one day, one night; north to Tolitoli there are boats twice monthly, Rp5000-5500; and to Pare Pare once in awhile, Rp3500-4000. Sail from Wani by *kapal layar* to Surabaya in about 9 days.

DONGGALA

By minibus from Palu 35 km over a winding coastal road, passing villages on stilts and night fishermen. Donggala is a small friendly Muslim port, pleasant to spend a few days in. Good walks. **sights:** There's a movie house just down the street from Peng. Anda. Climb Bale Hill to get a good view of Donggala's harbor of sleek sailing vessels. Little village on the top. One boatwright works in Donggala. Walk 3 km out to Tanjung Karang; glistening clear water with a panorama of giant sails and a long white beach, very relaxing. Restaurant Karang Ria with hostesses and cold Rp500 beers.

stay: Peng. Anda, Rp400, though central, must be the dumpiest hotel in all of Sulawesi; you fall through the floorboards on the way to the toilet and children peer at you from cracks underneath the building. Better deal and more private is Peng. Bruri, Rp550; take a left just after the bridge going into town from Palu, it's about 1½ km from the harbor. A clean, comfortable family-run place is Wisma Donggala, Rp2000 double, Rp2500 triple; meals cost Rp5-750. **eat:** The vegetable and fruit market, open everyday, is incredibly well-stocked for its size. Superkitsch Toko 39, complete with Charles Bronson calendar, has lots of most everything; try their hot Quaker Oats drink. Restaurant Dinda for Chinese food; one *cap cai kua* (Rp300) is enough for two. Gembira also specializes in Chinese food. Lots of places to eat.

from Donggala: Catch motorboats north to Sabang. Sometimes small ships chug across to Balikpapan and to Samarinda (East Kalimantan) from Donggala. Ask the Sriwijaya Lines or the P.T. Indrapura office on the waterfront about ships to Ujung Pandang; at least one ship weekly, Rp10,450, takes 3 days. For Ujung Pandang it's cheaper to get on a ship only as far as Pare Pare (Rp4000), then from Pare Pare (cheap *losmens*), it's Rp1150 by bus south to Ujung Pandang. P.T. Indrapura also has ships weekly to: Surabaya, Rp17,200, 4-5 days; Jakarta, Rp21,150; and about twice a month to Manado, Rp14,250, two days.

SOUTH CELEBES

(SULAWESI SELATAN)

Tired of Bali getting the lion's share of the tourist business, South Celebes is starting to go tourist crazy now with grandiose plans for an international airport, tourist villages, nightclubs, massage parlors, golf clubs, plus big souvenir shops in all the main towns. **Barombang:** A resort 20 km south of Ujung Pandang; sandy white beaches, palms, crystal water and an incredible range of shells. Rent canoes or small *prahus*. Get there soon before the tourist developers move in. Try Jeneponto Vino, a wine made from *lontar* palms. **Gua Mampu:** A bat cave 48 km from Bone where stalagmites form figures of animals and people. **Bantimurung:** A quiet resort 40 km from Ujung Pandang. Go first to Maros, then take a *bemo*. Nature reserve, cliffside caves, a 15 m high waterfall, and hundreds of species of colorful butterflies, some very rare like the Birdwing which has a wingspan as wide as your hand. Stay in cheap bungalows. **Maros:** There's a

new telecommunications center here, an American engineer will explain to you some of the equipment. Unusual rocks in this area. **Birta Ria:** 64 km south of Ujung Pandang. Climb down a bamboo ladder from a plateau to reach the beach. **Malino and Cikorok:** Cool hill resorts S.E. of Ujung Pandang. Malino is 760 m above sea level. Stay in the guest-houses or with families for perhaps Rp1000 at night. Tues. & Sun. are market days in Malino; it's a pleasant walk to the waterfall 4 km south of town. Use these resorts as a base for 2-3 hour walks through pine forests to *kampungs* in the hills. **Sengkang:** A small town near Lake Tempe. See home silk weaving produced here. Losmen Merdeka is filthy and although the other *losmen* is Rp1000, it's much cleaner. Losmen Sederhana, run by Chinese people, Rp350, is OK. People in the Bugis fishing villages on the lake will also put you up. **isolated societies:** Hunter-gatherer cultures (approx.

Saroako: *International Nickel Co. (Inco) has made the biggest single foreign non-oil investment in Indonesia so far: $850 million. Inco built a winding 52 km all-weather road through dense mountain rainforest to reach their mine site from the port area of Malili. They have made hugh infrastructure investments in airfields, hundreds of prefabricated houses for employees, schools, roads, power stations, and training programs for the local help. Inco built a complete nickel smelting plant on jungle-cleared land, and a second plant with a capacity of 35 million lbs. a year is close to being finished. These plants, which incorporate the most advanced smelting technology, transform the muddy ore with its 2.4% nickel content into a fine dusty matte containing 70% nickel. By the middle of 1978 they will be producing 100 million lbs. of nickel matte annually out of both plants, about 8% of world production.*

12,000), which don't live in permanent settlements, still exist in the southeast: the Toalas and the Toramanus in Rantebulan, Mambi subdistrict and in Tubi, Mambi subdistrict, Tutalla District; the Tanan Toa people (5000) live in Kajang subdistrict, Bulukumba District; the Onto People (2300) in Banta Eng subdistrict, Bantaeng District; the Tolampuna in Padangmalua Limbong subdistrict, Buwu District, only 200 left. Some of these groups show surviving evidences of the Veddoid culture, one of the first civilizations to occur in these islands 10,000 to 15,000 years ago.

THE BUGIS AND MAKASSANS

The Bugis and Makassans of the southwestern arm of Sulawesi have essentially the same language and culture. Celebrated for their coarseness, these peoples are the most *kasar* in the whole archipelago. Even the children. If you have a child they will pinch it to make it cry, or lob stones into your *becak* as you're riding past. To each other they do not behave this way; only to caucasoid strangers who can't do anything but take it. In Ujung Pandang in mid-1976, after having manhandled a pickpocket they had caught, 3 French travelers were critically stabbed. To understand this hostility towards the white man it helps to remember that in the early part of this century thousands of Bugis and Makassans were killed in retaliation for the death of a few Dutch soldiers during the Dutch pacification of the island. In this notorious 'Westerling Massacre', people were bundled together in groups of 50 and shot; 30,000 people died.

history: Known as the Sea Gypsys, the Bugis and Makassans have always been extraordinary shipbuilders, sailors, merchants, slaverunners, adventurers, warriors, and pirates. Just look at how the women dress to see their history. The Bugis were the first seafarers to visit Australia, sailing for hundreds of years in their traditional triangular masted *Lambere* as far as the Kimberleys and Arnhem Land to fish for Chinese delicacies. They left many loan words with the Australian aboriginal tribes of the Gulf of Carpentaria. South Celebes was a Majapahit province in the 14th Century, and a formidable naval power in the 16th Century, fighting great territorial sea battles. The most feared pirates of the Java Sea, the Bugis hunted their prey in packs, their ships armed with cast-bronze bow rammers shaped like dragons' gullets. When Torres visited New Guinea in 1603, he met Makassan traders there. South Celebes came under Portugese influence in 1625, who in turn were driven out by the Dutch in about 1667. Islam first entered South Celebes at Gowa, the most powerful early Makassan state, relatively late-only at the end of the 17th

Century. Makassar was from the 17th Century to the 19th Century the main harbor settlement for the King of Gowa whose actual capital was 10 km inland. Makassar directly dominated and exploited Sumbawa during the 17th Century and during the 18th Century this coastal kingdom became a political power in the Riau archipelago, large areas of Sumatra, maintaining colonies in Singapore and on Borneo, and trading with India, China, Philippines, Burma and Cambodia. This wealth and influence persisted until Dutch control was consolidated in 1905 when Holland's forces conquered the rest of Celebes, whereupon the Dutch treated the kings of Gowa like vassals. **literature:** The Bugis and Makassans are famous for their chanted heroic epic poems told by a storyteller who accompanies himself on a 2-stringed lute played with a bow. The *I Caligo Cycle* is a mythical account of the past which has become literature. Gods, ancestors, heaven and earth, the whole cosmological order are related. Diaries and journals were made fashionable under Portugese influence. **dance:** *Pattuddu* is performed by 6-8 teenagers. See the Bugis *Pajogo* and the *Pajaga,* and the stately court dance, *Pakarena.* All are being updated for tourists.

PRAHU

The Bugis and Makassans are the most skilful boat builders and sailors in Indonesia. Life is symbolized by sails. They don't use compasses or sextants when they sail and claim they can *smell* coral reefs. Steersmen sit outside the hull so if they fall asleep they'll plunge overboard instead of crashing the *prahu* on a reef. There's little distinction between captain and crew. Their *prahus* are usually forward tilting, square-bowed, have great oar-like rudders and seven sails balooning from very high masts. In a really big wind many of the larger *prahus* have to drop their gigantic sails. Some of the cargo freighters rigged up like schooners weigh up to 250 tons, they could measure 30 m from steam to stern and up to 15 m wide. Often there's a galley, a small shithouse hanging over the back, and two rooms, fore and aft. In South Celebes there's a central rudder but most other locales use one or two long heavy oars which trail astern. Some *prahus* can sail as fast as 30 km an hour in a good wind. An ocean-going two master with 7 sails can sail from Ujung Pandang to Jakarta fully loaded with 4 tons of copra in only 5 days. Some 30 ton boats carry loads that are heavier than the ship's deadweight.

types of prahus: Some designs reflect Portugese influence (palari) with giant rectangular sails. There are many other kinds: *pinisi* with different sizes and number of sails, *jarangka* and *sande* (big outriggers), etc. Racing *prahus* have one or two outriggers and carry a remarkably large sail whose width is twice the hull's length (8 m) and whose height is 20 times the beam. These very fast wild-flying one foot wide boats can turn in just a few seconds with their outriggers clear out of the water. Under sail they have the grace of a bird.

prahu-building: Bugis *prahus* are built virtually everywhere where there are Bugis people, which includes all of coastal Sulawesi. Whole communities of shipwrights, sailors and carpenters are involved in building them. Watch your boat grow from a pile of teak logs into a highly seaworthy strong vessel, said to the last 20-25 years. The work takes place on a palm-shaded beach and the shipwrights have about 8 tools between them, age old equipment including a giant wooden mallet. The only modern tools used are metal augers and steel blades. Long straight planks are hewn from solid teak logs from Kalimantan. Boats are built in cradles of scaffolding with round wooden bottoms and big broad beams ribbed like a whale. No iron is used, the entire hull is planked and fastened by long iron-woods pegs, then the frames are pegged to it. Deadeyes are carved from blocks of teak. Chaulking is shreds of paper bark poked into the cracks. Any modifications you want to make during the building could send the builders into total confusion and extend perhaps two months onto the completion of the job. So have them build it traditional, the way they know how. Belowdecks will be *all* modification. Bunks, tables, galley, proper floorboards and cupboards are totally unfamiliar to Indonesians who design their *prahus* to carry copra, stinking dried fish, timber, and live turtles to Java. Native sailors sleep and eat on deck in good or bad weather and bunks below are useless because of the odor or lack of space. Sails are made of cotton cloth from India, about US$75 for the mainsail. Unless you want to sail sideways, order a full-length keel. Ballast is 4 tons of rocks. Jakarta has the cheapest motors in Indonesia; a *prahu* usually fits a 33 horsepower, though most (about 30,000 in South Celebes) are motorless because of the cost, lack of spare parts and repair difficulties. Buy reef charts at the *syahbandar's* in Surabaya– *Peta Ichtisar Dari Kepulauan Indonesia: Bagian Barat, Bagian Timur* (two parts). Although the labor itself is extraordinary cheap (shipwrights earn Rp1500 a day), the cost of a *prahu* isn't cheap because of all the miscellaneous incidentals and extra expenses. Indonesians are lovely people but very difficult to do business with. There could be crooked dealing, rotten timber, incompetent workmanship, bribes to immigration officials, police and harbour authorities. Figure on US$3000-4000. **note:** The port of Melaka on the west coast of peninsular Malaysia is reported to be the most expedient place to build a Malaysian-style sailing vessel, just as cheap and less irksome than having a vessel built in Indonesia.

Bangkok March 22, 1977

Dear Mr. Dalton,

Been reading your latest traveler's notes and felt compelled to write this letter after reading page 62 where you said, 'Buy a teakwood hull for about US$3000'. Did you buy a boat? ... probably not or you wouldn't have suggested it. It's a bummer. We bought a boat and so did one of our friends. He ended up smashed on the rocks at Sumba and we ended up about US$3000 lighter in the pocket. It's a drag. You have to employ workers on a daily rate. You get a time ... cost quote and you have to double it, it takes at least twice as long and costs twice as much. US$3 a day for the carpenters plus US$2 a day for labourers seems like nothing and it's gone up lately since the French have moved in on the scene. US$3 seems fair until you start paying it out everyday. You're supposed to throw in a packet of cigarettes each day too. If you've got 3 carpenters it ends up at US$70 a week and believe me it takes many weeks. Would you believe it takes 10 men one day to paint half a side of a 10 meter boat (that's if you watch them). When you start getting a bit frantic and say it has to be ready in 3 weeks they say yes yes it will be then make sure it's minus a roof or something. It takes about 3 to 4 months to build a simple cabin. This usually means flying to Singapore for a new visa because your boat's got only half a cabin and you can't sail it anywhere. Like what happened to us.

Also 99% of the boats aren't teak. The people say oh yes jati jati bagus but they're not they're some wood they call labung but that doesn't matter because teak's not so good below the water line. It rots and gets full of worms. Equipment for your boat is cheap in Singapore, but hell you got to try to smuggle it back through customs because there's huge taxes in Indonesia on things like textiles (sails). Then you go back and find out it's the wrong time of the year for sailing anyway. We've heard so many disaster stories associated with prahus. Indonesian waters are some of the most dangerous in the world. The Lombok Straits are feared by even the best sailors. Another couple we know bought a boat. They were really experienced sailors. They actually got where they were going, Singapore, and ended up sitting there for about 4 months and selling theirs at a loss. They could have just as easily sailed back to Bali and sold it for 3 times the price they got to some innocent Australian fresh off the plane. But they swore they'd never sail it anywhere again.

It's the best way to stuff up your trip. Apart from the original cost you have to pay the headman of the village 10% of the cost of the boat, the harbormaster 10%, and the guy who arranges the deal 10%. So your US$3000 boat soon becomes your US$4000 boat straight off. If you have to mention boats tell people to go down to the harbor and look at them. Maybe pretend they're going to buy one and have a few test runs then go off and fantasize and dream a bit. Don't say buy one unless you really want to screw someone's trip. I could fill this writing pad with the odds against anyone ending up with a good deal.

Elizabeth Roshby

UJUNG PANDANG

Capital of South Celebes, for hundreds of years known as Makassar. Largest and busiest commercial center in all of East Indonesia. Makassar Bay has spectacularly beautiful sunsets. There are many florist shops, and deer even graze over the city. **getting there:** Hasanudin Airport is 20 km from the city. Garuda and Merpati fly to Ujung Pandang twice weekly from Bali; try for a student's discount. Or take Bouraq from Surabaya or from Kalimantan. **transport:** *Bemos* travel only a few main roads so *becaks* are the only way to get around except for walking. Depending upon how far, anything from Rp100-250. Older drivers are cheaper.

stay: Cheapest is Peng. Maros, Jl. Seram, Rp500; dingy and smelly, better to sleep out on the sidewalk in a howling monsoon. Hotel Nusantara, Rp600, with reliefs of giraffes on the walls and tanks of tropical fish, has a nice 2nd floor public sitting room over the street; harbor is only 1 km away. Many travelers stay in Hotel Alaska, Jl. Sun gaisaddang 52, Rp1100 single, Rp1650 double with private toilet and bath. Losmen Linggarjati, just off Jl. Sombu Opu opposite the mosque, is Rp900; see the ocean from some rooms. The Ramayana, Jl. G. Bawarkarang 121, is expensive at Rp1800 and up for a standard room, meals are about Rp650.

eat: There are diverse and surprising markets with hundreds of different kinds of live fish, eels, crab, squid, prawns , lobster, grilled over open fires. Cheaper food is in excellent night markets. The stalls behind the big day market start up at 6 pm; *mie rebus,* Rp100, cakes, Rp15. Visit Pasar Baru for all kinds of fruits and vegetables (6 different kinds of eggplant). Expect to spend Rp800-1000 for a meal in the restaurants. Asia Baru Restaurant, Jl. Salahutu 2, has a good reputation for seafood in a town that's famous for it. Try *baronang* fish, barbecued squid (cumi cumi), Rp650, or giant prawns at Rp400 each. Also good is Makassar boiled fish in spiced sauce (pulu mara). Empang, Jl. Siau, has Indonesian food and baked fish (ikan bakar) at its best. Try *soto makassar,* a savory super-nutritious soup made from buffalo guts; find it in *warungs* all over town. Lots of good ice juice places. On Jl. Sulawesi 185 is a little Chinese place serving a big portion of good *mie goreng,* Rp300. On Jl. Timur, fresh apples Rp125 each and grapes for Rp2250 a kilo. There are well-stocked grocery stores on Jl. Sulawesi selling 56 kinds of fresh-baked biscuits and cookies in glass jars, Australian cheese and wine, Dutch chocolates. There's about 7 separate brands of the sweet peach-like drink, *marquisha,* in Ujung Pandang; Rp500 a bottle.

sights: The tourist office (Kantor Parawisata) for South Celebes is located on Jl. A. Yani 2, just around the side of the Governor's building; they'll give you a booklet, maps and spot-on information. See the world's last remaining fleet of sailing ships at Paotare Harbor; swift black-hulled schooners whose designs haven't changed since Genghis Khan. Indonesians still pay homage at the tomb of Diponegoro, Indonesia's first nationalist leader who fought the Dutch on Java for 5 years (1830-35), was tricked into negotiations and arrested and sent to Ujung Pandang in exile until his death. There are some riotously ornate Chinese temples down on Jl. Sulawesi. **Fort Rotterdam:** Right in the center of the city. The original buildings were built in 1545 by a King of Gowa. It was a stronghold of Hasanudin, ruler of Makassar, until he was defeated in 1667, then occupied by the Dutch, renamed and rebuilt in classic 17th Century fortress architecture. The crumbling, blackened buildings are now being restored. Take in the museum inside the fort, a really fine collection on 3 floors; Rp50 entrance. Especially outstanding for musical instruments and old China. Also visit the Sungguminasa Museum on the southern outskirts of the city. **THR** (People's Amusement Park): A bummer. Bugis children are unbelievably ill-bred and rude to visitors; vibes of a real port-town. **Seashell Museum:** Visit C.L. Bundt (and his 16 squealing barking dauchunds) at his seashell Museum on Jl. Mochtar 15 A. It contains 200 different kinds of shells, plus there's a 41 year old orchid gardens. Orchids sell for Rp350, up to Rp15,000 for the Moon Orchid.

miscellaneous: For entertainment, visit the rollicking seamens' bars down on the waterfront; Bugis women, *Kupu Kupu Malam* (Night Butterflies), will keep you company for Rp3-5000 a night. Queen's Massage Parlour is the most favored by expats who have been in Ujung Pandang for a few years. Pay Rp3,200 to the gent at the desk, further negotiations with the young lady herself. Seaview Hotel not recommended for health reasons. Wisma Ria is the cheapest disco. Drop by Kiosk Bali for the sunset. It has a nice 3rd floor patio where they serve beer, fishball soup and snacks. Not that expensive. Semarang Kiosk is on a 2nd floor terrace, nice view and soft music. If you're starved for reading material, pay a call at Toko Baru on Jl. Balai Kota where they have a good selection of 2nd hand books in English, Newsweek, Time, etc. Check different banks for different rates of exchange, there could be a big difference; most are on Jl. Nusantara. Tennis anyone? Go to the military police barracks and find a partner, some fine players. Or just go to the courts on Jl. Sam Ratulangi and hang around until someone offers you a game. *Kantor imigrasi* is on Jl. Seram 8-12, near the harbor. If you

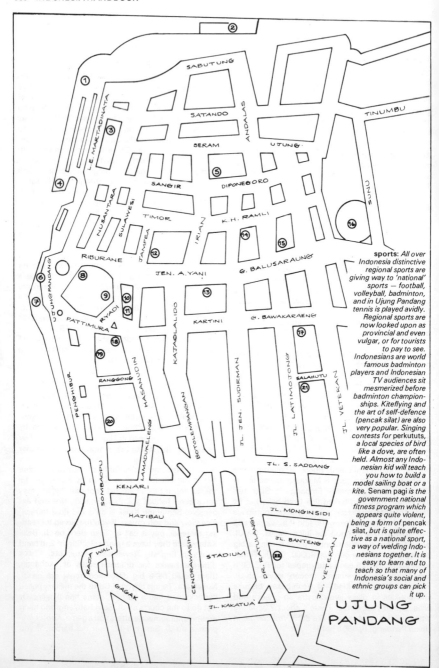

sports: *All over Indonesia distinctive regional sports are giving way to 'national' sports — football, volleyball, badminton, and in Ujung Pandang tennis is played avidly. Regional sports are now looked upon as provincial and even vulgar, or for tourists to pay to see. Indonesians are world famous badminton players and Indonesian TV audiences sit mesmerized before badminton championships. Kiteflying and the art of self-defence (pencak silat) are also very popular. Singing contests for perkututs, a local species of bird like a dove, are often held. Almost any Indonesian kid will teach you how to build a model sailing boat or a kite. Senam pagi is the government national fitness program which appears quite violent, being a form of pencak silat, but is quite effective as a national sport, a way of welding Indonesians together. It is easy to learn and to teach so that many of Indonesia's social and ethnic groups can pick it up.*

UJUNG PANDANG

want a 4th, 5th and 6th month (but no more than 6 months), get it here. Costs Rp4000 for your 4th month; shouldn't take more than a couple of hours to get it.

UJUNG PANDANG

1. *harbor*
2. *Paotare Harbor*
3. *Immigration Department*
4. *prahu harbor*
5. *Diponegoro's grave*
6. *Taman Bahari Restaurant*
7. *boats to Kayangan and Lai Lai*
8. *Fort Roterdam*
9. *Post Office*
10. *Governor's Office*
11. *Bank Rakyat Indonesia*
12. *Hilman Restaurant*
13. *Kareobesi Square*
14. *bus station*
15. *Grand Mosque*
16. *Hasanudin University*
17. *Bamboo Den Restaurant*
18. *C.V. Kanebo Souvenir Shop*
19. *Wisma Ria Bar and Restaurant*
20. *Bundt's Orchid and Seashell Museums*
21. *Asia Baru Seafood Restaurant*
22. *tennis courts*

---

crafts: Ujung Pandang is a big metalcrafts center where exquisite filigree Kendari style silverware is sold. Gowanese are known for their brilliant brasswork; brass bells and candle holders from Kuningan look almost Tibetan. Bugis and Makassan women bedeck themselves out in jewelry and much of a family's wealth is invested in womens' adornments. The traditional *kebaya* of the Buginese is called *baju bodo;* the older the woman, the darker the color. Jalan Sombaopu is chock full of shops selling gold and silverware, old coins, tortoise shell bracelets, Tanah Toraja crafts, alligator skin, horn artifacts, Bone woven goods, leather wallets, shell necklaces. C.V. Kanebo, on the corner of Jl. Pattimura and Jl. Somba Opu, has crafts from all over Indonesia. The Central Market contains spice stalls, colorful silk cloth (85% of Indonesia's silk is produced in this province), unique utensils. In Bone on the east coast, the most unusual baskets and boxes are made out of orchid fibres. Salayar Island, off the south coast, has much of its traditional technology such as fish traps, spearguns, spinning wheels, still intact. Woven *lontar* hats are made in Jeneponto. Bugis flutes look like recorders. Mandar farming communities make earthenware pots. The Bugis produce probably the most attractively ornamented pottery in Indonesia with the top half or two thirds of the dishes and bowls engraved with flowers, leafs, human and animal motifs and figures. Hawkers come round to the hotels in Ujung Pandang to flog 'antique' Chinese porcelain; let the buyer beware.

from Ujung Pandang: Good road maps in Toko Baru. Nitour, Jl. Lamadukeleng 2, offers tours for the man with little time. **bemos:** from the *bemo* station to Bantimurung, Rp275, one hour, leaving practically all the time. To Barombang, Rp350; to the airport, Rp200; to Malino, Rp600. **flights:** Besides Merpati, there are Mandala Airlines, Jl. Hos. Cokroaminoto 25, and Bouraq, Jl. Hos. Cokroaminoto 5, plus agents all over town. Cheapest is to fly Mandala; to Jakarta (via Surabaya), Rp27,750. Merpati flights to Ambon in the Moluccas Islands, Rp28,500. If the airline picks you up at your hotel it'll cost Rp1250 to the airport 25 km away at Mandai. **buses:** To Torajaland, hitching is fairly easy on the main roads either as a paying passenger or free. The best bus company for Torajaland is Liman Express, Jl. Paiya 25; open 8 am-9 pm. A beautiful journey through the hills, like Switzerland in the summer. Buy your ticket and reserve a seat the day before. Leaves for Rantepao at 7 am and 7 pm, Rp1500, takes 10-12 hours. If you can't get on with Liman, try Lita Co., Jl. G. Merapi, or Berlian Co., Jl. Candrawasi. A bus company to Rantepao also operates out of Bone, on the east coast. **alternative routes to Rantepao:** Get a lift on a boat to Pare Pare, then it's 4 hours more by bus. Or take a bus to Palopo for Rp2100, 390 km, 12 hours, and approach Rantepao from the east. **other destinations and prices:** By bus to Pare Pare Rp1150, 4 hours, twice daily; to Polewali, Rp1450, where you can get transport on to Mamasa (see 'Torajaland'); to Bone, Rp1000, 4-5 hours, twice daily; to Sengkang, Rp1250, 240 km. **to Salayar Island:** A traditional island off the south coast. Take bus first to Bulukumba, Rp950, 3-4 hours. From Bulukumba board a motorboat to Benteng on Salayar, Rp200, 6 hours. Stay in Losmen Salayar in Benteng. **motorbikes:** Rent a motorbike privately for about Rp1250-1500 a day in Ujung Pandang and take it up to Tanah Toraja because in Rantepao it costs up to Rp500 an hour, or Rp3500 per day. Ask around hotels for someone who wants to rent their bike out.

from Ujung Pandang by ship: There are over 25 shipping companies in this port town, most located in the crowded streets around the harbor. Some of the larger companies have ships to Europe, Hong Kong, Taiwan, Burma, Japan, and North America. Pelni has ships to: Kupang, Rp14,250, twice monthly; Bitung, Rp22,150, 2-3 times monthly; Kendari, Rp13,750, once a month; Tahuna (Sangir Islands), Rp24,000, takes 10 days; Jayapura, Irian Jaya, Rp31,100, 5 times a month. **prahus:** Paotare Harbor is about 4 km north of the main square. From Paotare you can catch *prahus* to anywhere in East Indonesia. See the helpful guys in the customs office. Sometimes there are *prahus* to Bima, Flores, Rp9000. From Bima it's easier to get to Kupang or to Komodo Island. Sailing vessels leave from Samudra Harbor is well. **kapal motor:** At least 5 times a month motorized 100 ton vessels leave for Balikpapan, Rp4000, 2 days, 2 nights if you're lucky; if not, 5-6 days. Check Samudra Harbor, Biro Perjalanan Office, for boat info or to buy tickets for the Pelni boat Larma Satu which sails to Balikpapan weekly, Rp6-7000, takes 2-3 days. (From Pare Pare, north, boats to Balikpapan are cheaper at Rp3500-4000.) Boats also from Samudra Harbor to: Gorontalo, Rp11,000; Bitung North Celebes, Rp15,000 (Pelni's price is Rp 22,000!), takes 5 days. For Gorontalo, try the Kebun Agung which gives a student discount. Costs only Rp9000. Go straight to the captain. Other *kapal motors to* Surabaya, Donggala (rare), Banjarmasin (Rp3-3500), take 2-3 days.

islands near Ujung Pandang: Take a tent and visit some fine deserted beaches and peaceful fishing villages on islands out in Makassar Bay. Sundays are very crowded. Most are reachable within one hour by *prahu* or 15 minutes by motorboat from the seawall in Ujung Padang. From Terminal Kayangan just past Wisma Ria to Kayangan Island, it's Rp100. Go down a side alley and catch a motorboat also to Lai Lai Island, Rp100; or to Samalona, Rp1000 each way. There are just 2 families on Samalona; stay with them for only Rp250 full board. On Sunday the scores of wide sails of bright painted craft out in the bay look like butterflies on the wing. From Samalona hop further to Barancadi; there are other islands even further out.

PARE PARE

A port 55 km north of Ujung Pandang. **stay:** Cheapest beds are at Peng. Murni, Rp500, close to the bus company and shipping offices; upstairs is breezier and quieter. Refresh yourself in the cake and ice juice shop on the opposite corner. Big, rambling, dark Hotel Siswa, Jl. Patompo, is Rp1750. **eat:** Good *mie kua* places are on Jl. Lasinrang. On the same street is a fruit market. Restaurant Asia is a fancy priced rip-off (horrible chicken in tomato sauce). Warung Merennu, Jl. Hasanudin, has good soups and *gado2*, Rp200. Sampurna, Jl. Bau Massepe, also is a bargain place. A floating restaurant (specializing in seafood of course) is Angin Mamiri on Jl. Pingir Laut right over the sea.

from Pare Pare: Buses from Pare Pare leave for Polewali north, Rp600, 3 hours; Rantepao in the highlands, Rp850, a half day trip. To Ujung Pandang it's faster to take the bus, Rp1150, rather than the boat. There are at least 4 shipping companies based in Pare Pare: Berita, Cahaya, Watampone, Tanjung Manis. All have daily boats (except Fri.) to the east coast of Kalimantan. Some boats travel all the way to Jambi, South Sumatra, twice monthly, Rp 20,200. Before embarking for anywhere you'll have to clear with the customs police in the Pare Pare docks, but all they actually want to do is to meet you for their own entertainment; perhaps mutual.

vicinity of Pare Pare: Pallengo is a small shipbuilding town on stilts 20 km south of Pare Pare. Have a small but fine *prahu* (one masted with one triangular sail) built here. In Bone the boats are much larger but roughly built.

SOUTHEAST PENINSULA

Kendari: This capital of S.E. Celebes lies in a very fertile district on the lower right leg of this amoeba-shaped island. There's a Japanese nickel project here. **getting there:** Take a boat from Palopo to Kolaka, Rp3000-3500, 1-2 days. Or from Bajoa, by *bemo* 6 km north of Bone on the coast opposite Ujung Padang, catch a W W II landing craft, 1 night, to Kolaka. Stay in Losmen Teluk Bone in Kolaka, Rp500; they also serve food and drink. From Kolaka take a bus to Kendari, Rp 1500 125 km. **stay:** Many cheap *losmens* in Kendari. **crafts:** Known for its fine silver, and quite inexpensive gold crafts. Some of the most intricate filigree work imaginable is spun from cobweb-like silver threads: brooches, necklaces, lizards with emerald eyes, even large fruit bowls. **from Kendari:** Fly with Merpati to Ujung Pandang for Rp17,250, or to Surabaya, Rp33,450.

Bajau People: A nomadic, boat-dwelling shore people usually living around Bugis settlements on the remote coasts of the eastern peninsula along the Gulf of Bone, the Straits of Tioro and Butung, the island of Wowoni, Kendari Bay, and northwards to the Salabangka Islands. Outstanding swimmers, they are able to dive so deep that more ignorant Sulawesians believe they have gills like fish. Children are thrown into the sea to make them downproof. The Bajau use trident harpoons and bamboo spears to hunt the giant stringray, sometimes employing the poisonous spine as a point for a dagger. They are dead accurate with these implements. The Bajau are masters of a cross-legged defensive art adapted to fighting on boats or in very cramped quarters.

Wangi Wangi: An island in the Kepulauan Tukangbesi group. Take a ship (or *kapal layar*) leaving every 10 days or so from Ujung Pandang; has all classes accommodation. A beautiful lagoon surrounds the *kampung* of Wangi Wangi with only a 5 m wide, 2 m deep entrance, though inside the lagoon itself it's 5 m deep. There are 2 cafes in the village where beer is sold, village girls do the *joget,* guitars strum into the night. Have a Bugis boat built for 1-1½ million *rupiah;* several foreigners have had trad boats built here. Catch *kapal motors* carrying goods to Ambon from Wangi Wangi. **vicinity of Wangi Wangi:** Just outside of town, enter a hole in the ground down through an underground cavern with a cool freshwater spring, the only one in the area. About a 1½ hour walk from the *kampung* there's a rock in a cave which has a gold color and is thought to disappear and reappear (tidal?). Other caves in the vicinity as well. It's a two hour walk to the lighthouse from Wangi Wangi village. There are some splendid lagoons to explore on nearby islands.

the Dutch in Indonesia: *By governing through local leaders, this tiny mercantile seafaring nation on the other side of the world in the cold North Atlantic came to dominate this sprawling archipelago in the Java Sea for over 350 years. The Dutch established the first estate crops and thus the first economic wealth of Indonesia. They used the considerable wealth generated from the Indonesian land to increase agricultural export and trade, and also to support manufacturing development in Holland. They upset the ecological balance by introducing new health schemes so Indonesians lived longer. Population growth in Indonesia for 100 years after 1830 was stupendous (growing to 60 million). By bringing to bear their organizational skills, technology, European education, egalitarian ideas, and ideologies, the Dutch finally made themselves superfluous and brought about their own extinction in the area.*

TORAJALAND

A magnificent rugged mountain country 340 km north of Ujung Pandang in South Sulawesi Province. The hotsprings in this region are said to have wonderous curative effects. Stay away from Torajaland during vacation time in Europe, July and August. It really gets flooded out with sometimes 400-500 French tourists, not travelers, overrunning Rantepao just long enough to buy up all the woodcarvings and other handicrafts. Little groups of kids even sing 'Aleuette' to you in perfect chorus for a handout. See rented jeeps loaded down with tourists careen around the peaceful countryside. Pacto and the 12 Objectives have arrived. Dec. is the next busiest time. **climate:** A delightful, cool highland climate. The dry season is April-November, though it rains sporadically; could start out cloudy, then it clears during the day. The wet season is Dec. - March.

getting there: Bad roads and the absence of an airport preserve this area from the fate that overtook Bali. By bus (Liman, Express, Jl. Paiya 25, Ujung Pandang), it's Rp1500 from Ujung Pandang, a 10-12 hour ride. The road leads from the southern plain northward over fantastically shaped limestone mountains, fertile valleys, lush vegetation, high peaks and terraces to Rantepao, then down again like a corkscrew to Palopo on the east coast. Ir Torajaland use either Makale (fewer tourists) or Rantepao as your base.

THE TORAJAS

Population 320,000. These proto-Malayan peoples came originally from Indochina. Legend says that their ancestors arrived in a storm from the western seas, pulled their splintered boats ashore, and used them as roofs. Today their houses are shaped like ships and they're all facing north in the direction of their origin. Steps leading up to the front porch are remnants of ships' ladders. Before the Dutch came in 1905, the Torajas were one of the fiercest and most remote people in all of Indonesia. Their skill in using spears was uncanny, able to pin small animals and birds at 15 m and impale a man at 30 m. They once lived in small walled fortress villages on top of hills, resembling European medieval castles (see some 400 year old remains at Pangala' and at Pontiko). There was much suspicion within Torajan communities between each of its members. Villagers who were suspected of witchcraft or sorcery were tried by a cultic ordeal. Their fingers were forced into burning pitch: if the hand burned, they were found guilty and were sold to other villagers for beheading. Only women and transvestites could become witchdoctors. When the Dutch moved them down into the valleys and introduced taxes, diseases, agriculture, and Christianity, the old family structure started to break down. Although buffaloes have now replaced human heads at sacrifices and the old religion has been much watered down from the original, very strong *adat* continues to be practiced in Torajaland. There still exist 3 classes of Torajas. *Tokapua* are the noblemen. They generally have longer hair, wear special turbans and loincloths, and employ servants. Although only about 5% of the population, the *Tokapua* own most of the land. The *Tomokaka* are the middle class tradesmen, 25% of the Torajas. Then there are the common people, the *Tobuda*, who are farmers and sharecroppers, about 7 out of every 10 Torajas.

religion: The old religion is called *Aluk Todolo* whose followers still make up about 50% of the population. Another 45% of Torajas are Christian (35% Protestant and 10% Catholic). Muslims make up the remaining 5% of the total. In the early 1900's when the Dutch prohibited headhunting (for pacification purposes) and the ceremony of cleansing the bones (for sanitation purposes), the whole religious structure of the Torajas came toppling down. Whereas missionaries before had been entirely unsuccessful, they were then able to immediately acquire large numbers of converts. Now every Sunday thunderous, moving choral singing (somewhat like Maori-singing) resounds from the wooden churches of Tilanga, Lemo and Rantepao. But the older people still believe most strongly in the ceremonies of the ancestors and strong animist rites are even carried over into Christian burials, a real mixture of the two religions. Sacrifices (rambu) are carried out in honor of the gods, *Tuka* is performed for housewarming and harvest ceremonies, also the *Maro* ritual is still practiced in order to erase evil spells. The hereafter, called *Puya*, is where everyone will live under the same conditions as he or she did on earth. This is why every Torajan tries to get wealthy. Souls of animals will follow their masters into heaven, thus the animal sacrifices. They *live* for death.

funerals: Torajaland is famous for two things, its great natural beauty and its funerals. Though rain buckets down every afternoon at around 4 pm, Aug., Sept. and Oct. are the best months for funerals in Torajaland; you can practically go out everyday to see one. A family's wealth is accumulated for a lifetime, then most of it is spent on staging the finest, most elaborate funeral they can afford, a strange blending of solemnity and celebration. A man's worth and prestige is in fact determined by how many buffaloes are slaughtered at his final burial, often taking place years after his 'first' burial. For there are two funerals held when a person dies, one immediately after death and the other at a later date when all the right offerings can be made and all the relatives can be assembled. After the initial burial, the putrefied bones are dug

up and cleansed for their spiritual life. Until this second funeral, the spirit of the deceased is considered very dangerous. In olden times, required offerings for the final burial were freshly severed human heads. After the funeral the heads were hung in the *rumah adat* and in the houses of the closest kin. You can still find old heads in some houses. Funerals are held in special ceremonial fields (rante) where tall circular stones stand. Many villages have *rante*, but especially good ones are in Lo'ko'mata, Bori, and at Sullukang. Buildings are constructed around this field especially for the funeral and burned afterwards. Here is where the sacrifices take place. Today buffaloes and pigs are slaughtered. It's the little boys privilege to catch the arterial blood from neck, and they get covered in it. Spotted buffaloes are the most prized for sacrifices; they could cost up to Rp350,000. The 2nd day of a funeral is the most interesting because all the relatives of the dead arrive, bearing gifts. If it's a *raja*, sometimes as many as 10,000 people attend the funeral and as many as 200 buffaloes are sacrificed. There are numerous ways to bury the final remains. Hanging Graves (erong) are wood-carved coffins supported on scaffolding high on cliffs or in caves. The best are at Tambolang, Alla, Kete', Mengkepe and Pala'tokke. Another form of burial is the *liang*, sunken holes high up in cliffs, which take up to 3 years to carve out of the cliffside with iron poles. *Liang* are the ideal grave because they are safe from thieves (as sometimes gold and money are buried with the wealthy) and wild animals. Every corpse buried in the cliff face has its 'double' on a rock or wooden gallery on the outside. These statues (tautau) show the sex of the deceased but usually not their likeness. Best places to see *tau-tau* are Kete', Pana, Lo'ko'mata, Lemo, Londa, and Sullukang. *Kaburan*, another kind of grave (found in Salu) look almost like a Mayan structure, a white top with a window into which you put the coffin.

Feast of the Dead: A happy festive occasion. The corpse is kept company by professional mourners so it won't become lonely during the orgiastic feasting and buffalo sacrifices. There are kick fights, buffalo duels, and dancing and singing while carrying the *prahu*-shaped coffin. Athletic pall bearers throw the tightly rolled body bundle over their shoulders and climb up an almost vertical pole of bamboo notched with toe holes. Every face looks up, then the body is stuffed inside the cliff *liang*.

conduct: When attending a funeral give food, cigarettes, perfume, soap, etc., for this means that you share in their grief. When you go to ceremonies, don't sit in any areas that have been prepared or roped off for other guests unless invited to do so. Guys should wear shirts and pants; women full tops with sleeves or long dresses. Longish shorts and *sarungs* are also acceptable. Don't take a guide along because the Torajas are put more at ease if you are alone; guides tend to tell too many tall stories.

dance: In Pana, tourists are asked to join in circle-dances, and local dances are even held in the Rantepao marketplace. Dances are mostly cere-monial, the *Ma'gellu* (or *Pa'gellu*) being perhaps the most serene. Three to five or more teenage girls wearing beaded costumes stretch out slender arms and flutter fingers while advancing and retreating towards the audience. In the *Manganda* perform-ance a group of men wear gigantic headdresses of silver coins, bulls' horns and black velvet, accom-panied by a bell and the voice of the leader. These headdresses are so heavy that the dance lasts only a few minutes. The *Maro* Dance rite is held when a sick person must be purified. There are harvest ceremonies, the *Manimbong* and *Ma'bugi*. The *Pa'daobulan* is danced by a group of teenagers wearing long white dress. The *Mabua* is a major ceremony taking place at 12 year intervals, a dance spiritually and ecologically invaluable to the

A Torajan funeral. The deceased raja is pictured in the background.

Torajas. Months of work are involved getting ready for this night long ritual, i.e. preparing a ceremonial field, costumes, and miniature implements of every-day life. There are stately female singers, festival poles, war yells, and bonfires of exploding bamboo stalks. Priests wearing water buffalo headdresses rush about a sacred tree. It concludes with a mock copulation with a buffalo. **music:** The bamboo flute is the favorite Torajan instrument, played at funerals and harvests, and also out of sheer joy. Schoolboys and girls play lively foot-tapping flute music. Hear flutes at their best in the Pa'bas (in Pana) performance, a mild sort of Incan sound. There are short transverse flutes as well as long ones, all decorated in the old style with poker work, beautifully engraved and colored. Sometimes re-sonating cones made out of buffalo horn are also used. Other instruments are fashioned from palm leaves and there are also Torajan jaw's harps. Though their singing is monotonous and restricted to just a few notes, songs include chants, poetic love songs, mourners' songs, etc. The singer is fre-quently accompanied by one-stringed lutes played with a bow. **games:** *Sisemba* kick fights are seen from late June to early Aug., a terrifying recrea-tional sport when old and young men fly into the air, sometimes knocking each other unconscious. *Takro* is a ball game using a rattan ball which is kicked and bounced (with only the head) over a bamboo stick about 1 m high and fixed parallel to the ground. Played something like volleyball, but with only 2 or 3 players.

crafts: Torajan crafts are very similar to Dayak art of Borneo, mostly two dimensional and not very dynamic, yet some crafts make striking wall hang-ings. Toraja is very much a bamboo culture: roofs, water carriers, cooking vessels, engraved and deco-rated cases used for carrying small objects. Lime cases and bamboo flutes are covered with intricate black designs burnt in with a hot iron. If you go out to the villages themselves (such as Kete' Kesu), buy flutes for Rp 25, bamboo necklaces for Rp125, and carved murals for Rp4-600. In the interiors expert pottery is made. Mesolithic bark-clothing (*tapa* or *fuyus*) of the Celebes-Moluccas areas reached a finesse unknown anywhere else in the world and were worn until quite recent times. Made out of inner barks, the bast was soaked in water up to 2 weeks, then beaten until soft and flexibile. Small pieces were felted into large ones, eliminating the need for seams. You can still find old examples in the hinterlands.

fabrics: Sa'dan is the weaving center. All the de-signs seen in Torajan houses are also seen in their fabrics. Human figures are so cleverly interwoven into strict geometrical patterns that only an expert can pick out the figures from the lines. Much Tora-jan weaving is very similar to the weaving of Latin America (Guatemala), in the texture of the cloth and in the designs and even the colors: red, white, yellow and black. Some beautiful *sarungs*. Reddish *ikat*-weaving with black and blue patterns is found. Expensive oganically dyed *ikat*-blankets take up to 3 months to make; the best come from Makki, Rongkong and Seko, Rp20-30,000. Those found in the shops of Rantepao are artificially dyed and cost Rp7000, Rp8000, and Rp9000. Artificially dyed ones in the villages are cheaper at Rp2000, Rp3000, and Rp4000.

architecture: Torajas are known for their re-markable dwellings, quite similar to the Batak build-ings of North Sumatra. These houses, richly carved and painted, have sweeping roofs like huge slope-prowed vessels riding in a sea of tropical foilage. In some villages where the houses and granaries stand in rows it feels like you're in the middle of a fleet of ships floating on the wind. The buffalo is the symbol of fertility, strength and protection from evil, so the gables of Torajan houses are often deco-rated with buffalo horns. Family status is shown by the number of horns at the entrance of the house. Geometrical patterns on structures are in black, red and white and are so perfect and symmetrical that they seem to have been precisely measured (they weren't). All designs come out evenly no matter how large or small the surface covered. Designs on the houses all represent some aspect of the festivals of *Aluk Todolo*. Only certain people are allowed to place certain designs on their houses. Pushed on rails, these dwellings can be moved from place to place. At the village of Marante, Palawa', Nanggala, see some impressive *adat* houses (but greedy kids are a nuisance). In each village seek out the *Tongkonan* house which is the focus of religious activity, usually richly ornamented and built solely by the tongue and groove construction. At the completion of each new dwelling there's an elaborate housewarming feast of buffalo meat and pork to which the whole village is invited, a joyful time when women dance with scarves. Now only 5% of the people actually live in the trad houses and, like a model wild west town for a movie set, Pacto Tours has begun constructing them especially for the tourist trade.

souvenirs: The only souvenir shops are in Rantepao and in Makale. Crafts are more expensive in the tourist season, July and August. Torajan woodcarving ability is legendary; good pieces (and other handicrafts) are found at Mambuliling. See ironsmiths make knives with traditional tools at La'bo near Bulukan. Find gold necklaces with quartz-like beads, *pao;* some cost up to Rp90,000. Hats are sold in the leprosy village near Rantepao, Rp750, or Rp4000 for the very fine ones. Go to Tonga village for inexpensive bamboo and wood crafts. Ba'tan for *tuak* and eel containers. Pana for model Torajan houses and ships, Rp3-3500 (in the souvenir shops in Rantepao they ask Rp7000). Last minute souvenir

shopping at Ujung Pandang airport. **markets:** Markets take place at Sangalla, Mengkendek, Rembon, Sa'dan and Buntao on different days of the week. Market day in Makale and Rantepao is every 6 days when country people with their goods and wears stream in and out of town all day long. Buy basketware (nase), Rp3-400; flat sifting baskets of attractive woven colors, Rp125; clay water pots, Rp100; work and dress hats, Rp1500 -4000.

food: Great coffee is grown in this region, especially around Pangala'. Special Torajan food, *pa'piong,* is anything cooked in bamboo sections like rice in coconut milk, or meat and vegetables in buffalo or pigs' blood. Fish and vegetables are also very popular. A typical Torajan breakfast is *songkolo.* Made up of sticky rice, *lombok* (chili) and coconut, it usually sells for Rp75 a package. Also try the sweet snack *baje,* fried coconut with brown sugar. *Balok* (Torajan for *tuak* or palm wine) is often drunk at Torajan ceremonies. Transported in long bamboo stalks, *balok* is drunk all day long out in the *padi* instead of water. A mild mellow booze, the same milky color as Mexican *pulque,* you feel more stoned than drunk. There are 3 varieties: the sweet, medium sweet, and the sour. The more sour variety is always redder; it has had more coconut skin added. For the real *balok,* go to eastern Toraja to the Batualu and Rantebua areas; all these little villages sell it for Rp500 for a whole bamboo pipe full.

trekking: Since the roads in Torajaland are so bone-jarring in vehicles, walking is more suitable, and because of the mud and rocks, you'll need good footwear to hike. It's always a good idea to take

Rantepao market

water with you. Carry a flashlight in case you get caught walking at night-time. If you're going into the mountains, take salt, sugar, and betelnut to the villages as a friendly offering. One of the best items to take out to distant *kampungs* on the long walks is medicine — for them and you — especially antibiotics for carbunkles and skin infections. Hire guides in Rantepao; for two guides perhaps Rp500 per day plus you pay for their food en route. If alone, there are always people around to ask the way. This is provided you speak Indonesian, otherwise it's definitely a handicap. There are coffee and tea stands in most villages where you can get refreshments after walking. Spend the night in the *Tongkonan* house virtually anywhere in Torajaland. Or ask the *kepala kampung* about accommodation. Give the lady of the house Rp4-600 per day for food. Although some *kampungs* will on occasion slaughter a chicken for you, don't expect much more than brown rice straight from the *padi* and vegetables such as *sayur labuk* (pumpkin) and cucumber.

RANTEPAO

A focal point for tourists visiting Torajan villages and sites, right in the center of their traditional territory. The police will come around personally to your hotel room and collect the 'tourist tax' of Rp1000; institutionalized rotteness. Cash money in Bank Rakyat opposite the post office. It only takes a couple of days to get to know your way around this small town. See western and Indonesian films at the Apollo Bioskop, Rp200. There are tailors opposite the Apollo cinema who'll make up anything for you, traditional designs or otherwise. Magic mushrooms (blue meanies) are around the outskirts of Rantepao; got to look for them.

stay: A nice clean place is Wisma Pola by the soccerfield, Rp500, and they have rooms to accommodate four. Losmen Flora, behind a brilliant flowering tree, is also Rp500; clean, opposite the mosque yet quiet. Losmen Peng. Harapan is opposite Restaurant Rachmat, above a souvenir shop, Rp500; clean and as central as you can get but the clanging ironsmith will drive you batty. Wisma Maria (speak to Roy, he's quite informed) is the most expensive hotel in town, but very comfortable. Losmen Palawa, Rp600-1000, has nice rooms with toilets. Peng. Ria, Jl. Mapanuki 18, is Rp500; dark and out-of-the-way, but the wood is gorgeous. Wisma Rosa, Rp1500 with a *mandi* in each room, is on the edge of town on a country road with village people going by 25 m in front of your porch all day long.

eat: Restaurant Segar is cheap; eat excellently for Rp250-300. It's right next to the Pentecostal church ·

(beautiful singing on Sundays!). Restaurant Rachmat has a menu in 5 languages including Japanese; you're not the first. Good food, but on the expensive side. Misiliana Restaurant Art Shop (and a *losmen* upstairs) has good food as well, about the same prices as Rachmat. The 3 *warungs* opposite Misiliana are much cheaper; *soto ayam*, Rp75; *nasi telur* and *campur*, Rp100, etc. Try special Torajan food in the *warungs* in the marketplace: steamed rice, buffalo meat, pig fat, vegetables, chilies, *tuak*. Ne Pande is open everyday but has a bigger selection on market day. Try *bale* and *lada* (fish and chilies). Visit the dog market. At nights go to the *tuak* places near the Apollo Theatre; jamming every evening with young guitarists and tourists.

transport: Jeeps rent for Rp12,000-15,000 per day. Between 6-7 people it works out cheaper; see Restaurant Rachmat. For motorbikes, go to Ajui Chinese store or Studio Foto Hibar behind Ajui's Rp2500-3000 for a 90 cc or Rp3500-4000 for a 100 cc per day. The most economical is to rent an old bus, the same ones that you see go all over the countryside, for Rp10,000 the whole day (6 am-5 pm); cheaper than taxis and you can fit comfortably up to 20 people in one. A chartered minibus also costs Rp10,000 per day. Have an Indonesian do the bargaining. Toko Abadi rents bicycle for Rp500 per day.

from Rantepao: Starting at 9 am buses leave all day long heading over the mountain to the harbor town of Palopo, Rp500 (but Rp600 coming back because you ascend). Buses and vans leave all the time up to 9 pm for Makale, 17 km to the south, Rp100. You can get to the northern towns of Palawa, Pangli and Sa'dan easier on Rantepao's market day; Rp150 by jeeps and old trucks which leave constantly to these northern villages, returning each hour until nightfall. For Ujung Pandang take Liman Express, Rp1500, 10 hours; their office is in the northern end of town. **to Enrekang:** A twisting road leads from Rantepao deep into the mountains high above the valleys, a panavision technicolor trip passing craggy limestone ridges honeycombed with caves. In some places streams are half a mile below the road, other spots they roll along together. See young girls playing flutes while walking along the roadsides. Try *baje kotu* (coconut candy) at Kotu on the way.

VICINITY OF RANTEPAO

It's no sense buying the Rp1000 all-inclusive ticket at Wisma Maria to get into the approximately 8 tourist sites around Rantepao because often there won't be anyone at the entrance gates to collect your tickets. Many sites are reachable by just one or two hour walks from Rantepao but these are super-touristy and often thronged with kids asking for money and candy ('minta uang, kasih gula'). As a rule children of Torajaland are very relaxed (and talkative) except for those in these tourist villages near Rantepao. It's a real drag in places like Palawa' and Marante, and grownups just egg them on. At some sites you could be asked to sign a visitor's book and to give a donation of Rp100-250. Given are the directions, various sites, and distances from Rantepao.

SOUTHEAST

Bokin: A nice view from here covering the whole southeast portion of Torajaland. Few tourists.

Buntao: 15 km. Old graves and *tau tau*. A Beautiful approach from Paniki. *Bemos* go here, but infrequently.

Kete' Kesu: 4 km. A characteristic Torajan village where many artifacts are for sale; outstanding wooden and bamboo carvings. See the *kepala desa's* house. 100 m behind the village are scattered skulls and bones over old rotted hardwood coffins with dragon motifs on them.

Lemo: 12 km. More dramatic than Londa and one of the easiest to get to. On the way to Lemo on the left-hand side there's a church to visit on Sunday morning; exuberant singing. Join in or just sit outside and listen. The best *tau tau* are to be seen at Lemo; 60 statues and 30 funerary niches carved into solid rock. Standing like spectators on balconies outside deep pockets where the dead are buried, the wide-eyed doubles lean on the railings. These realistic puppets are protected by thick paint. Climb the crag at the side until almost level with the staring bright eyes, their bodies clothed in vivid checks and bandana colors. Their clothing, worn by sun, wind and rain, is changed periodically. Some have traveling sacks for their trip to the Land of Souls.

Londa: 6 km. Old cave graves, a balcony of effigies, heaps of wooden coffins, bones. Little girls with smoking torches or flashlights will lead you through the catacombs.

Pala' tokke: 9 km. A long scenic walk. Two 800 year old hanging graves here and some skulls lying about in an almost Ethiopian setting. Kids playing flutes. The villagers will take you up the cliffs, 20 minutes walk. No charge; could give the guide a ballpoint pen or something.

liang *at Lemo*

Randan Batu: 11 km. Graves, and a knifesmith lives here.

Sangga Langi: 3 km. Houses are built against a cliff; once served as a fortress.

Sullukang: A very old secluded village about 3 km past Kete' Kesu. This amazingly tranquil island *kampung* has menhirs, graves and statues. The statues are seated in a shack overlooking the village; hard to get a good photo. Not often visited.

skulls at Kete' Kesu

Tembamba: 17 km. A mountain pass village 3 km beyond Buntao with old graves and an awesome panorama.

Tilanga: 9 km. A cool fresh clear blue water natural swimming hole. Free entry. On Sundays they sell fruit. Take a *bemo* to the turnoff, then walk 2 km from the highway down the road to Lemo. By the time you get to Tilanga you're ready for it.

SOUTHWEST

Buntupune: 2 km. An old traditional village.

Mandoe: 6 km, right off the main highway. Guesthouse. One km from Mandoe at Alang Alang there's good fishing from the bridge.

Salu: 15 km. There are good places to swim near a bamboo bridge over the river flowing through this village.

Siguntu: A traditional, seldom visited village. Nice rice barns and a great view looking out towards Singki and Rantepao (although you can't actually see Rantepao).

SOUTH

Dulang: 8 km. Old graves, *tau tau* (statues).

Pa'baisenan: 8 km. Graves of children in a large tree. If a child dies before teething, his coffin is hung in a tree.

Singki Hill: In the south part of Rantepao. Turn 100 m after the crossroads and just head for the big rock. A short but precipitous climb. See the whole of Rantepao from the top.

EAST

Marante: 6 km. A very typical Torajan village with graves and old statues.

Nanggala: 15 km. 14 traditional rice barns, the best you'll see. Besides serving the function of storing rice (on the 2nd floor), these buildings are also used for ceremonies. Guests are received on the first floor. They'll ask for a donation.

Tandung: 17 km. A most spectacular area with pine forests, 18 m high bamboo, and a gorgeous lake.

NORTH

Bori: A good *rante* (circle of megaliths) place for funeral ceremonies.

Palawa': 9 km. An old village.

Pangli: 7 km. A stone statue here has the likeness of a dead man, one Pong Massangka, carved on it.

Parinding: 7 km. Old houses. Nice walk to here and back to Rantepao.

Sa'dan: A village and weaving center. Go past the woman in the first house on the right after the bridge. Her prices for cloth are nearly the same as in Rantepao and she'll even try to charge you for *looking* at a loom. Go instead 2 km uphill to Tenun where you can actually see the weavers at work. They'll bring out the real old fabrics, shawls, and family heirlooms. Bargain as if you don't want it (even if you do).

woman weaving in Tenun

WALKS FROM RANTEPAO

A quite unknown short walk: Go down the same road as Losmen Flora 200 m to the river, then you come to a path. See an overgrown, eerie, watery cliff 200 m beyond at the base of which are very old tombs. **roundtrip to Alang Alang:** Cross the bridge south of town on the road to Singki and walk about 4 km to Alang Alang. Cross another bridge and turn north towards Rantepao again, walk 2 km, turn right, visit the Londa burial caves, then return to the main highway and catch a *bemo* Rp50 back to Rantepao.

the Nanggala walk: Head for Palopo by bus, get off at the Nanggala turnoff, Rp100, then walk 1½ km to Nanggala. See the best examples of rice barns here, beautifully preserved. It's a fantastic walk 10 km from Nanggala to Paniki over an arid mountainous area; some jungle and leeches. Constantly ask people along the way how to get to Paniki. This track seldom has visitors and buffaloes bolt at the smell of you. From Paniki, it's a shorter picturesque walk into Buntao. Could catch a *bemo* to Rantepao from Buntao or walk on a cobblestoned road to the highway where you can hitch a ride back. A good hard day's walk. If you continue on to Bokin, more good views.

roundtrip via Pangli and Parinding: Not many hills on this walk. Head north first 9 km to Pangli, then cut in to Bori where you can see the megalith circle. From Bori head through lovely ricefields back to Rantepao by way of Parinding. Go real early on market day so you can walk back to Rantepao with droves of villagers carrying their wares. **Rantepao-Makula' walk:** A level hike of 25 km. From Rantepao walk 1 km south to the Pertamina gas station, then turn east (left) and follow this path 6 km when you'll come to a fork in the road. Turn right here and carry on through Randan Batu. Bathe in the hotsprings at Makula. From Makula take the track heading directly north west to Makale. On the way see the carved figures in a cliff at Suaya. From Makale, take a *bemo* back to Rantepao, Rp100.

LONG DISTANCE HIKES FROM RANTEPAO

Penanian: 14 km. Here there are 200 year old houses with giant sized pillars. **hotsprings:** At Dole, Buntukasisi, Rantekaotoang. **Mt. Mamullu:** 8 km from the highway. See nearly the whole Torajan valley and a 100 m waterfall. **Rura:** In the Bambanpuang Valley; another destroyed palace. **Simbuang Province:** Visit this valley 2½ days walk from Rantepao for really old houses and more authentic sights than in the vicinity of Rantepao. Take a guide, the tracks are quite hard to find. **Nosu Valley:** A 2100 m high valley 4 days walk north from Rantepao. Torajan mountain dwellers, who are into chanting and circle dancing, moved up here 800 years ago (relatively recently). **Batutumonga:** 30 km north of Rantepao. Cross the bridge and turn left. Very rough road to Batutumonga. From the main road it takes 3 hours to reach this high-altitude village on the slopes of Mt. Sesean, but it's definitely worth the exertion. Beautiful view overlooking the whole place. Stay in the guesthouse, Rp200 a night. Eat down in the *warung,* Rp300 a meal. From the village it's a further 2 hour hike to the summit of Mt. Sesean. Get an early start.

Pangala': An area of expert dancers 18 km N.W. of Rantepao. Take the track between Pangala' and Bittuang 40 km, then on to Malale another 40 km. **Pana:** 34 km north of Rantepao. Incredible old burial·caves and stone graves in a bamboo forest here. These quite distinct graves are 350 meters before Pana on the right coming from Rantepao. The coffins are at eye-level. Chanting all night. It's equally as picturesque a hike from Batutumonga to Pana. **Lempo:** 25 km. Between Batutumonga and Deri. 100 sets of buffalo horns are displayed on an

adat house. **Paredean:** 30 km. See all the way to the ocean.

for Mamasa: Up and down hills all the way. There are two appraoches. One is from Pangala', 18 km north of Rantepao. Spend the night here with the *kepala desa*, get up at 5 am and walk 25 km all the next day to Bittuang. The other approach is by *bemo* from Rantepao Rp100 to Makale, then from Makale by jeep Rp500 to Bittuang. Stay with the coffee seller near the market or with the *kepala*

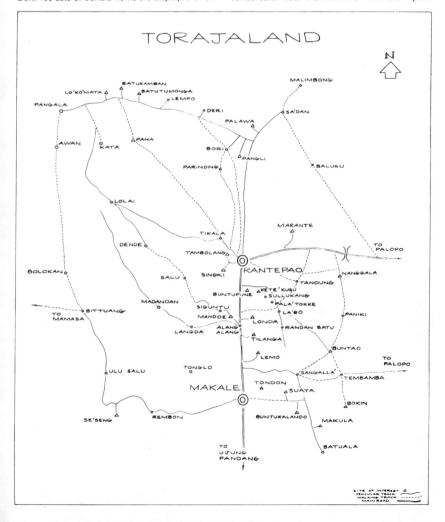

desa (his son's a thief) in Bittuang. From Bittuang to Mamasa it's 58 km, a 2-3 days walk. At the end of the first day stay with the headman at Punding, 18 km from Bittuang. Maybe even make it about 30 km to Timbaan, a tiny settlement and a place to sleep. Then the next day do the remainder to Mamasa. Not many tourists go this way and in Mamasa the army may trouble you for a *surat jalan* which they say you should've gotton in Polewali before starting out for Mamasa. Mamasa is not officially on the tourist trail yet. Try to meet the superior of the one who confronts you, and explain your situation to him.

MAKALE

17 km south of Rantepao. Makale overlooks a lotus lake and there's a good bazaar. Fewer tourists stay here than in Rantepao. Many good day-walks in the vicinity and the *bemo* and bus connections for Torajaland and to the south are frequent. **stay:** Losmen Merry is like a freak's Waldorf Astoria; very nice lounge, big canopy beds, Rp500. Wisma Hasanudin, Jl. Pong Tiku, charges Rp1500-2000. Wisma Maria, Jl. Ratulangi, is quite popular; Rp2000. **walks from Makale:** Walk up the highway 4 km north of Makale, turn east to Sangalla' and walk 8 km where you'll find the turn south to Makula', a natural swimming pool and hotsprings. Spend the night at the resthouse in Makula. On the way back to Makale see the king's house at Buntukalando and the king's grave and statue at Suaya. **Buntukalando:** Near Sangalla'. A king's palace and a big ceremonial field surrounded by bamboo houses. See the 'museum' of royal possessions, and the *Tongkonan* house. Torajan handicrafts are very cheap: handsome handwoven blankets (sedo nandi orrindun lolal) for Rp5000-5500. Each piece has a religious significance. Also bamboo and woodcarvings. **Tondon:** From this village it's an easy walk to the Gua Erong graves. **Kandora:** 5 km. An old palace on top of a mountain. **Banua Puan Marinding:** Another old ruined palace 8 km south of Mengkendek. **Pa'tengko:** 20 km south. Rice terraces and lovely mountain scenery. **for Mamasa:** Walk to Rembon where there's a marketplace and a sweeping panorama, then on to Se'seng for its natural swimming pool. Next hike to Bittuang (a total of 60 km from Makale) where there's a *losmen* to rest up in before continuing on to Mamasa, a 2-3 day walk from Bittuang. Or take the jeep, Rp500, that leaves daily or every other day from Makale to Bittuang.

MAMASA

The West Torajan culture of Mamasa district is considerably less exploited than the cultures found around Rantepao. The road to Mamasa is pure hell.

This is why Mamasa is the way it is, a quiet little town high in the mountains, cold when the evening mist sets in. Immaculately clean, even the market. Bring cash, there are no banks. See Ray Pwatapana, a regency officer, who really knows the area well. **vicinity of Mamasa:** Walk to Orbua, 6 km, for 200 year old *adat* houses. No corrugated iron here, the old ways still exist. Visit Rambu Seratu hot medicinal springs on the Toliwali Road, a pretty walk.

getting there: Pare Pare is Rp1150 by bus from Ujung Pandang. From Pare Pare take bus to Polewali, Rp600. Or take a bus direct from Ujung Pandang to Polewali for Rp1450. Stay overnight in Polewali at Peng. Polmas, Rp250, or with the *kepala desa.* No matter where you stay, always take your valuables with you, even when you go to the *mandi.* The police chief might come around personally to check your passport. The next day, if you're lucky, there will be a jeep up to Mamasa. If not, may have to wait around for a couple of days. The driver may try to overcharge you up to Rp2500, but knock him down to Rp1500. Afterall, it's only 70 km. Jeeps sometimes break down on the way, then you must walk in.

stay and eat: Peng. Pasangrahan is Rp250. Wisma Mamasa is on top of a hill; only Rp250 including coffee, wicker chairs and a patio. You usually have the place all to yourself under a mountain. Eat *nasi antur* (green beans, buffalo meat, and rice) in the town restaurant near the police station for Rp300; delicious. Or eat *nasi padang* food in the market *warungs*, Rp175 for a big meal. Avoid the other restaurants.

crafts: *Sambu* blankets are produced around Mamasa; they cost Rp7000 (Rp13,000 in Rantepao). Some of these 8 m long cloths take 7 years to complete on a loom consisting of just sticks stuck in the ground. Several west Torajan clans use a bronze-casting tecnhique called the lost wax process (cire perdue) which originated in southwest Europe in the 8th and 9th Centuries, then traveled through Central Asia and China by way of the Dongson Culture. Copper work is done by only a few specialized groups living in the north who make small human and animal figures, pendants, balls, coiled ornaments (sanggori), jewelry and bracelets. Deep in the interior tribespeople still produce pottery by means of a neolithic beating-technique.

from Mamasa: If you have a lot of gear hire horses in Mamasa for Rp2000 a day (they ask at first Rp8000 a day). To Makale there's a long 5 day walk, and a shorter one of 3 days. Be sure to get info first either from the people at Wisma Mamasa or at the *warungs* in the market. To Bittuang (where there are river crocodiles), it's a 70 km 3 day walk. From Mamasa the first 20 km is uphill, then about 16 km down, then up about 3 km to Punding. From Punding it's a gradual climb for 10 km, a steep climb 3 km, then descend down to Bittuang for 6 km. On this difficult winding trail you pass through a splendid country of waterfalls and mountain scenery. During the wet you have to get up and start walking early before the afternoon rains. Wear boots, not rubber sandals. From Bittuang, it's possible to take a jeep Rp500 down to Makale leaving approximately 2 pm each day or every other day. Sometimes the bridge is down on the way. **for Polewali:** Travel 12 hours downhill not on a road but on a dry riverbed full of boulders: literally get sores on your ass. The jeep may spend the night in a *kampung* along the way.

GALUMPANG AND RONGKONG

Visit the aboriginal Toala people in the mountains east of Galumpang, a one week walk from Rantepao through the jungles. A superstitious people who wear unique clothing, the Toalas are also found around the Poso area but are more unpredictable. In the tranquil village of Makki, Rong-

kong and Seko north of Palanga' live the modern Toala. **getting there:** One way to reach them is by bus first to Palopo then on to Sabang by car for Rp300 (Rp500 if you have many supplies). Walk from Sabang to Rongkong in 1 ½ days, from Rongkong to Seko in another 3 days, then from Seko to Galumpang a further 2 days. Another way is to follow the river to Galumpang, on to Makki and Seko, then circle back to Rongkong and Sabang. Notice what the monkies eat, that's what you should eat. **crafts:** Rongkong and Galumpang are centers for the woven arts, each town representing different styles. These cloths-of-the-dead are wrapped around corpses, a dowry for a bride must contain at least one piece, and they could also be used as part-payment for a murder.

from Galumpang: To Rantepao it's a 6 day walk on a difficult track with only huts to stay in, no *kampungs*. Lots of mud and mountains, big rivers, snakes, wild orchids, and huge salamandar-like lizards. You have to bring food and supplies with you. There's an alternative mountain trek from Galumpang to Tamlea from where you can take a river-boat down to Mamuju. Then trek from Mamuju to Mamasa. This will take you in all about 4 weeks. Slippery, muddy and hot, a tortuous but beautiful walk.

on the road from Rantepao to Palopo

PALOPO

Rp500 from Rantepao by bus. On this 62 km road pass over a mountain pine forest. During the rains there could be more than 20 landslides blocking

your way. Stay in the *pasangrahan* at Battang which overlooks the deep gorge down to the plain on which Palopo is located; Rp400 per night. Exotic butterflies in Battang sell for Rp150-1000. Good meals in Warung Puncak, Rp150. Look for brown sugar candy. Palopo is Muslim, another 'Hellow mister!' town. The streets are filled with *becaks* with the drivers sleeping in them, and at midday a cop dozes on the porch of the police station. The view from the end of the 2 km long pier is stupendous. **stay and eat:** A cheap town to stay in with good seafood. Losmen Marlia, Jl. Kartini, is a fun place; Rp300 without a window, Rp350 with a window. There are many *losmens* such as Peng. Muncul (Rp350), Peng. Lima (Rp350), and Rismaria (Rp350). Rumah Makan Bambooden, Jl. Kartini, has alright food. A cozier place is right opposite it at Chinese-run Kios Mini Indah; try the *sate* and *es buah.* **vicinity of Palopo:** Climb G. Balandai, 5 km from town, a one hour's walk. Songka Beach is 5 km or Rp200 by *becak.* Plywood Beach is 11 km from Palopo or Rp100 by *bemo.*

from Palopo by boat: There are two shipping companies in Palopo, P.T. Ramanyaga, Jl. Pelita 1; and P.M. Aman Jaya, close to the harbor. They each have boats leaving for Malili nightly, Rp1100-1250 deck class. Passenger cabins cost extra Rp500-1000. Sometimes it's a very rough trip. There are also boats to Kolaka from where you can go overland to Kendari. **by bus:** Take a bus to Wotu, Rp750, then do the walk up to Tomini Bay. Catch Liman or Damri Express from Palopo, to: Ujung Pandang, Rp1650, leaving daily at 7 am; Sengkang, Rp1250; Pare Pare, Rp1500. The Rante-

pao buses leave from out of town a bit but you can easily walk to the depot. The charge to Rantepao is Rp600 because it's a high climb. Most buses for Rantepao leave in the morning, the last bus leaves at around 6 pm.

to the Bay of Tomini and beyond: Take the bus from Palopo Rp600 to Masamba. Then walk from Masamba to Lake Poso in 3 days through a mountain pass and forest; quite easy, goes slowly up and slowly down. You might get a lift on trucks with roadbuilders. From the south end of Lake Poso to the north end of the lake, it's Rp500 by boat. From Tentena, on top of the lake, to Poso it's Rp750 by minibus. From Poso to Parigi, 7 hours by boat, Rp2000, leaving every 2-3 days. From Parigi to to Palu, take a bus Rp1500. From Palu to Donggala, Rp200-250 by minibus. From Donggala get a *kapal motor* over to East Kalimantan or by ship down to Ujung Pandang or to Pare Pare. From Poso to Manado there are boats for Rp13,000, but not that regular. You might have to take up to 3 different boats to reach Manado. Or catch a boat just over to Gorontalo, then go overland and by coaster up the west coast of the northern peninsula to Manado, or take a boat or ship from Poso up to Bitung on the east coast of Sulawesi Utara, then by van across the peninsula to Manado, Rp300.

THE MOLUCCAS

INTRODUCTION

First discovered and most famous of all Indonesian islands, today the Moluccas are the most undiscovered and least developed. These islands were the original 'Spice Islands' of Dutch Colonial history. Their fabulous wealth changed the power balance of the world. This 25th Province of Indonesia stretches over an area 50% greater than Kalimantan, yet all its islands, large and small, make up less than 4% of the total land area of Indonesia. Maluku is a transition zone between Asian and Australian flora and fauna as well as between the human cultures of the Indonesian archipelago and those of Melanesian and New Guinea. Only about 1.2 million people live here, many of them skilled seafarers. Animists live in the interiors. The skindiving from Ambon up to Ternate is unbelievable.

Bring your own snorkle and fins. **transport:** There are only about 1600 km of roads with less than 160 km paved. In the outer island areas, expect to walk. Although it's more expensive than Java and Bali to travel through these eastern islands you'll often be offered a place to stay with a family (Indecost) for much less.

the land: Maluku's approximately 1000 islands are surrounded by coral reefs and deep seas which only add to their geographical remoteness. The islands vary in size from tiny atolls, the tops of submerged volcanoes, up to Halmahera, Buru and Ceram, each over 4000 sq km. The best known, Ternate, Tidore, Banda and Ambon, range from 40-480 sq km respectively. Wild rugged mountainous

interiors are found on most islands with tropical jungles, evergreen forests, active volcanoes. Lying right in the middle of the 'Ring of Fire', Maluku is a volatile territory geophysically with 70 eruptions in the last 400 years. All the spices which first made these islands famous are still major crops: cloves, nutmeg, cocoa, and coffee. Rice cultivation is found on Ceram. The sago palm provides not only food, but its fronds are also used to thatch huts while the leaf midrib is used to build walls and ceilings. In some villages a festival is held each year to celebrate the end of a good sago harvest. In Maluku are some of the richest fishing grounds in Indonesia, especially for shrimp and tuna; its surrounding oceans are being criminally farmed by the Japanese. **climate:** The wet season everywhere else in Indonesia is Oct.-April. But in Maluku the wet season is April through to July. The sea is too rough during this time for small boats. The best season to visit is Sept.-Mar. when the seas are calm and inter-island shipping is more frequent. This is also the fishing season, which means good eats.

flora and fauna: Many endemic species of animals and plants are found here. In the 17th Century G.E. Rumph wrote his great book on the native flora of Maluku. In the 19th Century A.R. Wallace developed his theory of evolution here, which later greatly influenced Darwin's work. The wildlife, especially the birds, begin to show more affinity to New Guinea species. There are many kinds of honeyeaters, cockatoos, the famous racket-tailed kingfisher, the giant red-crested Moluccan cockatoo, and even one species of the Bird of Paradise. The region is well known for its parikeets and other vividly-colored birds such as black-capped, purple, red, and green lories. On Ceram, there are dazzling white fruit pigeons. In all of these eastern islands people keep lorikeets and King Parrots as pets. See them on front porches, in houses, *warungs,* everywhere. The Aru Islands have marsupials.

history: Nutmegs and cloves have brought trade to these islands since at least 300 B.C. They were definitely known by Chinese, Indians and Arabs long before the Portugese 'discovered' them in 1498. The Moluccas were always treated as satellites by various Javanese Kingdoms and port cities on the north Java coast: the 13th Century Singosari dynasty prospered hugely on the spice trade with the Moluccas. From the 14th Century the islands were dominated by Muslim sultans on Ternate. It was these 'East Indies' islands Columbus meant to find when he accidently and unknowingly discovered the Americas in 1492, calling the inhabitants 'Indians'. In the 16th Century the Portugese navigator Albuquerque captured a Javanese pilot who owned an outstanding map of all the smaller islands north of Java. By 1512 the Portugese were in the

Moluccas in force and converted the inhabitants to Catholicism. Magellan's crews arrived here mad with joy in 1521, the land they had sought for 27 months. Beginning in the 17th Century the Dutch tried to create a world monopoly of the valuable nutmeg, cinnamon, mace and clove trade in this region and imposed a system of forced cultivation in Maluku which remained for hundreds of years. To drive out the British and to achieve a monopoly the Dutch Governor General Coen decided on armed conquest of Ambon, Ternate, and the Banda Islands. Monopoly was achieved purely through ruthlessness and forced subjugation. Production was reduced to keep profits high and all the islanders were made to buy foodstuffs from the Company. Finally the British and French smuggled out specimens and succeeded in planting clove and nutmeg trees in their colonies in India and Africa, breaking the back of the monopoly. Gradually the spice trade began to decline in importance and by the end of the 18th Century the Moluccas had become an economic backwater. Ambon, Ternate and the Bandas were opened up to foreign shipping in 1854, but it wasn't until 1863 when a liberal constitution was brought in Holland when forced cultivation at last ceased and all monopolies were terminated.

dance and music: Maluku has a rich traditional music, and many popular Indonesian folk songs originated here. The special type of *gamelan* played here is called *totebuang.* Bamboo flutes are played unceasingly by schoolkids. In the *Gaba-Gaba* Dance (or the *Bamboo Gila* Dance), 4 bamboo poles placed crosswise are clicked together. Dancers step between and around the bamboo poles without ever getting their feet caught while the tempo gradually speeds up. Also performed is the slow and hypnotic Handkerchief Dance.

eat: The main diet is a meal extracted from the heart of the sago palm, a plant which grows wild. Sago bread comes in the form of a giant waffle. A unique native dish of this region is *papeta,* made by first pulverizing and straining the pulp from the trunk of the sago palm. This 'flour' is boiled up to form a viscous jelly-like tasteless mass to be eaten hot. *Papeta* has the consistency of, and even looks like, wallpaper paste. If you don't swallow it straightaway you think you're drowning. Thankfully, *papeta* is often served with fish curry soup which somewhat improves the taste. There are many varieties of bananas of matchless flavor throughout these islands including one tiny species which grows to maturity in only 7 months (pisang tuju bulon), up to the gargantuan (½ m long) *pisang raja* which Amboinese women are not permitted to eat because it is thought that it will wreck their marriage.

CENTRAL MOLUCCAS

(MALUKU TENGAH)

getting there: Garuda flies from Surabaya to Ambon via Ujung Pandang everyday, Rp50,000. Merpati propjets do this same flight twice a week for Rp40,000. Mandala also does a weekly flight from Surabaya for Rp40,000. From Manado, North Celebes, fly first to Ternate with Bouraq (Rp 12,500), then with Merpati to Ambon (Rp17,000) Other alternatives: take a Pelni boat or tramp freighter from Jakarta or Surabaya to Ambon; or board a ship from Bitung, North Celebes, to Ternate, Rp7-8000.

AMBON ISLAND

Celebrations commemorating the founding of this city (in 1575) take place each September 17th. Once the most colonized part of Indonesia, Dutch is still spoken here as a 2nd and in some cases even as a first language by many families. An individualistic and proud people, the Amboinese are wont to speak their minds. The local name for Ambon Island is Nusa Yapoono which means Pulau Embon. *Embun* means 'cloud' in Indonesian; the island is most always enclosed by fog and mist. A very striking people, the Amboinese have mixed with Portugese, Malayans, Javanese, and the Dutch, creating a sort of creole Moluccan culture.

the land: The island is divided in 2 parts: Hitu is the northern peninsula and Leitimor is the southern peninsula. Passo, lying on the isthmus that separates the two peninsulas, is Ambon's capital (though not its largest) city. The soil is rich. People don't plant anything, they just watch it grow. It's green everywhere you turn, whole hills are covered in rhododendrums. Cloves are still big business here. A kilo of harvested cloves brings in about Rp6-7000; some trees yield up to 30 kilos. Javanese buy the harvests at fixed prices and return to Java to make *kretek* cigarettes, then come back to sell them. Clove feuds still occur when a farmer finds a thief in his trees, the tradition being to knife him to death. Visit a plantation. As a rancher would his cattle, the manager will lovingly tell you the exact yield, age and gender of each tree. Once planted, this tree takes 7 years to mature. **climate:** A beautiful but rainy island; a short rainy season of 4 months and a long one of 8 months. Rain falls with great dramatic violence. Oct. and April are unbearably hot.

history: The ancestors of the present inhabitants of Central Moluccan villages migrated from West Ceram or from Makian Island near Ternate no later than the 15th Century. These origins are evident in

the sago palm: *At 15 years and at a height of 6-9 m, a sago produces a single flower-spike. This means it's ready to harvest. Before the flower matures, the trunk is cut down and the pith carved out. If the fruit is allowed to ripen, the starchy core feeds it, leaving the tree trunk a hollow shell. Nowhere can such quantities of bread be had for such little labor. In a day a sago gatherer can hack out enough snowy-white starch to last his family for months. Sago bread or cakes, made from this sago flour, taste like sand in the mouth or hot sawdust, and this food has little nutrition. Sago leaves and branches are treacherously slippery to walk on and are sometimes used as a ruse in combats. At full maturity (60-70 years), the sago palm flowers for the first and the last time with a magnificent widely branching plume at the top. Then the plant dies.*

their myths, folkways and *adat*. Amboinese were first dominated by the Islamic Kingdom of Ternate to the north which forcibly eradicated headhunting, introduced a political rather than a tribal form of social organization, and carried Islam to some villages. Next came the Catholic Portugese, then the Calvinist Dutch Protestants, who each in turn converted the Amboinese to their own faiths. The Dutch also brought to these people misery, ruin, and slavery. To drive prices up they allowed each of the 400 inhabitants of Ambon Island only 125 clove trees. Such was the moral climate of the times that if the growers refused, they were simply killed. In the first 100 years of Dutch rule, ⅓ of Ambon's inhabitants were wiped out. The Amboinese today are really into parades and marches, goosestepping and arms swinging, while crisply calling out cadence. This love of military spectacle is inherited from the Dutch who for centuries used Amboinese soldiers to help them police the archipelago, paying Amboinese mercenaries much higher wages than what other Indonesian soldiers received. Ambon city has been flattened by bombs 3 times since Worth War II. After independence and before republican forces could be sent out to replace the Dutch Colonial Army, the 'Republic of South Moluccas' seceeded from Indonesia. This group gained its greatest support from the Christians of Ambon, who share so little ethnically or spiritually with the Javanese. Resistence was finally crushed by Nov. 1950, although there was sporadic guerila fighting on the neighboring island of Ceram until 1968. The Javanese can't forget that this island once revolted against their Java-centralist government and now the Javanese are sitting on Ambon; the top 6 positions are Javanese-filled. There were only 9 Dutch policemen here before the war, but now it takes thousands of Javanese soldiers to occupy and control the island. The less you say about politics anywhere on Ambon, the better. Very strict security is enforced in these islands which lie so close to Buru Island to the west where, since 1969, thousands of Indonesian communists have been sent to hack a life for themselves out of the jungle.

village life: Most Amboinese live in small villages (negeri) made up of several local patrilineal kingroups (mata rumah) which form the village class system. Each important lineage belongs to a sacred spring, a sacred stone, has an honorific title, and maintains its own cultivated plots (dati) outside the villages. From this native elite are picked the village ruler (called by the pompous title of *raja*) and also the village priest (mauwang) whose function is to ensure plentiful harvests by placating the founding ancestors who first cleared the land. Many central Moluccan villages employ different traditional officers who help govern each village: there are heads of the *soa* (administrative subdistricts), the Lord of the Land (Tuan Tanah), the *adat*-chief, the war leader (*kapitan*, now a purely ceremonial office), the chief of the forest police (kepala kewang), and the village messenger (marinyo).

religion: Since Islam is the state religion, most public offices are filled by Muslims. There are many *hajis* on the island and you constantly hear loudspeaker calls to prayer from the mosques. Or else choruses of Christian singers. Though half the villages are Christian and half are Muslim, they are nearly identical culturally speaking. If you scratch the skin of a Muslim or a Christian, you find *adat*. The old *pela* system found here is a ritual, mythical-based form of truce between villages which were once at war. There are over 50 different kinds of *pela* in force. This strong unwritten system makes it easier for Christians and Muslims to co-exist. Sometimes Christians help their Muslim neighbors build a mosque and Muslims help their Christian neighbors build a church. On occasion you find both a mosque and a church in the same *kampung*.

transport: It's a small island and no bus trip anywhere is more than Rp350 except to the airport, Rp1000-1250. Ask questions at the bus station in Ambon about the place you want to go; usually the drivers come from the village where the bus is going. Although Amboinese speak their own dialect of Indonesian, you won't have any trouble communicating. But you'll be completely at the mercy of the villagers: if you want a drink of water, you got to ask for it. It's essential that you first pay a call to the *raja* of the village if he's there. The *raja* often lives in Ambon City and only visits his village when his presence is absolutely required. Some villages won't give you food or put you up without the *raja's* permission, but this is rare. Most villages will accommodate you; the people aren't as paranoid as the police. In Christian areas don't wear a *kain* or a *sarung*, but in Muslim areas they'll love it if you do.

ruins and old buildings: There are at least 40 ruins of old fortresses (benteng) on Ambon Island. If you're going to do a lot of walking around ruins, first contact the *camat* in Passo, the administrative center of the island. With a letter from him you can stay for free in places that get only one white visitor a year. Since a fort could be hallowed ground, people may deny that they have forts in their villages even if they do. Always ask first before wandering around out-areas so that the ancestors won't be disturbed in their shrines. While crawling over old forts be quite careful of treacherous land coral. **Ambon city:** At Benteng is a fortress; you must ask permission from the military installation there and it's a hassle. On the waterfront is ancient

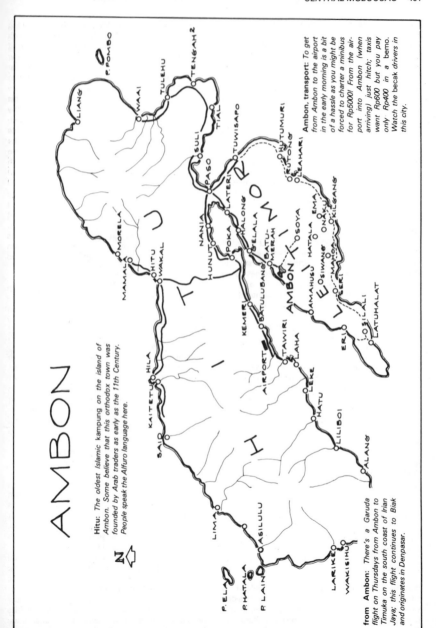

AMBON

Hitu: The oldest Islamic kampung on the island of Ambon. Some believe that this orthodox town was founded by Arab traders as early as the 11th Century. People speak the Alfuro language here.

from Ambon: There's a Garuda flight on Thursdays from Ambon to Timuka on the south coast of Irian Jaya; this flight continues to Biak and originates in Denpasar.

Ambon, transport: To get from Ambon to the airport in the early morning is a bit of a hassle as you might be forced to charter a minibus for Rp5000! From the airport into Ambon (when arriving) just hitch; taxis want Rp600 but you pay only Rp400 in a bemo. Watch the becak drivers in this city.

Fort Victoria built by the Dutch in 1605. Now it's an army camp and you have to get a letter from the Education Department or the Tourist Bureau to see it; there's just a gate left. Also Benteng Brusthede, close to the pier. **Benteng Hatunuk:** Another fortress near the little village of Batu Kasang. **Hila:** A fastastically contorted *banyan* tree grips the whole insides of a Portuguese fort in this village. Just the blockhouse, watchtowers and cannons left. The oldest church on Ambon is also here with a Dutch inscribed plaque. The entire village and its 300 screaming kids adopts you. Walk along a dreamy pebble beach where the giant island of Ceram looms in the distance. Kids will paddle you down the coast for more ruins. Reach the clove plantations by climbing high up in the hills behind Hila. Catch *prahus* from Hila to Ceram. **Lima:** To prevent another devastating Hitu War the Dutch built Fort Rotterdam in Lima.

other sights: Visit the fishing village of Galela, the Sea Gardens off Pombo Island, long stretches of inviting deserted beaches at Natsepa, and a hotsprings at Talehu. **Batu Capeau:** In Airsolabar. An expensive bordello and a sometimes quiet beach here. **Gunung Nona:** But for *absolute* quiet, take a bus from Ambon out to Benteng and turn up to the Chinese cematary. Then climb for two hours to the top of this small mountain. **Latuhalat:** Coral reefs and good snorkling but beware of razor sharp coral. **Eman Latu:** Up the coast from Latuhalat, where you can see up to 15 m below water. Don't need a mask, just a snorkel. Or just stick your head under the water, it's like swimming inside an aquarium. **Kusukusu:** The largest cave on Ambon, well known and a fairly easy walk from the city of Ambon. **waterfall:** There's a fantastic waterfall between Naku and Batuitam. Take the road to Batuitam, cross the river, and then the next river has the waterfall. On top are big rocks where, it's explained, 'houses have turned to stone.' See the old things that belong to the *kapitan*. It's a 3 hour lonely eerie walk back to Ambon. **Waai:** On the east coast by bus 25 km, Rp300. A sacred pool over a 60 m waterfall here. Holy fish come from under the sea. A 10 year old girl calls a giant eel by thumping on the water, then feeds it eggs. **Mamala:** This north coast district practice a sport called *sapulidi*, or broom-fighting, using palm fibres tied to a stick as the only weapon. **Naku and Hatalia:** In these two villages live Portuguese descendents. See dances exactly as were danced in 16th and 17th Century Portugal.

Soya: 2 hours walk uphill from Ambon behind the city through a countryside full of steep sided valleys, rainy hills covered in buffalo grass, jungle, palm groves, and higher up, Amboina conifers. See women carrying trays of coconuts and bananas on their heads down red clay paths. Soya has long traditions and an air of mysticism. The old church here was built by the Portuguse in 1817. On top of the mountain there's a foot high sacred stone chair believed to be where the first king sat, plus a water urn that never goes dry. If someone is going to leave the *negeri* they usually take a little water from this jar to guard themselves wherever they go. This mountain is also worth seeing for the view from the top, taking in the long inlet that separates the two peninsulas of the island. **from Soya:** It's a nice walk further up the mountain to Gunung Serimau. On the walk from Soya to Ema you pass a point on G. Serimau where you can see the whole south coast. Ema is a friendly village on top of the mountain.

Rutong: From Ambon a 24 km walk to this village on the south coast of Leitimor facing Ceram. Pass down avenues of eucalyptus trees, over rolling rhododendrum blanketed hills, dense forests with beautiful mauve orchids growing out of giant tree trunks, clear streams at the bottom of ravines. At last there's a chain of hills before the coast and an incredible panorama of the Banda Sea and long sweeping stretches of yellow beaches. Then descend down to the village. **from Rutong:** Hire a *kapal layar* or a motorboat to take you from Rutong to Passo, passing limestone cliffs and caves, tiny bays, sea gardens of pink coral, amber gold seaweed, and multi-colored tropical fish on the way. So quiet.

Alang: A Christian village on the southwestern tip of the island. For over 400 years Alang has guarded the entrance to Ambon Bay. A popular way to get here is by sea in an outrigger canoe, except during the 'east season' April-July when high winds and waves make this approach hazardous. Alang sits unsteadily on the rocky terraced slopes rising steeply from the bright green sea. Because of the lack of level space, its houses are built very close together on just a few streets. Nutmeg and cloves, its main crops, are found in the groves and gardens back in the heavily wooded hills behind the village. Also known for its *kanari* nuts. Listen to the choirs and flute orchestras in the large well cared for church with great rough-hewn beams; it was remodeled in the 1830's by a Dutch minister. People in this village love to sing, especially folk songs.

KOTA AMBON

Ambon city, 56 km from the airport, Rp1000-1250 by *bemo,* is a highly composite collection of closely-knit *kampungs* where people have come together from various islands to live. Food, accommodation and transport are as expensive as Jakarta. Euros usually come here for a reason. You see straight travelers on fieldwork who sterilize their drinking glasses onboard their yachts or guys from universities who tramp around the Central Moluccan islands in khaki shorts and safari shirts, intently studying pre-Christian archaeology or endemic species of water rats. A very musical island, there are 80-100 flute bands in Ambon. You hear Alice Cooper and Deep Purple in taxi buses, guitars played on porches, everyone owns and exchanges casettes. Marching bands galore, and down on the harbor a Sunday night brass band. Ambon is also one of the few places in Indonesia where you see drunks on the street, especially while staggering home yourself at 2 or 3 am. There are back room places where you can get loaded on *sopi* (Rp25 a shot) or brandy and advokat (Rp50 per glass). Get a good buzz for all of Rp100, then repair to the Gogona Nite Club where you can have a drink with the head of the secret police. Cold Bintang beer (Rp500), strobe lights, hostesses and Indonesian rock groups; open until 3 am. **transport:** Made up of only 3-4 main streets, there's nowhere too far to walk in this city. **imigrasi:** It's polite to report to *imigrasi* where they play Perry Como records; bring a photo. Visa extensions, Rp2000. Don't say that you're a student because they won't give you an extension. They'll ask where your papers are and if you show them it'll be even worse. They don't want you to study anything unless you have permission from LIPI in Jakarta and LIPI will run your ass off for 3 weeks getting it. Just say that you're a post office clerk or an *orang turis.*

stay: Ask the taxi drivers about the latest cheap places. Hotel Etma down a little lane (Gang Violeta) off Jl. Tulukabessy, Rp1500. Hotel Silalou, behind the Fakultas Keguruan (Teacher's College) on Jl. Sedapmalam 41, has singles for Rp2000. Kampung Markida Hotel is also reasonable. Hotel Anggrek, an old Colonial hotel on Jl. Yani, has new rooms with A.C. Good meals included in the price; Rp4000 single, Rp9000 double. Hotel Wisata, Jl. Mardika, and the Ramayana, Jl. Batumeja, have AC rooms for Rp6000 double. Or ask around if a family will provide you with room and board (Indecost). *Inde-*

cost is the best all-around accommodation; figure on about Rp1500 per day.

eat: Expensive. Even rice is imported. Fruits are high too (*durian,* Rp300, but very good flavor). Try Amboinese sweet-sour sauce (coloh-coloh) made with a citrus base and red chilies; it's especially piquant with baked fish. Many *warungs* serve meals such as *nasi campur,* etc., for Rp150-200. *Bakmie* wagons peddle soup for Rp100. Fresh tuna fish is lovely but fish is generally expensive too. The ice used in ice drinks isn't very clean, it might give you the shits. Try sweet-sour nutmeg (pala-gula), Rp5 for a little bag. This island's *sopi* is a god-awful potent palm wine. The best is made in Latere. Some *sopi* has a two month old deer fetus in the jar, *sopi rusa;* supposedly has curative and strengthening powers.

sights: The hero with the upraised sword in the town park fought against Dutch oppression. The top of his sword has been cut off by a low-flying army helicopter. The statue is located on the spot where this guerilla terrorist was hanged by the Dutch. Talk with Father Rutgus who's been in the Moluccas for almost 30 years (mostly in South Moluccas). He might take you to see his pride and joy, the hospital he built. Contact the Officer for Tourism, Mr. Oratmangun, Kantor Gubernor, Jl. Pattimura, who can answer your questions and he could make it easier for you to visit places that present bureacratic difficulties. Oratmangun has a travel booklet on the Moluccas Islands and sells postcards, about the only ones available and expensive. To see the new and growing Museum Siwalima contact Mr. Mailoa at the Education Dept. (PDK); it has pottery, Tanimbar carvings, Irianese artifacts, etc.

crafts: Seaweed bracelets (akar bahar) cost Rp500; cheaper on Bali. This is the source however for pretty tortoise shell: bracelets run Rp5-600, rings Rp250-300, hair clasps about Rp500. Polished *kayu besi,* Rp600. Ships are built completely out of cloves here with little men on deck, oars and lanterns; asking price Rp5-6000. *Gigi durung* (seacow teeth), Rp300. Great Ming platters, Rp50-60,000; the Nalulu people of Ceram have loads of 16th Century Ming cheaper, but you have to hike for it. Stuffed sea turtles, Rp3-10,000. Big bottle of Johnny Walker, Rp3000. Buru Island is the origin of *kayuputih* oil. But it's very cheap here on Ambon at Rp150-200 for a small bottle, Rp750-850 for a large bottle. For handwoven fabrics each Moluccan island has retained its own artistic style, motifs and dyeing methods. The tribes of Ceram make the finest woven crafts.

boats from Ambon: During the monsoon season (May-July) sea travel is restricted in South Moluccas. March-April is the best time to travel by boat in South Moluccas (Banda, Kai and Tanimbar Islands). Clove boats to east Ceram and other Central and North Moluccan ports mostly happen during the clove season Sept.-Dec. when the seas are calm. **for Ceram:** At Hila on Ambon catch *prahus* to Ceram from 1-5 pm for Rp600-1000; takes 2-3 hours to places like Waiputu, Luhu (bigger town) and Waijase. Or take motorized *prahus* for Rp350, takes 1 hour. **ships:** Ask the harbormaster (syahbandar) in Ambon city about boats to Fak Fak (Irian Jaya), Banda, and other islands. The M.V. Duren and the M.V. Bido when not in repair sail north to Ternate. Pelni, whose office is on the harbor, has ships to Irian Jaya via Sorong, Manokwari, Biak, then to Jayapura, Rp21,250, once monthly. Other Pelni prices, to: Kai Islands to the south, Rp14,000 round trip; Ujung Pandang (Celebes), Rp15,750; Surabaya, Rp22,400; Tanjung Priok (Jakarta), Rp25,600. Check Berdikari Shipping Lines, they have boats to Halmahera and to other northern islands. Also Berdikari has boats from Ambon to: Tual, Rp6500; Elat, Rp7800; Banda, Rp3500; Dobo, Rp9500; Saumlaki, Rp11,200; Kisar, Rp13,500- all one-way fares. **missionary boat:** The missions operate boats south costing as much as Rp21,000 but they stop in many of the small islands. At the Bishop's house in Ambon contact Monsigneur A. Sol. He'll tell you about the ship Bakti. It usually sails once monthly from Ambon to Kai, 45 hours, from Kai to Aru in one night, then to Dobo (capital of the Aru Islands), another 50 hours, a total of 644 km. It stops in Dobo 2 days and in Kai for one day. At 8 knots per hour, it takes 7-10 days in all. Costs Rp18,000 round trip. **flights:** Flights to Ternate with Merpati operate at least 3 times a week and cost Rp22,500 plus Rp800 airport tax. Plenty of space unless there's a football game or something special on. Other Merpati flights to: Kai Islands, twice weekly, Rp22,500; Amahai City (Ceram), once weekly, Rp12,500; Ujung Pandang (Celebes), twice weekly, Rp28,500. Mandala Airlines could have cheaper flights by Rp2000-3000 with service just as good. The airport is 56 km from Kota Ambon, Rp1000-1250 by *bemo*.

Saparua: A small isle east of Ambon. Get a boat from Tulehu to Saparua, 3 hours, Rp3-400. Boats to Saparua also leave from Waai, Rp350-400. In the city of Saparua there's a big market each Wed. and Saturday. Visit the old Dutch fort of Duurstede with its battlements and rusty cannons pointing over the rocky shore. There's one other ruin and a 17th Century church. Because of an age-old feud two villages on this small island set fire to each other once a year. At Ouw, a big pottery center turns out most of the island's earthenware. **vicinity of Saparua:** There are ruins of Portugese fortifications on the island of Haruku between Saparua and Ambon, about 7 km to the east of Ambon.

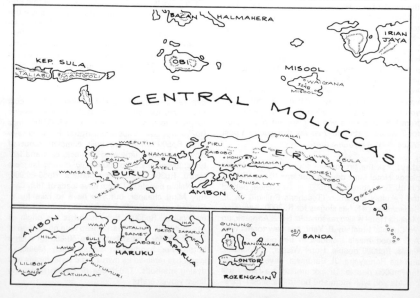

CERAM

The least known of the Moluccas but has an oil-field on the east coast. A very wooded and mountainous island, mountains rise up to 2750 m and the highest peak in the center is 3000 m. Ceram is swampy in the north, steep and rocky along the southern shoreline. The island has different weather entirely from Ambon's; if it's clear on Ceram, it's probably rainy on Ambon. The original Bandicoot and some endemic species of bats and flying foxes are found here. Its birdlife is the most colorful of all the Moluccan islands. Ceram's southern coast is one of the most densely populated areas of the Moluccas with 60-125 people per sq km. Very dense Christian area.

getting there: The easiest is just to fly from Kota Ambon to Amahai, Rp12,500. Or from Waai (Ambon Island) get boats to Kamal, Nurue, Waisamu, Hatusua, Kairatu (on west coast of Ceram). From Tulehu (Ambon) there are boats to Seruawan, Tihulale, Kamarian (Rp450), Rumahkai, Latu (west coast of Ceram), Liang, Waraka, Makariki, Masohi, Amahai, Sepa, Ruta, Tamilau, Tehoru (south coast of Ceram). **transport:** You have to walk on Ceram, there are few cars. You need 3 months to really get into it. To get around coastal villages take *prahus* along the coasts. Few travelers seldom make it over to the east which is quite remote and inaccessible except for Australian housewives discussing laundering problems at the Bula Oil Center. When you arrive in villages you must usually rely on the church people to put you up.

sights: The ancient Dutch fort of Kambelo (built in 1616) is on the west end of the western peninsula (Little Ceram). There's a completely ethnic Javanese village on the far west coast. At Waisamu, the Kupukupu Malam, a butterfly with a one foot wing-span, flaps along the shore at night. In the village of Kararian, southwestern Ceram, the male war dance *Jakalele* is still practiced. Though a native Moluccan dance, it's also found in Sulawesi.

the Alfuro: Ceram is an ethnologically rich island. In the east live the tribes, the west part of the island has more Malays. Inland villages are completely different than coastal; more courteous and friendlier to outsiders. Just get away from the coasts and you'll find hunter-gatherers: Nalulu Borera, Nalulu Rohua, Nalulu Halmalau, Nalulu Wataul, Nalulu Galisuru. The Alfuros (a group to which the Nalulus belong) are found in the interiors of all the larger Moluccan islands, the original inhabitants of the area who were pushed into the forests by incoming Malayan peoples at a much later date. The name Alfuro stems from the Portugese word *fora* or 'outsider' for when the Portugese arrived in the late 16th Century they saw these people living only in the mountain regions. The Ceramese Alfuro were former war-like headhunters. Heads were given in essence to the Lord of the Heavens in the form of concentric circles symbolizing the sun. Today they are the best stick and staff fighters in Indonesia and the bow and arrow is still quite common. The first man to go around the world was a dark Alfuro slave named Henry, a member of Magellan's crew whom Magellan had taken to Europe on his first voyage. Indigenous aboriginal crafts are still made in the interior of Ceram where tribes produce vivid handwoven articles.

walks on Ceram: Get a boat first from Talehu (Ambon) to Kairatu on Ceram for Rp500. From Kairatu the walk to Honitetu is fairly easy, but get ready for some climbing if you want to go any further inland. Another walk: First take the Merpati flight from Kota Ambon to Amahai, Rp12,500, then start along the fascinating coastal track from Amahai all the way to Tehoru. You'll find isolated tribal villages about 30 km north of Japutih; allow 3 weeks for this trip. **the Paliano walk:** First to Tehoru, then take a *prahu* across the bay (if you try to walk, you have to cross an estuary), then Paliano is just a half-day walk uphill.

BURU ISLAND

A primitively beautiful 2000 sq km island lying over 3000 km from Jakarta. Buru is surrounded by coral barriers and covered in inpenetrable eucalyptus forests and elephant grass. Many of its rivers, such as the Wai Apu south of Namlea, have densely overgrown banks with crocodiles, swarms of mosquitos, and insects the size of shuttlecocks. Until 1969 cannibalism was still practiced deep in the interior. In the western part is 670 m high Lake Wakolo, 60 km around. Buru produces timber and *kayuputih* oil. The main town is Namlea, a dusty village on the northeast coast composed of natives, Arabs, Chinese and Javanese. Some *transmigrasi* schemes have been set up here. Isolated aboriginal tribes of the Rana, Waeloa, Waetenum, and Waejapo people number about 5000 and are dying out. These Alfuro aboriginals can cut 30 banana tree stalks with one hack of their razor-sharp *parangs* (cleavers). **getting there:** Buru lies far from air and shipping routes. You have to have special permission from the Commander in Chief of the Moluccas Islands in Kota Ambon to get on this island, so forget it.

the prisoners: Since 1969 Buru has been a rehabilitation center for political detainees suspected of complicity in the nearly successful coup staged by Indonesia's communists in 1965. It's now a forbidden island, sealed off from the rest of Indonesia by the *Kopkamtib* (state security agency). This giant center holds 13,000 prisoners and is divided into 20 separate units, each containing 500-600 males, some with their wives and children. Each unit is built much like a Javanese village with churches, mosques, low houses with corrugated iron roofs, and a soccer or volleyball field on the outskirts. There's a meeting hall where prisoners are assembled for compulsory indoctrination lectures to replace communist ideology with the government's *Panca Sila* philosophy. Detainees are ordered to believe in god and must faithfully attend a church or a mosque; hundreds of communist voices singing 'Jesus is my Shepherd' resound eerily through the Buru jungles. There are no watchtowers or barbed wire, and the guards aren't armed. There are as well no newspapers, movies, radios or TV. Buru is an ideal isle of exile. Thirty-eight prisoners escaped in 1974 only to perish in the jungles within days. Many writers, artists and other intellectuals are confined to the camps including Subronto Admojo, 49, one of Indonesia's leading composer-conductors; Basuki Effendi, 47, Indonesia's foremost film director before his arrest in 1965 (now a camp violinist and instrument-maker); and Indonesia's greatest prose-writer, Pramoedya Ananta Toer, imprisoned without a trial after the abortive coup, another 'prisoner of conscience'. Many of these 'B-category' prisoners have been detained 10 years without a trial, but recently *Kopkamtib* announced that all prisoners in this category would be released by the end of 1978. But the government has spent millions to make Buru viable and the prisoners won't be taken back to Java again after liberation. 'Release' only means that they will live on this remote island until they die.

BANDA ISLANDS

Nine small islands with active volcanoes 160 km S.E. of Ambon. In 1619 the ruthless 31 year old Dutch Governor General, Jan Pieterszoon Coen, exterminated the indigenous population of these islands in order to acquire control of the nutmeg trade. Idyllic Stevonish islands, the haunt of anthropologists and for those seeking a journey into the 19th Century. The two main islands are close together and you can get around them easily by *prahu*. It's not difficult to make arrangements to stay with a family. *Mako-Mako* and *Maru-Maru* dances are held on occasions in the Bandas.

Bandanaira: The main port of the Banda Islands perched on the edge of a gigantic dead crater, the wharf facing 665 m Gunung Api. A sleepy port town with old Portugese houses and churches speaking of history, its population is made up of Javanese, Makassans and Arabs. There are two old forts. Belgica is only 500 m from the harbor. From the roof you get a sweeping view over the whole town, the volcano, and the nutmeg groves. Also visit Fort Nassau with its overgrown crumbling walls. See the lovely old Protestant church. There's a Christian and a Chinese cemetary near the church with aged lichen-covered inscriptions; probably one of the best collections of old tombstones in all of Indonesia. **vicinity of Bandanaira:** Walk to mouldy thick-walled compounds of the nutmeg plantations in shady forests. It's said that nutmeg can only grow within the sound of the sea. Wade in the famous sea gardens of the Bandas with their dull blue starfish and bright blue fish swimming over fans of delicate coral. Visit Fort Hollandia on Lonthoir Island. There's another fortress on Ay Island. The Pinju Islands in the Banda Sea are nesting grounds for giant sea turtles.

SOUTHEAST MOLUCCAS

(MALUKU TENGGARA)

All the southwest and southeast Moluccan islands are rather culturally homogenous. Most communities in the islands between Alor and Kai are divided into 3 fixed hereditary status-groups, the aristocrats, commoners and slaves. The aristocrats are often of mixed Malay-indigenous origin, the commoners of indigenous races, while the slaves were (are) imported from New Guinea. Life is very much centered around boats and some villagers are even laid out like a boat seen from above. They subsist on sago and from the produce of their dry-rice cultivation, rice being the main diet on the islands between Alor and Tanimbar and the former on the other islands.

KAI ISLANDS

The Kais are a forgotten place where the government puts in very little money. They comprise two

fairly large and many tiny islands covering about 900 sq km and have approximately 20,000 inhabitants. Tual, on an island near Kai Kecil, is the administrative center and the capital of the province.

getting there: If flying in you land at Dumatuban Airport in the town of Langgur. Langgur lies on P. Kai Kecil and you must cross a 100 m long bridge to reach Tual which lies 5 km away on P. Dullah. Another way is by boat: first fly to Kaimana on the southern coast of Irian Jaya from Nabire (Rp17,000), from Biak (Rp30,000), or from Ambon. Then from Kaimana take a *kapal motor* or sailing *prahu* to Tual, P. Dullah, for Rp2500. On the way the boat sometimes stops in the Mengawitu Islands. A lot of trade goes on between Kaimana and the Kais so boats are frequent. Also the ship Bakti leaves from Ambon once monthly for the Kais, Rp-18,000 round trip.

Kai Islands: *Two Merpati flights a week from Ambon to Kai, Tuesday and Fridays, Rp20,000. On arrival you have to pay Rp1000 for some vague registration at the police in Tual, no way to get around it. The best place to stay is the Catholic mission (Pasturan) 200 m from the airport in Langgur, Kai Kecil; pay Rp1500 for food and sleep. Also try Penginapan Merinah in Tual, main town and port of Kai Kecil. There are about 15 Dutch missionaries and teachers here, though very few of them speak English; use Indonesian. Quite a few roads on this island but no public transport; borrow a bicycle from the mission. Not very much to do in Kai except waiting for ships. You can get a ship to almost anyplace in South Moluccas if you hang around long enough, a month or so. The mission has ships to Aru, Tanimbar, Babar, Wetar, Kisar and Surabaya. Ships to Ambon and Banda are more frequent. In the wet season May-August there are very few boats.*

KAI ISLANDS

Kai Besar: *From Langgur there is a daily boat to Elat on Kai Besar, 3-4 hours. Very few roads on Kai Besar so you have to walk. There are a few villages on this island which are said to be Hindu. The population of Kai actually decreases because of the high incidence of malaria and cholera. 300 villagers died of the latter disease the first 6 months of this year — do not drink the water. You will probably catch malaria here even if you take tablets against it, but the hospital in Langgur will cure you.*

South of Langgur there's an island shaped like a boat; the natives believe their ancestors came from Bali by that boat.

Kai Besar (or Great Kai): This is the largest island in the Kais, about 80 km long and very narrow. Kai Besar is quite mountainous with the highest mountain being Gunung Dab. In Banda-Elat and Eli on Kai Besar live the descendants of the survivors of the Dutch genocide on the Banda Islands in the 17th Century. They are of Muslim faith. They build fine boats and produce woodcarvings and silver and goldwork. Most villages on the east coast of Kai Besar are animistic. Ohilim is situated in the hinterland on a small hill, a very primitive *kampung gunung* which shows signs of influence from the Aru Islands. Ohewait on the east coast is a sacred village with a square in the middle of it surrounded by big stones. A footpath connects this village with the west coast.

Nuhuroa: In the Kai Kecil Islands. Villages consist of big houses containing several nuclear families. In the villages large squatting wood statues representing ancestors are found and around the villages are thick stone walls for defensive purposes. Satean on Nuhuroa has a stone shaped like a ship by which the inhabitants believe their ancestors came from Bali. On Nuhuroa a few groups of a hunting and gathering people remain. The people of the island Ur are quite different from other Kai people, keeping themselves isolated and are very traditional minded. They have, however, a kind of marriage-exchange system with the nearby island of Kai-Tanimbar.

arts and crafts: Damp clay vessels are painted with a yellow coloring matter which turns to a red-dish tone when fired; very finely decorated with sensuous beautiful shapes. Also *nitu*-statues (soul-of-the-dead). Kai is one of the best places to have a sailing or motorized *prahu* built, between 5 and 200 tons. No rip-offs because the missions run the ship wharves. The Kai Islands are the most musical of the Moluccas; pretty songs are constructed diatonically and sung in various meters even up to 5 quarters meter.

ARU ISLANDS

The Aru Islands consist of many large and small low flat swampy islands, as the Kais. Dobo, on Wamar Island, is the capital of the district; see the commemorative column to Yos Sudarso who perished in the battle of Trikora while the Indonesians were attempting to capture Irian Jaya from the Dutch. The culture of Kepulauan Aru is of similar character as the Kais but in the interior a primitive nomadic culture of Papuan and Australian origin is found. Pearls and mother-of-pearl are its main products. The Arus have many deer, cassowaries, kangaroos, and even one species of the Bird of Paradise. It was in these islands in the 1850's where the great naturalist-explorer Alfred Russel Wallace was forced to recuperate from inflamed insect bites and write down for the first time all his thoughts on the faunal differences which he had observed during 7 years of travel. He and Darwin jointly announced to the world their Theory of Evolution in London in 1858, but because Darwin had emphasized man's evolution more he received the lion's share of the fame.

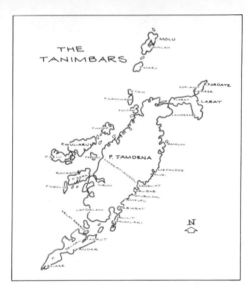

THE
TANIMBARS

N

crafts: The Catholics are trying to revive native pottery here. Very striking painted and engraved clay dishes and pots are produced in the Arus. There are also cave paintings. Large squatting ancestor statues are set up in centers or at entrances of villages and on mountaintops.

THE TANIMBARS

15 m long whales are found in the waters around these islands. The Tanimbars are made up of about 60 islands composed of a mix of peoples: Irianese, Negritos, and Orang Maluku. Saumlaki is the largest town on the main island of Jamdena. In Saumlaki there's a nice mission where you can always get a bed or take a bath. Visit the delightful harbormaster and the chief of police. Odilon, the amicable Chinese merchant, you will no doubt run into. He'll tell you how simple the people are, yet so happy.

from Saumlaki: Walk up the east coast of Jamdena (the main island) through the coastal villages. But take care; herds of wild bulls kill about 15 people a year on this island. From Saumlaki catch *prahus* to the southern island of Selaru and its main town of Adaut for two packs of tobacco. Selaru is a poor island, low and bushy. There's not a lot of food; meals of only rice and dried fish cost Rp150-350. Trade a bottle of beer for a seaweed bracelet (akhar bahar). **by boat:** About every 1½ months a small mission boat bedecked with flags departs Saumlaki for Babar, Kisar, Sermata, etc. Sometimes another boat sails to Aru and Kai. A boat also leaves for Ambon once every 3 weeks or so from Saumlaki.

crafts: The art of the peoples of Tanimbar and Alor Islands can be traced back as far as the ornamental Dongson-style of Annam. This style incorporates numerous oriental motifs, seen in their small carved wooden ancestor statues. Also woven *sarungs* and scarves are produced that look similar to those produced on Sumba and Timor but actually the colors and motifs are quite different. Herman De Vries in Saumlaki has a large collection of carvings (praying figures), books and notes. De Vries possesses a great knowledge of South Maluku, and is especially expert in the motifs used in this area. He's also lived in Agats, Irian Jaya, for 4 years.

other sights: On some islands in the Tanimbars the Alfuro aborigines practice a shark cult. Alfuros go into the sea to feed the sharks, supposedly man-eaters, then come out unharmed. Blowpipes are still used, but only as a hunting weapon. These Alfuro are some of the best spearmen in Indonesia. **Arui-Bab:** A village on the east coast of Jamdena. There's a long boat-shaped stone platform here where members of the village council sit for deliberations. It's an ancient custom for village elders to occupy ancestral stone seats, indicating their origins and reinforcing their authority to rule. **Leti Islands:** East of Timor. Here people worship the male sun god Upulero and the female earth goddess Upunisa who are regarded as being married. Rain is looked upon as this god's sperm. *Porka*-festivals are held every few years with phallic rites (also on Moa and Lakor Islands). On Leti and Lakor, religious sculptures are made totally unique in shape.

Ternate Harbor

NORTH MOLUCCAS

(MALUKU UTARA)

TERNATE ISLAND

A circular island only 9 km in diameter of 40 sq km, made up almost entirely of 3 main volcanic peaks rising to 1830 m. **history:** Famed in history for its spices, Ternate is still one of the main sources of cloves. During the 14th and 16th Centuries the sultans of Ternate ruled over their Moluccan empire from Ternate town. The Portugese, seeking commercial control over this spice island, moved in to commence business. But when they did away with the sultan the island revolted, causing the Portugese to lose their hopes of prosperous trade. The hatred generated by this murder eventually cost them the East Indies. The Spainards, who founded Manila in 1570, moved south and captured the Portugese garrison in Ternate in 1574, extending their power even further. Fearing a Spanish attack from the Philippines, the Dutch opportunistically moved in and nearly succeeded in setting up a monopoly of the spice trade here.

TERNATE CITY

This town has clung to the side of a smoking volcano since 1600. Though Ambon is more cosmopolitan, Ternate is more relaxing (except for the earth tremors at night). The streets are empty by 8 pm. This city is 90% orthodox Muslim. Young schoolgirls in white veils and sky-blue blouses are frequently seen in the streets. The populace is really into marching groups — women, men and children of all ages. Change money only at Bank Dagang Negara, Jl. Nukula; none of the other banks trust travelers checks. Better yet, bring enough cash because it's a hassle and takes time (you have to have an interview with the bank manager to get your money). **getting there:** Although Ba Ullah airport is quite near the city you must pay Rp500-750 to get into town. You're very much a visitor on Ternate and you spend half a day reporting to bureacrats. Upon landing at the airport you must pay the police for some nameless registration, Rp250. Report to *imigrasi* next, then to the local police station for another stamp and pay another Rp250, then you've officially arrived.

stay: Cheapest is Anang Arief's house, Jl. Babullah SK2/27, at Rp750 single. Register with the *kepala kampung,* Rp100. If you don't desire family life, there's Hotel Massa, Rp1500. Or comfortable small family hotel Peng. Sejahtera, Jl Lawa Mena 21; Rp3000 full room and board, or Rp2000 just for sleeping. Rent a room in town for a year, Rp30,000.

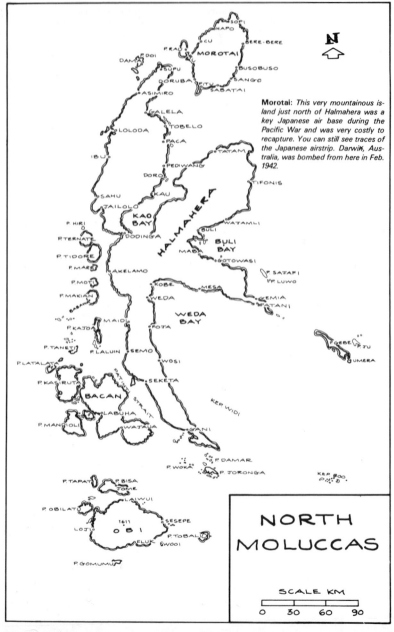

N

SOPI
HAPO
CU
BERE-BERE
P.RAU
MOROTAI
DAM DOI
BUSOBUSO
SUPU
ORUBA SANGO
PITU
SABATAI
ASIMIRO

Morotai: *This very mountainous island just north of Halmahera was a key Japanese air base during the Pacific War and was very costly to recapture. You can still see traces of the Japanese airstrip. Darwin, Australia, was bombed from here in Feb. 1942.*

GALELA
LOLODA
TOBELO
PACA
IBU
TATAM
PEDIWANG
DORO
TIFONIS
SAHU
KAU
JAILOLO
KAO
BAY
P. HIRI
WATAMLI
P.TERNATE
DODINGA
BULI
HALMAHERA
BULI
BAY
P.TIDORE
MABA
P.MARE
GOTOWASI
AKELAMO
P.MOTI
P. SAJAFI
KOBE
MESA
P LUWO
P.MAKIAN
WEDA
BABANG
GEMIA
PATANI
MAIDI
WEDA
BAY
P.KAJOA
FOJA
GEBE
P.TANETI
P JU
P.LALUIN
SEMO
GUMERA
P.LATALATA
WOSI
P.KASIRUTA
SEKETA
PATI STRAIT
BACAN
KEP WIDI
STRAIT
LABUHA
P.MANGOLI
WAJAUA
GANI
P.DAMAR
P.WOKA
KEP BOO
P. JORONGA
P.TARA
P.BISA
JORE
LAIWUI
P.OBILAT
1611
SESEPE
LOJI
O B I
P.TOBAL
FLUK
GWOI
P.GOMUMU

NORTH MOLUCCAS

SCALE KM

0   30   60   90

eat: Try *ikan bakar* (roasted fish) with *coloh-coloh* sauce, a specialty here. Lots of good places to eat such as Anugerah next to the mattress shop in front of the Taxi Terminal; meals for Rp150-250. A good hole in the wall is opposite Massa Hotel; quite filling *mie kuah* for Rp200. For hot sweet soya sauce with green fruit cocktail (ruyak), Rp50-75, *gado2*, cakes, and nonalcoholic drinks, go to the *warung* without-a-name in Kampung Makasar. It lies in a garden leaping with exotic plants (which are for sale). Orange, *durian* and chocolate ice milk at swank Garuda Restaurant in the city.

sights: Try to see the *Soja-Soja* Dance if you hear of it, performed by 13 men. Visit the palace of the dead sultan above the town with rewarding views over the harbor. Now a poor museum, it's intriguing if you use your imagination. Weather permitting, boxing matches are held in Ternate when hundreds converge on Stadiun Boksing to watch amateurs slug it out; a wheel hub is used as the bell. Like a stage comedy, hilarity convulses the audience. Ternate versus Ambon grudge fights are the most side-splitting. Oriental deference is paid to the losers. Pay a call at a casino shack packed with men right in the middle of town where a wild kind of roulette is played. A man lets out a shot and hurls a great foot-long chicken feather dart at a spinning dartboard; buy Rp1000 worth of paper chips first and give it a try.

crafts: Because they come from Ambon, tortoise shell bracelets are dear at Rp1000-1250. Stuffed civet cats, Rp7500. *Kulit mutiara* (mother-of-pearl) jewelry is higher quality and cheaper than Ambon. At Pasar Sayur you can buy a green, red, or dazzling white *Kakatua Raja* (King Parrot) from Halmahera; asking price Rp13,000. In Ternate one can pick up enough fragments of old Chinese ceramics on the side of the roads to fill a plastic bag in 5 minutes; set these pieces in silver rings and pendants, very striking.

old forts and ruins: There are more forts per sq inch in and around Ternate city than in any other locale in Indonesia; they once guarded the clove plantations. Benteng Oranye is right in the middle of the city. Toloko is in Dufa-Dufa; this structure is in such splendid condition that you can still read a 16th Century Portugese official seal on it.

TERNATE TOWN

1. the harbor
2. imigrasi
3. Sriwijaya Shipping Co.
4. Stasiun Polisi
5. Stadium Boksing
6. Kantor Bupati
7. pasar
8. stasiun bemo
9. rumah sakit
10. Anang Arief's losmen

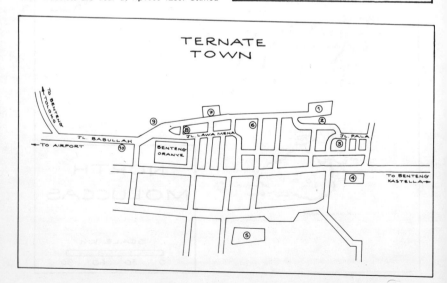

Benteng Oranye

Fort Kastella

Kayu Merah is just before entering Kalumata. Kota Janji lies after Kalumata. Kastella is about a 15 minute busride down a lovely road to Castela, Rp100. This wrecked fortification with its gateways still standing is covered in trees and mould. Dates from Magellan's time. Goats walk along its moss-grown walls. There's yet another well-preserved Portugese fortress called Sao Palolo on the island.

from Ternate by ship: Ask the *syahbandar* when the ship Duren is in. It sails 4 times monthly on a week long tour all over Halmahera Island to the north via Jailolo, Ibu, Morotai, Galela and Tobelo; round trip Rp7500. There are many other ships out of Ternate going in all directions (except north).

Berdikari Shipping Co., Jl. Komplex PKK, has ships to Ambon. Pelni boats sail from Ternate to: Bitung, Donggala and Ujung Pandang (Celebes). On the ship Tobelo (or on the Tokala, a better ship), it's 14 hours to Bitung (North Celebes); either one of these sails 2 times a month for Rp9000 to Bitung. Don't book, just pay when the ship arrives. Cheaper than Pelni is Sriwijaya Shipping Co., Jl. Pala; the Lamatang sails to Bitung. North Celebes, Rp7800. Other Sriwijaya fares to: Tobelo Rp7200, 19 hours; Galela, Rp7200, daily; Doruba, Rp7000 once monthly; Surabaya, Rp21,750; Jakarta, Rp26,750. **flights:** There's no Mandala Airlines office here, only Merpati which has a 28 minute flight to: Galela (Halmahera), Rp14,500; Manado (Celebes), 4

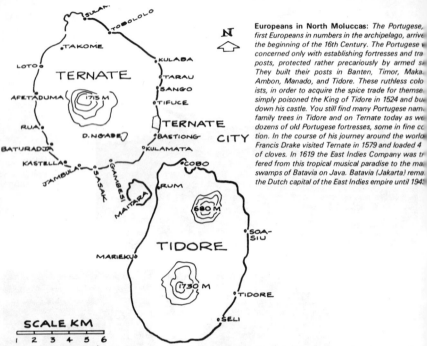

Europeans in North Moluccas: *The Portugese, first Europeans in numbers in the archipelago, arrive the beginning of the 16th Century. The Portugese w concerned only with establishing fortresses and tra posts, protected rather precariously by armed s They built their posts in Banten, Timor, Maka, Ambon, Manado, and Tidore. These ruthless colo ists, in order to acquire the spice trade for themse simply poisoned the King of Tidore in 1524 and bu down his castle. You still find many Portugese nam family trees in Tidore and on Ternate today as we dozens of old Portugese fortresses, some in fine c tion. In the course of his journey around the worl Francis Drake visited Ternate in 1579 and loaded 4 of cloves. In 1619 the East Indies Company was tr fered from this tropical musical paradise to the ma swamps of Batavia on Java. Batavia (Jakarta) rema the Dutch capital of the East Indies empire until 194*

SCALE KM
1 2 3 4 5 6

times weekly, Rp16,250; Poso (Celebes), twice weekly, Rp45,500.

vicinity of Ternate City: Inland there are two lakes, Laguna and Tolire, covered in lotus flowers and quite inviting. The leprosy village of Sorofo can be visited. **Ternate Mountain:** A 5 km walk from town takes you to the 350 year old Cengkih Afu (clove) tree on the slope of this mountain. Approximately 30 m high, 3 men can't join their arms around it. This tree yields up to 150 kilos of cloves each year. There are others nearly as huge in the vicinity. It's quite dangerous further up on the rim of this volcano with a sheer drop down into its cavernous crater. If you throw a rock into it, no sound. At the top you must walk on hot marble-sized stones. So wrote explorers on the ship 'The Challenger' over 100 years ago, and it's still true today. **Batu Hangus** (Burnt Corner): Where a river of lava plowed its way down to the sea in the 18th Century. A Japanese memorial stands nearby. The ocean shore around this coast has a slight bluish tint to it. Only about 2 m deep, direct sunlight goes straight to the bottom where you see black lava piled upon black sand, with white coral on top of this. No sharks while diving, but don't go very far out because of lethally strong currents. **volcano:** To charter a boat to see the volcano on P. Maitara in Ternate Bay it costs as much as Rp20,000; try

negotiating with a fisherman to take you out to it for less.

Tidore: A circular 50 sq km island right next to Ternate. Climb Puncak Tidore, a 1730 m volcano with superimposed peaks usually covered in clouds. A big market takes place in Rum each Sunday when people from Ternate, Soa-Siu, Makian and Halmahera arrive to buy and sell. The old walled town of Tidore sits on the eastern side of the island. **getting there:** Motorboats leave all the time from Ternate harbor, Rp150, to Rum. Then it's ½ hour by public taxi to Tidore city. **stay:** In Soa Siu, the cheapest is Peng. Fattah Hoom, Rp1000 a night. Old fort nearby. Good eating places.

Bacan Island: South of Ternate 140 km by sea. In the village of Labuha shark fins cut through the water in the harbor where village boys swim. Walk up to old decrepit Fort Barnevald which has a moat around it that used to be filled with crocodiles. None of the villagers know the history of the fort, it's just there. There's only 16 motorbikes in the whole town, but several good roads. Good cocoa here. For hundreds of years Bacan has been known for its transparent stones, Rp7000 first offer. Climb Sibela volcano.

HALMAHERA

The largest island of the Moluccas. In shape and geography just a smaller version of Celebes with 4 elongated peninsulas enclosing 3 large bays. The isthmus connecting the northern peninsula is only 8 km wide. Each of the peninsulas on Halmahera have mountains over 900-1500 m high on them. All 17 language groups in Indonesia belong to the Malayo-Polynesian family group except for one on Halmahera which is as yet unclassified, a member of the widely divergent Papuan dialects. The approximately 30 tribes of Halmahera have remained in their history untouched by the more sophisticated sultanate islands of East Indonesia such as Ternate and Tidore. Neither have they been exploited by competing merchant fleets. Thus, much of their traditional culture is intact.

Tobelo: Stay at Losmen Gunung Kawi close to the harbor and the market. There's a large hospital here run by a church group (Gereja Masehi Injili Halmahera) which also runs a coconut plantation on the side. **vicinity of Tobelo:** It's about a 30 km walk to aboriginal villages. The Tobelo, Galela and Tabau tribes in the northern part of the island produce amazingly intricate plaited mats and decorated bark fabrics which are given as marriage gifts or used at mortuary festivities. Sleeping mats almost 2 m long are made of *pandanus* leaves. Some pieces take years to complete, especially the ornamental display mats.

others: At Jailolo are unusual *adat* houses. **Kao Bay:** Find many downed Japanese planes in the jungle and amphibian tanks on the beach at Kao Bay. Go first to Dodinga, 2 hours by motorboat from Ternate, then it's one hour's walk to Babeneigo. Next take a small boat from Babeneigo to Kao Bay. Many pearl divers live in this area. **Weda:** Asbestos is produced in here. **Loloda:** There's a magnesium mine run by a joint local government-Japanese venture. **Morotai:** Fly into Pitustrep Airport. A big copra-producing island with tens of thousands of coconut palms waving in the wind. Other main crops include chocolate, *damar,* and rattan (in that order). Morotai was a big Japanese airbase during WWII.

Glory of the Seas *(conus gloriamaris): The world's most expensive shell is found in Indonesia, this cone by the name of Glory of the Seas. Usually sells for US$400-750, depending on the size and how fine the specimen is. For over 200 years this shell was the rarest, costliest, most coveted in the world. Its long spire and finely reticulated color pattern made it so lovely and elegant that to see one was a privilege, to hold one was an honor. The earliest record of the species was found in the collection of a Dutchman in 1757. The Hoehler specimen, found in the Solomon Islands, was bought for US$2000 in 1963. The theft of a Glory of the Seas was the central theme in a novel written by Miss Fanny Steele, and numerous papers have been written on it. There are only about 50 specimens known to exist in the world. They have been stolen, crushed to pieces by jealous owners, lost. See one in the British Museum or in the Academy of Natural Sciences, Philadelphia. Now certain shells of the mollusc family are considered ·rarer.*

SULA ISLANDS

An island group S.W. of Maluku Utara. Ricefields on these islands. On Obi and Sula are Japanese and Filipino timber companies. **Taliabu Island:** In the eastern part and in the interior N.E. of Bobong are the Kadai, Mangai and Sibojo people. The villages of Kadai and Mange have beautiful houses with *atap* roofs. **Mangole:** Get a ship from Ternate for Rp4-5000 to Sanana on Sanana Island, then take a small motorboat to Dofa on Mangole Island. **from the Sulas:** From Bobong on Taliabu Island, ships operate further to Banggai, Kep. Banggai, then from the Banggai Islands get a *kapal motor* on to Kendari or Luwuk, Celebes.

IRIAN JAYA

(WEST NEW GUINEA)

INTRODUCTION

Irian Jaya is Indonesia's most spectacular region for tourism. It's the biggest and and most intact natural history museum in existence- all 260,000 sq km of it (the same size as Spain or California). This province comprises roughly the whole western half of the island of New Guinea, the 2nd largest island in the world after Greenland, and makes up 22% of the total land surface of Indonesia. It's the least visited, the emptiest, the most remote Indonesian island. Only a million people live here and its capital, Jayapura, is 3520 km from Jakarta. Decades behind Java, it is the least economically developed territory of Indonesia. *Note:* The best map of Irian Jaya is *Nederlands Nieuw-Guinea,* 1:1,750,000 published by Topografisk, Delft 1956.

getting there: No special clearance is required now to enter Irian Jaya and only in certain areas and under certain circumstances must you report to the police station to obtain a *surat jalan* (travel permit). If you want to go to this territory the Indonesian consulate in the country you get your visa in might ask to see adequate travelers cheques before issuing you a visa. The weekly Garuda flight from Surabaya to Biak costs Rp68,000. From Biak there are connecting flights to Jayapura. Merpati flies to Biak from Ambon. Cheapest of all is to fly into Jayapura from Papua New Guinea. If you pay for all your Papua New Guinea and Irian Jaya flights in Australia it could work out cheaper still.

the land: 80% covered in forests and dense jungle. Although it has an unusual lack of wildlife, Irian Jaya has wilder landscapes, more impenetrable and treacherous jungle than any other tropical region, including the Amazon Valley and Africa. Several small pockets of unexplored territory are left and maps are still difficult to find. There are thousands of miles of brilliant white sand beaches lined with coconut palms, wild forest streams plunging down rockfaces, snowfields, torquoise and green colored lakes strewn with glacial rock and debris, heaths and yellow marshes with head high grass, stands of pine trees, wild sugar cane meadows, casuarina groves, moss carpeted forests with bright flowers growing all over them.

There will be silences you will remember. The greater part is mountainous with a high central backbone extending for 640 km. The highest peak, Gunung Jayawijaya, is 5490 m, and 10 others are over 4900 m; some mountains are so high that planes must fly between them to avoid turbulence. Although situated just 40 degrees below the equator, some mountaintops are permanently covered in snow, often over 90 m deep. This system of central ranges compares in structure and relief to the Swiss Alps, but the communication problems here are much more immense. High mountain regions are broken up by coarse grassy valleys and rainforests. Soil is generally poor in the south, but rich in the north. In the shallow south and southwest, heavy rainfall year round has created a mosaic river system that snakes through hundreds of miles of vast mangrove swamps and tidal forests. The most untouched part of Irian Jaya is between Wamena and the border of P.N.G.- no government posts, no missions, just you and them and the jungle.

fauna: Freshwater and terrestial vertebrate fauna are not abundant. Animals are nearly all of the Australian type, particularly N.E. Australia. Many species occur in one locale of Irian Jaya but not in another, possibly due to the difference in the amount of rainfall between the lowlands and the highlands. There are possums, cuscus, bandicoots, bats, rats, mice, snakes, tortoises, crocodiles, frilled lizards and giant monitor lizards. Irian Jaya has the world's largest tree-climbing water rat. Tadpoles with flattened heads suck onto the rocks of fast-flowing streams. The spiny anteater is a nocturnal marsupial with a long beak-like snout, small black eyes, a powerful set of claws, no tail and no teeth, but a very long thin tongue on which it catches ants, termites and other insects. It has one exit for both solid and liquid excreta; the only other animal like it is the platypus, which is missing in New Guinea. Other marsupials include possums which vary in size from the mouselike flying possums to the furry cuscus, the largest of the possum family. Tree kangaroos with grey brown coats live in the higher regions. There are more than 650 species of birds, including plumed herons and other lowland birds, kingfishers and honeyeaters, lovely green pigeons, lories, bee-eaters. The male Bower Bird dances and parades before females on a dancing ground made of a layer of moss surrounded by a 1 m high wall also made of moss and brightly decorated with flower petals, leaves, fruit and berries. The territory also has fabulously colored butterflies, some very rare. To fish in the rivers of New Guinea, such as the Digul, is like fishing in the sea. Many groups of freshwater fish in Irian Jaya are descended from seafish (sawfish, garfish). Sharks are even found in inland Yamur Lake. There are also seasnakes near Tanah Merah, and prawns in shallow ocean waters south of the province. In the highlands, however, the freshwater streams and lakes are nearly empty of fish except those artifically introduced at Wamena. Many natives have never seen fish, only eels and freshwater crayfish.

climate: Hot and humid on the coastal fringes. Mountain areas in the interior above 1800 m have a warm day temperature but severe frosts at night. In these highlands during Aug. and Sept., it's gloomy, misty and cold. Often the clouds gather so thick that it feels like night. In the north May-Oct. is the drier season, with May being the hottest month. South Irian Jaya has a well-defined dry season; in Meruake sometimes it doesn't rain for 5 months. Waterfalls during the wet are up to 100 m high.

history: The Negritos settled New Guinea first, beginning perhaps 30,000 years ago. Some believe that the original mountain Papuans came from the great plains to the south or even as far away as Australia; features and languages have many similarities with the Australian aboriginals. During neo-

Bird of Paradise *(Paradisea Apoda): For many years it was believed that they needed no feet since they never landed on earth but flew always in the sunlight. Papuans call them 'Birds of the Gods', and the Bird of Paradise is pictured on the national flag of P.N.G. A spectacular example of over-adaption to species specific evolution, the Bird of Paradise averages 430-460 mm from the tip of its beak to its tail with ½ m sprays of luxurious tail feathers and plumes underneath the wings. The Yellow Bird of Paradise uses its long golden plumes as a display-tree. Some species display in groups, though you only see this phenomenon in the wilderness. Some decorate nests with cast-off skins of snakes. These birds are difficult to catch sight of through the thick vegetation where they roost. Tremendous acrobats, they fly up very suddenly, alarmed and frantic, then when settled down again make a dull heavy noise. They all have a common silken rustling of wings. The Great Bird of Paradise has a mythological appearance: a rich coffee-brown body, fine straw-yellow feathers crowning its head, metallic emerald-green throat, golden-orange feathers, black middle tail feathers, a blue beak, and red eyes! The female bird of each species, although of very discerning taste, is usually drab brown all over and quite plain.*

lithic times came the Melanesians from the east. They brought with them the bow and arrow, the axe blade, pottery, crop plants, the calendar, cowrie shells for money, tatooing, betel-chewing, decorative woodcarving, outrigger canoes and seagoing vessels, mens' and womens' clubhouses, ritualized cannibalism and warfare. Throughout its history, European navigators could only see high snowy peaks from their ships from the coasts and not believe it, thinking they were clouds. Up until well into this century maps of Netherlands New Guinea had great white patches in the center showing that no white man had ever penetrated. The discovery and coastal exploration of West New Guinea came about because of the Moluccan spice trade. The first Dutch ship, captained by William Janz, reached the mainland in 1605; nine of his crew were eaten by tribesmen while fetching fresh water. The Spanish, British and Germans all tried to establish colonies here until the territory came into Dutch possession in the 19th Century. The Dutch government stubbornly hung on to Irian Jaya right up until 1962, twelve years after the rest of Indonesia had been handed over to Indonesians. It was the one last pearl in their former island empire. The Indonesians based their claim to the territory because it had once come under the Sultan of Tidore's suzerainty. They also argued that all the former Netherlands East Indies was promised to the Indonesian Republic by truce agreements. In Sukarno's *konfrontasi* campaign to oust the Dutch more than 2000 Indonesian soldiers were parachuted into wild jungle or put ashore in various parts of the Dutch-held territory with the intention of leading Irianese villagers in rebellion and sabotage against the Dutch. Hundreds were captured and killed; you can see some of the graves in Jayapura. Most of Indonesia's military forays into the conflict area ended in disaster; it was more world opinion that forced the Dutch out. The so-called New York Agreement between Holland and Indonesia in 1962 called for the Irianese to be given an opportunity to vote so that their joining the Indonesian republic be 'an act of free choice'. But in the year this vote was to have been held (1969), Jakarta waived the referendum and selected only 1025 delegates to do the voting. All these government appointed representatives, plied with favors and promises, voted to join Indonesia without a single dissenting vote. The Indonesians failed to consult the remaining 800,000 or so people in the interior because of the very real communication difficulties. In Aug. 1969, Irian Jaya became a part of Indonesia.

politics: Small ragtag forces of Free Papua guerillas, who believe that the Irianese are Melanesian and not Asian, have been fighting for the freedom of Irian since 1963 when this former Dutch colony was handed over to the Indonesian republic. These guerillas (OFM) are based in dense jungle lowlands near the northernmost joint boundary of Papua New Guinea around the Membarano River region. There are ambushes of Indonesian army patrols and district officials are now and then assassinated, but most incidents are successfully hushed up. Today the OFM is very much contained and doesn't constitute a threat to the present Indonesian administration. But foreigners aren't allowed to buy air tickets to the Highlands this year (1977) because of political troubles brought on by the elections in May. In fact, on 17 May 1977 Indonesian troops were dropped into the Baliem to quell uprisings in which 30 Irianese and 6 policemen were killed. Danis attacked police posts with spears and pounded stakes into airfields to prevent reinforcements from landing. Indonesians have used a combination of military repression, tight political control, economic development, buying off Irianese radicals with offers of rewards and status, as well as stepping up their nationalistic education policy, all aimed at instilling in the Irianese a sense of belonging to the Indonesian nation. The Indonesian government claims to be spending more money per capita in Irian Jaya than in any of its outer provinces. But Irian Jaya's average population is only 6 people per sq km and most of the money goes to improve transportation and communication links so as to solidify the political infrastructure and to make it easier for the military to control the province. Much emphasis is put on education with about ⅓ of the civil service employed by the Education Department. Cendrawasih University in Jayapura was one of the first projects the Indonesians completed. Vocational schools for high school age students are being built or expanded and a trickle of Irianese are sent to Java for technical training. Indonesians generally have a paternalistic attitude towards Irianese; they are enforcing change too quickly. A high ranking Indonesian general has even spoken of civilizing the natives 'if neccesary, at the point of a bayonet'. In Wamena in the Baliem Valley a naked Dani tribesman must put on clean shorts and a clean shirt before he goes to the police station for work details or for inquiries.

economy: The mineral, petroleum, forest and ocean resources of Irian Jaya are being criminally and harshly exploited with little benefit to the Irianese people. The Javanese have laid big plans for Irian Jaya's inland and offshore wealth and the Japanese are robbing its deepwater seas north by paying off influential politicians. Not only political positions but most economic enterprises are filled by outsiders and the Irianese as a rule get very little spinoff from foreign investments. Native sons aren't employed by these companies except as laborers; their personnel are drawn from the outside. Irian Jaya is the only province in all of Indonesia which has gold, uranium, copper, and perhaps even more oil resources than Sumatra. New oil rigs are opened up practically every week. Copper deposits at Tembagapura in the Ertsberg Mountains in the south-central region are reported to be among the largest in the world. They started with nothing in the middle of the Stone Age and the American Freeport Copper Co. has put over US$280 million into the project so far. Tramways were laid to carry ore through the mountains; a processing mill, a port, and a 112 km road were built. This province also produces rattan, copra and the finest and widest variety of timber in Indonesia including ironwood (kayu besi) on the coasts which is tough, weather and borer resistant. But marketing problems keep the timber industry in its infant stages.

the people: Papuans are spread throughout the whole territory in small clans kept separate by terrain, dialect and customs. They have little ethnic, linguistic, historic or spiritual relationship with other Indonesians. There's a giddy variety of tribes and virtually hundreds of languages with no one language intelligible to more than 150,000 people. Some only 2000 people speak. Only the areas around Manokwari on the eastern coast of Vogelkop (Bird's Head), the Schouten Islands in Geelvink Bay, the northern coast near Jayapura, and several fertile highland valleys (Paniai Lakes and the Baliem) have relatively high population densities. Some inland valleys have 10-15 people per sq km, though most parts have less than 6 people per sq km, or are totally uninhabited. Indonesians from Celebes, Java, the Moluccas and many other islands live in trading and fishing communities and in oil centers along the coasts, river mouths and on satellite islands. They have mixed with the original Papuans of the island and have had more contact with foreigners, particularly since WW II. The 800,000 Irianese who live in the central mountain regions have generally more complex social, spiritual and family structures than the coastal peoples. Negritos of the purest blood, and little known very isolated pygmy tribes, still live in the rough Pegunungan Sudirman Mountains, some raising crops and pigs as high as 3000 m.

missionaries: Over 200 missionaries are at work in Irian Jaya, more than any other locale in Indonesia. Protestant missionaries are active in building hospitals and clinics while Catholics concentrate more on agricultural projects and schooling. Both have had schools here for the last 20 years. Just in the last 3 years has Indonesia set up its own schools in the highland regions. The missionaries have made their mistakes. In the early days the natives

developed a taste for American missionary flesh, especially of the fanatic Protestant breed, of whom a few were consumed in the 60's and even the 70's. Some tribes used war arrows made from ground down metal Christian crosses given to them by the missionaries. In 1956 a violent uprising took place at Obano because these 'soldiers of God' had thoughtlessly brought in hundreds of thousands of cowrie shells for trading in order to establish their settlements, drastically undercutting the value of the shells and wrecking the local economy. The young men would age the new shells in battery acid, thereby usurping the privileges of the older chiefs. Dutch troops had to be called in and more than 200 tribesmen were killed by mortar fire. Several missionary groups have been known to go into the interiors with penicillin to clear up stubborn cases of yaws in 10 days, these pre-industrial natives attributing this 'miracle' to Jesus. Missionaries have also used their prior knowledge of a solar eclipse to bring about mass confessions of sin. There has always been conflict between the elders who want to hold onto the mysticism of the old religion and the young who are taking up Christianity. There was a war in Nibsan in Jan. 1975 when two Catholic priests were killed. One group sought refuge in the church and it was burned down and only the priests' heads were left. Read some 'missionary classics' (see 'Booklist') before you go; valuable for background for seeing how the missionaries think, since they are such important change agents between the Irianese and the Indonesian army and officials. **missionary organizations:** CAMA-Christian Missionary Alliance; RBMU-Regions Beyond Missionary Alliance; UFM-Unevangelized Fields Mission; ABM-Australian Baptist Mission; APEM-Asian Pacific Christian Mission; TEAM-Evangelical Alliance Mission; ZGK-Netherlands Reformed Church; Summer Institutes of Linguistic Studies; Wycliff Bible Translators; and finally the Christian Literature Crusade.

coastal transport: Try oil carrying, oil survey or oil rig supply ships for a free ride, especially in the petroleum-rich north; they ply between Manokwari, Sorong and Biak. From Jayapura there are small boats carrying rice and equipment back and forth along the northern coast. BUMA are private contractors who carry supplies and dynamite; they also take passengers, often packing as many as 200 people onboard. BUMA operates about 100 boats on the southern coastline, 20 boats in the Agats area alone. They also have offices in Fak Fak, Merauke, Sorong, and Biak. **by air:** Because the construction of roads are of such staggering expense, planes are about the only means of travel inside the province; but are costly. The cheapest is to utilize missionary aircraft. MAF means 'Missionary Aviation Fellowship' (Protestant air service) and

AMA means 'Associated Missions Aviation' (Roman Catholic air service). Both are very helpful. MAF alone has 185 airstrips all over Irian Jaya. They often use *stol* (short takeoff and landing planes) aircraft which can land almost anywhere. **hiking:** Quite tortuous but possible. You are faced with an excruciatingly difficult terrain with jagged limestone pinnacles and deep gorges with fiercely running torrents. In the south you must slog your way through equatorial swamps and jungles. In 1961 the son of one of the richest men in the world, David Rockefeller, died on the southern coast of Irian Jaya by drowning, was eaten by crocodiles or natives.

Cape Abba, Irian Jaya: *On the southern shore of Teluk Bintuni. There are many caves and galleries in this area with rock wall drawings done by prehistoric artists 400-1000 years ago in high coastal cliffs accessible only by sea. The Abba cave has one whole wall covered in silhouttes of hands with red ochre spat around them. A wild chaotic multi-colored collection of stencilled footprints, figures of men and sea animals, crescent moons, solar eclipses and the sun, lizard gods, fish, turtles, birds, boats. Some are hauntingly drawn, others just scribbled.*

IRIAN JAYA

✱ AIRFIELD STRIP

⊙ DIVISION SEAT

○ DISTRICT SEAT

SCALE KM

0	50	100	150	200

Freeport Copper Co.: *Located at Tembag-
pura, N.E. of Kokonau. This company
spending S$280 million to mine a gigantic ou
cropping of ore-bearing rock at an altitude
3532 m above sea level. The mine site sits on
ledge with mountains to the north and a shee
787 m drop to the south. They had to lowe
men and equipment by helicopter to build firs
a settlement, then laid a hard gravel roa
through 112 km of mangrove swamps fro
the sea to Tembagapura. The 787 m to th
mine site is covered by one of the longes
single-span aerial tramways in the world
Some 7500 tons of ore are transported daily t
a smelting plant where they are concentrate
from 2.4% copper to 32%. Then the ore is ser
112 km to the sea by pipeline. The actual cop
per output is 400,000 lbs. a day, and anothe
nearby deposit at least as large as the first w
soon be tapped. The first deposit will be gon
in 6 more years.*

Sorong: *Prepare yourself for a few heavy rip-offs in Sorong. The airport, Jefman, is on an island 32 km off Sorong. It costs Rp5000 to charter a dugout canoe to town. It's powered by two 40 hp outboarders and the trip is more than dangerous in the rough seas — not recommended. From Sorong to the airport is even more expensive, Rp10,000. A helicopter costs Rp16,000 one way. At 11 am the MS Merauke leaves the harbor of Sorong for the airport. Takes 1½ hours and costs Rp1000; it goes back in the afternoon. Change money at Bank Exim next to Pelni office. There's a few expensive night clubs with Manado hostesses around Hotel Cenderawasih.*

THE NORTHERN PROVINCES

(JAYAPURA, CENDRAWASIH AND MANOKWARI)

JAYAPURA

Pop. 30,000 On the N.E. coast of the territory. A tropical town with a brilliant blue harbour surrounded by perpetually green hills. Most houses are built on the slopes of the hills, while the administrative portion lies in a flat area between them. Access roads are cut out of steep rock walls. Lights of ships out in the harbor at night. A river with a wrecked car in it drains to the sea. Jayapura is dead from 12-4 pm when most shops and offices are closed. The *imigrasi* here will give a 4th or even 5th month extension without too much hassle or money. Change money at the Impor-Expor Bank. Paradiso Bar down on the harbor is where the night life is. Cold Heineken beer at Rp300. To dance with Manado hostesses, get a fistful of dance tickets at Rp150 each. **getting there:** The airport is at Lake Sentani, 40 km from Jayapura, one hour's drive. Even if 5 or 6 share a minibus, it will cost about Rp500 apiece to get into the city. Instead walk 10 minutes to Sentani village and get a *bemo* into Jayapura for Rp250-300. Tell the driver you want to get off at Losmen Lawo, the cheapest. **transport:** Get around by taking taxis (yellow licence plates) for Rp50-75. Watch the drivers, they cunningly lie about distances. Hitching is quite easy in and around the city.

stay: Agrapura Hotel just on the crest of the hill before descending into town, is Rp2500. Losmen Hamadijaya, Rp2000, is in a neighborhood of thousands of children and floating kites. Nearby is Hamadi Beach with its washed up rusted American assault boats from the WW II landings. Losmen Lawo, Jl. Sulawesi 22, is the latest cheap place, only Rp1000. Hotel Negara, Dok V. Jl. Trikora (on the other side of town) offers standard rooms for Rp6000 or *ekonomi*-rooms, Rp4500. They give a student discount of 40-50% off the Rp4500 rooms. For long term stay at Bali Toko, Rp12,000 a month, but no food.

eat: Really expensive food because most of it is imported from Surabaya. Irresistable fruit is sometimes available but even. a simple *es buah* costs Rp250. Most meals cost Rp300-400. Some places have *nasi campur* and *gado2* for Rp150-200. It's cheaper to buy a big loaf of bread, tinned cheese and fish, oleo, peanut butter, eggs and coffee. Pasar Malam, two blocks in back of the Impor-Expor Bank, is open from 5-11 pm; many eating tents here with charcoal grilled fish and vegetables, Rp250-300- about the best deal in town. Pasar Sentral down from Losmen Hamadi is also good for eats. Go early in the morning when the farmers are unloading; bring small change to buy big bunches of bananas, papayas (red inside), and other fruit cheaper. In Pasar Sentral, the taxi drivers eat at Ekasari next to Sumatran Restoran; has a fixed priced menu, and a lorikeet.

sights: Go to the end of the line with a bus to Ankasa, Rp50. Buses leave every hour until noon, then no buses until 4 pm. Bus goes up the mountain; get off and walk around, good views of the city. Take a taxi Rp75 to Bestiji, an indonesiazation of the name of a wartime American military base, 'Base G'. From Bestiji walk down to a partially deserted beach. During WW II, General MacArthur made his headquarters for awhile in Jayapura on a hill overlooking the beautiful harbor. You can still see his old command post, the huts now being used as headquarters for a fish farming pond. **crafts:** On Lake Sentani intricate panels are carved with raised surfaces painted black and white. Teluk Yos Sudarso is well known for its bark paintings of fish and monitor lizards; also woodcarving in the round showing kneeling and standing figures.

from Jayapura: To see the outstanding map of Irian Jaya in the Pertamina Office on Dock 8, ask Mr. Siragar. **by boat:** Slow Melanesian rice boats sail out of Jayapura to Biak for Rp5000 and up. But they take as long as 5 days; you can walk faster. Sorong and Ambon are easier places to get boats from. **ships:** The Kowera Office on the harbor arranges sea travel; see Mr. John. Pelni ships to Surabaya (Rp45,000) or to Ujung Pandang (Rp 35,000) depart Jayapura every week or 10 days. This is a nice trip and a relaxed way to experience outer island Indonesia. Moving real slow it takes 9-10 days to Surabaya and 13-14 days to Ujung Pandang. There are calls at Manokwari, Sorong, Ternate, Bitung, Pare Pare (on west coast of Celebes), spending 1-2 days at sea, then 1 or 2 days to walk around in port. But you never know when the ship is leaving so you have to hang around; departing times keep on being put off.

flights from Jayapura: Often the missionaries have cheaper air fares into the interior than the

NORTH IRIAN JAYA 425

commercial airlines. Ask at MAF (Protestant missions) or AMA (Catholic missions); both their headquarters are at Sentani Airport. To fetch hamburger, milk and eggs for the American missionaries, MAF operates a once a week (usually on Saturday) flight from Sentani to Vanimo and then on to Wewak (P.N.G.). At only Rp4000 this is the cheapest way (except for walking) to get to or from P.N.G. Depends on their free space and on the weight of the cargo if they can take you or not. From Sentani you could possibly get on a missionary flight to Australia which picks up spare parts for their aircraft, but planes leave no more than once a month. AMA at Sentani has fairly regular flights to the Star Mountains (Ok Sibil) and Agats via Wamena. For these inland flights the missionaries mostly use Cessna single engine aircraft. On Merpati flights ride in mainly Twin Otters and DHC turbo-prop stol-aircraft, or in some cases even old Dakotas and Fokker Friendships full of cabbages, goats, chickens and soldiers with sten guns. To Wamena it's Rp12,500, 4 times weekly. Since you don't get a discount buying round trip, just buy a one way ticket. You might be able to get a cheaper ride back with a returning missionary aircraft or even a free ride with a charter. Merpati to Merauke, Rp38,875, twice weekly. On this flight south you pass right over the glacial covered central mountain spine, an experience you won't forget. Dress warm. For Tanah Merah fly first to Merauke then on to Tanah Merah for another Rp19,000. **others:** Walk to Vanimo (P.N.G.)? The police in Wewak say it's OK but the P.N.G. customs people, whose first post is in Wewak, say it's for forbidden since too many Irianese arrive illegally in Vanimo seeking better living conditions and job opportunities. You may be arrested by the D.C. But some people manage it. Boats from Jayapura to Vanimo are quite rare.

BIAK

Known as *Kota Karang* (Town of Coral). Hot and bright, like sugar and water. For travelers, just a way station place with a big Indonesian naval base, 10 admirals, and an international airport. Walk easily from the airport into town; taxi is Rp750. See the fish market; giant tropical fish. Biak is a major bird-smuggling center. Pasar Panir sells (illegally) Bird of Paradise skins from Serui on the island of Japen, Rp15-20,000 asking price. Also live lorikeets and ravens (Rp6500) from other New Guinea islands. Don't rely upon the *imigrasi* in Biak, they tell you to go to Jayapura. **getting there:** The Merpati office in Ujung Pandang will grant student concessions but only on return fares. If you're flying Merpati from Ujung Pandang (or from Java) to Biak and proceeding to another destination within Irian Jaya the day after, then Merpati will put you up for

free in a hotel in Biak. You only need a written confirmation.

vicinity of Biak: Take a taxi Rp250, 26 km to the town of Bosneck on the east coast. A beautiful beach, the first Dutch capital of Biak. If you want to see where the Americans poured aviation gas and TNT down a hole and incinerated alive thousands of Japanese soldiers, go to the Japanese caves in the limestone hills to see the skeletons. For this you must charter a 4-wheel drive jeep taxi (Rp1500) for the road through the bush, then climb a steep mountain. **Korim Beach:** On the north coast 40 km by taxi bus, Rp400. Ride through tropical landscapes of Melanesian hill villages, tunnels of butterflies, and tall dead trees with wild orchids perched on top. Fruit for sale at roadside stalls along the way. Sleep in the house on the beach, on the beach itself, or ask the *kepala kampung* for a bed.

from Biak by ship: Book for ships at the Pelni Office; at P.T. Fajar, opposite the Merpati office; or at the Jayawijaya Shipping Lines, Jl. Tuan Bonjol. Pelni fares from Biak to: Sorong, Rp27,000; Jakarta, Rp67,000; Donggala, Celebes, Rp34,250. The cargo tramp steamer Tolando comes in from Jakarta, then on to Ambon from Biak (Rp24,500) once monthly; sometimes does the Morotai trip as well. Go straight up to the captain to pay. **prahus:** Get-*prahus* with outboard motors (one drum of petrol takes you there and back) to the traditional island of Japen; not in touch with the world. Also *prahus* to Manokwari via Nufor Island, Rp7,200, 280 km. The Monsoons being in Aug. and last 1 ½-2 months; there are more ships when the seas are not so rough. **flights:** In Biak, Merpati grants student discounts even on one-way fares. If you want to take boats from here on out, try trading in your Merpati air ticket for an M.C.O. which can be used towards the purchase of another ticket later. Merpati flights from Biak to: Manokwari, Rp18,450, 4 weekly; Sorong, Rp33,250, twice weekly; Fak Fak, Rp35,600. It's cheaper to fly Merpati to the island of Japen than going by chartered boat. See Cor at Wisma Panagia to arrange the charter of a Piper Aztec, maximum 5 people, about US$210 per hour to Merauke, Asmat, etc. (but can't land one at Agats).

MANOKWARI PROVINCE

Arfak: On the Bird's Head peninsula (Vogelkop in Dutch) in the N.W. corner of Irian Jaya. Exotic butterfly country. The inhabitants along this north coast of Irian Jaya are a striking mixture of Irianese, Buginese, Filipino, and Chinese peoples. There has also been much contact with people of the Moluccas to the west; the native languages here have a connection with those of northern and southern

the flying fox *(kalong): The most impressive of Indonesia's fruit bats. The largest have a wingspan of 1.67 m (5½ ft.). The kalong has a dog-like face with a long snout, sparkling eyes, and pricked up ears. Its head is covered in golden fur while the body fur is dark. In some species the genital area is covered only in black skin, and their genitalia is quite human in appearance, giving rise to many of its nicknames in Irian* *Jaya. Kalongs live in big colonies. In the day they hang motionless at the tops of the tallest rainforest trees, but at sunset they slowly form a long column and fly off to feed. At night troops swoop down upon the fruit trees, squeaking, biting, fighting, copulating, feeding among the branches, a memorable sight in the beam of a flashlight.*

Halmahera. Along the coasts many picturesque small towns with fishing and sawmill operations. Though remote from the main sea routes, this province has many natural harbors. The English built a fort at Dore in 1790 but so many died of beriberi and starvation that they pulled out by 1795. The Arfak tribe were the most notorious headhunters of western New Guinea. Often ancestor's skulls were worn as charms or else kept in an honored part of the house. This tribe fought the Japanese (and ate them) with rifles dropped by air from allied planes.

Manokwari: Though only covering a small area, the land in this district is very rich and populated. Mountains come right down to the sea. Very nice climate. The Irianese here are mostly Christians. Many Indonesian civil servants. An agricultural college, Catholic missionary, and a navy repair yard. Stay at PNK Wisma, Rp8000 or else Manokwari Hotel, Rp5000 and very bad- not even running water, no food, and you get to walk up a steep hill. Buy food before you ascend. **from Manokwari:** Rent a small Masda car, Rp1500 an hour. In Manokwari itself good roads, but terrible once you leave town.

Sorong: A big Pertamina oil base. Produces with its 10,000 laborers about 24,000 barrels a day. Pertamina actually spends money here, all other

places they only take. In front of Sorong a beautiful seaside but not much else to see or do. Many bars with Manado waitresses. Texas oilmen drinking whisky in cafes. Smelly market. Giant stuffed sea turtles, Rp2700-7500. **stay:** Sorong Hotel, airconditioned. Or the Beach Hotel is Rp7500 with breakfast. Tony's Yappen's guesthouse is on the pier close to the boats and the Chinese bar; has 5 rooms at Rp1500 per night, pretty good for Sorong prices. He's trying to build more rooms and to put in proper washroom facilities, to cater for low-budget travelers, but he's having a hard time because he's West Irianese, and the Javanese in Sorong don't like to see the local people getting on. Tony speaks English. Eat in the Chinese bar next door. After drinking in the noisy bar, most sailors spend the night at Tony's.

from Sorong: Merpati flies from Sorong to Fak Fak every other Wed., Rp19,000. Because of oil exploration and survey ships this is one of the best places to get ships. To Fak Fak, around Rp10,000. About once a month Pelni ships from Java stop first here, then go east or south. To the Salawati Islands charter a longboat without floats (2 engines), Rp25-30,000. On this north coast outboard motors are given as the dowry price so if you want to start a family bring a Johnson or an Evinrue.

SOUTHERN COAST

Cape Abba: Marvelous cave drawings can be seen in this area, which can only be approached by sea. In these paintings the artists show their very close relationship with sea animals and the cosmos. See the hornbill with its ribs x-rayed. **Sosorra Caves:** Near the small coastal village of Furur there are charcoal paintings of ships, the moon, and setting suns. At the entrance to this sacred cave is the village's hallowed stone, and inside is a freshwater spring with a nearby altar for offerings. Magic atmosphere. View other rock paintings at Risatot, Arjuni Island, Dury Cave, Warmerai Island; also at Kokas, Kaimana, Arjuna Bay, Humboldt Bay.

Marind-Anim: This tribe has much the same belief-system as the Toba Batak of North Sumatra. Known for their dances. The *Dema-gari* dancer wears a magnificent headdress colored white with an inner border of red and an outer fringe of black; it symbolizes the sun. Their *Ezam-huzum* rite increases fertility and is dramatized by male and female dancers re-enacting the meeting of clan ancestors.

The Mimika: This tribe lives in semi-permanent villages in the swampy country between the Miratha and Setakwa Rivers on the southwest coast. During the rains the Mimika all live in their villages, but at the beginning of the dry season the young marrieds move inland to harvest sago swamps, while the old people remain to grow vegetables and to tend the children. The Mimika erect great thick totem poles up to 12 m high carved with arabesques and demonic human figures. The tree is stuck in the ground upside down with the roots sticking up like a banner. Large 2 m wide decorative fan-shaped symbols (gari) are made from sago palm fronds. The animist Mimika believe in supernatural, nonpersonal spirits who live deep in the forest. Babies don't happen as a result of male and female intercourse but enter the womb of the mother through the navel (puser). Movement is life. If a man faints or is dying his friends and relatives frantically manipulate his limbs in order to bring life back to his body.

Merauke: Merpati flies from Jayapura for Rp38,875. A drab forlorn town in the southeastern coastal area. With its dry spells, the climate here is different from that of other parts of Irian Jaya. Stay in the reasonably priced Government Guesthouse. **vicinity of Merauke:** Inland there are sago palm swamps and white barked eucalyptus trees.

Landscapes are very similar to Australia with giant antheaps 4-5 m high, kangaroos thumping through the shrub, wild pigs and deer. During the dry season, drive through large savannahs with 1-2 m high elephant grass, kingfishers, flocks of wild cranes, storks, wild horses, unclaimed cattle. In shrub forests, cassowaries. Up the Maro River to the village of Erambo see herons, sandpipers, wimbrels, parrots and crowned pigeons as large as geese fly overhead. Red eyes of crocodiles shine in flashlight rays at night (for eating, boil the hind legs and tail; tastes like fishy chicken). Take a riverboat from Merauke to Tanah Merah, over 300 km up-river.

Bian River: The 1 week long *Imo* rite is held by the people of the Bian River. It is performed inside a burning circle of fire over which a bamboo pole is heated until it explodes, signalling the start of wild singing and dancing by the males. Then the mythical ancestor figures in the shape of 3 crocodiles-*Dema Imo, Dav* and *UK-* are destroyed in the fire. A wooden platform is erected in the ceremonial area from which banana, sugar cane and sweet potatoes are suspended. Three dimensional art is seen best in their headhunter's war club. **Kolepon Island** (formerly Frederick-Hendrik Island): Off the southwest coast. Can be reached by small boat from Mapi and Merauke. There's a government station in Kimaam on the Selat Marianne Strait. Most villages are inaccessible during the dry season (June-Oct.). The island is very flat and swampy so the natives live on artificial islands where they grow yams and other root crops.

CASUARINA COAST

A swampy stretch of coast in southeast Irian Jaya between the Barai and Obais Rivers. So named because of its huge casuarina trees, an Australasian species with jointed leafless branches. At dusk the sky fills with thousands of flying foxes which swarm down to feed on trees at the smell of ripe fruit. Here lives the largest of the New Guinea parrots, the *Kakatua Raja,* or King Parrot. At night trees are brilliantly lit by fireflies. Some of the most untouched tribes of New Guinea live here. Once known for their cannibalism, now only practiced in the remote hinterlands. Human meat is prepared like pig meat. In fact, humans are called 'long pigs', though human flesh is juicier than the drier pig flesh. The body is cut up into pieces by women and roasted over a fire.

The Asmat: A tribespeople who live along the Casuarina Coast. Untouched by civilization until recent years. Dutch outposts, missionary settlements and foreign expeditions finally made inroads into this isolated culture during the 50's and 60's. Vast mangrove, sago, and bamboo forests crowd the swampland environment which is home for approximately 35,000 Asmat scattered in 100 odd villages. In the coastal villages of Basiem and Agats, homes are built on pilings. Catwalks or log paths are necessary to cope with the spongy terrain and an estimated 200 inches (5080 mm) of yearly rainfall. Upriver, these Irianese live in houses up to 27-28 m long, or sometimes build houses in the treetops. Wifeswapping (*papisj*-system) is practiced by some groups. Knives and necklaces are made from the thigh bones and vertebrae of the giant cassowary bird. The Asmat paddle long narrow canoes with 3 m paddles while standing up. Fish and shrimp are caught in large hoop nets. They live on sago (their staple diet), mussels, snails, and collect fat insect larvae from decaying stumps of sago palms to be later eaten to the accompaniment of throbbing drums and ritual dances. These larval feasts could last up to two weeks. Dead ancestors' spirits are invited to attend festivities, but only for a night after which they are driven away. Almost every household article is given the name of a dead person. Implements of war are also named after dead relatives to remind the owner of his obligation to take revenge. In the upper river reaches, tribes wrap their dead in bark and lay them out on scaffolding only a few meters away from the house. The bodies are left there to rot until only the skeleton is left. Then the bones are brought into the house. A man will wear the skull of his mother around his neck in order that she give him protection in death as she did in life.

river travel: Could be very hazardous because unbelievably strong river currents cut away at the banks and carry trees and chunks of earth with

them. River banks are choked with bush, trees, ferns, gnarled roots and flowers. Going upriver there are unforgettable sights of freshwater turtles, crocodiles, white herons, Indian sea eagles, kingfishers, parrots, and slow-flapping hornbills. Pick out the red flowering trees hidden among other trees. See little villages hugging the rivers, houses usually on stilts. Live with the natives without payment. When villagers are unhappy in one location they just pack up the whole village and shift to another, so don't ever expect a village you've heard about to be there anymore.

Pirimopon: A coastal village subject to drastic tidal floods. Huts are built on stilts up to 6 m high. Totem poles lie abandoned on the shore. Over 200 years ago Capt. Cook attempted to land here but decided against it because of the hostility of the natives. He died in 1779 because he wasn't as cautious with Hawaiian natives. The book *Peace Child* was written about the villages north of Pirimopon. It describes a people who practice a religion which worships treachery; when the story of Judas is read to them out of the Bible, they cheer and clap. **Yaosakor:** Located at the branch of the River Eilanden. Go up to the BUMA (shipping agent) and they'll put you up. There's a Catholic mission here and a Protestant airfield (MAF) with a floatplane which can be hired out. Chinese work in this area hunting crocodiles.

AGATS

The missionaries own a timber mill here and they've raised wooden walkways all over the town which have now fallen into disrepair and are quite dangerous in places. Not very good *warungs*, just shops with seats outside. A can of coke or FN soda costs Rp400. **getting there:** The Ewer airstrip near Agats on the Per River can only take stol-aircraft like Islanders or small Cessnas and won't accommo-

an Asmat dwelling: *The Asmat are a semi-nomadic people who live on the southwest coast of Irian Jaya in extensive river country of low, muddy land covered in eternally green forests. Since stone doesn't exist in their region, knives and daggers are made from cassowary leg bones, spears and arrows are fashioned from bamboo and wood-mesolithic age practices. They carve large squatting ancestor figures with upward bent arms and other 3-dimensional wood carvings. The Asmat are greatly feared because of their headhunting, cannibalism, and unending tribal warfare in former times.*

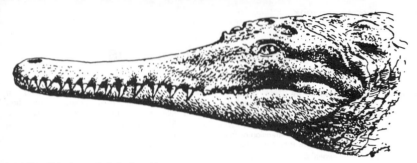

crocodiles: *This giant reptile is distributed from the Asian mainland to northern Australia. Maximum length is 9 m. The crocodile of Irian Jaya is quite distinct. In Africa crocodiles lay their eggs in mud, usually in two layers with sand in between. The heat of the sun hatches the eggs. But since the ivers of New Guinea are often surrounded in dense forests* *right down to the water's edge, the sun's heat can't be used. So New Guinea crocodiles drag leaves and plants together and lay their eggs in the center of a 0.610 m high heap. The heat of the mouldering vegetation hatches their eggs. The female usually lays on top or at the side to guard the eggs. These crocodiles, if not hunted with firearms, prey on man.*

date Aztecs. AMA flies from Wamena to Agats about once a month for Rp7-8000. Best to organize this flight first at their Sentani headquarters in Jaya-pura. Otherwise Agats is really hard to get to. It's possible to walk from Wamena all the way to the south coast (to Agats) by just following the Baliem River south. You run into extensive sago swamps but after a few days you can find *a prahu* down to the coast. **from Agats:** Get on with the mis-sionaries who operate motorized *prahus* which travel upriver.

Asmat arts and crafts: There's a quite unique museum of woodcarvings, weaponry, etc. run by the Catholics in Agats. This whole estuary region is an area of art lovers. Famous woodcarvings made from ironwood (kayu besi) produced around this coastal village include hafts for stone axes, 1-2 m shields, copulating figurines, solid wood human heads, arabesque panels. *Prahus* are painted in bright colors and ornamented with superb carvings. Much of the Asmats' very original art is symbolic of warfare, headhunting and warrior-ancestor venera-tion. Tribal warfare now is outlawed and nearly ex-tinct and the disappearance of warrior life has threatened to curtail the artistic production of the people. For example, their huge *bis* (ancestor poles) were carved solely to commemorate forebears mighty in battle. Fortunately in 1969 under a project financed by the United Nations to revive the local handicrafts, old master carvers were located in each major village and encouraged to train young carvers of promise. A purchasing depot was set up at Agats where good quality carvings were brought in from outlying villages and sorted, selected for display, and purchased from the carvers for cash or barter goods. Some spectacular pieces of Irian art are housed in the Museum of Primitive Art on West 54th St. in New York City.

OTHERS

Kaimana: A very small place and everything is very expensive. Stay at the mission station, Rp1500 a day with food, or at the *pasangrahan*. The mission has maps of the area for some interesting walks in the surrounding jungle, though there are very few native villages left. Walk all the way to Teluk Bin-tuni in about 1 week. Every 2nd week there's a Merpati flight to Sorong via Fak Fak, Rp20,875 plus Rp1000 to go by truck to the airport on a very bad road. Sometimes the mission airlines AMA has a Cessna to Nabire from where you can get planes to Enaratoli and Biak. In the dry season there's a small boat to Kokonau on the south coast where there's a mission station. From Kokonau you can go to Enaratoli by plane or to Agats by small boat.

Fak Fak: An uninteresting place. The airport here has an insane runway which is about 100 m too short for the plane to take off properly and the plane actually falls some 50 m after take off before it gains altitude again. Heart failure.

sea transport: The Pelni ship MS Beligo makes the Merauke-Sorong run once a month. This ship stops at really out-of-the-way places like Agats, Pirimopon, Mimika, Kaimana, Fak Fak, and Teluk Bintuni, taking more than 2 weeks to Sorong from Merauke. The Beligo also calls at Tual, Kai Islands; Tual-Kaimana is Rp3000, 18 hours. As the ship is overcrowded with people traveling to Sorong to work there, conditions can be pretty filthy. You'll be hard pressed to find a place to sleep and the food and the toilets are in the usual Pelni fashion.

THE EASTERN HIGHLANDS

Kiwirok Valley: Reached by following the Ok Bon River when not in flood. People here speak the Kiwirok dialect as well as the Papua New Guinea dialect used in the adjacent territory. Many villagers in this remote area have no comprehension of Irian Jaya as a separate nation from P.N.G. and for that matter 'Papua New Guinea' doesn't mean much to them either. Children are named after the rivers of the region: *Ok Tysop* (boy) and *Ok Bon* (a girl) Irianese here are usually friendly towards the *kaga-wok* (white man). **from Kiwirok:** A trek leads up to Tayesigin at 2200 m then on to the village of Tomkadin on Mt. Tomka, a ridge parallel to the northern Ok Bon only 9 km from P.N.G.

Tanah Merah (Red Clay): In the Southern Division. Called Boven Digul by the Dutch, originally this was a very large internment camp built on a malarial swamp. In 1926, many of the Communist leaders of the Madiun Rebellion were sent here by the Dutch. During revolutionary times (1926-48), notable Indonesian political personalities were exiled here- Hatta, Bondan, Sukarno- and many others. There have never been any escapees; they were invariably eaten by cannibals or died before they ever reached the coast. The present Indonesian government imprisons most opponents to its regime on Buru Island, Maluku, and Nusa Kambangan, off Cilicap, southern Java. **getting there:** Fly from Merauke. Alternatively, it takes about 3 days from the mouth of the Digul River by boat. **from Tanah Merah:** Kawakit, a region of steep valleys and raging rivers, is two days by boat upriver from Tanah Merah but only one day back. Wambons, the tribespeople of this area, are very shy and suspicious. From Kawakit it's a one month trek to the jungles of Katem. Hazy tracks. Along the western bank of the East Digul in a northerly direction from Katem, inhabitants still live in tree houses built as high as 15 m above the ground.

Mt. Antares: Over 3660 m high. Follow the Ok Bon River to its source. A cold but spectacular region of narrow ravines, trees with sharp thorns growing on the trunks, purple and pink rhododendrums, brightly colored spotted tree frogs, tree kangaroos with black stripes down their backs, and many species of insects found nowhere else. There are no tracks up these slopes because the Ok Bon Valley people consider this mountain *alut* (taboo); the spirits of their departed ancestors live there. Pass through a moss-covered fairytale enchanted forest filled with mist, thick cushions of ferns and

fungi, creepers trailing down trees, clinging fog splintered by sunlight, damp air smelling of rotting wood. Silence. Just the tinkle of water drops. No wind. Mysterious atmosphere and not to be traveled through alone; could sink into moss up to your waist.

SIBIL VALLEY

The Sibil Valley has the Orion Range for its northern boundary, the Tamal Mountain Ridge lies to the south, and the Digul Mountains to the southwest. Few white men have ever seen this area where rock villages are built on bare mountain ridges. The most explosively colorful airfield in New Guinea is here, surrounded by yellow African marigolds in full bloom. The valley is located in a limestone region with many deep water-filled sink holes with frogs (kol) and small birds swimming on their surface. Night moths and beetles extraordinaire. When it rains heavily in the west part of the valley the Ok Sibil becomes a wild muddy river which rushes through a cleft in the mountains and finally disappears down a hole in the ground only 2 meters wide.

The Sibillers: Their home is east of the Zigibi Range in a system of mountains the Dutch called the Star Mountains, the highest ridges and summits named after stars and constellations, Leo, Orion, etc. Sibillers have dark brown to light colored skin, in actuality the same people east and west of the international border. Women wear little aprons of rushes that look like scrubbing brushes. The men have small builds but are too large to be called pygmies. Body ornamentation includes armbands of pig tusks and orchid bark, chains of grass, parrot beaks, strings upon strings of dogs' teeth, and cowrie shells which are negotiable currency and a part of the bride price. Also worn are bamboo discs in the earlobes, Bird of Paradise headdresses, headbands of possum skins, sticks, rats' ribs, shells, buttons, bright feathers, and heads of rhinoceros beetles with the antenna sticking up are stuck through pierced noses. To show their eligibility for marriage, men wear clumps of clay weighing up to 2 kilos in their hair. Starting with their left little finger and by using their own body as an abacus, Sibillers can count up to 27. Sometimes the skeletons of fish and skulls of mammals are hung on the ceilings of their houses. Sibillers don't believe in natural death: you're either murdered or taken by witchcraft. Dead bodies are wrapped in leaves and tied upright in a tree. The family then sits amongst the branches to lament their loss until the stench drives them away.

Sibil War: When Sibillers go to war people could die in the process, but it's more like a festival or a sporting event. A war could be caused by women-stealing, a death due to witchcraft that must be avenged, boundary trespasses, etc. Both sides customarily agree as to when the war is to begin and the two parties clear the battleground together. As a neighborly gesture men from villages friendly to the warring *kampungs* also take part. As in all formal occasions, the combatants are brightly decorated with their faces painted red with pigs' fat and earth. Wars and waged only with stone war clubs and bows and arrows that have special tips for use against humans. The ability to dodge arrows and spears receives more praise than brave charges.

Zigibi: In this area there's a 4880 m limestone ridge from where you can see northwards over the whole East Digul River, the Antares mountain chain, and even distant snowcapped Puncak Mandala is sometimes visible. Hiking in this area is over some nearly impossible terrain. **Dilmot:** Over the East Digul near Dilmot is a suspension bridge more than 80 m long. **Um Bak:** Between Tulo and Kogonmedip. The Valley of the Giant Pisang Trees. These mammoth-stemmed banana trees grow up to 12-15 m high; the fruit is inedible. **Lambinime:** 30 minutes walk from this village is a rattan suspension bridge over a river 55 m below. If someone gets terrified and stuck in the middle Irianese start throwing stones and shouting to get him to rush to the other side safely. There are wild fabulous landscapes in this region with mossy green tangled woodlands and rushing dangerous rivers. Further north is the Valley of the Waterfalls tumbling out of the jungle into gorges; some you can't even hear or see where they fall. **Puncak Mandala:** One of the four New Guinea summits of eternal snow, mist, high wind and cold. Papuans maintain gardens on this mountain up to 2000 m. On the way up there are bare-sloping faces of limestone rock and alpine meadows. Higher up still, icicles hang on your tent. Antarctic landscapes.

flying over the mountainous backbone of New Guinea

THE CENTRAL HIGHLANDS

These highlanders still live a stone-age existence, slashing and burning forests to grow sweet potatoes and other vegetables, and terracing and cultivating mountain slopes that lie at an angle of 45 or even 50 degrees, far above the frost line to 2600 m and even up to 2800 m. They have for centuries constructed arduous irrigation systems in their tribal areas. Fields are generally cleared by the men, though planting and harvesting are done by the women. Each wife has her own garden plot. The pig is all important in the tribe's ceremonial and economic life and it's a crucial part of their social organization. Parts of the pig are used in ornamentation and for making tools. It's essential for feasts and as payment of personal debts. Tribal reparations are made with pigs to avoid war. The mens' main interests are pigs and woman, his status determined by how many of each he owns. A fat pig and a new wife cost about the same amount of cowrie shells. Like family members, when it gets dark the pigs wait outside the huts for the women to return home from the fields. You could even see women walking down roads with a piglet on one breast and a human baby on the other. Unlike most places in Indonesia, the highland Irianese don't look upon you as superior to them in any way. They accept you as you are. They have absolutely no eye avoidance when they look at you; they haven't been taught any complexes yet. Known for their yard-wide grins, they let out little yelps of delight, walk with you through the valley, take you back to their villages, play a bamboo jaw's harp for your entertainment. Blonde hair could fill the natives of the remote interior with amazement, wanting to keep locks of it for decoration. They stroke a white person's hair because it's so soft and smooth, lifting up pant legs to make sure you're white and hairy underneath. Your arms and legs get pinched mercilessly to see if you're real and not a ghost. When you shave or brush your teeth Irianese could run away thinking that you've gone made with foam coming out of your mouth. There are as well very wicked men among these people. Some valleys you just don't go into, you're never sure if you're going to be greeted with arrows or with laughter. In your wanderings in the interior bear in mind that 4 Dutch families were killed and eaten southeast of the Baliem Valley at Soba and Ninia as recently as Christmas 1974. Headhunting and cannibalism were once a rife but now have been all but stamped out by the Indonesian government and by the efforts of the missionaries.

crafts: Woodcarving and other crafts are much

less affected by commercialism than in the P.N.G. half of the island. **noken:** The womens' string bag of the Irian Jaya uplands is made out of rolled bark fibres; often dyed in red and purple stripes. In it the women carry sweet potatoes, babies, piglets and tools all at once. When empty it's worn over the shoulders and down the back to keep them warm in the cold mornings and evenings. **koteka** (peka pipes): A yellow penis gourd from 75 cm up to ½ m long made from the outer rinds of an elongated pumpkin-like fruit; common all the way from Telefomin on the Sepik River in P.N.G. to Teluk Bintuni, south of the Bird's Head. Men wear no clothing except this penis sheath which emphasizes their nakedness all the more. Each man has a wardrobe of several sizes and shapes, what he feels like wearing that day. Each *koteka* is carefully fashioned to fit the contour of a man's stomach. A very short *koteka* is used when a man goes into battle, a very large one for festive times. Sometimes decorated on top with a tassel of fur or a spiky cacoon. In some mountain tribes it's also used as a betelnut container. **kowar:** A decorated box sculpted by some tribes in which a human skull is kept; serves a typical ancestor worship function.

fighting, hunting and domestic implements: The following implements will be offered 'for sale' to you by the natives from the moment you step out of the plane in the highlands. Game arrows are smooth but war arrows have rows of small barbs which are difficult to remove. Some tribes use latex to attach bone barbs so that when the arrow is removed an infection will set in. Arrows have a very long shaft made of light cane to steady it in flight. Often the head and foreshaft of a spear or an arrow is carved in one piece from a hardwood. Negritos use the smallest bows, about 1.50 m long, while Papuans use bows over 1.85 m. Armguards protect the skin against the rattan bowstring. Spears are occasionally found 4 to 4.50 m long and as thick as a man's wrist; a hunter hurls himself to the ground in order to throw it with maximum thrust. Uplanders make stone axes by cracking a cliff-face with fire high on a scaffold or by hammering on cold rock; methods at least 30,000 years old. Women use digging sticks with which they find tubers and grubs, and are expected to use them for defence if surprised in their fields by enemy warriors.

TRAVEL IN THE INTERIOR

There's excellent motorcycle country in Wamena, Karnbaga, Mulia and Kangima. Try to hitch a ride with an oil company or geo-mapping helicoptor. **photography:** Pack in silica gel with your excess film and camera to prevent mildew. Take along a UV filter to help subdue sub-tropical glare. Low fine-grained films should be used as the light intensity in the highlands is quite high. **hiking:** The danger of hiking in the interior lies not with meeting poisonous snakes or insects, or hostile natives. The danger is in the harshness of the terrain and climate. If you trek you'll be rained on constantly, you'll fall and strain muscles and nerves, you'll slip down paths and steep rockfaces, wobble over slippery dangerous bridges, go hungry and thirsty. Take light clothing but also a warm sweater for highland mornings as well as windproof and waterproof gear. Shorts are the most comfortable to hike in. For higher altitudes you have to dress like a Himalayan mountain climber. Take a mosquito net (kelambu) for at night there are millions of insects. Use strong thick leather gloves to protect hands against sharp thorns on stems of treeferns and while tackling needle-like limestone ridges. Take along a hat and sunglasses or you'll be sorry. Unless you're Iranese, nature doesn't provide enough for you to live off the land. If you're not prepared to eat mainly sweet potatoes and juicy egg-shaped cucumbers, then food you must carry with you. The red fruit of the *pandanus* palm contains a fatty oil which tastes somewhat like pork fat; to many natives a delicacy but to most Europeans disagreeable. Large bugs, which emit a penetrating smell to Europeans, are eaten by the Iranese as tasty morsels. Sugar cane is very stimulating and thirst-quenching.

carriers: Hire carriers at central highland villages such as Tiom and Ilaga. For the longer treks you might need 20 or more. Bear in mind, the difference between you and them is immense. They are naked, build and eat only what they need, speak a different language, walk differently, even urinate differently. You are pink-skinned, dressed up in clothes, your equipment comes out of packs and your food out of tins. Use matches, steel axeheads, salt, razors, raincoats, mirrors, watches, whetstones, palmfulls of colored beads, and 100 *rupiah* notes plus the cost of their food as payment. A headman for the party, acting as arbitrator and guide, should be paid extra. Always remember the payback system'; whatever is given to you, you must give something in return– a steel axe head for a pig, some beads for a service, etc. Don't ever overpay or you'll bring about a devaluation and play havoc with the local economy. You'll find it could be difficult to get porters for mountain trekking because they're afraid of leaving their own village and immediate surroundings. It's often taboo for them to climb a mountain, believing that it will fall down

and crush them; it's also the forbidden home of ancestors. Never force carriers to walk later than they think because this could cause disturbances and desertion as well as over-exposure to all if caught in heavy cold rain. Mountain Iranese know best where good shelter and plentiful firewood can be found. They can build huts from tree trunks and branches within minutes and light fires without matches in complete darkness with soaking wet wood. Iranese are proud people, not servants. They won't wait on you hand and foot. A contract is made at the start for them to carry so much for so long to such and such a place for an agreed payment and that's that. Small boys and young men will fetch water, light fires, cook breakfast, erect tents, but not the older men.

river-crossings: Iranese cross rivers by throwing rocks in them to make better footholds in the strong currents. They get across larger rivers by simply cutting down trees and letting them crash over them. With an axe as the only tool they can build a crazily constructed bridge out of rattan and branches in only 30 minutes strong enough to hold 20 people on it at once. Sometimes a bridge is just a single strand of rattan with two strands somewhat higher to serve as hand ropes. For suspension bridges an arrow shoots the first *liana* fibre across, then more lines are hauled across until rivers up to 60 m wide are spanned. A high scaffold is first mounted like on a high diving board. Swaying violently, the middle of the bridge almost touches the river. Then it's like climbing up a mountain.

ILAGA REGION

Halfway between Enarotali and the Baliem Valley, the crossroads of the Central Highlands where traders from the east and west meet. Home of the strange Uhunduni tribe and the western Danis. Firesaws are still used to ignite tinder in this area. Surrounded by towering peaks, the jungle in this region is really lush with its tangle of bush, fallen tree trunks, and moor orchids everywhere you look. 600 million fossils are found in the area. **the Uhundunis:** Living in secluded valleys they raise pigs, cultivate struggling gardens, fight wars, are polygamous, and dwell in stone houses. They're the underdogs of all the tribes, looked down upon by the Danis, Monis and Ekagi alike. Uhundunis appease spirits by offering up pigs' blood and by planting certain trees along village paths. They love to sing chants; one person sings the melody, one person harmonizes and carries the main words of the song, while the rest join in responses to phrases somewhat like 'Old MacDonald Had a Farm'.

vicinity of Ilaga: Near Mulia, 80 km north of Ilaga at the end of a treacherous track, is the Ya-Li-

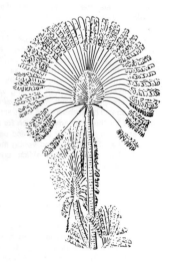

the Traveller's Palm: *Looks like a peacock's tail in shape. Its spreading fan points due east/west and its trunk has a great supply of water in it, so a traveler can both quench his thirst and also find his way.*

Me Quarry. Fire is used here to split the stone off the quarry cliffs for making axes, a practice which sets this culture apart as one of the last remaining paleolithic civilizations on earth. Taking up to 3 months to sharpen against a special rock, the stone becomes so smooth and shiny that you can see your face in it. Buy these same axes in Wamena for Rp500-Rp6000. Another quarry is at Karnbaga. **Swart Valley:** An extremely mountainous district N.W. of the Baliem Valley. The lower part of this valley is overgrown with tall grass, while higher up are continuous primeval forests. Small orchids grow high in the trees. Huts are scattered all over the mountain slopes. The dead are burned in the squatting position in this region.

PANIAI LAKES

Glorious scenery. Discovered by a Dutch flier, Wissel, in 1936 while making an aerial survey for an oil company. Three enchanted lakes are entirely surrounded by blue mountains. The most spectacular, Lake Paniai, is 24 km long and 18 km wide with sloping hills rising up from it. There are two other smaller olive-green lakes. None of them contain fish, only freshwater shrimp. No mosquitoes here. Women seine at night from log boats, building fires in them to keep warm. Paniai Lake has waves but

no current. A heavy mist comes in low over its waters in the early morning and from 9 am clouds start to obscure the mountain walls around the lake. The surface is calm until 11 am when a strong wind sweeps across it and breakers crash against the shore. This area is the home of the Moni and the Ekagi tribes. The Ekagi (or Kapaukus) are a healthy, muscular, black-skinned pygmoid people less than 1.50 m short. One of the first Europeans who visited Paniai described tham as 'childlike, carefree, undependable, selfish, deceitful, transparent, credulous, superstitious, fairly industrious, timid, but not without racial pride'.

getting there: Enarotali is a town on a high plateau near the lakes. AMA operates a fortnightly flight from Wamena (no fixed price) to Enarotali and vice versa. Best is to arrange this flight at Sentani Airport (40 km from Jayapura). Another way to get to Enarotali is from Nabire. Biak to Nabire daily flights cost Rp19,000. There are also boats from Biak to Nabire, Rp4-5000. It's cheaper if you just buy a through ticket on a flight from Biak all the way to Enarotali, Rp22,000, with a stopover in Nabire. **from Enarotali:** AMA Catholic airlines operates flights from Enarotali and from Nabire to Ilaga, Kokonau, Mimika, Timuka, and Agats.

THE BALIEM VALLEY

Discovered by a wealthy American explorer during his botanical and zoological expeditions of the New Guinea highlands in 1938. You can still see the debris of his campsite today on a 3000 m lake plateau. Its discoverer first reported that this mile-high valley appeared to be inhabited by a lost civilization. When the clouds cleared, the expedition members beheld a vast a beautifully tended garden of checkerboard squares with neat stone fences, clean cut networks of canals, and meticulously terraced mountain slopes. (Read of this discovery in the March 1941 issue of *National Geographic*). Baliem received world publicity in 1945 when a sightseeing plane out of wartime Hollandia crashed and its survivors had to be rescued in a daring glider operation. An American nurse in this group called the valley a Shangri La. The first to go in and settle were missionaries by amphibian landing on the Baliem River in 1954. The Grand Valley of the Baliem River is 72 km long by 16-32 km wide. It is inhabited by tribes of neolithic ex-warrior farmers, the Dani people, who number over 100,000. The Baliem River runs like a snake through the valley, supplying water for the Danis' intricate irrigation systems. Danis don't store or plant seeds but plant instead vegetative parts such as sprouts, tubers, rootstocks, and slips. Sweet potatoes, ginger, yams, cucumbers, banana stalks, and tobacco are also grown. Droughts and pests are infrequent. There are no dangerous animals and disease is rare. The valley has magnificent scenery and great tourist potential.

getting there: Land or water routes to the Baliem are nearly impossible. Access is only down one air corridor into the valley, a 300 m escarpment in the northern pass. The plane flies through it and there it is. Either fly from Jayapura, the easiest, or else fly from the south coast from Kokonau, more difficult to arrange. There's a village, a government post, and an airstrip at Wamena in the southern part of the Grand Valley, the focal point for most tourists. Before you fly into the Baliem, change your money at a bank in Jayapura into stacks of red 100 *rupiah* notes. This is the only denomination the Danis accept. Only the chief recognizes the value of a Rp1000 note. In Wamena, get change at the Catholic Mission near the Pertamina Hotel.

climate: High bracing weather. The temperature is mild. Rainfall is moderate. The wettest month is Nov. and the driest are Jan. and February. Sept. through Oct. is the season of high winds (over 80 km an hour). Wind rises in the afternoon. It's fre-

quently cloudy except in the early morning when it's bright and all the surrounding mountains are in clear view.

accommodation: There are hotels in Wamena, but expensive. If you hike out to a Dani village, be sure that you're invited to enter their U-shaped compound otherwise it's like walking into a stranger's living room. Sleep as a guest in the hot smoky *honnay* (mens' roundhouse) which looks like a giant beehive. No furniture. Straw is spread over the floor and in the center a pit fire always burns. Ceilings are black with soot. About 1½ m above is the 2nd floor for sleeping. Charms, tools, fetishes, weapons are also kept there. Sleep in this smoky top section as the cooler bottom room is unbearably thick with mosquitoes. Anywhere in the valley where you see a corrugated iron roof, this means that it's the home of an Indonesian school teacher or a missionary and you can probably stay there. There are village school teachers at Kurima and at Woogi; they are quite glad to see you and they can speak English. Better to stay at Catholic missions in the Baliem rather than the Protestant ones (especially CAMA) since they enjoy better relations with the natives and aren't so rabid. Expect to pay about Rp1000 for food and bed at the missions.

getting about: Using Wamena as a base you could spend a solid month just taking walks. Don't check in at Wamena's *kantor polisi* if you're going on a long trek, they won't let you go if you tell them beforehand. Many parts of the valley are very muddy so have someone carry your luggage, or else fall in mud ditches. If you employ porters for walks in the valley don't pay more than Rp200 a day to each man. You don't have to give them food (unless it's a long walk) because the villagers you stay with will feed them. It's getting more difficult and expensive to find Dani guides; they're holding out for more bread. They could be especially difficult to acquire for the longer distances because they're afraid that they'll be killed by hostile tribes. Pick your villages. In general most where Protestant missionaries went in, native crafts have been obliterated long ago in great fetish-burning confessionals. In Catholic villages they've been retained and even encouraged. For any information about the interior see Broder Karel at the Catholic Mission in Wamena; he's been in Irian Jaya for 26 years. A trail bike here would be ideal. A Zuzuki Fan Fan on Java costs Rp175,000 but you must pay another Rp175,000 to have it transported to Irian Jaya. For long-distance charters, the Catholic mission in

Wamena has 2 planes available. All the mission stations have their own airfields and each has 2-3 flights a month bringing supplies down from Jayapura. So if you just stick around you can catch a flight back to Jayapura cheaper than Merpati.

THE DANIS

Melanesians with negroid features and dark brown skins. No one knows their origin. Danis (in Indonesian termed: *Lannys*) are no longer cannibals; people eastwards are (Soba, Ninia). Dani tribes practice a high degree of social organization, a quite sophisticated from of agriculture, and an advanced engineering skill in constructing rattan bridges and dwellings. They have a complicated system of trading and bartering, importing Bird of Paradise feathers, *scere*-bird plumes, cowrie shells, or the finest spear-wood from distant villages. Their traditional home is the Baliem Vally deep in the highlands of New Guinea. There are no seasons in the Baliem so the Danis spend most of their lives working in the fields, always cleaning, draining, pruning vines, weeding beds, and scooping up the rich soil to put on their gardens. No clothing is worn except

grass skirts and tubelike yellow gourds up to ½ m long, hairnets, necklaces of cowrie shells, and armbands of pigs' scrotums which they believe ward off ghosts. Danis don't believe in washing but smear their bodies with a mixture of soot, pig grease, or red or white clay to keep themselves warm in their often cold climate. In the chilly mornings Dani men stand with their arms wrapped around their necks to keep warm. The loincloths of other tribes and clothing of white men are repugnant and rude to them. Dani men put ballpoint pens, drinking straws, boar tusks, or pieces of tin cans through their noses. Through their ears anything from cigarettes to diaper pins. On festive occasions (and formerly for battles), the men wear the most elaborate adornments such as headdresses of cassowary whisks, white egret feathers, anklets of parrot feathers, looking like they're going to take flight! Though it's being taught on a small scale, Indonesian isn't widely spoken here and the population is in large happily illiterate. They speak two dialects of one language, both spoken with the speed of machinegun fire. Danis have the gentlest handshake you'll ever experience, and appear fearless– their most striking characteristic. Their

---

USEFUL DANI WORDS

nayak	hello for man	nogo	sleep
lauk	hello for woman	ndanda	long way, far
nayak lak	hello for men	lek	no
lauk nayak	hello for women	kani	fire
hat komalan	where are you going?	kanangda	hasty shelter or hut
eka	how much?	tuan	white man
merema	how much?	ap	father
eka	red Rp100 note	sike	arrow
yi	river	pusie	axe
yenengena	lake	honnay	mens' hut
dugundugu	mountain area	yokol	grass skirt
an (or) ena	me	yungal	a married woman's skirt
hat	you	tali	a single woman's grass skirt
nait	I don't like	cege	spear
nan	food	batu ye	stone chisel
wam	pig	holim, koteka	penis-gourd
hipere	sweet potato pulp	jum, noken	net bag
hipere ka	sweet potato leaf	petari	hair net
etai	feast, ceremony	pakaiat	one
koulai	come here	pere	two
gebeh	go away	henawan	three
hano	good, beautiful	ekamonowo	four
weak	ugly	isaliko	five
nelekan	see	wayoawa	six
awo	soon	ekalimowa	seven
imay	here	sawirowa	eight
paybi	long time coming	opalvewa	nine
nawok	start walking, get moving	lumoluwa	ten

strength is phenomenal. Watch one run through the forest barefoot or walk 20 km with a man on his shoulders. Seven Javanese men can't hold a Dani down on the ground.

Dani warfare: Much broken up into fierce clans, the Danis up to about 10 years ago practiced what the anthropologists call ritual-warfare, which means that they regularly faced each other in formal battle. Now the Indonesian government and the missionaries have nearly eliminated all warfare between tribes. Chiefs now have less and less of a basis for their authority; they became chiefs partly because they were fearsome and skilled warriors. Watch-towers once stood along the perimeters of the garden areas so that the no-mans-land beyond could be watched and enemy raids seen before they happened. Each tower was the responsibility of those men who had gardens in the immediate vicinity. During the day, while the women worked in the gardens, men took turns as sentries in the towers. Messages and challenges were yodelled from one tower to the other. Now all these watch-towers have been torn down by the Indonesian authorities. The Danis did not fight a war (weem) for an ideology or in order to annex land or to dominate people but only to avenge ghosts of dead warriors. Often battles, between one alliance in the valley against another, were called out in the mornings. If the battle was not called off because of rain about 200 men would enjoy the fight. If a Dani did not want to fight he was not called a coward or made to suffer. Sallys were highly ritualistic, not intended to wreak carnage, and fighting on the same front line seldom lasted for more than 10-15 minutes. Rarely did a man die, and then only if he was clumsy or stupid. If a death did occur, the enemy plugged the rectum and ventral base of the penis of the dead man with grass to prevent bad magic. The main force stood relaxedly on a hill nearby watching the battle, smoking cigarettes, gossiping, and meeting friends who had come from other areas to participate. When darkness came and the battle was almost over, the warriors of each side would hurl abuse and taunts at each other, causing much laughter between them. When they learned later that an enemy had died of wounds they went out and congregated on hilltops to sing in pitched victorious choruses and yodels, sounding like cheers from a football stadium.

village life: Danis live in villages with U-shaped courtyards. Straw-thatched dome-roofed family dwellings are grouped around the open space. A typical settlement has a surrounding wall to keep in livestock and long tunnel-like connecting passages between houses to avoid moving outdoors on cold nights. Nearby are taro, tobacco and banana gardens. Gourd vines grow under the roofs. Dani buildings are held together with only rattan vines or elephant grass (logob). Roofs are made of the bark of the juniper tree or hard leaves of the *pandanus* palm which are interlocked into each other like roof tiles, making the structures virtually waterproof and windproof. A village contains a ritual mens' house (iwool) which only the initiated may enter. The round grass mens' house (honnay) is used for sleeping naked at night, all feet pointed towards the fire. A small door, which gives the only light, is closed with heavy wooden slats. The *honnay* are designated for all men and boys over 8 years old. The women, children, and pigs live in the long womens' houses (wew umah). Inside, heated rocks are placed around to sit on. Dani babies aren't weaned until 4 or 5 years old and during all that time on the breast a man may not sleep with his wife. Polygamy is thought to have evolved because of this custom. Until they get married, Dani girls wear grass skirts as are found in the Pacific islands. When a man buys a wife the bridegroom's village drapes the bride with a married womens' skirt made of seeds strung together. This skirt is worn just below the abdomen and held in place by callouses on her thighs. Though her breasts are exposed, her buttocks is always scrupulously covered. She also wears a long warmth-giving net bag around her head and down her back. Babies, piglets, belongings, and food are all caried together in it. There are no regular eating times, the Danis eat when they are hungry. Steamed or roasted sweet potatoes are 90% of their diet, eaten skin and all at least twice a day. Danis eat almost anything else they can lay their hands on; roots, dragonfly larvae, mice, raw tadpoles, frogs, caterpillars, spiny anteater and other marsupials' entrails. Slaughter by tying them to a stake and shooting them with arrows, pigs' flesh is eaten with vegetables cooked in the ground in big pits covered by hot stones and steaming grass. Pig is eaten only on festival occasions such as mass marriages (a gigantic pig banquet will be held in the Baliem in 1982). Try to get in on one of these pig feasts which usually coincide with the ripening of taro roots which are served with the steamed pork. Danis smash bones with rocks to get at the marrow, suck flesh from the jaws, nibble at vertebrae, gnaw at the kidneys- the whole pig vanishes. No knives or forks or cooking vessels are used, just round water gourds. Spoons are made out of the pelvis bones of pigs. Malaria is treated with pigs' blood. The word for pigs' fat may not be pronounced in the presence of women; it's a man's prerogative. A Dani man's status is reckoned by how many pigs and wives he owns. Pigs take their rightful place around the fire and human babies must compete with hungry piglets for mother's

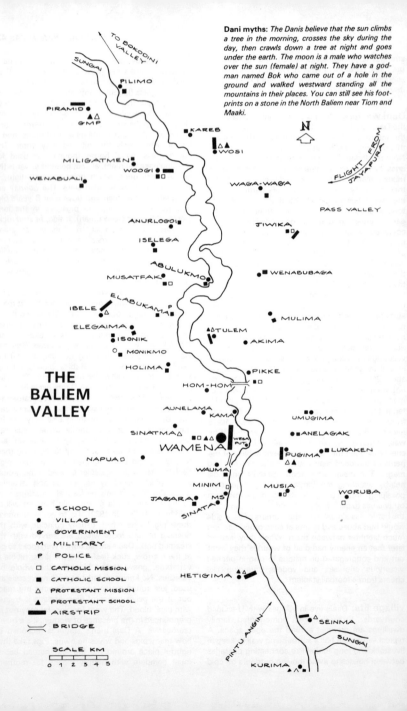

Dani myths: *The Danis believe that the sun climbs a tree in the morning, crosses the sky during the day, then crawls down a tree at night and goes under the earth. The moon is a male who watches over the sun (female) at night. They have a god-man named Bok who came out of a hole in the ground and walked westward standing all the mountains in their places. You can still see his footprints on a stone in the North Baliem near Tiom and Maaki.*

TO BOKODINI VALLEY

SUNGAI

PILIMO

PIRAMID
GMP

KAREB

WOSI

MILIGATMEN

WOOGI

WENABUALI

WAGA-WAGA

N

FLIGHT FROM JAYAPURA

PASS VALLEY

ANURLOGOI

ISELEGA

JIWIKA

ABULUKMO

MUSATFAK

WENABUBAGA

IBELE

ELABUKAMA   P

MULIMA

ELEGAIMA

ISONIK

TULEM

AKIMA

MONIKMO

HOLIMA

PIKKE

THE BALIEM VALLEY

HOM-HOM

AUNELAMA

KAMA

UMUGIMA

SINATMAA

WAMENA

WESA PUTU

ANELAGAK

PUGIMA   LUKAKEN

NAPUA

WAUMA

MINIM

MUSIA

WORUBA

JAGARA   MS

SINATA

S   SCHOOL
•   VILLAGE
G   GOVERNMENT
M   MILITARY
P   POLICE
□   CATHOLIC MISSION
■   CATHOLIC SCHOOL
△   PROTESTANT MISSION
▲   PROTESTANT SCHOOL
▬   AIRSTRIP
⌣   BRIDGE

HETIGIMA

SEINMA

SUNGAI

SCALE KM
0 1 2 3 4 5

PINTU ANGIN

KURIMA

milk. **death:** After a death the whole village is crying. Women smear their upper bodies and faces with mud to show their grief. Female relatives of the dead, starting at 12-13 years old, once had their fingers amputated up to the 2nd joint. The wound was dressed in banana leaves and husks and bound with a mixture of clay and ashes. It was then proudly displayed around the village. Though this practice is prohibited now, you'll notice many fingerless women over 25 years old.

WAMENA

This settlement, like Katmandhu, is surrounded by mountain ranges, some of the peaks snowcapped. The plane fare from Jayapura is over US$30 but it is money well spent. If any tourists ever visit Wamena it comes in bursts- 30 Germans at a time or 20 Dutchmen, etc. See the odd one or two Javanese tourists or *pegawi* getting their pictures taken while grinning beside wily spear-holding natives in front of Hotel Negara. Stock up on film in Jayapura where it's cheaper. In Wamena market, they scalp you on everything. There's even a beat radio station in Wamena.

stay: A bit of a problem, it's too dear. Hotel Negara is Rp5500 per person and it's a real hole. Pertamina runs the finest deluxe hotel in all of East Indonesia here; only US$45 singles or US$70 doubles; each unit is named after a tribe and each toilet has a Japanese garden. Much cheaper is Art Losmen run by Arnold Maun at Rp1000 per head. Take the road to Akima, it's 300 m past the market on the left. Arnold knows about the Baliem Valley and can give advice about artifacts. Lovely outhouses and lily ponds with shit-eating fish in back of his *losmen*.

eat: Buy Baliem Valley wild bee honey (madu) for about Rp1000 per big jar; smoky, thick or thin. A whole string of 12-15 fish from a Dani costs Rp4-

DISTANCES FROM WAMENA

Wamena	— Hom	2 hrs.	walking time
"	— Minimo	4 km	1 hour
"	— Sinata	4 km	1 hour
"	— Napua	8 km	2 hours
"	— Hepoba	8 km	2 hours
"	— Pugima	8 km	2 hours
"	— Holelama	8 km	2 hours
"	— Kururu	20 km	5 hours
"	— Asologima	32 km	8 hours
"	— Piramid	28 km	7-8 hours

500; cook them up yourself. Good sugar donuts are for sale all over town, Rp50. A friendly place is Ujung Kali behind Hotel Negara; most dishes in this *warung* must be ordered the day or morning before; great *gado2*. Or eat at the small restaurant behind Kommando Distrik Militer, but they seldom have all that you see on the menu. Settle price of each dish-before you eat, as they tend to overcharge. On the wall check out the framed photo of Wyn Sergeant, a female journalist from California who arrived in the Baliem in 1974 to make a film of the Danis. While here she married a Dani chieftan, Hukum Hearek, and it is said that she tried to start a war between two tribes in order to make a film of it. She also accused Indonesian officials of beating Danis (quite true). The Indonesians, who are still a bit tender over their administration of Irian, were not amused and promptly threw her out.

crafts: Tourism preserves and develops Dani carfts and also serves to introduce a cash economy to the people. Danis are enthusiastic craftsmen, designers of tools and dwellings, also of shells, feathers and other organic articles for self-adornment and for sale. Men in this society are the creators, women are the producers. Powerful warriors who killed in battle sit for hours making skirts or delicate orchid fibre necklaces for their wives. Bone awls and needles are used for weaving. Spiders are harvested in the forest, their elaborate webs hung around the throat in unique woven patterns (rarely found). Purchase stone axe blades (kapak) in Wamena for Rp500-2000, the price depending upon the size and the labor involved in making it. Black stone is the hardest and considered the finest. Although these axes cost up to Rp75,000 on Java, they are much too expensive in the Wamena market. Wait instead for Dani men to approach you, which they do often. Look for *sekan* (or *tetngen*), thin rattan handwoven bracelets that take 1-2 hours to make and cost Rp100 in outlying villages. *Noken* (bark string bags) are cheapest (Rp500) at the village of Wesa Put right behind the airport in the small workshop on the right just before the village. Ask for Daniel. The only way to make sure that you're buying a true *bark* string bag is to buy a grimy sweat-soaked one from a passing Dani woman. At Negara Hotel Restoran John S. Wolff sells handicrafts and implements such as tomohawks, axes, bows and arrows, hats, grass skirts (*yungal* or *yokal*) and *noken*. If you go out to the villages these same articles are considerably cheaper. To send artifacts back from Wamena do it through MAF or the Protestant air service. They get your stuff back safely to Australia by air freight.

short walks in the Baliem: A short easy walk from Wamena is to the rickety old Hepuba Hang-bridge: just follow the airstrip south, then down a path over rocks polished by bare-feet; good swimming. **Akima:** At the end of a 3-hour walk from Wamena is the famous smoked shrunken mummy in Akima. Pay only Rp100-150 for the boat across the river on the way. For foreigners to see the mummy Rp500, for Indonesians Rp200. This mummy is not for sale, not even an arm; it's the chief's grandfather. These are the Soka people so don't call them Danis. If you give the chief (the slender lively man in swim trunks) clothes, you could stay here indefinitely. **Hetagima saltwells:** Banana stems are first beaten dry of fluid, then put in a pool to soak up the brine; see women carry up to 70 kilo sections of stem back to be dried and then burned. The ashes are then collected and used as salt. Saltwells are also found at Jiwika. **Kurima:** At the entrance of the gorge, 3 hour's walk from Wamena; a high rockface drops down into a roaring river below. **Woogi:** Splendid dances, like the wedding ceremony dance, are held here. To take photos of a funeral or dancing it's best manners to pay perhaps Rp1-2000. But if you pay individuals for their pictures then all the Danis will want money- man, woman and child. It'll blow it.

Jiwika: Stay with a Dutch missionary here for Rp1000 per day full board. Meet Kurulu, chief of the Jiwika confederation of villages which covers all the land between Jiwika and Uwosilimo, the paramount chief of the eastern side of the Baliem River. His first wife and two sons were killed out in a field by a raiding party. So he started a war, captured the murderers, and ate them. If you ask him how they tasted, he'll smile. Memories are long. Recently when the men of Jiwika wanted to open up new gardens it was necessary for them to fetch some tools in Wamena. No porters could be obtained for the trek to Wamena because the tribesmen feared for their lives. 10 years ago the tribe around Wamena was their enemy! Sometimes as long as 5 or 8 years after a group of tribes had been defeated they would recover, rally, and secretly plan revenge. When the time came these usually peaceful men would become bestial, attacking villages at night, burning down huts, raping women, and killing as many men and boys as they could find. Famine, starvation, and sickness followed.

longer walks from Wamena: In the eastern limits of the valley one day's walk from Wamena is a deep grove of casuarina trees rising over 30 m in a region of tree kangaroos and huge tree-climbing rats. **Piramid:** Named after a mountain here shaped like a pyramid. About a 7-9 hour walk on a vehicular road to this mission station and airstrip. Beautiful panorama. Continue on to the Bokondini Valley, a northern extension of the Baliem. A Japanese millionaire is offering Rp1 million for an extremely rare butterfly inhabiting this area which flies very high, is jet black, with two orange spots on its wings. **Hometo:** Lying on the main trail between the Paniai Lakes and the Baliem Valley, a 5 day walk to this land of the Moni people. **Trikora Mountain Range:** About a 5 day trek. Most people only make it halfway up it's so slippery and hazardous. The peak is no longer permanently snowcapped. **Soba and Ninia:** The center of cannibal activity, though the missionaries have opened a clinic and are spreading good vibes. It's a one week walk from Wamena, or fly it in 15 minutes on a MAF charter for Rp19,000 or round trip about Rp25,000. Catholic aircraft aren't allowed to land in Ninia. At Soba, see a 1000 year old house and a 200 m high waterfall.

Chiefs (Kepala Suku) of the Baliem Valley

area	chief
Kalabaga	Kokik Hilapok
Elagaima	Johan Kossi
Hobikiak	Togolik Hobikussi
Mukokoh	Kwalian Matuan
Togima	Ekklowak
Ohenna	Inyayoto Wammu
Walessi	Muswarek Jaleget
Hetegima	Hukum Hearek
Jiwika	Kurulu

APPENDIX A

BAHASA INDONESIA

I. Grammar. Some basic rules:
A. No articles are used in Indonesian. *Teman* means 'a friend' or 'the friend'.
B. To make a noun plural, just double the noun. *Teman-teman* means 'friends'.
   1. It's often written *teman2*. This doubling is only necessary if it's not obvious from the context that a plural is meant.
   2. Otherwise just use the singular. *Dua orang* means two people and *seratus rupiah* means one hundred rupiahs.
C. There are no complex verb tenses. To indicate time, important adverbs are used, such as:
   1. *sudah* or *telah* — 'already' or something finished and done with.
   2. *belum* — that which is going to happen or perhaps never will happen; translated as 'not yet'.
   3. *akan* — means roughly 'will' to show the future.
D. Word order: subject — verb — object.
   1. Construct a sentence like this: *Saya sangat gembira berjumpa kamu.* (I am very glad to meet you.)
   2. Or *Saya senang sekali bertemu dengan Ali.* (I'm very glad to meet Ali.)
E. The possessive is formed by putting the personal pronoun after the noun.
   1. *teman saya,* my friend.
   2. Adjectives also come after the noun they modify: *mobil biru,* a blue car.

II. Pronouns. Use the polite forms in the following cases:
A. When speaking to an older man use *Bapak,* father, or with an older woman *Ibu,* mother.
B. When speaking to people your own age who aren't your friends, use *saudara* for males or *saudari* for females.
C. With *becak* drivers, *warung* owners, etc., use *Abang,* or in West Java and Central Java use *Mas.*
D. *Nyonya* is the polite form when speaking to a married woman and *Nona* when speaking to an unmarried woman.
E. Forms of address like *Tuan, Nona* and

Nyonya aren't used that much by Indonesians but are recommended for use by foreigners. *Tuan* is used over the phone by Indonesians when they don't know who it is they are talking to.
F. For people with whom you are already familiar, just use the person's name in place of 'you' or formal forms of address.

III. Other pronouns:

I	*saya*
you	*kamu* (to a child) or *saudara, saudari, anda* or the person's name (to an adult)
he, she	*dia*
we	*kami* (not including the listener)
we	*kita* (including the listener)
you (plural)	*saudara2* or *anda*
they	*mereka*
Mr. or Sir	*Tuan, Bapak 'Pak, Mas, Abang, Bung*
Mrs.	*Nyonya, Ibu*
Miss	*Nona*

IV. Pronounciation

Indonesian is a non-tonal language written in the roman alphabet using phonetic spelling. Bear in mind that there are many regional variations though these differences occur more iin intonation than in pronounciation. Talk fast; you are more likely to be understood. The accent usually falls on the second to the last syllable, but it's not as strong as in English.

a	is prounounced like a as in father: (akan)
ai	pronounced like i as in climb: *lain* (other) and *sampai* (arrive)
e	two ways: as in hay, or else it's stressed, a halfway sound between bet and bath.
c or tj	is pronounced very hard but a little softer than in chicken. *Cari* (look for or seek) and *kacang* (nut). Tj is the old spelling, which has been superseded by c.
u or oe	like oo as in book or like the u in put. Never as in mud. *Belum* (not yet).
	either short, as in pin, or a bit longer

	as in street. *Tiba-tiba* (to arrive suddenly); *babi* (pig).
y	as in yes or you. *Saya* (me).
kh	softly aspirated like soft 'ch' in German, not as harsh as in Loch Ness. *Kusus* (special) and *kabar* (news).
ng	as in singer, but never as in danger or dingo. *Bunga* (flower); *penginapan* (hotel).
ngg	like the ng in dingo. *Minggu* (week); *tinggi* (high).
r	always roll your r's. *Beras* (rice); *memberi* (give).
j	in the new spelling, j has replaced the old dj and is pronounced as in the word jump. *Bekerja* (work); *jalan* (street).
g	as in the word go.
h	is often soft. *Hitam* (black); *lihat* (see).
s	always like the s as in pass. Never like the English z.

V. Conversation

The following statements and questions are addressed to strangers:

thank you (very much)
 terima kasih (banyak2)
you're welcome
 terima kasih kembali
this, that
 ini, itu (after the noun)
yes, no
 ya, tidak (with an adjective or a verb); *bukar* (with a noun)
good morning (before 10 am)
 selamat pagi
good afternoon or evening
 selamat sore
good night
 selamat malam
good night (going to bed)
 selamat tidur
goodbye (to a person staying)
 selamat tinggal
goodbye (to a person going)
 selamat jalan
welcome
 selamat datang
please come in
 silakan masuk
excuse me
 permisi, maaf
please sit down
 silakan duduk
Can you speak English?
 Apahkah saudara dapat berbahasa Inggris?
please speak slowly

 Tolong bicara pelan2
What is your name?
 Siapa nama saudara?
My name is ...
 Nama saya ...
I understand.
 Saya mengerti.
I don't understand.
 Saya kurang mengerti.
I speak only a little Indonesian.
 Saya bisa bicara sedikit. Saya kurang pandai.
Where do you come from (Mr., Mrs.)?
 Dari mana saudara (saudari) *datang?*
I come from the house.
 Saya datang dari rumah.
I come from ... (Poland)
 Saya datang dari ... (Poland)
How do you do? How are you?
 Apa kabar?
I'm fine. Thank you.
 Kabar baik. Terima kasih.
I beg your pardon.
 Mohonkau saya. Saya minta maaf.
 Or simply, *Maaf.*
Do you smoke?
 Apakah saudara suka merokok?
What is this called in Indonesian?
 Apa namanya dalam Bahasa Indonesia?
What is this (that) called in Indonesian?
 Apa yang katakan ini? Apa yang dikatakan itu?
I am very glad to meet you.
 Saya senang bertemu dengan saudara.
What is your address?
 Apakah alamat anda?
Where do you live?
 Dimana saudara tinggal?
How old are you?
 Umur saudara berapa?
Where shall we go?
 Mau kemana kita?
I do not have ...
 Saya tidak punyai ...
All the best.
 Selamat.
I love you.
 Saya cinta padamu.
Would you like to spend the night with me?
 Mau bermalam sama saya?
That's right.
 Betul.
more than
 lebih dari pada
you like
 engkau suka
OK
 baik, baiklah
Where can I buy some grass?
 Dimana bisa saya beli ganja?

drunk/stoned
  mabuk/mabuk ganja
to long for ...
  ingin akan
What is it?
  Apakah? Apa ini?
What time does it start?
  Jam berapa mulai?

VI. Finding your way

How's it going, are you tired?
  Bagaimana, lelah?
Yes, I'm rather tired.
  Ya, agak lelah.
Well then, let us have a rest as relaxedly as possible.
  Nah, mari kita istirahat saja seenak-enaknya.
Where is the toilet?
  Dimana ada kamar kecil?
  Dimana ada weseyna?
I want to urinate/defecate.
  Saya mau kencing (or *buang air kecil*)/*berak* (or *buang air besar*).
I'll be a little while.
  Akan sedikit lama.
Don't worry.
  Tidak usah takut apa2.
Turn to the left.
  Belok kekiri.
Turn to the right.
  Belok kekanan.
Where do you want to go?
  Mau kemana?
I want to go to ...
  Saya mau ke ...
Where am I?
  Dimana saya?
to, in, from
  ke, di or *dalam, dari*
Stop here.
  Stop disini. Berhenti disini.
mosque, church, street
  mesjid, gereja, jalan
How many kilometers?
  Berapa kilometer jauhnya?
slow down, slowly.
  pelan2 (perlahan-lahan)
I don't want it, thank you.
  Saya tidak mau, terima kasih.
I'll be back in 5 minutes.
  Saya akan kembali lima menit lagi.
Where is the (train) station?
  Dimana stasiun (kereta api)?
What is this village called?
  Desa ini, apa namanya?
Where is the post office?
  Dimana kantor pos?
Where is the airport?
  Dimana lapangan terbang?

Where is the restaurant?
  Dimana restoran?
What street is this?
  Apakah nama jalan ini?
Wait here.
  Tunggulah disini.
Is there a lot to interest tourists around here?
  Apakah ada banyak pemandangan untuk pelancong yang baik disini?
Where do I get the boat to Balikpapan?
  Darimanakah dapat saya naik kapal ke Balikpapan?
Where are the buses for Bogor?
  Dimana stasiun bis ke Bogor?
left, right, straight on
  kiri, kanan, terus
house, office, shop
  rumah, kantor, toko
cross here (road sign)
  Menyeberang disini.
petrol, car, train
  benzin, mobil, kereta api

VII. Accommodation

Where is a hotel? *Losmen?*
  Ada hotel dimana? Dimana hotelnya? Dimana ada losmen?
Which is the best hotel (or *losmen*)?
  Dimana ada hotel (losmen) *yang terbaik?*
I've just arrived.
  Saya baru datang.
How much for one night?
  Berapa harganya satu malam?
Two (three) of us, one room.
  Dua (tiga) *orang, satu kamar.*
One person, one room.
  Satu orang, satu kamar.
What time do I have to check out?
  Jam berapa harus saya daftar untuk keluar?
How much does it cost?
  Berapa harganya? Berapa rupiah?
Where is the bath?
  Dimana ada kamar mandi?
Please wash these clothes
  Tolong cuci pakaian ini.
travelers cheques
  trapel cek
mosquito, mosquito coils
  nyamuk, obat nyamuk
very early
  pagi2
Is there a ... window?
  Ada ... jendela?
bed, room, eat
  tempat tidur, kamar, makan
table, chair, blanket
  meja, kursi, selimut

dirty, smelly
kotor, bau kurang baik

VIII. Food

tea or coffee?
teh atau kopi?

It's delicious
Enak sekali or *enak saja*

sweet black coffee
kopi manis

sweet coffee with milk
kopi susu manis

coffee without sugar or milk
kopi pahit

bread, meat, fish
roti, daging, ikan

milk, water, tea
susu, air, teh

Bring me coffee.
Ambil satu kopi.

restaurant
rumah makan or *restoran*

one serving
satu porsi

cook
masak

breakfast
makan pagi/sarapan

lunch
makan siang

dinner
makan malam

IX. At the market

from the market
dari pasar

What are you making?
Apa yang di buat? Bikin apa disini?

fixed price
harga pas

How much is it?
Berapa harganya?

It's too expensive.
Itu terlalu mahal. Itu mahal sekali.

Do you have a cheaper one?
Ada yang lebih murah?

Can you come down in price?
Bisa saudara kurangkan harganya?
Harap turun sedikit? Harap turun harganya?

What is this?
Apakah ini?

I'll take it.
Saya akan ambil ini.

there is, there is not
ada, tidak ada

as much again
sekali lagi

little, not much

sedikit

I'll come back later.
Saya akan kembali lagi.

I don't want to buy anything today, thanks.
Saya tidak mau beli apa2 hari ini, terima kasih.

on top of, in front of
diatas/dimuka

big and little
besar dan kecil

for sale
untuk dijual

Give it to me.
Berikan saya itu.

X. Numbers

one	*satu*
two	*dua*
three	*tiga*
four	*empat*
five	*lima*
six	*enam*
seven	*tujuh*
eight	*delapan*
nine	*sembilan*
ten	*sepuluh*
eleven	*sebelas*
twelve	*duabelas*
thirteen	*tigabelas*
fourteen	*empatbelas*
fifteen	*limabelas*
sixteen	*enambelas*
seventeen	*tujuhbelas*
one hundred	*seratus*
537	*limaratus tigapuluh tujuh*
one thousand	*seribu*
1944	*seribu sembilanratus empatpuluh empat*

XI. Time

What time is it?	*Jam berapa sekarang?*
Six o'clock.	*Jam enam.*
Half-past three.	*Setengah empat* (Or half-to-four).
It's twenty to nine.	*Jam sembilan kurang duapuluh menit.*
It's ten past one.	*Jam satu lewat sepuluh menit.*
It's eleven thirty.	*Jam setengah duabelas.*
now	*sekarang*
in a little while	*sebentar lagi*
later	*nanti*
already	*sudah*
not yet	*belum*

it won't happen, it won't come about,
it's not going to happen
tidak jadi

very flexible schedule, very approximately
jam karet (rubber time)

APPENDIX B

HINDU LEGENDS

THE MAHABHARATA

Sometimes called the *Barata-yuddha*. Critics have called this ancient Indian poem a history because of its naturalistic descriptions. But it is also the finest, most comprehensive Indian epic, containing fragments on Hindu meditation, as well as representing the quintessence of all philosophies among all the Sanskrit books. This epic poem is about a civil war in the legendary state of Bharat in India which took place over 2500 years ago. The half-real, half-divine god-populated magical world of this great Hindu story has awakened the same awe in Indonesians as the legends and literature of ancient Rome and Greece awoke in Renaissance man. A truly monumental work (90,000 stanzas), it's the longest single poem in world literature. No translations of this 20 volume epic (of 1000 pages each volume) is as yet correct or comprehensive enough. Pundits differ on every *sloka* (stanza). There has been only one authoritative commentary of the giant work: *Bharat Bhau Deep*, written in Sanskrit by Neelkanthji Maharaj, out of print since 1933.

the Indonesian version: Using the original Indian story as the prototype, the *Mahabharata* was composed on Java in the 10th and 12th Centuries by the order of kings. For at least 1000 years in Indonesia, the struggle between the Pandavas and the Korawas has served as an abundant source of mythology and inspiration for the arts and literature. Used as the central theme of *wayang* dramas, the story has been continuously re-worked, adapted and expanded to suit the needs of specific regional tastes. On Java and Bali it is performed as a shadow play and classical dance. In West Java, in *wayang golek*. Most Indonesian court poems were translated from the most popular episodes of this voluminous work. Ardjuna and Bima are the favorite heroes. Ardjuna, for his ability to charm and conquer women and for his superior power in combat, and the giant Bima (God of Wind) for his fearlessness and physical might. The enemy Korawas are always shown with monstrous shapes. Often the various heroes have different names according to the state in their lives, their activity, the name of the kingdom or tribe, father's name, etc., which

makes it confusing to follow each character. From Java the poem has penetrated into the literature of the outer Indonesian islands as well.

the Mahabharata story: Infused with many embellishments over the centuries, the original story is based on a historical war between two neighboring tribes, the Pandavas and the Korawas, which took place around the 9th Century B.C. These two families were in constant rivalry and the epic describes all the events day by day. The five Pandava brothers are continually proving superior to their cousins, the 99 Korawas, all sons of a blind king. The Korawas, filled with jealousy and hatred, set out to destroy the Pandavas, at one time lighting their house on fire. There is an archery contest in which Arjuna wins over all rivals, then a disastrous dice game which forces the Pandavas into exile in the forest for 12 years. All the bad blood culminates finally in the 18 day battle, 'The Great Battle of the Bharatas', which takes place between the two holy rivers, the Ganges and the Yumma. Great courage and tragedy is shown by both sides and in the end many brave warriors die and there's a great horse sacrifice. *Bhagavad Gita* is one of the *Mahabharata's* most beautiful and most famous chapters, a prelude to the great battle, describing Ardjuna's dialogue with his mentor and charioteer Krishna (an incarnation of Vishnu), to whom he turns in anguish at the prospect of having to slay all his kinsmen and closest teachers. This moment of intense introspection and self-scrutiny before the battle is called either 'Ardjuna's Despondency' or 'Ardjuna's Hesitation'.

THE RAMAYANA

A 3rd Century B.C. poem which records events taking place a thousand years before it was written. The story represents the eternal conflict of good and evil and the eventual triumph of good. A passage in the 2nd Century A.D. version mentions Indonesia (Yavadvipa) and describes it as having 7 kingdoms. Episodes from the Old Javanese genre (which the *Ramayana* was translated into) serve as the basis for modern ballet, puppet shadow theatre, and classical dance dramas all over present-day Indonesia. The *Ramayana* is the literary counterpart to such masterpieces of Javanese architecture and sculpture as Borobudur, Candi Prambanan and Panataran, plus many other temples on which you can see the story depicted in reliefs and carvings. Outside of Yogya, Central Java, view episodes from the story of Rama performed (wayang orang) during the 4 nights of the full moon each month in the dry season. In West Java the characters live on in the theatre of round puppets.

the Ramayana story: The story takes place in the Himalayas and opens as Rama, a boy-child-terror-prodigy is winning archery competitions and cleaning demons out of hermitages. He won his beautiful lady super-seductress Sita by his skill with the bow and arrow. The king's wicked wife demands that Rama, Sita, and his devoted brother Laksmana be sent into exile in order to put her own son on the throne. Because of an old promise the king must comply. Cheated of their throne and banished to the deep forest for 14 years, the three of them live with saints and hermits. The 10-headed giant-demon Rawana's sister one day wanders through the forest and catches sight of Rama, falling in love with him instantly. But Rama repulses her advances and she returns to Langka (Ceylon) to complain to her brother, the King of Demons. Rawana sends a servant in the shape of a beautiful golden deer who lures Rama away with Sita's urging in order to kill it. Laksmana hears cries of

pain and gives chase. While they're both gone, Rawana arrives and abducts Sita, flying into the air back to his palace in Langka. A legendary bird, Garuda, dies while trying to rescue her from the demon's clutches. Then, with the help of the white monkey general Hunuman, the search begins. Hunuman sends his monkey armies in all four directions into the world to find her. Meanwhile in Langka, the captured Sita refuses all Rawana's advances despite his tricks and threats. Hunuman finds Sita and tries to set her free. On his way back to India the monkey general sets Rawana's capital on fire with his tail (this episode is a favorite *lakon* in *wayang* plays). Hunuman's monkey armies then invade Langka, throwing boulders into the sea to build a causeway. After a 12 year war with many fierce battles, Rama finally kills Rawana with a magic arrow. Sita is reunited, but then Rama puts her faithfulness to test by an ordeal of fire. Satisfied, they all fly back to their Himalayan Kingdom in dead Rawana's flying chariot. There, Rama ousts his half brother and assumes his rightful kingship and everyone lives happily ever after. In some versions, Rama, still doubting his wife's reputation, banishes her. She lives in the woods, giving birth to two sons. When Rama repents and asks her to return, she refuses and disappears into the earth. The poet, Valmiki, who wrote the oldest version, takes the two sons as apprentices and Rama eventually makes it to heaven where he regains his original shape as Vishnu.

THE HINDU GODS

Rama: Rama is Vishnu as an *avatar* (incarnation) and represents the ideal Hindu, a gentle husband, a noble prince, a kindly king, and most significantly, a brave leader while under suppression. Sita, Rama's wife and an incarnation of Lakshmi, symbolizes the ideal Hindu wife who always remains devoted to her husband.

Brahma: The great Hindu God of Creation who carries a sceptre and various other symbols. From his four heads sprang the *Vedas,* four books written in a complex poetic style. These books of Aryan sacred hymns and verses have an age named after them. Laid down by priests during the Vedic Age of India (1500-500 B.C.), they record Aryan religious beliefs and practices.

Shiva: The Hindu God of Destruction. Shiva has many aspects: the intense ascetic, the demon-killer with a headdress of skulls and snakes wound around him, as the Lord of Creation dancing in a

circle of divine fire, as the male symbol of fertility. Shiva's followers have a slightly ascetic bias. The cult also has a strong sexual emphasis noted in its emblem, the phallus (lingga) and especially in the mystical sexual union of Shiva and his wife, Durga. Some of Hinduism's other gods are a result of the union of Shiva and Durga, bearing sons such as the elephant-god Ganesha. Shiva's mount is a bull, Nandi, also an old fertility symbol. Nandi is Shiva's constant companion, servant, musician. Shiva wears Nandi's emblem, the crescent moon, on his brow.

Parvati: Shiva's wife, the daughter of the Himalayan mountains and the sister of the Ganges. With love she lured Shiva from his asceticism. She represents the unity of the gods and goddesses, of man and woman. This mystical consort of Shiva's comes in different forms: Uma, a mild goddess of light and beauty; Durga, a ferocious 10-armed goddess who rides a tiger and battles demons; Kali,

Hinduism's most terrible goddess with an insatiable lust for blood sacrifices. She often appears blood-smeared, swarming with snakes, wearing necklaces of her son's skulls. Each of these manifestations personify her divine power.

Vishnu: The Preserver or Guardian of the World. To many Hindus, Vishnu is the Universal God. Whenever mankind needs help, this benevolent god appears on earth as an *avatar* or some sort of living god reincarnated. It's generally believed that 9 *avatars* have already appeared, with one to go to be called Kalkin who'll be riding a white horse. Statues of Vishnu usually hold four symbols: a discus, a conch shell, a mace, and a lotus.

Garuda: Vishnu's mount, the symbol of the old Javanese Majapahit Kingdom, and now Indonesia's official state seal. He is the mythological golden white-faced eagle which came out of the period of the gradual Indianization of the Indonesian culture (2nd Century to the 16th Century) when new motifs such as *nagas* (serpents) and *makaras* (fishes with elephantine bodies) were appearing. Garuda is one of the manifestations of the Hindu god Vishnu; he carries the god on his flashing gold back. Garuda is the king of all the things that fly. He has the body of a man, but with wings, head, claws, and the beak of a massive bird. This bird-like sun-principle hates everything that's evil and swallows it up. Sometimes mistaken for the fire god Agni, Garuda stands for creative energy. Being an eater of serpents, snake bite victims appeal to him.

the clowns: See front cover. Having been given old Javanese names, the clowns are thought to be survivors of an ancient ancestor cult. Semar is special, usually the servant of the hero, very ugly with tired rheumatic eyes and a big rear end. He gives wise counsel to the hero in awkward situations and can sometimes work powerful magic and destroy demons. At times Semar is even a reincarnation of a deity. He represents the motherly quality of tenderhearted wisdom. Petruk, with his long nose and perpetual grin, represents intellectual power plus cheerfulness. Gareng, lame and deformed, represents firmness of will, care, honesty, concentration, and contentment.

OTHER INDONESIANIZED LEGENDS

Ardjuna Wiwaha: A story used in Javanese dance drama patterned after the *Mahabharata* Hindu epic. First translated into Old Javanese by Mpu Kanwa in 1035 A.D. during the famous King Airlangga's reign. The story is an allegory of Airlangga's own life, who himself was a great ascetic living for many years in the wilderness of East Java, meditating to gain strength and accumulate wisdom. A demon king, Niwatakawaca, is bent on overthrowing all the gods of Indra's heaven. Like Achilles, his invulnerability is flawed by one secret spot. The gods appoint Ardjuna to vanquish him. Ardjuna is found in deep meditation inside of a mountain in the Himalayas. In order to test his strength and to prove his steadfastness, Shiva sends 7 lovely heavenly nymphs to tempt him by dancing near him, but his concentration doesn't fail him and Ardjuna remains unaffected by their alluring gestures. Shiva also visits him to test his ability and worthiness in battle. Then Indra himself appears in the form of an old weak holy man, to see if Ardjuna truly wants to save the world or else cop out and go into nirvana. Ardjuna satisfies them and the gods enlist his help to destroy the demons who are ravaging the heavens. Ardjuna travels to the titan's kingdom. A beautiful nymph accomplice tricks the demon king into revealing his one weak spot while Ardjuna watches invisibly. The titan finds out and a great battle takes place between all the monsters and giants and the gods. Ardjuna plays dead. While the demon is laughing at him and mocking him on the ground, Ardjuna shoots a magic arrow through his tongue (the secret spot) while the laughing mouth is open. As a reward for vanquishing the monster, Ardjuna is allowed to spend 7 months in 7 golden pavilions with the 7 nymphs who originally tried to tempt him during his meditations. Finally, exhausted, he returns to earth to his overjoyed people.

the Panji cycle: These are mythological love stories full of suspense, setbacks, and the romances of a culture hero. This cycle developed in East Java about 500 years ago, but could have derived from an earlier sun and moon myth, woven into the recorded history of East Java. Candra Kirono is the name of a royal princess whom Panji is deeply in love with, but loses her on their wedding night. He is like an East Javanese Ardjuna, a great lover, superb warrior, the ideal noble prince. According to East Javanese legend, this prince forged the first *kris*. He always wore it and the weapon was symbolic of his supernatural powers. Panji was also an excellent *gamelan* player and gongsmith. This popular story appeared in Java in the 14th Century (as a reaction against Indian influence?), spreading widely throughout Indonesia and even on to Malaysia, Thailand, and Cambodia, where its heroes go under different names.

the 7 fairies: A widespread tale in the Indonesian archipelago is the legend of a number of fairies, usually 7, who descend from heaven to bathe, leaving their clothing hidden nearby, returning to their abode every morning before sunrise. Always one of the fairies, often the youngest and most beautiful, is unable to find her clothing and is thereby forced to remain on earth, marrying the man who has hidden her clothes. After some years pass and they have several children, she invariably finds out that it was her husband who hid the clothes, forces him to return them to her, and flies away. This legend has been recorded in different versions in such places as Madura, North Celebes, Sumatra, and Irian Jaya. It's also found in European fairytales, and is thought to have originated from the *Thousand and One Nights*.

APPENDIX C

MOUNTAIN CLIMBING IN INDONESIA

Volcanoes which are active are easier to climb since open sand or rock covers them instead of the climber having to bushwack through dense forests. Older non-active volcanoes have had time to develop forested growth, and usually have old shrines or temples on top of them. Active Semeru on Java has heavy forests and native stands on the way up because it's not as populated, but Merbabu has been totally cleaned out of wood (for firewood or to make charcoal) and just thorny bush remains. Also around Merapi most forests have been cut. Usually there's no water above 750 m, except on the older volcanoes of Java like Merbabu or Arjuna (has water even at 2400 m) where there's water higher On newer volcanoes there's just sand, no water, so carrying a canteen is essential (especially on Java).

BALI

Mt. Abang: 2152 m. Start from Penelokan. Follow a paved road which begins a little way out of Penelokan for 5 km along the crater's rim to a junction. At this junction there's a road to the right that goes down to Besakih, but just continue on the trail right along the rim of the caldera and up the mountain. Duration: one-half or one day's walk.

Mt. Agung: 3142 m. Climb it from Besakih Temple (950 m). Make sure you get water at Besakih Temple as that's the last place you can get it. Take a track from the right side of the temple straight up the mountain. After about 1½ km there's another pagoda-like temple to the left of the path and from there on up it gets steeper. You can crash at the temple that's 1½ km up (there's nobody around and it's really quiet) or crash at Besakih. Duration: if you start out at 11 am you can get half way up Mt. Agung and back down again by 2 pm; to the top it's an easy one day climb, return.

EAST JAVA

Mt. Arjuna: 3344 m. From the village of Pandaan, take a *bemo* or minibus to Tretes hill station (750 m). Immediately above Tretes one will find a cobblestone paved trail; take this one and not the

one to the water creek. It's a very good highly used trail which leads to the summit. Mt. Arjuna has pine forests higher up and beautiful meadows. At 1600 m there's water and one small bush hut with just a roof, only a rain shelter. The trail continues to another water source at a sulphur mining camp at 2450 m and leads up to near the summit where there's a sulphur quarry. Duration: from Tretes to the top it would be a long day, up and back.

Mt. Lawu: 3265 m. Approach Mt. Lawu from Madiun or Solo on the road from Sarangan to Tawangmangu. Go to the village of Cemorosewu (1840 m elevation) where there are two radio TV antennae. The trail begins 300 m to the west of Cemorosewu, immediately west of the bridge. A very good well used trail continues to the summit from there. The trail encircles the mountain and the final ascent is actually from the northeast. There are several huts plus emergency shelters on the way up: the 1st hut is at 2400 m, the 2nd at 2850 m, and the 3rd at 3100 m. A *darma* (pilgrims' hut) is at 3125 m elevation and there's another little shelter only 2 m from the summit. A shrine with baskets of flowers, and remnants of old temples and terracing are near the top.

Mt. Semeru: 3677 m. Highest peak on Java. Mt. Semeru could be very active, booming. From Lumajang, take the road towards Pronojiwo. 5 km east of Pronojiwo there's a town called Supit Orang at 750 m. From here there's a dirt road up about 1 km towards the mountain to the town of Supit Orang II. Then from Supit Orang II up to Kamera (800 m elevation) it's approximately 2 km. There's traffic on these roads, the village truck, etc. At Kamera there are a lot of roads criss-crossing, but keep to the main trail to a point 200 m north towards the mountain, then turn and walk 300 m east of the main trail where there's a spring, the last chance for water. Then the trail goes up a slight slope for 2 km through sugar-cane at all different stages of maturity. Cut some and take it up the mountain with you for quick, pure and natural energy. At 1200 m, the highest portion of the sugar-cane cultivation, the trail ends. The best and easiest route from here right up through the forest is a dry creek bed. There are some bath-sized potholes in this creek bed which could contain water (it could also be stagnant). At 1700 m you emerge from the forest. See new volcanic flows coming down. Here you can camp right near the gully. Your tent is safe, nobody is around. To get to the summit simply go up the right side of the avalanche gully of lava straight to the top. Duration: for a fit person, two days from Supit Orang; for an unfit person, three days.

CENTRAL JAVA

Mt. Merapi: 2911 m. One of Indonesia's most active volcanoes. With at least an emission a year, this volcano regularly belches out hot clouds 1000 m above the crater and hot ashes that spill on the nearby town of Magelang. Merapi last erupted in 1931, triggering strong tremors and causing heavy loss of life. From Solo or Yogya take a bus to the Kartosuro junction, then from there to Boyolali by big bus for Rp50. From Boyolali up to Cepogo it costs Rp100 (Rp50 going down). From Cepogo to Selo (1500 m elevation) it's Rp75 and also Rp50 coming down. Maybe sleep in the *pasar* in Selo or somebody might put you up. You may leave your pack at the police station. All food necessary could be bought in Selo. There's a guide who lives 100 m west of the police station though you don't really need one. 600 m up the road (west) from the police station and school is another road (with a sign post) called Jalan Merapi. There s also a well here where people fill up their water jugs The last water is at

this junction at Jalan Merapi. From that point at the sign the road goes straight up towards the mountain peak for 1½ km. At the end of that road, turn to the left on a trail which continually ascends and stay on the ridge right up to the summit. Duration: it's an easy one day climb up and back from Selo.

Mt. Merbabu: 3142 m. From Selo, 100 m to the east of the police station, there's a dirt road branching from the main road called Jalan Merbabu (see the sign). This dirt road continues for 2 km in a northerly direction to two small villages at 1650 m. From here there are two possibilities: either follow the creek right along the water course to the top of a very prominant ridge (this is an eroded volcano with one long ridge jutting out of it), or in the village examine the hillside directly to the west and pick out the trail up to the hogsback. Once you're on this ridge trail, it leads right up to the summit and to a series of small peaks. Many woodcutters use this ridge trail, they made it. Don't get off on any of the many other trails, stay on this mountain ridge. Duration: Merbabu is one long day's climb up and back from Selo.

Mt. Slamet: 3427 m. From Purwokerto, there's a road going to Baturaden hill station. From Baturaden, a route leading to the top can be found. If one knows the trail it's usually just a one day climb.

Mt. Sumbing: 3371 m. From Magelang, get to Kaliangkrik hill station from where the trail straight up to the summit begins. Sumbing is one long day's climb up and back from Kaliangkrik.

INDONESIA BY RAIL

Indonesia is a natural for train buffs. Where else in the world can you see the last surviving Hannomag heavy Mallets? Or ride the last steam-hauled urban tramway on earth? Watch 90 year old 2.4.0s hauling 260 tons up steep gradients on a diet of teak? Travel with wood-burning rack and pinion tank engines into Sumatra's mountains? Railroads are concentrated mainly on the 830 mile (1335 km) long island of Java, the equivalent of a wildlife sanctuary for rare engines with 700 active steam locomotives made up of no less than 69 classes. Three separate networks also exist on Sumatra, and on Madura Island there's an intriguing rail line. Steam on passenger trains is largely confined to E. Java, but steam may be seen on freights almost everywhere. No steam engines were ever built in Java, and those running are almost all of unique design from European manufacturers. With the exception of relatively modern Krupp 1962 engines, these makes do not exist outside of Indonesia and enthusiasts

travel the world to see them. Indonesia's modern railway boasts the fastest streamlined limited expresses in S.E. Asia with AC and sleeping cars (from Jakarta: the overnight Bima to Surabaya, the Parahiyangan to Bandung in 2½ hrs. and the Gunung Jati, 136 miles to Cirebon in 2½ hrs). These all run on narrow gauge (3 ft., 6 inches) at speeds of 74 miles an hour, extremely fast for narrow gauge. **see:** A living railway museum is located at beautiful hilly Ambarawa in C. Java, where a Swiss-built cogwheel tank loco hauls a vintage train up to Bedono (915 m altitude). PJKA (Indonesian State Railways) is based at Bandung, W. Java, but by far the most fascinating yard of all is at Madiun in E. Java where steam engines are overhauled (line-ups often exceed 100 locomotives). Officials are quite cooperative and will even move engines out of the big shed for you to photograph. *Note:* get a hold of the excellent brochure 'See Java by Train' from the tourist office.

BOOKLIST

INTRODUCTORY BOOKS

DEIONGH, R.C. *Indonesia: Yesterday and Today.* Sydney, I. Novak, 1973. A short book on culture, politics, natural resources, ethnic groups, history.

GARNAUNT, ROSS and CHRIS MANNING. *Irian Jaya.* Canberra, Aust., A.N.U. Press, 1974. The most recent facts.

GRANT, BRUCE. *Indonesia.* 2nd ed., Zion, Ill., Melbourne University through International Scholarly Book Service, 1968. An account of the post-coup (1965) Sukarno Era Indonesia by an Australian writer.

LUCAS, CHRISTOPHER. *Indonesia is a Happening.* New York, Walker/Weatherhill, 1970. Journalist giving an interesting but improbable idea of the diversity of these islands. Good try.

McVEY, R.T., ed. *Indonesia: Its People, its Society, its Culture.* Rev. ed., New Haven, Human Relations Area Files, 1967. A major work of informative essays on Indonesian society.

NEILL, WILFRED T. *Twentieth-Century Indonesia.* New York and London, Columbia University Press, 1973. Very thorough survey of Indonesia's environment, history and culture. Really lets you see the place. Includes brilliantly written flora, fauna, and sealife chapters.

POOLE, F.K. *Indonesia.* New York, F. Watts, 1971. A lucid survey of the country's land, history, politics, everyday life, culture, religion, with very little sweet-talking. Deceptively well-written under the guise of a 'kid's book'

SPEED, FRANK. *Indonesia Today.* Sydney, Angus & Robertson, 1971. Sobre, cautious, accurate.

STEINBERG, DAVID, ed. *In Search of S.E. Asia.* New York, Praeger Publishers, 1971. Written by six leading S.E. Asian scholars in the U.S.A. Deals with the period from 1800 to present. The best introductory social history of S.E. Asia yet published.

WILLIAMS, MASLYN. *Five Journeys from Jakarta: Inside Sukarno's Indonesia.* New York, Morrow, 1965. Travel, political and social commentary. Sensitive feeling for the people. View-from-the-top as an honored journalist guest of officials, administrators, generals.

HISTORY

AZIZ, MUHAMMAD ABDUL. *Japanese Colonialism and In-*

donesia. The Hague, M. Nijhoff, 1955. An historical study on the Japanese occupation of Indonesia.

BENDA, HARRY J. *The Cresent and the Rising Sun: Indonesian Islam Under the Japanese Occupation 1942-1945.* The Hague, W. van Hoeve, 1958. An excellent tretise on Islam in Indonesia, studied from its first appearance in the islands. The war years are given the most detailed treatment.

CAMPBELL, DONALD MACLAINE. *Java: Past and Present.* 2 vols. London, W. Heinemann, 1915. Describes old Javanese customs in vivid detail, such as tiger-spearing (rampong).

DAY, CLIVE. *The Dutch in Java.* New York, Oxford University Press, 1966. Inspiring to read; makes you really interested in the period, though some portions are historically inaccurate.

DAY, C. *The Policy and Administration of the Dutch in Java.* New York, MacMillan, 1904. A critical study of Dutch colonial policy.

DEFRANCA, PINTO. *Portugese Influences in Indonesia.* Djakarta, Gunung Agung, 1970. The author has traveled widely for this unique material.

DEKKER, DOUWES. *Max Havelaar.* New York and Heinemann, London, London House and Maxwell, 1967. First published in 1860. The 'Uncle Tom's Cabin' of the Dutch Colonial Period. Describes the exploitation of the Javanese peasant under the control of the rapacious Dutch Colonial policy and the greedy Javanese regents in the time of the infamous *Cultuur Stelsel* period. This book did more to bring this period to an end than any other efforts. Takes place in Lebok District, W. Java.

DURRANT, A.E. *PNKA Power Parade: Indonesian Steam Locomotives.* Continental Railway Circle, 1974. About Indonesia's amazing and varied antiquated rolling stock. The whole island of Java is a living museum of antique trains.

HALL, D.G. *A History of S.E. Asia.* London, MacMillan, 1955. This work is especially valuable for visualizing Indonesia in its larger setting. The chapters on Indonesia are comprehensive and reliable.

HUGHES, JOHN. *Indonesian Upheaval.* New York, Fawcett Publications, 1967. A report of a coup that misfired, a titan who fell. One of the best newspaper report-type accounts of the 1965 coup, but an unfair interpretation. Hughes is a communist hater and his book typifies a mid-fifties preoccupation with the red bogeyman: '... communists being communists ...' But the material, once rid of its bias, is valuable and is written in a suspenseful tight style.

KILGOUR, RON. *Background to Indonesia.* Auckland, N.Z.,

Graphic Educational Publications, 1966. Excellent introduction to the history of Indonesia. A pithy 129 pages.

MOSSMAN, JAMES. *Rebels in Paradise*. London, Jonathon Cape, 1961. About Indonesia's Civil War (1958) in which North Celebes and Sumatra declared themselves separate states. War, Indonesian-style. A clear window onto the Indonesian character. Expertly written.

PALMIER, L.H. *Indonesia*. 1965. Good straight-forward history from Indian influences right up through nationalism and the events of the 60's. Covers also the economy and contemporary arts. Compels you to read further.

PALMIER, L.H. *Indonesia and the Dutch*. London, Oxford University Press, 1962.

PALMIER, L.H. *Social Status and Power in Java*. London, Athlone Press, 1960.

RAFFLES, THOMAS S. *The History of Java*. 2 vols. London, Black, Parbury, and Allen, 1965. A monumental work written in the early 19th Century between the Napoleonic Wars by the English Governor-General. Includes a description of Raffles' times in Indonesia.

REID, ANTHONY. *The Contest for North Sumatra: Acheh, the Netherlands and Britain, 1858-1898*. Kuala Lumpur, Oxford University Press, 1970.

REID, A. *The Indonesian National Revolution*. Hawthorn, Vic., Longman, Aust., 1974. Concise account of the Indonesian Revolution and the formation of the Indonesian state.

TANTRI, K'TUT. *Revolt in Paradise*. London, Heinemann, 1960. A passionate book by a young British-Born American woman who went to Bali in the 30's, was adopted by a Balinese *raja*, thrown in prison and tortured by the Japanese, and fought with Indonesian guerilla fighters for independence against the Dutch after the war.

VAN HEEKEREN, H.R. *The Stone Age of Indonesia*. Amsterdam, M. Nijhoff, 1958. One of the best studies of Indonesia's prehistory. See also the companion volume, *The Bronze Age of Indonesia* by Van Heekeren.

VLEKKE, BERNARD. *Nusantara: A History of Indonesia*. Rev. ed., Chicago, Quadrangle Press, 1960. A standard well-prepared, condensed history ending with the Japanese invasion in the early 40's.

WERTHEIM, WILLEM F. *Indonesian Society in Transition*. W.G. Kolf, 1956. A neo-marxist who gives a balanced objective view of Indonesia's post-war development. A major figure in Dutch-marxist scholarship on Indonesia.

ZAINU'DDIN, AILSA. *A Short History of Indonesia*. Melbourne, Aust., Cassell, 1968. Written by an Islamic scholar. Used as a high school textbook in Australia. Good.

ART

ALISJAHBANA, SUTAN TAKDIR. *Indonesia: Social and Cultural Revolution*. England, Oxford University Press, 1966.

BODROGI, TIBOR. *Art of Indonesia*. London, Academy Editions, 1973. Gives a detailed geographical, chronological description. Even finds a cultural pattern in this incredible jumble of cultures and islands called 'Indonesia'.

DRAEGER, DONN. *Weapons and Fighting Arts of the Indonesian Archipelago*. Rutland Vt., C.E. Tuttle, 1972. If this is your trip, this book is not only well-researched and written, but it's the only one on the subject. Good travel anecdotes.

GORIS, R. *Bali Atlas Kebudajaan: Cults and Customs*. Ministry of Education and Culture, Government of Indonesia, Jakarta, 1953. See Chapter V, 'A New Era in Art', Bonnet, R.

GRAPAPP, SELAND W. *Balinese Painting and the Wayang Tradition*. Artibus Asia (29), 1967. Very thorough-going information.

HOLT, CLAIRE. *Art in Indonesia: Continuities and Change*. Ithaca, N.Y., Cornell University Press, 1967. The best you can get hold of on this very broad subject. A modern classic written more for the student of art than for the academic. Covers her personal observations and researches while exploring Java and Bali's ancient ruins, as well as their contemporary performing and plastic arts.

HOLT, C. *Dance Quest in Celebes*. Paris, Les Archives Internationales de la Dance, 1939.

KEMPERS, BERNET. Ancient Indonesian Art. Amsterdam, D.P.J. van der Peet, 1959. The be-all, end-all, book for this subject; over 350 pages. Very scholarly, spot on info. Know your Hindu mythology before starting, otherwise filled with nonsense words.

KUNST, JAAP. *Music in Java: Its History, its Theory, its Technique*. The Hague, Nijhoff, 1949. For more about *wayang*. A superb study.

LOSCIN, CECELIA and LEANDRO. *Oriental Ceramics*. See Willetts, William under 'Art'.

McPHEE, COLIN. *Music in Bali*. New Haven, Yale University Press, 1966. A study in the form and instrumental organization in Balinese orchestral music. Good descriptive outline. As definitive as Kunst's *Music in Java*.

Paintings and Statues from the Collection of President Sukarno of the Republic of Indonesia. Publishing Committee of the Collection of Paintings and Statues of President Sukarno. 3 vols. Tokyo, Japan, Toppan. You can readily see the preoccupation Sukarno had with Asian women. This collection is in the President's Palace at Bogor.

SURYOBRONGTO, B.P. *The Classical Yogyanese Dance*. 1970. For further information on Javanese dance.

TIRTAAMIDJAYAJA, N. *Batik: Pattern and Motif*. Jakarta, Djambatan, 1966. Everything you ever wanted to know about *batik*: history, development, present day methods, most common designs and their origins, uses, regional differences, etc. Illustrations throughout.

WAGNER, FRITS. *The Art of Indonesia*. New York, Crown, 1959.

WAGNER, F. *The Art of an Island Group*. Useful general

account covering art, literature, dance and drama from prehistoric times to Independence. Flowery, art auction tone, but some broad-view insights clearly put.

WILLETTS, WILLIAM. *Ceramic Art of S.E. Asia.* Singapore, S.E. Asia Ceramics Society, 1971. Though hard to get hold of, this book (and the Loscins' *Oriental Ceramics*) are the best books on the subject with ample color illustrations, what and what not to look for.

ZOETE and SPIES. *Dance and Drama in Bali.* New York, Harper and Brothers, 1939. Best available introduction.

ZWITSER, FRANS. *Bali: An Adventure in Cultural Ecology.* Explains an exhibition in the Kosmos Building in Amsterdam of modern examples of traditional Balinese paintings.

LITERATURE

ALI, A. *The Flaming Earth: Poems from Indonesia.* Karachi, Friends of the Indonesian People Society, 1949. An anthology of the best of the fiery nationalist poets. Includes translations of the works of Chairil Anwar and Rivai Apin. Lauded as one of the most successful anthologies of Indonesian poetry in English yet published.

AVELING, HARRY. *Contemporary Indonesian Poetry.* Brisbane, Aust., Queensland University Press, 1975. Poems in Indonesian and English by such modern poets as Rendra, Rosidi, Heraty, Sastrowardjo, Ismail. 'Contemporary' claims to contain the best present-day poetry from Indonesia.

BANDOPADHYAYA, MANIK. *Padma River Boatman.* Brisbane, Aust., Queensland University Press, 1975.

BRANDON, JAMES. *On Thrones of Gold: Three Javanese Shadow Plays.* Cambridge, Mass., Harvard University Press, 1967. Good handling of traditional Javanese *lakon.*

JOAQUIN, NICK. *Tropical Gothic.* Brisbane, Aust., Queensland University Press.

KARTINI, RADEN. *Letters of a Javanese Princess.* New York, A.A. Knopf, 1920. One of the earliest modern Indonesian literary masterpieces, written (in Dutch) by the daughter of the Regent of Rembang, the first Indonesian Nationalist. Kartini argued that all Indonesian women have a right to be educated, but not to the exclusion of their domestic duties. Vivid atmosphere of Javanese court life at the turn of the century.

LUBIS, MOCHTAR. *Twilight in Jakarta.* London, Hutchinson, 1963. Basically about political corruption in post-independence (1950's) Indonesia. One of the best documents of daily life in the capital, especially its underbelly: the *becak* drivers, the derelicts, the prostitutes. Finished in 1957, a year after he was jailed by Sukarno. This book goes on and off the ban list. Lubis was rearrested in Feb. 1974.

MASON, VICTOR. *The Haughty Toad And Other Tales From Bali.* Selected and re-told by Victor Mason. Illustrated by artists of Pengosekan, Bali. Paul Hamlyn. P.T. Bali Art Print, Sanur, Bali. 1975.

MIHARJA, ACHIDIST. *Athesis.* A novel about the philosophical clash of western and Indonesian cultures during the 40's.

Perspective of Indonesia. A supplement to the 'Atlantic Monthly', 1956. Includes translations of stories by Pramudya Ananta Toer, Armijh Pane, Mochtar Lubis, Asrul Sani, Idrus and Achdiat Karta Mihardja; also poems by Chairil Anwar, Amir Hamzah, Takdir Alisjahbana, and Rivai Apin.

RAFFEL, BURTON. ed. *An Anthology of Modern Indonesian Poetry.* Berkeley, Calif., University of California Press, 1964.

RAFFEL, B. ed. *The Development of Modern Indonesian Poetry.* Albany, Suny Press, 1967.

RAFFEL, B. ed. *Poems of Chairil Anwar.* Albany, Suny Press, 1970. The translations are faced on the opposite page by *Bahasa Indonesia* texts.

TOER, PRAMOEDYA ANANTA. *A Heap of Ashes.* Brisbane, Aust. Queensland University Press.

WARD. PHILIP. *Indonesian Traditional Poetry.* New York, Oleander Press, 1975. An annotated anthology of Indonesia's folk chants and ritual songs in English and the regional languages.

WIGMORE, L. ed. *Span: An Adventure in Asian and Australian Writing.* Melbourne, F.W. Cheshire, 1958. Articles and stories by ten Indonesian writers, including Sitor Situmorang and Pramudya Ananta Toer.

WINSTEDT, R.A. *A History of Classical Malay Literature.* Fair Lawn, N.J., Oxford University Press, 1970.

TRAVEL

All Asia Guide. 9th completely revised edition. Far Eastern Economic Review. Ltd., Hong Kong. 1976.

BRONGERSMA, L.D. and VENEMA. *To the Mountains of the Stars.* London, Hodder & Stoughton, 1962. A Dutch expedition into the highlands of West New Guinea (Irian Jaya).

CONRAD, JOSEPH. *Alamayer's Folly: A Story of an Eastern River and Tales of Unrest.* London, E. Benn, 1895. Although written over 75 years ago, this book still captures the feel of Borneo's great rivers and its people.

EPTON, NINA. *The Palace and the Jungle.* London, Oldbourne Press, 1955. A cultural travelogue of Java and its mystics by the proper Englishwoman traveling over the globe.

GERST, TOM. *Indonesia in Pictures.* New York, Sterling Pub., 1970. Broad treatment, but a good introductory book.

GREENFIELD, DARBY. *A Traveler's Guide: Java and Sumatra.* Cambridge, England, The Oleander Press, 1975. Very thorough, highly personalized account of travel through Java and Sumatra with the emphasis on history and art.

HARRER, HEINRICH. *I Come from the Stone Age.* London, R. Hart-Davis, 1964. A famous explorer's account of his expedition to West New Guinea. Maps and color illustrations.

HITT, RUSSELL T. *Cannibal Valley.* London, Hodder & Stoughton, 1962. The experiences of missionaries in the Baliem, Enarotali, and Ilaga regions of West New Guinea from 1954 when they first arrived to the late 50's.

HOBMAN, BOB. *The Pitfalls of Yachtbuilding* (in Indonesia). 'Modern Boating', November, 1975.

HOEFER, HANS. *Guide to Bali.* Singapore, APA Publications, 1973. High souvenir value with its beautiful color pictures.

HOEFER, H. and PETER HUTTON. *Guide to Java.* Singapore, APA Publications, 1975. Many of the routes are meant for the private automobile. Memorable photography.

IMBER, WALTER. *Indonesia.* Bern, Kummerly & Frey, 1973. Written in German. Fantastic photos. Brings you there.

KOOIKER, HUNT. *Bali By Bicycle.* Singapore, Cosmic Dragon Publications, 1977. 'If you feel that the number of miles you cover is not as important as how you relate to each mile, read this book. With the help of two *bemo* rides to scale the central mountains, you can accomplish a beautiful, mostly level or downhill, 200 km circle trip of Bali by bicycle. Try the quiet wonder of an island which is being overrun by speeding tour buses and roaring motorcycles.'

MICKELSON, E.H. *God Can.* 1966. A missionary's battle for souls in West New Guinea.

MILLER, CHARLES C. *Black Borneo.* London, Museum Press, 1946. Sensationalist scholar-cum-adventurer style.

MODIGILIANI, *Batacchi Indipendenti.* A lavish survey of the Batak culture of North Sumatra written in the 19th Century. A great thick dusty book of travel and adventure; loving detail. Its pen and ink drawings will hypnotize you.

PALMOS, FRANK and PAT PRICE. *Indonesia Do-it-Yourself.* Indonesia, Palmii, 1975. Reads like a newspaper with attention-grabbing headlines above vignettes of Indonesian culture, difficulties while traveling, grandfatherly advise, anecdotes about the bureaucracy. The majority of the hotels recommended are A$12-20 per day.

RICHARDSON, DON. *Peace Child.* 1974. Takes place on southern coasts of West New Guinea. About a people who worship Judas as their savior.

SOUTER, GAVIN, *New Guinea: The Last Unknown.* Sydney, Aust., Angus and Robertson, 1963. Useful historical, geographical, cultural and political background on the whole island of New Guinea.

TEMPLE, PHILIP. *Nawok.* London, J.M. Dent, 1962. A New Zealand expedition (1961) into Irian Jaya's highest mountains.

WALLACE, A.R. *The Malay Archipelago: The Land of the Orang Utan and the Bird of Paradise.* New York, Dover, 1962. A reprint of the 1869 classic. Represents 7 years of research by this great British naturalist on the flora, fauna and ethnology of numerous islands. Still a brilliant and exhaust-

ive travelogue. Much of Indonesia is still as this book describes.

WHEELER, TONY. *S.E. Asia on a Shoestring.* Melbourne. Aust., Lonely Planet Pub., 1977. This 240 page book makes you an instant mini-expert on twelve countries. Very concise and useful.

WILLIAMS, GLEN. *Guide to Yogyakarta.* Yogyakarta, Kanisius, 1975. The best available guide on the 'tourist triangle' (Solo-Yogya-Dieng) of Central Java. Smothering detail.

WOLDENDORP, RICHARD (photographer). Text by A.H. JOHNS & Y. JOHNS. *Indonesia.* Melbourne, T. Nelson, 1972. Paints a fine picture in the 50 page introduction. Big black picture book (probably expensive).

POLITICS

ADAMS, C. *Sukarno: An Autobiography as Told to Cindy Adams,* New York, Bobbs-Merril, 1966. Shows conditions in Indonesia during Dutch rule. Makes you feel Sukarno's charisma, his demogogic energy jumps from every page.

JONES, HOWARD PALFREY. *Indonesia: the Possible Dream.* New York, Harcourt Brace Jovanovich, 1971. An ambassador's book. Worthwhile to read how the US diplomatic corps views the potential of this country.

KNOWLES, RUTH S. *Indonesia Today: The Nation that Helps Itself.* Los Angeles, Nash Publications, 1973. The story told by a petroleum specialist of how President Suharto and a team of free-market economic advisors encouraged foreign investment in post-coup Indonesia to develop its rich natural resources.

LEGGE, JOHN DAVID. *Indonesia.* Englewood Cliffs, N.J., Prentice-Hall, 1965.

LEGGE, J.D. *Sukarno.* London, Allen Lane, 1972. A biography by an Asian expert at Monash University. Melbourne. Gives also some flashes into a wide spectrum of Javanese life, while suggesting that Sukarno represented the archetypical Javanese character.

POLOMKA, PETER. *Indonesia Since Sukarno.* Harmondsworth, Middlesex, Penguin Books, 1971. His treatment of the Muslim religion and Javanese village life is well-done. Best known for the chapter called 'The Invisible Government' which examines the secret service.

PYE, LUCIEN, W. *Politics of S.E. Asia.* Princeton, N.J., Princeton University Press, 1960. Read the article 'The Neotraditional Accommodation to Political Independence' by Ruth Willner; it compares modern Indonesian politics with the 8th Century Mataram Empire. Enlightening.

PYE, L.W. *Southeast Asia's Political Systems.* Englewood Cliffs, N.J., Prentice-Hall, 1967.

ROEDER, O.G. *The Smiling General.* Jakarta, Gunung Agung, 1969. Fawning biography of President Suharto.

Some useful information.

TOER, PRAMUDYA ANANTA. *Korupsi*. A revealing account of this all-pervading facet of life in Indonesia.

ANTHROPOLOGY

COVARRUBIAS, M. *Island of Bali*. New York, Knopf, 1956. Written by a Mexican painter who lived and worked in Belaluan, Bali, for two years in the 30's collecting material for this artistic classic of traditional Balinese culture, the scope of which makes fascinating reading. Covarrubias was one of the first to call what the Balinese were living and creating 'art'. He did the drawings, his wife did the photographs.

GEDDES, W.R. *Nine Dayak Nights*. Melbourne, Oxford University Press, 1957. Dayak society as a layman sees it.

GEERTZ, CLIFFORD. *Agricultural Involution*. Berkeley, Pub. for the Assoc. for Asian Studies by University of Calif. Press, 1963. A study of the breakdown of Javanese traditional agricultural communities during colonial times.

GEERTZ, C. *The Religion of Java*. Illinois, Free Press of Glencoe, 1961. Still a goldmine of highly readable details of Javanese values and customs. Pare, E. Java ('Mojokuto') was his working model.

GEERTZ, C. *The Social History of an Indonesian Town*. Cambridge, Mass., Massachusetts Institute of Technology, Center for International Studies, 1965.

GEERTZ, HILDRED. *The Javanese Family: A Study of Kinship and Socialization*. New York, Free Press, 1961.

KOENTJARANINGRAT. ed. *Villages in Indonesia*. Ithaca, New York, Cornell University Press, 1967. A collection of comprehensive surveys of 13 villages all over Indonesia. First hand experiences by Indonesian, Dutch and American authors, most of them anthropologists. Though sometimes very dry reading, it's a part of the way in realizing Indonesia's giddy ethnic variegation.

LOEB, EDWIN M. *Sumatra: Its History and People*. Kuala Lumpur, Malaysia, Oxford University Press, 1974. The first authoritative ethnological work written on the peoples of Sumatra, their ritual and social anthropology. An old fashioned, American-school anthropological text. Outstanding preparation; enables you to be more perceptive once you get there.

MURDOCK, G.P. ed. *Social Structure in S.E. Asia*. New York, Free Press, 1965. See 'The Iban of Western Borneo', J.D. Freeman. Survey of community structure of the Iban Dayaks who live in both Sarawak (East Malaysia) and Kalimantan (Indonesia).

SIEGEL, JAMES. *The Rope of God*. Berkeley, Calif., Univ. of Calif. Press, 1969. An account of Acehnese society and attitudes. Conscientious doctorate-style of writing.

SINGARIMBUNG, MASTRI. *Kinship, Descent and Alliance Among the Karo Batak*. Berkeley, Calif., Univ. of Calif. Press, 1975. History of the Karo, their *rumah adat*, agriculture, etc. Both anecdotal and anthropological. Written by a Karo

Batak for the lay which makes it easy reading though the parts on kinship are involved.

SNOUCH HURGRONJE, CHRISTIAN. Translated by O'Sullivan. *The Acehnese*. Jakarta. 1906. Ideal preparation for this northernmost Sumatran province.

TOBING. *The Structure of the Toba Batak Belief in the High God*. South and Southeast Celebes Institute for Culture, 1956. Very specialist topic, quite thorough. He is a Toba Batak himself who studied at the University of Leyden, Heidelberg and Utrecht.

NATURAL SCIENCES

BUNNING, E. *Der Tropishe Regenwald*. A description of characteristic plants found in tropical forests written by an authority on rainforests. Goes straight to the core; readable and usable.

BUNNING, E. *In den Waldern Nordsumatras Bonn*.

GALDIKAS-BRINDAMOUR, BIRUTE. *Orangutans, Indonesia's People of the Forest*. 'National Geographic', October, 1975. Her study area was 23 sq km of the Tanjung Puting Reserve near Kumai, S. Kalimantan. She exploded a number of long-standing myths about orangutans.

KING, BENT and EDWARD C. DICKENSON. *A Field Guide to the Birds of South East Asia*. London, W. Collins, 1975.

KLOPPENBURG-BERSTEEGH, J. *Indische-Planten en haar Beneeskracht*. Semarang, Van Dor, 1907. A book on Indonesian plants and their curative powers. Widely refered to in the early part of this century, especially by the Eurasian community who had a great belief in the magical powers of herbs and plants.

MISSEN, G.J. *Viewpoint on Indonesia*. Melbourne, T. Nelson, 1972. A geographical study. Informative how Indonesian landforms and agricultural practices have been changed by history.

RICHARDS, P.W. *The Tropical Rainforest*. Cambridge, The University Press, 1952. 5th ed. Absolutely scientific, this book covers the rainforests world-wide. All the information you'll need: humidity, rainfall, soil, and the most typical plants of each region. Emphasis on ecology. A handbook.

RIPLEY, S.D. *Tropical Asia Flora and Fauna*. Time Life series: Wonder of Nature, 1966. Great photographs.

SMYTHIES, BERTRAM E. *The Birds of Borneo*. Edinburgh, Oliver and Boyd, 1960. About 1000 species of birds on this island. A gem of a book.

WHITMORE, T.C. *Tropical Rainforest of the Far East*. Oxford, Carendon Press, 1975. Specializes in the eastern rainforest.

LANGUAGE

ALMATSIER, A.M. *How to Master Bahasa Indonesia*. Jakarta, Penerbit Djambatan, 1974. 4th printing. A short-term course for English-speaking foreigners. Rp1000-1250.

ECHOLS AND SHADDILY. *Dictionary.* Ithaca and London, Cornell University Press, 1975. Available in Indonesia for Rp2000-2500 which is cheaper than Australia where it costs A$8. Excellent. Available in both the Indonesian to English and the English to Indonesian versions.

HADIAT DKK. *Manusia dan Lingkungannya.* Bandung, C.V. Rosda. A series: Man and His Surroundings.

HALIAN, BAIDILAH. B.A. DKK. *Bahasa Kita.* Bandung, Remadja Karya C.V., 1976. A good series of books used to teach Indonesian children *Bahasa Indonesia* in school.

HENDRATA, H. *A-L Course in Bahasa Indonesia.* Aust., Hendrata, 1975. Used throughout Australian schools as a basic text. Only the instructions to the lessons are in English. There are three books in this series: Part 1A, Part 1B, and Part 2.

HUTAGALUNG, AMIN and FLASH GORDON. *Practical Indonesian: A Guide to Basic Communication.* Hak Pengarang Dilindungi Undang-Undang. Expensive at Rp500, but a unique phrase book especially for the newcomer and traveler. The page devoted to bargaining techniques is invaluable.

JOHNS, YOHANNI. *Bahasa Indonesia: Longkah Baru.* Canberra, Australian National University, 1975. Probably the most competant teach-yourself-book on the market.

KWEE, JOHN B. *Teach Yourself Indonesian.* London, English Universities Press, 1965.

MCGARRY and SUMARYONA. *Learn Indonesian, Books I & II.* Australia, Modern Indonesian Publications, 1975. A standard, recommended book.

Topical Dictionary: Indonesia. Sydney, McGraw Hill, 1975. Includes words of everyday use: bribe, mate, etc. Handy.

GLOSSARY

acar—cucumber pickles, often with pineapple and chilies.

adat—traditional law or custom; unwritten rules of behaviour covering such matters as inheritance rights, ownership of land, cooking, eating, courtship, ceremonies of birth, marriage and death, times and methods of sowing rice, building houses, praying for rain. *Adat* is the real law of the land, the oldest and most respected.

Airlangga—an East Javanese hermit-king who ruled from 1019-1049 A.D. during the Golden Age of Indonesian history.

air panas—hotsprings, medicinal springs, or health spa.

alun2—the main town square, playing field, and town park where public meetings, festivals and sports events take place. Facing the *alun2* are the public buildings: mosque, church, local government offices, post office, banks, schools.

alus—a term used to describe the most refined cultural traits in real life as well as in characters in the *wayang* theatre forms; all gestures, judgements, behaviour or temperments which are refined, smooth, gracious, pure, polite, noble, subtle, civilized, sophisticated, exquisite.

Amir Hamzah—the Prophet Mohammed's uncle. These stories were derived from 7th Century Persian history. During the rise of Islam on Java in the 15th Century, the Amir Hamzah tales became Indonesianized. They tell of battles, wars, and love affairs of the warrior-missionaries (see: 'wali') of Java. Stories from this play make up the most popular *wayang golek* episodes in Central and West Java.

angklung—a neolithic rattle instrument used mostly in West Java by the Sundanese to accompany folk dances. Hollow bamboo tubes cut to graduated lengths are freely suspended in a wooden frame. When the frame is shook these tubes hit each other, producing a strange tinkling zylophonic sound. The melody decides how many instruments are needed; one *angklung* to each note, each note in a different pitch. Each player shakes his own instrument when it's his turn to play his note.

anoa—a timid animal that resembles a miniature buffalo, its horns sloping straight back from its head. Indigenous only to the high mountain forests of Celebes.

apam—a thick doughy pancake, spread with sugar and crushed nuts or coconut and folded over.

arak—distilled rice brandy; burns with a blue flame when lit. Rp200 a bottle in the markets.

Arjuna Wiwaha—a play composed by Mpu Kanwa in 1035 A.D. One of its more famous scenes describes the hero Arjuna meditating in the Himalayas to gain strength. To test his strength, Shiva sends heavenly nymphs to dance near him, but his concentration doesn't fail him. This play, inspired by the Hindu *Mahabharata* epic poem, was first translated into Old Javanese during the reign of King Airlangga who himself was a great ascetic and lived for many years in the wilderness meditating and gathering wisdom.

asli—native, original, authentic; also could mean high-born or noble.

asram—a student dormitory or student flats. Only in its broadest sense does it mean 'school' in Indonesian.

asuransi—insurance.

atap—palm thatch.

Atoni—the native peoples of Indonesian Timor living mainly in the inland mountain areas.

AUS—Australian Union of Students. An organization which provides cheap student flights all over the world with main offices in Singapore, Kuala Lumpur and Bangkok. Any tertiary level student may utilize AUS if they show a legitimate student's ID card. Its Indonesian-bound charters are heavily booked during the Australian University break, December through January.

badak—Java or Sumatran rhinoceros.

bahasa—language; dialect.

Bahasa Indonesia—Indonesian; the *lingua franca* of Indonesia, the national language.

bajigur—a delicious drink made of coconut milk, thickened with rice and sweetened condensed milk.

Bali Aga—Aboriginal pre-Hindu inhabitants of Bali.

banteng—the wild cattle of Indonesia. Looks like a cow but has longer limbs. In both sexes the rump is white, darkening to tawny-red in the cows and calves, deep black in the older bulls. *Banteng* graze on cooler well-drained foothills and grasslands and usually travel in herds of one or two bulls with several cows and their young. Lone misfit bulls rejected from the herd can be dangerous, so stay clear. The *banteng* symbolizes freedom and nationalism for the masses.

banyan tree — a fig or waringan tree with writhing arteries which spread out 10-15 m. Also Buddah's Bo Tree under which he received enlightenment. Its sturdy trunk, umbrella-shaped crown and cool shade symbolize physical protection and divine blessing and this tree is found on Indonesia's coat of arms. The *banyan* is believed to never die, replenishing itself from seedlings which drop from its branches. It may never be cut down for powerful spirits may dwell in it.

bapak — father, headman, leader, male teacher, department head, boss.

Barata-yuddha — a poem masterpiece begun by the court poet Mpu Sedah in 1157 A.D. dealing with a tremendous 18 day epic battle in Indian mythology between two family groups, the 5 Pandava brothers (the Five Senses of Man) pitted against the evil of their hundreds of cousins, the Korawas. The most popular stories and figures of the *wayang* plays of today are based directly on this involved Javanized story.

Barong Dance — the most violent and dramatic of Balinese dances; used often as an exorcism. Two demonic characters, *Rangda* and the *Barong*, feature in this mythological story. Also called the 'Kris Dance' (see 'Dance on Bali').

Batak — a proto-Malayan people of North Sumatra; one of the Ancient Peoples of Indonesia.

batik — a traditional way of decorating cloth made by wax-resist 'negative' painting. Hot wax is applied to the cloth on parts intended to be left blank. When the cloth is dipped in the color dye, the part which is not covered in wax becomes dyed. Next, the wax is dissolved in boiling water and scraped off, leaving the desired patterns on the dyed and undyed sections. This process of coating and dyeing is repeated many times to create a multi-colored design or to create certain effects. The term has also come to include hand-stamped (cap) technique and has even been expanded to include machine printed *batik* patterns on cloth, though this is not *batik* in the strict sense of the word. Java is the most renowned for this art and *batik* might have originated here. The most outstanding *batik* centers are Yogya, Solo, Tasikmalaya, and the whole north coast of Java between Cirebon and Semarang.

becak — Indonesia's bicycle trishaw. Carries two or more. Rarely used for distances longer than 2-4 km. Average cost is Rp50-150.

Bedaya Dance — a sedate court dance of the Central Javanese *kratons*; also seen in the palaces of a few river kingdoms of East Kalimantan. This dance dates back to the ancient Majapahit and Sriwijaya Empires and is traditionally performed by nine women costomed and adorned as brides. Related to the sultan, they are part of the sacred regalia of the court. The *Bedaya* was inspired by a 17th Century love affair between a sultan and the South Sea Goddess, Nyai Loro Kidul. Seldom made public; attend by invitation only.

bemo (or *becak motor* in full) — a 3 or 4 wheeled, usually 250 cc. small covered vehicle. The driver sits in front with one passenger and there are seats in the back for 6-8 passengers and their wares. Usually cost Rp25-50 for a 2-5 km ride. Often much cheaper to charter than taxis.

bendi (or 'dog carts') — a versatile horse-drawn two wheeled cart; a gig. They're not fast or comfortable but they're cheap, about Rp50 a km or less. A *bendi* offers the best visibility for sightseeing and has a canopy to ward off the sun or the rain. Used mostly in West Sumatra.

benteng — an old fortress, either Portuguese, Dutch, Indonesian or English.

bersih desa — an annual village cleansing festival which takes place after the harvest to rid a town of evil.

bhikku (female: *bhikksuni*) — the Pali form for 'religious hermit'. On Java it means 'a Hindu or Buddhist teacher'.

Bhinneka Tunggal Ika — an old Sanskrit term attributed to a 13th Century poet and now Indonesia's official motto, meaning 'We are many, but we are one.' Or, to use a more common translation, 'Unity in diversity.' The 14th Century Majapahit prime minister, Gadjah Mada, was the first to use this modern Indonesian phrase.

Bima — a warrior-lover of the Hindu *Ramayana* epic poem, one of the 5 Pandava brothers, the biggest and the baddest, the black-headed giant hero. Also the name of a fast air conditioned train that runs between Surabaya and Jakarta.

bis malam — special, fast, bit more expensive buses which travel long distances at night on Java, Bali, South Celebes and Sumatra.

blimbing (or 'star fruit') — a crispy, watery, thirst-quenching sour fruit which looks like a starfish. Usually yellow, but there are white and green varieties too. Wedged pieces smoothed over with salt is one favorite way to eat *blimbing*. In the dry season, *blimbings* are sweeter.

bonze — a Buddhist monk.

Bouraq — an Indonesian airlines which flies to many out-of-the-way places on Sulawesi, Kalimantan, and Nusa Tenggara; also Ambon and Ternate in Maluku; and by charter to Davao and Zamboanga in the Philippines.

Brahma—the four-headed Hindu God of Creation who gave birth to the Hindu castes. Brahma appears in white robes and rides a goose. Once thought to be the greatest and most revered out of all the Hindu gods because he set the universe in motion, he faded in importance with the rise of Shiva and Vishnu. Brahma was seldom worshipped in Indonesia.

Brahmin—the highest Hindu caste.

brem—fiery Balinese wine made from fermented black rice; tastes a bit like sweet Sherry and should be served cold.

bubur—Indonesian porridge. Very soft semi-liquid food made from rice, coconut or beans. Served usually in a glass with ice or sometimes steaming hot in a bowl. Comes in all shapes: snake-like curls, balls, pellets, or a pulpy mash. Colors range from bright green to chartreuse. Quite cheap; a common *kampung* dessert.

bupati—a local native chief or government district officer appointed by the Minister of Internal Affairs. The Dutch called them 'regents' and governed through them and even today the *bupati's* area of jurisdiction is translated as 'regency'. *Bupati* is the embodiment of traditional elite culture and the chief form for rural popular political focus. In the larger towns his function can now be compared to the position of mayor.

camat—civilian assistant head of a district; or second in command after the *bupati.*

candi—a Hindu or Buddhist tomb-temple. The term is commonly applied to all ancient monuments and ruins on Java and Sumatra, irrespective of their particular purpose or religion.

canting—an implement used for drawing (waxing) *batik* designs. Similar in function to a rudimentary fountain pen but hot wax is used instead of ink. Has a short bamboo handle and a tiny kettle on one end with a spout on the bottom where the wax comes out.

cap—a tin or copper stamp used in the hand-stamped *batik* process. *Cap*-printed *batik* is still waxed and dyed but the process is most usually less time-consuming (and thus usually less expensive) than hand-drawn *batik* (batik tulis).

cap cai—Indonesian vegetable and/or meat chop suey.

cella—a niche in an ancient stone temple in which a divinity, or his or her symbol, or a reincarnated king, nobleman or noblewoman is placed.

ciku—a sweet, soft fruit, shaped like an egg, brown in color on the outside and on the inside. To eat it, the skin must be sliced off. You'll find that its smooth flesh almost melts in your mouth. Be careful of the smooth doe-eyed stones inside.

Colt (pronounced 'Kol')—a Japanese-made (Mitibushi) van. Used all over Indonesia to transport passengers quickly from town to town. About Rp50 more expensive than buses but faster, the closest thing to an 'express' service you can get.

copra—the meat of a coconut that is pried loose from its shell and dried in the sun until it looks like soles of shoes, curled by the heat and tinged with mould. Coconut oil, which is extracted from copra, is used in such products as cooking oil, beauty lotion, soap, nitroglycerin.

cuscus—a nocturnal marsupial with soft fur, sharp claws and teeth, which lives a solitary existence except during the mating season. By day their pupils look like a vertical line. The female is frequently one-colored grey brown and males are spotted. The *cuscus* keeps to the trees where it lives on leaves and fruits. Found in Irian Jaya, its satellite islands, and in the Moluccas.

dagob—the highest pinnacle of a stupa.

dalang—the *wayang*-puppeteer who either manipulates the puppets and speaks the words, or else narrates a plot for live actors. The *dalang* is the playwright, producer, director, athletic, prompter, compere, singer and poet who jokes, cues the *gamelan,* philosophizes, impersonates. In essence, he is the star of the show. Traveling from village to village, the *dalang* is called upon to perform *wayang* on occasions of crisis events in peoples' lives such as births, circumcisions, marriages, or to exorcize evil spirits. He has a ready wit and weaves political commentary into each *wayang* performance. The *dalang's* reputation also depends upon his *sakti* (magic power).

Damar Wulan—a Majapahit hero and East Javanese theatre *lakon.*

datu—a Batak (an ethnic group of North Sumatra) medicine man, priest, auger, or physician.

dermaga—pier; loading-stage; quay-wall.

desa—a small village with an agrarian economy. On Java, a *desa* consists of farmhouses, barns, community meeting places, ricefields, fishponds, forests, houses. On Bali, a *desa* also consists of the central square, temples, market, *waringan* tree and an alarm-drum tower.

Dewi Sri—the Rice Goddess. From the time of rice-planting to the harvesting, ceremonies are held all over Java and Bali in honor of this animistic deity.

dokar—a light, two-wheeled horse carriage; usually there are two seats for 4-6 passengers.

duku—Ping-pong sized fruits, sweet with a sour tinge. Each wedge of the translucent white flesh is enclosed in a light brown shell, containing a greenish hard center which might taste bitter if you took too deep a bite. To open, just squeeze.

dukun—there are many gradations of these village doctors. A *dukun* could be any of the following: folk doctor, witch doctor, black magic advocate, herbalist, druggist, village healer using incantations, ritual specialist (employing simple prayers or amulets), chronicler, bard, diviner, or conjurors and spiritual leaders of great prestige. There are *dukuns* who place spells on people from a distance or on the spot, some who use water for a symbolic cleansing of the spirit. Many have a considerable fund of practical knowledge from which to draw and many are skilled at massage, osteopathy, and healing by faith. Also, many are quacks.

durian—the outside of this odorous fruit is spiked and looks like the back of an anteater. It's the only fruit that tigers eat, cracking it open with their claws. The inside consists of 3 or 4 compartments where the cream-colored fruit surrounds large pods. Suck the mushy oozy custard-like pulp from the pods. The taste is indescribable. You either love it with a passion or can't stand to be in the same room with it. Tastes like onions and peaches, camembert cheese, dates and nectarines, brandied eggnog with radishes, vanilla ice cream and onions, and other such wild combinations. Definitely an acquired taste. *Durian* grows on the boughs of a great tree like an oak and when it's in season the tree looks like it's full of green-spiked American footballs. The *durian* ripens and falls usually between Jan. and March (*durians* have killed people when they've fallen from trees). Costs Rp100-300 per fruit. Alcohol and durian together will make you deathly sick.

erong—graves which are hung from high cliffs in Torajaland, South Celebes.

es—ice. Could also mean sweet frozen fruit-flavored water on a stick, Rp5-25.

es buah—a mixture of fruit with shaved ice and/or sweetened condensed milk, coconut, *bubur,* and chocolate syrup on top.

es juice—a combination of fruit, crushed ice and sweet syrup mixed in a blender. Ask for your own combinations of exotic fruits, i.e. pineapple and banana, papaya and banana, etc. Some spike their *es juice* with liquor.

fahombe—a stone-jumping sport of the Niah Islanders (on Nias off the west coast of Sumatra), an activity once used to train warriors for battle and to prove a young man's fitness to take a wife. Now a tourist spectacle which you must hire to see.

gado2—a national wide dish of steamed green

beans, soya beans, potatoes, cabbage or bean sprouts and covered in a rich tangy peanut sauce.

Galungan—a festival of Bali during which the gods come down to visit the island for a week. Celebrated also by the Balinese community of Yogya, Central Java.

gamelan—a Javanese or Balinese percussion-type orchestra. Sounds soft, floating, liquid, sometimes clashing. Made up mainly of bronze and wooden xylophones shaped like discs, cylinders, keys or bulbous hollow bowls beaten with hammers. A chorus of singers (pesinden), drums, flutes, gongs, and sometimes bamboo rattle instruments (anklung) accompany the *gamelan*. The *gamelan's* tonal systems (*slendro* and *pelog*) are entirely different from western tuning systems. Traditional *gamelan* consists of up to 75 instruments played by 30 musicians. There are some 15 different kinds of *gamelan* for dramas, concerts, funerals, processions, festivals and other events.

Ganesha—in Hindu mythology, the fat-bellied elephant-headed son of Shiva; the Household God, or God of Prosperity. Beloved Ganesha is wise, thoughtful, well-versed in the scriptures, worshipped before every undertaking to assure success.

gang—alleyway, small lane, path, or street.

ganja—marijuana, cannabis.

garuda—a legendary bird like a combination eagle and supernatural roc, it carries the Hindu god Vishnu. Garuda tried to rescue Sita midflight during her abduction by the devil king Rawana, but dies in the attempt. You see this episode from the *Ramayana* enacted often in *wayang* shows. Garuda is a common motif in Indonesian art, the bird is as well the official emblem of the Indonesian Republic. Garuda is also the name of the government-run international airlines.

genggong—a Balinese jaw's harp.

ginseng—an organic Chinese drink that gives energy; made from a root shaped like a man.

gotong royong—village socialism. A traditional village practice of mutual cooperation; an agreement to work together especially in regards to planting, irrigating and harvesting. This is the actual force that gets a new school built, a local industry started, an irrigation canal dug — not a masterplan from Jakarta. *Gotong royong* is also used to organize feasts and festivals or even for carrying the dead to the graveyard. It's encouraged by the present government because it helps fight inflation.

gringsing—on Bali, a weaving design, the so-called 'flaming cloth'.

gunung—mountain. G. Merapi means Mount

Merapi.

gunungan—the triangular symbol of the *wayang* theatre which is set in the middle of the stage when the play begins and ends. It could also be the link that connects the different parts of the play. The *gunungan* represents the world cosmic order, harmony and peace with nature. By its motions or the angle in which it is set, it shows the mood of the next scene. In its center there's a small house suggesting the inward life of man·and to both sides are giants, symbolizing consience. The huge conical mounds of rice and vegetables carried in procession in Solo and Yogya — derived from the sacred Hindu World Mountain (Mahameru) — are also called *gunungan*.

guru—in the Indonesian sense it means anyone who teaches anything.

haji—a Muslim man who has made the pilgrimmage to Mecca; he wears the white skullcap called a *peci*. *Hajah* is the feminine form. When *Haji* preceeds a person's name, the word is also used as a title, i.e. Tuan *Haji* Idrus (or female, *Puan Hajah*). *Haj* is the noun and refers to the actual pilgrimmage made, about 40,000 Indonesians each year. Before the prospective *haji* leaves, he must show the village headman his family's ability to support itself in his absence; usually only wealthy men can afford to make the trip. He must also take a short written test on religious and state affairs.

Hari Raya (or *Idul Fitri*)—the Islamic New Year. Ear-splitting firecrackers everywhere. These one or two days of festivities end the monthlong Muslim fast, *Ramadan*. Celebrated by Muslims all over Indonesia, there are massprayers in mosques and crowded public places, followed by visits among relatives and friends when new clothes are worn and gifts are exchanged.

helicak—a small motorized 3-wheeled miniature vehicle which carries 5-8 passengers and makes a whining sputtering sound like a Honda. In Jakarta a *helicak* could be a *becak* with a ·motor scooter engine fitted to its frame, sheltered by a plastic bubble in front of the motorcycle in which the passenger is protected from the sun and rain. Average fare, Rp150-600.

Hinayana Buddhism—also called Theravada Buddhism, or the 'Lesser Vehicle' because of the narrowness of its tenets. This is the more fundamentalist Buddhist school which believes that you must get your own house in order before you're ready to spread the light of Buddhism to other people. An outerworldly form of monasticism, this sect promises the bliss of extinction for only yourself if after many incarnations a man achieves enlightenment. *Hinayana* (theravadic) Buddhism originated in South India, then spread to Ceylon, Burma, Thailand and the rest of Southeast Asia, but it never really caught on in Indonesia. Its canon is in Pali.

hukum tua—in Minahasa, North Celebes, the head of the village; the *kepala desa.*

ibu—mother. Also a deferential or affectionate title used when addressing any older woman such as a landlady, washerwoman, or *warung* cook.

ikan bakar—baked fish.

ikat—a tie-dye technique used to decorate fabrics whereby segments of the thread are bound and dyed before the weaving begins. The whole process results in a highly unusual and colorful overall design. Thin coconut fibres are wound tightly around cotton thread to prevent the bound parts from absorbing the color when it's dipped into the dye bath. By changing the wrappings after dyeing, various colors and patterns can be applied to the unwoven threads. *Ikat* can be applied to the warp, the weft, or both (very rare). In western and Central Java, and in Aceh (North Sumatra), *ikat* of the warp is employed. In East Java, South Bali, Central and South Sumatra, and the coastal areas of Borneo, *ikat* of the weft is prefered.

imigrasi—the immigration department or office. They give up to 5 one-month visa extensions, then you must leave the country, re-enter, and begin the process again of acquiring a visa extension each month.

istana—a palace or castle. Usually preceeds a proper name, i.e. Istana Bogor.

jambu-air—a juicy, pink, light green or white bell-shaped fruit about the size of a large strawberry. The whole fruit is edible. A popular way of eating *jambu-air* is to break it by squeezing it between the palms of the hands and then dipping the pieces into a mixture of black soya sauce, sugar, and sliced red chilies.

jambu-batu—the quava fruit. Eat the green outer layer, the pulp, or the whole.

jamu—herbal medicine made from a mixture of roots, barks, and grasses, usually steeped in hot water and drunk. Some *jamus* are applied directly on the skin, or simply eaten.

jeruk—this term is applicable to all citrus fruits. In some parts of Indonesia it means orange or mandarin, but in other parts a grapefruit or a lemon.

joget—social, not religious, dancing.

kabupaten—*bupati's* (regent's or mayor's) house,

residence, office.

kain—a length of material worn by both men and women about 2.75 m long and 1.20 m wide, fastened at the waist by a sash. A *kain* is what the western-dressed civil servant changes into when he or she gets home from work. *Kain kebaya* is the native costume of Indonesian women.

kakawin—a classical poetic style of ancient Javanese courts.

kala—literally 'badness' or 'evil' but in the figurative sense the demon himself who invisibly causes evil; a symbol of courseness and malice. He haunts desolate places like the seashores. the deep forests, dangerous parts of villages such as the cemetary or the crossroads. They can go into peoples' bodies and make them idiotic or insane. A *kala*-head is the carved stone head of a monster over temple gates and recesses to ward off demonic forces by magic means; looks like a stylized lion's head.

Kalimantan—an Indonesian territory south of Sarawak, Brunei, and Sabah; that part of the island of Borneo which is controlled by Indonesia.

kamar mandi—bathroom, washroom.

kampung—a village, neighborhood, homestead family, or migrant living compound in the city or country. In the cities, *kampungs* are really villages transplanted into the metropolis, each one reflecting the ethnic background and origins of its inhabitants. This poor man's sector often covers a large city area, and is made up of hundreds of shanties and hovels separated by narrow lanes or footpaths, very crowded and often without paved roads or electricity. Sometimes up to 3000 people are jammed together to form a single housing unit with just palm matting walls between each other.

kancil—also called the 'mouse-deer'. The *kancil* is not a true deer and has no antlers. Predators are kept at bay with sharp canine teeth. Smallest of all hoofed cud-chewing mammals, it stands no more than ½ m at the shoulders. The *kancil* has a soft brown coat and undersides. In folk tales, the *kancil* is represented as a shy, cunning creature, seemingly helpless but uses trickery to outwit and get the better of stronger enemies.

kantor—office.

Kantor Parawisata—tourist office.

kapal laut—a seagoing vessel; a ship.

kapal motor—a small motorized vessel capable of traveling along coasts, up rivers, and across channels or straits.

kapok—a silky waxy fibre taken from the pods of the *kapok* tree which grows on higher slopes. *Kapok* resists vermin and moisture and is as good as cork as a filler for life preservers. Oil from its seeds is used in munitions, food, soap.

karma—a Hindu belief that says that our destiny will be determined by the sum total of all our actions, good and bad, in all preceeding lives and that our destiny will also depend on the effect of the *karma* of others upon it. *Karma* is the total impact of all previous deeds and thoughts of the self.

kasar—a term used to describe rough, uncivilized, ungracious, unfit, impolite, coarse, blunt traits or attributes in objects, people or skills. Also could mean in poor taste. Includes things like poorly played music, stupid jokes, cheap pieces of cloth, blotchy paintings.

kauman—the orthodox Islamic quarter of a city; known for its strict adherence to Muslim customs and traditions.

kawi (or Old Javanese)—the classical literary language of early Javanese and Balinese poetry. Nine out of ten words in it are Sanskrit (*kawi* means 'poet'). Very rich, flowery and archaic; well-suited for singing and chanting and musical meter. *Kawi* is now kept more alive and best preserved on Bali rather than on Java.

kayu besi—ironwood.

kayuputih oil—a cure-all panacea. Drink diluted or rub on full strength for stomachaches, headcolds, rashes, etc. Smells and tastes horrid so you know it's gotta be good for you.

kebaya—a Chinese long-sleeved blouse with shaped bodice worn by Indonesian women. Most commonly made of cotton (the wealthy sometimes use silk, velvet or brocade), it has a feminine decolletage and fine embroidered hand-done edges. Some are very old.

Kecak—a seated choral dance drama by Balinese men. Often called the 'Monkey Dance' because of its characteristic staccato chorus ('chaka, chaka, chaka') with the dancers' arms shooting up and bodies contorting like in a voodoo rite.

Kediri—a town in East Java; also the name of an East Javanese Dynasty (1049-1222 A.D.) known mainly for its poetry. Though there is little in any of its writings which tell of contemporary historical events, such a large number of literary works were produced that this period is known as Indonesia's Golden Age of Literature. The *Barata-yuddha* was written by a Kediri poet. Few permanent monuments remain of this period.

kelapa—coconut. Has the widest variety of uses: food, drink, oil, wood, leaves for thatching, fibre for matting, its shells made into water vessels and dippers.

kemban—women's neckerchief or breastcloth.

Ken Arok—an historical 13th Century Central Javanese King about whom a classic of *kawi* literature was written; the story of 'The Magic Kris'. This rapist-bandit-charmer-parvenu became ruler by murdering the king, then marrying his beautiful wife. It's a story of intrigue, assassinations, curses and black magic—a high drama of medieval Java and Asian politics.

kepala desa—village leader or headman. Other names for the *kepala desa* are: *lurah, kepala kampung, kepala negeri* and *penghulu kampung.*

Ketoprak—a Javanese folk play. Though this village entertainment has less polished dancing than *wayang orang*, it's now so popular that it rivals *wayang orang* in costuming, staging and music. Its stories are based on Javanese history, ballads such as the *Panji* love-tales, the wooing of the Majapahit queen, and the fall of the rebel prince Arya Penangsang. A popular compromise between the classical and modern styles, the acting is basically realistic with extempore songs and everyday language used. There could even be red-fezzed officers; anything that might make a hit. Actors improvise freely, particularly in the humorous scenes.

klotok—a specialized river craft of Kalimantan. Has an outboard motor and sounds like a chorus of bullfrogs ('klotok, klotok, klotok').

kolintang—a wooden zylophonic orchestra. Sounds somewhat like *gamelan*. Found in Minahasa, North Celebes.

Konfrontasi—the period (1962-1965) when Sukarno's regime threatened Malaysia with military intervention because of Malaysia's neocolonialist policies. Indonesian armed raiders were put ashore on the Malaysian peninsula and attacks were launched from Kalimantan into British administered northern Borneo. *Konfrontasi* ended abruptly with Sukarno's overthrow in 1965.

korupsi—corruption, graft.

kraton—a small walled and fortified palace city. Derived in part from India, *kratons* were the supreme centers of religious worship in the Hindu-Javanese system of rule. *Kratons* and not the villages became the bearers of Hinduism and Islam in Indonesia. These court cities have always been a sanctuary for the best musicians, *dalangs,* dancing masters and artisans, as well as being the first producers of Indonesian handicrafts. Stimulated by the Indian masterpieces, writing and literature also developed in the *kratons*. Structures of the past, they are now more or less museums. The highest ranking are located in the heart of Java in the sultanate cities of Yogya and Solo.

kretek—Indonesian sweet clove-flavored cigarettes. Named after the sound they make when smoked. Invented by an asthmatic. Like smoking dessert.

kris—a Javanese or Balinese double-edged dagger. Designed for thrusting, its blade twists and winds like a snake. Simultaneously a weapon,

an ornament, a cultic object (said to have magic powers), and the finest example of Indonesian metalcrafts. Average length is 300-500 mm (12-20 inches) though the Balinese *kris* is often straighter and longer (over 1 meter) than the Javanese models. The *pamor* work on the blade is achieved by forging alternate layers of meteorite and ordinary iron, one shining bright and the other dull. *Kris* passed down through the family are now used only in formal ceremonial occasions.

Krishna—a popular Hindu god who could lift elephants at 4 years old; he later became a magnificent warrior and a great lover.

kroncong—gentle melancholy music played in Nusa Tenggara (Southeastern Islands) and in Jakarta. Derived from the popular lute music of 16th Century Portugal.

krupuk—fried prawn or fish crisps; Indonesian bread. Looks like a giant misshapen cracker. The most famous come from the Sitoarjo area of Surabaya and measure up to 380 mm across.

Kuda Kepang (*kuda,* horse; *kepang,* plaited bamboo)—a folk play trance dance performed by men simulating the actions of horses and riding flat hobby horses made of painted bamboo. The 'horse' nibbles at hay and laps water from a pail. There are 4, 6, or 8 riders, several musicians, plus other masked figures. Whips crack and steel pipes are beaten with a hammer. A medicine-man brings the riders out of it. This play is known in West Java as *Kuda Lumping,* in Southwest Java as *Kuda Ebleg,* around Yogya as *Jatilan,* and in East Java as *Reyog* or *Ludruk.*

kulkul—a drum tower found in Javanese and Balinese villages which sounds the alarm or calls people to meetings.

number of beats	meanings
• • • • • •	rampuk kampak (bandits)
• • • • •	kecurian royokoyo (theft of livestock)
• • • •	bencana alam (natural catastrophe)
• • • ⁻ • • •	kebakaran (fire)
• • ⁻ • •	pencurian barang (theft of personal property)
• • • • • •	menemukan mayat, caruk, atau gantung (a death, murder, manslaughter, or suicide)

ladang—slash and burn shifting cultivation. Using very simple tools such as a digging stick and an axe, plots are first cleared by burning, then crops (most often upland rice, sweet potato and corn) are cultivated on the ashes for several years. The farmer then shifts and clears a new plot, leaving the old one to fallow for a period of 2-20 years. Vegetation then restores and regenerates the earth, when he or his descendants return and begin the cycle once again.

lakon—the content or plot of a *wayang* dramatic play. It's like the first draft of a scenario; very standardized. *Lakon* includes an organized listing of scenes, what follows what and who follows who, where the action is going to occur, names of the leading characters and what they talk about and why. Seldom is there any written dialogue. There are four main groups of scripts: early history, Arjuna cycle, Rama cycle, Pandava cycle.

Leberan (also known as *Hari Raya*)—a religious holiday which follows the one month fast, *Ramadan* (or *Puasa* in Indonesian). During this religious celebration people customarily get new clothes, old quarrels are forgotten, cards and gifts are exchanged, families are reunited, there are endless rounds of visits, new friends are made, graves of ancestors are visited, employers pay their workers a bonus, etc.

Legong—a classical Balinese dance performed by two young girls. Training begins at 4 or 5 years old; they retire at around 13 years or once they begin menstruation. Considered by many the most beautiful and graceful of the Balinese dance ballets.

liana—a species of palm tree whose fibers are used in binding. It grows virtually anywhere, though it is hard to keep as an indoor plant. Quite expensive, about Rp10,000 for one band.

liang—graves which have been hewn out of cliffs by the Torajas of South Celebes.

lingga—a Hindu religious symbol in the form of an upright stone phallus-shaped column. *Lingga* is a symbol of virility and manliness, a monument of Shiva and of male potency. *Yoni* is the female counterpart, a vagina shaped symbol of fertility.

LIPI (Lembaga Ilmu Pengetahra Indonesia)—a government association based in Jakarta which appraises, then approves or disapproves, a foreign student's application for study or research in Indonesia.

longbot—a long thin motorized river craft capable of high speeds; sometimes propelled by as many as 3 outboard motors. Used in Kalimantan.

longsat—a small round fruit with a yellowish white skin and sweet white meat.

lontar—a species of palm tree. Life giving, especially in the eastern part of the archipelago, providing food, shelter, utensils, and ornaments. Much Indonesian literature and history has been inscribed over the years on strips of this palm, shaped like rulers about 25 mm wide and 300 mm long. Volumes are made by threading them together with a string, like venetian blinds. Texts and pictures are engraved with an iron stylus and filled in with a mixture of soot and oil, showing up very effectively against the yellowish background of the palm leaf. The eastern equivalent of the papyrus reed sheets of 4000 B.C., these brilliant examples of illustrative art are inscribed with elegant Sanskrit-like characters and depict stories, such as of Rama and Sita.

lontong—glutinous rice wrapped in *pandanus* leaves.

Loro Ratu Kidul—the South Sea goddess; said to be the legendary wife of a 16th Century Mataram ruler. Still venerated along the south coast of Java.

losmen—rooms to let. Found in even the smallest towns. Cheaper than hotels but equally as adequate. On Bali, *losmens* are usually native style houses, a family-run inn.

Ludruk—a theatre form (created this century) popular in the big cities of Indonesia. Comparable to musical comedy or burlesque shows of the west. Both male and female roles are mostly played by male actors. Plots are often based on conflicts arising out of the generation gap, thwarted love, and other dilemmas of modern life. Many satirical allusions to contemporary events. Surabaya and East Java are the main centers.

lurah—this term is used on Java. It means a village head elected traditionally by secret ballot by all over 18 who've lived continuously for a minimum of of 3 months in a village. Ballots are in the form of palm leaf ribs (lidi); a bamboo tube serves as a ballot box. First among equals, the *lurah* must mediate at meetings to see that a decision is reached so that everyone comes to some agreement. They aren't paid but are given village land which they cultivate as long as they hold office. Once these local leaders were the only officials to be elected by the people, but now they are beginning to be appointed by the government and paid a salary.

lurik—a locally made finely woven striped textile of Yogya, Central Java; often used as cheaper *batik* material.

Maengket Dance—a Minahasan (North Celebes) courting or house warming dance.

Mahabharata—a Hindu epic containing 100,000 couplets; the longest epic poem in the world. Tells of a tremendous 18 day battle between two family groups in the legendary state of Bharat in the Vedic Age in India (1500-500 B.C.). Translated into the high language of *kawi* in the Middle Ages, this Indian masterpiece plays a gigantic part in Indonesian literature, art and theatre.

Mahayana Buddhism — with its many relics, rosaries, liturgies, Bodhisattva-saints for future Buddahhood, this dramatic, ritualistic form of Buddhism has been likened to Mediterranean Christianity. It teaches that those who reach salvation (bodhi) stand on the edge of nirvana, but must renounce it so that they may confer it upon other human beings. Thus it is called the 'Greater Vehicle'. From North India, this form found its way further north into Tibet, China, Mongolia and Japan. Then it was carried by the Chinese down into Vietnam. A version of it, Tantricism, has had great influence on Java and South Sumatra.

Majapahit — an ancient East Javanese empire which held power over much of Indonesia from 1292-1398 A.D. and was finally dissolved by Islamic princes around 1520 A.D. Majapahit was the mightiest indigenous kingdom in Indonesia's history.

makan asli — native cuisine; a native dish.

makara — a formalized animal figure in old Javanese sculpture; the Asian zodiac sign of cancer.

maleo — the jungle-fowl; some species lay their eggs in black volcanic sand on beaches.

Maluku — the Moluccas Islands; 1000 islands scattered between Celebes and New Guinea.

mambruk (or Crown Pigeon) — a large bluish grey bird with a purplish brown breast, wings marked by 2 transverse bars, and a tuft of finely ramified feathers on its head; found only in the Moluccas Islands and in Irian Jaya. Poor fliers, they live and forage mostly on the ground in the forests or feed in marshes along the coast, flying up to trees only to roost or when disturbed, but always into low stunted trees. Papuans eat the *mambruk* and its crest feathers are very much in demand so this bird is now a protected species.

mandala — an ancient magic circle or shrine designed for meditation. Has its historical source in India. Also the name of an army-owned and run interisland airlines.

mandau — the traditional sword of Dayak tribes in Kalimantan.

mandi — a cement, palm or bamboo structured bathroom with a big cement tub in it from which you throw water over yourself with a dipper, elephant-fashion. The tub is not meant to be jumped into and its water is not for drinking.

mangosteen — a round purple-black skinned fruit with a whorl of green sepals on the top. Inside, white, sweet-sour juicy segments huddle together into a ball. Try it while you can. Mangosteens come into season about the same time as the *durian*; it counteracts the heatiness brought about by eating too much of the high-protein *durian*.

martabak — a thin doughed fried Arabian pancake stuffed with meat, egg and/or vegetables. About 100 times better than a Chico Roll. Sold over the counter at foodstalls for around Rp100. Eaten with green chilies (lombok), slices of cucumber, and a cold Bintang Beer.

MAS — Malaysian Airlines System.

mascrochan — banana crepe, usually found on Java.

Mataram — a Hindu empire which reached its apogee in the 16th and 17th Centuries, represented today in the sultanates of Yogya and Solo. Though it professed Islam, Mataram retained a Hindu-Buddhist state structure. Some of Mataram's kings are buried in highly venerated royal tombs at Imogiri and at Kota Gede, near Yogya, Central Java.

Menak Jonggo — a deadly enemy of the Majapahit hero Damar Wulan; a very evil literary character. These 'Arabian Tales' are used as a central theme in *wayang golek*.

menhir — a prehistoric monument consisting of one large upright stone.

merdeka — freedom.

Merpati — an Indonesian government-run airlines which mainly operates domestic flights; Merpati offers the most extensive network of any of the domestic airlines.

meru — a Javanese (and Buddhist) mountain-of-heaven. The legend of this sacred mountain originates in India. *Meru* is also a pagoda-like roof made of thatch found on Bali.

mesin becak — a motorcycle for hire that has a side car; a motorized *becak*.

mesjid — mosque.

mie — noodles.

mie goreng — fried noodles with meat and/or vegetables; for Rp100 extra it's topped with a fried, boiled or scrambled egg.

muezin — in the Islamic world, these men call the people to prayer from high towers on the mosques. In many places they have been replaced by loudspeakers which reach longer distances than the human voice, startling you awake at 4 or 5 am.

muncak — a small graceful variety of deer found on Timor and Java. Also called the 'barking deer'.

naga — a Hindu mythological serpent regarded as charged with magic powers. Most snake symbols, encountered frequently in S.E. Asia, are derived from this legendary creature. To augment its power the blade of the *kris* also resembles a snake.

nangka — jackfruit. A sweet, refreshing, fibrous, segmented fruit weighing up to 20 kilos. On the tree it hangs like a heavy green water-bag. Upon cutting open the thick, tough outer layer, the golden-yellow pulpy fruit is found to be juicy and chewy at the same time. The seeds taste like chestnuts when boiled in brine. A cousin of the *nangka* family is the *cempedak* which is smaller and creamier in texture.

nasi—rice.

nasi campur—a combination of eggs, vegetables, meat or fish and sauce on top of a heap of steamed rice; a good bargain meal all over Indonesia.

nasi padang—rice with many side dishes, usually quite spicy hot (pedas). This style of cooking originates in West Sumatra but is now found everywhere in Indonesia. The best deal for your rupes in Indonesian-style restaurants.

nasi pecel—a breakfast dish similar to *gado2* with boiled vegies such as papaya leaves, tapioca, bean sprouts, string beans, fried *tahu* (soybean cake) and *tempe,* plus there could be fresh cucumbers, soybeans, coconut shavings, peanuts, and peanut sauce on top.

negeri—district.

Negritos—the first known human inhabitants of Indonesia, entering the archipelago about 30,000 years ago. A pygmy people similar to African negroids in facial features but have thicker wooly hair, rounder heads, and smaller statures. Genetic traces of this pygmy stock are still detectable all over Indonesia, particularly on New Guinea and nearby islands.

oplet—a small (4-cylinder) Datsun or Ford covered pick-up truck with side benches used to transport passengers in cities for short distances cheaply. In Sumatra, an *oplet* is a small bus seating about 25 or more people.

orang laut—aboriginal nomadic sea gypsys or fishermen.

orangutan—'Man of the Forest'; a great ape claimed to have the closest resemblance to man. There are two different species, one native to Kalimantan, while the other inhabits Sumatra. The orangutan has a distinctive flat nose with sunken eyes, a 1½ meter armspan, and red hair which grows very long on its shoulders and sides. Ungainly on the ground, it lives mainly in the tree tops where it builds a sleeping platform. Eats fruit, young plants and leaves. Found in expensive-to-get-to Kutai Reserve in East Kalimantan, around Pundu in South Kalimantan, the Loeser Reserve (North Sumatra), or 4 hours by bus from Medan at Bukit Lawang Reserve, North Sumatra.

owa—this monkey is easily recognizable because its face is ringed by hood of fine tufted white hair. The *owa* are fantastic tree climbers with long spider-like arms, have a shrill, piercing call, and are tailless. Grey, yellowish, brown and black varieties are found in Sumatra. In Kalimantan and in West Java the grey *owa* occurs more frequently.

pala—a sweet-sour fruit which comes from the nutmeg tree of the Moluccas Islands and North Celebes.

pamong—in Solo, Central Java, a 'guide' for spiritual development. Could also mean caretaker, supporter, mentor, educator, teacher.

panakawans—grotesque figures found in *wayang* performances to give comic relief. Semar and his two (sometimes four) sons Petruk and Gareng, Bagong and Nala are the equivalent to the medieval court jesters, sort of scholar disciples of the heroes. With their paunches, short legs, flat noses and flabby breasts, they are a distinctive Javanese addition to the Hindu epics. Sometimes the *panakawans* are able to work powerful magic and destroy demons. They can take surprising liberties with the gods, beating them, mocking them, even throwing the great god Brahma down a well.

Panca Sila—a Sanskrit phrase meaning 'The Five Principles' put forth in 1945 by Sukarno to provide the philosophical basis of the Republic. They are: belief in one of the four great universal religions, nationalism, Indonesian-style 'guided' democracy, humanitarianism, and a just and prosperous society. Surmounted by a proud eagle, you can see the *Panca Sila* plaque at the entrance archways of even the smallest villages the width and breadth of Indonesia. These principles are meant to be a point of social and political reference, a touchstone for the state, and national education is aimed at producing citizens who are morally responsible to the principles.

pandanus—leaves of a species of tree native to Indonesia. Used in building, making utensils, wrapping, or for clothing.

Pandava—a family whose members are the main protaganists in the age-old Hindu epic poem, the *Mahabharata.*

Panji Cycle—an extensive cycle of Javanese stories of many different written and oral versions. Originates in the 15th Century. The stories focus on Panji's reunion with his elusive bride Candra Kirono (Radiant Ray of the Moon) whom he loses on their wedding night. She is a princess of Kediri and he is like an East Javanese Arjuna. The stories are full of mysterious vanishings, transformations, reawakenings, disguises, adventures. The vowel rhymes are based on the Indonesian language and are more in tune with the native ear than the courtly *kakawin* poetry. Staged often at wedding parties, this cycle serves as themes for mask plays (topeng) and for some puppet plays.

pantun—a traditional form of poetry, a four-lined verse consisting of alternating, roughly rhyming lines. Although the first and second lines some-time appear completely disconnected in meaning from the third and fourth, there is almost invariably a link of some sort, traceable through the faintest nuance of thought or deli-cately shadowed in a string of words. Generally, the first two lines describe a place: where a man and a girl met, a *kampung,* a moonlit beach, streams, long grass in fields. The next two con-tain the story, the idea, the feeling, the essence. These quatrains could be very passionate or bitterly cynical. So many symbols are employed in a *pantun* that a great deal is said in a very small space.

parang — chopping knife; machete, cleaver.

pasangrahan — government lodge or forestry hut which might accept travelers for a modest price or for free. Sometimes a *pasangrahan* is a com-mercial venture, a hotel.

pasar — market. For much of rural Indonesia the whole focus and center of a village. The *pasar* is also a socializing center.

pasirir — royalty.

pas jalan (or *surat jalan*) — a travel permit. See *'surat jalan'.*

peci (or *kopiah*) — an Indonesian felt or velvet cap, usually black; an Islamic religious symbol of tradition and power. The *peci* could also be worn by non-Muslims since it's also a national symbol of Indonesia and of the Malaysian cul-ture.

pedanda — a high priest of the Bali-Hindu religion.

pegawai — a white collar worker; functionary, staff or employee. Most often a civil servant or a government official.

Pelni — the state shipping line of Indonesia with an extensive interisland network. Reasonably-priced.

pencak silat — the Indonesian national self-defence art, a sort of stylized combat. It's both a lethal fighting skill and a graceful art form. *Silat* refers more to the physical side of it whereas *pencak* is an art; when *pencak* is combined with *silat,* it's deadly training. Though *pencak silat* is in-digenous to Indonesia and reflects an Indone-sian flavor, it is a product of a synthesis of many fighting arts with its origins mainly in China. This virulent combative system is designed for both empty-handed combat and is also based on the use of weapons. When practiced with percussion accompaniment it looks like dance and in fact many dances have borrowed move-ments from it and vice versa. In some *pencak silat* dance forms daggers or spears are used to create a spellbinding effect by staging ferocious and spectacular mock battles. There are 157 re-corded styles with numerous regional differ-ences: foot tactics on Sumatra, hand tactics in East Java and on Bali, and so on.

pendopo — a traditional, ornate, open-air pillared pavilion with a low pyramidal overhanging roof usually found in a *kraton* or in front of a Java-nese nobleman's house. Serves for audiences, receptions and celebrations accompanied by entertainments. Nowadays, many productions of amateur dance associations are performed on *pendopos.*

penghulu — a headman in a Batak village of North Sumatra. This term is also used in Sumbawan villages.

penginapan (Peng.) — a cheap hotel with plain facilities.

perkutut — a Javanese singing bird which looks like a dove with a pale blue head and rosy breast. Highly valued (up to Rp50,000) by the Javanese and Chinese who enter them in con-tests to determine the outstanding songbird of the village or district. A Javanese saying goes 'Happiness is a home, a wife, and a singing bird.'; their mythology claims that selection and care of the right *perkutut* will result in good luck. Outside houses on Java there's often a 8 m high pole on top of which is a brilliantly colored *perkutut* in a cage, trilling blithely. The bird is hoisted by pully to the top of the pole at dawn, then hauled down again at dusk when people start lighting flickering oil lamps.

Pertamina — Indonesia's mammoth state-owned, state-run — and recently nearly bankrupt — oil company.

pikulan — a pole which looks like the bow of an archer and rests on the shoulders of a labourer or a peddler on the move. Cans, wares, bricks, water, and other burdens are suspended from each end. A man can carry up to 50 kilos with a *pikulan.* All you hear is just his feet rhythmically hitting the mud as he pads by.

pisang — banana.

PKI — Partai Komunis Indonesia. The Communist Party of Indonesia exercised considerable social and political power in Indonesia during the later years of the Sukarno regime (1960-65). Dissolved on 12 March, 1966, by order of Pre-sidential (Suharto) Decree.

plangi — a tie-dye technique for decorating cloth practiced in Lombok, Palembang (South Suma-tra), and in the eastern districts of Java and Bali. In this very attractive process, the motifs are first drawn or stamped on the fabric (some-times on silk), then the figures are sketched in outline by using a tacking thread. When the threads are pulled tight small loops come up. When the fabric is dipped into the dye vat, the areas that were covered with the string don't absorb the dye, forming a design according to the pattern stitched. Many colors and a broad range of shades can be applied on the one fabric. This technique probably reached Indonesia by way of India.

P.N.G. — Papua New Guinea. A new country whose territory makes up roughly the whole eastern half of the island of New Guinea. It shares an international border with the Indonesian territory of Irian Jaya.

polisi — police.

prahu — a swift, strong, all wooden sailing boat or outrigger of Malay origin. Often built entirely without metal or nails, a *prahu* shows a very high level of traditional technology. Some weigh as much as 250 tons.

priyayi — the established aristocratic administrative class of Java. This upper middle class is roughly the successor of the old Hindu Satriya caste and today they are senior officials, officers in the armed forces, presidents of corporations, professors at state-run universities, doctors, lawyers, engineers, architects, politicians, writers; generally the intelligentsia and the new business group. To be a manufacturer or an industrialist is not *priyayi* and it's generally considered more dignified to work for the government. Distasteful and dishonorable manual occupations are left to the minority groups. Now the term tends to be used more to describe a cultured person or cultured behaviour.

puak — tribe, ethnic group.

pura — an old or new Balinese terraced temple consisting of 3 tiers enclosed by walls. A gateway, often lavishly decorated, leads to the terraces. The third terrace is usually the most sacred where you find recesses for offerings, shrines, and *meru*-roofed structures.

puri — on Bali, a palace of a prince.

pusaka — sacred heirlooms passed down from dynasty to dynasty or from generation to generation in families.

raja — a prince, lord or king. On Bali it may still be used to refer to male Hindu royalty. On Ambon, Central Moluccas, a *raja* is the aristocratic head of a village or district. In Indonesian Timor, a *raja* is the head of one of the 10 traditional Atoni princedoms.

raksasa — a mythical giant from Hindu mythology, like the European Gog and Magog. Sculptures and reliefs of *raksasa* figures are often seen guarding entrances to temples, erected on either side of the gates. Fierce, moustached, armed with a large club, with long canine teeth sticking out through the cheeks like wild boar's teeth, he wards off evil forces.

Ramadan (or *Puasa*) — the Muslim month of fasting which takes place on the 9th month of the Javanese-Muslim calendar. From dawn to dusk everyday devout Muslims abstain from drinking, eating, sex, and other earthly pleasures. They get up at 3 or 4 am and eat their first meal which must last them through all the daylight hours. The fast is broken each sunset with the firing of a cannon, a whistle, a siren, or by beating the mosque drum. The intensity and spiritual tension builds up as the month progresses. At the appearance of the new moon the month of fasting is over.

Ramayana — an Indian epic poem containing 18 books and 24,000 verses divided into 500 songs, all about an Aryan King of the Indian Vedic Age. The hero Rama (Vishnu reincarnated) defeats the wicked King Rawana of Ceylon who has stolen his woman and who is generally troubling the world. This story is known throughout S.E. Asia and all over Muslim Indonesia wherever Hindu culture had previously penetrated. The Ramayana provides the story line for almost all Indonesian theatricals as well as inspiring much of its art: fabric design, painting, sculpture, etc. Shops, companies, trains, toothbrushes are named after its characters and you can see reliefs depicting this story on ancient temples throughout Java and Bali. Written over 2000 years ago, this epic is as old as Homer's *Iliad* and it also incorporates the same legend: the abduction of a great beauty followed by a terrible war to rescue her. The oldest Javanese version in *kawi* was perhaps written around the 10th Century A.D. in Central Java; it's the oldest and longest poem in Old Javanese literature, much embellished by the poet Yogiswara's imagination. He used many different sources and many more stanzas than are found in the original by the sage poet Valmiki.

rambutan — a hairy red-skinned ping pong sized fruit with sweet white juicy meat; tastes like a big very sweet grape.

rante — a special field for funeral ceremonies in Torajaland, South Celebes.

rattan (Indo.: *rotan*) — a tough pliable vine from which handicrafts and furniture are made. (Stuffed cushions and upholstery are far too hot for Indonesia's climate.) Grows hundreds of feet in length.

rawon — rice with spiced sauce. Some versions are a spicy hot beef or buffalo meat soup with fried onions sprinkled on top and served with *lontong*.

rebab — a one-stringed violin of Arab-Persian origin.

reflesia — a giant flower of Sumatra which blooms only in October. Named after the first and only English Governor-General of Indonesia, Sir Stamford Raffles.

rendang — spiced beef in a thick rich sauce made from Minangkabau recipes of West Sumatra. Traveling food; can last without refrigeration for as long as a month. Could be very spicy hot.

Rendra — a Central Javanese poet and dramatist

born in 1935. Writes only in Indonesian.

rempeyek—round crisps with peanuts that have been fried in coconut oil.

Reyog—form of *wayang topeng,* a masked dance with a small number of performers including a ferocious tiger with a peacock standing on top of it, a red warrior figure, a giant. Often big heavy decorated headpieces are worn. This spiritually-involved 4 hour long trance-dance is not commonly seen, but is very popular. Ponorogo, Central Java, is one of the centers.

Riau Daratan—that portion of the Riau Province which is located on the east coast of the Sumatran mainland; eastern-central Sumatra.

ristaffel—means literally 'rice table' in Dutch. A sort of tropical smorgasbord, a banquet specialty. Though the food is Indonesian, the way of presenting it is Dutch. Plan to overeat. Boiled rice is the base with 20-40 individual spicy side dishes: meat, fish, eggs, and vegetables in various curries and sauces, dried pickled fruit and fresh fruit, tasty small dried fish, dried coconuts and nuts, and on and on.

ronde—a warm Javanese drink sold in *warungs* and by street vendors, made from ginger syrup, peanuts, fruit slices (kolang kaling), one ladle of hot water, and yellow balls of glutinous rice at the bottom of the bowl or glass. Many variations on the theme. Costs Rp15-20, with egg, Rp100.

rumah adat—a traditional and authentic native-style house, usually old.

rumah makan—eating place, restaurant, cafe.

rumah sakit—hospital or clinic.

rupiah—the Indonesian monetary unit: US$1 = Rp410-415.

sago—a starchy, low protein food extracted from a type of palm, the staple diet of the rural populations of the eastern island groups of Indonesia. Sago is relatively tasteless, but plentiful and indestructable. Stems are cut off the palm and then slivers of it are beaten with water until a pulp is made. When washed, the fibres float away and a flour remains. A single palm trunk will yield hundreds of kilos of sago in return for a day's work. The pith resists mould and can be kept up to 12 months.

salak—a pear-shaped soury fruit with a snake-like skin; comes from a palm tree. To avoid tartness, peel the inner membrane before eating.

sambal—a hot spicy chili sauce whose basic ingredients are fresh chilies, garlic, sugar, salt, vinegar, and onions.

sambur (or *rusa*)—a deer with a set of 3-pointed antlers related to the European red deer and the American wapati.

sampan—a small sailboat used over short distances in western Indonesia.

samping—a knee-length blouse.

samsara—a Hindu concept meaning 'woes of life'.

Sangyang Dedari—a famous Balinese trance-dance performed by 2 young girls who dance in unison on top of mens' shoulders.

santri—a Muslim who embraces the ethics and values of orthodox Islam and commerce. Historically, these devout Muslims have been merchants and traders.

sarung—a *kain* with both ends sewn together; worn by men, women and children. Worn with a tight sheath-like effect, the slack of this long loose tubular-shaped step-in skirt is folded and tucked in. A *sarung* is ultra-chic when worn by a Javanese *priyayi* woman, ultra useful when worn by workers of the land. It is excellently suited for carrying, sheltering and binding. Indonesian men's *sarungs* often have simple designs, mostly combinations of stripes and checks. Indonesian women generally wear ones with more floral, intricate and colorful designs.

sate—a national Indonesian dish much like *kebab* found throughout the Arab world. Chicken, beef, mutton, seafood or entrails (the Chinese prepare it with pork) are threaded on thin bamboo skewers and grilled over a charcoal fire. After roasting, *sate* is often served with a sharp peanut sauce. *Sate* sellers carry their kitchen on their shoulders, balanced on a *pikulan*. For you he sets his kitchen down, fans the charcoal embers, prepares *sate* according to your taste, then jogs off looking for more customers. Some of the best *sate* in Indonesia is served by these street vendors.

sawah—wet fields artificially constructed (often terraced) and continuously cultivated with a specialized crop. The crop is most often rice.

sawo—a fruit shaped like a potato; has the texture and flavour of sweet bread.

Seketan Week—Mohammed's Birthday. Celebrated with special ceremonies and festivals in Yogya and Solo, Central Java. There are big fairs, continuous prayer, processions carrying beehive shaped 'mountains of rice', and a parade of royal guards and palace officials.

semadi—mystico-magical meditation. First discovered 4000 years ago in India by yogis who learned how to control breathing in order to increase awareness. Many other techniques have since been developed by other practictioners. In Java *semadi* is used to bring about total enlightenment and this state is still aspired to by Indonesian political leaders who seek to increase their insight, influence, and earthly powers, usually through their mystical gurus or *pamongs.* The rewards of *semadi* were recorded in the 11th Century classical poem, Arjuna Wiwaha. The main center in Indonesia is Solo, Central Java.

Serimpi—any of the dances of the Central Javanese palace courts which are characterized by fluttering scarves and straight-backed dancers. Dating from Hindu times, this is the basic classical dance of Javanese women. *Serimpi* is performed by groups of even numbers and lasts for about 45 minutes. Very similar to the temple dances of South India, the *Serimpi* dancer appears straight even when leaning, the spine never bends or arches; she performs with smooth stateliness, intricate hand movements, bird-like gestures of head and neck. Only girls of noble birth could take part until 1918 when the Krida Beksa Wirama School was founded in Yogya, partly with the idea of spreading the knowledge beyond the *kraton* in order to preserve the Javanese spiritual heritage against the pressures of western modernism and materialism.

serow (or *kambing utan*)—the goat antelope of Sumatra, the Indonesian equivalent of the goral of S.E. Asia, the chamo of Europe, and the Rocky Mountain Big Horn of North America. Adapted to life in high mountain areas, this wild goat is short-horned and long-legged with pointed hoofs.

shaman—wizard, priest, exorcist, medicine man or woman.

Shiva—in the Hindu galaxy of gods this is one of the mightiest, the Destroyer of the World. Shiva is still the most venerated of the gods of India, the one you really have to worry about because of his destructiveness. The Shiva cult has a strong sexual tone since the world of gods and of men was brought about by Shiva's sexual union with Durga, his mystical consort. His emblem is the phallus (lingga). In Indonesia he also has the form of the supreme teacher, Maha Guru, or the supreme god, Maha Dewa.

siamang—a black monkey found on Sumatra and across the straits of Melaka in West Malaysia. It's difficult to tell the *siamang* apart from the *owa*, but the *siamang's* throat puffs up when it cries out.

Simalungun—one of the 5 main Batak clans of eastern North Sumatra.

Singosari—an ancient ruthless Javanese dynasty whose official faith was the Buddhist-Shivaite syncretism. Though it ruled for only 71 years (1222-1293 A.D.), Singosari initiated a new sculptural style in its temple reliefs, the so-called *wayang kulit* style.

sirih—betelnut. These scarlet seeds are chewed mostly by older people all over Indonesia; the teeth become rust-colored after years of chewing. Betelnut is a naturally occuring alkaloid, very similar to psylocybin, which mimes the action of acetocholin which is a neuro-transmitter, and when activated causes a mild euphoric stimulating state: in other words, it gives you a buzz when you chew it. Betelnut could also serve important ritual functions in restoring harmony and peace between individuals or a community. Considered the equivalent of European snuff. *Sirih* has been chewed in Indonesia for over 2500 years.

slendang (on Bali, called *kamben cerik*)—a long narrow shawl or shoulder cloth; also may be worn around the breast. The *slendang* is worn folded or wound, without requiring any tailoring or fasteners. It could be used as a sling for carrying babies and burdens on the back, serve as a cushion for a heavy basket on the head, but is generally thrown over one shoulder, or wrapped around the head.

songket—a gold-threaded fabric woven by the floating-weft technique.

sopi—an alcoholic drink; Indonesian gin. *Sopi manis* is liqueur.

soto—a spicy soup found all over Indonesia. Served with rice or *lontong*, soybean sprouts, chicken, mutton or beef, and garnished with fried or green onions.

soto madura—a rich coconut milk soup full of noodles, bean sprouts and other vegetables, and chicken.

spetboat—a long motorboat with an outboard motor used in western Indonesia.

Sriwijaya—an empire which flourished in southern Sumatra near present-day Palembang during the 12th Century.

stanplatz—a bus, *oplet, bemo*, Colt or taxi station; an assembly point for all of these conveyances. Taken from the Dutch, the word is still widely used on Java.

stempel—a long narrow river craft of Kalimantan which travels at a good speed and rides so close to the water that you often get wet.

stupa—a bell-shaped burial place for the remains or relics of Buddah or one of his disciples, or of Buddhists. Originally, *stupas* were burial mounds of prehistoric origin, but when they were built over Buddhists they became this symbol. These memorial shrines are the surviving reminders in India and in Indonesia of early Buddhism. A *stupa* is recognized by its characteristic *harmika* (stonebox) and *catra* (umbrella) structures, usually hemispheric in shape. The mounds or domes themselves are usually bare, but railings, gateways and galleries surrounding them are ornate and sometimes covered in carved panels.

subak—the village water board in South Balinese villages which controls the flow of water, canal building, drainage, maintainance; this association also settles disputes and polices the dams.

Subud—a religious, commercial, non-denominational association (but embraces much Islamic philosophy) on Java. Subud has other centers all over the world.

Sulawesi—Celebes.

suling—flute.

Sunan—the title of a *wali* and the name of his burial place. See *'walis'*.

Sundanese—the main ethnic group of West Java. Fifteen per cent of all Indonesians, the Sundanese are the next largest single group of Indonesians after the Javanese. They generally practice a more orthodox form of Islam than the Javanese of Central and East Java.

surat jalan—a letter that you could be required to carry to present on demand to army, police, immigration or customs officials in the outer islands of Indonesia (Maluku, and in some areas of Irian Jaya, Nusa Tenggara and Kalimantan). Obtain it from the local police station.

syahbandar—the harbormaster. The word dates from the 14th Century Hindu kingdom of Majapahit when it employed Muslims as *shahbandars*, or chiefs, of some of their ports. *Syahbandars* are found in every port in Indonesia where there are ships, from Wangi Wangi to Telukdalam. See him about boats to anywhere, when they are expected to arrive and how much you may expect to pay for your passage.

tanuk—tapir. A prehistoric pig-like animal that still exists in the forests of Sumatra and Kalimantan. Predominantly black with white hindquarters, it reaches a length of 2.15 to 2.40 m, yet only stands about 0.914 m high; it weighs up to 450 kg. The young have white or yellow spots and stripes on a brownish hide. Its nose and lips are longer than a pig's and movable, resembling a short trunk, thus it's sometimes called *babi gajah* or the elephant-pig. Along seashores it's called *kuda air* (water horse) because an excited male will gallop about like a stallion, tossing its head and whinnying. Its flesh tastes like beef. Giant herds of nomadic tapirs used to roam across Asia, Europe and the Americas, but are now confined to S.E. Asia, Central and South America.

tau-tau—lifesized statues that represent deceased persons and are placed on balconies outside cliffside graves in Torajaland, South Celebes; a custom of the Toraja people.

tegalan—a permanent, dry (not irrigated) garden or field. Planted with rice during the wet season and maize, cassava, sweet potatoes, groundnuts, chili peppers, and vegetables during the dry season. This system is used in areas that can't be irrigated, depending on rain for its water.

tempe—a protein-rich cake made from fermented soybeans.

tenunan—machine woven *kain ikat*.

Tongkonan—a special ceremonial house used for religious activities, burials, marriages, and also for sleeping. Built by upper class Torajas of Torajaland, .South Celebes.

transmigrasi—government resettlement programs aimed at depopulating Java and Bali by relocating Javanese and Balinese individuals or communities in the outer islands to build farming colonies.

trapel cek—travelers cheque.

tritik—a textile-decorating process in which designs are stitched on the fabric then the thread is pulled tightly so that only the exposed areas are dyed, leaving the areas underneath the threads and tucks colorless until restitched in a different pattern or re-dyed. While the *ikat* technique is applied to the thread before weaving, the *tritik* method is used for dyeing an already woven or finished piece of fabric. The finest *tritik* is produced in Solo, Central Java.

tuak—rice, palm (arin), or sago beer. *Tuak* is most often made from a kind of glutinous rice. The grain is first cooked, cooled and then mixed with a number of powdered roots and yeasts and finally put into a large earthenware jar to brew. No water is added at first as the fermentation begins. But before the brew is actually served both water and sugar are added to dilute the mash.

tugbot—a long, flat-bottomed, motorized, slow river craft with a shelter; used in Kalimantan.

ulos—an oblong fabric made by the *ikat* process worn in the Bataklands of North Sumatra by both men and women. Dull deep colors are characteristic.

Vishnu—in the Hindu panthenon of gods, Vishnu functions as the Guardian of the World. Vishnuism attaches great value on the service and love of god, thereby achieving identity of existence with him. On Java, kings and other historical personages (such as Sukarno) were frequently regarded as incarnations of Vishnu. This Hindu god was personified symbolically (avatar) in many creatures such as fish, tortoises, and in the Hindu epics in Krishna and Rama.

wadian—female shaman in the Dayak regions of Kalimantan.

walis—the nine legendary holy men who introduced Islam into Java; worshipped as saints. Their graves, indicated by the title *Sunan,* are looked upon as sacred places and are in main located on mountaintops.

waringan—a *banyan* (fig) tree.

waruga—pre-Christian Minahasan (North Celebes) burial sacrophagi shaped like prisms.

warung—a poor man's restaurant; a food stall.

Many also sell drinks, cigarettes, food, coffee and *sirih.*

wayang—a dramatic puppet theatre: In the strict sense it means flat leather-carved rod puppets of the shadow play, but in its broad sense it could mean any dramatic performance. When used as a noun, the type and *lakon* of the *wayang* performance is indicated by a qualifying worde which follows: *wayang orang, wayang golek, wayang kulit, wayang purwa,* and so on. The word *wayang* could also refer to the *wayang* theatre set up in a village or town. *Wayang* stories are usually filled with kings, queens, gods, heroes, and comical ugly servants who are semi-divine. The plot consists of love, war, treachery, deceit, with truth and loyalty always winning over evil in the end. Indonesian *wayang* is distinct because its technical equipment is inspired by the native environment.

wayang beber—a long linen or paper roll painted with various *wayang* scenes which is unrolled from one rod to another while the *dalang* comments on each of the scenes. The width of each roll is about 508 mm with the length varying from 2½-2¾ m. Usually 7 or 8 rolls are required for a story whose themes are usually from *wayang purwa, gedok* or *klitik* stories. The paintings on the scrolls are the last stragglers of Hindu-Javanese painting, now practically a lost art except in Solo where *beber* scrolls are still made. The box containing the rolls and equipment is the object of reverence, with healing and purifying powers attributed to it. This form of *wayang* is now nearly extinct and very rarely performed.

wayang golek—3-dimensional costumed wooden puppets. Rods, not strings, are used to manipulate them. The head of the puppet, supported by a wooden spindle which runs through the body, is rotatable. In this form, there might be as many as 100 characters. Unknown on Bali.

wayang kulit—2-dimensional (flat) leather shadow puppets found all over Bali and Java, and in Javanese settlements overseas. This traveling puppet theatre is the true shadow play. Puppets are cut out of polished and gilded buffalo leather (kulit) or goatskin. The only movable parts are its arms jointed at the elbow and shoulders; each hand is connected to a long rod moved by the *dalang* who also speaks the parts. An oil lamp or an electric bulb throws their grotesque shadows on a screen. The audience may sit before the screen and view the shadows, or sit behind and watch the actual pup-

pets. The plots are based on Indian mythology blended with Indonesian history, to bring about a content all their own. In pre-Hindu times, the puppets were portraits of deceased ancestors with whom the ancient Javanese would commune during the performance.

wayang orang—traditional live human theatre performed throughout Java and Bali. These dance dramas take place on a platform in a theatre with actors and actresses wearing elaborate costuming with or without masks (topeng). Dancers are made up to look like *wayang kulit* puppets, even simulating movements of the shadow figures and relying on the same stylized gestures to convey emotion, displaying extraordinary control and discipline. The dancers themselves recite the text, the *dalang* playing only a minor part. The repertory is most often based on the *Ramayana* and *Mahabharata* epic Hindu poems. This form has been steadily refined in Solo and Yogya over the past 200 years, and reached its perfection during the 1930's when opulent full-scale performances would sometimes last 72 hours. See *wayang orang* at the Prambanan Ramayana Festival which takes place near Yogya May to Oct..

wayang topeng—live dance plays whose actors and actresses wear wooden, brightly colored, expressive masks; up to 80 are in one complete set. The human performer bites into a leather strap to hold the mask in place. All dancers are usually men who speak or sing their own parts, the characters most often based on the stories of the *Panji* cycle. The *topeng* center is around Malang, East Java, but in other places on Java this form is a dying art. On Bali, however, *topeng* is still going strong.

wok—a round semi-spherical Chinese quick-frying or steaming pan.

YHA—Youth Hostel Association. In Indonesia Youth Hostels are usually a more expensive type of accommodation than cheap hotels or *losmens.*

yoni—a stylized vagina usually carved out of stone; the Hindu symbol of female life-giving force.

Zamrud—an Indonesian airlines which operates in Nusa Tenggara; their main office is on Jl. Gadjah Mada, Denpasar, Bali.

zirzak—custard apple. Rich, sweet-sour flavor, and creamy texture. It tastes so good, but don't overeat, it'll give you a bellyache.

INDEX

using the index: The letters a, b, c or d following a page number indicate the approximate position of the index entry on that page. Thus 120b refers to the lower half of the left-hand column of page 120. Page numbers in bold type followed by a bold typed *c, i* or *m* refer to a caption, illustration or map on that page which contains information about the index entry. Boldfaced *c* could also refer to lists, tables, charts, legends; *i* also refers to photographs.

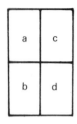

a	c
b	d

Abang, Mt., N. Bali, 220d, 449b

Abba, Cape, Irian Jaya, cave drawings of, *421ci*, 427a

Acehnese people, Aceh: religion of, 6b, 24c, 324bc; crafts, 30a, 325ab; legends, *117c;* society, 324cd; music, dance and games, 324d, 325a; business practices, 326a; mentioned, 306d, 313

Aceh Province, northern Sumatra: history of, 6b, 261b, 295b, 300b, 324ab; events, 27c, 324d, 325a; traveling in, 261cd; getting there, 262c, 294cd, 304d, 305a; *geudeu-geudeu* game, 325a

Adat (village law): definition of, 20ab; obligations, 20ab, 26a; functions, 20b

Adonara Island, Nusa Tenggara, 236ab; getting there, 239a

Affandi, painter, 119c, *188c*

Agats, Irian Jaya: from, 420d; getting there, 425ad, 434d; general, 428a, 429ad

Agriculture: systems used, 2, *252c;* products of, 17a; affects, 19d; and volcanoes, *222ci*

Agung, Mt., E. Bali: general, 183c, 204ab, 206c, 449b; view of, 207a, 220bd; mentioned, 201a, 204d

Airlangga, King of E. Java, *53c,* 67d, 151d, 447b

Airlines, networks of Indonesian air carriers, 42b

Airmadidi, N. Celebes, *116c,* 366c

Alas, Sumbawa: 251b; getting there, 258a; from, 258a

Alcoholic beverages of Indonesia. See Brews, native

Alfuro people, aboriginals of Moluccas: general, 19b, 405bc; religion of, 23cd; weaving, 405c; of Buru, 405d; of Tanimbar, 409d

Alor Island, Nusa Tenggara: getting there, 171c, 232c, 233a, 236c; *228m, 235m;* crafts of, 409c; mentioned, 232a, 407a

AMA (Associated Missions Aviation),

of Irian Jaya, 420d, 425a

Amahai, Ceram, C. Moluccas: 405ab; getting there, 404c, 405c

Ambarawa, C. Java: railway museum of, 102b; mentioned, 102d

Ambarita, N. Sumatra: 312a, 313c, 314a; general, 316b-d

Ambon, C. Moluccas: history of, 7d, 398c, 399ad, 400d; people, 7d, 232a, 398-99 *passim*; religions, 23b, 26c, 400c; crafts, 29d, 412bc; eat, 36d; getting there, 171bc, 343a, 383c, 399a, *407c,* 409b, 413d, 425c; general, 399a-404cd; climate, 399c, 405a; transportation on, 400cd, *401c,* 403b; forts of, 400d, 402a; *401m, 404m;* from, *401c,* 404a-c, 407c, *407c,* 417b, 424d; sights, 402ab

Ambon City, Ambon, 403a-404c

Amir Hamzah stories: dance themes from, 66b; in *wayang,* 71ab

Amlapura, E. Bali: stay, 193d, 206ac; from, 206b; vicinity of, 206bc; getting there, 218c, 224c, 225d; mentioned, 224d

Ampana, C. Celebes, getting there, 360c, 370cd *passim*

Ampenan, Lombok: getting there, 219a, 224d, 232c, 251b, 256b, 257c; from, 254b, 255c, 256a; transport in, 254b; general, 255a-56a; stay, 255ac; vicinity of, 255c-56a; *257m*

Amurang, N. Celebes, 368d

Ancient sculpture: of Sumatra, 55c, 264d, 266bc; of N. Celebes, *116c-17c,* 366ac; of Pasemah, 269d-70a; stelae of Nias, 298cd; of the Batak, 309d, *314i;* of C. Celebes, *374ci*

Ancient temples of Indonesia. See Temples of Indonesia

Angklung: definition of, 64d; performances, 87d

Animal life of Indonesia: waterbuffalo (kerbau), 3a, *172ci;* mousedeer (kancil), 73a, *189c;* tigers, 73a, 263ab, 268 *passim,* 282b, 287a, *294i;* gibbons,

73a, *356c;* rhinoceros, 73ab, *252c,* 273d, 326c; general, 92ac, 124a, 167b, 170c, *252-53c,* 289bc, 345c; Komodo lizard, 124a, 242a-d *passim, 243ci;* mandril monkey, 124a; orangutan, 124a, *299i,* 299b-300b, 305c, 323cd, *333ci, 345ci; babirusa,* 170c, *264ci,* 359b; elephants, 261a, 265bd; *anoa,* 170c, 289c, 359b, *364ci;* crocodiles, *189c,* 244c, 263a, 268c, 305a, *429ci; toke* lizard, *241c;* pangolin, *248ci;* dhole (ajak), *252c;* Black Crested Baboon, *260i,* 260d, 359b; *beruk* monkey, *288ci,* 298c, 359b, *364ci; serow,* 289c; butterflies and other insects, 305ac, 320b, 329d, 376a, 395d, 423d, 430b, 440c; frogs of Borneo, *329ci;* primates of Borneo, *355ci;* flying fox, *426ci.* *See also* Wildlife parks of Indonesia; Birdlife of Indonesia; Lizards of Indonesia

Antares, Mt., Irian Jaya: 430bc; 431ac *passim*

Antiques: general, 29bd; purchase of, 138a, 444. *See also* Chinese porcelain

Apo Kayan region, E. Kalimantan, 348b, 354b

Arabian people: on Java, *53c;* on Sumatra, 268a, 300c; in C. Moluccas, 405d, 406c

Arabian influences: in Moluccan history, *116-17c,* 398b; in Indonesian art, *189c;* in Timor's history, 232a; in Aceh, 325bc; in superstition, *350c*

Arabian language: influences on Indonesian literature, 7 *passim;* uses of in Aceh, 325bd; in N. Celebes, 368b

Ardjuna Wiwaha, legend of: as *wayang* theme, 68b; explanation of, 447b-d

Arfak, Irian Jaya: general, 425d, 426a; people of, 426b

Arjuna, Hindu hero: as character of *wayang,* 69c; in hermit cave carvings, 155a; adventures of in temple art, 165b; in classical dance, 172c, 173a; as hero in *Mahabharata,* 445cd

Arjuna, Mt., E. Java, 162c, 164a, 449

Arjuna Temple, Dieng Plateau, C. Java, **55c, 109c**

Army, Indonesian: political functions of, 13ac; position in Indonesia, 14ab; during war of independence, 14ab, **53c;** self-appointed task of, 14ab, **114c;** museum, 82d, 83ab

Art, ancient. *See* Temples of Indonesia; Ancient sculpture

Aru Islands, S.E. Moluccas: fauna of, 398b; getting there, 404c, **407c,** 409b; from, 408a; general, 408a-409a; **408m**

ASKI (music conservatory): of Solo, 139ab; of Bali, 218b; of W. Sumatra, 282d

Asmat, Irian Jaya: getting there, 425d; people of, 428 *passim,* 429d; dwelling, **429ci;** arts and crafts, 429bd

ASRI (school of fine art), 28a, 121ab

Atapupu, W. Timor: getting there, 232c; from, 233a; general, 233ab

Atoni people, W. Timor: general, 230ac; of Kupang, 232a

Australia: fauna of, 3b, **252-53c,** 417d; investment in Indonesia, 18ab; duty and shipping to, 28d; visas to Indonesia from, 49b, 50cd; history, 78a, **116c-17c;** getting there, 85bc, 219a; aborigines of, **117c,** 227c, 418c; influences on the Kais, 408c; from, 417b; mentioned, 80d

Babar, Babar Islands, getting there, **407c,** 409b

Babi guling: recipe for, **189c;** 201c, 217d

Bacan Island, N. Moluccas, 414d

Badas Harbor, Sumbawa: getting there, 219c; general, 251d

Badui people, W. Java: history of, 75 *passim;* getting there, 75cd

Bagansiapiapi, E. Sumatra, 273d-74b

Bahasa Indonesia: literature in, 9b, 21bc, 106c, 188c, 272b, 287d, 288a, 306b; as political vehicle, 10a, 21b; extent of us, 21; as spoken by Javanese, 21a; history of, 21bc, **116c;** philology, 21c; learning, 21d; courses in, 22ac; books, 22a; grammar, 22c, 23ac, 441; spelling of, 23c; spoken by Bataks, 306b; general, 441a-44d; mentioned, 60b

Bahau Dayak tribe, E. Kalimantan: **346c;** crafts of, 347b

Bahau River, E. Kalimantan, 352c, 353c, 354a

Bajang Ratu Temple, E. Java, 148a, 149c

Bajau people, S. Celebes, 382d

Balauring, Lembata, 234d, 235a

Bali: the land, 3c, 177, 178cd, 254b; religion of, 5 *passim,* 23b, 26c, 178bc, 182ab, 183, **213i,** 256d; festivals, 26b, 183 *passim,* **213ci;** crafts, 28a, 29d, 30a, 184b, 186b-87d, 200c, **208ci,** 217d-18a, 403d; foods, 36c, **188c,** 194a; health in, 44b; legends, **117c,** '

182c-83a, 205b; getting there, 124c, 125a, 162a, 171d, 172a, 178a, 233a, 343a; history of, 178 *passim,* 201d, 254c; temples, 183c, **184i, 208ci,** 217d, 218a; art, 182c-92d, **225ci;** sculpture, 184d-85a, 200b; painting, 185a-86c, 200b; dances, 190-92d, 198c; music, 190ab; dance study, 190d, 191a; accommodation in, 193d, 194a; climate of, 195cd; transport, 194cd-95, **210-11c; 197m;** museums, 200ab, **217c,** 217d-18a; architecture, **208ci, 210-11c,** 256c; from, 213b; mentioned, 165d, **189c,** 227b, **241c,** 259d, 376a, 384b. *See also* Pura

Bali Aga people, N. Bali: weaving of, 29c; 220d; 222c

Baliem River, Irian Jaya: mentioned, 440b

Baliem Valley, Irian Jaya: discovery, 435a; agricultural practices of, 435ab; climate, 435bc; accommodation, 435cd; getting around, 435d, 436a; **438m;** walks, 439d, 440a; getting there, 345bc; chiefs of, **440c;** mentioned, 419d, 420ab, 433d

Balikpapan, E. Kalimantan: getting there, 171bc, 172c, 338bc, 341a, 344a, 352d, 353a, 370c, 374c, 375c, 382a; transport in, 329d, 341ab; from, 330d, 341d, 343a, 352a; general, 341a-43a; mentioned, 327a, 337b

Balinese people: customs of, 181cd, 182c; of Lombok, 254bc; in Celebes, 367c; in the Kais, 408a; mentioned, 157c

Baluran Game Park, E. Java, 165cd

Banda Aceh, northern Sumatra: getting there, 304d, 325c; history of, 324b; general, 325b-26c; vicinity of, 326bc; mentioned, 326b

Banda Islands, C. Moluccas: history of, **117c,** 398c; volcanoes, 237c; land area, 397c; getting there, 404a, **407c;** general, 406c-d; sealife of, 406d

Bandanaira, Bandas, 406cd

Bandung, W. Java: arts and crafts of, **74c,** 87d, 88a; getting there, 84cd, 94c, 97d, 104d, 124d, 141b; general, 85c-90b; **86m, 89m;** mentioned, 77b, 142b, 194b

Bangka Island, Riau: people of, 20d, 273b; general, 264bc

Bangkalan, Madura: getting there, 157a; bullraces of, 173c

Bangko, S. Sumatra: getting there, 269ab; mentioned, 268b

Bangli, S. Bali: crafts of, 187a; general, 202d-203d; **203m;** getting there, 220b; mentioned, 223a

Banjarmasin, S. Kalimantan: getting there, 327b, 337b, 340c, 343b, 347c, 353a, 374c, 382a; general, 337b-39b; from, 338 *passim,* 339b, 339bc; vicinity, 339b, mentioned, 327a, 330d,

336a

Banjunglincir, S. Sumatra, getting there, 267a, 268cd

Banten, W. Java: history of, 7d, **53c,** 73d, 97d, 269b; religion of, 24c; general, 73d-75a; stay, 73d; influence on S. Sumatra, 269b

Bantimurung, S. Celebes: 376a; getting there, 381c

Banyuniba Temple, C. Java, 134d, **144c**

Banyuwangi, E. Java: getting there, 157a, 162a, 171d, 218c; general, 165d-67b; vicinity of, 167b; mentioned, 125a, 165c, 167ac

Barabai, S. Kalimantan: getting there, 336b, 339b, 343b; stay, 336b; mentioned, 330d, 337b

Barito River, S. Kalimantan: travel on, 339b, 347c; general, 340a; mentioned, 330b, 337b

Baron Beach, C. Java, 127c

Barong Dance, Bali: 66d; 134d; **191ci;** 191cd, 192a; origin of, 196d; performance, 203a, 209a, 218b; mentioned, 354b

Batak people, N. Sumatra: history of, 4d, 8a, 306c-307b, 310c, 314b, **369c;** crafts, 28a, 29d, **305i, 306i,** 309ad, **314i, 319i;** architecture, 82b, **308i,** 308ac, 313cd, 387d; legends, **117c;** music and dance, 276a, 307c, 308d-309a, 310d-11a; traditional culture, 307a; warfare, 307ab; events, 307d, 318cd; genealogy, 307d, 308a; kinship system, 307d, 308a; religion, 307 *passim;* markets, 310b; mentioned, 264ab, 268a, 300c. *See also* Karo Batak people; Simalungun Batak tribe

Batam Island, Riau: getting there, 272b, 275d; economy of, 272d

Batanghari River, Sumatra, 263a, 268a

Batik: history of, 7b, 29c, 60d; motifs of, 28c, **61ci,** 61d, 62a, 175a; batik tulis (hand-drawn), 28cd, **29ci,** 61ab, 60cd-62a; colors, 28cd, 62ac; batik painting, 28d; batik cap (stamped), 61bc; batik madura, 62a; batik solo, 62a, 97c, 137d, 138a; galleries, factories and shops of Yogya, 62a, **119c,** **114c,** 118 *passim,* 119ac; in wayang, 72a; batik cirebon, 97bc; batik indramayu, 97c; batik pekalongan, 97c, 99bc; batik tulungagung, 154c; of Bali, 186b, 187cd; of C. Celebes, 374a; mentioned, 60a, **188c,** 374a

Batu, E. Java: resort of, 162cd; vicinity of, 162d, 164a; mentioned, 148c

Batu, N. Celebes: waruga of, **116c;** music of, 360b

Batuan, C. Bali: crafts of, 187a; tour to, 213b

Batubulan, C. Bali: crafts of, 187a; temple of, 196b; tour to, 213b

Batukau, Mt., C. Bali, 202cd

Batur, Mt., N. Bali: views of, 202d; area

of, **221m;** general, 221 *passim;* stay, 221ac; climbing it, 221c, 223b; mentioned, 223c

Batur Lake, N. Bali: view of, 220b; area of, **221m;** general, 221c-22c

Batusangkar, W. Sumatra: 282d, 284a; bullfights of, 293c

Batutulis, W. Java, 75c, **92ci,** 93b, 328a

Bawamatalua, S. Nias, 297d, 298 *passim*

Bawean Bird Park, E. Java, 167b

Bayat, C. Java, 141d, 142a

Bedaya Dance: 65b, 66c; performance of, 139ac; of E. Kalimantan, 344d

Bedugal, N. Bali: tour to, 213b; 223cd

Bedulu, C. Bali, mentioned, 196d, 201d

Belahan, ancient bathing place, E. Java, **53c,** 147a, 151d, **152c**

Belawan, port of, N. Sumatra: getting there, 171c; from, 276a; exports from, 300c

Bengkulu, S. Sumatra: from, 263d, 269cd; general, 269b-d; getting there, 280b

Benoa Harbor, S. Bali: boat-buying in, 194d; getting there, 208c, 218c; from, 219c; mentioned, 207d

Benuaq Dayak group, E. Kalimantan: location and remarks, 346c; crafts of, 347ab

Berahu Temple, E. Java, 148a

Berau, E. Kalimantan: getting there, 344b, 352a

Besakih Temple complex, E. Bali: **177i;** general, 182c, 204ab; tour to, 213b; getting there, 220d, 449b; mentioned, 151d

Betelnut: uses of, **267ci;** mentioned, **225c**

Betelnut palm. *See* Arecoid (arenga) palm

Biak, Irian Jaya: people of, 19c; getting there, **401c,** 404a, 417b, 424d, 425bc; from, 407c, 417b, 425cd, 434d; general, 425b-d; mentioned, 420

Billiton, Riau: history of, 272c; people of, 273b

Bima: *Mahabharata* hero, 69b, 70c, 445b; temples dedicated to, 146 *passim;* in Balinese temple art, 202b

Bima, Sumbawa: getting there, 219a, 224d, 232c, 240a, 251d, 254d, 382a; people of, 249b; general, 249d-51b; vicinity of, 251a

Bima Temple, Dieng, C. Java, **55c,** 106c, **109c**

Bintauna, N. Celebes: from, 364a; getting there, 368b

Birdlife of Indonesia: general, 73a, 75a, 167b, **252c-53c, 258c;** herons, 73a, 75a, **252c;** hornbill, 73a, 268c, **353ci;** ibis, 75a, **253c;** *perkutut,* 124a, **252c-53c;** cormerares, 167b; pelicans, 167b; Bird of Paradise, **253c,** 398b, 408c, **418ci;** drongo, **258i;** *Kakatua Raja* (King Parrot), 412c, 427d. *See*

also Wildlife parks of Indonesia

Bird Markets of Indonesia, 80cd, **110c,** 124a

Bittuang, S. Celebes: getting there, 393ac, 394b, 395a; from, 394ab

Bitung, N. Celebes: getting there, 171c, 364a, 368b, 370b, 382a, 396c, 413bd, 424d; from, 360d, 364a, 366d, 399a

Black magic: on Java, 151b, 155a; in C. Moluccas, 402b

Blitar, E. Java: getting there, 84d, 162a; general, 155d-56c; temples, 156bc; vicinity of, 156c; mentioned, 155ab

Bogor, W. Java: getting there, 84d, 89d; general, 91a-94a, **253c;** stay, 91c; vicinity of, **92cm, 93cm,** 93bd; palace (Istana Bogor) of, 92c, 93a; botanical gardens of, 93ac; mentioned, 73b, 75c

Bohorok, N. Sumatra, 299b, 305c

Bondowoso, E. Java: area of, 167c, **168m;** mentioned, 54b, 165b, 167bc

Bone, S. Celebes: crafts of, 381b; from, 381d; getting there, 381d; *prahu*-building of, 382c

Bonnet, Rudolph: painting of, 185c; residence of, 200d

Bontong, E. Kalimantan: getting there, 343a; general, 344c; mentioned, 344b

Bori, Torajaland, S. Celebes: *rante* of, 385c; description, 391d; getting there, 392b

Borneo: plants of, 3d, **328ci,** 345c, **348-49ci;** population of, **59c,** 327a; legends of, **117c;** history of, 284d, 352a, 377c; mentioned, **252c,** 358c. *See also* Kalimantan

Borobudur, C. Java: vandalism of, 7b, 144d; restoration, 55ac, 130cd; getting there, 112a, 127d; history of, 125c, 127d, 128ab; general, 127d-31a, **129ci;** location of, 128bc, **129c;** shape, 128cd, **129c;** basreliefs, 130ab, 334a; Buddah-niches, 130bc; complex, 131a; compared, 133c; mentioned, 125c, 134a, **283c**

Botanical Gardens of Bogor, W. Java. *See* Bogor, botanical gardens of

Boyolali, C. Java: 125cd, 141d, 450a

Brahma: temple dedicated to, 133b; in Balinese religion, 181c, 182a; Hindu God, 446b; mentioned, 69a

Brahmanism: history of, 5c; art of, 54c, 328ac

Brantas River, E. Java, 156b, 160a, 164a

Brastagi, N. Sumatra: getting there, 304d, 310a, 311d, 317ac; general, 318d-20c; crafts of, 319b; stay, 319bd; from, 320b, 323c; vicinity of, 320bc

Bratan Lake, N. Bali: tour to, 213b; mentioned, 223cd

Brews, native: *arak,* 194b; *brem,* 194b; *tuak,* 194b, 209c, 233d-34a, 388c; *sopi,* 229c, 403 *passim*

Bromo, Mt., E. Java: *Kasada* Festival,

26d, 158ab, **350c;** compared, 142c; getting there, 157a, 158c, 162a, 171d; general, 157d-59c; **159m;** climbing it, 159c, 164b; mentioned, 90b

Bronze Age: of Irian Jaya, **117c;** of Bali, 201d; of Alor, 236cd; mentioned, **351c**

Buddah: ancient sculptures of, 122c, 123c, **124c,** 130bc, **131i,** 359bc; mentioned, 131c, 209b. *See also* Buddhism

Buddhism: history of, 5, 134c; modifications, 26bc; conduct towards, 32b; on Java, 52bc, **350c;** Theravedic, 102b; in art, **114c,** 127d, 128ab, 133cd, 147d, 165b, 170b, **189c,** 305a; Mahayana, **116-17c, 131c;** in Solo, 140a; meditation techniques, 140d; on Bali, 206c, 226cd; in Sumatra, 261a, 264c; in N. Celebes, 360d; mentioned, **129c, 282c.** *See also* Mahayana Buddhism

Bugis people, S. Celebes: in Timor, 233a; in Kalimantan, 344c; crafts of, 345bc, 381bc; boatwrights, 374c, 375a, 383a; general, 377a-78c; history of, 377bc; dance, 377c; literature of, 377c; dress, 381b; in Irian Jaya, 425d

Bukit Barisan, Sumatra, 260a, 269cd, 280a

Bukit Lawang, N. Sumatra: getting there, 299b, 320c; general, 299b-300b

Bukit Peninsula, S. Bali: view of, 203d; general, 208ac

Bukittinggi, W. Sumatra: crafts of, 30a, 289cd; getting there, 259d, 263cd, 264a, 273c, 280bd, 304d, 310a; from, 264a, 279b, 289d, 291a, 310c; transport, 272b; museum of, 285b; general, 288c-92a; stay, 288cd, 289a; sights, 289bc, 291c; vicinity of, 291bc; **291c, 290m;** bullfights, 293c; mentioned, 267c, 282c, 285d

Bullfights: of E. Java, 167b; of Madura, 173c; of W. Sumatra, **292c**

Bullraces: of Madura, 175 *passim;* of Negara, W. Bali, 193c.

Bunta, C. Celebes, getting there, 370cd

Buntao, S. Celebes: market of, 388c; general, 390a; getting there, 392b

Buntukalando, S. Celebes, 394b

Bureacracy, Indonesian-style: 14d, 15a; salaries of, 18d; dealing with, 31ab

Buru Island, C. Moluccas: land area of, 397c; political prisoners of, 400b, 405d-406b, 430b; general, 405d-406b; getting there, 405d

Cakranegara, Lombok: getting there, 254ad, 255c; general, 256a-c; stay and eat, 256b, 257c; vicinity of, 256b; from, 256bc, 257c

Campuan, C. Bali, 200c-201a

Car rental in Indonesia. *See* Transport in Indonesia, car rental

Casuarina Coast, Irian Jaya, 427d-29c

Catholicism in Indonesia: general, 23b, 26c; on Lembata, 235a, 236c; on Flores, 237bc; in the Kais, *407c;* in Irian Jaya, 420 *passim,* 421a, 435cd

Cave drawings. See Rock paintings

Celebes (Sulawesi): natural resources of, 17a, 18a; weaving, 29a; accommodation, 35c; history, 54b, 359 *passim;* getting there, 171bc, 343a, 359d; flora, 359b; the land, 359b, 395ac; transport, 359d; *363m;* fauna of, *364ci;* mentioned, 420b

Celuk, S. Bali: crafts of, 185a, 187ab; tour to, 213b; mentioned, 218d, 219a

Central Celebes: transport, 360c; crafts of, *371i; 371m, 372-73m;* isolated societies of, 373c, 374a

Central Java: religion of, 25c; archaeology, 54b-55c *passim, 144-45cm, 144c,* 147bc; ceremonies, 63a; dances, 65b-67a *passim; wayang* forms, 67a-72b *passim; 103m;* antiquities of, *144-45cm*

Central Moluccas: getting there, 399a; the land, 399c; *404m*

Cepogo, C. Java: getting there, 450a; from, 450a; mentioned, 141d

Ceram, C. Moluccas: history of, *117c,* 400b; people, 235a, 399d; land, 397c, 398a, 405a; getting there, 402a, 404ab, 405ab; general, 405a-d; sights of, 405b; transport, 405b; walks, 405cd; mentioned, 402d

Ceta Temple, C. Java, 144d, 146d

Chinese communists, influence in Indonesia, 11cd

Chinese communities: general, 20cd; religions of, 23b, 360d; in Riau, 273a; in Sumatra, 274b, 300c; in W. Kalimantan, 356ab; on Buru, 405d; of Irian Jaya, 425d, 428d

Chinese influence: in Cirebon art, 97bc; in Timor's history, 230a; in Sumatra's history, 261a; in Kalimantan art, 334b; in Moluccan history, 398c; mentioned, 189c

Chinese porcelain: general, 29b; of Jakarta, 82cd; Solo, 138a; Madura, 176a; Sumba, 246bc; Banjarmasin, 338a; S. Celebes, 381c; Ambon, 403d; mentioned, *53c, 252c. See also* Pottery

Christianity: political power of, 23b, 25c; influences on Islam, 24a; modifications of, 26 *passim, 53c;* in Moluccas, *117c;* on Enggano, 271d; on Nias, 296a; among the Batak, 309b, 318b; in Kalimantan, 331c

Ciamis, W. Java: regency of, *76m;* mentioned, 98c

Cianjur Regency, W. Java, *94m*

Ciawi, W. Java, 94a

Cibodas, Mt., historical remains on, *93c*

Cibodas, W. Java, *94c*

Cilicap, W. Java, 77ac, 430b

Cipanas, palace of (Istana Cipanas), W. Java, 94a

Cirebon, W. Java: history of, 6c, 8d, 95d, 97d; *batik* of, 62a, 97bc; getting there, 84d, 89d; general, 95b-97d; transport in, 95d; stay, 96ac, 97a; *96m; kratons* of, 96c, 97ab; arts and crafts of, 97bc; from, 97d; regency of, *98m*

Civil War (1958), 11b, 15c

Cockfighting: of W. Java, 89b; Balinese-style, 183d, 193bc, *193i;* of Kalimantan, 334a

Coen, Jan Pieterszoon, Dutch Governor-General: in Moluccas, 398c, 406c; in Jakarta, *53c*

Communist Party of Indonesia. See PKI

Cook, James: in Pulau Seribu, W. Java, 82a; Irian Jaya, 428c

Corruption: extent of, *12c, 18i;* causes, 18cd; practices, 18cd, 48c, 49a, 167d, 242d

Crafts: buying and trading, 28b, 444; weaving, 28d, 29ac, 205d, 391d; carving, 29d, 30a, 184d-85a, 334d, 345a, 403d; plaiting, *30i,* 30bc, 439d; silverworking, 30a, 125ab, 187 *passim,* 234a, 287d, 291d, 281b, 382d; history of, 52d, 54a; import of, *189c;* jewelry of Kalimantan, 338a; *tapa* bark clothing, 387b. *See also* Pottery; Chinese porcelain

Culik, E. Bali: getting there, 206b; panorama, 224d

Culture Period, Dutch, 8cd, 54a, *91c*

Cycling in Indonesia. See Transport in Indonesia, cycling

Daik, Lingga, Riau: getting there, 275d, 278a; palace ruins of, 276c

Dalang: general, 67d, 68d, 69a, *120c,* 198bc; performance of, *120i,* 151a, *255ci;* training of, 121b, *122c;* mentioned, 70d, 71 *passim,* 138b

Dance: hire, 66a, 298bc; classical Javanese, 65-67a, *122c, 144c,* 173a, 188c, 190b; general, *188c;* Balinese, 190b-92d. See also *Bedaya, Kuda Kepang, Legong, Reyog, Sangyang Dedari, Serimpi*

Dani people, Irian Jaya: ghosts and spirits of, 351c; general, 419d, 435ab, 436a-39a; customs of, 436ac, 437d, 439a; language, *436c,* 436c; warfare, 437ab; dwellings, 437c; myths, *438c;* crafts, 439cd; mentioned, 433d, 435b. *See also* Irian Jaya Highlands

Dayak arts and crafts: weaving of, 29ac, 334c; antiques, 29b; plaiting, 30bc, 334bc; metalurgy, *188c,* 334d, 335a; general, 334b-35c, 345 *passim;* 347a; beadwork, 334cd; sculpture, 334d; skin-tatooing, 334ac, *337ci;* bamboo, 335c; mentioned, *252c,* 387b

Dayak people, Kalimantan: general,

327a, 331a-35c, *346c, 349c;* travel among, 330b, 336ac, *350c;* history of, 331b; society, 331bc; religion, 331cd-32a; 'headhunting, 332ac; longhouses, 332b-333b, 336ac, 347c; Ship of the Dead cult, *332ci,* 332c; medicine-women of, 333bd; music and dance, 333d, 334a, 339d; of E. Kalimantan, *346c,* 352b, 354cd; of W. Kalimantan, 356d, 358d

Demak, C. Java: history of, 6c; events of, 27b; general, 102c; mosque of, 102c; mentioned, 142a

Dempo, Mt., S. Sumatra, 267c, 269d, 270a

Denpasar, Bali: getting there, 104d, 157a, 172c, 206b, 224c, 233a, 251b; stay, 193d, 215d, 217 *passim;* transport, 195c, 218bc; general, 215d-19d; *216m;* sights of, 217d, 218a; crafts, 218ab; from, 219 *passim,* 254ab; mentioned, 80d, 167a, 177d, 178a, 181b, 221a, 227d

Dewi Sri. See Rice Goddess

Dieng Plateau, C. Java: *55ci;* general, 106a-109c, *116c;* temples, 106bc; *144d;* stay and eat, 106cd; other ruins, 106d; vicinity of, 109ac; *109m;* mentioned, 54b

Digul River, Irian Jaya: fauna of, 418a; description, 430b, 431a

Diponegoro, Prince, sultan of Yogya: revolt of, 9ab, 135ab, 138d; monument, 123a; hideaway, 127b, 151a; grave, 379c, *380m, 381c*

Dobo, Arus: getting there, 404ac; description, 409c

Donggala, C. Celebes: getting there, 171c, 344a, 353a, 370c, 374c, 382c, 396c, 413d, 435c; general, 375 *passim;* sights of, 375ab; stay, 375c; from, 375cd, 396c

Dongson Culture, influence of: in W. Torajaland, 394d; in the Tanimbars, 409c; mentioned, 334b

Dumai, E. Sumatra (Riau): getting there, 260a, 278a; transport, 272b

Durga: sculpture of, 153a, 139d; on temple art, 154b; statue of, *182i;* in Balinese dance, 192a

Dutch colonisers: general, 6-11, 14a, 15a, 21b, 52c, *53c,* 54a, 59d, 71d, 72a, 78ab, 135ab, 154a, *383ci;* in conflict with Portugese, 7 *passim;* during war of independence, 8a, 97d, 110ad, 202bd, 299a, 369c; agricultural policies, 8cd, *53c,* 93c; during WW II, 9d; on Java, *53c,* 85d, 90b, *91c,* 92c, 93ac, *110c, 114c, 252-53c;* on Sumatra, *116c,* 269bc, 272d, 300b, 306c, 307a, 313ab, 324ab; in Irian Jaya, *117c,* 408c, 419ab, 420c, 430a; on Bali, 178c, 220a, 223b; coins of, *188c;* Nusa Tenggara, 230ad, 234d, 237bc, 249c; in Celebes, 360ab, *369c,* 377bc, 379c, 384d, 385a; in Moluccas, 397a,

399b, 400ab, 408a, 410b; mentioned, *116c, 189c*

East Java: the land, 51d, 252c; archaeology of, *53c,* 147, 148c, *149m,* 151d, *152c, 153m,* 155a-c, 202b, 310c; theatre forms, 63d, 71b; dances, 66d, 67a, 151c; *150m;* whip-fighting, 153c, 154a; heroes of, 447 *passim,* 448a; literature, 447-48a

East Kalimantan: getting there, 39b, 358a, 370c, 382c, 396c; economy, 328c; history of, 328c; *342m;* Dayak tribes, 346c, 352b, 354cd; Dayak crafts, 347ab; river towns, 347b-48b

Eastern Sumatra (Riau Daratan): ethnic makeup of, 20d; transport in, 272bc; general, 272c-74b; history of, 272c

East Timor: history of, 7d; war in, 13c; general, 227a-c; getting there, 233b; mentioned, 233a

Economy of Indonesia: Freeport Copper Co., 15d, 400a, *422c;* natural resources, 15d-17a, *16-17m,* 272d, 273a, 300c, *376c;* foreign investment, 17ac, 18ab, 77c, 372a-73c, 376c, 419d; history of, 17c, 18a

Education systems in Indonesia: 18d; under the Dutch, 9a

Ekagi people, Irian Jaya, 433d, 434d

Elat, Kais, getting there, 404a, *407c*

Enarotali, Irian Jaya: getting there, 434d; mentioned, 433d

Ende, W. Flores: getting there, 171c, 219c, 224d, 232c, 240a; fighting systems of, 206bc; from, 234b, 240a, 246c; stay, 240a; vicinity of, 240a

Enggano, off S. Sumatra: dwelling of, *270i;* general, 270c-71d

English: the general, 7d-8a; influences, 8a; during war of independence, 10c; on Java, *52c,* 93a, 110ab, 111c, 113b, 128b, 167d, 168a; on Sumatra, 268bd, 272d; in Moluccas, 398c; mentioned, *116c*

Exchange rates for Indonesian currency, 39ac, 48a, 312c

Fak Fak, Irian Jaya: getting there, 404a, 425d, 426d; from, 420d

Fauna of Indonesia. *See* Animal life of Indonesia

Five Principles, the. *See* Panca Sila

Flights, travel by in Indonesia. *See* Transport in Indonesia, flights

Flora of Indonesia. *See* Plantlife of Indonesia

Flores, Nusa Tenggara: religions of, 23b, 26b, 237bc; from, 44c; people of, 227c, 235a, 237bc; customs, 227d; general, 237a-41d; history of, 237a; the land, 237a; music and dance, 237d; *238-39m;* crafts, 238a, 240c; transport, 238ac, 239a-41d; accommodation, 238c; mentioned, 227a

Folk Doctors (dukuns): general, 26c,

46d, 47a, 60c; function in dance, 67a; of E. Java, 151b; of Bali (balian), 193a; of the Karos, 318cd; midwives, *186i, 350c*

Foreign investments in Indonesia. *See* Economy

Free Papua Movement (OFM), Irian Jaya, 419bc

Fretilin, independence movement of E. Timor, 228ac

Gadjah Mada University, Yogya, C. Java, *114c,* 123bc

Galumpang, C. Celebes, 394ac

Gamelan: history of, 6c, 7b, 142a, *351c;* Javanese, 60a, 64 *passim,* 139b, 190a, *220c,* 447d; general, *65ci,* 70c; used by *dalangs,* 68d, *120c, 225ci);* in *wayang orang,* 71d; performances, 83d, 112c, 113d, *114c,* 115a, *122c,* 139ab, 151a; royal, 118a; buying instruments of, 138bc; instrument-making, 139b, 151b; Balinese, 181a, 183b, 190a, 191c, 200bc, 367c; in Kalimantan, 333d; Moluccan-style (totebuang), 398d; mentioned, 60c, 175bc

Ganesha, sculpture of, 135a, *189c*

Garuda: airlines of, 42d; designs, 63c; statues of, 151d; depicted in temple art, 165b; Hindu god, 447ac

Garut, W. Java: general, *53c,* 90cd; getting there, 89d; *91cm;* mentioned, 75d, 90b

Gayo Highlands, Aceh: people of, 326c; general, 326cd

Gede, Mt., W. Java, 94c, 95a

Gedong Sono temple complex, C. Java, 102d, 104a

Gelgel, E. Bali, 204c

Gerta Gosa courthouse, E. Bali: general, 204c; tour to, 213b; mentioned, 183c

Gianyar, S. Bali: crafts of, 187a; general, 196b; vicinity of, 196bd; tour to, 213b; getting there, 218c, 220b

Gilamanuk, W. Bali: from, 178a; getting there, 178a, 218d, 224c; mentioned, 167a

Gitgit, N. Bali: tour to, 213b; description, 223d; getting there, 224c

Gorontalo, N. Celebes: from, 360c, 370 *passim;* getting there, 367a, 374a, 382a, 396c; general, 368-70d; stay and eat, 370a; vicinity of, 370ab

Gotong royong: concept and political uses of, 11b; general, 14cd, 300a

Government in Indonesia: provinces of, *12-13m;* history, 12a, *53c;* foundation, 12c; unification, 12c, 13a, *380c;* Indonesian-style democracy, *13c,* 14c; Peoples' Representative Council, 25a. *See also* Corruption, *Panca Sila* 379c

Greece: influence in Indonesian art, *189c;* writers of, about Indonesia,

116c, 328a

Gresik, E. Java: getting there, 172a; general, 173ab; mentioned, 138d

Gua Gadjah, cave monastery, C. Bali: crafts of, 187b; general, 198a, 202b; *202i*

Gua Kembang, E. Kalimantan: Hindu sculpture of, 245a; general, 348b

Gunung Gangsir Temple, E. Java, 156b, 164b

Gunung Kawi, E. Java, 162b

Gunung Kawi temple complex, C. Bali: *196i;* general, 198a; getting there, 200d

Gunungsitoli, N. Nias: getting there, 294c, 295a, 298a, 326a; stay, 298c; from, 298cd

Gunung Wukir, C. Java, 131d, 133a

Halmahera, N. Moluccas, flora and fauna of, 227b, 412c; land area, 397c; getting there, 404a, 413b; general, 415a-c; crafts of, 415c; mentioned, 414d

Haranggaol, N. Sumatra: getting there, 310a; market of, 310b; general, 316d

Hari Raya: special foods of, 38c; general, 27a-b; mentioned, 76c

Hatta, Mohammad: political life, 10a, 25c; in Irian Jaya, 430a

Hamengku Buwana, sultan of Yogya, *114c,* 115 *passim, 142c*

Hermits' caves, E. Java: general, *53c,* 154d-55a, 152c; mentioned, 202b

Hilismaetano, S. Nias, 297d, 298c

Hinduism: archaeology, 1d, *53c,* 82cd, 90d, 106cd, 146a, 164cd, 173a, 310bc, 348b, 354bd; history in Indonesia, 5-7 *passim,* 23b, 134c, 182a, 185b; modifications of, 26bc, *351c;* influence on Indonesian arts and crafts, 28d, 67d, 68 *passim,* 69a, 147cd, 182a, 185ab; Bali-Hindu religion, 178b; definition of, 182ab; history on Bali, 204a, *351c;* history in Nusa Tenggara, 229c, 237a; history on Sumatra, 264c, 271b, *283c,* 287ab, 306d; in the Kais, *407c*

Hitu, Ambon: history of, *116-17c, 401c;* peninsula of, 399c

Hutagodang, N. Sumatra, getting there, 310ab

Iban Dayaks, W. Kalimantan, 334b, 356c, 358c

Ijen Crater, E. Java, *166m,* 167 *passim, 252c*

Ikat: of the Bali Aga, 29c; Gresik, 173b; Lembata, 234b; of the Dayaks, 356c; Torajaland, 387c; mentioned, 227d. *See also Ikat* Sumba

Ikat Sumba: weaving of, *245ci,* 245b-45c; colors, 246a; motifs, 246c; purchase and selling, 246b; compared, 334c; mentioned, 409d. *See also Ikat*

Ilaga Region, Irian Jaya: vicinity of, 433d, 434b; getting there, 434d

Immigration department: 31ab, 50 *passim;* on Java, 78c, 84a, 168c; on Bali, 194bc; in Nusa Tenggara, 227d, 254d; in Sumatra, *280c,* 301c; in Celebes, 359d; in Irian Jaya, 424a

Immunizations, for Indonesia, 44b

Imogiri, C. Java: events of, 27a; getting there, 124b; general, 125bc

Independence Day (Proklamasi Kemerdekaan), 27c, *98c*

Indian (Hindu) influences: 5-7 *passim;* in epics used in *wayang,* 68b, 70c, 71b, 139d, 144c; on Java, 92c, 93c, *116c, 129c;* in Indonesian art, 106c, *114c,* 189c; dance, 188c; ancient sculpture of E. Kalimantan, 328a; superstition, *350c;* sculpture of ancient Celebes, 359bc; in Moluccas, 398b. *See also* Ramayana; *Mahabharata;* Temples of Indonesia

Indramayu: *batik* of, 97c; getting there, 97d

Indrokilo Temple, E. Java, 156b, 164d

Inobonto, N. Celebes: getting there, 367a; stay, 368b; from, 368bd

Irian Jaya: the land, 1b, *351c,* 417b, 421ac, 430bc, *431ci;* fauna of, 3d, 417-18a, 428ac, 430c; liberation, 11bc, 81a, 98ac; natural resources, 15d, 17a, 18a; travel in, 42d, 420d, 421ac, 428c, 431c, 432b-33d; history of, *117c,* 147b, 416c-19-19b, 425c; getting there, 343a, 364a, 382a, 417b, 426d; legends, *351c,* 427a, 448c; people of, 409b, 419d, 420ab, 425bd, 428a; climate, 418c; economy, 419d, 420a, 433b; missionaries, 420 *passim;* maps, *422-23m,* 424d. *See also* Dani people; Irian Jaya Highlands

Irian Jaya Highlands: people of, *253c, 351c,* 432ab, 433d, 436a-39a; politics in, 419c; crafts of, 432 *passim,* 439cd; cannibals of, 436a, 440d; mentioned, 433d. *See also* Dani people

Islam: history of, 5-7 *passim,* 9 *passim,* 23d, 24b, 148a; influences on art, 7b, 60d, 68a, 71c, *114c,* 173a; political parties of, 9cd, 25a; practices of, in Indonesia, 23-26 *passim,* 135c; definition, 24 *passim;* rituals, 24b, 26ab; obligations to, 24bd, 59d; mysticism, 25-27 *passim;* and *adat,* 25a-26d, 286c; festivals of, *100c, 105c. See also* Islamic penetration; Islamic High Saints

Islamic High Saints: general, 5d, 60d, 141d, 142a, 173b, *351c;* Falatehan of Cirebon, 97d; Sunan Muria of Kudus, 104d; Kalidjaga, 142a; Sunan Giri, 173b, 176c

Islamic penetration: into Indonesia, general, 6d, 24d, 25a, 259cd; in Java, 52d, *53c,* 95b, *116c, 141d,* 142a, *351c;* in Sumbawa, 249ab; in Sumatra, 259cd, 264c, 271d, 285b, 307cd, 309b, 318b; in Ambon, 400a. *See also* Islam, history of

Istana Negara (Presidential Palace), *78c,* 82b

Jagaraga Temple, N. Bali, 224d

Jago Temple, E. Java, 152d, 164bd, 165a

Jailolo, Halmahera: getting there, 412b; *adat* houses of, 416c

Jakarta, W. Java: history of, 7d, *53c,* 77d, 78ab, 82c; events, 27b; from, 43c, 84-85 *passim,* 264b, 265d, 272b, 337b, 341a, *357c;* museums of, *53c,* 78c, 82 *passim,* 83a, 359c; general, 77c-85c; people of, 78b, *350c;* transport, 78bc; antique shops and markets of, *78c,* 80cd, 81a; cultural center, *78c, 83ci,* 83cd; stay, 78c, 80ab; *79m;* eat, 80bc; mosques and churches, 83b; arts and crafts, 83cd; getting there, 97d, 104d, 124cd, 141d, 171d, 172ac, 218cd, 259d, 262c, 266cd, 268b, 269b, 273c, 276ab, 280bc, 288d, 304c, 339a, 343a, 356b, 364a, 375d, 381c, 413d, 425c; mentioned, 95a, 230d, 246b, 274b, 306b, 378c, 403a, 405d, 417a

Jalatunda, ancient bathing place, E. Java, *53c,* 152ac, *152c*

Jambi, S. Sumatra: history of, 261a; from, 261c, 262c, 268bd, 272b, 279b; getting there, 263c, 266d, 267ad, 269b, 280b, 382c; general, 268a-69b *passim;* stay, 268a; vicinity of, 268ab; mentioned, 264b

Japanese, the, in Indonesia: general, 8ab, 9d, 101c, *189c;* during WW II, 9d, 21b, *100c, 117c, 188c,* 426b; during war of independence, 10 *passim;* investment of, 17c, 18a, 398a, 419d

Japen Island, Irian Jaya: Bird of Paradise, 425b; getting there, 425d

Java, history of: Hindu influence, 5 *passim;* general, 6-10 *passim,* 51b, 52bc, *53cm,* 54b-55c, *55d, 117c, 126c, 129c,* 133a, *144c,* 178ab, *253c,* 261b; colonial, 8-11 *passim,* 398b; Java War, the (19th C.), 9ab. *See also* Dutch colonisers; Prehistoric man

Java: land of, 3c, 51 *passim,* 52a, *146i,* 259bc, 264cd; ethnic make-up, 20cd; religion, 25c, 60bc, *131c;* events, 26b; food, 36c, 215d; transport, 42c, 51bc; flora and fauna, 52ab, *252c;* climate, 52b; population, 58a-59c, *59c, 103c,* 264c; customs, 59d, 60ab; *batik,* 60c-62c, 374a; speech levels of, 60ab; folk drama and *wayang,* 63cd, 64a, 184bc, *188c;* dance, 65b-67a, 190b; getting there, 213b, 224cd, 226b, 232c, 276ab, 280d, 304bc, 343a, 344a, 356b, 381c, 424b, 425c; literature of, *225c,* 445bc; mentioned, *116-17c, 119c,* 185c, 189c, 259d, 278c, 286a, 417a, 433d. *See also* Batik; Java, history of

Javanese people: aristocracy of, 59d, 60ab; customs of, 59d-60c, 181b; in Sumatra, 263b, 264cd, 268a; of Kalimantan, 327a; of Moluccas, 399bc, 400ab, 405d, 406c; of Irian Jaya, 420b; mentioned, 271b, 439a

Java Sea, the: general, 51d, 90c, 173a, 223b; mentioned, 116c, *152-53c;* Loro Nyai Kidul, 66bc, 127ac, *142c*

Jawi Temple, E. Java, *152c,* 164b, 165b

Jayapura, Irian Jaya: getting there, 171b, 404a, 417b, 424ab, 436a; general, 424a-25b; stay, 424b; transport in, 424b; from, 424d-25b, 427b, 436a, 439a; mentioned, 80d, 417a, 434d, 435b

Jayawijaya, Mt., Irian Jaya, 253c, 417c, *117c*

Jepara, C. Java: general, 105ac-106a; stay, 105c; woodcarving, 105c

Jiwika, Irian Jaya, Baliem, 440b

Kabanjahe, N. Sumatra: getting there, 310a; general, 323c-d; vicinity of, 323c; mentioned, 320 passim, 323a

Kai Islands, S.E. Moluccas: people of, 235a; getting there, 404ac *passim, 407c,* 407c; *407m;* Kai Besar, *407c,* 408a; general, *407c,* 407a-408c; Kai Kecil, 407c; arts and crafts, 408b; fauna of, 408c; mentioned, 408c

Kaimana, Irian Jaya: from, *407c;* rock paintings of, 427a, 429cd

Kain: for comfort, 44d; of W. Timor, 230b; W. Kalimantan, 356c; C. Moluccas, 400d; mentioned, 69b, 188c

Kalabahi, Alor: getting there, 224d, 232c; general, 236b

Kalasan Temple, C. Java: 133d, 134ab, *144c,* 265d; mentioned, 147c

Kalimantan: the land, 17a, 327ad, 328a, 345cd, 347a, 397a; religions of, 26cd, 331d, 332a; crafts, 28d, 29a, 30a, 334b-35c, 338a, 347ab; accommodation, 35c; travel in, 42d, 43c, 329d, 330, 336ac, 345cd, 347a, *350c,* 353a, 358; history, 54b, *116c,* 328ac; getting there, 171b, 327 *passim, 327cm,* 343ab, 348a; climate of, 328a; economy, 328c; flora, 328c-29b; fauna, 329 *passim, 329ci,* 344bc, *355ci,* visas for, 329d; *330m;* from, 379a

Kaliurang, C. Java: getting there, 124b; general, 125d-26c

Kamal, Madura, 173c, 175d

Kandangan, E. Java: getting there, 148c, 153c, 162d

Kandangan, S. Kalimantan, 336c

Kapuas River, W. Kalimantan: general, 356a, 356d-58a; mentioned, 356c

Karangasem, E. Bali. *See* Amlapura, E. Bali

Karang Bolong, W. Java: 75a

Karang Bolong, C. Java, birds' nest soup, 99cd

Karo Batak people, N. Sumatra: general, 306a, 318a-20d; religion of, 306d; script, 309a; kinship system, 318bc; ceremonies, 318c; events of, 318cd; architecture, 320d, 323a. *See also* Batak people

Karo Highlands, N. Sumatra: getting there, 310a; mentioned, 305c, 318a

Kartini, Raden: writer, 9b; gravesite of, 27d, 102c; Kartini Day Celebrations, 27d; birthplace of, 106a

Kartosuro, C. Java: getting there, 124b; ruins of, 141d; from, 450a

Kawah Lake, E. Java, 167bc

Kawakit region, Irian Jaya, 430b

Kawar Lake, N. Sumatra, 320c

Kayan Dayak tribe, E. Kalimantan, crafts, 335ac

Kayan River, E. Kalimantan, 348b, 353a, 358d

Kayuputih oil: uses, 45c; source, 403d

Kecak Dance, Bali: general, 191c; performances of, 203a, 212d, 218b

Kedaton, Temple, E. Java, 54b, 147c, *152c*

Kediri, E. Java: vicinity of, *53c*, 153c, 154a; general, 152c-54a; getting there, 160d, 162a

Kediri Kingdom, E. Java: general, 5c, *53c*, 154a; mentioned, 52b

Kedisan, N. Bali, 220 *passim*, 221cd, 222a

Kefannanu, W. Timor, 232c

Keli Mutu, Mt., Flores: general, 240ab; climbing it, 240c

Kelud, Mt., E. Java, 156b

Ken Angrok, Javanese legend, 121c, 172c, 173a

Kendari, S.E. Celebes: transport, 359c; getting there, 370b, 382 passim, 416c; crafts of, 381b; general, 382c-d

Kenyah Dayak tribe, E. Kalimantan: crafts of, 335c; location and remarks, *346c;* general, 353c

Kerinci, Mt., S. Sumatra, 85b, 263a

Kerinci Lake, S. Sumatra: getting there, 268b, 280b; general, 268d-69b; sights of, 269a

Ketapang, E. Java, getting there, 165d, 167a, 172a, 178a, 356d

Kete' Kesu, Torajaland, S. Celebes: *liang* of, 385c; crafts, 387b; general, 390a; gravesite of, *391i;* mentioned, 390d

Ketoprak: general, 63d, 64a; performance of, 102a, 115d, 121c, 160a; mentioned, 188c

Ketungau River, W. Kalimantan, 358cd

Kidal Temple, E. Java, 147c, 152d, 164b, 165a-b

Kintamani, N. Bali: passion fruit, 194a; getting there, 200cd, 218c; general, 223 *passim*

Kisar, Leti Islands: getting there, 404a, *407c,* 409b; people of, 232a

Kiwirok Valley, Irian Jaya, 430a

Klungkung, E. Bali: crafts of, 187b; his-

tory, 203b, general, 204b-d; tour to, 213b; getting there, 218c; mentioned, 183c, 185c, 196b, 206ac

KOKAR, 191a, 280a

Kokonau, Irian Jaya: getting there, 434d; from, 435b

Kolepon Island, S. Irian Jaya, 427d

Komodo dragon. See Animal life of Indonesia, Komodo lizard

Komodo Island, Nusa Tenggara: getting there, 219cd, 241ac, 242d, 244ab, 251ab, 382a; general, 242a-44d; *243m;* sights of, 244cd; mentioned, 251a

Konfrontasi campaign (1962-65): history of, 11c, 156a; in Riau's economy, 272d; in Irian Jaya, 419b

Koran, the: origin of, 23d; contents of, 24ab; conduct towards, 32a; mentioned, 60c, 324c

Kota Baru, W. Sumatra: crafts of, 289d; getting there, 291a; from, 291c

Kota Gadang, W. Sumatra, 289d, 291 *passim*

Kota Gede, C. Java: events of, 27a; getting there, 112a; silver-working, 125ab; from, 327c

Kota Kinabalu, Sabah, E. Malaysia: getting there, 327b, 343a, 355a; from, 343a

Kotamobagu, N. Celebes: getting there, 364a; general, 367a-c; from, 367ac, 368b

Krakatoa volcano, W. Java: 73bc, *116c;* getting there, 73c, 263b, 280d; explosion of, *253c,* 298a

Kraton courts, Java: history of, 5d, 7d, *53c, 116c,* 134c; *gamelan* and dance, 65bd, 66a, *110c, 122c;* of Yogya, *114ci,* 115a, *115c;* attendants, *114c, 119c;* of Solo, 135b, *137c,* 138c-39ac; mentioned, 66c

Kretek: use of, 36d; of Kudus, 104cd; 136c; of Solo, 140b; source of, 399c

Kris: general, *62ci,* 62c-63c; buying, *62c,* 138bc; in ceremonies of C. Java, 63a, *114c;* making, 63b; design, 63bc; of Diponegoro, 123a; examples of, 138bc, 139d; of Madura, 176a; in E. Javanese legends, 447d; mentioned, 60c, 69b

Kris Dance. See Barong Dance

Kroe Region, S. Sumatra, weaving of, 29c, 264d

Kualakapuas, C. Kalimantan, 338c, 340cd

Kubu people, Sumatra: 19b, 264ab; religion of, 23c; in Jambi, 268a

Kucing, Sarawak: from, 327cd, *357c,* 365b; getting there, 329d, 343a, 352d; *Kuda Kepang* (Kuda Kopeng, Kuda Lumping): description, 66d, 67a; performances, 101d, 121b; buying plaited hobbyhorses, 123c; of E. Java, 151c

Kudus, C. Java, 104a-105a, *105m*

Kupang, W. Timor: getting there, 171c, 219ac, 224d, 239c, 246c, 251a, 381d-82a *passim;* general, 230d-33a *passim;* history of, 230d; stay and eat, 232a; from, 232c, 233a; mentioned, 227d, 232a, 233b

Kurima, Irian Jaya: stay, 435c; description, 440a

Kusamba, E. Bali: from, 205a; mentioned, 204cd

Kuta village, S. Bali: crafts of, 187cd; stay, 193d, 194a, 209d-10b, 212a; general, 208c-213b; *210-11m;* from, 212d, 213ab, 219d; getting there, 217c; mentioned, 177d, 178a, 185a, 198b, 207b, 215d, 220a, 224a

Kutacane, Aceh, 305c, 311d, 320d, 326d

Kutai Game Reserve, E. Kalimantan, 344bc

Kwandang, N. Celebes: getting there, 364a, 368b; from, 370a; vicinity of, 370b

Labuhan, W. Java, 73bc

Labuhanbajo, Flores: getting there, 232c, 238a, 251a; general, 241 *passim,* from, 241ab, 242d; mentioned, 244b

Labuhan Lombok, E. Lombok: getting there, 254b, 255c, 256b; from, 257c, 258a; general, 257c, 258a

Ladang, agricultural system of, 2 *passim,* 227b, 229c, 260b, 358b

Lagundi, S. Nias, 298a

Lahad Datu, Sabah: getting there, 327b, 354d; from, 327c, 354d

Lamalerap, S. Lembata: whale-hunting, 235ac; mentioned, 236a

Lampung District, S. Sumatra: archaeological remains of, 264d; fabrics of, 264d; people of, 264cd

Langgur, Kais, *407c,* 407c

Language of Indonesia. See Bahasa Indonesia

Larantuka, E. Flores: getting there, 224d, 232c; from, 234bc, 239ac

Lawu, Mt., C. Java: crater of, 145a; climbing it, 145c, 146a, 449cd; mentioned, 115d, 141d, 142bc, 151b

Leberan, celebration of, 27ab, 304a

Legian, S. Bali: stay, 193d, 213d, 214a, 215 *passim;* getting there, 212d; general, 213c-15d; *214m;* mentioned, 209a

Legong Dance-Ballet, Bali: general, 192ab; origin of, 198b; performance, 212d; dancers in stone carving, 218a; mentioned, 192c

Lembang, W. Java, 89d, 90a

Lembar, W. Lombok: getting there, 207c, 251ad, 254a; from, 255c

Lembata, Island of: general, 234a-35c; getting there, 234b

Lemo, Torajaland, S. Celebes: *liang* of, 385d, *390i;* general, 390c

Leti Islands, S.E. Moluccas: woodcrafts of, 30a; religion of, 409d

Leuser Nature Reserve, N. Sumatra, 305c, 326c

Liang graves: definition of, 385cd; examples of, 385d, 390c, *390i*

Limboto Lake, N. Celebes, 370ab *passim*

Lingga, N. Sumatra: getting there, 320b; general, 323a

Lingga Island, Riau: getting there, 275d, 276c; boat-building, 278c

LIPI, 50ab, 403b

Literature of Indonesia: 9b, 21b, *22c, 53c,* 116c, 154a, *188-89c,* 255a, 287d-88a, 306b, 445b-48c

Lizards of Indonesia: gekko, *241c;* toke (cikcik), *241ci;* Komodo, 242a-44d *passim, 243ci;* Kalimantan, *329c*

Lombok, Nusa Tenggara: getting there, 171c, 207ac, 218c, 219c, 233a, 254ab; general, 254a-58a; weaving, 254d, 256b; *257m;* mentioned, 227ad

Londa, Torajaland, S. Celebes: *tau-tau* of, 385d; general, 390c

Longbagun, E. Kalimantan, 347a, 348a

Longiram, C. Kalimantan: getting there, 343b; general, 347d

Longkemuat, E. Kalimantan, 348b, 352c

Longnawan, E. Kalimantan: getting there, 327d, 343b; general, 344a, 348b, 352d

Longpahanghai, E. Kalimantan: getting there, 347a; general, 348a

Lontar books: examples of, 218a, 224a; mentioned, 165b

Lontar palm: used in W. Timor, 229c; *255ci*

Loro Nyah Kidul, 66bc, 127ac, *142c*

Lovina Beach, N. Bali: general, 225d-26c; stay, 226ab

Lowolava, Lembata: getting there, 234b, 239a; general, 234d

Lubuklinggau, S. Sumatra: getting there, 262c, 263cd, 264a, 268d, 269b, 280b, 288d, 291a; from, 263d, 264a

Ludruk theatre form: 63d; performance of, 121cd, 143a; mentioned, *188c*

Luwuk, C. Celebes: getting there, 370cd, 416c

Madiun, W. Java: revolt of, *53c,* 430a; getting there, 141d, 144c, 171d; general, 156cd; from, 449c; mentioned, 143a, 145c, 146a

Madura Island: getting there, 157a, 173c; general, 173b-76c

MAF, Protestant airlines: in Kalimantan, 358d; Irian Jaya, 425a

Magelang, C. Java: getting there, 123a, 124b; from, 450d; mentioned, 450a

Magellan, Ferdinand: crew of, *117c;* voyage around the world, 398c, 405c

Mahabharata epic, the: depicted in temple art, *53c,* 152a, 154b, 165a; adaption into Javanese literature, 68bc, 447b; in cave paintings, 154d,

155a; history of, 445ab; Indonesian version, 445bc; story of, 445cd; mentioned, 146a

Mahakam River, E. Kalimantan: travel on, 343bc, 344ab; general, 344c, 345c-48b *passim; 348-49m;* getting there, 357b, 358bc; mentioned, 329a, 330b

Mahayana Buddhism: history of in Indonesia: 5 *passim, 116c, 131c;* colony, 206c; in Palembang, 265d, 266a. See also Buddhism

Majapahit Empire: history of, 5cd, 146ac, 147d, 155b, 157c, 167d, 178b; relics, *53c,* 148c; *kris,* 63c; general, 147b-48a *passim; kraton, 149m;* on Bali, 181c; on Sumatra, 270a; symbol of, 447a; mentioned, 52b

Makale, Torajaland, S. Celebes: getting there, 372b, 389d, 392c, 393a, 394d-95a *passim;* stay, 394a; general, 394ab

Makassan people: religion of, 26c; history of, *117c,* 227d, 377bc; general, 249ab, 377a-78c, 406c; dance, 377c; literature, 377c; crafts, 381bc

Makassar. See Ujung Pandang

Malang, E. Java: getting there, 141b, 148c, 153c, 157a, 159c, 172a, 218d; general, 160a-62b; stay, 160bc; from, 160d, 162a; *161m, 163m;* vicinity of, 162ab, 164-65b

Malay civilization: language of, 21bc; people, 189c, 263b, 399b; history, 272cd

Malili, C. Celebes: general, 359d, 372ab; getting there, 360c, 396a; stay and eat, 372a; from, 372ab, 373a

Malino, S. Celebes: 376c; getting there, 381c

Mamasa, Torajaland, S. Celebes: getting there, 363c, 381d, 394bc, 395c; from, 385a; general, 393c, 394a, 394b-95a

Manado, N. Celebes: events of, 27c, 360d, 363b; getting there, 353a, 360d, 368d, 370c, 374a, 375d, 396c; transport in, 359d, 360d; general, 360c-64c; stay and eat, 363d-64a; from, 364ac, 366a, 367a, 399a; history of, *369c*

Mandailing Batak tribe, N. Sumatra: general, 306a, 310b; religion of, 307c; mentioned, 310c. See also Batak people

Mandala, Mt., Irian Jaya, 431c

Mandau sword, of the Dayaks, E. Kalimantan, *188c,* 333d, 335a, 345b

Maninjau Lake, W. Sumatra: general, 282c, 292a-94a; getting there, 291c, 292ab; stay, 292b; vicinity of, 292b, 294a

Manokwari, Irian Jaya: getting there, 404a, 424d, 425c; province of, 425d-26d; from, 426b; mentioned, 240a, 420d

Mantingan, C. Java, 7b, 105c-106a

passim

Mas, C. Bali: general, 184d; crafts of, 187b; tour to, 213b

Matana Lake, C. Celebes, 373ac

Matapura, S. Kalimantan: general, 336a; mentioned, 337b, 338a

Mataram, Lombok: getting there, 254a; from, 254d

Mataram Empire, C. Java: history of, *53c,* 110a, *117c;* general, 105a, 135a, 141d; kings of, 125c; relics, 139cd; mentioned, 52b, 73d

Maumere, Flores: getting there, 172c, 219a, 224d, 232c, 240b; general, 239c; mentioned, 239a

Medan, N. Sumatra: events of, 27b, 302d, 304a; getting there, 85ab, 259d, 260a, 262c, 263c, 266d, 272b, 275d, 276b, 280bd, 300d, 310a, 311d, 320b, 326a; from, 279b, 304b-305a, 325c; general, 300b-305c; stay, 300d, 302a; sights of, 302 *passim,* 304b; *303cm;* vicinity of, 305a; mentioned, 265b

Melanesia: people of, 227c, 234b, 436a-39a; influence on Maluku, 397a

Menak Jonggo Leno, story of, 68b, 167b, 172c, 173a

Mendut Temple, C. Java: general, 131 *passim,* 133a, *144d*

Mengwi, C. Bali: getting there, 202d, 223d; mentioned, 218d

Mengwi, C. Bali: getting there, 202d, 223d; mentioned, 218d

Mentawais, W. Sumatra: general, 284a-d; getting there, 284a

Merak, W. Java: 84c, 266d; mentioned, 73b

Merapi, Mt., C. Java: general, 125cd, 291c; getting there, 125cd, 126ac, 167c; climbing it, 450ab; mentioned, 115d, 128b, 151b, 282b, 285d, 449a

Merauke, Irian Jaya: from, 420d, 427cd *passim,* 430b; getting there, 425 *passim;* general, 427bc

Merbabu, Mt., C. Java: general, 102d, 151b, 450c; mentioned, 128b, 449a

Mimika people, Irian Jaya, 427b

Minahasa, N. Celebes: language of, 21a; religions, 23b; history, *117c,* 359d, 360ab, 365d, 366a; legends, *117c;* people, 360c; sights, 366ac; travel in, 368b

Minangkabaus, W. Sumatra: history of, 6b, 232d, *283c,* 284a, 285bc; general, 24c, 263b, 282b, 285a-88a, 300c, 306b, *369c;* architecture of, 88c, *285i, 286ci;* music and dance, 282d, 287 *passim,* 288a, 294c; *merantau,* 285d, 286ac; customs, 286c; religion, 286c-87a; spirits and health, 287b; crafts, 287d, 289cd, 291cd, 292a; mentioned, 19ab, 279a, 306d

Minerals. See Natural resources of Indonesia; Oil

Missionaries in Indonesia: general, 23b; health clinics of, 45a, 289d, 435c, 440d; of Nusa Tenggara, 234cd,

235a, 236a, 237bc, 238c, 240d; stay with, 238c, 435cd; of Sumatra, 307c; of Kalimantan, 352d; in Maluku's history, 400a; organizations of, 420 *passim*, 435 *passim*. *See also* Transport, missionary

Mohammed: preachings of, 6, 7ab; life, 23d; birthday, 27c, 156c

Mojokerto, E. Java: museum of, 147a, 151a; general, 147a-b; getting there, 171d, 172a; mentioned, 148c

Moluccas Islands: history of, 7d, *117c*, 398bcc; the land, 17a, 397c, 398a; stay, 35c, 403bc, 409b, 410d; getting there, 171b, 381c, 424d; flora, fauna and sealife of, 227b, *253c*, 398ab, 408c, 409d, 412c; *397m*; general, 397a-98d; transport in, 397c; climate of, 398a; dance and music, 398cd; people, 420b, 425d, 426b

Morotai, N. Moluccas: general, *411cm*, 415c; getting there, 413b, 425cd

Mountain climbing, in Indonesia, 1b, 82d, 90b, 94ac, 106b, 125c-26c, 142bc, 145c, 146a, 151c-52c, 157d-59c, 165b, 269a, 291c, 366d, 449a-50d

Muarakaman, E. Kalimantan: crafts of, 347b; general, 347c, 348b

Muaro Takus, W. Sumatra, ruins of, 280b, 282b, *283ci*

Muntilan, C. Java: getting there, 124b; mentioned, 131d

Muntok, E. Sumatra, 264bc

Music of Indonesia: derivations, 7c, 83d; of Java, 64a-d, *65ci*, 190ab; instruments of, *65ci*, *88ci*; kroncong, 83d, 121c; of Bali, 190ab, 200c, 201c; Flores, 237d; Sumatra, 261bc, 266c, 282d, 287bc, 296a, 308c-309a; of the Dayaks, 334a; N. Celebes (kolintang), 360b, 365b; Torajaland, S. Celebes, 387a

Musi River, S. Sumatra, 265b, 266d, 267ac

Muslims. *See* Islam

Mysticism: Sufism, 24b, 26c, 60c; on Java, *25c*, *351c*; general, 26cd; as practiced by *dalangs*, 68d, *225ci*; ritual feasts (selamatan), 66a, 67b; meditation, 140-41b; meditator of *raksasa*, *226i*; as practiced in *pencak silat*, *278c*. *See also* Black magic; Spiritual disciplines

Nabire, Irian Jaya: from, 407c, 434d; getting there, 434d

Nainggolan, N. Sumatra, 312a

Nanggala, S. Celebes: *adat* houses of, 388a; general, 391c; getting there, 392b

Narmada, Lombok, 256bc

National Museum, Jakarta, W. Java, *78c*, 82cd, 83d

Natural resources, of Indonesia: minerals, 15d, 264b, 269d, 336a, 376c,

416c, 419d, 420a, *422c*; *16-17m*; timber, 16c, 17a, *342c*; rubber, 356a. *See also* Oil

Ndau, Isle of, Nusa Tenggara, 234ac

Negara, W. Bali, 193c

Negrito people: history of, 4bc; of Timor, 230a; of the Tanimbars, 409b; Irian Jaya, 420b, 432d; mentioned, 227c

New Guinea: sculpture of, *189c*; fauna of, 253c, 397a, 417c; compared, 327a; influence on Maluku, 397a, 407a; history, 418c-19b *passim*; people and tribes of, 426b, 427d

Nganjuk, E. Java, 154a, 172c

Ngawen Temple, C. Java, 131cd, 144c

Nias, Isle of: sculpture of, *188i*, *296i*, 296 *passim*, 298cd; getting there, 294c, 295a; general, 295a-98d; people of, 295 *passim*; transport on, 295ab; culture of, 295bc; history, 295bc; music and dance, 296a; religion, 296a

North Bali: the land, 178d; buying crafts in, 186d; architecture of, 217d, 218a; temple art of, 220a

North Celebes: history of, 11b, 15c, 360ab; fauna, 359b; economy, 360a; music and dance, 360b; transport in, 360bc; *369m*; travel in, 396c; legends of, 448c

North Moluccas: *411m*, *412m*, *414m*; history of, 415c

North Sumatra: economy of, 259b, 300c; travel in, 261cd, 262cd, 304c; general, 299a-323d; *301m*; architecture of, *308i*; mentioned, 295b

Nosu Valley, Torajaland, S. Celebes, 392d

Nufor Island, Irian Jaya, getting there, 425d

Nunukan, E. Kalimantan: general, 352c, 354cd; getting there, 353a, 354cd; from, 354c; stay, 354c

Nusa Dua, S. Bali: 208c; mentioned, 157a, 207d

Nusa Penida Island, off E. Bali: general, 204d-205b; view of, 206d

Nusa Tenggara: weaving of, 28d; getting there, 171bc, 219a, 224cd; general, 227; the land, 227a; climate of, 227b; flora and fauna, 227b; crafts, 227d; travel in, 227d; *228-29m*

Oeleelheue, N. Sumatra, 326b

Oil: of Sumatra, 259b, 265b, 272d, 273a; companies of E. Kalimantan, 341cd; of Irian Jaya, 419d, 420ad

Orangutan Rehabilitation Centers, N. Sumatra: Bukit Lawang, 299 passim; Ketembe, 305c, 323cd

Orion Range, Irian Jaya, 430c

Pacet, resort of, E. Java, 148c, 152c

Pacitan, C. Java: getting there, 141bd, 151c, 154d; general, 149a-51b; vicinity of, 151ab

Padang, W. Sumatra: getting there, 85c, 259d, 262c, 263cd, 264a, 266cd, 273c, 279b, 291a, 297d, 304cd, 311d; vicinity of, *116c*, 280d, 282ab; from, 264a, 268d, 269ab, 273b, 280 *passim*, 295a, 310c; transport in, 272b, 279b; general, 279a-82b; stay, 279b; sights of, 280a; *281cm*; mentioned, 285d

Padangbai, E. Bali: general, 207ac; getting there, 218c, 251d, 255c, 256a; from, 219c, 254a; mentioned, 205c

Padanglawas, temples of, N. Sumatra: general, 310bc; getting there, 310c

Padangpanjang, W. Sumatra: getting there, 280b, 291a; general, 282cd; bullraces of, *293c*

Pagai Islands, off W. Sumatra, 294d

Pagimana, C. Celebes, getting there, 360c, 370cd passim

Pajajaran Kingdom, W. Java, 5c, 75c, *92c*, 93bd, 95b, 97d

Palangkaraya, C. Kalimantan: general, 331a, 340 passim; getting there, 338c; from, 340c; mentioned, 336a, 337b

Palembang, S. Sumatra: getting there, 84c, 85c, 261c, 262c, 263cd, 264a, 265bd, 268bc, 280bd, 304c, 311d; history of, *116c*, 261a, 265d; sights, 263a, 266bc; from, 264b, 266cd, 269b, 279b; general, *265m*, 265b-67a; dances of, 266a, 287b; fabrics, 266a; stay and eat, 266a; museum of, 266bc; vicinity of, 267ac; mentioned, 264b, 269c, *350c*

Palopo, C. Celebes: getting there, 371b, 372b, 381d, 389d, 395c; from, 372a, 382c, 396ac; stay and eat, 395a; general, 395b-96c; vicinity of, 396a; mentioned, 392b

Palu, C. Celebes: getting there, 352d, 370c, 396c; transport, 359d; general, 374a-b; stay, 374b; from, 375a, 396c

Pamekasan, Madura, 175d

Pameungpeuk Bay, W. Java, 89d, 90cd

Pana, S. Celebes: *liang* of, 385d; dance, 386a; music, 387a; crafts, 388b; general, 393a

Panakawans: general, *119ci*; in Javanese legend, 447c. *See also* cover illustration

Panataran Temple complex, E. Java: general, *152c*, 155a-c; *155i*

Panca Sila, political philosophy, 5d, *10ci*, 12ac, 406a

Pandaan, E. Java: 72a, 165b, 171d, 172c, 173a, 449b

Pangala', Torajaland, S. Celebes: history of, 384d; coffee, 388c; general, 393a; from, 393c

Pangandaran, W. Java: *76c*; general, 76c-77c; getting there, 77a; from, 77bc

Pangkalan Brandan, N. Sumatra, 299a

Pangrango, Mt., W. Java, 94ac, 95a

Paniai Lakes, Irian Jaya: general, 420a, 434bd; getting there, 434d; mentioned, 440c

Panjalu Lake and Nature Reserve, W. Java, 76a, 98c

Panjang, S. Sumatra, getting there, 84c, 263b, 266d

Panji cycle, tales used in wayang, E. Java, 68b, 70b, 138b, 447d, 448a

Papandayan, Mt., W. Java, crater of, 76a, 90bc

Papua New Guinea: from, 50cd, 417b; land of, 417ad; Bird of Paradise, 418ci; crafts, 432c; mentioned, 419c, 430a

Papuan people: history of, 117c; of E. Indonesia, 230ab, 234b, 237ab, 258c, 408c; of Irian Jaya, 418c, 419a, 420ab, 432d

Parangkusomo, C. Java, 115d, 127c, 142c

Parangtritis, C. Java: general, 126c-27b; vicinity of, 127bc; 142c; mentioned, 115d

Pare, E. Java, 153a, 154a

Pare Pare, S. Celebes: from, 327b, 394c; getting there, 370c, 375 passim, 381d, 396ac, 424d; general, 382b-c

Parigi subdistrict, C. Celebes: getting there, 360c, 370cd, 396c

Pasemah Highlands, S. Sumatra, 266b, 269d-70a

Pasir Putih, E. Java: getting there, 157a; general, 157bc

Passo, Ambon: general, 399c, 400c; getting there, 402d

Pasuruan, E. Java, 157b

Pawon Temple, C. Java, 131ac, 144c

Payakumbuh, W. Sumatra: getting there, 280b; general, 282d; bullraces of, 293c

Pejeng, C. Bali: general, 201d; mentioned, 183c, 202bc, 205b

Pekalongan, C. Java: textiles of, 28c, 99a, 99b-c; getting there, 89d, 97d, 109c; general, 99a-c

Pekanbaru, E. Sumatra: getting there, 259b, 275d, 276b, 278ac, 280bd, 291a, 304c, 311b; transport, 272b; general, 273b-74b; stay, 273bc; from, 273c; vicinity of, 273d; mentioned, 194b, 273a

Pelabuhanratu, W. Java, 95ac

Peliatan, C. Bali: stay, 193d; general, 201 passim

Pematang Purba, N. Sumatra, 310a, 323d

Penang, Malaysia, getting there, 259d, 260a, 304bc

Penanggungan, C. Java, 53c, 141d, 151c-52c

Pencak silat: as dance form, 90d, 287cd; Ponorogo-style, 151b; Madura-style, 173d, 174c; general, 188c, 278ci; of Sumatra, 278ci, 278cd; political uses of, 380c; mentioned, 60a

Penelokan, N. Bali: getting there, 200d;

general, 220 passim; stay, 220cd; vicinity of, 220d, 221m, 221a; mentioned, 218d, 221d, 223a, 449b

Penestanan, C. Java: painting style of, 186c; stay, 193d; getting there, 200c; general, 201ab

Pengosekan, C. Bali, 200c passim

Penulisan, N. Bali, 223b

Pertamina: development and collapse of, 16ac; for cheap petrol, 41b; airlines of, 268c; in E. Sumatra, 273ad; history of, 299a; in Balikpapan, 343a

Philippines, the: getting there, 42d, 43a, 219a, 343a, 352d, 353a, 355ac, 364c; Fillipinos of Irian Jaya, 425d; pirates, 284d; mentioned, 53c, 366d

Pithecanthropus erectus. See Prehistoric man

PKI, Communist Party of Indonesia: 11cd, 53c, 99d, 116c, 135b, 156d, 358c

Plantlife of Indonesia: general, 3cd, 93ac, 252-53c; rainforest trees, 3d, 259a, 260c, 342c; forests, 16c, 227a, 259ab, 398a, 417b, 449a; coconut palm, 36a, 367ci; kapok tree, 52d; pandanus, 75d, 182c, 415c, 437c; orchids, 93c, 328c, 345c, 348-49ci; banyan tree, 201b, 252c; sago palm, 227c, 398d, 399ci, 427b, 428a, 429b; bamboo, 232ci, 335c, 335ci, 398d; nipah palm, 233b, 338ci; lontar palm, 233d-34a, 255ci; mango tree, 252c; reflesia, 253c, 260c, 269c, 282b, 291d; corpse plant, 260c; strangler fig, 260c; wait-a-minute vine, 260c; arecoid palm, 267i, 367i; ironwood (kayu besi) tree, 328c; pitcher plant, 328c; Tree Ferns, 328ci, 353a, 379d; teakwood tree, 328c, 378c; veiled lady, 329a; kanari tree, 402d; travelers' palm, 434ci

Plaosan Temple, C. Java, 134 passim, 144c

Polewali, S. Celebes: from, 363c, 394c; getting there, 381d, 382c, 394c, 395a

Ponorogo, E. Java, 151bc

Pontianak, W. Kalimantan: transport in, 329d; getting there, 338d, 343a, 356b; general, 356a-58a passim; from, 356b, 357c, 358a; stay, 356b; vicinity of, 356bc

Population of Indonesia, 15b, 58-9m, 58a-9c, 103c

Portugese colonisers: general, 7bc; in Nusa Tenggara, 26b, 229c, 230d, 234b, 235d, 236a, 237 passim, 238a, 239a; in Riau, 274d, 325b; in Celebes, 359cd, 360a, 377bd; in Moluccas, 398bc, 399a, 402bc, 405c, 406c, 410b

Poso, C. Celebes: getting there, 360c, 370 passim, 374a, 396c; from, 371m, 371a, 396c

Pottery: general, 29b; of Majelang, 76a; Madura, 175a, 176a; S. Celebes, 381bc; Kais, 408bc; Arus, 409a. See

also Chinese porcelain

Prahus: carving of, 28a, 103c, 332c; 38i; of the Bugis and Makassans, 44c, 377d-78d; of Java, 123a, 138d, 139d; use in Dayak death ceremonies, 332c; types of, 377d, 378a; prahu-building, 378 passim, 378c; use in Torajan death ceremonies, 385d; in the Kais, 408c; of the Asmat, 429d

Prambanan Plain Temple complex, C. Java: 132m; general, 133a-35a, 144c

Prambanan Temple, C. Java: dance festival of, 72a, 121d, 122a; reliefs of, 117c, 133 passim; crafts of, 123c; getting there, 124b; mentioned, 147c

Prapat, N. Sumatra: getting there, 288d, 291a, 300d, 302a, 304cd, 310a, 316c, 320b; general, 311b-12a; stay, 311bc; 312m, 313c

Prehistoric man: 4b, 51a, 88c, 141cim, 142b, 151b

Pringapus Temple, C. Java, 102d, 144d

Probolinggo, E. Java: getting there, 124c, 162a, 171d, 172a; general, 156d-57b; from, 157a, 158b

Proklamasi Kemerdekaan. See Independence Day

Pulau Telo, getting there, 295a

Punan people, E. Kalimantan, 19b, 335c, 346d, 352bc

Puncak Pass, W. Java: getting there, 89d; hiking, 94cm; general, 94c

Puntadewa Temple, Dieng, C. Java, 55ci, 109c

Pura: Puseh, C. Bali, 196b; Gaduh, C. Bali, 196bd; Bukit, C. Bali, 196d; Dalem, C. Bali, 196d; Panataran Sasih, C. Bali, 201d; Kebo Edan, C. Bali, 202b; Puser Ing Jagat, C. Bali, 202b; Kehen, C. Bali, 202d, 203d; Luhur, C. Bali, 202c; Batukuning, Nusa Penida, 205a; Ped, Nusa Penida, 205a; Sekenan, S. Bali, 213b; Ulu Watu, S. Bali, 213b; Sukawana, N. Bali, 223b; Beji, N. Bali, 224d, 225b; Medruwe Karang, N. Bali, 225b

Purwakarta, W. Java, 90d, 91a

Purwodadi Botanical Gardens, E. Java, 164b

Purwokerto, C. Java: getting there, 89d; vicinity of, 99cd; from, 450c

Putussibau, W. Kalimantan, getting there, 356d, 358a

Raffles, Sir Stamford: 8a; on Java, 93a; on Sumatra, 269b; in Riau, 274d; mentioned, 116c

Ramadan, 24b, 26d, 27a

Ramayana epic poem: history of, 5a, 445d, 446a; used in wayang, 68b, 71ab, 446bc; dance, 121cd, 191c; depicted in temple art, 133c, 155bc; story of, 446; mentioned, 71d, 106c, 225c

Ramayana Ballet, 121d-22a, 139a, 188c, 218b

Rangda, the witch: general, 182d, 191cd, 192a; portrayed in temple art, 224d

Rangkasbitung, W. Java, 75ad

Rantauprapat, N. Sumatra, 305a

Rantepeo, S. Celebes: getting there, 372b, 381cd, 392bc, 395c, 396c; market of, 386a, *388i*, 388c, 389d; weaving, 387c, 391d; from, 388a, 389d, 392a, 392d-94a; general, 389a-94a; transport in, 389c; vicinity of, 389d-92c, 391b, 394b, *395i*; mentioned, 359d, 384b, 391b, 393ac, 394a

Ratu Baka Temple complex, C. Java, 134cd, *144c*

Rembang, C. Java, 27d, 102c, *103c*, 106a

Rendang, E. Bali: *salak* of, 194a; getting there, 206b, 220d

Reo, Flores: getting there, 224d, 232c, 238a, 239c, 241ab; general, 240d-41b *passim*

Reyog Dance, Java: general, 66d, 151bc; performance of, 101d

Riau: people of, 20bc, 272d, 273ab; history of, *116c*, 272cd, 274d, 377c; getting there, 272ab; transport in, 272bc; scuba diving, 276d; *274m, 275c, 277m;* outer islands of, 278a

Rice: history of, 19d; uses of in ceremonies, *120c;* general, *126ci*

Rice Goddess (Dewi Sri), 3c, 19d, 26b, 27d

Rinjani, Mt., Lombok: view of, 220b; general, 256d-57c; getting there, 256d, 257a, 258a

Rock paintings: of S. Celebes, *117c;* Arus, 409a; Irian Jaya, *421ci*, 427a

Rongkong, Torajaland, S. Celebes,: *ikat*-weaving of, 387c; general, 395a-c

Roongurni Huta, N. Sumatra: burial urn of, 314a; *317m*

Roti, Nusa Tenggara: crafts of, 28a, 233b; getting there, 233a, 234c; general, 233b-34a; *lontar* culture of, 233d

Rotinese people: general, 233 *passim;* origin of, 233b; mentioned, 233a

Ruteng, W. Flores: getting there, 219a, 233a, 238a, 239c, 241a, 251b; general, 240d

Sabah, E. Malaysia, from, *327cm*. See *also* Kota Kinabalu; Lahad Datu; Sandakan; Tawau

Sa'dan, Torajaland, S. Celebes: general, 387bc, 389d, 391d; market of, 388c

Sailendra Kingdom: construction of Borobudur, 128a; princes of, 134bd; on Sumatra, 261a; mentioned, 5c

Sajiwan Temple, C. Java, 134c

Salak, Mt., W. Java, 93d, 94a

Salatiga, C. Java: language study in,

22ac; general, 102cd; University of, 102cd; stay, 102d; getting there, 141b

Salawati Islands, Irian Jaya, getting there, 426d

Salayar Island, S. Celebes: 381b, getting there, 381d

Samarinda, E. Kalimantan: getting there, 171c, 339bc, 343ab, 352d, 353a, 374c, 375c; transport in, 343c; general, 343c-44b; stay, 343cd; sights of, 343d, 344a; weaving, 343d, 344a; from, 344 *passim,* 347c, 352ac; mentioned, 327a, 330d, 337b

Sambas, W. Kalimantan: getting there, 276a; general, 356c

Sambisari Temple, C. Java, 133d, 134a, 135a

Samosir Island, N. Sumatra: general, 310d, 313a-17c, *315c;* getting there, 312a; visa extensions on, 313b; dope, 313bc, *315c;* stay and eat, 313cd; old graves and tombs, 313d, 314a; *315m*

Sandakan, Sabah: getting there, 327b, 354d; from, 327c, 354d;

Sangeh Monkey Forest, C. Bali, 202cd

Sangiran, C. Java, site of prehistoric man, 4b, *141cm,* 142b

Sangir Islands, off N. Celebes: 171b, 366cd; getting there, 364ac, 364c, *366m,* 366cd

Sangsit, N. Bali, 213b, 224d, 225b

Sangyang Dedari Trance Dance, Bali: general, 192c, 212d; performance of, 223a; mentioned, 191c

Sanskrit: used in Indonesian language, 5, 26a; *kawi,* 67b, 72d; in Mahayana Buddhism, 131c; mentioned, *350c.*

Sanur Beach, S. Bali: general, 207b-d; getting there, *217c, 218c*

Saparua, C. Moluccas, 404cd

Sape, E. Sumbawa: getting there, 241a, 251b; general, 242d, 244a; from, 249c, 251a

Sapudi Islands, 176c

Sarangan, E. Java: general, 142c, 143ac, 144ac; stay, 143c, 144a; from, 144c, 449c; vicinity of, 145a, 146 *passim;* mentioned, 146a

Sarawak, E. Malaysia: from, *357c;* mentioned, 348b, 356a. See *also* Kucing, Sarawak.

Sari Temple, C. Java, 133d, 134ab, *144c*

Sarung: uses of, 32b, 33c, 44d; of Flores, 239c; Lombok, 256b; of S. Sumatra, 264d; E. Kalimantan, 343d, 344a; C. Moluccas, 400d; mentioned, 60d, 71a

Sawah, 2d, 3ac, *126ci, 207i,* 230b, 264c, 366c

Sawu Island, Nusa Tenggara: dance and music of, *189c;* getting there, 233a, 247a; general, 234c; weaving of, 246c

Sculpture, ancient. See Ancient sculpture

Sealife of Indonesia: coral reefs, 73a, 82a, 208ac, 272a, 276d, 278ac, 402ab, 414b; fish, *81i,* 170c, *176i, 253c,* 272a, 406d, *415c, 440i;* marine reptiles, 244c; seashells, *176i, 216c, 415ci, 440i*

Sea, travel by, in Indonesia. See Transport, sea; *Prahus*

Seketan Festival, C. Java, 115cd, 123b, 139c

Seko, S. Celebes: from, 395c; getting there, 395c; mentioned, 374a

Selaru Island, Tanimbars, 409b

Selecta, E. Java: hotsprings, *151c;* general, 162d, 164a

Selo, C. Java: general, 450a; getting there, 450a; mentioned, 141d

Semarang, C. Java: getting there, 84bd, 89d, 97d, 124b, 162a, 171d, 218c, 339a; history of, 99d; general, 99d-102c; festivals of, *100c; 100m;* sights of, 101 *passim,* 102bc; transport in, 101a; stay, 101ab; theatre and dance, 101d, 102a; crafts, 102a; from, 102ab, 337b, 341a; temples in the vicinity, 102d

Semeru, Mt., E. Java: 162c, 167c, 449a; climbing it, 449d, 450a

Sendangduwar, E. Java, art of, 7a, 173a

Sengkang, S. Celebes: general, 376c; getting there, 381d, 396a

Sentani Airport, Irian Jaya, from, 424ab, 425a, 434d

Serang, E. Java, 73bd, 156c

Serangan, Turtle Island, E. Bali, 207d, 208a

Serimpi Dance: general, 66b; performance of, 121c, 139a; mentioned, 139c

Seririt, N. Bali: getting there, 224c; mentioned, 225d, 226c

Sewu Temple, C. Java, 134ab, *144c*

Ship of the Dead cult: in S. Sumatra, 264d; Kalimantan, *332ci,* 332c

Shipping: facilities for in Indonesia, 28d, 30cd; companies, 43cd; importing, *289c*

Shiva: Indonesian version of, 5c; temples dedicated to, *53c,* 133b, 213b; general, 69ab, 446bd; portrayed in temple art, 106c, *129c,* 165b; Shivaite influences in temple art, 131a, 154b, 165b; sculpture of, 139d; in Balinese religion, 182a; wife of (Parvati), 446d, 447a; mentioned, 447b

Siak River, E. Sumatra, 275d, 273b

Siantar, N. Sumatra: getting there, 304cd; general, 309b-10b; stay and eat, 309c; crafts, 309d; from, 310a; vicinity of, 310ab; mentioned, 311b, 323d

Sibayak, Mt., N. Sumatra, 305c, 320c, 323 *passim*

Siberut Island, Mentawais: getting there, 284ad; people of, 284b

Sibil people, Irian Jaya, *351c,* 430d,

431a

Sibolga, W. Sumatra: getting there, 291a, 310a, 326a; general, 294 *passim,* 311d; stay, 294a; from, 294cd, 295a; visa extensions in, *301c*

Simalungun Batak tribe, N. Sumatra: people of, 306a, 309ab, 310a; religion, 309b; museum of, 309cd

Simanindo, N. Sumatra: getting there, 312a; general, 316d, 319a; mentioned, 317a

Simeulue Island, off N.W. Sumatra, 284d, 294cd, 326a

Sinabung, Mt., N. Sumatra, 320c

Singapore: from, 39 *passim,* 259d, 272a, 327b, 356b; visas in, 50cd; getting there, 171bc, 264c, 266d, 268bc, 273c, 275d, 276ab, 280d, 304bc, 343a, 345d, 355a

Singaraja, N. Bali: crafts of, 186d, 224b; stay, 193d, 224ab; getting there, 206b, 207a, 218cd; tour to, 213b; general, 219d, 223d-25b; sights, 224b; from, 224cd, 242d; vicinity of, 224d, 225b; mentioned, 181b, 204a, 225b, 226c

Singarak Lake, W. Sumatra, 282cd

Singkawang, W. Kalimantan, *330c,* 356 *passim*

Singkep Island, Riau: general,, 264b; history of, 272d; getting there, 278a

Singosari Dynasty, E. Java: history of, *53c,* 155ab, 165ab, 398b; mentioned, 5c, 52b

Singosari Temple, E. Java, *117c,* 147c, 152d, 164cd

Sintang, W. Kalimantan, *357c,* 358cd

Sipisopiso Waterfall, N. Sumatra: getting there, 320d; mentioned, *301c*

Situbondo, E. Java: bullfights of, 167b; getting there, 167c

Slamet, Mt., C. Java, 99c, 450c

Solo, C. Java: religions of, 26c; events, 27a, 139c; antiques, 29b, 63c; *kratons* of, 54a, 135b, 137c, 138c-39c; getting there, 84bd, 124b, 144c, 151a; history, 125bc, 135ab; general, 135a-42b; stay, 135cd; *136m, 141m, 142-43m;* museum, *137c,* 139cd; Sriwedari theatre, *137c,* 139d, 140a; crafts, 138 *passim;* sights, 140a; from, 141bd, 449c, 450a; mentioned, 54a, 110a, 140 *passim*

Solok, W. Sumatra: vicinity of, *116c;* getting there, 280b; general, 282c; bullraces of, *293c*

Solor Archipelago: getting there, 171c, 239a; general, 235c-36b; *235m;* mentioned, 232a, 238a

Solo River, C. Java: general, 135c, 138d, 142ab; *252-53c;* mentioned, 141c

Songgoriti Hotsprings, E. Java: general, 162d, 164a; mentioned, *150c*

Sonobudoyo Museum, Yogya, C. Java, 71c, *110c,* 122c, 123a

Soroako, C. Celebes: getting there, 372 *passim;* from, 372c, 373a; vicinity of, 373ab; INCO, *376c*

Sorong, Irian Jaya: getting there, 404a, 420d, 424d, 425cd; from, 420d, 424d, 426d; general, *423c,* 426b-d; stay, 426d

South Kalimantan: land of, 328a, *336m,* 336a, 337b, 339b; transport in, 338ab, 347c

South Moluccas, getting there, 404a, *407c*

South Nias: general, 295a, 296c, 297b-98d; music and dance of, 296a; *297m*

South Sumatra: getting there, 259d, 262c; travel in, 262 *passim;* fauna of, 263a; the land, 263a; people of, 263b, 264ab; textiles, 264d; economy, 265b; flora, 267c; special foods of, *350c*

Soviet influence in Indonesia, 11c, 83b, 198a

Spanish, the: in N. Celebes, 360a; in N. Moluccas, 410b

Spies, Walter, painter, Bali, 185c, 200d

Spiritual disciplines: of the Badui, 75 *passim;* Semarang (kebatinan), 102b; Solo, 140c-41b; Bali, 206c, 226c; *226i. See also* Mysticism; Black magic

Sports of Indonesia, 380c. *See also* Surfing in Indonesia; Bullfights

Sriwijaya Empire: general, 5c, 21b, 261ab, 265d, 266a, 285b; history of, *166c*

Stupas in Indonesia: Borobudur, 127d-31a, *129ci;* Sumberawan, 164d; Muaro Takus, 280b, 282b, *283ci. See also* Temples of Indonesia

Suharto, President: military career, 11d; term of office, 13c; family of, 18c; views, 25a; attempted overthrow, 25c; mentioned, 75a, 109ac, *189c*

Sukabumi Regency, *95m*

Sukamade Beach, E. Java: general, 167b; reserve of, 167b; *252c*

Sukaraja, Lombok: weaving center of, 254d; getting there, 256b

Sukarno, President: political career of, 9cd, 11, 88ac, 156ab, 249d; during war of independence, 10 *passim,* 11c; during WW II, 10 *passim;* assassination attempts on, 25a; in Irian Jaya, 430a; mentioned, 83b, 93a, *188-89c*

Sukuh Temple, C. Java: sculpture of, 82c; general, *144c,* 146 *passim;* compared, 146c, 205b

Sula Islands, N. Moluccas: *416m;* general, 416ac; from, 416c

Sulawesi. *See* Celebes

Sullukang, Torajaland, S. Celebes: general, 385c, 390b; *tau-tau* of, 385d

Sultan Agung: general, 66c; tomb of, 125c

Sumatra: the land, 1b, 94a, 259 *passim,* 260ab; history of, 6b, 11bc, 54b, *116c,* 261ab, 271b, 283c, 377c; travel

in, 42cd, 261d-62d; getting there, 84c, 171bc, 259d; flora and fauna, *252c,* 260cd, 326c; architecture, 259b, *286ci,* 287ab; music and dance, 261b, 287b, 310d; climate, 261d; crafts, *262ci;* legends of, 448c

Sumba Island, Nusa Tenggara: event of, 26d, 248a; antiques, 29b; dance, *188c;* general, 245a-48c; travel in, 245c; *246-47m;* crafts of, 246bc; architecture, 247ac; mentioned, 227b, 234a. *See also* Ikat Sumba

Sumbawa Island, Nusa Tenggara: from, 44c; getting there, 219c, 233a, 256b; general, 249a-51d; people, 249bc; travel, 249c; *250m;* mentioned, 227ad

Sumbawa Besar, Sumbawa: getting there, 207c, 224d, 232c, 251a, 254d, 257cd, 258a; from, 246c, 251cd; general, 251 *passim;* mentioned, 227d

Sumberawan Temple, E. Java, 164d

Sumedang, W. Java: getting there, 89d; general, 90d

Sumenep, Madura: getting there, 157a; general, 175d, 176a; vicinity of, 176c

Sundanese people: textiles of, 28c; architecture, 76c; music and dance, 83d, *88ci;* general, 85cd, 95b, 268a; history of, 85d; ramfights, 90ab; festivals, *98c;* mentioned, 89b

Sungaipenuh, S. Sumatra: getting there, 268b, 280b; general, 268d-69b

Surabaya, E. Java: Battle of, 10c; from, 43c, 171 *passim,* 172a, 234b, 327b, 337b, 341a, 359d, 379a, 399a, 417b; getting there, 84bd, 89d, 104d, 124cd, 141b, 147b, 157a, 162a, 213b, 218cd, 219b, 224cd, 232c, 233a, 251a, 339a, 343a, 344a, 353a, 370bc, 375 *passim,* 382a, 404a, *407c,* 413d, 424d; general, 167d-73b; history of, 167d, 168a; transport in, 168ab; stay, 168bc; *169m;* sights of, 170bc, 253c; museums, 170c; vicinity of, 172c, 173a; mentioned, 148c, 158a, *252-53c*

Surawana Temple, E. Java: general, 147c, *152c,* 154b; basrelief from, *148i*

Surfing in Indonesia, *197c, 209b,* 298a. *See also* Sports of Indonesia

Tahulandang, Sangir, 366d

Tahuna, Sangir: general, 366d; getting there, 382a

Takingeun, Aceh, 326 *passim*

Talaut, 366d

Taliabu Island, Sulas, 416ac

Taman Sari, Yogya, C. Java, *116c,* 119d-21a

Tambora, Mt., Sumbawa, 249a

Tampaksiring, C. Bali: crafts of, 187a; general, 196d; mentioned, 198a

Tanah Lot, S. Bali, 213ab

Tanah Merah, Irian Jaya: fauna of, 418a; general, 425b, 430a; getting there, 427c, 430b; from, 430b; men-

tioned, 120d
Tandano Lake, N. Celebes, 365d
Tanimbar Islands, S.E. Moluccas: crafts of, 403d, 409cd; general, 404a, 409 *passim;* getting there, **407c; 409m;** sights of, 409d; mentioned, 407a
Tanjung Isui, E. Kalimantan: getting there, 344b; general, 347bc
Tanjungkarang, S. Sumatra: visa renewal in, 84a; from, 262c, 263cd; general, 263cd; getting there, 280b
Tanjung Pinang, Bintan Island, Riau: from, 39cd, 259d, 272bc, 275cd, 276ad, 278ac; getting there, 39cd, 85b, 259d, 262c, 264b, 266d, 272ab, 273c; **274m, 275c;** general, 274b-76b; stay, 274d; sights of, 274bc
Tanjung Redep, E. Kalimantan, 344b, 352a
Tanjung Selor, E. Kalimantan: general, 353ac; from, 353c; mentioned, 330d
Tapaktuan, Aceh: getting there, 294cd; general, 326a
Tarakan, E. Kalimantan: getting there, 171bc, 172c, 338c, 343a, 344ab; 352ac; general, 352c-53a; stay, 352d
Tasikmalaya, W. Java: general, 75d, 76a, 77a; getting there, 89d, 124d; museum of, 98a
Tawangmangu, C. Java: getting there, 141b; general, 142bc; mentioned, 143a, 144c, 146a, 449c
Tawar Lake, N. Sumatra, 313bc, 326cd
Tawau, Sabah: getting there, 327bc, 329d, 343a, 354c; from, 327c, 343a, 352c, 354d, 355ac
Telaga Warna Lake, W. Java, 94c
Telukbetung, S. Sumatra, 263b
Teluk Bintuni, Irian Jaya, mentioned, **351c, 421c,** 429d, 432c
Telukdalam, Nias: from, 284a, 297d, 298a; getting there, 289cd, 294c, 295a; stay and eat, 297bd
Tembagapura, Irian Jaya, 420a
Tembilahan, E. Sumatra (Riau): ruins of, 276c; mentioned, 274d
Temples of Indonesia: on Java, general, 54b-d; construction, 54d, 55a; reliefs of, 55bc; restoration, 55c; C. Java, 106a-9d, 127d, *132m,* 135a, **144-45cm, 146i,** 146, **155i,** 155 passim; E. Java, 147b-48d, 151c-52c, **152-53cm,** 154b, 155a-c, 156bc, 164b-65b; Bali, **184i, 196i, 208ci;** Sumatra, **283cm,** 305a. See also Stupas in Indonesia
Tenganan, E. Bali, 205b-206a
Tenggarong, E. Kalimantan: general, 328c, 344c-45c; sights of, 344d, 345a; stay and eat, 344d; crafts of, 345 passim; from, 345c, 347cd; mentioned, 330d
Tengger Mts., E. Java, 157d-59c, *350c*
Tengger people, E. Java: religion of, 26d, *350c;* general, 157cd, 158a
Tentena, C. Celebes: getting there, 371a, 374a, 396c; from, 374a, 396c

Terlukai, Riau: general, 276cd; getting there, 278a
Ternate, town of, Ternate: general, 410b-14d; getting there, 410d; stay, 410d; *412cm;* crafts, 412bc; *413i;* vicinity of, 414bd; from, 416c
Ternate Island, N. Moluccas: Islam of, 24c; getting there, 364c, 370b, 399a, 404ac, 424d; land of, 397c; history, 398c, 410b, 415a; old forts, 412c, *413i;* from, 413d, 414b, 415c; **414m;** mentioned, 399d
Thousand Islands. See Pulau Seribu.
Tianyar, E. Bali, getting there, 206b, 224c
Tidore, N. Moluccas: the land, 397c; **414m;** getting there, 414d; stay and eat, 414c; history of, 415a
Tigawangi Temple, E. Java, **152c,** 154b
Tikus Temple, ancient bathing place, E. Java, 148a, *149c*
Timor, Nusa Tenggara: the land, 1b, 228c, 229a; people of, 19c, 227c, 230ab; climate, 227b, 229ac; history, 229c, 230a; crafts, 230bc; horses, 230c; mentioned, 227ab, 249a
Timuka, Irian Jaya, getting there, *401c,* 434d
Tirtagangga Water Palace, E. Bali: general, 206d, 207a; mentioned, 206c
Toba Lake, N. Sumatra, 306a, 310d, 311a
Tobelo, Halmahera: getting there, 413bd; vicinity of, 415ac
Togian Islands, Tomini Bay, C. Celebes, 359b
Tomini Bay, C. Celebes, getting there, 360c, 370cd passim, 396ac
Tomohon, N. Celebes: general, 364c-66a; getting there, 364c, 365b; vicinity of, 365bd, 366a
Tomok, N. Sumatra: stay and eat, 313c, 314bc; graves of, 313d; crafts of, 314b; general, 314bc; from, 314d; getting there, 316c, 317c
Tongging, N. Sumatra, *301c,* 320bc
Torajaland, S. Celebes: getting there, 381cd, 384b; general, *384i,* 394a-95c, *393m;* climate of, 384b; *liang* graves, 385cd, 390c, *390i;* conduct, 385d, 386a; markets of, 388c; trekking in, 388d-89a, 394d, 395a
Toraja people, S. Celebes: origins of, 4d; religions, 26d, 385ab; crafts, 28a, 387b, 388ac, 394b; music and dance, *350c,* 386a-87a; funeral customs of, *351c,* 371a, 385bd, *386i,* 390c; games, *351c,* 387ab; headhunting, *351c;* general, 384d-88c; classes of, 385a; types of graves, 385bd; architecture, *387i,* 387d, 388a, 389a, 394b; fabrics, 387bc, 391d; festivals, 388a; food, 388c
Tosari, E. Java: from, 158bc, 164b; getting there, 159c
Towuti Lake, C. Celebes, 373ac

Toya Peka, Nusa Penida, 205a
Transmigrasi schemes: in the outer islands, 15c; S. Sumatra, 264cd; N. Celebes, 367c; Buru, 405d
Transport in Indonesia: hitching, 41b; motorcycles, 41cd; cycling, 41d, 42a; *bemo,* 42a; bus, 42b, 261d-62d; car rental, 42b; Colt, 42bc; *oplet,* 42bc; train, 42bc; flights, 42d, 43a; maps, 43a; sea, 43cd, 44ac, 377d-78d, *378c,* 408c; comfort, 44d, 45a; *becak,* 170a; missionary, 232c, 234b, 238c, 352a; 404 passim, 420d, 421a; finding your way, 443
Tretes, E. Java: getting there, 148c, 449bc; general, 173a
Trinil, C. Java, *141c*
Trolojo Cemetary, E. Java, 148a, *149c*
Trowulan, E. Java: museum of, *53c,* 147d, 148a; getting there, 147b; general, 147d-48c, 152d; transport around, 148ac; from, 148c; *149m;* mentioned, 162d
Trunyan, E. Bali: *221m;* getting there, 222a; general, 222ac
Tual, Kais: getting there, 404a, 407c; mentioned, *407c*
Tuban, E. Java: getting there, 171d, 172a; mentioned, 173a
Tukangbesi Island group, 393a
Tuk2, N. Sumatra: general, 314d-16b; stay and eat, 314d; mentioned, 314a
Tulungagung, E. Java: general, *53c,* 154c-55a; getting there, 156c

Ubud, C. Bali: arts of, 185b, 186c, 200 *passim;* museum, 185d, 198c, 200ab; crafts, 187b, 200bc; dance study, 191a, 212d; stay, 193d, 198bc; general, 198b-200d; *199m;* from, 200cd; getting there, *217c,* 218cd; mentioned, 221a, 224a
Ujung, E. Bali: waterpalace of, 206a; getting there, 206b
Ujung Kulon Game Reserve, W. Java: general, 73ab; getting there, 73b
Ujung Pandang, S. Celebes: getting there, 85c, 171bc, 172ac, 219a, 233a, 338c, 353a, 359d, 360d, 370 passim, 375c, 379a, 382c, 389d, 396ac, 399a, 404ac, 413d; from, 327b, 341a, 381c-82b, 394c, 425b; transport, 359d, 379a; general, 379a-82b, *380m, 381c;* stay, 379ab; crafts of, 379cd, 381bc, 388bc; seashell museum, 379cd; sights, 379cd; vicinity of, 382ab; mentioned, 194b, 329d, 376c, 382c, 384ab
Uludanu Temple, N. Bali, 223c
Ulu Watu, S. Bali: crafts of, 187d; description, 208a; getting there, 218c

Vanimo, Papua New Guinea, getting there, 425ab
Veddoid people, S. Celebes: general, 19bc; culture, 377a; mentioned, 227c

Village life in Indonesia, 2ab, 20ab, 27d, 32d, 33ab, 34bc, *47*

Visas: extensions, 31ab, 50 *passim;* for Indonesia, 49bc; types of, 49d, 50ab. See also Immigration department

Vishnu: in Indonesia, general, 5d, 447a; statues of, *53c*, 82c, 147a, 151d; in temple art, 104a; temples dedicated to, 133b, 156c; in Balinese religion, 182a; in sculpture, 185a; mentioned, 69a, 447c

Volcanoes: benefits of, 1d; belts of, 16d; religious significance of, 23b, 157d-59c, *350c;* of Java, 51d, 52b, 90bc, 115d, 151b, 156b; of Indonesia, *222ci,* 227a, 397c, 398a, 449a-50d *passim;* mentioned, 88c, 89c

Waai, Ambon: general, 402b; from, 405b

Waicak Day, 130d, 131a

Waigeo Island, *253c*

Waingapu, Sumba: getting there, 172c, 219a, 224d, 232c, 233a, 240a, 241b, 246c; general, 234c; from, 247a; mentioned, 246b

Wallace, Sir Alfred Russel: Wallace Line, 227b, 258ac; general, 258ac, *345c;* in the Moluccas, 398ab, 408cd

Wamena, Irian Jaya: events of, 27c; general, 418a, 435b, 439a-c, 440c; getting there, 425a; from, 434d, 435d, *439c,* 439d-40d; stay, 435c, 439ab; eat, 439bc; crafts of, 439cd

War of Independence: general, 9a-11a; in Yogya, 110ab; in Surabaya, 167d, 168a; in Bali, 202d, 204d; in Sumatra, 299a; in Celebes, 377ab; mentioned, *350c*

Wayang: history of, 7b, 67d, *351c;* plots (lakon), 19c, 67bc, 68ab, 69a, 70bc, 445b, 446c; and religion, *25c,* 142a; characters of, 31c, 67c, *67i, 68i,* 69

passim, 70i, 72i, 113ci, 119ci; general, 60a, *67i, 113c;* Javanese, 67a-72d; *113c, 114c,* 121b, 139a, 264d; forms of, 68bc, 83d; introductory, 82d

Wayang beber: making of, 138ab; performance of, 151a

Wayang golek: puppets, 70d, 71a, 123ad; plots of, 71ab, 445b; performances, 82d, 83d, 87d, 121b, *188c*

Wayang kulit: puppets, *25i,* 29d, 70ab, 72a, *120c,* 123d, 138c, 187b; history of, 69d, *351c; dalang,* 70c, *120i;* performances, 82d, 83d, 115a, 121b; *lakon, 120c;* of Bali, 184b, 203ab, 218b, *225ci;* mentioned, 72a, *188c*

Wayang orang: general, 70d-72 *passim;* history of, 71d, 72a, 114c; dancers, 72 *passim;* plot, 72cd; performances, 83d, 87d, 101d, 102a, 121cd, 139d, 140ab; mentioned, 71b, 138b, *188c*

Wayang puppets: history of, 52d, 67d, 68a; buying, 88a, 138ab; depicted in temple art, 147bc, 154b, 165a; Balinese, 184b

Wayang topeng: general, 71b-c; history of, 71c, 142a, *351c;* plots, 71c; masks, 123a, 138b, 309d; performance, 160ab; Balinese, 184c; mentioned, 60c, 71c, *188c*

Welirang, Mt., E. Java, 152c, 164a, 173a

West Java: the land, 1b, *89c;* history of, 8c, 92 *passim, 93c,* 249d; people, 51ab; *74m;* ramfights, *89c,* 90ab

West Kalimantan: political unrest, 12c; economy, 356a; introduction, 356a; *357m;* mentioned, *116-17c*

West Sumatra: history of, 11b, 15c, *116c, 283c;* eat, 38a; transport in, 272bc; architecture of, *282c, 285i, 286ci; 292-93m;* customs of, *294c;* fauna, 305a

West Timor: *23m, 231m;* general, 228c-

33d; the land, 228c, 229a; climate of, 229ac; history, 229c-30a; crafts, 230bc; travel, 230c

Wetar, S.E. Moluccas, getting there, *407c*

Wildlife parks of Indonesia: 73ab, 76c-77b, 95c, 165ab, 167b, 242a-44d, 299b-300b, 305c, 320d, 326c, 344bc. See also Orangutan rehabilitation centers; Animal life of Indonesia

Women: in Indonesian society, 26a; in Indonesian history, *117c;* of Bali, 181cd; of Irian Jaya, 437cd

Wonogiri, E. Java: general, 151ab; mentioned, 115d

Wonosobo, C. Java, 99c, 106b

Work in Indonesia, 49ab, 84a

Wotu, C. Celebes: getting there, 360c, 371b, 396a; from, 374a

Yaosakor, Irian Jaya, 428d

Yeh Pulu, C. Bali, 201d

Yeh Sanih, N. Bali, 225bd

Yogya, C. Java: history of, 10c, 11a, *111c, 117c,* 125bc, 128b; crafts and markets, 30a, 123cd, 234a, *252-53c;* batik, 62a, *114c,* 118 *passim;* theatre forms, 63d, 64a; dance and *gamelan* of, 66ab, 121bc, *122c;* getting there, 84bd, 89d, 141bd, 157a, 162a, 171d, 172a, 213b, 218c, 219a; *110-11m, 142-43m;* general, 110a-25a; *kratons* of, 110a, 113a-18b, *114c, 115c,* 121c; transport in, 110b, 112a; stay, 112 *passim;* festivals of, *114c,* 115b-18b; museums, 122ac, 123a; mosques and churches, 123b; from, 124b-25a, 450a; mentioned, 54a, 77d, 105c

Zamboanga, Philippines, getting there, 343a, 353a, 364c

Zigibi Range, Irian Jaya, *351c,* 430d, 431ac